1994/95 Edition

ORIGINAL PRONOUNCEMENTS

ACCOUNTING STANDARDS
as of June 1, 1994

VOLUME II
AICPA Pronouncements
FASB Interpretations
FASB concepts Statements
FASB Technical Bulletins
Topical Index/Appendixes

 Financial Accounting Standards Board

IRWIN

Burr Ridge, Illinois
Boston, Massachusetts
Sydney, Australia

Notice to Users of the *Original Pronouncements*

This year's edition of the Financial Accounting Standards Board's (FASB) *Original Pronouncements* has been updated to include the following new pronouncements:

FAS 116: Accounting for Contributions Received and Contributions Made

Statement 116 addresses the accounting for contributions received and made by all business enterprises and not-for-profit organizations. Statement 116 requires that contributions received, including unconditional promises to give, are recognized as revenues when received at their fair values. Contributions made, including unconditional promises to give, are recorded as expenses when made at their fair values. Conditional promises to give are recognized when the conditions are substantially met.

Not-for-profit organizations are further required to distinguish between contributions received that increase permanently restricted net assets, temporarily restricted net assets, and unrestricted net assets, and to recognize expirations of donor restrictions

FAS 117: Financial Statements of Not-for-Profit Organizations

Statement 117 establishes standards for general-purpose external financial statements provided by not-for-profit organizations. Not-for-profit organizations are required to present a statement of financial position, a statement of activities, and a statement of cash flows. According to Statement 117, organizations should classify net assets and revenues, expenses, gains, and losses based on whether they are restricted by donors.

FTB 94-1: Application of Statement 115 to Debt Securities Restructured in a Troubled Debt Restructuring

FTB 94-1 clarifies that FASB Statement No. 115, *Accounting for Certain Investments in Debt and Equity Securities,* applies to a loan that was restructured in a troubled debt restructuring involving a modification of terms if the restructured loan meets the definition of a security in Statement 115.

Acknowledgments

Judith A. Noë, FASB project manager, compiled the *Original Pronouncements* with the assistance of Deborah L. Monroe, FASB assistant project manager. Dorothy D. Lomazzo provided production assistance in the preparation of these volumes.

Norwalk, Connecticut
June 1994

Timothy S. Lucas
Director of Research and
Technical Activities

FOREWORD

This volume contains the following materials issued by the American Institute of Certified Public Accountants or its committees through June 1973 and by the Financial Accounting Standards Board (FASB) to June 1, 1994:

- Accounting Research Bulletins
- Accounting Principles Board Opinions
- Interpretations of Accounting Research Bulletins and Accounting Principles Board Opinions
- FASB Interpretations
- FASB Statements of Financial Accounting Concepts
- FASB Technical Bulletins

A companion volume (Volume I) contains the Statements of Financial Accounting Standards issued by the FASB from its inception in 1973 to June 1, 1994.

A shading technique is used to alert the reader when paragraphs containing accounting standards have been amended or superseded. All terms and sentences that have been deleted or replaced are shaded. Paragraphs and subparagraphs that have been amended simply by the addition of terms, sentences, or new footnotes are marked with a vertical solid bar in the left margin alongside the paragraph or subparagraph.

The appendixes and Topical Index in this volume refer to pronouncements contained in both volumes.

Appendix B presents a schedule of all amended and superseded standards. In addition, a status page at the beginning of each pronouncement identifies (a) the source of those changes, (b) other pronouncements affected by that pronouncement, and (c) the principal effective date. The status page also identifies, where applicable, other interpretive pronouncements and releases that further clarify that pronouncement. Pronouncements that have been completely superseded and may no longer be applied are omitted from this volume; however, a status page is retained for those omitted pronouncements. Because pronouncements may have delayed effective dates, the reader may wish to refer to Appendix C to determine when the change is effective.

The Topical Index includes references to the material contained in both volumes of the *Original Pronouncements* and, in addition, includes references to material included in the *Current Text*, the *EITF Abstracts* (a summary of proceedings of the FASB Emerging Issues Task Force), and other supplemental guidance published by the FASB in the form of question-and-answer Special Reports and published articles. (Please refer to the Introduction to the Topical Index for additional details and guidance on the use of this Index.)

Accounting Research Bulletins and Opinions of the Accounting Principles Board continue in effect until amended or superseded by Statements of Financial Accounting Standards issued by the FASB.

Volume II

ORIGINAL PRONOUNCEMENTS
(as of June 1, 1994)

TABLE OF CONTENTS

COMMITTEE ON
ACCOUNTING PROCEDURE

Accounting Research Bulletins

ACCOUNTING RESEARCH BULLETINS

TABLE OF CONTENTS

FOREWORD TO ACCOUNTING RESEARCH BULLETINS

SEPTEMBER 1961

The committee on accounting procedure and the committee on terminology of the American Institute of Certified Public Accountants were superseded on September 1, 1959, by the Accounting Principles Board. At its first meeting, on September 11, 1959, the Board approved the following resolution:

> The Accounting Principles Board of the American Institute of Certified Public Accountants on September 1, 1959, assumed the responsibilities of the former committees on accounting procedure and on terminology. During its existence, the committee on accounting procedure issued a series of accounting research bulletins and the committee on terminology issued a series of accounting terminology bulletins. In 1953, the first forty-two of the accounting research bulletins were revised, restated, or withdrawn and appeared as Accounting Research Bulletin No. 43 and Accounting Terminology Bulletin No. 1. Since 1953, other bulletins have been issued, the last accounting research bulletin being No. 51 and the last terminology bulletin being No. 4.
>
> The Accounting Principles Board has the authority, as did the predecessor committees, to review and revise any of these bulletins and it plans to take such action from time to time.
>
> Pending such action and in order to prevent any misunderstanding meanwhile as to the status of the existing accounting research and terminology bulletins, the Accounting Principles Board now makes public announcement that these bulletins should be considered as continuing in force with the same degree of authority as before.

Included in this volume[1] are Accounting Research Bulletin No. 43 (a revision and restatement of previous Bulletins) and Bulletins No. 44 to 51 in the form in which they were originally published. These are all of the bulletins which were in force at September 1, 1959, and, up to the date of this publication,[2] none of them has been revised or revoked by any action of the Accounting Principles Board.

---

[1]Accounting Research and Terminology Bulletins, Final Edition, 1961, American Institute of Certified Public Accountants.

[2]September 1961.

Accounting Research Bulletin No. 43
Restatement and Revision of Accounting
Research Bulletins

STATUS

Issued: June 1953

Effective Date: June 1953 (replaced ARBs issued September 1939-January 1953)

Affects: No other pronouncements

Affected by: Chapter 1A, paragraph 1 amended by FAS 111
Chapter 1B; Chapter 3A, paragraph 10; Chapter 5, paragraph 7; Chapter 7B, paragraph 6; Chapter 9C; Chapter 10B; Chapter 12, paragraphs 12 and 18; and Chapter 15, paragraph 12 amended by APB 6
Chapter 2A, paragraph 3 amended by APB 20
Chapter 2B and Chapter 8 superseded by APB 9
Chapter 3A, paragraph 4 amended by FAS 115
Chapter 3A, paragraph 6(g) amended by APB 21 and FAS 111
Chapter 3A, paragraph 8 amended by FAS 6
Chapter 3A, paragraph 7 amended by FAS 78
Chapter 3A, footnote 4 superseded by FAS 6
Chapter 3B superseded by APB 10
Chapter 5, paragraphs 1 through 9 superseded prospectively by APB 17
Chapter 5, paragraphs 5, 6, 8, and 9, and footnote 1; Chapter 10A, paragraph 19; Chapter 10B, paragraphs 15 and 17; Chapter 12, paragraph 21; and Chapter 15, paragraphs 7 and 17 amended by APB 9
Chapter 5, paragraphs 8 and 10 amended by FAS 44
Chapter 5, paragraph 10 superseded prospectively by APB 16
Chapter 6 superseded by FAS 5
Chapter 7A, paragraph 10 amended by FAS 111
Chapter 7C superseded by ARB 48
Chapter 9B superseded by APB 6
Chapter 9C, paragraph 5 amended by FAS 96 and FAS 109
Chapter 9C, paragraphs 11 through 13 amended by APB 11
Chapter 9C, paragraphs 11 through 13 superseded by FAS 96 and FAS 109
Chapter 10A, paragraph 19 amended by APB 9 and FAS 111
Chapter 10B superseded by APB 11, FAS 96, and FAS 109
Chapter 11B, paragraph 8 superseded by APB 11, FAS 96, and FAS 109
Chapter 11B, paragraph 9 and footnotes 3 and 4 amended by APB 9
Chapter 11B, paragraph 9 amended by FAS 111
Chapter 11B, footnotes 3 and 4 superseded by FAS 111
Chapter 12, paragraph 5 amended by FAS 8 and FAS 52
Chapter 12, paragraphs 7 and 10 through 22 superseded by FAS 8 and FAS 52
Chapter 12, paragraphs 8 and 9 superseded by FAS 94
Chapter 13A superseded by APB 8
Chapter 13B, paragraphs 6 through 14 and footnotes 2 and 3 amended by APB 25
Chapter 14 superseded by APB 5
Chapter 15, paragraph 11 amended by APB 11
Chapter 15 superseded by APB 26

Other Interpretive Pronouncements: AIN-ARB 43, Chapter 13B, Interpretation No. 1 (Superseded by APB 25)
FTB 85-1
FTB 85-6

Accounting Research Bulletin No. 43
Restatement and Revision of Accounting Research Bulletins

CONTENTS

PREFACE

Since its organization the American Institute of Accountants, aware of divergences in accounting procedures and of an increasing interest by the public in financial reporting, has given consideration to problems raised by these divergences. Its studies led it, in 1933, to make certain recommendations to the New York Stock Exchange which were adopted by the Institute in 1934. Further consideration developed into a program of research and the publication of opinions, beginning in 1938, in a series of Accounting Research Bulletins.

Forty-two bulletins were issued during the period from 1939 to 1953. Eight of these were reports of the committee on terminology. The other 34 were the result of research by the committee on accounting procedure directed to those segments of accounting practice where problems were most demanding and with which business and the accounting profession were most concerned at the time.

Some of these studies were undertaken to meet new business or economic developments. Some arose out of the war which ended in 1945 and the problems following in its wake. Certain of the bulletins were amended, superseded, or withdrawn as changing conditions affected their usefulness.

The purposes of this restatement are to eliminate what is no longer applicable, to condense and clarify what continues to be of value, to revise where changed views require revision, and to arrange the retained material by subjects rather than in the order of issuance. The terminology bulletins are not included. They are being published separately.

The committee has made some changes of substance, which are summarized in appendix B.

The several chapters and subchapters of this restatement and revision are to be regarded as a cancellation and replacement of Accounting Research Bulletins 1 through 42, excepting the terminology bulletins included in that series, which are being replaced by a separate publication.

Although the committee has approved the objective of finding a better term than the word *surplus* for use in published financial statements, it has used *surplus* herein as being a technical term well understood among accountants, to whom its pronouncements are primarily directed.

Committee on Accounting Procedure
June, 1953

Each section of Accounting Research Bulletin No. 43, entitled Restatement and Revision of Accounting Research Bulletins, *was separately adopted by the assenting votes of the twenty members of the committee except to the extent that dissents, or assents with qualification, are noted at the close of each section. Publication of the bulletin as a whole was approved by the assenting votes of all members of the committee, one of whom, Mr. Andrews, assented with qualification.*

Mr. Andrews assents to the publication of this bulletin only to the extent that it constitutes, with no changes in meaning other than those set forth in appendix B, a restatement of the bulletins previously issued by the committee and not mentioned in appendix C as having been omitted. He dissents from the statement contained in the preface that this bulletin is to be regarded as a cancellation of the previously issued bulletins; he regards it as beyond the power of the committee to cancel its previous statements, which in his view inescapably remain authoritative expressions as at the date of their utterance.

Committee on Accounting Procedure (1952-1953)

Paul K. Knight,	Perry Mason	William W. Werntz
Chairman	Edward F. McCormack	Edward B. Wilcox
Frederick B. Andrews	John Peoples	Raymond D. Willard
Frank S. Calkins	Maurice E. Peloubet	Robert W. Williams
H. A. Finney	John W. Queenan	Karl R. Zimmermann
Roy Godfrey	Walter L. Schaffer	
Thomas G. Higgins	C. Aubrey Smith	Carman G. Blough,
John A. Lindquist	C. Oliver Wellington	*Director of Research*

INTRODUCTION

Accounting and the Corporate System

1. Accounting is essential to the effective functioning of any business organization, particularly the corporate form. The test of the corporate system and of the special phase of it represented by corporate accounting ultimately lies in the results which are produced. These results must be judged from the standpoint of society as a whole—not merely from that of any one group of interested persons.

2. The uses to which the corporate system is put and the controls to which it is subject change from time to time, and all parts of the machinery must be adapted to meet changes as they occur. In the past fifty years there has been an increasing use of the corporate system for the purpose of converting into readily transferable form the ownership of large, complex, and more or less permanent business enterprises. This evolution has brought in its train certain uses of the processes of law and accounting which have led to the creation of new controls, revisions of the laws, and reconsideration of accounting procedures.

3. As a result of this development, the problems in the field of accounting have increasingly come to be considered from the standpoint of the buyer or seller of an interest in an enterprise, with consequent increased recognition of the significance of the income statement and a tendency to restrict narrowly charges and credits to surplus. The fairest possible presentation of periodic net income, with neither material overstatement nor understatement, is important, since the results of operations are significant not only to prospective buyers of an interest in the enterprise but also to prospective sellers. With the increasing importance of the income statement there has been a tendency to regard the balance sheet as the connecting link between successive income statements; however this concept should not obscure the fact that the balance sheet has significant uses of its own.

4. This evolution has also led to a demand for a larger degree of uniformity in accounting. *Uniformity* has usually connoted similar treatment of the same item occurring in many cases, in which sense it runs the risk of concealing important differences among cases. Another sense of the word would require that different authorities working independently on the same case should reach the same conclusions. Although uniformity is a worthwhile goal, it should not be pursued to the exclusion of other benefits. Changes of emphasis and objective as well as changes in conditions under which business operates have led, and doubtless will continue to

lead, to the adoption of new accounting procedures. Consequently diversity of practice may continue as new practices are adopted before old ones are completely discarded.

Applicability of Committee Opinions

5. The principal objective of the committee has been to narrow areas of difference and inconsistency in accounting practices, and to further the development and recognition of generally accepted accounting principles, through the issuance of opinions and recommendations that would serve as criteria for determining the suitability of accounting practices reflected in financial statements and representations of commercial and industrial companies. In this endeavor, the committee has considered the interpretation and application of such principles as appeared to it to be pertinent to particular accounting problems. The committee has not directed its attention to accounting problems or procedures of religious, charitable, scientific, educational, and similar non-profit institutions, municipalities, professional firms, and the like. Accordingly, except where there is a specific statement of a different intent by the committee, its opinions and recommendations are directed primarily to business enterprises organized for profit.

Voting Procedure in Adopting Opinions

6. The committee regards the representative character and general acceptability of its opinions as of the highest importance, and to that end has adopted the following procedures:

a. Any opinion or recommendation before issuance is submitted in final form to all members of the committee either at a meeting or by mail.
b. No such opinion or recommendation is issued unless it has received the approval of two-thirds of the entire committee.
c. Any member of the committee dissenting from an opinion or recommendation issued under the preceding rule is entitled to have the fact of his dissent and his reasons therefor recorded in the document in which the opinion or recommendation is presented.

7. Before reaching its conclusions, the committee gives careful consideration to prior opinions, to prevailing practices, and to the views of professional and other bodies concerned with accounting procedures.

Authority of Opinions

8. Except in cases in which formal adoption by the Institute membership has been asked and secured,

the authority of opinions reached by the committee rests upon their general acceptability. The committee recognizes that in extraordinary cases fair presentation and justice to all parties at interest may require exceptional treatment. But the burden of justifying departure from accepted procedures, to the extent that they are evidenced in committee opinions, must be assumed by those who adopt another treatment.

9. The committee contemplates that its opinions will have application only to items material and significant in the relative circumstances. It considers that items of little or no consequence may be dealt with as expediency may suggest. However, freedom to deal expediently with immaterial items should not extend to a group of items whose cumulative effect in any one financial statement may be material and significant.

Opinions Not Retroactive

10. No opinion issued by the committee is intended to have a retroactive effect unless it contains a statement of such intention. Thus an opinion will ordinarily have no application to a transaction arising prior to its publication, nor to transactions in process of completion at the time of publication. But while the committee considers it inequitable to make its statements retroactive, it does not wish to discourage the revision of past accounts in an individual case if it appears to be desirable in the circumstances.

The Company and Its Auditors

11. Underlying all committee opinions is the fact that the accounts of a company are primarily the responsibility of management. The responsibility of the auditor is to express his opinion concerning the financial statements and to state clearly such explanations, amplifications, disagreement, or disapproval as he deems appropriate. While opinions of the committee are addressed particularly to certified public accountants whose problem it is to decide what they may properly report, the committee recommends similar application of the procedures mentioned herein by those who prepare the accounts and financial statements.

Chapter 1

PRIOR OPINIONS

Section A—Rules Adopted by Membership

Below are reprinted the six rules adopted by the membership of the Institute in 1934, the first five of which had been recommended in 1933 to the New York Stock Exchange by the Institute's committee on cooperation with stock exchanges.

1. Unrealized profit should not be credited to income account of the corporation either directly or indirectly, through the medium of charging against such unrealized profits amounts which would ordinarily fall to be charged against income account. Profit is deemed to be realized when a sale in the ordinary course of business is effected, unless the circumstances are such that the collection of the sale price is not reasonably assured. An exception to the general rule may be made in respect of inventories in industries (such as packing-house industry) in which owing to the impossibility of determining costs it is a trade custom to take inventories at net selling prices, which may exceed cost.

2. Capital surplus, however created, should not be used to relieve the income account of the current or future years of charges which would otherwise fall to be made thereagainst. This rule might be subject to the exception that where, upon reorganization, a reorganized company would be relieved of charges which would require to be made against income if the existing corporation were continued, it might be regarded as permissible to accomplish the same result without reorganization provided the facts were as fully revealed to and the action as formally approved by the shareholders as in reorganization.

3. Earned surplus of a subsidiary company created prior to acquisition does not form a part of the consolidated earned surplus of the parent company and subsidiaries; nor can any dividend declared out of such surplus properly be credited to the income account of the parent company.

4. While it is perhaps in some circumstances permissible to show stock of a corporation held in its own treasury as an asset, if adequately disclosed, the dividends on stock so held should not be treated as a credit to the income account of the company.

5. Notes or accounts receivable due from officers, employees, or affiliated companies must be shown separately and not included under a general heading such as notes receivable or accounts receivable.

6. If capital stock is issued nominally for the acquisition of property and it appears that at about the same time, and pursuant to a previous agreement or understanding, some portion of the stock so issued is donated to the corporation, it is not permissible to treat the par value of the stock nominally issued for the property as the cost of that property. If stock so donated is subsequently sold, it is not permissible to treat the proceeds as a credit to sur-

plus of the corporation.

Section B—Opinion Issued by Predecessor Committee

1. Following an inquiry made by the New York Stock Exchange, a predecessor committee on accounting procedure in 1938 issued the following report:

"Profits or Losses on Treasury Stock"

2. "The executive committee of the American Institute of Accountants has directed that the following report of the committee on accounting procedure, which it received at a meeting on April 8, 1938, be published, without approval or disapproval of the committee, for the information of members of the Institute:

To the Executive Committee,
American Institute of Accountants:

3. "This committee has had under consideration the question regarding treatment of purchase and sale by a corporation of its own stock, which was raised during 1937 by the New York Stock Exchange with the Institute's special committee on cooperation with stock exchanges.

4. "As a result of discussions which then took place, the special committee on cooperation with stock exchanges made a report which was approved by the committee on accounting procedure and the executive committee, and a copy of which was furnished to the committee on stock list of the New York Stock Exchange. The question raised was stated in the following form:

5. "'Should the difference between the purchase and resale prices of a corporation's own common stock be reflected in earned surplus (either directly or through inclusion in the income account) or should such difference be reflected in capital surplus?'

6. "The opinion of the special committee on cooperation with stock exchanges reads in part as follows:

7. "'Apparently there is general agreement that the difference between the purchase price and the stated value of a corporation's common stock purchased and retired should be reflected in capital surplus. Your committee believes that while the net asset value of the shares of common stock outstanding in the hands of the public may be increased or decreased by such purchase and retirement, such transactions relate to the capital of the corporation

and do not give rise to corporate profits or losses. Your committee can see no essential difference between (a) the purchase and retirement of a corporation's own common stock and the subsequent issue of common shares, and (b) the purchase and resale of its own common stock.'

8. "This committee is in agreement with the views thus expressed; it is aware that such transactions have been held to give rise to taxable income, but it does not feel that such decisions constitute any bar to the application of correct accounting procedure as above outlined.

9. "The special committee on cooperation with stock exchanges continued and concluded its report with the following statement:

10. "'Accordingly, although your committee recognizes that there may be cases where the transactions involved are so inconsequential as to be immaterial, it does not believe that, as a broad general principle, such transactions should be reflected in earned surplus (either directly or through inclusion in the income account).'

11. "This committee agrees with the special committee on cooperation with stock exchanges, but thinks it desirable to point out that the qualification should not be applied to any transaction which, although in itself inconsiderable in amount, is a part of a series of transactions which in the aggregate are of substantial importance.

12. "This committee recommends that the views expressed be circulated for the information of members of the Institute."

Chapter 2

FORM OF STATEMENTS

Section A—Comparative Financial Statements

1. The presentation of comparative financial statements in annual and other reports enhances the usefulness of such reports and brings out more clearly the nature and trends of current changes affecting the enterprise. Such presentation emphasizes the fact that statements for a series of periods are far more significant than those for a single period and that the accounts for one period are but an instalment of what is essentially a continuous history.

2. In any one year it is ordinarily desirable that the balance sheet, the income statement, and the surplus statement be given for one or more preceding years as well as for the current year. Footnotes, explanations, and accountants' qualifications which

appeared on the statements for the preceding years should be repeated, or at least referred to, in the comparative statements to the extent that they continue to be of significance. If, because of reclassifications or for other reasons, changes have occurred in the manner of or basis for presenting corresponding items for two or more periods, information should be furnished which will explain the change. This procedure is in conformity with the well recognized principle that any change in practice which affects comparability should be disclosed.

3. It is necessary that prior-year figures shown for comparative purposes be in fact comparable with those shown for the most recent period, or that any exceptions to comparability be clearly brought out.

4. Circumstances vary so greatly that it is not practicable to deal here specifically with all situations. The independent accountant should, however, make very clear what statements are included within the scope of his report.

Section B—Combined Statement of Income and Earned Surplus

1. Attention has already been called in the introduction to the increased significance attributed to the income statement by users of financial statements and to the general tendency to regard the balance sheet as the connecting link between successive income statements. It therefore becomes important to consider the problems presented by the practice of combining the annual income statement with the statement of earned surplus.

2. The combining of these two statements, where possible, will often be found to be convenient and desirable. Where this presentation is contemplated, however, certain considerations should be borne in mind if undesirable consequences are to be avoided.

Advantages of the Combined Statement

3. Over the years it is plainly desirable that all costs, expenses, and losses, and all profits of a business, other than decreases or increases arising directly from its capital-stock transactions, be included in the determination of income. If this principle could in practice be carried out perfectly, there would be no charges or credits to earned surplus except those relating to distributions and appropriations of final net income. This is an ideal upon which all may agree, but because of conditions impossible to foresee it often fails of attainment. From time to time charges and credits are made to surplus which clearly affect the cumulative total of income for a series of years, although their exclusion from the

income statement of a single year is justifiable. There is danger that unless the two statements are closely connected such items will be overlooked, or at any rate not given full weight, in any attempt on the part of the reader to compute a company's long-run income or its income-earning capacity.

4. There is a marked tendency to exaggerate the significance of the net income for a single year, particularly the degree to which the net income can be identified exclusively with that year. In so far as the combined form calls attention to the character of the income statement as a tentative instalment in the long-time financial results it serves a useful purpose.

5. To summarize, the combined income and earned surplus statement serves the purpose of showing in one statement both the earnings applicable to the particular period and modifications of earned surplus on a long-run basis. It distinguishes current charges and credits related to a company's more usual or typical business operations from material extraordinary charges and credits[1] which may have arisen during the period by placing them in different sections of a continuous statement.

Disadvantages and Limitations

6. In the combined statement, net income for the year appears somewhere within the statement and not at the end. Such wording and arrangement should be used as will make this item unmistakably clear and leave the reader in no doubt as to the point at which the net income has been determined.

7. While it is true that the net income amount, when expressed as earnings per share, is often given undue prominence and its significance exaggerated, there nevertheless remain the responsibility for determination of net income by sound methods and the duty to show it clearly. The adoption of the combined statement provides no excuse for less care in distinguishing charges and credits to income from charges and credits to surplus than would be required if separate statements of income and surplus were presented. Failure to exercise care in the use of this form of statement would immediately discredit it.

Chapter 3

WORKING CAPITAL

Section A—Current Assets and Current Liabilities

1. The working capital of a borrower has always been of prime interest to grantors of credit; and

---

[1]See chapter 8, paragraphs 11, 12, and 13.

bond indentures, credit agreements, and preferred stock agreements commonly contain provisions restricting corporate actions which would effect a reduction or impairment of working capital. Many such contracts forego precise or uniform definitions and merely provide that current assets and current liabilities shall be determined in accordance with generally accepted accounting principles. Considerable variation and inconsistency exist, however, with respect to their classification and display in financial statements. In this section the committee discusses the nature of current assets and current liabilities with a view toward a more useful presentation thereof in financial statements.

2. The committee believes that, in the past, definitions of current assets have tended to be overly concerned with whether the assets may be immediately realizable. The discussion which follows takes cognizance of the tendency for creditors to rely more upon the ability of debtors to pay their obligations out of the proceeds of current operations and less upon the debtor's ability to pay in case of liquidation. It should be emphasized that financial statements of a going concern are prepared on the assumption that the company will continue in business. Accordingly, the views expressed in this section represent a departure from any narrow definition or strict *one year* interpretation of either current assets or current liabilities; the objective is to relate the criteria developed to the operating cycle of a business.

3. Financial position, as it is reflected by the records and accounts from which the statement is prepared, is revealed in a presentation of the assets and liabilities of the enterprise. In the statements of manufacturing, trading, and service enterprises these assets and liabilities are generally classified and segregated; if they are classified logically, summations or totals of the *current* or *circulating* or *working* assets, hereinafter referred to as *current assets,* and of obligations currently payable, designated as *current liabilities,* will permit the ready determination of working capital. *Working capital,* sometimes called *net working capital,* is represented by the excess of current assets over current liabilities and identifies the relatively liquid portion of total enterprise capital which constitutes a margin or buffer for meeting obligations within the ordinary operating cycle of the business. If the conventions of accounting relative to the identification and presentation of current assets and current liabilities are made logical and consistent, the amounts, bases of valuations, and composition of such assets and liabilities and their relation to the total assets or capital employed will provide valuable data for credit and management purposes and afford a sound basis for comparisons from year to year. It is recognized that there may be exceptions, in special cases, to certain of the inclusions and exclusions as set forth in this section.

When such exceptions occur they should be accorded the treatment merited in the particular circumstances under the general principles outlined herein.

4. For accounting purposes, the term *current assets* is used to designate cash and other assets or resources commonly identified as those which are reasonably expected to be realized in cash or sold or consumed during the normal operating cycle of the business. Thus the term comprehends in general such resources as (a) cash available for current operations and items which are the equivalent of cash; (b) inventories of merchandise, raw materials, goods in process, finished goods, operating supplies, and ordinary maintenance material and parts; (c) trade accounts, notes, and acceptances receivable; (d) receivables from officers, employees, affiliates, and others, if collectible in the ordinary course of business within a year; (e) instalment or deferred accounts and notes receivable if they conform generally to normal trade practices and terms within the business; (f) marketable securities representing the investment of cash available for current operations; and (g) prepaid expenses such as insurance, interest, rents, taxes, unused royalties, current paid advertising service not yet received, and operating supplies. Prepaid expenses are not current assets in the sense that they will be converted into cash but in the sense that, if not paid in advance, they would require the use of current assets during the operating cycle.

5. The ordinary operations of a business involve a circulation of capital within the current asset group. Cash is expended for materials, finished parts, operating supplies, labor, and other factory services, and such expenditures are accumulated as inventory cost. Inventory costs, upon sale of the products to which such costs attach, are converted into trade receivables and ultimately into cash again. The average time intervening between the acquisition of materials or services entering this process and the final cash realization constitutes an *operating cycle.* A one-year time period is to be used as a basis for the segregation of current assets in cases where there are several operating cycles occurring within a year. However, where the period of the operating cycle is more than twelve months, as in, for instance, the tobacco, distillery, and lumber businesses, the longer period should be used. Where a particular business has no clearly defined operating cycle, the one-year rule should govern.

6. This concept of the nature of current assets contemplates the exclusion from that classification of such resources as: (a) cash and claims to cash which are restricted as to withdrawal or use for other than current operations, are designated for expenditure in the acquisition or construction of noncurrent

assets, or are segregated[1] for the liquidation of long-term debts; (b) investments in securities (whether marketable or not) or advances which have been made for the purposes of control, affiliation, or other continuing business advantage; (c) receivables arising from unusual transactions (such as the sale of capital assets, or loans or advances to affiliates, officers, or employees) which are not expected to be collected within twelve months; (d) cash surrender value of life insurance policies; (e) land and other natural resources; (f) depreciable assets; and (g) long-term prepayments which are fairly chargeable to the operations of several years, or deferred charges such as unamortized debt discount and expense, bonus payments under a long-term lease, costs of rearrangement of factory layout or removal to a new location, and certain types of research and development costs.

7. The term *current liabilities* is used principally to designate obligations whose liquidation is reasonably expected to require the use of existing resources properly classifiable as current assets, or the creation of other current liabilities. As a balance-sheet category, the classification is intended to include obligations for items which have entered into the operating cycle, such as payables incurred in the acquisition of materials and supplies to be used in the production of goods or in providing services to be offered for sale; collections received in advance of the delivery of goods or performance of services[2]; and debts which arise from operations directly related to the operating cycle, such as accruals for wages, salaries, commissions, rentals, royalties, and income and other taxes. Other liabilities whose regular and ordinary liquidation is expected to occur within a relatively short period of time, usually twelve months, are also intended for inclusion, such as short-term debts arising from the acquisition of capital assets, serial maturities of long-term obligations, amounts required to be expended within one year under sinking fund provisions, and agency obligations arising from the collection or acceptance of cash or other assets for the account of third persons.[3]

8. This concept of current liabilities would include estimated or accrued amounts which are expected to be required to cover expenditures within the year for known obligations (a) the amount of which can be determined only approximately (as in the case of provisions for accruing bonus payments) or (b) where the specific person or persons to whom payment will be made cannot as yet be designated (as in the case of estimated costs to be incurred in connection with guaranteed servicing or repair of products already sold). The current liability classification, however, is not intended to include a contractual obligation falling due at an early date which is expected to be refunded,[4] or debts to be liquidated by funds which have been accumulated in accounts of a type not properly classified as current assets, or long-term obligations incurred to provide increased amounts of working capital for long periods. When the amounts of the periodic payments of an obligation are, by contract, measured by current transactions, as for example by rents or revenues received in the case of equipment trust certificates or by the depletion of natural resources in the case of property obligations, the portion of the total obligation to be included as a current liability should be that representing the amount accrued at the balance-sheet date.

9. The amounts at which various current assets are carried do not always represent their present realizable cash values. Accounts receivable net of allowances for uncollectible accounts, and for unearned discounts where unearned discounts are considered, are effectively stated at the amount of cash estimated as realizable. However, practice varies with respect to the carrying basis for current assets such as marketable securities and inventories. In the case of marketable securities where market value is less than cost by a substantial amount and it is evident that the decline in market value is not due to a mere temporary condition, the amount to be included as a current asset should not exceed the market value. The basis for carrying inventories is stated in chapter 4. It is important that the amounts at which current assets are stated be supplemented by

---

[1]Even though not actually set aside in special accounts, funds that are clearly to be used in the near future for the liquidation of long-term debts, payments to sinking funds, or for similar purposes should also, under this concept, be excluded from current assets. However, where such funds are considered to offset maturing debt which has properly been set up as a current liability, they may be included within the current asset classification.

[2]Examples of such current liabilities are obligations resulting from advance collections on ticket sales, which will normally be liquidated in the ordinary course of business by the delivery of services. On the contrary, obligations representing long-term deferments of the delivery of goods or services would not be shown as current liabilities. Examples of the latter are the issuance of a long-term warranty or the advance receipt by a lessor of rental for the final period of a ten-year lease as a condition to execution of the lease agreement.

[3]Loans accompanied by pledge of life insurance policies would be classified as current liabilities when, by their terms or by intent, they are to be repaid within twelve months. The pledging of life insurance policies does not affect the classification of the asset any more than does the pledging of receivables, inventories, real estate, or other assets as collateral for a short-term loan. However, when a loan on a life insurance policy is obtained from the insurance company with the intent that it will not be paid but will be liquidated by deduction from the proceeds of the policy upon maturity or cancellation, the obligation should be excluded from current liabilities.

[4]There should, however, be full disclosure that such obligation has been omitted from the current liabilities and a statement of the reason for such omission should be given. Cf note 1.

information which reveals, for temporary investments, their market value at the balance-sheet date, and for the various classifications of inventory items, the basis upon which their amounts are stated and, where practicable, indication of the method of determining the cost—e.g., *average cost, first-in first-out, last-in first-out*, etc.

One member of the committee, Mr. Mason, assented with qualification to adoption of section A of chapter 3.

Mr. Mason does not accept the view implied in paragraph 6 that unamortized debt discount is an asset. Also, referring to paragraph 9, he believes that the market value is the most significant figure in connection with marketable securities held as temporary investments of cash, and would prefer to show such securities in the accounts at their market value, whether greater or less than cost. He would accept as an alternative the use of cost in the accounts with market value shown parenthetically in the balance sheet.

Section B—Application of United States Government Securities against Liabilities for Federal Taxes on Income

1. It is a general principle of accounting that the offsetting of assets and liabilities in the balance sheet is improper except where a right of set-off exists. An example of such exception was the showing of United States Treasury Tax Notes, Tax Series A-1943 and B-1943, as a deduction from the liability for federal taxes on income, which the committee approved in 1942.

2. In view of the special nature of the terms of the 1943 tax notes, the intention of the purchaser to use them to pay federal income taxes could be assumed, since he received no interest or other advantage unless they were so used. Some purchasers doubtless viewed their purchase of the notes as being, to all intents and purposes, an advance payment of the taxes.

3. In the absence of evidence of a contrary intent, it was considered acceptable, and in accordance with good accounting practice, to show the notes in the current liability section of the balance sheet as a deduction from federal taxes on income in an amount not to exceed the accrued liability for such taxes. The full amount of the accrued liability was to be shown with a deduction for the tax payment value of the notes at the date of the balance sheet.

4. It also was recognized as clearly proper to show the notes in the current asset section of the balance sheet as any other temporary investments are shown. If at the balance-sheet date or at the date of

the independent auditor's report there was evidence that the original intent was changed, the notes were to be shown in the current asset section of the balance sheet.

5. Government securities having restrictive terms similar to those contained in the 1943 tax series notes are no longer issued, although certain other types of government securities have since been issued which are acceptable in payment of liabilities for federal taxes on income. However, because of the effect on the current position of large tax accruals and the related accumulations of liquid assets to meet such liabilities, many companies have adopted the practice of acquiring and holding government securities of various issues in amounts related to the estimated tax liability. In their financial statements these companies have often expressed this relationship by showing such securities as a deduction from the tax liability, even though the particular securities were not by their terms acceptable in payment of taxes. If the government securities involved may, by their terms, be surrendered in payment of taxes, the above practice clearly falls within the principle of the permissive exception described in paragraph 1. The committee further believes that the extension of the practice to include the offset of other types of United States government securities, although a deviation from the general rule against offsets, is not so significant a deviation as to call for an exception in an accountant's report on the financial statements.

6. Suggestions have been received that similar considerations may be advanced in favor of the offset of cash or other assets against the income and excess profits tax liability or against other amounts owing to the federal government. In the opinion of the committee, however, any such extension or application of the exception, recognized as to United States government securities and liabilities for federal taxes on income, is not to be regarded as acceptable practice.

One member of the committee, Mr. Calkins, assented with qualification to adoption of section B of chapter 3.

Mr. Calkins does not approve the concluding sentence of paragraph 5, which states that the offset of other types of United States Government securities, although a deviation from the general rule against offsets, is not so significant a deviation as to call for an exception in an accountant's report. He believes that the significance of such a deviation is a matter for judgment based on the facts of a particular case; that the broader language of the statement constitutes a condonation of the practice of offsetting against tax liabilities United States Government obligations which are not by their terms acceptable in payment of federal taxes; and that the condonation of such a practice is inconsistent with the opinion of the committee expressed in paragraph 6, with which he agrees, that cash and other assets should not be offset against liabilities for federal taxes.

Chapter 4

INVENTORY PRICING

1. Whenever the operation of a business includes the ownership of a stock of goods, it is necessary for adequate financial accounting purposes that inventories be properly compiled periodically and recorded in the accounts.[1] Such inventories are required both for the statement of financial position and for the periodic measurement of income.

2. This chapter sets forth the general principles applicable to the pricing of inventories of mercantile and manufacturing enterprises. Its conclusions are not directed to or necessarily applicable to noncommercial businesses or to regulated utilities.

Statement 1

The term *inventory* is used herein to designate the aggregate of those items of tangible personal property which (1) are held for sale in the ordinary course of business, (2) are in process of production for such sale, or (3) are to be currently consumed in the production of goods or services to be available for sale.

Discussion

3. The term *inventory* embraces goods awaiting sale (the merchandise of a trading concern and the finished goods of a manufacturer), goods in the course of production (work in process), and goods to be consumed directly or indirectly in production (raw materials and supplies). This definition of inventories excludes long-term assets subject to depreciation accounting, or goods which, when put into use, will be so classified. The fact that a depreciable asset is retired from regular use and held for sale does not indicate that the item should be classified as part of the inventory. Raw materials and supplies purchased for production may be used or consumed for the construction of long-term assets or other purposes not related to production, but the fact that inventory items representing a small portion of the total may not be absorbed ultimately in the production process does not require separate classification. By trade practice, operating materials

and supplies of certain types of companies such as oil producers are usually treated as inventory.

Statement 2

A major objective of accounting for inventories is the proper determination of income through the process of matching appropriate costs against revenues.

Discussion

4. An inventory has financial significance because revenues may be obtained from its sale, or from the sale of the goods or services in whose production it is used. Normally such revenues arise in a continuous repetitive process or cycle of operations by which goods are acquired and sold, and further goods are acquired for additional sales. In accounting for the goods in the inventory at any point of time, the major objective is the matching of appropriate costs against revenues in order that there may be a proper determination of the realized income. Thus, the inventory at any given date is the balance of costs applicable to goods on hand remaining after the matching of absorbed costs with concurrent revenues. This balance is appropriately carried to future periods provided it does not exceed an amount properly chargeable against the revenues expected to be obtained from ultimate disposition of the goods carried forward. In practice, this balance is determined by the process of pricing the articles comprised in the inventory.

Statement 3

The primary basis of accounting for inventories is cost, which has been defined generally as the price paid or consideration given to acquire an asset. As applied to inventories, cost means in principle the sum of the applicable expenditures and charges directly or indirectly incurred in bringing an article to its existing condition and location.

Discussion

5. In keeping with the principle that accounting is primarily based on cost, there is a presumption that inventories should be stated at cost. The definition of cost as applied to inventories is understood to mean acquisition and production cost,[2] and its determination involves many problems. Although principles for the determination of inventory costs may be easily stated, their application, particularly to such inventory items as work in process and

---

[1] Prudent reliance upon perpetual inventory records is not precluded.

[2] In the case of goods which have been written down below cost at the close of a fiscal period, such reduced amount is to be considered the cost for subsequent accounting purposes.

finished goods, is difficult because of the variety of problems encountered in the allocation of costs and charges. For example, under some circumstances, items such as idle facility expense, excessive spoilage, double freight, and rehandling costs may be so abnormal as to require treatment as current period charges rather than as a portion of the inventory cost. Also, general and administrative expenses should be included as period charges, except for the portion of such expenses that may be clearly related to production and thus constitute a part of inventory costs (product charges). Selling expenses constitute no part of inventory costs. It should also be recognized that the exclusion of all overheads from inventory costs does not constitute an accepted accounting procedure. The exercise of judgment in an individual situation involves a consideration of the adequacy of the procedures of the cost accounting system in use, the soundness of the principles thereof, and their consistent application.

Statement 4

Cost for inventory purposes may be determined under any one of several assumptions as to the flow of cost factors (such as first-in first-out, average, and last-in first-out); the major objective in selecting a method should be to choose the one which, under the circumstances, most clearly reflects periodic income.

Discussion

6. The cost to be matched against revenue from a sale may not be the identified cost of the specific item which is sold, especially in cases in which similar goods are purchased at different times and at different prices. While in some lines of business specific lots are clearly identified from the time of purchase through the time of sale and are costed on this basis, ordinarily the identity of goods is lost between the time of acquisition and the time of sale. In any event, if the materials purchased in various lots are identical and interchangeable, the use of identified cost of the various lots may not produce the most useful financial statements. This fact has resulted in the development of general acceptance of several assumptions with respect to the flow of cost factors (such as *first-in first-out, average,* and *last-in first-out*) to provide practical bases for the measurement of periodic income.[3] In some situations a reversed mark-up procedure of inventory pricing, such as the retail inventory method, may be both

practical and appropriate. The business operations in some cases may be such as to make it desirable to apply one of the acceptable methods of determining cost to one portion of the inventory or components thereof and another of the acceptable methods to other portions of the inventory.

7. Although selection of the method should be made on the basis of the individual circumstances, it is obvious that financial statements will be more useful if uniform methods of inventory pricing are adopted by all companies within a given industry.

Statement 5

A departure from the cost basis of pricing the inventory is required when the utility of the goods is no longer as great as its cost. Where there is evidence that the utility of goods, in their disposal in the ordinary course of business, will be less than cost, whether due to physical deterioration, obsolescence, changes in price levels, or other causes, the difference should be recognized as a loss of the current period. This is generally accomplished by stating such goods at a lower level commonly designated as *market*.

Discussion

8. Although the cost basis ordinarily achieves the objective of a proper matching of costs and revenues, under certain circumstances cost may not be the amount properly chargeable against the revenues of future periods. A departure from cost is required in these circumstances because cost is satisfactory only if the utility of the goods has not diminished since their acquisition; a loss of utility is to be reflected as a charge against the revenues of the period in which it occurs. Thus, in accounting for inventories, a loss should be recognized whenever the utility of goods is impaired by damage, deterioration, obsolescence, changes in price levels, or other causes. The measurement of such losses is accomplished by applying the rule of pricing inventories at *cost or market, whichever is lower.* This provides a practical means of measuring utility and thereby determining the amount of the loss to be recognized and accounted for in the current period.

Statement 6

As used in the phrase *lower of cost or market*[4] the term *market* means current replacement cost

---

[3]Standard costs are acceptable if adjusted at reasonable intervals to reflect current conditions so that at the balance-sheet date standard costs reasonably approximate costs computed under one of the recognized bases. In such cases descriptive language should be used which will express this relationship, as, for instance, "approximate costs determined on the first-in first-out basis," or, if it is desired to mention standard costs, "at standard costs, approximating average costs."

[4]The terms *cost or market, whichever is lower* and *lower of cost or market* are used synonymously in general practice and in this chapter. The committee does not express any preference for either of the two alternatives.

(by purchase or by reproduction, as the case may be) except that:

(1) Market should not exceed the net realizable value (i.e., estimated selling price in the ordinary course of business less reasonably predictable costs of completion and disposal); and
(2) Market should not be less than net realizable value reduced by an allowance for an approximately normal profit margin.

Discussion

9. The rule of *cost or market, whichever is lower* is intended to provide a means of measuring the residual usefulness of an inventory expenditure. The term *market* is therefore to be interpreted as indicating utility on the inventory date and may be thought of in terms of the equivalent expenditure which would have to be made in the ordinary course at that date to procure corresponding utility. As a general guide, utility is indicated primarily by the current cost of replacement of the goods as they would be obtained by purchase or reproduction. In applying the rule, however, judgment must always be exercised and no loss should be recognized unless the evidence indicates clearly that a loss has been sustained. There are therefore exceptions to such a standard. Replacement or reproduction prices would not be appropriate as a measure of utility when the estimated sales value, reduced by the costs of completion and disposal, is lower, in which case the realizable value so determined more appropriately measures utility. Furthermore, where the evidence indicates that cost will be recovered with an approximately normal profit upon sale in the ordinary course of business, no loss should be recognized even though replacement or reproduction costs are lower. This might be true, for example, in the case of production under firm sales contracts at fixed prices, or when a reasonable volume of future orders is assured at stable selling prices.

10. Because of the many variations of circumstances encountered in inventory pricing, Statement 6 is intended as a guide rather than a literal rule. It should be applied realistically in the light of the objectives expressed in this chapter and with due regard to the form, content, and composition of the inventory. The committee considers, for example, that the retail inventory method, if adequate markdowns are currently taken, accomplishes the objectives described herein. It also recognizes that, if a business is expected to lose money for a sustained period, the inventory should not be written down to offset a loss inherent in the subsequent operations.

Statement 7

Depending on the character and composition of the inventory, the rule of *cost or market, whichever is lower* may properly be applied either directly to each item or to the total of the inventory (or, in some cases, to the total of the components of each major category). The method should be that which most clearly reflects periodic income.

Discussion

11. The purpose of reducing inventory to *market* is to reflect fairly the income of the period. The most common practice is to apply the *lower of cost or market* rule separately to each item of the inventory. However, if there is only one end-product category the cost utility of the total stock—the inventory in its entirety—may have the greatest significance for accounting purposes. Accordingly, the reduction of individual items to *market* may not always lead to the most useful result if the utility of the total inventory to the business is not below its cost. This might be the case if selling prices are not affected by temporary or small fluctuations in current costs of purchase or manufacture. Similarly, where more than one major product or operational category exists, the application of the *cost or market, whichever is lower* rule to the total of the items included in such major categories may result in the most useful determination of income.

12. When no loss of income is expected to take place as a result of a reduction of cost prices of certain goods because others forming components of the same general categories of finished products have a market equally in excess of cost, such components need not be adjusted to market to the extent that they are in balanced quantities. Thus, in such cases, the rule of *cost or market, whichever is lower* may be applied directly to the totals of the entire inventory, rather than to the individual inventory items, if they enter into the same category of finished product and if they are in balanced quantities, provided the procedure is applied consistently from year to year.

13. To the extent, however, that the stocks of particular materials or components are excessive in relation to others, the more widely recognized procedure of applying the *lower of cost or market* to the individual items constituting the excess should be followed. This would also apply in cases in which the items enter into the production of unrelated products or products having a material variation in the rate of turnover. Unless an effective method of classifying categories is practicable, the rule should

be applied to each item in the inventory.

14. When substantial and unusual losses result from the application of this rule it will frequently be desirable to disclose the amount of the loss in the income statement as a charge separately identified from the consumed inventory costs described as *cost of goods sold.*

Statement 8

The basis of stating inventories must be consistently applied and should be disclosed in the financial statements; whenever a significant change is made therein, there should be disclosure of the nature of the change and, if material, the effect on income.

Discussion

15. While the basis of stating inventories does not affect the over-all gain or loss on the ultimate disposition of inventory items, any inconsistency in the selection or employment of a basis may improperly affect the periodic amounts of income or loss. Because of the common use and importance of periodic statements, a procedure adopted for the treatment of inventory items should be consistently applied in order that the results reported may be fairly allocated as between years. A change of such basis may have an important effect upon the interpretation of the financial statements both before and after that change, and hence, in the event of a change, a full disclosure of its nature and of its effect, if material, upon income should be made.

Statement 9

Only in exceptional cases may inventories properly be stated above cost. For example, precious metals having a fixed monetary value with no substantial cost of marketing may be stated at such monetary value; any other exceptions must be justifiable by inability to determine appropriate approximate costs, immediate marketability at quoted market price, and the characteristic of unit interchangeability. Where goods are stated above cost this fact should be fully disclosed.

Discussion

16. It is generally recognized that income accrues only at the time of sale, and that gains may not be anticipated by reflecting assets at their current sales prices. For certain articles, however, exceptions are permissible. Inventories of gold and silver, when there is an effective government-controlled market at a fixed monetary value, are ordinarily reflected at selling prices. A similar treatment is not uncommon for inventories representing agricultural, mineral,

and other products, units of which are interchangeable and have an immediate marketability at quoted prices and for which appropriate costs may be difficult to obtain. Where such inventories are stated at sales prices, they should of course be reduced by expenditures to be incurred in disposal, and the use of such basis should be fully disclosed in the financial statements.

Statement 10

Accrued net losses on firm purchase commitments for goods for inventory, measured in the same way as are inventory losses, should, if material, be recognized in the accounts and the amounts thereof separately disclosed in the income statement.

Discussion

17. The recognition in a current period of losses arising from the decline in the utility of cost expenditures is equally applicable to similar losses which are expected to arise from firm, uncancelable, and unhedged commitments for the future purchase of inventory items. The net loss on such commitments should be measured in the same way as are inventory losses and, if material, should be recognized in the accounts and separately disclosed in the income statement. The utility of such commitments is not impaired, and hence there is no loss, when the amounts to be realized from the disposition of the future inventory items are adequately protected by firm sales contracts or when there are other circumstances which reasonably assure continuing sales without price decline.

One member of the committee, Mr. Wellington, assented with qualification, and two members, Messrs. Mason and Peloubet, dissented to adoption of chapter 4.

Mr. Wellington objects to footnote (2) to statement 3. He believes that an exception should be made for goods costed on the *last-in first-out* (LIFO) basis. In the case of goods costed on all bases other than LIFO the reduced amount (market below cost) is cleared from the accounts through the regular accounting entries of the subsequent period, and if the market price rises to or above the original cost there will be an increased profit in the subsequent period. Accounts kept under the LIFO method should also show a similar increased profit in the subsequent period, which will be shown if the LIFO inventory is restored to its original cost. To do otherwise, as required by footnote (2), is to carry the LIFO inventory, not at the lower of cost or current market, but at the lowest market ever known since the LIFO method was adopted by the company.

Mr. Mason dissents from this chapter because of

its acceptance of the inconsistencies inherent in *cost or market whichever is lower.* In his opinion a drop in selling price below cost is no more of a realized loss than a rise above cost is a realized gain under a consistent criterion of realization.

Mr. Peloubet believes it is ordinarily preferable to carry inventory at not less than recoverable cost, and particularly in the case of manufactured or partially manufactured goods which can be sold only in finished form. He recognizes that application of the *cost or market* valuation basis necessitates the shifting of income from one period to another, but objects to unnecessarily accentuating this shift by the use, even limited as it is in this chapter, of reproduction or replacement cost as *market* when such cost is less than net selling price.

Chapter 5

INTANGIBLE ASSETS

1. This chapter deals with problems involved in accounting for certain types of assets classified by accountants as intangibles, specifically, those acquired by the issuance of securities or purchased for cash or other consideration. Such assets may be purchased or acquired separately for a specified consideration or may be purchased or acquired, together with other assets, for a lump-sum consideration without specification by either the seller or the purchaser, at the time of purchase, of the portions of the total price which are applicable to the respective assets thus acquired. In dealing with the intangible assets herein considered, important questions arise as to the initial carrying amount of such assets, the amortization of such amount where their term of existence is definitely limited or problematical, and their write-down or write-off at some later time where there is a substantial and permanent decline in the value of such assets. These questions involve basic accounting principles of balance-sheet presentation and income determination and this chapter is designed to promote a fuller consideration of those principles. It does not, however, deal with the problems of accounting for intangibles developed in the regular course of business by research, experimentation, advertising, or otherwise.

Classification of Intangibles

2. The intangibles herein considered may be broadly classified as follows:

a. Those having a term of existence limited by law, regulation, or agreement, or by their nature (such as patents, copyrights, leases, licenses, franchises for a fixed term, and goodwill as to which there is evidence of limited duration);
b. Those having no such limited term of existence and as to which there is, at the time of acquisition, no indication of limited life (such as goodwill generally, going value, trade names, secret processes, subscription lists, perpetual franchises, and organization costs).

3. The intangibles described above will hereinafter be referred to as type (a) and type (b) intangibles, respectively. The portion of a lump-sum consideration deemed to have been paid for intangible elements when a mixed aggregate of tangible and intangible property is acquired, or the excess of a parent company's investment in the stock of a subsidiary over its equity in the net assets of the subsidiary as shown by the latter's books at the date of acquisition, in so far as that excess would be treated as an intangible in consolidated financial statements of the parent and the subsidiary, may represent intangibles of either type (a) or type (b) or a combination of both.

Initial Carrying Amount

4. The initial amount assigned to all types of intangibles should be cost, in accordance with the generally accepted accounting principle that assets should be stated at cost when they are acquired. In the case of non-cash acquisitions, as, for example, where intangibles are acquired in exchange for securities, cost may be considered as being either the fair value of the consideration given or the fair value of the property or right acquired, whichever is the more clearly evident.

Amortization of Intangibles

Type (a)

5. The cost of type (a) intangibles should be amortized by systematic charges in the income statement over the period benefited, as in the case of other assets having a limited period of usefulness. If it becomes evident that the period benefited will be longer or shorter than originally estimated, recognition thereof may take the form of an appropriate decrease or increase in the rate of amortization or, if such increased charges would result in distortion of income, a partial write-down may be made by a charge to earned surplus.

Type (b)

6. When it becomes reasonably evident that the term of existence of a type (b) intangible has become limited and that it has therefore become a type (a) intangible, its cost should be amortized by systematic charges in the income statement over the estimated remaining period of usefulness. If, however, the period of amortization is relatively short so that misleading inferences might be drawn as a result of inclusion of substantial charges in the income state-

ment a partial write-down may be made by a charge to earned surplus,[1] and the rest of the cost may be amortized over the remaining period of usefulness.

7. When a corporation decides that a type (b) intangible may not continue to have value during the entire life of the enterprise it may amortize the cost of such intangible by systematic charges against income despite the fact that there are no present indications of limited existence or loss of value which would indicate that it has become type (a), and despite the fact that expenditures are being made to maintain its value. Such amortization is within the discretion of the company and is not to be regarded as obligatory. The plan of amortization should be reasonable; it should be based on all the surrounding circumstances, including the basic nature of the intangible and the expenditures currently being made for development, experimentation, and sales promotion. Where the intangible is an important income-producing factor and is currently being maintained by advertising or otherwise, the period of amortization should be reasonably long. The procedure should be formally approved and the reason for amortization, the rate used, and the shareholders' or directors' approval thereof should be disclosed in the financial statements.

Write-off of Intangibles

8. The cost of type (b) intangibles should be written off when it becomes reasonably evident that they have become worthless. Under such circumstances the amount at which they are carried on the books should be charged off in the income statement or, if the amount is so large that its effect on income may give rise to misleading inferences, it should be charged to earned surplus.[1] In determining whether an investment in type (b) intangibles has become or is likely to become worthless, consideration should be given to the fact that in some cases intangibles acquired by purchase may merge with, or be replaced by, intangibles acquired or developed with respect to other products or lines of business and that in such circumstances the discontinuance of a product or line of business may not in fact indicate loss of value.

Limitation on Write-off of Intangibles

9. Lump-sum write-offs of intangibles should not be made to earned surplus immediately after acquisition, nor should intangibles be charged against capital surplus. If not amortized systematically, intangibles should be carried at cost until an event has taken place which indicates a loss or a limitation on the useful life of the intangibles.

Purchase of Subsidiary's Stock or Basket Purchase of Assets

10. A problem arises in cases where a group of intangibles or a mixed aggregate of tangible and intangible property is acquired for a lump-sum consideration, or when the consideration given for a stock investment in a subsidiary is greater than the net assets of such subsidiary applicable thereto, as carried on its books at the date of acquisition. In this latter type of situation there is a presumption that the parent company, in effect, placed a valuation greater than their carrying amount on some of the assets of the subsidiary in arriving at the price it was willing to pay for its investment therein. The parent corporation may have (a) paid amounts in excess of carrying amounts for specific assets of the subsidiary or (b) paid for the general goodwill of the subsidiary. In these cases, if practicable, there should be an allocation, as between tangible and intangible property, of the cost of the mixed aggregate of property or of the excess of a parent's investment over its share of the amount at which the subsidiary carried its net assets on its books at the date of acquisition. Any amount allocated to intangibles should be further allocated to determine, if practicable, a separate cost for each type (a) intangible and for at least the aggregate of all type (b) intangibles. The amounts so allocated to intangibles should thereafter be dealt with in accordance with the procedures outlined in this chapter.

Chapter 6

CONTINGENCY RESERVES

[Totally superseded; refer to the status page of this pronouncement.]

---

[1]See chapter 8, paragraphs 11, 12, and 13.

(This page intentionally left blank.)

Chapter 7

CAPITAL ACCOUNTS

Section A—Quasi-Reorganization or Corporate Readjustment (Amplification of Institute Rule No. 2 of 1934)

1. A rule was adopted by the Institute in 1934 which read as follows:

> "Capital surplus, however created, should not be used to relieve the income account of the current or future years of charges which would otherwise fall to be made thereagainst. This rule might be subject to the exception that where, upon reorganization, a reorganized company would be relieved of charges which would require to be made against income if the existing corporation were continued, it might be regarded as permissible to accomplish the same result without reorganization provided the facts were as fully revealed to and the action as formally approved by the shareholders as in reorganization."[1]

2. Readjustments of the kind mentioned in the exception to the rule fall in the category of what are called quasi-reorganizations. This section does not deal with the general question of quasi-reorganizations, but only with cases in which the exception permitted under the rule of 1934 is availed of by a corporation. Hereinafter such cases are referred to as readjustments. The problems which arise fall into two groups: (a) what may be permitted in a readjustment and (b) what may be permitted thereafter.

Procedure in Readjustment

3. If a corporation elects to restate its assets, capital stock, and surplus through a readjustment and thus avail itself of permission to relieve its future income account or earned surplus account of charges which would otherwise be made thereagainst, it should make a clear report to its shareholders of the restatements proposed to be made, and obtain their formal consent. It should present a fair balance sheet as at the date of the readjustment, in which the adjustment of carrying amounts is reasonably complete, in order that there may be no continuation of the circumstances which justify charges to capital surplus.

4. A write-down of assets below amounts which are likely to be realized thereafter, though it may result in conservatism in the balance sheet at the readjustment date, may also result in overstatement of earnings or of earned surplus when the assets are subsequently realized. Therefore, in general, assets should be carried forward as of the date of readjustment at fair and not unduly conservative amounts, determined with due regard for the accounting to be employed by the company thereafter. If the fair value of any asset is not readily determinable a conservative estimate may be made, but in that case the amount should be described as an estimate and any material difference arising through realization or otherwise and not attributable to events occurring or circumstances arising after that date should not be carried to income or earned surplus.

5. Similarly, if potential losses or charges are known to have arisen prior to the date of readjustment but the amounts thereof are then indeterminate, provision may properly be made to cover the maximum *probable* losses or charges. If the amounts provided are subsequently found to have been excessive or insufficient, the difference should not be carried to earned surplus nor used to offset losses or gains originating after the readjustment, but should be carried to capital surplus.

6. When the amounts to be written off in a readjustment have been determined, they should be charged first against earned surplus to the full extent of such surplus; any balance may then be charged against capital surplus. A company which has subsidiaries should apply this rule in such a way that no consolidated earned surplus survives a readjustment in which any part of losses has been charged to capital surplus.

7. If the earned surplus of any subsidiaries cannot be applied against the losses before resort is had to capital surplus, the parent company's interest in such earned surplus should be regarded as capitalized by the readjustment just as surplus at the date of acquisition is capitalized, so far as the parent is concerned.

8. The effective date of the readjustment, from which the income of the company is thereafter determined, should be as near as practicable to the date on which formal consent of the stockholders is given, and should ordinarily not be prior to the close of the last completed fiscal year.

Procedure after Readjustment

9. When the readjustment has been completed, the company's accounting should be substantially similar to that appropriate for a new company.

10. After such a readjustment earned surplus previously accumulated cannot properly be carried

---

[1]See chapter 1A, paragraph 2.

forward under that title. A new earned surplus account should be established, dated to show that it runs from the effective date of the readjustment, and this dating should be disclosed in financial statements until such time as the effective date is no longer deemed to possess any special significance.

11. Capital surplus originating in such a readjustment is restricted in the same manner as that of a new corporation; charges against it should be only those which may properly be made against the initial surplus of a new corporation.

12. It is recognized that charges against capital surplus may take place in other types of readjustments to which the foregoing provisions would have no application. Such cases would include readjustments for the purpose of correcting erroneous credits made to capital surplus in the past. In this statement the committee has dealt only with that type of readjustment in which either the current income or earned surplus account or the income account of future years is relieved of charges which would otherwise be made thereagainst.

Section B—Stock Dividends and Stock Split-ups

1. The term *stock dividend* as used in this section refers to an issuance by a corporation of its own common shares to its common shareholders without consideration and under conditions indicating that such action is prompted mainly by a desire to give the recipient shareholders some ostensibly separate evidence of a part of their respective interests in accumulated corporate earnings without distribution of cash or other property which the board of directors deems necessary or desirable to retain in the business.

2. The term *stock split-up* as used in this chapter refers to an issuance by a corporation of its own common shares to its common shareholders without consideration and under conditions indicating that such action is prompted mainly by a desire to increase the number of outstanding shares for the purpose of effecting a reduction in their unit market price and, thereby, of obtaining wider distribution and improved marketability of the shares.

3. This chapter is not concerned with the accounting for a distribution or issuance to shareholders of (a) shares of another corporation theretofore held as an investment, or (b) shares of a different class, or (c) rights to subscribe for additional shares or (d) shares of the same class in cases where each shareholder is given an election to receive cash or shares.

4. The discussion of accounting for stock dividends and split-ups that follows is divided into two parts. The first deals with the problems of the recipient. The second deals with the problems of the issuer.

As to the Recipient

5. One of the basic problems of accounting is that of income determination. Complete discussion of this problem is obviously beyond the scope of this chapter. Basically, income is a realized gain and in accounting is recognized, recorded, and stated in accordance with certain principles as to time and amount.

6. In applying the principles of income determination to the accounts of a shareholder of a corporation, it is generally agreed that the problem of determining his income is distinct from the problem of income determination by the corporation itself. The income of the corporation is determined as that of a separate entity without regard to the equity of the respective shareholders in such income. Under conventional accounting concepts, the shareholder has no income solely as a result of the fact that the corporation has income; the increase in his equity through undistributed earnings is no more than potential income to him. It is true that income earned by the corporation may result in an enhancement in the market value of the shares, but until there is a distribution, division, or severance of corporate assets, the shareholder has no income. If there is an increase in the market value of his holdings, such unrealized appreciation is not income. In the case of a stock dividend or split-up, there is no distribution, division, or severance of corporate assets. Moreover, there is nothing resulting therefrom that the shareholder can realize without parting with some of his proportionate interest in the corporation.

7. The foregoing are important points to be considered in any discussion of the accounting procedures to be followed by the recipient of a stock dividend or split-up since many arguments put forward by those who favor recognizing stock dividends as income are in substance arguments for the recognition of corporate income as income to the shareholder as it accrues to the corporation, and prior to its distribution to the shareholder; the acceptance of such arguments would require the abandonment of the *separate entity* concept of corporation accounting.

8. The question as to whether or not stock dividends are income has been extensively debated; the arguments pro and con are well known.[1] The situation cannot be better summarized, however, than in

[1]See, for instance, Freeman, "Stock Dividends and the New York Stock Exchange," *American Economic Review,* December, 1931 (pro), and Whitaker, "Stock Dividends, Investment Trusts, and the Exchange," *American Economic Review,* June, 1931 (con).

the words approved by Mr. Justice Pitney in *Eisner v. Macomber,* 252 U.S. 189, wherein it was held that stock dividends are not income under the Sixteenth Amendment, as follows:

> "A stock dividend really takes nothing from the property of the corporation and adds nothing to the interests of the stockholders. Its property is not diminished and their interests are not increased . . . the proportional interest of each shareholder remains the same. The only change is in the evidence which represents that interest, the new shares and the original shares together representing the same proportional interests that the original shares represented before the issue of the new ones."

9. Since a shareholder's interest in the corporation remains unchanged by a stock dividend or split-up except as to the number of share units constituting such interest, the cost of the shares previously held should be allocated equitably to the total shares held after receipt of the stock dividend or split-up. When any shares are later disposed of, a gain or loss should be determined on the basis of the adjusted cost per share.

As to the Issuer

Stock dividends

10. As has been previously stated, a stock dividend does not, in fact, give rise to any change whatsoever in either the corporation's assets or its respective shareholders' proportionate interests therein. However, it cannot fail to be recognized that, merely as a consequence of the expressed purpose of the transaction and its characterization as a *dividend* in related notices to shareholders and the public at large, many recipients of stock dividends look upon them as distributions of corporate earnings and usually in an amount equivalent to the fair value of the additional shares received. Furthermore, it is to be presumed that such views of recipients are materially strengthened in those instances, which are by far the most numerous, where the issuances are so small in comparison with the shares previously outstanding that they do not have any apparent effect upon the share market price and, consequently, the market value of the shares previously held remains substantially unchanged. The committee therefore believes that where these circumstances exist the corporation should in the public interest account for the transaction by transferring from earned surplus to the category of permanent capitalization (represented by the capital stock and capital surplus accounts) an amount equal to the fair value of the additional shares issued. Unless this is done, the amount of earnings which the shareholder may believe to have been distributed to him will be left, except to the extent otherwise dictated by legal requirements, in earned surplus subject to possible further similar stock issuances or cash distributions.

11. Where the number of additional shares issued as a stock dividend is so great that it has, or may reasonably be expected to have, the effect of materially reducing the share market value, the committee believes that the implications and possible constructions discussed in the preceding paragraph are not likely to exist and that the transaction clearly partakes of the nature of a stock split-up as defined in paragraph 2. Consequently, the committee considers that under such circumstances there is no need to capitalize earned surplus, other than to the extent occasioned by legal requirements. It recommends, however, that in such instances every effort be made to avoid the use of the word *dividend* in related corporate resolutions, notices, and announcements and that, in those cases where because of legal requirements this cannot be done, the transaction be described, for example, as a *split-up effected in the form of a dividend.*

12. In cases of closely-held companies, it is to be presumed that the intimate knowledge of the corporations' affairs possessed by their shareholders would preclude any such implications and possible constructions as are referred to in paragraph 10. In such cases, the committee believes that considerations of public policy do not arise and that there is no need to capitalize earned surplus other than to meet legal requirements.

13. Obviously, the point at which the relative size of the additional shares issued becomes large enough to materially influence the unit market price of the stock will vary with individual companies and under differing market conditions and, hence, no single percentage can be laid down as a standard for determining when capitalization of earned surplus in excess of legal requirements is called for and when it is not. However, on the basis of a review of market action in the case of shares of a number of companies having relatively recent stock distributions, it would appear that there would be few instances involving the issuance of additional shares of less than, say, 20% or 25% of the number previously outstanding where the effect would not be such as to call for the procedure referred to in paragraph 10.

14. The corporate accounting recommended in paragraph 10 will in many cases, probably the majority, result in the capitalization of earned surplus in an amount in excess of that called for by the laws of the state of incorporation; such laws generally require the capitalization only of the par value of the shares issued, or, in the case of shares without par value, an amount usually within the discretion of the board of directors. However, these legal requirements are, in effect, minimum requirements and do not prevent the capitalization of a larger amount per share.

Stock Split-ups

15. Earlier in this chapter a stock split-up was defined as being confined to transactions involving the issuance of shares, without consideration moving to the corporation, for the purpose of effecting a reduction in the unit market price of shares of the class issued and, thus, of obtaining wider distribution and improved marketability of the shares. Where this is clearly the intent, no transfer from earned surplus to capital surplus or capital stock account is called for, other than to the extent occasioned by legal requirements. It is believed, however, that few cases will arise where the aforementioned purpose can be accomplished through an issuance of shares which is less than, say, 20% or 25% of the previously outstanding shares.

16. The committee believes that the corporation's representations to its shareholders as to the nature of the issuance is one of the principal considerations in determining whether it should be recorded as a stock dividend or a split-up. Nevertheless, it believes that the issuance of new shares in ratios of less than, say, 20% or 25% of the previously outstanding shares, or the frequent recurrence of issuances of shares, would destroy the presumption that transactions represented to be split-ups should be recorded as split-ups.

Three members of the committee, Messrs. Knight, Calkins, and Mason, assented with qualification, and one member, Mr. Wilcox, dissented to adoption of section B of chapter 7.

Mr. Knight assents with the qualification that he believes the section should recognize the propriety of treating as income stock dividends received by a parent from a subsidiary. He believes the section should have retained from the original Bulletin No. 11 the statement, "It is recognized that this rule, under which the stockholder has no income until there is a distribution, division, or severance, may require modification in some cases, or that there may be exceptions to it, as, for instance, in the case of a parent company with respect to its subsidiaries. . . ."

Messrs. Calkins and Mason approve part one, but believe part two is inconsistent therewith in that the former concludes that a stock dividend is not income to the recipient while the latter suggests accounting procedures by the issuer based on the assumption that the shareholder may think otherwise. They believe it is inappropriate for the corporate entity to base its accounting on considerations of possible shareholder reactions. They also

believe that part two deals with matters of corporate policy rather than accounting principles and that the purpose sought to be served could be more effectively accomplished by appropriate notices to shareholders at the time of the issuance of additional shares.

Mr. Wilcox dissents from the recommendations made both as to the recipient and as to the issuer. He believes that, with proper safeguards, stock dividends should be regarded as marking the point at which corporate income is to be recognized by shareholders, and denies that the arguments favoring this view are in substance arguments for the recognition of corporate income as income to the shareholder as it accrues to the corporation. He believes that the arguments regarding severance and maintenance of proportionate interest are unsound, and cannot logically be invoked as they are in this section, since they are widely ignored with respect to distributions of securities other than common stock dividends. Mr. Wilcox believes the recommendations as to the issuer are inconsistent with the rest of the section, involve arbitrary distinctions, hamper or discourage desirable corporate actions, result in meaningless segregation in the proprietorship section of balance sheets, and serve no informative purpose which cannot be better served by explanatory disclosures. He therefore also dissents from the omission of requirements for information and disclosures which were contained in the original Bulletin No. 11 issued in September, 1941.

Section C—Business Combinations

1. Whenever two or more corporations are brought together, or combined, for the purpose of carrying on in a single corporation the previously conducted businesses, the accounting to give effect to the combination will vary depending upon whether there is a continuance of the former ownership or a new ownership.[1] This section (a) differentiates these two types of corporate combinations, the first of which is designated herein as a *pooling of interests* and the second as a *purchase;* and (b) indicates the nature of the accounting treatment appropriate to each type.

2. For accounting purposes, the distinction between a pooling of interests and a purchase is to be found in the attendant circumstances rather than in the legal designation as a merger or a consolidation, or in legal considerations with respect to availability of net assets for dividends, or provisions of the Internal Revenue Code with respect to income taxes. In a pooling of interests, all or substantially all of the equity interests in predecessor corporations continue, as such, in a surviving corporation[1] which

---

[1] When the shares of stock in the surviving corporation that are received by the several owners of one of the predecessor companies are not substantially in proportion to their respective interests in the predecessor company, a new ownership or purchase of such company is presumed to result.

may be one of the predecessor corporations, or in a new one created for the purpose. In a purchase, on the other hand, an important part or all of the ownership of the acquired corporation is eliminated. A plan or firm intention and understanding to retire capital stock issued to the owners of one or more of the corporate parties, or substantial changes in ownership occurring immediately before or after the combination, would also tend to indicate that the combination is a purchase.

3. Other factors to be taken into consideration in determining whether a purchase or a pooling of interests is involved are the relative size of the constituent companies and the continuity of management or power to control the management. Thus, a purchase may be indicated when one corporate party to a combination is quite minor in size in relation to the others, or where the management of one of the corporate parties to the combination is eliminated or its influence upon the management of the surviving corporation is very small. Other things being equal, the presumption that a pooling of interests is involved would be strengthened if the activities of the businesses to be combined are either similar or complementary. No one of these factors would necessarily be determinative, but their presence or absence would be cumulative in effect.

4. When a combination is deemed to be a purchase the assets purchased should be recorded on the books of the acquiring company at cost, measured in money or the fair value of other consideration given, or at the fair value of the property acquired, whichever is more clearly evident. This is in accordance with the procedure applicable to accounting for purchases of assets.

5. When a combination is deemed to be a pooling of interests, the necessity for a new basis of accountability does not arise. The carrying amounts of the assets of the constituent companies, if stated in conformity with generally accepted accounting principles and appropriately adjusted when deemed necessary to place them on a uniform basis, should be carried forward; and earned surpluses of the constituent companies may be carried forward. However, any adjustment of assets or of surplus which would be in conformity with generally accepted accounting principles in the absence of a combination would be equally so if effected in connection with a pooling of interests. If one party to such a combination had been acquired by purchase as a subsidiary by another such party prior to the origin of a plan of combination, the parent's share of the earned surplus of the subsidiary prior to such acquisition should not be included in the earned surplus account of the pooled companies.

6. Because of the variety of conditions under which a pooling of interests may be carried out it is not practicable to deal with the accounting presentation except in general terms. A number of problems will arise. For example, the stated capital of the surviving corporation in a pooling of interests may be either more than, or less than, the total of the stated capital of the predecessor corporations. In the former event the excess should be deducted first from the total of any other contributed capital (capital surplus), and next from the total of any earned surplus of the predecessors, while in the latter event the difference should appear in the balance sheet of the surviving corporation as other contributed capital (capital surplus), analogous to that created by a reduction in stated capital where no combination is involved.

7. When a combination results in carrying forward the earned surpluses of the constituent companies, statements of operations issued by the continuing business for the period in which the combination occurs and for any preceding period should show the results of operations of the combined interests.

Chapter 8

INCOME AND EARNED SURPLUS

1. The purpose of this chapter is to recommend criteria for use in identifying material extraordinary charges and credits which may in some cases and should in other cases be excluded from the determination of net income and to recommend methods of presenting these charges and credits.

2. In dealing with the problem of selecting the most useful form of income statement, the danger of understatement or overstatement of income must be recognized. An important objective of income presentation should be the avoidance of any practice that leads to income equalization.

3. Attention is directed to certain facts which serve to emphasize that the word *income* is used to describe a general concept, not a specific and precise thing, and that the income statement is based on the concept of the *going concern*. It is at best an interim report. Profits are not fundamentally the result of operations during any short period of time. Allocations to fiscal periods of both charges and credits affecting the determination of net income are, in part, estimated and conventional and based on assumptions as to future events which may be invalidated by experience. While the items of which this is true are usually few in relation to the total number of transactions, they sometimes are large in relation to the other amounts in the income statement.

4. It must also be recognized that the ultimate dis-

tinction between *operating* income and charges and *non-operating* gains and losses, terms having considerable currency in the accounting profession, has not been established. The former are generally defined as recurrent features of business operation, more or less normal and dependable in their incidence from year to year; the latter are generally considered to be irregular and unpredictable, more or less fortuitous and incidental. The committee is also mindful that the term *net income* has been used indiscriminately and often without precise, and most certainly without uniform, definition in the financial press, investment services, annual reports, prospectuses, contracts relating to compensation of management, bond indentures, preferred stock dividend provisions, and many other places.

5. In the committee's view, the above facts with respect to the income statement and the income which it displays make it incumbent upon readers of financial statements to exercise great care at all times in drawing conclusions from them.

6. The question of what constitutes the most practically useful concept of income for the year is one on which there is much difference of opinion. On the one hand, net income is defined according to a strict proprietary concept by which it is presumed to be determined by the inclusion of all items affecting the net increase in proprietorship during the period except dividend distributions and capital transactions. The form of presentation which gives effect to this broad concept of net income has sometimes been designated the *all-inclusive* income statement. On the other hand, a different concept places its principal emphasis upon relationship of items to the operations, and to the year, excluding from the determination of net income any material extraordinary items which are not so related or which, if included, would impair the significance of net income so that misleading inferences might be drawn therefrom. This latter concept would require the income statement to be designed on what might be called a *current operating performance* basis, because its chief purpose is to aid those primarily interested in what a company was able to earn under the operating conditions of the period covered by the statement.

7. Proponents of the *all-inclusive* type of income statement insist that annual income statements taken for the life of an enterprise should, when added together, represent total net income. They emphasize the dangers of possible manipulation of the annual earnings figure if material extraordinary items may be omitted in the determination of income. They also assert that, over a period of years, charges resulting from extraordinary events tend to exceed the credits, and the omission of such items has the effect of indicating a greater earning performance than the corporation actually has exhibited. They insist that an income statement which includes all income charges or credits arising during the year is simple to prepare, is easy to understand, and is not subject to variations resulting from the different judgments that may be applied in the treatment of individual items. They argue that when judgment is allowed to enter the picture with respect to the inclusion or exclusion of special items, material differences in the treatment of borderline cases develop and that there is danger that the use of *distortion* as a criterion may be a means of accomplishing the equalization of income. With full disclosure of the nature of any special or extraordinary items, this group believes the user of the financial statements can make his own additions or deductions more effectively than can the management or the independent accountant.

8. Those who favor the *all-inclusive* income statement largely assume that those supporting the *current operating performance* concept are mainly concerned with establishing a figure of net income for the year which will carry an implication as to future earning capacity. Having made this assumption, they contend that income statements should not be prepared on the *current operating performance* basis because income statements of the past are of only limited help in the forecasting of the earning power of an enterprise. This group also argues that items reflecting the results of unusual or extraordinary events are part of the earnings history of the company, and accordingly should be given weight in any effort to make financial judgments with respect to the company. Since a judgment as to the financial affairs of an enterprise should involve a study of the results of a period of prior years, rather than of a single year, this group believes that the omission of material extraordinary items from annual income statements is undesirable since there would be a greater tendency for those items to be overlooked in such a study.

9. On the other hand, those who advocate the *current operating performance* type of income statement generally do so because they are mindful of the particular business significance which a substantial number of the users of financial reports attach to the income statement. They point out that, while some users of financial reports are able to analyze a statement and eliminate from it those unusual and extraordinary items that tend to distort it for their purposes, many users are not trained to do so. Furthermore, they contend, it is difficult at best to report in any financial statement sufficient data to afford a sound basis upon which the reader who does not have an intimate knowledge of the facts can make a well-considered classification. They consider it self-evident that management and the independent auditors are in a better position than

outsiders to determine whether there are unusual and extraordinary items which, if included in the determination of net income, may give rise to misleading inferences as to current operating performance. Relying on the proper exercise of professional judgment, they discount the contention that neither managements nor the independent auditors, because of the absence of objective standards to guide them, have been able to decide consistently which extraordinary charges and credits should be excluded in determining earning performance. They agree it is hazardous to place too great a reliance on the net income as shown in a single annual statement and insist that a realistic presentation of current performance must be taken for what it is and should not be construed as conveying an implication as to future accomplishments. The net income of a single year is only one of scores of factors involved in analyzing the future earnings prospects or potentialities of a business. It is well recognized that future earnings are dependent to a large extent upon such factors as market trends, product developments, political events, labor relationships, and numerous other factors not ascertainable from the financial statements. However, this group insists that the net income for the year should show as clearly as possible what happened in that year under that year's conditions, in order that sound comparisons may be made with prior years and with the performance of other companies.

10. The advocates of this *current operating performance* type of statement join fully with the so-called *all-inclusive* group in asserting that there should be full disclosure of all material charges or credits of an unusual character, including those attributable to a prior year, but they insist that disclosure should be made in such manner as not to distort the figure which represents what the company was able to earn from its usual or typical business operations under the conditions existing during the year. They point out that many companies, in order to give more useful information concerning their earning performance, make a practice of restating the earnings of a number of prior years after adjusting them to reflect the proper allocation of items not related to the years in which they were first reported. They believe that material extraordinary charges or credits may often best be disclosed as direct adjustments of surplus. They point out that a charge or credit in a material amount representing an unusual item not likely to recur, if included in the computation of annual net income, may be so distorting in its results as to lead to unsound judgments with respect to the current earning performance of the company.

11. The committee has indicated elsewhere[1] that in its opinion it is plainly desirable that over the years all profits and losses of a business be reflected in net income, but at the same time has recognized that, under appropriate circumstances, it is proper to exclude certain material charges and credits from the determination of the net income of a single year, even though they clearly affect the cumulative total of income for a series of years. In harmony with this view, **it is the opinion of the committee that there should be a general presumption that all items of profit and loss recognized during the period are to be used in determining the figure reported as net income. The only possible exception to this presumption relates to items which in the aggregate are material in relation to the company's net income and are clearly not identifiable with or do not result from the usual or typical business operations of the period.** Thus, only extraordinary items such as the following may be excluded from the determination of net income for the year, and they should be excluded when their inclusion would impair the significance of net income so that misleading inferences might be drawn therefrom:[2]

a. Material charges or credits (other than ordinary adjustments of a recurring nature) specifically related to operations of prior years, such as the elimination of unused reserves provided in prior years and adjustments of income taxes for prior years;
b. Material charges or credits resulting from unusual sales of assets not acquired for resale and not of the type in which the company generally deals;
c. Material losses of a type not usually insured against, such as those resulting from wars, riots, earthquakes, and similar calamities or catastrophes except where such losses are a recurrent hazard of the business;
d. The write-off of a material amount of intangibles;[3]
e. The write-off of material amounts of unamortized bond discount or premium and bond issue expenses at the time of the retirement or refunding of the debt before maturity.

12. The following, however, should be excluded from the determination of net income under all circumstances:

a. Adjustments resulting from transactions in the company's own capital stock;
b. Amounts transferred to and from accounts properly designated as surplus appropriations, such

[1]See chapter 2(b), paragraph 3.

[2]See chapter 10(b) with respect to the allocation of income taxes.

[3]See chapter 5, paragraphs 8 and 9, for conditions under which a material portion or the entire amount of intangibles described therein as type (b) may be written off.

as charges and credits with respect to general purpose contingency reserves;

c. Amounts deemed to represent excessive costs of fixed assets, and annual appropriations in contemplation of replacement of productive facilities at higher price levels;[4] and

d. Adjustments made pursuant to a quasi-reorganization.

13. Consideration has been given to the methods of presentation of the extraordinary items excluded in the determination of net income under the criteria set forth in paragraph 11. One method is to carry all such charges and credits directly to the surplus account with complete disclosure as to their nature and amount. A second method is to show them in the income statement after the amount designated as net income. Where the second method is used, misconceptions are likely to arise as to whether earnings for the period are represented by the amount actually designated as net income or by the final, and often more prominent, amount shown on the income statement after deduction or addition of material extraordinary items excluded from the determination of net income. Having in mind the possibility of such misconceptions where the second method is employed, the committee believes that the first method more clearly portrays net income. It should be noted that the Securities and Exchange Commission, in its revised Regulation S-X issued in December, 1950, made provision in item 17 of Rule 5-03 for the addition to or deduction from net income or loss, at the bottom of income statements filed with the Commission, of items of profit and loss given recognition in the accounts during the period and not included in the determination of net income or loss. The change in Rule 5-03 does not affect the determination of the amount to be reported as net income or earnings for the year. Furthermore, the additions or deductions at the foot of the income statement after determination of net income are equivalent to direct credits or charges to earned surplus. In view of the foregoing, and although the committee strongly prefers the first method, it considers the second method of presentation described above to be acceptable provided care is taken that the figure of net income is clearly and unequivocally designated so as not to be confused with the final figure in the income statement. Thus it is imperative that the caption of the final figure should precisely describe what it represents, e.g., *net income and special items, net income and refund of 1945 excess profits taxes, net loss and special items,* or *profit on sale of subsidiary less net loss.* A company may use the first method of presentation in one statement and the second method in another like statement covering the same fiscal period. The

committee wishes to make clear that neither of the above-described methods of presentation precludes the use of the combined statement of income and earned surplus.[5] However, where such combined statement is utilized, the committee's preference is that the figure of net income be followed immediately by the surplus balance at the beginning of the period. It is also the committee's opinion that deduction of the single item of dividends from net income on the income statement would not be subject to misconception.

14. In its deliberations concerning the nature and purpose of the income statement, the committee has been mindful of the disposition of even well-informed persons to attach undue importance to a single net income figure and to *earnings per share* shown for a particular year. The committee directs attention to the undesirability in many cases of the dissemination of information in which major prominence is given to a single figure of *net income* or *net income per share.* However, if such income data are reported (as in newspapers, investors' services, and annual corporate reports), the committee strongly urges that any determination of *income per share* be related to the amount designated in the income statement as net income and that where material extraordinary charges or credits have been excluded from the determination of net income, the corresponding total or per-share amount of such charges and credits also be reported separately and simultaneously. In this connection the committee earnestly solicits the cooperation of all organizations, both governmental and private, engaged in the compilation of business earnings statistics from annual reports.

Chapter 9

DEPRECIATION

Section A—Depreciation and High Costs

1. In December, 1947, the committee issued Accounting Research Bulletin No. 33, dealing with the subject of depreciation and high costs. In October, 1948, it published a letter to the membership reaffirming the opinion expressed in the bulletin.

2. The subject is one of continuing importance. The committee once more expresses its approval of the basic conclusions asserted in both publications, but in view of the many requests received for further consideration of various aspects of the problem has placed the subject on its agenda for further study.

---

[4]See chapter 9(a) and dissents thereto.
[5]See chapter 2(b).

3. Accounting Research Bulletin No. 33 read as follows:

4. "The American Institute of Accountants committee on accounting procedure has given extensive consideration to the problem of making adequate provision for the replacement of plant facilities in view of recent sharp increases in the price level. The problem requires consideration of charges against current income for depreciation of facilities acquired at lower price levels.

5. "The committee recognizes that business management has the responsibility of providing for replacement of plant and machinery. It also recognizes that, in reporting profits today, the cost of material and labor is reflected in terms of 'inflated' dollars while the cost of productive facilities in which capital was invested at a lower price level is reflected in terms of dollars whose purchasing power was much greater. There is no doubt that in considering depreciation in connection with product costs, prices, and business policies, management must take into consideration the probability that plant and machinery will have to be replaced at costs much greater than those of the facilities now in use.

6. "When there are gross discrepancies between the cost and current values of productive facilities, the committee believes that it is entirely proper for management to make annual appropriations of net income or surplus in contemplation of replacement of such facilities at higher price levels.

7. "It has been suggested in some quarters that the problem be met by increasing depreciation charges against current income. The committee does not believe that this is a satisfactory solution at this time. It believes that accounting and financial reporting for general use will best serve their purposes by adhering to the generally accepted concept of depreciation on cost, at least until the dollar is stabilized at some level. An attempt to recognize current prices in providing depreciation, to be consistent, would require the serious step of formally recording appraised current values for all properties, and continuous and consistent depreciation charges based on the new values. Without such formal steps, there would be no objective standard by which to judge the propriety of the amounts of depreciation charges against current income, and the significance of recorded amounts of profit might be seriously impaired.

8. "It would not increase the usefulness of reported corporate income figures if some companies charged depreciation on appraised values while others adhered to cost. The committee believes, therefore, that consideration of radical changes in accepted accounting procedure should not be under-

taken, at least until a stable price level would make it practicable for business as a whole to make the change at the same time.

9. "The committee disapproves immediate writedowns of plant cost by charges against current income in amounts believed to represent excessive or abnormal costs occasioned by current price levels. However, the committee calls attention to the fact that plants expected to have less than normal useful life can properly be depreciated on a systematic basis related to economic usefulness."

10. The letter of October 14, 1948, was addressed to the members of the Institute and read as follows:

11. "The committee on accounting procedure has reached the conclusion that no basic change in the accounting treatment of depreciation of plant and equipment is practicable or desirable under present conditions to meet the problem created by the decline in the purchasing power of the dollar.

12. "The committee has given intensive study to this problem and has examined and discussed various suggestions which have been made to meet it. It has solicited and considered hundreds of opinions on this subject expressed by businessmen, bankers, economists, labor leaders, and others. While there are differences of opinion, the prevailing sentiment in these groups is against any basic change in present accounting procedures. The committee believes that such a change would confuse readers of financial statements and nullify many of the gains that have been made toward clearer presentation of corporate finances.

13. "Should inflation proceed so far that original dollar costs lose their practical significance, it might become necessary to restate all assets in terms of the depreciated currency, as has been done in some countries. But it does not seem to the committee that such action should be recommended now if financial statements are to have maximum usefulness to the greatest number of users.

14. "The committee, therefore, reaffirms the opinion it expressed in Accounting Research Bulletin No. 33, December, 1947.

15. "Any basic change in the accounting treatment of depreciation should await further study of the nature and concept of business income.

16. "The immediate problem can and should be met by financial management. The committee recognizes that the common forms of financial statements may permit misunderstanding as to the amount which a corporation has available for distribution in the form of dividends, higher wages, or

lower prices for the company's products. When prices have risen appreciably since original investments in plant and facilities were made, a substantial proportion of net income as currently reported must be reinvested in the business in order to maintain assets at the same level of productivity at the end of a year as at the beginning.

17. "Stockholders, employees, and the general public should be informed that a business must be able to retain out of profits amounts sufficient to replace productive facilities at current prices if it is to stay in business. The committee therefore gives its full support to the use of supplementary financial schedules, explanations or footnotes by which management may explain the need for retention of earnings."

Six members of the committee, Messrs. Andrews, Peloubet, Peoples, Smith, Wellington, and Williams, dissented to adoption of section A of chapter 9.

The six dissenting members object to the reprinting, in this section, of Bulletin No. 33 of December, 1947, and the reaffirming letter of October 14, 1948. That bulletin was issued to check the extension of certain then-emerging practices and it was successful in that purpose. However, Bulletin No. 33 contains assertions which are not now appropriate and should be eliminated, notably:

   a. "An attempt to recognize current prices in providing depreciation . . . would require the serious step of formally recording appraised current values . . . and consistent depreciation charges based on the new values" (par. 7 of this section).

Those dissenting believe this is not the only method which may be followed—a conclusion also reached by the Study Group on Business Income (see page 61 of its report).[1]

   b. ". . . consideration of radical changes in accepted accounting procedure should not be undertaken, at least until a stable price level would make it practicable for business as a whole to make the change at the same time." (par. 8)

This statement virtually precludes changes in accounting practice in so far as the monetary unit is concerned and is inconsistent with the paragraphs on Accounting and the Corporate System in the introduction to this volume.

   c. The warnings (in paragraphs 5, 6, 16 and 17) to management as to the use of profits.

Such warnings are irrelevant; it is no part of the accountant's function to tell management what it may or may not properly do with income after it has been determined.

Those dissenting believe that acceptable accounting practices should comprehend financial statements to stockholders, employees, and the public designed to reflect those concepts of cost and net income which are recommended in paragraph 5 to management in determining product costs, prices, and business policies. They question whether net income can properly be so designated if appropriations therefrom, as suggested in paragraph 6, are needed to preserve capital invested in plant.

They believe that plant may continue to be carried in the balance sheet at historical cost with deduction for depreciation based thereon. In addition to historical depreciation, a supplementary annual charge to income should be permitted with corresponding credit to an account for property replacements and substitutions, to be classified with the stockholders' equity. This supplementary charge should be in such amount as to make the total charge for depreciation express in current dollars the exhaustion of plant allocable to the period. The supplementary charge would be calculated by use of a generally accepted price index applied to the expenditures in the years when the plant was acquired. The last sentence of paragraph 7 would then be no longer valid; the usefulness of financial statements would be enhanced without sacrifice of presently existing comparability

Section B—Depreciation on Appreciation

1. Historically, fixed assets have been accounted for on the basis of cost. However, fixed assets in the past have occasionally been written up to appraised values because of rapid rises in price levels, to adjust costs in the case of bargain purchases, etc. In some of these instances companies have continued to compute depreciation on the basis of cost.

---

[1]Study Group on Business Income, *Changing Concepts of Business Income,* New York: The Macmillan Co., 1952, 160 pp.

2. When appreciation has been entered on the books income should be charged with depreciation[1] computed on the written-up amounts. A company should not at the same time claim larger property valuations in its statement of assets and provide for the amortization of only smaller amounts in its statement of income. When a company has made representations as to an increased valuation of plant, depreciation accounting and periodic income determination thereafter should be based on such higher amounts.

Three members of the committee, Messrs. Calkins, Lindquist, and Mason, assented with qualification to adoption of section B of chapter 9.

Messrs. Calkins, Lindquist, and Mason believe that, as a matter of consistency, where increased property valuations have been entered on the books the credit item should be treated as permanent capital and would therefore not be available for subsequent transfer to earned surplus as *realized* through depreciation or sale.

Section C—Emergency Facilities: Depreciation, Amortization and Income Taxes

Certificates of Necessity

1. Section 124A of the Internal Revenue Code, which was added by the Revenue Act of 1950, provides for the issuance of certificates of necessity under which all or part of the cost of so-called *emergency facilities* may be amortized over a period of 60 months for income-tax purposes. In many cases, the amounts involved are material, and companies are faced with the problem of deciding whether to adopt the 60-month period over which the portions of the cost of the facilities covered by certificates of necessity may be amortized for income-tax purposes as the period over which they are to be depreciated in the accounts.

2. Thinking on this question apparently has become confused because many so-called *percentage certificates* have been issued covering less than the entire cost of the facility. This fact, together with the fact that the probable economic usefulness of the facility after the close of the five-year amortization period is considered by the certifying authority in determining the percentage covered by these certificates, has led many to believe that the percentage used represents the government's conclusion as to the proportion of the cost of the facility that is not expected to have usefulness at the end of five years.

3. In some cases, it is apparent that the probable lack of economic usefulness of the facility after the close of the amortization period must constitute the principal if not the sole basis for determining the percentage to be included in the certificate. However, it must be recognized that the certifying authority has acted under orders to give consideration also to a variety of other factors to the end that the amount certified may be the minimum amount necessary to secure expansion of industrial capacity in the interest of national defense during the emergency period. Among the factors required to be considered in the issuance of these certificates, in addition to loss of useful value, are (a) character of business, (b) extent of risk assumed (including the amount and source of capital employed, and the potentiality of recovering capital or retiring debt through tax savings or pricing), (c) assistance to small business and promotion of competition, (d) compliance with government policies (e.g., dispersal for security), and (e) other types of incentives provided by government, such as direct government loans, guaranties, and contractual arrangements.

Depreciation Considerations

4. The argument has been advanced from time to time that, since the portion of the cost of properties covered by certificates of necessity is amortized over a five-year period for income-tax purposes, it is necessary to follow the same procedure in the accounts. Sound financial accounting procedures do not necessarily coincide with the rules as to what shall be included in "gross income," or allowed as a deduction therefrom, in arriving at taxable net income. It is well recognized that such rules should not be followed for financial accounting purposes if they do not conform to generally accepted accounting principles. However, where the results obtained from following income-tax procedures do not materially differ from those obtained where generally accepted accounting principles are followed, there are practical advantages in keeping the accounts in agreement with the income-tax returns.

5. The cost of a productive facility is one of the costs of the services it renders during its useful economic life. Generally accepted accounting principles require that this cost be spread over the expected useful life of the facility in such a way as to allocate it as equitably as possible to the periods during which services are obtained from the use of the facility. This procedure is known as depreciation accounting, a system of accounting which aims to distribute the cost or other basic value of tangible capital assets, less salvage (if any), over the estimated useful life of the unit (which may be a group of assets) in a systematic and rational manner. It is a process of allocation, not of valuation.

---

[1]The word *depreciation* is here used in its ordinary accounting sense and not as the converse of *appreciation*.

6. The committee is of the opinion that from an accounting standpoint there is nothing inherent in the nature of emergency facilities which requires the depreciation or amortization of their cost for financial accounting purposes over either a shorter or a longer period than would be proper if no certificate of necessity had been issued. Estimates of the probable useful life of a facility by those best informed in the matter may indicate either a shorter or a longer life than the statutory 60-month period over which the certified portion of its cost is deductible for income-tax purposes.

7. In determining the proper amount of annual depreciation with respect to emergency facilities for financial accounting purposes, it must be recognized that a great many of these facilities are being acquired primarily for what they can produce during the emergency period. To whatever extent it is reasonable to expect the useful economic life of a facility to end with the close of the amortization period the cost of the facility is a proper cost of operation during that period.

8. In determining the prospective usefulness of such facilities it will be necessary to consider their adaptability to post-emergency use, the effect of their use upon economic utilization of other facilities, the possibility of excessive costs due to expedited construction or emergency conditions, and the fact that no deductions for depreciation of the certified portion will be allowable for income-tax purposes in the post-amortization years if the company elects to claim the amortization deduction. The purposes for which emergency facilities are acquired in a great many cases are such as to leave major uncertainties as to the extent of their use during the amortization period and as to their subsequent usefulness—uncertainties which are not normally encountered in the acquisition and use of operating facilities.

9. Consideration of these factors, the committee believes, will in many cases result in the determination of depreciation charges during the amortization period in excess of the depreciation that would be appropriate if these factors were not involved. Frequently they will be so compelling as to indicate the need for recording depreciation of the cost of emergency facilities in the accounts in conformity with the amortization deductions allowable for income-tax purposes. However, the committee believes that when the amount allowed as amortization for income-tax purposes is materially different from the amount of the estimated depreciation, the latter should be used for financial accounting purposes.

10. In some cases, certificates of necessity cover facilities which the owner expects to use after the emergency period in lieu of older facilities. As a result the older facilities may become unproductive

and obsolete before they are fully depreciated on the basis of their previously expected life. In such situations, the committee believes depreciation charges to income should be determined in relation to the total properties, to the end that sound depreciation accounting may be applied to the property accounts as a whole.

Recognition of Income Tax Effects

11. In those cases in which the amount of depreciation charged in the accounts on that portion of the cost of the facilities for which certificates of necessity have been obtained is materially less than the amount of amortization deducted for income-tax purposes, the amount of income taxes payable annually during the amortization period may be significantly less than it would be on the basis of the income reflected in the financial statements. In such cases, after the close of the amortization period the income taxes will exceed the amount that would be appropriate on the basis of the income reported in the statements. Accordingly, the committee believes that during the amortization period, where this difference is material, a charge should be made in the income statement to recognize the income tax to be paid in the future on the amount by which amortization for income-tax purposes exceeds the depreciation that would be allowable if certificates of necessity had not been issued. The amount of the charge should be equal to the estimated amount by which the income tax expected to be payable after the amortization period exceeds what would be so expected if amortization had not been claimed for income-tax purposes in the amortization period. The estimated amount should be based upon normal and surtax rates in effect during the period covered by the income statement with such changes therein as can be reasonably anticipated at the time the estimate is made.

12. In accounting for this deferment of income taxes, the committee believes it desirable to treat the charge as being for additional income taxes. The related credit in such cases would properly be made to an account for deferred income taxes. Under this method, during the life of the facility following the amortization period the annual charges for income taxes will be reduced by charging to the account for deferred income taxes that part of the income tax in excess of what would have been payable had the amortization deduction not been claimed for income-tax purposes in the amortization period. By this procedure the net income will more nearly reflect the results of a proper matching of costs and revenues.

13. There are those who similarly recognize the necessity for giving effect to the amount of the deferred income taxes but who believe this should be

accomplished by making a charge in the income account for additional amortization or depreciation. They would carry the related credit to an accumulated amortization or depreciation account as a practical means of recognizing the loss of future deductibility of the cost of the facility for income-tax purposes. If this procedure is followed the annual charges for depreciation will be correspondingly reduced throughout the useful life of the facility following the amortization period. Although this procedure will result in the same amount of net income as the procedure outlined in paragraph 12, and therefore may be considered as acceptable, the committee regards the paragraph 12 procedure as preferable. In any circumstances, there should be disclosure of the procedures followed.

Chapter 10

TAXES

Section A—Real and Personal Property Taxes

1. The purpose of this section is to draw attention to the problems involved in accounting for real and personal property taxes and to present some of the considerations which enter into a determination of their accounting treatment.

Legal Liability for Property Taxes and Treatment for Income-Tax Purposes

2. Unlike excise, income, and social security taxes, which are directly related to particular business events, real and personal property taxes are based upon the assessed valuation of property (tangible and intangible) as of a given date, as determined by the laws of a state or other taxing authority. For this reason the legal liability for such taxes is generally considered as accruing at the moment of occurrence of some specific event, rather than over a period of time. Whether such legal accrual should determine the accounting treatment is a question to be discussed later. Tax laws, opinions of attorneys, income-tax regulations, and court decisions have mentioned various dates on which certain property taxes are said to accrue legally. Among them are the following:

a. Assessment date,
b. Beginning of taxing authority's fiscal year,
c. End of taxing authority's fiscal year,
d. Date on which tax becomes a lien on the property,
e. Date tax is levied,
f. Date or dates tax is payable,
g. Date tax becomes delinquent,
h. Tax period appearing on tax bill.

3. Most of the foregoing dates are mentioned in tax laws. In a given case several of these dates may coincide.

4. The date to be applied in a particular case necessarily requires reference to the law and court decisions of the state concerned. Where the matter has been litigated, it has often been held that property taxes become a liability at the point of time when they become a lien. The general rule, however, is that such taxes accrue as of the date on which they are assessed. The position of the Bureau of Internal Revenue is that generally property taxes accrue on the assessment date, even if the amount of the tax is not determined until later.

5. A practical aspect of the legal liability for property taxes must be considered when title to property is transferred during the taxable year. As stated above, the assessment date generally determines accrual. But as between vendor and vendee, the Supreme Court[1] has laid down the rule that the lien date, or the date of personal obligation, controls and that where a transfer occurs after either of those dates, the purchaser is not entitled to deduct the taxes for income-tax purposes.

6. Adjustments on account of property taxes paid or accrued are frequently incorporated in agreements covering the sale of real estate, which determine the question for the individual case as between the buyer and seller, though they are not necessarily controlling for income-tax purposes.

7. Although pro-rata accrual of property taxes has been permitted by some courts, the generally accepted rule seems to be that such taxes accrue in a lump sum on one date and not ratably over the year.

Accounting for Property Taxes

Accrual accounting

8. Accounting questions arise as to (1) when the liability for real and personal property taxes should be recorded on the books of a taxpayer keeping his accounts on the accrual basis and (2) the amounts to be charged against the income of respective periods. Here again, the decision is influenced by the particular circumstances of each tax. Such terms as *assessment date* and *levy date* vary in meaning in the different jurisdictions; and while there is sufficient agreement about assessment date to furnish a basis for the general legal rule already mentioned, it does not necessarily follow that the legal rule should determine the accounting treatment.

9. Determination of the liability for the tax often

---

[1] *Magruder v. Supplee*, 316 U.S. 394 (1942).

proceeds by degrees, the several steps being taken at appreciable intervals of time. For example, while it is known that the owner of real property is liable, with respect to each tax period, for a tax on property owned on the assessment date, the amount of the tax may not be fixed until much later. There is sometimes reluctance toward recording liabilities of indeterminate amount, especially such items as property taxes, and a preference for recording them when the amount can be computed with certainty. While this consideration is one which occasionally leads to the mention of taxes in footnotes as contingent liabilities, the inability to determine the exact amount of taxes is in itself no justification for failure to recognize an existing tax liability.

10. In practice, real and personal property taxes have been charged against the income of various periods, as indicated below:

a. Year in which paid (cash basis),
b. Year ending on assessment (or lien) date,
c. Year beginning on assessment (or lien) date,
d. Calendar or fiscal year of taxpayer prior to assessment (or lien) date,
e. Calendar or fiscal year of taxpayer including assessment (or lien) date,
f. Calendar or fiscal year of taxpayer prior to payment date,
g. Fiscal year of governing body levying the tax,
h. Year appearing on tax bill.

11. Some of these periods may coincide, as when the fiscal year of the taxing body and that of the taxpayer are the same. The charge to income is sometimes made in full at one time, sometimes ratably on a monthly basis, sometimes on the basis of prior estimates, adjusted during or after the period.

12. The various periods mentioned represent varying degrees of conservatism in accrual accounting. Some justification may be found for each usage, but all the circumstances relating to a particular tax must be considered before a satisfactory conclusion is reached.

13. Consistency of application from year to year is the important consideration and selection of any of the periods mentioned is a matter for individual judgment.

Basis considered most acceptable

14. Generally, the most acceptable basis of providing for property taxes is monthly accrual on the taxpayer's books during the fiscal period of the taxing authority for which the taxes are levied. The books will then show, at any closing date, the appropriate accrual or prepayment.

15. It may be argued that the entire amount of tax should logically be accrued by the lien date. Advocates of this procedure vary from those who would accrue the tax by charges to income during the year ending on the lien date, to those who urge setting up the full tax liability on the lien date and charging the amount thereof to income during the subsequent year. However, the basis described in the preceding paragraph is held by the majority of accountants to be practical and satisfactory so long as it is consistently followed.

Treatment in Financial Statements

Balance sheet

16. An accrued liability for real and personal property taxes, whether estimated or definitely known, should be included among the current liabilities. Where estimates are subject to a substantial measure of uncertainty the liability should be described as estimated.

Income statement

17. While it is sometimes proper to capitalize in property accounts the amount of real estate taxes applicable to property which is being developed for use or sale, these taxes are generally regarded as an expense of doing business. They may be (a) charged to operating expenses; (b) shown as a separate deduction from income; or (c) distributed among the several accounts to which they are deemed to apply, such as factory overhead, rent income, and selling or general expenses.

18. In condensed income statements appearing in published reports, the amounts of real and personal property taxes, however charged in the accounts, are rarely shown separately. They are frequently combined with other taxes but not with taxes on income.

19. Since the liability for property taxes must frequently be estimated at the balance-sheet date, it is often necessary to adjust the provision for taxes of a prior year when their amount has been ascertained. These adjustments should ordinarily be made through the income statement, either in combination with the current year's provision or as a separate item in the income statement. Such adjustments should not be made in the surplus account, except under the conditions set forth in chapter 8, paragraphs 11, 12, and 13.

One member of the committee, Mr. Wellington, assented with qualification to adoption of section A of chapter 10.

Mr. Wellington objects to the statement in paragraph 15 that the basis described in paragraph 14 is held by the majority of accountants to be practical and satisfactory so long as it is consistently followed. In his opinion, the most logical practice is to accrue the entire amount of tax at the lien date, with a corresponding charge to an account such as *taxes unexpired* which will then be reduced pro rata, as outlined in the latter part of the second sentence of paragraph 15.

Section B—Income Taxes

1. This section deals with a number of accounting problems which arise in the reporting of income and excess-profits taxes (hereinafter referred to as *income taxes*) in financial statements. The problems arise largely where (a) material items entering into the computation of taxable income are not included in the income statement and where (b) material items included in the income statement do not enter into the computation of taxable income. The section does not apply where there is a presumption that particular differences between the tax return and the income statement will recur regularly over a comparatively long period of time.

2. Basic difficulties arise in connection with the accounting for income taxes where there are material and extraordinary differences between the taxable income upon which they are computed and the income for the period determined in accordance with generally accepted accounting principles. For example, provisions may be made in the income statement for possible losses not yet realized but requiring recognition under generally accepted accounting principles, such losses, however, being deductible for tax purposes only when they occur. On the other hand, deductions may be taken in the tax return which are not included in the income statement, such as charges against an estimated liability account created in a prior period. Likewise, gains subject to income tax may not be included in the income statement, as, for instance, a gain on the sale of property credited to surplus. Also, credits in the income statement may not be includible in taxable income, as when an unneeded past provision for an estimated liability is restored to income.

3. In some cases the transactions result in gains; in others they result in losses or net costs. If all the effects of the transactions (including their effect on income tax) were reflected in the income statement the income would, of course, be increased where the transactions result in a gain and reduced where they result in a loss or net cost. But where the effects are not all reflected in the income statement, and that statement indicates only the income tax actually payable, exactly the opposite effect is produced— where the special transactions result in a gain the net income is reduced; and where they result in a loss, or net cost, the net income is increased. Such results ordinarily detract from the significance or usefulness of the financial statements.

4. Financial statements are based on allocations of receipts, payments, accruals, and various other items. Many of the allocations are necessarily based on assumptions, but no one suggests that allocations based on imperfect criteria should be abandoned in respect of expenses other than income taxes, or even that the method of allocation should always be indicated. Income taxes are an expense that should be allocated, when necessary and practicable, to income and other accounts, as other expenses are allocated. What the income statement should reflect under this head, as under any other head, is the expense properly allocable to the income included in the income statement for the year.

5. In cases in which transactions included in the surplus statement but not in the income statement increase the income tax payable by an amount that is substantial and is determinable without difficulty, as in the case of a gain credited to surplus, an allocation of income tax between the two statements would ordinarily be made. Objection to allocation in other cases, as where a loss is charged to surplus, has been made on the ground that the amount shown for income taxes in the income statement would be increased beyond the amount of the tax estimated to be actually payable. Further objection has been made on the ground that the amount attributable to accounts other than income is not reasonably determinable.

6. The committee sees no objection to an allocation which results in the division of a given item into two parts one of which is larger than the item itself and is offset by the smaller. The argument that the effect of the special transactions on the amount of tax is not identifiable is usually without substantial merit. The difficulties encountered in allocation of the tax are not greater than those met with in many other allocations of expenses. The allocation procedure recommended here does not, of course, contemplate a determination of the tax effect attributable to every separate transaction. In the committee's view, all that is necessary in making an allocation is to consider the effect on taxes of those special transactions which are not included in the income statement.

7. The cases that are likely to call for allocation are those in which transactions affecting the income tax in a manner which would have a distorting effect on net income are included in (a) surplus accounts, (b) deferred-charge accounts, or (c) estimated liability and similar accounts. Methods of applying the allocation principle in these instances are set forth below.

Methods of Applying the Allocation Principle

Computation of tax effect

8. In most cases, it is appropriate to consider the tax effect as the difference between the tax payable with and without including the item in the amount of taxable income. In certain cases the tax effect attributable to a particular transaction for the purposes indicated above may be computed directly as in the case of transactions subject to the capital gains tax. There may also be cases in which it will be appropriate to use a current over-all effective rate or, as in the case of deferred income, an estimated future tax rate. The estimated rate should be based upon normal and surtax rates in effect during the period covered by the income statement with such changes therein as can be reasonably anticipated at the time the estimate is made.

Credits to surplus

9. Where an item resulting in a material increase in income taxes is credited to surplus, the portion of the provision for income taxes which is attributable to such item should, under the principle of allocation, be charged thereto. The committee suggests, however, that the provision for income taxes estimated as due be shown in the income statement in full and that the portion thereof charged to surplus be shown on the income statement either (a) as a separate deduction from the actual tax or (b) as a separate credit, clearly described.

Charges to surplus

10. Where an item resulting in a material reduction in income taxes is charged to surplus, the principle of allocation may be applied in the income statement in either of two ways: (a) the provision for income taxes may be shown as if the item in question were not deductible (the total amount of tax estimated to be due for the year being indicated) or (b) a special charge representing the portion of such item equal to the tax reduction resulting therefrom may be separately shown. In either case the amount charged to surplus is reduced accordingly.

Deferred-charge and estimated liability accounts

11. The principle of allocation applies also where an item resulting in a material reduction in income taxes is charged to or carried forward in a deferred-charge account or charged to an estimated liability account.

12. The deduction for tax purposes in a given year of an item which is carried to or remains in a

deferred-charge account will involve a series of charges in future income statements for amortization of the deferred charge, and these charges will not be deductible for tax purposes. In the period in which the item is taken as a deduction for tax purposes a charge should be made in the income statement of an amount equal to the tax reduction, in the manner set forth above with respect to charges to surplus, with a corresponding credit in the deferred-charge account. Thereafter amortization of the deferred charge should be based on the amount as adjusted by such tax reduction.

13. Where an item resulting in a material reduction in income taxes is charged to an estimated liability account the principle of allocation may be applied in the income statement in any of three ways: (a) the current provision for income taxes may be shown as if the item in question were not deductible (the total amount of tax estimated to be due for the year being indicated), or (b) a charge may be included for a portion of such item equal to the tax reduction resulting therefrom, or (c) the item in question may be charged in the income statement and a credit made in the income statement representing a portion of the estimated liability account equal to the excess of such item over the related tax reduction.

Special treatment

14. Where the treatments recommended above are considered to be not practicable, the amount of taxes estimated to be actually payable for the year may be shown in the income statement, provided that the pertinent facts, including the amount of the increase or decrease attributable to other accounts, are clearly disclosed either in a footnote or in the body of the income statement.

Additional Taxes and Refunds

15. Adjustments of provisions for income taxes of prior periods, as well as any refunds and any assessments of additional amounts, should be included in the income statement unless they are so material as to have a distorting effect on net income;[1] in such event they may be charged or credited to surplus with indication as to the period to which they relate.

Carry-back of Losses and Unused Excess-Profits Credits

16. While claims for refund of income taxes ordinarily should not be included in the accounts prior to approval by the taxing authorities, a claim based on the carry-back provisions of the Internal Revenue Code presumably has as definite a basis as has the computation of income taxes for the year.

[1]See chapter 8, paragraphs 11, 12, and 13.

Therefore, amounts of income taxes paid in prior years which are refundable to the taxpayer as the result of the carry-back of losses or unused excess-profits credits ordinarily should be included in the income statement of the year in which the loss occurs or the unused excess-profits credit arises. Either of two treatments is acceptable: (a) the amount of taxes estimated to be actually payable for such year may be shown in the income statement, with the amount of the tax reduction attributable to the amounts carried back indicated either in a foot-note or parenthetically in the body of the income statement; or (b) the income statement may indicate the results of operations without inclusion of such reduction, which reduction should be shown as a final item before the amount of net income for the period.

Carry-forward of Losses and Unused Excess-Profits Credits

17. Where taxpayers are permitted to carry forward losses or unused excess-profits credits, the commit-tee believes that, as a practical matter, in the prepa-ration of annual income statements the resulting tax reduction should be reflected in the year to which such losses or unused credits are carried. Either of two treatments is acceptable: (a) the amount of taxes estimated to be actually payable for such year may be shown in the income statement, with the amount of the tax reduction attributable to the amounts car-ried forward indicated either in a footnote or paren-thetically in the body of the income statement; or (b) the income statement may indicate the results of operations without inclusion of such reduction, which reduction should be shown as a final item before the amount of net income for the period. However, where it is believed that misleading inferences would be drawn from such inclusion, the tax reduction should be credited to surplus.

Disclosure of Certain Differences between Taxable and Ordinary Income

18. If, because of differences between accounting for tax and accounting for financial purposes, no income tax has been paid or provided as to certain significant amounts credited to surplus or to income, disclosure should be made. However, if a tax is likely to be paid thereon, provision should be made on the basis of an estimate of the amount of such tax. This rule applies, for instance, to profits on instalment sales or long-term contracts which are deferred for tax purposes, and to cases where unrealized appreciation of securities is taken into the accounts by certain types of investment companies.

Two members of the committee, Messrs. Wel-lington and Werntz, assented with qualification to adoption of section B of chapter 10.

Mr. Wellington objects to paragraph 17, as he believes that the amount of the reduction in tax of the later year is due to the operations of the prior year, is in effect an adjustment of the net income or net loss previously reported, and, unless it is rela-tively not significant, should not be included in the income of the current year but should be credited to surplus. In an income statement for several years, he would show this credit to surplus as an addition to the income previously reported for the prior year, with suitable explanation.

Mr. Werntz does not agree with some of the rea-soning, particularly paragraph 6, and certain of the conclusions contained in this section. While he believes that in many cases a difference in treatment of items for tax and financial purposes preferably requires a specialized charge or credit in the income account, so that neither a double benefit nor a dou-ble deduction results, he believes that the charge or credit may not always be mandatory and should ordinarily be described in terms of the item involved rather than as *taxes.*

Chapter 11

GOVERNMENT CONTRACTS

Section A—Cost-Plus-Fixed-Fee Contracts

1. This section deals with accounting problems aris-ing under cost-plus-fixed-fee contracts, hereinafter referred to as CPFF contracts.

Summary Statement

2. Fees under CPFF contracts may be credited to income on the basis of such measurement of partial performance as will reflect reasonably assured real-ization. One generally acceptable basis is delivery of completed articles. The fees may also be accrued as they are billable, under the terms of the agreements, unless such accrual is not reasonably related to the proportionate performance of the total work or ser-vices to be performed by the contractor from incep-tion to completion.

3. Where CPFF contracts involve the manufacture and delivery of products, the reimbursable costs and fees are ordinarily included in appropriate sales or other revenue accounts. Where such contracts involve only services, or services and the supplemen-tal erection of facilities, only the fees should ordi-narily be included in revenues.

4. Unbilled costs and fees under such contracts are ordinarily receivables rather than advances or inven-tory, but should preferably be shown separately from billed accounts receivable.

5. Offsetting of government advances on CPFF

contracts by, or against, amounts due from the government on such contracts is acceptable only to the extent that the advances may under the terms of the agreement be offset in settlement, and only if that is the treatment anticipated in the normal course of business transactions under the contract. In case of offset, the amounts offset should be adequately disclosed.

Discussion

6. Contracts in the CPFF form are used (a) for the manufacture and delivery of various products, (b) for the construction of plants and other facilities, and (c) for management and other services. Under these agreements contractors are reimbursed at intervals for their expenditures and in addition are paid a specified fixed fee. Payments on account of the fees (less 10% or other amount which is withheld until completion) are made from time to time as specified in the agreements, usually subject to the approval of the contracting officer. In most cases the amount of each payment is, as a practical matter, determined by the ratio of expenditures made to the total estimated expenditures rather than on the basis of deliveries or on the percentage of completion otherwise determined.

7. The agreements provide that title to all material applicable thereto vests in the government as soon as the contractor is reimbursed for his expenditures or, in some cases, immediately upon its receipt by the contractor at his plant even though not yet paid for. The contractor has a custodianship responsibility for these materials, but the government usually has property accountability officers at the plant to safeguard government interests.

8. The contracts are subject to cancellation and termination by the government, in which event the contractor is entitled to reimbursement for all expenditures made and an equitable portion of the fixed fee.

9. The government frequently makes advances of cash as a revolving fund or against the final payment due under the agreement.

Major accounting problems

10. There are a number of basic accounting problems common to all CPFF contracts. This section deals with the four most important, which are:

a. When should fees under such contracts be included in the contractor's income statement?
b. What amounts are to be included in sales or revenue accounts?
c. What is the proper balance-sheet classification of unbilled costs and fees?

d. What is the proper balance-sheet treatment of various items, debit and credit, identified with CPFF contracts?

a. When should fees under such contracts be included in the contractor's income statement?

11. It is recognized that income should be recorded and stated in accordance with certain accounting principles as to time and amount; that profit is deemed to be realized when a sale in the ordinary course of business is effected unless the circumstances are such that collection of the sales price is not reasonably assured; and that delivery of goods sold under contract is normally regarded as the test of realization of profit or loss.

12. In the case of manufacturing, construction, or service contracts, profits are not ordinarily recognized until the right to full payment has become unconditional, i.e., when the product has been delivered and accepted, when the facilities are completed and accepted, or when the services have been fully and satisfactorily rendered. This accounting procedure has stood the test of experience and should not be departed from except for cogent reasons.

13. It is, however, a generally accepted accounting procedure to accrue revenues under certain types of contracts and thereby recognize profits, on the basis of partial performance, where the circumstances are such that total profit can be estimated with reasonable accuracy and ultimate realization is reasonably assured. Particularly where the performance of a contract requires a substantial period of time from inception to completion, there is ample precedent for pro-rata recognition of profit as the work progresses, if the total profit and the ratio of the performance to date to the complete performance can be computed reasonably and collection is reasonably assured. Depending upon the circumstances, such partial performance may be established by deliveries, expenditures, or percentage of completion otherwise determined. This rule is frequently applied to long-term construction and other similar contracts; it is also applied in the case of contracts involving deliveries in instalments or the performance of services. However, the rule should be dealt with cautiously and not applied in the case of partial deliveries and uncompleted contracts where the information available does not clearly indicate that a partial profit has been realized after making provision for possible losses and contingencies.

14. CPFF contracts are much like the type of contracts upon which profit has heretofore been recognized on partial performance, and accordingly have at least as much justification for accrual of fee before final delivery as those cited. The risk of loss

is practically negligible, the total profit is fairly definite, and even on cancellation, pro-rata profit is still reasonably assured.

15. The basic problem in dealing with CPFF contracts is the measure of partial performance, i.e., whether fees thereunder should be accrued under the established rules as to partial deliveries or percentage of completion otherwise determined, or whether, in view of their peculiar terms with respect to part payments, the determination of amounts billable by continuous government audit, and the minimum of risk carried by the contractor, the fees should be accrued as they are billable.

16. Ordinarily it is acceptable to accrue the fees as they become billable. The outstanding characteristic of CPFF contracts is reimbursement for all allowable costs, plus payment of a fixed fee for the contractor's efforts. Delivery of the finished product may not have its usual legal significance because title passes to the government prior thereto and the contractor's right to partial payment becomes unconditional in advance thereof; deliveries are not necessarily, under the terms of the agreement, evidence of the progress of the work or of the contractor's performance. Amounts billable indicate reasonably assured realization, possibly subject to renegotiation, because of the absence of a credit problem and minimum risk of loss involved. The fee appears to be earned when allowable costs are incurred or paid and the fee is billable. Finally, accrual on the basis of amounts billable is ordinarily not a departure from existing rules of accrual on the basis of partial performance, but rather a distinctive application of the rule for determining percentage of completion.

17. Judgment must be exercised in each case as to whether accrual of the fee when billable is preferable to accrual on the usual basis of delivery or of percentage of completion otherwise determined. While the approval of the government as to amounts billable would ordinarily be regarded as objective evidence, factors may exist which suggest an earlier or later accrual. Such factors include indications of substantial difference between estimated and final cost, as where preparatory or tooling-up costs were much more than estimated, raw material needs were greatly and unduly anticipated by advance purchases, or delays in delivery schedules or other circumstances suggest that costs are exceeding estimates. While such factors are normally considered by the government and billings for fees may be temporarily adjusted to safeguard against too early proportionate payment, the contractor, in accruing income, should also consider them, particularly when any substantial lag exists between expenditures and billings and audit thereof. In such cases, the presumption may be that the fee will not be found to be billable when the charges are presented, and conservatism in accrual will be necessary. Excess costs may be indicated in some cases to such an extent that accrual of fee before actual production would be unwise. Where such a situation exists the usual rule of deliveries or percentage of completion may be a preferable method of accruing the fee.

18. There are further questions as to whether the fee may be accrued as it is billed rather than as it becomes billable and whether accrual should be on the basis of the full fee or the full fee less the amount withheld. As to the first question, it seems obvious that when accrual in relation to expenditures is otherwise suitable it should be on the basis of amounts billable, since such matters as clerical delays in assembling data for billing should not affect the income statement. As to the second question, accrual on the basis of 100% of the fee is ordinarily preferable since, while payment of the balance depends on complete performance, such completion is to be expected under ordinary circumstances. Care must be exercised, of course, to provide for possible non-realization where there is doubt as to the collection of claimed costs or of the fee thereon.

b. What amounts are to be included in sales or revenue accounts?

19. This problem is whether sales or revenue as reported in the income statement should include reimbursable costs and the fee, or the fee alone. The answer to this question depends upon the terms of the contract and upon judgment as to which method gives the more useful information.

20. Some CPFF contracts are service contracts under which the contractor acts solely in an agency capacity, whether in the erection of facilities or the management of operations. These appear to call for inclusion in the income statement of the fee alone. In the case of supply contracts, however, the contractor is more than an agent. For instance, he is responsible to creditors for materials and services purchased; he is responsible to employees for salaries and wages; he ordinarily uses his own facilities in carrying out his agreement; his position in many respects is that of an ordinary principal. In view of these facts, and the desirability of indicating the volume of his activities, it appears desirable to include reimbursable costs, as well as fees, in sales or revenues.

c. What is the proper balance-sheet classification of unbilled costs and fee?

21. The principal reason for the existence of unbilled costs at any date is the time usually required, after receipt of material or expenditures

for labor, etc., to assemble data for billing. The right to bill usually exists upon expenditure or accrual, and that right unquestionably represents a receivable rather than an advance or inventory. There is nevertheless a difference in character between billed items and unbilled costs and distinction should be made between them on the balance sheet.

d. What is the proper balance-sheet treatment of various items, debit and credit, identified with CPFF contracts?

22. In statements of current assets and current liabilities, amounts due to and from the same person are ordinarily offset where, under the law, they may be offset in the process of collection or payment. An advance received on a contract is, however, usually not offset unless it is definitely regarded as a payment on account of contract work in progress, in which event it will be shown as a deduction from the related asset. An advance on a CPFF contract usually is made for the purpose of providing a revolving fund and is not ordinarily applied as a partial payment until the contract is completed or nears completion. It therefore appears to be preferable to offset advances on CPFF contracts against receivables in connection with the contracts only when it is expected that the advances will be applied in payment of those particular charges. In any case, amounts offset should be clearly disclosed.

Section B—Renegotiation

1. This section[1] deals with certain aspects of the accounting for those government contracts and subcontracts which are subject to renegotiation.

2. Where such contracts constitute a substantial part of the business done, the uncertainties resulting from the possibilities of renegotiation are usually such that appropriate indication of their existence should be given in the financial statements.

3. It is impossible to lay down general rules which can be applied satisfactorily in all cases. Here, as elsewhere in accounting, there must be an exercise of judgment which should be based on experience and on a clear understanding of the objective to be attained. That objective is to present the fairest possible financial statements, and at the same time make clear any uncertainties that limit the significance of such statements.

4. In keeping with the established accounting principle that provision should be made in financial statements for all liabilities, including reasonable

estimates for liabilities not accurately determinable, provision should be made for probable renegotiation refunds wherever the amount of such refunds can be reasonably estimated. Thus, in cases where experience of the company or of comparable companies with renegotiation determinations is available and would make a reasonable estimate practicable, provision in the income account for an estimated refund affecting the current year's operations is called for. In cases in which a reasonable estimate cannot be made, as where the effect of a new or amended renegotiation act cannot be foretold within reasonable limits or where a company is facing renegotiation for the first time and no reliable precedent is available, disclosure of the inability, because of these circumstances, to determine renegotiation effects and of the consequent uncertainties in the financial statements is necessary.

5. In addition to any provision made in the accounts, disclosure by footnote or otherwise may be required as to the uncertainties, their significance, and the basis used in determining the amount of the provision, such as the prior years' experience of the contractor or of similar contractors if their experience is available and is used, renegotiation discussions relating to the current year, etc. Such disclosure may be helpful in informing shareholders or other interested persons as to the company's status under the renegotiation law. It should also be recognized that, if conditions change, the results of a prior-year determination or settlement are not, in most cases, indicative of the amount probably refundable for the current year.

Treatment in Financial Statements

6. Provisions made for renegotiation refunds should be included in the balance sheet among the current liabilities.

7. Accounting treatment in the income statement should conform to the concept that profit is deemed to be realized when a sale in the ordinary course of business is effected, unless the circumstances are such that collection of the sales price is not reasonably assured.[2] Renegotiation refunds are commonly referred to as involving a refund of "excessive profits"; realistically, however, renegotiation involves an adjustment of the original contract or selling price. Since a provision for renegotiation refund indicates that the collection, or retention, of the selling price is not reasonably assured, the provision should preferably be treated in the income statement as a deduction from sales. Because of the interrelationship of renegotiation and taxes on income, the provision for

---

[1]The comments in this section are considered to be applicable also to price redetermination estimated to result in retroactive price reduction.
[2]See chapter 1, rule 1.

such taxes should then be computed accordingly.

8. The amount refundable is, however, generally a net amount, i.e., allowance is made for any taxes on income which may have been paid or assessed thereon. Therefore, as an alternative to the presentation indicated in the preceding paragraph, the provision for renegotation refund may be shown as a charge in the income statement, separately from the provision for taxes on income, or in combination therewith.

Renegotiation Refunds for Prior Years

9. A further question arises where a renegotiation refund applicable to a particular year is made in an amount materially different from the provision made in the financial statements originally issued for such year. The committee recommends that the difference between the renegotiation refund and the provision therefor be shown as a separate item in the current income statement, unless such inclusion would result in a distortion of the current net income, in which event the adjustment should be treated as an adjustment of earned surplus.[3] Where an adjustment of earned surplus is made there should be appropriate disclosure of the effect of the adjustment on the prior year's net income. The committee believes that a major retroactive adjustment of the provision made for a renegotiation refund can often best be disclosed by presenting a revised income statement for the prior year, either in comparative form in conjunction with the current year's financial statements[4] or otherwise, and it urges that this procedure be followed.

Section C—Terminated War and Defense Contracts

1. This section deals with problems involved in accounting for fixed-price war and defense supply contracts terminated, in whole or in part, for the convenience of the government. It does not deal specifically with terminated cost-plus-fixed-fee contracts nor with contracts for facilities or services. However, the conclusions reached herein may serve as guides for the accounting applicable to such special contracts. Terminations for default of the contractor involve problems of a different nature and are not considered here.

2. Except where the text clearly indicates otherwise, the term *contractor* is used to denote either a prime contractor or a subcontractor, and the term *contract* to denote either a prime contract or a subcontract.

Summary Statement

3. The profit of a contractor on a fixed-price supply contract terminated for the convenience of the government accrues as of the effective date of termination.

4. Those parts of the termination claim which are reasonably determinable should be included in financial statements after termination; when the total of the undeterminable elements is believed to be material, full disclosure of the essential facts should be made, by footnote or otherwise.

5. Under ordinary circumstances the termination claim should be classified as a current asset and unless the amount is relatively small should be separately disclosed.

6. Advances received on the contract before its termination may be shown in financial statements after termination as a deduction from the claim receivable and should be appropriately explained. Loans negotiated on the security of the termination claim, however, should be shown as current liabilities.

7. All of the contractor's own cost and profit elements included in the termination claim are preferably accounted for as a sale and if material in amount should be separately disclosed. The costs and expenses chargeable to the claim may then be given their usual classification in the accounts.

8. When inventory items whose costs are included in the termination claim are subsequently reacquired by the contractor the reacquisition value of those items should be recorded as a purchase and applied, together with other disposal credits, against the termination claim receivable.

9. So called *no-cost* settlements—those in which the contractor waives the right to make a claim—result in no transaction which could be reflected in sales. The costs applicable to the contract may be given their usual classification in the accounts; the inventory retained should not be treated as a purchase but should be accounted for according to the usual methods and standards applicable to inventories.

Discussion

10. Termination of war and defense contracts for the convenience of the government is a means of adjusting the production of materials to the varying requirements of the military services. Since termina-

---

[3]See chapter 8, paragraphs 11, 12, and 13.
[4]See chapter 2(a).

tions transfer active contracts in process of execution into claims in process of liquidation, they, like contract renegotiations and cost-plus-fixed-fee contracts, may have important effects on the financial statements of defense contractors.

When profit accrues

11. An important problem involved in accounting for the effect of terminations is that of determining the time at which profit earned on the contract should be recognized. This problem is similar to that described in other sections of this chapter on renegotiation and cost-plus-fixed-fee contracts in that it involves accrual at a specific date of an element of profit whose original measurement may be difficult and will require informed judgment, and whose final amount may not be determined until some future period.

12. Three dates have been mentioned as dates for the determination of profit from terminated contracts: (a) the effective date of termination; (b) the date of final settlement; and (c) some intermediate date, such as that on which the claim is finally prepared or filed. The effective date of termination is the date at which the contractor acquires the right to receive payment on the terminated portion of the contract. This date is also, of the three, the one most objectively determined.

13. Under the accrual basis of accounting recognition is given to revenues and expenses, to the fullest extent possible, in the period to which they relate. Profit on a contract of sale is ordinarily taken into account upon delivery or performance. However, as stated in section A of this chapter it is a generally accepted accounting procedure to accrue revenues under certain types of contracts, and thereby recognize profits, on the basis of partial performance where the circumstances are such that total profit can be estimated with reasonable accuracy and ultimate realization is reasonably assured. Thus, the accrual of profit under a cost-plus-fixed-fee contract is recognized as the fee becomes billable rather than when it is actually billed. Upon termination of a contract the contractor acquires a claim for fair compensation; the government reserves the option of acquiring any of the inventories for which the contractor makes claim under the terminated contract. Except to effect settlements and to protect and dispose of property, the expenses of which are reimbursable, the contractor need perform no further service under a terminated contract in order to enforce his claim. It follows that any profit arising out of such a contract accrues at the effective date of termination and, if the amount can be reasonably ascertained, should be recorded at that time.

Determination of claim

14. Practical application of the accrual principle to the accounting for terminated war and defense contracts rests upon the possibility of making a reasonable estimate of the amount of the termination claim before its final determination by settlement. This involves two principal considerations: (1) whether the costs of the contractor can be determined with reasonable accuracy and (2) whether the amount of profit to be realized can be estimated closely enough to justify inclusion in the accounts.

15. The various acts and regulations, including a statement of principles for determining costs and certain termination cost memorandums, describe in general terms the costs and expenses which are to be taken into account in arriving at fair compensation, as well as certain costs which are not allowable, and establish uniform termination policies and procedures.

16. While the total claim, and particularly the profit allowance, is subject to negotiation, the termination articles provide for a formula settlement allowing definite percentages of profit based on costs in the event of the failure of negotiations. This in effect fixes a minimum expectation of profit allowance since the formula percentages have also been recognized by regulation as a basis of negotiating settlement in the event of failure by the parties to agree on any other basis. The same regulations give other guides for estimating a fair profit allowance, which in some cases may be greater than the amount computed by the formula percentages. When the contractor, because of lack of prior negotiation experience or uncertainty as to the application of the principles of these regulations to a particular case, is unable to determine a more appropriate profit allowance, he may accrue the minimum amount determined by the formula percentages.

17. The profit to be included in the accounts of the contractor upon termination is the difference between (a) the amount of his recorded claim and (b) the total of the inventory, deferred and capitalized items, and other costs applicable to the terminated contract as they are currently included in his accounts. This profit may exceed the amount specified as profit in the claim because costs applicable to the terminated portion of the contract may be allowable in the claim even though they may have been properly written off as incurred in prior periods.

18. In some cases it will be impossible to make a reasonable estimate of a termination claim in time for inclusion in the financial statements of the

period in which the termination occurs. Effect may then be given in the statements to those parts of the termination claim which are determinable with reasonable certainty and disclosure made, by footnote or otherwise, of the status of the remainder.

19. When the contractor's claim includes items of known controversial nature it should be stated at the amount estimated to be collectible. When a particular termination claim or part thereof is so uncertain in amount that it cannot be reasonably estimated, it is preferable not to give effect to that part of the claim in the financial statements; but if the total of such undeterminable elements is material, the circumstances should be disclosed in statements issued before the removal of the uncertainty. In an extreme case involving undeterminable claims, consideration should be given to delaying the issuance of financial statements until necessary data are available.

Presentation in financial statements

20. Termination has the effect of converting an active contract in process into a claim, or, from an accounting standpoint, from inventories and other charges into an account receivable. This receivable arises in the regular course of business; it is part of the working capital; and in view of the provisions made for financial assistance to the contractor during the period of termination, collection in large part may be expected within a relatively short time. The termination claim should therefore be classified as a current asset, unless there is an indication of extended delay, such as serious disagreement pointing to probable litigation, which would exclude it from this classification.

21. Although a claim may be composed of several elements representing reimbursable items of special equipment, deferred charges, inventories, and other items, as well as claims for profit, it is preferable to record the claim in one account. When the total of termination claims is material it should be disclosed separately from other receivables. It is also desirable to segregate claims directly against the government from claims against other contractors where the amounts are significant.

22. To assure adequate financial assistance to contractors, the acts provide in some cases for partial payments and in others for such payments or guaranteed loans from the effective date of termination until final settlement. Partial payments are, of course, to be recorded as reductions of the termination claim receivable. Termination loans, on the other hand, are definite liabilities to third parties, even though guaranteed in whole or in part by the government, and accordingly should be shown in

the balance sheet as liabilities, with appropriate cross-reference to the related claim or claims. When a terminated contract is one on which advance payments had previously been received, the financial statements of the contractor issued before final collection of the claim ordinarily should reflect any balance of those advances disclosed as deductions from the claim receivable.[1] Financial statements issued before the termination claim is recorded should disclose, by footnote or otherwise, the relationship of such liabilities to a possible termination claim receivable.

23. Ordinarily, a termination will result in the cessation of a contractor's activity through which materials or services have been supplied under the contract and of the related transactions which have been reflected in the contractor's income accounts as sales and cost elements. In effect, termination policies and procedures provide a basis upon which the contractor's costs in process may become the elements of a final sale under the terminated portion of the contract. Accordingly, the amount of the contractor's termination claim representing his cost and profit elements should be treated as a sale and the costs and expenses chargeable to the claim given their usual classification in the income statement. Because these termination sales are of a special type, their financial results should not be appraised in the same manner as are those of regular sales and they should, if material in amount, be separately disclosed in the income statement. Any items which the contractor chooses to retain without claim for cost or loss are, of course, not sold but remain as inventory or deferred charges in the contractor's accounts.

Claims of subcontractors

24. The term *subcontractor's claims* as used in connection with terminated contracts refers to those obligations of a contractor to a subcontractor which arise from the subcontractor's costs incurred through transactions which were related to the contract terminated but did not result in the transfer of billable materials or services to the contractor before termination. Other obligations of a contractor to a subcontractor, arising through transactions by which materials or services of the subcontractor are furnished or supplied to the contractor, are considered to be liabilities incurred in the ordinary course of business and are not included in the term *claims of subcontractors*.

25. The termination articles provide that, following the termination of a contract, the contractor shall settle, with the approval or ratification of the contracting officer when necessary, all claims of sub-

---

[1] See chapter 11(a), paragraph 22.

contractors arising out of the termination; and that the contractor shall be paid, as part of his settlement, the cost of settling and paying claims arising out of the stoppage of work under subcontracts affected by the termination. While a contractor ordinarily is liable to his subcontractors or suppliers for such obligations, the amounts due them are an element in his termination claim and often are not paid to them until after his claim has been settled. He often has no control over the filing of subcontractors' claims and may not know their amount until some time after the termination date or even until some time after he has filed and received payment for his own claim.

26. The possibility that a contractor may suffer loss through failure to recover the amount of his liability on subcontractors' claims arises principally from overcommitments, errors in ordering, and similar causes. Provision should be made in his accounts for losses of this character which are known or believed to be probable.

27. Although the principle that liabilities may not be offset against assets in the financial statements is generally approved by accountants, there is no general agreement as to the accounting treatment to be accorded subcontractors' claims which are expected to be fully recoverable. To the extent that a subcontractor's claim is considered to be unrecoverable no difference of opinion exists; the liability should be recorded and provision made for any contemplated loss. The difference of opinion relates to those subcontractors' claims which are deemed to be fully recoverable.

28. Some accountants believe that the effect of the various acts and regulations is to establish a relationship between the claims of subcontractors and the resulting right of the contractor under his own termination claim which differs from an ordinary commercial relationship and justifies their omission from the accounts. Recoverable subcontractors' claims are thus said to be in the nature of contingent liabilities, which are customarily omitted from the accounts except where a loss is expected. Contingent liabilities may be disclosed in the financial statements without recording them as assets and liabilities, and even when they are recorded it is customary accounting practice to show them on the balance sheet as deductions from the related contingent assets so that no effect upon financial ratios and relationships results.

29. Other accountants believe that the nature of an obligation to a subcontractor is that of an ordinary liability, even though it may arise through the termination of a war or defense contract, and that the contractor's termination claim receivable, although related to the subcontractor's claim, is to be accounted for independently as an asset. This group believes that all subcontractors' claims, to the extent that they are reasonably ascertainable, should be recorded in the accounts and displayed in the contractor's balance sheet as current liabilities, and that the amounts recoverable by the contractor should be included in his termination claim receivable. To the extent that the amounts of subcontractors' claims are not reasonably determinable, disclosure by footnote or otherwise in the financial statements is believed to be adequate.

30. Because of the merits and prevalence of these alternative views, the committee expresses no preference for either treatment and considers either to be acceptable.

Disposal credits

31. Disposal credits are amounts deducted from the contractor's termination claim receivable by reason of his retention, or sale to outsiders, of some or all of the termination inventory for which claim was made. In the case of items retained, either as scrap or for use by the contractor, the amount of the credit is determined by agreement between the contractor and a representative of the government. The sale of inventory items by the contractor is likewise subject to approval by the government, except as permitted by regulation. Since the amount of the contractor's termination claim, as already indicated, is properly recorded as a sale, any elements included in that claim for items of inventory retained by the contractor are, in effect, reacquired by him and should be treated as purchases at the agreed value. Amounts received for items sold to others with the approval of the government are collections for the account of the government and should be applied in reduction of the claim receivable. Obviously inventories or other items that are retained by the contractor after termination without claim for loss should not be included as an element of the termination claim.

No-cost settlements

32. A contractor whose contract is terminated may prefer to retain the termination inventory for use in other production or for disposal at his own risk. For these or other reasons the contractor may prefer to make no claim against the government or a higher-tier contractor. In the case of such no-cost settlements there is no sale of inventory or other items to the government and therefore no occasion to accrue any profit arising out of the termination. The costs otherwise applicable to the contract should be given their usual treatment in the accounts. Items of inventory or other property retained, having been previously recorded, will, of course, require no charge to purchases but should be treated in accordance with the usual procedures applicable to such assets.

Chapter 12

FOREIGN OPERATIONS AND FOREIGN EXCHANGE

1. The recommendations made in this chapter apply to United States companies which have branches or subsidiaries operating in foreign countries.

2. Since World War I foreign operations have been influenced to a marked degree by wars, departures from the gold standard, devaluations of currencies, currency restrictions, government regulations, etc.

3. Although comparatively few countries in recent years have had unrestricted currencies and exchanges, it is nevertheless true that many companies have been doing business in foreign countries having varying degrees of restrictions; in some cases they have been carrying on all operations regarded as normal, including the transmission of funds. In view of the difficulties mentioned above, however, the accounting treatment of assets, liabilities, losses, and gains involved in the conduct of foreign business and to be included or reflected in the financial statements of United States companies requires careful consideration.

4. A sound procedure for United States companies to follow is to show earnings from foreign operations in their own accounts only to the extent that funds have been received in the United States or unrestricted funds are available for transmission thereto. Appropriate provision should be made also for known losses.

5. Any foreign earnings reported beyond the amounts received in the United States should be carefully considered in the light of all the facts. The amounts should be disclosed if they are significant, and they should be reserved against to the extent that their realization in dollars appears to be doubtful.

6. As to assets held abroad, the accounting should take into consideration the fact that most foreign assets stand in some degree of jeopardy, so far as ultimate realization by United States owners is concerned. Under these conditions it is important that especial care be taken in each case to make full disclosure in the financial statements of United States companies of the extent to which they include significant foreign items.

7. Where more than one foreign exchange rate is in effect, care should be exercised to select the one most clearly realistic and appropriate in the circumstances.

Consolidation of Foreign Subsidiaries

8. In view of the uncertain values and availability of the assets and net income of foreign subsidiaries subject to controls and exchange restrictions and the consequent unrealistic statements of income that may result from the translation of many foreign currencies into dollars, careful consideration should be given to the fundamental question of whether it is proper to consolidate the statements of foreign subsidiaries with the statements of United States companies. Whether consolidation of foreign subsidiaries is decided upon or not, adequate disclosure of foreign operations should be made.

9. The following are among the possible ways of providing information relating to such foreign subsidiaries:

a. To exclude foreign subsidiaries from consolidation and to furnish (1) statements in which only domestic subsidiaries are consolidated and (2) as to foreign subsidiaries, a summary in suitable form of their assets and liabilities, their income and losses for the year, and the parent company's equity therein. The total amount of investments in foreign subsidiaries should be shown separately, and the basis on which the amount was arrived at should be stated. If these investments include any surplus of foreign subsidiaries and such surplus had previously been included in consolidated surplus, the amount should be separately shown or earmarked in stating the consolidated surplus in the statements here suggested. The exclusion of foreign subsidiaries from consolidation does not make it acceptable practice to include intercompany profits which would be eliminated if such subsidiaries were consolidated.

b. To consolidate domestic and foreign subsidiaries and to furnish in addition the summary described in (a)(2) above.

c. To furnish (1) complete consolidated statements and also (2) consolidated statements for domestic companies only.

d. To consolidate domestic and foreign subsidiaries and to furnish in addition parent company statements showing the investment in and income from foreign subsidiaries separately from those of domestic subsidiaries.

Losses and Gains on Foreign Exchange

10. Realized losses or gains on foreign exchange should be charged against or credited to operations.

11. Provision should be made, ordinarily by a charge against operations, for declines in translation

value of foreign net current and working assets (unrealized losses). Unrealized gains should preferably be carried to a suspense account, except to the extent that they offset prior provisions for unrealized losses, in which case they may be credited to the account previously charged.

Translation of Assets, Liabilities, Losses, and Gains

Balance Sheet

12. Fixed assets, permanent investments, and long-term receivables should be translated into dollars at the rates prevailing when such assets were acquired or constructed. When large items are purchased for United States dollars (or from the proceeds of sale of such dollars), the United States dollar cost will, of course, be used. If, however, the purchase is made in some foreign currency (obtained from earnings or borrowings), then the cost of the assets should be the equivalent of the amount of foreign currency in United States dollars, at the rate of exchange prevailing at the time payment is made. An exception to the foregoing general principle might be made where fixed assets, permanent investments, or long-term receivables were acquired shortly before a substantial and presumably permanent change in the exchange rate with funds obtained in the country concerned, in which case it may be appropriate to restate the dollar equivalents of such assets to the extent of the change in the related debt.

13. In consolidating or combining the accounts, depreciation should be computed on the amount of fixed assets as expressed in United States dollars, even though for purposes of local taxation it may be impossible to show the foreign currency equivalent of the full amount of depreciation on the foreign statements.

14. Cash, accounts receivables, and other current assets, unless covered by forward exchange contracts, should be translated at the rate of exchange prevailing on the date of the balance sheet.

15. Inventory should follow the standard rule of *cost or market, whichever is lower* in dollars. Where accounts are to be stated in which the question of foreign exchange enters and the inventory is not translated at the rate of exchange prevailing on the date of the balance sheet, as is usually done with current assets, the burden of proof is on those who wish to follow some other procedure.

16. There are, however, undoubtedly many cases where the cost or a portion of the cost of an article was incurred when the foreign currency was at a substantially higher rate of exchange than existed on the closing day of the financial period. In many cases such an asset could not be replaced for the amount in foreign currency at which it appears in the records of the branch or subsidiary company. In some cases the replacement price in foreign currency would undoubtedly have increased since the fall in exchange, and it would be inequitable to treat *the lower of cost or market* as a mere translation at the closing rate of the foreign currency cost price, where the article could now be replaced only at a much higher amount in foreign currency. Where the selling price obtainable in dollars, after deducting a reasonable percentage to cover selling and other local expenses, exceeds the cost of the article in dollars at the rate prevailing as of the date of purchase, such original dollar equivalent may be considered as the cost for purposes of inventory.

17. Current liabilities payable in foreign currency should be translated into dollars at the rate of exchange in force on the date of the balance sheet.

18. Long-term liabilities and capital stock stated in foreign currency should not be translated at the closing rate, but at the rates of exchange prevailing when they were originally incurred or issued. This is a general rule, but an exception may exist in respect to long-term debt incurred or capital stock issued in connection with the acquisition of fixed assets, permanent investments, or long-term receivables a short time before a substantial and presumably permanent change in the exchange rate. In such instances it may be appropriate to state the long-term debt or the capital stock at the new rate and proper to deal with the exchange differences as an adjustment of the cost of the assets acquired.

Profit and Loss Statement

19. The operating statements of foreign branches or subsidiaries, or of domestic corporations conducting their business in foreign currencies (buying, selling, and manufacturing), should preferably, where there have been wide fluctuations in exchange, be translated at the average rate of exchange applicable to each month or, if this procedure would involve too much labor, on the basis of a carefully weighted average.

20. Where a major change in an exchange rate takes place during a fiscal year, there may be situations in which more realistic results will be obtained if income computed in foreign currencies is translated for the entire fiscal year at the new rates in effect after such major fluctuation. This procedure would have the practical advantage of making unnecessary a cutoff at the date of the change in the exchange rate. Where dividends have been paid prior to a major change in the exchange rate, out of earnings of the current fiscal year, that portion of the income for the year should be considered as having been

earned at the rate at which such dividend was paid irrespective of the rates used in translating the remainder of the earnings.

21. While the possibility of losses from currency devaluation may ordinarily be considered to be a risk inherent in the conduct of business in foreign countries, the world-wide scope and unprecedented magnitude of devaluations that have occurred in recent years are such that they cannot be regarded as recurrent hazards of business. Accordingly, exchange adjustments arising from such extraordinary developments, if so material in amount that their inclusion in the income statement would impair the significance of net income to an extent that misleading inferences might be drawn therefrom, appear to be of such nature that they might appropriately be charged to surplus.

* * * * * *

22. The foregoing is no more than a brief résumé of the generally accepted principles pertaining to the treatment of foreign exchange as applied to the statements of accounts of American corporations. The practical problems which arise in their application should receive careful consideration in each case.

Two members of the committee, Messrs. Lindquist and Mason, assented with qualification to adoption of chapter 12.

Mr. Lindquist believes that the accounting indicated in paragraph 11 for unrealized losses and gains arising from exchange fluctuations should be consistent for losses and gains to the extent that they result from normal temporary fluctuations in exchange rates.

Mr. Mason does not approve the inconsistent treatment of unrealized losses and unrealized gains from exchange fluctuations. He would prefer to defer them both. He also believes that long-term receivables and long-term liabilities should be translated at current rates.

Chapter 13

COMPENSATION

Section A—Pension Plans: Annuity Costs Based on Past Service

1. This section deals with the accounting treatment of costs arising out of past service which are incurred under pension plans involving payments to outside agencies such as insurance companies and trustees. Self-administered and informal plans which do not require payments to outside agencies are not dealt with because of their special features and lack of uniformity. The principles set forth herein, however, are generally applicable to those plans as well.

2. Charges with respect to pension costs based on past service have sometimes been made to surplus on the ground that such payments are indirectly compensation for services and that since the services upon which computation of the payments is based were performed in the past, the compensation should not be permitted to affect any period or periods other than those in which the services involved were performed. In other cases all annuity costs based on past service have been charged to income in the period of the plan's inauguration as a current cost of originating the plan. In still other cases the position has been taken that a pension plan cannot bring the hoped-for benefits in the future unless past as well as future services are given recognition and, accordingly, annuity costs based on past service have been spread over a period of present and future years. The last method is the one permitted under provisions of the Internal Revenue Code.[1]

3. The committee believes that, even though the calculation is based on past service, costs of annuities based on such service are incurred in contemplation of present and future services, not necessarily of the individual affected but of the organization as a whole, and therefore should be charged to the present and future periods benefited. This belief is based on the assumption that although the benefits to a company flowing from pension plans are intangible, they are nevertheless real. The element of past service is one of the important considerations in establishing pension plans, and annuity costs measured by such past service contribute to the benefits gained by the adoption of a plan. It is usually expected that such benefits will include better employee morale, the removal of superannuated employees from the payroll, and the attraction and retention of more desirable personnel, all of which should result in improved operations.

4. The committee, accordingly, is of the opinion that:

a. Costs of annuities based on past service should be allocated to current and future periods; however, if they are not sufficiently material in amount to distort the results of operations in a single period, they may be absorbed in the current year;

b. Costs of annuities based on past service should not be charged to surplus.

---

[1] See IRC Sec. 23(p)(1)(A).

5. This opinion is not to be interpreted as requiring that charges be made to income rather than to reserves previously provided, or that recognition be given in the accounts of current or future periods to pension costs written off prior to the issuance of an opinion on this subject.

Section B—Compensation Involved in Stock Option and Stock Purchase Plans

1. The practice of granting to officers and other employees options to purchase or rights to subscribe for shares of a corporation's capital stock has been followed by a considerable number of corporations over a period of many years. To the extent that such options and rights involve a measurable amount of compensation, this cost of services received should be accounted for as such. The amount of compensation involved may be substantial and omission of such costs from the corporation's accounting may result in overstatement of net income to a significant degree. Accordingly, consideration is given herein to the accounting treatment of compensation represented by stock options or purchase rights granted to officers and other employees.[1]

2. For convenience, this section will discuss primarily the problems of compensation raised by stock option plans. However, the committee feels that substantially the same problems may be encountered in connection with stock purchase plans made available to employees, and the discussion below is applicable to such plans also.

Rights Involving Compensation

3. Stock options involving an element of compensation usually arise out of an offer or agreement by an employer corporation to issue shares of its capital stock to one or more officers or other employees (hereinafter referred to as grantees) at a stated price. The grantees are accorded the right to require issuance of the shares either at a specified time or during some determinable period. In some cases the grantee's options are exercisable only if at the time of exercise certain conditions exist, such as that the grantee is then or until a specified date has been an employee. In other cases, the grantees may have undertaken certain obligations, such as to remain in the employment of the corporation for at least a specified period, or to take the shares only for investment purposes and not for resale.

Rights Not Involving Compensation

4. Stock option plans in many cases may be intended not primarily as a special form of compensation but rather as an important means of raising capital, or as an inducement to obtain greater or more widespread ownership of the corporation's stock among its officers and other employees. In general, the terms under which such options are granted, including any conditions as to exercise of the options or disposal of the stock acquired, are the most significant evidence ordinarily available as to the nature and purpose of a particular stock option or stock option plan. In practice, it is often apparent that a particular option or plan involves elements of two or more of the above purposes. Where the inducements are not larger per share than would reasonably be required in an offer of shares to all shareholders for the purpose of raising an equivalent amount of capital, no compensation need be presumed to be involved.

5. Stock purchase plans also are frequently an integral part of a corporation's program to secure equity capital or to obtain widespread ownership among employees, or both. In such cases, no element of compensation need be considered to be present if the purchase price is not lower than is reasonably required to interest employees generally or to secure the contemplated funds.

Time of Measurement of Compensation

6. In the case of stock options involving compensation, the principal problem is the measurement of the compensation. This problem involves selection of the date as of which measurement of any element of compensation is to be made and the manner of measurement. The date as of which measurement is made is of critical importance since the fair value of the shares under option may vary materially in the often extended period during which the option is outstanding. There may be at least six dates to be considered for this purpose: (a) the date of the adop-

---

[1]Bulletin 37, "Accounting for Compensation in the Form of Stock Options," was issued in November, 1948. Issuance of a revised bulletin in 1953 and its expansion to include stock purchase plans were prompted by the very considerable increase in the use of certain types of option and purchase plans following the enactment in 1950 of Section 130A of the Internal Revenue Code. This section granted specialized tax treatment to employee stock options if certain requirements were met as to the terms of the option, as to the circumstances under which the option was granted and could be exercised and as to the holding and disposal of the stock acquired thereunder. In general, the effect of Section 130A is to eliminate or minimize the amount of income taxable to the employee as compensation and to deny to the issuing corporation any tax deduction in respect of such restricted options. In 1951, the Federal Salary Stabilization Board issued rules and regulations relating to stock options and purchase rights granted to employees whereby options generally comparable in nature to the restricted stock options specified in Section 130A might be considered for its purposes not to involve compensation, or to involve compensation only in limited amounts.

tion of an option plan, (b) the date on which an option is granted to a specific individual, (c) the date on which the grantee has performed any conditions precedent to exercise of the option, (d) the date on which the grantee may first exercise the option, (e) the date on which the option is exercised by the grantee, and (f) the date on which the grantee disposes of the stock acquired.

7. Of the six dates mentioned two are not relevant to the question considered in this bulletin—cost to the corporation which is granting the option. The date of adoption of an option plan clearly has no relevance, inasmuch as the plan per se constitutes no more than a proposed course of action which is ineffective until options are granted thereunder. The date on which a grantee disposes of the shares acquired under an option is equally immaterial since this date will depend on the desires of the individual as a shareholder and bears no necessary relation to the services performed.[2]

8. The date on which the option is exercised has been advocated as the date on which a cost may be said to have been incurred. Use of this date is supported by the argument that only then will it be known whether or not the option will be exercised. However, beginning with the time at which the grantee may first exercise the option he is in effect speculating for his own account. His delay has no discernible relation to his status as an employee but reflects only his judgment as an investor.

9. The date on which the grantee may first exercise the option will generally coincide with, but in some cases may follow, the date on which the grantee will have performed any conditions precedent to exercise of the option. Accordingly this date presents no special problems differing from those to be discussed in the next paragraph.

10. There remain to be considered the date on which an option is granted to a specific individual and the date on which the grantee has fulfilled any conditions precedent to exercise of the option. When compensation is paid in a form other than cash the *amount* of compensation is ordinarily determined by the fair value of the property which was agreed to be given in exchange for the services to be rendered. The time at which such fair value is to be determined may be subject to some difference of opinion but it appears that the date on which an option is granted to a specific individual would be the appropriate point at which to evaluate the cost to the employer, since it was the value at that date which the employer may be presumed to have had in mind. In most of the cases under discussion, more-

over, the only important contingency involved is the continuance of the grantee in the employment of the corporation, a matter very largely within the control of the grantee and usually the main objective of the grantor. Under such circumstances it may be assumed that if the stock option were granted as a part of an employment contract, both parties had in mind a valuation of the option at the date of the contract; and accordingly, value at that date should be used as the amount to be accounted for as compensation. If the option were granted as a form of supplementary compensation otherwise than as an integral part of an employment contract, the grantor is nevertheless governed in determining the option price and the number of shares by conditions then existing. It follows that it is the value of the option at that time, rather than the grantee's ultimate gain or loss on the transaction, which for accounting purposes constitutes whatever compensation the grantor intends to pay. The committee therefore concludes that in most cases, including situations where the right to exercise is conditional upon continued employment, valuation should be made of the option as of the date of grant.

11. The date of grant also represents the date on which the corporation foregoes the principal alternative use of the shares which it places subject to option, i.e., the sale of such shares at the then prevailing market price. Viewed in this light, the *cost* of utilizing the shares for purposes of the option plan can best be measured in relation to what could then have been obtained through sale of such shares in the open market. However, the fact that the grantor might, as events turned out, have obtained at some later date either more or less for the shares in question than at the date of the grant does not bear upon the measurement of the compensation which can be said to have been in contemplation of the parties at the date the option was granted.

Manner of Measurement

12. Freely exercisable option rights, even at prices above the current market price of the shares, have been traded in the public markets for many years, but there is no such objective means for measuring the value of an option which is not transferable and is subject to such other restrictions as are usually present in options of the nature here under discussion. Although there is, from the standpoint of the grantee, a value inherent in a restricted future right to purchase shares at a price at or even above the fair value of shares at the grant date, the committee believes it is impracticable to measure any such value. As to the grantee any positive element may, for practical purposes, be deemed to be largely or

---

[2]This was the date on which income or gain taxable to the grantee may arise under Section 130A. Use of this date for tax purposes is doubtless based on considerations as to the ability of the optionee to pay taxes prior to sale of the shares.

wholly offset by the negative effect of the restrictions ordinarily present in options of the type under discussion. From the viewpoint of the grantor corporation no measurable cost can be said to have been incurred because it could not at the grant date have realized more than the *fair value* of the optioned shares, the concept of fair value as here used encompassing the possibility and prospect of future developments. On the other hand, it follows in the opinion of the committee that the value to the grantee and the related cost to the corporation of a restricted right to purchase shares at a price *below* the fair value of the shares at the grant date may for the purposes here under discussion be taken as the excess of the then fair value of the shares over the option price.

13. While market quotations of shares are an important and often a principal factor in determining the fair value of shares, market quotations at a given date are not necessarily conclusive evidence.[3] Where significant market quotations cannot be obtained, other recognized methods of valuation have to be used. Furthermore, in determining the fair value of shares for the purpose of measuring the cost incurred by a corporation in the issuance of an option, it is appropriate to take into consideration such modifying factors as the range of quotations over a reasonable period and the fact that the corporation by selling shares pursuant to an option may avoid some or all of the expenses otherwise incurred in a sale of shares. The absence of a ready market, as in the case of shares of closely-held corporations, should also be taken into account and may require the use of other means of arriving at fair value than by reference to an occasional market quotation or sale of the security.

Other Considerations

14. If the period for which payment for services is being made by the issuance of the stock option is not specifically indicated in the offer or agreement, the value of the option should be apportioned over the period of service for which the payment of the compensation seems appropriate in the existing circumstances. Accrual of the compensation over the period selected should be made by means of charges against the income account. Upon exercise of an option the sum of the cash received and the amount of the charge to income should be accounted for as the consideration received on issuance of the stock.

15. In connection with financial statements, disclosure should be made as to the status of the option or plan at the end of the period of report, including the number of shares under option, the option price, and the number of shares as to which options were exercisable. As to options exercised during the period, disclosure should be made of the number of shares involved and the option price thereof.

One member of the committee, Mr. Mason, assented with qualification to adoption of section B of chapter 13. One member, Mr. Knight, did not vote.

Mr. Mason assents only under the assumption that if an option lapses after the grantee becomes entitled to exercise it, the related compensation shall be treated as a contribution by the grantee to the capital of the grantor.

Chapter 14

DISCLOSURE OF LONG-TERM LEASES IN FINANCIAL STATEMENTS OF LESSEES

[Totally superseded; refer to the status page of this pronouncement.]

Chapter 15

UNAMORTIZED DISCOUNT, ISSUE COST, AND REDEMPTION PREMIUM ON BONDS REFUNDED

[Totally superseded; refer to the status page of this pronouncement.]

---

[3] Whether treasury or unissued shares are to be used to fulfill the obligation is not material to a determination of value.

(This page intentionally left blank.)

Appendix A

**LIST OF ACCOUNTING RESEARCH
BULLETINS WITH CROSS-REFERENCES**

The following is a chronological list of Account-

ing Research Bulletins 1 through 42, which are now superseded. It indicates the chapter of the restatement containing each former bulletin, or portion thereof, as revised.

No.	Date Issued		Title	Restatement Chapter Number
1	Sept.,	1939	General Introduction and Rules Formerly Adopted ...	Introduction and Chap. 1
2	Sept.,	1939	Unamortized Discount and Redemption Premium on Bonds Refunded	15
3	Sept.,	1939	Quasi-Reorganization or Corporate Readjustment— Amplification of Institute Rule No. 2 of 1934........	7A
4	Dec.,	1939	Foreign Operations and Foreign Exchange	12
5	April,	1940	Depreciation on Appreciation.....................	9B
6	April,	1940	Comparative Statements.........................	2A
7	Nov.,	1940	Reports of Committee on Terminology............	*
8	Feb.,	1941	Combined Statement of Income and Earned Surplus ..	2B
9	May,	1941	Report of Committee on Terminology..............	*
10	June,	1941	Real and Personal Property Taxes	10A
11	Sept.,	1941	Corporate Accounting for Ordinary Stock Dividends..	7B
12	Sept.,	1941	Report of Committee on Terminology..............	*
13	Jan.,	1942	Accounting for Special Reserves Arising out of the War..................................	**
14	Jan.,	1942	Accounting for United States Treasury Tax Notes.....	3B
15	Sept.,	1942	The Renegotiation of War Contracts	11B
16	Oct.,	1942	Report of Committee on Terminology..............	*
17	Dec.,	1942	Post-War Refund of Excess-Profits Tax.............	**
18	Dec.,	1942	Unamortized Discount and Redemption Premium on Bonds Refunded (Supplement)	15
19	Dec.,	1942	Accounting under Cost-Plus-Fixed-Fee Contracts.....	11A
20	Nov.,	1943	Report of Committee on Terminology..............	*
21	Dec.,	1943	Renegotiation of War Contracts (Supplement)	11B
22	May,	1944	Report of Committee on Terminology..............	*
23	Dec.,	1944	Accounting for Income Taxes.....................	10B
24	Dec.,	1944	Accounting for Intangible Assets	5
25	April,	1945	Accounting for Terminated War Contracts	11C
26	Oct.,	1946	Accounting for the Use of Special War Reserves	**
27	Nov.,	1946	Emergency Facilities	9C
28	July,	1947	Accounting Treatment of General Purpose Contingency Reserves	6
29	July,	1947	Inventory Pricing	4
30	Aug.,	1947	Current Assets and Current Liabilities: Working Capital......................................	3A
31	Oct.,	1947	Inventory Reserves	6
32	Dec.,	1947	Income and Earned Surplus......................	8
33	Dec.,	1947	Depreciation and High Costs	9A
34	Oct.,	1948	Recommendation of Committee on Terminology—Use of Term "Reserve"	*
35	Oct.,	1948	Presentation of Income and Earned Surplus	8
36	Nov.,	1948	Pension Plans: Accounting for Annuity Costs Based on Past Services	13A
37	Nov.,	1948	Accounting for Compensation in the Form of Stock Options.............................	13B
38	Oct.,	1949	Disclosure of Long-Term Leases in Financial Statements of Lessees	14

*Terminology bulletins published separately.
**Withdrawn. See explanation ff. in Appendix C.

*Terminology bulletins published separately.
**Withdrawn. See explanation ff. in Appendix C.

Appendix B

CHANGES OF SUBSTANCE MADE IN THE COURSE OF RESTATING AND REVISING THE BULLETINS

1. Restatement and revision of the Accounting Research Bulletins involved numerous changes in wording, amounting in some cases to complete rewriting, but most of these changes were made in the interest of clarification, condensation, or elimination of material no longer pertinent. Changes in substance where necessary were made and are set forth below by chapters. Particular attention is called to the comments respecting the application of government securities against liabilities for federal taxes on income, write-offs of intangibles, and the treatment of refunds of income taxes based on the carry-back of losses and unused excess-profits credits.

Applicability of Bulletins

2. In Bulletin No. 1 no general comment was made as to the applicability of the committee's pronouncements other than to state that they should not be regarded as applicable to investment trusts. That statement has been omitted. A new statement of applicability appears in the introduction, which indicates that, in general, the committee's opinions should be regarded as applicable primarily to business enterprises organized for profit. The statement reads as follows:

3. "The principal objective of the committee has been to narrow areas of difference and inconsistency in accounting practices, and to further the development and recognition of generally accepted

accounting principles, through the issuance of opinions and recommendations that would serve as criteria for determining the suitability of accounting practices reflected in financial statements and representations of commercial and industrial companies. In this endeavor, the committee has considered the interpretation and application of such principles as appeared to it to be pertinent to particular accounting problems. The committee has not directed its attention to accounting problems or procedures of religious, charitable, scientific, educational, and similar non-profit institutions, municipalities, professional firms, and the like. Accordingly, except where there is a specific statement of a different intent by the committee, its opinions and recommendations are directed primarily to business enterprises organized for profit."

Current Assets and Current Liabilities—Chapter 3, Section A

4. A comment has been included under current assets to the effect that the description of the basis of pricing inventories should include an indication of the method of determining the cost—e.g., *average cost, first-in first-out, last-in first-out,* etc.

Application of United States Government Securities Against Liabilities for Federal Taxes on Income—Chapter 3, Section B

5. In Bulletin No. 14 the committee expressed approval of the offsetting of United States Treasury Tax Notes, Tax Series A-1943 and B-1943, against liabilities for federal taxes on income in the balance sheet, provided that at the date of the balance sheet or of the independent auditor's report there was no evidence of an intent not to surrender the notes in payment of the taxes. Government securities having

restrictive terms similar to those contained in the 1943 tax series are no longer issued but certain other types of government securities have since been issued which, by their terms, may be surrendered in payment of liabilities for federal taxes on income. In section B of chapter 3 the committee sanctions the offsetting of these securities against liabilities for federal taxes on income. It also expresses the opinion that extension of the practice to include the offset of other types of United States government securities, although a deviation from the general rule against offsets, is not so significant a deviation as to call for an exception in an accountant's report on the financial statements.

Intangible Assets—Chapter 5

6. Bulletin No. 24, which was published in 1944, stated the committee's belief that the long accepted practice of eliminating type (b) intangibles (i.e., intangibles with no limited term of existence and as to which there is, at the time of acquisition, no indication of limited life) against any existing surplus, capital or earned, even though the value of the asset was unimpaired, should be discouraged, especially if proposed to be effected by charges to capital surplus.

7. In chapter 5 the committee expresses the opinion that lump-sum write-offs of type (b) intangibles should in no case be charged against capital surplus, should not be made against earned surplus immediately after acquisition, and, if not amortized systematically, should be carried at cost until an event has taken place which indicates a loss or a limitation on the useful life of the intangibles.

Contingency Reserves—Chapter 6

8. In chapter 6 the opinion is expressed that the preferable balance-sheet treatment of general purpose contingency reserves (a subject not specifically covered in Bulletins Nos. 28 and 31) is to show them under stockholders' equity.

Quasi-Reorganization or Corporate Readjustment—Chapter 7, Section A

9. Bulletin No. 3 stated that a readjustment of accounts through quasi-reorganization calls for the opening of a new earned surplus account dating from the effective date of the readjustment, but made no reference to the length of time such dating should continue. Section A of chapter 7 states that "... this dating should be disclosed in financial statements until such time as the effective date is no longer deemed to possess any special significance."

Business Combinations—Chapter 7, Section C

10. The opinions expressed in Bulletin No. 40 have been amplified to indicate that any adjustment of assets or of surplus which would be in conformity with generally accepted accounting principles in the absence of a combination would be equally acceptable if effected in connection with a pooling of interests.

Income Taxes—Chapter 10, Section B

11. In connection with the presentation of allocated income taxes in the income statement, the committee recognizes the possibility of disclosure in a footnote or in the body of the income statement in special cases when the recommended presentation is not considered to be practicable. The revision also contains a statement that in some cases the use of a current over-all effective tax rate or, as in the case of deferred income, an estimated future tax rate may be appropriate in computing the tax effect attributable to a particular transaction.

12. In the old bulletin the committee recommended that where tax reductions result from the carryforward of losses or unused excess-profits credits, the income statement indicate the results of operations without inclusion of such reduction, which reduction should be shown as a final item before the amount of net income for the period, except that where there is substantial reason to believe that misleading inferences might be drawn from such inclusion the tax reduction might be credited to surplus. Section B of chapter 10 adds an alternative treatment whereby the amount of taxes estimated to be actually payable for the year may be shown in the income statement, with the amount of the tax reduction attributable to the amounts carried forward indicated either in a footnote or parenthetically in the body of the income statement.

13. The opinion was expressed in the previous bulletin that claims for refunds of income taxes based on the carry-back of losses or unused excess-profits credits should be credited to income, except that under certain circumstances they might be credited to surplus. Section B of chapter 10 expresses the opinion that they should be carried to income. This may be done either by indicating in the income statement for the year the results of operations before application of the claim for refund, which should then be shown as a final item before the amount of net income, or by charging income with the amount of taxes estimated to be actually payable for the year and showing the amount of the reduction attributable to the carry-back in a footnote or parenthetically in the body of the income statement.

Renegotiation of Government Contracts—Chapter 11, Section B

14. The committee has modified the recommendations made in Bulletin No. 21 respecting the methods to be used in disclosing the renegotiation status and the provision or lack of provision for refund in relation to prior year settlements. It believes that individual judgment should determine which cases require disclosure of the basis of determining the amount provided. The committee has also indicated that the comments in section B of chapter 11 are applicable to price redetermination estimated to result in retroactive price reduction.

Foreign Operations and Foreign Exchange—Chapter 12

15. In Bulletin No. 4 it was stated that a safe course to follow is to take earnings from foreign operations into the accounts of United States companies only to the extent that funds have been received in the United States. In chapter 12 these words are added: "or unrestricted funds are available for transmission thereto."

16. An exception is noted in chapter 12 to the general rule of translating long-term liabilities and capital stock stated in foreign currency at the rate of exchange prevailing when they were originally incurred or issued. The exception relates to long-term debt incurred or stock issued in connection with the acquisition of fixed assets, permanent investments, or long-term receivables a short time before a substantial and presumably permanent change in the exchange rate. The opinion is expressed that in such instances it may be appropriate to state the long-term debt or the capital stock at the new rate and proper to deal with the exchange differences as an adjustment of the cost of the assets acquired.

17. The revision also takes into consideration the possibility that in some situations more realistic results will be obtained by translating income for the entire fiscal year at the new rates in effect after such major fluctuation. Where dividends have been paid prior to a major change in the exchange rate, out of earnings of the current fiscal year, that portion of the income for the year should be considered as having been earned at the rate at which such dividend was paid irrespective of the rates used in translating the remainder of the earnings.

18. Consideration is also given to the matter of devaluation losses arising from world-wide readjustment, as to which the committee comments that where they are so material that their inclusion in the income statement would impair the significance of net income to an extent that misleading inferences

might be drawn therefrom, consideration may appropriately be given to charging them to surplus.

19. The three preceding paragraphs relate to changes which, in part, give recognition to recommendations made in a statement entitled *Accounting Problems Arising from Devaluation of Foreign Currencies* issued as a research memorandum in November, 1949.

Unamortized Discount, Issue Cost, and Redemption Premium on Bonds Refunded—Chapter 15

20. When Bulletin No. 2 was issued the committee considered three methods of writing off unamortized discount on refunded bonds (including issue cost and redemption premium):

a. Write-off by a direct charge to earned surplus in the year of refunding;
b. Amortization over the remainder of the original life of the issue retired; or
c. Amortization over the life of the new issue.

21. Methods (a) and (b) were at that time approved as acceptable practice, with a comment that, with a continuance of the shift in emphasis from the balance sheet to the income account, method (b) might well become the preferred procedure. Method (c) was stated to be unacceptable except where such treatment was authorized or prescribed by a regulatory body to whose jurisdiction the accounting corporation was subject, or had been adopted by the company prior to the publication of Bulletin No. 2.

22. In chapter 15 a write-off in full in the year of refunding is stated to be acceptable. The committee believes, however, that the charge should be to income rather than earned surplus, unless the net income figure would thereby be so distorted as to invite misleading inferences. It further believes that any write-off made to earned surplus should be limited to the excess of the unamortized discount over the reduction of current taxes to which the refunding gives rise.

23. Distribution of the charge, by systematic charges against income, over the remainder of the original life of the bonds refunded (method (b)) is stated in chapter 15 to be the preferred method, conforming more closely than any other to current accounting opinion. When this method is adopted an amount equal to the reduction in current income tax resulting from the refunding should be deducted in the income statement, and the remainder should be apportioned over the future period.

24. Amortization over the life of the new issue,

unless it is less than the remaining life of the old issue, is stated to be an unacceptable practice.

Appendix C

BULLETINS NOT INCLUDED IN THE RESTATEMENT AND REVISION

1. Accounting Research Bulletins No. 13, *Accounting for Special Reserves Arising out of the War,* and No. 26, *Accounting for the Use of Special War Reserves,* are not included in the restatement. Those bulletins were formally withdrawn by the committee in July, 1951, by the issuance of addenda. At that time the committee commented that, "in the light of subsequent developments of accounting procedures, these bulletins should no longer be relied upon as a basis for the establishment and use of reserves."

2. Bulletin No. 17, *Post-War Refund of Excess-Profits Tax,* is withdrawn because it no longer has applicability under present tax laws.

3. Bulletins Nos. 7, 9, 12, 16, 20, 22, 34, and 39, which were issued as recommendations of the committee on terminology, are being published separately.

Accounting Research Bulletin No. 44
Declining-balance Depreciation

STATUS

Issued: October 1954

Effective Date: October 1954

Affects: No other pronouncements

Affected by: Superseded by ARB 44 (Rev.)

Accounting Research Bulletin No. 44 (Revised) Declining-balance Depreciation

(Supersedes Accounting Research Bulletin No. 44 Issued in October 1954)

STATUS

Issued: July 1958

Effective Date: July 1958

Affects: Supersedes ARB 44

Affected by: Paragraph 3 amended by APB 20
Paragraphs 4, 5, 7, and 10 superseded by APB 11
Paragraphs 8 and 9 superseded by FAS 71
Paragraph 9 superseded by APB 6
Letter—superseded by APB 11, FAS 96, and FAS 109
Superseded by FAS 96 and FAS 109

(The next page is 64.)

Accounting Research Bulletin No. 45
Long-Term Construction-Type Contracts

STATUS

Issued: October 1955

Effective Date: October 1955

Affects: No other pronouncements

Affected by: No other pronouncements

Accounting Research Bulletin No. 45
Long-Term Construction-Type Contracts

1. This bulletin is directed to the accounting problems in relation to construction-type contracts in the case of commercial organizations engaged wholly or partly in the contracting business. It does not deal with cost-plus-fixed-fee contracts, which are discussed in Chapter 11, Section A, of Accounting Research Bulletin No. 43*, other types of cost-plus-fee contracts, or contracts such as those for products or services customarily billed as shipped or rendered. In general the type of contract here under consideration is for construction of a specific project. While such contracts are generally carried on at the job site, the bulletin would also be applicable in appropriate cases to the manufacturing or building of special items on a contract basis in a contractor's own plant. The problems in accounting for construction-type contracts arise particularly in connection with long-term contracts as compared with those requiring relatively short periods for completion.

2. Considerations other than those acceptable as a basis for the recognition of income frequently enter into the determination of the timing and amounts of interim billings on construction-type contracts. For this reason, income to be recognized on such contracts at the various stages of performance ordinarily should not be measured by interim billings.

GENERALLY ACCEPTED METHODS

3. Two accounting methods commonly followed by contractors are the percentage-of-completion method and the completed-contract method.

Percentage-of-Completion Method

4. The percentage-of-completion method recognizes income as work on a contract progresses. The committee recommends that the recognized income be that percentage of estimated total income, either:

a. that incurred costs to date bear to estimated total costs after giving effect to estimates of costs to complete based upon most recent information, or

b. that may be indicated by such other measure of progress toward completion as may be appropriate having due regard to work performed.

Costs as here used might exclude, especially during the early stages of a contract, all or a portion of the cost of such items as materials and subcontracts if it appears that such an exclusion would result in a more meaningful periodic allocation of income.

5. Under this method current assets may include costs and recognized income not yet billed, with respect to certain contracts; and liabilities, in most cases current liabilities, may include billings in excess of costs and recognized income with respect to other contracts.

6. When the current estimate of total contract costs indicates a loss, in most circumstances provision should be made for the loss on the entire contract. If there is a close relationship between profitable and unprofitable contracts, such as in the case of contracts which are parts of the same project, the group may be treated as a unit in determining the necessity for a provision for loss.

7. The principal advantages of the percentage-of-completion method are periodic recognition of income currently rather than irregularly as contracts are completed, and the reflection of the status of the uncompleted contracts provided through the current estimates of costs to complete or of progress toward completion.

8. The principal disadvantage of the percentage-of-completion method is that it is necessarily dependent upon estimates of ultimate costs and consequently of currently accruing income, which are subject to the uncertainties frequently inherent in long-term contracts.

Completed-Contract Method

9. The completed-contract method recognizes income only when the contract is completed, or substantially so. Accordingly, costs of contracts in process and current billings are accumulated but there are no interim charges or credits to income other than provisions for losses. A contract may be regarded as substantially completed if remaining costs are not significant in amount.

10. When the completed-contract method is used, it may be appropriate to allocate general and adminis-

---

**Restatement and Revision of Accounting Research Bulletins,* American Institute of Accountants, 1953.

trative expenses to contract costs rather than to periodic income. This may result in a better matching of costs and revenues than would result from treating such expenses as period costs, particularly in years when no contracts were completed. It is not so important, however, when the contractor is engaged in numerous projects and in such circumstances it may be preferable to charge those expenses as incurred to periodic income. In any case there should be no excessive deferring of overhead costs, such as might occur if total overhead were assigned to abnormally few or abnormally small contracts in process.

11. Although the completed-contract method does not permit the recording of any income prior to completion, provision should be made for expected losses in accordance with the well established practice of making provision for foreseeable losses. If there is a close relationship between profitable and unprofitable contracts, such as in the case of contracts which are parts of the same project, the group may be treated as a unit in determining the necessity for a provision for losses.

12. When the completed-contract method is used, an excess of accumulated costs over related billings should be shown in the balance sheet as a current asset, and an excess of accumulated billings over related costs should be shown among the liabilities, in most cases as a current liability. If costs exceed billings on some contracts, and billings exceed costs on others, the contracts should ordinarily be segregated so that the figures on the asset side include only those contracts on which costs exceed billings, and those on the liability side include only those on which billings exceed costs. It is suggested that the asset item be described as "costs of uncompleted contracts in excess of related billings" rather than as "inventory" or "work in process," and that the item on the liability side be described as "billings on uncompleted contracts in excess of related costs."

13. The principal advantage of the completed-contract method is that it is based on results as finally determined, rather than on estimates for unperformed work which may involve unforeseen costs and possible losses.

14. The principal disadvantage of the completed-contract method is that it does not reflect current performance when the period of any contract extends into more than one accounting period and under such circumstances it may result in irregular recognition of income.

Selection of Method

15. The committee believes that in general when estimates of costs to complete and extent of progress toward completion of long-term contracts are reasonably dependable, the percentage-of-completion method is preferable. When lack of dependable estimates or inherent hazards cause forecasts to be doubtful, the completed-contract method is preferable. Disclosure of the method followed should be made.

COMMITMENTS

16. In special cases disclosures of extraordinary commitments may be required, but generally commitments to complete contracts in process are in the ordinary course of a contractor's business and are not required to be disclosed in a statement of financial position. They partake of the nature of a contractor's business, and generally do not represent a prospective drain on his cash resources since they will be financed by current billings.

The statement entitled "Long-Term Construction-Type Contracts" was adopted unanimously by the twenty-one members of the committee, of whom two, Mr. Coleman and Mr. Dixon, assented with qualification.

Mr. Coleman and Mr. Dixon do not approve the statements in paragraphs 6 and 11 as to provisions for expected losses on contracts. They believe that such provisions should be made in the form of footnote disclosure or as a reservation of retained earnings, rather than by a charge against revenues of the current period.

Mr. Coleman also questions the usefulness of the refinement of segregating the offset costs and billings by character of excess as set forth in the second sentence of paragraph 12. He suggests that a more useful alternative would be to show in any event total costs and total billings on all uncompleted contracts (a) with the excess shown either as a current asset or a current liability, and (b) with a supporting schedule indicating individual contract costs, billings, and explanatory comment.

NOTES

(See Introduction to *Accounting Research Bulletin No. 43*.)

1. Accounting Research Bulletins represent the considered opinion of at least two-thirds of the members of the committee on accounting procedure, reached on a formal vote after examination of the subject matter by the committee and the research department. Except in cases in which formal adoption by the Institute membership has been asked and secured, the authority of the bulletins rests upon the general acceptability of opinions so reached.

2. *Opinions of the committee are not intended to be retroactive unless they contain a statement of such intention. They should not be considered applicable to the accounting for transactions arising prior to the publication of the opinions. However, the committee does not wish to discourage the revision of past accounts in an individual case if the accountant thinks it desirable in the circumstances. Opinions of the committee should be considered as applicable only to items which are material and significant in* the relative circumstances.

3. *It is recognized also that any general rules may be subject to exception; it is felt, however, that the burden of justifying departure from accepted procedures must be assumed by those who adopt other treatment. Except where there is a specific statement of a different intent by the committee, its opinions and recommendations are directed primarily to business enterprises organized for profit.*

Committee on Accounting Procedure (1954-1955)

John A. Lindquist,
  Chairman
Gordon S. Battelle
Garrett T. Burns
Robert Caldwell, Jr.
Almand R. Coleman
Robert L. Dixon
L. T. Flatley

Thomas D. Flynn
Clifford V. Heimbucher
Harry D. Hopson
Donald R. Jennings
William L. Keating
Colin MacLennan
H. W. Maloy
John K. McClare

John Peoples
Weldon Powell
Walter R. Staub
Ross T. Warner
William W. Werntz
Edward B. Wilcox

Carman G. Blough,
  Director of Research

Accounting Research Bulletin No. 46
Discontinuance of Dating Earned Surplus

STATUS

Issued: February 1956

Effective Date: February 1956

Affects: No other pronouncements

Affected by: No other pronouncements

Accounting Research Bulletin No. 46
Discontinuance of Dating Earned Surplus

1. Paragraph 10 of Chapter 7(a), *Quasi-Reorganization or Corporate Readjustment,* of Accounting Research Bulletin No. 43, *Restatement and Revision of Accounting Research Bulletins,* reads as follows:

> After such a readjustment earned surplus previously accumulated cannot properly be carried forward under that title. A new earned surplus account should be established, dated to show that it runs from the effective date of the readjustment, and this dating should be disclosed in financial statements until such time as the effective date is no longer deemed to possess any special significance.

2. The committee believes that the dating of earned surplus following a quasi-reorganization would rarely, if ever, be of significance after a period of ten years. It also believes that there may be exceptional circumstances in which the discontinuance of the dating of earned surplus could be justified at the conclusion of a period less than ten years.

The statement entitled "Discontinuance of Dating Earned Surplus" was adopted by the assenting votes of twenty members of the committee. One member, Mr. Keating, did not vote.

NOTES

(See Introduction to *Accounting Research Bulletin* No. 43.)

1. Accounting Research Bulletins represent the considered opinion of at least two-thirds of the members of the committee on accounting procedure, reached on a formal vote after examination of the subject matter by the committee and the research department. Except in cases in which formal adoption by the Institute membership has been asked and secured, the authority of the bulletins rests upon the general acceptability of opinions so reached.

2. Opinions of the committee are not intended to be retroactive unless they contain a statement of such intention. They should not be considered applicable to the accounting for transactions arising prior to the publication of the opinions. However, the committee does not wish to discourage the revision of past accounts in an individual case if the accountant thinks it desirable in the circumstances. Opinions of the committee should be considered as applicable only to items which are material and significant in the relative circumstances.

3. It is recognized also that any general rules may be subject to exception; it is felt, however, that the burden of justifying departure from accepted procedures must be assumed by those who adopt other treatment. Except where there is a specific statement of a different intent by the committee, its opinions and recommendations are directed primarily to business enterprises organized for profit.

Committee on Accounting Procedure (1955-1956)

John A. Lindquist, *Chairman*	Carl H. Forsberg	Walter R. Staub
Gordon S. Battelle	LeVerne W. Garcia	Ross T. Warner
Garrett T. Burns	Donald R. Jennings	William W. Werntz
Robert Caldwell	William L. Keating	Edward B. Wilcox
Almand R. Coleman	Homer L. Luther	James B. Willing
Robert L. Dixon	John K. McClare	
L.T. Flatley	John Peoples	Carman G. Blough, *Director of Research*
Thomas D. Flynn	Weldon Powell	

Accounting Research Bulletin No. 47
Accounting for Costs of Pension Plans

STATUS

Issued: September 1956

Effective Date: September 1956

Affects: No other pronouncements

Affected by: Superseded by APB 8

Accounting Research Bulletin No. 48
Business Combinations

STATUS

Issued: January 1957

Effective Date: January 1957

Affects: Supersedes ARB 43, Chapter 7C

Affected by: Paragraphs 5 and 6 amended by APB 6
     Paragraph 12 amended by APB 10
     Superseded by APB 16

Accounting Research Bulletin No. 49
Earnings per Share

STATUS

Issued: April 1958

Effective Date: April 1958

Affects: No other pronouncements

Affected by: Superseded by APB 9

Accounting Research Bulletin No. 50
Contingencies

STATUS

Issued: October 1958

Effective Date: October 1958

Affects: No other pronouncements

Affected by: Superseded by FAS 5

ARB 51

Accounting Research Bulletin No. 51
Consolidated Financial Statements

STATUS

Issued: August 1959

Effective Date: August 1959

Affects: No other pronouncements

Affected by: Paragraphs 2, 3, and 19 through 21 superseded by FAS 94
Paragraph 6 amended by FAS 71
Paragraphs 7 and 8 superseded by APB 16
Paragraph 10 amended by FAS 58
Paragraph 16 superseded by APB 23
Paragraph 17 amended by APB 11
Paragraph 17 superseded by FAS 96
Paragraph 17 reinstated by FAS 109
Paragraphs 19 and 20 amended by APB 10
Paragraphs 19 through 21 amended by APB 18
Footnote 1 superseded by FAS 111

Other Interpretive Pronouncements: AIN-ARB 51, Interpretation No. 1 (Superseded by FAS 111)
FTB 85-2

Accounting Research Bulletin No. 51
Consolidated Financial Statements

PURPOSE OF CONSOLIDATED STATEMENTS

1. The purpose of consolidated statements is to present, primarily for the benefit of the shareholders and creditors of the parent company, the results of operations and the financial position of a parent company and its subsidiaries essentially as if the group were a single company with one or more branches or divisions. There is a presumption that consolidated statements are more meaningful than separate statements and that they are usually necessary for a fair presentation when one of the companies in the group directly or indirectly has a controlling financial interest in the other companies.

CONSOLIDATION POLICY

2. The usual condition for a controlling financial interest is ownership of a majority voting interest, and, therefore, as a general rule ownership by one company, directly or indirectly, of over fifty per cent of the outstanding voting shares of another company is a condition pointing toward consolidation. However, there are exceptions to this general rule. For example, a subsidiary should not be consolidated where control is likely to be temporary, or where it does not rest with the majority owners (as, for instance, where the subsidiary is in legal reorganization or in bankruptcy). There may also be situations where the minority interest in the subsidiary is so large, in relation to the equity of the shareholders of the parent in the consolidated net assets, that the presentation of separate financial statements for the two companies would be more meaningful and useful. However, the fact that the subsidiary has a relatively large indebtedness to bondholders or others is not in itself a valid argument for exclusion of the subsidiary from consolidation. (Also, see Chapter 12 of Accounting Research Bulletin No. 43 for the treatment of foreign subsidiaries.)

3. In deciding upon consolidation policy, the aim should be to make the financial presentation which is most meaningful in the circumstances. The reader should be given information which is suitable to his needs, but he should not be burdened with unnecessary detail. Thus, even though a group of companies is heterogeneous in character, it may be better to make a full consolidation than to present a large number of separate statements. On the other hand, separate statements or combined statements would be preferable for a subsidiary or group of subsidiaries if the presentation of financial information concerning the particular activities of such subsidiaries would be more informative to shareholders and creditors of the parent company than would the inclusion of such subsidiaries in the consolidation. For example, separate statements may be required for a subsidiary which is a bank or an insurance company and may be preferable for a finance company where the parent and the other subsidiaries are engaged in manufacturing operations.

4. A difference in fiscal periods of a parent and a subsidiary does not of itself justify the exclusion of the subsidiary from consolidation. It ordinarily is feasible for the subsidiary to prepare, for consolidation purposes, statements for a period which corresponds with or closely approaches the fiscal period of the parent. However, where the difference is not more than about three months, it usually is acceptable to use, for consolidation purposes, the subsidiary's statements for its fiscal period; when this is done, recognition should be given by disclosure or otherwise to the effect of intervening events which materially affect the financial position or results of operations.

5. Consolidated statements should disclose the consolidation policy which is being followed. In most cases this can be made apparent by the headings or other information in the statements, but in other cases a footnote is required.

CONSOLIDATION PROCEDURE GENERALLY

6. In the preparation of consolidated statements, intercompany balances and transactions should be eliminated. This includes intercompany open account balances, security holdings, sales and purchases, interest, dividends, etc. As consolidated statements are based on the assumption that they represent the financial position and operating results of a single business enterprise, such statements should not include gain or loss on transactions among the companies in the group. Accordingly, any intercompany profit or loss on assets remaining within the group should be eliminated; the concept usually applied for this purpose is gross profit or loss. (See also paragraph 17.) However, in a regulated industry where a parent or subsidiary manufactures or constructs facilities for other companies in the consolidated group, the foregoing is not intended to require the elimination of intercompany profit to the extent that such profit is substantially equivalent to a reasonable return on investment

ordinarily capitalized in accordance with the established practice of the industry.

ELIMINATION OF INTERCOMPANY INVESTMENTS

7. Where the cost to the parent of the investment in a purchased[1] subsidiary exceeds the parent's equity in the subsidiary's net assets at the date of acquisition, as shown by the books of the subsidiary, the excess should be dealt with in the consolidated balance sheet according to its nature. In determining the difference, provision should be made for specific costs or losses which are expected to be incurred in the integration of the operations of the subsidiary with those of the parent, or otherwise as a result of the acquisition, if the amount thereof can be reasonably determined. To the extent that the difference is considered to be attributable to tangible assets and specific intangible assets, such as patents, it should be allocated to them. Any difference which cannot be so applied should be shown among the assets in the consolidated balance sheet under one or more appropriately descriptive captions. When the difference is allocated to depreciable or amortizable assets, depreciation and amortization policies should be such as to absorb the excess over the remaining life of related assets. For subsequent treatment of intangibles, see Chapter 5 of Accounting Research Bulletin No. 43.

8. In general, parallel procedures should be followed in the reverse type of case. Where the cost to the parent is less than its equity in the net assets of the purchased subsidiary, as shown by the books of the subsidiary at the date of acquisition, the amount at which such net assets are carried in the consolidated statements should not exceed the parent's cost. Accordingly, to the extent that the difference, determined as indicated in paragraph 7, is considered to be attributable to specific assets, it should be allocated to them, with corresponding adjustments of the depreciation or amortization. In unusual circumstances there may be a remaining difference which it would be acceptable to show in a credit account, which ordinarily would be taken into income in future periods on a reasonable and systematic basis. A procedure sometimes followed in the past was to credit capital surplus with the amount of the excess; such a procedure is not now considered acceptable.

9. The earned surplus or deficit of a purchased[1] subsidiary at the date of acquisition by the parent should not be included in consolidated earned surplus.

10. When one company purchases two or more blocks of stock of another company at various dates and eventually obtains control of the other company, the date of acquisition (for the purpose of preparing consolidated statements) depends on the circumstances. If two or more purchases are made over a period of time, the earned surplus of the subsidiary at acquisition should generally be determined on a step-by-step basis; however, if small purchases are made over a period of time and then a purchase is made which results in control, the date of the latest purchase, as a matter of convenience, may be considered as the date of acquisition. Thus there would generally be included in consolidated income for the year in which control is obtained the postacquisition income for that year, and in consolidated earned surplus the postacquisition income of prior years, attributable to each block previously acquired. For example, if a 45% interest was acquired on October 1, 1957 and a further 30% interest was acquired on April 1, 1958, it would be appropriate to include in consolidated income for the year ended December 31, 1958, 45% of the earnings of the subsidiary for the three months ended March 31, and 75% of the earnings for the nine months ended December 31, and to credit consolidated earned surplus in 1958 with 45% of the undistributed earnings of the subsidiary for the three months ended December 31, 1957.

11. When a subsidiary is purchased during the year, there are alternative ways of dealing with the results of its operations in the consolidated income statement. One method, which usually is preferable, especially where there are several dates of acquisition of blocks of shares, is to include the subsidiary in the consolidation as though it had been acquired at the beginning of the year, and to deduct at the bottom of the consolidated income statement the preacquisition earnings applicable to each block of stock. This method presents results which are more indicative of the current status of the group, and facilitates future comparison with subsequent years. Another method of prorating income is to include in the consolidated statement only the subsidiary's revenue and expenses subsequent to the date of acquisition.

12. Where the investment in a subsidiary is disposed of during the year, it may be preferable to omit the details of operations of the subsidiary from the consolidated income statement, and to show the equity of the parent in the earnings of the subsidiary prior to disposal as a separate item in the statement.

13. Shares of the parent held by a subsidiary should not be treated as outstanding stock in the consolidated balance sheet.

---

[1] See Accounting Research Bulletin No. 48, *Business Combinations,* for the difference in treatment between a purchase and a pooling of interests.

MINORITY INTERESTS

14. The amount of intercompany profit or loss to be eliminated in accordance with paragraph 6 is not affected by the existence of a minority interest. The complete elimination of the intercompany profit or loss is consistent with the underlying assumption that consolidated statements represent the financial position and operating results of a single business enterprise. The elimination of the intercompany profit or loss may be allocated proportionately between the majority and minority interests.

15. In the unusual case in which losses applicable to the minority interest in a subsidiary exceed the minority interest in the equity capital of the subsidiary, such excess and any further losses applicable to the minority interest should be charged against the majority interest, as there is no obligation of the minority interest to make good such losses. However, if future earnings do materialize, the majority interest should be credited to the extent of such losses previously absorbed.

INCOME TAXES

16. When separate income tax returns are filed, income taxes usually are incurred when earnings of subsidiaries are transferred to the parent. Where it is reasonable to assume that a part or all of the undistributed earnings of a subsidiary will be transferred to the parent in a taxable distribution, provision for related income taxes should be made on an estimated basis at the time the earnings are included in consolidated income, unless these taxes are immaterial in amount when effect is given, for example, to dividend-received deductions or foreign-tax credits. There is no need to provide for income tax to the parent company in cases where the income has been, or there is evidence that it will be, permanently invested by the subsidiaries, or where the only likely distribution would be in the form of a tax-free liquidation.

17. If income taxes have been paid on intercompany profits on assets remaining within the group, such taxes should be deferred or the intercompany profits to be eliminated in consolidation should be appropriately reduced.

STOCK DIVIDENDS OF SUBSIDIARIES

18. Occasionally, subsidiary companies capitalize earned surplus arising since acquisition, by means of a stock dividend or otherwise. This does not require a transfer to capital surplus on consolidation, inasmuch as the retained earnings in the consolidated financial statements should reflect the accumulated earnings of the consolidated group

not distributed to the shareholders of, or capitalized by, the parent company.

UNCONSOLIDATED SUBSIDIARIES IN CONSOLIDATED STATEMENTS

19. There are two methods of dealing with unconsolidated subsidiaries in consolidated statements. Whichever method is adopted should be used for all unconsolidated subsidiaries, subject to appropriate modification in special circumstances. The preferable method, in the view of the committee, is to adjust the investment through income currently to take up the share of the controlling company or companies in the subsidiaries' net income or net loss, except where the subsidiary was excluded because of exchange restrictions or other reasons which raise the question of whether the increase in equity has accrued to the credit of the group. (Adjustments of the investment would also be made for "special" debits or credits shown on the income statements of the unconsolidated subsidiaries below the net income for the period, and for similar items shown in the schedule of earned surplus.) The other method, more commonly used at present, is to carry the investment at cost, and to take up income as dividends are received; however, provision should be made for any material impairment of the investment, such as through losses sustained by the subsidiaries, unless it is deemed to be temporary. When the latter method is followed, the consolidated statements should disclose, by footnote or otherwise, the cost of the investment in the unconsolidated subsidiaries, the equity of the consolidated group of companies in their net assets, the dividends received from them in the current period, and the equity of the consolidated group in their earnings for the period; this information may be given in total or by individual subsidiaries or groups of subsidiaries.

20. Whichever method of dealing with unconsolidated subsidiaries is followed, if there is a difference between the cost of the investment and the equity in net assets at the date of acquisition, appropriate recognition should be given to the possibility that, had the subsidiaries been consolidated, part of such difference would have been reflected in adjusted depreciation or amortization. Also, appropriate recognition should be given to the necessity for an adjustment for intercompany gains or losses on transactions with unconsolidated subsidiaries. If sales are made to unconsolidated subsidiaries and the investment in the subsidiaries is carried at cost plus the equity in undistributed earnings, an elimination of unrealized intercompany gains and losses should be made to the same extent as if the subsidiaries were consolidated. The same applies where intercompany sales are made by the un-

consolidated subsidiaries. If, however, the investment is carried at cost, it is not necessary to eliminate the intercompany gain on sales to such subsidiaries, if the gain on the sales does not exceed the unrecorded equity in undistributed earnings of the unconsolidated subsidiaries. If such gain is material, it should be appropriately disclosed. Where the sales are made by the unconsolidated subsidiaries to companies included in the consolidated group, the intercompany gains or losses should be eliminated in arriving at the amount of the equity in the undistributed earnings of the unconsolidated subsidiaries which will be disclosed in a footnote or otherwise. (See paragraph 19.)

21. Where the unconsolidated subsidiaries are, in the aggregate, material in relation to the consolidated financial position or operating results, summarized information as to their assets, liabilities and operating results should be given in the footnotes or separate statements should be presented for such subsidiaries, either individually or in groups, as appropriate.

COMBINED STATEMENTS

22. To justify the preparation of consolidated statements, the controlling financial interest should rest directly or indirectly in one of the companies included in the consolidation. There are circumstances, however, where combined financial statements (as distinguished from consolidated statements) of commonly controlled companies are likely to be more meaningful than their separate statements. For example, combined financial statements would be useful where one individual owns a controlling interest in several corporations which are related in their operations. Combined statements would also be used to present the financial position and the results of operations of a group of unconsolidated subsidiaries. They might also be used to combine the financial statements of companies under common management.

23. Where combined statements are prepared for a group of related companies, such as a group of unconsolidated subsidiaries or a group of commonly controlled companies, intercompany transactions and profits or losses should be eliminated, and if there are problems in connection with such matters as minority interests, foreign operations, different fiscal periods, or income taxes, they should be treated in the same manner as in consolidated statements.

PARENT-COMPANY STATEMENTS

24. In some cases parent-company statements may be needed, in addition to consolidated statements, to indicate adequately the position of bondholders and other creditors or preferred stockholders of the parent. Consolidating statements, in which one column is used for the parent company and other columns for particular subsidiaries or groups of subsidiaries, often are an effective means of presenting the pertinent information.

The statement entitled, "Consolidated Financial Statements" was unanimously adopted by the twenty-one members of the committee, of whom nine, Messrs. Bedford, Dunn, Graese, Graham, Halvorson, Hoyler, Kent, Powell, and Werntz, assented with qualification.

Mr. Bedford objects to the provision in paragraph 2 that ownership of over fifty per cent of the outstanding voting stock is the general rule governing consolidation policy. He believes the over fifty per cent ownership requirement is at best only one of several criteria evidencing the existence of a consolidated entity.

Messrs. Graese and Hoyler do not agree with the statement made in the last sentence of paragraph 8. Mr. Graese believes there are cases in which the crediting of a capital surplus account with the "excess credit" will result in a more appropriate presentation of consolidated operations and financial position, particularly in (but not limited to) situations where the acquisition of control of the subsidiary has been accomplished over an extended period of time or where there are acquisitions of minority interest at a date considerably after obtaining control. Mr. Hoyler is of the opinion that there have been, and probably will be, circumstances under which credits to capital surplus of the excesses referred to in this paragraph will be appropriate.

Messrs. Halvorson and Werntz object to the relative emphasis given to the recommendations in paragraph 10, which they believe should be reversed. They believe that the date of the purchase which results in control should generally be considered to be the date of acquisition; however, if a limited number of purchases are made over a period of time pursuant to a plan or program which culminates in control, they agree that the earned surplus of the subsidiary at acquisition may be determined on a step-by-step basis.

Mr. Halvorson disagrees with the recommendation in paragraph 18. In his view, the usual subsidiary is a closely held corporation, and consequently is under no pressure to declare stock dividends and is under no compulsion to follow the "fair value" method of accounting for them if it does. If it does capitalize earned surplus by means of a stock dividend or otherwise, particularly "otherwise," he feels that it must have been done with a purpose relating to its financial position, at the direction of, and with the acquiescence of, the parent company, and that the capitalization should carry through into the consolidated surplus accounts. If the subsidiary is one in which there is a publicly held minority interest, and a stock dividend is issued and accounted for on a fair-value basis in the manner of an independent publicly owned corporation, the accounting for earned surplus in respect of the majority interest would be the same as that for the minority interest, and again he believes that the capitalization should follow through into the consolidated surplus accounts. Mr. Powell also disagrees with the conclusion expressed in this paragraph. He believes that if a parent causes a subsidiary to freeze a part or all of its earned surplus through the payment of a stock dividend or otherwise, thus making such surplus unavailable for ordinary dividends, it should follow a similar procedure on consolidation.

Mr. Kent believes the consolidation policy section is deficient since it fails to restrict the increasing practice of not including certain subsidiaries in consolidated financial statements. He suggests that the bulletin may possibly result in further increasing such practice as a consequence of the preference expressed in paragraph 19 for the inclusion of the equity in earnings of unconsolidated subsidiaries in consolidated statements. It is his belief that in the usual situation a full consolidation policy as implied in paragraph 1 is generally preferable, supplemented by such summarized financial information, in footnotes or otherwise, as may be appropriate.

Messrs. Dunn and Graham believe that the "preferable" method in paragraph 19 should be recognized as the only acceptable method of dealing with unconsolidated subsidiaries in consolidated statements, and that the method which carries the investment in unconsolidated subsidiaries at cost, and takes up as income only the dividends received, should be discontinued as rapidly as is practicable. They feel that the "preferable" method conforms to the purpose of consolidated statements as set forth in paragraph 1—to present the results of operations and the financial position essentially as if the group were a single company, and that its uniform adoption would increase the comparability of the financial statements of different companies, and would avoid the possibility of manipulation of reported

consolidated earnings through the control of dividends received by the parent.

Mr. Dunn believes that paragraph 20 should require the elimination of intercompany gain on sales to unconsolidated subsidiaries if the failure to do so would have a material effect on the reported consolidated income, regardless of whether the gain on intercompany sales exceeds the unrecorded equity in undistributed earnings of the unconsolidated subsidiaries.

NOTES

(See Introduction to *Accounting Research Bulletin* No. 43.)

1. Accounting Research Bulletins represent the considered opinion of at least two-thirds of the members of the committee on accounting procedure, reached on a formal vote after examination of the subject matter by the committee, the technical services department, and the director of research. Except in cases in which formal adoption by the Institute membership has been asked and secured, the authority of the bulletins rests upon the general acceptability of opinions so reached.

2. Opinions of the committee are not intended to be retroactive unless they contain a statement of such intention. They should not be considered applicable to the accounting for transactions arising prior to the publication of the opinions. However, the committee does not wish to discourage the revision of past accounts in an individual case if the accountant thinks it desirable in the circumstances. Opinions of the committee should be considered as applicable only to items which are material and significant in the relative circumstances.

3. It is recognized also that any general rules may be subject to exception; it is felt, however, that the burden of justifying departure from accepted procedures must be assumed by those who adopt other treatment. Except where there is a specific statement of a different intent by the committee, its opinions and recommendations are directed primarily to business enterprises organized for profit.

Committee on Accounting Procedure (1958-59)

William W. Werntz, *Chairman*	Newman T. Halvorson	Weldon Powell
Norton M. Bedford	Charles A. Hoyler	Samuel L. Ready
Garrett T. Burns	Donald R. Jennings	Walter R. Staub
Keith W. Dunn	Ralph E. Kent	William J. von Minden
Carl M. Esenoff	George W. Lafferty	Edward B. Wilcox
Clifford E. Graese	John F. Macha	Delmar G. Wilsey
Willard J. Graham	John K. McClare	
	Herbert E. Miller	Carman G. Blough, *Director of Research*

ACCOUNTING PRINCIPLES BOARD

Opinions

APB OPINIONS

TABLE OF CONTENTS

Table of Contents

APB Opinion No. 1
New Depreciation Guidelines and Rules

STATUS

Issued: November 1962

Effective Date: November 1962

Affects: No other pronouncements

Affected by: Paragraphs 1, 5, and 6 and footnote 1 amended by APB 11
Paragraph 7 superseded by FAS 71
Superseded by FAS 96 and FAS 109

(The next page is 88.)

APB Opinion No. 2
Accounting for the "Investment Credit"

STATUS

Issued: December 1962

Effective Date: December 1962

Affects: No other pronouncements

Affected by: Paragraphs 13 and 17 amended by APB 4
             Paragraph 16 superseded by FAS 109
             Addendum superseded by FAS 71
             Paragraph 17 superseded by FAS 71

Other Interpretive Pronouncements: FIN 25 (Superseded by FAS 96 and FAS 109)
                                       FIN 32 (Superseded by FAS 96 and FAS 109)
                                       FTB 81-2 (Superseded by FAS 96 and FAS 109)

APB Opinion No. 2
Accounting for the "Investment Credit"

1. The Revenue Act of 1962 provides for an "investment credit" which, in general, is equal to a specified percentage of the cost of certain depreciable assets acquired and placed in service after 1961. It is subject to certain statutory limitations and the amount available in any one year is used to reduce the amount of income tax payable for that year. The full amount of the investment credit is treated for income tax purposes as a reduction in the basis of the property. An investment credit once allowed is subject to recapture under certain circumstances set forth in the statute.

2. Some decision as to the nature of the investment credit, i.e., as to the *substance* of its essential characteristics, if not indispensable, is of great significance in a determination of its accounting treatment. We believe there can be but one useful conclusion as to the nature of the investment credit and that it must be determined by the weight of the pertinent factors.

3. Three concepts as to the substance of the investment credit have been considered by the Board: (a) subsidy by way of a contribution to capital; (b) reduction in taxes otherwise applicable to the income of the year in which the credit arises; and (c) reduction in a cost otherwise chargeable in a greater amount to future accounting periods.

4. There is no significant disagreement with the view that the investment credit is a factor which influences the determination of net income. The basic accounting issue before us therefore is not whether the investment credit increases net income but, rather, the accounting period(s) during which it should be reflected in the operating statement. Resolution of the accounting issue, in large part, rests upon the accounting principles relative to the realization of income. This is true for both regulated and nonregulated companies. (See paragraph 17 of this Opinion.)

5. **Subsidy by way of a contribution to capital.** This concept, in our opinion, is the least rational because it runs counter to the conclusion that the investment credit increases the net income of some accounting period(s).

6. **Tax reduction.** The argument for this concept essentially is that since the investment credit is made available by the Revenue Act of 1962 it is in substance a selective reduction in taxes related to the taxable income of the year in which the credit arises.

7. A refinement of the tax reduction concept advocates that 48% of the investment credit (the maximum extent to which the credit normally can increase net income, assuming that the income tax rate is 52%) should be recorded as a reduction of tax expense of the year in which the credit arises; the balance of 52% should be deferred to subsequent accounting periods, as provided in Chapter 10B of *Accounting Research Bulletin No. 43*, because of the statutory requirement that the basis of the property be reduced for tax purposes by the amount of the investment credit.

8. The General Rule of section 38 of the Revenue Act of 1962 provides that

> There shall be allowed, as a credit against the tax imposed by this chapter, the amount determined under sub-part B of this part.

The tax code has traditionally distinguished between exclusions from taxable income (which affect the computation of taxes payable on taxable income of the period) and credits to be applied to reduce taxes otherwise applicable to such taxable income (which do not enter into such computation). In our view the relevant materials support the interpretation that the investment credit is an administrative procedure to permit the taxpayer to withhold the cash equivalent of the credit from taxes otherwise payable and that it is not an element entering into the computation of taxes related to income of the period.

9. **Cost reduction.** We believe that the interpretation of the investment credit as a reduction in or offset against a cost otherwise chargeable in a greater amount to future accounting periods is supported by the weight of the pertinent factors and is based upon existing accounting principles.

10. In reaching this conclusion we have evaluated the pertinent portions of the legislative history of the investment credit, which we regard as significant but not decisive. We also evaluated the pertinent provisions of the Revenue Act of 1962 which, as earlier stated, require that the investment credit be treated as a reduction in the basis of the property which gives rise to the credit and which contain recapture and other provisions the effect of which is to make realization of the credit dependent to some degree on future events.

11. The investment credit under certain circumstances is transferable to the lessee of qualified property. We regard it as significant that in such

cases the rules and regulations of the Treasury require the lessee to reduce his taxable deduction for rent over a four, six, or eight year period, depending upon the useful life category of the property.

12. In concluding that the cost reduction concept is based upon existing accounting principles we attach substantial weight to two points in particular. First, in our opinion, earnings arise from the use of facilities, not from their acquisition. Second, the ultimate realization of the credit is contingent to some degree on future developments. Where the incidence of realization of income is uncertain, as in the present circumstances, we believe the record does not support the treatment of the investment credit as income at the earliest possible point of time. In our opinion the alternative choice of spreading the income in some rational manner over a series of future accounting periods is more logical and supportable.

CONCLUSIONS

13. We conclude that the allowable[1] investment credit should be reflected in net income over the productive life of acquired property and not in the year in which it is placed in service.

14. A number of alternative choices for recording the credit on the balance sheet has been considered. While we believe the reflection of the allowable credit as a reduction in the net amount at which the acquired property is stated (either directly or by inclusion in an offsetting account) may be preferable in many cases, we recognize as equally appropriate the treatment of the credit as deferred income, provided it is amortized over the productive life of the acquired property.

15. We believe it preferable that the statement of income in the year in which the allowable investment credit arises should be affected only by the results which flow from the accounting for the credit set forth in paragraph 13. Nevertheless, reflection of income tax provisions, in the income statement, in the amount payable (that is, after deduction of the allowable investment credit) is appropriate provided that a corresponding charge is made to an appropriate cost or expense (for example, to the provision for depreciation) and the treatment is adequately disclosed in the financial statements of the first year of its adoption.

16. An investment credit should be reflected in the financial statements only to the extent that it has been used as an offset against income tax liability. Under the statute, unused investment credits may be carried back or forward to other years. The accounting for these carrybacks and carryforwards should be consistent with the provisions of *Accounting Research Bulletin No. 43,* Chapter 10B, "Income Taxes," paragraphs 16 and 17. The amount of a carryback of unused investment credit may be set up as an asset (a claim for refund of income taxes) and be added to the allowable investment credit in accounting for the effect of the credit in the year in which the property is placed in service. A carryforward of unused investment credit should ordinarily be reflected only in the year in which the amount becomes "allowable," in which case the unused amount would not appear as an asset. Material amounts of unused investment credits should be disclosed.

17. Authorities having jurisdiction over regulated business may require that the investment credit be accounted for in some manner not consistent with the conclusions expressed in this Opinion. We have previously stated our position on the issues involved in such a case (*The Journal of Accountancy,* December 1962, page 67—reprinted as an Addendum to this Opinion). The position there taken is intended to permit the so-called "flow through" treatment only in those circumstances where the standards described in that statement are met.

The Opinion entitled "Accounting for the 'Investment Credit'" was adopted by the assenting votes of fourteen members of the Board, of whom one, Mr. McEachren, assented with qualification. Messrs. Bevis, Black, Cannon, Powell, Tippit, and Walker dissented.

Mr. McEachren agrees with the conclusion that the investment credit should be reflected in net income over the productive life of acquired property but disagrees with the inclusion of paragraphs 9, 10, and 12 to the extent that they argue that the investment credit is a reduction of cost. Whether or not it is a reduction of cost is a question with many ramifications and subject to different interpretations under differing circumstances and in any event is not relevant to the matter here involved. He believes that the fundamental basis for the conclusion in paragraph 13 is that "earnings arise from the use of facilities; not from their acquisition."

Messrs. Bevis, Powell, and Tippit believe that the pertinent factors preponderantly support the views that the investment credit is in substance a reduction in income taxes. They consider that the generally accepted accounting principles applicable (including the pronouncements of the former Committee on Accounting Procedure, especially those relating to the accounting for income taxes and to the reporting of income, which are still in

[1] The first $25,000 of income tax payable plus 25% of the remainder. See paragraph 16 for treatment of unused investment credits.

effect) preponderantly support the treatment of the investment credit as a reduction of the provision for current income taxes in the year in which the credit arises. They believe specifically, that the generation of taxable income for the year in and by itself, rather than the future productive use of the related property, effects the realization of the credit. They point out that opinions received by the Board from practitioners and businessmen make it clear that the "48-52" method discussed in paragraph 7 of the Opinion has at least as wide acceptance among these groups as the method sponsored by the majority of the Board. They believe that, in the circumstances, the "48-52" method must also be considered to have substantial authoritative support and, therefore, to be generally acceptable.

Messrs. Black and Cannon dissent from the conclusion that there is only one acceptable accounting treatment of the investment credit. While not objecting to reflecting the investment credit over the productive life of the acquired property, they believe that it would be preferable to defer only that part of the credit (52%) equivalent to the increased taxes in future years arising from the reduction in the tax base of the property acquired.

Mr. Walker concurs with the method set forth in the Opinion as the preferred basis for treatment of the investment credit, but it is his opinion that, with adequate disclosure, it should be considered an acceptable alternative to reduce the taxes of the year in which the credit arises by an appropriate portion of such credit.

NOTE

Unless otherwise indicated Opinions present the considered opinion of at least two-thirds of the members of the Accounting Principles Board, reached on a formal vote after examination of the subject matter. Except where formal adoption by the Council or the membership of the Institute has been asked and secured, the authority of the opinions rests upon their general acceptability. While it is recognized that general rules may be subject to exception, the burden of justifying departures from the Board's recommendations must be assumed by those who adopt other practices. Recommendations of the Board are not intended to be retroactive, nor applicable to immaterial items.

ADDENDUM

Accounting Principles for Regulated Industries

The following statement, referred to in paragraph 17 of the Opinion and approved by the Board, originally appeared in *The Journal of Accountancy*, December 1962, p. 67:

1. The basic postulates and the broad principles of accounting comprehended in the term "generally accepted accounting principles" pertain to business enterprises in general. These include public utilities, common carriers, insurance companies, financial institutions, and the like that are subject to regulation by government, usually through commissions or other similar agencies.

2. However, differences may arise in the application of generally accepted accounting principles as between regulated and nonregulated businesses, because of the effect in regulated businesses of the rate-making process, a phenomenon not present in nonregulated businesses. Such differences usually concern mainly the time at which various items enter into the determination of net income in accordance with the principle of matching costs and revenues. For example, if a cost incurred by a regulated business during a given period is treated for rate-making purposes by the regulatory authority having jurisdiction as applicable to future revenues, it may be deferred in the balance sheet at the end of the current period and written off in the future period or periods in which the related revenue accrues, even though the cost is of a kind which in a nonregulated business would be written off currently. However, this is appropriate only when it is clear that the cost will be recoverable out of future revenues, and it is not appropriate when there is doubt, because of economic conditions or for other reasons, that the cost will be so recoverable.

3. Accounting requirements not directly related to the rate-making process commonly are imposed on regulated businesses by orders of regulatory authorities, and occasionally by court decisions or statutes. The fact that such accounting requirements are imposed by the government does not necessarily mean that they conform with generally accepted accounting principles. For example, if a cost, of a kind which in a nonregulated business would be charged to income, is charged directly to surplus pursuant to the applicable accounting requirements of the regulatory authority, such cost nevertheless should be included in operating expenses or charged to income, as appropriate in financial statements intended for use by the public.

4. The financial statements of regulated businesses other than those prepared for filing with the government for regulatory purposes preferably should be based on generally accepted accounting principles (with appropriate recognition of rate-making considerations as indicated in paragraph 2) rather than on systems of accounts or other accounting requirements of the government.

5. *Generally Accepted Auditing Standards* lists

four standards of reporting, the first of which says that "The report shall state whether the financial statements are presented in accordance with generally accepted principles of accounting." In reporting on the financial statements of regulated businesses, the independent auditor should observe this standard and should deal with material variances from generally accepted accounting principles (with appropriate recognition of rate-making considerations as indicated in paragraph 2), if the financial statements reflect any such variances, in the same manner as in his reports on nonregulated businesses.

Accounting Principles Board (1962-1963)

Weldon Powell, *Chairman*	Arthur M. Cannon	Herbert E. Miller
Gordon S. Battelle	W. A. Crichley	C. A. Moyer
Herman W. Bevis	Walter F. Frese	Ira A. Schur
William M. Black	Ira N. Frisbee	Leonard Spacek
Carman G. Blough	Thomas G. Higgins	Hassel Tippit
Joseph Campbell	Alvin R. Jennings	Wilbert A. Walker
	John W. McEachren	John H. Zebley, Jr.

APB Opinion No. 3
The Statement of Source and Application of Funds

STATUS

Issued: October 1963

Effective Date: October 1963

Affects: No other pronouncements

Affected by: Superseded by APB 19

APB Opinion No. 4 (Amending No. 2)
Accounting for the "Investment Credit"

STATUS

Issued: March 1964

Effective Date: March 1964

Affects: Amends APB 2, paragraphs 13 and 17

Affected by: No other pronouncements

Other Interpretive Pronouncements: AIN-APB 4, Interpretations No. 1 through 6 (Interpretations No. 4 and 6 superseded by FAS 96 and FAS 109 and Interpretation No. 5 superseded by FAS 111)
FIN 25 (Superseded by FAS 96 and FAS 109)
FIN 32 (Superseded by FAS 96 and FAS 109)
FTB 81-2 (Superseded by FAS 96 and FAS 109)

APB Opinion No. 4 (Amending No. 2)
Accounting for the "Investment Credit"

1. In December 1962 this Board issued Opinion No. 2, "Accounting for the 'Investment Credit.'" In this Opinion we said:

> Some decision as to the nature of the investment credit, i.e., as to the *substance* of its essential characteristics, if not indispensable, is of great significance in a determination of its accounting treatment. We believe there can be but one useful conclusion as to the nature of the investment credit and that it must be determined by the weight of the pertinent factors. (paragraph 2)

2. The Opinion listed the possible interpretations which the Board had considered:

> Three concepts as to the substance of the investment credit have been considered by the Board: (a) subsidy by way of a contribution to capital; (b) reduction in taxes otherwise applicable to the income of the year in which the credit arises; and (c) reduction in a cost otherwise chargeable in a greater amount to future accounting periods. (paragraph 3)

3. After noting the arguments in favor of each, the Board said:

> We believe that the interpretation of the investment credit as a reduction in or offset against a cost otherwise chargeable in a greater amount to future accounting periods is supported by the weight of the pertinent factors and is based upon existing accounting principles. (paragraph 9)

4. The Board concluded (paragraph 13) that the investment credit "should be reflected in net income over the productive life of acquired property and not in the year in which it is placed in service."

5. In January 1963 the Securities and Exchange Commission issued *Accounting Series Release No. 96* in which it reported that in recognition of the substantial diversity of opinion among responsible persons in the matter of accounting for the investment credit the Commission would accept statements in which the credit was accounted for either as this Board concluded in Opinion No. 2 or as a reduction in taxes otherwise applicable to the year in which the credit arises. The Commission has recently reconsidered and reaffirmed that position.

6. The Board's review of experience since the issuance of Opinion No. 2 shows that the investment credit has been treated by a significant number of companies as an increase in net income of the year in which the credit arose.

7. The Revenue Act of 1964 eliminates the requirement imposed by the Revenue Act of 1962 that the investment credit be treated for income tax purposes as a reduction in the basis of the property to which the credit relates.

CONCLUSIONS

8. It is the conclusion of this Board that the Revenue Act of 1964 does not change the essential nature of the investment credit and, hence, of itself affords no basis for revising our Opinion as to the method of accounting for the investment credit.

9. However, the authority of Opinions of this Board rests upon their general acceptability. The Board, in the light of events and developments occurring since the issuance of Opinion No. 2, has determined that its conclusions as there expressed have not attained the degree of acceptability which it believes is necessary to make the Opinion effective.

10. In the circumstances the Board believes that, while the method of accounting for the investment credit recommended in paragraph 13 of Opinion No. 2 should be considered to be preferable, the alternative method of treating the credit as a reduction of Federal income taxes of the year in which the credit arises is also acceptable.

11. The Board emphasizes that whichever method of accounting for the investment credit is adopted, it is essential that full disclosure be made of the method followed and amounts involved, when material.

The Opinion entitled "Accounting for the 'Investment Credit'" was adopted by the assenting votes of fifteen members of the Board, of whom eight, Messrs. Bevis, Crichley, Frese, Higgins, Jennings, Queenan, Tippit and Trueblood assented with qualification. Messrs. Armstrong, Blough, Moonitz, Moyer and Spacek dissented.

Messrs. Crichley and Trueblood believe that, under the Revenue Act of 1964, there is considerable theoretical support for regarding the investment credit as a selective reduction in taxes. Accordingly, they do not necessarily regard amortization of the investment credit over the life of acquired properties as the "preferable method." They believe that the alternative method is preferable, but agree that recognition of both methods is necessary and desirable under existing conditions.

Mr. Frese assents to the conclusions in this Opinion, and to its publication, because he believes developments and circumstances summarized in paragraphs 5, 6, and 9 leave the Board no other practical choice. He desires, however, to express his strong preference for the conclusion of the Board in Opinion No. 2 because he believes it conforms with the basic concept, which has long been generally accepted, that income should be recognized as it is earned through the use of assets and not as an immediate result of their acquisition.

Messrs. Higgins and Jennings assent to Opinion No. 4 and its publication only because they believe the action of the SEC, reported in paragraph 5, and the consequences recited in paragraph 6, leave no other practicable choice. They believe that the Revenue Act of 1964 does not alter the soundness of the conclusion stated in Opinion No. 2 that the investment credit should be reflected in net income over the productive life of acquired property and not in the year in which such property is placed in service. They believe further that the present action recognizing the alternative treatment as acceptable is illogical (for the reasons given in the first sentence of Mr. Moonitz's dissent) and is tantamount to taking no position. They observe that paragraph 17 of Opinion No. 2 is still effective and, accordingly, that the alternative method of treating the credit as a reduction of Federal income tax of the year in which the credit arises is improper and should be unacceptable in those instances where Section 203(e) of the Revenue Act of 1964 effectively requires the credit to be reflected in net income over the productive life of the property.

Mr. Queenan, joined by Messrs. Bevis and Tippit, assents to the Opinion because he continues to believe that the investment credit constitutes a reduction in income tax expense in the year in which the credit arises. In view of the substantial support of the cost-reduction concept, he does not object to inclusion of the credit in net income over the life of the acquired property, but believes that the order of preference expressed in paragraph 10 should be reversed.

Mr. Armstrong dissents from Opinion No. 4. He agrees that the Revenue Act of 1964 does not change the essential nature of the investment credit and agrees with the conclusions expressed in Opinion No. 2. He disagrees with paragraph 10 of Opinion No. 4 wherein an alternative method of treating the credit is recognized as being acceptable, thereby adding one more to the list of principles for which there are a variety of acceptable methods yielding substantially different results in comparable situations.

Mr. Blough dissents from this opinion because he believes the conclusion reached in Opinion No. 2 "that the allowable investment credit should be reflected in net income over the productive life of acquired property and not in the year in which it is placed in service" was and is sound. The fact that there is substantial support for treating the investment credit as an increase in net income of the year in which the credit arose is not a sound reason, in his opinion, for this Board to retreat from a position which it still considers to be "preferable." He does not believe the Board can carry out its major responsibility "to determine appropriate practice and to narrow the areas of difference and inconsistency in practice" if it withdraws its influence from the support of its considered opinion whenever that opinion is not immediately accepted by all influential persons.

Mr. Moonitz dissents to paragraph 10 of Opinion No. 4 because while it is conceivable that the tax reduction method may be right, or that cost reduction may be right, or that both are wrong and some other unspecified possibility right, the investment credit cannot be two different things at one and the same time. As between the two methods set forth in paragraph 10, he believes that accounting principles compel the treatment of the investment credit as a selective reduction in tax available to those who meet the conditions laid down in the statute. The method preferred by the majority of the Board permits identical items bought from the same supplier at identical prices to be recorded at different "costs" depending upon the tax status of the purchaser and not upon the conditions prevailing in the transaction between buyer and seller. Alternatively the method preferred by the majority of the Board permits the balance sheet to include a "deferred credit to income" that cannot be classified as part of the interest of owners, creditors, government, employees, or any other recognizable group. He concludes that the effect of Opinion No. 4 can only be the direct opposite of the Board's ultimate objective of narrowing the areas of difference in practice.

Mr. Moyer believes that Opinion No. 4 should not have been issued, as it carries the strong implication that Opinions of the Board always should follow existing practices. He believes that progress cannot be made under such a policy.

Mr. Spacek dissents from the conclusion in paragraph 10. He believes this Opinion illustrates the accounting profession's complete failure in its responsibility to establish accounting principles that will provide reliable financial statements that are comparable among companies and industries, for use of the public in making personal investment decisions. He states there is no justification for sanctioning two contradictory practices to accommodate

SEC and other regulatory bodies and some CPAs who have approved reporting the investment credit as, in effect, profit from acquisition rather than from use of property. This flouts Congress' clear intent in granting the investment credit, "to reduce the net cost of acquiring depreciable property." Alternative procedures under this Opinion can increase by up to 25 per cent the earnings otherwise reported. In this Opinion and in SEC's stated position, Mr. Spacek finds no word of concern for the investor, to whose protection both CPAs and SEC supposedly are dedicated. He believes this Opinion approves accounting of the type that precipitated the 1929 financial crisis, and that history is being repeated by actions of the very authorities created to prevent such catastrophes. He feels this breakdown in safeguards created to protect investors has resulted from fragmentation of responsibility for establishing accounting principles, and the only remedy is to create a Federally established Court of Accounting Principles with a prescribed basis for its

decisions; this court would be independent of the profession and regulatory commissions, and its decisions would be binding on all, thus rescuing investors from their present abandonment.

NOTE

Opinions present the considered opinion of at least two-thirds of the members of the Accounting Principles Board, reached on a formal vote after examination of the subject matter. Except where formal adoption by the Council or the membership of the Institute has been asked and secured, the authority of the opinions rests upon their general acceptability. While it is recognized that general rules may be subject to exception, the burden of justifying departures from the Board's recommendations must be assumed by those who adopt other practices. Recommendations of the Board are not intended to be retroactive, nor applicable to immaterial items.

Accounting Principles Board (1963-1964)

Alvin R. Jennings, *Chairman*	Ira N. Frisbee Thomas G. Higgins	John W. Queenan Ira A. Schur
Marshall S. Armstrong	LeRoy Layton	Leonard Spacek
Herman W. Bevis	Maurice Moonitz	Hassel Tippit
Carman G. Blough	C. A. Moyer	Robert M. Trueblood
W. A. Crichley	Louis H. Penney	Wilbert A. Walker
Walter F. Frese	John Peoples	Robert E. Witschey

APB Opinion No. 5
Reporting of Leases in Financial Statements of Lessee

STATUS

Issued: September 1964

Effective Date: September 1964

Affects: Supersedes ARB 43, Chapter 14

Affected by: Paragraphs 14, 20, and 23 amended by APB 31
Paragraphs 16 through 18 superseded by APB 31
Paragraph 21 amended by APB 11
Superseded by FAS 13

(This page intentionally left blank.)

APB Opinion No. 6
Status of Accounting Research Bulletins

STATUS

Issued: October 1965

Effective Date: For fiscal periods beginning after December 31, 1965

Affects: Amends ARB 43, Chapter 1B
Amends ARB 43, Chapter 3A, paragraph 10
Amends ARB 43, Chapter 5, paragraph 7
Amends ARB 43, Chapter 7B, paragraph 6
Supersedes ARB 43, Chapter 9B
Amends ARB 43, Chapter 9C
Amends ARB 43, Chapter 10B
Amends ARB 43, Chapter 12, paragraphs 12 and 18
Amends ARB 43, Chapter 15, paragraph 12
Supersedes ARB 44 (Rev.), paragraph 9
Amends ARB 48, paragraphs 5 and 6

Affected by: Paragraphs 12(c) and 22 superseded by APB 16
Paragraph 15 superseded by APB 17
Paragraph 16 amended by FAS 111
Paragraph 18 superseded by FAS 8
Paragraph 18 superseded by FAS 52
Paragraph 19 superseded by APB 26
Paragraph 20 superseded by FAS 71 and FAS 109
Paragraphs 21 and 23 and footnotes 7 and 8 superseded by APB 11 and FAS 109
Paragraph 22 superseded by FAS 109

Other Interpretive Pronouncements: FTB 85-6

APB Opinion No. 6
Status of Accounting Research Bulletins

1. On October 2, 1964, Council of the Institute adopted recommendations[1] requiring that departures from accounting principles accepted in Board Opinions and Accounting Research Bulletins be disclosed in footnotes to financial statements or in independent auditors' reports when the effect of any such departure on the financial statements is material. This requirement is applicable to financial statements for fiscal periods that begin after December 31, 1965.

2. Concurrently, in a related action,[1] Council directed the Accounting Principles Board to review all Accounting Research Bulletins prior to December 31, 1965, and determine whether any of them should be revised or withdrawn.

3. In accordance with this directive, the Board has reviewed all outstanding Accounting Research Bulletins. These consist of Numbers 43 (including Preface, Introduction and Appendices) through 51,[2] except:

a. Chapter 7C of ARB 43, which was superseded in 1957 by ARB 48;
b. Chapter 14 of ARB 43, which was superseded in 1964 by Board Opinion 5; and
c. ARB 44, which was superseded in July 1958 by ARB 44 (Revised).

For convenience, individual chapters and subchapters of Accounting Research Bulletin No. 43 are, at times, referred to as "Bulletins" in this Opinion.

4. A number of matters currently under study or planned for study by the Board are directly related to matters discussed in the Bulletins. It is the present intention of the Board to make some of these subjects of Opinions as soon as practicable. Accordingly, the language, form and substance of some of the Bulletins may be changed at a later date.

5. Nevertheless, the Board believes that the considerations which gave rise to the conclusions set forth in some of the Bulletins may no longer apply with the same force as when the Bulletins were issued, and that, pending further consideration by the Board, it should revise certain of the Bulletins in order to obviate conflicts between present accepted practice and provisions of outstanding Bulletins which would otherwise require unwarranted disclosure under the action of Council.[3]

6. The Board's review at this time, accordingly, was confined primarily to substantive matters in the Bulletins, and the revisions set forth in this Opinion are made in the light of currently accepted practices followed in preparing financial statements and reporting upon them. In addition, it has approved revisions designed to clarify parts of some of the Bulletins and to express its conclusions on certain matters not covered specifically in the Bulletins.

7. In making its review, the Board has interpreted the disclosure requirement approved by Council to apply, with equal force, to departures from the provisions of Accounting Research Bulletins and Board Opinions that relate not only to accounting principles followed in the preparation of the financial statements but also to the form and content of financial statements and to the disclosure of information. For purposes of carrying out Council's requirement, the Board construes the term "accounting principles" to include not only principles and practices, but also the methods of applying them.[4]

8. Some Accounting Research Bulletins and Board Opinions contain expressions of preference as to accounting principles, including form and content of financial statements and the disclosure of information, although other principles are stated to be acceptable. Under these circumstances, when one of the principles accepted in the Bulletin or Opinion is applied in financial statements, disclosure of a departure from the *preferred* principle is not required. On the other hand, the language of some Accounting Research Bulletins and Board Opinions indicates that one or more specified principles are acceptable, and, directly or by implication, that others are not. In such cases, departures from the *specified* principles must be disclosed.

9. The Preface and Appendices of ARB 43 explain what revisions the Committee on Accounting Proce-

---

[1] Special Bulletin, *Disclosure of Departures From Opinions of Accounting Principles Board,* October 1964. (Reprinted in Appendix A of this Opinion.)

[2] ARB Nos. 1-42 were cancelled and replaced by ARB 43, and by Accounting Terminology Bulletin No. 1, both issued in 1953.

[3] Special Bulletin, *Disclosure of Departures From Opinions of Accounting Principles Board,* October 1964. (Reprinted in Appendix A of this Opinion.)

[4] Statement on Auditing Procedure No. 33, *Auditing Standards and Procedures,* paragraph 2, page 40.

dure made to previously issued Bulletins and why certain revisions were made; therefore, the Board considers this material to be primarily of historical value. With respect to the Introduction, paragraph 8 has been expanded as to disclosure requirements by the action of Council on October 2, 1964.[5]

10. The following paragraphs (12 through 23) of this Opinion set forth the Board's conclusions as to the extent to which currently outstanding Bulletins should be revised at this time. Except for these revisions, these and all other currently existing Bulletins continue in full force and effect without change.

BULLETINS REVISED

11. The following Bulletins are revised, in part, by this Opinion.

ARB 43, Chapter 1B—Treasury Stock

12. The Board considers that the following accounting practices, in addition to the accounting practices indicated in Chapter 1B, are acceptable, and that they appear to be more in accord with current developments in practice:

a. When a corporation's stock is retired, or purchased for constructive retirement (with or without an intention to retire the stock formally in accordance with applicable laws):

   i. *an excess of purchase price over par or stated value* may be allocated between capital surplus and retained earnings. The portion of the excess allocated to capital surplus should be limited to the sum of (a) all capital surplus arising from previous retirements and net "gains" on sales of treasury stock of the same issue and (b) the prorata portion of capital surplus paid in, voluntary transfers of retained earnings, capitalization of stock dividends, etc., on the same issue. For this purpose, any remaining capital surplus applicable to issues fully retired (formal or constructive) is deemed to be applicable prorata to shares of common stock. Alternatively, the excess may be charged entirely to retained earnings in recognition of the fact that a corporation can always capitalize or allocate retained earnings for such purposes.

   ii. *an excess of par or stated value over purchase price* should be credited to capital surplus.

b. When a corporation's stock is acquired for purposes other than retirement (formal or constructive), or when ultimate disposition has not yet been decided, the cost of acquired stock may be shown separately as a deduction from the total of capital stock, capital surplus, and retained earnings, or may be accorded the accounting treatment appropriate for retired stock, or in some circumstances may be shown as an asset in accordance with paragraph 4 of Chapter 1A of ARB 43. "Gains" on sales of treasury stock not previously accounted for as constructively retired should be credited to capital surplus; "losses" may be charged to capital surplus to the extent that previous net "gains" from sales or retirements of the same class of stock are included therein, otherwise to retained earnings.

c. Treasury stock delivered to effect a "pooling of interests" should be accounted for as though it were newly issued, and the cost thereof should receive the accounting treatment appropriate for retired stock.

13. Laws of some states govern the circumstances under which a corporation may acquire its own stock and prescribe the accounting treatment therefor. Where such requirements are at variance with paragraph 12, the accounting should conform to the applicable law. When state laws relating to acquisition of stock restrict the availability of retained earnings for payment of dividends or have other effects of a significant nature, these facts should be disclosed.

ARB 43, Chapter 3A—Current Assets and Current Liabilities

14. The following paragraph is added to this chapter:

   10. Unearned discounts (other than cash or quantity discounts and the like), finance charges and interest included in the face amount of receivables should be shown as a deduction from the related receivables.

ARB 43, Chapter 5—Intangible Assets

15. The last sentence of paragraph 7 of Chapter 5 is deleted.

ARB 43, Chapter 7B—Stock Dividends and Stock Split-Ups

16. The Board is of the opinion that paragraph 6 should not be construed as prohibiting the equity method of accounting for substantial intercorporate investments. This method is described in paragraph 19 of ARB 51.

[5]Special Bulletin, *Disclosure of Departures From Opinions of Accounting Principles Board*, October 1964. (Reprinted in Appendix A of this Opinion.)

ARB 43, Chapter 9B—Depreciation on Appreciation

17. Paragraphs 1 and 2 are deleted and the following paragraph is substituted for them:

   1. The Board is of the opinion that property, plant and equipment should not be written up by an entity to reflect appraisal, market or current values which are above cost to the entity. This statement is not intended to change accounting practices followed in connection with quasi-reorganizations[6] or reorganizations. This statement may not apply to foreign operations under unusual conditions such as serious inflation or currency devaluation. However, when the accounts of a company with foreign operations are translated into United States currency for consolidation, such write ups normally are eliminated. Whenever appreciation has been recorded on the books, income should be charged with depreciation computed on the written up amounts.

   Mr. Davidson agrees with the statement that at the present time "property, plant and equipment should not be written up" to reflect current costs, but only because he feels that current measurement techniques are inadequate for such restatement. When adequate measurement methods are developed, he believes that both the reporting of operations in the income statement and the valuation of plant in the balance sheet would be improved through the use of current rather than acquisition costs. In the meanwhile, strong efforts should be made to develop the techniques for measuring current costs.

ARB 43, Chapter 12—Foreign Operations and Foreign Exchange

18. Paragraphs 12 and 18 state that long-term receivables and long-term liabilities should be translated at historical exchange rates. The Board is of the opinion that translation of long-term receivables and long-term liabilities at current exchange rates is appropriate in many circumstances.

ARB 43, Chapter 15—Unamortized Discount, Issue Cost, and Redemption Premium on Bonds Refunded

19. Paragraph 12 is amended to read as follows:

   12. The third method, amortization over the life of the new issue, is appropriate under circumstances where the refunding takes place because of currently lower interest rates or anticipation of higher interest rates in the future. In such circumstances, the expected benefits justify spreading the costs over the life of the new issue, and this method is, therefore, acceptable. Paragraph 11 of this chapter is applicable when this method is adopted.

ARB 44 (Revised)—Declining-balance Depreciation

20. Pending further study, paragraph 9 is revised to read as follows:

   9. When a company subject to rate-making processes adopts the declining-balance method of depreciation for income tax purposes but adopts other appropriate methods for financial accounting purposes in the circumstances described in paragraph 8, and does not give accounting recognition to deferred income taxes, disclosure should be made of this fact.

   Messrs. Donald J. Bevis, Catlett, Layton, Moonitz, Penney, Schur, and Weston do not agree with paragraph 20 of this Opinion because it deletes a requirement in paragraph 9 of Accounting Research Bulletin No. 44 (Revised) for the disclosure of information they consider to be essential in financial statements. Paragraph 9 has required full disclosure of the effect ". . . arising out of the difference between the financial statements and the tax returns when the declining-balance method is adopted for income-tax purposes but other appropriate methods are used for financial accounting purposes" in the case of companies which (pursuant to paragraph 8) are not required to give accounting recognition to such differences. The intent of paragraph 20 of this Opinion is to continue the requirement for disclosure of the accounting practice followed but to omit the previous requirement for disclosure of the effect of the practice. Thus, in their opinion, the Accounting Principles Board is inappropriately sponsoring the viewpoint that investors and other users of financial statements should be told of the practice but need not be furnished the information to judge its significance.

21. The letter of April 15, 1959, addressed to the members of the Institute by the Committee on Accounting Procedure, interpreting ARB 44 (Revised), is continued in force.

---

[6]See Accounting Research Bulletin No. 43, Chapter 7A, *Quasi-Reorganization or Corporate Readjustment.*

ARB 48—Business Combinations

22. The Board believes that Accounting Research Bulletin No. 48 should be continued as an expression of the general philosophy for differentiating business combinations that are purchases from those that are poolings of interests, but emphasizes that the criteria set forth in paragraphs 5 and 6 are illustrative guides and not necessarily literal requirements.

Deferred Income Taxes

23. Provisions for deferred income taxes may be computed either (a) at the tax rate for the period in which the provision is made (the so-called "deferred credit" approach) or (b) at the tax rate which it is estimated will apply in the future (the so-called "liability" approach).[7]

a. Under the deferred credit method, the accumulated balance is not adjusted for changes in tax rates subsequent to the year of provision. Accordingly, the deferred amount is allocated to (drawn down in) the future periods based on the recorded tax benefit, which may be at a rate different from the then current rate.
b. Under the liability method, the accumulated balance is adjusted for changes in tax rates subsequent to the year of provision.[8] Accordingly, the deferred amount after adjustment is allocated to (drawn down in) the future periods based on the then current tax rates.

All provisions of Accounting Research Bulletins and Board Opinions in conflict with this paragraph are modified accordingly, including Chapter 9C and Chapter 10B of ARB 43 and ARB 44 (Revised).

EFFECTIVE DATE OF THIS OPINION

24. This Opinion shall be effective for fiscal periods that begin after December 31, 1965. However, the Board encourages earlier application of the provi-

sions of this Opinion.

The Opinion entitled "Status of Accounting Research Bulletins" was adopted unanimously by the twenty-one members of the Board, of whom one, Mr. Davidson, assented with qualification as to paragraph 17 and seven, Messrs. Donald J. Bevis, Catlett, Layton, Moonitz, Penney, Schur, and Weston assented with qualification as to paragraph 20.

NOTES

Opinions present the considered opinion of at least two-thirds of the members of the Accounting Principles Board, reached on a formal vote after examination of the subject matter.

Except as indicated in the succeeding paragraph, the authority of the Opinions rests upon their general acceptability. While it is recognized that general rules may be subject to exception, the burden of justifying departures from Board Opinions must be assumed by those who adopt other practices.

Action of Council of the Institute (Special Bulletin, Disclosure of Departures From Opinions of Accounting Principles Board, *October 1964) provides that:*

a. *"Generally accepted accounting principles" are those principles which have substantial authoritative support.*
b. *Opinions of the Accounting Principles Board constitute "substantial authoritative support."*
c. *"Substantial authoritative support" can exist for accounting principles that differ from Opinions of the Accounting Principles Board.*

The Council action also requires that departures from Board Opinions be disclosed in footnotes to the financial statements or in independent auditors' reports when the effect of the departure on the financial statements is material.

Unless otherwise stated, Opinions of the Board are not intended to be retroactive. They are not intended to be applicable to immaterial items.

Accounting Principles Board (1965-1966)

Clifford V. Heimbucher, *Chairman*	Sidney Davidson	John Peoples
Marshall S. Armstrong	Philip L. Defliese	John W. Queenan
Donald J. Bevis	Walter F. Frese	Ira A. Schur
Herman W. Bevis	LeRoy Layton	Hassel Tippit
George R. Catlett	Oral L. Luper	Wilbert A. Walker
W. A. Crichley	Maurice Moonitz	Frank T. Weston
	Robert J. Murphey	Robert E. Witschey
	Louis H. Penney	

---

[7]For a discussion of this subject see Accounting Research Study No. 7, *Inventory of Generally Accepted Accounting Principles for Business Enterprises,* p. 114.

[8]See Accounting Research Bulletin No. 43, Chapter 8, paragraph 11.

Appendix A

SPECIAL BULLETIN

Disclosure of Departures From Opinions of Accounting Principles Board

To Members of the American Institute of Certified Public Accountants

The Council of the Institute, at its meeting October 2, 1964, unanimously adopted recommendations that members should see to it that departures from Opinions of the Accounting Principles Board (as well as effective Accounting Research Bulletins issued by the former Committee on Accounting Procedure) are disclosed, either in footnotes to financial statements or in the audit reports of members in their capacity as independent auditors.

This action applies to financial statements for fiscal periods beginning after December 31, 1965.

The recommendations adopted by Council are as follows:

1. "Generally accepted accounting principles" are those principles which have substantial authoritative support.

2. Opinions of the Accounting Principles Board constitute "substantial authoritative support."

3. "Substantial authoritative support" can exist for accounting principles that differ from Opinions of the Accounting Principles Board.

4. No distinction should be made between the Bulletins issued by the former Committee on Accounting Procedure on matters of accounting principles and the Opinions of the Accounting Principles Board. Accordingly, references in this report to Opinions of the Accounting Principles Board also apply to the Accounting Research Bulletins.[1,2]

5. If an accounting principle that differs materially in its effect from one accepted in an Opinion of the Accounting Principles Board is applied in financial statements, the reporting member must decide whether the principle has substantial authoritative support and is applicable in the circumstances.

a. If he concludes that it does not, he would either qualify his opinion, disclaim an opinion, or give an adverse opinion as appropriate. Requirements for handling these situations in the reports of members are set forth in generally accepted auditing standards and in the Code of Professional Ethics and need no further implementation.

b. If he concludes that it does have substantial authoritative support:
   (1) he would give an unqualified opinion and
   (2) disclose the fact of departure from the Opinion in a separate paragraph in his report or see that it is disclosed in a footnote to the financial statements and, where practicable, its effects on the financial statements.* Illustrative language for this purpose is as follows:

> The company's treatment of (describe) is at variance with Opinion No.____ of the Accounting Principles Board (Accounting Research Bulletin No.____ of the Committee on Accounting Procedure) of the American Institute of Certified Public Accountants. This Opinion (Bulletin) states that (describe the principle in question). If the Accounting Principles Board Opinion (Accounting Research Bulletin) had been followed, income for the year would have been increased (decreased) by $____ , and the amount of retained earnings at (date) increased (decreased) by $____ . In our opinion, the company's treatment has substantial authoritative support and is an acceptable practice.

> *   *   *

> If disclosure is made in a footnote, the last sentence might be changed to read: In the opinion of the independent auditors, ____, the company's treatment has substantial authoritative support and is an acceptable practice.

6. Departures from Opinions of the Accounting Principles Board which have a material effect should be disclosed in reports for fiscal periods that begin:

---

[1]This is in accord with the following resolution of the Accounting Principles Board at its first meeting on September 11, 1959:

"The Accounting Principles Board has the authority, as did the predecessor committee, to review and revise any of these Bulletins (published by the predecessor committee) and it plans to take such action from time to time.

"Pending such action and in order to prevent any misunderstanding meanwhile as to the status of the existing accounting research and terminology bulletins, the Accounting Principles Board now makes public announcement that these bulletins should be considered as continuing in force with the same degree of authority as before."

[2]The Terminology Bulletins are not within the purview of the Council's resolution nor of this report because they are not statements on accounting principles.

*In those cases in which it is not practicable to determine the approximate effect on the financial statements, this fact should be expressly stated.

a. After December 31, 1965, in the case of existing Bulletins and Opinions;

b. After the issue date of future Opinions unless a later effective date is specified in the Opinion.

7. The Accounting Principles Board should review prior to December 31, 1965, all Bulletins of the Committee on Accounting Procedure and determine whether any of them should be revised or withdrawn.

8. The Accounting Principles Board should include in each Opinion a notation that members should disclose a material departure therefrom.

9. The failure to disclose a material departure from an Accounting Principles Board Opinion is deemed to be substandard reporting.† The Practice Review Committee should be instructed to give its attention to this area and to specifically report to Council the extent of deviations from these recommendations.

10. The Committee on Professional Ethics and the Institute's legal counsel have advised that the present By-Laws and Code of Professional Ethics would not cover an infraction of the above recommendations. Whether the Code of Professional Ethics should be amended is a question which should be studied further.‡

*   *   *

As indicated in the above text, Council's action is not intended to have the force and effect of a rule of ethics, but rather that of a standard of reporting practice, deviations from which should have the attention of the Practice Review Committee.

Yours truly,
Thomas D. Flynn, *President*

---

†In discussion at the Council meeting it was explained that the phrase "substandard reporting" was used in the sense of reporting practices not in conformity with recommendations of the Council.

‡By order of the Council a special committee is now reviewing the entire matter of the status of Opinions of the Accounting Principles Board, and the development of accounting principles and practices for the purpose of recommending to Council a general statement of philosophy, purpose and aims in this area.

APB Opinion No. 7
Accounting for Leases in Financial Statements of Lessors

STATUS

Issued: May 1966

Effective Date: For fiscal periods beginning after December 31, 1966

Affects: No other pronouncements

Affected by: Paragraph 8 amended by APB 27
Paragraph 12 superseded by APB 27
Superseded by FAS 13

Other Interpretive Pronouncement: AIN-APB 7, Interpretation No. 1 (Superseded by FAS 111)

APB Opinion No. 8
Accounting for the Cost of Pension Plans

STATUS

Issued: November 1966

Effective Date: For fiscal periods beginning after December 31, 1966

Affects: Supersedes ARB 43, Chapter 13A
Supersedes ARB 47

Affected by: Paragraph 31 amended by FAS 74
Paragraph 46 superseded by FAS 36
Superseded by FAS 87

Other Interpretive Pronouncements: AIN-APB 8, Interpretations No. 1 through 28 (Superseded by FAS 111)
FIN 3 (Superseded by FAS 87)
FTB 81-3 (Superseded by FAS 111)
FTB 87-1 (Superseded by FAS 106)

(The next page is 125.)

APB Opinion No. 9
Reporting the Results of Operations

I—Net Income and the Treatment of Extraordinary Items and Prior Period Adjustments
II—Computation and Reporting of Earnings per Share

STATUS

Issued: December 1966

Effective Date: For fiscal periods beginning after December 31, 1966

Affects: Supersedes ARB 43, Chapter 2B
Amends ARB 43, Chapter 5, paragraphs 5, 6, 8, and 9 and footnote 1
Supersedes ARB 43, Chapter 8
Amends ARB 43, Chapter 10A, paragraph 19
Amends ARB 43, Chapter 10B, paragraphs 15 and 17
Amends ARB 43, Chapter 11B, paragraph 9 and footnotes 3 and 4
Amends ARB 43, Chapter 12, paragraph 21
Amends ARB 43, Chapter 15, paragraphs 7 and 17
Supersedes ARB 49

Affected by: Paragraph 6 amended by APB 13
Paragraph 17 amended by APB 30 and FAS 111
Paragraph 18 amended by APB 20 and FAS 16
Paragraph 20 amended by APB 20
Paragraphs 20 through 22, footnote 2, paragraph 29, and Exhibits A through D superseded by APB 30
Paragraphs 23 and 24 superseded by·FAS 16
Paragraph 25 superseded by APB 20
Paragraphs 30 through 51, footnotes 6 through 9, and Exhibit E superseded by APB 15

Other Interpretive Pronouncements: AIN-APB 9, Interpretations No. 1 and 2 (Interpretation No. 2 superseded by FAS 111)
FTB 85-2

APB Opinion No. 9
Reporting the Results of Operations

I—Net Income and the Treatment of Extraordinary Items and Prior Period Adjustments
II—Computation and Reporting of Earnings Per Share

CONTENTS

INTRODUCTION

1. The American Institute of Certified Public Accountants, through its boards and committees, reviews from time to time the form and content of financial statements to determine how their usefulness may be improved. This Opinion is the result of a review of present practice in the reporting of the results of operations of business entities.

2. This Opinion supersedes (a) Chapter 2B, *Combined Statement of Income and Earned Surplus* of Accounting Research Bulletin No. 43; (b) Chapter

8, *Income and Earned Surplus* of Accounting Research Bulletin No. 43; and (c) Accounting Research Bulletin No. 49, *Earnings per Share*. It also modifies Chapter 5, *Intangible Assets* (paragraphs 5, 6, 8 and 9); Chapter 10A, *Real and Personal Property Taxes* (paragraph 19); Chapter 10B, *Income Taxes* (paragraphs 15 and 17); Chapter 11B, *Government Contracts—Renegotiation* (paragraph 9); Chapter 12, *Foreign Operations and Foreign Exchange* (paragraph 21); and Chapter 15, *Unamortized Discount, Issue Cost, and Redemption Premium on Bonds Refunded* (paragraphs 7 and 17) of Accounting Research Bulletin No. 43 to the extent the paragraphs indicated specify a particular treatment within income or retained earnings.

3. This Opinion (a) concludes that net income should reflect all items of profit and loss recognized during the period except for prior period adjustments, with extraordinary items to be shown separately as an element of net income of the period, (b) specifies the criteria to be used in determining which items, if any, recognized during the current period are to be considered extraordinary items, (c) specifies the criteria to be used in determining which items, if any, recognized during the current period are to be considered prior period adjustments and excluded from net income for the current period and (d) specifies the statement format and terminology to be used and the disclosures to be made when extraordinary items or prior period adjustments are present.

4. This Opinion also specifies the method of treating extraordinary items and prior period adjustments in comparative statements for two or more periods, specifies the disclosures required when previously issued statements of income are restated and recommends methods of presentation of historical, statistical-type financial summaries which include extraordinary items or are affected by prior period adjustments. In Part II, this Opinion specifies how earnings per share and dividends per share should be computed and reported.

5. For convenience, the term *net income* is used herein to refer to either net income or net loss. Similarly, *net income per share* or *earnings per share* is used to refer to either net income (or earnings) per share or net loss per share.

Applicability

6. This Opinion applies to general purpose statements which purport to present results of operations in conformity with generally accepted accounting principles. Investment companies, insurance companies and certain nonprofit organizations have developed income statements with formats different from those of the typical commercial entity described herein, designed to highlight the peculiar nature and sources of their income or operating results. The portion of this Opinion which requires that net income be presented as one amount does not apply to such entities. A committee of the American Institute of Certified Public Accountants is in the process of recommending a format for the income statement of commercial banks. Until such recommendation has been given and until the Board has taken a position thereon, this Opinion is not applicable to commercial banks.

I—Net Income and the Treatment of Extraordinary Items and Prior Period Adjustments

DISCUSSION

General

7. Business entities have developed a reporting pattern under which periodic financial statements are prepared from their accounting records to reflect the financial position of the entity at a particular date and the financial results of its activities for a specified period or periods. The statement of income and the statement of retained earnings (separately or combined) are designed to reflect, in a broad sense, the "results of operations."

8. A problem in reporting the results of operations of a business entity for one or more periods is the treatment of extraordinary items and prior period adjustments. This Opinion discusses the nature of events and transactions which might be considered "extraordinary," establishes related criteria which the Board feels are reasonable and practicable, and specifies the method and extent of disclosure of such items in the financial statements. The Opinion also discusses the various types of adjustment which might be considered to be proper adjustments of the recorded results of operations of prior periods and establishes criteria which the Board feels are reasonable and practicable for the relatively few items which should be so recognized.

Historical Background

General

9. There is considerable diversity of views as to whether extraordinary items and prior period adjustments should enter into the determination of net income of the period in which they are recognized. When Accounting Research Bulletin No. 32 was issued in December 1947, as well as when it was reissued in June 1953 as Chapter 8 of Accounting Research Bulletin No. 43, two conflicting viewpoints had attracted considerable support. The paragraphs which follow summarize the discussion of these two viewpoints contained in Chapter 8.

Current Operating Performance

10. Under one viewpoint, designated *current operating performance,* the principal emphasis is upon the ordinary, normal, recurring operations of the entity during the current period. If extraordinary or prior period transactions have occurred, their

inclusion might impair the significance of net income to such an extent that misleading inferences might be drawn from the amount so designated.

11. Advocates of this position believe that users of financial statements attach a particular business significance to the statement of income and the "net income" reported therein. They point out that, while some users are able to analyze a statement of income and to eliminate from it those prior period adjustments and extraordinary items which may tend to impair its usefulness for their purposes, many users are not trained to do this. They believe that management (subject to the attestation of the independent auditors) is in a better position to do this, and to eliminate the effect of such items from the amount designated as net income.

12. Advocates of this position also point out that many companies, in order to give more useful information concerning their earnings performance, restate the earnings or losses of affected periods to reflect the proper allocation of prior period adjustments. They believe therefore that items of this type may best be handled as direct adjustments of retained earnings or as "special items" excluded from net income of the current period. They feel that extraordinary items of *all* types may often best be disclosed as direct adjustments of retained earnings, since this eliminates any distortive effect on reported earnings.

All Inclusive

13. Under the other viewpoint, designated *all inclusive,* net income is presumed to include all transactions affecting the net increase or decrease in proprietorship equity during the current period, except dividend distributions and transactions of a capital nature.

14. Proponents of this position believe that the aggregate of such periodic net incomes, over the life of an enterprise, constitutes total net income, and that this is the only fair and complete method of reporting the results of operations of the entity. They believe that extraordinary items and prior period adjustments are part of the earnings history of an entity and that omission of such items from periodic statements of income increases the possibility that these items will be overlooked in a review of operating results for a period of years. They also stress the dangers of possible manipulation of annual earnings figures if such items may be omitted from the determination of net income. They believe that a statement of income including all such items is easy to understand and less subject to variations resulting from different judgments. They feel

that, when judgment is allowed to determine whether to include or exclude particular items or adjustments, significant differences develop in the treatment of borderline cases and that there is a danger that the use of "extraordinary" as a criterion may be a means of equalizing income. Advocates of this theory believe that full disclosure in the income statement of the nature of any extraordinary items or prior period adjustments during each period will enable the user of a statement of income to make his own assessment of the importance of the items and their effects on operating results.

Decisions of Committee on Accounting Procedure—Subsequent Developments

15. The committee on accounting procedure (predecessor of the Accounting Principles Board) did not embrace either of these viewpoints in its entirety in issuing its first Accounting Research Bulletin on this subject in December 1947. Instead, the committee stated ". . . it is the opinion of the committee that there should be a general presumption that all items of profit and loss recognized during the period are to be used in determining the figure reported as net income. The only possible exception to this presumption in any case would be with respect to items which in the aggregate are materially significant in relation to the company's net income and are clearly not identifiable with or do not result from the usual or typical business operations of the period. Thus, only extraordinary items such as the following may be excluded from the determination of net income for the year, and they should be excluded when their inclusion would impair the significance of net income so that misleading inferences might be drawn therefrom:. . . ."[1] The list of items which followed consisted of material charges or credits, other than ordinary adjustments of a recurring nature, (a) specifically related to operations of prior years, (b) resulting from unusual sales of assets not acquired for resale and not of the type in which the company usually deals, (c) resulting from losses of a type not usually insured against, (d) resulting from the write-off of a material amount of intangibles or a material amount of unamortized bond discount or premium and expense. The language quoted above was continued substantially unchanged in the 1953 *Restatement and Revision of Accounting Research Bulletins,* becoming Chapter 8 of ARB No. 43.

16. Since the issuance of these guidelines for the determination of net income, developments in the business and investment environment have increased the emphasis on, and interest in, the financial reporting format of business entities and the nature of the amount shown as net income therein. As a result of the widespread and increasing

---

[1]Accounting Research Bulletin No. 32, *Income and Earned Surplus.*

dissemination of financial data, often in highly condensed form, to investors and potential investors, suggestions have been made that the criteria for the determination of the amount to be reported as net income, insofar as it is affected by extraordinary items and prior period adjustments, should be reexamined.

OPINION

Summary

17. The Board has considered various methods of reporting the effects of extraordinary events and transactions and of prior period adjustments which are recorded in the accounts during a particular accounting period. The Board has concluded that net income should reflect all items of profit and loss recognized during the period with the sole exception of the prior period adjustments described below. *Extraordinary items* should, however, be segregated from the results of ordinary operations and shown separately in the income statement, with disclosure of the nature and amounts thereof. The criteria for determination of extraordinary items are described in paragraph 21 below.

18. With respect to *prior period adjustments,* the Board has concluded that those rare items which relate directly to the operations of a specific prior period or periods, which are material and which qualify under the criteria described in paragraphs 23 and 25 below should, in single period statements, be reflected as adjustments of the opening balance of retained earnings. When comparative statements are presented, corresponding adjustments should be made of the amounts of net income (and the components thereof) and retained earnings balances (as well as of other affected balances) for all of the periods reported therein, to reflect the retroactive application of the prior period adjustments. (See paragraph 26 for required disclosures of prior period adjustments.)

19. The Board has concluded that the above approach to the reporting of the results of operations of business entities will result in the most meaningful and useful type of financial presentation. The principal advantages are: (a) inclusion of all operating items related to the current period, with segregation and disclosure of the extraordinary items, (b) a reporting of current income from operations free from distortions resulting from material items directly related to prior periods and (c) proper retroactive reflection in comparative financial statements of material adjustments relating directly to prior periods. In reaching its conclusion, the Board recognizes that this approach may involve (a) occasional revision of previously-reported net income

for prior periods to reflect subsequently recorded material items directly related thereto, (b) difficulty in segregating extraordinary items and items related to prior periods and (c) the possibility that disclosures regarding adjustments of opening balances in retained earnings or of net income of prior periods will be overlooked by the reader.

Income Statement Presentation

20. Under this approach, the income statement should disclose the following elements:

> Income before extraordinary items
> Extraordinary items
>   (less applicable income tax)
> Net income

If the extraordinary items are few in number, descriptive captions may replace the caption *extraordinary items* and related notes. In such cases, the first and last captions shown above should nonetheless appear. Similarly, even though material extraordinary items may net to an immaterial amount, they should be positioned and disclosed as indicated above, and the first and last captions shown above should appear. If there are no extraordinary items, the caption *net income* should replace the three captions shown above. The amount of income tax applicable to the segregated items should be disclosed, either on the face of the income statement or in a note thereto. (The amount of prior period adjustments and the amount of income tax applicable thereto should also be disclosed, as outlined in paragraph 26.) Illustrative examples of the treatment of such items in financial statements appear herein as Exhibits A through D.

Criteria for Extraordinary Items Related to the Current Period

21. The segregation in the income statement of the effects of events and transactions which have occurred during the current period, which are of an extraordinary nature and whose effects are material requires the exercise of judgment. (In determining materiality, items of a similar nature should be considered in the aggregate. Dissimilar items should be considered individually; however, if they are few in number, they should be considered in the aggregate.) Such events and transactions are identified primarily by the nature of the underlying occurrence. They will be of a character significantly different from the typical or customary business activities of the entity. Accordingly, they will be events and transactions of material effect which would not be expected to recur frequently and which would not be considered as recurring factors in any evaluation of the ordinary operating processes of the business. Examples of extraordinary items,

assuming that each case qualifies under the criteria outlined above, include material gains or losses (or provisions for losses) from (a) the sale or abandonment of a plant or a significant segment of the business,[2] (b) the sale of an investment not acquired for resale, (c) the write-off of goodwill due to unusual events or developments within the period, (d) the condemnation or expropriation of properties and (e) a major devaluation of a foreign currency. As indicated above, such material items, less applicable income tax effect, should be segregated, but reflected in the determination of net income.

22. Certain gains or losses (or provisions for losses), regardless of size, do not constitute extraordinary items (or prior period adjustments) because they are of a character typical of the customary business activities of the entity. Examples include (a) write-downs of receivables, inventories and research and development costs, (b) adjustments of accrued contract prices and (c) gains or losses from fluctuations of foreign exchange. The effects of items of this nature should be reflected in the determination of income before extraordinary items. If such effects are material, disclosure is recommended.

Criteria for Prior Period Adjustments

23. Adjustments related to prior periods—and thus excluded in the determination of net income for the current period—are limited to those material adjustments which (a) can be specifically identified with and directly related to the business activities of particular prior periods, and (b) are not attributable to economic events occurring subsequent to the date of the financial statements for the prior period, and (c) depend primarily on determinations by persons other than management and (d) were not susceptible of reasonable estimation prior to such determination. Such adjustments are rare in modern financial accounting. They relate to events or transactions which occurred in a prior period, the accounting effects of which could not be determined with reasonable assurance at that time, usually because of some major uncertainty then existing. Evidence of such an uncertainty would be disclosure thereof in the financial statements of the applicable period, or of an intervening period in those cases in which the uncertainty became apparent during a subsequent period. Further, it would be expected that, in most cases, the opinion of the reporting independent auditor on such prior period would have contained a qualification because of the uncertainty. Examples are material, nonrecurring adjustments or settlements of income taxes, of renegotiation proceedings

or of utility revenue under rate processes. Settlements of significant amounts resulting from litigation or similar claims may also constitute prior period adjustments.

24. Treatment as prior period adjustments should not be applied to the normal, recurring corrections and adjustments which are the natural result of the use of estimates inherent in the accounting process. For example, changes in the estimated remaining lives of fixed assets affect the computed amounts of depreciation, but these changes should be considered prospective in nature and not prior period adjustments. Similarly, relatively immaterial adjustments or provisions for liabilities (including income taxes) made in prior periods should be considered recurring items to be reflected in operations of the current period. Some uncertainties, for example those relating to the realization of assets (collectibility of accounts receivable, ultimate recovery of deferred costs or realizability of inventories or other assets), would not qualify for prior period adjustment treatment, since economic events subsequent to the date of the financial statements must of necessity enter into the elimination of any previously-existing uncertainty. Therefore, the effects of such matters are considered to be elements in the determination of net income for the period in which the uncertainty is eliminated. Thus, the Board believes that prior period adjustments will be rare.

25. A change in the application of accounting principles may create a situation in which retroactive application is appropriate. In such situations, these changes should receive the same treatment as that for prior period adjustments. Examples are changes in the basis of preparing consolidated financial statements or in the basis of carrying investments in subsidiaries (e.g., from cost to the equity method).

Disclosure of Prior Period Adjustments and Restatements of Reported Net Income

26. When prior period adjustments are recorded, the resulting effects (both gross and net of applicable income tax) on the net income of prior periods should be disclosed in the annual report for the year in which the adjustments are made.[3] When financial statements for a single period only are presented, this disclosure should indicate the effects of such restatement on the balance of retained earnings at the beginning of the period and on the net income of the immediately preceding period. When financial statements for more than one period are presented, which is ordinarily the preferable procedure,[4] the

---

[2]Operating results prior to the decision as to sale or abandonment should not be considered an element of the extraordinary gain or loss.

[3]The Board recommends disclosure, in addition, in interim reports issued during that year subsequent to the date of recording the adjustments.

[4]See ARB No. 43, Chapter 2A, *Form of Statements—Comparative Financial Statements.*

disclosure should include the effects for each of the periods included in the statements. Such disclosures should include the amounts of income tax applicable to the prior period adjustments. Disclosure of restatements in annual reports issued subsequent to the first such post-revision disclosure would ordinarily not be required.

Historical Summaries of Financial Data

27. It has become customary for business entities to present historical, statistical-type summaries of financial data for a number of periods—commonly five or ten years. The Board recommends that the format for reporting extraordinary items described in paragraph 20 be used in such summaries. The Board further recommends that, whenever prior period adjustments have been recorded during any of the periods included therein, the reported amounts of net income (and the components thereof), as well as other affected items, be appropriately restated, with disclosure in the first summary published after the adjustments.

Capital Transactions

28. The Board reaffirms the conclusion of the former committee on accounting procedure that the following should be excluded from the determination of net income or the results of operations under all circumstances: (a) adjustments or charges or credits resulting from transactions in the company's own capital stock,[5] (b) transfers to and from accounts properly designated as appropriated retained earnings (such as general purpose contingency reserves or provisions for replacement costs of fixed assets) and (c) adjustments made pursuant to a quasi-reorganization.

Illustrative Statements

29. Examples of financial statements illustrating applications of the Board's conclusions appear as Exhibits to this Opinion. The illustrative income statements are prepared in "single-step" form. The "multi-step" form is also acceptable. Regardless of the form used, the income statement should disclose revenues (sales), and the elements mentioned in paragraph 20 above should be clearly disclosed in the order there indicated.

II—Computation and Reporting of Earnings per Share

Introduction

30. Statistical presentations of periodic "net income per share," "net loss per share" or "earnings per share" are commonly used in prospectuses, proxy material and annual reports to stockholders, and in the compilation of business earnings data for the press, statistical services and other publications.[6] When presented in conjunction with formal financial statements for a number of periods, such information can be useful, together with other data, in evaluating the past operating performance of a business entity and attempting to form an opinion as to its future potential.

OPINION

General

31. The Board believes that earnings per share data are most useful when furnished in conjunction with a statement of income. Accordingly, the Board strongly recommends that earnings per share be disclosed in the statement of income.

32. It is the Board's opinion that the reporting of per share data should disclose amounts for (a) income before extraordinary items, (b) extraordinary items, if any, (less applicable income tax) and (c) net income—the total of (a) and (b). (See paragraph 20—Part I.) The Board believes that not only will this reporting format increase the usefulness of the reports of results of operations of business entities, but that it will also help to eliminate the tendency of many users to place undue emphasis on one amount reported as earnings per share. Illustrative examples of various methods of disclosure of per share data are included in Exhibits A to E herein.

Computations for Single Periods

General

33. When used without qualification, *earnings per share* refers to the amount of earnings applicable to each share of common stock or other residual security outstanding.[7] When more than one class of

---

[5]See paragraph 12 of APB Opinion No. 6, *Status of Accounting Research Bulletins.*

[6]See Paragraph 5.

[7]When, as occasionally occurs in business combinations, an agreement exists to issue additional shares at a future date without additional consideration and without other significant conditions precedent (such as the attainment of specified levels of earnings), such shares are normally reflected in the balance sheet. These shares should be considered as outstanding for purposes of computing per share earnings data.

common stock is outstanding, or when an outstanding security has participating dividend rights with the common stock, or when an outstanding security clearly derives a major portion of its value from its conversion rights or its common stock characteristics, such securities should be considered "residual securities" and not "senior securities" for purposes of computing earnings per share. Appropriate consideration should be given to any senior dividend rights or interest relating to such securities, and to any participation provisions. (See also paragraph 49.) In order to compute earnings per share properly, consideration should be given to shares outstanding which are senior to the common stock, and to changes in the common and senior shares during the period. Procedures for doing so are outlined below. The term *common,* when used in this and subsequent paragraphs, includes "residual securities" as defined above.

Treatment of Senior Shares Outstanding

34. The term *earnings per share* should not be used with respect to outstanding shares of senior securities (e.g., preferred stock) in view of their limited dividend rights. In such cases it is often informative to show the number of times or the extent to which the dividend requirements of senior securities have been earned ("earnings coverage"), but such information should not be designated as earnings per share.

35. The claims of senior shares on earnings should be deducted from net income (and also from income before extraordinary items, if an amount therefor appears in the statement) before computing per share amounts applicable to residual securities. Therefore, in arriving at earnings applicable to common stock, provision should be made for cumulative preferred dividends for the period, whether or not earned. (In the case of a net loss, the amount of the loss should be increased by any cumulative preferred dividends for the period.) When cumulative preferred dividends are in arrears, the per share and aggregate amounts thereof should be disclosed. When preferred dividends are cumulative only if earned, no adjustment of this type is required, except to the extent of income available therefor. When preferred dividends are in no way cumulative, only the amount of such dividends declared during the period should be deducted. In all cases, the effect that has been given to dividend rights of senior securities in arriving at the earnings per share of residual securities should be disclosed.

Changes in Common or Senior Shares during the Period

36. The computation of earnings per share should

be based on the weighted average number of shares outstanding during the period. Minor increases and decreases in the number of common shares outstanding during the period may be disregarded; under these conditions, the computation may be based on the number of common shares outstanding at the end of the period. For purposes of determining the number of shares outstanding, reacquired shares (including treasury stock) should be excluded. Major increases or decreases should be taken into consideration as discussed below.

37. When common shares are issued to acquire a business in a transaction which is accounted for as a purchase, the computation should be based on a weighted average of the shares outstanding during the period. When a business combination is accounted for as a pooling of interests, the computation should be based on the aggregate of the weighted average outstanding shares of the constituent businesses (adjusted to equivalent shares of the surviving business) determined in accordance with the provisions herein. This difference in treatment reflects the fact that, in a purchase, the results of operations of the acquired business are included in the statement of income only from the date of acquisition; whereas, in a pooling of interests, the results of operations are combined for the entire period. In the case of reorganizations, the computations should be based on an analysis of the particular transaction according to the criteria contained herein.

38. When senior stock or debt is converted into common stock during a period, earnings per share should be based on a weighted average of the number of shares outstanding during the period. Use of a weighted average makes unnecessary any adjustments with respect to interest or other related factors. Dividends on preferred stock applicable to the period prior to conversion should be handled in accordance with paragraph 35 above. Supplementary pro forma computations of earnings per share, showing what the earnings would have been if the conversion had taken place at the beginning of the period, should be furnished if the effect of conversion is material, as outlined in paragraph 41 below.

39. When the number of shares outstanding increases as a result of a stock dividend or stock split,[8] or decreases as a result of a reverse split, without significant proceeds or disbursements, the computation should give retroactive recognition to an appropriate equivalent change in capital structure for the entire period. When a decrease in the number of shares outstanding results from acquisition of treasury stock or from a transaction other than a reverse split, the computation should be

---

[8]See ARB No. 43, Chapter 7B, *Capital Accounts—Stock Dividends and Stock Split-Ups.*

based on a weighted average of the number of shares outstanding during the period.

Changes in Common or Senior Shares after Close of Period

40. When changes in common stock due to stock splits or reverse splits take place after the close of the period but before completion and issuance of the financial report, the per share computations should be based on the new number of shares, on a pro forma basis, since the reader's primary interest is presumed to be related to the current capitalization. Similar considerations apply to stock dividends, although a relatively small stock dividend may be disregarded. When per share computations reflect changes in the number of shares after the close of the period, this fact should be disclosed. It is usually not satisfactory to show two amounts of earnings per share under these circumstances.

41. When senior stock or debt is converted into common stock after the close of the period but before completion and issuance of the financial report, supplementary pro forma computations of earnings per share, showing what the earnings would have been if the conversion had taken place at the beginning of the latest period, should be furnished if the effect is material. In making these computations, dividends paid on the senior securities converted should not be deducted from the historical net income for the period; interest and related expenses on the debt converted, less applicable income tax, should be added to the historical net income of the period. The bases of these supplementary computations should be disclosed.

42. Occasionally a sale of common stock for cash is scheduled to occur after the close of the period but before completion and issuance of the financial report. When a portion or all of the proceeds of the sale are to be used to retire preferred stock or debt, supplementary pro forma computations of earnings per share should be furnished to show what the earnings would have been for the latest period if the retirement had taken place at the beginning of that period, if the effect is material. The average number of shares outstanding to be used in the computation should include those whose proceeds are to be used to retire the preferred stock or debt. The basis of these supplementary computations should be disclosed.

Contingent Changes and Dilution[9]

43. Under certain circumstances, earnings per share may be subject to dilution in the future if existing contingencies permitting issuance of common shares eventuate. Such circumstances include contingent changes resulting from the existence of (a) outstanding senior stock or debt which is convertible into common shares, (b) outstanding stock options, warrants or similar agreements and (c) agreements for the issuance of common shares for little or no consideration upon the satisfaction of certain conditions (e.g., the attainment of specified levels of earnings following a business combination). If such potential dilution is material, supplementary pro forma computations of earnings per share should be furnished, showing what the earnings would be if the conversions or contingent issuances took place. The Board strongly recommends that such per share data be disclosed in the statement of income. The methods of computation should follow those outlined in the preceding paragraphs. When increased earnings levels are a condition of issuance, as in (c) above, such earnings should be given appropriate recognition in the computation of potential dilution. (See also paragraph 49.)

44. The fact that the relationship between current market and conversion prices makes conversion or other contingent issuance unlikely in the foreseeable future is not sufficient basis for omission of the disclosure of the pro forma earnings per share data described in paragraph 43. Disclosure of the current conditions would, nonetheless, normally be desirable.

Computations for Two or More Periods (Including Historical, Statistical-Type Summaries in Annual Reports to Stockholders)

45. The criteria governing the computations of earnings per share for two or more periods, while generally conforming with those outlined above for single periods, vary somewhat depending on the nature and purpose of the presentation in which they appear. Variations in the capitalization structure of the entity during the periods may have substantial effects on earnings per share, and comparisons of such data without adequate explanations may tend to be misleading. Furthermore, unless such earnings statistics are presented in conjunction with financial statements and with other historical information, the usefulness of per share data in evaluating the past operating performance of a business entity and attempting to form an opinion as to its future potential is limited.

46. Annual reports to stockholders are generally considered to be primarily historical in nature. Thus, although a trend has developed in recent years

---

[9]Paragraphs 43 and 44 do not apply to securities which, because of their characteristics, are accorded the treatments described in paragraph 33 or in note 7 thereto.

to include statistical-type summaries of financial data for a number of years, the main emphasis in the financial statements themselves has been on the results of the broad business activities of the entity during the current year as compared with those of the immediately preceding year. Accordingly, the computations of earnings per share in annual reports to stockholders, whether related to the formal financial statements in comparative form for two years or to the historical summaries covering a period of years, should usually be based on the capitalization structure existing during each period. The computation for each year should therefore follow the criteria outlined in paragraphs 33 through 44 above. The principal exception to this practice of avoiding retroactive recomputations for changes in the capitalization structure occurs when a pooling of interests has occurred. Since the earnings of the pooled entities are combined for all periods, the capital structure used to compute earnings per share for all periods should reflect appropriate recognition of the securities issued in the pooling transaction. Other exceptions to this treatment are the result of (a) stock splits or reverse splits, and (b) stock dividends, including those in recurring small percentages which in the aggregate become material during the periods involved. In these situations the methods outlined in paragraphs 39 and 40 above should be followed for all of the periods involved. When changes in the capitalization structure of the types described in paragraphs 41 and 42 above occur after the close of the last period, or when contingencies exist (see paragraphs 43 and 44), supplementary pro forma computations for the latest period, as a minimum, should be furnished.

47. In those cases in which net income of a prior period has been restated as a result of a prior period adjustment during the current period, any earnings per share data should be based on the restated amount of net income. The effect of the restatement, expressed in per share terms, should be disclosed.

48. The Board recommends that management be guided by the methods outlined in paragraphs 45, 46 and 47 herein for computing and reporting earnings per share in historical, statistical-type summaries contained in annual reports to stockholders.

Other

49. The Board recognizes that it is impracticable, in this Opinion, to discuss all the possible conditions and circumstances under which it may be necessary or desirable to compute earnings per share. However, when situations not expressly covered in this Opinion occur, they should be dealt with in accordance with the guidelines and criteria outlined herein. Such determinations require careful consid-

eration of all the facts, and the exercise of judgment. The resulting earnings per share data should reflect a realistic evaluation of all the attendant circumstances. In all unusual cases, the basis of the computations should be disclosed.

Dividends per Share

50. Dividends constitute historical facts and usually are so reported. However, in certain cases, such as those affected by stock dividends or splits or reverse splits, the presentation of dividends per share should be made in terms of the current equivalent of the number of shares outstanding at the time of the dividend, so that dividends per share and earnings per share will be stated on a comparable basis. A disclosure problem exists in presenting data as to dividends per share following a pooling of interests. If the dividend policies of the constituent companies were different, a combination of dividends declared may be misleading, even though the per share data are expressed in shares of the continuing company. In such cases, it is usually preferable to disclose the dividends declared per share by the principal constituent and to disclose, in addition, either the amount per equivalent share or the total amount for each period for the other constituent, with appropriate explanations of the circumstances. When dividends per share are presented on other than an historical basis, the basis of presentation should be disclosed.

Illustrative Statements

51. Examples illustrating the inclusion of per share data in financial statements in accordance with the Board's recommendations are shown in Exhibits A, B, D and E.

EFFECTIVE DATE

52. This Opinion shall be effective for fiscal periods beginning after December 31, 1966. However, where feasible the Board recommends earlier compliance with this Opinion. The Board also strongly recommends that, in comparative statements in which one or more periods are subject to this Opinion, the provisions of the Opinion be applied to all periods appearing therein.

The Opinion entitled "Reporting the Results of Operations" was adopted unanimously by the twenty members of the Board, of whom five, Messrs. Biegler, Catlett, Frese, Halvorson and Walker, assented with qualification.

Mr. Biegler assents to the issuance of this Opinion because he believes that the usefulness of the income statement to the investor is enhanced when all items of profit and loss relating to the period are included in the determination of net income and the results of the ordinary, recurring operations of a business are reported separately from extraordinary items. He believes that the caption described in paragraph 20 as "Income before extraordinary items" can best meet the needs of investors for an index of the results of and trends in ordinary recurring operations when there is excluded therefrom those gains or losses which are extraordinary because of the combination of rarity in the circumstances giving rise thereto and the abnormal size thereof. Accordingly, he dissents from the conclusion stated in paragraph 22 that certain types of gains or losses, *regardless of size,* must be reflected in the determination of "income before extraordinary items." He believes that the quality of being extraordinary can be derived from rarity or extreme infrequency in size, as well as from the nature of a transaction or event.

Mr. Catlett does not agree that the criteria for prior period adjustments as set forth in paragraphs 23 and 24 of this Opinion are established on a proper basis. He considers that the nature of the adjustment and the factors which cause it are controlling, and that any material item which is in fact applicable to, and a correction of, a prior period should be accounted for as an adjustment of that period. He believes that there are cases in which prior period adjustments are appropriate with respect to questions involving realization of assets, such as receivables, inventories and property. He is of the opinion (1) that the Board is establishing arbitrary rules to discourage or prohibit prior period adjustments rather than determining appropriate principles to be followed in reviewing the nature of the items involved, and (2) that the inclusion in the current period's net income of a material item which is really applicable to a prior period results in the financial statements for two periods being in error.

Mr. Walker, joined by Mr. Frese, recognizes that the Opinion attempts to set up the criteria to restrict the number of items deemed to be prior period adjustments which are to be excluded from net income of the year and thrown back to prior years by restating opening balances of retained earnings. He nevertheless feels that such treatment will result in continuing controversy and will be confusing to users of financial statements. He believes that such treatment should not be mandatory, but rather should be left to the judgment of the managements who have the primary responsibility for proper presentation to stockholders. He therefore recommends that the so-called "all inclusive" statement of income—consistently followed—and with adequate disclosure of material special items (including extraordinary and prior period items) should be permissive.

Mr. Halvorson concurs in the qualified assent expressed by Mr. Walker in respect of the mandatory exclusion of prior period adjustments from the current statement of income, and extends his qualification to the mandatory determination of an arbitrary "income before extraordinary items" within the determination of net income.

NOTES

Opinions present the considered opinion of at least two-thirds of the members of the Accounting Principles Board, reached on a formal vote after examination of the subject matter.

Except as indicated in the succeeding paragraph, the authority of the Opinions rests upon their general acceptability. While it is recognized that general rules may be subject to exception, the burden of justifying departures from Board Opinions must be assumed by those who adopt other practices.

Action of Council of the Institute (Special Bulletin, Disclosure of Departures From Opinions of Accounting Principles Board, *October 1964) provides that:*

a. *"Generally accepted accounting principles" are those principles which have substantial authoritative support.*
b. *Opinions of the Accounting Principles Board constitute "substantial authoritative support."*
c. *"Substantial authoritative support" can exist for accounting principles that differ from Opinions of the Accounting Principles Board.*

The Council action also requires that departures from Board Opinions be disclosed in footnotes to the financial statements or in independent auditors' reports when the effect of the departure on the financial statements is material.

Unless otherwise stated, Opinions of the Board are not intended to be retroactive. They are not intended to be applicable to immaterial items.

Accounting Principles Board (1966-1967)

Clifford V. Heimbucher, *Chairman*	Joseph P. Cummings	John K. McClare
Marshall S. Armstrong	Sidney Davidson	Robert J. Murphey
Donald J. Bevis	Philip L. Defliese	Louis H. Penney
John C. Biegler	Walter F. Frese	John W. Queenan
George R. Catlett	Newman T. Halvorson	Wilbert A. Walker
W. A. Crichley	LeRoy Layton	Frank T. Weston
	Oral L. Luper	Robert E. Witschey

EXHIBITS

Illustrative Statements

The following examples illustrate the treatment of extraordinary items and prior period adjustments in financial statements. The format of the statements is illustrative only, and does not necessarily reflect a preference by the Accounting Principles Board for the format or for the intermediate captions shown. See Part I—paragraph 20 as to certain final captions. The statements do not include customary disclosures, such as the amount of depreciation expense for the period, which are not considered pertinent to the subject matter of this Opinion.

The illustrative examples, in comparative form, are as follows:

	Exhibit
Statement of Income and Retained Earnings	A
Statement of Income...................	B
Statement of Retained Earnings..........	C
Statement of Income—Five Years	D
Disclosures of per share data when senior securities are outstanding or material potential dilution exists	E

Exhibit A

STATEMENT OF INCOME AND RETAINED EARNINGS

Years Ended December 31, 1967 and December 31, 1966

	1967	1966
		(Note 2)
Net sales	$84,580,000	$75,650,000
Other income	80,000	100,000
	84,660,000	75,750,000
Cost and expenses—		
Cost of goods sold	60,000,000	55,600,000
Selling, general and administrative expenses	5,000,000	4,600,000
Interest expense	100,000	100,000
Other deductions	80,000	90,000
Income tax	9,350,000	7,370,000
	74,530,000	67,760,000
Income before extraordinary items	10,130,000	7,990,000
Extraordinary items, net of applicable income tax of $1,880,000 in 1967 (Note 1)	(2,040,000)	(1,280,000)
Net Income	8,090,000	6,710,000
Retained earnings at beginning of year—		
As previously reported	28,840,000	25,110,000
Adjustments (Note 2)	(3,160,000)	(1,760,000)
As restated	25,680,000	23,350,000
	33,770,000	30,060,000
Cash dividends on common stock—		
$.75 per share	4,380,000	4,380,000
Retained earnings at end of year	$29,390,000	$25,680,000
Per share of common stock—		
Income before extraordinary items	$1.73	$1.37
Extraordinary items, net of tax	(.34)	(.22)
Net income	$1.39	$1.15

Note 1

During 1967 the Company sold one of its plants at a net loss of $2,040,000, after applicable income tax reduction of $1,880,000. During 1966 the Company sold an investment in marketable securities at a loss of $1,280,000, with no income tax effect.

Note 2

The balance of retained earnings at December 31, 1966 has been restated from amounts previously reported to reflect a retroactive charge of $3,160,000 for additional income taxes settled in 1967. Of this amount, $1,400,000 ($.24 per share) is applicable to 1966 and has been reflected as an increase in tax expense for that year, the balance (applicable to years prior to 1966) being charged to retained earnings at January 1, 1966.

Exhibit B

STATEMENT OF INCOME

Years Ended December 31, 1967 and December 31, 1966

	1967	1966
		(Note 2)
Net sales	$84,580,000	$75,650,000
Other income	80,000	100,000
	84,660,000	75,750,000
Cost and expenses—		
Cost of goods sold	60,000,000	55,600,000
Selling, general and administrative expenses	5,000,000	4,600,000
Interest expense	100,000	100,000
Other deductions	80,000	90,000
Income tax	9,350,000	7,370,000
	74,530,000	67,760,000
Income before extraordinary items (per share: 1967—$1.73; 1966—$1.37)	10,130,000	7,990,000
Extraordinary items, less applicable income tax in 1967 (Note 1) (per share: 1967—$(.34); 1966—$(.22))	(2,040,000)	(1,280,000)
Net income (per share: 1967—$1.39; 1966—$1.15)	$ 8,090,000	$ 6,710,000

Note 1

During 1967 the Company sold one of its plants at a net loss of $2,040,000, after applicable income tax reduction of $1,880,000. During 1966 the Company sold an investment in marketable securities at a loss of $1,280,000, with no income tax effect.

Note 2

The balance of retained earnings at December 31, 1966 has been restated from amounts previously reported to reflect a retroactive charge of $3,160,000 for additional income taxes settled in 1967. Of this amount, $1,400,000 ($.24 per share) is applicable to 1966 and has been reflected as an increase in tax expense for that year, the balance (applicable to years prior to 1966) being charged to retained earnings at January 1, 1966.

Exhibit C

STATEMENT OF RETAINED EARNINGS

Years Ended December 31, 1967 and December 31, 1966

	1967	1966
Retained earnings at beginning of year—		
As previously reported	$28,840,000	$25,110,000
Adjustments (Note 2)	(3,160,000)	(1,760,000)
As restated	25,680,000	23,350,000
Net income	8,090,000	6,710,000
	33,770,000	30,060,000
Cash dividends on common stock— $.75 per share	4,380,000	4,380,000
Retained earnings at end of year	$29,390,000	$25,680,000

(See accompanying notes appearing on statement of income, Exhibit B.)

Exhibit D

STATEMENT OF INCOME

For the Five Years Ended December 31, 1967

	1963	1964	1965	1966	1967
	(In thousands of dollars)				
Net sales	$67,100	$66,700	$69,300	$75,650	$84,580
Other income	80	80	60	100	80
	67,180	66,780	69,360	75,750	84,660
Costs and expenses:					
Cost of goods sold	48,000	47,600	49,740	55,600	60,000
Selling, general and administrative expenses	4,300	4,200	4,500	4,600	5,000
Interest expense	120	100	90	100	100
Other deductions	80	80	60	90	80
Income tax	7,340	7,400	7,490	7,370	9,350
	59,840	59,380	61,880	67,760	74,530
Income before extraordinary items	7,340	7,400	7,480	7,990	10,130
Extraordinary items, net of applicable income tax (Note A)	—	760	—	(1,280)	(2,040)
Net income (Note B)	$ 7,340	$ 8,160	$ 7,480	$ 6,710	$ 8,090
Per share of common stock:					
Income before extraordinary items	$1.26	$1.27	$1.28	$1.37	$1.73
Extraordinary items, net of income tax	—	$ .12	—	$ (.22)	$ (.34)
Net income	$1.26	$1.39	$1.28	$1.15	$1.39

NOTE A

The extraordinary items consist of the following: 1964—gain as a result of condemnation of idle land, less applicable income tax of $254,000; 1966—loss on sale of investment in marketable securities, with no income tax effect; 1967—loss on sale of plant, less applicable income tax reduction $1,880,000.

NOTE B

The amounts of net income for 1963, 1964 and 1966 have been restated from amounts previously reported to reflect additional income taxes for such years settled in 1967. These retroactive adjustments reduced net income for such years by $860,000 ($.15 per share), $900,000 ($.15 per share) and $1,400,000 ($.24 per share), respectively, as follows:

	1963	1964	1966
	(In thousands of dollars)		
Previously reported	$8,200	$9,060	$8,110
Adjustments	860	900	1,400
As adjusted	$7,340	$8,160	$6,710

Exhibit E

DISCLOSURES OF PER SHARE DATA WHEN SENIOR SECURITIES ARE OUTSTANDING OR MATERIAL POTENTIAL DILUTION EXISTS

Senior securities outstanding

When senior securities are outstanding, per share data are preferably shown in the format illustrated in Exhibit A, that is, in a table at the bottom of the income statement and not against the captions of the statement itself. The preferred method is illustrated below:

Per share earnings applicable to common stock (Note X)

Earnings before extraordinary items	$1.23	$ .87
Extraordinary items, net of tax	(.34)	(.22)
Earnings applicable to common stock	$ .89	$ .65

Note X

Per share data are based on the average number of common shares outstanding during each year, after recognition of the dividend requirements ($2,920,000) on the 5% preferred stock.

Material potential dilution exists—convertible preferred stock

Under these conditions, the basic and supplementary per share data are preferably shown at the bottom of the income statement, as in Exhibit A, with an additional note, as follows:

Per share earnings applicable to common stock (Note X)

Earnings before extraordinary items	$1.23	$ .87
Extraordinary items, net of tax	(.34)	(.22)
Earnings applicable to common stock	$ .89	$ .65

Pro forma per share of common stock, reflecting conversion (Note Y)

Income before extraordinary items	$ .99	$ .78
Extraordinary items, net of tax	(.20)	(.12)
Net income	$ .79	$ .66

Note X

Per share data are based on the average number of common shares outstanding during each year, after recognition of the dividend requirements ($2,920,000) on the 5% preferred stock.

Note Y

The pro forma per share data are based on the assumption that the outstanding 5% preferred shares were converted into common shares at the conversion ratio in effect at December 31, 1967, reflecting the 4,380,000 shares issuable on conversion and eliminating the preferred dividend requirements.

**Material potential dilution exists—
convertible debt, no preferred stock**

Under these conditions, the basic and supplementary per share data are preferably shown at the bottom of the income statement, as in Exhibit A, with an additional note, as follows:

Per share of common stock

Income before extraordinary items	$1.73	$1.37
Extraordinary items, net of tax	(.34)	(.22)
Net income	$1.39	$1.15

Pro forma per share of common stock, reflecting conversion (Note M)

Income before extraordinary items	$1.53	$1.21
Extraordinary items, net of tax	(.31)	(.19)
Net income	$1.22	$1.02

Note M

The pro forma per share data are based on the assumption that the 5 1/2% convertible debentures outstanding at December 31, 1967 were converted into common shares at the conversion rate in effect at that date, reflecting the 800,000 shares issuable on conversion and eliminating the related interest on the convertible debentures (less applicable income tax) of $50,000.

APB Opinion No. 10
Omnibus Opinion—1966

Consolidated Financial Statements
Poolings of Interest—Restatement of Financial Statements
Tax Allocation Accounts—Discounting
Offsetting Securities Against Taxes Payable
Convertible Debt and Debt Issued with Stock Warrants
Liquidation Preference of Preferred Stock
Installment Method of Accounting

STATUS

Issued: December 1966

Effective Date: For fiscal periods beginning after December 31, 1966

Affects: Supersedes ARB 43, Chapter 3B
      Amends ARB 48, paragraph 12
      Amends ARB 51, paragraphs 19 and 20

Affected by: Paragraphs 2 through 4 and footnotes 1 through 5 superseded by APB 18
      Paragraph 5 and footnote 6 superseded by APB 16
      Paragraphs 8 and 9 amended by APB 12
      Paragraphs 8 and 9 superseded by APB 14
      Paragraph 11(b) amended by FAS 111

Other Interpretive Pronouncements: FTB 88-2 (Superseded by FIN 39)
                FIN 39

APB Opinion No. 10
Omnibus Opinion—1966

Consolidated Financial Statements
Poolings of Interest—Restatement of Financial Statements
Tax Allocation Accounts—Discounting
Offsetting Securities Against Taxes Payable
Convertible Debt and Debt Issued with Stock Warrants
Liquidation Preference of Preferred Stock
Installment Method of Accounting

INTRODUCTION

1. This is the first of a series of Opinions which the Board expects to issue periodically containing:

a. Amendments of prior Opinions of the Accounting Principles Board and Accounting Research Bulletins of its predecessor, the committee on accounting procedure, as appear necessary to clarify their meaning or to describe their applicability under changed conditions.

b. Affirmation of accounting principles and methods which have become generally accepted through practice and which the Board believes to be sound, and when it desires to prevent the possible development of less desirable alternatives.

c. Conclusions as to appropriate accounting principles and methods on subjects not dealt with in previous pronouncements and for which a separate Opinion is not believed to be warranted.

CONSOLIDATED FINANCIAL STATEMENTS

(Amendment to *Accounting Research Bulletin* No. 51)

2. Paragraph 1 of ARB No. 51 states that "There is a presumption that consolidated statements . . .

are usually necessary for a fair presentation when one of the companies in the group directly or indirectly has a controlling financial interest in the other companies." The usefulness of consolidated financial statements has been amply demonstrated by the widespread acceptance of this form of financial reporting. A research study on the broader subject of accounting for intercorporate investments is now in process which will encompass the matters covered in ARB No. 51. Pending consideration of that study the Board has adopted the following amendments to ARB No. 51.

3. If, in consolidated financial statements, a domestic subsidiary is not consolidated,[1] the Board's opinion is that, unless circumstances are such as those referred to in paragraph 2 of ARB No. 51,[2] the investment in the subsidiary should be adjusted for the consolidated group's share of accumulated undistributed earnings and losses since acquisition.[3] This practice is sometimes referred to as the "equity" method. In reporting periodic consolidated net income, the earnings or losses of the unconsolidated subsidiary (or group of subsidiaries) should generally be presented as a separate item.[4] The amount of such earnings or losses should give effect to amortization, if appropriate, of any difference between the cost of the investment and the equity in net assets at date of acquisition and to any

---

[1] This paragraph modifies paragraphs 19 and 20 of ARB 51 insofar as they relate to domestic subsidiaries. An accounting research study on the subject of foreign investments and operations is in process. The Board has deferred consideration of the treatment of foreign subsidiaries in consolidated financial statements until the study is published. In the meantime, the provisions of Chapter 12 of ARB 43 (as amended by paragraph 18 of APB Opinion No. 6 and by paragraphs 17, 21 and 22 of APB Opinion No. 9) continue in effect.

The Board has also deferred consideration of the treatment of jointly owned (50 per cent or less) companies pending completion of the study on accounting for intercorporate investments.

[2] "For example, a subsidiary should not be consolidated where control is likely to be temporary, or where it does not rest with the majority owners (as, for instance, where the subsidiary is in legal reorganization or in bankruptcy)."

[3] Cumulative undistributed earnings at the effective date of this Opinion should be reflected, with a corresponding adjustment of retained earnings, and reported as a prior period adjustment resulting from a retroactive change in the application of an accounting principle; where the results of operations of prior periods would be materially affected, they should be restated. See paragraph 25 of APB Opinion No. 9.

[4] Extraordinary items and prior period adjustments may require treatment in accordance with APB Opinion No. 9 if, on a consolidated basis, such items would be material in relation to consolidated net income. Thus, consolidated income before extraordinary items and consolidated net income would be the same as if the unconsolidated subsidiary were fully consolidated.

elimination of intercompany gains or losses that would have been made had the subsidiary been consolidated. If desired, dividends received by members of the consolidated group from the unconsolidated subsidiary may be shown parenthetically or by footnote. (See also paragraph 21 of ARB 51, which relates to disclosure of assets and liabilities of unconsolidated subsidiaries.)

4. The Board is of the opinion that, in the preparation of consolidated financial statements for periods subsequent to the effective date of this Opinion, the accounts of all subsidiaries (regardless of when organized or acquired) whose principal business activity is leasing property or facilities to their parents or other affiliates should be consolidated. The Board believes that the "equity" method, referred to in paragraph 3, which directs its emphasis primarily to recognizing results of operations of the enterprise as a whole, is not adequate for fair presentation in the case of these subsidiaries because of the significance of their assets and liabilities to the consolidated financial position of the enterprise.[5]

Messrs. Catlett and Davidson do not agree with paragraph 4 of this Opinion. They believe that the Board should not use this piecemeal pronouncement on consolidation principles to attempt to overcome some of the basic deficiencies in Opinion No. 5. A subsidiary of the type referred to in paragraph 4 represents one of several possible approaches to financing by means of leases, and in many such cases the noncancellable leases from the parent company are the principal security for the funds borrowed by the subsidiary; such leases, in effect, are obligations to outside lenders. The consolidation of such a subsidiary would increase further the existing confusion and lack of comparability between companies in the financial reporting of lease obligations, because the consolidation might involve (1) leases entered into prior to the effective date of Opinion No. 5, and (2) leases in which there is not the creation of a significant equity for the lessee in the property. They consider that the better solution to this problem would be for Opinion No. 5 to be revised to provide that material amounts payable under noncancellable leases should be shown as obligations (discounted to present value) in the balance sheets of all lessee companies.

POOLINGS OF INTERESTS—RESTATEMENT OF FINANCIAL STATEMENTS

5. Paragraph 12 of ARB No. 48 is amended to read as follows:

12. When a combination is considered to be a pooling of interests,[6] statements of results of operations issued by the continuing business for the period in which the combination occurs should include the combined results of operations of the constituent interests for the entire period in which the combination was effected. Similarly, if the pooling is consummated at or shortly after the close of the period, and before financial statements of the continuing business are issued, the financial statements should, if practicable, give effect to the pooling for the entire period being reported; in this case, information should also be furnished as to revenues and earnings of the constituent businesses for all periods presented. Results of operations, balance sheets and other historical financial data of the continuing business for periods (including interim periods) prior to that in which the combination was effected, when presented for comparative purposes, should be restated on a combined basis. In order to show the effect of poolings upon their earnings trends, companies may wish to provide reconciliations of amounts of revenues and earnings previously reported with those currently presented. Combined financial statements of pooled businesses should be clearly described as such, and disclosure should be made that a business combination has been treated as a pooling.

TAX ALLOCATION ACCOUNTS—DISCOUNTING

6. Accounting Research Study No. 9, *Interperiod Allocation of Corporate Income Taxes,*[7] deals with the allocation of income taxes among accounting periods when revenues and expenses are reported for financial accounting purposes in different

---

[5]The Board is giving further consideration to the accounting treatment of lease transactions. In the meantime, it has deferred expressing an opinion on the inclusion in consolidated financial statements of companies organized in connection with leasing transactions in which the equity interest, usually nominal at the time of organization, is held by third parties, but in which the principal lessee, through options or by similar devices, possesses or has the power to obtain the economic benefits of ownership from the lease arrangements. (This deferment does not affect the applicability of paragraph 12 of APB Opinion No. 5.)

[6]Accounting Research Study No. 5 on *A Critical Study of Accounting for Business Combinations* has been published, and another research study on accounting for goodwill is in process. The Board plans to reconsider the entire subject of accounting for business combinations after the latter study is published.

[7]Accounting Research Studies are not statements of this Board or of the American Institute of Certified Public Accountants, but are published for the purpose of stimulating discussion on important accounting issues.

periods than they are for income tax purposes. The Board is presently giving attention to this general subject with a view to issuing an Opinion on it. One of the questions now being considered is whether certain long-term tax allocation accounts should be determined on a discounted basis as recommended in the Study. Pending further consideration of this subject and the broader aspects of discounting as it is related to financial accounting in general and until the Board reaches a conclusion on this subject, it is the Board's opinion that, except for applications existing on the exposure date of this Opinion (September 26, 1966) with respect to transactions consummated prior to that date, deferred taxes should not be accounted for on a discounted basis.

Messrs. Davidson and Weston do not agree with the conclusion of the Board that further use of the discounting (or present value) technique in measuring the current cost of deferred income taxes is not acceptable, pending further consideration of this subject by the Board. They point out that Accounting Research Study No. 9 concluded that this method is required whenever the interest factor is significant. They recognize that the Board is attempting to prevent the development of an alternative practice until it has had an opportunity to consider the subject matter thoroughly and form an opinion thereon. On the other hand, the Board has required use of the discounting technique in measuring the present value of obligations due in the future in (a) the capitalization of leases (Opinion No. 5—paragraph 15) and (b) the accrual of pension costs (Opinion No. 8—paragraphs 23 and 42). They find it difficult to reconcile these inconsistent positions of the Board on similar questions of measurement. Furthermore, they believe that the Board is creating an unwise precedent by outlawing potential developments in practice which may be preferable to those presently in use, with the sole justification that the Board is not yet properly prepared to evaluate the merits of the developing practice. This position would, in the opinion of Messrs. Davidson and Weston, be detrimental to the sound development of accounting principles and practices through experience, which, in their considered view, is an effective means by which accounting techniques can be improved.

OFFSETTING SECURITIES AGAINST TAXES PAYABLE

7. Chapter 3B, entitled *Working Capital— Application of United States Government Securities Against Liabilities for Federal Taxes on Income,* of Accounting Research Bulletin No. 43 is withdrawn in its entirety. The following Chapter 3B, entitled *Offsetting Securities Against Taxes Payable,* is substituted in its place:

1. It is a general principle of accounting that the offsetting of assets and liabilities in the balance sheet is improper except where a right of setoff exists. Accordingly, the offset of cash or other assets against the tax liability or other amounts owing to governmental bodies is not acceptable except in the circumstances described in paragraph 3 below.

2. Most securities now issued by governments are not by their terms designed specifically for the payment of taxes and, accordingly, should not be deducted from taxes payable on the balance sheet.

3. The only exception to this general principle occurs when it is clear that a purchase of securities (acceptable for the payment of taxes) is in substance an advance payment of taxes that will be payable in the relatively near future, so that in the special circumstances the purchase is tantamount to the prepayment of taxes. This occurs at times, for example, as an accommodation to a local government and in some instances when governments issue securities that are specifically designated as being acceptable for the payment of taxes of those governments.

CONVERTIBLE DEBT AND DEBT ISSUED WITH STOCK WARRANTS

8. A portion of the proceeds received for bonds or other debt obligations which are convertible into stock, or which are issued with warrants to purchase stock, is ordinarily attributable to the conversion privilege or to the warrants, a factor that is usually reflected in the stated interest rate. In substance, the acquirer of the debt obligation receives a "call" on the stock. Accordingly, the portion of the proceeds attributable to the conversion feature or the warrants should be accounted for as paid-in capital (typically by a credit to capital surplus); however, as the liability under the debt obligation is not reduced by such attribution, the corresponding charge should be to debt discount. The discount so recognized (or the reduced premium if the proceeds exceed the face amount of the debt obligation) should thereafter be accounted for in accordance with Chapter 15 of ARB No. 43 as amended by paragraph 19 of APB Opinion No. 6 and by paragraph 17 of APB Opinion No. 9. Upon conversion, the related unamortized debt discount should be accounted for as a reduction of the consideration for the securities being issued.

9. The discount or reduced premium, in the case of convertible debt obligations, may ordinarily be measured as the difference between the price at

which the debt was issued and the estimated price for which it would have been issued in the absence of the conversion feature. Warrants are frequently traded and their fair value can usually be determined by market prices at the time the debt is issued; accordingly, proceeds of the issue can be allocated in proportion to the relative market values of the debt obligations and warrants.

LIQUIDATION PREFERENCE OF PREFERRED STOCK

10. Companies at times issue preferred (or other senior) stock which has a preference in involuntary liquidation considerably in excess of the par or stated value of the shares. The relationship between this preference in liquidation and the par or stated value of the shares may be of major significance to the users of the financial statements of those companies and the Board believes it highly desirable that it be prominently disclosed. Accordingly, the Board recommends that, in these cases, the liquidation preference of the stock be disclosed in the equity section of the balance sheet in the aggregate, either parenthetically or "in short," rather than on a per share basis or by disclosure in notes.

11. In addition, the financial statements should disclose, either on the face of the balance sheet or in notes pertaining thereto:

a. the aggregate or per share amounts at which preferred shares may be called or are subject to redemption through sinking fund operations or otherwise;

b. as called for by paragraph 35 of APB Opinion No. 9, the aggregate and per share amounts of arrearages in cumulative preferred dividends.

INSTALLMENT METHOD OF ACCOUNTING

12. Chapter 1A of ARB No. 43, paragraph 1, states that "Profit is deemed to be realized when a sale in the ordinary course of business is effected, unless the circumstances are such that the collection of the sale price is not reasonably assured." The Board reaffirms this statement; it believes that revenues should ordinarily be accounted for at the time a transaction is completed, with appropriate provision for uncollectible accounts. Accordingly, it concludes that, in the absence of the circumstances[8] referred to above, the installment method of recog-

nizing revenue is not acceptable.

EFFECTIVE DATE OF THIS OPINION

13. This Opinion shall be effective for fiscal periods beginning after December 31, 1966 and does not have retroactive effect except as indicated in paragraphs 3, 4, 5 and 6. However, earlier application is encouraged.

The Opinion entitled "Omnibus Opinion—1966" was adopted unanimously by the twenty members of the Board, of whom two, Messrs. Catlett and Davidson, assented with qualification as to paragraph 4 and two, Messrs. Davidson and Weston, assented with qualification as to paragraph 6.

NOTES

Opinions present the considered opinion of at least two-thirds of the members of the Accounting Principles Board, reached on a formal vote after examination of the subject matter.

Except as indicated in the succeeding paragraph, the authority of the Opinions rests upon their general acceptability. While it is recognized that general rules may be subject to exception, the burden of justifying departures from Board Opinions must be assumed by those who adopt other practices.

Action of Council of the Institute (Special Bulletin, Disclosure of Departures from Opinions of Accounting Principles Board, *October, 1964) provides that:*

a. *"Generally accepted accounting principles" are those principles which have substantial authoritative support.*

b. *Opinions of the Accounting Principles Board constitute "substantial authoritative support."*

c. *"Substantial authoritative support" can exist for accounting principles that differ from Opinions of the Accounting Principles Board.*

The Council action also requires that departures from Board Opinions be disclosed in footnotes to the financial statements or in independent auditors' reports when the effect of the departure on the financial statements is material.

Unless otherwise stated, Opinions of the Board are not intended to be retroactive. They are not intended to be applicable to immaterial items.

---

[8]The Board recognizes that there are exceptional cases where receivables are collectible over an extended period of time and, because of the terms of the transactions or other conditions, there is no reasonable basis for estimating the degree of collectibility. When such circumstances exist, and as long as they exist, either the installment method or the cost recovery method of accounting may be used. (Under the cost recovery method, equal amounts of revenue and expense are recognized as collections are made until all costs have been recovered, postponing any recognition of profit until that time.)

APB Opinion No. 11
Accounting for Income Taxes

STATUS

Issued: December 1967

Effective Date: For fiscal periods beginning after December 31, 1967

Affects: Amends ARB 43, Chapter 9C, paragraphs 11 through 13
Supersedes ARB 43, Chapter 10B
Supersedes ARB 43, Chapter 11B, paragraph 8
Amends ARB 43, Chapter 15, paragraph 11
Supersedes ARB 44 (Rev.), paragraphs 4, 5, 7, and 10
Supersedes ARB 44 (Rev.) Letter Dated April 15, 1959
Amends ARB 51, paragraph 17
Amends APB 1, paragraphs 1, 5, and 6 and footnote 1
Amends APB 5, paragraph 21
Supersedes APB 6, paragraphs 21 and 23 and footnotes 7 and 8

Affected by: Paragraph 6 amended by APB 28
Paragraph 6 amended by FAS 60 and FAS 71
Paragraphs 38, 39, and 41 superseded by APB 23
Paragraph 40 superseded by FAS 9
Paragraph 49 amended by APB 16
Paragraph 57 amended by FAS 37
Superseded by FAS 96 and FAS 109

Other Interpretive Pronouncements: AIN-APB 11, Interpretations No. 1 through 25 (Superseded by FAS 96 and FAS 109)
FIN 22 (Superseded by FAS 96 and FAS 109)
FIN 25 (Superseded by FAS 96 and FAS 109)
FIN 32 (Superseded by FAS 96 and FAS 109)
FTB 82-1
FTB 83-1 (Superseded by FAS 96 and FAS 109)
FTB 84-2 (Superseded by FAS 96 and FAS 109)
FTB 84-3 (Superseded by FAS 96 and FAS 109)
FTB 86-1 (Superseded by FAS 96 and FAS 109)
FTB 87-2

Other Interpretive Release: FASB *Highlights,* "Task Force Addresses Accounting for Corporate Alternative Minimum Tax," May 26, 1987

(The next page is 162.)

APB Opinion No. 12
Omnibus Opinion—1967

Classification and Disclosure of Allowances
Disclosure of Depreciable Assets and Depreciation
Deferred Compensation Contracts
Capital Changes
Convertible Debt and Debt Issued with Stock Warrants
Amortization of Debt Discount and Expense or Premium

STATUS

Issued: December 1967

Effective Date: For fiscal periods beginning after December 31, 1967

Affects: Amends APB 10, paragraphs 8 and 9

Affected by: Paragraph 6 amended by FAS 87 and FAS 106
Paragraphs 11 through 15 and footnote 2 superseded by APB 14
Footnote 1 superseded by FAS 106 and FAS 111

APB Opinion No. 12
Omnibus Opinion—1967

Classification and Disclosure of Allowances
Disclosure of Depreciable Assets and Depreciation
Deferred Compensation Contracts
Capital Changes
Convertible Debt and Debt Issued with Stock Warrants
Amortization of Debt Discount and Expense or Premium

INTRODUCTION

1. This is the second of a series of Opinions which the Board expects to issue periodically containing:

a. Amendments of prior Opinions of the Accounting Principles Board and Accounting Research Bulletins of its predecessor, the committee on accounting procedure, as appear necessary to clarify their meaning or to describe their applicability under changed conditions.
b. Affirmation of accounting principles and methods which have become generally accepted through practice and which the Board believes to be sound, and when it desires to prevent the possible development of less desirable alternatives.
c. Conclusions as to appropriate accounting principles and methods on subjects not dealt with in previous pronouncements and for which a separate Opinion is not believed to be warranted.

CLASSIFICATION AND DISCLOSURE OF ALLOWANCES

2. Although it is generally accepted that accumulated allowances for depreciation and depletion and asset valuation allowances for losses such as those on receivables and investments should be deducted from the assets to which they relate, there are instances in which these allowances are shown among liabilities or elsewhere on the credit side of the balance sheet.

3. It is the Board's opinion that such allowances should be deducted from the assets or groups of assets to which the allowances relate, with appropriate disclosure.

DISCLOSURE OF DEPRECIABLE ASSETS AND DEPRECIATION

4. Disclosure of the total amount of depreciation expense entering into the determination of results of operations has become a general practice. The balances of major classes of depreciable assets are also generally disclosed. Practice varies, however, with respect to disclosure of the depreciation method or methods used.

5. Because of the significant effects on financial position and results of operations of the depreciation method or methods used, the following disclosures should be made in the financial statements or in notes thereto:

a. Depreciation expense for the period,
b. Balances of major classes of depreciable assets, by nature or function, at the balance-sheet date,
c. Accumulated depreciation, either by major classes of depreciable assets or in total, at the balance-sheet date, and
d. A general description of the method or methods used in computing depreciation with respect to major classes of depreciable assets.

DEFERRED COMPENSATION CONTRACTS

6. APB Opinion No. 8, *Accounting for the Cost of Pension Plans,* applies to deferred compensation contracts with individual employees if such contracts, taken together, are equivalent to a pension plan. The Board believes that other deferred compensation contracts should be accounted for individually on an accrual basis. Such contracts customarily include certain requirements such as continued employment for a specified period and availability for consulting services and agreements not to compete after retirement, which, if not complied with, remove the employer's obligations for future payments. The estimated amounts[1] to be paid under each contract should be accrued in a systematic and rational manner over the period of active employment from the time the contract is entered into, unless it is evident that future services expected to be received by the employer are com-

---

[1]The amounts to be accrued periodically should result in an accrued amount at the end of the term of active employment which is not less than the then present value of the estimated payments to be made.

mensurate with the payments or a portion of the payments to be made. If elements of both current and future services are present, only the portion applicable to the current services should be accrued.

7. Some deferred compensation contracts provide for periodic payments to employees or their surviving spouses for life with provisions for a minimum lump-sum settlement in the event of the early death of one or all of the beneficiaries. The estimated amount[1] of future payments to be made under such contracts should be accrued over the period of active employment from the time the contract is entered into. Such estimates should be based on the life expectancy of each individual concerned (based on the most recent mortality tables available) or on the estimated cost of an annuity contract rather than on the minimum payable in the event of early death.

8. At the effective date of this Opinion, amounts[1] pertaining to deferred compensation contracts with employees actively employed, which amounts have not been accrued in a manner consistent with the provisions of the Opinion, should be accrued over the employee's remaining term of active employment. For purposes of transition, these amounts may be accrued over a period of up to ten years if the remaining term of active employment is less than ten years.

CAPITAL CHANGES

9. Paragraph 7 of APB Opinion No. 9, *Reporting the Results of Operations,* states that "The statement of income and the statement of retained earnings (separately or combined) are designed to reflect, in a broad sense, the 'results of operations'." Paragraph 28 of APB Opinion No. 9 states that certain capital transactions ". . . should be excluded from the determination of net income or the results of operations under all circumstances." Companies generally have reported the current year's changes in stockholders' equity accounts other than retained earnings in separate statements or notes to the financial statements when presenting both financial position and results of operations for one or more years. A question has arisen as to whether, because of the language of APB Opinion No. 9, changes in stockholders' equity accounts other than retained earnings are required to be reported.

10. When both financial position and results of operations are presented, disclosure of changes in the separate accounts comprising stockholders' equity (in addition to retained earnings) and of the changes in the number of shares of equity securities

during at least the most recent annual fiscal period and any subsequent interim period presented is required to make the financial statements sufficiently informative. Disclosure of such changes may take the form of separate statements or may be made in the basic financial statements or notes thereto.

CONVERTIBLE DEBT AND DEBT ISSUED WITH STOCK WARRANTS

11. Paragraphs 8 and 9 of APB Opinion No. 10 call for certain accounting treatment, effective for periods beginning after December 31, 1966, for proceeds received for debt securities convertible into stock or issued together with warrants to purchase stock. Since the issuance of that Opinion, the Board has observed developments in the use of securities of this character and experiences in the application of those paragraphs of the Opinion. In addition, the Board has received views of interested parties relative to the nature of these securities and the problems in implementing the paragraphs. These observations and views have suggested that because certain aspects of these instruments, particularly in the case of convertible debentures, raise difficult estimation and other problems, further study is needed in this area. Also, because of the actual or potential equity nature of these instruments, the relationship between the accounting for the proceeds and the treatment of "residual" securities in the determination of earnings per share has created problems which need to be studied further. For these reasons, the Board is temporarily suspending the effectiveness of paragraphs 8 and 9 of Opinion No. 10 retroactively to their effective date.

12. In the meantime, the Board is studying further the accounting treatment of the various types of convertible and participating securities in relation to the determination of results of operations and earnings per share, including the residual aspects of such securities, and plans to issue a separate Opinion on this subject by December 31, 1968. It should be noted, however, that some issues of convertible debt securities may presently be residual securities and should be treated as such for the purpose of determining earnings per share as provided in paragraph 33 of APB Opinion No. 9, regardless of the suspension referred to above.

13. Pending issuance of the new Opinion, the accounting treatment set forth in paragraphs 8 and 9 of Opinion No. 10 is considered to be an acceptable practice.

[1]The amounts to be accrued periodically should result in an accrued amount at the end of the term of active employment which is not less than the then present value of the estimated payments to be made.

14. Since the paragraphs being suspended were effective for fiscal periods beginning after December 31, 1966, the Board may decide to have the new Opinion effective on a retroactive basis for such fiscal periods.

15. Those entities which otherwise are or would be subject to the accounting requirements of paragraphs 8 and 9 of Opinion No. 10 (by virtue of having issued, during a fiscal period beginning after December 31, 1966, convertible debt or debt with stock warrants) may elect, as a result of this suspension, not to adopt such accounting treatment. If an entity so elects, the Board has concluded that, until issuance of its Opinion with respect to the treatment of such securities, a dual presentation of earnings per share of common stock should be furnished on the face of the statement of income. This dual presentation should disclose (a) earnings per share computed in accordance with Opinion No. 9, based on average shares outstanding during the period and (b) earnings per share computed on the assumption that *all* conversions and contingent issuances[2] had taken place. (The bases for each of these computations should be disclosed.) These computations should be described somewhat as follows:

Earnings per share of common
stock—
Based on average shares
outstanding during the period $X.XX
Based on assumption of conversion
or exercise of all outstanding
convertible securities, options
and warrants $X.XX

The purpose of the dual presentation is to recognize and emphasize the complex nature of these securities, including the existence of equity security characteristics, and the possibility that conversion of the security or exercise of options or of warrants may affect earnings per share of common stock. In addition, disclosure should be made that the provisions of the proposed new Opinion may be required to be applied retroactively in financial statements for fiscal periods beginning after December 31, 1966. Such disclosure should include an estimate, if reasonably determinable, of the effect upon net income of retroactive application of paragraphs 8 and 9 of Opinion No. 10. This disclosure should be made in total and on a per-share basis.

Messrs. Armstrong and Layton concur with the temporary suspension of paragraphs 8 and 9 of Opinion No. 10, but do not agree with paragraph 14 and the disclosures required in the last three sentences of paragraph 15 above, since they believe that retroactive application of any new Opinion on the subject should not be required. They therefore object to the disclosures implying the possibility of retroactive application and further believe that such disclosures will create unnecessary uncertainties in the minds of readers of financial statements.

Mr. Halvorson concurs with paragraphs 11, 12 and 13 suspending the effectiveness of paragraphs 8 and 9 of APB Opinion No. 10, but he believes the suspension should be unconditional and therefore disagrees with paragraph 14 implying retroactive application of a new Opinion and with paragraph 15 attaching conditions to the suspension.

Mr. Luper dissents from the section of this Opinion entitled "Convertible Debt and Debt Issued with Stock Warrants" (paragraphs 11-15) because he does not agree with the conclusions in paragraphs 14 and 15. He believes that the statement in paragraph 14 that the Board may decide to require retroactive treatment for a new Opinion to be issued in the future establishes an unsound precedent. In his view the Board should not require that its Opinions be accorded retroactive treatment because such action introduces a condition of instability in financial reporting standards—a condition that, from a business viewpoint, is inimical to both those who prepare and those who use financial statements.

Mr. Luper regards the further requirement in paragraph 15 that issuers of financial statements shall state, under the conditions given, that their reported net income and earnings per share may be revised subsequently because of possible conclusions to be included in an Opinion not yet formulated by the Board is an unreasonable intrusion on the responsibilities of such issuers.

AMORTIZATION OF DEBT DISCOUNT AND EXPENSE OR PREMIUM

16. Questions have been raised as to the appropriateness of the "interest" method of periodic amortization of discount and expense or premium on debt (i.e., the difference between the net proceeds, after expense, received upon issuance of debt and the amount repayable at its maturity) over its term. The objective of the interest method is to arrive at a periodic interest cost (including amortization) which will represent a level effective rate on the sum of the face amount of the debt and (plus or minus) the unamortized premium or discount and expense at the beginning of each period. The difference between the periodic interest cost so calculated and the nominal interest on the outstanding amount of the debt is the amount of periodic amortization.

17. In the Board's opinion, the interest method of amortization is theoretically sound and an acceptable method.

[2]See Opinion No. 9, paragraph 43.

EFFECTIVE DATE OF THIS OPINION

18. As indicated in paragraph 11, the effectiveness of paragraphs 8 and 9 of Opinion No. 10 is temporarily suspended retroactively to their effective date. In other respects, this Opinion shall be effective for fiscal periods beginning after December 31, 1967. However, the Board encourages earlier application of the provisions of this Opinion.

All portions of the Opinion entitled "Omnibus Opinion—1967" were adopted by the twenty members of the Board, except as follows: Messrs. Armstrong and Layton assented with qualification as to paragraph 14 and the last three sentences of paragraph 15 and Mr. Halvorson assented with qualification as to paragraphs 14 and 15. Mr. Luper dissented as to paragraphs 11-15.

NOTES

Opinions present the considered opinion of at least two-thirds of the members of the Accounting Principles Board, reached on a formal vote after examination of the subject matter.

Except as indicated in the succeeding paragraph, the authority of the Opinions rests upon their general acceptability. While it is recognized that general rules may be subject to exception, the burden of justifying departures from Board Opinions must be assumed by those who adopt other practices.

Action of Council of the Institute (Special Bulletin, Disclosure of Departures From Opinions of Accounting Principles Board, *October 1964) provides that:*

a. *"Generally accepted accounting principles" are those principles which have substantial authoritative support.*
b. *Opinions of the Accounting Principles Board constitute "substantial authoritative support."*
c. *"Substantial authoritative support" can exist for accounting principles that differ from Opinions of the Accounting Principles Board.*

The Council action also requires that departures from Board Opinions be disclosed in footnotes to the financial statements or in independent auditors' reports when the effect of the departure on the financial statements is material.

Unless otherwise stated, Opinions of the Board are not intended to be retroactive. They are not intended to be applicable to immaterial items.

Accounting Principles Board (1966-1967)

Clifford V. Heimbucher, *Chairman*	W. A. Crichley	Oral L. Luper
Marshall S. Armstrong	Joseph P. Cummings	John K. McClare
Donald J. Bevis	Sidney Davidson	Robert J. Murphey
John C. Biegler	Philip L. Defliese	Louis H. Penney
Milton M. Broeker	Walter F. Frese	John W. Queenan
George R. Catlett	Newman T. Halvorson	Wilbert A. Walker
	LeRoy Layton	Frank T. Weston

APB Opinion No. 13
Amending Paragraph 6 of APB Opinion No. 9, Application to Commercial Banks

STATUS

Issued: March 1969

Effective Date: For fiscal periods beginning after December 31, 1968

Affects: Amends APB 9, paragraph 6

Affected by: No other pronouncements

APB Opinion No. 13
Amending Paragraph 6 of APB Opinion No. 9,
Application to Commercial Banks

1. In December, 1966 this Board issued Opinion No. 9, *Reporting the Results of Operations.* That Opinion did not apply to financial statements of commercial banks for reasons expressed in the last two sentences of paragraph 6, which stated:

"A committee of the American Institute of Certified Public Accountants is in the process of recommending a format for the income statement of commercial banks. Until such recommendation has been given and until the Board has taken a position thereon, this Opinion is not applicable to commercial banks."

2. The last two sentences of paragraph 6 of APB Opinion No. 9 are deleted and such Opinion as hereby amended is therefore applicable to financial statements issued by commercial banks for fiscal periods beginning after December 31, 1968.

The Opinion entitled "Amending Paragraph 6 of APB Opinion No. 9, Application to Commercial Banks" was adopted unanimously by the eighteen members of the Board.

NOTES

Opinions present the considered opinion of at least two-thirds of the members of the Accounting Principles Board, reached on a formal vote after examination of the subject matter.

Except as indicated in the succeeding paragraph, the authority of the Opinions rests upon their general acceptability. While it is recognized that general rules may be subject to exception, the burden of justifying departures from Board Opinions must be assumed by those who adopt other practices.

Action of Council of the Institute (Special Bulletin, Disclosure of Departures from Opinions of Accounting Principles Board, *October, 1964) provides that:*

a. *"Generally accepted accounting principles" are those principles which have substantial authoritative support.*
b. *Opinions of the Accounting Principles Board constitute "substantial authoritative support."*
c. *"Substantial authoritative support" can exist for accounting principles that differ from Opinions of the Accounting Principles Board.*

The Council action also requires that departures from Board Opinions be disclosed in footnotes to the financial statements or in independent auditors' reports when the effect of the departure on the financial statements is material.

Unless otherwise stated, Opinions of the Board are not intended to be retroactive. They are not intended to be applicable to immaterial items.

Accounting Principles Board (1969)

LeRoy Layton, *Chairman*	Joseph P. Cummings	Charles T. Horngren
Marshall S. Armstrong	Sidney Davidson	Louis M. Kessler
Kenneth S. Axelson	Philip L. Defliese	Oral L. Luper
Donald J. Bevis	Newman T. Halvorson	J. S. Seidman
Milton M. Broeker	Emmett S. Harrington	George C. Watt
George R. Catlett	Charles B. Hellerson	Frank T. Weston

APB Opinion No. 14
Accounting for Convertible Debt and Debt Issued with Stock Purchase Warrants

STATUS

Issued: March 1969

Effective Date: For fiscal periods beginning after December 31, 1966

Affects: Supersedes APB 10, paragraphs 8 and 9
Supersedes APB 12, paragraphs 11 through 15 and footnote 2

Affected by: No other pronouncements

Other Interpretive Pronouncement: AIN-APB 26, Interpretation No. 1

APB Opinion No. 14
Accounting for Convertible Debt and Debt Issued
with Stock Purchase Warrants

INTRODUCTION

1. Paragraphs 8 and 9 of APB Opinion No. 10[1] stated that a portion of the proceeds received for convertible debt or debt issued with stock purchase warrants is ordinarily attributable to the conversion feature or to the warrants and should therefore be accounted for as paid-in capital. Since the issuance of that Opinion, the Board has observed the experiences of issuers of these securities in applying those paragraphs. In addition, interested parties have expressed their views as to the nature of these securities and the problems of implementing the principles discussed in those paragraphs. The observations and views indicated that dealing with certain aspects of these securities, particularly convertible debentures, involved difficult problems which warranted further study. In December 1967, the Board, therefore, temporarily suspended the effectiveness of paragraphs 8 and 9 of the APB Opinion No. 10 retroactively to their effective date and established specific requirements for earnings per share data to be included in income statements. (See paragraphs 11 through 15 of APB Opinion No. 12.)

2. Since then the Board has reexamined the characteristics of convertible debt and debt issued with stock purchase warrants to determine whether the accounting called for by paragraphs 8 and 9 of APB Opinion No. 10 should be reinstated. This Opinion results from that study and sets forth the conclusions reached by the Board. Accordingly, this Opinion supersedes paragraphs 8 and 9 of APB Opinion No. 10 and paragraphs 11 through 15 of APB Opinion No. 12.

CONVERTIBLE DEBT

Discussion

3. Convertible debt securities discussed herein are those debt securities which are convertible into common stock of the issuer or an affiliated company at a specified price at the option of the holder and which are sold at a price or have a value at issuance not significantly in excess of the face amount. The terms of such securities generally include (1) an interest rate which is lower than the issuer could establish for nonconvertible debt, (2) an initial conversion price which is greater than the market value of the common stock at time of issuance, and (3) a conversion price which does not decrease except pursuant to antidilution provisions. In most cases such securities also are callable at the option of the issuer and are subordinated to nonconvertible debt.

4. Convertible debt may offer advantages to both the issuer and the purchaser. From the point of view of the issuer, convertible debt has a lower interest rate than does nonconvertible debt. Furthermore, the issuer of convertible debt securities, in planning its long-range financing, may view convertible debt as essentially a means of raising equity capital. Thus, if the market value of the underlying common stock increases sufficiently in the future, the issuer can force conversion of the convertible debt into common stock by calling the issue for redemption. Under these market conditions, the issuer can effectively terminate the conversion option and eliminate the debt. If the market value of the stock does not increase sufficiently to result in conversion of the debt, the issuer will have received the benefit of the cash proceeds to the scheduled maturity dates at a relatively low cash interest cost.

5. On the other hand, the purchaser obtains an option to receive either the face or redemption amount of the security or the number of common shares into which the security is convertible. If the market value of the underlying common stock increases above the conversion price, the purchaser (either through conversion or through holding the convertible debt containing the conversion option) benefits through appreciation. He may at that time require the issuance of the common stock at a price lower than the current market price. However, should the value of the underlying common stock not increase in the future, the purchaser has the protection of a debt security. Thus, in the absence of default by the issuer, he would receive the principal and interest if the conversion option is not exercised.

6. Differences of opinion exist as to whether convertible debt securities should be treated by the issuer solely as debt or whether the conversion option should receive separate accounting recognition at time of issuance. The views in favor of each of these two concepts are contained in the following paragraphs.

[1] Effective for fiscal periods beginning after December 31, 1966.

7. The most important reason given for accounting for convertible debt solely as debt is the inseparability of the debt and the conversion option. A convertible debt security is a complex hybrid instrument bearing an option, the alternative choices of which cannot exist independently of one another. The holder ordinarily does not sell one right and retain the other. Furthermore the two choices are mutually exclusive; they cannot both be consummated. Thus, the security will either be converted into common stock or be redeemed for cash. The holder cannot exercise the option to convert unless he forgoes the right to redemption, and vice versa.

8. Another reason advanced in favor of accounting for convertible debt solely as debt is that the valuation of the conversion option or the debt security without the conversion option presents various practical problems. In the absence of separate transferability, values are not established in the marketplace, and accordingly, the value assigned to each feature is necessarily subjective. A determination of the value of the conversion feature poses problems because of the uncertain duration of the right to obtain the stock and the uncertainty as to the future value of the stock obtainable upon conversion. Furthermore, issuers often claim that a subjective valuation of a debt security without the conversion option but with identical other terms (which are usually less restrictive on the issuer and less protective of the holder than those of nonconvertible debt) is difficult because such a security could not be sold at a price which the issuer would regard as producing an acceptable cost of financing. Thus, when the attractiveness to investors of a convertible debt security rests largely on the anticipated increased value of the issuer's stock, the conversion feature may be of primary importance, with the debt feature regarded more as a hedge than as the principal investment objective. Many proponents of the single-element view believe that the practical problems of determining separate values for the debt and the conversion option should not be controlling for purposes of determining appropriate accounting but such problems should be given consideration, particularly if valid arguments exist for each of the two accounting concepts identified in paragraph 6.

9. The contrary view is that convertible debt possesses characteristics of both debt and equity and that separate accounting recognition should be given to the debt characteristics and to the conversion option at time of issuance. This view is based on the premise that there is an economic value inherent in the conversion feature or call on the stock and that the nature and value of this feature should be recognized for accounting purposes by the is-

suer. The conversion feature is not significantly different in nature from the call represented by an option or warrant, and sale of the call is a type of capital transaction. The fact that the conversion feature coexists with certain debt characteristics in a hybrid security and cannot be sold or transferred separately from these senior elements or from the debt instrument itself does not constitute a logical or compelling reason why the values of the two elements should not receive separate accounting recognition. Similar separate accounting recognition for disparate features of single instruments is reflected in, for example, the capitalization of long-term leases—involving the separation of the principal and interest elements—and in the allocation of the purchase cost in a bulk acquisition between goodwill and other assets.

10. Holders of this view also believe that the fact that the eventual outcome of the option available to the purchaser of the convertible debt security cannot be determined at time of issuance is not relevant to the question of reflecting in the accounting records the distinguishable elements of the security at time of issuance. The conversion option has a value at time of issuance, and a portion of the proceeds should therefore be allocated to this element of the transaction. The remainder of the proceeds is attributable to the debt characteristics, and should be so recognized for accounting purposes.

11. Holders of this view also believe that the difficulties of implementation—which are claimed by some to justify or to support not recognizing the conversion option for accounting purposes—are not insurmountable and should not govern the conclusion. When convertible debt securities are issued, professional advisors are usually available to furnish estimates of values of the conversion option and of the debt characteristics, which values are sufficiently precise for the purpose of allocating the proceeds. If a nonconvertible debt security could not be sold at an acceptable price, the value of the conversion option is of such material significance that its accounting recognition, even on the basis of an estimate, is essential.

Opinion

12. The Board is of the opinion that no portion of the proceeds from the issuance of the types of convertible debt securities described in paragraph 3 should be accounted for as attributable to the conversion feature. In reaching this conclusion, the Board places greater weight on the inseparability of the debt and the conversion option (as described in paragraph 7) and less weight on practical difficulties.

DEBT WITH STOCK PURCHASE WARRANTS

Discussion

13. Unlike convertible debt, debt with detachable warrants to purchase stock is usually issued with the expectation that the debt will be repaid when it matures. The provisions of the debt agreement are usually more restrictive on the issuer and more protective of the investor than those for convertible debt. The terms of the warrants are influenced by the desire for a successful debt financing. Detachable warrants often trade separately from the debt instrument. Thus, the two elements of the security exist independently and may be treated as separate securities.

14. From the point of view of the issuer, the sale of a debt security with warrants results in a lower cash interest cost than would otherwise be possible or permits financing not otherwise practicable. The issuer usually cannot force the holders of the warrants to exercise them and purchase the stock. The issuer may, however, be required to issue shares of stock at some future date at a price lower than the market price existing at that time, as is true in the case of the conversion option of convertible debt. Under different conditions the warrants may expire without exercise. The outcome of the warrant feature thus cannot be determined at time of issuance. In either case the debt must generally be paid at maturity or earlier redemption date whether or not the warrants are exercised.

15. There is general agreement among accountants that the proceeds from the sale of debt with stock purchase warrants should be allocated to the two elements for accounting purposes. This agreement results from the separability of the debt and the warrants. The availability of objective values in many instances is also a factor. There is agreement that the allocation should be based on the relative fair values of the debt security without the warrants and of the warrants themselves at time of issuance. The portion of the proceeds so allocated to the warrants should be accounted for as paid-in capital. The remainder of the proceeds should be allocated to the debt security portion of the transaction. This usually results in issuing the debt security at a discount (or, occasionally, a reduced premium).

Opinion

16. The Board is of the opinion that the portion of the proceeds of debt securities issued with detachable stock purchase warrants which is allocable to the warrants should be accounted for as paid-in capital. The allocation should be based on the relative fair values of the two securities at time of issuance.[2] Any resulting discount or premium on the debt securities should be accounted for as such.[3] The same accounting treatment applies to issues of debt securities (issued with detachable warrants) which may be surrendered in settlement of the exercise price of the warrant. However, when stock purchase warrants are not detachable from the debt and the debt security must be surrendered in order to exercise the warrant, the two securities taken together are substantially equivalent to convertible debt and the accounting specified in paragraph 12 should apply.

17. When detachable warrants are issued in conjunction with debt as consideration in purchase transactions, the amounts attributable to each class of security issued should be determined separately, based on values at the time of issuance.[2] The debt discount or premium is obtained by comparing the value attributed to the debt securities with the face amount thereof.

OTHER TYPES OF DEBT SECURITIES

Opinion

18. The Board recognizes that it is not practicable in this Opinion to discuss all possible types of debt with conversion features, debt issued with stock purchase warrants, or debt securities with a combination of such features. Securities not explicitly discussed in this Opinion should be dealt with in accordance with the substance of the transaction. For example, when convertible debt is issued at a substantial premium, there is a presumption that such premium represents paid-in capital.

EFFECTIVE DATE OF THIS OPINION

19. This Opinion is effective for fiscal periods beginning after December 31, 1966.[4] However, if a

---

[2] The time of issuance generally is the date when agreement as to terms has been reached and announced, even though the agreement is subject to certain further actions, such as directors' or stockholders' approval.

[3] See Chapter 15 of ARB No. 43 (as amended by paragraph 19 of APB Opinion No. 6 and paragraph 17 of APB Opinion No. 9) and paragraphs 16 and 17 of APB Opinion No. 12.

[4] This was the effective date of paragraphs 8 and 9 of APB Opinion No. 10 which were temporarily suspended by paragraphs 11-15 of APB Opinion No. 12. The latter Opinion stated that the Board might decide to have the Opinion resolving this question apply retroactively to fiscal periods beginning after December 31, 1966.

portion of the proceeds of a convertible debt issue covered by paragraph 12 was allocated to the conversion feature for periods beginning before January 1, 1969 that accounting may be continued with respect to such issues.

20. Material adjustments resulting from adoption of this Opinion which affect periods beginning prior to January 1, 1969 should be treated as prior period adjustments (see paragraphs 23 and 25 of APB Opinion No. 9).

The Opinion entitled "Accounting for Convertible Debt and Debt Issued with Stock Purchase Warrants" was adopted by the assenting votes of fourteen members of the Board, of whom two, Messrs. Halvorson and Luper, assented with qualification. Messrs. Cummings, Davidson, Seidman and Weston dissented.

Mr. Halvorson assents to the publication of the Opinion, but dissents to paragraph 19 insofar as it requires the recommended accounting for detachable warrants to be made retroactive to January 1, 1967, and also dissents to paragraph 12 because he believes that, as a matter of principle, there are circumstances under which an issuer should be permitted, or even required, to account for a part of the proceeds of convertible debt as being attributable to the conversion feature.

Mr. Luper assents to the issuance of this Opinion but dissents to paragraph 19 which makes this Opinion effective for fiscal periods beginning after December 31, 1966. He believes that it is unsound for the Board to require that an Opinion be applied retroactively because such requirement causes a condition of instability in financial reporting standards.

Messrs. Cummings, Davidson, Seidman, and Weston dissent from the conclusion set forth in paragraph 12 of this Opinion, for the reasons set forth in paragraphs 9 through 11. They believe that, by ignoring the value of the conversion privilege and instead using as a measure solely the coupon rate of interest, the Opinion specifies an accounting treatment which does not reflect the true interest cost. The resulting error can be demonstrated by comparing the simultaneous sale of debt securities by two issuers—one with a prime credit rating, so that it can obtain financing by means of non-convertible debt; the other with an inferior credit rating, so that

it can obtain financing at an acceptable rate only by means of a conversion option added to its debt. The coupon rate of interest on the debt of the prime rated issuer may be the same as, or higher than, the rate on the convertible debt of the other issuer. To conclude under these conditions, as the Opinion does, that the cost of this financing for the prime rated issuer is equal to or greater than that of the inferior rated issuer is to belie economic reality. Furthermore, while the debt obligation and the conversion feature coexist in a hybrid instrument, such fact is not a logical reason for failing to account separately for their individual values.

NOTES

Opinions present the considered opinion of at least two-thirds of the members of the Accounting Principles Board, reached on a formal vote after examination of the subject matter.

Except as indicated in the succeeding paragraph, the authority of the Opinions rests upon their general acceptability. While it is recognized that general rules may be subject to exception, the burden of justifying departures from Board Opinions must be assumed by those who adopt other practices.

Action of Council of the Institute (Special Bulletin, Disclosure of Departures from Opinions of Accounting Principles Board, *October, 1964) provides that:*

a. *"Generally accepted accounting principles" are those principles which have substantial authoritative support.*

b. *Opinions of the Accounting Principles Board constitute "substantial authoritative support".*

c. *"Substantial authoritative support" can exist for accounting principles that differ from Opinions of the Accounting Principles Board.*

The Council action also requires that departures from Board Opinions be disclosed in footnotes to the financial statements or in independent auditors' reports when the effect of the departure on the financial statements is material.

Unless otherwise stated, Opinions of the Board are not intended to be retroactive. They are not intended to be applicable to immaterial items.

Accounting Principles Board (1969)

LeRoy Layton,	Joseph P. Cummings	Charles T. Horngren
Chairman	Sidney Davidson	Louis M. Kessler
Marshall S. Armstrong	Philip L. Defliese	Oral L. Luper
Kenneth S. Axelson	Newman T. Halvorson	J. S. Seidman
Donald J. Bevis	Emmett S. Harrington	George C. Watt
Milton M. Broeker	Charles B. Hellerson	Frank T. Weston
George R. Catlett		

APB Opinion No. 15
Earnings per Share

STATUS

Issued: May 1969

Effective Date: For fiscal periods beginning after December 31, 1968

Affects: Supersedes APB 9, paragraphs 30 through 51, footnotes 6 through 9, and Exhibit E

Affected by: Paragraph 5 amended by FAS 111
Paragraph 13 amended by APB 20
Paragraph 13 and footnote 8 amended by APB 30
Paragraph 33 and footnote 10 amended by FAS 55
Paragraph 33 and footnotes 9 and 10 superseded by FAS 85
Paragraph 35 amended by FAS 85
Paragraph 45 amended by FAS 21
Appendix C, Exhibit B amended by FAS 111
Appendix D, definition of cash yield superseded by FAS 85

Other Interpretive Pronouncements: AIN-APB 15, Interpretations No. 1 through 102 (Interpretations
No. 13 and 16 superseded by FAS 96 and FAS 109,
Interpretations No. 34 and 35 superseded by FAS 85, and
Interpretation No. 38 superseded by FAS 111)
AIN-APB 20, Interpretations No. 1 and 2
FIN 28
FIN 31

APB Opinion No. 15
Earnings per Share

CONTENTS

INTRODUCTION

1. Earnings per share data are used in evaluating the past operating performance of a business, in forming an opinion as to its potential and in making investment decisions. They are commonly presented in prospectuses, proxy material and reports to stockholders. They are used in the compilation of business earnings data for the press, statistical services and other publications. When presented with formal financial statements, they assist the investor in weighing the significance of a corporation's current net income and of changes in its net income from period to period in relation to the shares he holds or may acquire.

2. In view of the widespread use of earnings per share data, it is important that such data be computed on a consistent basis and presented in the most meaningful manner. The Board and its prede-

cessor committee have previously expressed their views on general standards designed to achieve these objectives, most recently in Part II of APB Opinion No. 9, *Reporting the Results of Operations.*

3. In this Opinion the Board expresses its views on some of the more specific aspects of the subject, including the guidelines that should be applied uniformly in the computation and presentation of earnings per share data in financial statements. Accordingly, this Opinion supersedes Part II (paragraphs 30-51) and Exhibit E of APB Opinion No. 9. In some respects, practice under APB Opinion No. 9 will be changed by this Opinion.

4. Computational guidelines for the implementation of this Opinion are contained in Appendix A. Certain views differing from those adopted in this Opinion are summarized in Appendix B. Illustrations of the presentations described in this Opinion

are included in the Exhibits contained in Appendix C. Definitions of certain terms as used in this Opinion are contained in Appendix D.

APPLICABILITY

5. This Opinion applies to financial presentations which purport to present results of operations of corporations in conformity with generally accepted accounting principles and to summaries of those presentations, except as excluded in paragraph 6. Thus, it applies to corporations whose capital structures include only common stock or common stock and senior securities and to those whose capital structures also include securities that should be considered the equivalent of common stock[1] in computing earnings per share data.

6. This Opinion does not apply to mutual companies that do not have outstanding common stock or common stock equivalents (for example, mutual savings banks, cooperatives, credit unions, and similar entities); to registered investment companies; to government-owned corporations; or to nonprofit corporations. This Opinion also does not apply to parent company statements accompanied by consolidated financial statements, to statements of wholly-owned subsidiaries, or to special purpose statements.

HISTORICAL BACKGROUND

7. Prior to the issuance of APB Opinion No. 9, earnings per share were generally computed by dividing net income (after deducting preferred stock dividends, if any) by the number of common shares outstanding. The divisor used in the computation usually was a weighted average of the number of common shares outstanding during the period, but sometimes was simply the number of common shares outstanding at the end of the period.

8. ARB No. 49, *Earnings per Share,* referred to "common stock or other residual security;" however, the concept that a security other than a common stock could be the substantial equivalent of common stock and should, therefore, enter into the computation of earnings per share was seldom followed prior to the issuance of APB Opinion No. 9. Paragraph 33 of APB Opinion No. 9 stated that earnings per share should be computed by reference to common stock and other residual securities and defined a residual security as follows:

"When more than one class of common stock is outstanding, or when an outstanding security has participating dividend rights with the common stock, or when an outstanding security clearly derives a major portion of its value from its conversion rights or its common stock characteristics, such securities should be considered 'residual securities' and not 'senior securities' for purposes of computing earnings per share."

9. APB Opinon No. 9 also stated in part (paragraph 43) that:

"Under certain circumstances, earnings per share may be subject to dilution in the future if existing contingencies permitting issuance of common shares eventuate. Such circumstances include contingent changes resulting from the existence of (a) outstanding senior stock or debt which is convertible into common shares, (b) outstanding stock options, warrants or similar agreements and (c) agreements for the issuance of common shares for little or no consideration upon the satisfaction of certain conditions (e.g., the attainment of specified levels of earnings following a business combination). If such potential dilution is material, supplementary pro forma computations of earnings per share should be furnished, showing what the earnings would be if the conversions or contingent issuances took place."

Before the issuance of APB Opinion No. 9 corporations had rarely presented pro forma earnings per share data of this type except in prospectuses and proxy statements.

10. Under the definition of a residual security contained in paragraph 33 of APB Opinion No. 9, residual status of convertible securities has been determined using the "major-portion-of-value" test at the time of the issuance of the security and from time to time thereafter whenever earnings per share data were presented. In practice this test has been applied by comparing a convertible security's market value with its investment value, and the security has been considered to be residual whenever more than half its market value was attributable to its common stock characteristics at time of issuance. Practice has varied in applying this test subsequent to issuance with a higher measure used in many cases. Thus, a convertible security's status as a residual security has been affected by equity and debt market conditions at and after the security's issuance.

---

[1]APB Opinion No. 9 referred to certain securities as *residual* securities, the determination of which was generally based upon the market value of the security as it related to investment value. In this Opinion, the Board now uses the term *common stock equivalents* as being more descriptive of those securities other than common stock that should be dealt with as common stock in the determination of earnings per share.

11. Application of the residual security concept as set forth in paragraph 33 of APB Opinion No. 9 has raised questions as to the validity of the concept and as to the guidelines developed for its application in practice. The Board has reviewed the concept of residual securities as it relates to earnings per share and, as a result of its own study and the constructive comments on the matter received from interested parties, has concluded that modification of the residual concept is desirable. The Board has also considered the disclosure and presentation requirements of earnings per share data contained in APB Opinion No. 9 and has concluded that these should be revised.

OPINION

Presentation on Face of Income Statement

12. The Board believes that the significance attached by investors and others to earnings per share data, together with the importance of evaluating the data in conjunction with the financial statements, requires that such data be presented prominently in the financial statements. The Board has therefore concluded that earnings per share or net loss per share data should be shown on the face of the income statement. The extent of the data to be presented and the captions used will vary with the complexity of the company's capital structure, as discussed in the following paragraphs.

13. The reporting of earnings per share data should be consistent with the income statement presentation called for by paragraph 20 of APB Opinion No. 9. Earnings per share amounts should therefore be presented for (a) income before extraordinary items and (b) net income. It may also be desirable to present earnings per share amounts for extraordinary items, if any.

Simple Capital Structures

14. The capital structures of many corporations are relatively simple—that is, they either consist of only common stock or include no potentially dilutive convertible securities, options, warrants or other rights that upon conversion or exercise could in the aggregate dilute[2] earnings per common share. In these cases, a single presentation expressed in terms such as *Earnings per common share* on the face of the income statement (based on common shares outstanding and computed in accordance with the provisions of paragraphs 47-50 of Appendix A) is the appropriate presentation of earnings per share data.

Complex Capital Structures

15. Corporations with capital structures other than those described in the preceding paragraph should present two types of earnings per share data (dual presentation) with equal prominence on the face of the income statement. The first presentation is based on the outstanding common shares and those securities that are in substance equivalent to common shares and have a dilutive[2] effect. The second is a pro-forma presentation which reflects the dilution[2] of earnings per share that would have occurred if *all* contingent issuances of common stock that would individually reduce earnings per share had taken place at the beginning of the period (or time of issuance of the convertible security, etc., if later). For convenience in this Opinion, these two presentations are referred to as "primary earnings per share" and "fully diluted earnings per share,"[3] respectively, and would in certain circumstances discussed elsewhere in this Opinion be supplemented by other disclosures and other earnings per share data. (See paragraphs 19-23.)

Dual Presentation

16. When dual presentation of earnings per share data is required, the primary and fully diluted earnings per share amounts should be presented with equal prominence on the face of the income statement. The difference between the primary and fully diluted earnings per share amounts shows the maximum extent of potential dilution of current earnings which conversions of securities that are not common stock equivalents could create. If the capital structure contains no common stock equivalents, the first may be designated *Earnings per common share—assuming no dilution* and the second *Earnings per common share—assuming full dilution*. When common stock equivalents are present and dilutive, the primary amount may be designated *Earnings per common and common equivalent share*. The Board recognizes that precise designations should not be prescribed; corporations should be free to designate these dual presentations in a manner which best fits the circumstances provided they are in accord with the substance of this Opinion. The term *Earnings per common share* should not be used without appropriate qualification except under the conditions discussed in paragraph 14.

Periods Presented

17. Earnings per share data should be presented for all periods covered by the statement of income or

[2]Any reduction of less than 3% in the aggregate need not be considered as dilution in the computation and presentation of earnings per share data as discussed throughout this Opinion. In applying this test only issues which reduce earnings per share should be considered. In establishing this guideline the Board does not imply that a similar measure should be applied in any circumstances other than the computation and presentation of earnings per share data under this Opinion.

[3]APB Opinion No. 9 referred to the latter presentation as "supplementary pro forma earnings per share."

summary of earnings. If potential dilution exists in any of the periods presented, the dual presentation of primary earnings per share and fully diluted earnings per share data should be made for all periods presented. This information together with other disclosures required (see paragraphs 19-23) will give the reader an understanding of the extent and trend of the potential dilution.

18. When results of operations of a prior period included in the statement of income or summary of earnings have been restated as a result of a prior period adjustment, earnings per share data given for the prior period should be restated. The effect of the restatement, expressed in per share terms, should be disclosed in the year of restatement.

Additional Disclosures

Capital Structure

19. The use of complex securities complicates earnings per share computations and makes additional disclosures necessary. The Board has concluded that financial statements should include a description, in summary form, sufficient to explain the pertinent rights and privileges of the various securities outstanding. Examples of information which should be disclosed are dividend and liquidation preferences, participation rights, call prices and dates, conversion or exercise prices or rates and pertinent dates, sinking fund requirements, unusual voting rights, etc.

Dual Earnings per Share Data

20. A schedule or note relating to the earnings per share data should explain the bases upon which both primary and fully diluted earnings per share are calculated. This information should include identification of any issues regarded as common stock equivalents in the computation of primary earnings per share and the securities included in the computation of fully diluted earnings per share. It should describe all assumptions and any resulting adjustments used in deriving the earnings per share data.[4] There should also be disclosed the number of shares issued upon conversion, exercise or satisfaction of required conditions, etc., during at least the most recent annual fiscal period and any subsequent interim period presented.[5]

21. Computations and/or reconciliations may

sometimes be desirable to provide a clear understanding of the manner in which the earnings per share amounts were obtained. This information may include data on each issue of securities entering into the computation of the primary and fully diluted earnings per share. It should not, however, be shown on the face of the income statement or otherwise furnished in a manner implying that an earnings per share amount which ignores the effect of common stock equivalents (that is, earnings per share based on outstanding common shares only) constitutes an acceptable presentation of primary earnings per share.

Supplementary Earnings per Share Data

22. Primary earnings per share should be related to the capital structures existing during each of the various periods presented.[6] Although conversions ordinarily do not alter substantially the amount of capital employed in the business, they can significantly affect the trend in earnings per share data. Therefore, if conversions during the current period would have affected (either dilutively or incrementally) primary earnings per share if they had taken place at the beginning of the period, supplementary information should be furnished (preferably in a note) for the latest period showing what primary earnings per share would have been if such conversions had taken place at the beginning of that period (or date of issuance of the security, if within the period). Similar supplementary per share earnings should be furnished if conversions occur after the close of the period but before completion of the financial report. It may also be desirable to furnish supplementary per share data for each period presented, giving the cumulative retroactive effect of all such conversions or changes. However, primary earnings per share data should not be adjusted retroactively for conversions.

23. Occasionally a sale of common stock or common stock equivalents for cash occurs during the latest period presented or shortly after its close but before completion of the financial report. When a portion or all of the proceeds of such a sale has been used to retire preferred stock or debt, or is to be used for that purpose, supplementary earnings per share data should be furnished (preferably in a note) to show what the earnings would have been for the latest fiscal year and any subsequent interim period presented if the retirement had taken place at the beginning of the respective period (or date of

---

[4]These computations should give effect to all adjustments which would result from conversion: for example, dividends paid on convertible preferred stocks should not be deducted from net income; interest and related expenses on convertible debt, less applicable income tax, should be added to net income, and any other adjustments affecting net income because of these assumptions should also be made. (See paragraph 51.)

[5]See also paragraphs 9 and 10 of APB Opinion No. 12.

[6]See paragraphs 48-49 and 62-64 for exceptions to this general rule.

issuance of the retired security, if later). The number of shares of common stock whose proceeds are to be used to retire the preferred stock or debt should be included in this computation. The bases of these supplementary computations should be disclosed.[7]

Primary Earnings per Share

24. If a corporation's capital structure is complex and either does not include common stock equivalents or includes common stock equivalents which do not have a dilutive effect, the primary earnings per share figures should be based on the weighted average number of shares of common stock outstanding during the period. In such cases, potential dilutive effects of contingent issuances would be reflected in the fully diluted earnings per share amounts. Certain securities, however, are considered to be the equivalent of outstanding common stock and should be recognized in the computation of primary earnings per share if they have a dilutive effect.

Nature of Common Stock Equivalents

25. The concept that a security may be the equivalent of common stock has evolved to meet the reporting needs of investors in corporations that have issued certain types of convertible and other complex securities. A common stock equivalent is a security which is not, in form, a common stock but which usually contains provisions to enable its holder to become a common stockholder and which, because of its terms and the circumstances under which it was issued, is in substance equivalent to a common stock. The holders of these securities can expect to participate in the appreciation of the value of the common stock resulting principally from the earnings and earnings potential of the issuing corporation. This participation is essentially the same as that of a common stockholder except that the security may carry a specified dividend or interest rate yielding a return different from that received by a common stockholder. The attractiveness of this type of security to investors is often based principally on this potential right to share in increases in the earnings potential of the issuing corporation rather than on its fixed return or other senior security characteristics. With respect to a convertible security, any difference in yield between it and the underlying common stock as well as any other senior characteristics of the convertible security become secondary. The value of a common stock equivalent is derived in large part from the value of the common stock to which it is related, and changes in its value tend to reflect changes in the value of the common stock. Neither conversion nor the imminence of conversion is necessary to cause a security to be a common stock equivalent.

26. The Board has concluded that outstanding convertible securities which have the foregoing characteristics and which meet the criteria set forth in this Opinion for the determination of common stock equivalents at the time they are issued should be considered the equivalent of common stock in computing primary earnings per share if the effect is dilutive. The recognition of common stock equivalents in the computation of primary earnings per share avoids the misleading implication which would otherwise result from the use of common stock only; use of the latter basis would place form over substance.

27. In addition to convertible debt and convertible preferred stocks, the following types of securities are or may be considered as common stock equivalents:

Stock options and warrants (and their equivalents) and stock purchase contracts—should always be considered common stock equivalents (see paragraphs 35-38).

Participating securities and two-class common stocks—if their participation features enable their holders to share in the earnings potential of the issuing corporation on substantially the same basis as common stock even though the securities may not give the holder the right to exchange his shares for common stock (see paragraphs 59 and 60).

Contingent shares—if shares are to be issued in the future upon the mere passage of time (or are held in escrow pending the satisfaction of conditions unrelated to earnings or market value) they should be considered as outstanding for the computation of earnings per share. If additional shares of stock are issuable for little or no consideration upon the satisfaction of certain conditions they should be considered as outstanding when the conditions are met (see paragraphs 61-64).

Determination of Common Stock Equivalents at Issuance

28. The Board has concluded that determination of whether a convertible security is a common stock equivalent should be made only at the time of issuance and should not be changed thereafter so long as the security remains outstanding. However, convertible securities outstanding or subsequently issued with the same terms as those of a common stock equivalent also should be classified as common stock equivalents. After full consideration of whether a convertible security may change its status as a common stock equivalent subsequent to issuance, including the differing views which are set forth in Appendix B hereto, the Board has con-

[7]There may be other forms of recapitalization which should be reflected in a similar manner.

cluded that the dilutive effect of any convertible securities that were not common stock equivalents at time of their issuance should be included only in the fully diluted earnings per share amount. This conclusion is based upon the belief (a) that only the conditions which existed at the time of issuance of the convertible security should govern the determination of status as a common stock equivalent, and (b) that the presentation of fully diluted earnings per share data adequately discloses the potential dilution which may exist because of changes in conditions subsequent to time of issuance.

29. Various factors should be considered in determining the appropriate "time of issuance" in evaluating whether a security is substantially equivalent to a common stock. The time of issuance generally is the date when agreement as to terms has been reached and announced, even though subject to certain further actions, such as directors' or stockholders' approval.

No Anti-Dilution

30. Computations of primary earnings per share should not give effect to common stock equivalents or other contingent issuance for any period in which their inclusion would have the effect of increasing the earnings per share amount or decreasing the loss per share amount otherwise computed.[8] Consequently, while a security once determined to be a common stock equivalent retains that status, it may enter into the computation of primary earnings per share in one period and not in another.

Test of Common Stock Equivalent Status

31. *Convertible securities.* A convertible security which at the time of issuance has terms that make it for all practical purposes substantially equivalent to a common stock should be regarded as a common stock equivalent. The complexity of convertible securities makes it impractical to establish definitive guidelines to encompass all the varying terms which might bear on this determination. Consideration has been given, however, to various characteristics of a convertible security which might affect its status as a common stock equivalent, such as cash yield at issuance, increasing or decreasing conversion rates, liquidation and redemption amounts, and the conversion price in relation to the market price of the common stock. In addition, consideration has been given to the

pattern of various nonconvertible security yields in recent years, during which period most of the existing convertible securities have been issued, as well as over a longer period of time. Many of the characteristics noted above, which in various degrees may indicate status as a common stock equivalent, are also closely related to the interest or dividend rate of the security and to its market price at the time of issuance.

32. The Board has also studied the use of market price in relation to investment value (value of a convertible security without the conversion option) and market parity (relationship of conversion value of a convertible security to its market price) as means of determining if a convertible security is equivalent to a common stock. (See discussion of investment value and market parity tests in Appendix B.) It has concluded, however, that these tests are too subjective or not sufficiently practicable.

33. The Board believes that convertible securities should be considered common stock equivalents if the cash yield to the holder at time of issuance is significantly below what would be a comparable rate for a similar security of the issuer without the conversion option. Recognizing that it may frequently be difficult or impossible to ascertain such comparable rates, and in the interest of simplicity and objectivity, the Board has concluded that a convertible security should be considered as a common stock equivalent at the time of issuance if, based on its market price,[9] it has a cash yield of less than $66^2/_3\%$ of the then current bank prime interest rate.[10] For any convertible security which has a change in its cash interest rate or cash dividend rate scheduled within the first five years after issuance, the lowest scheduled rate during such five years should be used in determining the cash yield of the security at issuance.

34. The Board believes that the current bank prime interest rate in general use for short-term loans represents a practical, simple and readily available basis on which to establish the criteria for determining a common stock equivalent, as set forth in the preceding paragraph. The Board recognizes that there are other rates and averages of interest rates relating to various grades of long-term debt securities and preferred stocks which might be appropriate or that a more complex approach could be adopted. However, after giving consideration to various

---

[8]The presence of a common stock equivalent together with extraordinary items may result in diluting income before extraordinary items on a per share basis while increasing net income per share, or vice versa. If an extraordinary item is present and a common stock equivalent results in dilution of either income before extraordinary items or net income on a per share basis, the common stock equivalent should be recognized for all computations even though it has an anti-dilutive effect on one of the per share amounts.

[9]If no market price is available, this test should be based on the fair value of the security.

[10]If convertible securities are sold or issued outside the United States, the most comparable interest rate in the foreign country should be used for this test.

approaches and interest rates in this regard, the Board has concluded that since there is a high degree of correlation between such indices and the bank prime interest rate, the latter is the most practical rate available for this particular purpose.

35. *Options and warrants (and their equivalents).* Options, warrants and similar arrangements usually have no cash yield and derive their value from their right to obtain common stock at specified prices for an extended period. Therefore, these securities should be regarded as common stock equivalents at all times. Other securities, usually having a low cash yield (see definition of "cash yield", Appendix D), require the payment of cash upon conversion and should be considered the equivalents of warrants for the purposes of this Opinion. Accordingly, they should also be regarded as common stock equivalents at all times. Primary earnings per share should reflect the dilution that would result from exercise or conversion of these securities and use of the funds, if any, obtained. Options and warrants (and their equivalents) should, therefore, be treated as if they had been exercised and earnings per share data should be computed as described in the following paragraphs. The computation of earnings per share should not, however, reflect exercise or conversion of any such security[11] if its effect on earnings per share is anti-dilutive (see paragraph 30) except as indicated in paragraph 38.

36. Except as indicated in this paragraph and in paragraphs 37 and 38, the amount of dilution to be reflected in earnings per share data should be computed by application of the "treasury stock" method. Under this method, earnings per share data are computed as if the options and warrants were exercised at the beginning of the period (or at time of issuance, if later) and as if the funds obtained thereby were used to purchase common stock at the average market price during the period.[12] As a practical matter, the Board recommends that assumption of exercise not be reflected in earnings per share data until the market price of the common stock obtainable has been in excess of the exercise price for substantially all of three consecutive months ending with the last month of the period to which earnings per share data relate. Under the treasury stock method, options and warrants have a dilutive effect (and are, therefore, reflected in earnings per share computations) only when the average market price of the common stock obtainable upon exercise during the period exceeds the exercise price of the options or warrants. Previously reported earnings per share amounts should not be retroactively

adjusted, in the case of options and warrants, as a result of changes in market prices of common stock. The Board recognizes that the funds obtained by issuers from the exercise of options and warrants are used in many ways with a wide variety of results that cannot be anticipated. Application of the treasury stock method in earnings per share computations is not based on an assumption that the funds will or could actually be used in that manner. In the usual case, it represents a practical approach to reflecting the dilutive effect that would result from the issuance of common stock under option and warrant agreements at an effective price below the current market price. The Board has concluded, however, that the treasury stock method is inappropriate, or should be modified, in certain cases described in paragraphs 37 and 38.

37. Some warrants contain provisions which permit, or require, the tendering of debt (usually at face amount) or other securities of the issuer in payment for all or a portion of the exercise price. The terms of some debt securities issued with warrants require that the proceeds of the exercise of the related warrants be applied toward retirement of the debt. As indicated in paragraph 35, some convertible securities require cash payments upon conversion and are, therefore, considered to be the equivalent of warrants. In all of these cases, the "if converted" method (see paragraph 51) should be applied as if retirement or conversion of the securities had occurred and as if the excess proceeds, if any, had been applied to the purchase of common stock under the treasury stock method. However, exercise of the options and warrants should not be reflected in the computation for the period specified in paragraph 36 either (a) the market price of the related common stock exceeds the exercise price or (b) the security which may be (or must be) tendered is selling at a price below that at which it may be tendered under the option or warrant agreement and the resulting discount is sufficient to establish an effective exercise price below the market price of the common stock that can be obtained upon exercise. Similar treatment should be followed for preferred stock bearing similar provisions or other securities having conversion options permitting payment of cash for a more favorable conversion rate from the standpoint of the investor.

38. The treasury stock method of reflecting use of proceeds from options and warrants may not adequately reflect potential dilution when options or warrants to acquire a substantial number of common shares are outstanding. Accordingly, the Board

---

[11]Reasonable grouping of like securities may be appropriate.

[12]For example, if a corporation has 10,000 warrants outstanding, exercisable at $54 and the average market price of the common stock during the reporting period is $60, the $540,000 which would be realized from exercise of the warrants and issuance of 10,000 shares would be an amount sufficient to acquire 9,000 shares; thus 1,000 shares would be added to the outstanding common shares in computing primary earnings per share for the period.

has concluded that, if the number of shares of common stock obtainable upon exercise of outstanding options and warrants in the aggregate exceeds 20% of the number of common shares outstanding at the end of the period for which the computation is being made, the treasury stock method should be modified in determining the dilutive effect of the options and warrants upon earnings per share data. In these circumstances all the options and warrants should be assumed to have been exercised and the aggregate proceeds therefrom to have been applied in two steps:

a. As if the funds obtained were first applied to the repurchase of outstanding common shares at the average market price during the period (treasury stock method) but not to exceed 20% of the outstanding shares; and then

b. As if the balance of the funds were applied first to reduce any short-term or long-term borrowings and any remaining funds were invested in U.S. government securities or commercial paper, with appropriate recognition of any income tax effect.

The results of steps (a) and (b) of the computation (whether dilutive or anti-dilutive) should be aggregated and, if the net effect is dilutive, should enter into the earnings per share computation.[13]

Non-Recognition of Common Stock Equivalents in Financial Statements

39. The designation of securities as common stock equivalents in this Opinion is solely for the purpose of determining primary earnings per share. No changes from present practices are recommended in the accounting for such securities, in their presentation within the financial statements or in the manner of determining net assets per common share. Information is available in the financial statements and elsewhere for readers to make judgments as to the present and potential status of the various securities outstanding.

Fully Diluted Earnings per Share

No Anti-Dilution

40. The purpose of the fully diluted earnings per share presentation is to show the maximum potential dilution of current earnings per share on a prospective basis. Consequently, computations of fully diluted earnings per share for each period should exclude those securities whose conversion, exercise or other contingent issuance would have the effect of increasing the earnings per share amount or decreasing the loss per share amount[14] for such period.

---

[13]The following are examples of the application of Paragraph 38:

Assumptions:	Case 1	Case 2
Net income for year	$ 4,000,000	$ 2,000,000
Common shares outstanding	3,000,000	3,000,000
Options and warrants outstanding to purchase equivalent shares	1,000,000	1,000,000
20% limitation on assumed repurchase	600,000	600,000
Exercise price per share	$15	$15
Average and year-end market value per common share to be used (see paragraph 42)	$20	$12
Computations:		
Application of assumed proceeds ($15,000,000):		
Toward repurchase of outstanding common shares at applicable market value	$12,000,000	$ 7,200,000
Reduction of debt	3,000,000	7,800,000
	$15,000,000	$15,000,000
Adjustment of net income:		
Actual net income	$ 4,000,000	$ 2,000,000
Interest reduction (6%) less 50% tax effect	90,000	234,000
Adjusted net income (A)	$ 4,090,000	$ 2,234,000
Adjustment of shares outstanding:		
Actual outstanding	3,000,000	3,000,000
Net additional shares issuable (1,000,000 − 600,000)	400,000	400,000
Adjusted shares outstanding (B)	3,400,000	3,400,000
Earnings per share:		
Before adjustment	$1.33	$ .67
After adjustment (A ÷ B)	$1.20	$ .66

[14]See footnote 8.

When Required

41. Fully diluted earnings per share data should be presented on the face of the statement of income for each period presented if shares of common stock (a) were issued during the period on conversions, exercise, etc., or (b) were contingently issuable at the close of any period presented and if primary earnings per share for such period would have been affected (either dilutively or incrementally) had such actual issuances taken place at the beginning of the period or would have been reduced had such contingent issuances taken place at the beginning of the period. The above contingencies may result from the existence of (a) senior stock or debt which is convertible into common shares but is not a common stock equivalent, (b) options or warrants, or (c) agreements for the issuance of common shares upon the satisfaction of certain conditions (for example, the attainment of specified higher levels of earnings following a business combination). The computation should be based on the assumption that all such issued and issuable shares were outstanding from the beginning of the period (or from the time the contingency arose, if after the beginning of the period). Previously reported fully diluted earnings per share amounts should not be retroactively adjusted for subsequent conversions or subsequent changes in the market prices of the common stock.

42. The methods described in paragraphs 36-38 should be used to compute fully diluted earnings per share if dilution results from outstanding options and warrants; however, in order to reflect maximum potential dilution, the market price at the close of the period reported upon should be used to determine the number of shares which would be assumed to be repurchased (under the treasury stock method) if such market price is higher than the average price used in computing primary earnings per share (see paragraph 30). Common shares issued on exercise of options or warrants during each period should be included in fully diluted earnings per share from the beginning of the period or date of issuance of the options or warrants if later; the computation for the portion of the period prior to the date of exercise should be based on market prices of the common stock when exercised.

Situations Not Covered in Opinion

43. The Board recognizes that it is impracticable to cover all possible conditions and circumstances that may be encountered in computing earnings per share. When situations not expressly covered in this Opinion occur, however, they should be dealt with in accordance with their substance, giving cognizance to the guidelines and criteria outlined herein.

Computational Guidelines

44. The determination of earnings per share data required under this Opinion reflects the complexities of the capital structures of some businesses. The calculations should give effect to matters such as stock dividends and splits, business combinations, changes in conversion rates, etc. Guidelines which should be used in dealing with some of the more common computational matters are set forth in Appendix A hereto.

EFFECTIVE DATE

45. This Opinion shall be effective for fiscal periods beginning after December 31, 1968 for all earnings per share data (primary, fully diluted and supplementary) regardless of when the securities entering into computations of earnings per share were issued, except as described in paragraph 46 as it relates to primary earnings per share. The Board recommends that (a) computations for periods beginning before January 1, 1969 be made for all securities in conformity with the provisions of this Opinion and (b) in comparative statements in which the data for some periods are subject to this Opinion and others are not, the provisions of the Opinion be applied to all periods—in either case based on the conditions existing in the prior periods.

46. In the case of securities whose time of issuance is prior to June 1, 1969 the following election should be made as of May 31, 1969 (and not subsequently changed) with respect to all such securities for the purpose of computing primary earnings per share:

a. determine the classifications of all such securities under the provisions of this Opinion, or

b. classify as common stock equivalents only those securities which are classified as residual securities under APB Opinion No. 9 regardless of how they would be classified under this Opinion.

If the former election is made, the provisions of this Opinion should be applied in the computation of both primary and fully diluted earnings per share data for all periods presented.

The Opinion entitled "Earnings per Share" was adopted by the assenting votes of fifteen members of the Board, of whom five, Messrs. Axelson, Davidson, Harrington, Hellerson and Watt, assented with qualification. Messrs. Halvorson, Seidman and Weston dissented.

Messrs. Axelson and Watt dissent to the requirement in paragraphs 35 and 36 that options and warrants whose exercise price is at or above the market price of related common stock at time of issuance be taken into account in the computation of *primary* earnings per share. They believe that this destroys the usefulness of the dual presentation of primary and fully diluted earnings per share by failing to disclose the magnitude of the contingency arising from the outstanding warrants and options and is inconsistent with the determination of the status of convertible securities at time of issuance only. Therefore, they concur with the comments in paragraph 86. They also dissent to the 20 percent limitation in paragraph 38 on use of the treasury stock method of applying proceeds from the assumed exercise of options and warrants because such limitation is arbitrary and unsupported and because of the inconsistency between this limitation and the Board's conclusion expressed in paragraph 36 that use of the treasury stock method "is not based on an assumption that the funds will or could actually be used in that manner." Further, they dissent to the requirement in paragraphs 63 and 64 that the computation of *primary* earnings per share take into account shares of stock issuable in connection with business combinations on a purely contingent basis, wholly dependent upon the movement of market prices in the future.

Mr. Davidson assents to the issuance of this Opinion because he believes that practice under Part II of APB Opinion No. 9 has been so varied that clarification of APB Opinion No. 9 is necessary. He agrees with the concept of common stock equivalents, but dissents to the conclusion that convertible securities can be classified as common stock equivalents only by consideration of conditions prevailing at the time of their issuance (paragraph 28). He believes that in determining common stock equivalency, current conditions reflected in the market place are the significant criterion (paragraphs 74-77). The use of the investment value method (paragraphs 79-81) adequately reflects these current conditions.

Mr. Davidson also dissents to the use of the bank prime rate for the cash-yield test (paragraphs 33-34). It does not differentiate among types of securities issued nor the standing of the issuers.

Mr. Harrington assents to the issuance of the Opinion; however, he dissents from paragraphs 36, 37 and 38. He believes it is inconsistent in computing fully diluted earnings per share to measure potential dilution by the treasury stock method in the case of most warrants and to assume conversion in the case of convertible securities. This inconsistency, in his view, results in required recognition of potential dilution attributable to all convertible securities; and, at the same time through the use of the treasury stock method, permits understatement or no recognition of potential dilution attributable to warrants. He further believes that the potential dilution inherent in warrants should be recognized in fully

diluted earning per share, but need not be recognized in primary earnings per share, when the exercise price exceeds the market price of the stock.

Mr. Hellerson assents to the issuance of this Opinion because he believes the Board has an obligation to resolve without further delay the implementation problems raised by Part II of APB Opinion No. 9 which have been greatly extended by the characteristics of a number of the securities issued since the release of that Opinion. However, he dissents from the mandatory requirement that earnings per share be shown on the face of the income statement as prescribed in paragraphs 12 through 16 and paragraph 41. The accounting profession has taken the position, and in his view rightly so, that fair presentation of financial position and results of operations requires the presentation of certain basic financial statements supplemented by disclosure of additional information in the form of separate statements or notes to the basic financial statements. Fair presentation is achieved by the whole presentation, not by the specific location of any item. This principle was most recently restated by the Board in paragraph 10 of APB Opinion No. 12 on capital changes as follows: "Disclosure of such changes may take the form of separate statements or may be made in the basic financial statements or notes thereto." Accordingly, it is his view that, although the Opinion should require dual presentation of earnings per share, it should not specify that the presentation must be made on the face of the income statement and thereby dignify one figure above all others.

Mr. Halvorson dissents to the Opinion because he believes the subject matter is one of financial analysis, not accounting principles, and that any expression by the Accounting Principles Board on the subject should not go beyond requiring such disclosure of the respective rights and priorities of the several issues of securities which may be represented in the capital structure of a reporting corporation as will permit an investor to make his own analysis of the effects of such rights and priorities on earnings per common share. Mr. Halvorson agrees that certain nominally senior securities are the equivalent of common shares under certain circumstances, but believes that the determination of common-stock equivalence is a subjective one which cannot be accommodated within prescribed formulae or arithmetical rules, although it can be facilitated by disclosure of information which does fall within the bounds of fair presentation in conformity with generally accepted accounting principles. Mr. Halvorson believes that a corporation should not be denied the right to report factually determined earnings per weighted average outstanding common share on the face of the income statement as a basis against which to measure the potential dilutive effects on earnings per share of senior issues, and that from such basis the investor may make such pro forma calculations of common-stock equivalence as he believes best serve his purpose.

Mr. Seidman dissents for the reasons set forth in paragraphs 72, 73, 92 and 93, dealing with the invalidity and inconsistent application of the concept of common stock equivalents. He adds: (1) It is unsound for the determination of earnings per share to depend on the fluctuations of security prices. It is even more unsound when an increase in security prices can result in a decrease in earnings per share, and vice versa. These matters arise under this Opinion since it calls for earnings per share based on cash yield of convertibles, comparison of stock and exercise prices of options and warrants, and no antidilution. (2) It is erroneous to attribute earnings to securities that do not currently and may never share in those earnings, particularly when part or all of those earnings may have already been distributed to others as dividends. (3) It does not serve the interests of meaningful disclosure when, as in paragraph 21, the Opinion bans showing on the face of the income statement any reference to the amount of earnings per share in relation to the one factual base, namely the number of shares actually outstanding, and instead fashions from various surmises what it calls "primary earnings per share". (4) It is baffling to say, as does this Opinion, that convertible debt is debt in the statement of earnings but is common stock equivalent in the statement of earnings per share; and that dividends per share are based on the actual number of shares outstanding, while earnings per share are based on a different and larger number of shares.

Mr. Weston dissents to the issuance of this Opinion because he believes it represents a significant retrogression in terms of the purpose of the Accounting Principles Board. The residual security concept, which has been successfully and appropriately applied to convertible securities during the period since issuance of APB Opinion No. 9, has, in this Opinion, been so restricted as to be meaningless for all practical purposes with respect to such securities. Accordingly, computations of primary earnings per share data under the provisions of this Opinion (paragraph 28 in particular) will not properly reflect the characteristics of those convertible securities which are currently the substantial equivalent of common stock—and are so recognized in the marketplace—which did not qualify for residual status at their date of issuance—possibly years previously. Such disregard of basic principles is a disservice to investors, who have a right to view the primary earnings per share data computed under this Opinion as a realistic attribution of the earnings of the issuer to the various complex elements of its capital structure based on the economic realities of today—not those existing years ago.

Mr. Weston also disagrees with the conclusions contained in paragraphs 33, 36, 39 and 51.

NOTES

Opinions present the considered opinion of at least two-thirds of the members of the Accounting Principles Board, reached on a formal vote after examination of the subject matter.

Except as indicated in the succeeding paragraph, the authority of the Opinions rests upon their general acceptability. While it is recognized that general rules may be subject to exception, the burden of justifying departures from Board Opinions must be assumed by those who adopt other practices.

Action of Council of the Institute (Special Bulletin, Disclosure of Departures from Opinions of the Accounting Principles Board, *October, 1964) provides that:*

a. *"Generally accepted accounting principles" are those principles which have substantial authoritative support.*

b. *Opinions of the Accounting Principles Board constitute "substantial authoritative support."*

c. *"Substantial authoritative support" can exist for accounting principles that differ from Opinions of the Accounting Principles Board.*

The Council action also requires that departures from Board Opinions be disclosed in footnotes to the financial statements or in independent auditors' reports when the effect of the departure on the financial statements is material.

Unless otherwise stated, Opinions of the Board are not intended to be retroactive. They are not intended to be applicable to immaterial items.

Accounting Principles Board (1969)

LeRoy Layton, *Chairman*	Joseph P. Cummings	Charles T. Horngren
	Sidney Davidson	Louis M. Kessler
Marshall S. Armstrong	Philip L. Defliese	Oral L. Luper
Kenneth S. Axelson	Newman T. Halvorson	J. S. Seidman
Donald J. Bevis	Emmett S. Harrington	George C. Watt
Milton M. Broeker	Charles B. Hellerson	Frank T. Weston
George R. Catlett		

Appendix A

COMPUTATIONAL GUIDELINES

CONTENTS

Appendix A

COMPUTATIONAL GUIDELINES

The Board has adopted the following general guidelines which should be used in the computation of earnings per share data.

47. *Weighted average.* Computations of earnings per share data should be based on the weighted average number of common shares and common share equivalents outstanding during each period presented. Use of a weighted average is necessary so that the effect of increases or decreases in outstanding shares on earnings per share data is related to the portion of the period during which the related consideration affected operations. Reacquired shares should be excluded from date of their acquisition. (See definition in Appendix D.)

48. *Stock dividends or splits.* If the number of common shares outstanding increases as a result of a stock dividend or stock split[15] or decreases as a result of a reverse split, the computations should give retroactive recognition to an appropriate equivalent change in capital structure for all periods presented. If changes in common stock resulting from stock dividends or stock splits or reverse splits have been consummated after the close of the period but before completion of the financial report, the per share computations should be based on the new number of shares because the readers' primary

interest is presumed to be related to the current capitalization. When per share computations reflect such changes in the number of shares after the close of the period, this fact should be disclosed.

49. *Business combinations and reorganizations.* When shares are issued to acquire a business in a transaction accounted for as a purchase, the computation of earnings per share should give recognition to the existence of the new shares only from the date the acquisition took place. When a business combination is accounted for as a pooling of interests, the computation should be based on the aggregate of the weighted average outstanding shares of the constituent businesses, adjusted to equivalent shares of the surviving business for all periods presented. This difference in treatment reflects the fact that in a purchase the results of operations of the acquired business are included in the statement of income only from the date of acquisition, whereas in a pooling of interests the results of operations are combined for all periods presented. In reorganizations, the computations should be based on analysis of the particular transaction according to the criteria contained in this Opinion.

50. *Claims of senior securities.* The claims of senior securities on earnings of a period should be deducted from net income (and also from income before extraordinary items if an amount therefor appears in the statement) before computing earnings per share. Dividends on cumulative preferred senior securities, whether or not earned, should be

---

[15]See ARB No. 43, Chapter 7B, *Capital Accounts—Stock Dividends and Stock Split Ups.*

deducted from net income.[16] If there is a net loss, the amount of the loss should be increased by any cumulative dividends for the period on these preferred stocks. If interest or preferred dividends are cumulative only if earned, no adjustment of this type is required, except to the extent of income available therefor. If interest or preferred dividends are not cumulative, only the interest accruable or dividends declared should be deducted. In all cases, the effect that has been given to rights of senior securities in arriving at the earnings per share should be disclosed.

51. *Use of "if converted" method of computation.* If convertible securities are deemed to be common stock equivalents for the purpose of computing primary earnings per share, or are assumed to have been converted for the purpose of computing fully diluted earnings per share, the securities should be assumed to have been converted at the beginning of the earliest period reported (or at time of issuance, if later). Interest charges applicable to convertible securities and non-discretionary adjustments that would have been made to items based on net income or income before taxes—such as profit sharing expense, certain royalties, and investment credit— or preferred dividends applicable to the convertible securities should be taken into account in determining the balance of income applicable to common stock. As to primary earnings per share this amount should be divided by the total of the average outstanding common shares and the number of shares which would have been issued on conversion or exercise of common stock equivalents.[17] As to fully diluted earnings per share this amount should be divided by the total of the average outstanding common shares plus the number of shares applicable to conversions during the period from the beginning of the period to the date of conversion and the number of shares which would have been issued upon conversion or exercise of any other security which might dilute earnings.

52. The if converted method recognizes the fact that the holders of convertible securities cannot share in distributions of earnings applicable to the common stock unless they relinquish their right to senior distributions. Conversion is assumed and earnings applicable to common stock and common stock equivalents are determined before distributions to holders of these securities.

53. The if converted method also recognizes the fact that a convertible issue can participate in earnings, through dividends or interest, either as a senior security or as a common stock, but not both. The

two-class method (see paragraph 55) does not recognize this limitation and may attribute to common stock an amount of earnings per share less than if the convertible security had actually been converted. The amount of earnings per share on common stock as computed under the two-class method is affected by the amount of dividends declared on the common stock.

54. *Use of "two-class" method of computation.* Although the two-class method is considered inappropriate with respect to the securities described in paragraph 51, its use may be necessary in the case of participating securities and two-class common stock. (See paragraphs 59-60 for discussion of these securities.) This is the case, for example, when these securities are not convertible into common stock.

55. Under the two-class method, common stock equivalents are treated as common stock with a dividend rate different from the dividend rate on the common stock and, therefore, conversion of convertible securities is not assumed. No use of proceeds is assumed. Distributions to holders of senior securities, common stock equivalents and common stock are first deducted from net income. The remaining amount (the undistributed earnings) is divided by the total of common shares and common share equivalents. Per share distributions to the common stockholders are added to this per share amount to arrive at primary earnings per share.

56. *Delayed effectiveness and changing conversion rates or exercise prices.* In some cases, a conversion option does not become effective until a future date; in others conversion becomes more (or less) advantageous to the security holder at some later date as the conversion rate increases (or decreases), generally over an extended period. For example, an issue may be convertible into one share of common stock in the first year, 1.10 shares in the second year, 1.20 shares in the third year, etc. Frequently, these securities receive little or no cash dividends. Hence, under these circumstances, their value is derived principally from their conversion or exercise option and they would be deemed to be common stock equivalents under the yield test previously described. (See paragraph 33 of this Opinion.)[18] Similarly, the right to exercise options or warrants may be deferred or the exercise price may increase or decrease.

57. *Conversion rate or exercise price to be used— primary earnings per share.* The conversion rate or exercise price of a common stock equivalent in effect during each period presented should be used in computing primary earnings per share, with the

---

[16]The per share and aggregate amounts of cumulative preferred dividends in arrears should be disclosed.

[17]Determined as to options and warrants by application of the method described in paragraphs 36-38 of this Opinion.

[18]An increasing conversion rate should not be accounted for as a stock dividend.

exceptions stated hereinafter in this paragraph. Prior period primary earnings per share should not be restated for changes in the conversion ratio or exercise price. If options, warrants or other common stock equivalents are not immediately exercisable or convertible, the earliest effective exercise price or conversion rate if any during the succeeding five years should be used. If a convertible security having an increasing conversion rate is issued in exchange for another class of security of the issuing company and is convertible back into the same or a similar security, and if a conversion rate equal to or greater than the original exchange rate becomes effective during the period of convertibility, the conversion rate used in the computation should not result in a reduction in the number of common shares (or common share equivalents) existing before the original exchange took place until a greater rate becomes effective.

58. *Conversion rate or exercise price to be used— fully diluted earnings per share.* Fully diluted earnings per share computations should be based on the most advantageous (from the standpoint of the security holder) conversion or exercise rights that become effective within ten years following the closing date of the period being reported upon.[19] Conversion or exercise options that are not effective until after ten or more years may be expected to be of limited significance because (a) investors' decisions are not likely to be influenced substantially by events beyond ten years, and (b) it is questionable whether they are relevant to current operating results.

59. *Participating securities and two-class common.* The capital structures of some companies include:

a. Securities which may participate in dividends with common stocks according to a predetermined formula (for example, two for one) with, at times, an upper limit to the extent of participation (for example, up to but not beyond a specified amount per share).
b. A class of common stock with different dividend rates or voting rights from those of another class of common stock, but without prior or senior rights.

Additionally, some of these securities are convertible into common stock. Earnings per share computations relating to certain types of participating securities may require the use of the two-class method. (See paragraphs 54-55.)

60. Because of the variety of features which these securities possess, frequently representing combina-

tions of the features referred to above, it is not practicable to set out specific guidelines as to when they should be considered common stock equivalents. Dividend participation does not *per se* make a security a common stock equivalent. A determination of the status of one of these securities should be based on an analysis of all the characteristics of the security, including the ability to share in the earnings potential of the issuing corporation on substantially the same basis as the common stock.

61. *Issuance contingent on certain conditions.* At times, agreements call for the issuance of additional shares contingent upon certain conditions being met. Frequently these conditions are either:

a. the maintenance of current earnings levels, or
b. the attainment of specified increased earnings.

Alternatively, agreements sometimes provide for immediate issuance of the maximum number of shares issuable in the transaction with some to be placed in escrow and later returned to the issuer if specified conditions are not met. For purposes of computing earnings per share, contingently returnable shares placed in escrow should be treated in the same manner as contingently issuable shares.

62. If attainment or maintenance of a level of earnings is the condition, and if that level is currently being attained, the additional shares should be considered as outstanding for the purpose of computing both primary and fully diluted earnings per share. If attainment of increased earnings reasonably above the present level or maintenance of increased earnings above the present level over a period of years is the condition, the additional shares should be considered as outstanding only for the purpose of computing fully diluted earnings per share (but only if dilution is the result); for this computation, earnings should be adjusted to give effect to the increase in earnings specified by the particular agreements (if different levels of earnings are specified, the level that would result in the largest potential dilution should be used). Previously reported earnings per share data should not be restated to give retroactive effect to shares subsequently issued as a result of attainment of specified increased earnings levels. If upon expiration of the term of the agreement providing for contingent issuance of additional shares the conditions have not been met, the shares should not be considered outstanding in that year. Previously reported earnings per share data should then be restated to give retroactive effect to the removal of the contingency.

63. The number of shares contingently issuable

---

[19]The conversion rate should also reflect the cumulative effect of any stock dividends on the preferred stock which the company has contracted or otherwise committed itself to issue within the next ten years.

may depend on the market price of the stock at a future date. In such a case, computations of earnings per share should reflect the number of shares which would be issuable based on the market price at the close of the period being reported on. Prior period earnings per share should be restated if the number of shares issued or contingently issuable subsequently changes because the market price changes.

64. In some cases, the number of shares contingently issuable may depend on both future earnings and future prices of the shares. In that case, the number of shares which would be issuable should be based on both conditions, that is, market prices and earnings to date as they exist at the end of each period being reported on. (For example, if (a) a certain number of shares will be issued at the end of three years following an acquisition if earnings of the acquired company increase during those three years by a specified amount and (b) a stipulated number of additional shares will be issued if the value of the shares issued in the acquisition is not at least a designated amount at the end of the three-year period, the number of shares to be included in the earnings per share for each period should be determined by reference to the cumulative earnings of the acquired company and the value of the shares at the end of the latest period.) Prior-period earnings per share should be restated if the number of shares issued or contingently issuable subsequently changes from the number of shares previously included in the earnings per share computation.

65. *Securities of subsidiaries.* At times subsidiaries issue securities which should be considered common stock equivalents from the standpoint of consolidated and parent company financial statements for the purpose of computing earnings per share. This could occur when convertible securities, options, warrants or common stock issued by the subsidiary are in the hands of the public and the subsidiary's results of operations are either consolidated or reflected on the equity method. Circumstances in which conversion or exercise of a subsidiary's securities should be assumed for the purpose of computing the consolidated and parent company earnings per share, or which would otherwise require recognition in the computation of earnings per share data, include those where:

As to the Subsidiary

a. Certain of the subsidiary's securities are common stock equivalents in relation to its own common stock.
b. Other of the subsidiary's convertible securities, although not common stock equivalents in relation to its own common stock, would enter into the computation of its fully diluted earnings per share.

As to the Parent

a. The subsidiary's securities are convertible into the parent company's common stock.
b. The subsidiary issues options and warrants to purchase the parent company's common stock.

The treatment of these securities for the purpose of consolidated and parent company reporting of earnings per share is discussed in the following four paragraphs.

66. If a subsidiary has dilutive warrants or options outstanding or dilutive convertible securities which are common stock equivalents from the standpoint of the subsidiary, consolidated and parent company primary earnings per share should include the portion of the subsidiary's income that would be applicable to the consolidated group based on its holdings and the subsidiary's primary earnings per share. (See paragraph 39 of this Opinion.)

67. If a subsidiary's convertible securities are not common stock equivalents from the standpoint of the subsidiary, only the portion of the subsidiary's income that would be applicable to the consolidated group based on its holdings and the fully diluted earnings per share of the subsidiary should be included in consolidated and parent company fully diluted earnings per share. (See paragraph 40 of this Opinion.)

68. If a subsidiary's securities are convertible into its parent company's stock, they should be considered among the common stock equivalents of the parent company for the purpose of computing consolidated and parent company primary and fully diluted earnings per share if the conditions set forth in paragraph 33 of this Opinion exist. If these conditions do not exist, the subsidiary's convertible securities should be included in the computation of the consolidated and parent company fully diluted earnings per share only.

69. If a subsidiary issues options or warrants to purchase stock of the parent company, they should be considered common stock equivalents by the parent in computing consolidated and parent company primary and fully diluted earnings per share.

70. *Dividends per share.* Dividends constitute historical facts and usually are so reported. However, in certain cases, such as those affected by stock dividends or splits or reverse splits, the presentation of dividends per share should be made in terms of the current equivalent of the number of common shares outstanding at the time of the dividend. A disclosure problem exists in presenting data as to dividends per share following a pooling of interests. In such cases,

it is usually preferable to disclose the dividends declared per share by the principal constituent and to disclose, in addition, either the amount per equivalent share or the total amount for each period for the other constituent, with appropriate explanation of the circumstances. When dividends per share are presented on other than an historical basis, the basis of presentation should be disclosed.

Appendix B

SUMMARY OF DIFFERING VIEWPOINTS

CONTENTS

Appendix B

SUMMARY OF DIFFERING VIEWPOINTS

This Appendix contains a summary of various viewpoints on a number of matters relating to the computation of earnings per share data, which viewpoints differ from the conclusions of the Board as stated in this Opinion. The views in this Appendix therefore do not represent the views of the Board as a whole.

Common Stock Equivalent or Residual Concept

71. This Opinion concludes (paragraph 26) that, for purposes of computing primary earnings per share, certain securities should be considered the equivalent of common stock. The Opinion further concludes (paragraph 28) that such treatment—as to convertible securities—should be based on a determination of status made at the time of issuance of each security, based on conditions existing at that date and not subsequently changed. Viewpoints which differ from those conclusions are based on a number of positions, which are summarized below.

Concept Has No Validity

72. Some believe there should be no such category as "common stock equivalent" or "residual" security, and hence no such classification as "primary" earnings per share including such securities. They contend that the common stock equivalent or residual security concept involves assumptions and arbitrary, intricate determinations which result in figures of questionable meaning which are more likely to confuse than enlighten readers. They advocate that earnings per share data be presented in a tabulation—as part of the financial statements—which first discloses the relationship of net income and the number of common shares actually outstanding and then moves through adjustments to determine adjusted net income and the number of common shares which would be outstanding if all conversions, exercises and contingent issuances took place. Under this approach, all the figures involved would be readily determinable, understandable and significant. Such information, together with the other disclosures required in this Opinion regarding the terms of securities, would place the reader in a position to make his own judgment regarding prospects of conversion or exercise and the resulting impact on per share earnings. Accounting should not make or pre-empt that judgment.

73. Until convertible securities, etc., are in fact converted, the actual common stockholders are in control, and the entire earnings could often be distributed as dividends. The conversions, exercises and contingent issuances may, in fact, never take

place. Hence, the reporting as "primary" earnings per share of an amount which results from treating as common stock securities which are not common stock is, in the view of some, improper.

Concept Has Validity Both At
Issuance and Subsequently

74. Some who believe in the validity of the common stock equivalent or residual concept feel that the status of a security should be determined not only at the time of its issuance but from time to time thereafter. Securities having the characteristics associated with residual securities—among other things the ability to participate in the economic benefits resulting from the underlying earnings and earnings potential of the common stock through the right of their holders to become common stockholders—do change their nature with increases and decreases in the market value of the common stock after issuance. These securities are designed for this purpose, and therefore, in certain circumstances, they react to changes in the earnings or earnings potential of the issuer just as does the common stock. Furthermore, although many such securities are issued under market and yield conditions which do not place major emphasis at the time of issuance on their common stock characteristics, both the issuer and the holder recognize the possibility that these characteristics may become of increasing significance if, and when, the value of the underlying common stock increases. The limitation of the residual concept for convertible securities to "at issuance only" disregards these significant factors. (For example, a convertible security with a cash yield of 4% at time of issuance [assumed to be in excess of the yield test for common stock equivalent status in this Opinion] may well appreciate in value subsequent to issuance, due to its common stock characteristics, to such an extent that its cash yield will drop to 2% or less. It seems unsound to consider such a security a "senior security" for earnings per share purposes at such later dates merely because its yield at date of issuance—possibly years previously—was 4%. This seems particularly unwise when the investment community evaluates such a security currently as the substantial equivalent of the common stock into which it is convertible.) Thus, the "at issuance only" application of the residual security concept is, in the opinion of some, illogical and arbitrary. In connection with the computation of earnings per share data, this approach disregards current conditions in reporting a financial statistic whose very purpose is a reflection of the *current* substantive relationship between the earnings of the issuer and its complex capital structure.

75. Furthermore, the adoption of the treasury stock method to determine the number of shares to be considered as common stock equivalents under

outstanding options and warrants (see paragraphs 36-38) is apparent recognition of the fact that market conditions subsequent to issuance should influence the determination of the status of a security. Thus, the conclusions of the Opinion in these matters are inconsistent.

76. As for the contention that use of the residual concept subsequent to issuance has a "circular" effect—in that reported earnings per share influences the market, which, in turn, influences the classification status of a security, which, in turn, influences the computation of earnings per share, which, in turn, influences the market—analysts give appropriate recognition to the increasing importance of the common stock characteristics of convertible securities as the market rises or falls. It seems only appropriate that a computation purporting to attribute the earnings of a corporation to the various components of its capital structure should also give adequate recognition to the changing substance of these securities. Thus, the movement of securities in and out of residual status subsequent to their issuance is a logical and integral part of the entire concept.

77. As for the contention that the dual presentation of earnings per share data required by this Opinion appropriately reflects the dilutive effect of any convertible securities which were not residual at time of issuance but which might subsequently be considered as residual, the disclosure of "fully-diluted" earnings per share data is aimed at *potential* (i.e., possible future) dilution; for issuers with securities having extremely low yields of the levels described in the preceding paragraph, the dilution has already taken place—these common stock equivalents are being so traded in the market, and any method which does not reflect these conditions results in an amount for "primary earnings per share" which may be misleading. Furthermore, whenever an issuer has more than one convertible security outstanding, the effect of even the "potential" dilution of such "residual" securities is not appropriately reflected in any meaningful manner in the fully-diluted earnings per share amount, since its impact is combined with that of other convertible securities of the issuer which may not currently be "residual".

Criteria and Methods for Determination
of Residual Status

78. This Opinion concludes (paragraph 33) that a cash yield test—based on a specified percentage of the bank prime interest rate—should be used to determine the residual status of convertible securities, and that options and warrants should be considered residual securities at all times. Viewpoints differing from those conclusions and supporting other criteria or methods are summarized below.

Convertible Securities

79. *Investment value method.* As explained in paragraphs 8-11 of this Opinion, a previous Opinion specified a relative value method for the determination of the residual status of a security. In practice the method has been applied by comparing the market value of a convertible security with its "investment value", and by classifying a security as residual at time of issuance if such market value were 200% or more of investment value, with certain practical modifications of this test subsequent to time of issuance to assure the substance of an apparent change in status and to prevent frequent changes of status for possible temporary fluctuations in the market.

80. The establishment of investment values for convertible securities involves considerable estimation, and frequently requires the use of experts. Published financial services report estimates of investment value for many, but not all, convertible securities. Most convertible securities are issued under conditions which permit a reasonable estimate of their investment values. In addition, reference to the movements of long-term borrowing rates for groups of issuers with similar credit and risk circumstances—or even reference to general long-term borrowing rates—can furnish effective evidence for an appropriate determination of the investment value of a convertible security subsequent to its issuance. As in many determinations made for accounting purposes, estimates of this nature are often necessary. The necessity of establishing some percentage or level as the line of demarcation between residual and non-residual status is common to all methods under consideration—including the market parity test and various yield tests—and appears justifiable in the interest of reasonable consistency of treatment, both for a single issuer and among issuers.

81. The investment value method is somewhat similar to the cash yield method specified in paragraph 33 of this Opinion. However, the latter method has two apparent weaknesses, in the view of those who support the investment value method. In the first place, it does not differentiate between issuers—that is, it is based on the same borrowing rate for all issuers, without regard for their credit ratings or other risks inherent in their activities. Second, it is based on the current bank prime interest rate, which is essentially a short-term borrowing rate. The relationship between this rate—assuming that it is constant in all sections of the country at any given time—and the long-term corporate borrowing rate may fluctuate to such an extent that the claimed ease of determination may be offset by a lack of correlation. The investment value method, based on the terms of each issue and the status of each issuer, is

thus considered by some to be a more satisfactory method.

82. *Market parity method.* This method compares a convertible security's market value with its conversion value. In general, if the two values are substantially equivalent and in excess of redemption price, the convertible security is considered to be "residual".

83. The market parity method has the advantage, as compared to the investment value method, of using amounts that usually are readily available or ascertainable, and of avoiding estimates of investment value. More importantly, in the view of some, the equivalence of values is clearly an indication of the equivalence of the securities, while a comparison of relative values of the characteristics of a security is an indication of its status only if arbitrary rules, such as the "major portion of value" test, are used. In similar vein, the yield test also requires the establishment of a point at which to determine residuality. On the other hand, a practical application of the market parity test would also require the establishment of a percentage relationship at which to determine residual status, due to the many variables involved and the need for consistent application. Also, the call or redemption price of a convertible security has an effect on the point at which market parity is achieved.

84. *Yield methods.* There are various other methods of determining the residual nature of a convertible security based on yield relationships. Each of these is based on a comparison of the cash yield on the convertible security (based on its market value) and some predetermined rate of yield (based on other values, conditions or ratings). The discussion of the various methods contained in this Opinion comprehends the advantages and disadvantages of these other methods.

Options and Warrants

85. As explained in paragraphs 35-38 of this Opinion, options and warrants should be regarded as common stock equivalents at all times; the "treasury stock method" should be used in most cases to determine the number of common shares to be considered the equivalent of the options and warrants; and the number of common shares so computed should be included in the computation of both the "primary" and "fully-diluted" earnings per share (assuming a dilutive effect). Viewpoints which differ from those conclusions and support other treatments or other methods of measurement are summarized below.

86. *Exclusion from computation of primary earnings per share.* In this Opinion the Board has for the

first time considered options and warrants to be common stock equivalents at all times and, because of the treasury stock method of computation established, the primary earnings per share will in some cases be affected by the market price of the stock obtainable on exercise, rather than solely by the economics of the transaction entered into. Some believe that this produces a circular effect in that the reporting of earnings per share may then influence the market which, in turn, influences earnings per share. They believe that earnings per share should affect the market and not vice versa. They point out that the classification of convertible debentures and convertible preferred stocks is determined at time of issuance only and consequently subsequent fluctuations in the market prices of these securities do not affect primary earnings per share. Therefore, they believe that the dual, equally prominent presentation of primary and fully diluted earnings per share is most informative when the effect of options and warrants, other than those whose exercise price is substantially lower than market price at time of issuance, is included only in the fully diluted earnings per share which would be lower than primary earnings per share and thus would emphasize the potential dilution.

87. *Determination of equivalent common shares.* Some believe that the "treasury stock method" described in paragraph 36 of this Opinion is unsatisfactory and that other methods are preferable. Under one such method the number of equivalent shares is computed by reference to the relationship between the market value of the option or warrant and the market value of the related common stock. In general, it reflects the impact of options and warrants on earnings per share whenever the option or warrant has a market value, and not only when the market price of the related common stock exceeds the exercise price (as does the treasury stock method).

88. *Measurement of effect of options and warrants.* Some believe that the effect of outstanding options and warrants on earnings per share should be computed by assuming exercise as of the beginning of the period and assuming some use of the funds so attributed to the issuer. The uses which have been suggested include application of such assumed proceeds to (a) reduce outstanding short or long term borrowings, (b) invest in government obligations or commercial paper, (c) invest in operations of the issuer or (d) fulfill other corporate objectives of the issuer. Each of these methods is felt by some to be the preferable approach. Many who support one of these methods feel that the "treasury stock method" is improper since (a) it fails to reflect any dilution unless the market price of the common stock exceeds the exercise price, (b) it assumes a hypothetical purchase of treasury stock which in many

cases—due to the significant number of common shares involved—would either not be possible or be possible only at a considerably increased price per share, and (c) it may be considered to be the attribution of earnings assumed on the funds received—in which case the earnings rate for each issuer is a function of the price-earnings ratio of its common stock and is thus similar in result to an arbitrary assumption of a possibly inappropriate earnings rate.

89. Some believe that no increment in earnings should be attributed to the funds assumed to be received upon the exercise of options and warrants, particularly if such instruments are to be reflected in the computation of primary earnings per share, since the funds were not available to the issuer during the period.

Computational Methods—Convertible Securities

90. This Opinion concludes (paragraph 51) that the "if converted" method of computation should be used for primary earnings per share when convertible securities are considered the equivalent of common stock. Some believe that this method does not properly reflect the actual circumstances existing during the period, and favor, instead, the so-called "two-class" method of computation. (See paragraphs 54-55.) Under the latter method, securities considered common stock equivalents are treated as common shares with a different dividend rate from that of the regular common shares. The residual security concept is based on common stock equivalence without the necessity of actual conversion; therefore, this method properly recognizes the fact that these securities receive a preferential distribution before the common stock—and also share in the potential benefits of the undistributed earnings through their substantial common stock characteristics in the same way as do the common shares. These securities are designed to achieve these two goals. Those who favor this method believe that the "if converted" method disregards the realities of what occurred during the period. Thus, in their view, the "if converted" method is a "pro-forma" method which assumes conversion and the elimination of preferential distributions to these securities; as such, it is not suitable for use in the computation of *primary earnings per share data,* since the assumed conversions did not take place and the preferential distributions did take place.

91. Those who favor the "two-class" method point out that it is considered appropriate in the case of certain participating and two-class common situations. In their view, the circumstances existing when common stock equivalents are outstanding are similar; therefore, use of this method is appropriate.

Recognition of Common Stock Equivalents in the Financial Statements

92. This Opinion concludes (paragraph 39) that the designation of securities as common stock equivalents is solely for the purpose of determining primary earnings per share; no changes from present practice are recommended in the presentation of such securities in the financial statements. Some believe, however, that the financial statements should reflect a treatment of such securities which is consistent with the method used to determine earnings per share in the financial statements. Accordingly, convertible debt considered to be a common stock equivalent would be classified in the balance sheet in association with stockholders' equity—either under a separate caption immediately preceding stockholders' equity, or in a combined section with a caption such as "Equity of common stockholders and holders of common stock equivalents". In the statement of income and retained earnings, interest paid on convertible debt considered a common stock equivalent would be shown as a "distribution to holders of common stock equivalents", either following the caption of "net income" in the statement of income or grouped with other distributions in the statement of retained earnings.

93. Some believe that the inconsistency of the positions taken on this matter in this Opinion is clearly evident in the requirement (paragraph 66) that, when a subsidiary has convertible securities which are common stock equivalents, the portion of the income of the subsidiary to be included in the consolidated statement of income of the parent and its subsidiaries should be computed disregarding the effect of the common stock equivalents, but that the computation of the primary earnings per share of the parent should reflect the effect of these common stock equivalents in attributing the income of the subsidiary to its various outstanding securities. This inconsistent treatment is, in the opinion of some, not only illogical but misleading.

Appendix C

ILLUSTRATIVE STATEMENTS

The following exhibits illustrate the disclosure of earnings per share data on the assumption that this Opinion was effective for all periods covered. The format of the disclosure is illustrative only, and does not necessarily reflect a preference by the Accounting Principles Board.

Exhibit A. This exhibit illustrates the disclosure of earnings per share data for a company with a simple capital structure (see paragraph 14 of this Opinion). The facts assumed for Exhibit A are as follows:

	Number of Shares	
	1968	*1967*
Common stock outstanding:		
Beginning of year	3,300,000	3,300,000
End of year	3,300,000	3,300,000
Issued or acquired during year	None	None
Common stock reserved under employee stock options granted	7,200	7,200
Weighted average number of shares	3,300,000	3,300,000

NOTE: Shares issuable under employee stock options are excluded from the weighted average number of shares on the assumption that their effect is not dilutive (see paragraph 14 of this Opinion).

EXHIBIT A
EXAMPLE OF DISCLOSURE OF EARNINGS PER SHARE
Simple Capital Structure

(Bottom of Income Statement)	Thousands Except per share data	
	1968	*1967*
Income before extraordinary item	$ 9,150	$7,650
Extraordinary item—gain on sale of property less applicable income taxes	900	—
Net Income	$10,050	$7,650
Earnings per common share:		
Income before extraordinary item	$ 2.77	$ 2.32
Extraordinary item	.28	—
Net Income	$ 3.05	$ 2.32

Exhibit B. This exhibit illustrates the disclosure of earnings per share data for a company with a complex capital structure (see paragraph 15 of this Opinion). The facts assumed for Exhibit B are as follows:

Market price of common stock. The market price of the common stock was as follows:

Average Price:	1968	1967	1966
First quarter	50	45	40
Second quarter	60	52	41
Third quarter	70	50	40
Fourth quarter	70	50	45
December 31 closing price	72	51	44

Cash dividends. Cash dividends of $0.125 per common share were declared and paid for each quarter of 1966 and 1967. Cash dividends of $0.25 per common share were declared and paid for each quarter of 1968.

Convertible debentures. 4% convertible debentures with a principal amount of $10,000,000 due 1986 were sold for cash at a price of 100 in the last quarter of 1966. Each $100 debenture was convertible into two shares of common stock. No debentures were converted during 1966 or 1967. The entire issue was converted at the beginning of the third quarter of 1968 because the issue was called by the company.

These convertible debentures were not common stock equivalents under the terms of this Opinion. The bank prime rate at the time the debentures were sold in the last quarter of 1966 was 6%. The debentures carried a coupon interest rate of 4% and had a market value of $100 at issuance. The cash yield of 4% was not less than 66 2/3% of the bank prime rate (see paragraph 33 of this Opinion). Cash yield is the same as the coupon interest rate in this case only because the market value at issuance was $100.

Convertible preferred stock. 600,000 shares of convertible preferred stock were issued for assets in a purchase transaction at the beginning of the second quarter of 1967. The annual dividend on each share of this convertible preferred stock is $0.20. Each share is convertible into one share of common stock. This convertible stock had a market value of $53 at the time of issuance and was therefore a common stock equivalent under the terms of this Opinion at the time of its issuance because the cash yield on market value was only 0.4% and the bank prime rate was 5.5% (see paragraph 33 of this Opinion).

Holders of 500,000 shares of this convertible preferred stock converted their preferred stock into common stock during 1968 because the cash dividend on the common stock exceeded the cash dividend on the preferred stock.

Warrants. Warrants to buy 500,000 shares of common stock at $60 per share for a period of five years were issued along with the convertible preferred stock mentioned above. No warrants have been exercised. (Note that the number of shares issuable upon exercise of the warrants is less than 20% of outstanding common shares; hence paragraph 38 is not applicable.)

The number of common shares represented by the warrants (see paragraph 36 of this Opinion) was 71,428 for each of the third and fourth quarters of 1968 ($60 exercise price × 500,000 warrants = $30,000,000; $30,000,000 ÷ $70 share market price = 428,572 shares; 500,000 shares − 428,572 shares = 71,428 shares). No shares were deemed to be represented by the warrants for the second quarter of 1968 or for any preceding quarter (see paragraph 36 of this Opinion) because the market price of the stock did not exceed the exercise price for substantially all of three consecutive months until the third quarter of 1968.

Common stock. The number of shares of common stock outstanding were as follows:

	1968	1967
Beginning of year	3,300,000	3,300,000
Conversion of preferred stock	500,000	—
Conversion of debentures	200,000	—
End of year	4,000,000	3,300,000

Weighted average number of shares. The weighted average number of shares of common stock and common stock equivalents was determined as follows:

	1968	1967
Common stock:		
Shares outstanding from beginning of period	3,300,000	3,300,000
500,000 shares issued on conversion of preferred stock; assume issuance evenly during year	250,000	—
200,000 shares issued on conversion of convertible debentures at beginning of third quarter of 1968	100,000	—
	3,650,000	3,300,000
Common stock equivalents:		
600,000 shares convertible preferred stock issued at the beginning of the second quarter of 1967, excluding 250,000 shares included under common stock in 1968	350,000	450,000
Warrants: 71,428 common share equivalents outstanding for third and fourth quarters of 1968, i.e., one-half year	35,714	—
	385,714	450,000
Weighted average number of shares	4,035,714	3,750,000

The weighted average number of shares would be adjusted to calculate fully diluted earnings per share as follows:

	1968	1967
Weighted average number of shares	4,035,714	3,750,000
Shares applicable to convertible debentures converted at the beginning of the third quarter of 1968, excluding 100,000 shares included under common stock for 1968	100,000	200,000
Shares applicable to warrants included above	(35,714)	—
Shares applicable to warrants based on year-end price of $72 (see paragraph 42 of this Opinion)	83,333	—
	4,183,333	3,950,000

Income before extraordinary item and net income would be adjusted for interest expense on the debentures in calculating fully diluted earnings per share as follows:

| | *Thousands* | | |
	Before adjustment	*Interest, net of tax effect*	*After adjustment*
1967: Net income	$10,300	$208	$10,508
1968:			
Income before extraordinary item	12,900	94	12,994
Net income	13,800	94	13,894

NOTES: (a) Taxes in 1967 were 48%; in 1968 they were 52.8%.

(b) Net income is before dividends on preferred stock.

EXHIBIT B
EXAMPLE OF DISCLOSURE OF EARNINGS PER SHARE
Complex Capital Structure

| | *Thousands Except per share data* | |
(Bottom of Income Statement)	*1968*	*1967*
Income before extraordinary item	$12,900	$10,300
Extraordinary item—gain on sale of property less applicable income taxes	900	—
Net Income	$13,800	$10,300
Earnings per common share and common equivalent share (note X):		
Income before extraordinary item	$ 3.20	$ 2.75
Extraordinary item	.22	—
Net Income	$ 3.42	$ 2.75
Earnings per common share—assuming full dilution (note X):		
Income before extraordinary item	$ 3.11	$ 2.66
Extraordinary item	.21	—
Net Income	$ 3.32	$ 2.66

EXHIBIT C

Example of Note X* to Exhibit B

The $0.20 convertible preferred stock is callable by the company after March 31, 1972 at $53 per share. Each share is convertible into one share of common stock.

During 1968, 700,000 shares of common stock were issued on conversions: 500,000 shares on conversion of preferred stock and 200,000 on conversion of all the 4% convertible debentures.

Warrants to acquire 500,000 shares of the company's stock at $60 per share were outstanding at the end of 1968 and 1967. These warrants expire March 31, 1972.

Earnings per common share and common equivalent share were computed by dividing net income by the weighted average number of shares of common stock and common stock equivalents outstanding during the year. The convertible preferred stock has been considered to be the equivalent of common stock from the time of its issuance in 1967. The number of shares issuable on conversion of preferred stock was added to the number of common shares. The number of common shares was also increased by the number of shares issuable on the exercise of warrants when the market price of the common stock exceeds the exercise price of the warrants. This increase in the number of common shares was reduced by the number of common shares which are assumed to have been purchased with the proceeds from the exercise of the warrants; these purchases were assumed to have been made at the average price of the common stock during that part of the year when the market price of the common stock exceeded the exercise price of the warrants.

Earnings per common share and common equivalent share for 1968 would have been $3.36 for net income and $3.14 for income before extraordinary item had the 4% convertible debentures due 1986 been converted on January 1, 1968. (These debentures were called for redemption as of July 1, 1968 and all were converted into common shares.)

Earnings per common share—assuming full dilution for 1968 were determined on the assumptions that the convertible debentures were converted and the warrants were exercised on January 1, 1968. As to the debentures, net earnings were adjusted for the interest net of its tax effect. As to the warrants, outstanding shares were increased as described above except that purchases of common stock are assumed to have been made at the year-end price of $72.

Earnings per common share—assuming full dilution for 1967 were determined on the assumption that the convertible debentures were converted on January 1, 1967. The outstanding warrants had no effect on the earnings per share data for 1967, as the exercise price was in excess of the market price of the common stock.

Appendix D

DEFINITIONS OF TERMS

There are a number of terms used in discussion of earnings per share which have special meanings in that context. When used in this Opinion they are intended to have the meaning given in the following definitions. Some of the terms are not used in the Opinion but are provided as information pertinent to the subject of earnings per share.

Call price. The amount at which a security may be redeemed by the issuer at the issuer's option.

Cash yield. The cash received by the holder of a security as a distribution of accumulated or current earnings or as a contractual payment for return on the amount invested, without regard to the par or face amount of the security. As used in this Opinion the term "cash yield" refers to the relationship or ratio of such cash to be received annually to the market value of the related security at the specified date. For example, a security with a coupon rate of 4% (on par of $100) and a market value of $80 would have a cash yield of 5%.

---

*The following disclosure in the December 31, 1968 balance sheet is assumed for this note:

	1968	1967
Long-term debt:		
4% convertible debentures, due 1986	—	$10,000,000
Stockholders' equity (note x):		
Convertible voting preferred stock of $1 par value, $0.20 cumulative dividend. Authorized 600,000 shares; issued and outstanding 100,000 shares (600,000 in 1967)	$ 100,000	$ 600,000
(Liquidation value $22 per share, aggregating $2,200,000 in 1968 and $13,200,000 in 1967)		
Common stock of $1 par value per share. Authorized 5,000,000 shares; issued and outstanding 4,000,000 shares (3,300,000 in 1967)	4,000,000	3,300,000
Additional paid-in capital	XXX	XXX
Retained earnings	XXX	XXX
	$XXX	$XXX

Common stock. A stock which is subordinate to all other stocks of the issuer.

Common stock equivalent. A security which, because of its terms or the circumstances under which it was issued, is in substance equivalent to common stock.

Contingent issuance. A possible issuance of shares of common stock that is dependent upon the exercise of conversion rights, options or warrants, the satisfaction of certain conditions, or similar arrangements.

Conversion price. The price that determines the number of shares of common stock into which a security is convertible. For example, $100 face value of debt convertible into 5 shares of common stock would be stated to have a conversion price of $20.

Conversion rate. The ratio of (a) the number of common shares issuable upon conversion to (b) a unit of a convertible security. For example, a preferred stock may be convertible at the rate of 3 shares of common stock for each share of preferred stock.

Conversion value. The current market value of the common shares obtainable upon conversion of a convertible security, after deducting any cash payment required upon conversion.

Dilution (Dilutive). A reduction in earnings per share resulting from the assumption that convertible securities have been converted or that options and warrants have been exercised or other shares have been issued upon the fulfillment of certain conditions. (See footnote 2.)

Dual presentation. The presentation with equal prominence of two types of earnings per share amounts on the face of the income statement—one is primary earnings per share; the other is fully diluted earnings per share.

Earnings per share. The amount of earnings attributable to each share of common stock. For convenience, the term is used in this Opinion to refer to either net income (earnings) per share or to net loss per share. It should be used without qualifying language only when no potentially dilutive convertible securities, options, warrants or other agreements providing for contingent issuances of common stock are outstanding.

Exercise price. The amount that must be paid for a share of common stock upon exercise of a stock option or warrant.

Fully diluted earnings per share. The amount of current earnings per share reflecting the maximum dilution that would have resulted from conversions, exercises and other contingent issuances that individually would have decreased earnings per share and in the aggregate would have had a dilutive effect. All such issuances are assumed to have taken place at the beginning of the period (or at the time the contingency arose, if later).

"If converted" method. A method of computing earnings per share data that assumes conversion of convertible securities as of the beginning of the earliest period reported (or at time of issuance, if later).

Investment value. The price at which it is estimated a convertible security would sell if it were not convertible, based upon its stipulated preferred dividend or interest rate and its other senior security characteristics.

Market parity. A market price relationship in which the market price of a convertible security and its conversion value are approximately equal.

Option. The right to purchase shares of common stock in accordance with an agreement, upon payment of a specified amount. As used in this Opinion, options include but are not limited to options granted to and stock purchase agreements entered into with employees. Options are considered "securities" in this Opinion.

Primary earnings per share. The amount of earnings attributable to each share of common stock outstanding, including common stock equivalents.

Redemption price. The amount at which a security is required to be redeemed at maturity or under a sinking fund arrangement.

Security. The evidence of a debt or ownership or related right. For purposes of this Opinion it includes stock options and warrants, as well as debt and stock.

Senior security. A security having preferential rights and which is not a common stock or common stock equivalent, for example, nonconvertible preferred stock.

Supplementary earnings per share. A computation of earnings per share, other than primary or fully diluted earnings per share, which gives effect to conversions, etc., which took place during the period or shortly thereafter as though they had occurred at the beginning of the period (or date of issuance, if later).

Time of issuance. The time of issuance generally is the date when agreement as to terms has been reached and announced, even though such agreement is subject to certain further actions, such as directors' or stockholders' approval.

Treasury stock method. A method of recognizing the use of proceeds that would be obtained upon exercise of options and warrants in computing earnings per share. It assumes that any proceeds would be used to purchase common stock at current market prices. (See paragraphs 36-38).

"Two-class" method. A method of computing primary earnings per share that treats common stock equivalents as though they were common stocks with different dividend rates from that of the common stock.

Warrant. A security giving the holder the right to purchase shares of common stock in accordance with the terms of the instrument, usually upon payment of a specified amount.

Weighted average number of shares. The number of shares determined by relating (a) the portion of time within a reporting period that a particular number of shares of a certain security has been outstanding to (b) the total time in that period. Thus, for example, if 100 shares of a certain security were outstanding during the first quarter of a fiscal year and 300 shares were outstanding during the balance of the year, the weighted average number of outstanding shares would be 250.

APB Opinion No. 16
Business Combinations

STATUS

Issued: August 1970

Effective Date: For business combinations initiated after October 31, 1970

Affects: Supersedes prospectively ARB 43, Chapter 5, paragraph 10
Supersedes ARB 48
Supersedes ARB 51, paragraphs 7 and 8
Supersedes APB 6, paragraphs 12(c) and 22
Supersedes APB 10, paragraph 5 and footnote 6
Amends APB 11, paragraph 49

Affected by: Paragraph 6 superseded by FAS 71
Paragraph 87 amended by FAS 96 and FAS 109
Paragraph 88 amended by FAS 38, FAS 87, FAS 96, FAS 106, and FAS 109
Paragraph 89 superseded by FAS 96 and FAS 109
Paragraph 96 amended by FAS 79
Paragraph 99 amended by FAS 10
Footnote 13 superseded by FAS 87

Other Interpretive Pronouncements: AIN-APB 16, Interpretations No. 1 through 39
FIN 4
FIN 9
FIN 21
FIN 25 (Superseded by FAS 96 and FAS 109)
FTB 81-2 (Superseded by FAS 96 and FAS 109)
FTB 85-5

APB Opinion No. 16
Business Combinations

CONTENTS

SUMMARY

Problem

1. A business combination occurs when a corporation and one or more incorporated or unincorporated businesses are brought together into one accounting entity. The single entity carries on the activities of the previously separate, independent enterprises.

2. Two methods of accounting for business combinations—"purchase" and "pooling of interests"—have been accepted in practice and supported in pronouncements of the Board and its predecessor, the Committee on Accounting Procedure. The accounting treatment of a combination may affect significantly the reported financial position and net income of the combined corporation for prior, current, and future periods.

3. The Director of Accounting Research of the Amercan Institute of Certified Public Accountants has published two studies on accounting for business combinations and the related goodwill: Accounting Research Study No. 5, *A Critical Study of Accounting for Business Combinations,* by Arthur R. Wyatt and Accounting Research Study No. 10, *Accounting for Goodwill,* by George R. Catlett and Norman O. Olson.[1] The two studies describe the origin and development of the purchase and pooling of interests methods of accounting for business combinations.The studies also cite the supporting authoritative pronouncements and their influences on accounting practices and evaluate the effects of practices on financial reporting.

Scope and Effect of Opinion

4. The Board has considered the conclusions and recommendations of Accounting Research Studies Nos. 5 and 10, the discussions of the need for and appropriateness of the two accepted methods of accounting for business combinations, and proposals for alternative accounting methods. It has also observed the present treatments of combinations in various forms and under differing conditions. The Board expresses in this Opinion its conclusions on accounting for business combinations.

5. This Opinion covers the combination of a corporation and one or more incorporated or unincorporated businesses; both incorporated and unincorporated enterprises are referred to in this Opinion as companies. The conclusions of this Opinion apply equally to business combinations in which one or more companies become subsidiary corporations, one company transfers its net assets to another, and each company transfers its net assets to a newly formed corporation. The acquisition of some or all of the stock held by minority stockholders of a subsidiary is not a business combination, but paragraph 43 of this Opinion specifies the applicable method of accounting. The term business combination in this Opinion excludes a transfer by a corporation of its net assets to a newly formed substitute corporate entity chartered by the existing corporation and a transfer of net assets or exchange of shares between companies under common control (control is described in paragraph 2 of ARB No. 51), such as between a parent corporation and its subsidiary or between two subsidiary corporations of the same parent. This Opinion does not specifically discuss the combination of a corporation and one or more unincorporated businesses or of two or more unincorporated businesses, but its provisions should be applied as a general guide.

6. This Opinion applies to regulated companies in accordance with the provisions of the Addendum to APB Opinion No. 2, *Accounting for the "Investment Credit,"* 1962.

7. The conclusions of this Opinion modify previous views of the Board and its predecessor committee. This Opinion therefore supersedes the following Accounting Research Bulletins (ARB) and Opinions of the Accounting Principles Board (APB):

ARB No. 43, Chapter 5, *Intangible Assets,* paragraph 10.

ARB No. 48, *Business Combinations.*

ARB No. 51, *Consolidated Financial Statements,* paragraphs 7 and 8.

APB Opinion No. 6, *Status of Accounting Research Bulletins,* paragraphs 12c and 22.

APB Opinion No. 10, *Omnibus Opinion— 1966,* paragraph 5.

---

[1]Accounting research studies are not pronouncements of the Board or of the Institute but are published for the purpose of stimulating discussion on important accounting matters.

Since this Opinion supersedes those existing pronouncements, paragraph 87 of this Opinion should be substituted for the reference to ARB No. 51 in paragraph 49 of APB Opinion No. 11.

Conclusions

8. The Board concludes that the purchase method and the pooling of interests method are both acceptable in accounting for business combinations, although not as alternatives in accounting for the same business combination. A business combination which meets specified conditions requires accounting by the pooling of interests method. A new basis of accounting is not permitted for a combination that meets the specified conditions, and the assets and liabilities of the combining companies are combined at their recorded amounts. All other business combinations should be accounted for as an acquisition of one or more companies by a corporation. The cost to an acquiring corporation of an entire acquired company should be determined by the principles of accounting for the acquisition of an asset. That cost should then be allocated to the identifiable individual assets acquired and liabilities assumed based on their fair values; the unallocated cost should be recorded as goodwill.

BACKGROUND

Present Accounting and Its Development

Development of Two Methods

9. Most business combinations before World War II were classified either as a "merger," the acquisition of one company by another, or as a "consolidation," the formation of a new corporation. Accounting for both types of combinations generally followed traditional principles for the acquisition of assets or issuance of shares of stock. The accounting adopted by some new corporations was viewed as a precedent for the combining of retained earnings and of amounts of net assets recorded by predecessor corporations as retained earnings and net assets of a new entity.

10. Emphasis shifted after World War II from the legal form of the combination to distinctions between "a continuance of the former ownership or a new ownership" (ARB No. 40, paragraph 1). New ownership was accounted for as a purchase; continuing ownership was accounted for as a pooling of interests. Carrying forward the stockholders' equity, including retained earnings, of the constituents became an integral part of the pooling of interests method. Significant differences between the purchase and pooling of interests methods accepted today are in the amounts ascribed to assets and liabilities at the time of combination and income reported for the combined enterprise.

Purchase Method[2]

11. The purchase method accounts for a business combination as the acquisition of one company by another. The acquiring corporation records at its cost the acquired assets less liabilities assumed. A difference between the cost of an acquired company and the sum of the fair values of tangible and identifiable intangible assets less liabilities is recorded as goodwill. The reported income of an acquiring corporation includes the operations of the acquired company after acquisition, based on the cost to the acquiring corporation.

Pooling of Interests Method[2]

12. The pooling of interests method accounts for a business combination as the uniting of the ownership interests of two or more companies by exchange of equity securities. No acquisition is recognized because the combination is accomplished without disbursing resources of the constituents. Ownership interests continue and the former bases of accounting are retained. The recorded assets and liabilities of the constituents are carried forward to the combined corporation at their recorded amounts. Income of the combined corporation includes income of the constituents for the entire fiscal period in which the combination occurs. The reported income of the constituents for prior periods is combined and restated as income of combined corporation.

13. The original concept of pooling of interests as a fusion of equity interests was modified in practice as use of the method expanded.[3] The method was first applied in accounting for combinations of affiliated corporations and then extended to some combinations of unrelated corporate ownership interests of comparable size. The method was later accepted for most business combinations in which common

---

[2]This Opinion refers to the "purchase method of accounting" for a business combination because the term is widely used and generally understood. However, the more inclusive terms "acquire" (to come into possession of) and "acquisition" are generally used to describe transactions rather than the more narrow term "purchase" (to acquire by the payment of money or its equivalent). The broader terms clearly encompass obtaining assets by issuing stock as well as by disbursing cash and thus avoid the confusion that results from describing a stock transaction as a "purchase." This Opinion does not describe a business combination accounted for by the pooling of interests method as an "acquisition" because the meaning of the word is inconsistent with the method of accounting.

[3]The origin, development, and application of the pooling of interests method of accounting are traced in Accounting Research Study No. 5 and summarized in Accounting Research Study No. 10.

stock was issued. New and complex securities have been issued in recent business combinations and some combination agreements provide for additional securities to be issued later depending on specified events or circumstances. Most of the resulting combinations are accounted for as poolings of interests. Some combinations effected by both disbursing cash and issuing securities are now accounted for as a "part purchase, part pooling."

14. Some accountants believe that the pooling of interests method is the only acceptable method for a combination which meets the requirements for pooling. Others interpret the existing pronouncements on accounting for business combinations to mean that a combination which meets the criteria for a pooling of interests may alternatively be accounted for as a purchase.

Appraisal of Accepted Methods of Accounting

15. The pooling of interests method of accounting is applied only to business combinations effected by an exchange of stock and not to those involving primarily cash, other assets, or liabilities. Applying the purchase method of accounting to business combinations effected by paying cash, distributing other assets, or incurring liabilities is not challenged. Thus, those business combinations effected primarily by an exchange of equity securities present a question of choice between the two accounting methods.

16. The significantly different results of applying the purchase and pooling of interests methods of accounting to a combination effected by an exchange of stock stem from distinct views of the nature of the transaction itself. Those who endorse the pooling of interests method believe that an exchange of stock to effect a business combination is in substance a transaction between the combining stockholder groups and does not involve the corporate entities. The transaction therefore neither requires nor justifies establishing a new basis of accountability for the assets of the combined corporation. Those who endorse the purchase method believe that the transaction is an issue of stock by a corporation for consideration received from those who become stockholders by the transaction. The consideration received is established by bargaining between independent parties, and the acquiring corporation accounts for the additional assets at their bargained—that is, current—values.

Purchase Method

17. The more important arguments expressing the advantages and disadvantages of the purchase method and some of the practical difficulties experienced in implementing it are summarized in para-

graphs 18 to 26.

18. *An acquisition.* Those who favor the purchase method of accounting believe that one corporation acquires another company in almost every business combination. The acquisition of one company by another and the identities of the acquiring and acquired companies are usually obvious. Generally, one company in a business combination is clearly the dominant and continuing entity and one or more other companies cease to control their own assets and operations because control passes to the acquiring corporation.

19. *A bargained transaction.* Proponents of purchase accounting hold that a business combination is a significant economic event which results from bargaining between independent parties. Each party bargains on the basis of his assessment of the current status and future prospects of each constituent as a separate enterprise and as a contributor to the proposed combined enterprise. The agreed terms of combination recognize primarily the bargained values and only secondarily the costs of assets and liabilities carried by the constituents. In fact, the recorded costs are not always known by the other bargaining party.

20. Accounting by the purchase method is essentially the same whether the business combination is effected by distributing assets, incurring liabilities, or issuing stock because issuing stock is considered an economic event as significant as distributing assets or incurring liabilities. A corporation must ascertain that the consideration it receives for stock issued is fair, just as it must ascertain that fair value is received for cash disbursed. Recipients of the stock similarly appraise the fairness of the transaction. Thus, a business combination is a bargained transaction regardless of the nature of the consideration.

21. *Reporting economic substance.* The purchase method adheres to traditional principles of accounting for the acquisition of assets. Those who support the purchase method of accounting for business combinations effected by issuing stock believe that an acquiring corporation accounts for the economic substance of the transaction by applying those principles and by recording:

a. All assets and liabilities which comprise the bargained cost of an acquired company, not merely those items previously shown in the financial statements of an acquired company.
b. The bargained costs of assets acquired less liabilities assumed, not the costs to a previous owner.
c. The fair value of the consideration received for stock issued, not the equity shown in the financial statements of an acquired company.

d. Retained earnings from its operations, not a fusion of its retained earnings and previous earnings of an acquired company.
e. Expenses and net income after an acquisition computed on the bargained cost of acquired assets less assumed liabilities, not on the costs to a previous owner.

22. *Defects attributed to purchase method.* Applying the purchase method to business combinations effected primarily by issuing stock may entail difficulties in measuring the cost of an acquired company if neither the fair value of the consideration given nor the fair value of the property acquired is clearly evident. Measuring fair values of assets acquired is complicated by the presence of intangible assets or other assets which do not have discernible market prices. Goodwill and other unidentifiable intangible assets are difficult to value directly, and measuring assets acquired for stock is easier if the fair value of the stock issued is determinable. The excess of the value of stock issued over the sum of the fair values of the tangible and identifiable intangible assets acquired less liabilities assumed indicates the value of acquired unidentified intangible assets (usually called goodwill).

23. However, the fair value of stock issued is not always objectively determinable. A market price may not be available for a newly issued security or for securities of a closely held corporation. Even an available quoted market price may not always be a reliable indicator of fair value of consideration received because the number of shares issued is relatively large, the market for the security is thin, the stock price is volatile, or other uncertainties influence the quoted price. Further, the determinable value of one security may not necessarily indicate the fair value of another similar, but not identical, security because their differences affect the value—for example, the absence of registration or an agreement which restricts a holder's ability to sell a security may significantly affect its value.

24. Those who oppose applying the purchase method to some or most business combinations effected by stock also challenge the theoretical merits of the method. They contend that the goodwill acquired is stated only by coincidence at the value which would be determined by direct valuation. The weakness is attributed not to measurement difficulties (direct valuation of goodwill is assumed) but to the basis underlying an exchange of shares of stock. Bargaining in that type of transaction is normally based on the market prices of the equity securities. Market prices of the securities exchanged are more likely to be influenced by anticipated earning capacities of the companies than by evaluations of individual assets. The number of shares of stock issued in a business combina-

tion is thus influenced by values attributed to goodwill of the acquirer as well as goodwill of the acquired company. Since the terms are based on the market prices of both stocks exchanged, measuring the cost of an acquired company by the market price of the stock issued may result in recording acquired goodwill at more or less than its value determined directly.

25. A related argument is that the purchase method is improper accounting for a business combination in which a relatively large number of shares of stock is issued because it records the goodwill and fair values of only the acquired company. Critics of purchase accounting say that each group of stockholders of two publicly held and actively traded companies evaluates the other stock, and the exchange ratio for stock issued is often predicated on relative market values. The stockholders and management of each company evaluate the goodwill and fair values of the other. Purchase accounting is thus viewed as illogical because it records goodwill and values of only one side of the transaction. Those who support this view prefer that assets and liabilities of both companies be combined at existing recorded amounts, but if one side is to be stated at fair values, they believe that both sides should be recorded at fair values.

26. Criticism of the purchase method is directed not only to the theoretical and practical problems of measuring goodwill in combinations effected primarily by stock but also to accounting after the combination for goodwill recorded by the purchase method. Present accounting for goodwill, which often has an indeterminate useful life, is cited as an example of lack of uniformity because selecting among alternative methods of accounting is discretionary.

Pooling of Interests Method

27. The more important arguments expressing the advantages and disadvantages of the pooling of interests method and some of the practical difficulties experienced in implementing it are summarized in paragraphs 28 to 41.

28. *Validity of the concept.* Those who support the pooling of interests method believe that a business combination effected by issuing common stock is different from a purchase in that no corporate assets are disbursed to stockholders and the net assets of the issuing corporation are enlarged by the net assets of the corporation whose stockholders accept common stock of the combined corporation. There is no newly invested capital nor have owners withdrawn assets from the group since the stock of a corporation is not one of its assets. Accordingly, the net assets of the constituents remain intact but com-

bined; the stockholder groups remain intact but combined. Aggregate income is not changed since the total resources are not changed. Consequently, the historical costs and earnings of the separate corporations are appropriately combined. In a business combination effected by exchanging stock, groups of stockholders combine their resources, talents, and risks to form a new entity to carry on in combination the previous businesses and to continue their earnings streams. The sharing of risks by the constituent stockholder groups is an important element in a business combination effected by exchanging stock. By pooling equity interests, each group continues to maintain risk elements of its former investment and they mutually exchange risks and benefits.

29. A pooling of interests transaction is regarded as in substance an arrangement among stockholder groups. The fractional interests in the common enterprise are reallocated—risks are rearranged among the stockholder groups outside the corporate entity. A fundamental concept of entity accounting is that a corporation is separate and distinct from its stockholders. Elected managements represent the stockholders in bargaining to effect a combination, but the groups of stockholders usually decide whether the proposed terms are acceptable by voting to approve or disapprove a combination. Stockholders sometimes disapprove a combination proposed by management, and tender offers sometimes succeed despite the opposition of management.

30. Each stockholder group in a pooling of interests gives up its interests in assets formerly held but receives an interest in a portion of the assets formerly held in addition to an interest in the assets of the other. The clearest example of this type of combination is one in which both groups surrender their stock and receive in exchange stock of a new corporation. The fact that one of the corporations usually issues its stock in exchange for that of the other does not alter the substance of the transaction.

31. *Consistency with other concepts.* Proponents of pooling of interests accounting point out that the pooling concept was developed within the boundaries of the historical-cost system and is compatible with it. Accounting by the pooling of interests method for business combinations arranged through the issuance of common stock is based on existing accounting concepts and is not an occasion for revising historical costs. Both constituents usually have elements of appreciation and of goodwill which are recognized and offset, at least to some extent, in setting a ratio of exchange of stock. The bargaining which occurs usually reflects the relative earning capacities (measured by historical-cost accounts) of the constituents and frequently recog-

nizes the relative market values of the two stocks, which in turn reflect earning capacity, goodwill, or other values. Accounting recognizes the bargaining by means of the new number of shares outstanding distributed in accordance with the bargained ratio, which has a direct effect on earnings per share after the combination.

32. *Usefulness of the concept.* Those who favor the pooling of interests method of accounting believe that the economic substance of a combination is best reflected by reporting operations up to the date of the exchange of stock based on the same historical-cost information used to develop the separate operating results of each constituent. Also, informative comparison with periods prior to the business combination is facilitated by maintaining historical costs as the basis of reporting combined operations subsequent to the combination.

33. *Application of the concept.* It has been observed that criteria for distinguishing between a pooling and a purchase have eroded over the years and that present interpretations of criteria have led to abuse. However, most accountants who support the pooling concept believe that criteria can be redefined satisfactorily to eliminate abuses. It is their view that the pooling of interests method of accounting for business combinations is justifiable on conceptual grounds and is a useful technique and therefore should be retained.

34. Some proponents of pooling of interests accounting support a restriction on the difference in size of combining interests because a significant sharing of risk cannot occur if one combining interest is minor or because a meaningful mutual exchange does not occur if the combination involves a relatively small number of shares. Most, however, believe that there is no conceptual basis for a size restriction and that establishing a size restriction would seriously impair pooling of interests accounting.

35. *Defects attributed to pooling of interests method.* Those who oppose the pooling of interests method of accounting doubt that the method is supported by a concept. In their view it has become essentially a method of accounting for an acquisition of a company without recognizing the current costs of the assets, including goodwill, underlying the transaction. The concept of a pooling of interests was described in general terms in the past—for example, as a continuity of equity interests or as a combination of two or more interests of comparable size. The descriptions tend to be contradictory. For example, accountants do not agree on whether or not relative size is part of the pooling of interests concept. Attempts to define the concept in terms of broad criteria for applying the method have also been unsuccessful.

36. Indeed, many opponents of the pooling of interests method of accounting believe that effective criteria cannot be found. The concept of a uniting or fusing of stockholder groups on which pooling of interests accounting is based implies a broad application of the method because every combination effected by issuing stock rather than by disbursing cash or incurring debt is potentially a pooling of interests unless the combination significantly changes the relative equity interests. However, so broad an application without effective criteria results in applying the pooling of interests method to numerous business combinations which are clearly in economic substance the acquisition of one company by another.

37. Some critics point out that the method was first applied to combining interests of comparable size and that pronouncements on business combinations have never sanctioned applying pooling of interests accounting to all or almost all business combinations effected by exchanging stock. All pronouncements have indicated that a large disparity in the size of the combining interests is evidence that one corporation is acquiring another.

38. Other criteria restricting application of pooling of interests accounting, such as those prohibiting future disposals of stock received and providing for continuity of management, were added to the size restriction. Those criteria have, however, tended to strengthen the view that one corporation acquires another because they are unilateral, that is, they are applied only to the stockholders and management of the "acquired" company.

39. The most serious defect attributed to pooling of interests accounting by those who oppose it is that it does not accurately reflect the economic substance of the business combination transaction. They believe that the method ignores the bargaining which results in the combination by accounting only for the amounts previously shown in accounts of the combining companies. The acquiring corporation does not record assets and values which usually influence the final terms of the combination agreement with consequent effects on subsequent balance sheets and income statements. The combined earnings streams, which are said to continue after a pooling of interests, can continue unchanged only if the cost of the assets producing those earnings is identical for the acquiring corporation and the acquired company. That coincidence rarely occurs because the bargaining is based on current values and not past costs.

40. Pooling of interests accounting is also challenged because the amount of assets acquired less liabilities assumed is recorded without regard to the number of shares of stock issued. The result does not reflect the presumption that a corporation issues stock only for value received and, in general, the greater the number of shares issued, the larger the consideration to be recorded.

41. Traditional principles of accounting for acquisitions of assets encompass all business combinations because every combination is effected by distributing assets, incurring liabilities, issuing stock, or some blend of the three. Those who oppose the pooling of interests method believe that a departure from the traditional principles is justified only if evidence shows that financial statements prepared according to other principles better reflect the economic significance of a combination. In their opinion, the characteristics of a business combination do not justify departing from traditional principles of accounting to accommodate the pooling of interests method.

OPINION

Applicability of Accounting Methods

42. The Board finds merit in both the purchase and pooling of interests methods of accounting for business combinations and accepts neither method to the exclusion of the other. The arguments in favor of the purchase method of accounting are more persuasive if cash or other assets are distributed or liabilities are incurred to effect a combination, but arguments in favor of the pooling of interests method of accounting are more persuasive if voting common stock is issued to effect a combination of common stock interests. Therefore, the Board concludes that some business combinations should be accounted for by the purchase method and other combinations should be accounted for by the pooling of interests method.

43. The Board also concludes that the two methods are not alternatives in accounting for the same business combination. A single method should be applied to an entire combination; the practice now known as part-purchase, part-pooling is not acceptable. The acquisition after the effective date of this Opinion of some or all of the stock held by minority stockholders of a subsidiary—whether acquired by the parent, the subsidiary itself, or another affiliate—should be accounted for by the purchase method rather than by the pooling of interests method.

44. The Board believes that accounting for business combinations will be improved significantly by specifying the circumstances in which each method should be applied and the procedures which should be followed in applying each method. The distinctive conditions which require pooling of interests

accounting are described in paragraphs 45 to 48, and combinations involving all of those conditions should be accounted for as described in paragraphs 50 to 65. All other business combinations should be treated as the acquisition of one company by another and accounted for by the purchase method as described in paragraphs 66 to 96.

Conditions for Pooling of Interests Method

45. The pooling of interests method of accounting is intended to present as a single interest two or more common stockholder interests which were previously independent and the combined rights and risks represented by those interests. That method shows that stockholder groups neither withdraw nor invest assets but in effect exchange voting common stock in a ratio that determines their respective interests in the combined corporation. Some business combinations have those features. A business combination which meets *all* of the conditions specified and explained in paragraphs 46 to 48 should be accounted for by the pooling of interests method. The conditions are classified by (1) attributes of the combining companies, (2) manner of combining interests, and (3) absence of planned transactions.

46. *Combining companies.* Certain attributes of combining companies indicate that independent ownership interests are combined in their entirety to continue previously separate operations. Combining virtually all of existing common stock interests avoids combining only selected assets, operations, or ownership interests, any of which is more akin to disposing of and acquiring interests than to sharing risks and rights. It also avoids combining interests that are already related by substantial intercorporate investments.

The two conditions in this paragraph define essential attributes of combining companies.

a. Each of the combining companies is autonomous and has not been a subsidiary or division of another corporation within two years before the plan of combination is initiated.

A plan of combination is initiated on the earlier of (1) the date that the major terms of a plan, including the ratio of exchange of stock, are announced publicly or otherwise formally made known to the stockholders of any one of the combining companies or (2) the date that stockholders of a combining company are notified in writing of an exchange offer. Therefore, a plan of combination is often initiated even though consummation is subject to the approval of stockholders and others.

A new company incorporated within the preceding two years meets this condition unless the company is successor to a part of a company or to a company that is otherwise not autonomous for this condition. A wholly owned subsidiary company which distributes voting common stock of its parent corporation to effect the combination is also considered an autonomous company provided the parent corporation would have met all conditions in paragraphs 46 to 48 had the parent corporation issued its stock directly to effect the combination.

Divestiture of assets to comply with an order of a governmental authority or judicial body results in an exception to the terms of this condition. Either a subsidiary divested under an order or a new company which acquires assets disposed of under an order is therefore autonomous for this condition.

b. Each of the combining companies is independent of the other combining companies.

This condition means that at the dates the plan of combination is initiated and consummated the combining companies hold as intercorporate investments no more than 10 percent in total of the outstanding voting common stock of any combining company.[4] For the percentage computation, intercorporate investments exclude voting common stock that is acquired after the date the plan of combination is initiated in exchange for the voting common stock issued to effect the combination. Investments of 10 percent or less are explained in paragraph 47-b.

47. *Combining of interests.* The combining of existing voting common stock interests by the exchange of stock is the essence of a business combination accounted for by the pooling of interests method. The separate stockholder interests lose their identities and all share mutually in the combined risks and rights. Exchanges of common stock that alter relative voting rights, that result in preferential claims to distributions of profits or assets for some common stockholder groups, or that leave significant minority interests in combining companies are incompatible with the idea of mutual sharing. Similarly, acquisitions of common stock for assets or debt, reacquisitions of outstanding stock for the purpose of exchanging it in a business combination, and other transactions that reduce the common stock interests are contrary to the idea of combining existing stockholder interests. The seven conditions in this paragraph relate to the exchange to effect the combination.

a. The combination is effected in a single transac-

---

[4]An exception for common stock held on October 31, 1970 is explained in paragraph 99.

tion or is completed in accordance with a specific plan within one year after the plan is initiated.

Altering the terms of exchange of stock constitutes initiation of a new plan of combination unless earlier exchanges of stock are adjusted to the new terms.[5]

A business combination completed in more than one year from the date the plan is initiated meets this condition if the delay is beyond the control of the combining companies because proceedings of a governmental authority or litigation prevents completing the combination.

b. A corporation offers and issues only common stock with rights identical to those of the majority of its outstanding voting common stock[6] in exchange for substantially all of the voting common stock interest of another company at the date the plan of combination is consummated.

The plan to issue voting common stock in exchange for voting common stock may include, within limits, provisions to distribute cash or other consideration for fractional shares, for shares held by dissenting stockholders, and the like but may not include a pro rata distribution of cash or other consideration.

Substantially all of the voting common stock means 90 percent or more for this condition. That is, after the date the plan of combination is initiated, one of the combining companies (issuing corporation) issues voting common stock in exchange for at least 90 percent of the voting common stock of another combining company that is outstanding at the date the combination is consummated. The number of shares exchanged therefore excludes those shares of the combining company (1) acquired before and held by the issuing corporation and its subsidiaries at the date the plan of combination is initiated, regardless of the form of consideration,[7] (2) acquired by the issuing corporation and its subsidiaries after the date the plan of combination is initiated other than by issuing its own voting common stock, and (3) outstanding after the date the combination is consummated.

An investment in stock of the issuing corporation held by a combining company may prevent a combination from meeting this condition even though the investment of the combining company is not more than 10 percent of the outstanding stock of the issuing corporation (paragraph 46-b). An investment in stock of the issuing corporation by another combining company is the same in a mutual exchange as an investment by the issuing corporation in stock of the other combining company—the choice of issuing corporation is essentially a matter of convenience. An investment in stock of the issuing corporation must be expressed as an equivalent number of shares of the investor combining company because the measure of percent of shares exchanged is in terms of shares of stock of the investor company. An investment in 10 percent or less of the outstanding voting common stock of the issuing corporation affects the measure of percent of shares exchanged in the combination as follows:

The number of shares of voting common stock of the issuing corporation held by the investor combining company at the date the plan is initiated plus shares it acquired after that date are restated as an equivalent number of shares of voting common stock of the investor combining company based on the ratio of exchange of stock in the combination.

The equivalent number of shares is deducted from the number of shares of voting common stock of the investor combining company exchanged for voting common stock of the issuing corporation as part of the plan of combination.

The reduced number of shares is considered the number exchanged and is compared with 90 percent of the outstanding voting common stock of the investor combining company at the date the plan is consummated to determine whether the terms of condition 47-b are met.

Since the number of shares of voting common stock exchanged is reduced for an intercorporate investment in voting common stock of the issuing corporation, the terms of condition 47-b may not be met even though 90 percent or more of the outstanding common stock of a combining company is exchanged to effect a combination.

A combination of more than two companies is evaluated essentially the same as a combination of two companies. The percent of voting common stock exchanged is measured separately for each combining company, and condition 47-b is met if 90 percent

---

[5]However, an adjustment after the effective date of this Opinion in the terms of exchange in a plan of combination initiated before and consummated after the effective date always constitutes initiation of a new plan. The one year specified in this condition is measured, therefore, from the date of adjustment of terms and all other conditions are evaluated for the new plan. (Paragraph 97 describes the application of this Opinion to a plan of combination initiated before the effective date of this Opinion and consummated later in accordance with the terms of exchange prevailing on the effective date.)

[6]A class of stock that has voting control of a corporation is the majority class.

[7]An exception for common stock held on October 31, 1970 is explained in paragraph 99.

or more of the voting common stock of each of the several combining companies is exchanged for voting common stock of the issuing corporation. The number of shares exchanged for stock of the issuing corporation includes only shares exchanged by stockholders other than the several combining companies themselves. Thus, intercorporate investments in combining companies are included in the number of shares of stock outstanding but are excluded from the number of shares of stock exchanged to effect the combination.

A new corporation formed to issue its stock to effect the combination of two or more companies meets condition 47-b if (1) the number of shares of each company exchanged to effect the combination is not less than 90 percent of its voting common stock outstanding at the date the combination is consummated and (2) condition 47-b would have been met had any one of the combining companies issued its stock to effect the combination on essentially the same basis.

Condition 47-b relates to issuing common stock for the common stock interests in another company. Hence, a corporation issuing stock to effect the combination may assume the debt securities of the other company or may exchange substantially identical securities or voting common stock for other outstanding equity and debt securities of the other combining company. An issuing corporation may also distribute cash to holders of debt and equity securities that either are callable or redeemable and may retire those securities. However, the issuing corporation may exchange only voting common stock for outstanding equity and debt securities of the other combining company that have been issued in exchange for voting common stock of that company during a period beginning two years preceding the date the combination is initiated.

A transfer of the net assets of a combining company to effect a business combination satisfies condition 47-b provided all net assets of the company at the date the plan is consummated are transferred in exchange for stock of the issuing corporation. However, the combining company may retain temporarily cash, receivables, or marketable securities to settle liabilities, contingencies, or items in dispute if the plan provides that the assets remaining after settlement are to be transferred to the corporation issuing the stock to effect the combination. Only voting common stock may be issued to effect the combination unless both voting common stock and other stock of the other combining company are outstanding at the date the plan is consummated. The combination may then be effected by issuing all voting common stock or by issuing voting common and

other stock in the same proportions as the outstanding voting common and other stock of the other combining company. An investment in 10 percent or less of the outstanding voting common stock of a combining company held by another combining company requires special computations to evaluate condition 47-b. The computations and comparisons are in terms of the voting common stock of the issuing corporation and involve:

Stock issued for common stock interest. The total number of shares of voting common stock issued for all of the assets[8] is divided between those applicable to outstanding voting common stock and those applicable to other outstanding stock, if any, of the combining company which transfers assets (transferor company).

Reduction for intercorporate investments. The number of issued shares of voting common stock applicable to the voting common stock interests of the transferor combining company is reduced by the sum of (1) the number of shares of voting common stock of the issuing corporation held by the transferor combining company at the date the plan of combination is initiated plus shares it acquired after that date and (2) the number of shares of voting common stock of the transferor combining company held by the issuing corporation at the date the plan of combination is initiated plus shares it acquired after that date. The shares of the transferor combining company are restated as the equivalent number of shares of voting common stock of the issuing corporation for this purpose. Restatement is based on the ratio of the number of shares of voting common stock of the transferor combining company which are outstanding at the date the plan is consummated to the number of issued shares of voting common stock applicable to the voting common stock interests.

Comparison with 90 percent. The reduced number of shares of stock issued is compared with 90 percent of the issued number of shares of voting common stock applicable to voting common stock interests to determine if the transfer of assets meets the terms of condition 47-b.

c. None of the combining companies changes the equity interest of the voting common stock in contemplation of effecting the combination either within two years before the plan of combination is initiated or between the dates the combination is initiated and consummated; changes in contemplation of effecting the combination may include distributions to stockholders and additional issuances, exchanges, and retirements of securities.

---

[8]Including (for this computation) stock of the issuing corporation held by the transferor combining company.

Distributions to stockholders which are no greater than normal dividends are not changes for this condition. Normality of dividends is determined in relation to earnings during the period and to the previous dividend policy and record. Dividend distributions on stock of a combining company that are equivalent to normal dividends on the stock to be issued in exchange in the combination are considered normal for this condition.

d. Each of the combining companies reacquires shares of voting common stock only for purposes other than business combinations, and no company reacquires more than a normal number of shares between the dates the plan of combination is initiated and consummated.

Treasury stock acquired for purposes other than business combinations includes shares for stock option and compensation plans and other recurring distributions provided a systematic pattern of reacquisitions is established at least two years before the plan of combination is initiated. A systematic pattern of reacquisitions may be established for less than two years if it coincides with the adoption of a new stock option or compensation plan. The normal number of shares of voting common stock reacquired is determined by the pattern of reacquisitions of stock before the plan of combination is initiated.

Acquisitions by other combining companies of voting common stock of the issuing corporation after the date the plan of combination is initiated are essentially the same as if the issuing corporation reacquired its own common stock.

e. The ratio of the interest of an individual common stockholder to those of other common stockholders in a combining company remains the same as a result of the exchange of stock to effect the combination.

This condition means that each individual common stockholder who exchanges his stock receives a voting common stock interest exactly in proportion to his relative voting common stock interest before the combination is effected. Thus no common stockholder is denied or surrenders his potential share of a voting common stock interest in a combined corporation.

f. The voting rights to which the common stock ownership interests in the resulting combined corporation are entitled are exercisable by the stockholders; the stockholders are neither deprived of nor restricted in exercising those rights for a period.

This condition is not met, for example, if shares of common stock issued to effect the combination are transferred to a voting trust.

g. The combination is resolved at the date the plan is consummated and no provisions of the plan relating to the issue of securities or other consideration are pending.

This condition means that (1) the combined corporation does not agree to contingently issue additional shares of stock or distribute other consideration at a later date to the former stockholders of a combining company or (2) the combined corporation does not issue or distribute to an escrow agent common stock or other consideration which is to be either transferred to common stockholders or returned to the corporation at the time the contingency is resolved.

An agreement may provide, however, that the number of shares of common stock issued to effect the combination may be revised for the later settlement of a contingency at a different amount than that recorded by a combining company.

48. *Absence of planned transactions.* Some transactions after a combination is consummated are inconsistent with the combining of entire existing interests of common stockholders. Including those transactions in the negotiations and terms of the combination, either explicitly or by intent, counteracts the effect of combining stockholder interests. The three conditions in this paragraph relate to certain future transactions.

a. The combined corporation does not agree directly or indirectly to retire or reacquire all or part of the common stock issued to effect the combination.

b. The combined corporation does not enter into other financial arrangements for the benefit of the former stockholders of a combining company, such as a guaranty of loans secured by stock issued in the combination, which in effect negates the exchange of equity securities.

c. The combined corporation does not intend or plan to dispose of a significant part of the assets of the combining companies within two years after the combination other than disposals in the ordinary course of business of the formerly separate companies and to eliminate duplicate facilities or excess capacity.

Subsidiary Corporation

49. Dissolution of a combining company is not a condition for applying the pooling of interests method of accounting for a business combination. One or more combining companies may be subsidiaries of the issuing corporation after the combination is consummated if the other conditions are met.

Application of Pooling of Interests Method

50. A business combination which meets all of the

conditions in paragraphs 45 to 48 should be accounted for by the pooling of interests method. Appropriate procedures are described in paragraphs 51 to 65.

Assets and Liabilities Combined

51. The recorded assets and liabilities of the separate companies generally become the recorded assets and liabilities of the combined corporation. The combined corporation therefore recognizes those assets and liabilities recorded in conformity with generally accepted accounting principles by the separate companies at the date the combination is consummated.

52. The combined corporation records the historical-cost based amounts of the assets and liabilities of the separate companies because the existing basis of accounting continues. However, the separate companies may have recorded assets and liabilities under differing methods of accounting and the amounts may be adjusted to the same basis of accounting if the change would otherwise have been appropriate for the separate company. A change in accounting method to conform the individual methods should be applied retroactively, and financial statements presented for prior periods should be restated.

Stockholders' Equity Combined

53. The stockholders' equities of the separate companies are also combined as a part of the pooling of interests method of accounting. The combined corporation records as capital the capital stock and capital in excess of par or stated value of outstanding stock of the separate companies. Similarly, retained earnings or deficits of the separate companies are combined and recognized as retained earnings of the combined corporation (paragraph 56). The amount of outstanding shares of stock of the combined corporation at par or stated value may exceed the total amount of capital stock of the separate combining companies; the excess should be deducted first from the combined other contributed capital and then from the combined retained earnings. The combined retained earnings could be misleading if shortly before or as a part of the combination transaction one or more of the combining companies adjusted the elements of stockholders' equity to eliminate a deficit; therefore, the elements of equity before the adjustment should be combined.

54. A corporation which effects a combination accounted for by the pooling of interests method by distributing stock previously acquired as treasury stock (paragraph 47-d) should first account for those shares of stock as though retired. The issuance of the shares for the common stock interests of the

combining company is then accounted for the same as the issuance of previously unissued shares.

55. Accounting for common stock of one of the combining companies which is held by another combining company at the date a combination is consummated depends on whether the stock is the same as that which is issued to effect the combination or is the same as the stock which is exchanged in the combination. An investment of a combining company in the common stock of the issuing corporation is in effect returned to the resulting combined corporation in the combination. The combined corporation should account for the investment as treasury stock. In contrast, an investment in the common stock of other combining companies (not the one issuing stock in the combination) is an investment in stock that is exchanged in the combination for the common stock issued. The stock in that type of intercorporate investment is in effect eliminated in the combination. The combined corporation should account for that investment as stock retired as part of the combination.

Reporting Combined Operations

56. A corporation which applies the pooling of interests method of accounting to a combination should report results of operations for the period in which the combination occurs as though the companies had been combined as of the beginning of the period. Results of operations for that period thus comprise those of the separate companies combined from the beginning of the period to the date the combination is consummated and those of the combined operations from that date to the end of the period. Eliminating the effects of intercompany transactions from operations before the date of combination reports operations before and after the date of combination on substantially the same basis. The effects of intercompany transactions on current assets, current liabilities, revenue, and cost of sales for periods presented and on retained earnings at the beginning of the periods presented should be eliminated to the extent possible. The nature of and effects on earnings per share of nonrecurring intercompany transactions involving long-term assets and liabilities need not be eliminated but should be disclosed. A combined corporation should disclose in notes to financial statements the revenue, extraordinary items, and net income of each of the separate companies from the beginning of the period to the date the combination is consummated (paragraph 64-d). The information relating to the separate companies may be as of the end of the interim period nearest the date that the combination is consummated.

57. Similarly, balance sheets and other financial information of the separate companies as of the

beginning of the period should be presented as though the companies had been combined at that date. Financial statements and financial information of the separate companies presented for prior years should also be restated on a combined basis to furnish comparative information. All restated financial statements and financial summaries should indicate clearly that financial data of the previously separate companies are combined.

Expenses Related to Combination

58. The pooling of interests method records neither the acquiring of assets nor the obtaining of capital. Therefore, costs incurred to effect a combination accounted for by that method and to integrate the continuing operations are expenses of the combined corporation rather than additions to assets or direct reductions of stockholders' equity. Accordingly, all expenses related to effecting a business combination accounted for by the pooling of interests method should be deducted in determining the net income of the resulting combined corporation for the period in which the expenses are incurred. Those expenses include, for example, registration fees, costs of furnishing information to stockholders, fees of finders and consultants, salaries and other expenses related to services of employees, and costs and losses of combining operations of the previously separate companies and instituting efficiencies.

Disposition of Assets After Combination

59. A combined corporation may dispose of those assets of the separate companies which are duplicate facilities or excess capacity in the combined operations. Losses or estimated losses on disposal of specifically identified duplicate or excess facilities should be deducted in determining the net income of the resulting combined corporation. However, a loss estimated and recorded while a facility remains in service should not include the portion of the cost that is properly allocable to anticipated future service of the facility.

60. Profit or loss on other dispositions of assets of the previously separate companies may require special disclosure unless the disposals are part of customary business activities of the combined corporation. Specific treatment of a profit or loss on those dispositions is warranted because the pooling of interests method of accounting would have been inappropriate (paragraph 48-c) if the combined corporation were committed or planned to dispose of a significant part of the assets of one of the combining companies. The Board concludes that a combined corporation should disclose separately a profit or loss resulting from the disposal of a significant part of the assets or a separable segment of the previously separate companies, provided

the profit or loss is material in relation to the net income of the combined corporation, and

the disposition is within two years after the combination is consummated.

The disclosed profit or loss, less applicable income tax effect, should be classified as an extraordinary item.

Date of Recording Combination

61. A business combination accounted for by the pooling of interests method should be recorded as of the date the combination is consummated. Therefore, even though a business combination is consummated before one or more of the combining companies first issues its financial statements as of an earlier date, the financial statements issued should be those of the combining company and not those of the resulting combined corporation. A combining company should, however, disclose as supplemental information, in notes to financial statements or otherwise, the substance of a combination consummated before financial statements are issued and the effects of the combination on reported financial position and results of operations (paragraph 65). Comparative financial statements presented in reports of the resulting combined corporation after a combination is consummated should combine earlier financial statements of the separate companies.

62. A corporation may be reasonably assured that a business combination which has been initiated but not consummated as of the date of financial statements will meet the conditions requiring the pooling of interests method of accounting. The corporation should record as an investment common stock of the other combining company acquired before the statement date. Common stock acquired by disbursing cash or other assets or by incurring liabilities should be recorded at cost. Stock acquired in exchange for common stock of the issuing corporation should, however, be recorded at the proportionate share of underlying net assets at the date acquired as recorded by the other company. Until the pooling of interests method of accounting for the combination is known to be appropriate, the investment and net income of the investor corporation should include the proportionate share of earnings or losses of the other company after the date of acquisition of the stock. The investor corporation should also disclose results of operations for all prior periods presented as well as the entire current period as they will be reported if the combination is later accounted for by the pooling of interests

method. After the combination is consummated and the applicable method of accounting is known, financial statements issued previously should be restated as necessary to include the other combining company.

Disclosure of a Combination

63. A combined corporation should disclose in its financial statements that a combination which is accounted for by the pooling of interests method has occurred during the period. The basis of current presentation and restatements of prior periods may be disclosed in the financial statements by captions or by references to notes.

64. Notes to financial statements of a combined corporation should disclose the following for the period in which a business combination occurs and is accounted for by the pooling of interests method.

a. Name and brief description of the companies combined, except a corporation whose name is carried forward to the combined corporation.
b. Method of accounting for the combination— that is, by the pooling of interests method.
c. Description and number of shares of stock issued in the business combination.
d. Details of the results of operations of the previously separate companies for the period before the combination is consummated that are included in the current combined net income (paragraph 56). The details should include revenue, extraordinary items, net income, other changes in stockholders' equity, and amount of and manner of accounting for intercompany transactions.
e. Descriptions of the nature of adjustments of net assets of the combining companies to adopt the same accounting practices and of the effects of the changes on net income reported previously by the separate companies and now presented in comparative financial statements (paragraph 52).
f. Details of an increase or decrease in retained earnings from changing the fiscal year of a combining company. The details should include at least revenue, expenses, extraordinary items, net income, and other changes in stockholders' equity for the period excluded from the reported results of operations.
g. Reconciliations of amounts of revenue and earnings previously reported by the corporation that issues the stock to effect the combination with the combined amounts currently presented in financial statements and summaries. A new corporation formed to effect a combination may instead disclose the earnings of the separate companies which comprise combined earnings for prior periods.

The information disclosed in notes to financial statements should also be furnished on a pro forma basis in information on a proposed business combination which is given to stockholders of combining companies.

65. Notes to the financial statements should disclose details of the effects of a business combination consummated before the financial statements are issued but which is either incomplete as of the date of the financial statements or initiated after that date (paragraph 61). The details should include revenue, net income, earnings per share, and the effects of anticipated changes in accounting methods as if the combination had been consummated at the date of the financial statements (paragraph 52).

Application of Purchase Method

Principles of Historical-Cost Accounting

66. Accounting for a business combination by the purchase method follows principles normally applicable under historical-cost accounting to recording acquisitions of assets and issuances of stock and to accounting for assets and liabilities after acquisition.

67. *Acquiring assets.* The general principles to apply the historical-cost basis of accounting to an acquisition of an asset depend on the nature of the transaction:

a. An asset acquired by exchanging cash or other assets is recorded at cost—that is, at the amount of cash disbursed or the fair value of other assets distributed.
b. An asset acquired by incurring liabilities is recorded at cost—that is, at the present value of the amounts to be paid.
c. An asset acquired by issuing shares of stock of the acquiring corporation is recorded at the fair value of the asset[9]—that is, shares of stock issued are recorded at the fair value of the consideration received for the stock.

The general principles must be supplemented to apply them in certain transactions. For example, the fair value of an asset received for stock issued may not be reliably determinable, or the fair value of an asset acquired in an exchange may be more reliably determinable than the fair value of a noncash asset given up. Restraints on measurement have led to the practical rule that assets acquired for other than cash, including shares of stock issued, should be stated at "cost" when they are acquired and "cost"

---

[9]An asset acquired may be an entire entity which may have intangible assets, including goodwill.

may be determined either by the fair value of the consideration given or by the fair value of the property acquired, whichever is the more clearly evident."[10] "Cost" in accounting often means the amount at which an entity records an asset at the date it is acquired whatever its manner of acquisition, and that "cost" forms the basis for historical-cost accounting.

68. *Allocating cost.* Acquiring assets in groups requires not only ascertaining the cost of the assets as a group but also allocating the cost to the individual assets which comprise the group. The cost of a group is determined by the principles described in paragraph 67. A portion of the total cost is then assigned to each individual asset acquired on the basis of its fair value. A difference between the sum of the assigned costs of the tangible and identifiable intangible assets acquired less liabilities assumed and the cost of the group is evidence of unspecified intangible values.

69. *Accounting after acquisition.* The nature of an asset and not the manner of its acquisition determines an acquirer's subsequent accounting for the cost of that asset. The basis for measuring the cost of an asset—whether amount of cash paid, fair value of an asset received or given up, amount of a liability incurred, or fair value of stock issued—has no effect on the subsequent accounting for that cost, which is retained as an asset, depreciated, amortized, or otherwise matched with revenue.

Acquiring Corporation

70. A corporation which distributes cash or other assets or incurs liabilities to obtain the assets or stock of another company is clearly the acquirer. The identities of the acquirer and the acquired company are usually evident in a business combination effected by the issue of stock. The acquiring corporation normally issues the stock and commonly is the larger company. The acquired company may, however, survive as the corporate entity, and the nature of the negotiations sometimes clearly indicates that a smaller corporation acquires a larger company. The Board concludes that presumptive evidence of the acquiring corporation in combinations effected by an exchange of stock is obtained by identifying the former common stockholder interests of a combining company which either retain or receive the larger portion of the voting rights in the combined corporation. That corporation should be treated as the acquirer unless other evidence clearly indicates that another corporation is the acquirer. For example, a substantial investment of one company in common stock of another before the combination may be evidence that the investor is the acquiring corporation.

71. If a new corporation is formed to issue stock to effect a business combination to be accounted for by the purchase method, one of the existing combining companies should be considered the acquirer on the basis of the evidence available.

Determining Cost of an Acquired Company

72. The same accounting principles apply to determining the cost of assets acquired individually, those acquired in a group, and those acquired in a business combination. A cash payment by a corporation measures the cost of acquired assets less liabilities assumed. Similarly, the fair values of other assets distributed, such as marketable securities or properties, and the fair value of liabilities incurred by an acquiring corporation measure the cost of an acquired company. The present value of a debt security represents the fair value of the liability, and a premium or discount should be recorded for a debt security issued with an interest rate fixed materially above or below the effective rate or current yield for an otherwise comparable security.

73. The distinctive attributes of preferred stocks make some issues similar to a debt security while others possess common stock characteristics, with many gradations between the extremes. Determining cost of an acquired company may be affected by those characteristics. For example, the fair value of a nonvoting, nonconvertible preferred stock which lacks characteristics of common stock may be determined by comparing the specified dividend and redemption terms with comparable securities and by assessing market factors. Thus although the principle of recording the fair value of consideration received for stock issued applies to all equity securities, senior as well as common stock, the cost of a company acquired by issuing senior equity securities may be determined in practice on the same basis as for debt securities.

74. The fair value of securities traded in the market is normally more clearly evident than the fair value of an acquired company (paragraph 67). Thus, the quoted market price of an equity security issued to effect a business combination may usually be used to approximate the fair value of an acquired company after recognizing possible effects of price fluctuations, quantities traded, issue costs, and the like (paragraph 23). The market price for a reasonable period before and after the date the terms of the acquisition are agreed to and announced should be considered in determining the fair value of securities issued.

75. If the quoted market price is not the fair value of stock, either preferred or common, the consideration received should be estimated even though

---

[10]ARB No. 24; the substance was retained in slightly different words in Chapter 5 of ARB No. 43 and ARB No. 48.

measuring directly the fair values of assets received is difficult. Both the consideration received, including goodwill, and the extent of the adjustment of the quoted market price of the stock issued should be weighed to determine the amount to be recorded. All aspects of the acquisition, including the negotiations, should be studied, and independent appraisals may be used as an aid in determining the fair value of securities issued. Consideration other than stock distributed to effect an acquisition may provide evidence of the total fair value received.

76. *Costs of acquisition.* The cost of a company acquired in a business combination accounted for by the purchase method includes the direct costs of acquisition. Costs of registering and issuing equity securities are a reduction of the otherwise determinable fair value of the securities. However, indirect and general expenses related to acquisitions are deducted as incurred in determining net income.

Contingent Consideration

77. A business combination agreement may provide for the issuance of additional shares of a security or the transfer of cash or other consideration contingent on specified events or transactions in the future. Some agreements provide that a portion of the consideration be placed in escrow to be distributed or to be returned to the transferor when specified events occur. Either debt or equity securities may be placed in escrow, and amounts equal to interest or dividends on the securities during the contingency period may be paid to the escrow agent or to the potential security holder.

78. The Board concludes that cash and other assets distributed and securities issued unconditionally and amounts of contingent consideration which are determinable at the date of acquisition should be included in determining the cost of an acquired company and recorded at that date. Consideration which is issued or issuable at the expiration of the contingency period or which is held in escrow pending the outcome of the contingency should be disclosed but not recorded as a liability or shown as outstanding securities unless the outcome of the contingency is determinable beyond reasonable doubt.

79. Contingent consideration should usually be recorded when the contingency is resolved and consideration is issued or becomes issuable. In general, the issue of additional securities or distribution of other consideration at resolution of contingencies based on earnings should result in an additional element of cost of an acquired company. In contrast, the issue of additional securities or distribution of other consideration at resolution of contingencies based on security prices should not change the recorded cost of an acquired company.

80. *Contingency based on earnings.* Additional consideration may be contingent on maintaining or achieving specified earnings levels in future periods. When the contingency is resolved and additional consideration is distributable, the acquiring corporation should record the current fair value of the consideration issued or issuable as additional cost of the acquired company. The additional costs of affected assets, usually goodwill, should be amortized over the remaining life of the asset.

81. *Contingency based on security prices.* Additional consideration may be contingent on the market price of a specified security issued to effect a business combination. Unless the price of the security at least equals the specified amount on a specified date or dates, the acquiring corporation is required to issue additional equity or debt securities or transfer cash or other assets sufficient to make the current value of the total consideration equal to the specified amount. The securities issued unconditionally at the date the combination is consummated should be recorded at that date at the specified amount.

82. The cost of an acquired company recorded at the date of acquisition represents the entire payment, including contingent consideration. Therefore, the issuance of additional securities or distribution of other consideration does not affect the cost of the acquired company, regardless of whether the amount specified is a security price to be maintained or a higher security price to be achieved. On a later date when the contingency is resolved and additional consideration is distributable, the acquiring corporation should record the current fair value of the additional consideration issued or issuable. However, the amount previously recorded for securities issued at the date of acquisition should simultaneously be reduced to the lower current value of those securities. Reducing the value of debt securities previously issued to their later fair value results in recording a discount on debt securities. The discount should be amortized from the date the additional securities are issued.

83. Accounting for contingent consideration based on conditions other than those described should be inferred from the procedures outlined. For example, if the consideration contingently issuable depends on both future earnings and future security prices, additional cost of the acquired company should be recorded for the additional consideration contingent on earnings, and previously recorded consideration should be reduced to current value of the consideration contingent on security prices. Similarly, if the consideration contingently issuable depends on later settlement of a contingency, an increase in the cost of acquired assets, if any, should be amortized over the remaining life of the assets.

84. *Interest or dividends during contingency period.* Amounts paid to an escrow agent representing interest and dividends on securities held in escrow should be accounted for according to the accounting for the securities. That is, until the disposition of the securities in escrow is resolved, payments to the escrow agent should not be recorded as interest expense or dividend distributions. An amount equal to interest and dividends later distributed by the escrow agent to the former stockholders should be added to the cost of the acquired assets at the date distributed and amortized over the remaining life of the assets.

85. *Tax effect of imputed interest.* A tax reduction resulting from imputed interest on contingently issuable stock reduces the fair value recorded for contingent consideration based on earnings and increases additional capital recorded for contingent consideration based on security prices.

86. *Compensation in contingent agreements.* The substance of some agreements for contingent consideration is to provide compensation for services or use of property or profit sharing, and the additional consideration given should be accounted for as expenses of the appropriate periods.

Recording Assets Acquired and Liabilities Assumed

87. An acquiring corporation should allocate the cost of an acquired company to the assets acquired and liabilities assumed. Allocation should follow the principles described in paragraph 68.

First, all identifiable assets acquired, either individually or by type, and liabilities assumed in a business combination, whether or not shown in the financial statements of the acquired company, should be assigned a portion of the cost of the acquired company, normally equal to their fair values at date of acquisition.

Second, the excess of the cost of the acquired company over the sum of the amounts assigned to identifiable assets acquired less liabilities assumed should be recorded as goodwill. The sum of the market or appraisal values of identifiable assets acquired less liabilities assumed may sometimes exceed the cost of the acquired company. If so, the values otherwise assignable to noncurrent assets acquired (except long-term investments in marketable securities) should be reduced by a proportionate part of the excess to determine the assigned values. A deferred credit for an excess of assigned value of identifiable assets over cost of an acquired company (sometimes called "negative goodwill") should not be recorded unless those assets are reduced to zero value.

Independent appraisals may be used as an aid in determining the fair values of some assets and liabilities. Subsequent sales of assets may also provide evidence of values. The effect of taxes may be a factor in assigning amounts to identifiable assets and liabilities (paragraph 89).

88. General guides for assigning amounts to the individual assets acquired and liabilities assumed, except goodwill, are:

a. Marketable securities at current net realizable values.
b. Receivables at present values of amounts to be received determined at appropriate current interest rates, less allowances for uncollectibility and collection costs, if necessary.
c. Inventories:
   (1) Finished goods and merchandise at estimated selling prices less the sum of (a) costs of disposal and (b) a reasonable profit allowance for the selling effort of the acquiring corporation.
   (2) Work in process at estimated selling prices of finished goods less the sum of (a) costs to complete, (b) costs of disposal, and (c) a reasonable profit allowance for the completing and selling effort of the acquiring corporation based on profit for similar finished goods.
   (3) Raw materials at current replacement costs.
d. Plant and equipment: (1) to be used, at current replacement costs for similar capacity[11] unless the expected future use of the assets indicates a lower value to the acquirer, (2) to be sold or held for later sale rather than used, at current net realizable value, and (3) to be used temporarily, at current net realizable value recognizing future depreciation for the expected period of use.
e. Intangible assets which can be identified and named, including contracts, patents, franchises, customer and supplier lists, and favorable leases, at appraised values.[12]
f. Other assets, including land, natural resources, and nonmarketable securities, at appraised values.
g. Accounts and notes payable, long-term debt, and other claims payable at present values of amounts to be paid determined at appropriate current interest rates.
h. Liabilities and accruals—for example, accruals

---

[11]Replacement cost may be determined directly if a used asset market exists for the assets acquired. Otherwise, the replacement cost should be approximated from replacement cost new less estimated accumulated depreciation.

[12]Fair values should be ascribed to specific assets; identifiable assets should not be included in goodwill.

for pension cost,[13] warranties, vacation pay, deferred compensation—at present values of amounts to be paid determined at appropriate current interest rates.

i. Other liabilities and commitments, including unfavorable leases, contracts, and commitments and plant closing expense incident to the acquisition, at present values of amounts to be paid determined at appropriate current interest rates.

An acquiring corporation should record periodically as a part of income the accrual of interest on assets and liabilities recorded at acquisition date at the discounted values of amounts to be received or paid. An acquiring corporation should not record as a separate asset the goodwill previously recorded by an acquired company and should not record deferred income taxes recorded by an acquired company before its acquisition. An acquiring corporation should reduce the acquired goodwill retroactively for the realized tax benefits of loss carryforwards of an acquired company not previously recorded by the acquiring corporation.

89. The market or appraisal values of specific assets and liabilities determined in paragraph 88 may differ from the income tax bases of those items. Estimated future tax effects of differences between the tax bases and amounts otherwise appropriate to assign to an asset or a liability are one of the variables in estimating fair value. Amounts assigned to identifiable assets and liabilities should, for example, recognize that the fair value of an asset to an acquirer is less than its market or appraisal value if all or a portion of the market or appraisal value is not deductible for income taxes. The impact of tax effects on amounts assigned to individual assets and liabilities depends on numerous factors, including imminence or delay of realization of the asset value and the possible timing of tax consequences. Since differences between amounts assigned and tax bases are not timing differences (APB Opinion No. 11, *Accounting for Income Taxes,* paragraph 13), the acquiring corporation should not record deferred tax accounts at the date of acquisition.

Amortization of Goodwill

90. Goodwill recorded in a business combination accounted for by the purchase method should be amortized in accordance with the provisions in paragraphs 27 to 31 of APB Opinion No. 17, *Intangible Assets*.

Excess of Acquired Net Assets Over Cost

91. The value assigned to net assets acquired should not exceed the cost of an acquired company because the general presumption in historical-cost based accounting is that net assets acquired should be recorded at not more than cost. The total market or appraisal values of identifiable assets acquired less liabilities assumed in a few business combinations may exceed the cost of the acquired company. An excess over cost should be allocated to reduce proportionately the values assigned to noncurrent assets (except long-term investments in marketable securities) in determining their fair values (paragraph 87). If the allocation reduces the noncurrent assets to zero value, the remainder of the excess over cost should be classified as a deferred credit and should be amortized systematically to income over the period estimated to be benefited but not in excess of forty years. The method and period of amortization should be disclosed.

92. No part of the excess of acquired net assets over cost should be added directly to stockholders' equity at the date of acquisition.

Acquisition Date

93. The Board believes that the date of acquisition of a company should ordinarily be the date assets are received and other assets are given or securities are issued. However, the parties may for convenience designate as the effective date the end of an accounting period between the dates a business combination is initiated and consummated. The designated date should ordinarily be the date of acquisition for accounting purposes if a written agreement provides that effective control of the acquired company is transferred to the acquiring corporation on that date without restrictions except those required to protect the stockholders or other owners of the acquired company—for example, restrictions on significant changes in the operations, permission to pay dividends equal to those regularly paid before the effective date, and the like. Designating an effective date other than the date assets or securities are transferred requires adjusting the cost of an acquired company and net income otherwise reported to compensate for recognizing income before consideration is transferred. The cost of an acquired company and net income should therefore be reduced by imputed interest at an appropriate current rate on assets given, liabilities incurred, or preferred stock distributed as of the transfer date to acquire the company.

94. The cost of an acquired company and the values assigned to assets acquired and liabilities assumed should be determined as of the date of acquisition. The statement of income of an acquiring corpora-

---

[13]An accrual for pension cost should be the greater of (1) accrued pension cost computed in conformity with the accounting policies of the acquiring corporation for one or more of its pension plans or (2) the excess, if any, of the actuarially computed value of vested benefits over the amount of the pension fund.

tion for the period in which a business combination occurs should include income of the acquired company after the date of acquisition by including the revenue and expenses of the acquired operations based on the cost to the acquiring corporation.

Disclosure in Financial Statements

95. Notes to the financial statements of an acquiring corporation should disclose the following for the period in which a business combination occurs and is accounted for by the purchase method.

a. Name and a brief description of the acquired company.
b. Method of accounting for the combination— that is, by the purchase method.
c. Period for which results of operations of the acquired company are included in the income statement of the acquiring corporation.
d. Cost of the acquired company and, if applicable, the number of shares of stock issued or issuable, and the amount assigned to the issued and issuable shares.
e. Description of the plan for amortization of acquired goodwill, the amortization method, and period (APB Opinion No. 17, paragraphs 27 to 31).
f. Contingent payments, options, or commitments specified in the acquisition agreement and their proposed accounting treatment.

Information relating to several relatively minor acquisitions may be combined for disclosure.

96. Notes to the financial statements of the acquiring corporation for the period in which a business combination occurs and is accounted for by the purchase method should include as supplemental information the following results of operations on a pro forma basis:

a. Results of operations for the current period as though the companies had combined at the beginning of the period, unless the acquisition was at or near the beginning of the period.
b. Results of operations for the immediately preceding period as though the companies had combined at the beginning of that period if comparative financial statements are presented.

The supplemental pro forma information should as a minimum show revenue, income before extraordinary items, net income, and earnings per share. To present pro forma information, income taxes, interest expense, preferred stock dividends, depreciation and amortization of assets, including

goodwill, should be adjusted to their accounting bases recognized in recording the combination. Pro forma presentation of results of operations of periods prior to the combination transaction should be limited to the immediately preceding period.

EFFECTIVE DATE

97. The provisions of this Opinion shall be effective to account for business combinations initiated[14] after October 31, 1970. Business combinations initiated before November 1, 1970 and consummated on or after that date under the terms prevailing on October 31, 1970 (paragraph 47-a) may be accounted for in accordance with this Opinion or the applicable previous pronouncements of the Board and its predecessor committee.

98. The provisions of this Opinion should not be applied retroactively for business combinations consummated before November 1, 1970.

99. If a corporation holds as an investment on October 31, 1970 a minority interest in or exactly 50 percent of the common stock of another company and the corporation initiates after October 31, 1970 a plan of combination with that company, the resulting business combination may be accounted for by the pooling of interests method provided

the combination is completed within five years after October 31, 1970 and
the combination meets all conditions specified in paragraphs 45 to 48, except that
  (i) the minority interest in the voting common stock of the combining company held on October 31, 1970 may exceed 10 percent of the outstanding voting common stock of the combining company (paragraph 46-b), and
  (ii) the corporation which effects the combination issues voting common stock for at least 90 percent of the outstanding voting common stock interest, as described in paragraph 47-b, of the other combining company not already held on October 31, 1970 (rather than 90 percent of all of the common stock interest of the combining company).

The investment in common stock held on October 31, 1970 should not be accounted for as treasury stock or retired stock at the date of the combination. Instead, the excess of cost over the investor corporation's proportionate equity in the net assets of the combining company at or near the date the stock investment was acquired should be allocated to identifiable assets of the combining company at the

[14]Initiated is defined in paragraph 46-a whether the combination is accounted for by the pooling of interests method or by the purchase method.

date the combination is consummated on the basis of the fair values of those assets at the combination date. The unallocated portion of the excess should be assigned to an unidentified intangible asset (goodwill) and should be accounted for according to applicable previous pronouncements of the Board and its predecessor committee. The cost of goodwill should not be amortized retroactively but may be amortized prospectively under the provision of APB Opinion No. 17, paragraph 35. If the cost of the investment is less than the investor's equity in the net assets of the combining company, that difference should reduce proportionately the recorded amounts of noncurrent assets (except long-term investments in marketable securities) of the combining company.

The Opinion entitled "Business Combinations" was adopted by the assenting votes of twelve members of the Board. Messrs. Broeker, Burger, Davidson, Horngren, Seidman, and Weston dissented.

Messrs. Broeker, Burger, and Weston dissent to issuance of this Opinion because they believe that it is not a sound or logical solution of the problem of accounting for business combinations. They believe that, except for combinations of companies whose relative size is such as to indicate a significant sharing of ownership risks and benefits, business combinations represent the acquisition or purchase of one company by another and that accounting should reflect that fact. While they agree that the criteria specified in this Opinion for the pooling of interests method represent, in most cases, an improvement over present criteria in practice, this action does not, in their opinion, represent a substantive response by the Accounting Principles Board to the overall problem.

Messrs. Davidson, Horngren, and Seidman dissent to the Opinion because it seeks to patch up some of the abuses of pooling. The real abuse is pooling itself. On that, the only answer is to eliminate pooling. Paragraphs 35 to 41 set forth some of the defects of pooling. The fundamental one is that pooling ignores the asset values on which the parties have traded, and substitutes a wholly irrelevant figure—the amount on the seller's books. Such nonaccounting for bargained acquisition values permits the reporting of profits upon subsequent disposition of such assets when there really may be less profit or perhaps a loss. Had the assets been acquired from the seller for cash, the buyer's cost would be the amount of the cash. Acquisition for stock should make no difference. The accounting essence is the amount of consideration, not its nature. Payment in cash or stock can be a matter of form, not substance. Suppose the seller wants cash. The buyer can first sell stock and turn over the proceeds to the seller, or the seller can take stock and promptly sell

the stock for cash.

The following deal with some arguments made in the Opinion for pooling: (1) Pooling is described in paragraph 28 as a fusion resulting from "pooling equity interests". But it is the sort of fusion where a significant exchange transaction takes place. The seller parts with control over its assets and operations. In return the buyer issues stock representing an interest in its assets and operations. That interest has value and is a measure of the cost of the acquisition to the buyer. (2) Paragraph 29 declares that pooling is really a transaction among the stockholders. That just is not the fact. The buyer is always a company. (3) Paragraph 25 decries purchase accounting because it results in a write-up of only seller's assets. There is no write-up. There is only a recording of cost to the buyer. That cost is measured by the value of the assets acquired from the seller. (4) Pooling is said to avoid the difficulty of valuing assets or stock (paragraph 22). Difficulty of valuation should not be permitted to defeat fair presentation. Besides, the parties do determine values in their bargaining for the amount of stock to be issued.

Some say that to eliminate pooling will impede mergers. Mergers were prevalent before pooling, and will continue after. Accounting does not exist to aid or discourage mergers, but to account for them fairly. Elimination of pooling will remove the confusion that comes from the coexistence of pooling and purchase accounting. Above all, the elimination of pooling would remove an aberration in historical-cost accounting that permits an acquisition to be accounted for on the basis of the seller's cost rather than the buyer's cost of the assets obtained in a bargained exchange.

NOTES

Opinions of the Accounting Principles Board present the conclusions of at least two-thirds of the members of the Board, which is the senior technical body of the Institute authorized to issue pronouncements on accounting principles.

Board Opinions are considered appropriate in all circumstances covered but need not be applied to immaterial items.

Covering all possible conditions and circumstances in an Opinion of the Accounting Principles Board is usually impracticable. The substance of transactions and the principles, guides, rules, and criteria described in Opinions should control the accounting for transactions not expressly covered.

Unless otherwise stated, Opinions of the Board are not intended to be retroactive.

Council of the Institute has resolved that Institute members should disclose departures from Board Opinions in their reports as independent auditors when the effect of the departures on the financial statements is material or see to it that such departures are disclosed in notes to the financial statements and, where practicable, should disclose their effects on the financial statements (Special Bulletin, Disclosure of Departures from Opinions of the Accounting Principles Board, *October 1964). Members of the Institute must assume the burden of justifying any such departures.*

Accounting Principles Board (1970)

LeRoy Layton,	George R. Catlett	Charles B. Hellerson
Chairman	Joseph P. Cummings	Charles T. Horngren
Kenneth S. Axelson	Sidney Davidson	Oral L. Luper
Donald J. Bevis	Philip L. Defliese	J. S. Seidman
Milton M. Broeker	Newman T. Halvorson	George C. Watt
Leo E. Burger	Robert Hampton, III	Frank T. Weston
	Emmett S. Harrington	

APB Opinion No. 17
Intangible Assets

STATUS

Issued: August 1970

Effective Date: For intangible assets acquired after October 31, 1970

Affects: Supersedes prospectively ARB 43, Chapter 5, paragraphs 1 through 9
Supersedes APB 6, paragraph 15

Affected by: Paragraph 6 amended by FAS 2
Paragraph 7 superseded by FAS 71
Paragraphs 29 through 31 amended by FAS 72
Paragraph 30 amended by FAS 96 and FAS 109
Paragraph 31 amended by APB 30

Other Interpretive Pronouncements: AIN-APB 17, Interpretations No. 1 and 2
FIN 9

APB Opinion No. 17
Intangible Assets

CONTENTS

SUMMARY

Problem

1. An enterprise may acquire intangible assets from others or may develop them itself. Many kinds of intangible assets may be identified and given reasonably descriptive names, for example, patents, franchises, trademarks, and the like. Other types of intangible assets lack specific identifiability. Both identifiable and unidentifiable assets may be developed internally. Identifiable intangible assets may be acquired singly, as a part of a group of assets, or as part of an entire enterprise, but unidentifiable assets cannot be acquired singly. The excess of the cost of an acquired company over the sum of identifiable net assets, usually called goodwill, is the most common unidentifiable intangible asset.

2. Accounting for an intangible asset involves the same kinds of problems as accounting for other long-lived assets, namely, determining an initial carrying amount, accounting for that amount after

acquisition under normal business conditions (amortization), and accounting for that amount if the value declines substantially and permanently. Solving the problems is complicated by the characteristics of an intangible asset: its lack of physical qualities makes evidence of its existence elusive, its value is often difficult to estimate, and its useful life may be indeterminable.

3. The Director of Accounting Research of the American Institute of Certified Public Accountants has published Accounting Research Study No. 10, *Accounting for Goodwill,* by George R. Catlett and Norman O. Olson.[1] The study emphasizes accounting for goodwill acquired in a business combination but also discusses accounting for goodwill developed internally. The study cites the supporting authoritative pronouncements and their influences on accounting practices and evaluates the effects of practices on financial reporting.

Scope and Effect of Opinion

4. The Board has considered the conclusions and

---

[1]Accounting research studies are not pronouncements of the Board or of the Institute but are published for the purpose of stimulating discussion on important accounting matters.

recommendations of Accounting Research Study No. 10, the discussions of the appropriateness of accepted methods of accounting for intangible assets, and proposals for alternative accounting procedures. The Board expresses in this Opinion its conclusions on accounting for intangible assets.

5. This Opinion covers the accounting for both identifiable and unidentifiable intangible assets that a company acquires, including those acquired in business combinations. "Company" in this Opinion refers to both incorporated and unincorporated enterprises. The conclusions of the Opinion apply to intangible assets recorded, if any, on the acquisition of some or all of the stock held by minority stockholders of a subsidiary company. This Opinion also covers accounting for costs of developing goodwill and other unidentifiable intangible assets with indeterminate lives.

6. The provisions of this Opinion apply to costs of developing identifiable intangible assets that a company defers and records as assets. Some companies defer costs incurred to develop identifiable intangible assets while others record the costs as expenses as incurred. Certain costs, for example, research and development costs and preoperating costs, present problems which need to be studied separately. The question of deferral of those costs is beyond the scope of this Opinion.

7. This Opinion applies to regulated companies in accordance with the provisions of the Addendum to APB Opinion No. 2, *Accounting for the "Investment Credit,"* 1962.

8. The conclusions of this Opinion modify previous views of the Board and its predecessor, the Committee on Accounting Procedure. This Opinion therefore supersedes the following Accounting Research Bulletin (ARB) and Opinion of the Accounting Principles Board (APB):

ARB No. 43, Chapter 5, *Intangible Assets,* except paragraph 10 which is superseded by APB Opinion No. 16, *Business Combinations.*

APB Opinion No. 6, *Status of Accounting Research Bulletins,* paragraph 15.

Conclusions

9. The Board concludes that a company should record as assets the costs of intangible assets acquired from others, including goodwill acquired in a business combination. A company should record as expenses the costs to develop intangible assets which are not specifically identifiable. The Board also concludes that the cost of each type of intangible asset should be amortized by systematic

charges to income over the period estimated to be benefited. The period of amortization should not, however, exceed forty years.

BACKGROUND

Bases of Classification

10. Various intangible assets differ in their characteristics, their useful lives, their relations to operations, and their later dispositions. Intangible assets may be classified on several different bases:

Identifiability—separately identifiable or lacking specific identification.

Manner of acquisition—acquired singly, in groups, or in business combinations or developed internally.

Expected period of benefit—limited by law or contract, related to human or economic factors, or indefinite or indeterminate duration.

Separability from an entire enterprise—rights transferable without title, salable, or inseparable from the enterprise or a substantial part of it.

Present Accounting

Accounting for Costs at Acquisition

11. Present principles of accounting for intangible assets are generally similar to those for tangible, long-lived assets such as property, plant, and equipment. Intangible assets acquired from other entities are recorded at cost when acquired. Costs incurred to develop specifically identifiable intangible assets are often recorded as assets if the periods of expected future benefit are reasonably determinable. Costs of developing other intangible assets are usually recorded as expenses when incurred.

Accounting for Deferred Costs After Acquisition

12. Intangible assets have been divided into two classes for purposes of accounting for their costs: (a) those with a determinable term of existence because it is limited by law, regulation, or agreement, or by the nature of the asset, and (b) those having no limited term of existence and no indication of limited life at the time of acquisition. The cost of a type (a) intangible asset is amortized by systematic charges to income over the term of existence or other period expected to be benefited. The cost of a type (b) intangible asset may be treated in either of two ways: (1) the cost may be retained until a limit on the term of existence or a loss of value is evident, at which time the cost is amortized systematically over the estimated remaining term of existence or, if

worthless, written off as an extraordinary item in the income statement, or (2) the cost may be amortized at the discretion of management by charges to income even though no present evidence points to a limited term of existence or a loss of value.

13. The cost of an intangible asset, including goodwill acquired in a business combination, may not be written off as a lump sum to capital surplus or to retained earnings nor be reduced to a nominal amount at or immediately after acquisition (ARB No. 43, Chapter 5, and APB Opinion No. 9).

Criticism of Present Practice

14. Present accounting for goodwill and other unidentifiable intangible assets is often criticized because alternative methods of accounting for costs are acceptable. Some companies amortize the cost of acquired intangible assets over a short arbitrary period to reduce the amount of the asset as rapidly as practicable, while others retain the cost as an asset until evidence shows a loss of value and then record a material reduction in a single period. Selecting an arbitrary period of amortization is criticized because it may understate net income during the amortization period and overstate later net income. Retaining the cost as an asset is criticized because it may overstate net income before the loss of value is recognized and understate net income in the period of write-off.

Appraisal of Alternative Procedures

Cost of Intangible Assets

15. The cost of intangible assets acquired either singly or in groups, including intangible assets acquired in a business combination, from other businesses or individuals is determined by general principles of the historical-cost basis of accounting. The costs of developing goodwill and other intangible assets with indeterminate lives are ordinarily not distinguishable from the current costs of operations and are thus not assignable to specific assets.

Treatment of Costs

16. Costs of intangible assets which have fixed or reasonably determinable terms of existence are now amortized by systematic charges to income over their terms of existence. Differences of opinion center on the amortization of acquired intangible assets with lives which cannot be estimated reliably either at the date of acquisition or perhaps long after, for example, goodwill and trade names.

17. The literature on business combinations and goodwill, including Accounting Research Study No. 10, *Accounting for Goodwill,* contains at least four possible accounting treatments of goodwill and similar intangible assets:

a. Retain the cost as an asset indefinitely unless a reduction in its value becomes evident.
b. Retain the cost as an asset but permit amortization as an operating expense over an arbitrary period.
c. Retain the cost as an asset but require amortization as an operating expense over its estimated limited life or over an arbitrary but specified maximum and minimum period.
d. Deduct the cost from stockholders' equity at the date acquired.

18. *Arguments for nonamortization.* The two of the four accounting proposals which do not involve amortization of goodwill as an operating expense are based in part on the contention that goodwill value is not consumed or used to produce earnings in the same manner as various property rights, and therefore net income should not be reduced by amortization of goodwill. Further, net income should not be reduced by both amortization of goodwill and current expenditures that are incurred to enhance or maintain the value of the acquired intangible assets. All methods of amortizing goodwill are criticized as arbitrary because the life of goodwill is indefinite and an estimated period of existence is not measurable.

19. The basis for proposing that the cost of goodwill be retained as an asset until a loss in value becomes evident is that the cost incurred for acquired goodwill should be accounted for as an asset at the date acquired and in later periods. The cost should not be reduced as long as the value of the asset is at least equal to that cost.

20. The basis for proposing that the cost of goodwill be deducted from stockholders' equity at the date acquired is that the nature of goodwill differs from other assets and warrants special accounting treatment. Since goodwill attaches only to a business as a whole and its value fluctuates widely for innumerable reasons, estimates of either the terms of existence or current value are unreliable for purposes of income determination.

Accounting on the Historical-Cost Basis

21. All assets which are represented by deferred costs are essentially alike in historical-cost based accounting. They result from expenditures or owners' contributions and are expected to increase revenue or reduce costs to be incurred in future periods. If future benefit or the period to be benefited is questionable, the expenditure is usually treated as a current expense and not as a deferred cost. Associating deferred costs with the revenue or

period to which they are expected to relate is a basic problem in historical-cost based accounting both in measuring periodic income and in accounting for assets. The basic accounting treatment does not depend on whether the asset is a building, a piece of equipment, an element of inventory, a prepaid insurance premium, or whether it is tangible or intangible. The cost of goodwill and similar intangible assets is therefore essentially the same as the cost of land, buildings, or equipment under historical-cost based accounting. Deducting the cost of an asset from stockholders' equity (either retained earnings or capital in excess of par or stated value) at the date incurred does not match costs with revenue.

22. Accounting for the cost of a long-lived asset after acquisition normally depends on its estimated life. The cost of assets with perpetual existence, such as land, is carried forward as an asset without amortization, and the cost of assets with finite lives is amortized by systematic charges to income. Goodwill and similar intangible assets do not clearly fit either classification; their lives are neither infinite nor specifically limited, but are indeterminate. Thus, although the principles underlying present practice conform to the principles of accounting for similar types of assets, their applications have led to alternative treatments. Amortizing the cost of goodwill and similar intangible assets on arbitrary bases in the absence of evidence of limited lives or decreased values may recognize expenses and decreases of assets prematurely, but delaying amortization of the cost until a loss is evident may recognize the decreases after the fact.

A Practical Solution

23. A solution to this dilemma is to set minimum and maximum amortization periods. This accounting follows from the observation that few, if any, intangible assets last forever, although some may seem to last almost indefinitely. Allocating the cost of goodwill or other intangible assets with an indeterminate life over time is necessary because the value almost inevitably becomes zero at some future date. Since the date at which the value becomes zero is indeterminate, the end of the useful life must necessarily be set arbitrarily at some point or within some range of time for accounting purposes.

OPINION

Acquisition of Intangible Assets

24. The Board concludes that a company should record as assets the costs of intangible assets acquired from other enterprises or individuals. Costs of developing, maintaining, or restoring

intangible assets which are not specifically identifiable, have indeterminate lives, or are inherent in a continuing business and related to an enterprise as a whole—such as goodwill—should be deducted from income when incurred.

25. *Cost of intangible assets.* Intangible assets acquired singly should be recorded at cost at date of acquisition. Cost is measured by the amount of cash disbursed, the fair value of other assets distributed, the present value of amounts to be paid for liabilities incurred, or the fair value of consideration received for stock issued as described in paragraph 67 of APB Opinion No. 16.

26. Intangible assets acquired as part of a group of assets or as part of an acquired company should also be recorded at cost at date of acquisition. Cost is measured differently for specifically identifiable intangible assets and those lacking specific identification. The cost of identifiable intangible assets is an assigned part of the total cost of the group of assets or enterprise acquired, normally based on the fair values of the individual assets. The cost of unidentifiable intangible assets is measured by the difference between the cost of the group of assets or enterprise acquired and the sum of the assigned costs of individual tangible and identifiable intangible assets acquired less liabilities assumed. Cost should be assigned to all specifically identifiable intangible assets; cost of identifiable assets should not be included in goodwill. Principles and procedures of determining cost of assets acquired, including intangible assets, are discussed in detail in paragraphs 66 to 89 of APB Opinion No. 16, *Business Combinations.*

Amortization of Intangible Assets

27. The Board believes that the value of intangible assets at any one date eventually disappears and that the recorded costs of intangible assets should be amortized by systematic charges to income over the periods estimated to be benefited. Factors which should be considered in estimating the useful lives of intangible assets include:

a. Legal, regulatory, or contractual provisions may limit the maximum useful life.
b. Provisions for renewal or extension may alter a specified limit on useful life.
c. Effects of obsolescence, demand, competition, and other economic factors may reduce a useful life.
d. A useful life may parallel the service life expectancies of individuals or groups of employees.
e. Expected actions of competitors and others may restrict present competitive advantages.
f. An apparently unlimited useful life may in fact be indefinite and benefits cannot be reasonably projected.

g. An intangible asset may be a composite of many individual factors with varying effective lives.

The period of amortization of intangible assets should be determined from the pertinent factors.

28. The cost of each type of intangible asset should be amortized on the basis of the estimated life of that specific asset and should not be written off in the period of acquisition. Analysis of all factors should result in a reasonable estimate of the useful life of most intangible assets. A reasonable estimate of the useful life may often be based on upper and lower limits even though a fixed existence is not determinable.

29. The period of amortization should not, however, exceed forty years. Analysis at the time of acquisition may indicate that the indeterminate lives of some intangible assets are likely to exceed forty years and the cost of those assets should be amortized over the maximum period of forty years, not an arbitrary shorter period.

30. *Method of amortization.* The Board concludes that the straight-line method of amortization—equal annual amounts—should be applied unless a company demonstrates that another systematic method is more appropriate. The financial statements should disclose the method and period of amortization. Amortization of acquired goodwill and of other acquired intangible assets not deductible in computing income taxes payable does not create a timing difference, and allocation of income taxes is inappropriate.

31. *Subsequent review of amortization.* A company should evaluate the periods of amortization continually to determine whether later events and circumstances warrant revised estimates of useful lives. If estimates are changed, the unamortized cost should be allocated to the increased or reduced number of remaining periods in the revised useful life but not to exceed forty years after acquisition. Estimation of value and future benefits of an intangible asset may indicate that the unamortized cost should be reduced significantly by a deduction in determining net income (APB Opinion No. 9, paragraph 21). However, a single loss year or even a few loss years together do not necessarily justify an extraordinary charge to income for all or a large part of the unamortized cost of intangible assets. The reason for an extraordinary deduction should be disclosed.

Disposal of Goodwill

32. Ordinarily goodwill and similar intangible assets cannot be disposed of apart from the enterprise as a whole. However, a large segment or separable group of assets of an acquired company or the entire acquired company may be sold or otherwise liquidated, and all or a portion of the unamortized cost of the goodwill recognized in the acquisition should be included in the cost of the assets sold.

EFFECTIVE DATE

33. The provisions of this Opinion shall be effective to account for intangible assets acquired after October 31, 1970. Intangible assets recognized in business combinations initiated before November 1, 1970 and consummated on or after that date under the terms prevailing on October 31, 1970[2] may be accounted for in accordance with this Opinion or Chapter 5 of ARB No. 43 and APB Opinion No. 9.

34. The provisions of this Opinion should not be applied retroactively to intangible assets acquired before November 1, 1970, whether in business combinations or otherwise.

35. The Board encourages the application on a prospective basis to all intangible assets held on October 31, 1970 of the provisions in paragraphs 27 to 31 of this Opinion which require amortization of all intangible assets. Unless the provisions of this Opinion are applied prospectively, the accounting for intangible assets held on October 31, 1970 should be in accordance with Chapter 5 of ARB No. 43 as modified by APB Opinion No. 9.

The Opinion entitled "Intangible Assets" was adopted by the assenting votes of thirteen members of the Board. Messrs. Burger, Catlett, Davidson, Hellerson, and Horngren dissented.

Mr. Catlett dissents to this Opinion because he believes that goodwill should never be shown as an asset in the balance sheet and should never be amortized as a charge to income. In his view, goodwill, regardless of the form of consideration paid for it, reflects values brought about by investor expectations attributable to a multitude of factors. Such values fluctuate frequently and widely, and the changes do not occur in any rational, predictable manner. Thus, there is no continuing relationship between the value of goodwill and its cost. Goodwill does not have a demonstrable useful life; and its expiration, if any, cannot be related on any logical basis to the operating revenues of particular periods. If goodwill values from an earlier date and for only a portion of a combined company, and the arbitrary

---

[2]Paragraphs 46-a and 47-a of APB Opinion No. 16, *Business Combinations,* define date initiated and describe the effect of changes in terms of a plan of combination.

amortization of such values, are reflected in financial statements, an unwarranted responsibility is placed upon investors to make proper allowance for this mis-statement of assets and distortion of earnings in appraising the earning power and the value of the combined company, including all of its goodwill, on a current basis. Mr. Catlett believes that the lack of recognition by the Accounting Principles Board of the true nature of goodwill, as discussed in Accounting Research Study No. 10, has resulted in conclusions which adversely affect the development of sound accounting principles far beyond the accounting for goodwill. He also believes this Opinion demonstrates in a dramatic manner the urgent need for the Accounting Principles Board to define clearly the objectives of financial statements if it is to deal successfully with basic accounting problems.

Messrs. Burger, Davidson, Hellerson, and Horngren dissent to the required amortization of goodwill and other intangible assets (for example, perpetual franchises) having indeterminate lives. Whether amortization is appropriate depends on the particular circumstances of each case, including the evidence of increases or decreases in the value of such assets. In some cases, the facts may indicate maintenance or enhancement rather than diminution of value of the intangibles. In such cases, amortization is inappropriate. In other cases, the useful life may be determinable; then the cost should be amortized by systematic charges to income over the estimated period of usefulness. In all cases, the amortization of intangible assets should be based on professional judgment, rather than arbitrary rules.

NOTES

Opinions of the Accounting Principles Board present the conclusions of at least two-thirds of the members of the Board, which is the senior technical body of the Institute authorized to issue pronouncements on accounting principles.

Board Opinions are considered appropriate in all circumstances covered but need not be applied to immaterial items.

Covering all possible conditions and circumstances in an Opinion of the Accounting Principles Board is usually impracticable. The substance of transactions and the principles, guides, rules, and criteria described in Opinions should control the accounting for transactions not expressly covered.

Unless otherwise stated, Opinions of the Board are not intended to be retroactive.

Council of the Institute has resolved that Institute members should disclose departures from Board Opinions in their reports as independent auditors when the effect of the departures on the financial statements is material or see to it that such departures are disclosed in notes to the financial statements and, where practicable, should disclose their effects on the financial statements. (Special Bulletin, Disclosure of Departures from Opinions of the Accounting Principles Board, *October 1964). Members of the Institute must assume the burden of justifying any such departures.*

Accounting Principles Board (1970)

LeRoy Layton, *Chairman*	George R. Catlett	Charles B. Hellerson
Kenneth S. Axelson	Joseph P. Cummings	Charles T. Horngren
Donald J. Bevis	Sidney Davidson	Oral L. Luper
Milton M. Broeker	Philip L. Defliese	J. S. Seidman
Leo E. Burger	Newman T. Halvorson	George C. Watt
	Robert Hampton, III	Frank T. Weston
	Emmett S. Harrington	

APB Opinion No. 18
The Equity Method of Accounting for Investments in Common Stock

STATUS

Issued: March 1971

Effective Date: For fiscal periods beginning after December 31, 1971

Affects: Amends ARB 51, paragraphs 19 through 21
Supersedes APB 10, paragraphs 2 through 4 and footnotes 1 through 5

Affected by: Paragraphs 1, 16, 17, 19, 19(a), and 20(d) amended by FAS 94
Paragraphs 14 and 20(c) and footnotes 1, 3, and 4 superseded by FAS 94
Paragraph 15 and footnote 5 superseded by FAS 13
Paragraph 19(d) amended by APB 30
Paragraph 19(j) and footnote 11 superseded by APB 23
Paragraph 19(l) amended by FAS 115
Paragraph 19(m) amended by FAS 58

Other Interpretive Pronouncements: AIN-APB 18, Interpretations No. 1 through 3
FIN 35
FTB 79-19

APB Opinion No. 18
The Equity Method of Accounting for Investments in Common Stock

INTRODUCTION

1. The Accounting Principles Board expresses in this Opinion its views on the equity method of accounting for investments in common stock. This Opinion clarifies the applicability of the equity method of accounting (paragraph 6b) to investments in common stock of subsidiaries and extends the applicability of the equity method of accounting to investments in common stock of corporate joint ventures and certain other investments in common stock. The Opinion also applies to investments reported in parent-company financial statements when such statements are prepared for issuance to stockholders as the financial statements of the primary reporting entity.[1] This Opinion supersedes paragraphs 2, 3 and 4 of APB Opinion No. 10 and amends paragraphs 19, 20 and 21 of Accounting Research Bulletin No. 51 to the extent that they relate to the equity method of accounting.[2]

2. This Opinion does not apply to investments in common stock held by (a) investment companies registered under the Investment Company Act of 1940 or investment companies which would be included under the Act (including small business investment companies) except that the number of stockholders is limited and the securities are not offered publicly, or (b) nonbusiness entities, such as estates, trusts and individuals. The Opinion also does not apply to investments in common stock other than those described in the Opinion.

3. Several terms are used in this Opinion as indicated:

a. "Investor" refers to a business entity that holds an investment in voting stock of another company.
b. "Investee" refers to a corporation that issued voting stock held by an investor.
c. "Subsidiary" refers to a corporation which is controlled, directly or indirectly, by another corporation. The usual condition for control is ownership of a majority (over 50%) of the outstanding voting stock. The power to control may also exist with a lesser percentage of ownership, for example, by contract, lease, agreement with other stockholders or by court decree.
d. "Corporate joint venture" refers to a corpora-

tion owned and operated by a small group of businesses (the "joint venturers") as a separate and specific business or project for the mutual benefit of the members of the group. A government may also be a member of the group. The purpose of a corporate joint venture frequently is to share risks and rewards in developing a new market, product or technology; to combine complementary technological knowledge; or to pool resources in developing production or other facilities. A corporate joint venture also usually provides an arrangement under which each joint venturer may participate, directly or indirectly, in the overall management of the joint venture. Joint venturers thus have an interest or relationship other than as passive investors. An entity which is a subsidiary of one of the "joint venturers" is not a corporate joint venture. The ownership of a corporate joint venture seldom changes, and its stock is usually not traded publicly. A minority public ownership, however, does not preclude a corporation from being a corporate joint venture.
e. "Dividends" refers to dividends paid or payable in cash, other assets, or another class of stock and does not include stock dividends or stock splits.
f. "Earnings or losses of an investee" and "financial position of an investee" refer to net income (or net loss) and financial position of an investee determined in accordance with accounting principles generally accepted in the United States.

DISCUSSION

4. Paragraph 1 of Accounting Research Bulletin No. 51 states that: "There is a presumption that consolidated statements are more meaningful than separate statements and that they are usually necessary for a fair presentation when one of the companies in the group directly or indirectly has a controlling financial interest in the other companies." Consolidated financial statements combine the assets, liabilities, revenues and expenses of subsidiaries with the corresponding items of the parent company. Intercompany items are eliminated to avoid double counting and prematurely recognizing income. Consolidated financial statements report the financial position and results of operations of the parent com-

---

[1] Accounting research studies on the broader subjects of accounting for intercorporate investments and foreign operations are now in process and will encompass the matters on parent-company financial statements and on consolidated financial statements covered in ARB No. 51 and in ARB No. 43, Chapter 12, as amended.

[2] This Opinion amends APB Statement No. 4, *Basic Concepts and Accounting Principles Underlying Financial Statements of Business Enterprises,* to the extent that it relates to the equity method of accounting.

pany and its subsidiaries as an economic entity. In practice, consolidation has been limited to subsidiary companies, although under certain circumstances valid reasons may exist for omitting a subsidiary from consolidation.[3]

5. Investments are sometimes held in stock of companies other than subsidiaries, namely corporate joint ventures and other noncontrolled corporations. These investments are usually accounted for by one of two methods—the cost method or the equity method. While practice varies to some extent, the cost method is generally followed for most investments in noncontrolled corporations, in some corporate joint ventures, and to a lesser extent in unconsolidated subsidiaries, particularly foreign. The equity method is generally followed for investments in unconsolidated domestic subsidiaries, some corporate joint ventures and some noncontrolled corporations. An adaptation of the cost method, the lower of cost or market, has also been followed for investments in certain marketable securities if a decline in market value is evidently not a mere temporary condition.

6. A summary of the two principal methods of accounting for the investments in common stock discussed in this Opinion follows:

a. *The cost method.* An investor records an investment in the stock of an investee at cost, and recognizes as income dividends received that are distributed from net accumulated earnings of the investee since the date of acquisition by the investor. The net accumulated earnings of an investee subsequent to the date of investment are recognized by the investor only to the extent distributed by the investee as dividends. Dividends received in excess of earnings subsequent to the date of investment are considered a return of investment and are recorded as reductions of cost of the investment. A series of operating losses of an investee or other factors may indicate that a decrease in value of the investment has occurred which is other than temporary and should accordingly be recognized.

b. *The equity method.* An investor initially records an investment in the stock of an investee at cost, and adjusts the carrying amount of the investment to recognize the investor's share of the earnings or losses of the investee after the date of acquisition. The amount of the adjustment is included in the determination of net income by the investor, and such amount reflects adjustments similar to those made in preparing consolidated statements including adjustments to eliminate intercompany gains and losses, and to amortize, if appropriate, any difference between

investor cost and underlying equity in net assets of the investee at the date of investment. The investment of an investor is also adjusted to reflect the investor's share of changes in the investee's capital. Dividends received from an investee reduce the carrying amount of the investment. A series of operating losses of an investee or other factors may indicate that a decrease in value of the investment has occurred which is other than temporary and which should be recognized even though the decrease in value is in excess of what would otherwise be recognized by application of the equity method.

7. Under the cost method of accounting for investments in common stock, dividends are the basis for recognition by an investor of earnings from an investment. Financial statements of an investor prepared under the cost method may not reflect substantial changes in the affairs of an investee. Dividends included in income of an investor for a period may be unrelated to the earnings (or losses) of an investee for that period. For example, an investee may pay no dividends for several periods and then pay dividends substantially in excess of the earnings of a period. Losses of an investee of one period may be offset against earnings of another period because the investor reports neither in results of operations at the time they are reported by the investee. Some dividends received from an investee do not cover the carrying costs of an investment whereas the investor's share of the investee's earnings more than covers those costs. Those characteristics of the cost method may prevent an investor from reflecting adequately the earnings related to an investment in common stock—either cumulatively or in the appropriate periods.

8. Corporations have increasingly established or participated in corporate joint venture arrangements or taken substantial positions (but less than majority ownership) in other corporations. The significant increase in the number of intercorporate investments of less than majority ownership of voting stock has broadened interest in reflecting earnings from investments on a more timely basis than by receipt of dividends. Some hold that such investments should be accounted for at market value and that this basis of accounting is most appropriate, whether market value is lower than or higher than cost. Others hold that the equity method is the most appropriate basis of accounting for some or all investments of that type.

9. Under the market value method, an investor recognizes both dividends received and changes in market prices of the stock of the investee company as earnings or losses from an investment. Dividends

---

[3]See paragraphs 2 and 3 of ARB No. 51 and paragraph 8 of ARB No. 43, Chapter 12.

received are accounted for as part of income from the investment. In addition, an investor adjusts the carrying amount of its investment based on the market value of the investee's stock. Change in market value since the preceding reporting date is included in results of operations of the investor. Reporting of investments in common stock at market value (or at approximate fair value if market value is not available) is considered to meet most closely the objective of reporting the economic consequences of holding the investment. However, the market value method is now used only in special circumstances. While the Board believes the market value method provides the best presentation of investments in some situations, it concludes that further study is necessary before the market value method is extended beyond current practice.

10. Under the equity method, an investor recognizes its share of the earnings or losses of an investee in the periods for which they are reported by the investee in its financial statements rather than in the period in which an investee declares a dividend. An investor adjusts the carrying amount of an investment for its share of the earnings or losses of the investee subsequent to the date of investment and reports the recognized earnings or losses in income. Dividends received from an investee reduce the carrying amount of the investment. Thus, the equity method is an appropriate means of recognizing increases or decreases measured by generally accepted accounting principles in the economic resources underlying the investments. Furthermore, the equity method of accounting more closely meets the objectives of accrual accounting than does the cost method since the investor recognizes its share of the earnings and losses of the investee in the periods in which they are reflected in the accounts of the investee.

11. Under the equity method, an investment in common stock is generally shown in the balance sheet of an investor as a single amount. Likewise, an investor's share of earnings or losses from its investment is ordinarily shown in its income statement as a single amount.

12. The equity method tends to be most appropriate if an investment enables the investor to influence the operating or financial decisions of the investee.

The investor then has a degree of responsibility for the return on its investment, and it is appropriate to include in the results of operations of the investor its share of the earnings or losses of the investee. Influence tends to be more effective as the investor's percent of ownership in the voting stock of the investee increases. Investments of relatively small percentages of voting stock of an investee tend to be passive in nature and enable the investor to have little or no influence on the operations of the investee.

13. Some hold the view that neither the market value method nor the equity method is appropriate accounting for investments in common stock where the investor holds less than majority ownership of the voting stock. They would account for such investments at cost. Under that view the investor is not entitled to recognize earnings on its investment until a right to claim the earnings arises, and that claim arises only to the extent dividends are declared. The investor is considered to have no earnings on its investment unless it is in a position to control the distribution of earnings. Likewise, an investment or an investor's operations are not affected by losses of an investee unless those losses indicate a loss in value of the investment that should be recognized.

OPINION

14. The Board reaffirms the conclusion that investors should account for investments in common stock of unconsolidated domestic subsidiaries by the equity method in consolidated financial statements, and the Board now extends this conclusion to investments in common stock of all unconsolidated subsidiaries (foreign as well as domestic) in consolidated financial statements. The equity method is not, however, a valid substitute for consolidation and should not be used to justify exclusion of a subsidiary when consolidation is otherwise appropriate. The Board also concludes that parent companies should account for investments in the common stock of subsidiaries by the equity method in parent-company financial statements prepared for issuance to stockholders as the financial statements of the primary reporting entity.[4]

15. In APB Opinion No. 10, paragraph 4, the Board stated that the accounts of subsidiaries

---

[4]Paragraphs 2 and 3 of ARB No. 51 and paragraph 8 of ARB No. 43, Chapter 12, describe, among other things, the conditions under which a subsidiary should or might not be consolidated. The limitations on consolidation described in paragraph 2 of ARB No. 51 and paragraph 8 of ARB No. 43, Chapter 12, should also be applied as limitations to the use of the equity method. The Board has deferred further consideration of the treatment of foreign subsidiaries in consolidated statements and the treatment of all subsidiaries in parent-company statements that are not prepared for issuance to stockholders as the financial statements of the primary reporting entity until the accounting research studies on foreign operations and intercorporate investments are published. In the meantime, the provisions of Chapter 12 of ARB No. 43 (as amended by paragraph 18 of APB Opinion No. 6 and by paragraphs 17, 21 and 22 of APB Opinion No. 9) continue in effect. The conclusions in paragraph 14 of this Opinion apply to investments in foreign subsidiaries unless those companies are operating under conditions of exchange restrictions, controls or other uncertainties of a type that would affect decisions as to consolidation or application of the equity method; if those conditions exist, the cost method should be followed.

(regardless of when organized or acquired) whose principal business activity is leasing property or facilities to parent or other affiliated companies should be consolidated. The Board also concluded that the equity method is not adequate for fair presentation of those subsidiaries because their assets and liabilities are significant to the consolidated financial position of the enterprise. The Board reaffirms those conclusions.[5]

16. The Board concludes that the equity method best enables investors in corporate joint ventures to reflect the underlying nature of their investment in those ventures. Therefore, investors should account for investments in common stock of corporate joint ventures by the equity method, both in consolidated financial statements and in parent-company financial statements prepared for issuance to stockholders as the financial statements of the primary reporting entity.[6]

17. The Board concludes that the equity method of accounting for an investment in common stock should also be followed by an investor whose investment in voting stock gives it the ability to exercise significant influence over operating and financial policies of an investee even though the investor holds 50% or less of the voting stock. Ability to exercise that influence may be indicated in several ways, such as representation on the board of directors, participation in policy making processes, material intercompany transactions, interchange of managerial personnel, or technological dependency. Another important consideration is the extent of ownership by an investor in relation to the concentration of other shareholdings, but substantial or majority ownership of the voting stock of an investee by another investor does not necessarily preclude the ability to exercise significant influence by the investor. The Board recognizes that determining the ability of an investor to exercise such influence is not always clear and applying judgment is necessary to assess the status of each investment. In order to achieve a reasonable degree of uniformity in appli-

cation, the Board concludes that an investment (direct or indirect) of 20% or more of the voting stock of an investee should lead to a presumption that in the absence of evidence to the contrary an investor has the ability to exercise significant influence over an investee. Conversely, an investment of less than 20% of the voting stock of an investee should lead to a presumption that an investor does not have the ability to exercise significant influence unless such ability can be demonstrated. When the equity method is appropriate, it should be applied in consolidated financial statements and in parent-company financial statements prepared for issuance to stockholders as the financial statements of the primary reporting entity.[7]

18. An investor's *voting stock interest* in an investee should be based on those currently outstanding securities whose holders have present voting privileges. Potential voting privileges which may become available to holders of securities of an investee should be disregarded. An investor's *share of the earnings or losses* of an investee should be based on the shares of *common* stock held by an investor without recognition of securities of the investee which are designated as "common stock equivalents" under APB Opinion No. 15.[8]

19. *Applying the equity method.* The difference between consolidation and the equity method lies in the details reported in the financial statements. Thus, an investor's net income for the period and its stockholders' equity at the end of the period are the same whether an investment in a subsidiary is accounted for under the equity method or the subsidiary is consolidated (except as indicated in paragraph 19i). The procedures set forth below should be followed by an investor in applying the equity method of accounting to investments in common stock of unconsolidated subsidiaries, corporate joint ventures, and other investees which qualify for the equity method:

a. Intercompany profits and losses should be eliminated until realized by the investor or investee

---

[5]The Board is giving further consideration to the accounting treatment of lease transactions. In the meantime, it has deferred expressing an opinion on the inclusion in consolidated financial statements of leasing companies in which the equity interest, usually nominal at the time of organization, is held by third parties, but in which the principal lessee, through options or by similar devices, possesses or has the power to obtain the economic benefits of ownership from the lease arrangements. That deferment does not affect the applicability of paragraph 12 of APB Opinion No. 5.

[6]The equity method should not be applied to the investments described in this paragraph insofar as the limitations on the use of the equity method outlined in footnote 4 would be applicable to investments other than those in subsidiaries.

[7]The equity method should not be applied to the investments described in this paragraph insofar as the limitations on the use of the equity method outlined in footnote 4 would be applicable to investments other than those in subsidiaries.

[8]Paragraph 39 of APB Opinion No. 15 states: "The designation of securities as common stock equivalents in this Opinion is solely for the purpose of determining primary earnings per share. No changes from present practices are recommended in the accounting for such securities, in their presentation within the financial statements or in the manner of determining net assets per common share. Information is available in the financial statements and elsewhere for readers to make judgments as to the present and potential status of the various securities outstanding." Paragraphs 65-69 of that Opinion discuss the treatment of common stock equivalents of subsidiaries in computing earnings per share of a parent company. The provisions of those paragraphs also apply to investments in common stock of corporate joint ventures and investee companies accounted for under the equity method.

as if a subsidiary, corporate joint venture or investee company were consolidated.

b. A difference between the cost of an investment and the amount of underlying equity in net assets of an investee should be accounted for as if the investee were a consolidated subsidiary.[9]

c. The investment(s) in common stock should be shown in the balance sheet of an investor as a single amount, and the investor's share of earnings or losses of an investee(s) should ordinarily be shown in the income statement as a single amount except for the extraordinary items as specified in (d) below.

d. The investor's share of extraordinary items and its share of prior-period adjustments reported in the financial statements of the investee in accordance with APB Opinion No. 9 should be classified in a similar manner unless they are immaterial in the income statement of the investor.

e. A transaction of an investee of a capital nature that affects the investor's share of stockholders' equity of the investee should be accounted for as if the investee were a consolidated subsidiary.

f. Sales of stock of an investee by an investor should be accounted for as gains or losses equal to the difference at the time of sale between selling price and carrying amount of the stock sold.

g. If financial statements of an investee are not sufficiently timely for an investor to apply the equity method currently, the investor ordinarily should record its share of the earnings or losses of an investee from the most recent available financial statements. A lag in reporting should be consistent from period to period.

h. A loss in value of an investment which is other than a temporary decline should be recognized the same as a loss in value of other long-term assets. Evidence of a loss in value might include, but would not necessarily be limited to, absence of an ability to recover the carrying amount of the investment or inability of the investee to sustain an earnings capacity which would justify the carrying amount of the investment. A current fair value of an investment that is less than its carrying amount may indicate a loss in value of the investment. However, a decline in the quoted market price below the carrying amount or the existence of operating losses is not neces-

sarily indicative of a loss in value that is other than temporary. All are factors to be evaluated.

i. An investor's share of losses of an investee may equal or exceed the carrying amount of an investment accounted for by the equity method plus advances made by the investor. The investor ordinarily should discontinue applying the equity method when the investment (and net advances) is reduced to zero and should not provide for additional losses unless the investor has guaranteed obligations of the investee or is otherwise committed to provide further financial support for the investee.[10] If the investee subsequently reports net income, the investor should resume applying the equity method only after its share of that net income equals the share of net losses not recognized during the period the equity method was suspended.

j. The guides in paragraph 16 of ARB No. 51 for income taxes on undistributed earnings of subsidiaries in consolidation remain in effect as provided in paragraph 39 of APB Opinion No. 11 until the Board issues an Opinion on that subject. The guides should also apply (1) to investments in common stock of unconsolidated subsidiaries, corporate joint ventures,[11] and other investee companies accounted for by the equity method in consolidated financial statements and (2) to investments accounted for by the equity method in parent-company financial statements prepared for issuance to stockholders as the financial statements of the primary reporting entity.

k. When an investee has outstanding cumulative preferred stock, an investor should compute its share of earnings (losses) after deducting the investee's preferred dividends, whether or not such dividends are declared.

l. An investment in voting stock of an investee company may fall below the level of ownership described in paragraph 17 from sale of a portion of an investment by the investor, sale of additional stock by an investee, or other transactions and the investor may thereby lose the ability to influence policy, as described in that paragraph. An investor should discontinue accruing its share of the earnings or losses of the investee for an investment that no longer qualifies for the equity method. The earnings or losses that relate

---

[9]For investments made prior to November 1, 1970, the effective date of APB Opinion No. 17, investors are not required to amortize any goodwill in the absence of evidence that the goodwill has a limited term of existence; prospective amortization of such goodwill is encouraged.

[10]An investor should, however, provide for additional losses when the imminent return to profitable operations by an investee appears to be assured. For example, a material, nonrecurring loss of an isolated nature may reduce an investment below zero even though the underlying profitable operating pattern of an investee is unimpaired.

[11]Certain corporate joint ventures have a life limited by the nature of the venture, project or other business activity. Therefore, a reasonable assumption is that a part or all of the undistributed earnings of the venture will be transferred to the investor in a taxable distribution. Deferred taxes should be recorded at the time the earnings (or losses) are included in the investor's income in accordance with the concepts of APB Opinion No. 11.

to the stock retained by the investor and that were previously accrued should remain as a part of the carrying amount of the investment. The investment account should not be adjusted retroactively under the conditions described in this subparagraph. However, dividends received by the investor in subsequent periods which exceed his share of earnings for such periods should be applied in reduction of the carrying amount of the investment (see paragraph 6a).

m. An investment in common stock of an investee that was previously accounted for on other than the equity method may become qualified for use of the equity method by an increase in the level of ownership described in paragraph 17 (i.e., acquisition of additional voting stock by the investor, acquisition or retirement of voting stock by the investee, or other transactions). When an investment qualifies for use of the equity method, the investor should adopt the equity method of accounting. The investment, results of operations (current and prior periods presented), and retained earnings of the investor should be adjusted retroactively in a manner consistent with the accounting for a step-by-step acquisition of a subsidiary.

n. The carrying amount of an investment in common stock of an investee that qualifies for the equity method of accounting as described in subparagraph (m) may differ from the underlying equity in net assets of the investee. The difference should affect the determination of the amount of the investor's share of earnings or losses of an investee as if the investee were a consolidated subsidiary. However, if the investor is unable to relate the difference to specific accounts of the investee, the difference should be considered to be goodwill and amortized over a period not to exceed forty years, in accordance with APB Opinion No. 17.[12]

20. *Disclosures.* The significance of an investment to the investor's financial position and results of operations should be considered in evaluating the extent of disclosures of the financial position and results of operations of an investee. If the investor has more than one investment in common stock, disclosures wholly or partly on a combined basis may be appropriate. The following disclosures are generally applicable to the equity method of accounting for investments in common stock:

a. Financial statements of an investor should disclose parenthetically, in notes to financial statements, or in separate statements or schedules (1) the name of each investee and percentage of ownership of common stock, (2) the accounting policies of the investor with respect to investments in common stock,[13] and (3) the difference, if any, between the amount at which an investment is carried and the amount of underlying equity in net assets and the accounting treatment of the difference.

b. For those investments in common stock for which a quoted market price is available, the aggregate value of each identified investment based on the quoted market price usually should be disclosed. This disclosure is not required for investments in common stock of subsidiaries.

c. When investments in unconsolidated subsidiaries are, in the aggregate, material in relation to financial position or results of operations, summarized information as to assets, liabilities, and results of operations should be presented in the notes or separate statements should be presented for such subsidiaries, either individually or in groups, as appropriate.

d. When investments in common stock of corporate joint ventures or other investments of 50% or less accounted for under the equity method are, in the aggregate, material in relation to the financial position or results of operations of an investor, it may be necessary for summarized information as to assets, liabilities, and results of operations of the investees to be presented in the notes or in separate statements, either individually or in groups, as appropriate.

e. Conversion of outstanding convertible securities, exercise of outstanding options and warrants and other contingent issuances of an investee may have a significant effect on an investor's share of reported earnings or losses. Accordingly, material effects of possible conversions, exercises or contingent issuances should be disclosed in notes to the financial statements of an investor.[14]

EFFECTIVE DATE

21. This Opinion shall be effective for all fiscal periods beginning after December 31, 1971, and should be applied retroactively to all investments in common stock held during any portion of the

[12]For investments made prior to November 1, 1970, the effective date of APB Opinion No. 17, investors are not required to amortize any goodwill in the absence of evidence that the goodwill has a limited term of existence; prospective amortization of such goodwill is encouraged.

[13]Disclosure should include the names of any significant investee corporations in which the investor holds 20% or more of the voting stock, but the common stock is not accounted for on the equity method, together with the reasons why the equity method is not considered appropriate, and the names of any significant investee corporations in which the investor holds less than 20% of the voting stock and the common stock is accounted for on the equity method, together with the reasons why the equity method is considered appropriate.

[14]See footnote 8.

period for which results of operations are presented regardless of the date the investments were acquired. However, the Board encourages earlier application of the provisions of this Opinion. Adjustments resulting from a change in accounting method to comply with this Opinion should be treated as adjustments of prior periods, and financial statements presented for the periods affected should be restated appropriately.

The Opinion entitled "The Equity Method of Accounting for Investments in Common Stock" was adopted by the assenting votes of seventeen members of the Board, of whom five, Messrs. Broeker, Catlett, Hellerson, Horngren and Weston, assented with qualification. Mr. Halvorson dissented.

Mr. Broeker assents to the publication of the Opinion but dissents to paragraph 17 which provides for a different standard of qualification for equity accounting for investments that represent 20% or more of the voting stock of the investee from that required of those that represent less than 20%. He believes that in all instances where the investor does not own more than 50% of the voting control of the investee, the investor should always be required to demonstrate an ability to exercise significant influence over the operating and financial policies of an investee and that at no level of voting control under 51% should such significant influence be presumed to exist. He also dissents from paragraph 19(l) which does not provide for a retroactive adjustment to cost at the time a minority investment ceases to qualify under the equity method. He believes that a retroactive adjustment should be required similar to the accounting prescribed under 19(m) for investments at the time they first qualify for the equity method of accounting.

Messrs. Catlett and Horngren assent to the issuance of this Opinion because in their view it represents a step in the right direction. However, they do not agree with the arbitrary criterion of 20% combined with a variable test of "significant influence" in paragraph 17, because such an approach is not convincing in concept and will be very difficult to apply in practice. They believe that the equity method should be followed for all significant investments in common stock representing long-term business affiliations where consolidation of the financial statements is not appropriate. Messrs. Catlett and Horngren do not agree with the portions of paragraph 19 which require that consolidation practices be followed in determining the amount of income to be reported by the investor company under the equity method of accounting for investments in common stock of companies which are not subsidiaries. They believe that consolidation practices generally should be limited to parent-subsidiary relationships. In their view, where con-

solidation practices are not appropriate, the income reflected under the equity method by an investor company should be based on the reported income of the investee company. The approach taken in this Opinion will, in their judgment, make it difficult to improve the accounting for investments in common stock not accounted for under the equity method.

Mr. Hellerson assents to the issuance of this Opinion because it represents improved accounting for the type of investment described in it. However, he dissents from the permission granted in paragraph 19(g) to record earnings or losses based on the most recent available financial statements. It is his view that this paragraph should be comparable to paragraph 4 of ARB No. 51. Although he agrees with the discontinuance of the application of the equity method when the investment is reduced to zero, he believes that paragraph 20 should require disclosure of the periodic and accumulated losses. He also dissents to paragraph 19(m), as he believes that the method should only be applied prospectively from the date that it became applicable. Finally, reference is made to his qualified assent to Opinion No. 17 for his views on the amortization of goodwill prescribed in paragraphs 19(b) and (n).

Mr. Weston assents to issuance of this Opinion but he disagrees with the conclusion contained in paragraph 18 that an investor's share of the earnings or losses of an investee should be computed without regard to any securities of the investee which are common stock equivalents. This conclusion is inconsistent with the requirement in footnote 8 to paragraph 18 that such common stock equivalents be recognized in the computation of an investor's share of the earnings or losses of an investee to be reflected in the earnings per share of the investor.

Mr. Halvorson dissents to this Opinion for a number of reasons, some of which are: (1) the ability to exercise significant influence should be affirmatively demonstrated before the equity method is applicable to investments of 50% or less of voting stock, as opposed to the presumption in the Opinion that such ability exists at the 20% level in the absence of evidence to the contrary; (2) the asserted correspondence of the equity method with conventional accrual accounting is not supported by the discussion in the Opinion; (3) if the equity method is to be a generally accepted accounting principle, it should apply to parent-company financial statements regardless of the purpose of their issuance; (4) in cases where a so-called investee has common-stock equivalents or dilutive senior securities outstanding, the Opinion would require an investor to report equity in an amount greater than earnings per share attributable to the investment reported by the investee; and (5) at the time an investment qualifies for use of the equity method, a new reporting entity is created, and the accounts of the investor for periods prior to that time should not be adjusted retroactively to reflect an entity that did not exist.

NOTES

Opinions of the Accounting Principles Board present the conclusions of at least two-thirds of the members of the Board, which is the senior technical body of the Institute authorized to issue pronouncements on accounting principles.

Board Opinions are considered appropriate in all circumstances covered but need not be applied to immaterial items.

Covering all possible conditions and circumstances in an Opinion of the Accounting Principles Board is usually impracticable. The substance of transactions and the principles, guides, rules, and criteria described in Opinions should control the accounting for transactions not expressly covered.

Unless otherwise stated, Opinions of the Board are not intended to be retroactive.

Council of the Institute has resolved that Institute members should disclose departures from the Board Opinions in their reports as independent auditors when the effect of the departures on the financial statements is material or see to it that such departures are disclosed in notes to the financial statements and, where practicable, should disclose their effects on the financial statements (Special Bulletin, Disclosure of Departures from Opinions of the Accounting Principles Board, *October 1964). Members of the Institute must assume the burden of justifying any such departures.*

Accounting Principles Board (1971)

APB Opinion No. 19
Reporting Changes in Financial Position

STATUS

Issued: March 1971

Effective Date: For fiscal periods ending after September 30, 1971

Affects: Supersedes APB 3

Affected by: Paragraph 10 amended by APB 30
Superseded by FAS 95

Other Interpretive Pronouncements: AIN-APB 19, Interpretations No. 1 through 3 (Superseded by FAS 95)

(The next page is 244.)

APB Opinion No. 20
Accounting Changes

STATUS

Issued: July 1971

Effective Date: For fiscal years beginning after July 31, 1971

Affects: Amends ARB 43, Chapter 2A, paragraph 3
Amends ARB 44 (Rev.), paragraph 3
Amends APB 9, paragraphs 18 and 20
Supersedes APB 9, paragraph 25
Amends APB 15, paragraph 13

Affected by: Paragraph 3 amended by FAS 71 and FAS 95
Paragraph 4 amended by FAS 111
Paragraph 7 amended by FAS 111
Paragraph 9 amended by FAS 111
Paragraph 16 amended by FAS 111
Paragraph 27 amended by FAS 73
Paragraph 34 amended by FAS 58
Footnote 2 superseded by FAS 111
Footnote 4 amended by FAS 111
Footnote 5 superseded by FAS 32 and FAS 111
Footnote 9 superseded by FAS 16

Other Interpretive Pronouncements: AIN-APB 20, Interpretations No. 1 and 2
FIN 1
FIN 20
FTB 87-1 (Superseded by FAS 106)

APB Opinion No. 20
Accounting Changes

CONTENTS

INTRODUCTION

1. A change in accounting by a reporting entity may significantly affect the presentation of both financial position and results of operations for an accounting period and the trends shown in comparative financial statements and historical summaries. The change should therefore be reported in a manner which will facilitate analysis and understanding of the financial statements.

Scope of Opinion

2. This Opinion defines various types of accounting changes and establishes guides for determining the manner of reporting each type. It also covers reporting a correction of an error in previously issued financial statements.

3. The Opinion applies to financial statements which purport to present financial position, changes in financial position, and results of operations in conformity with generally accepted accounting principles. The guides in this Opinion also may be appropriate in presenting financial information in other forms or for special purposes. Companies in regulated industries may apply generally accepted accounting principles differently from nonregulated companies because of the effect of the rate-making process. This Opinion should therefore be applied to regulated companies in accordance with the provisions of the Addendum to APB Opinion No. 2.

4. This Opinion does not change the policy of the Board that its Opinions, unless otherwise stated, are not intended to be retroactive. Each published Opinion specifies its effective date and the manner

of reporting a change to conform with the conclusions of the Opinion. An industry audit guide prepared by a committee of the American Institute of Certified Public Accountants may also prescribe the manner of reporting a change in accounting principle. Accordingly, the provisions of this Opinion do not apply to changes made in conformity with such pronouncements issued in the past or in the future.

5. This Opinion reaffirms the provisions of previous Board Opinions that prescribe the manner of reporting a change in accounting principle, an accounting estimate, or reporting entity except for the following paragraphs of Accounting Research Bulletins (ARB) or Opinions of the Accounting Principles Board (APB):[1]

a. Paragraph 3 of Chapter 2, Section A, *Comparative Financial Statements,* of ARB No. 43 is amended to insert a cross reference to this Opinion. This Opinion identifies numerous accounting changes and specifies the manner of reporting each change.
b. Paragraph 20 of APB Opinion No. 9, *Reporting the Results of Operations,* and paragraph 13 of APB Opinion No. 15, *Earnings per Share,* are amended. This Opinion specifies an additional element in the presentation of the income statement.
c. Paragraph 25 of APB Opinion No. 9 is superseded. Although the conclusion of that paragraph is not modified, this Opinion deals more completely with accounting changes.

TYPES OF ACCOUNTING CHANGES

6. The term *accounting change* in this Opinion means a change in (a) an accounting principle, (b) an accounting estimate, or (c) the reporting entity (which is a special type of change in accounting principle classified separately for purposes of this Opinion). The correction of an error in previously issued financial statements is not deemed to be an accounting change.

Change in Accounting Principle

7. A change in accounting principle results from adoption of a generally accepted accounting principle different from the one used previously for reporting purposes. The term *accounting principle* includes "not only accounting principles and practices but also the methods of applying them."[2]

8. A characteristic of a change in accounting principle is that it concerns a choice from among two or more generally accepted accounting principles. However, neither (a) initial adoption of an accounting principle in recognition of events or transactions occurring for the first time or that previously were immaterial in their effect nor (b) adoption or modification of an accounting principle necessitated by transactions or events that are clearly different in substance from those previously occurring is a change in accounting principle.

9. Changes in accounting principle are numerous and varied. They include, for example, a change in the method of inventory pricing, such as from the last in, first out (LIFO) method to the first in, first out (FIFO) method; a change in depreciation method for previously recorded assets, such as from the double declining balance method to the straight line method;[3] a change in the method of accounting for long-term construction-type contracts, such as from the completed contract method to the percentage of completion method; and a change in accounting for research and development expenditures, such as from recording as expense when incurred to deferring and amortizing the costs. (Paragraph 11 covers a change in accounting principle to effect a change in estimate.)

Change in Accounting Estimate

10. Changes in estimates used in accounting are necessary consequences of periodic presentations of financial statements. Preparing financial statements requires estimating the effects of future events. Examples of items for which estimates are necessary are uncollectible receivables, inventory obsolescence, service lives and salvage values of depreciable assets, warranty costs, periods benefited by a deferred cost, and recoverable mineral reserves. Future events and their effects cannot be perceived with certainty; estimating, therefore, requires the exercise of judgment. Thus accounting estimates change as new events occur, as more experience is acquired, or as additional information is obtained.

11. *Change in estimate effected by a change in accounting principle.* Distinguishing between a change in an accounting principle and a change in an accounting estimate is sometimes difficult. For example, a company may change from deferring and amortizing a cost to recording it as an expense when incurred because future benefits of the cost

---

[1]This Opinion amends APB Statement No. 4, *Basic Concepts and Accounting Principles Underlying Financial Statements of Business Enterprises,* to the extent that it relates to reporting accounting changes.

[2]Statement on Auditing Procedure No. 33, *Auditing Standards and Procedures,* chapter 7, paragraph 2.

[3]A change to the straight line method at a specific point in the service life of an asset may be planned at the time the accelerated depreciation method is adopted to fully depreciate the cost over the estimated life of the asset. Consistent application of such a policy does not constitute a change in accounting principle for purposes of applying this Opinion. (Paragraph 5-d of APB Opinion No. 12 covers disclosure of methods of depreciation.)

have become doubtful. The new accounting method is adopted, therefore, in partial or complete recognition of the change in estimated future benefits. The effect of the change in accounting principle is inseparable from the effect of the change in accounting estimate. Changes of this type are often related to the continuing process of obtaining additional information and revising estimates and are therefore considered as changes in estimates for purposes of applying this Opinion.

Change in the Reporting Entity

12. One special type of change in accounting principle results in financial statements which, in effect, are those of a different reporting entity. This type is limited mainly to (a) presenting consolidated or combined statements in place of statements of individual companies, (b) changing specific subsidiaries comprising the group of companies for which consolidated financial statements are presented, and (c) changing the companies included in combined financial statements. A different group of companies comprise the reporting entity after each change. A business combination accounted for by the pooling of interests method also results in a different reporting entity.

Correction of an Error in Previously Issued Financial Statements

13. Reporting a correction of an error in previously issued financial statements concerns factors similar to those relating to reporting an accounting change and is therefore discussed in this Opinion.[4] Errors in financial statements result from mathematical mistakes, mistakes in the application of accounting principles, or oversight or misuse of facts that existed at the time the financial statements were prepared. In contrast, a change in accounting estimate results from new information or subsequent developments and accordingly from better insight or improved judgment. Thus, an error is distinguishable from a change in estimate. A change from an accounting principle that is not generally accepted to one that is generally accepted is a correction of an error for purposes of applying this Opinion.

VIEWS ON REPORTING CHANGES IN ACCOUNTING PRINCIPLES

14. An essential question in reporting a change in accounting principle is whether to restate the financial statements currently presented for prior periods to show the new accounting principle applied retroactively. A summary of differing views bearing on that question is:

a. Accounting principles should be applied consistently for all periods presented in comparative financial statements. Using different accounting principles for similar items in financial statements presented for various periods may result in misinterpretations of earnings trends and other analytical data that are based on comparisons. The same accounting principle therefore should be used in presenting financial statements of current and past periods. Accordingly, financial statements presented for prior periods in current reports should be restated if a reporting entity changes an accounting principle.

b. Restating financial statements of prior periods may dilute public confidence in financial statements and may confuse those who use them. Financial statements previously prepared on the basis of accounting principles generally accepted at the time the statements were issued should therefore be considered final except for changes in the reporting entity or corrections of errors.

c. Restating financial statements of prior periods for some types of changes requires considerable effort and is sometimes impossible. For example, adequate information may not be available to restate financial statements of prior periods if the method of recording revenue from long-term contracts is changed from the completed contract method to the percentage of completion method.

d. Restating financial statements of prior periods for some changes requires assumptions that may furnish results different from what they would have been had the newly adopted principle been used in prior periods. For example, if the method of pricing inventory is changed from the FIFO method to the LIFO method, it may be assumed that the ending inventory of the immediately preceding period is also the beginning inventory of the current period for the LIFO method. The retroactive effects under that assumption may be different from the effects of assuming that the LIFO method was adopted at an earlier date.

OPINION

Justification for a Change in Accounting Principle

15. The Board concludes that in the preparation of financial statements there is a presumption that an accounting principle once adopted should not be changed in accounting for events and transactions of a similar type. Consistent use of accounting principles from one accounting period to another enhances the utility of financial statements to users by facilitating analysis and understanding of comparative accounting data.

---

[4]Statement on Auditing Procedure No. 41, *Subsequent Discovery of Facts Existing at the Date of the Auditor's Report,* discusses other aspects of errors in previously issued financial statements.

16. The presumption that an entity should not change an accounting principle may be overcome only if the enterprise justifies the use of an alternative acceptable accounting principle on the basis that it is preferable. However, a method of accounting that was previously adopted for a type of transaction or event which is being terminated or which was a single, nonrecurring event in the past should not be changed. For example, the method of accounting should not be changed for a tax or tax credit which is being discontinued or for pre-operating costs relating to a specific plant. The Board does not intend to imply, however, that a change in the estimated period to be benefited for a deferred cost (if justified by the facts) should not be recognized as a change in accounting estimate. The issuance of an Opinion of the Accounting Principles Board that creates a new accounting principle, that expresses a preference for an accounting principle, or that rejects a specific accounting principle is sufficient support for a change in accounting principle. The burden of justifying other changes rests with the entity proposing the change.[5]

General Disclosure—A Change in Accounting Principle

17. The nature of and justification for a change in accounting principle and its effect on income should be disclosed in the financial statements of the period in which the change is made. The justification for the change should explain clearly why the newly adopted accounting principle is preferable.

Reporting a Change in Accounting Principle

18. The Board believes that, although they conflict, both (a) the potential dilution of public confidence in financial statements resulting from restating financial statements of prior periods and (b) consistent application of accounting principles in comparative statements are important factors in reporting a change in accounting principles. The Board concludes that most changes in accounting should be recognized by including the cumulative effect, based on a retroactive computation, of changing to a new accounting principle in net income of the period of the change (paragraphs 19 to 26) but that a few specific changes in accounting principles should be re-ported by restating the financial statements of prior periods (paragraphs 27 to 30 and 34 to 35).

19. For all changes in accounting principle except those described in paragraphs 27 to 30 and 34 to 35, the Board therefore concludes that:

a. Financial statements for prior periods included for comparative purposes should be presented as previously reported.
b. The cumulative effect of changing to a new accounting principle on the amount of retained earnings at the beginning of the period in which the change is made should be included in net income of the period of the change (paragraph 20).
c. The effect of adopting the new accounting principle on income before extraordinary items and on net income (and on the related per share amounts) of the period of the change should be disclosed.
d. Income before extraordinary items and net income computed on a pro forma basis[6] should be shown on the face of the income statements for all periods presented as if the newly adopted accounting principle had been applied during all periods affected (paragraph 21).

Thus, income before extraordinary items and net income (exclusive of the cumulative adjustment) for the period of the change should be reported on the basis of the newly adopted accounting principle. The conclusions in this paragraph are modified for various special situations which are described in paragraphs 23 to 30.

20. *Cumulative effect of a change in accounting principle.* The amount shown in the income statement for the cumulative effect of changing to a new accounting principle is the difference between (a) the amount of retained earnings at the beginning of the period of a change and (b) the amount of retained earnings that would have been reported at that date if the new accounting principle had been applied retroactively for all prior periods which would have been affected and by recognizing only the direct effects of the change and related income tax effect.[7] The amount of the cumulative effect should be shown in the income statement between the captions "extraordinary items" and "net income." The

---

[5]The issuance of an industry audit guide by a committee of the American Institute of Certified Public Accountants also constitutes sufficient support for a change in accounting principle (paragraph 4).

[6]The pro forma amounts include both (a) the direct effects of a change and (b) nondiscretionary adjustments in items based on income before taxes or net income, such as profit sharing expense and certain royalties, that would have been recognized if the newly adopted accounting principle had been followed in prior periods: related income tax effects should be recognized for both (a) and (b). Direct effects are limited to those adjustments that would have been recorded to restate the financial statements of prior periods to apply retroactively the change. The nondiscretionary adjustments described in (b) should not therefore be recognized in computing the adjustment for the cumulative effect of the change described in paragraph 20 unless nondiscretionary adjustments of the prior periods are actually recorded.

[7]See footnote 6.

cumulative effect is not an extraordinary item but should be reported in a manner similar to an extraordinary item. The per share information shown on the face of the income statement should include the per share amount of the cumulative effect of the accounting change.

21. *Pro forma effects of retroactive application.* Pro forma effects of retroactive application (paragraph 19-d including footnote 6) should be shown on the face of the income statement for income before extraordinary items and net income. The earnings per share amounts (primary and fully diluted, as appropriate under APB Opinion No. 15, *Earnings per Share*) for income before extraordinary items and net income computed on a pro forma basis should be shown on the face of the income statement. If space does not permit, such per share amounts may be disclosed prominently in a separate schedule or in tabular form in the notes to the financial statements with appropriate cross reference; when this is done the actual per share amounts should be repeated for comparative purposes. Pro forma amounts should be shown in both current and future reports for all periods presented which are prior to the change and which would have been affected. Appendix A illustrates the manner of reporting a change in accounting principle. If an income statement is presented for the current period only, the actual and the pro forma amounts (and related per share data) for the immediately preceding period should be disclosed.

22. The principal steps in computing and reporting the cumulative effect and the pro forma amounts of a change in accounting principle may be illustrated by a change in depreciation method for previously recorded assets as follows:

a. The class or classes of depreciable assets to which the change applies should be identified. (A "class of assets" relates to general physical characteristics.)

b. The amount of accumulated depreciation on recorded assets at the beginning of the period of the change should be recomputed on the basis of applying retroactively the new depreciation method. Accumulated depreciation should be adjusted for the difference between the recomputed amount and the recorded amount. Deferred taxes should be adjusted for the related income tax effects.

c. The cumulative effect on the amount of retained earnings at the beginning of the period of the change resulting from the adjustments referred to in (b) above should be shown in the income statement of the period of the change.

d. The pro forma amounts should give effect to the

pro forma provisions for depreciation of each prior period presented and to the pro forma adjustments of nondiscretionary items,[8] computed on the assumption of retroactive application of the newly adopted method to all prior periods and adjusted for the related income tax effects.

23. *Change in method of amortization and related disclosure.* Accounting for the costs of long-lived assets requires adopting a systematic pattern of charging those costs to expense. These patterns are referred to as depreciation, depletion, or amortization methods (all of which are referred to in this Opinion as methods of amortization). Various patterns of charging costs to expenses are acceptable for depreciable assets; fewer patterns are acceptable for other long-lived assets.

24. Various factors are considered in selecting an amortization method for identifiable assets, and those factors may change, even for similar assets. For example, a company may adopt a new method of amortization for newly acquired, identifiable, long-lived assets and use that method for all additional new assets of the same class but continue to use the previous method for existing balances of previously recorded assets of that class. For that type of change in accounting principle, there is no adjustment of the type outlined in paragraphs 19-22, but a description of the nature of the change in method and its effect on income before extraordinary items and net income of the period of the change, together with the related per share amounts, should be disclosed. If the new method of amortization is however applied to previously recorded assets of that class, the change in accounting principle requires an adjustment for the cumulative effect of the change and the provisions of paragraphs 15 to 22 should be applied.

25. *Pro forma amounts not determinable.* In rare situations the pro forma amounts described in paragraph 21 cannot be computed or reasonably estimated for individual prior periods, although the cumulative effect on retained earnings at the beginning of the period of change can be determined. The cumulative effect should then be reported in the income statement of the period of change in the manner described in paragraph 20. The reason for not showing the pro forma amounts by periods should be explained because disclosing those amounts is otherwise required and is expected by users of financial statements.

26. *Cumulative effect not determinable.* Computing the effect on retained earnings at the beginning of the period in which a change in accounting princi-

---

[8]See footnote 6.

ple is made may sometimes be impossible. In those rare situations, disclosure will be limited to showing the effect of the change on the results of operations of the period of change (including per share data) and to explaining the reason for omitting accounting for the cumulative effect and disclosure of pro forma amounts for prior years. The principal example of this type of accounting change is a change in inventory pricing method from FIFO to LIFO for which the difficulties in computing the effects of that change are described in paragraph 14-d.

27. *Special changes in accounting principle reported by applying retroactively the new method in restatements of prior periods.* Certain changes in accounting principle are such that the advantages of retroactive treatment in prior period reports outweigh the disadvantages. Accordingly, for those few changes, the Board concludes that the financial statements of all prior periods presented should be restated. The changes that should be accorded this treatment are: (a) a change from the LIFO method of inventory pricing to another method, (b) a change in the method of accounting for long-term construction-type contracts, and (c) a change to or from the "full cost" method of accounting which is used in the extractive industries.

28. The nature of and justification for a change in accounting principle described in paragraph 27 should be disclosed in the financial statements for the period the change was adopted. In addition, the effect of the change on income before extraordinary items, net income, and the related per share amounts should be disclosed for all periods presented. This disclosure may be on the face of the income statement or in the notes. Appendix B illustrates the manner of reporting a change in accounting principle retroactively by restating the statements of those prior periods affected. Financial statements of subsequent periods need not repeat the disclosures.

29. *Special exemption for an initial public distribution.* The Board concludes that in one specific situation the application of the foregoing provisions of this Opinion may result in financial statement presentations of results of operations that are not of maximum usefulness to intended users. For example, a company owned by a few individuals may decide to change from one acceptable accounting principle to another acceptable principle in connection with a forthcoming public offering of shares of its equity securities. The potential investors may be better served by statements of income for a period of years reflecting the use of the newly adopted

accounting principles because they will be the same as those expected to be used in future periods. In recognition of this situation, the Board concludes that financial statements for all prior periods presented may be restated retroactively when a company first issues its financial statements for any one of the following purposes: (a) obtaining additional equity capital from investors, (b) effecting a business combination, or (c) registering securities. This exemption is available only once for changes made at the time a company's financial statements are first used for any of those purposes and is not available to companies whose securities currently are widely held.

30. The company should disclose in financial statements issued under the circumstances described in paragraph 29 the nature of the change in accounting principle and the justification for it (paragraph 17).

Reporting a Change in Accounting Estimate

31. The Board concludes that the effect of a change in accounting estimate should be accounted for in (a) the period of change if the change affects that period only or (b) the period of change and future periods if the change affects both. A change in an estimate should not be accounted for by restating amounts reported in financial statements of prior periods or by reporting pro forma amounts for prior periods.[9]

32. A change in accounting estimate that is recognized in whole or in part by a change in accounting principle should be reported as a change in an estimate because the cumulative effect attributable to the change in accounting principle cannot be separated from the current or future effects of the change in estimate (paragraph 11). Although that type of accounting change is somewhat similar to a change in method of amortization (paragraphs 23 and 24), the accounting effect of a change in a method of amortization can be separated from the effect of a change in the estimate of periods of benefit or service and residual values of assets. A change in method of amortization for previously recorded assets therefore should be treated as a change in accounting principle, whereas a change in the estimated period of benefit or residual value should be treated as a change in accounting estimate.

33. *Disclosure.* The effect on income before extraordinary items, net income and related per share amounts of the current period should be disclosed for a change in estimate that affects several future periods, such as a change in service lives of

---

[9]Financial statements of a prior period should not be restated for a change in estimate resulting from later resolution of an uncertainty which may have caused the auditor to qualify his opinion on previous financial statements unless the change meets all the conditions for a prior period adjustment (paragraph 23 of APB Opinion No. 9).

depreciable assets or actuarial assumptions affecting pension costs. Disclosure of the effect on those income statement amounts is not necessary for estimates made each period in the ordinary course of accounting for items such as uncollectible accounts or inventory obsolescence; however, disclosure is recommended if the effect of a change in the estimate is material.

Reporting a Change in the Entity

34. The Board concludes that accounting changes which result in financial statements that are in effect the statements of a different reporting entity (paragraph 12) should be reported by restating the financial statements of all prior periods presented in order to show financial information for the new reporting entity for all periods.

35. *Disclosure.* The financial statements of the period of a change in the reporting entity should describe the nature of the change and the reason for it. In addition, the effect of the change on income before extraordinary items, net income, and related per share amounts should be disclosed for all periods presented. Financial statements of subsequent periods need not repeat the disclosures. (Paragraphs 56 to 65 and 93 to 96 of APB Opinion No. 16, *Business Combinations,* describe the manner of reporting and the disclosures required for a change in reporting entity that occurs because of a business combination.)

Reporting a Correction of an Error in Previously Issued Financial Statements

36. The Board concludes that correction of an error in the financial statements of a prior period discovered subsequent to their issuance (paragraph 13) should be reported as a prior period adjustment. (Paragraph 18 of APB Opinion No. 9 covers the manner of reporting prior period adjustments.)

37. *Disclosure.* The nature of an error in previously issued financial statements and the effect of its correction on income before extraordinary items, net income, and the related per share amounts should be disclosed in the period in which the error was discovered and corrected. Financial statements of subsequent periods need not repeat the disclosures.

Materiality

38. The Board concludes that a number of factors are relevant to the materiality of (a) accounting changes contemplated in this Opinion and (b) corrections of errors, in determining both the accounting treatment of these items and the necessity for disclosure. Materiality should be considered in relation to both the effects of each change separately and the combined effect of all changes. If a change or correction has a material effect on income before extraordinary items or on net income of the current period before the effect of the change, the treatments and disclosures described in this Opinion should be followed. Furthermore, if a change or correction has a material effect on the trend of earnings, the same treatments and disclosures are required. A change which does not have a material effect in the period of change but is reasonably certain to have a material effect in later periods should be disclosed whenever the financial statements of the period of change are presented.

Historical Summaries of Financial Information

39. Summaries of financial information for a number of periods are commonly included in financial reports. The summaries often show condensed income statements, including related earnings per share amounts, for five years or more. In many annual reports to stockholders, the financial highlights present similar information in capsule form. The Board concludes that all such information should be prepared in the same manner (including the presentation of pro forma amounts) as that prescribed in this Opinion for primary financial statements (paragraphs 15 to 38) because the summaries include financial data based on the primary financial statements. In a summary of financial information that includes an accounting period in which a change in accounting principle was made, the amount of the cumulative effect of the change that was included in net income of the period of the change should be shown separately along with the net income and related per share amounts of that period and should not be disclosed only by a note or parenthetical notation.

EFFECTIVE DATE

40. The provisions of this Opinion are effective for fiscal years beginning after July 31, 1971. However, the Board encourages application of the provisions of this Opinion in reporting any accounting changes included in fiscal years beginning before August 1, 1971 but not yet reported in financial statements issued for the year of the change.

The Opinion entitled "Accounting Changes" was adopted by the assenting votes of twelve members of the Board. Messrs. Catlett, Halvorson, Harrington, Kessler, Luper, and Watt dissented.

Messrs. Catlett, Kessler and Luper dissent to this Opinion because they believe that when a change in accounting principles is made the financial statements for prior periods should be restated on the same basis as those for the current period. The

Board has reached a similar conclusion in most previous Opinions, since such Opinions have encouraged or required retroactive treatment for recommended changes in accounting principles. They also believe that the cumulative adjustments applicable to prior periods arising from changes in accounting principles have no bearing upon the current results of operations and should not be included in the determination of net income for the current period. This Opinion recognizes that consistent use of accounting principles "enhances the utility of financial statements to users by facilitating analysis and understanding of comparative accounting data" and that changes in accounting principles should not be made unless the principle adopted is "preferable." Yet, when such changes are made, this Opinion places severe constraints on restatement and thus not only precludes "preferable" accounting for prior periods in many areas but also impairs the comparability of the financial statements.

Mr. Harrington and Messrs. Catlett, Kessler and Luper dissent to this Opinion because in their view the great divergence between the selective requirements for restatement in paragraphs 27, 29 and 34 and the general requirements for cumulative adjustments in paragraphs 19 and 24 is not based on any supportable rationale; and such general requirements will be confusing and will contribute far more to the dilution of public confidence in financial reporting than would the restatement of prior periods for all changes in accounting principles. Furthermore, Messrs. Catlett, Harrington and Luper are particularly concerned with the continuing tendency of the Board to attempt to eliminate alleged "abuses" by means of arbitrary rules and to use accounting requirements as a disciplinary tool rather than to establish standards for the most meaningful financial reports for investors and other users of financial statements. They believe that the cumbersome requirements of this Opinion will discourage improvements in accounting in numerous areas on which the Board will not issue Opinions for many years.

Mr. Halvorson dissents because he believes that all income and expense should be included in the income statement once and neither more nor less than once, and that this can really be achieved only if newly-adopted principles are applied prospectively. The cumulative adjustment required by the Opinion for most accounting changes ignores this cardinal tenet of reporting by effectively obscuring the result if the one-time inclusion is accommodated in the cumulative adjustment and completely negating the desired result when the cumulative adjustment requires duplication in the future of items already accounted for and reported in earlier periods. He believes that restatement ("actual" or pro forma) of information previously published in good faith will endanger the credibility of financial reporting and that availability of the cumulative-

adjustment device will minimize the disciplinary effect that accounting has on the issuers of financial statements. It should be sufficient to report the dollar effect of a change (the "inconsistency") in the year of change, and in a multi-period statement including the year of change to disclose the principle applied in each of the several included periods. It is the further view of Mr. Halvorson that the required pro forma presentation for past years cannot properly report the operating results for such years as they would have been if the newly-adopted principle had then been used, because reported operating results themselves have a compelling influence on non-accounting operating decisions in such areas as pricing and methods of financing, and the effect of such decisions cannot be arithmetically reconstructed to reflect the effect of what might have been.

Mr. Watt dissents to this Opinion because its conclusions are not in accord with his view that the best presentation is one that does not require excessive interpretation by the financial statement user. He believes that, with respect to accounting changes, it is more important for statements presented in comparative form to be comparable in detail than for historical continuity to be retained there; such continuity is important and changes to amounts previously reported can be adequately reconciled in the notes to financial statements. Thus, the presumption should be that, with respect to accounting changes, retroactive restatement is most desirable wherever statements are presented in comparative form. The exception to this would be where the change relates to items whose carrying amount involves a substantial valuation judgment. Mr. Watt is in agreement with the conclusion in the Opinion that depreciation lives of assets are an element of the estimation process and changes therein should be applied prospectively. He believes, however, that depreciation method changes, although conceptually accounting changes, are inextricably tied to subjective judgment of the periods of exhaustion of the useful lives of assets and therefore the selection of a method is usually the result of a composite decision involving both methods and estimated useful lives. Thus, it is his view that all changes in depreciation methods should be reflected prospectively. Similarly, accounting changes relating to the amortization of depletable costs, goodwill, preoperating and research and development cost, etc. should be reflected prospectively. This view as it relates to pension accruals is also consistent with that expressed in paragraph 47 of APB Opinion No. 8, *Accounting for the Cost of Pension Plans,* that a change in accounting method should be applied prospectively.

NOTES

Opinions of the Accounting Principles Board

present the conclusions of at least two-thirds of the members of the Board, which is the senior technical body of the Institute authorized to issue pronouncements on accounting principles.

Board Opinions are considered appropriate in all circumstances covered but need not be applied to immaterial items.

Covering all possible conditions and circumstances in an Opinion of the Accounting Principles Board is usually impracticable. The substance of transactions and the principles, guides, rules, and criteria described in Opinions should control the accounting for transactions not expressly covered.

Unless otherwise stated, Opinions of the Board are not intended to be retroactive.

Council of the Institute has resolved that Institute members should disclose departures from Board Opinions in their reports as independent auditors when the effect of the departures on the financial statements is material or see to it that such departures are disclosed in notes to the financial statements and, where practicable, should disclose their effects on the financial statements (Special Bulletin, Disclosure of Departures from Opinions of the Accounting Principles Board, *October 1964*). Members of the Institute must assume the burden of justifying any such departures.

Accounting Principles Board (1971)

Philip L. Defliese, *Chairman*	Robert L. Ferst	Louis M. Kessler
Donald J. Bevis	Newman T. Halvorson	Oral L. Luper
Milton M. Broeker	Robert Hampton, III	David Norr
Leo E. Burger	Emmett S. Harrington	George C. Watt
George R. Catlett	Charles B. Hellerson	Glenn A. Welsch
Joseph P. Cummings	Charles T. Horngren	Frank T. Weston

Appendix A

AN ILLUSTRATION OF REPORTING A CHANGE IN ACCOUNTING PRINCIPLE (PURSUANT TO PARAGRAPHS 19 TO 22)

41. ABC Company decides in 1971 to adopt the straight line method of depreciation for plant equipment. The straight line method will be used for new acquisitions as well as for previously acquired plant equipment for which depreciation had been provided on an accelerated method.

42. This illustration assumes that the direct effects are limited to the effect on depreciation and related income tax provisions and that the direct effect on inventories is not material. The pro forma amounts have been adjusted for the hypothetical effects of the change in the provisions for incentive compensation. The per share amounts are computed assuming that 1,000,000 shares of common stock are issued and outstanding, that 100,000 additional shares would be issued if all outstanding bonds (which are not common stock equivalents) are converted, and that the annual interest expense, less taxes, for the convertible bonds is $25,000. Other data assumed for this illustration are—

Year	Excess of Accelerated Depreciation Over Straight Line Depreciation	Effects of Change Direct, Less Tax Effect	Pro forma (Note A)
Prior to 1967	$ 20,000	$ 10,000	$ 9,000
1967	80,000	40,000	36,000
1968	70,000	35,000	31,500
1969	50,000	25,000	22,500
1970	30,000	15,000	13,500
Total at beginning of 1971	$250,000	$125,000	$112,500

43. The manner of reporting the change in two-year comparative statements is—

	1971	1970
Income before extraordinary item and cumulative effect of a change in accounting principle	$1,200,000	$1,100,000
Extraordinary item (description)	(35,000)	100,000
Cumulative effect on prior years (to December 31, 1970) of changing to a different depreciation method (Note A)	125,000	
Net Income	$1,290,000	$1,200,000

Per share amounts—
Earnings per common share—assuming no dilution:

	1971	1970
Income before extraordinary item and cumulative effect of a change in accounting principle	$ 1.20	$1.10
Extraordinary item	(0.04)	0.10
Cumulative effect on prior years (to December 31, 1970) of changing to a different depreciation method	0.13	
Net income	$ 1.29	$1.20

Earnings per common share—assuming full dilution:

	1971	1970
Income before extraordinary item and cumulative effect of a change in accounting principle	$ 1.11	$1.02
Extraordinary item	(0.03)	0.09
Cumulative effect on prior years (to December 31, 1970) of changing to a different depreciation method	0.11	
Net income	$ 1.19	$1.11

Pro forma amounts assuming the new depreciation method is applied retroactively—

	1971	1970
Income before extraordinary item	$1,200,000	$1,113,500
Earnings per common share—assuming no dilution	$1.20	$1.11
Earnings per common share—assuming full dilution	$1.11	$1.04
Net income	$1,165,000	$1,213,500
Earnings per common share—assuming no dilution	$1.17	$1.21
Earnings per common share—assuming full dilution	$1.08	$1.13

(See accompanying note to the financial statements)

NOTE A:

Change in Depreciation Method for Plant Equipment

Depreciation of plant equipment has been computed by the straight line method in 1971. Depreciation of plant equipment in prior years, beginning in 1954, was computed by the sum of the years digits method. The new method of depreciation was adopted to recognize . . . (state justification for change of depreciation method) . . . and has been applied retroactively to equipment acquisitions of prior years. The effect of the change in 1971 was to increase income before extraordinary item by approximately $10,000 (or one cent per share). The adjustment of $125,000 (after reduction for income taxes of $125,000) to apply retroactively the new method is included in income of 1971. The pro forma amounts shown on the income statement have been adjusted for the effect of retroactive application on depreciation, the change in provisions for incentive compensation which would have been made had the new method been in effect, and related income taxes.

44. The manner of reporting the change in five-year comparative statements is—

	1971	1970	1969	1968	1967
Income before extraordinary item and cumulative effect of a change in accounting principle	$1,200,000	$1,100,000	$1,300,000	$1,000,000	$800,000
Extraordinary item	(35,000)	100,000		40,000	
Cumulative effect on prior years (to December 31, 1970) of changing to a different depreciation method (Note A)	125,000				
Net income	$1,290,000	$1,200,000	$1,300,000	$1,040,000	$800,000
Earnings per common share—assuming no dilution:					
Income before extraordinary item and cumulative effect of change in accounting principle	$ 1.20	$1.10	$1.30	$1.00	$0.80
Extraordinary item	(0.04)	0.10		0.04	
Cumulative effect on prior years (to December 31, 1970) of changing to a different depreciation method	0.13				
Net income	$ 1.29	$1.20	$1.30	$1.04	$0.80
Earnings per common share—assuming full dilution:					
Income before extraordinary item and cumulative effect of change in accounting principle	$ 1.11	$1.02	$1.20	$0.93	$0.75
Extraordinary item	(0.03)	0.09		0.04	
Cumulative effect on prior years (to December 31, 1970) of changing to a different depreciation method	0.11				
Net income	$ 1.19	$1.11	$1.20	$0.97	$0.75
Pro forma amounts assuming the new depreciation method is applied retroactively:					
Income before extraordinary item	$1,200,000	$1,113,500	$1,322,500	$1,031,500	$836,000
Earnings per common share—assuming no dilution	$1.20	$1.11	$1.32	$1.03	$0.84
Earnings per common share—assuming full dilution	$1.11	$1.04	$1.23	$0.96	$0.78
Net income	$1,165,000	$1,213,500	$1,322,500	$1,071,500	$836,000
Earnings per common share—assuming no dilution	$1.17	$1.21	$1.32	$1.07	$0.84
Earnings per common share—assuming full dilution	$1.08	$1.13	$1.23	$1.00	$0.78

A note similar to Note A of this Appendix should accompany the five-year comparative income statement.

Appendix B

AN ILLUSTRATION OF REPORTING A SPECIAL CHANGE IN ACCOUNTING PRINCIPLE BY RESTATING PRIOR PERIOD FINANCIAL STATEMENTS (PURSUANT TO PARAGRAPHS 27 AND 28)

45. XYZ Company decides in 1971 to adopt the percentage of completion method in accounting for all of its long-term construction contracts. The company had used in prior years the completed contract method and had maintained records which are adequate to apply retroactively the percentage of completion method. The change in accounting principle is to be reported in the manner described in paragraphs 27 and 28 of this Opinion.

46. The direct effect of the change in accounting principle and other data assumed for this illustration are—

| Year | Pre-tax Income Reported by | | Difference in Income | |
	Percentage of Completion Method	Completed Contract Method	Direct	Less Tax Effect
Prior to 1967	$1,800,000	$1,300,000	$ 500,000	$ 250,000
1967	900,000	800,000	100,000	50,000
1968	700,000	1,000,000	(300,000)	(150,000)
1969	800,000	600,000	200,000	100,000
1970	1,000,000	1,100,000	(100,000)	(50,000)
Total at beginning of 1971	5,200,000	4,800,000	400,000	200,000
1971	1,100,000	900,000	200,000	100,000
Total	$6,300,000	$5,700,000	$ 600,000	$ 300,000

The per share amounts are computed assuming that 1,000,000 shares of common stock are issued and outstanding, that 100,000 additional shares would be issued if all outstanding bonds (which are not common stock equivalents) are converted, and that the annual interest expense, less taxes, for the convertible bonds is $25,000.

47. The manner of reporting the change in two-year comparative statements is—

Income Statement:

	1971	1970
		as adjusted (Note A)
Income before extraordinary item	$ 550,000	$ 500,000
Extraordinary item (description)		(80,000)
Net Income	$ 550,000	$ 420,000

Per share amounts:

Earnings per common share—assuming no dilution:

	1971	1970
Income before extraordinary item	$0.55	$0.50
Extraordinary item		(.08)
Net Income	$0.55	$0.42

Earnings per common share—assuming full dilution:

	1971	1970
Income before extraordinary item	$0.52	$0.47
Extraordinary item		(.07)
Net Income	$0.52	$0.40

Statement of Retained Earnings:

	1971	1970
		as adjusted (Note A)
Balance at beginning of year, as previously reported	$17,800,000	$17,330,000
Add adjustment for the cumulative effect on prior years of applying retroactively the new method of accounting for long-term contracts (Note A)	200,000	250,000
Balance at beginning of year, as adjusted	$18,000,000	$17,580,000
Net income	550,000	420,000
Balance at end of year	$18,550,000	$18,000,000

(See accompanying note to the financial statements)

NOTE A:

Change in Method of Accounting for Long-Term Contracts

The company has accounted for revenue and costs for long-term construction contracts by the percentage of completion method in 1971, whereas in all prior years revenue and costs were determined by the completed contract method. The new method of accounting for long-term contracts was adopted to recognize . . . (state justification for change in accounting principle) . . . and financial statements of prior years have been restated to apply the new method retroactively. For income tax purposes, the completed contract method has been continued. The effect of the accounting change on income of 1971 and on income as previously reported for 1970 is—

Effect on—	*Increase (Decrease)* 1971	1970
Income before extraordinary item and net income	$100,000	$(50,000)
Earnings per common share—assuming no dilution	$0.10	($0.05)
Earnings per common share—assuming full dilution	$0.09	($0.05)

The balances of retained earnings for 1970 and 1971 have been adjusted for the effect (net of income taxes) of applying retroactively the new method of accounting.

48. A note to a five-year summary of financial statements should disclose the effect of the change

on net income and related per share amounts for the periods affected in the following manner:

NOTE A:

Change in Method of Accounting for Long-Term Contracts

The company has accounted for revenue and costs for long-term construction contracts by the percentage of completion method in 1971, whereas in all prior years revenue and costs were determined by the completed contract method. The new method of accounting for long-term contracts was adopted to recognize . . . (state justification for change in accounting principle) . . . and financial statements of prior years have been restated to apply the new method retroactively. For income tax purposes, the completed contract method has been continued. The effect of the accounting change on net income as previously reported for 1970 and prior years is—

	1970	1969	1968	1967
Net income as previously reported	$470,000	$300,000	$500,000	$400,000
Adjustment for effect of a change in accounting principle that is applied retroactively	(50,000)	100,000	(150,000)	50,000
Net income as adjusted	$420,000	$400,000	$ 350,000	$450,000
Per share amounts:				
Earnings per common share—assuming no dilution:				
Net income as previously reported	$ 0.47	$0.30	$ 0.50	$0.40
Adjustment for effect of a change in accounting principle that is applied retroactively	(0.05)	0.10	(0.15)	0.05
Net income as adjusted	$ 0.42	$0.40	$ 0.35	$0.45
Earnings per common share—assuming full dilution:				
Net income as previously reported	$ 0.45	$0.30	$ 0.47	$0.38
Adjustment for effect of a change in accounting principle that is applied retroactively	(0.05)	0.09	(0.13)	0.05
Net income as adjusted	$ 0.40	$0.39	$ 0.34	$0.43

APB Opinion No. 21
Interest on Receivables and Payables

STATUS

Issued: August 1971

Effective Date: For transactions on or after October 1, 1971

Affects: Amends ARB 43, Chapter 3A, paragraph 6(g)

Affected by: Paragraphs 15 and 16 amended by FAS 34
Footnote 8 amended by FAS 96 and FAS 109

Other Interpretive Pronouncements: AIN-APB 21, Interpretation No. 1
FIN 2 (Superseded by FAS 15)

APB Opinion No. 21
Interest on Receivables and Payables

CONTENTS

INTRODUCTION

1. *Problem.* Business transactions often involve the exchange of cash or property, goods, or service for a note or similar instrument. The use of an interest rate that varies from prevailing interest rates warrants evaluation of whether the face amount and the stated interest rate of a note or obligation provide reliable evidence for properly recording the exchange and subsequent related interest. This Opinion sets forth the Board's views regarding the appropriate accounting when the face amount of a note does not reasonably represent the present value[1] of the consideration given or received in the exchange. This circumstance may arise if the note is noninterest bearing or has a stated interest rate which is different from the rate of interest appropriate for the debt at the date of the transaction. Unless the note is recorded at its present value in this circumstance the sales price and profit to a seller in the year of the transaction and the purchase price and cost to the buyer are misstated, and interest income and interest expense in subsequent periods are also misstated. The primary objective of this Opinion is to refine the manner of applying existing accounting principles in this circumstance. Thus, it is not intended to create a new accounting principle.

2. *Applicability.* The principles discussed in this Opinion are applicable to receivables and payables which represent contractual rights to receive money

or contractual obligations to pay money on fixed or determinable dates, whether or not there is any stated provision for interest, except as stated in paragraphs 3 and 4. Such receivables and payables are collectively referred to in this Opinion as "notes." Examples are secured and unsecured notes, debentures, bonds, mortgage notes, equipment obligations, and some accounts receivable and payable.

3. Except that paragraph 16 covering statement presentation of discount and premium is applicable in all circumstances, this Opinion is not intended to apply to:

a. receivables and payables arising from transactions with customers or suppliers in the normal course of business which are due in customary trade terms not exceeding approximately one year;

b. amounts which do not require repayment in the future, but rather will be applied to the purchase price of the property, goods, or service involved (e.g., deposits or progress payments on construction contracts, advance payments for acquisition of resources and raw materials, advances to encourage exploration in the extractive industries);

c. amounts intended to provide security for one party to an agreement (e.g., security deposits, retainages on contracts);

d. the customary cash lending activities and

---

[1] *Present value* is the sum of the future payments discounted to the present date at an appropriate rate of interest. The Appendix contains a description of the valuation process.

demand or savings deposit activities of financial institutions whose primary business is lending money;

e. transactions where interest rates are affected by the tax attributes or legal restrictions prescribed by a governmental agency (e.g., industrial revenue bonds, tax exempt obligations, government guaranteed obligations, income tax settlements); and

f. transactions between parent and subsidiary companies and between subsidiaries of a common parent.[2]

4. This Opinion is also not intended to apply to, and the Board is not presently taking a position[3] as to, the application of the present value measurement (valuation) technique to estimates of contractual or other obligations assumed in connection with sales of property, goods, or service, for example, a warranty for product performance. This Opinion does not alter the accounting for convertible debt securities described in APB Opinion No. 14, *Accounting for Convertible Debt and Debt Issued with Stock Purchase Warrants.*

5. Paragraph 16 of this Opinion amends paragraph 6(g) of Chapter 3A, *Current Assets and Liabilities* of Accounting Research Bulletin No. 43 which covers the balance sheet classification of unamortized debt discount.[4]

DISCUSSION

6. *Note received or issued for cash.* The total amount of interest during the entire period of a cash loan is generally measured by the difference between the actual amount of cash received by the borrower and the total amount agreed to be repaid to the lender. Frequently, the stated or coupon interest rate differs from the prevailing rate applicable to similar notes, and the proceeds of the note differ from its face amount. As the Appendix to this Opinion demonstrates, such differences are related to differences between the present value upon issuance and the face amount of the note. The difference between the face amount and the proceeds upon issuance is shown as either discount or premium, which is amortized over the life of the note.[5]

7. *Unstated rights or privileges.* A note issued solely for cash equal to its face amount is presumed to earn the stated rate of interest. However, in some cases the parties may also exchange unstated (or stated) rights or privileges, which are given accounting recognition by establishing a note discount or premium account. In such instances, the effective interest rate differs from the stated rate. For example, a corporation may lend a supplier cash which is to be repaid five years hence with no stated interest. Such a noninterest bearing loan may be partial consideration under a purchase contract for supplier products at lower than the prevailing market prices. In this circumstance, the difference between the present value of the receivable and the cash loaned to the supplier is appropriately regarded as an addition to the cost of products purchased during the contract term. The note discount is amortized as interest income over the five-year life of the note.

8. *Note received or issued in a noncash transaction.* A note exchanged for property, goods, or service represents two elements, which may or may not be stipulated in the note: (1) the principal amount, equivalent to the bargained exchange price of the property, goods, or service as established between the supplier and the purchaser and (2) an interest factor to compensate the supplier over the life of the note for the use of funds he would have received in a cash transaction at the time of the exchange. Notes so exchanged are accordingly valued and accounted for at the present value of the consideration exchanged between the contracting parties at the date of the transaction in a manner similar to that followed for a cash transaction. The difference between the face amount and the present value upon issuance is shown as either discount or premium, which is amortized over the life of the note.

9. *Determining present value.* If determinable, the established exchange price (which, presumably, is the same as the price for a cash sale) of property, goods, or service acquired or sold in consideration for a note may be used to establish the present value

---

[2]The Board has deferred consideration of the treatment of transactions between such companies pending consideration of the subject of reporting on components of a business enterprise and completion of the Accounting Research Study on intercorporate investments.

[3]In paragraph 6 of APB Opinion No. 10, *Omnibus—1966,* the Board concluded that deferred income taxes should not be accounted for on a discounted (present value) basis. That conclusion is not modified by this Opinion.

[4]This Opinion amends APB Statement No. 4, *Basic Concepts and Accounting Principles Underlying Financial Statements of Business Enterprises,* to the extent that it relates to recording and disclosing interest on receivables and payables.

[5]For example, if a bond is issued at a discount or premium, such discount or premium is recognized in accounting for the original issue. The coupon or stated interest rate is not regarded as the effective yield or market rate. Moreover, if a long-term noninterest bearing note or bond is issued, its net proceeds are less than face amount and an effective interest rate is based on its market value upon issuance. As the Appendix illustrates, the coupon or stated rate of interest and the face amount of a note or bond may *not* be the appropriate bases for valuation. The presumption that market values provide the evidence for valuation must be overcome before using coupon or stated rates and face or maturity amounts as the bases for accounting.

of the note. When notes are traded in an open market, the market rate of interest and market value of the notes provide the evidence of the present value. The above methods are preferable means of establishing the present value of the note.

10. If an established exchange price is not determinable and if the note has no ready market, the problem of determining present value is more difficult. To estimate the present value of a note under such circumstances, an applicable interest rate is approximated which may differ from the stated or coupon rate. This process of approximation is frequently called imputation, and the resulting rate is often called an imputed interest rate. Nonrecognition of an apparently small difference between the stated rate of interest and the applicable current rate may have a material effect on the financial statements if the face amount of the note is large and its term is relatively long.

OPINION

11. *Note exchanged for cash.* When a note[6] is received or issued solely for cash and no other right or privilege is exchanged, it is presumed to have a present value at issuance measured by the cash proceeds exchanged. If cash and some other rights or privileges are exchanged for a note, the value of the rights or privileges should be given accounting recognition as described in paragraph 7.

12. *Note exchanged for property, goods, or service.* When a note is exchanged for property, goods, or service in a bargained transaction entered into at arm's length, there should be a general presumption that the rate of interest stipulated by the parties to the transaction represents fair and adequate compensation to the supplier for the use of the related funds. That presumption, however, must not permit the form of the transaction to prevail over its economic substance and thus would not apply if (1) interest is not stated, or (2) the stated interest rate is unreasonable (paragraphs 13 and 14) or (3) the stated face amount of the note is materially different from the current cash sales price for the same or similar items or from the market value of the note at the date of the transaction. In these circumstances, the note, the sales price, and the cost of the property, goods, or service exchanged for the note should be recorded at the fair value of the property, goods, or services or at an amount that reasonably approximates the market value of the note, whichever is the more clearly determinable. That amount may or may not be the same as its face amount, and any resulting discount or premium should be accounted for as an element of interest over the life of the note (paragraph 15). In the absence of established exchange prices for the related property, goods, or service or evidence of the market value of the note (paragraph 9), the present value of a note that stipulates either no interest or a rate of interest that is clearly unreasonable should be determined by discounting all future payments on the notes using an imputed rate of interest as described in paragraphs 13 and 14. This determination should be made at the time the note is issued, assumed, or acquired; any subsequent changes in prevailing interest rates should be ignored.

13. *Determining an appropriate interest rate.* The variety of transactions encountered precludes any specific interest rate from being applicable in all circumstances. However, some general guides may be stated. The choice of a rate may be affected by the credit standing of the issuer, restrictive covenants, the collateral, payment and other terms pertaining to the debt, and, if appropriate, the tax consequences to the buyer and seller. The prevailing rates for similar instruments of issuers with similar credit ratings will normally help determine the appropriate interest rate for determining the present value of a specific note at its date of issuance. In any event, the rate used for valuation purposes will normally be at least equal to the rate at which the debtor can obtain financing of a similar nature from other sources at the date of the transaction. The objective is to approximate the rate which would have resulted if an independent borrower and an independent lender had negotiated a similar transaction under comparable terms and conditions with the option to pay the cash price upon purchase or to give a note for the amount of the purchase which bears the prevailing rate of interest to maturity.

14. The selection of a rate may be affected by many considerations. For instance, where applicable, the choice of a rate may be influenced by (a) an approximation of the prevailing market rates for the source of credit that would provide a market for sale or assignment of the note; (b) the prime or higher rate for notes which are discounted with banks, giving due weight to the credit standing of the maker; (c) published market rates for similar quality bonds; (d) current rates for debentures with substantially identical terms and risks that are traded in open markets; and (e) the current rate charged by investors for first or second mortgage loans on similar property.[7]

---

[6]Paragraphs 2, 3 and 4 describe the applicability of this Opinion.

[7]A theory has been advanced which states that no imputation of interest is necessary if the stated interest rate on a note receivable exceeds the interest cost on the borrowed funds used to finance such notes. The Board considers this theory unacceptable for reasons discussed in this Opinion.

15. *Amortization of discount and premium.* With respect to a note which by the provisions of this Opinion requires the imputation of interest, the difference between the present value and the face amount should be treated as discount or premium[8] and amortized as interest expense or income over the life of the note in such a way as to result in a constant rate of interest when applied to the amount outstanding at the beginning of any given period. This is the "interest" method described in and supported by paragraphs 16 and 17 of APB Opinion No. 12, *Omnibus Opinion—1967.* However, other methods of amortization may be used if the results obtained are not materially different from those which would result from the "interest" method.

16. *Statement presentation of discount and premium.* The discount or premium resulting from the determination of present value in cash or non-cash transactions is not an asset or liability separable from the note which gives rise to it. Therefore, the discount or premium should be reported in the balance sheet as a direct deduction from or addition to the face amount of the note. It should not be classified as a deferred charge or deferred credit. The description of the note should include the effective interest rate; the face amount should also be disclosed in the financial statements or in the notes to the statements.[9] Amortization of discount or premium should be reported as interest in the statement of income. Issue costs should be reported in the balance sheet as deferred charges.

EFFECTIVE DATE

17. This Opinion shall be effective for transactions entered into on or after October 1, 1971. The Board believes that the conclusions as to balance sheet presentation and disclosure in paragraph 16 should apply to transactions made prior as well as subsequent to the issuance of this Opinion. However, this Opinion is not intended to require the discounting of

notes existing on September 30, 1971 which were not previously discounted. Notes that were previously recorded in fiscal years ending before October 1, 1971 should not be adjusted. However, notes that have previously been recorded in the fiscal year in which October 1, 1971 occurs may be adjusted to comply with the provisions of this Opinion.

The Opinion entitled "Interest on Receivables and Payables" was adopted unanimously by the eighteen members of the Board.

NOTES

Opinions of the Accounting Principles Board present the conclusions of at least two-thirds of the members of the Board, which is the senior technical body of the Institute authorized to issue pronouncements on accounting principles.

Board Opinions are considered appropriate in all circumstances covered but need not be applied to immaterial items.

Covering all possible conditions and circumstances in an Opinion of the Accounting Principles Board is usually impracticable. The substance of transactions and the principles, guides, rules, and criteria described in Opinions should control the accounting for transactions not expressly covered.

Unless otherwise stated, Opinions of the Board are not intended to be retroactive.

Council of the Institute has resolved that Institute members should disclose departures from Board Opinions in their reports as independent auditors when the effect of the departures on the financial statements is material or see to it that such departures are disclosed in notes to the financial statements and, where practicable, should disclose their effects on the financial statements (Special Bulletin, Disclosure of Departures from Opinions of the Accounting Principles Board, October 1964). Members of the Institute must assume the burden of justifying any such departures.

Accounting Principles Board (1971)

Philip L. Defliese, *Chairman*	Robert L. Ferst	Louis M. Kessler
Donald J. Bevis	Newman T. Halvorson	Oral L. Luper
Milton M. Broeker	Robert Hampton, III	David Norr
Leo E. Burger	Emmett S. Harrington	George C. Watt
George R. Catlett	Charles B. Hellerson	Glenn A. Welsch
Joseph P. Cummings	Charles T. Horngren	Frank T. Weston

---

[8]Differences between the recognition for financial accounting purposes and income tax purposes of discount or premium resulting from determination of the present value of a note should be treated as timing differences in accordance with APB Opinion No. 11, *Accounting for Income Taxes.*

[9]Refer to the Appendix for illustrations of balance sheet presentation.

Appendix A

18. *Present value concepts.* Upon issuance of a note or bond, the issuer customarily records as a liability the face or principal amount of the obligation. Ordinarily, the recorded liability also represents the amount which is to be repaid upon maturity of the obligation. The value recorded in the liability account, however, may be different from the proceeds received or the present value of the obligation at issuance if the market rate of interest differs from the coupon rate of interest. For example, consider the issuance of a $1,000, 20-year bond which bears interest at 10% annually. If we assume that 10% is an appropriate market rate of interest for such a bond the proceeds at issuance will be $1,000. The bond payable would be recorded at $1,000 which represents the amount repayable at maturity and also the present value at issuance which is equal to the proceeds. However, under similar circumstances, if the prevailing market rate were more (less) than 10%, a 20-year 10% bond with a face amount of $1,000 would usually have a value at issuance and provide cash proceeds of less (more) than $1,000. The significant point is that, upon issuance, a bond is valued at (1) the present value of the future coupon interest payments *plus* (2) the present value of the future principal payments (face amount). These two sets of future cash payments are discounted at the prevailing market rate of interest (for an equivalent security) at the date of issuance of the debt. As the 8% and 12% columns show, premium or discount arises when the prevailing market rate of interest differs from the coupon rate:

	Assume prevailing market rate of		
	10%	*8%*	*12%*
1. Present value of annual interest payments of $100 (the coupon rate of 10% of $1,000) for 20 years	$ 851	$ 982	$747
2. Present value of payment of the face amount of $1,000 at the end of year 20	149	215	104
Present value and proceeds at date of issuance	$1,000	$1,197	$851

19. In the case of a $1,000 noninterest bearing 20-year note, where the prevailing market rate for comparable credit risks is 10%, the following valuation should be made:

1. Present value of no annual interest payments	$ 0
2. Present value of payment of the face amount of $1,000 at the end of year 20	149
Present value and proceeds at date of issuance	$149

Comparison of the results of the illustrations in paragraph 18 with the illustration above shows the significant impact of interest.

20. *Illustrations of balance sheet presentation of notes which are discounted.*

	December 31	
	1970	*1969*
Example 1—*Discount presented in caption*		
NOTE RECEIVABLE FROM SALE OF PROPERTY:		
$1,000,000 face amount, noninterest bearing, due December 31, 1975 (less unamortized discount based on imputed interest rate of 8%—1970, $320,000; 1969, $370,000)	$ 680,000	$ 630,000
Example 2—*Discount presented separately*		
NOTE RECEIVABLE FROM SALE OF PROPERTY:		
Noninterest bearing note due December 31, 1975	$ 1,000,000	$ 1,000,000
Less unamortized discount based on imputed interest rate of 8%	320,000	370,000
Note receivable less unamortized discount	$ 680,000	$ 630,000
Example 3—*Several notes involved*		
LONG-TERM DEBT (Note 1):		
Principal amount	$24,000,000	$24,000,000
Less unamortized discount	2,070,000	2,192,000
Long-term debt less unamortized discount	$21,930,000	$21,808,000

Note 1—Long-Term Debt
Long-term debt at December 31, 1970 consisted of the following:

	Principal	Unamortized Discount
6% subordinated debentures, due 1984 (discount is based on imputed interest rate of 7%)	$20,000,000	$ 1,750,000
6 1/2% bank loan, due 1973	3,000,000	—
Noninterest bearing note issued in connection with acquisition of property, due 1975 (discount is based on imputed interest rate of 8%)	1,000,000	320,000
Total	$24,000,000	$ 2,070,000

APB Opinion No. 22
Disclosure of Accounting Policies

STATUS

Issued: April 1972

Effective Date: For fiscal years beginning after December 31, 1971

Affects: No other pronouncements

Affected by: Paragraphs 6, 7, 8, and 12 amended by FAS 95
Paragraph 13 amended by FAS 2, FAS 8, and FAS 52
Footnote 2 amended by FAS 111

Other Interpretive Pronouncements: AIN-APB 22, Interpretation No. 1 (Superseded by FAS 111)
FTB 81-1 (Superseded by FAS 80)
FTB 82-1

APB Opinion No. 22
Disclosure of Accounting Policies

CONTENTS

INTRODUCTION

1. In recent years, a number of business enterprises have adopted the practice of including in their annual reports to shareholders a separate summary of the significant accounting policies followed in preparing the financial statements. This disclosure has been favorably received by users of financial statements and endorsed by organizations representing corporate business.

2. Practice by those entities that present summaries of accounting policies has varied considerably. Some present the summary of accounting policies as an integral part of the financial statements; others present it as supplementary information. In addition, both the nature and the degree of disclosure vary, and related guidelines are lacking.

3. Disclosure of accounting policies by those entities that do not present separate summaries has varied also. Some have included, in footnotes relating to particular items in the financial statements, descriptions of all significant accounting policies. Most entities, however, have disclosed no information as to certain significant accounting policies.

4. In view of the increasing recognition of the usefulness of disclosure of accounting policies, the Accounting Principles Board has considered whether this disclosure should be required in financial statements and whether guides should be established for the form and scope of disclosure. This Opinion sets forth the Board's conclusions.

DISCUSSION

5. Financial statements are the end product of the financial accounting process, which is governed by generally accepted accounting principles on three levels: pervasive principles, broad operating princi-

ples, and detailed principles.[1] Applying generally accepted accounting principles requires that judgment be exercised as to the relative appropriateness of acceptable alternative principles and methods of application in specific circumstances of diverse and complex economic activities. Although the combined efforts of professional accounting bodies, of business, and of the regulatory agencies have significantly reduced the number of acceptable alternatives and are expected to reduce the number further, judgment must nevertheless be exercised in applying principles at all three levels.

6. The *accounting policies* of a reporting entity are the specific accounting principles and the methods of applying those principles that are judged by the management of the entity to be the most appropriate in the circumstances to present fairly financial position, changes in financial position, and results of operations in accordance with generally accepted accounting principles and that accordingly have been adopted for preparing the financial statements.

7. The accounting policies adopted by a reporting entity can affect significantly the presentation of its financial position, changes in financial position, and results of operations. Accordingly, the usefulness of financial statements for purposes of making economic decisions about the reporting entity depends significantly upon the user's understanding of the accounting policies followed by the entity.

OPINION

Applicability

8. The Board concludes that information about the accounting policies adopted by a reporting entity is essential for financial statement users. When financial statements are issued purporting to present fairly financial position, changes in financial posi-

---

[1] See APB Statement No. 4, *Basic Concepts and Accounting Principles Underlying Financial Statements of Business Enterprises,* Chapters 6, 7, and 8. This Opinion amends Statement No. 4 insofar as it relates to disclosure of accounting policies.

tion, and results of operations in accordance with generally accepted accounting principles, a description of all significant accounting policies of the reporting entity should be included as an integral part of the financial statements. In circumstances where it may be appropriate to issue one or more of the basic financial statements without the others, purporting to present fairly the information given in accordance with generally accepted accounting principles, statements so presented should also include disclosure of the pertinent accounting policies.

9. The Board also concludes that information about the accounting policies adopted and followed by not-for-profit entities should be presented as an integral part of their financial statements.

10. The provisions of paragraphs 8 and 9 above are not intended to apply to unaudited financial statements issued as of a date between annual reporting dates (e.g., each quarter) if the reporting entity has not changed its accounting policies since the end of its preceding fiscal year.[2]

11. This Opinion does not supersede any prior pronouncement of the American Institute of Certified Public Accountants relating to disclosure requirements.

Content

12. Disclosure of accounting policies should identify and describe the accounting principles followed by the reporting entity and the methods of applying those principles that materially affect the determination of financial position, changes in financial position, or results of operations. In general, the disclosure should encompass important judgments as to appropriateness of principles relating to recognition of revenue and allocation of asset costs to current and future periods; in particular, it should encompass those accounting principles and methods that involve any of the following:

a. A selection from existing acceptable alternatives;
b. Principles and methods peculiar to the industry in which the reporting entity operates, even if such principles and methods are predominantly followed in that industry;
c. Unusual or innovative applications of generally accepted accounting principles (and, as applicable, of principles and methods peculiar to the industry in which the reporting entity operates).

13. Examples of disclosures by a business entity

commonly required with respect to accounting policies would include, among others, those relating to basis of consolidation, depreciation methods, amortization of intangibles, inventory pricing, accounting for research and development costs (including basis for amortization), translation of foreign currencies, recognition of profit on long-term construction-type contracts, and recognition of revenue from franchising and leasing operations. This list of examples is not all-inclusive.

14. Financial statement disclosure of accounting policies should not duplicate details (e.g., composition of inventories or of plant assets) presented elsewhere as part of the financial statements. In some cases, the disclosure of accounting policies should refer to related details presented elsewhere as part of the financial statements; for example, changes in accounting policies during the period should be described with cross-reference to the disclosure required by APB Opinion No. 20, *Accounting Changes,* of the current effect of the change and of the pro forma effect of retroactive application.

Format

15. The Board recognizes the need for flexibility in matters of format (including the location) of disclosure of accounting policies provided that the reporting entity identifies and describes its significant accounting policies as an integral part of its financial statements in accordance with the foregoing guides in this Opinion. The Board believes that the disclosure is particularly useful if given in a separate *Summary of Significant Accounting Policies* preceding the notes to financial statements or as the initial note. Accordingly, it expresses its preference for that format under the same or a similar title.

EFFECTIVE DATE

16. This Opinion shall be effective for fiscal years beginning after December 31, 1971. The Board, however, encourages earlier application of the provisions of this Opinion.

The Opinion entitled "Disclosure of Accounting Policies" was adopted unanimously by the eighteen members of the Board, of whom four, Messrs. Broeker, Burger, Norr and Watt assented with qualification.

Messrs. Broeker, Burger and Watt assent to the issuance of this Opinion because they believe it should enhance the usefulness of financial state-

---

[2]The Board recognizes also that it may be appropriate to omit disclosure of accounting policies in some other circumstances; for example, from financial statements restricted to internal use only (see Statement on Auditing Procedure No. 38, paragraphs 5 and 6) and from certain special reports in which incomplete or no financial presentations are made (see Statement on Auditing Procedure No. 33, Chapter 13, paragraphs 9 and 10).

ments to investors and other users. However, they qualify their assent because paragraph 10 does not require accounting policies to be disclosed in unaudited interim financial statements which are intended to present fairly financial position, changes in financial position, and results of operations in accordance with generally accepted accounting principles. They agree that the provisions of paragraphs 8 and 9 should not apply to incomplete or condensed financial data published periodically when no accounting policy has been changed. To say that there is a different degree of adequacy of disclosure as between unaudited interim financial statements that purport to present fairly financial position, changes in financial position, and results of operations in accordance with generally accepted accounting principles and audited interim financial statements that purport to present the same thing is an inconsistent and untenable position. Furthermore, they believe that it is entirely inconsistent for paragraph 10 to permit the omission of some disclosures from such unaudited interim financial statements while paragraph 11 calls for the inclusion of other disclosures required by prior pronouncements of the American Institute of Certified Public Accountants.

Messrs. Broeker, Burger and Watt, while not agreeing with paragraph 10, also believe that it should have made clear that, if the reporting entity has changed its accounting policies since the end of its preceding fiscal year, it should have to describe only those that were changed.

Mr. Norr assents to the issuance of this Opinion but feels that paragraph 12 does not go far enough. He believes that mere disclosure of accounting policies does not meet the needs of readers. Where alternatives exist he believes that standards must be created. Then deviations from standard must be indicated in order to measure the dollar impact on net income. In the absence of such alternatively derived net income figures he believes the user is not well served.

NOTES

Opinions of the Accounting Principles Board present the conclusions of at least two-thirds of the members of the Board, which is the senior technical body of the Institute authorized to issue pronouncements on accounting principles.

Board Opinions are considered appropriate in all circumstances covered but need not be applied to immaterial items.

Covering all possible conditions and circumstances in an Opinion of the Accounting Principles Board is usually impracticable. The substance of transactions and the principles, guides, rules, and criteria described in Opinions should control the accounting for transactions not expressly covered.

Unless otherwise stated, Opinions of the Board are not intended to be retroactive.

Council of the Institute has resolved that Institute members should disclose departures from Board Opinions in their reports as independent auditors when the effect of the departures on the financial statements is material or see to it that such departures are disclosed in notes to the financial statements and, where practicable, should disclose their effects on the financial statements (Special Bulletin, Disclosure of Departures from Opinions of the Accounting Principles Board, *October 1964). Members of the Institute must assume the burden of justifying any such departures.*

Accounting Principles Board (1972)

Philip L. Defliese,
  Chairman
Donald J. Bevis
Albert J. Bows
Milton M. Broeker
Leo E. Burger
Joseph P. Cummings

Robert L. Ferst
Oscar Gellein
Newman T. Halvorson
Robert Hampton, III
Donald J. Hayes
Charles B. Hellerson

Charles T. Horngren
Louis M. Kessler
David Norr
George C. Watt
Allan Wear
Glenn A. Welsch

APB Opinion No. 23
Accounting for Income Taxes—Special Areas

STATUS

Issued: April 1972

Effective Date: For fiscal periods beginning after December 31, 1971

Affects: Supersedes ARB 51, paragraph 16
Supersedes APB 11, paragraphs 38, 39, and 41
Supersedes APB 18, paragraph 19(j) and footnote 11

Affected by: Paragraph 2 amended by FAS 9
Paragraph 4 superseded by FAS 71
Paragraphs 9, 13, and 21 and footnotes 7 and 9 amended by FAS 96 and FAS 109
Paragraph 10 amended by FAS 96
Paragraph 10 superseded by FAS 109
Paragraphs 11, 14, and 24 and footnotes 4, 6, and 10 superseded by FAS 96 and FAS 109
Paragraph 17 amended by FAS 96
Paragraph 23 amended by FAS 109
Paragraphs 26 through 30 and footnote 11 superseded by FAS 60
Footnote 3 superseded by FAS 109

Other Interpretive Pronouncements: AIN-APB 23, Interpretation No. 1 (Superseded by FAS 96 and FAS 109)
FIN 22 (Superseded by FAS 96 and FAS 109)
FIN 29 (Superseded by FAS 96 and FAS 109)
FTB 84-2 (Superseded by FAS 96 and FAS 109)

APB Opinion No. 23
Accounting for Income Taxes—Special Areas

CONTENTS

INTRODUCTION

1. In December 1967 the Accounting Principles Board issued APB Opinion No. 11, *Accounting for Income Taxes,* but deferred modifying the practices of accounting for income taxes in five special areas identified in paragraphs 38 through 41 of that Opinion as requiring further study:

a. Undistributed earnings of subsidiaries
b. Intangible development costs in the oil and gas industry
c. "General reserves" of stock savings and loan associations
d. Amounts designated as "policyholders' surplus" by stock life insurance companies
e. Deposits in statutory reserve funds by United States steamship companies.

2. The Board has examined the characteristics of the tax consequences of transactions in the three special areas designated (a), (c), and (d) above and sets forth in this Opinion its conclusions on appropriate accounting treatments. The Board continues to defer conclusions on intangible development costs in the oil and gas industry pending the issuance of an Opinion on extractive industries. The Board also defers conclusions on deposits in capital construction funds or statutory reserve funds by United

States steamship companies until regulations covering the provisions of the Merchant Marine Act of 1970 are available; experience under the 1970 Act, which substantially modified the Merchant Marine Act of 1936, is now limited. The Board also expresses in this Opinion its conclusions on accounting for taxes on income from investments in corporate joint ventures accounted for by the equity method in accordance with APB Opinion No. 18, *The Equity Method of Accounting for Investments in Common Stock.* APB Opinion No. 24 covers accounting for taxes on income from investments in common stock accounted for by the equity method (other than subsidiaries and corporate joint ventures).

3. This Opinion supersedes paragraph 16 of Accounting Research Bulletin No. 51, *Consolidated Financial Statements* paragraphs 38, 39, and 41 of APB Opinion No. 11 and paragraph 19(j) of APB Opinion No. 18. Except as stated in the preceding sentence this Opinion does not modify APB Opinion No. 11.

4. This Opinion applies to financial statements which purport to present financial position, results of operations, and changes in financial position in conformity with generally accepted accounting principles. It does not apply to regulated industries in

those circumstances meeting the standards described in the Addendum to APB Opinion No. 2, *Accounting for the "Investment Credit."*

Discussion

5. In APB Opinion No. 11 the Board defined differences between taxable income and pretax accounting income as either timing differences or permanent differences and provided criteria for distinguishing between the differences. Timing differences are "Differences between the periods in which transactions affect taxable income and the periods in which they enter into the determination of pretax accounting income. Timing differences originate in one period and reverse or 'turn around' in one or more subsequent periods." Permanent differences are "Differences between taxable income and pretax accounting income arising from transactions that, under applicable tax laws and regulations, will not be offset by corresponding differences or 'turn around' in other periods." The Board also recognized that the tax consequences of a number of other transactions are somewhat similar to those of timing differences; however, the initial differences between taxable income and pretax accounting income related to the transactions may not reverse until indefinite future periods or may never reverse.

6. A timing difference arises when the initial difference between taxable income and pretax accounting income originates in one period and predictably reverses or turns around in one or more subsequent periods. The reversal of a timing difference at some future date is definite and the period of reversal is generally predictable within reasonable limits. Sometimes, however, reversal of a difference cannot be predicted because the events that create the tax consequences are controlled by the taxpayer and frequently require that the taxpayer take specific action before the initial difference reverses.

UNDISTRIBUTED EARNINGS OF SUBSIDIARIES

Discussion

7. Paragraph 16 of ARB No. 51, *Consolidated Financial Statements,* which is superseded by this Opinion, provided guides for interperiod allocation of income taxes that will be incurred at the date that previously undistributed earnings of subsidiaries are remitted to the parent company.[1] The concept of accruing income taxes for earnings included in consolidated income in accordance with ARB No. 51 has been applied inconsistently. Some believe that the only appropriate method is to accrue related deferred taxes substantially in accordance with paragraphs 36 and 37 of APB Opinion No. 11 while others believe that under the criteria set forth in ARB No. 51 a parent company need accrue related deferred taxes only if the transfer of earnings to the parent company in a taxable distribution is imminent or relatively certain. Disclosure of the accounting for income taxes on undistributed earnings of subsidiaries has often been inadequate. Some believe that the contingent liability for taxes that would be payable if the undistributed earnings of subsidiaries were remitted should be disclosed. In their view changing circumstances, often beyond the control of the parent company, may accelerate distribution of earnings of a subsidiary so that the parent company will incur a tax for which no provision has been made. They believe an inability to determine the exact amount of the tax that might be payable is in itself no justification for not accruing the best current estimate of the contingent liability. Others believe that instead the amount of undistributed earnings of subsidiaries for which a parent company has not accrued income taxes should be disclosed in notes to financial statements. In their view disclosure of a hypothetical tax which would be payable, assuming those earnings were distributed currently, implies a contradiction of the decision that it is not necessary to provide for income taxes on the earnings in the financial statements. They do not believe that such a hypothetical tax is normally a realistic quantification of the contingent taxes that would be incurred even if some portion of the undistributed earnings were remitted.

8. A domestic or foreign subsidiary remits earnings to a parent company after the parties consider numerous factors, including the following:

a. Financial requirements of the parent company
b. Financial requirements of the subsidiary
c. Operational and fiscal objectives of the parent company, both long-term and short-term
d. Remittance restrictions imposed by governments
e. Remittance restrictions imposed by lease or financing agreements of the subsidiary
f. Tax consequences of the remittance.

Remittance of earnings of a subsidiary may some-

---

[1]Paragraph 16 of ARB No. 51 stated: "When separate income tax returns are filed, income taxes usually are incurred when earnings of subsidiaries are transferred to the parent. Where it is reasonable to assume that a part or all of the undistributed earnings of a subsidiary will be transferred to the parent in a taxable distribution, provision for related income taxes should be made on an estimated basis at the time the earnings are included in consolidated income, unless these taxes are immaterial in amount when effect is given, for example, to dividend-received deductions or foreign-tax credits. There is no need to provide for income tax to the parent company in cases where the income has been, or there is evidence that it will be, permanently invested by the subsidiaries, or where the only likely distribution would be in the form of a tax-free liquidation."

times be indefinite because of the specific long-term investment plans and objectives of the parent company. Even in the absence of long-term investment plans, the flexibility inherent in the United States Internal Revenue Code may permit a parent company to postpone income taxes on the earnings of a subsidiary for an extended period or may permit the ultimate distribution to be taxed at special rates applicable to the nature of the distribution. Other circumstances may indicate that the earnings will probably be remitted in the foreseeable future. However, the parent company may control the events that create the tax consequences in either circumstance.

Opinion

9. The Board concludes that including undistributed earnings of a subsidiary[2] in the pretax accounting income of a parent company, either through consolidation or accounting for the investment by the equity method, may result in a timing difference, in a difference that may not reverse until indefinite future periods, or in a combination of both types of differences, depending on the intent and actions of the parent company.

10. *Timing difference.* The Board believes it should be presumed that all undistributed earnings of a subsidiary will be transferred to the parent company. Accordingly, the undistributed earnings of a subsidiary included in consolidated income (or in income of the parent company[3]) should be accounted for as a timing difference, except to the extent that some or all of the undistributed earnings meet the criteria in paragraph 12. Income taxes attributable to a timing difference in reporting undistributed earnings of a subsidiary should be accounted for in accordance with the provisions of APB Opinion No. 11 for interperiod allocation of taxes. Problems in measuring and recognizing the tax effect of a timing difference do not justify ignoring income taxes related to the timing difference. Income taxes of the parent company applicable to a timing difference in undistributed earnings of a subsidiary are necessarily based on estimates and assumptions. For example, the tax effect may be determined by assuming that unremitted earnings were distributed in the current period and that the parent company received the benefit of all available tax-planning alternatives and available tax credits and deductions.[4] The income tax expense of the parent company should also include taxes that would have been withheld if the undistributed earnings had been remitted as dividends.

11. The tax effect of a difference between taxable income and pretax accounting income attributable to losses of a subsidiary should be accounted for in accordance with the Board's conclusions on operating losses in paragraphs 44 through 50 of APB Opinion No. 11.

12. *Indefinite reversal criteria.* The presumption that all undistributed earnings will be transferred to the parent company may be overcome, and no income taxes should be accrued by the parent company, if sufficient evidence shows that the subsidiary has invested or will invest the undistributed earnings indefinitely or that the earnings will be remitted in a tax-free liquidation. A parent company should have evidence of specific plans for reinvestment of undistributed earnings of a subsidiary which demonstrate that remittance of the earnings will be postponed indefinitely. Experience of the companies and definite future programs of operations and remittances are examples of the types of evidence required to substantiate the parent company's representation of indefinite postponement of remittances from a subsidiary. If circumstances change and it becomes apparent that some or all of the undistributed earnings of a subsidiary will be remitted in the foreseeable future but income taxes have not been recognized by the parent company, it should accrue as an expense of the current period income taxes attributable to that remittance; income tax expense for such undistributed earnings should not be accounted for as an extraordinary item. If it becomes apparent that some or all of the undistributed earnings of a subsidiary on which income taxes have been accrued will not be remitted in the foreseeable future, the parent company should adjust income tax expense of the current period; such adjustment of income tax expense should not be accounted for as an extraordinary item.

13. *Change in investment.* An investment in common stock of a subsidiary may change so that it is no longer a subsidiary because the parent company sells a portion of the investment, the subsidiary sells additional stock, or other transactions affect the investment. If the remaining investment in common stock should be accounted for by the equity method, the investor should recognize income taxes on its share of current earnings of the investee company in accordance with the provisions of APB Opinion No. 24. If a parent company did not recognize income taxes on its equity in undistributed earnings

---

[2]The conclusions of the Board on undistributed earnings of a subsidiary also apply to the portion of the earnings of a Domestic International Sales Corporation (DISC) that is eligible for tax deferral.

[3]Paragraph 14 of APB Opinion No. 18.

[4]As the unused tax credits that are recognized by the parent in determining deferred income taxes on undistributed earnings of a subsidiary are subsequently realized, the initial reduction in deferred taxes should be reinstated at the then current rates in accordance with the provisions of APB Opinion No. 11.

of a subsidiary for the reasons cited in paragraph 12 (and the company in which the investment is held ceases to be a subsidiary), it should accrue as a current period-expense income taxes on undistributed earnings in the period that it becomes apparent[5] that any of those undistributed earnings (prior to the change in status) will be remitted; the accrual of those income taxes should not be accounted for as an extraordinary item. If a parent company recognized income taxes on its equity in undistributed earnings of a subsidiary, the amount of deferred income taxes of the parent attributable to undistributed earnings of the subsidiary should be considered in accounting for a disposition through sale or other transaction which reduces the investment.

14. *Disclosure.* Information concerning undistributed earnings of a subsidiary for which income taxes have not been accrued that should be disclosed in notes to financial statements includes:

a. A declaration of an intention to reinvest undistributed earnings of a subsidiary to support the conclusion that remittance of those earnings has been indefinitely postponed, or a declaration that the undistributed earnings will be remitted in the form of a tax-free liquidation, and

b. The cumulative amount of undistributed earnings on which the parent company has not recognized income taxes.[6]

INVESTMENTS IN CORPORATE JOINT VENTURES

Discussion

15. Corporate joint ventures, as defined in APB Opinion No. 18, are of two kinds: (1) those essentially permanent in duration and (2) those that have a life limited by the nature of the venture or other business activity. In APB Opinion No. 18 the Board concluded that the equity method of accounting best enables an investor in a corporate joint venture to recognize the underlying nature of the investment regardless of duration.

16. Unless characteristics indicate a limited life, a corporate joint venture has many of the characteristics of a subsidiary. The investors usually participate

in the management of the joint venture, consider the factors set forth in paragraph 8 above, and agree (frequently before forming the venture) as to plans for long-term investment, for utilizing the flexibility inherent in the United States Internal Revenue Code, and for planned remittances.

Opinion

17. The Board concludes that the principles applicable to undistributed earnings of subsidiaries (paragraphs 9, 10, 11, 12, and 13) also apply to tax effects of differences between taxable income and pretax accounting income attributable to earnings of corporate joint ventures that are essentially permanent in duration and are accounted for by the equity method.[7]

18. *Disclosure.* The disclosure requirements set forth in paragraph 14 also apply to earnings of corporate joint ventures.

"BAD DEBT RESERVES" OF SAVINGS AND LOAN ASSOCIATIONS

Discussion

19. Regulatory authorities require both stock and mutual savings and loan associations to appropriate a portion of earnings to general reserves[8] and to retain the reserves as a protection for depositors. Provisions of the United States Internal Revenue Code permit a savings and loan association to deduct an annual addition to a reserve for bad debts[8] in determining taxable income, subject to certain limitations. This annual addition permitted by the Code generally differs significantly from the bad debt experience upon which determination of pretax accounting income is based. Thus, taxable income and pretax accounting income of an association usually differ.

20. Although a general reserve determined according to requirements of the regulatory authorities is not directly related to a reserve for bad debts computed according to provisions of the United States Internal Revenue Code, the purposes and restrictions of each reserve are similar. Amounts of bad debt deductions for income tax purposes are includ-

---

[5]The change in the status of an investment would not by itself mean that remittance of these undistributed earnings should be considered apparent.

[6]Other disclosure requirements in paragraphs 56-64 of APB Opinion No. 11 may also apply. Disclosure of other matters such as available tax credits and deductions may be desirable.

[7]Certain corporate joint ventures have a life limited by the nature of the venture, project, or other business activity. Therefore, a reasonable assumption is that a part or all of the undistributed earnings of the venture will be transferred to the investor in a taxable distribution. Deferred taxes should be recorded, in accordance with the concepts of APB Opinion No. 11 at the time the earnings (or losses) are included in the investor's income.

[8]The terms *general reserves* and *reserve for bad debts* are used in the context of the special meaning these terms have in regulatory pronouncements and in the United States Internal Revenue Code.

able in taxable income of later years only if the bad debt reserves are used subsequently for purposes other than to absorb bad debt losses.

21. The term *pretax accounting income,* as used in this section, represents income or loss for a period, exclusive of related income tax expense, determined in conformity with generally accepted accounting principles. The term *taxable income,* as used in this section, represents pretax accounting income (a) adjusted for reversal of provisions for estimated losses on loans and property acquired in settlement of loans, and gains or losses on the sales of such property, and adjusted for permanent differences, and (b) after giving effect to the bad debt deduction allowable by the United States Internal Revenue Code assuming the applicable tax return were to be prepared based on such adjusted pretax accounting income.

22. Some believe that a difference between taxable income and pretax accounting income attributable to a bad debt reserve that is accounted for as part of the general reserve and undivided profits of a savings and loan association has attributes of a permanent or indefinite deferral of tax payments. In their view, a savings and loan association should not accrue income taxes on such differences. Others believe that this difference has the principal attributes of a timing difference as described in paragraphs 36 and 37 of APB Opinion No. 11. In effect, they believe that this difference is a Government-sponsored deferral of tax, that the Government has an equity in the savings and loan association to the extent of the deferred tax, and that it is inappropriate to include earnings in stockholders' equity without accruing income taxes which the association would incur if the earnings were distributed to stockholders or otherwise became subject to tax. In their view the savings and loan association should recognize deferred taxes on the difference.

Opinion

23. The Board concludes that a difference between taxable income and pretax accounting income attributable to a bad debt reserve that is accounted for as part of the general reserves and undivided profits of a savings and loan association[9] may not reverse until indefinite future periods or may never reverse. The association controls the events that create the tax consequence, and the association is required to take specific action before the initial difference reverses. Therefore, a savings and loan association should not provide income taxes on this

difference. However, if circumstances indicate that the association is likely to pay income taxes, either currently or in later years, because of known or expected reductions in the bad debt reserve, income taxes attributable to that reduction should be accrued as tax expense of the current period; the accrual of those income taxes should not be accounted for as an extraordinary item.

24. *Disclosure.* Information that should be disclosed in notes to financial statements of a savings and loan association concerning bad debt reserves that are accounted for as part of the general reserves and undivided profits includes:

a. The purposes for which the reserves are provided under the applicable rules and regulations and the fact that income taxes may be payable if the reserves are used for other purposes, and

b. The accumulated amount of the reserves for which income taxes have not been accrued.[10]

25. The disclosure requirements set forth in paragraph 24 also apply to a parent company of a savings and loan association accounting for that investment either through consolidation or by the equity method.

"POLICYHOLDERS' SURPLUS" OF STOCK LIFE INSURANCE COMPANIES

Discussion

26. The provisions of the United States Internal Revenue Code provide for the exclusion from taxable income of a stock life insurance company of amounts determined under a formula and the allocation of those amounts to policyholders' surplus until the total policyholders' surplus equals a specified maximum. The amounts excluded from taxable income and designated as policyholders' surplus are includable in taxable income of later years if the company elects to (a) distribute policyholders' surplus to stockholders as dividends, (b) transfer amounts from policyholders' surplus to shareholders' surplus designated for tax purposes as available for any business purpose, or (c) take, or if it fails to take, certain other specified actions (none of which usually occur).

27. Some believe that a difference between taxable income and pretax accounting income attributable to amounts designated as policyholders' surplus of a stock life insurance company has attributes of a per-

---

[9]Paragraph 38 of APB Opinion No. 11 indicated that the "general reserves" of stock savings and loan associations was a special area requiring further study. In practice the statement also has been applied to mutual savings and loan associations and mutual savings banks. The Board affirms that its conclusions in this Opinion apply to stock and mutual savings and loan associations and mutual savings banks.

[10]Other disclosure requirements in paragraphs 56-64 of APB Opinion No. 11 may also apply.

manent or indefinite deferral of tax payments. In their view, a stock life insurance company should not accrue income taxes on the difference between taxable income and pretax accounting income related to amounts designated as policyholders' surplus unless circumstances indicate that the insurance company is likely to pay income taxes, either currently or in future years, because of known or expected reductions in policyholders' surplus. Others believe that the difference has the principal attributes of a timing difference as described in paragraphs 36 and 37 of APB Opinion No. 11. In effect, they believe that the difference is a Government-sponsored deferral of tax, that the Government has an equity in the stock life insurance company to the extent of the deferred tax, and that it is inappropriate to include earnings in stockholders' equity without accruing income taxes which would be incurred by the stock life insurance company if those earnings were distributed to stockholders or otherwise became subject to tax. In their view the stock life insurance company should accrue deferred taxes on the difference.

Opinion

28. The Board concludes that a difference between taxable income and pretax accounting income attributable to amounts designated as policyholders' surplus of a stock life insurance company may not reverse until indefinite future periods or may never reverse. The insurance company controls the events that create the tax consequences and the company is generally required to take specific action before the initial difference reverses. Therefore, a stock life insurance company should not accrue income taxes on the difference between taxable income and pretax accounting income attributable to amounts designated as policyholders' surplus. However, if circumstances indicate that the insurance company is likely to pay income taxes, either currently or in later years, because of known or expected reductions in policyholders' surplus, income taxes attributable to that reduction should be accrued as a tax expense of the current period; the accrual of those income taxes should not be accounted for as an extraordinary item.

29. *Disclosure.* Information concerning amounts designated as policyholders' surplus of a stock life insurance company that should be disclosed in notes to financial statements includes:

a. The treatment of policyholders' surplus under the United States Internal Revenue Code and the fact that income taxes may be payable if the company takes certain specified actions, which should be appropriately described, and

b. The accumulated amount of the policyholders' surplus for which income taxes have not been accrued.[11]

30. The disclosure requirements set forth in paragraph 29 also apply to a parent company of a stock life insurance company accounting for that investment either through consolidation or by the equity method.

EFFECTIVE DATE

31. This Opinion shall be effective for all fiscal periods beginning after December 31, 1971. However, the Board encourages earlier application of the provisions of this Opinion.

32. The conclusions of the Board on accounting for income taxes on undistributed earnings of subsidiaries and corporate joint ventures represent a clarification of current practice. Accordingly, this Opinion should be applied retroactively to undistributed earnings of subsidiaries included in consolidated financial statements and to undistributed earnings applicable to unconsolidated subsidiaries and investments in corporate joint ventures accounted for by the equity method in accordance with APB Opinion No. 18. An adjustment resulting from a change in accounting method to comply with this Opinion should be treated as an adjustment of prior periods, and financial statements presented for the periods affected should be restated.

33. The conclusions of the Board on "bad debt reserves" of savings and loan associations and amounts designated as "policyholders' surplus" by stock life insurance companies agree generally with current practice. If application of this Opinion should result in a change in accounting principle, the adjustment should be treated as an adjustment of prior periods, and financial statements presented for the periods affected should be restated.

The Opinion entitled "Accounting for Income Taxes—Special Areas" was adopted by the assenting votes of fourteen members of the Board, of whom four, Messrs. Halvorson, Hellerson, Norr, and Watt, assented with qualification. Messrs. Bevis, Bows, Broeker, and Burger dissented.

Mr. Halvorson assents to the publication of this Opinion but believes that a company should be permitted to accrue taxes on differences between taxable income and pretax accounting income in any circumstances where management judgment so dictates and that the prohibition thereof expressed by the "should not" injunction in paragraphs 12, 23, and 28 will stifle what could be a desirable develop-

---

[11]Other disclosure requirements in paragraphs 56-64 of APB Opinion No. 11 may also apply.

ment in accounting. He further believes that the disclosure of the cumulative amount of untaxed earnings required by paragraphs 14, 24, and 29 should be coupled with a requirement to disclose the amount of such earnings for each period currently under report.

Mr. Hellerson assents to the issuance of this Opinion as he believes it does clarify and standardize the accounting in the areas encompassed by it. However, he qualifies his assent because of disagreement with the last two sentences of paragraph 12. It is his view that if undistributed earnings of a subsidiary on which income taxes have not been recognized are, in fact, remitted this may be prima facie evidence that the company's plans have changed and a tax on the remainder of the undistributed earnings which have not, in fact, been reinvested should be provided. He also disagrees with the final sentence in paragraph 12 which sanctions the reversal of a tax previously accrued. It is his view that any plans for reinvestment of undistributed earnings should be applied prospectively and not retroactively, i.e., the tax expense for the current and future periods should be affected. Further, it is his understanding that the thrust of the portion of the Opinion pertaining to undistributed earnings of subsidiaries is that all such undistributed earnings give rise to a timing difference for which comprehensive interperiod income tax allocation is required in accordance with APB Opinion No. 11, *Accounting for Income Taxes.* However, after giving effect to available tax-planning alternatives and available tax credits and deductions the resulting tax effect of the timing difference may be nil. He believes that paragraph 10, and particularly the second sentence thereof, does not clearly describe this thrust.

Mr. Norr assents to the publication of this Opinion but objects to the conclusions of paragraph 14(b). He believes that the most meaningful disclosure for the reader is the estimated amount of taxes that might be payable on undistributed earnings of the current period if such earnings were to be remitted currently taking into consideration all available tax-planning alternatives and available tax credits and deductions.

Mr. Watt assents to the issuance of this Opinion because it results in the accrual of only income taxes reasonably expected to be paid. However, he disagrees with the conclusions in paragraphs 12, 13, 23, and 28 that *in all cases* when circumstances change, income taxes not previously recognized or income taxes accrued but no longer required may never be accounted for as an extraordinary item. He believes that such adjustments should qualify as extraordinary in some cases based on a combination of extreme infrequency of occurrence and abnormal size. He further believes that this Opinion should not have an effective date prior to its issuance but instead should have been effective for fiscal periods beginning after December 31, 1972 to allow a reasonable time for preparation of information necessary to implement the Opinion.

Mr. Bevis dissents to this Opinion because he believes it contradicts the concepts of APB Opinion No. 11, *Accounting for Income Taxes.*

Messrs. Bows, Broeker, and Burger dissent to this Opinion because they believe the major conclusions relating to the omission of a requirement for providing deferred taxes are not supported in theory or logic by the provisions of the income tax laws. In their view, the Government sponsors a benefit by providing the use of tax funds during the deferment period (regardless of how long it may be), but it does not provide for the ultimate waiver of the taxes on those earnings. This Opinion validates a practice that they consider to be completely contrary to the underlying concepts of deferred tax accounting applicable to other businesses (APB Opinion No. 11) by sponsoring the idea that certain earnings may be accounted for on an accrual basis while the related income taxes are accounted for on the cash basis. They also believe that the accounting distinction provided in this Opinion for over 50% investors (no deferred income taxes) and in APB Opinion No. 24 for less than 50% investors (deferred taxes) is completely artificial.

NOTES

Opinions of the Accounting Principles Board present the conclusions of at least two-thirds of the members of the Board, which is the senior technical body of the Institute authorized to issue pronouncements on accounting principles.

Board Opinions are considered appropriate in all circumstances covered but need not be applied to immaterial items.

Covering all possible conditions and circumstances in an Opinion of the Accounting Principles Board is usually impracticable. The substance of transactions and the principles, guides, rules, and criteria described in Opinions should control the accounting for transactions not expressly covered.

Unless otherwise stated, Opinions of the Board are not intended to be retroactive.

Council of the Institute has resolved that Institute members should disclose departures from Board Opinions in their reports as independent auditors when the effect of the departures on the financial statements is material or see to it that such departures are disclosed in notes to the financial statements and, where practicable, should disclose their effects on the financial statements (Special Bulletin, Disclosure of Departures from Opinions of the Accounting Principles Board, *October 1964). Members of the Institute must assume the burden of justifying any such departures.*

Accounting Principles Board (1972)

Philip L. Defliese,
  Chairman
Donald J. Bevis
Albert J. Bows
Milton M. Broeker
Leo E. Burger
Joseph P. Cummings

Robert L. Ferst
Oscar Gellein
Newman T. Halvorson
Robert Hampton, III
Donald J. Hayes
Charles B. Hellerson

Charles T. Horngren
Louis M. Kessler
David Norr
George C. Watt
Allan Wear
Glenn A. Welsch

APB Opinion No. 24
Accounting for Income Taxes—Investments in Common Stock Accounted for by the Equity Method (Other than Subsidiaries and Corporate Joint Ventures)

STATUS

Issued: April 1972

Effective Date: For fiscal periods beginning after December 31, 1971

Affects: No other pronouncements

Affected by: Paragraph 3 superseded by FAS 71
            Superseded by FAS 96 and FAS 109

Other Interpretive Pronouncement: FIN 29 (Superseded by FAS 96 and FAS 109)

(The next page is 283.)

(This page intentionally left blank.)

APB Opinion No. 25
Accounting for Stock Issued to Employees

STATUS

Issued: October 1972

Effective Date: For awards granted after December 31, 1972

Affects: Amends ARB 43, Chapter 13B, paragraphs 6 through 14 and
     footnotes 2 and 3
    Supersedes AIN-ARB 43, Chapter 13B, Interpretation No. 1

Affected by: Paragraph 17 amended by FAS 96 and FAS 109

Other Interpretive Pronouncements: AIN-APB 25, Interpretation No. 1
                                      FIN 28
                                      FIN 38
                                      FTB 82-2

APB Opinion No. 25
Accounting for Stock Issued to Employees

CONTENTS

INTRODUCTION

Scope of Opinion

1. Many corporations have adopted various plans, contracts, and agreements to compensate officers and other employees by issuing to them stock of the employer corporation. Under traditional stock option and stock purchase plans an employer corporation grants options to purchase a fixed number of shares of stock of the corporation at a stated price during a specified period or grants rights to purchase shares of stock of the corporation at a stated price, often at a discount from the market price of the stock at the date the rights are granted. Stock options and purchase rights are normally granted for future services of employees. Accounting Research Bulletin No. 43, Chapter 13B, *Compensation Involved in Stock Option and Stock Purchase Plans* (1953), contains the principles of accounting for those plans (Reproduced in Appendix B).

2. Among traditional plans not described in Chapter 13B of ARB No. 43 are plans in which an employer corporation awards to employees shares of stock of the corporation for current or future services. Some corporations have replaced or supplemented traditional plans with more complex plans, contracts, and agreements for issuing stock. An arrangement may be based on variable factors that depend on future events; for example, a corporation may award a variable number of shares of stock or may grant a stock option with a variable option price. Other arrangements combine the characteristics of two or more types of plans, and some give an employee an election.

3. Accounting for employee services received as consideration for stock issued is included in an accounting research study[1] on stockholders' equity that is in process.

4. This Opinion deals with some aspects of accounting for stock issued to employees through both noncompensatory and compensatory plans (a plan is any arrangement to issue stock to officers and employees, as a group or individually). ARB No. 43, Chapter 13B, remains in effect for traditional stock option and stock purchase plans except that the measure of compensation is redefined in this Opinion. This Opinion recognizes certain practices that evolved after Chapter 13B of ARB No. 43 was adopted and applies the principles of that chapter to other plans in which the number of shares of stock that may be acquired by or awarded to an employee and the option or purchase price, if any, are known or determinable at the date of grant or award. It also specifies the accounting for (a) plans in which either the number of shares of stock or the option or purchase price depends on future events and (b) income tax benefits related to stock issued to employees through stock option, purchase, and award plans. Appendix A to the Opinion illustrates

---

[1] Accounting research studies are not pronouncements of the Board or of the Institute but are published for the purpose of stimulating discussion on important accounting matters.

measuring and accounting for compensation under typical plans.

Differing Views

5. Some accountants believe that compensation cost for all compensatory plans should be recorded at the date of grant or not later than the date of exercise. They believe that past experience and outside evidence of values can overcome difficulties in measuring compensation. Other accountants believe that compensation need not be recorded if an employee pays an amount that is at least equal to the market price of the stock at the date of grant and that problems in accounting for compensation plans pertain to plans in which the number of shares of stock or the option or purchase price cannot be determined until after the date of grant or award. Still other accountants, although they agree in principle with the first group, believe that progress will result from specifying the accounting for plans with variable factors but leaving Chapter 13B of ARB No. 43 in effect with modifications while the entire topic of accounting for compensation involving stock is studied.

6. Some accountants believe that a tax benefit attributable to compensation that is deductible in computing taxable income but is not recorded as an expense of any period results from a permanent difference. The benefit should therefore be recorded under paragraphs 33 and 34 of APB Opinion No. 11, *Accounting for Income Taxes,* as a reduction of income tax expense for the period that the benefit is received. Other accountants believe that the tax benefit results from issuing stock and should be accounted for as an adjustment of capital in addition to par or stated value of capital stock in accordance with paragraph 52 of APB Opinion No. 11.

OPINION

Noncompensatory Plans

7. Paragraphs 4 and 5 of Chapter 13B of ARB No. 43 describe stock option and stock purchase plans that may not be intended primarily to compensate employees. An employer corporation recognizes no compensation for services in computing consideration received for stock that is issued through noncompensatory plans. The Board concludes that at least four characteristics are essential in a noncompensatory plan: (a) substantially all full-time employees meeting limited employment qualifica-

tions may participate (employees owning a specified percent of the outstanding stock and executives may be excluded), (b) stock is offered to eligible employees equally or based on a uniform percentage of salary or wages (the plan may limit the number of shares of stock that an employee may purchase through the plan), (c) the time permitted for exercise of an option or purchase right is limited to a reasonable period, and (d) the discount from the market price of the stock is no greater than would be reasonable in an offer of stock to stockholders or others. An example of a noncompensatory plan is the "statutory" employee stock purchase plan that qualifies under Section 423 of the Internal Revenue Code.

Compensatory Plans

8. Plans that do not possess the four characteristics of noncompensatory plans are classified as compensatory plans. Since the major principles of Chapter 13B of ARB No. 43 are not changed, classification as a compensatory plan does not necessarily require that compensation cost be recognized.[2]

9. *Services as Consideration for Stock Issued.* The consideration that a corporation receives for stock issued through a stock option, purchase, or award plan consists of cash or other assets, if any, plus services received from the employee.

10. *Measuring Compensation for Services.* Compensation for services that a corporation receives as consideration for stock issued through employee stock option, purchase, and award plans should be measured by the quoted market price of the stock at the measurement date less the amount, if any, that the employee is required to pay. That is the principle in Chapter 13B of ARB No. 43 with two modifications: (a) the meaning of fair value of stock for compensatory plans is narrowed and (b) the measurement date for plans with a variable number of shares of stock or a variable option or purchase price is different.

a. *Quoted market price* is substituted for *fair value.* The Board acknowledges the conclusion in Chapter 13B that "market quotations at a given date are not necessarily conclusive evidence" of fair value of shares of stock but concludes that, for purposes of this Opinion, the unadjusted quoted market price of a share of stock of the same class that trades freely in an established market should be used in measuring compensation. An employee's right to acquire or receive

---

[2]All compensation arrangements involving stock, regardless of the name given, should be accounted for according to their substance. For example, an arrangement in which the consideration for stock issued to an employee is a nonrecourse note secured by the stock issued may be in substance the same as the grant of a stock option and should be accounted for accordingly. The note should be classified as a reduction of stockholders' equity rather than as an asset.

shares of stock is presumed to have a value, and that value stems basically from the value of the stock to be received under the right. However, the value of the right is also affected by various other factors, some of which tend to diminish its value and some of which tend to enhance it. Those opposing factors include a known future purchase price (or no payment), restrictions on the employee's right to receive stock, absence of commissions on acquisition, different risks as compared with those of a stockholder, tax consequences to the employee, and restrictions on the employee's ability to transfer stock issued under the right. The effects of the opposing factors are difficult to measure, and a practical solution is to rely on quoted market price to measure compensation cost related to issuing both restricted (or letter) and unrestricted stock through stock option, purchase, or award plans. If a quoted market price is unavailable, the best estimate of the market value of the stock should be used to measure compensation.

b. *The measurement date* for determining compensation cost in stock option, purchase, and award plans is the first date on which are known both (1) the number of shares that an individual employee is entitled to receive and (2) the option or purchase price, if any. That date for many or most plans is the date an option or purchase right is granted or stock is awarded to an individual employee and is therefore unchanged from Chapter 13B of ARB No. 43. However, the measurement date may be later than the date of grant or award in plans with variable terms that depend on events after date of grant or award.

Thus a corporation recognizes compensation cost for stock issued through compensatory plans unless the employee pays an amount that is at least equal to the quoted market price of the stock at the measurement date.

11. *Applying the measurement principle*—The following supplements paragraph 10 for special situations in some plans.

a. Measuring compensation by the cost to an employer corporation of reacquired (treasury) stock that is distributed through a stock option, purchase, or award plan is not acceptable practice. The only exception is that compensation cost under a plan with all the provisions described in paragraph 11(c) may be measured by the cost of stock that the corporation (1) reacquires during the fiscal period for which the stock is to be awarded and (2) awards shortly thereafter to employees for services during that period.

b. The measurement date is not changed from the grant or award date to a later date solely by pro-

visions that termination of employment reduces the number of shares of stock that may be issued to an employee.

c. The measurement date of an award of stock for current service may be the end of the fiscal period, which is normally the effective date of the award, instead of the date that the award to an employee is determined if (1) the award is provided for by the terms of an established formal plan, (2) the plan designates the factors that determine the total dollar amount of awards to employees for the period (for example, a percent of income), although the total amount or the individual awards may not be known at the end of the period, and (3) the award pertains to current service of the employee for the period.

d. Renewing a stock option or purchase right or extending its period establishes a new measurement date as if the right were newly granted.

e. Transferring stock or assets to a trustee, agent, or other third party for distribution of stock to employees under the terms of an option, purchase, or award plan does not change the measurement date from a later date to the date of transfer unless the terms of the transfer provide that the stock (1) will not revert to the corporation, (2) will not be granted or awarded later to the same employee on terms different from or for services other than those specified in the original grant or award, and (3) will not be granted or awarded later to another employee.

f. The measurement date for a grant or award of convertible stock (or stock that is otherwise exchangeable for other securities of the corporation) is the date on which the ratio of conversion (or exchange) is known unless other terms are variable at that date (paragraph 10b). The higher of the quoted market price at the measurement date of (1) the convertible stock granted or awarded or (2) the securities into which the original grant or award is convertible should be used to measure compensation.

g. Cash paid to an employee to settle an earlier award of stock or to settle a grant of option to the employee should measure compensation cost. If the cash payment differs from the earlier measure of the award of stock or grant of option, compensation cost should be adjusted (paragraph 15). The amount that a corporation pays to an employee to purchase stock previously issued to the employee through a compensation plan is "cash paid to an employee to settle an earlier award of stock or to settle a grant of option" if stock is reacquired shortly after issuance. Cash proceeds that a corporation receives from sale of awarded stock or stock issued on exercise of an option and remits to the taxing authorities to cover required withholding of income taxes on an award is not "cash paid to an employee to settle an earlier award of stock or to settle a grant of option" in measuring compensation cost.

h. Some plans are a combination of two or more types of plans. An employer corporation may need to measure compensation for the separate parts. Compensation cost for a combination plan permitting an employee to elect one part should be measured according to the terms that an employee is most likely to elect based on the facts available each period.

12. *Accruing Compensation Cost.* Compensation cost in stock option, purchase, and award plans should be recognized as an expense of one or more periods in which an employee performs services and also as part or all of the consideration received for stock issued to the employee through a plan. The grant or award may specify the period or periods during which the employee performs services, or the period or periods may be inferred from the terms or from the past pattern of grants or awards (ARB No. 43, Chapter 13B, paragraph 14; APB Opinion No. 12, *Omnibus Opinion—1967,* paragraph 6).

13. An employee may perform services in several periods before an employer corporation issues stock to him for those services. The employer corporation should accrue compensation expense in each period in which the services are performed. If the measurement date is later than the date of grant or award, an employer corporation should record the compensation expense each period from date of grant or award to date of measurement based on the quoted market price of the stock at the end of each period.

14. If stock is issued in a plan before some or all of the services are performed,[3] part of the consideration recorded for the stock issued is unearned compensation and should be shown as a separate reduction of stockholders' equity. The unearned compensation should be accounted for as expense of the period or periods in which the employee performs service.

15. Accruing compensation expense may require estimates, and adjustment of those estimates in later periods may be necessary (APB Opinion No. 20, *Accounting Changes,* paragraphs 31 to 33). For example, if a stock option is not exercised (or awarded stock is returned to the corporation) because an employee fails to fulfill an obligation, the estimate of compensation expense recorded in previous periods should be adjusted by decreasing compensation expense in the period of forfeiture.

16. *Accounting for Income Tax Benefits.* An employer corporation may obtain an income tax benefit related to stock issued to an employee through a stock option, purchase, or award plan. A corporation is usually entitled to a deduction for income tax purposes of the amount that an employee reports as ordinary income, and the deduction is allowable to the corporation in the year in which the amount is includable in the gross income of the employee. Thus, a deduction for income tax purposes may differ from the related compensation expense that the corporation recognizes,[4] and the deduction may be allowable in a period that differs from the one in which the corporation recognizes compensation expense in measuring net income.

17. An employer corporation should reduce income tax expense for a period by no more of a tax reduction under a stock option, purchase, or award plan than the proportion of the tax reduction that is related to the compensation expense for the period. Compensation expenses that are deductible in a tax return in a period different from the one in which they are reported as expenses in measuring net income are timing differences (APB Opinion No. 11, paragraphs 34 to 37), and deferred taxes should be recorded. The remainder of the tax reduction, if any, is related to an amount that is deductible for income tax purposes but does not affect net income. The remainder of the tax reduction should not be included in income but should be added to capital in addition to par or stated value of capital stock in the period of the tax reduction. Conversely, a tax reduction may be less than if recorded compensation expenses were deductible for income tax purposes. If so, the corporation may deduct the difference from additional capital in the period of the tax reduction to the extent that tax reductions under the same or similar compensatory stock option, purchase, or award plans have been included in additional capital.

18. A corporation may, either by cash payment or otherwise—for example, by allowing a reduction in the purchase price of stock—reimburse an employee for his action related to a stock option, purchase, or award plan that results in a reduction of income taxes of the corporation. The corporation should include the reimbursement in income as an expense.

19. *Disclosure.* ARB No. 43, Chapter 13B, specifies in paragraph 15 the disclosures related to stock option and stock purchase plans that should be made in financial statements.[5]

---

[3]State law governs the issuance of a corporation's stock including the acceptability of issuing stock for future services.

[4]A corporation may be entitled to a deduction for income tax purposes even though it recognizes no compensation expense in measuring net income.

[5]Other disclosure requirements are in Regulation S-X for financial statements filed with the Securities and Exchange Commission and in listing agreements of the stock exchanges for financial statements included in annual reports to stockholders.

EFFECTIVE DATE

20. This Opinion applies to all stock option, purchase, award, and bonus rights granted by an employer corporation to an individual employee after December 31, 1972 under both existing and new arrangements and to reductions of income taxes resulting from deductions as of a date after December 31, 1972 that are related to stock option, purchase, award, and bonus rights granted before as well as after the effective date of this Opinion.

The Opinion entitled "Accounting for Stock Issued to Employees" was adopted by the assenting votes of fifteen members of the Board, of whom six, Messrs. Cummings, Ferst, Hayes, Horngren, Norr, and Watt assented with qualification. Messrs. Bows, Gellein and Halvorson dissented.

Messrs. Cummings, Ferst and Watt assent to the issuance of this Opinion because it improves the accounting principles applicable to the measurement of compensation costs relating to some plans which have come into widespread use subsequent to the issuance of ARB No. 43, Chapter 13B. However, they disagree with the conclusion in paragraph 17 that the tax effects of a permanent difference (as defined in APB Opinion No. 11) in the amount of compensation expense recorded in the financial statements, if any, and the amount allowable for income tax purposes should be added to capital in addition to par or stated value of capital stock. The permanent difference arises as a result of the determination of compensation expense under generally accepted accounting principles in a manner differing from the determination of compensation expense by the taxing authorities. The tax effect of such difference is related, therefore, to an item affecting the determination of income and not to the amount of an employee's investment in the stock of the employer corporation. Accordingly, the tax effect should be reflected as a reduction of income tax expense.

Mr. Cummings also observes that the conclusions in paragraph 17 are inconsistent with those in paragraph 30 of APB Opinion No. 17 which proscribes allocation of income taxes as to the amortization of nondeductible intangible assets even though such intangible assets may have been acquired through issuance of stock.

Mr. Hayes assents to the publication of this Opinion because he believes it will serve to clarify and promote consistency in accounting for stock compensation arrangements not explicitly covered by previous pronouncements, including arrangements which have evolved in recent years. However, he disagrees with certain conclusions in paragraph 10. He disagrees with the conclusion in paragraph 10(b) that compensation under certain types of plans should be measured at a date subsequent to the date

an option or purchase right is granted or shares are awarded. He believes that the date of grant or award is the appropriate date for purposes of measuring compensation costs even though the number of shares that may be issued or the purchase price is not known at that time. Further, in his view, the measure of compensation resulting from issuance of a stock right should approximate the value of the right at the date it is conferred, and the effects of events or conditions subsequent to such date, including fluctuations in the value of optioned or awarded shares, should not affect compensation cost and, hence, an employer's net income.

Messrs. Ferst, Hayes and Watt disagree with the conclusion in paragraph 10(a) that the unadjusted quoted market price of a share of stock of the same class that trades freely in an established market should be used in measuring compensation in all arrangements where stock is issued to employees. They believe that a discount for the inability to trade restricted (or letter) stock is appropriate when employee rights or obligations which might affect the value of the stock are not present, for example, if at the date of issuance the employee has met all conditions of the award, including any obligations to perform services.

Mr. Horngren assents to the issuance of this Opinion because in his view it represents a step toward the desirable objective of attempting to measure all compensation costs. He believes that in all compensation plans the appropriate measure of the compensation is the value of the benefit at the time of its award. Whether the compensation has fixed or contingent terms should not cloud the basic objective of valuation at date of grant. Although he recognizes the difficulties of measurement, he disagrees with the valuation model in paragraph 10(b), which (1) frequently provides a measurement of zero for a fixed option at date of grant, and which (2) for some other option and award plans, provides a measurement dependent on changes in market values subsequent to the date of grant or award.

Mr. Norr assents to the publication of this Opinion but qualifies his assent because he believes that non-compensatory plans of paragraph 7 involve measurable value. He also believes that stock options where employees pay an amount equal to the quoted market at the measurement date are valuable privileges involving compensation costs in contrast to the position taken in the first sentence of paragraph 10. He believes that the measurement date of paragraph 10 should not be the grant date but rather the exercise date. He also believes that there should be no exception in paragraph 11(a) for Treasury stock purchases.

Mr. Bows dissents from this Opinion because in his view compensation costs of a company's stock option, bonus, or award plan should be measured at the grant or award date and not be altered by later developments (such as changing market prices for the company's stock) arising after the option, bonus, or award is granted. While subsequent market action (or some other variable) may affect the later value of the grant to the officer or employee, such developments provide no basis for altering the compensation cost incurred at the time the grant or award is made. Therefore, the conclusions of paragraphs 10(b) and 13 are inappropriate. Mr. Bows also believes the Opinion is inequitable because grants made under many plans will not result in recognition of compensation costs under this Opinion even though such grants convey valuable rights to officers and employees at the date of grant. The conclusions of paragraph 10 permit the value of those rights to escape measurement as compensation costs, while the cost of other rights must be recognized under the Opinion. He also believes that techniques are available to develop the information needed to estimate the value of all rights.

Mr. Gellein dissents from the Opinion because in his view compensation generally should be measured by the fair value of that which is given in exchange for services at the time it is given. He believes therefore that in any compensation plan where an option to acquire stock is awarded or other benefit is granted, the appropriate measure of the compensation is the value of the benefit (in the case of an option, the value of the call on the company's stock) at the time it is awarded. The periods in which this compensation should be recognized as an expense are the ones in which the employee services are rendered. Mr. Gellein recognizes that there are problems to be resolved in connection with the measurement of the value of stock options, but he believes that they can be resolved satisfactorily without undue delay. He recognizes, too, that the options granted and benefits given in certain rather recently adopted plans have value considerably in excess of that of conventional stock option plans, and believes that compensation commensurate with these values should be charged to income. He believes it inappropriate, however, to measure the compensation on the basis of changes in market value after the awards are made, as provided in paragraphs 10 and 13.

Mr. Halvorson believes that the Board is acting prematurely on a subject that presumably is being explored more comprehensively in an accounting research study now in progress and that the alleged abuses in accounting for stock compensation which the Opinion seeks to correct have been emphasized out of proportion to their real significance because of the abiding human concern and curiosity about executive compensation, which is a very different thing from the usually relatively immaterial accounting effect of the alleged abuses on results of operations and financial position. In respect of some specific aspects of the Opinion, Mr. Halvorson believes (1) that a convincing case cannot be made for the proposition that quoted market price is a fair measure of the value of stock issued subject to restrictions on the employee's privilege of selling or transferring the stock, despite the acknowledged existence of various factors which may or may not offset the difference in values. (The resort to "best estimate" in the Opinion for situations in which a quoted market price is unobtainable suggests that similar "best estimates" could be obtained for restricted shares.); (2) that the unearned compensation evidenced by stock issued before services are performed should appropriately be reported as a prepaid expense as opposed to the recommended reporting as a reduction of stockholders' equity; and (3) that any difference between compensation deductible in the computation of taxable income and the corresponding charge, if any, in determining book income is a permanent difference and that the resultant tax benefit should therefore be included as a component of income in conformity with the requirements of Opinion No. 11, not as a component of paid-in capital.

NOTES

Opinions of the Accounting Principles Board present the conclusions of at least two-thirds of the members of the Board, which is the senior technical body of the Institute authorized to issue pronouncements on accounting principles.

Board Opinions are considered appropriate in all circumstances covered but need not be applied to immaterial items.

Covering all possible conditions and circumstances in an Opinion of the Accounting Principles Board is usually impracticable. The substance of transactions and the principles, guides, rules, and criteria described in Opinions should control the accounting for transactions not expressly covered.

Unless otherwise stated, Opinions of the Board are not intended to be retroactive.

Council of the Institute has resolved that Institute members should disclose departures from Board Opinions in their reports as independent auditors when the effect of the departures on the financial statements is material or see to it that such departures are disclosed in notes to the financial statements and, where practicable, should disclose their effects on the financial statements (Special Bulletin, Disclosure of Departures From Opinions of the Accounting Principles Board, *October 1964). Members of the Institute must assume the burden of justifying any such departures.*

Appendix A

MEASURING AND ACCOUNTING FOR COMPENSATION UNDER TYPICAL PLANS (FOR ILLUSTRATION ONLY)

21. Corporations issue stock to officers and other employees through plans with a variety of names and a multiplicity of terms. Plans in which employees pay cash, either directly or through payroll withholding, as all or a significant part of the consideration for stock they receive, are commonly designated by names such as stock option, stock purchase, or stock thrift or savings plans. Plans in which employees receive stock for current or future services without paying cash (or with a nominal payment) are commonly designated by names such as stock bonus or stock award plans. Stock bonus and award plans are invariably compensatory. Stock thrift and savings plans are compensatory to the extent of contributions of an employer corporation. Stock option and purchase plans may be either compensatory or noncompensatory. The combination of terms in some plans tend to make various types of plans shade into one another, and an assigned name may not describe the nature of a plan.

22. This Appendix is organized according to the most vital distinction in the Opinion—compensatory plans are divided between plans in which the cost of compensation is measured at the date of grant or award and those in which the cost of compensation depends on events after the date of grant or award. Combination plans are described briefly in a final section.

Compensation Cost Measured at Date of Grant or Award

23. *Accounting.* Total compensation cost is measured by the difference between the quoted market price of the stock at the date of grant or award and the price, if any, to be paid by an employee and is recognized as expense over the period the employee performs related services. The sum of compensation and cash paid by the employee is the consideration received for the stock issued. Compensation cost related to an award of stock may be adjusted for a later cash settlement (paragraph 11(g)).

24. *Typical Plans with Fixed and Determinable Terms.* The characteristic that identifies plans in this group is that the terms fix and provide means for determining at the date of grant or award both the number of shares of stock that may be acquired by or awarded to an employee and the cash, if any, to be paid by the employee. Plans usually presume or provide that the employee perform current or future services. The right to transfer stock received is sometimes restricted for a specified period.

25. *Stock option and stock purchase plans*—Typical terms provide for an employer corporation to grant to an employee the right to purchase a fixed number of shares of stock of the employer corporation at a stated price during a specified period.

26. *Stock bonus or award plans*—Typical terms provide for an employer corporation to award to an employee a fixed number of shares of stock of the employer corporation without a cash payment (or with a nominal cash payment) by the employee. Often the award is specified as a fixed dollar amount but is distributable in stock with the number of shares determined by the quoted market price of the stock at the date of award, the effective date of award (paragraph 11(c)), or the date treasury stock is acquired (paragraph 11(a)).

Compensation Cost Measured at Other Than Date of Grant or Award

27. *Accounting.* Compensation cost is accounted for the same as for plans in the first group with one exception. The quoted market price used in the measurement is not the price at date of grant or award but the price at the date on which both the number of shares of stock that may be acquired by or awarded to an individual employee and the option or purchase price are known. Total compensation cost is measured by the difference between that quoted market price of the stock and the amount, if any, to be paid by an employee and is recognized as expense over the period the employee performs related services. The sum of compensation and cash paid by the employee is the consideration received for the stock issued. Compensation cost related to an award of stock may be adjusted for a later cash settlement (paragraph 11(g)).

28. Estimates of compensation cost are recorded before the measurement date based on the quoted market price of the stock at intervening dates. Recorded compensation expense between the date of grant or award and the measurement date may either increase or decrease because changes in quoted market price of the stock require recomputations of the estimated compensation cost.

29. *Typical Plans with Variable Terms.* The characteristic that identifies plans in this group is that the terms prevent determining at the date of grant or award either the number of shares of stock that may be acquired by or awarded to an employee or the price to be paid by the employee, or both. The indeterminate factors usually depend on events that are not known or determinable at the date of grant or award. Plans usually presume or provide that the employee perform current or future services. The right to transfer stock received is sometimes restricted for a specified period.

30. *Stock option and stock purchase plans*—Some terms provide for an employer corporation to grant to an employee the right to purchase shares of stock of the employer corporation during a specified period. The number of shares of stock, the option or purchase price, or both may vary depending on various factors during a specified period, such as market performance of the stock, equivalents of dividends distributed, or level of earnings of the employer corporation.

31. *Stock bonus or award plans*—Some terms provide for an employer corporation to award to an employee the right to receive shares of stock of the employer corporation but the number of shares is not determinable at the date of award. Often the award is specified as a fixed dollar amount but is distributable in stock with the number of shares of stock determined by the market price of the stock at the date distributed, or the award may be of an undesignated number of shares of stock and that number is to be determined by variable factors during a specified period.

32. The terms of some plans, often called *phantom stock* or *shadow stock* plans, base the obligations for compensation on increases in market price of or dividends distributed on a specified or variable number of shares of stock of the employer corporation but provide for settlement of the obligation to the employee in cash, in stock of the employer corporation, or a combination of cash and stock.

Combination and Elective Plans

33. *Accounting.* In general, compensation is measured for the separate parts of combination or elective plans. Compensation expense is the sum of the parts that apply. An employer corporation may need to measure compensation at various dates as the terms of separate parts become known. For example, if an employee is entitled to dividend equivalents, compensation cost is the sum of the costs measured at the dates the dividends are credited to the employee in accordance with the terms of the plan. If an employee may choose between alternatives, compensation expense is accrued for the alternative that the employee is most likely to elect based on the facts available at the date of accrual.

34. *Typical Combination and Elective Plans.* Some plans provide for an employer corporation to grant or award to an employee rights with more than one set of terms. Often an employee may elect the right to be exercised. The combination of rights may be granted or awarded simultaneously or an employee who holds a right may subsequently be granted or awarded a second but different right. The rights may run concurrently or for different periods. An illustration is: an employee holding an option to purchase a fixed number of shares of stock at a fixed price during a specified period is granted an alternative option to purchase the same number of shares at a different price or during a different specified period. Instead of a second option, the award may be the right to elect to receive cash or shares of stock without paying cash. Often the election to acquire or receive stock under either right decreases the other right. Plans combining rights are often called *tandem stock* or *alternate stock* plans; the second right may be of the type that is sometimes called a *phantom stock* plan.

Appendix B

REPRINT OF ACCOUNTING RESEARCH BULLETIN NO. 43, CHAPTER 13, COMPENSATION

Section B—Compensation Involved in Stock Option and Stock Purchase Plans

1. The practice of granting to officers and other employees options to purchase or rights to subscribe for shares of a corporation's capital stock has been followed by a considerable number of corporations over a period of many years. To the extent that such options and rights involve a measurable amount of compensation, this cost of services received should be accounted for as such. The amount of compensation involved may be substantial and omission of such costs from the corporation's accounting may result in overstatement of net income to a significant degree. Accordingly, consideration is given herein to the accounting treatment of compensation repre-

sented by stock options or purchase rights granted to officers and other employees.[1]

2. For convenience, this section will discuss primarily the problems of compensation raised by stock option plans. However, the committee feels that substantially the same problems may be encountered in connection with stock purchase plans made available to employees, and the discussion below is applicable to such plans also.

Rights Involving Compensation

3. Stock options involving an element of compensation usually arise out of an offer or agreement by an employer corporation to issue shares of its capital stock to one or more officers or other employees (hereinafter referred to as grantees) at a stated price. The grantees are accorded the right to require issuance of the shares either at a specified time or during some determinable period. In some cases the grantee's options are exercisable only if at the time of exercise certain conditions exist, such as that the grantee is then or until a specified date has been an employee. In other cases, the grantees may have undertaken certain obligations, such as to remain in the employment of the corporation for at least a specified period, or to take the shares only for investment purposes and not for resale.

Rights Not Involving Compensation

4. Stock option plans in many cases may be intended not primarily as a special form of compensation but rather as an important means of raising capital, or as an inducement to obtain greater or more widespread ownership of the corporation's stock among its officers and other employees. In general, the terms under which such options are granted, including any conditions as to exercise of the options or disposal of the stock acquired, are the most significant evidence ordinarily available as to the nature and purpose of a particular stock option or stock option plan. In practice, it is often apparent that a particular option or plan involves elements of two or more of the above purposes. Where the inducements are not larger per share than would reasonably be required in an offer of shares to all shareholders for the purpose of raising an equiva-

lent amount of capital, no compensation need be presumed to be involved.

5. Stock purchase plans also are frequently an integral part of a corporation's program to secure equity capital or to obtain widespread ownership among employees, or both. In such cases, no element of compensation need be considered to be present if the purchase price is not lower than is reasonably required to interest employees generally or to secure the contemplated funds.

Time of Measurement of Compensation

6. In the case of stock options involving compensation, the principal problem is the measurement of the compensation. This problem involves selection of the date as of which measurement of any element of compensation is to be made and the manner of measurement. The date as of which measurement is made is of critical importance since the fair value of the shares under option may vary materially in the often extended period during which the option is outstanding. There may be at least six dates to be considered for this purpose: (a) the date of the adoption of an option plan, (b) the date on which an option is granted to a specific individual, (c) the date on which the grantee has performed any conditions precedent to exercise of the option, (d) the date on which the grantee may first exercise the option, (e) the date on which the option is exercised by the grantee, and (f) the date on which the grantee disposes of the stock acquired.

7. Of the six dates mentioned two are not relevant to the question considered in this bulletin—cost to the corporation which is granting the option. The date of adoption of an option plan clearly has no relevance, inasmuch as the plan per se constitutes no more than a proposed course of action which is ineffective until options are granted thereunder. The date on which a grantee disposes of the shares acquired under an option is equally immaterial since this date will depend on the desires of the individual as a shareholder and bears no necessary relation to the services performed.[2]

8. The date on which the option is exercised has been advocated as the date on which a cost may be

[1]Bulletin 37, "Accounting for Compensation in the Form of Stock Options," was issued in November, 1948. Issuance of a revised bulletin in 1953 and its expansion to include stock purchase plans were prompted by the very considerable increase in the use of certain types of option and purchase plans following the enactment in 1950 of Section 130A of the Internal Revenue Code. This section granted specialized tax treatment to employee stock options if certain requirements were met as to the terms of the option, as to the circumstances under which the option was granted and could be exercised and as to the holding and disposal of the stock acquired thereunder. In general, the effect of Section 130A is to eliminate or minimize the amount of income taxable to the employee as compensation and to deny to the issuing corporation any tax deduction in respect of such restricted options. In 1951, the Federal Salary Stabilization Board issued rules and regulations relating to stock options and purchase rights granted to employees whereby options generally comparable in nature to the restricted stock options specified in Section 130A might be considered for its purposes not to involve compensation, or to involve compensation only in limited amounts.

[2]This is the date on which income or gain taxable to the grantee may arise under Section 130A. Use of this date for tax purposes is doubtless based on considerations as to the ability of the optionee to pay taxes prior to sale of the shares.

said to have been incurred. Use of this date is supported by the argument that only then will it be known whether or not the option will be exercised. However, beginning with the time at which the grantee may first exercise the option he is in effect speculating for his own account. His delay has no discernible relation to his status as an employee but reflects only his judgment as an investor.

9. The date on which the grantee may first exercise the option will generally coincide with, but in some cases may follow, the date on which the grantee will have performed any conditions precedent to exercise of the option. Accordingly this date presents no special problems differing from those to be discussed in the next paragraph.

10. There remain to be considered the date on which an option is granted to a specific individual and the date on which the grantee has fulfilled any conditions precedent to exercise of the option. When compensation is paid in a form other than cash the *amount* of compensation is ordinarily determined by the fair value of the property which was agreed to be given in exchange for the services to be rendered. The time at which such fair value is to be determined may be subject to some difference of opinion but it appears that the date on which an option is granted to a specific individual would be the appropriate point at which to evaluate the cost to the employer, since it was the value at that date which the employer may be presumed to have had in mind. In most of the cases under discussion, moreover, the only important contingency involved is the continuance of the grantee in the employment of the corporation, a matter very largely within the control of the grantee and usually the main objective of the grantor. Under such circumstances it may be assumed that if the stock option were granted as a part of an employment contract, both parties had in mind a valuation of the option at the date of the contract; and accordingly, value at that date should be used as the amount to be accounted for as compensation. If the option were granted as a form of supplementary compensation otherwise than as an integral part of an employment contract, the grantor is nevertheless governed in determining the option price and the number of shares by conditions then existing. It follows that it is the value of the option at that time, rather than the grantee's ultimate gain or loss on the transaction, which for accounting purposes constitutes whatever compensation the grantor intends to pay. The committee therefore concludes that in most cases, including situations where the right to exercise is conditional upon continued employment, valuation should be made of the option as of the date of grant.

11. The date of grant also represents the date on which the corporation foregoes the principal alternative use of the shares which it places subject to option, i.e., the sale of such shares at the then prevailing market price. Viewed in this light, the *cost* of utilizing the shares for purposes of the option plan can best be measured in relation to what could then have been obtained through sale of such shares in the open market. However, the fact that the grantor might, as events turned out, have obtained at some later date either more or less for the shares in question than at the date of the grant does not bear upon the measurement of the compensation which can be said to have been in contemplation of the parties at the date the option was granted.

Manner of Measurement

12. Freely exercisable option rights, even at prices above the current market price of the shares, have been traded in the public markets for many years, but there is no such objective means for measuring the value of an option which is not transferable and is subject to such other restrictions as are usually present in options of the nature here under discussion. Although there is, from the standpoint of the grantee, a value inherent in a restricted future right to purchase shares at a price at or even above the fair value of shares at the grant date, the committee believes it is impracticable to measure any such value. As to the grantee any positive element may, for practical purposes, be deemed to be largely or wholly offset by the negative effect of the restrictions ordinarily present in options of the type under discussion. From the viewpoint of the grantor corporation no measurable cost can be said to have been incurred because it could not at the grant date have realized more than the *fair value* of the optioned shares, the concept of fair value as here used encompassing the possibility and prospect of future developments. On the other hand, it follows in the opinion of the committee that the value to the grantee and the related cost to the corporation of a restricted right to purchase shares at a price *below* the fair value of the shares at the grant date may for the purposes here under discussion be taken as the excess of the then fair value of the shares over the option price.

13. While market quotations of shares are an important and often a principal factor in determining the fair value of shares, market quotations at a given date are not necessarily conclusive evidence.[3] Where significant market quotations cannot be obtained, other recognized methods of valuation have to be used. Furthermore, in determining the fair value of shares for the purpose of measuring the

---

[3] Whether treasury or unissued shares are to be used to fulfill the obligation is not material to a determination of value.

cost incurred by a corporation in the issuance of an option, it is appropriate to take into consideration such modifying factors as the range of quotations over a reasonable period and the fact that the corporation by selling shares pursuant to an option may avoid some or all of the expenses otherwise incurred in a sale of shares. The absence of a ready market, as in the case of shares of closely-held corporations, should also be taken into account and may require the use of other means of arriving at fair value than by reference to an occasional market quotation or sale of the security.

Other Considerations

14 If the period for which payment for services is being made by the issuance of the stock option is not specifically indicated in the offer or agreement, the value of the option should be apportioned over the period of service for which the payment of the compensation seems appropriate in the existing circumstances. Accrual of the compensation over the period selected should be made by means of charges against the income account. Upon exercise of an option the sum of the cash received and the amount of the charge to income should be accounted for as the consideration received on issuance of the stock.

15. In connection with financial statements, disclosure should be made as to the status of the option or plan at the end of the period of report, including the number of shares under option, the option price, and the number of shares as to which options were exercisable. As to options exercised during the period, disclosure should be made of the number of shares involved and the option price thereof.

One member of the committee, Mr. Mason, assented with qualification to adoption of section B of chapter 13. One member, Mr. Knight, did not vote.

Mr. Mason assents only under the assumption that if an option lapses after the grantee becomes entitled to exercise it, the related compensation shall be treated as a contribution by the grantee to the capital of the grantor.

APB Opinion No. 26
Early Extinguishment of Debt

STATUS

Issued: October 1972

Effective Date: For transactions on or after January 1, 1973

Affects: Supersedes ARB 43, Chapter 15
      Supersedes APB 6, paragraph 19

Affected by: Paragraphs 2 and 3(a) amended by FAS 15
              Paragraph 2 amended by FAS 71
              Paragraph 2 superseded by FAS 76
              Paragraph 2 amended by FAS 84
              Paragraph 3(a) superseded by FAS 76
              Paragraphs 3(c), 19, and 21 amended by FAS 76
              Paragraph 20 amended by APB 30
              Paragraph 20 amended by FAS 4

Other Interpretive Pronouncements: AIN-APB 26, Interpretation No. 1
                                     FTB 80-1

APB Opinion No. 26
Early Extinguishment of Debt

INTRODUCTION

1. Debt is frequently extinguished in various ways before its scheduled maturity. Generally, the amount paid upon reacquisition of debt securities will differ from the net carrying amount of the debt at that time. This Opinion expresses the views of the Accounting Principles Board regarding the appropriate accounting for that difference.

2. *Applicability.* This Opinion applies to the early extinguishment of all kinds of debt. It supersedes Chapter 15 of ARB No. 43 and Paragraph 19 of APB Opinion No. 6. However, this Opinion does not apply to debt that is converted pursuant to the existing conversion privileges of the holder. Moreover, it does not alter the accounting for convertible debt securities described in APB Opinion No. 14. This Opinion applies to regulated companies in accordance with the provisions of the Addendum to APB Opinion No. 2, *Accounting for the "Investment Credit,"* 1962.

3. *Definitions.* Several terms are used in this Opinion as follows:

a. *Early extinguishment* is the reacquisition of any form of debt security or instrument before its scheduled maturity except through conversion by the holder, regardless of whether the debt is viewed as terminated or is held as so-called "treasury bonds." All open-market or mandatory reacquisitions of debt securities to meet sinking fund requirements are early extinguishments.

b. *Net carrying amount* of debt is the amount due at maturity, adjusted for unamortized premium, discount, and cost of issuance.

c. *Reacquisition price* of debt is the amount paid on early extinguishment, including a call premium and miscellaneous costs of reacquisition. If early extinguishment is achieved by a direct exchange of new securities, the reacquisition price is the total present value of the new securities.

d. *Difference* as used in this Opinion is the excess of the reacquisition price over the net carrying amount or the excess of the net carrying amount over the reacquisition price.

DISCUSSION

4. *Current practice.* Early extinguishment of debt is usually achieved in one of three ways: use of existing liquid assets, use of proceeds from issuance of equity securities, and use of proceeds from issuing other debt securities. The replacement of debt with other debt is frequently called refunding.

5. Differences on nonrefunding extinguishments are generally treated currently in income as losses or gains. Three basic methods are generally accepted to account for the differences on refunding transactions:

a. Amortization over the remaining original life of the extinguished issue
b. Amortization over the life of the new issue
c. Recognition currently in income as a loss or gain.

Each method has been supported in court decisions, in rulings of regulatory agencies, and in accounting literature.

6. *Amortization over life of old issue.* Some accountants believe that the difference on refunding should be amortized over the remaining original life of the extinguished issue. In effect, the difference is regarded as an adjustment of the cash cost of borrowing that arises from obtaining another arrangement for the unexpired term of the old agreement. Therefore, the cost of money over the remaining period of the original issue is affected by the difference that results upon extinguishment of the original contract. Early extinguishment occurs for various reasons, but usually because it is financially advantageous to the issuer, for example, if the periodic cash interest outlay can be reduced for future periods. Accordingly, under this view the difference should be spread over the unexpired term of the original issue to obtain the proper periodic cost of borrowed money. If the maturity date of the new issue precedes the maturity date of the original issue, a portion of the difference is amortized over the life of the new debt and the balance of the difference is recognized currently in income as a loss or gain.

7. *Amortization over life of new issue.* Some accountants believe that the difference on refunding should be amortized over the life of the new issue if refunding occurs because of lower current interest rates or anticipated higher interest rates in the future. Under this view, the principal motivation for refunding is to establish a more favorable interest rate over the term of the new issue. Therefore, the expected benefits to be obtained over the life of the new issue justify amortization of the difference over the life of the new issue.

8. *Recognition currently in income.* Some accoun-

tants believe a difference on refunding is similar to the difference on other early extinguishments and should be recognized currently in income in the period of the extinguishment. This view holds that the value of the old debt has changed over time and that paying the call price or current market value is the most favorable way to extinguish the debt. The change in the market value of the debt is caused by a change in the market rate of interest, but the change has not been reflected in the accounts. Therefore, the entire difference is recorded when the specific contract is terminated because it relates to the past periods when the contract was in effect. If the accountant had foreseen future events perfectly at the time of issuance, he would have based the accounting on the assumption that the maturity value of the debt would equal the reacquisition price. Thus, no difference upon early extinguishment would occur because previous periods would have borne the proper interest expense. Furthermore, a call premium necessary to eliminate an old contract and an unamortized discount or premium relate to the old contract and cannot be a source of benefits from a new debt issue. For example, a larger (or smaller) coupon rate could have been set on the old issue to avoid an unamortized discount (or premium) at issuance. When such debt originally issued at par is refunded, few accountants maintain that some portion of past interest should be capitalized and written off over the remaining life of the old debt or over the life of the new debt.

9. Another argument in favor of current recognition of the difference as gain or loss is also related to market forces but is expressed differently. If debt is callable, the call privilege is frequently exercised when the market value of the bonds as determined by the current yield rate exceeds the call price. A loss or gain is recognized on extinguishing the debt because an exchange transaction occurs in which the call or current market value of the debt differs from its net carrying amount. For example, the market value of the debt ordinarily rises as the market rate of interest falls. If market values were recorded as the market rate of interest fluctuates, the changes in the market value of the debt would have been recorded periodically as losses or gains. The bond liability would not exceed the call price.

10. On the other hand, some accountants holding views opposing current recognition of the difference in income believe that recognizing the difference as gains or losses may induce a company to report income by borrowing money at high rates of interest in order to pay off discounted low-rate debt. Conversely, a large potential charge to income may discourage refunding even though it is economically desirable; the replacement of high cost debt with low cost debt may result in having to recognize a large loss. Thus, a company may show higher current income in the year of extinguishment while increasing its economic cost of debt and lower current income while decreasing its economic cost of debt. For these reasons, these accountants favor deferral.

11. *Extinguishment of convertible debt.* Accountants have expressed differing views regarding accounting for the extinguishment of convertible debt. In APB Opinion No. 14, which is directed in part to accounting for convertible debt at time of issue, the Board concluded that no portion of the proceeds from the issuance of the types of convertible debt securities defined in the Opinion should be accounted for as attributable to the conversion feature. In reaching that conclusion, the Board placed greater weight on the inseparability of the debt and conversion option and less weight on practical difficulties. The Board emphasized that a convertible debt security is a complex hybrid instrument bearing an option the alternative choices of which cannot exist independently of one another. The holder ordinarily does not sell one right and retain the other. Furthermore, the two choices are mutually exclusive; the holder cannot exercise the option to convert unless he foregoes the right to redemption, and vice versa. Therefore, APB Opinion No. 14 implies that (except for conversion) a difference on extinguishing convertible debt needs to be recognized in the same way as a difference on extinguishment of debt without conversion features.

12. The various views expressed on how to account for the extinguishment of convertible debt to some extent reflect the same attitudes as to the nature of the debt at time of issue as were considered in APB Opinion No. 14. Thus, some accountants believe that a portion of the proceeds at issuance is attributable to the conversion feature. If the convertible debt is later extinguished, the initial value of the conversion feature should then be recorded as an increase in stockholders' equity. The balance of the difference would, under that view of the transaction, be a gain or loss in income of the period of extinguishment.

13. Some accountants maintain that the intent of issuing convertible debt is to raise equity capital. A convertible debt is therefore in substance an equity security, and all the difference on extinguishing convertible debt should be an increase or decrease of paid-in capital.

14. Another view is that the market price that gives rise to the difference reflects both the level of interest rates on debt and the prices of the related common stock or both. Those expressing this view believe that if the effects of these factors can be identified at the time of extinguishment, the difference attributable to the interest rate should be accounted for as gain or loss in income, and that the

difference attributable to the market price of the issuer's common stock should be accounted for as an increase or decrease in paid-in capital.

15. Some accountants believe that the accounting for a difference on extinguishment of convertible debt depends on the nature of the security at the time of extinguishment. Events after time of issue may provide evidence that a convertible debt is either still debt in substance or equity in substance. Under this view the purchase price on extinguishment provides the best evidence as to whether the security is essentially debt or equity. Convertible debt that is selling below the call or redemption price at time of extinguishment is essentially debt; the difference should be a gain in current income. Moreover, if convertible debt has a coupon rate that exceeds the current market rate of interest and clearly causes the issue to trade at a premium as a debt instrument, the difference on extinguishment should be a loss in current income. On the other hand, if convertible debt is selling above the call or redemption price because of the conversion privilege, it is essentially a common stock. In effect, market forces have transformed a debt instrument into an equity security, and the extinguishment provides an explicit transaction to justify recognizing that the convertible debt is in substance a common stock equivalent. Those who hold this view believe that accounting should report the substance of the transaction rather than its form; convertible debt need not be converted into common stock to demonstrate that the extinguishment transaction is equivalent to a purchase of common stock for retirement.

16. *Economic nature of extinguishment.* In many respects the essential economics of the decision leading to the early extinguishment of outstanding debt are the same, regardless of whether such debt is extinguished via the use of the existing liquid assets, new equity securities, or new debt. That is, the decision favoring early extinguishment usually implies that the net present value of future cash inflows and outflows is maximized by extinguishing the debt now rather than by letting it run to maturity. The savings may be in lower cash interest costs on a new debt issue, in increased earnings per share of common stock if the assets are not earning the interest rate on the outstanding debt, or in some other form. The essential event is early extinguishment. Under this view, the difference is associated with extinguishing the existing debt and is accounted for the same regardless of how extinguishment is accomplished.

17. To illustrate that view, assume that three firms each have long-term debt outstanding with ten years remaining to maturity. The first firm may have excess cash and no investment opportunities that earn a rate of return higher than the cash savings that would ensue from immediately extinguishing the debt. The second firm may wish to replace the debt with a similar issue bearing a lower coupon rate. The third firm may have excessive debt and may want to replace the debt with a new issue of common stock. The underlying reason for the early extinguishment in all three cases is to obtain a perceived economic advantage. The relevant comparison in the replacement of debt with other debt is with the costs of other debt. The comparison in other cases is with other means of financing. The means by which the debt is extinguished have no bearing on how to account for the loss or gain.

OPINION

18. The following conclusions of the Board are based primarily on the reasoning in paragraphs 8, 9, 11, 16, and 17.

19. *Reduction of alternatives.* The Board concludes that all extinguishments of debt before scheduled maturities are fundamentally alike. The accounting for such transactions should be the same regardless of the means used to achieve the extinguishment.

20. *Disposition of amounts.* A difference between the reacquisition price and the net carrying amount of the extinguished debt should be recognized currently in income of the period of extinguishment as losses or gains and identified as a separate item.[1] The criteria in APB Opinion No. 9 should be used to determine whether the losses or gains are ordinary or extraordinary items. Gains and losses should not be amortized to future periods.

21. *Convertible debt.* The extinguishment of convertible debt before maturity does not change the character of the security as between debt and equity at that time. Therefore, a difference between the cash acquisition price of the debt and its net carrying amount should be recognized currently in income in the period of extinguishment as losses or gains.

EFFECTIVE DATE

22. This Opinion shall be effective for all extinguishments of debt occurring on or after January 1,

---

[1]If upon extinguishment of debt, the parties also exchange unstated (or stated) rights or privileges, the portion of the consideration exchanged allocable to such unstated (or stated) rights or privileges should be given appropriate accounting recognition. Moreover, extinguishment transactions between related entities may be in essence capital transactions.

1973. Extinguishment transactions are considered to be terminated events similar to that set forth in paragraph 16 of APB Opinion No. 20 and as such, extinguishments that were previously recorded in fiscal years ending before January 1, 1973 should not be adjusted. However, the accounting for refunding transactions that have been previously reported in the fiscal year in which December 31, 1972 occurs may be retroactively restated to comply with the provisions of this Opinion.

The Opinion entitled "Early Extinguishment of Debt" was adopted by the assenting votes of fifteen members of the Board, of whom three, Messrs. Cummings, Ferst, and Gellein, assented with qualification. Messrs. Defliese, Watt, and Wear dissented.

Messrs. Cummings and Ferst assent to the issuance of this Opinion because it will reduce alternatives in accounting for extinguishments of long-term debt which are fundamentally alike. They object, however, to the conclusion in paragraph 21 that extinguishment of convertible debt gives rise to an income charge for the entire difference between the acquisition price and its carrying amount under all circumstances. In their view when convertible debt is traded at amounts which are clearly attributable to the value of the securities into which it is convertible, the acquisition of such debt by the issuing company is in substance an acquisition of its treasury stock. Paragraph 21 mandates the unnecessary process of first converting the debt and then acquiring the stock in order to reflect the financial reality inherent in the transaction.

Mr. Gellein assents to issuance of the Opinion but disagrees with the conclusion expressed in paragraph 18 that all extinguishments of debt before scheduled maturities are fundamentally alike. He believes that some debt retirements which are accompanied by concurrent borrowings have economic purposes and results different from other debt retirements, and that the accounting should in these limited cases recognize these differences. Where a concurrent borrowing and retirement is planned, for example, to take advantage of a relatively low market rate of interest, or to avoid an anticipated increase, he believes that there is in substance a substitution of debt and that the "difference" between the reacquisition price and the net carrying amount of the retired debt should be charged or credited, as the case may be, to income over the remaining term of the retired debt. He believes that in such a situation the difference, whether charge or credit, arises from an economic circumstance and an action the result of which is to cause the periodic interest expense to be virtually unchanged during the remaining life of the retired debt. Amortizing the "difference" over the remaining life of the retired debt will show that result; the

accounting recommended in paragraph 19 will not.

Mr. Defliese dissents to this Opinion because it fails to require recognition of the economic effects associated with an early extinguishment of debt designed to yield a profit. In his view such a payment, whether from borrowed funds (debt refunding) or from working capital (equity refunding), is essentially in every case a refunding at a higher cost of money (over the remaining original term) than that of the debt being prepaid, equivalent to an arbitrage with a predetermined net profit consisting of the *difference* between the discount from par and the future increased interest differential. He believes that omission of a provision for this added interest cost overstates the profit in the year of prepayment and shifts the interest burden to future periods. When the added cost is not known, or cannot be reasonably estimated, the entire discount should be allocated ratably over the remaining original term to offset such cost, in which case the net profit is spread over the remaining term. Similarly, when debt is refunded at a premium in order to take advantage of lower current or future rates, the premium should be deferred and charged appropriately to the periods benefited.

Mr. Watt dissents to this Opinion for the reasons set forth in paragraphs 6 and 10, because it requires gain or loss to be recognized currently in income of a difference between the reacquisition price and the net carrying amount of the extinguished debt in a refunding situation. He also dissents, for the reason set forth in paragraph 15, because it requires a loss to be recognized on the retirement of a convertible debt that is obviously trading on its common stock characteristics. To him this Opinion is a classic example of narrowing alternative accounting principles in a limited area to a point where the use of different accounting principles to accommodate entirely different circumstances calling for different results has now been proscribed.

Mr. Wear dissents to this Opinion because, in his view, it does not develop a persuasive and convincing argument that all extinguishments of debt before scheduled maturities are fundamentally alike.

He believes there are important differences in refunding situations, for the reasons described in paragraph 6, and where convertible debt is involved, for the reasons set forth in paragraph 15.

NOTES

Opinions of the Accounting Principles Board present the conclusions of at least two-thirds of the members of the Board, which is the senior technical body of the Institute authorized to issue pronouncements on accounting principles.

Board Opinions are considered appropriate in all circumstances covered but need not be applied to immaterial items.

Covering all possible conditions and circumstances in an Opinion of the Accounting Principles
Board is usually impracticable. The substance of
transactions and the principles, guides, rules, and
criteria described in Opinions should control the
accounting for transactions not expressly covered.

Unless otherwise stated, Opinions of the Board
are not intended to be retroactive.

Council of the Institute has resolved that Institute
members should disclose departures from Board
Opinions in their reports as independent auditors
when the effect of the departures on the financial
statements is material or see to it that such departures are disclosed in notes to the financial statements and, where practicable, should disclose their
effects on the financial statements (Special Bulletin,
Disclosure of Departures from Opinions of the
Accounting Principles Board, October 1964). Members of the Institute must assume the burden of justifying any such departures.

Accounting Principles Board (1972)

Philip L. Defliese,
 Chairman
Donald J. Bevis
Albert J. Bows
Milton M. Broeker
Leo E. Burger

Joseph P. Cummings
Robert L. Ferst
Oscar Gellein
Newman T. Halvorson
Robert Hampton, III
Donald J. Hayes
Charles B. Hellerson

Charles T. Horngren
Louis M. Kessler
David Norr
George C. Watt
Allan Wear
Glenn A. Welsch

APB Opinion No. 27
Accounting for Lease Transactions by Manufacturer or Dealer Lessors

STATUS

Issued: November 1972

Effective Date: For transactions after December 31, 1972

Affects: Amends APB 7, paragraph 8
       Supersedes APB 7, paragraph 12

Affected by: Superseded by FAS 13

(This page intentionally left blank.)

APB Opinion No. 28
Interim Financial Reporting

STATUS

Issued: May 1973

Effective Date: For interim periods relating to fiscal years beginning after December 31, 1973

Affects: Amends APB 11, paragraph 6

Affected by: Paragraphs 2 and 33 amended by FAS 95
　　　　　　 Paragraphs 19 and 20 and footnotes 2 and 3 amended by FAS 96 and FAS 109
　　　　　　 Paragraph 27 and footnote 5 superseded by FAS 3
　　　　　　 Paragraph 31 amended by FAS 3

Other Interpretive Pronouncements: FIN 18
　　　　　　　　　　　　　　　　　　 FTB 79-9

APB Opinion No. 28
Interim Financial Reporting

CONTENTS

DISCUSSION

1. The purpose of this Opinion is to clarify the application of accounting principles and reporting practices to interim financial information, including interim financial statements and summarized interim financial data of publicly traded companies issued for external reporting purposes.

2. Interim financial information may include current data during a fiscal year on financial position, results of operations and changes in financial position. This information may be issued on a monthly or quarterly basis or at other intervals and may take the form of either complete financial statements or summarized financial data. Interim financial information often is provided for each interim period or on a cumulative year-to-date basis, or both, and for the corresponding periods of the preceding year.

3. APB Opinions and Accounting Research Bulletins make few specific references to the applicability of generally accepted accounting principles to financial statements for interim periods. A wide variety of practice exists in the application of accounting principles to interim financial information. This Opinion indicates the applicability of generally accepted accounting principles to interim financial information and indicates types of disclosures necessary to report on a meaningful basis for a period of less than a full year.

4. The determination of the results of operations on a meaningful basis for intervals of less than a full year presents inherent difficulties. The revenues of some businesses fluctuate widely among interim periods because of seasonal factors, while in other businesses heavy fixed costs incurred in one interim period may benefit other periods. In these situations, financial information for periods of less than a full year may be of limited usefulness. In other situations costs and expenses related to a full year's activities are incurred at infrequent intervals during the year and need to be allocated to products in process or to other interim periods to avoid distortion of interim financial results. In view of the limited time available to develop complete information, many costs and expenses are estimated in interim periods. For example, it may not be practical to perform extensive reviews of individual inventory items, costs on individual long-term contracts and precise income tax calculations for each interim period. Subsequent refinement or correction of these estimates may distort the results of operations of later interim periods. Similarly, the effects of disposal of a segment of a business and extraordinary, unusual or infrequently occurring events and transactions on the results of operations in an interim period will often be more pronounced than they will be on the results for the annual period. Special attention must be given to disclosure of the impact of these items on financial information for interim periods.

5. The variety of practice that exists in the presentation of interim financial information is partly attributable to differing views as to the principal objective of interim financial information.

a. Some view each interim period as a basic accounting period and conclude that the results of operations for each interim period should be determined in essentially the same manner as if the interim period were an annual accounting period. Under this view deferrals, accruals, and estimations at the end of each interim period are determined by following essentially the same principles and judgments that apply to annual periods.

b. Others view each interim period primarily as being an integral part of the annual period. Under this view deferrals, accruals, and estimations at the end of each interim period are affected by judgments made at the interim date as to results of operations for the balance of the annual period. Thus, an expense item that might be considered as falling wholly within an annual accounting period (no fiscal year-end accrual or deferral) could be allocated among interim periods based on estimated time, sales volume, productive activity, or some other basis.

6. Despite these differing views and limitations, periodic and timely financial information during a fiscal year is useful to investors and others. The principal objectives of this Opinion are to provide guidance on accounting and disclosure issues peculiar to interim reporting and to set forth minimum disclosure requirements for interim financial reports of publicly traded companies.[1] The Opinion is not intended to deal with unresolved matters of accounting related to annual reporting.

OPINION

Applicability

7. The Board has reviewed the applicability of APB Opinions and Accounting Research Bulletins in relation to the current practices followed in the preparation and reporting of interim financial information. The Board believes the accounting principles and reporting practices in the Opinions and Bulletins should apply to interim financial information in the manner set forth in this Opinion. The guides expressed in this Opinion are applicable whenever companies issue interim financial information.

8. This Opinion (a) outlines (Part I, paragraphs 9-29) the application of generally accepted accounting principles to the determination of income when interim financial information is presented, (b) provides (paragraphs 19 and 20) for the use of estimated effective income tax rates (thus modifying paragraph 6 of APB Opinion No. 11, *Accounting for Income Taxes*), and (c) specifies (Part II, paragraphs 30-33) certain disclosure requirements for

summarized financial information issued by publicly traded companies.

PART I

Standards for Determining Interim Financial Information

9. Interim financial information is essential to provide investors and others with timely information as to the progress of the enterprise. The usefulness of such information rests on the relationship that it has to the annual results of operations. Accordingly, the Board has concluded that each interim period should be viewed primarily as an integral part of an annual period.

10. In general, the results for each interim period should be based on the accounting principles and practices used by an enterprise in the preparation of its latest annual financial statements unless a change in an accounting practice or policy has been adopted in the current year (paragraphs 23-29). However, the Board has concluded that certain accounting principles and practices followed for annual reporting purposes may require modification at interim reporting dates so that the reported results for the interim period may better relate to the results of operations for the annual period. Paragraphs 12-20 set forth the modifications that are necessary or desirable at interim dates in accounting principles or practices followed for annual periods.

Revenue

11. Revenue from products sold or services rendered should be recognized as earned during an interim period on the same basis as followed for the full year. For example, revenues from long-term construction-type contracts accounted for under the percentage-of-completion method should be recognized in interim periods on the same basis followed for the full year. Losses projected on such contracts should be recognized in full during the interim period in which the existence of such losses becomes evident.

Costs and Expenses

12. Costs and expenses for interim reporting purposes may be classified as:

a. Costs associated with revenue—those costs that are associated directly with or allocated to the products sold or to the services rendered and

[1]A publicly traded company for purposes of this Opinion includes any company whose securities trade in a public market on either (1) a stock exchange (domestic or foreign) or (2) in the over-the-counter market (including securities quoted only locally or regionally). When a company makes a filing with a regulatory agency in preparation for sale of its securities in a public market it is considered a publicly traded company for this purpose.

which are charged against income in those interim periods in which the related revenue is recognized.

b. All other costs and expenses—those costs and expenses that are not allocated to the products sold or to the services rendered and which are charged against income in interim fiscal periods as incurred, or are allocated among interim periods based on an estimate of time expired, benefit received, or other activity associated with the periods.

Costs Associated with Revenue

13. Those costs and expenses that are associated directly with or allocated to the products sold or to the services rendered for annual reporting purposes (including, for example, material costs, wages and salaries and related fringe benefits, manufacturing overhead, and warranties) should be similarly treated for interim reporting purposes.

14. Practices vary in determining costs of inventory. For example, cost of goods produced may be determined based on standard or actual cost, while cost of inventory may be determined on an average, FIFO, or LIFO cost basis. While companies should generally use the same inventory pricing methods and make provisions for write-downs to market at interim dates on the same basis as used at annual inventory dates, the following exceptions are appropriate at interim reporting dates:

a. Some companies use estimated gross profit rates to determine the cost of goods sold during interim periods or use other methods different from those used at annual inventory dates. These companies should disclose the method used at the interim date and any significant adjustments that result from reconciliations with the annual physical inventory.

b. Companies that use the LIFO method may encounter a liquidation of base period inventories at an interim date that is expected to be replaced by the end of the annual period. In such cases the inventory at the interim reporting date should not give effect to the LIFO liquidation, and cost of sales for the interim reporting period should include the expected cost of replacement of the liquidated LIFO base.

c. Inventory losses from market declines should not be deferred beyond the interim period in which the decline occurs. Recoveries of such losses on the same inventory in later interim periods of the same fiscal year through market price recoveries should be recognized as gains in the later interim period. Such gains should not exceed previously recognized losses. Some market declines at interim dates, however, can reasonably be expected to be restored in the fiscal year. Such

temporary market declines need not be recognized at the interim date since no loss is expected to be incurred in the fiscal year.

d. Companies that use standard cost accounting systems for determining inventory and product costs should generally follow the same procedures in reporting purchase price, wage rate, usage or efficiency variances from standard cost at the end of an interim period as followed at the end of a fiscal year. Purchase price variances or volume or capacity cost variances that are planned and expected to be absorbed by the end of the annual period, should ordinarily be deferred at interim reporting dates. The effect of unplanned or unanticipated purchase price or volume variances, however, should be reported at the end of an interim period following the same procedures used at the end of a fiscal year.

All Other Costs and Expenses

15. Charges are made to income for all other costs and expenses in annual reporting periods based upon (a) direct expenditures made in the period (salaries and wages), (b) accruals for estimated expenditures to be made at a later date (vacation pay) or (c) amortization of expenditures that affect more than one annual period (insurance premiums, interest, rents). The objective in all cases is to achieve a fair measure of results of operations for the annual period and to present fairly the financial position at the end of the annual period. The Board has concluded that the following standards should apply in accounting for costs and expenses other than product costs in interim periods:

a. Costs and expenses other than product costs should be charged to income in interim periods as incurred, or be allocated among interim periods based on an estimate of time expired, benefit received or activity associated with the periods. Procedures adopted for assigning specific cost and expense items to an interim period should be consistent with the bases followed by the company in reporting results of operations at annual reporting dates. However, when a specific cost or expense item charged to expense for annual reporting purposes benefits more than one interim period, the cost or expense item may be allocated to those interim periods. (See paragraph 16.)

b. Some costs and expenses incurred in an interim period, however, cannot be readily identified with the activities or benefits of other interim periods and should be charged to the interim period in which incurred. Disclosure should be made as to the nature and amount of such costs unless items of a comparable nature are included in both the current interim period and in the corresponding interim period of the preceding year.

c. Arbitrary assignment of the amount of such costs to an interim period should not be made.

d. Gains and losses that arise in any interim period similar to those that would not be deferred at year end should not be deferred to later interim periods within the same fiscal year.

16. A complete listing of examples of application of the standards set forth in paragraph 15 is not practical; however, the following examples of applications may be helpful:

a. When a cost that is expensed for annual reporting purposes clearly benefits two or more interim periods (e.g., annual major repairs), each interim period should be charged for an appropriate portion of the annual cost by the use of accruals or deferrals.

b. When quantity discounts are allowed customers based upon annual sales volume, the amount of such discounts charged to each interim period should be based on the sales to customers during the interim period in relation to estimated annual sales.

c. Property taxes (and similar costs such as interest and rent) may be accrued or deferred at annual reporting date, to achieve a full year's charge of taxes to costs and expenses. Similar procedures should be adopted at each interim reporting date to provide an appropriate cost in each period.

d. Advertising costs may be deferred within a fiscal year if the benefits of an expenditure made clearly extend beyond the interim period in which the expenditure is made. Advertising costs may be accrued and assigned to interim periods in relation to sales prior to the time the service is received if the advertising program is clearly implicit in the sales arrangement.

17. The amounts of certain costs and expenses are frequently subjected to year-end adjustments even though they can be reasonably approximated at interim dates. To the extent possible such adjustments should be estimated and the estimated costs and expenses assigned to interim periods so that the interim periods bear a reasonable portion of the anticipated annual amount. Examples of such items include inventory shrinkage, allowance for uncollectible accounts, allowance for quantity discounts, and discretionary year-end bonuses.

Seasonal Revenue, Costs, or Expenses

18. Revenues of certain businesses are subject to material seasonal variations. To avoid the possibility

that interim results with material seasonal variations may be taken as fairly indicative of the estimated results for a full fiscal year, such businesses should disclose the seasonal nature of their activities, and consider supplementing their interim reports with information for twelve-month periods ended at the interim date for the current and preceding years.

Income Tax Provisions

19. In reporting interim financial information, income tax provisions should be determined under the procedures set forth in APB Opinion Nos. 11, 23, and 24. At the end of each interim period the company should make its best estimate of the effective tax rate expected to be applicable for the full fiscal year. The rate so determined should be used in providing for income taxes on a current year-to-date basis. The effective tax rate should reflect anticipated investment tax credits, foreign tax rates, percentage depletion, capital gains rates, and other available tax planning alternatives. However, in arriving at this effective tax rate no effect should be included for the tax related to significant unusual or extraordinary items that will be separately reported or reported net of their related tax effect in reports for the interim period or for the fiscal year.[2]

20. The tax effects of losses that arise in the early portion of a fiscal year (in the event carryback of such losses is not possible) should be recognized only when realization is assured beyond any reasonable doubt (paragraph 45 of APB Opinion No. 11). An established seasonal pattern of loss in early interim periods offset by income in later interim periods should constitute evidence that realization is assured beyond reasonable doubt, unless other evidence indicates the established seasonal pattern will not prevail. The tax effects of losses incurred in early interim periods may be recognized in a later interim period of a fiscal year if their realization, although initially uncertain, later becomes assured beyond reasonable doubt. When the tax effects of losses that arise in the early portions of a fiscal year are not recognized in that interim period, no tax provision should be made for income that arises in later interim periods until the tax effects of the previous interim losses are utilized.[3] Changes resulting from new tax legislation should be reflected after the effective dates prescribed in the statutes.

Disposal of a Segment of a Business and Extraordinary, Unusual, Infrequently Occurring and Contingent Items

21. Extraordinary items should be disclosed sepa-

[2]Disclosure should be made of the reasons for significant variations in the customary relationship between income tax expense and pre-tax accounting income, if they are not otherwise apparent from the financial statements or from the nature of the entity's business (see APB Opinion No. 11, paragraph 63).

[3]The tax benefits of interim losses accounted for in this manner would not be reported as extraordinary items in the results of operations of the interim period as is provided for in annual periods in paragraph 45 of APB Opinion No. 11.

rately and included in the determination of net income for the interim period in which they occur. In determining materiality, extraordinary items should be related to the estimated income for the full fiscal year. Effects of disposals of a segment of a business and unusual and infrequently occurring transactions and events that are material with respect to the operating results of the interim period but that are not designated as extraordinary items in the interim statements should be reported separately. In addition, matters such as unusual seasonal results, business combinations treated for accounting purposes as poolings of interests and acquisition of a significant business in a purchase should be disclosed to provide information needed for a proper understanding of interim financial reports. Extraordinary items, gains or losses from disposal of a segment of a business, and unusual or infrequently occurring items should not be prorated over the balance of the fiscal year.

22. Contingencies and other uncertainties that could be expected to affect the fairness of presentation of financial data at an interim date should be disclosed in interim reports in the same manner required for annual reports.[4] Such disclosures should be repeated in interim and annual reports until the contingencies have been removed, resolved, or have become immaterial.

Accounting Changes

23. Each report of interim financial information should indicate any change in accounting principles or practices from those applied in (a) the comparable interim period of the prior annual period, (b) the preceding interim periods in the current annual period and (c) the prior annual report.

24. Changes in an interim or annual accounting practice or policy made in an interim period should be reported in the period in which the change is made, in accordance with the provisions of APB Opinion No. 20, *Accounting Changes.*

25. Certain changes in accounting principle, such as those described in paragraphs 4 and 27 of APB Opinion No. 20, require retroactive restatement of previously issued financial statements. Paragraph 26 of APB Opinion No. 9, *Reporting the Results of Operations,* requires similar treatment for prior period adjustments. Previously issued financial statements must also be restated for a change in the reporting entity (see paragraphs 34-35 of APB Opinion No. 20) and for correction of an error (see paragraphs 36-37 of APB Opinion No. 20). Pre-

viously issued interim financial information should be similarly restated. APB Opinion Nos. 9 and 20 specify the required disclosures.

26. The effect of a change in an accounting estimate, including a change in the estimated effective annual tax rate, should be accounted for in the period in which the change in estimate is made. No restatement of previously reported interim information should be made for changes in estimates, but the effect on earnings of a change in estimate made in a current interim period should be reported in the current and subsequent interim periods, if material in relation to any period presented and should continue to be reported in the interim financial information of the subsequent year for as many periods as necessary to avoid misleading comparisons. Such disclosure should conform with paragraph 33 of APB Opinion No. 20.

27. A change in accounting principle or practice adopted in an interim period that requires an adjustment for the cumulative effect of the change to the beginning of the current fiscal year should be reported in the interim period in a manner similar to that to be followed in the annual report.[5] The cumulative effect of a change in accounting practice or policy should be calculated in an interim period by determining the effect of the change on the amount of retained earnings at the beginning of the annual period in which the interim period falls. The effect of the change from the beginning of the annual period to the period of change should be reported as a determinant of net income in the interim period in which the change is made. When the previously reported interim information is subsequently presented, it should be restated to give effect to the accounting change.

28. The Board recommends that, whenever possible, companies adopt any accounting changes during the first interim period of a fiscal year. Changes in accounting principles and practices adopted after the first interim period in a fiscal year tend to obscure operating results and complicate disclosure of interim financial information.

29. In determining materiality for the purpose of reporting the cumulative effect of an accounting change or correction of an error, amounts should be related to the estimated income for the full fiscal year and also to the effect on the trend of earnings. Changes that are material with respect to an interim period but not material with respect to the estimated income for the full fiscal year or to the trend of earnings should be separately disclosed in the interim period.

---

[4]The significance of a contingency or uncertainty should be judged in relation to annual financial statements. Disclosures of such items should include, but not be limited to, those matters that form the basis of a qualification of an independent auditor's report.

[5]Paragraphs 20-22 of APB Opinion No. 20 provide guidance on the determination of the cumulative effect of an accounting change. The first two sentences of paragraph 27 above apply the guides of paragraphs 20-22 to APB Opinion No. 20 to interim data.

PART II

Disclosure of Summarized Interim Financial Data by Publicly Traded Companies

30. The Board recognizes that many publicly traded companies[6] report summarized financial information to their securityholders at periodic interim dates in considerably less detail than that provided in annual financial statements. While this information provides securityholders with more timely information than would result if complete financial statements were issued at the end of each interim period, the timeliness of presentation may be partially offset by a reduction in detail in the information provided. As a result, the Board recognizes that certain guides as to minimum disclosure are desirable. When publicly traded companies report summarized financial information to their securityholders at interim dates (including reports on fourth quarters), the following data should be reported, as a minimum:[7]

a. Sales or gross revenues, provision for income taxes, extraordinary items (including related income tax effects), cumulative effect of a change in accounting principles or practices, and net income.
b. Primary and fully diluted earnings per share data for each period presented, determined in accordance with the provisions of APB Opinion No. 15, *Earnings Per Share.*
c. Seasonal revenue, costs or expenses (paragraph 18).
d. Significant changes in estimates or provisions for income taxes (paragraph 19).
e. Disposal of a segment of a business and extraordinary, unusual or infrequently occurring items (paragraph 21).
f. Contingent items (paragraph 22).
g. Changes in accounting principles or estimates (paragraphs 23-29).
h. Significant changes in financial position (paragraph 33).

When summarized financial data are regularly reported on a quarterly basis, the foregoing information with respect to the current quarter and the current year-to-date or the last twelve months to date should be furnished together with comparable data for the preceding year.

31. When interim financial data and disclosures are not separately reported for the fourth quarter, securityholders often make inferences about that quarter by subtracting data based on the third quarter interim report from the annual results. In the absence of a separate fourth quarter report or disclosure of the results (as outlined in paragraph 30) for that quarter in the annual report, disposals of segments of a business and extraordinary, unusual, or infrequently occurring items recognized in the fourth quarter, as well as the aggregate effect of year-end adjustments which are material to the results of that quarter (see paragraphs 4 and 17) should be disclosed in the annual report in a note to the annual financial statements.

32. Disclosure of the impact on the financial results for interim periods of the matters discussed in paragraphs 21-29 is desirable for as many subsequent periods as necessary to keep the reader fully informed. The Board believes there is a presumption that users of summarized interim financial data will have read the latest published annual report, including the financial disclosures required by generally accepted accounting principles and management's commentary concerning the annual financial results, and that the summarized interim data will be viewed in that context. In this connection, the Board encourages management to provide commentary relating to the effects of significant events upon the interim financial results.

33. The Board encourages publicly traded companies to publish balance sheet and funds flow data at interim dates since these data often assist securityholders in their understanding and interpretation of the income data reported. When condensed interim balance sheet information or funds flow data are not presented at interim reporting dates, significant changes since the last reporting period with respect to liquid assets, net working capital, long-term liabilities, or stockholders' equity should be disclosed.

EFFECTIVE DATE

34. This Opinion shall be effective for interim financial information issued for all interim periods relating to fiscal years beginning after December 31, 1973. However, the Board encourages earlier application of the provisions of this Opinion.

35. When interim financial data are presented for prior interim periods for comparative purposes, these data should be restated on a basis consistent with procedures newly adopted, or the effect on the prior interim period data had the newly adopted procedures been applicable for that period should be disclosed.

The Opinion entitled "Interim Financial Report-

---

[6]See footnote 1.

[7]It should be recognized that the minimum disclosures of summarized interim financial data required of publicly traded companies by Part II of this Opinion do not constitute a fair presentation of financial position and results of operations in conformity with generally accepted accounting principles.

ing" was adopted by the assenting votes of fourteen members of the Board, of whom two, Messrs. Horngren and Norr, assented with qualification. Messrs. Cummings, Halvorson, Hayes and Watt dissented.

Mr. Horngren assents to this Opinion because it provides a step in the right direction. However, he believes this Opinion does not resolve the differing views as to the principal objective of interim financial information, as described in paragraph 5. Until the principal objective is agreed upon, interim financial reporting will, in his opinion, continue to be too diverse.

Mr. Norr assents with qualification. He believes that income for publicly traded companies should be reported in the same detail as in the annual report. Illustrations of a few necessary items would be cost of goods sold, depreciation, and the investment tax credit. (Par. 30). He believes that the text of all releases accompanying interim reports should not depart from generally accepted accounting principles. In addition he believes that interim reports should explain variances from the comparable period of the prior year and should discuss material corporate developments. Thus explanations should be provided indicating the impact on net income of volume, prices, start-up costs or shifts in the line of business. He also believes that in most circumstances each interim period is a discrete period and that the Opinion encourages normalizing and smoothing income, concealing the actual level of activity.

Mr. Cummings dissents from Part I of this Opinion because he believes paragraphs 9 through 17 provide inadequate and inherently contradictory guidelines for the determination of income and expenses appropriate for interim reporting. He agrees with the concept expressed in paragraph 9 that each interim period should be viewed primarily as being an integral part of an annual period. However, he points out that succeeding paragraphs sanction inconsistent concepts which, for example, permit the recognition of costs in interim periods as incurred, or allocation based on an estimate of time expired, benefit received, or other associated activity. As a consequence, instead of establishing appropriate accounting principles to be followed in the preparation of interim financial reports, the lack of adequate guidelines must necessarily lead to confusion which can only serve to dilute investor confidence in and understanding of the financial accounting process.

Messrs. Halvorson, Hayes and Watt dissent from Part I of this Opinion because they believe that the essential concepts of accrual and deferral of costs and expenses that are applicable to annual periods are equally applicable to interim periods. They observe that any interim period is both a discrete accounting period and a fraction of an annual period in the same sense that an annual report is both a discrete accounting period and a segment of the period representing the life of the enterprise and they believe it is unnecessary to characterize an interim period as either of these things to the exclusion of the other for purposes of establishing appropriate accounting principles. In general, they believe that financial statements for any period (which is necessarily both a discrete period and a segment of a larger period) should reflect the events of that period. In their view the Opinion encourages normalizing income by arbitrarily normalizing expenses, thereby concealing actual results of operations of an interim period. In so doing, the Opinion ignores the fundamental concept of consistency by condoning the use of interim principles and practices inconsistent with accounting policies used in the preparation of annual financial statements. While they recognize that the shorter a reporting period the less useful it is as a predictive tool, they do believe that it is not a proper function of accounting to adjust the historical accounting for any period in order to produce purported results of operations more representative of other periods than the events of that period.

They believe paragraphs 9 through 17 provide inadequate and inherently contradictory guidelines for the determination of income and expenses appropriate for interim reporting. Relative to certain businesses subject to material seasonal variations, the admonition in paragraph 18 to "avoid the possibility that interim results with material seasonal variations may be taken as fairly indicative of the estimated results for a full fiscal year" gives no practical guidance to problems of income measurement in such businesses.

They believe that the problem which the Opinion should have covered is one of measuring income during periods representing fractions of annual or other cycles, a problem which is not peculiar to interim reports. In their view, a proper approach to this problem would recognize that many activities and events of a business occur in and are related to such annual or other cycles. Some are related to such cycles for physical reasons (e.g., the harvesting and marketing of agricultural products) and some by reason of custom, law or contract (e.g., annual bonuses and income taxes). Methods of accruing or deferring various costs and expenses relating to such cycles should be developed and they should be applied consistently during interim periods and in annual financial statements. Under this approach, there is no need or justification for accruals and deferrals in interim periods which are not also recognized at year end. Likewise, if the application of a previously accepted year-end accounting principle to interim periods is found to be inappropriate and another principle adopted, it should be necessary to change the principle applied at the year end to be consistent with the principle considered necessary for a fair presentation of results of operations for the interim period.

Messrs. Cummings, Halvorson, Hayes, and Watt dissent from Part II of this Opinion because it prescribes "minimum" disclosures of selected financial information without offering an understandable frame of reference. They observe that such minimum standards prescribe some disclosures not required when complete statements are presented and fail to prescribe others which are required when complete statements are presented. Since such summarized financial information is not intended to "present fairly" results of operations or financial position, they believe it is not appropriate for the Board to establish disclosure requirements for only a limited group of companies, namely publicly traded companies, which has the effect of simply regulating them and which will not result in consistent interim reports to securityholders and other users of financial statements of all companies. They observe that paragraph 31 of Part II requires disclosure of "disposals of a segment of a business and extraordinary, unusual or infrequently occurring items recognized in the fourth quarter, as well as the aggregate effect of year end adjustments which are material to the results of that quarter." To them it is inappropriate to require in annual financial statements disclosure of information relative solely to interim periods and irrelevant in a report of results of operations for a fiscal year. They believe also that this requirement creates an unreasonable burden on all parties involved in reporting annual results of operations, particularly since it offers no guidance for implementing the required disclosure of "the aggregate effect of year end adjustments."

NOTES

Opinions of the Accounting Principles Board present the conclusions of at least two-thirds of the members of the Board.

Board Opinions need not be applied to immaterial items.

Covering all possible conditions and circumstances in an Opinion of the Accounting Principles Board is usually impracticable. The substance of transactions and the principles, guides, rules, and criteria described in Opinions should control the accounting for transactions not expressly covered.

Unless otherwise stated, Opinions of the Board are not intended to be retroactive.

Rule 203 of the Institute's Rules of Conduct prohibits a member from expressing his opinion that financial statements are presented in conformity with generally accepted accounting principles if the statements depart in a material respect from such principles unless he can demonstrate that due to unusual circumstances application of the principles would result in misleading statements—in which case his report must describe the departure, its approximate effects, if practicable, and the reasons why compliance with the established principles would result in misleading statements.

Pursuant to resolution of Council, this Opinion of the APB establishes, until such time as they are expressly superseded by action of FASB, accounting principles which fall within the provisions of Rule 203 of the Rules of Conduct.

Accounting Principles Board (1973)

Philip L. Defliese, *Chairman*	Robert L. Ferst	Charles T. Horngren
Donald J. Bevis	Oscar S. Gellein	Louis M. Kessler
Albert J. Bows	Newman T. Halvorson	David Norr
Milton M. Broeker	Robert Hampton, III	George C. Watt
Leo E. Burger	Donald J. Hayes	Allan Wear
Joseph P. Cummings	Charles B. Hellerson	Glenn A. Welsch

APB Opinion No. 29
Accounting for Nonmonetary Transactions

STATUS

Issued: May 1973

Effective Date: For transactions after September 30, 1973

Affects: No other pronouncements

Affected by: Paragraph 4 amended by FAS 71
Paragraph 27 amended by FAS 96 and FAS 109

Other Interpretive Pronouncements: FIN 30
FTB 85-1

APB Opinion No. 29
Accounting for Nonmonetary Transactions

CONTENTS

INTRODUCTION

1. Most business transactions involve exchanges of cash or other monetary assets or liabilities[1] for goods or services. The amount of monetary assets or liabilities exchanged generally provides an objective basis for measuring the cost of nonmonetary assets or services received by an enterprise as well as for measuring gain or loss on nonmonetary assets transferred from an enterprise. Some transactions, however, involve either (a) an exchange with another entity (reciprocal transfer[1]) that involves principally nonmonetary assets or liabilities[1] or (b) a transfer of nonmonetary assets for which no assets are received or relinquished in exchange (nonreciprocal transfer[1]). Both exchanges and nonreciprocal transfers that involve little or no monetary assets or liabilities are referred to in this Opinion as nonmonetary transactions.

2. Questions have been raised concerning the determination of the amount to assign to a nonmonetary asset transferred to or from an enterprise in a nonmonetary transaction and also concerning the recognition of a gain or loss on a nonmonetary asset transferred from an enterprise in a nonmonetary transaction. Practice has varied; some nonmonetary transactions have been accounted for at the estimated fair value of the assets transferred and some at the amounts at which the assets transferred were previously recorded. This Opinion sets forth the views of the Board on accounting for nonmonetary transactions.

Definitions

3. The meanings of certain terms used in this Opinion are:

---

[1]See paragraph 3 of this Opinion for definitions of these terms.

a. *Monetary assets and liabilities* are assets and liabilities whose amounts are fixed in terms of units of currency by contract or otherwise. Examples are cash, short- or long-term accounts and notes receivable in cash, and short- or long-term accounts and notes payable in cash.[2]

b. *Nonmonetary assets and liabilities* are assets and liabilities other than monetary ones. Examples are inventories; investments in common stocks; property, plant and equipment; and liabilities for rent collected in advance.[2]

c. *Exchange* (or *exchange transaction*) is a reciprocal transfer between an enterprise and another entity that results in the enterprise's acquiring assets or services or satisfying liabilities by surrendering other assets or services or incurring other obligations.[3]

d. *Nonreciprocal transfer*[3] is a transfer of assets or services in one direction, either from an enterprise to its owners (whether or not in exchange for their ownership interests) or another entity or from owners or another entity to the enterprise. An entity's reacquisition of its outstanding stock is an example of a nonreciprocal transfer.

e. *Productive assets* are assets held for or used in the production of goods or services by the enterprise. Productive assets include an investment in another entity if the investment is accounted for by the equity method but exclude an investment not accounted for by that method. *Similar productive assets* are productive assets that are of the same general type, that perform the same function or that are employed in the same line of business.

Applicability

4. This Opinion does not apply to the following transactions:

a. A business combination accounted for by an enterprise according to the provisions of APB Opinion No. 16, *Business Combinations,*

b. A transfer of nonmonetary assets solely between companies or persons under common control, such as between a parent company and its subsidiaries or between two subsidiary corporations of the same parent, or between a corporate joint venture and its owners,

c. Acquisition of nonmonetary assets or services on issuance of the capital stock of an enterprise,[4] and

d. Stock issued or received in stock dividends and stock splits which are accounted for in accordance with ARB No. 43, Chapter 7B.

This Opinion applies to regulated companies in accordance with the Addendum to APB Opinion No. 2, *Accounting for the Investment Credit,* 1962 and it amends APB Statement No. 4, *Basic Concepts and Accounting Principles Underlying Financial Statements of Business Enterprises,* to the extent it relates to measuring transfers of certain nonmonetary assets. Some exchanges of nonmonetary assets involve a small monetary consideration, referred to as "boot," even though the exchange is essentially nonmonetary. This Opinion also applies to those transactions. For purposes of applying this Opinion, events and transactions in which nonmonetary assets are involuntarily converted (for example, as a result of total or partial destruction, theft, seizure, or condemnation) to monetary assets that are then reinvested in other nonmonetary assets are monetary transactions since the recipient is not obligated to reinvest the monetary consideration in other nonmonetary assets.

DISCUSSION

Present Accounting for Nonmonetary Transactions

5. *Nonreciprocal Transfers with Owners.* Some nonmonetary transactions are nonreciprocal transfers between an enterprise and its owners. Examples include (a) distribution of nonmonetary assets, such as marketable equity securities, to stockholders as dividends, (b) distribution of nonmonetary assets, such as marketable equity securities, to stockholders to redeem or acquire outstanding capital stock of the enterprise, (c) distribution of nonmonetary assets, such as capital stock of subsidiaries, to stockholders in corporate liquidations or plans of reorganization that involve disposing of all or a significant segment of the business (the plans are variously referred to as spin-offs, split-ups, and

---

[2]APB Statement No. 3, *Financial Statements Restated for General Price-Level Changes,* paragraphs 17-19 and Appendix B, contains a more complete explanation of monetary and nonmonetary items.

[3]APB Statement No. 4, *Basic Concepts and Accounting Principles Underlying Financial Statements of Business Enterprises,* paragraphs 180-183, contains a more complete explanation of exchanges and nonreciprocal transfers.

[4]The Board has deferred consideration of accounting for those transactions pending completion and consideration of Accounting Research Studies on intercorporate investments and stockholders' equity except to the extent they are covered in APB Opinion No. 25, *Accounting for Stock Issued to Employees.*

split-offs), and (d) distribution of nonmonetary assets to groups of stockholders, pursuant to plans of rescission or other settlements relating to a prior business combination, to redeem or acquire shares of capital stock previously issued in a business combination. Accounting for decreases in owners' equity that result from nonreciprocal nonmonetary transactions with owners has usually been based on the recorded amount of the nonmonetary assets distributed.

6. *Nonreciprocal Transfers with Other Than Owners.* Other nonmonetary transactions are nonreciprocal transfers between an enterprise and entities other than its owners. Examples are the contribution of nonmonetary assets by an enterprise to a charitable organization and the contribution of land by a governmental unit for construction of productive facilities by an enterprise. Accounting for nonmonetary assets received in a nonreciprocal transfer from an entity other than an owner has usually been based on fair value of the assets received while accounting for nonmonetary assets transferred to another entity has usually been based on the recorded amount of the assets relinquished.

7. *Nonmonetary Exchanges.* Many nonmonetary transactions are exchanges of nonmonetary assets or services with another entity. Examples include (a) exchange of product held for sale in the ordinary course of business (inventory) for dissimilar property as a means of selling the product to a customer, (b) exchange of product held for sale in the ordinary course of business (inventory) for similar product as an accommodation—that is, at least one party to the exchange reduces transportation costs, meets immediate inventory needs, or otherwise reduces costs or facilitates ultimate sale of the product—and not as a means of selling the product to a customer, and (c) exchange of productive assets—assets employed in production rather than held for sale in the ordinary course of business—for similar productive assets or for an equivalent interest in similar productive assets. Examples of exchanges in category (c) include the trade of player contracts by professional sports organizations, exchange of leases on mineral properties, exchange of one form of interest in an oil producing property for another form of interest, exchange of real estate for real estate. Accounting for nonmonetary assets acquired in a nonmonetary exchange has sometimes been based on the fair value of the assets relinquished and sometimes on the recorded amount of the assets relinquished.

Differing Views

8. Views of accountants differ as to appropriate accounting for all of the types of nonmonetary transactions described in paragraphs 5 to 7.

9. *Nonreciprocal Transfers of Nonmonetary Assets to Owners.* Some believe that accounting for nonreciprocal transfers of nonmonetary assets to owners should be based on the carrying amount of the nonmonetary assets transferred because only that method is consistent with the historical cost basis of accounting.

10. Others believe that accounting for transfers of nonmonetary assets to reduce certain owners' interests other than through a reorganization, liquidation, or rescission of a prior business combination should be based on the fair value of the nonmonetary assets distributed or the fair value of the stock representing the owners' equity eliminated, whichever is more clearly evident. In their view, disposing of the value represented by a nonmonetary asset is a significant economic event, and the unrecorded increase or decrease that has resulted in the value of the nonmonetary asset since its acquisition should be recognized.

11. Many who agree with accounting based on fair value for a nonreciprocal transfer of a nonmonetary asset that reduces certain owners' interests also believe that distributing a nonmonetary asset as an ordinary dividend (but not distributing a nonmonetary asset as a liquidating dividend or in a spin-off, reorganization or similar distributions) may be regarded as equivalent to an exchange with owners and therefore recorded at the fair value of the nonmonetary asset distributed, particularly if the dividend is distributable as either cash or the nonmonetary asset at the election of the owner. They believe that failure to recognize the fair value of nonmonetary assets transferred may both misstate the dividend and fail to recognize gains and losses on nonmonetary assets that have already been earned or incurred by the enterprise and should be recognized on distributing the assets for dividend purposes.

12. Others generally agree with the view that nonreciprocal transfers of nonmonetary assets to certain owners should be accounted for at fair value but believe that dividends and other prorata distributions to owners are essentially similar to liquidating dividends or distributions in spin-offs and reorganizations and should be accounted for at the recorded amount of the asset transferred.

13. *Nonreciprocal Receipts of Nonmonetary Assets.* Many believe that a nonmonetary asset received in a nonreciprocal transfer from other than owners should be recorded at fair value because fair value is the only value relevant to the recipient enterprise. Others believe that such nonmonetary assets should be recorded at a nominal value since fair value cannot be reasonably determined in view of performance obligations usually agreed to by the

recipient as a consideration for the transfer.

14. *Nonreciprocal Transfers of Nonmonetary Assets to Other Than Owners.* Some believe that accounting for a nonreciprocal transfer of a nonmonetary asset to an entity other than an owner should be based on the carrying amount of the asset transferred because only that method is consistent with the historical cost basis of accounting. Others believe that failure to recognize the fair value of a nonmonetary asset transferred may both understate (or overstate) expenses incurred and fail to recognize gains or losses on nonmonetary assets that have already been earned or incurred by the enterprise and should be recognized when the transfer of the asset is recognized as an expense.

15. *Exchange Transactions.* Some believe that accounting for an exchange of nonmonetary assets between an enterprise and another entity (an enterprise or individual acting in a capacity other than a stockholder of the enterprise) should be based on the fair values of the assets involved, while others believe that accounting for the exchange should be based on the carrying amount of the asset transferred from the enterprise. Those who advocate the former view believe it to be the only method consistent with the accounting principle that an asset acquired should be recorded at its cost as measured by the fair value of the asset relinquished to acquire it. Those advocating the latter view believe that revenue should be recognized only if an exchange involves monetary assets; therefore recognizing fair value is inappropriate unless a monetary asset is received in an exchange.

16. Many accountants who accept the concept that accounting for an exchange of nonmonetary assets should be based on fair value believe that problems of measurement and questions about the conditions for recognizing revenue require modification of the concept in two types of exchanges. They therefore conclude that:

a. Fair values should not be recognized if an enterprise exchanges product or property held for sale in the ordinary course of business for product or property to be sold in the same line of business. The emphasis in that exchange, in their view, is on developing economical ways to acquire inventory for resale to customers rather than on marketing inventory to obtain revenue from customers. Therefore, "swapping" inventories between enterprises that are essentially competitors and not customers of each other is merely an incidental early stage of an earning process, and revenue should not be recognized until the time of sale of the exchanged products

(in the same or another form) to a customer of the enterprise.

b. Fair value should not be recognized if an enterprise exchanges a productive asset for a similar productive asset or an equivalent interest in the same or similar productive asset. Therefore, revenue should not be recognized merely because one productive asset is substituted for a similar productive asset but rather should be considered to flow from the production and sale of the goods or services to which the substituted productive asset is committed.

17. *Fair Value Not Determinable.* General agreement exists that a nonmonetary transaction, regardless of form, should not be recorded at fair value if fair value is not determinable within reasonable limits. Major uncertainties concerning realizability of the fair value proposed to be assigned to a nonmonetary asset received in a nonmonetary transaction are indicative of an inability to determine fair value within reasonable limits. Some believe that only an exchange transaction between parties with essentially opposing interests provides an independent test of fair value to be used in measuring the transaction; therefore fair value is determinable within reasonable limits only in a negotiated exchange transaction. Others believe that fair value in a nonreciprocal transfer is also often determinable within reasonable limits and should be recognized in certain types of transactions.

OPINION

Basic Principle

18. The Board concludes that in general accounting for nonmonetary transactions should be based on the fair values[5] of the assets (or services) involved which is the same basis as that used in monetary transactions. Thus, the cost of a nonmonetary asset acquired in exchange for another nonmonetary asset is the fair value of the asset surrendered to obtain it, and a gain or loss should be recognized on the exchange. The fair value of the asset received should be used to measure the cost if it is more clearly evident than the fair value of the asset surrendered. Similarly, a nonmonetary asset received in a nonreciprocal transfer should be recorded at the fair value of the asset received. A transfer of a nonmonetary asset to a stockholder or to another entity in a nonreciprocal transfer should be recorded at the fair value of the asset transferred, and a gain or loss should be recognized on the disposition of the asset. The fair value of an entity's own stock reacquired may be a more clearly evident measure of the fair value of the asset distributed in a nonreciprocal

---

[5]See paragraph 25 for determination of fair value.

transfer if the transaction involves distribution of a nonmonetary asset to eliminate a disproportionate part of owners' interests (that is, to acquire stock for the treasury or for retirement).

19. The Board believes that certain modifications of the basic principle are required to accommodate problems of measurement and questions about the conditions for recognizing revenue. These modifications are specified in paragraphs 20 to 23.

Modifications of the Basic Principle

20. *Fair Value Not Determinable.* Accounting for a nonmonetary transaction should not be based on the fair values of the assets transferred unless those fair values are determinable within reasonable limits (paragraph 25).

21. *Exchanges.* If the exchange is not essentially the culmination of an earning process, accounting for an exchange of a nonmonetary asset between an enterprise and another entity should be based on the recorded amount (after reduction, if appropriate, for an indicated impairment of value) of the nonmonetary asset relinquished. The Board believes that the following two types of nonmonetary exchange transactions do not culminate an earning process:

a. An exchange of a product or property held for sale in the ordinary course of business for a product or property to be sold in the same line of business to facilitate sales to customers other than the parties to the exchange, and

b. An exchange of a productive asset not held for sale in the ordinary course of business for a similar productive asset or an equivalent interest in the same or similar productive asset (similar productive asset is defined in paragraph 3 and examples are given in paragraph 7).[6]

22. The exchanges of nonmonetary assets that would otherwise be based on recorded amounts (paragraph 21) may include an amount of monetary consideration. The Board believes that the recipient of the monetary consideration has realized gain on the exchange to the extent that the amount of the monetary receipt exceeds a proportionate share of the recorded amount of the asset surrendered. The portion of the cost applicable to the realized amount should be based on the ratio of the monetary consideration to the total consideration received (monetary consideration plus the estimated fair value of the nonmonetary asset received) or, if more clearly evident, the fair value of the nonmonetary asset transferred. The Board further believes that the entity paying the monetary consideration should not

recognize any gain on a transaction covered in paragraph 21 but should record the asset received at the amount of the monetary consideration paid plus the recorded amount of the nonmonetary asset surrendered. If a loss is indicated by the terms of a transaction described in this paragraph or in paragraph 21, the entire indicated loss on the exchange should be recognized.

23. *Nonreciprocal Transfers to Owners.* Accounting for the distribution of nonmonetary assets to owners of an enterprise in a spin-off or other form of reorganization or liquidation or in a plan that is in substance the rescission of a prior business combination should be based on the recorded amount (after reduction, if appropriate, for an indicated impairment of value) of the nonmonetary assets distributed. A prorata distribution to owners of an enterprise of shares of a subsidiary or other investee company that has been or is being consolidated or that has been or is being accounted for under the equity method is to be considered to be equivalent to a spin-off. Other nonreciprocal transfers of nonmonetary assets to owners should be accounted for at fair value if the fair value of the nonmonetary asset distributed is objectively measurable and would be clearly realizable to the distributing entity in an outright sale at or near the time of the distribution.

Applying the Basic Principle

24. The Board's conclusions modify to some extent existing practices as described in paragraphs 5 to 7. The conclusions are based on supporting reasons given in paragraphs 8 to 17.

25. Fair value of a nonmonetary asset transferred to or from an enterprise in a nonmonetary transaction should be determined by referring to estimated realizable values in cash transactions of the same or similar assets, quoted market prices, independent appraisals, estimated fair values of assets or services received in exchange, and other available evidence. If one of the parties in a nonmonetary transaction could have elected to receive cash instead of the nonmonetary asset, the amount of cash that could have been received may be evidence of the fair value of the nonmonetary assets exchanged.

26. Fair value should be regarded as not determinable within reasonable limits if major uncertainties exist about the realizability of the value that would be assigned to an asset received in a nonmonetary transaction accounted for at fair value. An exchange involving parties with essentially opposing interests is not considered a prerequisite to determining a fair value of a nonmonetary asset trans-

---

[6]The fact that an exchange of productive assets is not a taxable transaction for tax purposes may be evidence that the assets exchanged are similar for purposes of applying this Opinion.

ferred; nor does an exchange insure that a fair value for accounting purposes can be ascertained within reasonable limits. If neither the fair value of a nonmonetary asset transferred nor the fair value of a nonmonetary asset received in exchange is determinable within reasonable limits, the recorded amount of the nonmonetary asset transferred from the enterprise may be the only available measure of the transaction.

27. A difference between the amount of gain or loss recognized for tax purposes and that recognized for accounting purposes may constitute a timing difference to be accounted for according to APB Opinion No. 11, *Accounting for Income Taxes.*

Disclosure

28. An enterprise that engages in one or more nonmonetary transactions during a period should disclose in financial statements for the period the nature of the transactions, the basis of accounting for the assets transferred, and gains or losses recognized on transfers.[7]

EFFECTIVE DATE

29. This Opinion shall be effective for transactions entered into after September 30, 1973. Transactions recorded previously for a fiscal year ending before October 1, 1973 should not be adjusted. However, transactions recorded previously for a fiscal year that includes October 1, 1973 may be adjusted to comply with the provisions of this Opinion.

The Opinion entitled "Accounting for Nonmonetary Transactions" was adopted by the assenting votes of seventeen members of the Board, of whom three, Messrs. Hellerson, Horngren, and Norr, assented with qualification. Mr. Broeker dissented.

Messrs. Hellerson and Horngren assent to this Opinion because in their view it represents a step in the right direction. However, they disagree with Paragraph 22, which in substance creates a class of "part-monetary, part-nonmonetary" transactions having illogical accounting results. In their view, a significant amount of monetary consideration in a transaction makes the exchange in substance a monetary rather than a nonmonetary transaction. In short, if boot is significant, the exchange is no longer an exchange of similar products, property, or productive assets. Therefore, the transaction should be accounted for on the basis of the fair values of

the assets involved.

Mr. Norr assents with qualification. He is concerned with the opportunity for abuse that might arise through use of independent appraisals (Paragraph 25) and would limit the application of the Opinion to cases where clear objective evidence of third party values exist.

Mr. Broeker dissents to the issuance of this Opinion. In his view, the Opinion does not improve present accounting practice because the modifications and exceptions (Paragraphs 20 through 23) are so broad that (a) the general principle as defined in Paragraph 18 may apply only to a very narrow range of transactions and (b) interpretations of the Opinion could encourage alternative methods of accounting for similar transactions. He further believes that nonreciprocal transfers to owners do not generate profits and losses and therefore should be accounted for at carrying amounts of the nonmonetary assets transferred.

NOTES

Opinions of the Accounting Principles Board present the conclusions of at least two-thirds of the members of the Board.

Board Opinions need not be applied to immaterial items.

Covering all possible conditions and circumstances in an Opinion of the Accounting Principles Board is usually impracticable. The substance of transactions and the principles, guides, rules, and criteria described in Opinions should control the accounting for transactions not expressly covered.

Unless otherwise stated, Opinions of the Board are not intended to be retroactive.

Rule 203 of the Institute's Rules of Conduct prohibits a member from expressing his opinion that financial statements are presented in conformity with generally accepted accounting principles if the statements depart in a material respect from such principles unless he can demonstrate that due to unusual circumstances application of the principles would result in misleading statements—in which case his report must describe the departure, its approximate effects, if practicable, and the reasons why compliance with the established principles would result in misleading statements.

Pursuant to resolution of Council, this Opinion of the APB establishes, until such time as they are expressly superseded by action of FASB, accounting principles which fall within the provisions of Rule 203 of the Rules of Conduct.

---

[7]Paragraph 12 of ARB No. 51, *Consolidated Financial Statements*, includes additional disclosures that are preferred if a parent company disposes of a subsidiary during the year.

APB Opinion No. 30
Reporting the Results of Operations—
Reporting the Effects of Disposal of a Segment of
a Business, and Extraordinary, Unusual and Infrequently
Occurring Events and Transactions

STATUS

Issued: June 1973

Effective Date: For events and transactions after September 30, 1973

Affects: Amends APB 9, paragraph 17
    Supersedes APB 9, paragraphs 20 through 22 and 29, footnote 2, and
      Exhibits A through D
    Amends APB 15, paragraph 13 and footnote 8
    Amends APB 17, paragraph 31
    Amends APB 18, paragraph 19(d)
    Amends APB 19, paragraph 10
    Amends APB 26, paragraph 20
    Amends AIN-APB 9, Interpretation No. 1

Affected by: Paragraph 7 amended by FAS 96 and FAS 109
    Paragraph 20 amended by FAS 4 and FAS 101
    Paragraph 25 amended by FAS 16
    Footnote 8 amended by FAS 60 and FAS 83
    Footnote 8 superseded by FAS 97

Other Interpretive Pronouncements: AIN-APB 30, Interpretation No. 1
    FIN 27
    FTB 82-1
    FTB 84-2 (Superseded by FAS 96 and FAS 109)
    FTB 84-3 (Superseded by FAS 96 and FAS 109)
    FTB 85-1
    FTB 85-6

Reporting the Results of Operations—Reporting the Effects of
Disposal of a Segment of a Business, and Extraordinary, Unusual **APB 30**
and Infrequently Occurring Events and Transactions

APB Opinion No. 30
Reporting the Results of Operations—Reporting the Effects of
Disposal of a Segment of a Business, and Extraordinary, Unusual and
Infrequently Occurring Events and Transactions

CONTENTS

INTRODUCTION

1. In APB Opinion No. 9, *Reporting the Results of Operations,* issued in 1966, the Board concluded that net income for a period should reflect all items of profit and loss recognized during the period except for certain prior period adjustments. The Opinion further provided that *extraordinary items* should be segregated from the results of ordinary operations and shown separately in the income statement and that their nature and amounts should be disclosed.

2. Financial reporting practices in recent years indicate that interpreting the criteria for extraordinary items in APB Opinion No. 9 has been difficult and significant differences of opinion exist as to certain of its provisions. The Board is also concerned with the varying accounting treatments accorded to certain transactions involving the sale, abandonment, discontinuance, condemnation, or expropriation of a segment of an entity (referred to in this Opinion as disposals of a segment of a business).

3. The purposes of this Opinion are (1) to provide more definitive criteria for extraordinary items by clarifying and, to some extent, modifying the existing definition and criteria, (2) to specify disclosure requirements for extraordinary items, (3) to specify the accounting and reporting for disposal of a seg-

ment of a business, (4) to specify disclosure requirements for other unusual or infrequently occurring events and transactions that are not extraordinary items.

DISCUSSION

4. Some accountants believe that financial statements would be improved by presenting an all-inclusive income statement without separate categories for continuing operations, discontinued operations and extraordinary items. In their view, the use of arbitrary and subjectively defined categories tends to mislead investors and to invite abuse of the intended purposes of the classifications. They believe, therefore, that basically an income statement should reflect only the two broad categories, (a) revenue and gains and (b) expenses and losses. They also believe that investors would be better served by reporting separately the primary types of revenue and expense, including identification of items that are unusual or occur infrequently. Alternatively, sufficient information relating to those items should be otherwise disclosed to permit investors to evaluate their relevance. These accountants believe that such changes should be implemented at the present time.

5. Other accountants believe that the income statement is more useful if the effects of events or trans-

actions that occur infrequently and are of an unusual nature are segregated from the results of the continuing, ordinary, and typical operations of an entity. They also believe that the criteria for income statement classification should relate to the environment in which an entity operates. In their view the criteria in APB Opinion No. 9, paragraph 21, for determining whether an event or transaction should be reported as extraordinary lack precision. Accordingly, they conclude that the criteria should be clarified and modified to provide that to be classified as an extraordinary item an event or transaction should be both unusual in nature and infrequent in occurrence when considered in relation to the environment in which the entity operates. They also believe that to enhance the usefulness of the income statement (a) the results of continuing operations of an entity should be reported separately from the operations of a segment of the business which has been or will be discontinued and (b) the gain or loss from disposal of a segment should be reported in conjunction with the operations of the segment and not as an extraordinary item. They further believe that material events and transactions that are either unusual or occur infrequently, but not both, should be adequately disclosed.

6. Still other accountants agree in part with the views described in paragraph 5 but believe that a combination of infrequency of occurrence and abnormality of financial effect should also result in classifying an event or transaction as extraordinary.

APPLICABILITY

7. This Opinion supersedes paragraphs 20 through 22, paragraph 29 insofar as it refers to examples of financial statements, and Exhibits A through D of APB Opinion No. 9. It also amends paragraph 13 and footnote 8 of APB Opinion No. 15, *Earnings per Share,* insofar as this Opinion prescribes the presentation and computation of earnings per share of continuing and discontinued operations. This Opinion does not modify or amend the conclusions of APB Opinion No. 11, *Accounting for Income Taxes,* paragraphs 45 and 61, or of APB Opinion No. 16, *Business Combinations,* paragraph 60, with respect to the classification of the effects of certain events and transactions as extraordinary items. Prior APB Opinions that refer to the superseded paragraphs noted above are modified to insert a cross reference to this Opinion.[1]

OPINION

Income Statement Presentation and Disclosure

8. *Discontinued Operations of a Segment of a Business.* For purposes of this Opinion, the term *discontinued operations* refers to the operations of a segment of a business as defined in paragraph 13 that has been sold, abandoned, spun off, or otherwise disposed of or, although still operating, is the subject of a formal plan for disposal (see paragraph 14). The Board concludes that the results of continuing operations should be reported separately from discontinued operations and that any gain or loss from disposal of a segment of a business (determined in accordance with paragraphs 15 and 16) should be reported in conjunction with the related results of discontinued operations and not as an extraordinary item. Accordingly, operations of a segment that has been or will be discontinued should be reported separately as a component of income before extraordinary items and the cumulative effect of accounting changes (if applicable) in the following manner:

Income from continuing operations before income taxes[2]	$XXXX
Provision for income taxes	XXX
Income from continuing operations[2]	$XXXX
Discontinued operations (Note ____):	
Income (loss) from operations of discontinued Division X (less applicable income taxes of $ ____)	$XXXX
Loss on disposal of Division X, including provision of $ ____ for operating losses during phase-out period (less applicable income taxes of $ ____)	XXXX XXXX
Net Income	$XXXX

Amounts of income taxes applicable to the results of discontinued operations and the gain or loss from disposal of the segment should be disclosed on the face of the income statement or in related notes.

---

[1]This Opinion amends APB Statement No. 4, *Basic Concepts and Accounting Principles Underlying Financial Statements of Business Enterprises,* to the extent that it describes an extraordinary item.

[2]These captions should be modified appropriately when an entity reports an extraordinary item and/or the cumulative effect of a change in accounting principle in accordance with APB Opinion No. 20, *Accounting Changes.* The presentation of per share data will need similar modification.

Revenues applicable to the discontinued operations should be separately disclosed in the related notes.

9. Earnings per share data for income from continuing operations and net income, computed in accordance with APB Opinion No. 15, should be presented on the face of the income statement.[3] If presented, per share data for the results of discontinued operations and gain or loss from disposal of the business segment may be included on the face of the income statement or in a related note.

10. *Extraordinary Items.* The Board has also reconsidered the presentation of extraordinary items in an income statement as prescribed in APB Opinion No. 9, and reaffirms the need to segregate extraordinary items for the reasons given in paragraph 5 of this Opinion and paragraph 19 of APB Opinion No. 9.

11. In the absence of discontinued operations and changes in accounting principles, the following main captions should appear in an income statement if extraordinary items are reported (paragraphs 17-19 of APB Opinion No. 9):

Income before extraordinary items[4]	$XXX
Extraordinary items (less applicable income taxes of $____) (Note____)	XXX
Net income	$XXX

The caption *extraordinary items* should be used to identify separately the effects of events and transactions, other than the disposal of a segment of a business, that meet the criteria for classification as extraordinary as discussed in paragraphs 19-24. Descriptive captions and the amounts for *individual* extraordinary events or transactions should be presented, preferably on the face of the income statement, if practicable; otherwise disclosure in related notes is acceptable. The nature of an extraordinary event or transaction and the principal items entering into the determination of an extraordinary gain or loss should be described. The income taxes applicable to extraordinary items should be disclosed on the face of the income statement; alternatively disclosure in the related notes is acceptable. The caption *net income* should replace the three captions shown above if the income statement includes no extraordinary items.

12. Earnings per share data for income before extraordinary items and net income should be presented on the face of the income statement, as prescribed by APB Opinion No. 15.

Accounting for the Disposal of a Segment of a Business

13. For purposes of this Opinion, the term *segment of a business* refers to a component of an entity whose activities represent a separate major line of business or class of customer. A segment may be in the form of a subsidiary, a division, or a department, and in some cases a joint venture or other nonsubsidiary investee, provided that its assets, results of operations, and activities can be clearly distinguished, physically and operationally and for financial reporting purposes, from the other assets, results of operations, and activities of the entity. Financial statements of *current and prior* periods that include results of operations prior to the measurement date (as defined in paragraph 14) should disclose the results of operations of the disposed segment, less applicable income taxes, as a separate component of income before extraordinary items (see paragraph 8). The fact that the results of operations of the segment being sold or abandoned cannot be separately identified strongly suggests that the transaction should not be classified as the disposal of a segment of the business. The disposal of a segment of a business should be distinguished from other disposals of assets incident to the evolution of the entity's business, such as the disposal of part of a line of business, the shifting of production or marketing activities for a particular line of business from one location to another, the phasing out of a product line or class of service, and other changes occasioned by technological improvements. The disposal of two or more unrelated assets that individually do not constitute a segment of a business should not be combined and accounted for as a disposal of a segment of business.

14. *Definition of Measurement and Disposal Dates.* For purposes of applying the provisions of this Opinion, the *measurement date* of a disposal is the date on which the management having authority to approve the action commits itself to a formal plan to dispose of a segment of the business, whether by sale or abandonment. The plan of disposal should include, as a minimum, identification of the major assets to be disposed of, the expected method of disposal, the period expected to be required for completion of the disposal, an active program to find a buyer if disposal is to be by sale, the estimated results of operations of the segment from the

---

[3]The presence of a common stock equivalent or other dilutive securities together with income from continuing operations and extraordinary items may result in diluting one of the per share amounts which are required to be disclosed on the face of the income statement—i.e., income from continuing operations, income before extraordinary items and before the cumulative effect of accounting changes, if any, and net income—while increasing another. In such a case, the common stock equivalent or other dilutive securities should be recognized for all computations even though they have an anti-dilutive effect on one of the per share amounts.

[4]This caption should be modified appropriately when an entity reports the cumulative effect of an accounting change.

measurement date to the disposal date, and the estimated proceeds or salvage to be realized by disposal. For purposes of applying this Opinion, the *disposal date* is the date of closing the sale if the disposal is by sale or the date that operations cease if the disposal is by abandonment.

15. *Determination of Gain or Loss on Disposal of a Segment of a Business.* If a loss is expected from the proposed sale or abandonment of a segment, the estimated loss should be provided for at the measurement date.[5] If a gain is expected, it should be recognized when realized, which ordinarily is the disposal date. The determination of whether a gain or a loss results from the disposal of a segment of a business should be made at the measurement date based on estimates at that date of the net realizable value of the segment after giving consideration to any estimated costs and expenses directly associated with the disposal and, if a plan of disposal is to be carried out over a period of time and contemplates continuing operations during that period, to any estimated income or losses from operations. If it is expected that net losses from operations will be incurred between the measurement date and the expected disposal date, the computation of the gain or loss on disposal should also include an estimate of such amounts. If it is expected that income will be generated from operations during that period the computation of the gain or loss should include the estimated income, limited however to the amount of any loss otherwise recognizable from the disposal; any remainder should be accounted for as income when realized. The Board believes that the estimated amounts of income or loss from operations of a segment between measurement date and disposal date included in the determination of loss on disposal should be limited to those amounts that can be projected with reasonable accuracy. In the usual circumstance, it would be expected that the plan of disposal would be carried out within a period of one year from the measurement date and that such projections of operating income or loss would not cover a period exceeding approximately one year.[6]

16. Gain or loss from the disposal of a segment of a business should not include adjustments, costs, and expenses associated with normal business activities that should have been recognized on a going-concern basis up to the measurement date, such as adjustments of accruals on long-term contracts or write-down or write-off of receivables, inventories, property, plant, and equipment used in the business, equipment leased to others, deferred research and development costs, or other intangible assets. However, such adjustments, costs, and expenses which (a) are clearly a *direct* result of the decision to dispose of the segment and (b) are clearly not the adjustments of carrying amounts or costs, or expenses that should have been recognized on a going-concern basis prior to the measurement date should be included in determining the gain or loss on disposal. Results of operations before the measurement date should not be included in the gain or loss on disposal.

17. Costs and expenses *directly* associated with the decision to dispose include items such as severance pay, additional pension costs, employee relocation expenses, and future rentals on long-term leases to the extent they are not offset by sub-lease rentals.

18. *Disclosure.* In addition to the amounts that should be disclosed in the financial statements (paragraph 8), the notes to financial statements for the period encompassing the measurement date should disclose:

a. the identity of the segment of business that has been or will be discontinued,
b. the expected disposal date, if known (see paragraph 14),
c. the expected manner of disposal,
d. a description of the remaining assets and liabilities of the segment at the balance sheet date,[7] and
e. the income or loss from operations and any proceeds from disposal of the segment during the period from the measurement date to the date of the balance sheet.

For periods subsequent to the measurement date and including the period of disposal, notes to the financial statements should disclose the information listed in (a), (b), (c), and (d) above and also the information listed in (e) above compared with the prior estimates.

Criteria for Extraordinary Items

19. Judgment is required to segregate in the income statement the effects of events or transactions that are extraordinary items (as required by paragraph

---

[5]If financial statements for a date prior to the measurement date have not been issued, and the expected loss provides evidence of conditions that existed at the date of such statements and affects estimates inherent in the process of preparing them, the financial statements should be adjusted for any change in estimates resulting from the use of such evidence. (See Statement on Auditing Standards No. 1, *Codification of Auditing Standards and Procedures,* paragraph 560.03.)

[6]When disposal is estimated to be completed within one year and subsequently is revised to a longer period of time, any revision of the net realizable value of the segment should be treated as a change in estimate (see paragraph 25).

[7]Consideration should be given to disclosing this information by segregation in the balance sheet of the net assets and liabilities (current and noncurrent) of the discontinued segment. Only liabilities which will be assumed by others should be designated as liabilities of the discontinued segment. If the loss on disposal cannot be estimated within reasonable limits, this fact should be disclosed.

*Reporting the Results of Operations—Reporting the Effects of
Disposal of a Segment of a Business, and Extraordinary, Unusual* **APB 30**
and Infrequently Occurring Events and Transactions

11). The Board concludes that an event or transaction should be presumed to be an ordinary and usual activity of the reporting entity, the effects of which should be included in income from operations, unless the evidence clearly supports its classification as an extraordinary item as defined in this Opinion.

20. Extraordinary items are events and transactions that are distinguished by their unusual nature *and* by the infrequency of their occurrence. Thus, *both* of the following criteria should be met to classify an event or transaction as an extraordinary item:

a. *Unusual nature*—the underlying event or transaction should possess a high degree of abnormality and be of a type clearly unrelated to, or only incidentally related to, the ordinary and typical activities of the entity, taking into account the environment in which the entity operates. (See discussion in paragraph 21.)
b. *Infrequency of occurrence*—the underlying event or transaction should be of a type that would not reasonably be expected to recur in the foreseeable future, taking into account the environment in which the entity operates. (See discussion in paragraph 22.)

21. *Unusual Nature.* The specific characteristics of the entity, such as type and scope of operations, lines of business, and operating policies should be considered in determining ordinary and typical activities of an entity. The environment in which an entity operates is a primary consideration in determining whether an underlying event or transaction is abnormal and significantly different from the ordinary and typical activities of the entity. The environment of an entity includes such factors as the characteristics of the industry or industries in which it operates, the geographical location of its operations, and the nature and extent of governmental regulation. Thus, an event or transaction may be unusual in nature for one entity but not for another because of differences in their respective environments. Unusual nature is not established by the fact that an event or transaction is beyond the control of management.

22. *Infrequency of Occurrence.* For purposes of this Opinion, an event or transaction of a type not reasonably expected to recur in the foreseeable future is considered to occur infrequently. Determining the probability of recurrence of a particular event or transaction in the foreseeable future should take into account the environment in which an entity operates. Accordingly, a specific transaction of one entity might meet that criterion and a similar transaction of another entity might not because of different probabilities of recurrence. The past occurrence of an event or transaction for a particular entity provides evidence to assess the probability of recurrence of that type of event or transaction in the foreseeable future. By definition, extraordinary items occur infrequently. However, mere infrequency of occurrence of a particular event or transaction does not alone imply that its effects should be classified as extraordinary. An event or transaction of a type that occurs frequently in the environment in which the entity operates cannot, by definition, be considered as extraordinary, regardless of its financial effect.

23. Certain gains and losses should not be reported as extraordinary items because they are usual in nature or may be expected to recur as a consequence of customary and continuing business activities. Examples include:

a. Write-down or write-off of receivables, inventories, equipment leased to others, deferred research and development costs, or other intangible assets.
b. Gains or losses from exchange or translation of foreign currencies, including those relating to major devaluations and revaluations.
c. Gains or losses on disposal of a segment of a business.
d. Other gains or losses from sale or abandonment of property, plant, or equipment used in the business.
e. Effects of a strike, including those against competitors and major suppliers.
f. Adjustment of accruals on long-term contracts.

In rare situations, an event or transaction may occur that clearly meets both criteria specified in paragraph 20 of this Opinion and thus gives rise to an extraordinary gain or loss that includes one or more of the gains or losses enumerated above. In these circumstances, gains or losses such as (a) and (d) above should be included in the extraordinary item if they are a direct result of a major casualty (such as an earthquake), an expropriation, or a prohibition under a newly enacted law or regulation that clearly meets both criteria specified in paragraph 20. However, any portion of such losses which would have resulted from a valuation of assets on a going concern basis should not be included in the extraordinary items. Disposals of a segment of a business should be accounted for pursuant to paragraph 13 and presented in the income statement pursuant to paragraph 8 even though the circumstances of the disposal meet the criteria specified in paragraph 20.

24. *Materiality.* The effect of an extraordinary event or transaction should be classified separately in the income statement in the manner described in paragraph 11 if it is material in relation to income before extraordinary items or to the trend of annual earnings before extraordinary items, or is material

by other appropriate criteria. Items should be considered individually and not in the aggregate in determining whether an extraordinary event or transaction is material. However, the effects of a series of related transactions arising from a single specific and identifiable event or plan of action that otherwise meets the two criteria in paragraph 20 should be aggregated to determine materiality.

Adjustment of Amounts Reported in Prior Periods

25. Circumstances attendant to disposals of a segment of a business and extraordinary items frequently require estimates, for example, of associated costs and occasionally of associated revenue, based on judgment and evaluation of the facts known at the time of first accounting for the event. Each adjustment in the current period of a loss on disposal of a business segment or of an element of an extraordinary item that was reported in a prior period should not be reported as a prior period adjustment unless it meets the criteria for a prior period adjustment as defined in paragraph 23 of APB Opinion No. 9. An adjustment that does not meet such criteria should be separately disclosed as to year of origin, nature, and amount and classified separately in the current period in the same manner as the original item. If the adjustment is the correction of an error, the provisions of APB Opinion No. 20, *Accounting Changes,* paragraphs 36 and 37 should be applied.

Disclosure of Unusual or Infrequently Occurring Items

26. A material event or transaction that is unusual in nature or occurs infrequently but not both, and therefore does not meet both criteria for classification as an extraordinary item, should be reported as a separate component of income from continuing operations. The nature and financial effects of each event or transaction should be disclosed on the face of the income statement or, alternatively, in notes to the financial statements. Gains or losses of a similar nature that are not individually material should be aggregated. Such items should not be reported on the face of the income statement net of income taxes or in any manner inconsistent with the provisions of paragraphs 8 and 11 of this Opinion or in any other manner that may imply that they are extraordinary items. Similarly, the earnings per share effects of those items should not be disclosed on the face of the income statement.[8]

EFFECTIVE DATE

27. This Opinion shall be effective for events and transactions occurring after September 30, 1973. Events and transactions that were reported as extraordinary items in statements of income for fiscal years ending before October 1, 1973 should not be restated, except that a statement of income including operations of discontinued segments of a business may be reclassified in comparative statements to conform with the provisions of Paragraphs 8 and 9 of this Opinion and the Board encourages such reclassification. In addition, the accounting for events and transactions that have been reported previously for the fiscal year in which September 30, 1973 occurs may be restated retroactively to comply with the provisions of this Opinion, and the Board encourages such restatement. Differences in classification of the effects of events and transactions in the financial statements of the current and any prior periods presented should be disclosed in notes to the financial statements.

The Opinion entitled "Reporting the Results of Operations" was adopted by the assenting votes of fifteen members of the Board, of whom three, Messrs. Horngren, Norr, and Welsch, assented with qualification. Messrs. Bows and Watt dissented.

Mr. Horngren assents to this Opinion because it provides somewhat more definitive criteria for pinpointing extraordinary items than have existed to date. However, he agrees with the substance of paragraph 4. Separate identification of abnormal, unusual, or infrequent items is the primary need. Whether these items are classified as extraordinary or ordinary is a secondary issue. Furthermore, he is unconvinced that any criteria can be formulated which provide a workable distinction between extraordinary and ordinary items.

Mr. Norr assents because he believes the Opinion will reduce the frequency of use of the extraordinary item category. In order to provide stewardship he believes all items should go through the income statement with supplemental disclosure of results of discontinued operations, paragraph 8. He believes that the criteria created in this Opinion for extraordinary items, unusual and infrequent (paragraphs 20-22), are subjective and unworkable. He does not believe earthquakes, expropriations or prohibitions under new laws (paragraph 23) are extraordinary. He believes that the extraordinary category has resulted in a proliferation of abuses, particularly

---

[8]Exceptions to the final two sentences of this paragraph are specified in the following AICPA industry audit guides: *Audits of Banks,* p. 36; *Audits of Fire and Casualty Insurance Companies,* p. 66; and *Audits of Stock Life Insurance Companies,* p. 89.

debits, comparable to direct entries to surplus. He believes the investor is best served by single line identification of unusual items. In that way there is stewardship for past events and the reader may predict which items may not recur. Thus, the subject of forecasting is a companion piece and is a vital adjunct to an all-inclusive income statement.

Mr. Welsch assents to the issuance of this Opinion because he believes it will reduce the differences in the classification of certain events and transactions as extraordinary. He also believes that it will reduce the varying accounting treatments accorded certain transactions involving the disposal of a segment of an entity. Mr. Welsch does not agree that the addition of another subjectively defined category and the attendant earnings per share complications will further serve the investor. He believes that the all-inclusive income statement, coupled with comprehensive disclosure requirements, would better serve the investor for the reasons given in Paragraph 4 of this Opinion. He believes this change should be implemented at the present time.

Mr. Bows dissents to this Opinion because in his view it will cause serious erosion and confusion in efforts to achieve an informative and proper presentation of results of operations. This deterioration will occur because ordinary operating results will be blurred by inclusion of nonoperating, unusual and nonrecurring items that affect net income for a given period. For example, material gains or losses from retirement of debt, from major devaluations, from sales of nonoperating capital assets, from major storms or floods, and from litigation unrelated to current operations are to be included in the determination of "income from continuing operations" rather than being set out separately on a net-of-tax basis below such operating results. The statement of income will present a distorted picture of ordinary operating results and thus will be less useful to readers than if ordinary operating results were clearly distinguished from truly extraordinary items on a net-of-tax basis and with a separate indication of their earnings per share effect.

Mr. Watt dissents to this Opinion because it virtually eliminates extraordinary items yet perpetuates the format which implies that only ordinary events and transactions are included in income before extraordinary items. To him the inclusion in "ordinary" income, for example, of expenses, net of tax, directly associated with the disposal of a business (and in the format required by paragraph 8), and gains and losses from sale or abandonment of a plant without adjustment for related income taxes (paragraph 23d), obscures current operating performance and will result in readers of financial statements questioning the usefulness of the complex format described in paragraph 8. He also believes that, in addition to the criteria for extraordinary items prescribed in paragraph 20, the Board should have recognized that the quality of being extraordinary can be derived from a combination of infrequency of occurrence (paragraph 20b) and abnormality of size, without regard to the nature of the event or transaction (paragraph 20a). This view is described in paragraph 6 of the Opinion.

NOTES

Opinions of the Accounting Principles Board present the conclusions of at least two-thirds of the members of the Board.

Board Opinions need not be applied to immaterial items.

Covering all possible conditions and circumstances in an Opinion of the Accounting Principles Board is usually impracticable. The substance of transactions and the principles, guides, rules, and criteria described in Opinions should control the accounting for transactions not expressly covered.

Unless otherwise stated, Opinions of the Board are not intended to be retroactive.

Rule 203 of the Institute's Rules of Conduct prohibits a member from expressing his opinion that financial statements are presented in conformity with generally accepted accounting principles if the statements depart in a material respect from such principles unless he can demonstrate that due to unusual circumstances application of the principles would result in misleading statements—in which case his report must describe the departure, its approximate effects, if practicable, and the reasons why compliance with the established principles would result in misleading statements.

Pursuant to resolution of Council, this Opinion of the APB establishes, until such time as they are expressly superseded by action of FASB, accounting principles which fall within the provisions of Rule 203 of the Rules of Conduct.

Accounting Principles Board (1973)

Philip L. Defliese, *Chairman*	Joseph P. Cummings	Charles B. Hellerson
Donald J. Bevis	Robert L. Ferst	Charles T. Horngren
Albert J. Bows	Oscar S. Gellein	Louis M. Kessler
Milton M. Broeker	Newman T. Halvorson	David Norr
Leo E. Burger	Robert Hampton, III	George C. Watt
	Donald J. Hayes	Glenn A. Welsch

APB Opinion No. 31
Disclosure of Lease Commitments by Lessees

STATUS

Issued: June 1973

Effective Date: For fiscal periods ending on or after December 31, 1973

Affects: Amends APB 5, paragraphs 14, 20, and 23
Supersedes APB 5, paragraphs 16 through 18

Affected by: Superseded by FAS 13

AMERICAN INSTITUTE OF CERTIFIED PUBLIC ACCOUNTANTS

Accounting Interpretations

1973 AICPA NOTICE REGARDING AICPA ACCOUNTING INTERPRETATIONS

The Institute staff has been authorized to issue interpretations of accounting questions having general interest to the profession. The purpose of the interpretations is to provide guidance on a timely basis without the formal procedures required for an APB Opinion and to clarify points on which past practice may have varied and been considered generally accepted. These interpretations, which are reviewed with informed members of the profession, are not pronouncements of the Board. However, members should be aware that they may be called upon to justify departures from the interpretations. Responsibility for their preparation rests with Richard C. Lytle, administrative director of the Accounting Principles Board. Unless otherwise stated, the Interpretations are not intended to be retroactive.

AICPA ACCOUNTING INTERPRETATIONS

TABLE OF CONTENTS

Table of Contents

Table of Contents

Table of Contents

Compensation Involved in Stock Option and Stock Purchase Plans: Unofficial Accounting Interpretations of Accounting Research Bulletin No. 43, Chapter 13B

STATUS

Issued: March 1971

Effective Date: March 1971

Affects: No other pronouncements

Affected by: Superseded by APB 25

Deferred Compensation Contracts: Unofficial Accounting Interpretations

STATUS

Issued: November 1970

Effective Date: November 1970

Affects: No other pronouncements

Affected by: Superseded by FTB 85-4

Consolidated Financial Statements: Accounting Interpretations of ARB No. 51

STATUS

Issued: February 1972

Effective Date: February 1972

Affects: No other pronouncements

Affected by: Interpretation No. 1 superseded by FAS 111

(This page intentionally left blank.)

Accounting for the Investment Credit: Accounting Interpretations of APB Opinion No. 4

STATUS

Issued: February 1972-March 1972

Effective Date: Interpretation No. 1—February 1972
                Interpretations No. 2 through 6—March 1972

Affects: No other pronouncements

Affected by: Interpretation No. 4 superseded by FAS 96 and FAS 109
             Interpretation No. 5 superseded by FAS 111
             Interpretation No. 6 superseded by FAS 96 and FAS 109

Accounting for the Investment Credit: Accounting Interpretations of APB Opinion No. 4

1. TAX CREDIT DISCLOSURE

Question—What disclosure is required in relation to accounting for the investment tax credit?

Interpretation—Paragraph 11 of APB Opinion No. 4 specifies that full disclosure of the method followed and amounts involved, when material, in accounting for the investment credit is essential. For this purpose, materiality should be measured in relation to the income tax provision, net income, and the trend of earnings. Generally, all amounts of investment credit should be revealed unless they are clearly insignificant.

[Issue Date: February, 1972]

2. TAX CREDIT DISCLOSURE (MODIFICATION)

Accounting Interpretation No. 1, (above) issued in February 1972 stated, "full disclosure of the method followed and amounts involved, when material, in accounting for the investment credit is essential. For this purpose, materiality should be measured in relation to the income tax provision, net income, and the trend of earnings. Generally, all amounts of investment credit should be revealed unless they are clearly insignificant." That Interpretation is reaffirmed, except for the foregoing references to materiality as it relates to disclosure of the *method*.

The 1971 Act and the Treasury releases require a taxpayer to disclose in financial reports the method of accounting used for the investment credit but no materiality guideline is given. Accordingly, until such time as a guideline may be issued, the *method* of accounting for the investment credit should be disclosed in all financial reports for taxable years ending after December 9, 1971 even though the *amount* is not material and is not disclosed and disclosure would not otherwise be required. If more than one *method* is used (for example, the deferral method for "old" credits and the flow-through method for "new" credits), all *methods* should be disclosed. The amounts may be omitted only if they are clearly insignificant.

[Issue Date: March, 1972]

3. ACCEPTABLE METHODS OF ACCOUNTING FOR INVESTMENT CREDITS UNDER 1971 ACT

Question—What methods may be used to account for investment credits allowable under the Revenue Act of 1971?

Interpretation—In a news release dated January 10, 1972, the Treasury Department interpreted the Act to mean that the flow-through and the deferral methods are the only acceptable methods to account for investment credits allowable under the 1971 Act for taxable years ending after December 9, 1971.

Under the flow-through method, the credit is reflected as a reduction of tax expense in the year it is recognized in the financial statements.

Under the deferral method, the credit is reflected as a reduction of tax expense ratably over the period during which the asset is depreciated and follows the depreciation method used for financial reporting purposes. The amortization period may be the specific life of each asset or the composite life of all depreciable assets. However, amortization over the period the asset must be held to avoid recapture of the credit rather than life of the asset is not acceptable because it is not based on depreciable life.

A financing institution may include the investment credit as part of the proceeds from leased property accounted for by the financing method and include it in determining the yield from the "loan" which is reflected in income over the term of the lease. However, the financing institution may account for the investment credit on property purchased for its own use by either the flow-through or the deferral method.

The investment credit may be passed through to a lessee for leased property. The lessee should account for the credit by whichever method is used for purchased property. If the deferral method is used and the leased property is not capitalized, the term of the lease, generally including renewal options which are reasonably expected to be exercised, is the period over which the credit should be amortized.

[Issue Date: March, 1972]

4. CHANGE IN METHOD OF ACCOUNTING FOR INVESTMENT CREDIT

Question—The Revenue Act of 1971 provides that a taxpayer need not use a particular method of accounting for the investment credit in financial reports subject to the jurisdiction of or made to any federal agency. However, once a method is adopted, a taxpayer may not under the Act change to another method unless the Secretary of the Treasury or his delegate consents. (Therefore, a taxpayer has a one-time "free choice" to select a method different from the one used in the past to account for the investment credit under the 1971 Act but must continue to use the method selected.) The Treasury Department issued news releases on December 21, 1971 and January 10, 1972 specifying December 10, 1971 as the effective date for the accounting requirements for the credit under the Act in financial reports issued by taxpayers and describing methods of accounting for it. How do the 1971 Act and the Treasury Department releases affect the application of APB Opinion No. 20 on Accounting Changes by taxpayers who change their method of accounting for the investment credit in financial reports issued to shareholders?

Interpretation—This Accounting Interpretation sets forth our understanding of how APB Opinion No. 20[1] should be applied under the Act and the Treasury releases in accounting and reporting for the investment credit in general purpose financial statements issued by companies subject to the jurisdiction of or making reports to federal agencies. These would include, for example, annual reports to shareholders and other investors under the jurisdiction of the SEC, ICC, CAB, SBA, etc. The conclusions of this Interpretation should be applied to all financial statements prepared in accordance with generally accepted accounting principles even though they are issued by companies whose financial reports are not under the jurisdiction of or who do not report to a federal agency. (It is our understanding that a tax return is not deemed a financial report to come under the provisions of the 1971 Act discussed in this Interpretation.) If anything in this Interpretation should conflict with any requirement issued by the Treasury, the requirement of the Treasury prevails for those financial statements.

"Old" Investment Credits

Paragraph 16 of APB Opinion No. 20 specifies that the previously adopted method of accounting for a tax credit which is being discontinued or terminated should not be changed. Therefore, the method of accounting used for investment credits previously reported in financial statements covering taxable years ending before December 10, 1971 should be continued for those credits in financial statements issued after December 9, 1971. Thus, an investment credit received in 1968 and accounted for by the deferral method should under APB Opinion

No. 20 continue to be amortized on the same basis as before even though the taxpayer elects to use the flow-through method under the one-time "free choice" to account for 1971 Act investment credits. Likewise, a 1968 investment credit which was accounted for by the flow-through method should not be reinstated, either by retroactive restatement or by a "catch-up" accounting change adjustment, even though the taxpayer elects the deferral method under the one-time "free choice" to account for 1971 Act investment credits.

Under paragraph 16 of APB Opinion No. 20, the "old" investment credit in the above examples is considered terminated as of December 9, 1971 in view of the Treasury Department releases. The adoption of a different method to account for 1971 Act investment credits under the one-time "free choice" is, therefore, considered similar to the adoption of a different method of amortization for newly acquired assets as provided by paragraph 24 of APB Opinion No. 20.

"New" Credits Arising Before Cutoff Date

An investment credit arising under the Revenue Act of 1971 but allowable in a taxable year ending before December 10, 1971 (for example, from property purchased in September 1971 by a taxpayer with a November 30 taxable year) may be accounted for either by the method used in prior years to account for the investment credit or by the method the taxpayer will use under the one-time "free choice." In these circumstances, those taxpayers who use the "old" method may exercise their one-time "free choice" in the following year. Those taxpayers who change to a different method for the 1971 Act credit should continue that method in accounting for investment credits allowable in following taxable years ending after December 9, 1971.

Carrybacks and Carryforwards

In practice, the investment credit is recognized in financial statements[2] by including it in the "with and without" computation of the tax effect of a timing difference which is specified by paragraph 36 of APB Opinion No. 11. This practice continues to be appropriate in taxable years ending after December 9, 1971 although the credit is a carryback or a carryforward for income tax purposes. Thus, when different methods are used to account for the credit in different years and carrybacks or carryforwards are involved, the method applicable to a particular credit is the method used for the year in which the credit is recognized in the financial statements.

Therefore, an investment credit arising from an investment made during a taxable year ending after

---

[1]APB Opinion No. 20 is effective for fiscal years beginning after July 31, 1971, but earlier application is encouraged.

[2]See AICPA Accounting Interpretation No. 18, "Investment Credit Carrybacks and Carryforwards," of APB Opinion No. 11, and paragraphs 45-48 and 53 of APB Opinion No. 11 for rationale.

December 9, 1971 but carried back to produce a refund from a taxable year ending prior to December 10, 1971 should be accounted for by the method selected under the one-time "free choice." An investment credit arising under prior Revenue Acts which has not been previously accounted for and which is allowable in a taxable year ending after December 9, 1971 (for example, from property purchased in 1968 for which all or part of the credit was carried forward to calendar 1971) should be accounted for by the method selected under the one-time "free choice."

The Treasury Department releases do not apply to investment credits which have been reported in annual income statements covering taxable years ending before December 10, 1971 even though the credits may be carried forward to reduce tax liability in years ending after December 9, 1971. Therefore, those investment credit carryforwards realized after that date should be accounted for in the normal manner by crediting the assets set up to recognize the investment credit carryforward or by restoring the deferred tax credit when the carryforward credit is realized.

An investment credit recognized in a carryforward year rather than in the year it arises should be included in the determination of income before extraordinary items in the carryforward year.

Consistency Exception in Auditor's Report

A change in the method of accounting for the investment credit (either by selection of a different method under the one-time "free choice" or later by permission of the Secretary of the Treasury or his delegate) would call for a consistency exception in an independent auditor's report if it has a material effect on the financial statements in the current year (see Accounting Interpretation No. 2 (page 340) on tax credit disclosure). The effect of the change under the one-time "free choice" should be disclosed in the manner specified by paragraph 24 of APB Opinion No. 20. The effect of a Treasury approved change should be disclosed in the manner specified by paragraph 21 of APB Opinion No. 20.

[Issue Date: March, 1972]

5. INVESTMENT CREDIT IS PRIOR PERIOD ADJUSTMENT

Question—The Revenue Act of 1971 allows an investment credit retroactively to some taxpayers whose fiscal years closed prior to enactment of the Act on December 10, 1971. To what accounting period does this credit belong?

Interpretation—An investment credit arising under the Revenue Act of 1971 and allowable in a taxable year ending before December 10, 1971 is considered to be an event of a fiscal year ending before December 10, 1971. If the financial statements have not yet been issued, they should be adjusted to reflect the credit as a type 1 subsequent event (see SAP No. 47). If the financial statements have already been issued, the credit should be treated as a prior period adjustment as described by paragraph 18 of APB Opinion No. 9 (see also paragraph 18 of APB Opinion No. 15).

The credit may be accounted for by the method used in prior years to account for the investment credit or by a different method. If a different method is used, that method should be used thereafter to account for investment credits allowable in following taxable years ending after December 9, 1971. (See Accounting Interpretation No. 4, page 340, on change in method of accounting for the investment credit.)

[Issue Date: March, 1972]

6. INVESTMENT CREDIT IN CONSOLIDATION

Question—The Revenue Act of 1971 specifies that a taxpayer shall not be required to use a particular method of accounting for the investment credit in reports subject to the jurisdiction of a federal agency. However, a taxpayer must continue to use the method adopted in all such reports subsequently issued unless consent to change is granted by the Secretary of the Treasury or his delegate. May different methods of accounting for the investment credit be adopted by the various legal entities that file separate income tax returns but are included in consolidated financial statements?

Interpretation—No, a single method of accounting for the investment credit should be adopted under the one-time "free choice" by a parent company and its subsidiaries in consolidated financial statements (including subsidiaries carried on the equity method) and other financial reports subject to the jurisdiction of or made to a federal agency.

[Issue Date: March, 1972]

Accounting for Leases in Financial Statements of Lessors: Accounting Interpretations of APB Opinion No. 7

STATUS

Issued: November 1971

Effective Date: November 1971

Affects: No other pronouncements

Affected by: Interpretation No. 1 superseded by FAS 111

AIN-APB8

Accounting for the Cost of Pension Plans:
Accounting Interpretations of APB Opinion No. 8

STATUS

Issued: 1968

Effective Date: 1968

Affects: No other pronouncements

Affected by: Interpretations No. 1 through 28 superseded by FAS 111

(The next page is 369.)

344

Reporting the Results of Operations: Unofficial Accounting Interpretations of APB Opinion No. 9

STATUS

Issued: February 1971-April 1971

Effective Date: Interpretation No. 1—February 1971
Interpretation No. 2—April 1971

Affects: No other pronouncements

Affected by: Interpretation No. 1 amended by APB 30
Interpretation No. 2 superseded by FAS 111

Reporting the Results of Operations: Unofficial Accounting Interpretations of APB Opinion No. 9

1. LOSSES CAUSED BY BANKRUPTCIES

Question—Recent railroad bankruptcies raise the question of whether companies holding receivables from these railroads should account for losses arising from charging off such assets as ordinary losses or as extraordinary losses in determining net income. The Interstate Commerce Commission has ruled that railroads must write off certain past due payments from other railroads (e.g., interline receivables) as extraordinary losses. Is this accounting treatment appropriate in the annual reports to railroads' shareholders and in the annual reports to shareholders of other (non-railroad) companies?

Interpretation—No, paragraph 22 of APB Opinion No. 9 specifies that, regardless of size, losses from receivables do *not* constitute extraordinary losses. The fact that the loss arises from a receivable from a company in bankruptcy proceedings does not alter this answer in any way.

Regulatory authorities often rule on the accounting treatment to be applied by companies under their jurisdiction. The above question is covered by paragraphs 3 and 4 of the Addendum to APB Opinion No. 2. An auditor should in his opinion take an exception to any loss from an interline receivable classified as an extraordinary item in a railroad's annual report to shareholders.

[Issue Date: February, 1971]

2. REV. RUL. ON LIFO INVENTORY OF SUB.

Question—Revenue Ruling 69-17, issued January 1969, permitted the use of the FIFO method for inventories in consolidated financial statements although the LIFO method was used by a subsidiary in its separate financial statements and in its income tax return. Revenue Ruling 70-457, issued August 31, 1970, revoked Revenue Ruling 69-17 to require LIFO in consolidation if used by the subsidiary in its income tax return. Technical Information Release 1048, issued October 8, 1970, extended the effective date of Revenue Ruling 70-457 so that it now applies to consolidated financial statements issued after August 31, 1971. How should the accounting change be reflected in consolidated financial statements when a company reverts to the LIFO method for the inventory of a subsidiary to comply with Revenue Ruling 70-57?

Interpretation—The Accounting Principles Board currently is considering a proposed Opinion on accounting changes.* A change from FIFO to LIFO after the effective date of that Opinion would be reported in accordance with the Opinion. In the meantime, the effect of such a change should be reflected as a retroactive adjustment of prior periods when the cost of inventories was determined under the FIFO (or another acceptable) method. The effect of the change on net income and earnings per share amounts should also be disclosed for each of the periods included in the financial statements for the year in which the adjustment is made. If only the current period is presented, this disclosure should indicate the effects of such restatement on the balance of retained earnings at the beginning of the period and on the net income and earnings per share of the immediately preceding period. These recommendations are consistent with paragraphs 25 and 26 of APB Opinion No. 9 and paragraph 18 of APB Opinion No. 15.

The effect of the change on fiscal year company statements should be reported in the first interim statements and quarterly earnings releases issued following the change.

In these cases, the auditor's opinion on financial statements reflecting such a retroactive adjustment would be governed by paragraphs 25 and 26 of Chapter 8 of SAP No. 33, which require reference to the change in the auditor's opinion.

[Issue Date: April, 1971]

---

*An exposure draft of a proposed Opinion entitled "Accounting Changes" was issued by the Board on January 20, 1971 for comment until May 15, 1971 from persons interested in financial reporting. Exposure Drafts are not Opinions of the Board unless adopted by the assenting votes of at least two-thirds of the members of the Board.

Accounting for Income Taxes:
Accounting Interpretations of APB Opinion No. 11

STATUS

Issued: 1969-March 1972

Effective Date: Interpretation No. 1—July 1970
    Interpretations No. 2 through 23—1969
    Interpretations No. 24 and 25—March 1972

Affects: No other pronouncements

Affected by: Interpretation No. 4 amended by FAS 71
    Interpretations No. 1 through 25 superseded by FAS 96 and
    FAS 109

Other Interpretive Pronouncements: FTB 83-1 (for Interpretation No. 8) (Superseded by FAS 96 and
    FAS 109)
    FTB 84-3 (for Interpretation No. 10) (Superseded by FAS 96 and
    FAS 109)

(The next page is 397.)

(This page intentionally left blank.)

Computing Earnings per Share:
Accounting Interpretations of APB Opinion No. 15

STATUS

Issued: July 1970-September 1971

Effective Date: Interpretations No. 1 through 101—July 1970
Interpretation No. 102—September 1971

Affects: No other pronouncements

Affected by: Part 1 amended by FAS 111
Interpretation No. 2 amended by FAS 111
Interpretation No. 10 superseded by FAS 111
Interpretations No. 13 and 16 superseded by FAS 96 and FAS 109
Interpretations No. 26, 30, and 33 amended by FAS 111
Interpretations No. 34 and 35 and footnote 21 superseded by FAS 85
Interpretations No. 36 and 37 amended by FAS 85
Interpretation No. 38 and footnote 22 superseded by FAS 111
Interpretation No. 56 amended by FAS 111
Interpretation No. 82 and footnotes 38 through 42 amended by FIN 31
Interpretation No. 92 amended by FAS 111

Computing Earnings per Share:
Accounting Interpretations of APB Opinion No. 15

CONTENTS

INTRODUCTION

Comparison of APB Opinions No. 9 and 15

APB Opinion No. 15, *Earnings per Share,* is an extension of the issues discussed in Part II, "Computation and Reporting of Earnings Per Share," of APB Opinion No. 9.

APB Opinion No. 9 included certain "residual" securities as the equivalent of common stock in earnings per share computations, established "supplementary pro forma" earnings per share for reporting what the effect on earnings per share would have been if all residual and contingently issuable securities had been issued, and strongly recommended that both earnings per share and supplementary pro forma earnings per share be disclosed in the income statement.

APB Opinion No. 15 supersedes Part II of APB Opinion No. 9, modifies the concept of residual securities and replaces the term *residual securities* with the new designation *common stock equivalents.* Under the Opinion, dilutive common stock equivalents are included with outstanding common stock in computing "primary" earnings per share. Common stock, dilutive common stock equivalents and other potentially dilutive securities are included in computing "fully diluted" earnings per share.

The Opinion requires that earnings per share be presented on the face of corporate income statements or summaries of such statements with both the primary and fully diluted amounts presented when potential dilution of earnings per share exists. Also, APB Opinion No. 15 specifically prohibits including anti-dilutive[1] securities in earnings per share computations (except in special situations to be discussed later) while APB Opinion No. 9 discussed dilution but did not specifically prohibit anti-dilution.

Interpretation of APB Opinion No. 15

These Unofficial Accounting Interpretations are intended to explain the provisions of APB Opinion No. 15. They do not in any way amend or modify the Opinion. They do not presume to answer all questions which might be raised in applying the Opinion but rather are addressed to questions raised since the Opinion was issued.

Some Interpretations are concerned with simple situations; others are concerned with rather complex situations. And just as APB Opinions are not neces-

---

[1] See Interpretation 5 for the definition of an anti-dilutive security.

sarily applicable to immaterial items, these Interpretations do not necessarily apply to immaterial items. In many cases the refinements described will be material, but in many other cases they will not. When the difference is not significant, the refinements need not be applied. For example, the quarterly share averaging procedure for options and warrants described in Interpretations 58-62 need not be used when the market price of common stock is stable throughout the year and always above the exercise price. In such a case the treasury stock method could be applied on an annual basis.

Although the Interpretations are not binding on Institute members, they reflect informed consideration of the situations posed and express what the Institute staff believes to be the preferred practices for earnings per share computations under the Opinion.

Arrangement

This section of Interpretations of APB Opinion No. 15 is divided into two parts. Part I is an overview of the Opinion. Although Part I summarizes the basic provisions of the Opinion, familiarity with the Opinion is assumed and terms used in the Opinion are not defined in this part. Part I also serves as a brief description of the underlying concepts of the Opinion. Part II contains definitional Interpretations followed by individual Interpretations in question and answer form. The Interpretations are numbered sequentially and are arranged generally in the order in which the topics appear in Part I. Exhibits follow Part II. A cross-reference table appears which lists each Opinion paragraph cited (as explained below) and the location of the citation.

Numbers appearing in brackets at the end of paragraphs indicate references (in numerical order) to paragraph numbers in APB Opinion No. 15 relevant to the material being discussed.

PART I: AN OVERVIEW OF APB OPINION NO. 15

Presentation of Earnings Per Share

The Opinion requires nearly all corporations[2] to report earnings per share data on the face of income statements or earnings summaries issued for periods beginning after December 31, 1968. Each presentation must include per share data for income or loss before extraordinary items (if extraordinary items are reported on the income statement) and per share data for net income or loss. Corporations with capital structures containing securities that do not, in the aggregate, dilute earnings per share 3% or more need present only earnings per common share. This exception for corporations whose securities do not dilute earnings per share by at least 3% is based upon the immateriality of dilution of less than 3%. In this Opinion the Board specified the point at which dilution becomes material rather than allowing different judgments to determine different levels of materiality. All other corporations are required to have the "dual" presentation of primary earnings per share and fully diluted earnings per share. All computations of earnings per share data are to be based on a weighted average of shares assumed to be outstanding during the period. [*12, 13, 14, 15, 47*]

Assumptions

Earnings per share computations for corporations with complex capital structures are based on various assumptions which are required by the Opinion. These assumptions are made to reflect (1) what a corporation's earnings per share would have been if common stock had been issued to replace all dilutive securities considered to be the equivalent of common stock and (2) the additional dilution which would have resulted if common stock had been issued to replace all of the corporation's other potentially dilutive securities.[3] [*20, 24-27, 41*]

Assumptions to be made are specified for exercise, conversion, and issuance of securities, prices to be used, and methods to be applied to reflect the dilution which would have resulted if the transactions and events underlying those assumptions had actually occurred. Although specific methods for applying the assumptions are designated, the Board realized that the events and transactions assumed for the computations might not actually occur. Rather, the Board specified the assumptions and the methods as a practical approach to obtaining comparable determinations of earnings per share. [*34, 36*]

Classification of Securities

The advent of securities which are not common stock in form but which enable their holders to obtain common stock modifies some of the traditional relationships among securities. While common stock is regarded as the basic equity security and nonconvertible preferred stock and nonconvertible debt are regarded as senior securities, those securities which enable their holders to obtain common stock are classified as either *common stock equivalents* or as *other potentially dilutive securities* for earnings per share computations. This classifica-

---

[2]See Interpretation 9 for the exceptions.

[3]See Interpretation 3 for the special context in which the term *other potentially dilutive securities* is used in these Unofficial Accounting Interpretations of APB Opinion No. 15. The term is not used in the Opinion.

tion is made at time of issuance and does not change thereafter.[4] [*25, 28, 41*]

A security is classified solely for purposes of determining earnings per share. The accounting for securities, their presentation in the financial statements, and the determination of book value per share are not affected by the classification of securities for earnings per share computations. [*39*]

Common stock equivalents are included in both primary and fully diluted earnings per share computations. Other potentially dilutive securities are included only in fully diluted earnings per share computations. However, common stock equivalents and other potentially dilutive securities are included in the *computations* only when their effect is dilutive. Both are excluded from the *computations* whenever their effect is anti-dilutive except in the situations described in the following paragraph. Thus, a security retains its status as a common stock equivalent or as an other potentially dilutive security after its classification has been determined, but it may enter earnings per share computations in one period and not in another period. [*15, 30*]

Anti-Dilutive Securities

Anti-dilutive securities are excluded from earnings per share computations unless (1) common stock was issued during the period on an anti-dilutive exercise or conversion or (2) a security is anti-dilutive in earnings per share for income before extraordinary items but is dilutive in earnings per share for net income or vice versa[5] or (3) an aggregate computation is required which has a net dilutive effect but which may include anti-dilutive securities or anti-dilutive computations.[6] All other anti-dilutive securities are excluded from earnings per share computations even when some anti-dilutive securities are included in the computation because of one or more of the above exceptions. In an aggregate computation, only when the net result is dilutive may anti-dilutive securities be included in the earnings per share computation. [*14, 30, 30 fn. 8, 38, 40, 41*]

Primary Earnings per Share

Primary earnings per share data are based upon outstanding common stock and common stock assumed to be outstanding to reflect the dilutive effect of common stock equivalents. Convertible securities which yield less than two-thirds of the bank prime interest rate at the time of issuance are classified as common stock equivalents. Convertible securities issued with the same terms as those of an outstanding common stock equivalent are classified as common stock equivalents regardless of their yield. Outstanding convertible securities which are not common stock equivalents become common stock equivalents if another convertible security with the same terms is issued and is classified as a common stock equivalent. [*28, 33*]

Convertible securities which allow or require the payment of cash at conversion are considered the equivalents of warrants. Options, warrants and their equivalents, stock purchase contracts, and certain agreements to issue common stock in the future are classified as common stock equivalents. Some participating securities and two-class common stocks are also classified as common stock equivalents. [*27, 37*]

Fully Diluted Earnings per Share

Fully diluted earnings per share data are based on outstanding common stock and common stock assumed to be outstanding to reflect the maximum dilutive effect of common stock equivalents and other potentially dilutive securities. Thus, convertible securities, options, warrants, stock purchase contracts, participating securities, two-class common stocks and agreements to issue stock in the future are included in the computation of fully diluted earnings per share. The difference between the primary and the fully diluted earnings per share amounts is the additional dilution resulting from other potentially dilutive securities outstanding. [*16, 40*]

Earnings Applicable to Common Stock

To compute earnings per share, net income must often first be adjusted to determine earnings applicable to common stock. The adjustments to net income do not in any way change reported net income but rather are made to compute the earnings for the period to which common stock has a claim. Corporations with nonconvertible preferred stock,

---

[4]Except as explained in Interpretations 29 and 30.

[5]Note that either primary earnings per share for net income or primary earnings per share for income before extraordinary items may be anti-dilutive when common stock equivalents are present together with extraordinary items. The common stock equivalents may have an anti-dilutive effect upon either of these amounts so long as the effect is dilutive upon the other amount. The same type of anti-dilution may be reflected *within* fully diluted earnings per share when common stock equivalents and other potentially dilutive securities are present together with extraordinary items. However, fully diluted earnings per share for net income would *not* be anti-dilutive with respect to primary earnings per share for net income unless the anti-dilution is caused by actual exercises or conversions.

[6]For example, an aggregate computation is required by Opinion paragraph 38 when the number of common shares issuable upon the exercise of all options, warrants, and their equivalents exceeds 20% of the number of common shares outstanding at the end of the period for which the computation is being made. An aggregate computation would also be made for an anti-dilutive option which must be exercised before a dilutive option may be exercised. (See Interpretation 49.)

for example, must deduct any preferred dividends paid, declared, or accumulated for the period in adjusting net income to determine earnings applicable to common stock. [*39, 50*]

Only dividends which are applicable to the period covered by the income statement would be deducted. Dividends declared or accumulated during a prior period and paid during the period covered by the income statement are not deducted since they were considered in computing earnings applicable to common stock during the prior period and their payment merely retires the liability.

Corporations with common stock equivalents or other potentially dilutive securities may have to make more complex adjustments or may not make some adjustments which would otherwise be made. For example, interest, less tax effect, on convertible bonds deducted in arriving at net income would be added back to net income to determine earnings applicable to common stock when the convertible bonds are assumed to be converted. Since dividends on convertible preferred stock are not deducted in arriving at net income, they would not be added back to net income to determine earnings applicable to common stock when convertible preferred stock is assumed to be converted. [*51, 52*]

Convertible Securities

Convertible securities are included in earnings per share computations under the "if converted" method. Under this method, the security is assumed to have been converted into common stock at the beginning of the period being reported upon (or time of issuance of the security, if later). The common stock which would have been issued upon conversion is considered outstanding from the date of the assumed conversion. Interest deductions applicable to convertible debt reduced by the income taxes attributable to such interest are added back to net income because the interest would not have been incurred if the debt had been converted into common stock. Nondiscretionary adjustments based on net income or income before taxes (for items such as profit sharing or royalty agreements, etc.) are recomputed after the interest adjustment is made. Any difference (less income tax) from the amount originally computed is also included in the adjusted net income. [*51*]

Convertible securities which *require* the payment of cash at conversion are considered the equivalent of warrants for computational purposes. Both the treasury stock method and the if converted method must be applied. Convertible securities which *permit* the payment of cash as an alternative at conversion are also considered the equivalent of warrants. But when conversion without the payment of cash would be more advantageous to the holder with this alternative, only the if converted method is applied. No proceeds would be received to which the

treasury stock method could be applied. [*35, 37*]

When conversion is not assumed because the result would be anti-dilutive, dividends declared for the period (or accumulated for the period even though not declared) are deducted from net income to determine earnings applicable to common stock. [*30, 40, 50*]

Options and Warrants

The basic method for including options and warrants and their equivalents in earnings per share computations is the treasury stock method. Under this method, exercise of options and warrants and their equivalents is assumed at the beginning of the period (or time of issuance, if later). Shares of common stock are assumed to be issued and the proceeds from exercise are assumed to be used to purchase common stock at the exercise date. Common stock outstanding is assumed to increase by the difference between the number of shares issued and the number of shares purchased. The provision against reflecting anti-dilution in earnings per share computations generally prohibits the assumption of exercise of any option or warrant or their equivalents when the assumed purchased price of the common stock is below the exercise price of the option or warrant. [*36, 42*]

The Opinion recommends as a practical matter that exercise not be assumed for earnings per share computations until the market price of the common stock has been higher than the exercise price for substantially all of three consecutive months ending with the last month of the period for which the share computation is being made. Thus, exercise need not be assumed until this three-month test has once been met. [*36*]

After the test has been met, however, an ending market price which is above the average market price is used for fully diluted computations if the result is dilutive. Therefore, options and warrants may be reflected in fully diluted earnings per share even though they are not reflected in primary earnings per share. Options and warrants may also be included in the computations in some periods but not be included in other periods. [*42*]

Some warrants require or permit the tendering of debt or other securities in payment of all or part of the exercise price. Upon the assumed exercise of such warrants, the debt or other securities are assumed to be tendered (unless tendering cash would be more advantageous to the warrant holder when permitted and the treasury stock method is applied). Interest, net of income tax, on any debt tendered is added back to net income. The treasury stock method is applied for proceeds assumed to be received in cash. [*37*]

The proceeds from the exercise of some warrants must be applied to retire debt under the terms of the debt. Upon the assumed exercise of such warrants, the proceeds are applied to purchase the debt at its market price rather than to purchase common stock under the treasury stock method. The treasury stock method is applied, however, for excess proceeds from the assumed exercise. Interest, net of income tax, on any debt assumed to be purchased is added back to net income.

Some convertible securities require or permit the payment of cash upon conversion and are considered the equivalent of warrants. The treasury stock method must be applied to purchase common stock from proceeds assumed to be received. The "if converted method" must also be applied for the convertible security.

The application of the treasury stock method is modified when the number of common shares which would be issued if all outstanding options and warrants and their equivalents were exercised exceeds 20% of the number of common shares outstanding at the end of the period. This 20% test is based only on common shares actually outstanding, not considering any assumed conversion or contingently issuable shares. [38]

When the 20% test is met, *all* options and warrants and their equivalents are assumed to be exercised (or converted) regardless of whether each would be dilutive or anti-dilutive. The treasury stock method is first applied to purchase no more than 20% of the number of common shares outstanding at the end of the period with the proceeds from exercise. The balance of any proceeds remaining after applying the treasury stock method is then applied to reduce any short-term or long-term debt of the issuer to the extent that the debt may be retired. Finally, any remaining balance of proceeds is assumed to be invested in U.S. government securities or commercial paper. Appropriate recognition is given to any necessary interest adjustments (and related income tax effect) for both debt retirement and investment in determining earnings applicable to common stock. [35, 38]

The results of the foregoing computations are then aggregated. If the net aggregate effect is dilutive, *all* of these computations enter into earnings per share computations. However, *all* are omitted if the net aggregate effect is anti-dilutive. (See Interpretation 74 for a description of the distinction between the 20% test and the 20% limitation.)

Delayed Effectiveness and Changing Rates or Prices

Some convertible securities are not convertible until a future date or their conversion rates may increase or decrease in the future. Similarly, some options or warrants are not exercisable until a future date or their exercise prices may increase or decrease in the future. [56]

For primary earnings per share computations, the conversion rate or exercise price in effect for the period presented is used. If the holder does not have the right to convert or exercise the security until after that period, the earliest effective conversion rate or exercise price during the five years following the close of the period is used. [57]

For fully diluted earnings per share computations, the most advantageous conversion rate or exercise price (to the security holder) becoming effective within ten years following the close of the period being reported upon is used. [58]

Other Securities

Although the Opinion does not describe in depth the treatment to be accorded to other types of securities, they were contemplated by the Opinion and some guidelines given. The earnings per share treatments of two-class common stock, participating securities, common stock issuable in the future upon the satisfaction of specified conditions, securities of subsidiaries, and options or warrants to purchase convertible securities are discussed in the Interpretations which follow in Part II. Situations or securities not expressly covered in the Opinion should be dealt with in accordance with their substance following the guidelines and criteria of the Opinion and these Unofficial Accounting Interpretations. [43]

Restatement of Previously Reported Data

The earnings per share amounts reported in a prior period generally will be reported at the same amounts when that prior period is included in a later comparative income statement. The Opinion specifically prohibits retroactive restatement (1) for changes in market prices of common stock when the treasury stock method has been applied for options and warrants, (2) when conversion rates of convertible securities or exercise prices of options or warrants change, (3) when convertible securities are actually converted, and (4) for primary earnings per share, when the number of shares issued upon the attainment of increased earnings levels differs from the number of shares previously considered outstanding. [22, 36, 41, 57, 62]

The Opinion requires retroactive restatement (1) to give effect to prior period adjustments,[7] (2) to give effect to stock dividends, stock splits, and reverse splits, including those occurring after the close of the period being reported upon, (3) to give effect to a pooling of interests, (4) to give effect to changes in the number of shares contingently issuable or issued when such changes are caused by changes in market prices of the stock, and (5) to give effect to a reduction in the number of shares con-

---

[7]As defined in paragraphs 23 and 24 of APB Opinion No. 9.

tingently issuable when the term of an agreement to issue additional shares expires and the conditions have not been met.[8] *[18, 48, 49, 62, 63]*

The Opinion recommends retroactive restatement of earnings per share data for periods beginning before January 1, 1969 when such data are presented in comparative income statements including a period beginning after December 31, 1968 and election "b" of Opinion paragraph 46 has been made. Retroactive restatement of such data is required, however, when election "a" of Opinion paragraph 46 has been made. Otherwise, part of the data would conform to the provisions of Part II of APB Opinion No. 9 which is superseded by APB Opinion No. 15. *[45, 46]*

Business Combinations and Reorganizations

A business combination accounted for as a purchase of another business should, in the weighted average of shares, give effect to additional securities issued only from the date of acquisition. Results of operations of the acquired business are also included in the statement of income only from the date of acquisition. *[49]*

In a pooling of two or more corporations, the weighted average outstanding securities of the constituent corporations adjusted to the equivalent securities of the surviving corporation should be used for the earnings per share computation for all periods presented. The results of operations of the constituent businesses are also combined for all periods presented.

After a reorganization or quasi-reorganization, the earnings per share computations should be based on an analysis of the particular transaction applying the guidelines of the Opinion.

Disclosure

Disclosure is required to explain the rights and privileges of the holders of the various securities outstanding; the bases upon which primary and fully diluted earnings per share were computed; the number of shares issued upon conversion, exercise or satisfaction of required conditions; and other information necessary for a clear understanding of the data presented. (For example, if the fully diluted amount is the same as the primary amount because certain anti-dilutive securities which are not com-

mon stock equivalents are omitted from the fully diluted computation, that fact would be disclosed.) *[15-16, 19, 20]*

Supplementary Data

Supplementary earnings per share data[9] are to be furnished for the latest period when conversion occurs and primary earnings per share would have increased or decreased at least 3% if the conversion had occurred at the beginning of the period. Supplementary data are also to be furnished when common stock or common stock equivalents are sold and the proceeds are used to retire preferred stock or debt. It may also be desirable to furnish supplementary earnings per share data for each period presented giving the cumulative retroactive effect of all such issuances. *[14 fn. 2, 22-23]*

Supplementary data show what primary earnings per share would have been if the situations described above had occurred at the beginning of the period being reported upon rather than during the period. Thus, supplementary data are helpful for reflecting the trend of earnings per share data when primary amounts are affected by an increase in the number of shares included in the computation without an increase in the capital employed in the business.

Effective Date

APB Opinion No. 15 is effective for fiscal periods beginning after December 31, 1968. Earnings per share must therefore be reported on the faces of all income statements for periods beginning January 1, 1969 and thereafter. Securities are to be classified under the provisions of the Opinion regardless of the time of issuance except that an election is granted for securities with a time of issuance prior to June 1, 1969 for computing primary earnings per share to either:

a. classify all such securities under the provisions of the Opinion, i.e., apply the Opinion retroactively regardless of when the securities were issued, or
b. classify all securities outstanding[10] at May 31, 1969 as common stock equivalents if they were residual securities under APB Opinion No. 9.

All securities subject to the election must be classified under election "a" or all securities must be clas-

---

[8]But note that restatement is prohibited for primary earnings per share when increased earnings levels are attained and shares are issued which were not previously considered outstanding for prior primary computations. (See point 4 in the preceding paragraph and Opinion paragraph 62.)

[9]Supplementary earnings per share data should not be confused with fully diluted earnings per share. As used in APB Opinion No. 15, "supplementary earnings per share data" are additional data which are disclosed in a note. (APB Opinion No. 9 used the term "supplementary pro forma earnings per share" to describe data which are described as "fully diluted earnings per share" in APB Opinion No. 15.)

[10]Securities no longer outstanding at May 31, 1969 are classified as common stock equivalents if they were residual securities under APB Opinion No. 9 at the statement date. This applies only for income statements for periods prior to May 31, 1969 when such income statements are subsequently included in comparative income statements after that date.

sified under election "b." The election may not be changed after it is made. Thus, the classification of all securities issued prior to June 1, 1969 once determined under election "a" or election "b" never change.[11] All securities with a time of issuance after May 31, 1969 must be classified under the provisions of APB Opinion No. 15. [*45, 46*]

Election "b" allows a corporation to ignore options and warrants issued before June 1, 1969 in primary earnings per share computations unless they were considered residual securities under APB Opinion No. 9. The election was provided because the Board has traditionally not made its Opinions retroactive. This Opinion therefore does not apply new rules to securities which were issued under a prior Opinion and which were already outstanding when APB Opinion No. 15 was issued.

The election applies only to primary earnings per share computations. Fully diluted earnings per share computations include all common stock equivalents and other potentially dilutive securities without regard to the election. However, supplementary pro forma earnings per share determined under APB Opinion No. 9 are not necessarily the same[12] as fully diluted earnings per share determined under APB Opinion No. 15. Therefore, the Board recommends that previously reported earnings per share data be restated when reported in comparative income statements including an earnings per share amount computed under the provisions of APB Opinion No. 15 if election "b" of Opinion paragraph 46 has been made. Restatement for all prior periods presented is accomplished by retroactively applying (1) the security classifications determined under election "b" and (2) the computational methods prescribed by APB Opinion No. 15. [*45, 46*]

Both primary and fully diluted earnings per share amounts for prior periods must be retroactively restated if election "a" of Opinion paragraph 46 has been made when the prior period data are reported in comparative income statements including earnings per share data computed under the provisions of APB Opinion No. 15.

PART II: UNOFFICIAL ACCOUNTING INTERPRETATIONS OF APB OPINION NO. 15

Definitional Interpretations

1. Security

The term *security* is used in APB Opinion No. 9, APB Opinion No. 15 and in these Interpretations in a broad context to include instruments not usually considered to be securities. Securities are usually thought of as being common stocks, preferred stocks (both nonconvertible and convertible), bonds (both ordinary and convertible), and warrants. In a broad context, the term *security* also includes all debt instruments, options to purchase stock (or other securities), stock purchase contracts, stock subscriptions, and agreements to issue stock (or other securities) at a future date. Several securities may be included in a single instrument, which may or may not be separable. [*27, 37*]

2. Common Stock Equivalents

A common stock equivalent is defined by the Opinion as: "A security which, because of its terms or the circumstances under which it was issued, is in substance equivalent to common stock." (See page 199.) A common stock equivalent is not common stock in form but rather derives a large portion of its value from its common stock characteristics or conversion privileges. Such a security typically contains provisions enabling its holder to become a common stockholder. Its value tends to change with changes in the value of the common stock to which it is related. Examples of common stock equivalents are: options and warrants, preferred stock or debt convertible into common stock if the stock or debt yields less than 66 2/3% of the bank prime interest rate at time of issuance, and agreements to issue common stock with the passage of time as the only condition to issuance. [*25, 27, 33, 35*]

---

[11]See Interpretations 29 and 30 for exceptions.

[12]Although pro forma earnings per share and fully diluted earnings per share could be the same, they might be different. Any differences would result principally from the anti-dilution provisions of APB Opinion No. 15 and from different computational methods for options and warrants.

3. Other Potentially Dilutive Securities

Other potentially dilutive securities is a term used in this Interpretation to designate a classification of securities which are similar to common stock equivalents but which for one reason or another do not meet the tests for common stock equivalents under the Opinion.[13] Other potentially dilutive securities are included only in fully diluted earnings per share computations while common stock equivalents are, in effect, included in both primary and fully diluted earnings per share computations.

Examples of other potentially dilutive securities are convertible senior securities (convertible preferred stock and convertible debt) and options or warrants issued prior to June 1, 1969 if election "b" of Opinion paragraph 46 is made[14] and the options or warrants were not classified as residual securities under APB Opinion No. 9. [*41, 46*]

4. Dilution—Dilutive Security

Dilution, as used in the Opinion, is a reduction of the amount which would otherwise be reported as earnings per share. A dilutive security is a security which results in a decrease in the amount reported as earnings per share. As explained in Interpretations 5 and 15, there is no dilution of net loss per share when a corporation reports a net loss on its income statement. [*14 fn. 2, 30, 40*]

A dilutive security increases the number of common shares which are considered to be outstanding during the period for which the earnings per share computation is being made. Thus, a dilutive security increases the denominator used in the earnings per share computation. Earnings applicable to common stock, the numerator in the computation, may also increase. But so long as the numerator increase per additional denominator share is less than earnings per outstanding share, the security will be dilutive. [*51*]

5. Anti-Dilution—Anti-Dilutive Security

Anti-dilution is an increase in the amount which would otherwise be reported as earnings per share or a decrease in the amount of the net loss per share. Anti-dilution therefore has an incremental effect on earnings per share data. An anti-dilutive security is a security which would result in an increase in the amount reported as earnings per share or a decrease in the amount reported as net loss per share. [*30, 40*]

When a net income is reported, an anti-dilutive option or warrant under the treasury stock method reduces the number of common shares considered outstanding during a period. Such options or warrants, if permitted to enter the computation, would increase earnings per share by reducing the denominator used. Anti-dilutive convertible debt would increase the denominator. However, its interest adjustment would increase earnings applicable to common stock, the numerator used in the computation, by a greater amount per additional share than earnings per share computed without assuming conversion. Any numerator increase per additional denominator share which is greater than earnings per share computed without assuming conversion would have an incremental effect on earnings per share and would be anti-dilutive. Convertible preferred stock is anti-dilutive when its dividend per common share obtainable upon conversion exceeds earnings per share computed without assuming conversion.

When a net loss is reported, exercise or conversion is not assumed.[15] Any computation is anti-dilutive which increases the number of shares considered outstanding during a period for which a net loss is reported. Exercise of options and warrants is not assumed since this would increase the number of shares considered outstanding. Likewise, conversion would increase the number of shares considered outstanding. In addition, the if converted adjustments for convertible debt would decrease the amount of the loss. Not deducting dividends on convertible preferred stock would also decrease the amount of the loss applicable to common stock.

6. Dual Presentation

The dual presentation has two groups of earnings per share data; one is primary earnings per share data and the other is fully diluted earnings per share data. Both must be presented with equal prominence on the face of the income statement. [*16*]

The dual presentation of primary and fully diluted earnings per share data should not be confused with the two earnings per share amounts which must be presented when a corporation reports extraordinary items on its income statement. Even when the dual presentation is not required, a corporation reporting extraordinary items must report (1) earnings per share for income before extraordinary items and (2) earnings per share for net

---

[13]The term is not used in the Opinion in this strict context. *Potentially dilutive securities,* as that term is used in the Opinion, includes common stock equivalents. (For example, see Opinion paragraph 14.) The Opinion discusses convertible senior securities which are not common stock equivalents and other contingent issuances which are not common stock equivalents. Securities which are *not* common stock equivalents but which enable their holders to obtain common stock are described in these Interpretations as *"other* potentially dilutive securities." Therefore, convertible senior securities described in the Opinion are classified as "other potentially dilutive securities" in these Interpretations.

[14]See Interpretation 46 for an explanation of why these options and warrants are not classified as common stock equivalents.

[15]See footnote 5 in Part I.

income. When the dual presentation is required, a corporation reporting extraordinary items must report both amounts for primary earnings per share and both amounts for fully diluted earnings per share. [*13*]

A corporation with no extraordinary items on its income statement would report only earnings per share for net income. But this must be reported for both primary and fully diluted earnings per share by a corporation when the dual presentation is required.

7. Primary Earnings per Share

Primary earnings per share is the amount of earnings attributable to each share of common stock outstanding and common stock assumed to be outstanding to reflect the dilutive effect of common stock equivalents. Primary earnings per share data include an earnings per share amount for income before extraordinary items and an earnings per share amount for net income. These data may also include an earnings per share amount for extraordinary items. [*13, 15*]

Primary earnings per share is used in the Opinion and in these Interpretations as a convenient means of designating the presentation of these data which must appear on the face of an income statement of a corporation when the dual presentation is required. Thus, "primary" is a communication tool used merely to identify this group of earnings per share data to be presented and is not suggested as a caption to be used on the income statement. The term "primary" is not intended in any way to attribute greater significance to this group of data than is attributed to the fully diluted data.

8. Fully Diluted Earnings per Share

Fully diluted earnings per share is the amount of earnings attributable to each share of common stock outstanding and common stock assumed outstanding to reflect the dilutive effect of common stock equivalents and other potentially dilutive securities. Fully diluted earnings per share data include an earnings per share amount for income before extraordinary items and an earnings per share amount for net income. These data may include an earnings per share amount for extraordinary items. [*13, 15*]

Fully diluted earnings per share is used in the Opinion and in these Interpretations as a convenient means of designating the presentation of these data which must appear on the face of an income statement of a corporation when the dual presentation is required. Thus, "fully diluted" is a communication tool used merely to identify this group of earnings per share data to be presented and is not suggested as a caption to be used on the income statement.

Applicability of the Opinion

9. Corporations and Financial Presentations Excepted

Q—Does the Opinion require all corporations to present earnings per share on all income statements?

A—All corporations which are not specifically excepted by the Opinion must present earnings per share on the face of any income statement or summary of such a statement for periods beginning after December 31, 1968.

The only corporations excepted from the provisions of the Opinion are:

1. Mutual companies without common stock or common stock equivalents outstanding (for example, mutual savings banks, cooperatives, credit unions, etc.).
2. Companies registered under the Investment Company Act of 1940.
3. Corporations owned by political subdivisions or municipal, county, state, federal or foreign governments.
4. Not-for-profit corporations (for example, colleges, universities, medical or scientific research entities, trade and professional associations, religious organizations, etc. which are incorporated). [*6*]

The Opinion applies to all financial presentations which purport to present results of operations in conformity with generally accepted accounting principles and to summaries of those presentations for all corporations except those listed above. However, the following financial presentations are also excepted from the provisions of the Opinion:

1. Parent company statements accompanying consolidated financial statements.
2. Statements of wholly owned subsidiaries.
3. Special purpose statements.

Special purpose statements (as described in Chapter 13 of Statements on Auditing Procedure No. 33) by definition are not prepared in accordance with generally accepted accounting principles. Special purpose statements are not, however, merely those prepared for specific purposes if they purport to present results of operations in conformity with generally accepted accounting principles. For example, SEC Form S-9 for registration of certain high-grade, nonconvertible, fixed-interest debt securities requires disclosure of ratios of earnings to fixed charges for each year in the summary (or statement) of earnings. Although the SEC does not require that earnings per share data be reported in Form S-9, this form is not a "special purpose statement." Earnings per share must therefore be reported under APB Opinion No. 15. [*5, 6*]

10. Closely Held Corporations

Q—Does the Opinion apply to closely held corporations?

A—Yes, closely held corporations which are not wholly owned subsidiaries of other corporations must report earnings per share on their income statements in accordance with the Opinion. A corporation whose stock is all owned by a single individual is not a wholly owned subsidiary. [5, 6]

11. Dilution Less Than 3%

Q—Must a corporation with few dilutive securities outstanding make the dual presentation? May such a corporation ignore the dilutive securities and report earnings per share based on common shares outstanding?

A—The required reporting of earnings per share data depends on the materiality of the amount of dilution produced by securities which enable their holders to obtain common stock in the future. Aggregate dilution from all such securities which is less than 3% of earnings per common share outstanding need not be reported for either primary or fully diluted earnings per share, since such dilution is not considered to be material. Thus, if both the primary and fully diluted amounts are more than 97% of earnings per common share outstanding, earnings per share may be based on only common shares outstanding. [14 fn. 2]

The 3% provision applies to fully diluted earnings per share compared to earnings per common share outstanding, not compared to primary earnings per share. Anti-dilutive securities are not dilutive by definition and should be excluded in computing aggregate dilution. The 3% provision also applies to the reporting of any other earnings per share information, such as supplementary data. Aggregate dilution of less than 3% generally should be reported when it is anticipated that earnings per share data for a period when the provision applies might subsequently be included in a comparative income statement in which the following period reflects dilution of 3% or more. Otherwise, dilution in the following period would appear greater than it in fact was. [15, 17]

The Board intended the 3% provision to provide relief from complex computations to corporations which would have insignificant dilution if all obligations to issue common stock in the future were fulfilled currently. This would be the case, for example, for a corporation which has no obligations to issue common stock except for a small amount of stock under options granted to its executives. [14 fn. 2]

12. 3% Test

Q—Is there a simple test which can be applied to determine if dilution would be at least 3%?

A—Yes. As a "rule of thumb," make both the primary and fully diluted computations whenever the number of additional common shares which must be assumed to be issued exceeds 3%[16] of the number of outstanding common shares. If the dilution produced by either computation is at least 3%, the dual presentation is required. [15]

Dilutive options and warrants are included in earnings per share computations under the treasury stock method, which produces incremental shares (as explained in Interpretation 51). The number of incremental shares the treasury stock method will produce can be approximated by applying a simple formula. Since stock options are the only obligations of many closely held corporations to issue common stock, the formula is useful when the test described above is to be applied and only options or warrants are considered. [36]

The following formula[17] will approximate the number of incremental shares which will result from applying the treasury stock method for options or warrants:

$$I = \frac{M - E}{M} \ (N)$$

Where:

I is the number of incremental shares which would be produced by the treasury stock method.

M is the market price (or fair value) per share of common stock.

E is the exercise price of the option or warrant per common share obtainable upon exercise.

N is the total number of shares obtainable on exercise.

Subject to the constraint[18] that M >E.

---

[16]Actually, the number of additional shares must be at least 3/97 (or 3.09 + %) of the number of outstanding common shares. If earnings applicable to common stock includes an "if converted" adjustment, a greater number of additional shares would be required to produce dilution of at least 3%. Thus, although the number of additional shares is not the only determinant of dilution, common shares assumed outstanding must increase more than 3% to produce dilution of at least 3%.

[17]The formula should not be used when Opinion paragraph 38 applies, i.e., when the number of common shares obtainable on the exercise of all options and warrants and their equivalents exceeds 20% of the number of common shares outstanding.

[18]The formula would not be used unless the market price is greater than the exercise price since the result could be anti-dilutive.

An example of the application of the formula follows. Assume that a corporation has granted options to its officers to purchase 10,000 shares of common stock at $6 per share and the common stock has a market price (or fair value) of $10 per share.

Applying the formula for the information given, the amounts to be substituted for the letters are:

I = unknown
M = $10
E = $6
N = 10,000

Therefore:

$$I = \frac{\$10 - \$6}{\$10}\,(10,000)$$

$$I = .4(10,000)$$

$$I = 4,000$$

If the 4,000 incremental shares exceeds 3% of the number of outstanding common shares, actual dilution would be computed to determine if dilution is at least 3%.

13. Subchapter S Corporations

Q—Does the Opinion apply to the financial statements of corporations electing under Subchapter S of Chapter 1 of the *Internal Revenue Code?*

A—Yes, such corporations must report earnings per share on the face of their income statements. Net income is computed without regard to taxes on that income which will be paid by stockholders rather than by the corporation. Undistributed earnings of the corporation taxed to the stockholders increase the stockholders' tax bases in the shares they own, but the number of shares outstanding does not increase unless the corporation issues additional shares. The amount per share of income tax the corporation would have paid in the absence of the Subchapter S election would be useful information to disclose. [5, 6]

14. Unaudited Financial Statements

Q—Does the Opinion apply to unaudited financial statements?

A—Yes. If a CPA is associated with an unaudited income statement which does not report earnings per share, the CPA should phrase his disclaimer of opinion on the statement in accordance with the provisions of either paragraph 5 or 6 of Statements on Auditing Procedure No. 38 or paragraph 6 of Statements on Auditing Procedure No. 42 as is

appropriate under the circumstances of the engagement. [5, 6]

Earnings per Share Presentation

15. Reporting Loss per Share

Q—Must net loss per share be reported?

A—Yes, net loss per share must be reported under the same requirements that earnings per share must be reported. Net loss per share, however, is based on outstanding common shares. Assuming exercise of options and warrants or conversion of convertible securities would be anti-dilutive since an increase in the number of shares assumed to be outstanding would reduce the amount of the loss per share.[19] The amount of the loss is increased by any dividends declared (or cumulative even though not declared) for the period on preferred stocks. [12, 50]

16. EPS for Extraordinary Items

Q—Must earnings per share be presented for extraordinary items?

A—No, although this presentation may generally be desirable. Paragraph 13 of APB Opinion No. 15 states that earnings per share data should be reported consistent with the income statement presentation required by paragraph 20 of APB Opinion No. 9. Thus, it would appear that earnings per share should be presented for (1) income before extraordinary items, (2) extraordinary items less applicable income tax, and (3) net income as required by APB Opinion No. 9 when an extraordinary item is reported on the income statement. This presentation is used in the example in Exhibit B of Appendix C of APB Opinion No. 15. [13, Exh. B]

However, paragraph 13 of APB Opinion No. 15 requires that earnings per share data be presented for only (1) income before extraordinary items and (2) net income. Although the two requirements appear to conflict, earnings per share need not be presented for extraordinary items. A reader of the financial statements can determine earnings per share for extraordinary items by subtraction if it is not reported.

Naturally, the earnings per share data will be more complete if an amount is reported for extraordinary items when such items are reported on the income statement. This presentation, although not required, may therefore be generally desirable. In some cases, reporting all three earnings per share amounts would be particularly helpful to the reader, such as in the situation described in Opinion footnote 8 (where the effect on either income before extraordinary items or on net income is anti-dilutive but is dilutive on the other). [30 fn. 8]

---

[19]See footnote 5 in Part I.

17. Simple Capital Structure

Q—What is a simple capital structure for purposes of computing earnings per share?

A—A corporation has a simple capital structure for purposes of computing earnings per share if during the period it had no securities outstanding (or agreements to issue securities) that in the aggregate dilute earnings per outstanding common share. *[14]*

18. Complex Capital Structure

Q—What is a complex capital structure for purposes of computing earnings per share?

A—A corporation has a complex capital structure for purposes of computing earnings per share if it has issued, in addition to common stock, securities which have a dilutive effect on earnings per outstanding common share. Among the securities which may have a dilutive effect are convertible preferred stock, convertible debt, options, warrants, participating securities, different classes of common stock, and agreements to issue such securities or shares of common stock in the future. *[15, 27, 41]*

As explained in Interpretation 11, if the aggregate dilution for the period produced by all such securities which are dilutive does not reduce earnings per outstanding common share by at least 3%, a corporation may be considered as having a simple capital structure for purposes of computing earnings per share. It may be desirable, however, to report the actual dilution in such a case, particularly if the period being reported upon might later be included in a comparative income statement which includes one or more periods with dilution of 3% or more. *[14, 14 fn. 2, 17]*

19. EPS for Simple and Complex Capital Structures

Q—How does the reporting of earnings per share data differ for corporations with simple capital structures and corporations with complex capital structures?

A—A corporation with a simple capital structure is required to have a single presentation of "earnings per common share" on the face of its income statement. A corporation with a complex capital structure is required to have a dual presentation of both primary and fully diluted earnings per share on the face of its income statement. *[14, 15]*

Exceptions which apply to corporations with simple capital structures are explained in Interpretation 20. An exception which applies to corporations with complex capital structures is explained in Interpretation 18.

20. Dual Presentation for Corporation with Simple Capital Structure

Q—Is a corporation with a simple capital structure ever required to have the dual presentation?

A—Yes, the dual presentation is required if common stock was issued during the period on exercise, conversion, etc. and primary earnings per share would have increased or decreased if the issuance had taken place at the beginning of the period. *[41]*

A corporation has a simple capital structure when it has no dilutive securities outstanding. If outstanding anti-dilutive securities are exercised or converted, however, such a corporation would be required to have the dual presentation if primary earnings per share would have been affected as described above. Thus the dual presentation may be required for a corporation with a simple capital structure to report the incremental effect of an anti-dilutive exercise or conversion. *[14, 41]*

Also, the dual presentation is required for all periods presented in a comparative income statement if it is required for any period. The dual presentation may therefore be required for one or more periods in a comparative income statement when the corporation had a simple capital structure. *[17]*

21. Primary v. Fully Diluted EPS

Q—How do fully diluted earnings per share differ from primary earnings per share?

A—Primary earnings per share computations include only common stock and dilutive common stock equivalents. Fully diluted earnings per share computations include common stock and dilutive common stock equivalents together with other potentially dilutive securities. Fully diluted earnings per share also include those exercises or conversions for which common stock was issued during the period whether their effect is dilutive or anti-dilutive. *[24, 41]*

Fully diluted earnings per share show the maximum potential dilution of all dilutive contractual obligations to issue common stock and their effect on current earnings per share on a prospective basis. The difference between primary and fully diluted earnings per share shows (1) the maximum extent of potential dilution of current earnings which would occur from the conversions of securities that are not common stock equivalents or the contingent issuance of common stock not included in the computation of primary earnings per share and (2) the effect of all issuances of common stock on exercises or conversions during the year as if the issuance had occurred at the beginning of the year. *[16, 40, 41]*

22. Captions for Earnings per Share Presentations

Q—What captions should be used for reporting earnings per share amounts in the dual presentation?

A—Precise designations are not prescribed by the Opinion except that the term "earnings per common share" should not be used unless a corporation has a simple capital structure or the term is appropriately qualified. The qualification is determined by whether the corporation has only common stock equivalents or also has other potentially dilutive securities. [16]

Listed below are five captions which might be used to designate earnings per share amounts. Following the captions is a table indicating the captions a corporation might use when it has various combinations of securities outstanding. The first two columns of the table indicate the combinations of securities a corporation might have. The numbers in the other three columns refer to the numbers listed beside the captions which might be used to designate the earnings per share amounts. For example, a corporation having both dilutive common stock equivalents and other potentially dilutive securities outstanding could designate the primary amounts "Earnings per common and common equivalent share" and could designate the fully diluted amounts "Earnings per common share—assuming full dilution."

Suggested earnings per share captions

1. Earnings per common share.
2. Earnings per common share—assuming no dilution.
3. Earnings per common share—assuming full dilution.
4. Earnings per common and common equivalent share. (If both dilutive and anti-dilutive common stock equivalents are present, the caption may be: Earnings per common and dilutive common equivalent share.)
5. Earnings per common share—assuming issuance of all dilutive contingent shares.

TABLE INDICATING USE OF EPS CAPTIONS

Common Stock Equivalents Present	Other Potentially Dilutative Securities Present	Caption for Single Presentation	Dual Presentation	
			Primary Caption	Fully Diluted Caption
No[a]	No[a]	1		
No[a]	Dilutive		2	3
No[a]	Anti-dilutive	1[b]		
Dilutive	No		4	3[c]
Dilutive	Dilutive		4	3
Dilutive	Anti-dilutive		4	5[b, c]
Anti-dilutive	No[a]	1[b]		
Anti-dilutive	Dilutive		2[b]	5[b]
Anti-dilutive	Anti-dilutive	1[b]		

Notes:
[a]Or dilution is less than 3% if such securities are present.
[b]In a note, disclose the existence of the anti-dilutive securities.
[c]Primary and fully diluted amounts will be the same.

23. Captions in Comparative Statements

Q—What presentation is required in a comparative income statement when a corporation has a simple capital structure in one period and a complex capital structure in another period?

A—The dual presentation is required for all periods presented if it is required for any period presented. Since the corporation had a complex capital structure in one period presented, the dual presentation is required for that period and for all other periods presented in the comparative income statement. [17]

In a comparative income statement the captions used should be appropriate for the most dilutive presentation. For example, if there were no common stock equivalents in one period, anti-dilutive common stock equivalents in one period, and dilutive common stock equivalents in another period in a comparative income statement, the primary amounts could have a designation such as "earnings per common and dilutive common equivalent share." Explanatory disclosure in a note may also be appropriate.

Computing Earnings per Share

24. Earnings Applicable to Common Stock

Q—How is "earnings applicable to common stock" determined for earnings per share computations?

A—For a corporation with a simple capital structure, earnings applicable to common stock is net income reduced by dividends declared or paid for the period to preferred stock. Cumulative preferred dividends for the current period not paid or declared also are deducted from net income in determining earnings applicable to common stock. However, preferred dividends which are cumulative only if earned are deducted only to the extent they are earned. Interest on debt need not be adjusted in determining earnings applicable to common stock since it was deducted in arriving at net income. [50]

For example, assume that a corporation has a net income of $6,000 and has 1,000 shares of common stock outstanding. Also outstanding are 1,000 shares of nonconvertible noncumulative preferred stock and $10,000 of 6% nonconvertible bonds. The corporation has a simple capital structure. If no dividends were paid on preferred stock, earnings applicable to common stock would be $6,000. Earnings per common share would be $6 per share ($6,000 net income divided by 1,000 common shares). The declaration of a dividend of $1 per share on preferred stock would result in earnings applicable to common stock of $5,000 ($6,000 net income less $1,000 for preferred dividends) and earnings per common share of $5 per share. The same result would be obtained if the dividend were cumulative and had not been declared. The same result would also be obtained whether or not the corporation paid (or declared) a dividend on common stock. [14, 50]

For a corporation with a complex capital structure, net income is reduced by dividends on nonconvertible preferred stock as described above. When the if converted method is applied for outstanding convertible securities, however, dividends for convertible preferred stock are not deducted from net income but other adjustments may be necessary. Under the if converted method, convertible dividends are not deducted when conversion is assumed, and interest (less applicable income tax) is added back to net income when convertible debt is assumed to be converted. [51]

For example, assume that a corporation has a net income of $6,000 and has 1,000 shares of common stock outstanding. Also outstanding are 1,000 shares of common stock equivalent convertible preferred stock (convertible one common share for each preferred share) and $10,000 of 6% convertible bonds (convertible three common shares for each $100 bond) which are not common stock equivalents. The corporation has a complex capital structure. Assume also that the corporation paid a $1 per share dividend on both common and preferred stock and the income tax rate is 22%. For primary earnings per share, earnings applicable to common stock is $6,000 and earnings per common and common equivalent share is $3 per share ($6,000 divided by 2,000 shares, composed of 1,000 common shares and 1,000 common equivalent shares from the assumed conversion of the convertible preferred stock). For fully diluted earnings per share, earnings applicable to common stock is $6,468 ($6,000 net income plus $600 interest less $132 additional tax payable if the interest had not reduced net income). Earnings per common share assuming full dilution is $2.81 per share ($6,468 divided by 2,300 shares; composed of 1,000 common shares, 1,000 common equivalent shares, and 300 shares from the assumed conversion of the convertible bonds). [15, 51]

25. Weighted Average of Shares Outstanding

Q—What is the effect on earnings per share computations of issuing common stock or other securities which may be converted or exercised to obtain common stock or of reacquiring common stock or such securities during a period?

A—Such issuances or reacquisitions of common stock or other securities during a period require that a weighted average of shares be computed for the denominator to be used in the earnings per share computations. A weighted average gives due consideration to all shares outstanding and assumed to have been outstanding during a period. Shares issued or retired during a period are weighted by the fraction of the period they were outstanding. The weighted number of shares is added to the number of shares outstanding for the entire period to obtain the weighted average number of shares outstanding during the period. [47]

For example, assume that a corporation had 100,000 common shares outstanding on January 1 and issued 6,000 additional common shares on March 1. The weighted average would be 102,000 shares for the quarter ending March 31 or 104,000 shares for the six months ending June 30 or 105,000 shares for the year ending December 31.

COMPUTATIONAL NOTES:
$$100,000 + 1/3 (6,000) = 102,000$$
$$100,000 + 4/6 (6,000) = 104,000$$
$$100,000 + 10/12 (6,000) = 105,000$$

The same answers would result if the 6,000 shares issued on March 1 were merely assumed to have been issued to reflect the dilutive effect of common stock equivalents issued on March 1. It should be noted that the number of shares in the weighted average for the quarter and for the year are different.

Reacquired shares are included in the weighted

413

average only for the time they were outstanding. For example, assume that a corporation had 100,000 shares outstanding on January 1 and reacquired 6,000 shares on March 1. The weighted average would be 98,000 shares for the quarter ending March 31 or 96,000 shares for the six months ending June 30 or 95,000 shares for the year ending December 31.

COMPUTATIONAL NOTES:

$$100,000 - \qquad 6,000 = 94,000$$
$$94,000 + 2/3 \ (6,000) = 98,000$$
$$94,000 + 2/6 \ (6,000) = 96,000$$
$$94,000 + 2/12 \ (6,000) = 95,000$$

The same answers would result if the 100,000 shares had included common stock equivalents and the corporation had reacquired 100 dilutive common stock equivalent convertible bonds (convertible 60 common shares for one bond) on March 1.

More complex methods for computing a weighted average could be used if the number of shares involved changes frequently, such as computing an average weighted by days. (See Exhibit 5, page 452.)

The weighted average discussed in the Opinion and in these Interpretations is technically an arithmetical mean average of shares outstanding and assumed to be outstanding for earnings per share computations. The most precise average would be the sum of the shares determined on a daily basis divided by the number of days in the period. Less precise averaging methods may be used, however, as illustrated above, if they produce reasonable results. But methods which introduce artificial weighting are not acceptable for computing a weighted average of shares for earnings per share computations. For example, the "Rule of 78" method, which weights shares for the first month of the year by 12 and weights shares for the last month of the year by 1, is not an acceptable method.

Retroactive recognition is given for all periods presented to any stock dividend, stock split or reverse split, including those occurring after the end of the period for which the computation is being made but before the statements are issued.

Convertible Securities

26. Classification and Assumed Conversion

Q—Which convertible securities are assumed to be converted for primary earnings per share computations and which are assumed to be converted for fully diluted earnings per share computations?

A—Convertible securities which are classified as common stock equivalents are assumed to be converted for both primary and fully diluted earnings per share computations. Convertible securities which are not common stock equivalents are classified as other potentially dilutive securities and are assumed to be converted only for fully diluted earnings per share computations. [*15, 31*]

Conversion is assumed for either computation only when the result is dilutive unless (1) the security is included in an aggregate computation which has a net dilutive effect or (2) for fully diluted earnings per share, common stock was issued during the period on an anti-dilutive conversion, that is, a conversion which would have had the effect of increasing earnings per share if it had occurred at the beginning of the period. When conversion is assumed, the if converted method is applied.[20] When conversion is not assumed because the result would be anti-dilutive, interest or dividends on the securities reduce the amount of earnings or increase the amount of loss otherwise applicable to common stock. [*30, 38, 40, 41, 50, 51*]

Most convertible securities are classified on the basis of their yield at time of issuance. (The exceptions are discussed in the following paragraphs of this Interpretation.) Under the yield test, convertible securities which yield less than 66 2/3% of the bank prime interest rate at time of issuance are common stock equivalents; those yielding at least 66 2/3% of the prime rate are other potentially dilutive securities. [*33*]

If a convertible security has a change scheduled in its interest or dividend rate within five years after issuance, its yield at issuance is considered to be the lowest scheduled rate within the five years. (See Interpretation 28 for the treatment of convertible securities which are not convertible until a future date.) A convertible security which would not otherwise be a common stock equivalent at time of issuance is classified as a common stock equivalent if it is issued with the same terms as those of an outstanding convertible security which is a common stock equivalent. [*28*]

Convertible securities issued prior to June 1, 1969 are classified by the issuer under one of two alternative elections specified in paragraph 46 of APB Opinion No. 15. (The election made applies to all securities issued before that date, not just to convertible securities.) Under election "a," all convertible securities issued prior to June 1, 1969 are classified as either common stock equivalents or other potentially dilutive securities under the provisions of APB Opinion No. 15. Under election "b," all convertible securities issued prior to June 1, 1969 which were classified as residual securities under APB Opinion No. 9 are classified as common stock equivalents; those which were classified as nonresidual securities are classified as other potentially dilutive securities. [*46*]

---

[20]See page 403 of Part I of this Interpretation and Opinion paragraph 51 for a description of the if converted method.

Convertible securities which require or permit the payment of cash upon conversion are considered the equivalents of warrants and are classified as common stock equivalents. (See Interpretation 71 for the treatment of such securities.) A few convertible participating securities are common stock equivalents for which the two-class method may be applied. (See Interpretation 87 for the treatment of such securities.) The if converted method is applied when any convertible security is assumed to be converted except for unusual cases when the two-class method is applied. [*35, 37, 51, 59*]

27. Time of Issuance

Q—What is the "time of issuance" of a convertible security?

A—"Time of issuance" is *generally* the date when agreement as to terms has been reached and announced even though subject to further actions, such as directors' or stockholders' approval. In this context, time of issuance is often referred to in financial jargon as the "handshake" date. Thus, time of issuance will usually precede the actual date of issuance of a security by some period which might be as long as several months or as short as a few hours. [*29*]

"Agreement as to terms" means that all of the terms have been set, not merely that the parties have reached an agreement in principle but the number of securities to be issued or the issue price is still to be determined at a later date. Agreement as to terms is reached when the parties are obligated to complete the transaction if it is ratified by the directors and/or stockholders, that is, neither party may legally terminate the agreement except for failure to receive approval from the directors or stockholders. The fact that the agreement is subject to a "favorable" ruling from the Treasury Department or a regulatory agency does not affect time of issuance so long as all of the terms of the agreement have been set.

The classification of a convertible security is determined at time of issuance and does not change when the security is actually issued except as discussed in Interpretation 29.

When time of issuance occurs before a year end but the agreement has not been approved by either the directors or stockholders before the financial statements are issued, the securities are not considered outstanding in the financial statements being issued or in earnings per share computations. (The securities are similar to a contingent issuance whose conditions are not currently being met.) [*62*]

28. Classification and Computation Not Always the Same

Q—Are convertible securities included in earnings per share computations at time of issuance?

A—Convertible securities are classified at time of issuance. Generally they are assumed to be converted for earnings per share computations from this date also. Although a convertible security is classified at time of issuance, in some cases it is not assumed to be converted for earnings per share computations until a later date. [*28, 51*]

If the conversion privilege is not effective during the period being reported upon, the length of time before the privilege becomes effective determines when the security is eligible for assumed conversion in earnings per share computations. Conversion is not assumed for either primary or fully diluted computations if the conversion privilege is not effective within ten years from the end of the period being reported upon. Conversion is assumed only for fully diluted computations if the conversion privilege is effective after five years but within ten years from the end of the period being reported upon. Conversion is assumed as if the security were immediately convertible if the conversion privilege is effective within five years from the end of the period being reported upon. [*57, 58*]

For example, assume that a corporation issued a debt security at the end of its 1969 reporting year that may be converted into common stock after twelve years (at the end of 1981). The security's yield at time of issuance requires that it be classified as a common stock equivalent. Conversion would not be assumed for 1969 or 1970 earnings per share computations (interest would reduce net income in 1970, however). Conversion would be assumed whenever the effect is dilutive for fully diluted computations beginning in 1971 and for both primary and fully diluted computations beginning in 1976. Thus, the security is classified at time of issuance but conversion is not assumed for earnings per share computations until later. [*28*]

Time of issuance and classification of a convertible security may precede the obligation to issue and actual issuance by as much as several months, but a convertible security is not considered outstanding in the interim until there is a valid obligation to issue the security. For example, assume that agreement as to terms for a business combination is reached and announced on December 1, 1969. Final approval by stockholders occurs on February 16, 1970 and a convertible security is to be issued March 2, 1970. Classification of the security is determined at December 1, 1969. The security would be omitted from 1969 earnings per share computations if the financial statements are issued before February 16, 1970, but the impending issuance would be disclosed.

If the business combination is accounted for as a purchase, the security would be considered outstanding from the date of the acquisition in 1970 earnings per share computations if the stockholders in fact ratify the agreement. If the business combination is accounted for as a pooling of interests, prior periods' earnings per share data would be retroactively restated in comparative income statements issued subsequently to reflect the security as outstanding for all periods presented. (See Part I, Page 405.) [*49*]

29. Change of Classification of Convertible Security

Q—When does the classification of a convertible security change?

A—A convertible security's classification is generally determined only at time of issuance and does not change thereafter. However, a change of classification (usually from other potentially dilutive security status to common stock equivalent status) may be required in two situations. These are when (1) an incorrect estimate of the security's value at time of issuance was made in the absence of a market price or (2) a common stock equivalent convertible security is issued with the same terms as an already outstanding convertible security which is not a common stock equivalent. (See Interpretation 30.) [*28, 29*]

If a convertible security does not have a market price at time of issuance, an estimate must be made of the security's fair value to apply the yield test. If the estimate of the security's value is too low, a convertible security which should be classified as a common stock equivalent might not be so classified. In such a case, the security would have to be reclassified as a common stock equivalent at actual issuance. Typically, an obviously incorrect estimate would be evidenced by materially higher market transactions for the security at actual issuance shortly after the time of issuance. [*29, 33 fn. 9*]

A change of the classification of the security would not be appropriate in such a case, however, if the higher market prices resulted from an external change over which the issuer had no control. (A general increase in the market prices of other securities might indicate an external change.) A change of the classification would also not be appropriate if convertible securities were sold for cash and the gross proceeds to the issuer were substantially equal to the total amount of the original fair value estimate for the securities. In this case, the total of the net amount received by the issuer plus brokerage commissions paid is approximately equal to the original estimate of fair value of the securities.

30. Change of Classification Is Mandatory

Q—Would convertible securities issued prior to June 1, 1969 and classified as other potentially dilutive securities under Opinion paragraph 46 become common stock equivalents if another convertible security is issued with the same terms after May 31, 1969 and is classified as a common stock equivalent? [*46*]

A—Yes, a change in classification is required by the second sentence of Opinion paragraph 28 for any outstanding convertible security which is not a common stock equivalent but which has the same terms as those of another convertible security being issued which is classified as a common stock equivalent at time of issuance. Thus, an outstanding convertible security which is not a common stock equivalent would be reclassified as a common stock equivalent if another convertible security is issued with the same terms and is classified as a common stock equivalent at time of issuance. [*28*]

Although this reclassification is an exception to the general rule that securities do not change status subsequent to time of issuance, reclassification is mandatory. All of a corporation's convertible securities issued with the same terms therefore are classified the same for earnings per share computations.

For example, assume that convertible securities were issued with the same terms on May 2, June 2, and July 2, 1969. Only the July 2 issue is a common stock equivalent if classification is based on yield at time of issuance because of an increase in the bank prime interest rate. Under Opinion paragraph 28, however, both the May 2 and June 2 issues become common stock equivalents also.

31. Definition of "Same Terms"

Q—What are the "same terms" (as used in the second sentence of Opinion paragraph 28) for the subsequent issuance of a convertible security?

A—The "same terms" are identical terms, not merely similar terms. Thus, any change in dividend or interest rates, conversion rates, call prices or dates, preferences in liquidation, etc. is a change in terms. Market price or issue price is not considered a "term." (See Interpretation 32.) [*28*]

32. Issue Price Is Not a "Term"

Q—Do different issue prices for different issuances of convertible securities constitute a change in "terms" if all other terms for the securities are the same?

A—No, different issue prices for convertible securities with the same terms otherwise is not a change in terms. Thus, two convertible securities issued at different prices but with the same stated dividend or interest rates, conversion rates, call prices and dates, preferences in liquidation, etc. have the same terms. [*28*]

33. Sale of Treasury Securities Is a New Issue

Q—Are convertible securities sold by an issuer from securities held as treasury securities to be classified as a new issue or as part of the original issue under the provisions of the second sentence of Opinion paragraph 28?

A—When convertible securities are acquired by the issuing corporation and subsequently reissued, they constitute a new issue with the same terms as the existing outstanding convertible security. The "new" issue's status (as a common stock equivalent or not) should be determined under both the common stock equivalent test and the provisions of the second sentence of Opinion paragraph 28. If deemed a common stock equivalent, the "new" issue could also affect the status of outstanding securities with the same terms as described in the second sentence of Opinion paragraph 28. For example, if the outstanding securities are not common stock equivalents and the reissued securities are common stock equivalents under the yield test (because of a change in market prices or the prime rate), the outstanding securities also become common stock equivalents. [*28*]

34. *Determining a Convertible Security's Cash Yield*

Q—Upon what return is a convertible security's cash yield based?

A—Cash yield for most convertible securities is based upon the stated amount of interest or dividends the security is scheduled to pay each year.[21] However, if the dividends on convertible preferred stock are not cumulative, yield might have to be based on some lesser amount, particularly if the stated amount appears impossible to pay. Low earnings or contractual provisions on outstanding debt, for example, might prohibit payment of the stated amount. The same would apply for preferred dividends which are cumulative only if earned. [*33*]

35. *Computing a Convertible's Cash Yield*

Q—How is a convertible security's cash yield at time of issuance computed?

A—Yield is a security's return expressed as a percentage of its value. For example, a $1,000 bond which is paying $45 annual interest to the holder and selling at 90 (i.e., $900) yields 5%

$$\left(\text{computed} \quad \frac{\$45}{\$900} \times 100 \right)$$

if the time factor to maturity is ignored. Although yield is generally computed to maturity, the yield test described in the Opinion for convertible securities

uses only the stated annual return expressed as a percentage of the security's market price (ignoring commissions and transfer taxes) at time of issuance. If the security does not have a market price at time of issuance, the test is based on the security's fair value. [*33*]

36. *Cash Yield of Convertible Security in a "Package"*

Q—How is the cash yield determined for a convertible security issued in a "package," i.e., a convertible security is one of two or more securities issued as a unit?

A—When two or more securities are issued as a unit, the unit price at time of issuance should be allocated to each security based on the relative fair values of the securities at time of issuance. For example, assume that a "package" consisting of one share of common stock, one share of convertible preferred stock, and one nonconvertible $100 bond with a detachable warrant is sold as a unit for a total price of $200. At time of issuance, fair values were $42 per share of common stock, $63 per share of convertible preferred stock, $99.75 per bond and $5.25 per warrant. The $200 unit amount would be allocated to each security as follows:

	Fair Value at Issuance	Percentage of Total	Allocated Amount of $200
Common stock	$ 42.00	20.0%	$ 40.00
Preferred stock	63.00	30.0	60.00
Bond	99.75	47.5	95.00
Warrant	5.25	2.5	5.00
Totals	$210.00	100.0%	$200.00

If the convertible preferred stock is scheduled to pay a dividend of $3.15 per share each year, it would yield 5.25%

$$\left(\text{computed} \quad \frac{\$3.15}{\$60.00} \times 100 \right)$$

[*33, fn. 9**]

37. *Property Included in Cash Yield*

Q—May the fair value of property to be paid as dividends or interest be included in computing cash yield since the Opinion specifically states only "cash"?

A—Yes, the fair value of property to be paid in lieu of cash may be included in computing the cash

---

[21]See Interpretation 26 for the amount to be used when a convertible security has a change of interest or dividends scheduled.
*Also see APB Opinion No. 14.

yield of a convertible security. The property so treated may include nonconvertible senior securities of the same company. But it may not include the same issue for which common stock equivalency is being determined. And it may not include securities of the issuer or its parent or subsidiary which are currently or potentially dilutive and enter into the computation of either primary or fully diluted earnings per share. [*33*]

For example, any common stock or common stock equivalent of the issuer and securities such as those described in Opinion paragraphs 59, 60, and 65-69 would not be considered property for this purpose. Also, "extra" dividends to be paid on convertible stock on a nonrecurring basis would not be considered in computing cash yield in conformity with the "lowest scheduled rate" provision of Opinion paragraph 33.

38. Prime Rate Used in Yield Test

Q—What bank prime interest rate should be used to determine the status of a convertible security as a common stock equivalent or not in applying the yield test when more than one rate is in effect in a country?

A—The prime interest rate in effect at the bank where the issuer borrows is used when more than one bank prime interest rate (or its equivalent in foreign[22] countries) is in effect in the U.S. If the issuer borrows from more than one bank and the different banks have different prime rates in effect, an average of the rates is used. If the issuer does not borrow from a bank where the prime interest rate is offered and more than one bank prime interest rate is in effect, an average of the rates would be used unless the issuer can show that the predominant rate is more appropriate than an average rate. [*34*]

39. Prior Period Prime Rates

Q—What source should be considered authoritative in determining the bank prime interest rate which was in effect in the U.S. during prior periods when applying election "a" of Opinion paragraph 46? [*46*]

A—The *Federal Reserve Bulletin* may be considered an authoritative source for determining the bank prime interest rate at any time. When a "split" prime rate is in effect, the provisions of Interpretation 38 are applied. For readers' convenience, the dates of changes in the prime rate and the rates in effect from 1954 through 1970 have been extracted and appear in Exhibit 2, page 448. [*34*]

40. Original Issue Premium or Discount on Convertible Securities

Q—What happens to original issue premium or discount when convertible securities are assumed to be converted and common stock is assumed to be issued for earnings per share computations?

A—Any original issue premium or discount amortized during the period (to compute the effective interest deducted from net income for a debt security) is eliminated from net income in arriving at earnings applicable to common stock. The unamortized original issue premium or discount balance at the date of assumed conversion (the ending balance plus the amount amortized during the period) is then ignored for earnings per share computations. The if converted method only assumes conversion of the securities; it does not assume retirement. The converted securities are assumed to be held by the issuer as treasury securities during the period being reported upon and balance sheet accounts related to those securities are not affected by the assumed conversion. Note that these assumptions are made only for earnings per share computations; the issuer's balance sheet and net income for the period are not affected in any way by the assumptions made for earnings per share computations. [*39, 51*]

41. No Anti-Dilution from Convertible Preferred Stock

Q—When is convertible preferred stock antidilutive and therefore not assumed to be converted for earnings per share computations?

A—Convertible preferred stock is anti-dilutive and conversion is not assumed[23] whenever the amount of the dividend paid or declared for the current period (or accumulated if not paid) per common share obtainable upon conversion exceeds the earnings per share amount computed without assuming conversion. [*30, 40, 50*]

For example, assume that a corporation had a net income of $1,500 and had 1,000 shares of common stock outstanding. Also outstanding were 1,000 shares of preferred stock convertible on a one-for-one basis and classified as a common stock equivalent. A $1 per share dividend was paid to the convertible shareholders. Assumption of conversion would be anti-dilutive in this case since earnings per outstanding common share is $.50 per share. (Earnings per common and common equivalent share would be $.75 per share if conversion were assumed.) Conversion would not be assumed, but rather the preferred dividend would be deducted to

---

[22]See *The Banker*, February 1969, p. 117 *ff.*, for a discussion of rates in foreign countries which are the equivalents of the U.S. bank prime interest rate.

[23]See Interpretation 44 for an exception when actual conversion occurs.

compute earnings applicable to common stock. Earnings per share would be computed on the basis of actual common stock outstanding. The same result would be obtained if the dividend were cumulative and not paid.

42. No Anti-Dilution from Convertible Debt

Q—When is convertible debt anti-dilutive and therefore not assumed to be converted for earnings per share computations?

A—Convertible debt is anti-dilutive and conversion is not assumed[24] whenever its interest (net of tax) per common share obtainable on conversion exceeds the earnings per share computed without assuming conversion. [30, 40, 50]

For example, assume that a corporation had a net income of $500 and had 1,000 shares of common stock outstanding. Also outstanding were 1,000 convertible bonds with a par value of $100 each paying interest at 3% per annum and convertible into one share of common stock each. Assume the bonds are classified as common stock equivalents and that the effective income tax rate is 50%. The earnings per common share outstanding (ignoring conversion of the bonds) is $.50 per share. Assuming conversion, $3,000 interest would be added back less $1,500 of additional income tax, resulting in a net increase of $1,500 and earnings applicable to common stock of $2,000. The $1.00 earnings per share for the 2,000 common and common equivalent shares would be anti-dilutive and conversion would therefore not be assumed.

43. Conversion Assumed for Primary Only

Q—When a common stock equivalent convertible security is assumed to be converted for primary earnings per share computations, must it also be assumed to be converted for fully diluted earnings per share computations?

A—Generally, a common stock equivalent convertible security is assumed to be converted for both computations. However, if fully diluted earnings per share would be increased by the assumed conversion, conversion would be assumed only for the primary earnings per share computation. Such a situation could occur if two convertible securities were outstanding and the dividend on one classified as a common stock equivalent exceeds fully diluted earnings per share but not primary earnings per share. [15, 31, 40]

For example, assume that a corporation had a net income of $9,500 and had 2,000 shares of common stock outstanding. Also outstanding were 1,000 shares of Class A convertible preferred stock which was a common stock equivalent and 1,500 shares of Class B convertible preferred stock which was not a common stock equivalent. The Class A paid a dividend of $2.50 per share and the Class B paid a dividend of $1 per share. Both are convertible into common on a one-for-one basis.

Primary earnings per share is $2.67 per share assuming conversion of the Class A convertible preferred ($9,500 − $1,500 = $8,000 earnings applicable to common divided by 3,000 shares). Fully diluted earnings per share would be $2.11 per share if conversion were assumed for both the Class A and Class B convertible preferred ($9,500 ÷ 4,500 shares). However, fully diluted earnings per share is $2.00 per share if conversion is assumed for only the Class B ($9,500 − $2,500 = $7,000 earnings applicable to common divided by 3,500 shares). The difference between $2.11 and $2.00 is caused by the incremental effect of assuming conversion of the Class A. Since the Class A dividend per common share obtainable upon conversion exceeds fully diluted earnings per share computed without assuming conversion, conversion would be anti-dilutive. (See Interpretation 41.) Therefore, primary earnings per share is reported at $2.67 per share and fully diluted earnings per share is reported at $2.00 per share since this is the maximum dilutive amount.

This example illustrates the fact that earnings per share amounts may be affected by changes either in the numerator or in the denominator used in the computation. Naturally, in some cases, both change.

44. If Converted Method at Actual Conversion

Q—Is the if converted method applied differently for primary and fully diluted earnings per share computations when actual conversion occurs?

A—When a common stock equivalent convertible security is converted during a period, the if converted method is applied from the beginning of the period[25] to the date of conversion for both primary and fully diluted earnings per share computations if the result is dilutive. [41]

If the result is anti-dilutive, however, conversion is not assumed for the primary computation. But when an actual conversion occurs during a period, conversion is assumed at the beginning[25] of the period for the fully diluted computation and the if converted method is applied, regardless of whether the result is dilutive or anti-dilutive. [30, 41]

Upon actual conversion, common stock issued is included in the weighted average of shares outstanding in both the primary and fully diluted computations from the date of conversion. The securities

---

[24]See Interpretation 44 for an exception when actual conversion occurs.

[25]For convertible securities issued and converted during the period, conversion is assumed only from time of issuance rather than from the beginning of the period.

tendered by the holder for conversion are thereafter considered to be retired. [47]

45. Securities Convertible into Other Convertible Securities

Q—How is a convertible security which is convertible into another convertible security included in earnings per share computations?

A—Such convertible securities enter earnings per share computations according to their provisions and their characteristics. [43]

A convertible security issued by a subsidiary which is convertible only into a parent company's convertible security is a senior security from the standpoint of the subsidiary, i.e., the yield test does not apply. For consolidated earnings per share computations, however, the subsidiary's security would be assumed to be converted into the parent's security. The parent's security would then be assumed to be converted under the if converted method (if the net result is dilutive). If the parent's convertible security is not a common stock equivalent, conversion of the parent's security would be assumed only for fully diluted computations. If it is a common stock equivalent, conversion of the parent's security would be assumed for both primary and fully diluted computations. (See Interpretation 93.)

Convertible securities which are convertible at the option of the holder into either another convertible security or a nonconvertible security are assumed to be converted into the security which would be more advantageous for the holder (but not if the result is anti-dilutive). If conversion is assumed into the other convertible security, that security is then assumed to be converted into common stock for earnings per share computations (but not if the net result is anti-dilutive). If conversion is assumed into the nonconvertible security, dividends which would have been applicable to the nonconvertible security, as if it had been outstanding, are deducted in determining earnings applicable to common stock. If converted adjustments may also be applicable. The classification (determined under the yield test) as a common stock equivalent or other potentially dilutive security of convertible securities which are convertible at the option of the holder as discussed in this paragraph determines whether conversion is assumed for both primary and fully diluted computations or only for fully diluted computations. [56, 58]

In some cases, the security which would be more advantageous for assumed conversion cannot be determined. This might be the case, for example, if the nonconvertible security pays a high dividend and the second convertible security has good prospects for an increase in its market price. If the more advantageous security to the holders cannot be determined, the computation should give effect to the greater earnings per share dilution.

Options and Warrants and Their Equivalents

46. Classification of Options and Warrants

Q—How are options, warrants and their equivalents classified for earnings per share computations?

A—Options, warrants and their equivalents are always common stock equivalents unless *all* of the following conditions are met: (1) they were issued prior to June 1, 1969 *and* (2) the issuer makes election "b" under paragraph 46 of APB Opinion No. 15 *and* (3) they were not classified as residual securities under APB Opinion No. 9. Options, warrants and other equivalents classified under this exception are not common stock equivalents but are other potentially dilutive securities and are included only in fully diluted earnings per share computations.[26] All other options, warrants and their equivalents are included in both primary and fully diluted earnings per share computations. [35, 42, 46]

47. No Anti-Dilution from Options and Warrants

Q—When are options and warrants anti-dilutive under the treasury stock method?

A—Generally, options and warrants are anti-dilutive whenever their exercise price exceeds the market price of the common stock obtainable on exercise. This is because application of the treasury stock method in such a case would reduce the number of common shares included in the computation which would increase the earnings per share amount. [36, 36 fn. 12]

The prohibition against anti-dilution in applying the treasury stock method recognizes the economic fact that an option or warrant would not be exercised if the exercise price were above the market price because the stock could be purchased in the market for less than it could be purchased by exercising the option or warrant. However, if for some reason options or warrants are exercised when the market price is below the exercise price, the market price at the exercise date is applied in the fully diluted computation for the exercised options or warrants for the period they were outstanding. (See Interpretation 62.) However, anti-dilution is not reflected in the primary computation prior to exercise. [30, 40, 42]

---

[26]These options and warrants would be common stock equivalents except for the fact that they were issued before APB Opinion No. 15 was released. The Opinion provides that they be classified as common stock equivalents only if the issuer elects to so classify them.

In special cases for which other methods are applied (see Opinion paragraphs 37 and 38), the factors which cause dilution or anti-dilution are, of course, different. These special cases are discussed in Interpretations 50 and 65-71. *[37, 38]*

48. Equivalents of Options and Warrants

Q—What kinds of securities are considered the equivalents of options and warrants and therefore always classified as common stock equivalents?

A—Stock purchase contracts, stock subscriptions not fully paid, deferred compensation plans providing for the issuance of common stock, and convertible debt and convertible preferred stock allowing or requiring the payment of cash at conversion (regardless of the yield of such convertible securities at time of issuance) are considered the equivalents of options or warrants. The treasury stock method should be applied for all of these securities unless their terms or the provisions of Opinion paragraphs 37 and 38 require that another method be applied for the computation of earnings per share. *[27, 35, 36, 37, 38]*

49. Grouping Options and Warrants

Q—May anti-dilutive options and warrants be grouped with dilutive options and warrants in applying the treasury stock method?

A—No, except in the special situations discussed below. *[30, 40]*
Footnote 11 of the Opinion allows reasonable grouping of like securities, i.e., options and warrants with the same exercise prices per common share to be issued. For example, it would be appropriate to group an option to purchase one share of common stock for $20 with a warrant to purchase two shares of common stock for $40. Assuming a market price of $15 per share for common stock, these options and warrants would not be grouped with a warrant to purchase one share of common stock for $10. *[35 fn. 11]*
If an aggregate computation is required, however, anti-dilutive and dilutive securities must be included in the same computation. Opinion paragraph 38 provides for an aggregate computation, for example. An anti-dilutive option which must be exercised before a dilutive option may be exercised must also be included in an aggregate computation. *[38]*
For example, assume an option is exercisable at $30 to purchase one share of common stock and a second option is exercisable at $10 to purchase one share of common stock *after* the first option is exercised. The two options would be grouped and considered as a "two-step" option to buy two shares of common stock for $40. Their aggregate effect would be dilutive whenever the market price of common stock exceeds $20 per share. An aggregate

computation would not be made for a dilutive option which must be exercised before an anti-dilutive option may be exercised, because the anti-dilutive option would not be exercised in such a situation.

50. Methods Used for Options and Warrants

Q—Since different methods are described for the treatment of options and warrants in the Opinion, in what order should the different methods be applied?

A—In determining the effect of options and warrants and their equivalents in earnings per share computations, apply Opinion paragraphs in the following order (to the extent that each is pertinent):

> Opinion paragraph 37
> Opinion paragraph 38
> Opinion paragraph 36

[36]
Opinion paragraph 37 applies to options and warrants or their equivalents (1) which either allow or require the tendering of debt at exercise or (2) whose proceeds from exercise must be applied to retire debt or other securities under the terms of those securities. Opinion paragraph 37 also applies to convertible securities which either allow or permit the payment of cash at conversion. Such convertibles are considered the equivalents of warrants. *[35, 37]*
Opinion paragraph 38 applies only when the number of common shares obtainable upon exercise of all outstanding options and warrants and their equivalents exceed 20% of the number of common shares outstanding at the end of the period. *[38]*
Opinion paragraph 36 (the treasury stock method) applies to all other options and warrants and their equivalents. *[36]*

51. Treasury Stock Method Reflects Dilution of Options and Warrants

Q—How does the treasury stock method reflect the dilutive effect of options and warrants?

A—The treasury stock method increases the number of shares assumed to be outstanding when the exercise price of an option or warrant is below the market price of common stock obtainable on exercise. The dilutive effect of the treasury stock method is demonstrated in the following example. *[36 fn. 12]*
Assume that a corporation earned $125,000 during a period when it had 60,000 shares of common stock outstanding. The common stock sold at an average market price of $20 per share during the period. Also outstanding were 10,000 warrants which could be exercised to purchase one share of common stock for $15 for each warrant exercised.

Earnings per common share *outstanding* would be $2.08 per share ($125,000 ÷ 60,000 shares).

Applying the treasury stock method, the 10,000 warrants would be assumed to have been exercised by their holders at the beginning of the period. Upon exercise, 10,000 shares of common stock would be assumed to have been issued by the corporation to the holders. The $150,000 proceeds (10,000 warrants at an exercise price of $15 per share) would be assumed to have been used by the corporation to purchase 7,500 shares ($150,000 ÷ $20 per share average market price) of common stock in the market on the exercise date. Common stock would therefore increase 2,500 shares.[27] (10,000 shares issued less 7,500 shares purchased results in 2,500 *incremental* shares.) A total of 62,500 shares would be considered as outstanding for the entire period. The amount to be reported as primary earnings per share would be $2.00 per share ($125,000 ÷ 62,500 shares), or dilution of $.08 per share. [*36*]

Fully diluted earnings per share would also be $2.00 per share if the ending market price of the common stock were $20 per share or less. But an ending market price above $20 per share would cause more dilution to be reflected in fully diluted earnings per share. For example, an ending market price of $25 per share would produce 4,000 incremental common shares[28] which would result in fully diluted earnings per share of $1.95 per share. Dilution would be $.13 per share from earnings per outstanding share and $.05 per share from primary earnings per share. [*42*]

52. Market Prices Used for Treasury Stock Method

Q—What market prices of common stock are used in applying the treasury stock method for options and warrants?

A—The average market price of common stock during each three-month quarter included in the period being reported upon is used to determine the number of incremental shares included in primary earnings per share computations. When a period of less than three months is being reported upon, the average market price during that period is used. [*36, Exh. B*]

The average market price during each three-month quarter included in the period being reported upon is also used to determine the number of incremental shares included in fully diluted earnings per share computations *unless* (1) the ending market price for the quarter is higher than the average market price or (2) options or warrants were exercised during the quarter. [*42, Exh. B*]

A higher ending market price for the quarter is used in fully diluted computations rather than the average market price. For the fully diluted year-to-date computation, the number of incremental shares produced by applying the ending market price is compared to the number of shares determined by computing a year-to-date weighted average of incremental shares included in the quarterly fully diluted computations. The number of incremental shares used in the fully diluted year-to-date computation is the greater of the number of incremental shares determined from the ending market price or from the weighted average of quarters. (See Interpretation 60 and Exhibit 4 for examples.)

When options or warrants are exercised, the market price on the exercise date is applied for the exercised options or warrants from the beginning of the year to the exercise date for fully diluted computations. Thus, the incremental share computations for quarters prior to the exercise date use the market price at the exercise date rather than the ending or average market price. (See Interpretations 61 and 62 for examples.)

In accordance with the anti-dilution provisions of the Opinion, exercise of options or warrants is not assumed for any quarter when the exercise price is higher than the market price determined for the computation (as described above) except when options or warrants have in fact been exercised. However, anti-dilutive options or warrants would be included in an aggregate computation resulting in a net dilutive effect. [*30, 38, 40, 42*]

Thus, options and warrants may be included in the computations in some quarters but not in other quarters. Also, options and warrants may be included in fully diluted earnings per share computations in a quarter when the ending market price is above the exercise price but not included in primary earnings per share computations for the quarter because the average market price is below the exercise price. [*30, 42*]

---

[27]The incremental number of shares may be more simply computed

$$\frac{\$20 - \$15}{\$20} \times 10,000 = 2,500$$ using the formula given in Interpretation 12.

[28]For fully diluted incremental shares, the computation would be

$$\frac{\$25 - \$15}{\$25} \times 10,000 = 4,000.$$

53. How Many Market Prices?

Q—How many market prices should be used to determine the average market price of common stock when applying the treasury stock method? [*36*]

A—As many market prices as are needed to compute a meaningful average would be used. [*36*]

Theoretically, every market transaction for a company's common stock (both the number of shares and the price per share) could be included in determining the average market price. For example, consider four transactions of: 100 shares at $10 per share, 60 shares at $11 per share, 30 shares at $12 per share, and 10 shares at $13 per share. The average of the four prices would be $11.50 (a simple average) but the average price for the 200 shares would be $10.75 per share (a weighted average).

As a practical matter, however, a simple average of monthly prices is adequate so long as prices do not fluctuate significantly. If prices fluctuate greatly, weekly or daily prices probably would be used. Only if volume of common shares traded and prices at which trades occurred both fluctuated significantly would it be necessary to compute a weighted average to obtain a meaningful average market price.

54. What Market Price to Use?

Q—Should the market price used in computing the average described in Interpretation 53 be the high, low, close or an average of high and low prices?

A—Generally, closing market prices would be adequate for use in computing the average market price. When prices fluctuate widely, however, an average of the high and low prices for the period the price represents (whether a month, week, or day) would usually produce a more representative price to be used. [*36*]

Perhaps more important than the price selected is that the particular price selected be used consistently unless it is no longer representative because of changed conditions. For example, a company using the closing price during several years of relatively stable market prices could change to an average of high and low prices if prices started fluctuating greatly and the closing market price would no longer produce a representative average market price. Likewise, a company using an average of high and low prices during several years of relatively stable volume could use an average weighted by the number of shares included in market transactions during the period if both prices and volume started fluctuating greatly and the simple average of high and low prices would no longer produce a representative average market price. Shorter periods would be more appropriate than longer periods in this case also, as noted in Interpretation 53.

Changing the price, period or method used in computing the average market price would only be done when it becomes obvious that a representative average market price would not be obtained if the change were not made. In the absence of changed conditions a change would not be made.

55. Over-the-Counter and Listed Stocks Not Traded

Q—What price should be used when applying the treasury stock method for an over-the-counter stock or a listed stock not traded?

A—If available, market prices at which trades occur would be used in applying the treasury stock method. For stocks traded over-the-counter, the actual trade prices may not be known. Bid and asked quotations generally are available, however, for both over-the-counter stocks and listed stocks not traded. [*36*]

The price which will be representative of the market price may have to be computed from the information available. An average of the bid and asked quotations might produce a representative price. In some cases, an average of quotations from several dealers could be used. Generally the method selected would be used consistently in the absence of actual market prices.

It should be noted that although bid quotations produce a conservative estimate of a stock's market value, asked quotations are more conservative for earnings per share computations. This is because a higher market price produces more incremental shares under the treasury stock method than does a lower price. Therefore, to obtain a conservative answer, the asked quotation would be used in applying the treasury stock method for listed common stocks not traded and for common stocks traded over the counter.

56. Fair Value Used If No Market Price

Q—How should the average market price be determined, to apply the treasury stock method for options and warrants, if a company's common stock is not traded (for example, for a closely held company with only options outstanding)?

A—When a company's common stock is not traded and market prices are therefore not available, the fair value per share of its common stock is used to apply the treasury stock method for options and warrants. [*33 fn. 9*]

Estimating the fair value of a share of common stock which is seldom, if ever, traded is often difficult. Various methods of valuation may be appropriate under different circumstances. While book value or liquidation value per share may provide some indication of fair value, these amounts usually would not be used without adjustment. Estimations based on replacement value or capitalized earnings value, however, might be used in determining fair value.

In some cases documents may be used as a basis for estimating the fair value of a company's common stock. Personal financial statements of stockholders prepared in accordance with *Audits of Personal Financial Statements* (An AICPA Industry Audit Guide published by the American Institute of CPAs in 1968) would present the estimated value of their stock ownership in the company. Buy and sell agreements contain provisions for determining the value of a stockholder's interest in a company in the event of death or retirement or withdrawal from participation in the company's activities. Estate tax valuations established for recently deceased stockholders may provide a basis for estimating the current value of a company's stock. Merger or sales negotiations entered into by the company and valuations or appraisals obtained by a stockholder or the company for credit purposes may provide established values appropriate for use in estimating the fair value of a company's common stock. A fair value estimate of the stock might also be projected currently from the relationship at the time of issuance of the warrant or option to earnings (on a per share basis) or to the book value of the common stock.

External sources may also be used to obtain a fair value estimate for a company's stock. Traded securities of other companies in the same industry, their price-earnings ratios, dividend yields, and the relationship of their market prices to book values per share may provide guidance for estimating the value of a stock which is not traded. In addition to the methods suggested above, articles in professional publications may suggest other valuation methods and provide more specific guidance for applying selected techniques (for example, see *The Journal of Accountancy,* August 1969, pages 35-47, and March 1966, pages 47-55). Revenue Ruling 59-60 also provides guidance for valuing stocks with no quoted market prices. In some instances, companies have engaged investment bankers to estimate the value of the common stock when management believed a fair value could not be obtained any other way.

When a fair value estimate is used in the absence of market prices for a company's common stock, this fact and the method used to estimate the fair value would be disclosed as required by Opinion paragraph 20. The disclosure would usually be contained in a note to the earnings per share amounts presented (such as the example in Exhibit C of Appendix C to the Opinion). [20]

57. Options and Warrants Outstanding Part of a Period

Q—How should dilutive options or warrants which are outstanding for only part of a period be treated for earnings per share computations?

A—Dilutive options or warrants which are issued during a period or which expire or are cancelled during a period are reflected in both primary and fully diluted earnings per share computations for the time they were outstanding during the period being reported upon. The common equivalent shares to be considered enter earnings per share computations as a weighted average as described in Opinion paragraph 47. [*36, 41, 47*]

For example, assume that a corporation whose financial reporting year ends on December 31 issued 100,000 warrants for one share each on October 8, 1969 with an exercise price of $10. Assume also an average market price for common stock during the intervening twelve-week period of $12 per share. Applying the treasury stock method for primary earnings per share computations for the fourth quarter, the 16,667 incremental shares

$$\left(\text{computed } \frac{\$12 - \$10}{\$12} \times 100,000 = 16,667 \right)$$

would be weighted 12/13, since they were outstanding for only twelve of the thirteen weeks during the quarter, and would represent 15,385 common shares (16,667 × 12/13) in the fourth quarter of 1969. In the annual earnings per share computation for 1969, these warrants would represent 3,846 common shares (15,385 ÷ 4).

If the market price at December 31, 1969 for common stock exceeded the $12 average market price, the higher market price would be used in computing fully diluted earnings per share to reflect maximum potential dilution as specified in Opinion paragraph 42. For a market price of common stock on December 31 of $12.50 per share, the shares to be added for the fourth quarter fully diluted earnings per share would be computed as follows:

$$\frac{\$12.50 - \$10}{\$12.50} \times 100,000 = 20,000$$

$$12/13 \times 20,000 = 18,462 \text{ shares.}$$

The shares to be added for 1969 annual fully diluted earnings per share in this case would be 4,615.

If the warrants described in the above example expired or were cancelled on March 25, 1970 and we assume an average market price for common stock during the twelve weeks then ended of $12, the same results as above would be obtained for primary earnings per share computations for the first quarter of 1970. That is, assumed exercise of the 100,000 warrants would produce 16,667 incremental shares weighted 12/13 and would represent 15,385 common shares in the first quarter of 1970. In the annual earnings per share computations for 1970, these warrants would represent 3,846 common shares.

If the market price of common stock on the *last day the warrants were outstanding* (March 25, 1970) exceeded the $12 average market price for the twelve-week period, the higher market price would be used in computing fully diluted earnings per share to reflect maximum dilution. For a market price of $12.50 on March 25, 1970 in this example, 18,462 shares would be added for the first quarter computations and 4,615 shares would be added for the 1970 annual computations in computing fully diluted earnings per share. [*42*]

Generally, options or warrants which expire or are cancelled will not affect earnings per share computations. The above examples are included only for those rare cases when they do. Most dilutive options and warrants will be exercised prior to expiration or cancellation. Anti-dilutive options and warrants do not enter earnings per share computations,[29] since they would not be exercised when common stock could be purchased for less in the market than through exercise. [*30, 40*]

When dilutive options or warrants expire or are cancelled during a period, it may also be desirable to furnish supplementary earnings per share data as described in Opinion paragraph 22, but previously reported earnings per share data would not be retroactively adjusted for expirations or cancellations of warrants or options. [*22*]

58. What Is a Period?

Q—What is a "period" as the term is used in the Opinion?

A—A "period" is the time for which net income is reported and earnings per share are computed.

However, when the treasury stock method or any method[30] requiring the computation of an average market price is used and the reporting period is longer than three months, a separate computation is made for each three-month period. [*Exh. B*]

If a period of less than a quarter is being reported upon, the average market price of common stock during the period encompassed by the income statement is used in applying the treasury stock methods. Other methods[30] requiring the use of average market prices also use the prices in effect during this shorter period.

59. Share Averaging

Q—When the reporting period is longer than three months and the treasury stock method is applied, how is the weighted average of shares computed for the reporting period?

A—A weighted average of shares is computed based on the average market prices during each three months included in the reporting period. Thus, if the period being reported upon is six months, nine months, or one year, a weighted average[31] of shares is computed for each quarter. The weighted averages for all quarters are then added together, and the resulting total is divided by the number of quarters to determine the weighted average for the period. [*Exh. B*]

Assume, for example, that a corporation had 25,000 shares of common stock outstanding during a year and also had granted options which resulted in the following incremental shares computed using the treasury stock method: 500 in the first quarter, none in the second quarter because they would have been anti-dilutive, 1,400 in the third quarter, and 1,000 in the fourth quarter. The weighted average of shares for the year could be computed either

$$25,500 + 25,000 + 26,400 + 26,000 = 102,900$$
$$102,900 \div 4 = 25,725$$

or

$$\frac{500}{4} + \frac{1,400}{4} + \frac{1,000}{4} = 725$$
$$725 + 25,000 = 25,725$$

60. Applying Ending and Average Market Prices

Q—How do the computations of primary and fully diluted earnings per share differ when the treasury stock method is applied for options and warrants and the ending market price of common stock is different from the average market price?

A—When the ending market price of common stock is higher than the average market price for the period, the ending market price is used for the fully diluted computation to reflect maximum potential dilution. The use of different market prices for primary and fully diluted earnings per share computations naturally results in different numbers of shares for the two computations. The use of a higher ending market price for fully diluted computations may also result in the assumption of exercise for fully diluted earnings per share but not for primary earnings per share. Year-to-date computations for fully diluted earnings per share may also be more complex when market prices of common stock increase and then decrease during the year, since the share computation is then made two ways and the greater number of shares is used in computing year-to-date

---

[29]Except in the unusual situations described in Opinion paragraph 38 and in footnote 6 in Part I.

[30]For example, see Interpretations 67, 70, 77 and 79.

[31]See Interpretation 25 and Exhibit 3 for examples of computing a weighted average.

fully diluted earnings per share. The above situations are illustrated in the following example. [42]

Assume stock options are outstanding to obtain 5,000 shares of common stock at an exercise price of $10 per share. Assume also the following average and ending market prices of common stock during the calendar year:

	Average Market Price	Ending Market Price
First quarter	$11.11	$12.00
Second quarter	9.75	11.00
Third quarter	13.89	14.00
Fourth quarter	12.50	13.00

For primary earnings per share, the treasury stock method would produce the following number of *incremental* shares to reflect the dilutive effect of the options:

	Primary Incremental Shares	
	Quarterly EPS	Year-to-Date EPS
First quarter	500(1)	500
Second quarter	—0—	250(2)
Third quarter	1,400(3)	633(4)
Fourth quarter	1,000(5)	725(6)

COMPUTATIONAL NOTES:

(1) $\dfrac{\$11.11 - \$10}{\$11.11} \times 5,000 = 500$

(2) $500 + 0 = 500.$ $\qquad 500 \div 2 = 250$

(3) $\dfrac{\$13.89 - \$10}{\$13.89} \times 5,000 = 1,400$

(4) $500 + 0 + 1,400 = 1,900.$ $1,900 \div 3 = 633$

(5) $\dfrac{\$12.50 - \$10}{\$12.50} \times 5,000 = 1,000$

(6) $500 + 0 + 1,400 + 1,000 = 2,900.$ $2,900 \div 4 = 725$

For fully diluted earnings per share, the treasury stock method would produce the following number of incremental shares to reflect the maximum dilutive effect of the options:

	Fully Diluted Incremental Shares	
	Quarterly EPS(1)	Year-to-Date EPS
First quarter	833	833
Second quarter	455(2)	644(3)
Third quarter	1,429	1,429(4)
Fourth quarter	1,154	1,154(5)

COMPUTATIONAL NOTES:

(1) Based on ending market price for each quarter.

(2) Note that the *average* market price for this quarter was anti-dilutive, so the computation is made only for fully diluted earnings per share.

(3) $833 + 455 = 1,288.$ $1,288 \div 2 = 644$
Use 644 weighted average since 644 is greater than 455 incremental shares based on ending market price.

(4) $833 + 455 + 1,429 = 2,717.$ $2,717 \div 3 = 906$
Use 1,429 incremental shares based on the ending market price since 1,429 is greater than 906.

(5) $833 + 455 + 1,429 + 1,154 = 3,871.$
$3,871 \div 4 = 968$
Use 1,154 incremental shares based on the ending market price since 1,154 is greater than 968.

Note that the two computations made for year-to-date fully diluted incremental shares may in some cases cause different market prices to be applied for the quarterly and year-to-date fully diluted computations. For example, assume that in the above illustration the average market price in the fourth quarter was $13 and the ending market price was $12.50. The $13 average market price would produce 1,154 incremental shares in the fourth quarter for both primary and fully diluted computations. In the annual fully diluted computation, however, the $12.50 ending market price would produce 1,000 incremental shares while the average number of shares for the four quarters would be only 968 (see computational note 5 above under fully diluted). Therefore the average market price would be used for the fourth quarter fully diluted computation and the ending market price would be used for the annual fully diluted computation.

A more comprehensive example of these points appears in Exhibit 4.

61. Treasury Stock Method at Exercise

Q—How is the treasury stock method applied for options and warrants which are exercised?

A—Common stock issued upon the exercise of options or warrants is included in the weighted average of outstanding shares from the exercise date. The treasury stock method is applied for exercised options or warrants from the beginning of the period to the exercise date. For primary earnings per share, the computation for the period prior to exercise is based on the average market price of common stock during the period the exercised options or warrants were outstanding (if the result is dilutive). Incremental shares are weighted for the period the options or warrants were outstanding and shares issued are weighted for the period the shares were outstanding. For fully diluted earnings per share, however, the computation for the period prior to exercise is based on the market price of common stock when the options or warrants were exercised regardless of whether the result is dilutive or anti-dilutive. Incremental shares are weighted for the period the options or warrants were outstanding and shares issued are weighted for the period the shares are outstanding. These situations are illustrated in the following example. [*42, 47*]

Assume stock options are outstanding to obtain 5,000 shares of common stock at an exercise price of $10 per share. Assume also the following average and ending market prices of common stock during the calendar year:

	Average Market Price	Ending Market Price
First quarter	$11.11	$12.00
Second quarter	9.75	11.00
Third quarter	13.89	14.00
Fourth quarter	12.50	13.00

Also assume that 1,000 options were exercised May 1 when the market price of common stock was $10.50 per share and another 1,000 options were exercised September 1 when the market price of common stock was $15 per share. The average market price from April 1 to May 1 was $11.25 and from July 1 to September 1 was $13.

For primary earnings per share, the treasury stock method would produce the following number of *incremental* shares to reflect the dilutive effect of the options:

Primary Incremental Shares		
	Quarterly EPS	Year-to-Date EPS
First quarter	500	500
Second quarter	37(1)	269(2)
Third quarter	994(3)	510(4)
Fourth quarter	600	533(5)

COMPUTATIONAL NOTES:
(1) 1/3 of 111 incremental shares for 1,000 options exercised May 1 (using $11.25 average market price for the period the options were outstanding). Remaining options are anti-dilutive.
(2) 500 + 37 = 537.   537 ÷ 2 = *269*
(3) 840 incremental shares for 3,000 options outstanding all of the quarter (exercise assumed at $13.89 average market price for the quarter) plus 2/3 of the 231 incremental

shares for 1,000 options outstanding for two months of the quarter (exercise assumed at $13 average market price for the period the options were outstanding). 840 + 154 = *994*
(4) 500 + 37 + 994 = 1,531.
$$1,531 \div 3 = 510$$
(5) 500 + 37 + 994 + 600 = 2,131.
$$2,131 \div 4 = 533$$

In addition, outstanding shares would increase as follows to reflect options *exercised* May 1 and September 1:

Increase in Outstanding Shares		
	Quarterly EPS	Year-to-Date EPS
First quarter	—0—	—0—
Second quarter	667(1)	333(2)
Third quarter	1,333(3)	667(4)
Fourth quarter	2,000(5)	1,000(6)

COMPUTATIONAL NOTES:
(1) 2/3 of 1,000 shares issued May 1 and outstanding for two months.
(2) 0 + 667 = 667.   667 ÷ 2 = *333*
(3) 1,000 shares issued May 1 plus 1/3 of 1,000 shares issued September 1.
(4) 667 + 1,333 = 2,000.   2,000 ÷ 3 = *667*
(5) 1,000 shares issued May 1 plus 1,000 shares issued September 1.
(6) 0 + 667 + 1,333 + 2,000 = 4,000.
$$4,000 \div 4 = 1,000$$

For fully diluted earnings per share, the treasury stock method would produce the following number of *incremental* shares to reflect the maximum dilutive effect of the options:

Fully Diluted Incremental Shares		
	Quarterly EPS	Year-to-Date EPS
First quarter	833	833
Second quarter	380(1)	548(2)
Third quarter	1,079(3)	1,174(4)
Fourth quarter	692(5)	930(6)

COMPUTATIONAL NOTES:
(1) 364 incremental shares for 4,000 options outstanding all of the quarter (using $11 ending market price) plus 1/3 of 48 incremental shares for 1,000 options exercised May 1 (using $10.50 market price at exercise date).

(2) $(667 + 48) + 380 = 1,095. 1,095 \div 2 = 548$. For the first quarter, 667 incremental shares for 4,000 options (using $12 ending market price) plus 48 incremental shares for 1,000 options exercised May 1 (using $10.50 market price at exercise date). See note 1 for second quarter. The incremental shares for the two quarters are then weighted.

(3) 857 incremental shares for 3,000 options outstanding all of the quarter plus 2/3 (333) = 222 incremental shares for 1,000 options exercised September 1 and outstanding two months.

(4) 857 incremental shares for 3,000 options outstanding for all of the three quarters based on $14 higher ending market price applied for all of the three quarters plus 4/9 (48) = 21 for the May 1 exercise plus 8/9 (333) = 296 for the September 1 exercise.

(5) Based on $13 market price and 3,000 options.

(6) $500 + 273 + 857 + 692 = 2,322$.

$$2,322 \div 4 = 581$$

incremental shares for 3,000 options outstanding for four quarters using market prices of $12, $11, $14 and $13 for the respective quarters for computing the weighted average of incremental shares. Since 692 incremental shares determined by applying the ending market price is greater than 581 weighted incremental shares, 692 is used. The 692 is increased by 4/12 (48) = 16 shares for the May 1 exercise plus 8/12 (333) = 222 for the September 1 exercise. $692 + 16 + 222 = 930$.

In addition, outstanding shares would increase by the same number of shares as illustrated for the primary earnings per share computation for the options *exercised* on May 1 and September 1, i.e., 667 shares in the second quarter, 1,333 in the third quarter, 2,000 in the fourth quarter, 333 for the first six months, 667 for the first nine months, and 1,000 for the year.

62. Anti-Dilutive Exercise

Q—Is the treasury stock method applied for options and warrants which are exercised when the market price is below the exercise price?

A—Options or warrants usually would not be exercised in such a situation. The common stock obtainable upon exercise could be purchased in the market for less than the exercise price. However, in those rare cases where such an exercise does occur, the treasury stock method is applied from the beginning of the year to the exercise date for fully diluted computations using the market price at the exercise date. The result will be anti-dilutive. [42]

For primary computations, the average market price from the beginning of the quarter to the exercise date is used, but only if the result is dilutive. Thus, when the average market price is less than the exercise price while the exercised options or warrants were outstanding, the exercised options or warrants are omitted from primary computations. [30, 36]

Common stock issued upon exercise is included in the weighted average of outstanding shares from the exercise date for both primary and fully diluted computations. Shares produced by the treasury stock method are included in the weighted average of outstanding shares for the time the exercised options or warrants were outstanding. [47]

For example, assume stock options are outstanding to obtain 5,000 shares of common stock at an exercise price of $10 per share. Assume also the following average and ending market prices of common stock during the calendar year.

	Average Market Price	Ending Market Price
First quarter	$11.11	$12.00
Second quarter	9.75	11.00
Third quarter	13.89	14.00
Fourth quarter	12.50	13.00

On June 1, 1,000 options were exercised when the market price of common stock was $9.50 per share. The average market price from April 1 to June 1 was $9.65 per share.

For primary earnings per share, the treasury stock method would produce the following number of *incremental* shares to reflect the dilutive effect of the options:

	Primary Incremental Shares	
	Quarterly EPS	Year-to-Date EPS
First quarter	500	500
Second quarter	—0—(1)	250
Third quarter	1,120(2)	540(3)
Fourth quarter	800	605(4)

COMPUTATIONAL NOTES:

(1) Average market price for both outstanding options and exercised options are anti-dilutive.

(2) 1,120 incremental shares for 4,000 options outstanding all of the quarter.

(3) $500 + 0 + 1,120 = 1,620$.

$$1,620 \div 3 = 540$$

(4) $500 + 0 + 1,120 + 800 = 2,420$.

$$2,420 \div 4 = 605$$

In addition, outstanding shares would increase as follows to reflect options *exercised* June 1:

Increase in Outstanding Shares

	Quarterly EPS	Year-to-Date EPS
First quarter	—0—	—0—
Second quarter	333(1)	167(2)
Third quarter	1,000(3)	444(4)
Fourth quarter	1,000(5)	583(6)

COMPUTATIONAL NOTES:
(1) 1/3 of 1,000 shares issued June 1 and outstanding for one month.
(2) 0 + 333 = 333.
    333 ÷ 2 = 167
(3) 1,000 shares issued June 1.
(4) 0 + 333 + 1,000 = 1,333.
    1,333 ÷ 3 = 444
(5) 1,000 shares issued June 1.
(6) 0 + 333 + 1,000 + 1,000 = 2,333.
    2,333 ÷ 4 = 583

For fully diluted earnings per share, the treasury stock method would produce the following number of *incremental* shares to reflect the maximum dilutive effect of the options:

Fully Diluted Incremental Shares

	Quarterly EPS	Year-to-Date EPS
First quarter	833	833
Second quarter	329(1)	472(2)
Third quarter	1,143(3)	1,114(4)
Fourth quarter	923(5)	901(6)

COMPUTATIONAL NOTES:
(1) 364 incremental shares for 4,000 options outstanding all of the quarter *less 2/3* (1,000 − 1,053) = − 35 to reflect the anti-dilutive effect of the exercise of 1,000 options outstanding 2 months during the quarter. 364 − 35 = 329
(2) (667 − 53) + (364 − 35) = 943. 943 ÷ 2 = 472. See note 1. For the first quarter, 667 incremental shares for 4,000 options are reduced by 53 anti-dilutive shares for 1,000 options exercised June 1. The net incremental shares for the two quarters are then weighted.
(3) 1,143 incremental shares for 4,000 options outstanding all of the quarter.

(4) 1,143 incremental shares for 4,000 options outstanding for all of the three quarters based on $14 higher ending market price applied for all of the three quarters *less* 5/9 (53) = − 29 for the June 1 anti-dilutive exercise.
(5) Based on $13 market price and 4,000 options.
(6) 667 + 364 + 1,143 + 923 = 3,097. 3,097 ÷ 4 = 774 incremental shares for 4,000 options outstanding for four quarters using market prices of $12, $11, $14 and $13 for the respective quarters for computing the weighted average of incremental shares. Since 923 incremental shares determined by applying the ending market price is greater than 774 weighted incremental shares, 923 is used. The 923 is decreased by 5/12 (− 53) = − 22 for the June 1 anti-dilutive exercise. 923 − 22 = 901.

In addition, outstanding shares would increase by the same number of shares as illustrated for the primary earnings per share computation for the options *exercised* on June 1, i.e., 333 shares in the second quarter, 1,000 shares in the third and fourth quarters, 167 shares for the first six months, 444 shares for the first nine months, and 583 shares for the year.

63. "Substantially All" of Three Months

Q—How long is "substantially all" of a three-month period and why should exercise of options and warrants not be assumed in applying the treasury stock method "until" the market price has exceeded the exercise price for such a period?

A—"Substantially all" is not defined in the Opinion. Following the recommendation[32] to not assume exercise before the three-month test is met (1) eliminates the need to make the computation until the market price has exceeded the exercise price for a significant period and (2) reduces "flip-flop" of options and warrants in and out of the computation because of the common stock's market price fluctuations above and below the exercise price. [36]
Presumably, eleven weeks would be substantially all of a thirteen-week quarter. Therefore, the computation would be made for any quarter after the market price has once been above the exercise price for any eleven weeks during a quarter.
Note that this is a one-time test. Exercise need not be assumed for the computations *until* the test has been met, not *unless* the test is met in a particular quarter. Thus, once the test is met, the average market price would be computed thereafter unless

---

[32]The Board recommended that exercise of options and warrants not be assumed for earnings per share data *until* the market price has been above the exercise price for *substantially all* of the three months ending with the month for which the computation is being made.

the market prices are clearly anti-dilutive.

The test applies for both primary and fully diluted computations. But after the test has once been met, an ending market price which is above the exercise price is used for the fully diluted computation even though the average market price is below the exercise price. [42]

This recommendation also applies to earnings per share computations for income statements prepared for periods which are less than a quarter. When applied to shorter periods, however, virtually all market prices in the shorter period should be above the exercise price or exercise need not be assumed. For a one-month statement, for example, the market prices during that month and for most of the two preceding months should be above the exercise price. [36]

64. Total of Quarters May Not Equal Annual EPS

Q—Are previously reported earnings per share data ever retroactively adjusted or restated for changes in the incremental number of shares computed using the treasury stock method?

A—No, retroactive adjustment or restatement of previously reported earnings per share data are not made when the incremental number of shares determined by applying the treasury stock method changes. The Board realized that the total of four quarters' earnings per share might not equal the earnings per share for the year when market prices change and the treasury stock method is applied. [36, 41]

Computations for each quarter or other period are independent. Earnings per share data would not either be restated retroactively nor adjusted currently to obtain quarterly (or other period) amounts to equal the amount computed for the year or year to date.

65. Unusual Warrants and Their Equivalents

Q—To what kinds of securities does Opinion paragraph 37 apply?

A—Opinion paragraph 37 must be applied for earnings per share computations for the following kinds of securities, all of which are classified as common stock equivalents:

1. Warrants which *require* the tendering of debt or other securities of the issuer or its parent or its subsidiary in full or partial payment of the exercise price.
2. Warrants which *permit* as an alternative the tendering of debt or other securities of the issuer or its parent or its subsidiary in full or partial payment of the exercise price.
3. Warrants whose proceeds from exercise must be applied toward the retirement of debt or other securities of the issuer. Such debt or other securities would have been issued with the warrants and the requirement to apply any proceeds toward retirement would usually be written into an indenture, making the requirement a contractual obligation.
4. Convertible securities which *require* the payment of cash upon conversion (regardless of their yield at time of issuance).
5. Convertible securities which *permit* the payment of cash as an alternative upon conversion, for example, to obtain a greater number of common shares than could be obtained from straight conversion (regardless of their yield at time of issuance). [37]

66. Securities Subject to Paragraph 37 Tests

Q—Are all of the securities listed in the preceding Interpretation subject to the two tests described in Opinion paragraph 37?

A—The two tests described in Opinion paragraph 37 are tests to determine whether certain warrants are dilutive or anti-dilutive. The "a" test is the usual test to determine if a warrant is dilutive. The "b" test is applied when securities can be tendered in lieu of cash to exercise a warrant. The computations to be made when either or both tests are met are described in Interpretations 67-70. [37]

The "a" test (the market price of the related common stock must exceed the exercise price of the warrant or the convertible security considered the equivalent of a warrant) applies to warrants (1) which require the tendering of debt, (2) which permit the tendering of debt, and (3) whose proceeds must be used to retire debt.

The "b" test (the security to be tendered is selling at enough discount to establish an effective exercise price below the market price of the common stock obtainable) applies only to the debt or other securities which must or may be tendered toward the exercise price of the warrant (the debt listed in 1 and 2 in Interpretation 65). The "b" test gives recognition to the possibility that a warrant holder could purchase debt in the market at a discount and exercise a warrant by tendering the debt at its face amount, thereby effecting the purchase of the common stock for less than its market price.

These tests are demonstrated in the following example. Assume that a warrant may be exercised to purchase two shares of common stock by tendering either $100 cash or a $100 face value debenture when market prices are $48 per common share, $94 per debenture, and $6 per warrant. The "a" test is not met (2 × $48 = $96 market price of common does not exceed the exercise price of $100 cash). The "b" test is met. (The $94 market price of the debenture is below the $96 market price for two shares of common. This may also be computed

$$\frac{\$94 \text{ market price of debenture}}{\$100 \text{ tender value of debenture}} \times$$

$50 exercise price per share = $47 effective exercise price per share.) Note that the market price of the warrant is not considered in either test.

The "a" and "b" tests apply to securities on an individual basis. However, when Opinion paragraph 38 applies (see Interpretations 72-74), the securities subject to these tests are included in the aggregate computation required by that paragraph whether their individual effect is dilutive or anti-dilutive. [*35, 38*]

67. Market Prices Used in Paragraph 37 Tests

Q—What market prices are used for the two tests described in Opinion paragraph 37?

A—The market prices used for these two tests and for the computations when the tests are met correspond to the market prices used for the treasury stock method (see Interpretations 52-56). Therefore, the computations are made for each quarter and the shares for the quarters are averaged for annual primary computations. [*37*]

The market price of common stock for both tests is the average market price during each three-month quarter included in the period being reported upon. The ending market price of common stock is used, however, for fully diluted earnings per share if the ending price is *higher* than the average price. [*42, Exh. B*]

For the "b" test, the average market price of the debt or other security during each three-month quarter included in the period being reported upon is used. The ending market price of the debt or other security is used, however, for fully diluted earnings per share if the ending price is *lower* than the average price. [*37*]

Usually, only one test will be met. In some cases, however, both tests will be met. Also, different tests may be met for primary and fully diluted computations. The computations to be made in these situations are explained in Interpretations 68 and 69. When neither test is met, these securities are not included in earnings per share computations unless Opinion paragraph 38 applies. [*35, 38*]

68. Computations for Warrants Requiring the Tendering of Debt

Q—What computations are made under the "a" and "b" tests specified in Opinion paragraph 37 for warrants which require that debt or other securities be tendered upon exercise?

A—If either the "a" or "b" test described in Interpretations 66 and 67 is met when debt or other securities *must* be tendered toward the exercise price, exercise of the warrants is assumed. The debt or other security is tendered at the amount it must be tendered (usually face amount). Interest, net of tax, on the debt is added back to net income in determining earnings applicable to common stock. Common stock is assumed to be issued on the exercise date. The treasury stock method is applied for any cash proceeds when cash is also to be tendered with the debt. The fact that both tests may sometimes be met does not affect the computations. [*37*]

69. Computations for Warrants Allowing the Tendering of Debt

Q—What computations are made under the "a" and "b" tests specified in Opinion paragraph 37 for warrants which permit the tendering of debt or other securities upon exercise?

A—The computations depend upon the test met. If both tests are met, the computations depend upon the alternatives available since some warrants and their equivalents provide two or more exercise or conversion alternatives to the holder. For example, a warrant may be exercisable by paying $60 cash to obtain one share of common stock or by tendering $100 face value debt to obtain two shares of common stock. In such a case, debt *may* be tendered but is not required to be tendered. [*37*]

When only the "a" test is met (because the debt or other security is selling for more than the amount for which it may be tendered), the treasury stock method is applied since the debt or other security would not be tendered toward exercise of the warrant or its equivalent.

When only the "b" test is met (the debt or other security which may be tendered is selling at enough discount to create an effective exercise price below the market price of the common stock), the procedures described in Interpretation 68 (for when debt or other securities *must* be tendered) are applied.

If *both* the "a" and "b" tests described above are met when debt or other securities *may* be tendered toward the exercise price or if two or more exercise or conversion alternatives meet one test (whether or not both tests are met), the computation should be based upon the alternative which meets the test and is more (or most) advantageous to the holder of the warrant or its equivalent. [*58*]

The "a" and "b" tests are applied for each quarter using the market prices specified in Interpretation 67. When either test is met, the computations are made for that quarter. Different tests may apply for different quarters in the period. The shares determined for each quarter are averaged for year-to-date primary computations. In fully diluted year-to-date computations, the greater of the average number of shares included in the fully diluted quarterly computations or the number of shares determined by applying ending market prices is used. [*Exh. B*]

70. Computations for Warrants Whose Proceeds Are Applied To Retire Debt

Q—How are warrants whose proceeds must be used to retire debt or other securities included in earnings per share computations?

A—When debt or other securities of the issuer require that the proceeds from the exercise of warrants or their equivalents be applied toward retirement of those securities, exercise of the warrants is assumed at the beginning of the period (or time of issuance, if later). The proceeds from exercise are assumed to have been used to purchase the securities to be retired at the date of assumed exercise. [*37*]

These computations are made on a quarterly basis. The shares determined for each quarter are averaged for annual earnings per share computations. The purchase price to be used is the average market price during each three-month quarter for the securities assumed to have been purchased. To reflect maximum potential dilution, the purchase price for the computation of fully diluted earnings per share is the market price of the securities to be retired at the end of the period if this price is *higher* than the average market price. [*42, Exh. B*]

Exercise of the warrants is not assumed for either primary or fully diluted earnings per share unless the market price of the related common stock exceeds the exercise price of the warrants.[33] When exercise is assumed and the proceeds from exercise are used to purchase securities to be retired, interest (net of tax) on any debt retired must be added back to net income in determining earnings applicable to common stock. Any excess amount from the assumed exercise of the warrants above the amount needed for the purchase of securities is used to purchase common stock under the treasury stock method. [*30, 37, 40*]

71. Treasury Stock Method for Convertibles

Q—How are convertible securities which require or permit the payment of cash at conversion included in earnings per share computations?

A—Convertible securities which require or permit the payment of cash at conversion are considered the equivalents of warrants and are therefore always[34] common stock equivalents. [*37*]

Convertible securities requiring the payment of cash are assumed to be converted at the beginning of the period (or time of issuance, if later) and the if converted method is applied. Proceeds from conversion are used to purchase common stock under the treasury stock method. Thus, the incremental number of shares assumed to be outstanding is the difference between the number of shares issued upon assumed conversion and the number of shares assumed purchased under the treasury stock method. If the net result of the aggregate computation of applying both the if converted method and the treasury stock method is dilutive, these computations are included in both primary and fully diluted earnings per share. The computations are not included, however, if the net result is anti-dilutive.[35] [*30, 40*]

Some convertible securities permit the payment of cash at conversion to obtain a more favorable conversion rate. The procedures described in the preceding paragraph are applied for such securities except that no proceeds are assumed to be received upon conversion whenever the amount of cash to be paid exceeds the market value of the additional shares obtainable. The treasury stock method therefore cannot be applied when this condition exists and only the if converted method is applied (if the result is dilutive).[35] [*37, 58*]

When several conversion alternatives exist (for example, permitting the payment of different amounts of cash for different conversion rates), the computation should give effect to the alternative which is most advantageous to the holder of the convertible security. [*58*]

72. Anti-Dilutive Options and Warrants Included

Q—When Opinion paragraph 38 applies (the number of common shares obtainable upon exercise of all options and warrants exceeds 20% of the number of common shares outstanding at the end of the period), are anti-dilutive options and warrants assumed to be exercised as well as dilutive options and warrants?

A—Yes, when Opinion paragraph 38 applies, all options and warrants and their equivalents are assumed to be exercised (or converted) whether they are dilutive or anti-dilutive. Under this exception to the general rule that computations should not give effect to anti-dilution, all of the computations specified in paragraphs 36, 37, and 38 are made and aggregated. If the net result is dilutive, all are included. If the net result is anti-dilutive, all are excluded. [*35, 36, 37, 38*]

---

[33]Exercise may be assumed, however, if Opinion paragraph 38 applies. See Interpretations 72-74.

[34]Unless issued before June 1, 1969 and classified under election "b" of Opinion paragraph 46.

[35]Conversion may be assumed even if the result is anti-dilutive when Opinion paragraph 38 applies. See Interpretations 72-74 and Opinion paragraphs 35 and 38.

73. No Order for Exercise

Q—When Opinion paragraph 38 applies and several issues of options and warrants with different exercise prices are outstanding, which options and warrants should be assumed to be exercised to obtain common stock under the treasury stock method, i.e., may anti-dilutive options and warrants be used in applying the treasury stock method or is the treasury stock method applicable only for dilutive options and warrants?

A—All options and warrants are assumed to be exercised when Opinion paragraph 38 applies without regard to whether the proceeds will be applied to purchase common stock under the treasury stock method or will be applied to the retirement of debt. Specific options or warrants are not to be allocated for the treasury stock method, but rather all options and warrants are assumed to be exercised and the number of common shares assumed to be repurchased under the treasury stock method may not exceed 20% of the number of common shares outstanding at the end of the period. [*38*]

74. Explanation of 20% Provision

Q—How is the 20% provision described in Opinion paragraph 38 applied?

A—20% is used in two ways in Opinion paragraph 38. First, a 20% *test* is applied[36] to outstanding common shares. If the 20% test is met, an aggregate computation is required and all options and warrants and their equivalents are assumed to be exercised. Then a 20% *limitation* is applied to the number of common shares purchased under the treasury stock method. [*38*]

Even though the 20% test is met, the number of shares purchased under the treasury stock method may be below the 20% limitation if the market price is high relative to the exercise price. For example, if 1,000,000 common shares and warrants to obtain 500,000 shares were outstanding, the 20% test would be met and the 20% limitation for the treasury stock method would be 200,000 shares. At an exercise price of $10 and a market price of $50, however, only 100,000 shares could be purchased under the treasury stock method.

Note that the 20% limitation applies only to shares assumed *purchased* under the treasury stock method. It does not apply to the number of incremental shares which results from the computation.

In the above example, 400,000 incremental shares resulted from the assumed issuance of 500,000 shares upon exercise and the assumed purchase of 100,000 shares under the treasury stock method.

In addition, some warrants and their equivalents for which the treasury stock method may not be applicable result in the assumed issuance of common stock. They are therefore included in applying the 20% test and are included in the aggregate computation if the test is met. For example, warrants whose proceeds must be used to retire debt are included in applying the 20% test and in the aggregate computation if the test is met. Only the proceeds in excess of the amount required for debt retirement would be eligible for the treasury stock method, however. Warrants assumed to be exercised by tendering debt or other securities would also be included in applying the 20% test and in the aggregate computation if the test is met. But only if both cash and debt or other securities were assumed tendered would there be any proceeds eligible for the treasury stock method. Convertible securities which require or permit the payment of cash at conversion are considered the equivalent of warrants. Such convertible securities would be included in applying the 20% test and in the aggregate computation if the test is met. [*35, 37, 38*]

Most convertible securities, however, (those which do *not* require or permit the payment of cash at conversion) are *not* included in applying the 20% test. Nor are other securities which are not options or warrants or their equivalents included in the 20% test. For example, the usual participating securities, two-class common stocks and common stock issuable when specified conditions are met are not included in the 20% test. [*27, 33*]

Securities which are not included in the 20% test are not included in the aggregate computation[37] described in Opinion paragraph 38. Thus, even if the net result of the aggregate computation is anti-dilutive and therefore not included in the earnings per share computation, other securities not included in the aggregate computation would be included in the earnings per share computations if they are dilutive. [*15, 38*]

75. Original Issue Premium or Discount

Q—What treatment is accorded to any original issue premium or discount when debt is assumed acquired under the provisions of Opinion paragraphs 37 and 38?

A—Original issue premium or discount is treated

---

[36] A corporation which has made election "b" of Opinion paragraph 46 would apply this test for both primary and fully diluted earnings per share computations, since the number of shares obtainable from options and warrants may differ for the two computations as described in Interpretation 81.

[37] However, convertible debt assumed to be retired with proceeds from exercise in excess of the amount required for applying the treasury stock method would be included in the aggregate computation and its interest would be eliminated as described in Opinion paragraph 51.

as specified in Interpretation 40, i.e., applicable premium or discount amortized during the period is eliminated from net income. Unamortized premium or discount is not included in earnings applicable to common stock and does not affect earnings per share. [*51*]

76. Redemption Premium or Discount

Q—What treatment is accorded to any redemption premium or discount when debt is assumed acquired under the provisions of Opinion paragraphs 37 and 38?

A—Redemption premium or discount, i.e., the difference between the purchase price and the "book" carrying amount of debt, is ignored for earnings per share computations. [*51*]

Redemption premium or discount could occur only when the proceeds from the assumed exercise of options and warrants are applied to purchase debt at the market price under the provisions of either Opinion paragraph 37 or paragraph 38. Redemption premium or discount is not included in earnings applicable to common stock and does not affect earnings per share.

Common shares are, of course, assumed to be issued for all options and warrants assumed to be exercised. [*36, 42*]

77. Debt Purchased Under Opinion Paragraph 38

Q—What debt may the issuer assume is purchased when the provisions of Opinion paragraph 38 apply?

A—The issuer may select any debt which is eligible to be retired for assumed purchase when the provisions of Opinion paragraph 38 apply. This includes convertible debt (both common stock equivalents and other potentially dilutive securities) except that convertible debt may not be assumed purchased if the purchase would be anti-dilutive (that is, result in less dilution). Debt is eligible to be retired when it either may be "called" or is trading and could be purchased in the market. [*30, 38, 40*]

The same debt is assumed purchased for both primary and fully diluted earnings per share computations. Different amounts of debt may be assumed purchased, however, since different market prices may have to be used for the primary and fully diluted computations for the treasury stock method. The average market price of the debt during each quarter for which the computations are made is used for both the primary and fully diluted computations under Opinion paragraph 38. [*38*]

78. Compensating Balances Excluded

Q—When Opinion paragraph 38 applies and a loan is assumed to be paid, what treatment is accorded to any compensating balance maintained for the loan?

A—A compensating balance maintained for a loan assumed to be paid is excluded from consideration in applying Opinion paragraph 38. Although a compensating balance increases the effective interest rate on a loan to the borrower, only the actual interest paid or accrued (less applicable income tax) is adjusted against net income for earnings per share computations. [*38*]

79. Investments Under Paragraph 38

Q—What securities are eligible for assumed purchase as investments when the provisions of Opinion paragraph 38 apply?

A—Only U.S. government securities and commercial paper are eligible for assumed purchase as investments when the provisions of Opinion paragraph 38 apply. Tax-exempt securities of state and local governments are not eligible. The same securities are assumed purchased as investments for both primary and fully diluted earnings per share computations. Different amounts may have to be assumed invested for primary and fully diluted computations, however. [*38*]

U.S. government securities, in the context of Opinion paragraph 38, are securities issued by the federal government, not merely securities guaranteed by the federal government. Typically the securities to be considered would be short-term securities, such as Treasury bills.

80. Debt Eligible Only While Outstanding

Q—When Opinion paragraph 38 applies and debt assumed purchased was actually outstanding only part of the period, may the assumed purchase apply for the entire period?

A—No, debt issued or retired during the period may be assumed purchased at its average market price under Opinion paragraph 38 only for the time the debt was actually outstanding. Since all computations under this paragraph are made on a quarterly basis, the issue or retirement typically affects only one quarter. An investment in U.S. government securities or commercial paper must be assumed for the time when debt was not outstanding and therefore could not be purchased. Any difference in interest (net of tax) between the debt and the investment naturally is reflected in earnings applicable to common stock. [*38*]

81. Computations May Differ for Primary and Fully Diluted when Paragraph 38 Applies

Q—Will Opinion paragraph 38 always apply for both primary and fully diluted computations if it applies to either?

A—No, in some cases Opinion paragraph 38 may apply for fully diluted computations but not for primary computations. This could occur when an issuer has made election "b" under Opinion paragraph 46 and the common shares obtainable upon exercise of options and warrants issued before June 1, 1969 exceed 20% of the common shares outstanding. Opinion paragraph 38 applies in such a case for fully diluted but not for primary computations because the options and warrants issued before June 1, 1969 are included only in fully diluted computations. [38, 46]

Even if the common shares obtainable upon exercise of options and warrants issued before June 1, 1969 do not exceed 20% of the outstanding common shares when election "b" is in effect, the subsequent issuance of additional options or warrants could cause Opinion paragraph 38 to apply for fully diluted but not for primary computations. In such a case, Opinion paragraph 38 would be applied only for fully diluted computations because options and warrants issued before June 1, 1969 would not be included in primary computations. [38, 46]

The computation of primary and fully diluted earnings per share would also differ if Opinion paragraph 38 applied for both computations, but the net result in primary is anti-dilutive and is dilutive in fully diluted. This could occur when the ending market price is above the exercise price but the average market price is below the exercise price. In such a case, the computations would be included only for determining fully diluted earnings per share. [30, 36, 38, 42]

82. Deferred Compensation Stock Option

Q—What treatment for earnings per share computations should be accorded to an employee deferred compensation plan with the compensation to be paid in stock?

A—Stock to be issued to an employee under a deferred compensation plan is considered a stock option. The time of issuance is the agreement date (or "date of grant"). The fact that the employee may not receive (or be able to sell) the stock until more than five or ten years from the statement date does not affect the computation. Accordingly, all shares to be issued are considered outstanding and the treasury stock method is applied to determine the incremental number of shares to be included in the earnings per share computations. The exercise amount of the option is the sum of the amount the employee must pay, the unamortized deferred compensation, and any tax benefit[38] credited to capital surplus. The exercise amount is divided by the market price[39] per share of the common stock to determine the number of shares assumed to be purchased. [29, 35, 36, 57, 58]

For primary earnings per share computations, the average unamortized deferred compensation for the period and the average market price of the issuer's common stock are used. For fully diluted earnings per share computations, the unamortized deferred compensation at the end of the period and, if higher than the average market price, the ending market price of the issuer's common stock are used.

For example, assume that on December 31, 1968[40] a corporation grants options to its president for the purchase of 6,000 shares of its common stock at $2 per share, with options for 1,000 shares exercisable each July 1 and January 1 for three years as partial compensation for services during the preceding six months. The shares issued cannot be sold within three years of the issue date. At time of the grant of the options (December 31, 1968[41]), the 6,000 shares have a fair value of $10 per share (the market price of common is $12 per share). Also assume that the fair value per share increases steadily during the three years at the rate of $1 per quarter (the market price of common increases $1.20) and the tax rate is 50%. (The corporation follows the

---

[38]The tax benefit is the "windfall" tax credit resulting from an increase in the market price of the stock between the date the plan is entered into and the date the compensation charge is deductible for tax purposes (based on market value of the stock when measurable). Since the compensation is charged on the financial statements against the period benefited, the tax related to the charge results in a timing difference for interperiod tax allocation. If the market price of the stock increases, the additional reduction in taxes is a permanent difference (i.e., a "windfall" gain). Some persons believe this difference should be credited to income while others believe it should be credited to capital surplus. (See pages 11-12 of *Accounting for Income Taxes: An Interpretation of APB Opinion No. 11* by Donald J. Bevis and Raymond E. Perry, AICPA, 1969). If credited to capital surplus, the "windfall" gain is considered part of the proceeds from the stock compensation plan which would be used to purchase stock under the treasury stock method.

[39]Fair value per share rather than market price is used if a restriction on the sale of the stock makes it worth less than the market price of freely trading stock. Fair value might be stated as a fraction or a percentage of market price. For example, if the restriction reduced the value approximately 1/6, a stock with a $12 market price would have a fair value of $10 per share (5/6 of $12).

[40]Plans entered into after April 21, 1969 are subject to the 1969 *Tax Reform Act*. Because the income tax treatment for such plans under this Act is different from that described in this Interpretation, many persons believe that use of such plans in the future will decrease substantially.

[41]This example assumes the corporation makes election "a" under Opinion paragraph 46. If election "b" were made, only the fully diluted computations would apply, since "time of issuance" of the options is the date of grant.

practice of crediting the "windfall" tax benefit to capital surplus.) The total compensation to be charged to expense over the three-year period is $48,000

$$\left\{ \frac{\$10}{\$12} \right\} \times \$12 =$$

$10 fair value reduced by the $2 option price results in $8 per share compensation multiplied by 6,000 shares$\left. \right\}$

At March 31, 1969, the unamortized deferred compensation is $44,000 ($48,000 − $4,000) and the windfall tax benefit is $3,600 ($1.20 × 6,000 = $7,200 increase in market multiplied by .50 tax rate). The total exercise price is $12,000 (6,000 × $2). For primary computations, averages of $46,000 unamortized deferred compensation and $1,800 windfall tax benefit plus the $12,000 total exercise price produce $59,800 "proceeds" for the total exercise amount. Dividing by the average fair value of $10.50 ($10 + $11 = $21 divided by 2) results in 5,695 shares assumed repurchased under the treasury stock method. Therefore, 305 incremental shares (6,000 − 5,695) are assumed to be outstanding for the first quarter in the primary computation. For fully diluted computations, 582 incremental shares are computed:

$$\$44,000 + \$3,600 + \$12,000 = \$59,600$$
$$\$59,600 \div \$11 = 5,418$$
$$6,000 - 5,418 = 582$$

At June 30, 1969, the second quarter primary computation would include 835 incremental shares and fully diluted would include 1,067 incremental shares computed:

$$\$42,000 + \$5,400 + \$12,000 = \$59,400$$
$$\$59,400 \div \$11.50 = 5,165$$
$$6,000 - 5,165 = 835$$
$$\$40,000 + \$7,200 + \$12,000 = \$59,200$$
$$\$59,200 \div \$12 = 4,933$$
$$6,000 - 4,933 = 1,067$$

On July 1, 1969, 1,000 shares would be issued to the president and are outstanding shares thereafter.[42] At September 30, 1969, the treasury stock method would produce 560 incremental shares for the third quarter primary and 769 incremental shares for fully diluted computed:

$$\$38,000 + \$7,500 + \$10,000 = \$55,500$$
$$\$55,500 \div \$12.50 = 4,440$$
$$5,000 - 4,440 = 560$$
$$\$36,000 + \$9,000 + \$10,000 = \$55,000$$
$$\$55,000 \div \$13 = 4,231$$
$$5,000 - 4,231 = 769$$

At December 31, 1969, the treasury stock method would produce 963 incremental shares for the fourth quarter primary and 1,143 incremental shares for fully diluted computed:

$$\$34,000 + \$10,500 + \$10,000 = \$54,500$$
$$\$54,500 \div \$13.50 = 4,037$$
$$5,000 - 4,037 = 963$$
$$\$32,000 + \$12,000 + \$10,000 = \$54,000$$
$$\$54,000 \div \$14 = 3,857$$
$$5,000 - 3,857 = 1,143$$

The deferred compensation payable in stock would produce the following shares of common stock to be included in the corporation's 1969 annual earnings per share computations:

	Primary Compu- tations	Fully Diluted Computations
Incremental shares from application of the treasury stock method:		
First quarter	305	1,067(1)
Second quarter	835	1,067
Third quarter	560	1,143(2)
Fourth quarter	963	1,143
Totals	2,663	4,420
Shares for weighted average (divide totals by 4)	666	1,105
Shares issued (1,000 ÷ 2)	500	500
Total shares	1,166	1,605

COMPUTATIONAL NOTES:
(1) 582 incremental shares computed for first quarter fully diluted not used in annual computation. 1,067 incremental shares based on $12 fair value at July 1 "exercise date" when the stock was issued.
(2) 769 incremental shares computed for third quarter fully diluted not used in annual computation. 1,143 incremental shares based on $14 ending fair value for the fourth quarter.

If the market or fair value of the stock should subsequently fall below the market value at the date of grant, the application of the treasury stock method would be anti-dilutive. In such a case, the treasury stock method would not be applied and any unissued shares would not be considered outstanding for earnings per share computations. [30, 40]

The procedures described above are also used for deferred compensation plans to be paid in stock

---

[42] The amount of the tax benefit for each share issued will be the lesser of the difference between the $2 exercise price and (1) the market price of the unrestricted stock when the restricted stock is issued or (2) the market price when restrictions lift. Changes in the windfall tax gain after the stock is issued are ignored in this computation since the compensation paid in stock is considered finalized upon issuance in this example.

which do not require the employee to make a payment to obtain the stock. In such plans, the option price is zero. The period for measuring compensation under such plans is generally the period over which the restrictions lift. Although the plans are different, the procedures described in this Interpretation are applied with the zero option price offset by an increase in the unamortized deferred compensation. Also, these procedures would be applied for earnings per share computations whether or not the plan has been recorded by the company prior to the issuance of the stock. [35, 36, 39]

Whether or not these procedures apply to "phantom" or "shadow" stock deferred compensation plans depends upon the nature of the plan. These plans may require the employer corporation to (1) either issue stock or pay cash for the stock's value to the employee at a future date or (2) pay the employee in cash at a future date for any increase in the stock's value. Most "phantom" stock plans are based on the employer corporation's stock but some of these plans are based on the stock of an unrelated corporation selected by the employee. Additionally, these plans may either be "funded" or "unfunded." Funding may be accomplished by periodically setting aside any cash to be paid out under the plan or by purchasing stock (which may subsequently be issued or sold to fulfill the plan) or, in the case of plans based on the employer corporation's stock, by reserving unissued or treasury shares.

Phantom stock deferred compensation plans based on the employer corporation's stock (or the stock of a parent or subsidiary corporation) are included in earnings per share computations under the procedures described above in this Interpretation. However, plans requiring the employer to pay cash rather than stock to the employee are an exception if stock will not be sold to provide the cash. Such plans affect earnings per share only through any compensation charged against net income, since the stock value determines the compensation amount and stock is not issued.

Phantom stock plans based on the stock of an unrelated corporation likewise affect earnings per share only through any compensation charged against net income, since the employer corporation's stock is in no way involved in the plan.

83. Stock Subscriptions Are Warrants

Q—How are stock subscriptions included in earnings per share computations?

A—Fully paid stock subscriptions are considered outstanding stock whether or not the shares have actually been issued. Partially paid stock subscriptions are considered the equivalents of warrants and are therefore always[43] common stock equivalents.

The unpaid balance is assumed to be proceeds used to purchase stock under the treasury stock method. [35]

The number of shares included in earnings per share computations for partially paid stock subscriptions is the difference between the number of shares subscribed and the number of shares assumed to be purchased under the treasury stock method.

The procedures described above are used for subscriptions to purchase convertible securities as well as for subscriptions to purchase common stock. Any incremental convertible securities resulting are then assumed to be converted into common stock if the result is dilutive (see Interpretation 84).

84. Options or Warrants to Purchase Convertible Securities

Q—What treatment is accorded options or warrants to purchase convertible securities?

A—Options or warrants to purchase convertible securities are assumed to be exercised to purchase the *convertible* security whenever the market price of both the convertible security and the common stock obtainable upon conversion are above the exercise price of the warrant. However, exercise is not assumed unless conversion of the *outstanding* convertible securities is also assumed. The treasury stock method is applied to determine the incremental number of convertible securities which are assumed to be issued and immediately converted into common stock. The if converted adjustments which would be applicable to the incremental convertible securities are ignored since the adjustments would be self-cancelling, i.e., any interest or dividends imputed to the incremental convertible securities would be cancelled in applying the if converted method. [30, 36, 40, 51]

For example, assume that a corporation issued 10,000 warrants exercisable to obtain its $100 par value 5% convertible debt. Each warrant may be exercised at $90 to obtain one convertible bond. Each bond is convertible into two shares of common stock. The market prices of the securities are $46 per common share and $95 per convertible bond. The warrants are dilutive (2 × $46 = $92 which is greater than the $90 exercise price).

Assumption of exercise would produce $900,000 proceeds, which would be used to purchase 9,474 convertible bonds, resulting in 526 incremental bonds. Conversion would be assumed and 1,052 shares of common (2 × 526 = 1,052) would be assumed issued to replace the 526 convertible bonds. [36]

If the market price of common were $45 per share or less, exercise would not be assumed (for example,

---

[43]Unless subscribed before June 1, 1969 and election "b" under Opinion paragraph 46 is made.

at $42 per share, 2 × $42 = $84 which is less than $90).

The classification of the convertible security as a common stock equivalent or other potentially dilutive security determines whether the incremental number of common shares enters primary and fully diluted or enters only fully diluted earnings per share computations. [33]

Two-Class Common Stock and Participating Securities

85. EPS Treatment of Two-Class and Participating Securities

Q—How are two-class common stocks and participating securities treated for earnings per share computations?

A—Two-class common is a term applied when a corporation has issued more than one class of common stock (for example, Class A and Class B). A participating security is a security eligible to participate in dividends with common stock; often a fixed amount is guaranteed to the participating security, then common is paid a dividend at the same rate, and the security participates with common on a reduced ratio thereafter. Classes of common stock other than "ordinary" common stock and the participating securities may be convertible into "ordinary" common stock or may be nonconvertible and may or may not be senior to common stock.

For example, some stocks may be designated as common stock (e.g., Class B Common), but their terms and conditions are equivalent to preferred stock (by limiting their voting rights or the amount of dividends they may receive and by giving them preferences in liquidation). If dividends are guaranteed in some way but limited in participation to a maximum for a particular class of common stock, that common stock is considered the equivalent of a senior security to the extent it is to share in earnings.

If dividend participation for a particular class of common stock is not limited but the participation is at a rate different from the "ordinary" common stock (for example, participating equally to some amount per share and partially participating thereafter), the two-class method is used. The two-class method is also used for participating preferred stock which is not limited as to participation in dividends with common stock. The two-class method is modified, however, when it is applied for a convertible security. (See Interpretation 87.) To be applied for a convertible security, the two-class method must result in greater dilution than would result from application of the if converted method. [54, 55]

A determination of the status of a two-class common stock or other participating security as a common stock equivalent or as an other potentially dilutive security is based on an analysis of all the characteristics of the security, including the ability to share in the earnings potential of the issuing corporation on substantially the same basis as the common stock. Dividend participation *per se* does not make such a security a common stock equivalent. [60]

The two-class method of computation for nonconvertible securities is discussed in Interpretation 86. The two-class method of computation for convertible securities is discussed in Interpretation 87.

86. Two-Class Method for Nonconvertible Securities

Q—How is the two-class method applied for nonconvertible securities?

A—The two-class method for nonconvertible securities is an earnings allocation formula which determines earnings per share for each class of common stock and participating security according to dividends paid and participation rights in undistributed earnings. [55]

Under the two-class method, net income is first reduced by the amount of dividends actually paid for the period to each class of stock and by the contractual amount of any dividends (or interest on participating income bonds) which must be paid (for example, unpaid cumulative dividends or dividends declared during the period and paid during the following period). The remaining unencumbered undistributed earnings is secondly allocated to common stock and participating securities to the extent each security may share in earnings. The total earnings allocated to each security is determined by adding together the amount allocated for dividends and the amount allocated for a participation feature.

This amount is divided by the number of outstanding shares of the security to which the earnings are allocated to determine the earnings per share for the security. For this computation, outstanding common stock (the "ordinary" class of common stock) includes the usual common stock equivalent securities assumed to be converted or exercised for primary computations and includes these securities and all other potentially dilutive securities assumed to be converted or exercised for fully diluted computations. Although reporting earnings per share for each class of security may be desirable, earnings per share must be reported for the "ordinary" class of common stock.

The application of the two-class method for a nonconvertible security is illustrated in the following example. Assume that a corporation had 5,000 shares of $100 par value nonconvertible preferred stock and 10,000 shares of $50 par value common stock outstanding during 1969 and had a net income of $65,000. The preferred stock is entitled to a non-cumulative annual dividend of $5 per share before any dividend is paid on common. After common has been paid a dividend of $2 per share, the preferred stock then participates in any additional dividends on a 40:60 *per share* ratio with common. That is, after preferred and common have been paid dividends of $5 and $2 per share respectively, preferred participates in any additional dividends at a rate of two-thirds of the additional amount paid to common on a per share basis. Also assume that for 1969 preferred shareholders have been paid $27,000 (or $5.40 per share) and common shareholders have been paid $26,000 (or $2.60 per share). Earnings per share for 1969 would be computed as follows under the two-class method for nonconvertible securities:

Net income		$65,000
Less dividends paid:		
Preferred	$27,000	
Common	26,000	53,000
Undistributed 1969 earnings		$12,000

Allocation of undistributed earnings:

To preferred:
$$\frac{.4(5,000)}{.4(5,000) + .6(10,000)} \times \$12,000 = \$3,000$$
$$\$3,000 \div 5,000 \text{ shares} = \$.60 \text{ per share.}$$

To common:
$$\frac{.6(10,000)}{.4(5,000) + .6(10,000)} \times \$12,000 = \$9,000$$
$$\$9,000 \div 10,000 \text{ shares} = \$.90 \text{ per share.}$$

Earnings per share amounts:

	Preferred Stock	Common Stock
Distributed earnings	$5.40	$2.60
Undistributed earnings	.60	.90
Totals	$6.00	$3.50

87. *Two-Class Method for Convertible Securities*

Q—How is the two-class method applied for convertible securities?

A—Most convertible two-class common stocks and other convertible participating securities are assumed to be converted and the if converted method is applied for earnings per share computations. The two-class method is rarely appropriate for such convertible securities and may be applied only when it results in greater dilution than would result from the if converted method. [*51, 54*]

When the two-class method is used for a convertible two-class common or other convertible participating security, net income is first allocated under the procedure described in Interpretation 86 for dividends for the current period which were paid or declared or are cumulative if not paid or declared. Conversion of the convertible two-class common and participating securities is then assumed, but adjustments to net income usually made for the if converted method are *not* made. Unencumbered undistributed earnings is divided by the total of all common shares outstanding and assumed outstanding from conversions and exercise. The resulting amount per share is added to the amount of the dividends per share allocated to each class of security to determine the earnings per share for each class of security. Although reporting earnings per share for each class of security may be desirable, earnings per share must be reported for the "ordinary" class of common stock. [*55*]

The application of the two-class method for a convertible security is illustrated in the following example. Assume that a corporation had 10,000 shares of Class A common stock (the "ordinary" common) and 5,000 shares of Class B common stock outstanding during 1969 and had a net income of $65,000. Each share of Class B is convertible into two shares of Class A. The Class B is entitled to a non-cumulative annual dividend of $5 per share. After Class A has been paid a dividend of $2 per share, Class B then participates in any additional dividends on a 40:60 *per share* ratio with Class A. For 1969 the Class A shareholders have been paid $26,000 (or $2.60 per share) and the Class B shareholders have been paid $27,000 (or $5.40 per share). Earnings per share for 1969 would be computed as follows:

Under the if converted method:

$$\frac{\$65,000}{20,000 \text{ shares*}} = \$3.25 \text{ per share}$$

*Conversion of Class B is assumed.

Under the two-class method for convertible securities:

Net income		$65,000
Less dividends paid:		
Class A common	$26,000	
Class B common	27,000	53,000
Undistributed 1969 earnings		$12,000

Allocation of undistributed earnings:

$$\frac{\$12,000}{20,000 \text{ shares}} = \$.60 \text{ per Class A share}$$

$$2(.60) = \$1.20 \text{ per Class B share.}$$

Earnings per share amounts:

	Class A	Class B
Distributed earnings	$2.60	$5.40
Undistributed earnings	.60	1.20
Totals	$3.20	$6.60

The two-class method may be used in this case since it results in greater dilution than the if converted method.

Securities Issuable Upon Satisfaction of Specified Conditions

88. Contingent Shares

Q—How is common stock contingently issuable or subject to recall classified and treated in earnings per share computations?

A—Common stock contingently issuable or subject to contingent recall is always[44] classified as a common stock equivalent unless it will be issued upon the mere passage of time and is therefore considered to be outstanding for both primary and fully diluted computations. Whether (1) the stock will be issued in the future upon the satisfaction of specified conditions, (2) the stock has been placed in escrow and part must be returned if specified conditions are not met, or (3) the stock has been issued but the holder must return part if specified conditions are not met does not affect the classification of contingent shares. [27, 61]

When certain conditions are not met, however, contingent shares are omitted from primary or from primary and fully diluted earnings per share computations. Typical examples of the conditions to be met for contingent shares are (1) the passage of time along with other conditions, (2) the maintenance of some level of earnings, (3) the attainment of some level of earnings, and (4) changes in market prices which modify the number of shares to be issued.

Contingent shares are included in both primary and fully diluted computations when the conditions for their issuance are currently being met. If additional shares would be contingently issuable if a higher earnings level were being attained currently, the additional shares are included only in fully diluted computations (giving effect to the higher earnings level) but only if dilution results. Con-

tingent shares based on (1) the attainment of increased earnings levels above the present earnings level or (2) the maintenance of increased earnings above the present level of earnings over a period of years are included only in fully diluted computations (giving effect to the higher earnings level) but only if dilution results. [62]

When contingent shares have been included in an earnings per share computation, they continue to be included in the computations in following periods until the expiration of the term of the agreement providing for the contingent issuance of additional shares. However, contingent shares are excluded from the computations whenever their effect would be anti-dilutive. [30, 40]

Prior period primary and fully diluted earnings per share should be retroactively restated whenever the number of shares issued or contingently issuable changes from the number of shares originally included in the computation. However, prior period earnings per share data are not retroactively restated for shares actually issued when the condition was the attainment of specified increased earnings levels and the shares were not previously considered outstanding. [62-64]

89. Time of Issuance for Contingent Issuances

Q—What is the time of issuance of a contingently issuable security?

A—The time of issuance of a contingently issuable security is the date when agreement to terms has been reached and announced even though subject to further actions, such as directors' or stockholders' approval. But, contingently issuable common stock is considered outstanding for earnings per share computations only when the terms become binding. (See Interpretations 27 and 28.) [29]

90. Market Price Conditions

Q—How do market price conditions affect the number of contingent shares included in earnings per share computations?

A—The number of contingently issuable shares may depend on market prices for an issuer's common stock. Generally, these market price conditions for contingent shares may be classified as (1) maximum future market price guarantees, (2) market prices for base number of shares to be determined, and (3) minimum future market price guarantees. Additionally, some agreements based on market prices for an issuer's common stock specify that no less than some minimum number of shares and/or no more than some maximum number of shares will

---

[44]Unless their time of issuance (see Interpretation 89) is prior to June 1, 1969 *and* the issuer makes election "b" of Opinion paragraph 46 *and* they were not considered residual securities under APB Opinion No. 9. Contingent shares meeting these three conditions are other potentially dilutive securities.

be issued regardless of market prices. [*63, 64*]

Conditions which guarantee a maximum future price provide "upside" assurance. That is, the issuer guarantees that the market price per share will increase to some stated amount within some time period. To the extent that the market price does not increase as guaranteed, the issuer agrees to issue additional shares or pay cash to make up the difference. Such a guarantee may extend to shares already issued as well as shares to be issued.

Conditions for market prices to determine the base number of shares to be issued may relate to periodic prices (such as the end of each year), an average of prices over some period, or some final price (such as at the end of five years). The conditions may also specify maximum or minimum market price guarantees.

Conditions which guarantee a minimum future price provide "downside" protection. That is, the issuer guarantees that the market price per share will not decrease below some stated amount within some time period. To the extent that the market price goes below that amount, the issuer agrees to issue additional shares or pay cash to make up the difference. Such a guarantee may extend to shares already issued as well as to shares to be issued.

When the number of contingently issuable shares depends on the future market price of an issuer's common stock, earnings per share computations reflect the number of shares which would be issuable based on the market price at the close of the period being reported upon. If a minimum and/or maximum number of shares is also specified, the number of shares determined from the market price at the close of the period would, if necessary, be adjusted to not less than the minimum nor more than the maximum number of shares so specified.

When additional shares are to be issued for an "upside" or a "downside" guarantee and the market price at the close of the period is less than the guaranteed price, earnings per share computations should give effect to the additional shares which would be issued.

The number of contingently issuable shares may differ for primary and fully diluted computations based upon earnings levels. But market price conditions do not cause different numbers of contingently issuable shares to be included in primary and fully diluted computations. Specifically, more shares are not included in fully diluted than in primary computations because of market price guarantees. A market price guarantee has the same effect on both computations. [*62, 63, 64*]

Prior period earnings per share would be retroactively restated if the number of shares issued or contingently issuable subsequently changes because of market price changes.

91. Earnings Conditions

Q—How does an earnings condition affect the number of contingent shares included in earnings per share computations?

A—Earnings conditions for the contingent issuance of common stock vary. Some earnings conditions determine the *total* number of shares to be issued, for example, one share for each $100 earned (1) each year for five years or (2) based on a formula, such as ten times the average annual earnings for five years. [*62, 64*]

Other earnings conditions determine the *additional* number of shares to be issued. Typically, additional shares are to be issued based on either (1) the *maintenance* of (a) the present level of earnings or (b) a higher level of earnings or (2) the *attainment* of (a) a higher level of earnings or (b) successively higher levels of earnings.

Earnings conditions may specify a minimum and/or a maximum number of shares to be issued regardless of earnings. Shares may be issued each year or only at the end of several years. Earnings conditions may apply to each year individually or may apply to all years on some cumulative or average basis. Various combinations of the earnings conditions described above may be contained in an agreement.

Some maximum number of shares may be issued initially (or placed in escrow) with the stipulation that unearned shares are to be returned to the issuer. Such plans specifying that shares are returnable are treated the same as contingently issuable shares for earnings per share computations. [*61*]

Because of the diversity of earnings conditions, stating general guidelines which will apply to all agreements is difficult. The number of shares included in earnings per share computations for an earnings agreement should conform to the provisions of Opinion paragraphs 62 and 64 and to the guidelines given below.

If shares would at some time be issuable based on the present level of earnings, the shares issuable based on that level of earnings projected to the end of the agreement are considered outstanding for both primary and fully diluted computations. If shares previously considered outstanding become unissuable (for example, because of a decline in earnings), previously reported earnings per share data would be retroactively restated when the term of the condition expires and it is determined that the shares will not be issued. [*62, 64*]

If additional shares would at some time be issuable if a level of earnings higher than the present level were attained, the additional shares issuable based on the higher level (or levels) projected to the end of the agreement are considered outstanding only for the fully diluted computation, giving effect to the higher earnings level. If different levels of earnings are specified, the level which results in the greatest dilution is used. If additional shares previously considered outstanding become unissuable (for example, because the higher earnings level is not maintained), previously reported earnings per share data would be retroactively restated when it is determined that the shares will not be issued. If in giving effect to the higher earnings level dilution does not result, the additional shares are not included in the computation. When such additional shares were not included in prior earnings per share computations but are subsequently issued (for example, because the higher earnings level was actually attained), previously reported earnings per share data are *not* retroactively restated.

When an earnings condition specifies a minimum and/or a maximum number of shares to be issued, no less than the minimum nor no more than the maximum number specified would be included in the earnings per share computations. If shares are issued each year and a total minimum and/or maximum number is specified, the minimum and/or maximum would be reduced by the number of shares issued.

92. Convertible Securities Contingently Issuable

Q—How are contingently issuable convertible securities treated for earnings per share computations?

A—Contingently issuable convertible securities are included in earnings per share computations under the guidelines described for convertible securities and the guidelines described for contingently issuable common stock. That is, additional convertible securities are assumed to be issued in conformity with the conditions specified for their issuance. (See Interpretations 88-91 for an explanation of how conditions affect the number of securities considered outstanding.) [*33, 51, 61-64*]

Time of issuance of the contingently issuable convertible securities is the date when agreement as to terms has been reached and announced. The classification of the contingently issuable convertible security as a common stock equivalent or other potentially dilutive security is determined at time of issuance based on its yield at that time[45] and does not change when the security is actually issued. A change in the bank prime interest rate or the market price of the security between the time of issuance and actual issuance of a contingently issuable convertible security has no effect on its classification.[46] [*29*]

Those contingently issuable convertible securities classified as common stock equivalents are included in both primary and fully diluted computations. However, such common stock equivalents based on

the attainment or maintenance of earnings above the present level are included only in fully diluted computations. Contingently issuable convertible securities classified as other potentially dilutive securities are included only in fully diluted computations. [*33, 62*]

When contingently issuable convertible securities are to be included in earnings per share computations, conversion of the additional securities is assumed. However, conversion is not assumed for the additional securities unless conversion is also assumed for their counterpart outstanding convertible securities. Interest or dividends are not imputed for the additional contingently issuable convertible securities since any imputed amount would be reversed by the if converted adjustments for assumed conversion. [*51*]

Parent and Consolidated Financial Statements

93. Securities Issued by Subsidiaries

Q—How do convertible securities and options and warrants issued by a subsidiary affect parent and/or consolidated earnings per share?

A—The effect of options and warrants and convertible securities issued by a subsidiary upon consolidated earnings per share (or parent company earnings per share when parent company statements are prepared as the primary financial statements using the equity method) depends upon whether the securities issued by the subsidiary to the public enable their holders to obtain common stock of the subsidiary company or common stock of the parent company. [*65*]

Securities issued by a subsidiary which enable their holders to obtain the subsidiary's common stock are included in computing the subsidiary's earnings per share data. These earnings per share data are then included in the parent or consolidated earnings per share computations based on the consolidated group's holdings of the subsidiary's securities. [*66-67*]

Options and warrants issued by a subsidiary which enable their holders to purchase parent company common stock are common stock equivalents[47] for parent or consolidated earnings per share computations. Securities of a subsidiary convertible into parent company common stock are classified as common stock equivalents or other potentially dilutive securities for parent or consolidated earnings per share computations under the yield test.[48] [*68-69*]

---

[45]Unless it has the same terms as the terms of an outstanding convertible security which is a common stock equivalent. A convertible security contingently issuable at May 31, 1969 would be classified under either election "a" or election "b" of Opinion paragraph 46.

[46]Except in the situations described in Interpretations 29 and 30.

[47]Unless issued prior to June 1, 1969 and the parent company makes election "b" specified by Opinion paragraph 46.

[48]See Interpretation 45 for a description of the treatment of a subsidiary security convertible into a parent company's convertible security.

The following example illustrates the earnings per share computations for a subsidiary's securities which enable their holders to obtain the subsidiary's common stock. Assume that a parent corporation had a net income of $10,000 from operations (excluding any dividends paid by the subsidiary), had 10,000 shares of common stock outstanding and had not issued any other securities. The parent corporation owned 900 of the common shares of a domestic subsidiary corporation and also owned 40 warrants and 100 shares of convertible preferred stock issued by the subsidiary. The subsidiary corporation had a net income of $3,600 and had outstanding 1,000 shares of common stock, 200 warrants exercisable to purchase 200 shares of its common at $10 per share (assume $20 average and ending market price for common), and 200 shares of preferred stock convertible into two of its common shares for each preferred share. The convertible preferred paid a dividend of $1.50 per share and is not a common stock equivalent. Assume that no intercompany eliminations or adjustments are necessary except for dividends. (Income taxes have been ignored in the following computations for simplicity.) [66-67]

EARNINGS PER SHARE FOR THE SUBSIDIARY

Primary earnings per share $3.00

Computed:

$$\frac{\$3,600^a - \$300^b}{1,000^c + 100^d}$$

[a]Subsidiary's net income.
[b]Dividends paid by subsidiary on convertible preferred stock.
[c]Shares of subsidiary's common stock outstanding.
[d]Incremental shares of subsidiary's common stock assumed outstanding applying the treasury stock method for warrants

$$\left(\text{computed } \frac{\$20 - \$10}{\$20} \times 200 \right)$$

Fully diluted earnings per share $2.40

Computed:

$$\frac{\$3,600^e}{1,000 + 100 + 400^f}$$

[e]Subsidiary's earnings applicable to common stock applying the if converted method for convertible preferred stock.
[f]Shares of subsidiary's common stock assumed outstanding from conversion of convertible preferred stock.

PARENT OR CONSOLIDATED EARNINGS PER SHARE

Primary earnings per share $1.29

Computed:

$$\frac{\$10,000^a + \$150^b + \$2,700^c + \$60^d}{10,000^e}$$

[66]
[a]Parent's net income.
[b]Dividends received by parent on subsidiary's convertible preferred stock.
[c]Parent's proportionate interest in subsidiary's earnings attributable to common stock, computed:
$\frac{900}{1,000}$ (1,000 shares × $3 per share).
[d]Parent's proportionate interest in subsidiary's earnings attributable to warrants, computed:
$\frac{40}{200}$ (100 incremental shares × $3 per share).
[e]Shares of parent's common stock outstanding.

Fully diluted earnings per share $1.27

Computed:

$$\frac{\$10,000 + \$2,160^f + \$48^g + \$480^h}{10,000}$$

[67]
[f]Parent's proportionate interest in subsidiary's earnings attributable to common stock, computed:
$\frac{900}{1,000}$ (1,000 shares × $2.40 per share).
[g]Parent's proportionate interest in subsidiary's earnings attributable to warrants, computed:
$\frac{40}{200}$ (100 incremental shares × $2.40 per share).
[h]Parent's proportionate interest in subsidiary's earnings attributable to convertible preferred stock, computed:
$\frac{100}{200}$ (400 shares from conversion × $2.40 per share).

The above computations apply only to earnings per share data. Parent or consolidated net income is determined in the usual manner as follows:

Parent net income from operations			$10,000
Subsidiary net income		$3,600	
Less minority interest:			
Preferred	$150[i]		
Common	330[j]	480	3,120
Parent or consolidated net income			$13,120

[39]
Computed:

[i]50% (200 preferred shares × $1.50 dividend per share).
[j]10% ($3,600 net income — $300 preferred dividends).

Note that parent or consolidated net income is not the basis for parent or consolidated earnings per share computations.

These computations would be different if the subsidiary's securities could be exercised or converted only to obtain the parent company's common stock. For example, assume the same facts as were given in the preceding illustration except (1) the warrants and convertible securities are all owned by outsiders, (2) the subsidiary's warrants are exercisable only to obtain parent company common stock, and (3) the subsidiary's preferred stock is convertible only into parent company common stock. [68-69]

EARNINGS PER SHARE FOR THE SUBSIDIARY

Primary earnings per share $3.30

Computed:
$$\frac{\$3,600 - \$300}{1,000}$$

Fully diluted earnings per share $3.30

Computed:
$$\frac{\$3,600 - \$300}{1,000}$$

PARENT OR CONSOLIDATED EARNINGS PER SHARE

Primary earnings per share $1.28

Computed:
$$\frac{\$10,000^a + \$2,970^b}{10,000^c + 100^d}$$

[68]

[a]Parent's net income.
[b]Parent's proportionate interest in subsidiary's earnings attributable to common stock, computed:
$\frac{900}{1,000}$ (1,000 shares × $3.30 per share).

[c]Shares of parent's common stock outstanding.
[d]Incremental shares of parent's common stock assumed outstanding applying the treasury stock method for warrants issued by subsidiary exercisable to obtain parent's common stock (computed $\frac{\$20 - \$10}{\$20} \times 200$).

Fully diluted earnings per share $1.26

Computed:
$$\frac{\$10,000 + \$2,970 + \$300^e}{10,000 + 100 + 400^f}$$

[69]

[e]Dividends paid by subsidiary on convertible preferred stock which would not have been received by outsiders if the subsidiary's preferred stock had been converted into parent's common stock at the beginning of the period.
[f]Shares of parent's common stock assumed outstanding from conversion of subsidiary's preferred stock convertible into parent's common stock.

Parent or consolidated net income would be determined as follows:

Parent or consolidated net income would be determined as follows:

Parent net income from operations		$10,000
Subsidiary net income	$3,600	
Less: Dividends on preferred stock	$300	
Minority common interest (10%)	330	630 2,970
Parent or consolidated net income		$12,970

[39]
Note that parent or consolidated net income is not the basis for parent or consolidated earnings per share computations.

Effects of Scheduled Changes

94. Changing Exercise Prices and Conversion Rates

Q—How do changes which may occur in exercise prices or conversion rates affect earnings per share computations?

A—Except as discussed in the next paragraph, if an exercise price or conversion rate is in effect during a period, that exercise price or conversion rate is used for primary computations. When no exercise price or conversion rate is in effect during a period, the earliest effective exercise price or conversion rate during the following five years is used for primary computations. The most advantageous exercise price or conversion rate available to the holder within ten years is always used for fully diluted computations. Previously reported earnings per share data are not restated for subsequent changes in the conversion rate or exercise price. [57, 58]

If a convertible security having an increasing conversion rate is issued in exchange for another class of security of the issuing company and is at some time convertible back into as many of the same or a similar security as was exchanged, the conversion rate used in the computation does not result in a reduction of the number of common shares (or common stock equivalents) existing before the exchange.

For example, assume that a corporation issued 100,000 shares of convertible preferred to officers and principal stockholders in exchange for 300,000 shares of common stock and each preferred share is convertible back into one common share the first year, two common shares the second year, three common shares the third year, and four common shares the fourth year and thereafter. The convertible preferred would be included as 300,000 common equivalent shares for primary earnings per share computations and 400,000 common equivalent shares for fully diluted earnings per share computations for the first three years and 400,000 common equivalent shares thereafter for both computations.

Election to Classify Outstanding Securities

95. Factors in Paragraph 46 Election

Q—What factors would be considered in classifying securities issued prior to June 1, 1969 under the elections provided in Opinion paragraph 46?

A—The following factors might be considered for elections "a" and "b" provided in Opinion paragraph 46:
1. The Opinion recommends restatement of prior periods' earnings per share data if election "b" is made and such data are included in financial statements issued after May 31, 1969, e.g., included in a comparative income statement. Restatement is not required under election "b." Although retroactive restatement is recommended, restatement may not greatly change previously reported earnings per share data. Such data therefore could be included in a comparative income statement without restatement and without a significant loss of comparability. [*46*]
If election "a" is made, however, all prior periods' earnings per share data must be retroactively recomputed and restated under the provisions of APB Opinion No. 15 when prior periods' data are subsequently presented.
2. APB Opinion No. 15 includes all options and warrants as common stock equivalents and establishes a test at issuance for convertible securities to determine their classification as common stock equivalents or not. APB Opinion No. 9 excluded the effect of options and warrants from the first EPS amount (unless they were classified as

residual securities) and allowed a convertible security to move from senior security to residual status and vice versa based on the value of its conversion rights and common stock characteristics.

Therefore, election "b" would generally exclude options and warrants issued before May 31, 1969 from primary earnings per share computations. Election "a," on the other hand, would cause convertible securities classified as residual under APB Opinion No. 9 at May 31, 1969 which would not be common stock equivalents at issuance under APB Opinion No. 15 to be reclassified as other potentially dilutive securities. If a corporation had options and warrants and convertible securities as described above, the effects of both types of securities would probably be considered in determining the election to be made.

96. Effect of New Issue of Common Stock Equivalents

Q—When securities are classified under election "b" of Opinion paragraph 46, can the classifications of those securities change in the future?

A—Generally, the classification of a security does not change after either election is made. However, convertible securities issued before June 1, 1969 would change from other potentially dilutive security status to common stock equivalent status if another convertible security is issued with the same terms which is a common stock equivalent as specified by the second sentence of Opinion paragraph 28. (See Interpretation 30.) [*28, 46*]

97. No Change for Options and Warrants

Q—Would outstanding options or warrants issued prior to June 1, 1969 classified as nonresidual securities under election "b" of Opinion paragraph 46 become common stock equivalents under the second sentence of Opinion paragraph 28 if another option or warrant were issued with the same terms after May 31, 1969?

A—No, such a change of classification applies only to convertible securities. Although this creates a difference of treatment between convertible securities and options and warrants, the Board was explicit in naming only convertible securities. [*28*]
Because warrants are often traded, identification of a warrant being exercised as having been issued "before" or "after" may be impossible. When an exercised warrant cannot definitely be identified as having been issued after May 31, 1969, exercise is assumed on a FIFO basis. That is, the first warrants issued are assumed to be the first exercised when specific identification is impossible. The same treatment applies for options, except options usually are not transferable and the specific option being exer-

cised can usually be identified.

98. Prior Period Restatement Recommended

Q—Must earnings per share reported under the provisions of APB Opinion No. 9 be restated under the provisions of APB Opinion No. 15?

A—When election "b" of Opinion paragraph 46 is made, the Opinion recommends that earnings per share amounts previously reported under APB Opinion No. 9 be restated so the previously outstanding securities conform to the classifications determined under election "b" when such amounts are reported in comparative income statements and election "b" applies to at least one period in the statement. To the extent that the Opinions differ, following this recommendation will have the effect of retroactively restating previously reported earnings per share amounts. [*45*]

If election "a" of paragraph 46 is made, APB Opinion No. 15 must be applied for all periods presented. [*46*]

If election "b" of paragraph 46 is made, some companies might prefer not to restate previously reported earnings per share amounts and such restatement is not required by APB Opinion No. 15. There may be cases, however, where the corporation or its auditor may believe that disclosure of the restated earnings per share data is particularly appropriate.

99. Is Prior Period Restatement Permitted?

Q—May prior period earnings per share amounts be retroactively restated other than when restatement is required, for example, for changes in the number of shares computed under the treasury stock method or when a convertible security being issued is determined to be a common stock equivalent and causes outstanding convertible securities with the same terms which were not common stock equivalents at issuance to also become common stock equivalents?

A—No, previously reported earnings per share amounts generally are retroactively restated only when restatement is required (see Part 1, page 404). Earnings per share data are not restated because of changes in the number of shares computed under the treasury stock method. Nor should primary earnings per share data be restated when a convertible security's classification changes because of the subsequent issuance of another convertible security with the same terms. [*28,36*]

Disclosure

100. Required Disclosure

Q—What information related to earnings per

share is required to be disclosed in addition to earnings per share data?

A—APB Opinion No. 15 requires disclosure of the following information:

1. Restatement for a prior period adjustment.
2. Dividend preferences.
3. Liquidation preferences.
4. Participation rights.
5. Call prices and dates.
6. Conversion rates and dates.
7. Exercise prices and dates.
8. Sinking fund requirements.
9. Unusual voting rights.
10. Bases upon which primary and fully diluted earnings per share were calculated. (The computations would not, however, appear upon the face of the income statement.)
11. Issues which are common stock equivalents.
12. Issues which are potentially dilutive securities.
13. Assumptions and adjustments made for earnings per share data.
14. Shares issued upon conversion, exercise, and conditions met for contingent issuances.
15. Recapitalization occurring during the period or before the statements are issued.
16. Stock dividends, stock splits or reverse splits occurring after the close of the period before the statements are issued.
17. Claims of senior securities entering earnings per share computations.
18. Dividends declared by the constituents in a pooling.
19. Basis of presentation of dividends in a pooling on other than a historical basis.
20. Per share and aggregate amount of cumulative preferred dividends in arrears.

[*18, 19, 20, 21, 23, 48, 50, 50 fn. 16, 70*]

101. Supplementary Data

Q—When must supplementary earnings per share data be furnished?

A—Supplementary earnings per share data must be furnished for the latest period when common stock is issued on conversion during the period or after the close of the period before the report is issued if primary earnings per share would have increased or decreased at least 3% if the issuance had occurred at the beginning of the period. It may also be desirable to furnish supplementary earnings per share data for each period presented giving the cumulative retroactive effect of all such issuances, but primary earnings per share as reported in those periods should not be retroactively adjusted. [*14 fn. 2, 22*]

Supplementary earnings per share data generally

would also be furnished whenever common stock or common stock equivalents have been sold for cash and the proceeds have been or are to be used to retire preferred stock or debt. The supplementary data would be furnished even though the sale occurred shortly after the close of the period but before completion of the financial report. [23]

When the issuance of a convertible security classified as a common stock equivalent causes outstanding convertible securities with the same terms classified as other potentially dilutive securities to be reclassified as common stock equivalents, supplementary earnings per share data may be useful to explain the change in classification. The supplementary data would show what previously reported primary earnings per share would have been if the convertible securities had been classified as common stock equivalents since issuance and thus reconstruct the primary earnings trend. Previously reported primary earnings per share would not be retroactively restated for prior periods in a comparative income statement because of such a change in classification. [22, 28]

Exhibit 1

DESCRIPTION OF UNOFFICIAL ACCOUNTING INTERPRETATION SERVICE

Reprinted from The CPA, September 1969, Page 6 from the Executive Vice President, Leonard M. Savoie

Unofficial Accounting Interpretations: an Institute service to the profession

The need for timely and consistent explanations of what constitutes good accounting practice has long been recognized by the Institute. The many Institute activities dedicated to this objective give evidence of this recognition. Since its inception the Accounting Principles Board has assumed the major responsibility for issuing authoritative statements on accounting principles through its official Opinions. It has increased its production of Opinions and is effectively fulfilling its responsibility.

Most subjects considered by the Board are controversial, thus requiring time for research and study by Board members. In spite of the dedication of Board members and their commitment to an unbelievable workload, there are more issues remaining to be treated in Opinions than have been dealt with thus far. Furthermore, an APB Opinion does not solve all problems; in fact, a new Opinion often opens up new areas calling for interpretation.

Audit guides and the pronouncements of other Institute technical committees often deal with questions which relate to matters of accounting principles in a specific area and may require interpretation.

In areas not covered by existing pronouncements, situations frequently arise where inconsistent practices seem likely unless the profession is guided into a preferable position. In such cases there may not be enough time for formal APB consideration.

All of these conditions point up the need for a timely informal interpretive service to provide guidance as to preferred accounting practices.

In response to this need, the executive committee with the APB's concurrence early this year authorized the staff to issue Unofficial Accounting Interpretations. Although the interpretations are to be issued without the formal procedures required for an APB Opinion, each interpretation must be approved for release by the executive vice president of the Institute and by the chairman of the Accounting Principles Board. The objective is to provide interpretations which will be sound and in conformity with the APB's intent when they relate to an Opinion. The interpretations will not be the personal views of the staff as to what an Opinion *should* have said but rather a statement of what the APB intended, based on records of the Board's deliberation and discussion with individual Board members. At times the Board itself may consider the issue and advise the staff in arriving at the interpretive position.

After the interpretation service was authorized, J. T. Ball, then the Institute's assistant director of examinations, was selected to fill the newly created position of research associate for accounting interpretations upon the completion of his duties for the May 1969 CPA examination. Mr. Ball will undertake the necessary research and consultation with informed members of the profession who have extensive experience in the problem areas to define the issues and arrive at tentative conclusions. He will prepare interpretations under the supervision of Richard C. Lytle, administrative director of the APB.

The interpretations are being published initially in the Accounting and Auditing Problems section of *The Journal of Accountancy.* (See J of A, July 69, p. 67 and Sept. 69, p. 70.) Plans are underway to integrate them into the loose-leaf edition of *APB Accounting Principles* in a section separate from Opinions but with co-ordinated indexing. Should the APB issue an Opinion on matters included in an Unofficial Accounting Interpretation, the superseded material would be withdrawn immediately.

The interpretation service will provide guidance on questions having general interest to the profession and will not respond to individual inquiries about specific accounting questions; *all individual inquiries should continue to be directed to the Institute's Technical Information Service.* Naturally, some TIS inquiries will probably point to the need for Unofficial Accounting Interpretations.

Although the interpretations are unofficial and tentative, they will be considered by the Institute to express preferred practices in the areas of financial reporting to which they relate. In view of the procedures under which the interpretations are to be developed and approved, Unofficial Accounting Interpretations may be relied upon by members of the profession in the absence of other authoritative pronouncements. We believe that this timely guidance will be greatly welcomed by all practicing CPAs.

Exhibit 2

U.S. BANK PRIME INTEREST RATES
(Source: Federal Reserve Bulletin)

Effective Date		Prime Rate (%)	66 2/3% of Prime Rate (%)
1954	January 1	3.25	2.17
	March 17	3.00	2.00
1955	August 4	3.25	2.17
	October 14	3.50	2.33
1956	April 13	3.75	2.50
	August 21	4.00	2.67
1957	August 6	4.50	3.00
1958	January 22	4.00	2.67
	April 21	3.50	2.33
	September 11	4.00	2.67
1959	May 18	4.50	3.00
	September 1	5.00	3.33
1960	August 23	4.50	3.00
1965	December 6	5.00	3.33
1966	March 10	5.50	3.67
	June 29	5.75	3.83
	August 16	6.00	4.00
1967	January 26-27	5.75(1)	3.83
	March 27	5.50	3.67
	November 20	6.00	4.00
1968	April 19	6.50	4.33
	September 25	6.25(2)	4.17
	November 13	6.25	4.17
	December 2	6.50	4.33
	December 18	6.75	4.50
1969	January 7	7.00	4.67
	March 17	7.50	5.00
	June 9	8.50	5.67
1970	February 25	8.50(3)	5.67
	March 25-26	8.00(4)	5.33

Notes:

(1) 5.75% predominant rate with 5.50% in effect at some banks.
(2) 6.25% predominant rate with 6% in effect at some banks.
(3) 8.50% predominant rate. Starting on February 25, 1970, however, and on several days thereafter, several small banks reduced their prime rates to 8%. At least one bank announced a 7 1/2% prime rate. (See Interpretation 38.)
(4) Many major banks reduced their prime rates to 8% on March 25 and others followed on March 26. The 8% rate was the predominant rate in effect the date this table was prepared (May 6, 1970).

Exhibit 3

EXAMPLES OF COMPUTING AVERAGE MARKET PRICES

An average market price may be computed various ways in applying the treasury stock method for options and warrants. (See Interpretations 53 and 54.) In first applying the treasury stock method, the computation depends upon the stability of the market price of the common stock.

In the following example, an average market price has been computed eight different ways for one quarter. First, the computation is based upon weekly prices. The weekly prices are then averaged to determine a monthly average, which is then aver-

aged to determine a quarterly average. (Although not illustrated, a quarterly average could also be computed by adding weekly prices and dividing by 13, thereby eliminating the computation of a monthly average.) In the second example, the computation is based upon monthly prices.

The "High-Low" computation is based upon an average of the high and low prices for the week or month. In the weighted averages, the market prices are weighted by the number of shares involved in the transactions.

Assume the following market transactions for a corporation's common stock during a three-month period:

	Week	High	Low	Close	Shares Traded
Month 1	1	21	19	20	300
	2	24	20	23	700
	3	24	22	22	500
	4	23	21	21	500
Month 2	5	26	22	23	1,000
	6	27	23	26	1,200
	7	29	27	28	1,500
	8	31	29	31	2,000
Month 3	9	28	26	26	2,500
	10	26	22	23	1,500
	11	24	22	22	1,000
	12	22	20	21	800
	13	20	20	20	500

Computing quarterly average from monthly averages based on weekly prices:

Week	Simple Averages High-Low	Simple Averages Close	Weighted Averages Shares	Weighted Averages High-Low	Weighted Averages Close
1	20	20	300	6,000	6,000
2	22	23	700	15,400	16,100
3	23	22	500	11,500	11,000
4	22	21	500	11,000	10,500
Month 1 totals	87	86	2,000	43,900	43,600
Divide by	4	4		2,000	2,000
Month 1 averages	21.75	21.50		21.95	21.80
5	24	23	1,000	24,000	23,000
6	25	26	1,200	30,000	31,200
7	28	28	1,500	42,000	42,000
8	30	31	2,000	60,000	62,000
Month 2 totals	107	108	5,700	156,000	158,200
Divide by	4	4		5,700	5,700
Month 2 averages	26.75	27.00		27.37	27.75
9	27	26	2,500	67,500	65,000
10	24	23	1,500	36,000	34,500
11	23	22	1,000	23,000	22,000
12	21	21	800	16,800	16,800
13	20	20	500	10,000	10,000
Month 3 totals	115	112	6,300	153,300	148,300
Divide by	5	5		6,300	6,300
Month 3 averages	23.00	22.40		24.33	23.54
Three month total	71.50	70.90		73.65	73.09
Divide by	3	3		3	3
Three month average	23.83	23.63		24.55	24.36

Computing quarterly averages from monthly prices:

	Simple Averages High-Low	Simple Averages Close	Weighted Averages Shares	Weighted Averages High-Low	Weighted Averages Close
Month 1	21.50	21.00	2,000	43,000	42,000
Month 2	26.50	31.00	5,700	151,050	176,700
Month 3	24.00	20.00	6,300	151,200	126,000
Quarterly total	72.00	72.00	14,000	345,250	344,700
Divided by	3	3		14,000	14,000
Quarterly average	24.00	24.00		24.66	24.62

Assuming an exercise price of $20 for options or warrants to purchase 10,000 shares, the above average market prices would produce the following incremental shares:

	Simple Averages High-Low	Simple Averages Close	Weighted Averages High-Low	Weighted Averages Close
Weekly prices	1,607	1,536	1,853	1,790
Monthly prices	1,667	1,667	1,890	1,877

Note: Computed

$$10,000 - \left(\frac{\$20 \times 10,000}{\text{average price}} \right) = \text{incremental shares}$$

Exhibit 4

APPLICATION OF THE TREASURY STOCK METHOD FOR OPTIONS AND WARRANTS

Assume 100,000 common shares are outstanding and 10,000 warrants are outstanding which are exercisable at $20 per share to obtain 10,000 common shares. Assume also the following market prices for common stock during a three-year period:

Market Prices Per Share of Common Stock

	Year 1		Year 2		Year 3	
Quarter	Average	Ending	Average	Ending	Average	Ending
1	$18*	$22	$24	$25	$20	$18
2	20*	21	22	21	18	22
3	22	19	20	19	24	21
4	24	23	18	17	22	25

*Assume market prices had been more than $20 for substantially all of a previous quarter.

Computation of Number of Incremental Shares by Quarters

Primary Earnings Per Share[1]

Quarter	Year 1	Year 2	Year 3
1	—0—	1,667	—0—
2	—0—	909	—0—
3	909	—0—	1,667
4	1,667	—0—	909

Fully Diluted Earnings Per Share

Quarter	Year 1	Year 2	Year 3
1	909(2)	2,000(2)	—0—
2	476(2)	909(1)	909(2)
3	909(1)	—0—	1,667(1)
4	1,667(1)	—0—	2,000(2)

(1) Based on average market price
(2) Based on ending market price

Note:
Computed

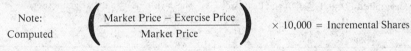

$$\left(\frac{\text{Market Price} - \text{Exercise Price}}{\text{Market Price}} \right) \times 10,000 = \text{Incremental Shares}$$

Number of Incremental Shares Included in Year-to-Date Weighted Average

Primary Earnings Per Share[1]

	Year 1	Year 2	Year 3
First quarter	—0—	1,667	—0—
Six months	—0—	1,288	—0—
Nine months	303	859	556
Year	644	644	644

Fully Diluted Earnings Per Share

	Year 1	Year 2	Year 3
First quarter	909(1)	2,000(1)	—0—(1)
Six months	693(1)	1,455(1)	909(2)
Nine months	765(1)	970(1)	859(1)
Year	1,304(2)	727(1)	2,000(2)

(1) Computed by adding incremental shares of each quarter included and dividing by number of quarters included in the year-to-date.
(2) Incremental shares for all quarters included based on ending market price.

Exhibit 5

DAYS BETWEEN TWO DATES

The table on page 453 is useful in computing a weighted average of shares outstanding when the number of shares outstanding changes frequently during the year. The table includes numbered days for two years; one day must be added after February 28 during leap year. Corporations reporting on a calendar year basis should use the first 366 numbers; all other corporations should use both tables.

Since the number of days between two dates is determined by subtraction, the number used for the last day of the year is the first day of the following year. That is, a corporation reporting on a calendar year having a stock transaction on June 20 should weight the shares outstanding before the transaction by 170 (determined 171 − 1 = 170) and the shares

outstanding after the transaction by 195 (determined 366 − 171 = 195). The 170 days before plus the 195 days after then equal 365 days. For leap year, corresponding computations would be 172 − 1 = 171 and 367 − 172 = 195, so 171 + 195 = 366.

An example of how to use the table follows. Assume a corporation reports on a fiscal year ending June 30. At July 1, 1969 the corporation had 100,000 shares of common stock outstanding. On August 25, 1969 the corporation distributed a 5% stock dividend to its shareholders. On September 18, 1969 the corporation purchased 525 shares of its stock. On April 8, 1970 the corporation issued 10,000 shares of its stock for cash. On May 21, 1970 the corporation split its stock 2-for-1.

The days to be used for weighting are:

Transaction Day	Number for Transaction Day	Number for Beginning Day	Days for Weighting
September 18, 1969	261	182	79
April 8, 1970	463	261	202
End of year	547	463	84
Total days			365

The August 25, 1969 stock dividend and the May 21, 1970 stock split are reflected retroactively in the weighted average of shares outstanding as computed below:

Date	Shares		Stock Dividend[49]	Stock Split[49]	Days Outstanding	Weighted Shares
7/ 1/69	outstanding	100,000	× 1.05 = 105,000	× 2 = 210,000 ×	79	= 16,590,000
9/18/69	purchase	(525)		× 2 = (1,050)		
				208,950 ×	202	= 42,207,900
4/ 8/70	issue	10,000		× 2 = 20,000 ×		
				228,950 ×	84	= 19,231,800
Totals					365	78,029,700

Weighted average number of shares outstanding:

$$\frac{78,029,700}{365} = 213,780$$

[49]Note that stock dividends and stock splits are retroactive adjustments rather than transactions to be weighted by the number of days a stock dividend or split was outstanding.

TABLE OF DAYS BETWEEN TWO DATES

Day in Month	January	February	March	April	May	June	July	August	September	October	November	December	Day in Month	January	February	March	April	May	June	July	August	September	October	November	December	Day in Month
1	1	32	60	91	121	152	182	213	244	274	305	335	1	366	397	425	456	486	517	547	578	609	639	670	700	1
2	2	33	61	92	122	153	183	214	245	275	306	336	2	367	398	426	457	487	518	548	579	610	640	671	701	2
3	3	34	62	93	123	154	184	215	246	276	307	337	3	368	399	427	458	488	519	549	580	611	641	672	702	3
4	4	35	63	94	124	155	185	216	247	277	308	338	4	369	400	428	459	489	520	550	581	612	643	673	703	4
5	5	36	64	95	125	156	186	217	248	278	309	339	5	370	401	429	460	490	521	551	582	613	643	674	704	5
6	6	37	65	96	126	157	187	218	249	279	310	340	6	371	402	430	461	491	522	552	583	614	644	675	705	6
7	7	38	66	97	127	158	188	219	250	280	311	341	7	372	403	431	462	492	523	553	584	615	645	676	706	7
8	8	39	67	98	128	159	189	220	251	281	312	342	8	373	404	432	463	493	524	554	585	616	646	677	707	8
9	9	40	68	99	129	160	190	221	252	282	313	343	9	374	405	433	464	494	525	555	586	617	647	678	708	9
10	10	41	69	100	130	161	191	222	253	283	314	344	10	375	406	434	465	495	526	556	587	618	648	679	709	10
11	11	42	70	101	131	162	192	223	254	284	315	345	11	376	407	435	466	496	527	557	588	619	649	680	710	11
12	12	43	71	102	132	163	193	224	255	285	316	346	12	377	408	436	467	497	528	558	589	620	650	681	711	12
13	13	44	72	103	133	164	194	225	256	286	317	347	13	378	409	437	468	498	529	559	590	621	651	682	712	13
14	14	45	73	104	134	165	195	226	257	287	318	348	14	379	410	438	469	499	530	560	591	622	652	683	713	14
15	15	46	74	105	135	166	196	227	258	288	319	349	15	380	411	439	470	500	531	561	592	623	653	684	714	15
16	16	47	75	106	136	167	197	228	259	289	320	350	16	381	412	440	471	501	532	562	593	624	654	685	715	16
17	17	48	76	107	137	168	198	229	260	290	321	351	17	382	413	441	472	502	533	563	594	625	655	686	716	17
18	18	49	77	108	138	169	199	230	261	291	322	352	18	383	414	442	473	503	534	564	595	626	656	687	717	18
19	19	50	78	109	139	170	200	231	262	292	323	353	19	384	415	443	474	504	535	565	596	627	657	688	718	19
20	20	51	79	110	140	171	201	232	263	293	324	354	20	385	416	444	475	505	536	566	597	628	658	689	719	20
21	21	52	80	111	141	172	202	233	264	294	325	355	21	386	417	445	476	506	537	567	598	629	659	690	720	21
22	22	53	81	112	142	173	203	234	265	295	326	356	22	387	418	446	477	507	538	568	599	630	660	691	721	22
23	23	54	82	113	143	174	204	235	266	296	327	357	23	388	419	447	478	508	539	569	600	631	661	692	722	23
24	24	55	83	114	144	175	205	236	267	297	328	358	24	389	420	448	479	509	540	570	601	632	662	693	723	24
25	25	56	84	115	145	176	206	237	268	298	329	359	25	390	421	449	480	510	541	571	602	633	663	694	724	25
26	26	57	85	116	146	177	207	238	269	299	330	360	26	391	422	450	481	511	542	572	603	634	664	695	725	26
27	27	58	86	117	147	178	208	239	270	300	331	361	27	392	423	451	482	512	543	573	604	635	665	696	726	27
28	28	59	87	118	148	179	209	240	271	301	332	362	28	393	424	452	483	513	544	574	605	636	666	697	727	28
29	29	...	88	119	149	180	210	241	272	302	333	363	29	394	...	453	484	514	545	575	606	637	667	698	728	29
30	30	...	89	120	150	181	211	242	273	303	334	364	30	395	...	454	485	515	546	576	607	638	668	699	729	30
31	31	...	90	...	151	...	212	243	...	304	...	365	31	396	...	455	...	516	...	577	608	...	669	...	730	31

CROSS-REFERENCE TABLE

In the following table, Opinion paragraphs, footnotes, and exhibits are listed in the first column followed by a citation to each Interpretation which references the Opinion paragraph, footnote, or exhibit. Citations in the second column refer to a page number in Part I. Citations in the third column refer to the number of an Interpretation in Part II.

APB Opinion No. 15 Paragraph Number	Part I Page Number	Part II Interpretation Number	Interpretation Subject
5		9	Corporations and Financial Presentations Excepted
5		10	Closely Held Corporations
5		13	Subchapter S Corporations
5		14	Unaudited Financial Statements
6		9	Corporations and Financial Presentations Excepted
6		10	Closely Held Corporations
6		13	Subchapter S Corporations
6		14	Unaudited Financial Statements
12	401		Presentation of Earnings per Share
12		15	Reporting Loss per Share
13	401		Presentation of Earnings per Share
13		6	Dual Presentation
13		7	Primary Earnings per Share
13		8	Fully Diluted Earnings per Share
13		16	EPS for Extraordinary Items
14	401		Presentation of Earnings per Share
14		3	Other Potentially Dilutive Securities
14		17	Simple Capital Structure
14		18	Complex Capital Structure
14		19	EPS for Simple and Complex Capital Structures
14		20	Dual Presentation for Corporation with Simple Capital Structure
14		24	Earnings Applicable to Common Stock
15	401		Presentation of Earnings per Share
15	401		Classification of Securities
15	405		Disclosure
15		7	Primary Earnings per Share
15		8	Fully Diluted Earnings per Share
15		11	Dilution Less Than 3%
15		12	3% Test
15		18	Complex Capital Structure
15		19	EPS for Simple and Complex Capital Structures
15		24	Earnings Applicable to Common Stock
15		26	Classification and Assumed Conversion
15		43	Conversion Assumed for Primary Only
15		74	Explanation of 20% Provision
16	402		Fully Diluted Earnings per Share
16	405		Disclosure
16		6	Dual Presentation
16		21	Primary v. Fully Diluted EPS
16		22	Captions for Earnings per Share Presentations
17		11	Dilution Less Than 3%
17		18	Complex Capital Structure
17		20	Dual Presentation for Corporation with Simple Capital Structure
17		23	Captions in Comparative Statements
18	404		Restatement of Previously Reported Data
18		100	Required Disclosure
19	405		Disclosure
19		100	Required Disclosure
20	401		Assumptions
20	405		Disclosure

APB Opinion No. 15 Paragraph Number	Part I Page Number	Part II Interpretation Number	Interpretation Subject
20		56	Fair Value Used If No Market Price
20		100	Required Disclosure
21		100	Required Disclosure
22	404		Restatement of Previously Reported Data
22	405		Supplementary Data
22		57	Options and Warrants Outstanding Part of a Period
22		101	Supplementary Data
23	405		Supplementary Data
23		100	Required Disclosure
23		101	Supplementary Data
24	401		Assumptions
24		21	Primary vs. Fully Diluted EPS
25	401		Assumptions
25	401		Classification of Securities
25		2	Common Stock Equivalents
26	401		Assumptions
27	401		Assumptions
27	402		Primary Earnings per Share
27		1	Security
27		2	Common Stock Equivalents
27		18	Complex Capital Structure
27		48	Equivalents of Options and Warrants
27		74	Explanation of 20% Provision
27		88	Contingent Shares
28	401		Classification of Securities
28	402		Primary Earnings per Share
28		26	Classification and Assumed Conversion
28		28	Classification and Computation Not Always the Same
28		29	Change of Classification of Convertible Security
28		30	Change of Classification is Mandatory
28		31	Definition of "Same Terms"
28		32	Issue Price is Not a "Term"
28		33	Sale of Treasury Securities is a New Issue
28		96	Effect of New Issue of Common Stock Equivalents
28		97	No Change for Options and Warrants
28		99	Is Prior Period Restatement Permitted?
28		101	Supplementary Data
29		27	Time of Issuance
29		29	Change of Classification of Convertible Security
29		82	Deferred Compensation Stock Option
29		89	Time of Issuance for Contingent Issuances
29		92	Convertible Securities Contingently Issuable
30	401		Classification of Securities
30	402		Anti-Dilutive Securities
30	403		Convertible Securities
30		4	Dilution—Dilutive Security
30		5	Anti-Dilution—Anti-Dilutive Security
30		26	Classification and Assumed Conversion
30		41	No Anti-Dilution From Convertible Preferred Stock
30		42	No Anti-Dilution From Convertible Debt
30		44	If Converted Method at Actual Conversion
30		47	No Anti-Dilution from Options and Warrants
30		49	Grouping Options and Warrants
30		52	Market Prices Used for Treasury Stock Method
30		57	Options and Warrants Outstanding Part of a Period
30		62	Anti-Dilutive Exercise

APB Opin-ion No. 15 Paragraph Number	Part I Page Number	Part II Inter-pretation Number	Interpretation Subject
36		81	Computations May Differ for Primary and Fully Diluted When Paragraph 38 Applies
36		82	Deferred Compensation Stock Option
36		84	Options or Warrants to Purchase Convertible Securities
36		99	Is Prior Restatement Permitted?
37	402		Primary Earnings per Share
37	403		Convertible Securities
37	403		Options and Warrants
37		1	Security
37		26	Classification and Assumed Conversion
37		47	No Anti-Dilution from Options and Warrants
37		48	Equivalents of Options and Warrants
37		50	Methods Used for Options and Warrants
37		65	Unusual Warrants and Their Equivalents
37		66	Securities Subject to Paragraph 37 Tests
37		67	Market Prices Used in Paragraph 37 Tests
37		68	Computations for Warrants Requiring the Tendering of Debt
37		69	Computations for Warrants Allowing the Tendering of Debt
37		70	Computations for Warrants Whose Proceeds Are Applied To Retire Debt
37		71	Treasury Stock Method for Convertibles
37		72	Anti-Dilutive Options and Warrants Included
37		74	Explanation of 20% Provision
37		75	Original Issue Premium or Discount
37		76	Redemption Premium or Discount
38	402		Anti-Dilutive Securities
38	403		Options and Warrants
38		12	3% Test
38		26	Classification and Assumed Conversion
38		47	No Anti-Dilution from Options and Warrants
38		48	Equivalents of Options and Warrants
38		49	Grouping Options and Warrants
38		50	Methods Used for Options and Warrants
38		52	Market Prices Used for Treasury Stock Method
38		57	Options and Warrants Outstanding Part of a Period
38		66	Securities Subject to Paragraph 37 Tests
38		67	Market Prices Used in Paragraph 37 Tests
38		70	Computations for Warrants Whose Proceeds Are Applied To Retire Debt
38		71	Treasury Stock Method for Convertibles
38		72	Anti-Dilutive Options and Warrants Included
38		73	No Order for Exercise
38		74	Explanation of 20% Provision
38		75	Original Issue Premium or Discount
38		76	Redemption Premium or Discount
38		77	Debt Purchased Under Paragraph 38
38		78	Compensating Balances Excluded
38		79	Investments Under Paragraph 38
38		80	Debt Eligible Only While Outstanding
38		81	Computations May Differ for Primary and Fully Diluted When Paragraph 38 Applies
39	401		Classification of Securities
39	402		Earnings Applicable to Common Stock
39		40	Original Issue Premium or Discount on Convertible Securities
39		82	Deferred Compensation Stock Option

APB Opin-ion No. 15 Paragraph Number	Part I Page Number	Part II Inter-pretation Number	Interpretation Subject
39		93	Securities Issued by Subsidiaries
40	402		Anti-Dilutive Securities
40	402		Fully Diluted Earnings per Share
40	403		Convertible Securities
40		4	Dilution—Dilutive Security
40		5	Anti-Dilution—Anti-Dilutive Security
40		21	Primary v. Fully Diluted EPS
40		26	Classification and Assumed Conversion
40		41	No Anti-Dilution From Convertible Preferred Stock
40		42	No Anti-Dilution From Convertible Debt
40		43	Conversion Assumed for Primary Only
40		47	No Anti-Dilution from Options and Warrants
40		49	Grouping Options and Warrants
40		52	Market Prices Used for Treasury Stock Method
40		57	Options and Warrants Outstanding Part of a Period
40		70	Computations for Warrants Whose Proceeds Are Applied To Retire Debt
40		71	Treasury Stock Method for Convertibles
40		77	Debt Purchased Under Paragraph 38
40		82	Deferred Compensation Stock Option
40		84	Options or Warrants to Purchase Convertible Securities
40		88	Contingent Shares
41	401		Assumptions
41	401		Classification of Securities
41	402		Anti-Dilutive Securities
41	404		Restatement of Previously Reported Data
41		3	Other Potentially Dilutive Securities
41		18	Complex Capital Structure
41		20	Dual Presentation for Corporation with Simple Capital Structure
41		21	Primary v. Fully Diluted EPS
41		26	Classification and Assumed Conversion
41		44	If Converted Method at Actual Conversion
41		57	Options and Warrants Outstanding Part of a Period
41		64	Total of Quarters May Not Equal Annual EPS
42	403		Options and Warrants
42		46	Classification of Options and Warrants
42		47	No Anti-Dilution from Options and Warrants
42		51	Treasury Stock Method Reflects Dilution of Options and Warrants
42		52	Market Prices Used for Treasury Stock Method
42		57	Options and Warrants Outstanding Part of a Period
42		60	Applying Ending and Average Market Prices
42		61	Treasury Stock Method at Exercise
42		62	Anti-Dilutive Exercise
42		63	"Substantially All" of Three Months
42		67	Market Prices Used in Paragraph 37 Tests
42		70	Computations for Warrants Whose Proceeds Are Applied To Retire Debt
42		76	Redemption Premium or Discount
42		81	Computations May Differ for Primary and Fully Diluted when Paragraph 38 Applies
43	404		Other Securities
43		45	Securities Convertible into Other Convertible Securities
45	404		Restatement of Previously Reported Data
45	405		Effective Date
45		98	Prior Period Restatement Recommended
46	404		Restatement of Previously Reported Data

APB Opinion No. 15 Paragraph Number	Part I Page Number	Part II Interpretation Number	Interpretation Subject
46	405		Effective Date
46		3	Other Potentially Dilutive Securities
46		26	Classification and Assumed Conversion
46		30	Change of Classification is Mandatory
46		39	Prior Period Prime Rates
46		46	Classification of Options and Warrants
46		71	Treasury Stock Method for Convertibles
46		74	Explanation of 20% Provision
46		81	Computations May Differ for Primary and Fully Diluted when Paragraph 38 Applies
46		82	Deferred Compensation Stock Option
46		83	Stock Subscriptions Are Warrants
46		88	Contingent Shares
46		92	Convertible Securities Contingently Issuable
46		93	Securities Issued by Subsidiaries
46		95	Factors in Paragraph 46 Election
46		96	Effect of New Issue of Common Stock Equivalents
46		97	No Change for Options and Warrants
46		98	Prior Period Restatement Recommended
47	401		Presentation of Earnings per Share
47		25	Weighted Average of Shares Outstanding
47		44	If Converted Method at Actual Conversion
47		57	Options and Warrants Outstanding Part of a Period
47		61	Treasury Stock Method at Exercise
47		62	Anti-Dilutive Exercise
48	404		Restatement of Previously Reported Data
48		100	Required Disclosure
49	404		Restatement of Previously Reported Data
49	405		Business Combinations and Reorganization
49		28	Classification and Computation Not Always the Same
50	402		Earnings Applicable to Common Stock
50	403		Convertible Securities
50		15	Reporting Loss per Share
50		24	Earnings Applicable to Common Stock
50		26	Classification and Assumed Conversion
50		41	No Anti-Dilution From Convertible Preferred Stock
50		42	No Anti-Dilution From Convertible Debt
50		100	Required Disclosure
51	402		Earnings Applicable to Common Stock
51	403		Convertible Securities
51		4	Dilution—Dilutive Security
51		24	Earnings Applicable to Common Stock
51		26	Classification and Assumed Conversion
51		28	Classification and Computation Not Always the Same
51		40	Original Issue Premium or Discount on Convertible Securities
51		74	Explanation of 20% Provision
51		75	Original Issue Premium or Discount
51		76	Redemption Premium or Discount
51		84	Options or Warrants to Purchase Convertible Securities
51		87	Two-Class Method for Convertible Securities
51		92	Convertible Securities Contingently Issuable
52	402		Earnings Applicable to Common Stock
54		85	EPS Treatment of Two-Class and Participating Securities
54		87	Two-Class Method for Convertible Securities
55		85	EPS Treatment of Two-Class and Participating Securities
55		86	Two-Class Method for Nonconvertible Securities

APB Opin-ion No. 15 Paragraph Number	Part I Page Number	Part II Inter-pretation Number	Interpretation Subject
55		87	Two-Class Method for Convertible Securities
56	404		Delayed Effectiveness and Changing Rates or Prices
56		45	Securities Convertible into Other Convertible Securities
57	404		Delayed Effectiveness and Changing Rates or Prices
57	404		Restatement of Previously Reported Data
57		28	Classification and Computation Not Always the Same
57		82	Deferred Compensation Stock Option
57		94	Changing Exercise Prices and Conversion Rates
58	404		Delayed Effectiveness and Changing Rates or Prices
58		28	Classification and Computation Not Always the Same
58		45	Securities Convertible into Other Convertible Securities
58		69	Computations for Warrants Allowing the Tendering of Debt
58		71	Treasury Stock Method for Convertibles
58		82	Deferred Compensation Stock Option
58		94	Changing Exercise Prices and Conversion Rates
59		26	Classification and Assumed Conversion
59		37	Property Included in Cash Yield
60		37	Property Included in Cash Yield
60		85	EPS Treatment of Two-Class and Participating Securities
61		88	Contingent Shares
61		91	Earnings Conditions
61		92	Convertible Securities Contingently Issuable
62	404		Restatement of Previously Reported Data
62		27	Time of Issuance
62		88	Contingent Shares
62		90	Market Price Condition
62		91	Earnings Conditions
62		92	Convertible Securities Contingently Issuable
63	404		Restatement of Previously Reported Data
63		88	Contingent Shares
63		90	Market Price Conditions
63		92	Convertible Securities Contingently Issuable
64		88	Contingent Shares
64		90	Market Price Conditions
64		91	Earnings Conditions
64		92	Convertible Securities Contingently Issuable
65		37	Property Included in Cash Yield
65		93	Securities Issued by Subsidiaries
66		37	Property Included in Cash Yield
66		93	Securities Issued by Subsidiaries
67		37	Property Included in Cash Yield
67		93	Securities Issued by Subsidiaries
68		37	Property Included in Cash Yield
68		93	Securities Issued by Subsidiaries
69		37	Property Included in Cash Yield
69		93	Securities Issued by Subsidiaries
70		100	Required Disclosure

APB Opin-ion No. 15 Footnote Number	Part I Page Number	Part II Inter-pretation Number	Interpretation Subject
2	405		Supplementary Data
2		4	Dilution—Dilutive Security
2		11	Dilution Less Than 3%
2		18	Complex Capital Structure

APB Opinion No. 15 Footnote Number	Part I Page Number	Part II Interpretation Number	Interpretation Subject
2		101	Supplementary Data
8	402		Anti-Dilutive Securities
8		16	EPS for Extraordinary Items
9		29	Change of Classification of Convertible Security
9		36	Cash Yield of Convertible Security in a "Package"
9		56	Fair Value Used If No Market Price
11		49	Grouping Options and Warrants
12		47	No Anti-Dilution from Options and Warrants
12		51	Treasury Stock Method Reflects Dilution of Options and Warrants
14	402		Anti-Dilutive Securities
16		100	Required Disclosure

APB Opinion No. 15 Exhibit	Part I Page Number	Part II Interpretation Number	Interpretation Subject
B		16	EPS for Extraordinary Items
B		52	Market Prices Used for Treasury Stock Method
B		58	What is a Period?
B		59	Share Averaging
B		67	Market Prices Used in Paragraph 37 Tests
B		69	Computations for Warrants Allowing the Tendering of Debt
B		70	Computations for Warrants Whose Proceeds Are Applied To Retire Debt
C		56	Fair Value Used If No Market Price

Computing Earnings Per Share: Accounting Interpretations of APB Opinion No. 15

102. TWO-CLASS METHOD FOR WARRANTS ISSUED BY REITs

Question—The capitalization of a real estate investment trust (REIT) includes shares of beneficial interest (common stock) and an equal number of warrants. This REIT is not subject to federal income tax with respect to the income it distributes to its shareholders because it distributes at least 90 percent of its annual taxable income (as defined by the *Internal Revenue Code*) and elects not to be taxed on the income distributed. How should this entity treat warrants in computing earnings per share under APB Opinion No. 15?

Interpretation—The "two-class" method of computing primary earnings per share should be used by any REIT which elects under the *Internal Revenue Code* not to be subject to tax on income distributed and which pays dividends equal to 90 percent or more of its taxable income. Under this method, dividends are deducted from net income and the remaining amount (the undistributed earnings) is allocated to the total of common shares and common share equivalents with use of warrant proceeds applied as described in paragraph 36 or 38. Per share distributions to common shareholders (total dividends divided by the weighted average of common shares outstanding) are added to this per share amount to determine primary earnings per share.

For example, the REIT described in the question above should compute primary earnings per share under the "two-class" method in conjunction with paragraph 38 of APB Opinion No. 15. Assume that this REIT has a net income of $1,000,000 and distributes $900,000 in dividends on 1,000,000 common shares outstanding. Warrants exercisable at $5 per share for 1,000,000 common shares are also outstanding. Assuming a market price of $23 per share for common and a 3 percent interest rate for debt and/or investments in commercial paper or U. S. government securities, primary earnings per share would be determined applying the two-class method and paragraph 38 as follows:

Net income		$1,000,000
Less dividends		900,000
Undistributed earnings		$ 100,000
Proceeds from the exercise of warrants:		
1,000,000 × $5	$5,000,000	
Purchase of treasury stock under paragraph 38-a		
200,000 shares × $23	4,600,000	
Balance to retire debt under paragraph 38-b	400,000	
Interest rate on debt retired	.03	
Interest adjustment		12,000
Adjusted undistributed earnings		$ 112,000
Common shares outstanding		1,000,000
Common shares assumed issued for warrants	1,000,000	
Less treasury stock purchased	200,000	
Incremental shares for warrants		800,000
Common and common equivalent shares		1,800,000
Primary earnings per share:		
Distributed earnings ($900,000 ÷ 1,000,000)		$ .90
Undistributed earnings ($112,000 ÷ 1,800,000)		.06
Total earnings per common and common equivalent share		$ .96

If the per share amount computed above had exceeded earnings per outstanding common share of $1.00 (computed: $1,000,000 ÷ 1,000,000 shares), the result would be anti-dilutive and primary earnings per share would be reported as $1.00 in accordance with paragraph 30.

The two-class method should not be used by an REIT in computing fully diluted earnings per share in order to reflect maximum potential dilution. Therefore, fully diluted earnings per share computed for the above example would be $.56 (computed: $1,012,000 ÷ 1,800,000 shares) applying only paragraph 38.

Although dividends declared after the close of the taxable year may be included in meeting the 90 percent requirement for federal income tax purposes, only dividends paid or declared during the period for which the computation is being made should be considered in applying the two-class method. However, a dividend declaration (or official company policy in lieu of actual declaration) before the close of the period stated as a percentage of taxable earnings (the amount to be determined after the close of the period) will be considered as being declared during the period if the dividend is paid by the date the financial statements are issued.

[Issue Date: September, 1971]

462

Business Combinations:
Accounting Interpretations of APB Opinion No. 16

STATUS

Issued: December 1970-March 1973

Effective Date: Interpretations No. 1 through 7—December 1970
Interpretations No. 8 through 17—April 1971
Interpretations No. 18 through 23—September 1971
Interpretations No. 24 and 25—November 1971
Interpretations No. 26 through 33—December 1971
Interpretations No. 34 and 35—January 1972
Interpretation No. 36—Effective for combinations consummated after May 31, 1972
Interpretation No. 37—November 1972
Interpretations No. 38 and 39—March 1973

Affects: No other pronouncements

Affected by: Interpretations No. 15, 17, and 24 amended by FAS 10
Interpretation No. 30 amended by FAS 111

Other Interpretive Pronouncement: FTB 85-5 (for Interpretations No. 11, 13, 26, and 39)

Business Combinations:
Accounting Interpretations of APB Opinion No. 16

1. RATIO OF EXCHANGE

Question—Paragraph 46-a of APB Opinion No. 16 defines the initiation date for a business combination as the earlier of (1) the date the major terms of a plan, including the ratio of exchange of stock, are announced publicly or otherwise formally made known to the stockholders of any one of the combining companies or (2) the date that stockholders of a combining company are notified in writing of an exchange offer. Does the announcement of a formula by which the ratio of exchange will be determined in the future constitute the initiation of a plan of combination?

Interpretation—Yes, the actual exchange ratio (1 for 1, 2 for 1, etc.) need not be known to constitute initiation of a business combination so long as the ratio of exchange is absolutely determinable by objective means in the future. A formula would usually provide such a determination.

A formula to determine the exchange ratio might include factors such as earnings for some period of time, market prices of stock at a particular date, average market prices for some period of time, appraised valuations, etc. The formula may include upper and/or lower limits for the exchange ratio and the limits may provide for adjustments based upon appraised valuations, audit of the financial statements, etc. Also, the formula must be announced or communicated to stockholders as specified by paragraph 46-a to constitute initiation.

If a formula is used after October 31, 1970 to initiate a business combination which is intended to be accounted for by the pooling of interests method, the actual exchange ratio would have to be determined by the consummation date and therefore no later than one year after the initiation date to meet the conditions of paragraph 47-a. Also, changing the terms after October 31, 1970 of a formula used to initiate a business combination before November 1, 1970 would constitute the initiation of a new plan of combination (see Opinion footnote 5).

[Issue Date: December, 1970]

2. NOTIFICATION TO STOCKHOLDERS

Question—Paragraph 46-a of APB Opinion No. 16 specifies that a business combination is initiated on the earlier of (1) the date major terms of a plan are formally announced or (2) the date that stockholders of a combining company are notified in writing of *an* exchange offer. Does communication in writing to a corporation's own stockholders that the corporation plans a future exchange offer to another company without disclosure of the terms constitute initiation of a business combination?

Interpretation—No. Paragraph 46-a defines "initiation" in terms of two dates. The first date is for the announcement of an exchange offer negotiated between representatives of two (or more) corporations. The second date is for a tender offer made by a corporation directly or by newspaper advertisement to the stockholders of another company. It is implicit in the circumstances of a tender offer that the plan is not initiated until the stockholders of the other company have been informed as to the offer and its major terms, including the ratio of exchange.

Therefore, in the second date specified for initiation in paragraph 46-a, *"a* combining company" refers to the company whose stockholders will tender their shares to the issuing corporation. *"An* exchange offer" means the major terms of a plan including the ratio of exchange (or a formula to objectively determine the ratio).

A corporation may communicate to its own stockholders its intent to make a tender offer or to negotiate on the terms of a proposed business combination with another company. However, intent to tender or to negotiate does not constitute "initiation." A business combination is not initiated until the major terms are "set" and announced publicly or formally communicated to stockholders.

[Issue Date: December, 1970]

3. INTERCORPORATE INVESTMENT EXCEEDING 10 PER CENT LIMIT

Question—Paragraph 46-b (the "independence" condition) of APB Opinion No. 16 states that the pooling of interests method of accounting for a business combination may not be applied if *at* the dates the plan of combination is initiated and consummated the combining companies hold as intercorporate investments more than 10 per cent in total of the outstanding voting common stock of any combining company. Would an intercorporate investment of 10 per cent or less *at* the initiation and consummation dates but exceeding 10 per cent *between* these dates (for example, through a cash purchase and subsequent sale of the voting common stock of a combining company) prohibit accounting for a business combination under the pooling of interests method?

Interpretation—Paragraph 46-b would not be met if *between* the initiation and consummation dates combining companies hold as intercorporate investments more than 10 per cent of the outstanding voting common stock of any combining company even though the intercorporate investments do not exceed 10 per cent *at* either the initiation or consummation date. Although the Opinion mentions only the initiation and consummation dates, intercorporate investments exceeding 10 per cent in the interim would violate the spirit of the independence condition and the business combination would be an acquisition accounted for under the purchase method. For the 10 per cent computation, however, intercorporate investments exclude voting common stock that is acquired after the date the plan of combination is initiated in exchange for the voting common stock issued to effect the combination.

[Issue Date: December, 1970]

4. CONSUMMATION DATE FOR A BUSINESS COMBINATION

Question—APB Opinion No. 16 in paragraphs 46 through 48 specifies certain conditions which require a business combination to be accounted for by the pooling of interests method. Among these conditions in paragraphs 46-b and 47-b are quantitative measurements which are to be made on the consummation date. When does the "consummation date" occur for a business combination?

Interpretation—A plan of combination is consummated on the date the combination is completed, that is, the date assets are transferred to the issuing corporation. The quantitative measurements specified in paragraphs 46-b and 47-b are, therefore, made on the date the combination is completed. If they and all of the other conditions specified in paragraphs 46 through 48 are met on that date, the combination must be accounted for by the pooling of interests method.

It should not be overlooked that paragraph 47-a states the plan of combination must be *completed* in accordance with a specific plan within one year after it is initiated unless delay is beyond the control of the combining companies as described in that paragraph. Therefore, ownership of the issuing corporation's common stock must pass to combining stockholders and assets must be transferred from the combining company to the issuing corporation within one year after the initiation date (unless the described delay exists) if the business combination is to be accounted for by the pooling of interests method. Physical transfer of stock certificates need not be accomplished on the consummation date so long as the transfer is in process.

If any of the conditions specified in paragraphs 46 through 48 are not met, a business combination is an acquisition which must be accounted for by the purchase method. Paragraph 93 specifies that the

date of acquisition should ordinarily be the date assets are received and other assets are given or securities are issued, that is, the consummation date. However, this paragraph allows the parties for convenience to designate the end of an accounting period falling between the initiation and consummation dates as the effective date for the combination.

The designated effective date is not a substitute for the consummation date in determining whether the purchase or pooling of interests method of accounting applies to the combination. In designating an effective date as some date prior to the consummation date, the parties would automatically be anticipating that the business combination would be accounted for as a purchase since paragraphs 51 and 61 specify that a business combination accounted for by the pooling of interests method must be recorded as of the date the combination is consummated.

[Issue Date: December, 1970]

5. POOLING NOT COMPLETED WITHIN ONE YEAR

Question—Paragraph 47-a of APB Opinion No. 16 specifies that a condition for a business combination to be accounted for by the pooling of interests method is for the combination to be completed in accordance with a specific plan within one year after the plan is initiated unless delay is beyond the control of the combining companies. This paragraph also indicates that new terms may be offered if earlier exchanges of stock are adjusted to the new terms. If completion of a business combination is delayed beyond one year, would the offering of new terms during the delay period meet the condition of paragraph 47-a for a business combination to be accounted for by the pooling of interests method?

Interpretation—New terms may be offered under the conditions of paragraph 47-a more than one year after the initiation date if delay in completion is beyond the control of the combining companies because of certain circumstances and earlier exchanges of stock are adjusted to the new terms (but see Opinion footnote 5 for plans in effect on October 31, 1970). However, the only delays permitted under paragraph 47-a are proceedings of a governmental authority and litigation.

Proceedings of a governmental authority for this purpose include deliberations by a federal or state regulatory agency on whether to approve or disapprove a combination where the combination cannot be effected without approval. They do *not* include registration of the securities with the SEC or a state securities commission. Litigation for this purpose means, for example, an antitrust suit filed by the Justice Department or a suit filed by a dissenting minority stockholder to prohibit a combination.

[Issue Date: December, 1970]

6. REGISTERED STOCK EXCHANGED FOR RESTRICTED STOCK

Question—The pooling of interests method of accounting for a business combination is required by APB Opinion No. 16 if the conditions specified in paragraphs 46 through 48 are met showing that stockholder groups have combined their rights and risks. Would the exchange of unrestricted voting common stock of the issuing corporation for the shares owned by a substantial common stockholder of a combining company whose stock was restricted as to voting or public sale indicate the conditions were not met if the stock issued could be sold immediately?

Interpretation—Stockholder groups have combined their rights and risks so long as stockholders holding substantially all classes of the voting common stock in the combining company receive shares of the majority class of voting common stock of the issuing corporation exactly in proportion to their relative voting common stock interest before the combination was effected. The fact that unrestricted voting common stock is exchanged for stock previously held in a voting trust would not negate accounting for a business combination by the pooling of interests method. Likewise, the fact that "registered" voting common stock of the issuing corporation is exchanged for "restricted" voting common stock of the combining corporation also would not negate accounting for a business combination by the pooling of interests method.

[Issue Date: December, 1970]

7. POOLING UNDER "OLD RULES"

Question—Paragraph 97 of APB Opinion No. 16 states that business combinations initiated before November 1, 1970 and consummated on or after that date under the terms prevailing on October 31, 1970 may be accounted for in accordance with APB Opinion No. 16 *or* the applicable previous pronouncements of the Board or its predecessor committee. Paragraph 97 also contains a reference to paragraph 47-a which, among other things, states that a combination must be completed within one year after the plan is initiated to be accounted for by the pooling of interests method. Does this mean a business combination initiated before November 1, 1970 must be consummated within one year after it was initiated to be accounted for as a pooling of interests under the "old rules"?

Interpretation—No, a business combination initiated before November 1, 1970 need only be consummated under the terms in effect on October 31, 1970 to be accounted for under the "old rules." There is no time limit for consummating the combination.

The reference to paragraph 47-a is intended to call attention to the discussion of a change in terms in that paragraph and to footnote 5 which specifies that an adjustment after October 31, 1970 in the terms of exchange in effect on October 31, 1970 always constitutes initiation of a new plan. A new plan of combination, naturally, would be subject to the provisions of APB Opinion No. 16.

To require a business combination initiated before November 1, 1970 to be consummated within one year after initiation would be retroactive application of APB Opinion No. 16. For example, a business combination initiated on December 31, 1969 would need to be consummated no later than December 31, 1970 if the Opinion were retroactive. The Opinion was not intended to be retroactive and retroactive application is in fact prohibited by paragraph 98 for business combinations consummated before November 1, 1970.

[Issue Date: December, 1970]

8. APPLYING PURCHASE ACCOUNTING

Question—APB Opinion No. 16 clearly applies when one corporation obtains at least 90 per cent of the voting common stock of another corporation, whether through a purchase or a pooling of interests. Does the Opinion also apply when one corporation acquires less than 90 per cent of the voting common stock of another corporation?

Interpretation—APB Opinion No. 16 discusses a 90 per cent "cutoff" (paragraph 47-b) only as one of the conditions to be met to account for a business combination by the pooling of interests method. If this condition—or any other condition in paragraphs 46 through 48—is not met, a business combination must be accounted for by the purchase method.

The Opinion does not create new rules for purchase accounting. The purchase section (paragraphs 66 through 96) merely discusses valuation techniques in much greater detail than is given in prior APB Opinions and Accounting Research Bulletins. Thus, APB Opinion No. 16 provides more guidance for the application of purchase accounting, whether the item purchased is an entire company, a major portion of the stock of a company or a manufacturing plant and regardless of whether the consideration given is cash, other assets, debt, common or preferred stock or a combination of these.

An investment by a corporation in the voting common stock of another company which does not meet the 90 per cent condition must be accounted for as a purchase. The purchase method of accounting applies even though the investment is acquired through an exchange of the voting common stock of the companies.

The acquisition by a corporation of voting control over another corporation creates a parent-subsidiary relationship. Generally, domestic subsidiaries either are consolidated or are included in consolidated financial statements under the equity method of accounting (see ARB No. 51 and APB Opinion No. 10).

Since a controlling interest is usually considered to be more than 50 per cent of the outstanding voting stock in another corporation, the fair value of the assets and liabilities of the subsidiary would be determined when control is acquired if the resulting subsidiary is either consolidated in the financial statements or included under the equity method of accounting. Also, APB Opinion No. 17 specifies the appropriate accounting for intangible assets, if any, recognized for these cases.

In addition, the subsequent acquisition of some or all of the stock held by minority stockholders of a subsidiary is accounted for by the purchase method (see paragraph 5 and 43 of APB Opinion No. 16). Thus, after a business combination has been completed or a controlling interest in a subsidiary has been obtained, the acquisition of some or all of the remaining minority interest is accounted for by the purchase method. The purchase method applies even though the minority interest is acquired through an exchange of common stock for common stock, including the acquisition of a minority interest remaining after the completion of a business combination accounted for by the pooling of interests method.

[Issue Date: April, 1971]

9. "TWO-YEAR" PROVISIONS AT EFFECTIVE DATE

Question—Paragraphs 46-a and 47-c of APB Opinion No. 16 specify conditions to be met for two years prior to the initiation of a business combination which is to be accounted for by the pooling of interests method. Since the Opinion applies to combinations initiated after October 31, 1970, must the conditions of paragraph 46-a (each company is autonomous) and paragraph 47-c (no changes in equity interests) be met for a combination initiated in November 1970 to be accounted for by the pooling of interests method?

Interpretation—No, a corporation which has had a change in the equity interest in its voting common stock or which was a division that was spun-off as a separate corporation prior to November 1, 1970 could be a party to a business combination initiated

on or after that date and meet the conditions for accounting by the pooling of interests method without regard to the two-year period.

[Issue Date: April, 1971]

10. EFFECT OF TERMINATION

Question—Paragraph 46-a of APB Opinion No. 16 defines the initiation of a plan of combination as the date the major terms of an exchange offer are announced publicly or communicated to stockholders even though the plan is still subject to approval of stockholders and others. What is the effect of termination of a plan of combination prior to approval by stockholders and the subsequent resumption of negotiations between the parties?

Interpretation—Paragraph 47-a specifies that a combination must be completed in accordance with *a specific plan*. Therefore, if negotiations are formally terminated after a plan has been initiated (as defined in paragraph 46-a), the subsequent resumption of negotiations always constitutes a new plan. Formal announcement of the major terms of the new plan constitutes a new initiation, even if the terms are the same as the terms of the old plan. Any shares of stock exchanged under the old plan become subject to the conditions of paragraphs 46-b and 47-b (the 10 per cent and 90 per cent tests) upon initiation of the new plan.

[Issue Date: April, 1971]

11. USE OF RESTRICTED STOCK TO EFFECT A BUSINESS COMBINATION

Question—Paragraph 47-b of APB Opinion No. 16 states as a condition for accounting for a business combination by the pooling of interests method that a corporation may issue only common stock with rights *identical* to those of the majority of its outstanding voting common stock in exchange for the voting common stock of another company. Would restrictions on the sale of the shares of common stock issued result in different rights for these shares?

Interpretation—The "rights" pertinent to paragraph 47-b are those involving relationships between stockholders and the corporation rather than between the stockholders and other parties. The "rights" therefore pertain to voting, dividends, liquidation, etc., and not necessarily to a stockholder's right to sell stock. Restrictions imposed on the sale of the stock to the public in compliance with governmental regulations do not ordinarily cause the "rights" to be different, but other restrictions may create different rights.

For example, voting common stock issued by a publicly held corporation to effect a business combination may be restricted as to public sale until a registration with the SEC or a state securities commission becomes effective. If a registration were in process or the issuing corporation agreed to register the stock subsequent to the combination, the rights of the stock would not be different because of the restriction.

However, a restriction imposed by the issuing corporation upon the sale of the stock in the absence of a governmental regulation would probably create different rights between previously outstanding and newly issued stock. Such a restriction might also indicate the previously separate stockholder groups would not be sharing the same risks in the business combination (see paragraph 45 and introductory statements in paragraphs 46 and 47). Likewise, a restriction upon the sale of the stock to anyone other than the issuing corporation or an affiliate would not meet the "absence of planned transactions" condition specified in paragraph 48-a.

[Issue Date: April, 1971]

12. WARRANTS MAY DEFEAT POOLING

Question—May a business combination be accounted for by the pooling of interests method if the issuing corporation exchanges voting common stock *and* warrants for the voting common stock of a combining company?

Interpretation—Paragraph 47-b of APB Opinion No. 16 specifies that in a business combination accounted for by the pooling of interests method a corporation may issue *only* common stock in exchange for at least 90 per cent of the common stock of another company. Therefore, a *pro rata* distribution of warrants of the issuing corporation to all stockholders of a combining company would not meet this condition and the business combination would be accounted for as a purchase.

In some cases, however, warrants may be used in a business combination accounted for by the pooling of interests method. Warrants (as well as cash or debt) could be used, for example, to acquire up to 10 per cent of the common stock of a combining company under paragraph 47-b and the combination could still qualify as a "pooling" so long as the common stock acquired plus other intercorporate investments plus any remaining minority interest would allow the 90 per cent test to be met.

Warrants may be issued in exchange for the combining company's outstanding preferred stock or debt.

The issuing corporation may exchange its warrants for the combining company's outstanding warrants. Any warrants issued could not provide for the

purchase of a greater number of shares than could be obtained if the warrants were exercised. For example, if the issuing corporation will exchange three of its common shares for each of the combining company's common shares outstanding and the combining company has warrants outstanding allowing the holders to purchase two common shares per warrant, each warrant issued in exchange for the outstanding warrants could provide for the purchase of no more than six of the issuing corporation's common shares. (It should be noted that warrants issued by either company in contemplation of effecting the combination might not meet the conditions of paragraph 47-c.)

[Issue Date: April, 1971]

13. TWO-CLASS COMMON FOR POOLING

Question—Paragraph 47-b of APB Opinion No. 16 specifies that a corporation must issue common stock "with rights identical to those of the majority class of its outstanding voting common stock" in a business combination which is to be accounted for by the pooling of interests method. Could the common stock issued be designated as a class of stock different from majority class (for example, Class A if the majority class has no class designation) and meet this condition?

Interpretation—Paragraph 47-b does not prohibit designating the common stock issued as a different class if it has *rights identical* to those of the majority class of outstanding voting common stock. Thus, the different class must have the same voting, dividend, liquidation, preemptive, etc., rights as the majority class with the stipulation that these rights cannot be changed unless a corresponding change is made in the rights of the majority class.

Issuing a different class of common stock with rights identical to other common stock would generally serve no useful purpose. It would be suspected that the parties might have secretly agreed that they would in the future change the rights of the different class to restrict voting; grant a preference in liquidation; or increase, guarantee or limit dividends.

[Issue Date: April, 1971]

14. CONTINGENT SHARES DEFEAT POOLING

Question—Paragraph 47-g of APB Opinion No. 16 specifies that in a business combination to be accounted for by the pooling of interests method a corporation may not (1) agree to issue additional shares of stock at a later date or (2) issue to an escrow agent shares which will later be transferred to stockholders or returned to the corporation.

Would this condition be met if the corporation issued some maximum number of shares to stockholders of the combining company under an agreement that part of the shares would be returned if future earnings are below a certain amount or the future market price of the stock is above a stipulated price?

Interpretation—No, contingent shares based on earnings, market prices and the like require a business combination to be accounted for as a purchase. Paragraph 47-g states that the combination must be "resolved at the date the plan is consummated."

The only contingent arrangement permitted under paragraph 47-g is for settlement of a contingency pending at consummation, such as the later settlement of a lawsuit. A contingent arrangement would also be permitted for an additional income tax liability resulting from the examination of "open" income tax returns.

[Issue Date: April, 1971]

15. PARAGRAPH 99 IS NOT MANDATORY

Question—APB Opinion No. 16 requires business combinations meeting the conditions of paragraphs 46 through 48 to be accounted for by the pooling of interests method and all other business combinations to be accounted for by the purchase method. However, paragraph 99 provides a "grandfather clause" permitting certain exceptions to the pooling conditions for business combinations which meet the conditions of that paragraph. Under paragraph 99 the accounting treatment is: (1) the excess of cost of the investment in common stock acquired prior to November 1, 1970 over equity in net assets when the stock investment was acquired is allocated to identifiable assets and goodwill regardless of the percentage of ownership on October 31, 1970 and (2) the pooling of interests method is applied for the common stock issued in the combination if the combination meets the conditions for accounting by the pooling of interests method. That is, the combination is accounted for as a "part-purchase, part-pooling." Is the application of paragraph 99 mandatory for a busines combination meeting the conditions of that paragraph?

Interpretation—No, the accounting described in paragraph 99 is an election available to an issuing corporation to apply the pooling of interests method to account for a business combination not otherwise meeting the conditions of paragraphs 46-b and 47-b. Paragraph 99 specifies "the resulting business combination *may* [emphasis added] be accounted for by the pooling of interests method provided. . . ."

Paragraph 99 applies only for intercorporate investments held at October 31, 1970 and to business combinations completed within five years after that date. The provision was inserted to avoid retroactivity by allowing pooling of interest accounting for a combination that would not have met the conditions of paragraphs 46-b and 47-b because an intercorporate investment held at October 31, 1970 then was near or exceeded 10 per cent of the outstanding voting common stock of the combining company.

A business combination meeting all of the conditions of paragraphs 46 through 48 as well as the conditions of paragraph 99 would be accounted for by the pooling of interests method. Paragraph 99 would not apply and the intercorporate investment would be accounted for as described in paragraph 55. A business combination meeting the conditions of paragraph 99 but not otherwise meeting the conditions of paragraphs 46-b and 47-b may either be accounted for as a "part-purchase, part-pooling" as described in paragraph 99 or as a purchase.

[Issue Date: April, 1971]

16. CHANGES IN INTERCORPORATE INVESTMENTS

Question—How do sales of investments in another corporation's voting common stock owned at October 31, 1970 and acquisitions of additional investments of the same class of stock after that date affect computations under the "grandfather clause" in paragraph 99 of APB Opinion No. 16?

Interpretation—Sales after October 31, 1970 of investments in another corporation's voting common stock which was owned at that date are always considered as reductions of the common stock to which the "grandfather clause" in paragraph 99 applies, in other words, on a first-in, first-out basis. This reduction is made even though the common stock sold is identified as having been acquired after October 31, 1970.

The "grandfather clause" in paragraph 99 does not apply to acquisitions after October 31, 1970 of voting common stock of the same class as was owned at that date. Any stock so acquired is therefore subject to the conditions of paragraphs 46-b and 47-b.

[Issue Date: April, 1971]

17. INTERCORPORATE INVESTMENT AT 10/31/70

Question—Paragraph 99 of APB Opinion No. 16 contains a "grandfather clause" which exempts minority interests held on October 31, 1970 from certain provisions of the Opinion in business combinations initiated and consummated within five years after that date. The paragraph is written in terms of an intercorporate investment owned by the corporation which effects the combination by issuing voting common stock. Does this paragraph also apply to stock of the issuing corporation which is owned by the other combining company on October 31, 1970?

Interpretation—Paragraph 99 was intended to exempt intercorporate investments owned on October 31, 1970 by all of the parties to the business combination in the circumstances described. Thus, stock of the issuing corporation which is owned by the other combining company on October 31, 1970 may be ignored in computing the 90 per cent condition described in paragraph 47-b.

For example, assume that on October 31, 1970 Baker Company owned 500,000 of the 3,000,000 shares of the voting common stock of Adam Corporation. Subsequently, Adam Corporation initiated a business combination by offering the stockholders of Baker Company one share of Adam common for each share of Baker common out-

standing. The combination was consummated in a single transaction within one year after initiation and within five years after October 31, 1970. Of the 1,000,000 Baker common shares outstanding at initiation and consummation, 950,000 shares were tendered to Adam Corporation. Assume also that the combination meets all of the conditions of paragraphs 46 through 48 to be accounted for by the pooling of interests method except the conditions of paragraph 46-b (no more than 10 per cent intercorporate investments) and paragraph 47-b (the 90 per cent condition).

Under paragraph 99 as interpreted here, the business combination may be accounted for by the pooling of interests method since the 500,000 Adam shares owned by Baker Company need not be considered in applying the conditions of paragraphs 46-b and 47-b. Under the pooling of interests method, the 500,000 Adam shares would become treasury stock of Adam Corporation as specified by paragraph 55.

[Issue Date: April, 1971]

Business Combinations:
Accounting Interpretations of APB Opinion No. 16

18. WHOLLY OWNED SUBSIDIARY

Question—Paragraph 46-a of APB Opinion No. 16 states that a wholly owned subsidiary may distribute voting common stock of its parent corporation in a "pooling" combination if its parent would have met all of the conditions in paragraphs 46-48 had the parent issued its stock directly to effect the combination. As a practical matter, a parent may be unable to own all of a subsidiary's stock. State laws generally require a certain number of the directors of a corporation to own some of the corporation's shares, so a parent would not legally own a few "qualifying directors' shares" registered in the names of "inside" directors. Also, even though a parent attempts to purchase all of a subsidiary's shares owned by outsiders, a few shareholders may never be located and others may refuse to sell their shares for a reasonable amount. If a parent company owns *substantially all* of the outstanding voting stock of a subsidiary, will the subsidiary be considered "wholly" owned for purposes of applying paragraph 46-a?

Interpretation—Yes, a subsidiary is considered "wholly" owned under paragraph 46-a if its parent owns substantially all of the subsidiary's outstanding voting stock. The subsidiary may therefore

"pool" with another company by distributing the parent company's voting common stock if the parent would have met the conditions of paragraphs 46-48 in a direct issuance.

What constitutes "substantially all" of a subsidiary's voting stock will vary according to circumstances. Generally, the shares not owned by the parent would be expected to be an insignificant number, such as qualifying directors' shares. A parent might also be considered as owning "substantially all" of a subsidiary's voting stock if the parent had attempted to buy all of the stock but some owners either could not be located or refused to sell a small number of shares at a reasonable price. In no case, however, would less than 90 percent be considered "substantially all" (see paragraph 47-b) and generally the percentage would be expected to be much higher.

The reason for using the subsidiary as the combining company would also be important in determining if "substantially all" of its voting stock is owned by the parent. A parent would be expected to own all but a few of its subsidiary's shares, other than qualifying directors' shares, in a combination in which either the parent or subsidiary could engage if the parent is to be considered as owning "substantially all" of its subsidiary's voting stock. A somewhat greater percentage of outside ownership would be acceptable in a combination between a subsidiary authorized to operate in a state where the parent is not authorized to operate and another company operating in that state. An even larger outside ownership (but not more than 10 percent) would be acceptable in a regulated industry (where a subsidiary in the industry—but not its parent outside the industry—could combine with another company in the industry) when a subsidiary engages in a combination that its parent could not undertake directly.

[Issue Date: September, 1971]

19. EQUITY AND DEBT ISSUED FOR COMMON BEFORE POOLING

Question—Paragraph 47-b of APB Opinion No. 16 states that the issuing corporation may exchange only voting common stock for outstanding equity and debt securities of the other combining company that have been issued in exchange for voting common stock of that company during a period beginning two years preceding the date a "pooling" combination is initiated. What is the purpose of this provision?

Interpretation—Paragraph 47-c of APB Opinion No. 16 prohibits accounting for a business combination by the pooling of interests method if equity and/or debt securities have been issued by a combining company in exchange for or to retire its voting common stock in contemplation of effecting the combination within two years before the plan of combination was initiated or between the dates of initiation and consummation. In paragraph 47-b, there is an implied presumption that all such transactions of the other combining company were made in contemplation of effecting a combination, thereby violating the condition of paragraph 47-c. However, the issuance of voting common stock of the issuing corporation to the holders of such equity and debt securities of the other combining company in exactly the same ratio as their former holdings of voting common stock of the other combining company will restore the holders of the securities to their former position and, hence, will "cure" the violation of the condition of paragraph 47-c.

[Issue Date: September, 1971]

20. TREASURY STOCK ALLOWED WITH POOLING

Question—Paragraph 47-d of APB Opinion No. 16 states as a condition for "pooling" that each of the combining companies may reacquire shares of voting common stock (as treasury stock) only for

purposes other than business combinations. Also, paragraphs 47-c and 47-d of APB Opinion No. 16 include provisions related to the reacquisition of treasury stock within two years prior to initiation and between initiation and consummation of a business combination which is planned to be accounted for by the pooling of interests method. For what purposes may treasury stock be reacquired during this period?

Interpretation—The statement "for purposes other than business combinations" means combinations initiated under APB Opinion No. 16 which are to be accounted for by the pooling of interests method. Therefore, acquisitions of treasury stock for specific purposes that are not related to a particular business combination which is planned to be accounted for by the pooling of interests method are not prohibited by the conditions of either paragraph 47-c or 47-d.

In the absence of persuasive evidence to the contrary, however, it should be presumed that all acquisitions of treasury stock during the two years preceding the date a plan of combination is initiated (or from October 31, 1970 to the date of initiation if that period is less than two years) and between initiation and consummation were made in contemplation of effecting business combinations to be accounted for as a pooling of interests. Thus, lacking such evidence, this combination would be accounted for by the purchase method regardless of whether treasury stock or unissued shares or both are issued in the combination.

The specific purposes for which treasury shares may be reacquired prior to consummation of a "pooling" include shares granted under stock option or compensation plans, stock dividends declared (or to be declared as a recurring distribution), and recurring distributions as provided in paragraph 47-d. Likewise, treasury shares reacquired for issuance in a specific "purchase" or to resolve an existing contingent share agreement from a prior business combination would not invalidate a concurrent "pooling." Treasury shares reacquired for these purposes should be either reissued prior to consummation or specifically reserved for these purposes existing at consummation.

To the extent that treasury shares reacquired within two years prior to initiation or between initiation and consummation have not been reissued or specifically reserved, an equivalent number of shares of treasury stock may be sold prior to consummation to "cure" the presumed violation of paragraphs 47-c and 47-d. If the number of shares not reserved or disposed of prior to consummation of a combination is material in relation to the number of shares *to be issued* to effect the combination, the combination should be accounted for by the purchase method.

Treasury shares reacquired more than two years

prior to initiation may be reissued in a "pooling." Also, "tainted" treasury shares purchased within two years prior to initiation or between intiation and consummation and not disposed of or reserved may be reissued in a "pooling" if not material in relation to the total number of shares issued to effect the combination. Treasury shares reissued in a "pooling" should be accounted for as specified in paragraph 54.

It should be noted that earnings and market price contingencies were permitted in both "purchases" and "poolings" under "old rules." These contingencies in a combination consummated under APB Opinion No. 16 require the combination to be accounted for as a "purchase." Although "liability-type" contingencies may exist in a "pooling" as specified in paragraph 47-g, treasury stock may not be reacquired to satisfy such a contingency.

[Issue Date: September, 1971]

21. POOLING WITH "BAILOUT"

Question—Paragraph 48-a of APB Opinion No. 16 specifies that a combined corporation may not agree to directly or indirectly retire or reacquire all or part of the common stock issued to effect a business combination and paragraph 48-b specifies that a combined corporation may not enter into financial arrangements for the benefit of the former stockholders of a combining company if a business combination is to be accounted for by the pooling of interests method. Would an arrangement whereby a third party buys all or part of the voting common stock issued to stockholders of a combining company immediately after consummation of a business combination cause the combination to not meet these conditions?

Interpretation—The fact that stockholders of a combining company sell voting common stock received in a business combination to a third party would not indicate failure to meet the conditions of paragraphs 48-a and 48-b. "Continuity of ownership interests," a criterion for a pooling of interests under ARB No. 48, is *not* a condition to account for a business combination by the pooling of interests method under APB Opinion No. 16. The critical factor in meeting the conditions of paragraphs 48-a and 48-b is that the voting common stock issued to effect a business combination remains outstanding outside the combined corporation without arrangements on the part of any of the corporations involving the use of their financial resources to "bailout" former stockholders of a combining company or to induce others to do so.

Either the combined corporation or one of the combining companies may assist the former stockholders in locating an unrelated buyer for their shares (such as by introduction to underwriters) so long as compensation or other financial inducements from the corporation are not in some way involved in the arrangement. If unregistered stock is issued, the combined corporation may also agree to pay the costs of initial registration.

[Issue Date: September, 1971]

22. DISPOSITION OF ASSETS TO COMPLY WITH AN ORDER

Question—As a condition to account for a business combination by the pooling of interests method, paragraph 48-c of APB Opinion No. 16 prohibits the planned disposal of a significant part of the assets of the combining companies within two years after the consummation date other than disposals in the ordinary course of business and eliminations of duplicate facilities or excess capacity. Likewise, paragraph 47-c prohibits a change in the equity interests of the voting common stock—such as through the "spin-off" of a division or a subsidiary—in contemplation of effecting a "pooling" combination either within two years before initiation or between initiation and consummation. Does a prior or a planned disposition of a significant part of the assets of a combining company to comply with an order of a governmental authority or judicial body constitute a violation of this condition?

Interpretation—No. The prior or planned disposition of a significant part of the assets of a combining company (even though in contemplation of effecting or planned subsequent to a combination) does not negate accounting for a business combination as a "pooling" if the disposition is undertaken to comply with an order of a governmental authority or judicial body or to avoid circumstances which, on the basis of available evidence, would result in the issuance of such an order. This is generally consistent with paragraph 46-a (autonomy of combining companies) which permits subsidiaries disposed of in compliance with an order of a governmental authority or judicial body to be considered autonomous for purposes of that condition.

Any gain or loss resulting from a disposal within two years after consummation of a pooling of interests should be accounted for in accordance with paragraph 59 and 60.

[Issue Date: September, 1971]

23. RETROACTIVE DISCLOSURE OF POOLING

Question—Paragraph 61 of APB Opinion No. 16 specifies that a business combination accounted for by the pooling of interests method should be recorded as of the date the combination is consummated. This paragraph prohibits a combining company from retroactively reflecting in the financial statements for the current year a combination consummated after the close of the year but before financial statements are issued. However, this paragraph requires a corporation to disclose *as supplemental information, in notes to financial statements or otherwise, the substance of a combination consummated before financial statements are issued and the effects of the combination on reported financial position and results of operations.* Could this disclosure be in the form of a statement with side-by-side columns reporting financial data for (1) the issuing corporation and (2) the combined corporations, and, perhaps, (3) the other combining company?

Interpretation—APB Opinion No. 16 does not prohibit the side-by-side columnar format described above, nor alternatively, does it prohibit an above-and-below columnar format. The term *or otherwise* included in paragraph 61 is sufficiently broad to permit disclosure of the information on the face of the financial statements in either side-by-side or above-and-below columns.

Because the Opinion prohibits retroactive pooling for a combination completed after the close of the year but before the financial statements are issued, however, the individual columns in the presentation should be separately identified as primary or supplemental information. That is, data for the issuing corporation would be identified as the primary financial statements and data for the combined corporation would be identified as supplemental information. If presented, data for the combining company would also be identified as supplemental information.

It might be noted that a side-by-side presentation will disclose information in greater detail than is required by paragraph 65 (which requires that only revenue, net income, earnings per share and the effects of anticipated changes in accounting methods be disclosed as if the combination had been consummated at the date of the financial statements). Although both paragraphs 61 and 65 specify disclosure in *notes* to the financial statements and paragraph 65 specifies only *note* disclosure without the *or otherwise* provision, this paragraph refers back to paragraph 61 so the columnar format is not prohibited by paragraph 65 as long as the information is properly identified as primary and supplemental.

Information for the combined corporation identified as supplemental information (as described above) would be reported as primary information in statements for the following period when the combination was consummated if comparative financial statements are presented. Reporting and disclosure requirements for the period when a business com-

bination is consummated and for prior periods are contained in paragraphs 51-58, 63 and 64.

Notes to the statements and other disclosures which are included in the statements are a part of the financial statements. Accordingly, the auditor's opinion—unless appropriately modified—would apply to disclosure (in notes to the statements or in columnar format) of the substance of a combination consummated after the close of the year but before the financial statements were issued. The auditor's opinion might be modified, however, to disclaim an opinion on the supplemental information if it had not been included in the auditor's examination.

[Issue Date: September, 1971]

24. "GRANDFATHER" FOR SUBSIDIARIES

Question—Paragraph 46-a of APB Opinion No. 16 prohibits use of pooling accounting for a business combination initiated after October 31, 1970 (the effective date of the Opinion) which involves an entity which was a "subsidiary." However, notes to the Opinion state the Opinion is not intended to be retroactive. Paragraph 46-a appears to impose a retroactive effect on subsidiaries with significant minority interests that may have been considering engaging in pooling combinations. Was this intended?

Interpretation—Paragraph 46-a was not intended to have the retroactive effect described above. Subsidiaries which had a *significant* outstanding minority interest at October 31, 1970 may take part in a pooling combination completed within five years after that date providing the significant minority also exists at the initiation of the combination. In addition, the combination must meet all of the other pooling conditions specified in paragraphs 46 through 48 both directly and indirectly (i.e., the parent company cannot take actions on behalf of the subsidiary that the subsidiary could not take itself).

For purposes of this Interpretation, a significant minority means that at least 20 percent of the voting common stock of the subsidiary is owned by persons not affiliated with the parent company.

This "grandfathering" is consistent with paragraph 99 of the Opinion and applies both to combinations where the subsidiary with a significant minority interest is the issuing corporation and those where it is the other combining company. However, it does not permit a pooling between a subsidiary and its parent.

[Issue Date: November, 1971]

25. ALL SHARES MUST BE EXCHANGED TO POOL

Question—Paragraph 47-b of APB Opinion No. 16 specifies that an issuing corporation must exchange only voting common stock for at least 90 percent of the voting common stock interest of a combining company to account for the combination as a pooling of interests. The paragraph permits cash or other consideration to be exchanged for the remaining shares or they may continue outstanding as a minority interest. Under paragraph 47-b, assuming the issuing corporation exchanges common stock for at least 90 percent of the common stock of the combining company, may an individual common shareholder of the combining company exchange some of his shares for shares of the issuing corporation and either retain the balance of his shares or sell the shares to the issuing corporation for cash?

Interpretation—If a business combination is to be accounted for as a pooling of interests, each common shareholder of the combining company must either agree to exchange *all* of his shares for common shares of the issuing corporation or refuse to exchange *any* of his shares.

It would be contrary to the "pooling" concept expressed in APB Opinion No. 16 for an individual shareholder of a combining company to exchange some of his shares and keep some of his shares in a pooling of interests or for the issuing corporation to exchange common stock for some of an individual shareholder's shares and pay cash for some of his shares. The "pooling" concept would be violated in these cases even though the issuing corporation exchanged its common stock for at least 90 percent of the common stock of the combining company as required by paragraph 47-b.

Theoretically two or more *entire* common stockholder groups join together as a single entity in a pooling of interests to share the combined risks and rights represented by the previously independent interests without the distribution of corporate assets to *any* of the common stockholders (see paragraph 45). Paragraph 46 states as an attribute of "pooling" that independent ownership interests are combined in their entirety. That paragraph indicates that combining only selected assets or ownership interests would be more akin to disposing of or acquiring interests than to sharing rights and risks. Paragraph 47 states that acquisitions of common stock for assets or debt and other transactions that reduce the common stock interest are contrary to the idea of combining existing stockholder interests.

The Opinion permits the theoretical concept of "pooling" to be modified only within strict limits to accommodate practical obstacles that may be encountered in many combinations. Thus, the 90 percent "test" in paragraph 47-b recognizes that, as a practical matter, some shareholders of a combining company may refuse to exchange their shares even though most shareholders agree to a combination.

Paragraph 47-b permits cash or other consideration to be distributed by the issuing corporation for shares held by these dissenting shareholders of the combining company. However, a shareholder who assents to exchange part of his shares can hardly be considered a dissenting shareholder.

In addition, the exchange by an individual shareholder of a combining company of only part of his shares for common stock of the issuing corporation would not meet paragraph 47-e. That paragraph states that each individual shareholder who exchanges his stock must receive a voting common stock interest in proportion to his relative voting common stock interest in the combining company before the combination.

Usually the determination of whether or not a shareholder of a combining company is exchanging all of his shares for common stock of the issuing corporation will be made at consummation. However, transactions prior to consummation between the issuing corporation and a shareholder of a combining company who exchanges shares at consummation may also preclude a "pooling." In the absence of persuasive evidence to the contrary, it should be presumed that the purchase was made in contemplation of effecting the combination (see paragraph 47-c) if the issuing corporation purchased shares of a combining company within two years prior to initiation and before consummation from a shareholder who also exchanges shares at consummation.

To overcome another purely practical problem, paragraph 47-b also allows cash or other consideration to be distributed by the issuing corporation in lieu of fractional shares. There is no essential difference between the payment of cash to a common shareholder for a fraction of a share and the payment of cash for some of his shares. Therefore, the payment of more than a reasonable amount of cash to a shareholder for a fractional share would also be contrary to the "pooling" concept expressed in the Opinion. Thus, the payment for fractional shares among shareholders must be reasonable in amount and should be proportional to each shareholder's fractional share interest.

[Issue date: November, 1971]

Business Combinations:
Accounting Interpretations of APB Opinion No. 16

26. ACQUISITION OF MINORITY INTEREST

Question—How should a corporation account for the acquisition of all or part of the minority interest of a subsidiary?

Interpretation—Paragraph 5 of APB Opinion No. 16 states, "The acquisition of some or all of the stock held by minority shareholders of a subsidiary is not a business combination, but paragraph 43 of this Opinion specifies the applicable method of accounting." Paragraph 43 states that the acquisition of some or all of the stock held by minority stockholders of a subsidiary—whether acquired by the parent, the subsidiary itself, or another affiliate—should be accounted for by the purchase method. Thus, purchase accounting applies when (a) a parent exchanges its common stock or assets or debt for common stock held by minority shareholders of its subsidiary, (b) the subsidiary buys as treasury stock the common stock held by minority shareholders, or (c) another subsidiary of the parent exchanges its common stock or assets or debt for common stock held by the minority shareholders of an affiliated subsidiary.

In addition, paragraph 46-b precludes pooling when the combining companies hold as intercorporate investments more than 10 percent of the outstanding voting common stock of any combining company (except when paragraph 99 applies, as discussed later). Therefore, pooling is precluded in the exchange by a subsidiary of its common stock for the outstanding voting common stock of its parent (usually referred to as a "downstream merger"). Instead, purchase accounting applies and the transaction should be accounted for as if the parent had exchanged its common stock for common stock held by minority shareholders of its subsidiary. (Whether a parent acquires the minority or a subsidiary acquires its parent, the end result is a single shareholder group, including the former minority shareholders, owning the consolidated net assets.) The same would be true if a new corporation exchanged its common stock for the common stock of the parent and the common stock of the subsidiary held by minority shareholders.

An exception to the requirement for purchase accounting in the acquisition of a minority interest may exist in some rare cases under paragraph 99. This paragraph permits pooling accounting to be elected on a "grandfather" basis under certain conditions, one condition being a combination in which one corporation owns no more than 50 percent of the voting *common* stock of the other combining

company. Since a parent company may control a subsidiary even though the parent owns less than 50 percent of the subsidiary's voting common stock (e.g., by owning voting preferred stock in addition to voting common stock—see paragraph 2 of ARB No. 51), the exchange by the parent of its voting common stock for the voting common stock of the subsidiary owned by outsiders could qualify for pooling accounting. However, it should be noted that paragraph 99 would require the parent to allocate the excess of the cost of its previously existing investment over its proportionate equity in the subsidiary's net assets to the subsidiary's identifiable assets (and to goodwill, if any) based on fair values at the consummation date.

[Issue Date: December, 1971]

27. ENTITIES UNDER COMMON CONTROL IN A BUSINESS COMBINATION

Question—Paragraph 5 of APB Opinion No. 16 states that the provisions of the Opinion should be applied as a general guide in a business combination involving one or more unincorporated businesses. Paragraph 46-a requires that each company in a pooling be autonomous and have not been a subsidiary or division for two years prior to initiation. How does the Opinion apply to a combination involving one entity controlled by one or a few individuals who control several other entities?

Interpretation—A proprietorship or a partnership may be a party to a business combination accounted for under APB Opinion No. 16 as stated in the first sentence of paragraph 5. Many of these entities are very similar, except for legal form of organization, to a closely held corporation. Often a single individual may own one or more proprietorships and also may own the controlling interest in one or more corporations and in addition may have an interest in one or more partnerships.

Considerable judgment will usually be required to determine the substance of a combination involving one (or more) of several companies under common control. For example, it may be necessary to look beyond the form of the legal organizations to determine substance when an unincorporated business or a closely held corporation owned by one or a few individuals who also control other entities is involved since the dividing lines may not be as "sharp" as they would be in publicly held corporations with wide ownership interests.

An individual who owns two separate businesses organized as corporations theoretically is a "parent" with two "subsidiaries." The same would be true if the businesses were organized as two proprietorships or as one proprietorship and one corporation. To apply paragraph 46-a to a combination involving one of these businesses, however, the relationship between the two businesses is more important than the fact that each business is theoretically a subsidiary, because paragraph 46-a precludes fragmenting a business and pooling only a part of the business. The following examples demonstrate these points.

If both businesses are grocery stores, a combination involving only *one* business should presumably be accounted for as a purchase because the two stores presumably are part of a single kind of business and the two separate legal organizations should be ignored.

On the other hand, if one business is a grocery store and the other is an automobile dealership, a combination involving only one business would be accounted for as a pooling of interests if all other conditions of paragraphs 46-48 are met because the individual is operating two unrelated businesses. In these examples, a "line of business" is an indicator of a single business.

Also, a combination involving two or more businesses owned by one individual must be accounted for by a single method. For example, if both the grocery store and the automobile dealership are to be combined with another unrelated company, one could *not* be a purchase and the other a pooling. (Paragraph 47-b discusses a combination of more than two companies and paragraph 43 states the two methods are not alternatives in accounting for the same combination.)

In general, the same guidelines apply to a business with a few owners rather than an individual owner. They would apply, for example, to two partnerships having the same partners, two closely held corporations having the same stockholders, or to a partnership and a closely held corporation whose stockholders are the partners in the partnership. If the various individuals are all members of one family, the effect may be the same (but is not always the same) as if there were only an individual owner rather than several partners and/or several stockholders.

Because the ratios of ownership of the different businesses may differ or the ownership groups may overlap but be different, however, several owners of different businesses create complexities which are not present if there is a single owner. Because of the diversity of the situations which might be encountered in practice, stating guidelines beyond those given above is impossible.

[Issue Date: December, 1971]

28. POOLING BY SUBSIDIARY OF PERSONAL HOLDING COMPANY

Question—A single individual may control other corporations (for federal income tax reasons) through a personal holding company. Paragraph 46-a requires that each company in a pooling be autonomous and have not been a subsidiary or division for two years prior to the initiation of a combination. Does this preclude a pooling by a corporation which is controlled by a personal holding company?

Interpretation—The legal form may sometimes be ignored in a combination involving a subsidiary of a personal holding company. Under paragraph 46-a a personal holding company is technically a parent corporation and the corporations it controls are technically subsidiaries. In many cases, a parent-subsidiary relationship does in fact exist and should be considered as such in applying paragraph 46-a if the personal holding company or any of its subsidiaries is involved in a business combination.

In other cases, a personal holding company is a convenience established for federal income tax reasons and the various "subsidiaries" are in fact operated by the "owners" as if the personal holding company did not exist. In a combination involving such a "subsidiary," the personal holding company may be disregarded and the various "subsidiaries" considered autonomous in applying paragraph 46-a. However, the guidelines described in Accounting Interpretation titled, "Entities Under Common Control in a Business Combination" should be applied in determining the appropriate method of accounting for the combination and all other conditions of paragraphs 46-48 must be met in a pooling.

[Issue Date: December, 1971]

29. OPTION MAY INITIATE COMBINATION

Question—Paragraph 46-a of APB Opinion No. 16 specifies the requirements for initiation of a business combination. Does an option to exchange substantially all of their shares at a future date (for example, three years hence) granted by the shareholders of a closely held company to another company constitute the initiation of a business combination?

Interpretation—An option that *requires* unilateral performance by either party or bilateral performance by both parties constitutes initiation. Thus, if one company is required to issue stock upon the tendering of shares by the shareholders of another company or if the shareholders are required to tender their shares upon demand, the date the option is granted is the initiation date. The combination must be consummated within one year thereafter to be accounted for by the pooling of interests method (see paragraph 47-a).

However, an agreement which grants only the right of "first refusal" does not constitute initiation. This would be the case, for example, where the stockholders of a closely held company agree to negotiate with one company before negotiating with any other company if the shareholders should in the future decide to consider entering into a business combination. Neither party may be obligated to perform, however, or to pay damages in the absence of performance.

The payment of cash or other consideration by either company for a "first refusal" agreement would also be contrary to the pooling concept expressed in APB Opinion No. 16. Individual shareholders, however, may pay cash to obtain the agreement so long as company resources are not directly or indirectly involved.

[Issue Date: December, 1971]

30. REPRESENTATIONS IN A POOLING

Question—Paragraph 47-g of APB Opinion No. 16 specifies that in a business combination accounted for as a pooling of interests there can be no agreement to contingently issue additional shares of stock or other consideration at a later date and no escrowing of shares until a contingency is resolved. This paragraph allows, however, revision of the number of shares issued upon the settlement of a contingency at an amount different from that recorded by a combining company. May an issuing company reserve or escrow some shares against the representations of the management of a combining company in a pooling?

Interpretation—Paragraph 47-g is intended to require purchase accounting when an earnings or market price contingency agreement is present in a business combination. However, this paragraph does not prohibit certain kinds of contingency agreements in a pooling so long as they provide for the sharing of rights and risks arising after consummation and are not in effect earnings or market price contingency agreements.

A contingency agreement which is not prohibited in a pooling may provide for the reservation by the issuing company of a portion of the shares being issued, the issuance of additional shares, the return of shares by former shareholders of the combining company, or the issuance of shares to an escrow agent who will subsequently transfer them to the former shareholders of the combining company or

return them to the issuing company. (Note that the former shareholders of the combining company must be able to vote any shares issued, reserved, or escrowed to meet the condition of paragraph 47-f.)

The most common type of contingency agreement *not* prohibited in a pooling by paragraph 47-g is the "general management representation" which is present in nearly all business combinations. In such a representation, management of a combining company typically warrants that the assets exist and are worth specified amounts and that all liabilities and their amounts have been disclosed. The contingency agreement usually calls for an adjustment in the total number of shares exchanged up to a relatively small percentage (normally about 10 percent) for variations from the amounts represented, but actual adjustments of the number of shares are rare.

A contingency agreement for a "general management representation" does not violate paragraph 47-g if it provides for a substantial sharing of rights and risks beginning with consummation and the complete sharing within a reasonable period of time. In this light, the contingency agreement is merely a device to provide time for the issuing company to determine that the representations are accurate so it does not share risks arising prior to consummation. Although the time required will vary with circumstances, these determinations should be completed within a few months following consummation of the combination. In any case, the maximum time should not extend beyond the issuance of the first independent audit report on the company making the representations following consummation of the combination. Thereafter, the combined shareholder interests share the risks of inventory obsolescence, collection of receivables, etc. However, if the complete sharing of risks is unduly delayed or if the risk sharing is not substantial at consummation, a "general management representation" may in effect indicate an earnings contingency agreement.

Paragraph 47-g specifically allows certain contingency agreements in a pooling to cover specific situations whose outcome cannot be reasonably determined at consummation and perhaps even for several years thereafter. (Contingencies of this type are described in paragraph 2 of ARB No. 50.) Although management of a combining company may make specific representations as to these contingencies that are known at the consummation of a pooling and as to those which may arise within a reasonable period thereafter, the combined shareholder interests are expected to share the risks and rights of all other contingencies if paragraph 47-g is to be met. Likewise, the former shareholders of a combining company must be able to vote any shares issued, reserved, or escrowed for a specific contingency until it is finally resolved if paragraph 47-f is to be met. The contingency agreement may provide, however, that any dividends during the contingency period on contingent shares "follow" the shares when the contingency is resolved.

It should also be noted that any change in the number of shares (as originally recorded for a pooling of interests) upon the final resolution of either a general or a specific representation contingency is recorded as an adjustment to stockholders' equity (see paragraph 53). The effect of the resolution of a contingency involving an asset or liability, whether or not previously recorded, is reflected currently in net income or as a prior period adjustment in accordance with APB Opinion No. 9. In no case may a contingency agreement for either a general or a specific representation in a pooling be used as a means of relieving current or prior net income of an amount which should be reflected therein.

[Issue Date: December, 1971]

31. EMPLOYMENT CONTINGENCIES IN A POOLING

Question—Paragraph 47-g of APB Opinion No. 16 stipulates that in a business combination accounted for as a pooling of interests there can be no agreement for contingent issuance of additional shares of stock or distribution of other consideration to the former stockholders of a combining company. Would the granting of an employment contract or a deferred compensation plan by the combined corporation to former stockholders of a combining company cause this condition to not be met?

Interpretation—An employment contract or a deferred compensation plan granted by the combined corporation to former stockholders of a combining company would not automatically constitute failure of paragraph 47-g. The critical factors would be the reasonableness of the arrangement and restriction of the arrangement to continuing management personnel. Generally, reasonable contracts or plans entered into for valid business purposes would meet paragraph 47-g. Substance, however, is more important than form.

As an example, the granting of employment contracts to former stockholders of a combining company who were active in its management and who will be active in management of the combined corporation would meet paragraph 47-g if the contracts are reasonable in relation to existing contracts granted by the issuing corporation to its management. However, the granting of employment contracts to former stockholders of a combining company who were not or will not be active in management probably indicates a contingent pay-out arrangement. Likewise, "consultant" contracts for former stockholders might also indicate a contingent pay-out arrangement.

Employment contracts and deferred compensation plans entered into by a combining company between the initiation and consummation dates may also cause a business combination to not meet paragraph 47-g. For example, a combining company may not enter into a "contingency-type" compensation agreement *in contemplation* of the combination and meet paragraph 47-g if the issuing corporation could not also enter into the same agreement under the paragraph.

[Issue Date: December, 1971]

32. STOCK OPTIONS IN A POOLING

Question—Paragraph 47-g of APB Opinion No. 16 states that in a business combination accounted for as a pooling of interests the combined corporation may not agree to contingently issue additional shares of stock to the former stockholders of a combining company. Would this condition be violated if the combined corporation granted stock options to these stockholders?

Interpretation—Generally, stock options granted by the combined corporation as current compensation to former stockholders of a combining company would not violate paragraph 47-g. That is, the former stockholders of a combining company who are employees or directors of the combined corporation may participate in a stock option plan adopted by the combined corporation for its employees and/or directors.

Paragraph 47-g would be violated, however, if the stock option plan in reality is an arrangement to issue additional shares of stock at a relatively low cost to these former stockholders of the combining company to satisfy a contingency agreement. Also, a stock option plan to accomplish the same result adopted by the combining company prior to consummation but *in contemplation* of the combination would not meet paragraphs 47-c and 47-g.

[Issue Date: December, 1971]

33. COSTS OF MAINTAINING AN "ACQUISITIONS" DEPARTMENT

Question—A corporation maintains an "acquisitions" department to find, evaluate, and negotiate with possible merger candidates. The president of the corporation also spends a considerable portion of his time negotiating business combinations. Cost records are excellent and the total cost is determined for each investigation and negotiation, whether it is successful or unsuccessful. What accounting is specified by APB Opinion No. 16 for these costs?

Interpretation—All "internal" costs associated

with a business combination are deducted *as incurred* in determining net income under APB Opinion No. 16. This answer applies to costs incurred for both "poolings" (see paragraph 58) and "purchases" (see paragraph 76). Naturally, costs incurred in unsuccessful negotiations are also deducted as incurred.

Paragraph 76 specifies that in a business combination accounted for by the purchase method the cost of a company acquired includes the *direct* costs of acquisition. These direct costs, however, are "out-of-pocket" or incremental costs rather than recurring internal costs which may be directly related to an acquisition. The direct costs which are capitalized in a purchase therefore include, for example, a finder's fee and fees paid to outside consultants for accounting, legal, or engineering investigations or for appraisals, etc. All costs related to effecting a pooling of interests, including the direct costs listed above, are charged to expense as specified in paragraph 58.

[Issue Date: December, 1971]

34. FORCED SALE OF STOCK

Question—A publicly held corporation wants to effect a business combination with a large closely held corporation and to account for the combination as a pooling of interests. Because management of the publicly held corporation prefers not to have a single stockholder owning a large block of its stock, the agreement to combine requires the majority stockholder of the closely held corporation to sell 25 percent of the voting common stock he receives immediately following consummation and to sell another 25 percent within one year thereafter. The stock is to be sold in public offerings and all of the shares will remain outstanding outside the combined corporation. Since APB Opinion No. 16 does not have the "continuity of ownership interests" criterion of ARB No. 48 as a condition for pooling, should this combination be accounted for as a pooling of interests or as a purchase?

Interpretation—The combination is a purchase because of the *requirement* imposed on a shareholder to sell some of the voting common stock received. Any requirement imposed on a stockholder (other than by a government authority) either *to sell* or *to not sell* stock received in a business combination is contrary to the pooling concept expressed in APB Opinion No. 16 of the sharing of rights and risks by the previously independent stockholder interests. While such a requirement does not violate any specific condition for pooling described in paragraphs 46-48, it violates the whole pooling concept of the Opinion.

[Issue Date: January, 1972]

35. REGISTRATION COSTS IN A PURCHASE

Question—If a company issues previously *registered* equity securities in a business combination accounted for by the purchase method, the fair value of the securities issued is credited to the capital accounts of the issuing corporation. However, if the securities issued have not been previously registered, paragraph 76 of APB Opinion No. 16 specifies that the costs of registering and issuing equity securities are a reduction of the otherwise determinable fair value of the securities. How should a corporation account for the costs of a registration which will not be undertaken until after the securities are issued?

Interpretation—A publicly held company issuing *un*registered equity securities in an acquisition with an agreement for subsequent registration should credit the fair value of the securities (the otherwise determinable fair value less registration costs) to its capital accounts. The present value of the estimated costs of registration should be accrued as a liability at the date of acquisition (see paragraph 88-h) with an immediate charge to the assets acquired (in most cases, to "goodwill"). Any difference between the actual costs of registration and the amount accrued at the payment date (the original accrual plus imputed interest) would be an adjustment to the recorded goodwill. Total assets (including goodwill) and total capital will thereby be recorded at the same amounts as if previously registered securities had been issued except for any difference in fair value ascribed to restrictions prohibiting sale of the securities at time of issuance.

Agreements for the subsequent registration of unregistered securities issued in business combinations often specify that the securities will be registered "piggyback" (that is, included in the registration of a planned future offering of other securities). In such a case, only the incremental costs of registering the equity securities issued in the acquisition would be accrued or subsequently charged to "goodwill" as described above and amortized prospectively over the remaining term of the period of amortization of the initial goodwill.

[Issue Date: January, 1972]

36. NO POOLING WITH WHOLLY OWNED SUBSIDIARIES

Question—Company A initiated a combination by making a tender offer for Company B which was at the time an independent company. Company C, which owned a large interest in but not control of Company B, subsequently and without Company A's knowledge purchased all of the remaining outstanding voting common stock of Company B and operated Company B as a wholly owned subsidiary. Within one year of the date Company A made the tender offer, Company C tendered all of the voting common stock of Company B to Company A in exchange for voting common stock of Company A at the ratio of exchange of the tender offer. Paragraph 46-a of APB Opinion No. 16 generally precludes accounting for a business combination by the pooling of interests method if one of the combining companies has been a subsidiary of another corporation within two years prior to initiation of the combination. Does the fact that Company B became a wholly owned subsidiary of Company C following initiation of the combination by Company A preclude pooling in this case?

Interpretation—Yes, pooling is precluded and Company A should account for the combination as a purchase. (Company C, in effect, sold its wholly owned subsidiary B to Company A.) Paragraph 46-a provides that a wholly owned subsidiary may pool only by distributing the stock of its parent company.

Although paragraph 46-a refers to not being a subsidiary "within two years before the plan of combination is initiated," the intent of the paragraph is that a combining company in a pooling has not been a subsidiary during a period beginning two years prior to initiation and ending at consummation of a combination.

[Effective for combinations consummated after May 31, 1972]

Business Combinations:
Accounting Interpretations of APB Opinion No. 16

37. COMBINATION CONTINGENT ON "BAILOUT"

Question—An accounting interpretation of APB Opinion No. 16, "Pooling with 'Bailout'," issued in September 1971 indicates that former shareholders of a combining company may sell voting common stock received in a business combination accounted for as a pooling of interests. Would the accounting for a combination be affected by the fact that its consummation is contingent upon the purchase by a third party or parties of all or part of the voting common stock to be issued in the combination?

Interpretation—Yes. A business combination should be accounted for as a purchase if its consummation is contingent upon the purchase by a third party or parties of *any* of the voting common stock to be issued. This would be the case, for example, if the parties to the combination have agreed that consummation of the combination will not occur until there is a commitment by a third party for a private purchase, a firm public offering, or some other form of a guaranteed market for all or part of the shares to be issued. Including such a contingency in the arrangements of the combination, either explicitly or by intent, would be considered a financial arrangement which is precluded in a pooling by paragraph 48-b of APB Opinion No. 16.

It should be noted that this accounting interpretation does not modify the previous interpretation, "Pooling with 'Bailout'," which states that shareholders may sell stock received in a pooling and that the corporation may assist them in locating an unrelated buyer for their shares. Although shareholders may sell stock received in a pooling, consummation of the business combination must first occur without regard to such a sale and cannot be contingent upon a firm commitment by the potential purchaser of the shares to be issued.

[Issue Date: November, 1972]

38. SEVERAL COMPANIES IN A SINGLE BUSINESS COMBINATION

Question—How does APB Opinion No. 16 apply when more than two companies are involved in a single business combination?

Interpretation—When more than two companies negotiate a combination which is contingent upon the mutual agreement by the several companies to the terms, the resulting combination is deemed a single business combination regardless of the number of companies involved. Each company must meet all of the conditions of paragraphs 46-48 if the combination is to be accounted for by the pooling of interests method. In particular, paragraphs 46-b and 47-b specify how the 10 percent and 90 percent tests should be made when more than two companies are involved in a single combination.

Paragraph 43 specifies that a single method should be applied to account for an entire combination. Therefore, if any condition in paragraphs 46-48 is not met by any company, the entire combination would be accounted for by the purchase method.

However, it should be noted that a corporation may be involved in more than one business combination at the same time and that different methods of accounting may apply to the different combinations.

[Issue Date: March, 1973]

39. TRANSFERS AND EXCHANGES BETWEEN COMPANIES UNDER COMMON CONTROL

Question—Paragraph 5 of APB Opinion No. 16 states the Opinion does not apply to a transfer of net assets or to an exchange of shares between companies under common control. What are some examples of the types of transactions excluded from the Opinion by this provision and what accounting should be applied?

Interpretation—In general, paragraph 5 excludes transfers and exchanges that do not involve outsiders. For example, a parent company may transfer the net assets of a wholly owned subsidiary into the parent company and liquidate the subsidiary, which is a change in legal organization but not a change in

the entity. Likewise, a parent may transfer its interest in several partially owned subsidiaries to a new wholly owned subsidiary, which is again a change in legal organization but not in the entity. Also, a parent may exchange its ownership or the net assets of a wholly owned subsidiary for additional shares issued by the parent's partially owned subsidiary, thereby increasing the parent's percentage of ownership in the partially owned subsidiary but leaving all of the existing minority interest outstanding.

None of the above transfers or exchanges is covered by APB Opinion No. 16. The assets and liabilities so transferred would be accounted for at historical cost in a manner similar to that in pooling of interests accounting.

It should be noted, however, that purchase accounting applies when the effect of a transfer or exchange is to acquire all or part of the outstanding shares held by the minority interest of a subsidiary (see paragraph 43). The acquisition of all or part of a minority interest, however acquired, is never considered a transfer or exchange by companies under common control. (See Interpretation No. 26 of APB Opinion No. 16, "Acquisition of Minority Interest.")

[Issue Date: March, 1973]

Intangible Assets:
Unofficial Accounting Interpretations
of APB Opinion No. 17

STATUS

Issued: April 1971-March 1973

Effective Date: Interpretation No. 1—April 1971
Interpretation No. 2—March 1973

Affects: No other pronouncements

Affected by: No other pronouncements

Intangible Assets:
Unofficial Accounting Interpretations of
APB Opinion No. 17

1. INTANGIBLE ASSETS

Question—APB Opinion No. 17 requires that intangible assets acquired after October 31, 1970 be amortized over a period not exceeding 40 years. Does this Opinion encourage the capitalization of identifiable internally developed intangible assets which have been generally charged to expense in the past?

Interpretation—APB Opinion No. 17 does not change present accounting practice for intangible assets in any way except to require that intangible assets acquired after October 31, 1970 be amortized. Paragraph 6 notes that the costs of some identifiable intangible assets are now capitalized as deferred assets by some companies while other companies record the costs as expenses when incurred. This paragraph also specifies that the question of whether the costs of identifiable internally developed intangible assets are to be capitalized or charged to expense is not covered by the Opinion. Therefore, the Opinion does not encourage capitalizing the costs of a large initial advertising campaign for a new product or capitalizing the costs of training new employees.

[Issue Date: April, 1971]

2. GOODWILL IN A STEP ACQUISITION

Question—Goodwill and other intangible assets acquired before November 1, 1970 (the effective date of APB Opinion No. 17) are not required to be amortized until their term of existence becomes limited (see Chapter 5 of ARB No. 43). APB Opinion No. 17 requires all intangible assets acquired after October 31, 1970 to be amortized. When a company purchases two or more blocks of voting common stock of another company at various dates before and after November 1, 1970 and eventually obtains control or the ability to exercise significant influence over operating and financial policies of the other company, how should the investor company subsequently account for any "goodwill" related to the investment?

Interpretation—When a company in a series of purchases on a step-by-step basis acquires either a subsidiary which is consolidated or an investment which is accounted for under the equity method, the company should identify the cost of each investment, the fair value of the underlying assets acquired and the goodwill for each step purchase. This process would then identify the goodwill associated with each step purchase made before November 1, 1970 or after October 31, 1970 for each investment.[1]

Goodwill associated with each step purchase acquired prior to November 1, 1970 should be accounted for in accordance with Chapter 5 of ARB No. 43 as amended by APB Opinion No. 9. Although amortization is not required in the absence of evidence that the goodwill has a limited term of existence, paragraph 35 of APB Opinion No. 17 encourages prospective amortization of such goodwill. Retroactive amortization is prohibited by paragraph 34.

Goodwill associated with each step purchase acquired after October 31, 1970 should be amortized in accordance with APB Opinion No. 17. The period of amortization may not exceed forty years as specified by paragraph 29.

[Issue Date: March, 1973]

---

[1]The accounting for a step acquisition of a subsidiary which is consolidated is described by paragraph 10 of ARB No. 51 (see also paragraphs 87, 93, and 94 of APB Opinion No. 16). As specified by paragraphs 19-b and 19-n of APB Opinion No. 18, similar procedures apply for a step acquisition of an investment carried under the equity method.

The Equity Method of Accounting for Investments in Common Stock: Accounting Interpretations of APB Opinion No. 18

STATUS

Issued: November 1971-February 1972

Effective Date: Interpretations No. 1 and 2—November 1971
Interpretation No. 3—February 1972

Affects: No other pronouncements

Affected by: Interpretation No. 1 amended by FAS 96 and FAS 109
Interpretation No. 2 amended by FAS 96, FAS 109, and FAS 111

The Equity Method of Accounting for Investments in Common Stock: Accounting Interpretations of APB Opinion No. 18

1. INTERCOMPANY PROFIT ELIMINATION UNDER EQUITY METHOD

Question—In applying the equity method of accounting, intercompany profits or losses on assets still remaining with an investor or investee should be eliminated, giving effect to any income taxes on the intercompany transactions. (See paragraph 19-a of APB Opinion No. 18 and paragraphs 6 and 17 of ARB No. 51.) Should all of the intercompany profit or loss be eliminated or only that portion related to the investor's common stock interest in the investee?

Interpretation—Paragraph 19 of APB Opinion No. 18 normally requires an investor's net income and stockholder's equity to be the same from application of the equity method as would result from consolidation. Because the equity method is a "one-line" consolidation, however, the details reported in the investor's financial statements under the equity method will not be the same as would be reported in consolidated financial statements (see paragraph 19-c). All intercompany transactions are eliminated in consolidation, but under the equity method intercompany profits or losses are normally eliminated only on assets still remaining on the books of an investor or an investee.

Paragraph 14 of ARB No. 51 provides for complete elimination of intercompany profits or losses in consolidation. It also states that the elimination of intercompany profit or loss may be allocated proportionately between the majority and minority interests. Whether all or a proportionate part of the intercompany profit or loss should be eliminated under the equity method depends largely upon the relationship between the investor and investee.

When an investor controls an investee through majority voting interest and enters into a transaction with an investee which is not on an "arm's length" basis, none of the intercompany profit or loss from the transaction should be recognized in income by the investor until it has been realized through transactions with third parties. The same treatment also applies for an investee established with the cooperation of an investor (including an investee established for the financing and operation or leasing of property sold to the investee by the investor) when control is exercised through guarantees of indebtedness, extension of credit and other special arrangements by the investor for the benefit of the investee, or because of ownership by the investor of warrants, convertible securities, etc. issued by the investee.

In other cases, it would be appropriate for the investor to eliminate intercompany profit in relation to the investor's common stock interest in the investee. In these cases, the percentage of intercompany profit to be eliminated would be the same regardless of whether the transaction is "downstream" (i.e., a sale by the investor to the investee) or "upstream" (i.e., a sale by the investee to the investor). The following examples illustrate how these eliminations might be made. The examples assume an investor owns 30 percent of the common stock of an investee, the investment is accounted for under the equity method, and the income tax rate to both the investor and the investee is 40 percent.

Assume an investor sells inventory items to the investee ("downstream"). At the investee's balance sheet date, the investee holds inventory for which the investor has recorded a gross profit of $100,000. The investor's net income would be reduced $18,000 to reflect a $30,000 reduction in gross profit and a $12,000 reduction in income tax expense. The elimination of intercompany profit might be reflected in the investor's balance sheet in various ways; for example, the investor might present $12,000 as a deferred tax charge (this is a "timing" difference under APB Opinion No. 11) and $30,000 as a deferred income credit. The income statement and balance sheet presentations will depend upon what is the most meaningful in the circumstances.

Assume an investee sells inventory items to the investor ("upstream"). At the investor's balance sheet date, the investor holds inventory for which the investee has recorded a gross profit of $100,000. In computing the investor's equity "pickup," $60,000 ($100,000 less 40% of income tax) would be deducted from the investee's net income and $18,000 (the investor's share of the intercompany gross profit after income tax) would thereby be eliminated from the investor's equity income. Usually, the investor's investment account would also reflect the $18,000 intercompany profit elimination, but the elimination might also be reflected in various other ways; for example, the investor's inventory might be reduced $18,000.

[Issue Date: November, 1971]

2. INVESTMENTS IN PARTNERSHIPS AND VENTURES

Question—Do the provisions of APB Opinion No. 18 apply to investments in partnerships and unincorporated joint ventures?

Interpretation—APB Opinion No. 18 applies only to investments in common stock of corporations and does not cover investments in partnerships and unincorporated joint ventures (also called undivided interests in ventures). Many of the provisions of the Opinion would be appropriate in accounting for investments in these unincorporated entities, however, as discussed below.

Partnership profits and losses accrued by investor-partners are generally reflected in their financial statements as described in paragraphs 19-c and 19-d. Likewise, most of the other provisions of paragraph 19 would be appropriate in accounting for a partnership interest, such as the elimination of intercompany profits and losses (see paragraph 19-a).

However, contrary to the provisions of paragraph 19-j (income taxes on undistributed earnings of subsidiaries), income taxes should be provided on the profits accrued by investor-partners regardless of the tax basis employed in the partnership return. The tax liabilities applicable to partnership interests relate directly to the partners, and the accounting for income taxes generally contemplated by APB Opinion No. 11 is appropriate.

Generally, the above discussion of partnerships would also apply to unincorporated joint ventures, particularly the elimination of intercompany profits and the accounting for income taxes. However, because the investor-venturer owns an undivided interest in each asset and is proportionately liable for its share of each liability, the provisions of paragraph 19-c may not apply in some industries. For example, where it is the established industry practice (such as in some oil and gas venture accounting), the investor-venturer may account in its financial statements for its *pro rata* share of the assets, liabilities, revenues, and expenses of the venture.

[Issue Date: November, 1971]

3. EARLY DISCLOSURE OF MATERIAL EQUITY ADJUSTMENT

Question—APB Opinion No. 18 requires the equity method of accounting to be applied for a qualifying investment in common stock for fiscal periods beginning after December 31, 1971. The Board encouraged earlier adoption of the Opinion. If a company owns an investment in 1971 for which it does not adopt the equity method until 1972 when the retroactive application will materially change the originally reported 1971 net income, should the amount of the change be disclosed in the 1971 financial statements when they are first issued?

Interpretation—Yes, as a minimum the company should disclose in its 1971 financial statements the effect later retroactive application of the equity method will have on 1971 net income. In fact, the company should consider adopting the equity method in 1971 even though not required to do so.

The Board issued this Opinion in March 1971 and provided a relatively long interval before its effective date because of the time required for companies to accumulate information, arrange for audits of investee companies, etc. Extenuating circumstances may therefore exist for not applying the equity method in 1971. However, any material effect of subsequent retroactive application should be disclosed in the 1971 financial statements.

[Issue Date: February, 1972]

486

Reporting Changes in Financial Position:
Accounting Interpretations of APB Opinion No. 19

STATUS

Issued: February 1972-June 1972

Effective Date: Interpretations No. 1 and 2—February 1972
             Interpretation No. 3—June 1972

Affects: No other pronouncements

Affected by: Interpretations No. 1 through 3 superseded by FAS 95

(The next page is 489.)

(This page intentionally left blank.)

Accounting Changes:
Accounting Interpretations of APB Opinion No. 20

STATUS

Issued: March 1973

Effective Date: March 1973

Affects: No other pronouncements

Affected by: No other pronouncements

Accounting Changes:
Accounting Interpretations of APB Opinion No. 20

1. CHANGING EPS DENOMINATOR FOR RETROACTIVE ADJUSTMENT TO PRIOR PERIOD

Question—Paragraph 27 of APB Opinion No. 20 specifies that certain accounting changes should be reported by retroactively restating all prior periods presented. Paragraph 28 requires that the effect of these changes on the prior periods' earnings per share amounts be disclosed. The anti-dilution prohibitions of paragraphs 30 and 40 of APB Opinion No. 15 require the exclusion from earnings per share computations of securities whose conversion, exercise, or other contingent issuance would have the effect of increasing the earnings per share amount or decreasing the loss per share amount. If these securities were originally included in the earnings per share computation in a prior period but would have been excluded if the retroactively restated amount had been reported in the prior period, should the securities be included or excluded when computing the restated earnings per share amount?

Interpretation—A retroactively restated earnings per share amount should always be computed as if the restated income or loss had been originally reported in the prior period. Common stock assumed to be issued for exercise, conversion, etc. and included in the original earnings per share denominator should, therefore, in circumstances such as those described below be excluded from the denominator in computing the restated earnings per share amount.

For example, assume that a corporation which reported $200,000 net income in the immediately preceding year changes its method of accounting for long-term construction-type contracts from the completed contract method to the percentage of completion method. In applying this change retroactively (see paragraph 27 of APB Opinion No. 20), the net income originally reported for the immediately preceding year is decreased $290,000 and restated as a net loss of $90,000. Further assume that in the prior year the corporation had 900,000 shares of common stock and 150,000 warrants outstanding for the entire year. Each warrant could be exercised to purchase one share of common stock for $10 while the market price of common was $30 throughout the year. Earnings per share were originally reported as $.20 based on $200,000 net income divided by a denominator of 1,000,000 common shares (900,000 shares outstanding plus 100,000 shares for warrants computed under the treasury stock method). The assumption of exercise of warrants is anti-dilutive when there is a loss, so the restated amount would be reported as a net loss

of $.10 per share based on $90,000 net loss divided by a denominator of 900,000 common shares outstanding.

Note that retroactive restatement could also cause securities originally determined to be anti-dilutive to become dilutive. For example, assume the same facts as given in the preceding illustration except a $90,000 net loss was originally reported and is restated as $200,000 net income. Exercise of the warrants would not have been assumed in the original per share computation because the result would have been anti-dilutive but would be assumed in computing the restated earnings per share because the result is dilutive.

Retroactive restatement may also cause the earnings per share numerator to change by an amount different from the amount of the retroactive adjustment. For example, assume that a corporation changes from the LIFO method of inventory pricing to the FIFO method, retroactively increasing net income for the immediately preceding year by $400,000 (see paragraph 27 of APB Opinion No. 20). Further assume that the corporation originally reported a net income of $800,000 in the prior year and had 800,000 shares of common stock outstanding. In addition, 200,000 shares of preferred stock were outstanding which were convertible into common stock on a one-for-one basis. The preferred stock is a common stock equivalent and paid a dividend of $1 per share. Earnings per share were originally reported as $.75 based on an earnings per share numerator of $600,000 ($800,000 net income less $200,000 preferred dividends) and a denominator of 800,000 common shares. The assumption of conversion in the original computation would have been anti-dilutive. Restated net income is $1,200,000 and restated earnings per share is $1.20 based on a numerator of $1,200,000 and a denominator of 1,000,000 shares (800,000 common shares outstanding plus 200,000 common shares for the assumed conversion of preferred stock). Although restatement increased net income and, therefore, the earnings per share numerator $400,000 in this case, the assumed conversion of the preferred stock increased the earnings per share numerator by another $200,000.

In addition to a retroactive adjustment for a change in accounting principle under paragraph 27 of APB Opinion No. 20, the guidelines given above in this Interpretation apply to (a) retroactive restatement under paragraphs 29 and 30 of APB Opinion No. 20, (b) restatement of prior periods for a change in the reporting entity as described in paragraphs 34 and 35 of APB Opinion No. 20, (c) the correction of an error in previously issued financial statements as described in paragraphs 36 and 37 of APB Opinion

No. 20, and (d) a prior period adjustment as described in paragraphs 18, 23, and 24 of APB Opinion No. 9. These guidelines will likewise apply whenever an APB Opinion requires that it be applied retroactively, including Opinions which may be issued in the future.

Also, these guidelines should be applied in computing the pro forma earnings per share amounts for the types of changes in accounting principle described in paragraph 19 of APB Opinion No. 20. Although these types of changes in accounting principle are not applied retroactively, paragraphs 19-d and 21 require that the pro forma effects of retroactive application be disclosed.

A change in the earnings per share denominator (and perhaps numerator) from that originally used in the computation may create certain complications in reporting the effect of a retroactive change. These complications may be illustrated by considering the data in the table below, given for the examples presented earlier in this Interpretation.

	Warrant Example	Convertible Preferred Stock Example
Net income as previously reported	$ 200,000	$ 800,000
Adjustment for retroactive change	(290,000)	400,000
Net income (loss) as adjusted	$ (90,000)	$1,200,000
Earnings per share amounts:		
As previously reported	$ .20[a]	$ .75[c]
Effect of retroactive change	(.30)	.45
As adjusted	$(.10)[b]	$1.20[d]

Computational Notes:
  (a) $200,000 ÷ (900,000 + 100,000) shares
  (b) $90,000 ÷ 900,000 shares
  (c) ($800,000−$200,000) ÷ 800,000 shares
  (d) $1,200,000 ÷ (800,000 + 200,000) shares

In both of the above examples, the earnings per share amounts shown for "effect of retroactive change" are computed by subtracting the previously reported amounts from the adjusted amounts. Determining the per share amount of the change by subtraction comprehends the effects of any necessary changes in the denominator and the numerator by reason of retroactive application.

[Issue Date: March, 1973]

2. EPS FOR "CATCH-UP" ADJUSTMENT

Question—Paragraph 20 of APB Opinion No. 20 requires the per share amount of the cumulative effect of most accounting changes (see paragraphs 18 and 19) to be shown on the face of the income statement similar to the manner in which an extraordinary item would be shown. Footnote 8 of APB Opinion No. 15 giving an exception to the anti-dilution prohibition in primary earnings per share computations, states that if an extraordinary item is present and a common stock equivalent results in dilution of either income before extraordinary items or net income on a per share basis, the common stock equivalent should be recognized for all computations. Footnote 14 gives a similar reference for fully diluted computations. How does reporting the cumulative effect of an accounting change in a manner similar to an extraordinary item affect the application of these two footnotes in computing earnings per share?

Interpretation—The cumulative effect of an accounting change (sometimes referred to as a "catch-up" adjustment) is considered the same as an extraordinary item, whether or not extraordinary items are present, in computing earnings per share. Therefore, a common stock equivalent which has a dilutive effect on the primary earnings per share computation for either (a) income before extraordinary items (if any) and the cumulative effect of a change in accounting principle or (b) net income should be recognized in all computations of primary earnings per share for the period. Likewise, a common stock equivalent or other potentially dilutive security which has a dilutive effect on the fully diluted earnings per share computation for either (a) income before extraordinary items (if any) and cumulative effect of a change in accounting principle or (b) net income should be recognized in all computations of fully diluted earnings per share for the period. Note that, under these exceptions to the anti-dilution prohibitions of APB Opinion No. 15, a common stock equivalent or other potentially dilutive security may have an anti-dilutive effect on either "a" or "b" but not on both. The per share amount of an extraordinary item or a "catch-up" adjustment is always computed by using the same denominator used to compute both the "a" and "b" earnings per share amounts.

However, the exceptions to the anti-dilution prohibitions do not permit an assumed exercise, conversion, etc. to cause fully diluted net income (loss) per share to be anti-dilutive in relation to primary net income (loss) per share. That is, the assumed exercise, conversion, etc. of a security may have an anti-dilutive effect within primary earnings per share or within fully diluted earnings per share, but the assumed exercise, conversion, etc. should not have the effect of increasing (decreasing) the fully diluted net income (loss) per share amount to more (less) than the primary net income (loss) per share amount. (See footnote 5, page 402, *Computing Earnings per Share*.)

Although the "catch-up" adjustment is considered the same as an extraordinary item in computing earnings per share, the earnings per share reporting requirement for the two items is different. APB Opinion No. 15 does not require that per share amounts be reported for extraordinary items, although this presentation may generally be desirable (see Interpretation 16 page 410, *Computing Earnings per Share*). Paragraph 20 of APB Opinion No. 20 does require per share data for a "catch-up" adjustment to be shown on the face of the income statement. Preferably, when both an extraordinary item and a "catch-up" adjustment are reflected in net income for a period, per share data for both should be presented on the face of the income statement.

[Issue Date: March, 1973]

Interest on Receivables and Payables:
Accounting Interpretations of APB Opinion No. 21

STATUS

Issued: June 1972

Effective Date: June 1972

Affects: No other pronouncements

Affected by: No other pronouncements

Interest on Receivables and Payables:
Accounting Interpretations of APB Opinion No. 21

1. ADVANCE NOT REQUIRING IMPUTATION

Question—APB Opinion No. 21 requires interest to be imputed for some rights to receive or obligations to pay money on fixed or determinable dates. In certain transactions, pipeline companies make advances to encourage exploration. These advances are satisfied by delivery of future production, but there is also a definite obligation to repay if the future production is insufficient to discharge the obligation by a definite date. Does APB Opinion No. 21 apply to such advances?

Interpretation—No, paragraph 3-b states that the Opinion is not intended to apply to "amounts which do not require repayment in the future, but rather will be applied to the purchase price of the property, goods, or service involved (e.g., deposits or progress payments on construction contracts, advance payments for acquisition of resources and raw materials, advances to encourage exploration in the extractive industries)." The advance described in the question above is covered by the exclusion in paragraph 3-b even though there may be an obligation to repay should the future production prove insufficient to discharge the obligation.

[Issue Date: June, 1972]

Disclosure of Accounting Policies:
Accounting Interpretations of APB Opinion No. 22

STATUS

Issued: November 1973

Effective Date: November 1973

Affects: No other pronouncements

Affected by: Interpretation No. 1 superseded by FAS 111

AIN-APB23

Accounting for Income Taxes—Special Areas: Accounting Interpretations of APB Opinion No. 23

STATUS

Issued: March 1973

Effective Date: March 1973

Affects: No other pronouncements

Affected by: Interpretation No. 1 superseded by FAS 96 and FAS 109

(The next page is 499.)

Accounting for Stock Issued to Employees: Accounting Interpretations of APB Opinion No. 25

STATUS

Issued: June 1973

Effective Date: June 1973

Affects: No other pronouncements

Affected by: Interpretation No. 1 amended by FAS 96 and FAS 109

Accounting for Stock Issued to Employees:
Accounting Interpretations of APB Opinion No. 25

1. STOCK PLANS ESTABLISHED BY A PRINCIPAL STOCKHOLDER

Question—Accounting for compensatory and noncompensatory stock option, purchase and award plans adopted by a corporation is discussed in APB Opinion No. 25 and ARB No. 43, Chapter 13B. Should a corporation account for plans or transactions ("plans"), if they have characteristics otherwise similar to compensatory plans adopted by corporations, that are established or financed by a principal stockholder (i.e., one who either owns 10% or more of the corporation's common stock or has the ability, directly or indirectly, to control or influence significantly the corporation)?

Interpretation—It is difficult to evaluate a principal stockholder's intent when he establishes or finances a plan with characteristics otherwise similar to compensatory plans generally adopted by corporations. A principal stockholder may be satisfying his generous nature, settling a moral obligation, or attempting to increase or maintain the value of his own investment. If a principal stockholder's intention is to enhance or maintain the value of his investment by entering into such an arrangement, the corporation is implicitly benefiting from the plan by retention of, and possibly improved performance by, the employee. In this case, the benefits to a principal stockholder and to the corporation are generally impossible to separate. Similarly, it is virtually impossible to separate a principal stockholder's personal satisfaction from the benefit to the corporation. Accounting Principles Board Statement No. 4, *Basic Concepts and Accounting Principles Underlying Financial Statements of Business Enterprises,* paragraph 127 states that "Financial accounting emphasizes the economic substance of

events even though the legal form may differ from the economic substance and suggest different treatment."

The economic substance of this type of plan is substantially the same for the corporation and the employee, whether the plan is adopted by the corporation or a principal stockholder. Consequently, the corporation should account for this type of plan when one is established or financed by a principal stockholder unless (1) the relationship between the stockholder and the corporation's employee is one which would normally result in generosity (i.e., an immediate family relationship), (2) the stockholder has an obligation to the employee which is completely unrelated to the latter's employment (e.g., the stockholder transfers shares to the employee because of personal business relationships in the past, unrelated to the present employment situation), or (3) the corporation clearly does not benefit from the transaction (e.g., the stockholder transfers shares to a minor employee with whom he has had a close relationship over a number of years).

This type of plan should be treated as a contribution to capital by the principal stockholder with the offsetting charge accounted for in the same manner as compensatory plans adopted by corporations.

Compensation cost should be recognized as an expense of one or more periods in accordance with the provisions of APB Opinion No. 25, paragraphs 12 through 15.

The corporation should account for tax benefits, if any, from this type of plan in accordance with the provisions of APB Opinion No. 25, paragraphs 16 through 18. If the corporation receives no tax benefit from this type of plan, but would have received such benefit had the plan been adopted by the corporation, the absence of such tax benefit is one of the variables in estimating the plan's cost to the corporation (see APB Opinion No. 16, paragraph 89).

[Issue Date: June, 1973]

Early Extinguishment of Debt:
Accounting Interpretations of APB Opinion No. 26

STATUS

Issued: March 1973

Effective Date: March 1973

Affects: No other pronouncements

Affected by: Interpretation No. 1 amended by FAS 111

Early Extinguishment of Debt:
Accounting Interpretations of APB Opinion No. 26

1. DEBT TENDERED TO EXERCISE WARRANTS

Question—APB Opinion No. 26 stipulates that gain or loss should be recognized currently in income when any form of debt security is reacquired by the issuer before its scheduled maturity except through conversion by the holder. Does this Opinion apply to debt tendered to exercise warrants which were originally issued with that debt but which were detachable?

Interpretation—APB Opinion No. 26 does not apply to debt tendered to exercise detachable war-

rants which were originally issued with that debt if the debt is permitted to be tendered towards the exercise price of the warrants under the terms of the securities at issuance. The tendering of the debt in such a case would be a conversion "pursuant to the existing conversion privileges of the holder" (see paragraph 2 of the Opinion).

APB Opinion No. 26 does not apply to a conversion of debt nor does the Opinion specify the accounting for conversion of debt. In practice, however, the carrying amount of the debt, including any unamortized premium or discount, is credited to the capital accounts upon conversion to reflect the stock issued and no gain or loss is recognized.

[Issue Date: March, 1973]

Reporting the Results of Operations: Accounting Interpretations of APB Opinion No. 30

STATUS

Issued: November 1973

Effective Date: November 1973

Affects: No other pronouncements

Affected by: No other pronouncements

Reporting the Results of Operations:
Accounting Interpretations of APB Opinion No. 30

1. ILLUSTRATION OF THE APPLICATION OF APB OPINION NO. 30

Question—As stated in paragraph 19 of APB Opinion No. 30, judgment is required to segregate in the income statement the effects of events or transactions that are extraordinary items. What factors must be considered in determining whether the effects of a particular event or transaction are extraordinary items or should otherwise be set forth in the income statement, and how are these factors applied in practice?

Interpretation—The first question which generally should be considered in determining the appropriate classification of profit or loss items which appear to be unusual, infrequently occurring or extraordinary is:

Does the event or transaction involve the sale, abandonment or other manner of disposal of a segment of a business as defined in paragraph 13 of the Opinion?

Discussion—As explained in paragraph 8 of the Opinion, results of discontinued operations of a segment of a business and any gain or loss from disposal of the segment should be reported separately in the income statement, but should not be designated as extraordinary items. The term "segment of a business" is defined in paragraph 13 of the Opinion as a component of an entity whose activities represent a separate major line of business or class of customer. The Opinion further provides guidelines for the determination of a segment of a business and distinguishes between the disposal of a segment and the disposal of assets incident to the evolution of an entity's business. The following are illustrative of disposals which should be classified as disposals of a segment of a business:

(1) A sale by a diversified company of a major division which represents the company's only activities in the electronics industry. The assets and results of operations of the division are clearly segregated for internal financial reporting purposes from the other assets and results of operations of the company.

(2) A sale by a meat packing company of a 25% interest in a professional football team which has been accounted for under the equity method. All other activities of the company are in the meat packing business.

(3) A sale by a communications company of all its radio stations which represent 30% of gross revenues. The company's remaining activities are three television stations and a publishing company. The assets and results of operations of the radio stations are clearly distinguishable physically, operationally and for financial reporting purposes.

(4) A food distributor disposes of one of its two divisions. One division sells food wholesale primarily to supermarket chains and the other division sells food through its chain of fast food restaurants, some of which are franchised and some of which are company-owned. Both divisions are in the business of distribution of food. However, the nature of selling food through fast food outlets is vastly different than that of wholesaling food to supermarket chains. Thus by having two major classes of customers, the company has two segments of its business.

Certain disposals would not constitute disposals of a segment of a business because they do not meet the criteria specified in the Opinion. For example, the following disposals should not be classified as disposals of a segment of a business:

(5) The sale of a major foreign subsidiary engaged in silver mining by a mining company which represents all of the company's activities in that particular country. Even though the subsidiary being sold may account for a significant percentage of gross revenue of the consolidated group and all of its revenues in the particular country, the fact that the company continues to engage in silver mining activities in other countries would indicate that there was a sale of a part of a line of business.

(6) The sale by a petrochemical company of a 25% interest in a petrochemical plant which is accounted for as an investment in a corporate joint venture under the equity method. Since the remaining activities of the company are in the same line of business as the 25% interest which has been sold, there has not been a sale of a major line of business but rather a sale of part of a line of business.

(7) A manufacturer of children's wear discontinues all of its operations in Italy which were composed of designing and selling children's wear for the Italian market. In the context of determining a segment of a business by class of customer, the nationality of customers or slight variations in product lines in order to appeal to particular groups are not determining factors.

(8) A diversified company sells a subsidiary which manufactures furniture. The company has

retained its other furniture manufacturing subsidiary. The disposal of the subsidiary, therefore, is not a disposal of a segment of the business but rather a disposal of part of a line of business. As discussed in paragraph 13 of the Opinion, such disposals are incident to the evolution of the entity's business.

(9) The sale of all the assets (including the plant) related to the manufacture of men's woolen suits by an apparel manufacturer in order to concentrate activities in the manufacture of men's suits from synthetic products. This would represent a disposal of a product line as distinguished from the disposal of a major line of business.

If it has been determined that the particular event or transaction is not a disposal of a segment of a business, then the criteria for extraordinary items classification should be considered. That is:

Does the event or transaction meet both criteria of *unusual nature* and *infrequency of occurrence?*

Discussion—Paragraphs 19-22 of the Opinion discusses the criteria of unusual nature and infrequency of occurrence of events or transactions taking into account the environment in which the entity operates. Paragraph 23 specifies certain gains or losses which should not be reported as extraordinary unless they are the direct result of a major casualty, an expropriation, or a prohibition under a newly enacted law or regulation that clearly meets both criteria for extraordinary classification. Events or transactions which would meet both criteria in the circumstances described are:

(10) A large portion of a tobacco manufacturer's crops are destroyed by a hail storm. Severe damage from hail storms in the locality where the manufacturer grows tobacco is rare.

(11) A steel fabricating company sells the only land it owns. The land was acquired ten years ago for future expansion, but shortly thereafter the company abandoned all plans for expansion and held the land for appreciation.

(12) A company sells a block of common stock of a publicly traded company. The block of shares, which represents less than 10% of the publicly-held company, is the only security investment the company has ever owned.

(13) An earthquake destroys one of the oil refineries owned by a large multi-national oil company.

The following are illustrative of events or transactions which do not meet both criteria in the circumstances described and thus should not be reported as extraordinary items:

(14) A citrus grower's Florida crop is damaged by frost. Frost damage is normally experienced every three or four years. The criterion of infrequency of occurrence taking into account the environment in which the company operates would not be met since the history of losses caused by frost damage provides evidence that such damage may reasonably be expected to recur in the foreseeable future.

(15) A company which operates a chain of warehouses sells the excess land surrounding one of its warehouses. When the company buys property to establish a new warehouse, it usually buys more land than it expects to use for the warehouse with the expectation that the land will appreciate in value. In the past five years, there have been two instances in which the company sold such excess land. The criterion of infrequency of occurrence has not been met since past experience indicates that such sales may reasonably be expected to recur in the foreseeable future.

(16) A large diversified company sells a block of shares from its portfolio of securities which it has acquired for investment purposes. This is the first sale from its portfolio of securities. Since the company owns several securities for investment purposes, it should be concluded that sales of such securities are related to its ordinary and typical activities in the environment in which it operates and thus the criterion of unusual nature would not be met.

(17) A textile manufacturer with only one plant moves to another location. It has not relocated a plant in twenty years and has no plans to do so in the foreseeable future. Notwithstanding the infrequency of occurrence of the event as it relates to this particular company, moving from one location to another is an occurrence which is a consequence of customary and continuing business activities, some of which are finding more favorable labor markets, more modern facilities, and proximity to customers or suppliers. Therefore, the criterion of unusual nature has not been met and the moving expenses (and related gains and losses) should not be reported as an extraordinary item. Another example of an event which is a consequence of customary and typical business activities (namely financing) is an unsuccessful public registration, the cost of which should not be reported as an extraordinary item. (For additional examples, see paragraph 23 of the Opinion.)

Disposals of part of a line of business, such as examples 5-9 of this Interpretation, should not be classified as extraordinary items. As discussed in paragraph 13 of the Opinion, such disposals are incident to the evolution of the entity's business and therefore the criterion of unusual nature would not be met.

Question—Paragraph 27 of the Opinion states that events and transactions that were reported as extraordinary items in statements of income for fiscal years ending before October 1, 1973 should not be restated except that a statement of income including operations of discontinued segments of a business that meet the paragraph 13 criteria may be reclassified in comparative statements to conform with the provisions of paragraphs 8 and 9 of the Opinion. If a gain or loss on such a disposal in a prior year had been classified as an extraordinary item but was not computed in the *manner* specified in paragraphs 15-17 of the Opinion, may the prior year income statements be reclassified and the gain or loss adjusted to comply with the provisions of the Opinion?

Interpretation—The Opinion specifically uses the term "reclassified" in paragraph 27 and makes direct reference to paragraphs 8 and 9 which describe the manner of reporting disposals of a segment of a business as defined in paragraph 13. While such reclassification is optional under the Opinion, there should not be a redetermination (restatement) of net income using the measurement principles specified in paragraphs 15-17. Since Opinions of the Board are not intended to be retroactive unless otherwise stated, the method of computing of the gain or loss on disposals of a segment should not be retroactively applied if it results in a change in net income of a prior year.

Question—Events or transactions which are not disposals of a segment of a business and are not extraordinary items may nevertheless be required to be reported as a separate component of income from continuing operations under the provisions of paragraph 26 of the Opinion. If a company sells a portion of a line of business which does not meet the definition of a segment of a business as defined in paragraph 13 of the Opinion, should the gain or loss be calculated using the measurement principles for determination of gain or loss on disposal of a segment of a business as prescribed in paragraphs 15-17 of the Opinion and how should the financial effects of such sale be reported?

Interpretation—The gain or loss on a sale of a portion of a line of business which is not a segment of a business as defined in paragraph 13 should be calculated using the same measurement principles as if it were a segment of a business (paragraphs 15-17 of the Opinion). Under the provisions of paragraph 26 of the Opinion, the amount of such gain or loss should be reported as a separate component of income from continuing operations. However, the gain or loss should not be reported on the face of the income statement net of income taxes or in any manner inconsistent with the provisions of paragraphs 8 and 11 of the Opinion which may imply that it is a disposal of a segment of the business. In addition, the earnings per share effect should not be disclosed on the face of the income statement. Revenues and related costs and expenses of the portion of the line of business prior to the measurement date should not be segregated on the face of the income statement but may be disclosed in the notes to the financial statements and such disclosure is encouraged. In addition, the notes to the financial statements should disclose, if known, those items specified in paragraph 18 of the Opinion.

The foregoing examples are illustrative. It should be recognized that all attendant circumstances, which can vary from those above, need to be considered in making the judgments required by APB Opinion No. 30.

[Issue Date: November, 1973]

FASB Interpretations

FASB INTERPRETATIONS (FIN)

TABLE OF CONTENTS

Table of Contents

Table of Contents

FASB Interpretation No. 1
Accounting Changes Related to the Cost of Inventory

an interpretation of APB Opinion No. 20

STATUS

Issued: June 1974

Effective Date: July 1, 1974

Affects: No other pronouncements

Affected by: No other pronouncements

FASB Interpretation No. 1
Accounting Changes Related to the Cost of Inventory

an interpretation of APB Opinion No. 20

INTRODUCTION

1. *Accounting Principles Board (APB) Opinion No. 20* specifies how changes in accounting principles should be reported in financial statements and what is required to justify such changes. Under that Opinion, the term *accounting principle* includes "not only accounting principles and practices but also the methods of applying them."

2. Paragraph 5 of Chapter 4 of *Accounting Research Bulletin No. 43* states "there is a presumption that inventories should be stated at cost," which is "understood to mean acquisition and production cost." It further states that "the exclusion of all overheads from inventory costs does not constitute an accepted accounting procedure."

3. Internal Revenue Service (IRS) Regulation 1.471—11, adopted in September 1973, specifies how certain costs should be treated in determining inventory costs for income tax reporting. Under IRS Reg. 1.471—11, some costs must be included in inventory or excluded from inventory for income tax reporting *regardless* of their treatment for financial reporting. Other costs must be included in inventory or excluded from inventory for income tax reporting *depending upon* their treatment for financial reporting, "but only if such treatment is not inconsistent with generally accepted accounting principles." Among the costs listed in IRS Reg. 1.471—11 in this last category are taxes other than income taxes, depreciation, cost depletion, factory administrative expenses, and certain insurance costs.

4. Taxable income and accounting income are based on common information about transactions of an enterprise. However, the objectives of income determination for Federal income taxation and the objectives of income determination for financial statements of business enterprises are not always the same.

INTERPRETATION

5. A change in composition of the elements of cost included in inventory is an accounting change. A company which makes such a change for financial reporting shall conform to the requirements of *APB Opinion No. 20*, including justifying the change on the basis of preferability as specified by paragraph 16 of *APB Opinion No. 20*. In applying *APB Opinion No. 20*, preferability among accounting principles shall be determined on the basis of whether the new principle constitutes an improvement in financial reporting and not on the basis of the income tax effect alone.

EFFECTIVE DATE

6. This Interpretation shall be effective on July 1, 1974.

This Interpretation was adopted by the unanimous vote of the seven members of the Financial Accounting Standards Board following submission to the members of the Financial Accounting Standards Advisory Council.

Marshall S. Armstrong, *Chairman*	Arthur L. Litke	Walter Schuetze
Donald J. Kirk	Robert E. Mays	Robert T. Sprouse
	John W. Queenan	

FASB Interpretation No. 2
Imputing Interest on Debt Arrangements Made under the Federal Bankruptcy Act

an interpretation of APB Opinion No. 21

STATUS

Issued: June 1974

Effective Date: For transactions after June 30, 1974

Affects: No other pronouncements

Affected by: Superseded by FAS 15

(This page intentionally left blank.)

FASB Interpretation No. 3
Accounting for the Cost of Pension Plans Subject to the Employee Retirement Income Security Act of 1974

an interpretation of APB Opinion No. 8

STATUS

Issued: December 1974

Effective Date: December 31, 1974

Affects: No other pronouncements

Affected by: Superseded by FAS 87

Other Interpretive Pronouncement: FTB 81-3 (Superseded by FAS 111)

FASB Interpretation No. 4
Applicability of FASB Statement No. 2 to Business Combinations Accounted for by the Purchase Method

an interpretation of FASB Statement No. 2

STATUS

Issued: February 1975

Effective Date: For business combinations initiated after March 31, 1975

Affects: No other pronouncements

Affected by: No other pronouncements

FASB Interpretation No. 4
Applicability of FASB Statement No. 2 to Business
Combinations Accounted for by the Purchase Method

an interpretation of FASB Statement No. 2

INTRODUCTION

1. The FASB has been asked to explain the applicability of *FASB Statement No. 2,* "Accounting for Research and Development Costs," to the cost of tangible and intangible assets to be used in research and development activities of an enterprise when those assets are acquired in a business combination accounted for by the purchase method.

2. Broad guidelines about the activities to be classified as research and development and the elements of costs to be identified with those activities are set forth in paragraphs 8-11 of *Statement No. 2.* Paragraph 12 of that Statement provides that research and development costs shall be charged to expense when incurred. However, some costs associated with research and development activities shall be capitalized if the item has alternative future uses in research and development or otherwise (see paragraphs 11(a) and 11(c) of *Statement No. 2*). The cost of materials consumed, the depreciation of equipment and facilities used, and the amortization of intangibles used in research and development activities are research and development costs.

3. *Statement No. 2* amends *APB Opinion No. 17,* "Intangible Assets," to exclude from the scope of that Opinion those research and development costs encompassed by the Statement but does not amend *APB Opinion No. 16,* "Business Combinations." Paragraph 34 of the Statement indicates that paragraph 11(c) is not intended to alter the conclusions in paragraphs 87-88 of *APB Opinion No. 16* regarding allocation of cost to assets acquired in a business combination accounted for by the purchase method.

INTERPRETATION

4. The intent of paragraph 34 of *Statement No. 2* is that the allocation of cost to the identifiable assets of an acquired enterprise shall be made in accordance with the provisions of *APB Opinion No. 16.* Therefore, costs shall be assigned to all identifiable tangible and intangible assets, including any *resulting from* research and development activities of the acquired enterprise or *to be used in* research and development activities of the combined enterprise. Identifiable assets *resulting from* research and development activities of the acquired enterprise might include, for example, patents received or applied for, blueprints, formulas, and specifications or designs for new products or processes. Identifiable assets *to be used* in research and development activities of the combined enterprise might include, for example, materials and supplies, equipment and facilities, and perhaps even a specific research project in process. In either case, the costs to be assigned under *APB Opinion No. 16* are determined from the amount paid by the acquiring enterprise and *not* from the original cost to the acquired enterprise.

5. The subsequent accounting by the combined enterprise for the costs allocated to assets[1] *to be used in* research and development activities shall be determined by reference to *Statement No. 2.* Paragraph 12 of *Statement No. 2* requires that costs identified with research and development activities shall be charged to expense when incurred unless the test of alternative future use in paragraph 11(a) or 11(c) is met. That requirement also applies in a business combination accounted for by the purchase method. Accordingly, costs assigned to assets to be used in a particular research and development project and that have no alternative future use shall be charged to expense at the date of consummation of the combination. Therefore, the accounting for the cost of an item to be used in research and development activities is the same under paragraphs 11 and 12 of *Statement No. 2,* whether the item is purchased singly, or as part of a group of assets, or as part of an entire enterprise in a business combination accounted for by the purchase method.

EFFECTIVE DATE AND TRANSITION

6. Because there have been varying interpretations of *Statement No. 2* with respect to the accounting for the cost of tangible and intangible assets covered by this Interpretation, the Board has concluded that it shall be effective as follows:

a. Application of this Interpretation to business combinations accounted for by the purchase method that are initiated[2] after March 31, 1975 is required.

---

[1] In this regard, paragraph 69 of *APB Opinion No. 16* states in part that: "The nature of an asset and not the manner of its acquisition determines an acquirer's subsequent accounting for the cost of that asset."

[2] See paragraph 46(a) of *APB Opinion No. 16* for the definition of "initiated."

b. Application of this Interpretation to business combinations accounted for by the purchase method that are initiated prior to April 1, 1975 and consummated after March 31, 1975 is encouraged but is not required. It may be applied selectively to those combinations.

c. Application of this Interpretation to business combinations accounted for by the purchase method that were initiated and consummated prior to April 1, 1975 is encouraged but is not required. If an enterprise chooses to apply this Interpretation to those combinations, it shall be applied retroactively as described in paragraphs 15 and 16 of *Statement No. 2* to *all* business combinations accounted for by the purchase method that were consummated prior to April 1, 1975.

7. This Interpretation shall not be applied prior to the initial application of *Statement No. 2*.

This Interpretation was adopted by the unanimous vote of the seven members of the Financial Accounting Standards Board following submission to the members of the Financial Accounting Standards Advisory Council.

Marshall S. Armstrong, *Chairman*
Oscar S. Gellein

Donald J. Kirk
Arthur L. Litke
Robert E. Mays

Walter Schuetze
Robert T. Sprouse

FASB Interpretation No. 5
Applicability of FASB Statement No. 2 to
Development Stage Enterprises

an interpretation of FASB Statement No. 2

STATUS

Issued: February 1975

Effective Date: March 31, 1975 for fiscal periods beginning on or after January 1, 1975

Affects: No other pronouncements

Affected by: Superseded by FAS 7

FASB Interpretation No. 6
Applicability of FASB Statement No. 2
to Computer Software

an interpretation of FASB Statement No. 2

STATUS

Issued: February 1975

Effective Date: For fiscal years beginning on or after April 1, 1975

Affects: No other pronouncements

Affected by: Paragraphs 3, 6, and 8 amended by FAS 86
Paragraphs 7 and 9 superseded by FAS 86

Other Interpretive Pronouncement: FTB 79-2 (Superseded by FAS 86)

FASB Interpretation No. 6
Applicability of FASB Statement No. 2
to Computer Software

an interpretation of FASB Statement No. 2

INTRODUCTION

1. The FASB has been asked to explain the applicability of *FASB Statement No. 2,* "Accounting for Research and Development Costs," to costs incurred to obtain or develop computer software.

2. Broad guidelines about the activities to be classified as research and development and the elements of costs to be identified with those activities are set forth in paragraphs 8-11 of *Statement No. 2.* Paragraph 12 of that Statement provides that research and development costs shall be charged to expense when incurred. However, some costs associated with research and development activities shall be capitalized if the item has alternative future uses in research and development or otherwise (see paragraphs 11(a) and 11(c) of *Statement No. 2).* The costs of materials consumed, the depreciation of equipment and facilities used, and the amortization of intangibles used in research and development activities are research and development costs.

3. Paragraph 31 of *Statement No. 2* states the following about the activities for which computer software is developed:

Computer software is developed for many and diverse uses. Accordingly, in each case the nature of the activity for which the software is being developed should be considered in relation to the guidelines in paragraphs 8-10 to determine whether software costs should be included or excluded [in research and development]. For example, efforts to develop a new or higher level of computer software capability intended for sale (but not under a contractual arrangement) would be a research and development activity encompassed by this Statement.

INTERPRETATION

4. Paragraph 8 of *Statement No. 2* defines research and development to include those activities aimed at developing or significantly improving a product or service (hereinafter "product") or a process or technique (hereinafter "process") whether the product or process is intended for sale or use. A process may be a system whose output is to be sold, leased, or otherwise marketed to others. A process also may be used internally as a part of a manufacturing activity or a service activity where the service itself is marketed. A process may be intended to achieve cost reductions as opposed to revenue generation. Paragraph 8(b) of *Statement No. 2,* however, specifically excludes from research and development activities "market research or market testing activities." Those activities were excluded because they relate to the selling function of an enterprise. Thus, while in the broadest sense of the word, a process may be used in all of an enterprise's activities, the Board's intent in *Statement No. 2* was that the acquisition, development, or improvement of a process by an enterprise for use in its selling or administrative activities be excluded from the definition of research and development activities.[1] To the extent, therefore, that the acquisition, development, or improvement of a process by an enterprise for use in its selling or administrative activities includes costs for computer software, those costs are not research and development costs. Examples of the excluded costs of software are those incurred for development by an airline of a computerized reservation system or for development of a general management information system.

Purchase or Lease of Software

5. Costs incurred to purchase or lease computer software developed by others are not research and development costs under *Statement No. 2* unless the software is for use in research and development activities. When software for use in research and development activities is purchased or leased, its cost shall be accounted for as specified by paragraphs 11(c) and 12 of *Statement No. 2.* That is, the cost shall be charged to expense as incurred unless the software has alternative future uses (in research and development or otherwise).

Internal Development of Software

6. An enterprise may undertake development of computer software internally for its own use or as a product or process to be sold, leased, or otherwise marketed to others for their use. If development is undertaken for the enterprise's own use, the software may be intended, for example, to be used in the research and development activities of the enterprise or as a part of a newly developed or significantly improved product or process.

---

[1]General and administrative costs are discussed in paragraphs 11(e) and 35 of *Statement No. 2.*

7. *Development of software as a product or process to be sold, leased, or otherwise marketed.* Accounting for the cost of developing software for others under a contractual arrangement is beyond the scope of *Statement No. 2,* because paragraph 2 of the Statement indicates that this is part of accounting for contracts in general. On the other hand, if the development of software is undertaken to create a new or significantly improved product or process without any contractual arrangement, costs incurred for *conceptual formulation or the translation of knowledge into a design* would be research and development costs (see paragraph 8 of *Statement No. 2*). Other costs, including those incurred for programming and testing software, are research and development costs when incurred in the search for or the evaluation of product or process alternatives or in the design of a pre-production model. On the other hand, costs for programming and testing are *not* research and development costs when incurred, for example, in routine or other on-going efforts to improve an existing product or adapt a product to a particular requirement or customer's need. Because the term *product* also encompasses services that are sold, leased, or otherwise marketed to others, this paragraph applies, for example, to costs incurred in developing software to be used by a data processing service bureau or a computer time-sharing company.

8. *Development of software to be used in research and development activities.* Developing or significantly improving a product or process that is intended to be sold, leased, or otherwise marketed to others is a research and development activity (see paragraph 8 of *Statement No. 2*). Similarly, developing or significantly improving a process whose output is a product that is intended to be sold, leased, or otherwise marketed to others is a research and development activity. Costs incurred by an enterprise in developing computer software internally for use in its research and development activities are research and development costs and, therefore, shall be charged to expense when incurred.[2] This includes costs incurred during all phases of software develop-

ment because all of those costs are incurred in a research and development activity.

9. *Development of software to be used as a part of a product or process.* An enterprise may undertake internal development of software as a part of a newly developed or significantly improved product or process that will be sold, leased, or otherwise marketed to others, or as a part of a process whose output is a product that will be sold, leased, or otherwise marketed to others. For example, a manufacturer of computerized typesetting machinery may undertake to develop and use software as a part of that machinery, or a medical laboratory may undertake to develop software for use in a newly developed analytical process. In those cases, costs incurred for *conceptual formulation or the translation of knowledge into a design* would be research and development costs (see paragraph 8 of *Statement No. 2*). Other costs, including those incurred for programming and testing software, are research and development costs when incurred in the search for or the evaluation of product or process alternatives or in the design of a pre-production model. On the other hand, costs for programming and testing are *not* research and development costs when incurred, for example, in routine or other on-going efforts to improve an existing product or process or adapt a product or process to a particular requirement or customer's need.

EFFECTIVE DATE AND TRANSITION

10. Because there have been varying interpretations of *Statement No. 2* with respect to costs of computer software, this Interpretation shall be effective for fiscal years beginning on or after April 1, 1975. Earlier application is encouraged, except that this Interpretation shall not be applied prior to initial application of *Statement No. 2.* Retroactive application of this Interpretation, as described in paragraphs 15 and 16 of *Statement No. 2,* to costs incurred in prior fiscal years is also encouraged but is not required.

This Interpretation was adopted by the unanimous vote of the seven members of the Financial Accounting Standards Board following submission to the members of the Financial Accounting Standards Advisory Council.

Marshall S. Armstrong, *Chairman*	Donald J. Kirk	Walter Schuetze
Oscar S. Gellein	Arthur L. Litke	Robert T. Sprouse
	Robert E. Mays	

---

[2]The alternative future use test does not apply to the internal development of computer software; paragraph 11(c) of *Statement No. 2* applies only to intangibles *purchased from others.*

FASB Interpretation No. 7
Applying FASB Statement No. 7 in Financial Statements of Established Operating Enterprises

an interpretation of FASB Statement No. 7

STATUS

Issued: October 1975

Effective Date: For fiscal periods beginning on or after January 1, 1976

Affects: No other pronouncements

Affected by: No other pronouncements

FASB Interpretation No. 7
Applying FASB Statement No. 7 in Financial Statements
of Established Operating Enterprises

an interpretation of FASB Statement No. 7

INTRODUCTION

1. The FASB has been asked to explain the applicability of *FASB Statement No. 7*, "Accounting and Reporting by Development Stage Enterprises," to an established operating enterprise's financial statements that include the financial statements of a development stage subsidiary or other investee either by consolidation or by the equity method,[1] in terms of the following questions:

a. Must the effect of a change in accounting principle adopted in the separate financial statements of a development stage subsidiary to conform to the provisions of *Statement No. 7* be reflected in the consolidated financial statements of an established operating enterprise that include the financial statements of that subsidiary?
b. If it is appropriate that the established operating enterprise's consolidated financial statements reflect the effect of its development stage subsidiary's change to a new principle of accounting adopted to conform to the provisions of *Statement No. 7*, how should the effect of the change be reported in the established operating enterprise's financial statements?

2. Paragraph 10 of *Statement No. 7* states:

> Financial statements issued by a development stage enterprise shall present financial position, changes in financial position, and results of operations in conformity with the generally accepted accounting principles that apply to established operating enterprises. . . . Generally accepted accounting principles that apply to established operating enterprises shall govern the recognition of revenue by a development stage enterprise and shall determine whether a cost incurred by a development stage enterprise is to be charged to expense when incurred or is to be capitalized or deferred. Accordingly, capitalization or deferral of costs shall be subject to the same assessment of recoverability that would be applicable in an established operating enterprise. For a development stage subsidiary or other investee, the recoverability of costs shall be assessed within the entity for which separate financial statements are being presented.

3. Paragraph 14 of *Statement No. 7* provides for initial application of the Statement as follows:

> This Statement shall be effective for fiscal periods beginning on or after January 1, 1976, although earlier application is encouraged. Thereafter, when financial statements, or financial summaries or other data derived therefrom, are presented for periods prior to the effective date of this Statement, they shall be restated, where necessary, to conform to the provisions of this Statement. Accordingly, any items that would have been accounted for differently by a development stage enterprise if the provisions of paragraph 10 had then been applicable shall be accounted for by prior period adjustment (described in paragraphs 18 and 26 of *APB Opinion No. 9*, "Reporting the Results of Operations").

Further, paragraph 1 of *Statement No. 7* states, in part, that "the transition requirements of this Statement are also applicable to certain established operating enterprises" and makes specific reference to paragraphs 14-16 of *Statement No. 7* by footnote.

INTERPRETATION

4. *Statement No. 7* does not address and does not alter generally accepted accounting principles for the preparation of consolidated financial statements. Therefore, *Statement No. 7* does not address the question of whether the effect of a change in accounting principle adopted in the separate financial statements of a development stage subsidiary to conform to the provisions of that Statement must be reflected in an established operating enterprise's consolidated financial statements that include the financial statements of the subsidiary. However, paragraph 10 of the Statement specifies that "capitalization or deferral of costs shall be subject to the same assessment of recoverability that would be applicable in an established operating enterprise" and further specifies that "for a development stage subsidiary or other investee, the recoverability of costs shall be assessed within the entity for which separate financial statements are being presented." In specifying that the same assessment of recovera-

---

[1]Hereinafter, in this Interpretation, the term *subsidiary* comprehends all *investees* that are accounted for by the equity method as described in *APB Opinion No. 18*, "The Equity Method of Accounting for Investments in Common Stock." Likewise, the term *consolidated financial statements* hereinafter comprehends the *equity method of accounting*.

bility be made, the Statement does not require that the results of that assessment must necessarily be the same. Further, the Statement does not affect any accepted practice in consolidation of financial statements where the results of an assessment of recoverability of a cost may be different (a) in the broader context of a consolidated enterprise and (b) in the context of a development stage subsidiary standing alone. Under any such accepted practice, a cost incurred by a development stage subsidiary could be assessed as recoverable within the consolidated enterprise and be capitalized or deferred in consolidated financial statements even though that cost is assessed as not being recoverable within a development stage subsidiary and, therefore, charged to expense in the separate financial statements of the development stage subsidiary.

5. Except in the circumstances described in the preceding paragraph, the effect of a development stage subsidiary's change in accounting principle to conform its accounting to the requirements of *Statement No. 7* generally would be reflected in an established operating enterprise's consolidated financial statements that include that subsidiary. When a development stage subsidiary adopts a new accounting principle to conform its accounting to the requirements of *Statement No. 7* and the effect of that subsidiary's accounting change is also reflected in an established operating enterprise's consolidated financial statements that include that subsidiary, the provisions of paragraph 14 of *Statement No. 7* apply. In that situation, the established operating enterprise's consolidated financial statements for periods prior to the period in which the subsidiary's accounting change is made and financial summaries and other data derived therefrom shall be restated by prior period adjustment. It should be noted that *Statement No. 7* does not address the question of how an established operating enterprise should report accounting changes adopted with respect to the revenue and costs related to activities of the parent company or any subsidiaries that are not in the development stage; that question is covered by *APB Opinion No. 20,* "Accounting Changes."

EFFECTIVE DATE

6. This Interpretation shall be effective for fiscal periods beginning on or after January 1, 1976, although earlier application is encouraged, except that it shall not be applied prior to initial application of *Statement No. 7.*

This Interpretation was adopted by the affirmative votes of five members of the Financial Accounting Standards Board following submission to the members of the Financial Accounting Standards Advisory Council. Mr. Mays and Mr. Schuetze dissented.

Mr. Mays and Mr. Schuetze dissent because, in their view, the response to the first of the two questions addressed is ambiguous and serves to create additional uncertainty as to the substance of paragraph 10 of *FASB Statement No. 7.*

If different conclusions as to recoverability can be justified on the basis that the two entities are making their assessments within different "contexts," as paragraph 4 attempts to rationalize, would not a development stage enterprise and an established operating enterprise always have different contexts for such assessments? How, then, they ask, is the development stage enterprise subject to "the same assessment of recoverability that would be applicable in an established operating enterprise" as required by paragraph 10 of the Statement? They find equivocal the explanation that although the assessments must be the same the conclusions may be different.

In their opinion, the only appropriate response to the question in paragraph 1(a) is to require that the effect of the change in principle and the assessment of recoverability in the development stage subsidiary be preserved and reflected in the consolidated financial statements in the same manner as in the subsidiary's financial statements.

Members of the Financial Accounting Standards Board:

Marshall S. Armstrong, *Chairman*	Donald J. Kirk	Walter Schuetze
Oscar S. Gellein	Arthur L. Litke	Robert T. Sprouse
	Robert E. Mays	

FIN8

FASB Interpretation No. 8
Classification of a Short-Term Obligation Repaid Prior to Being Replaced by a Long-Term Security

an interpretation of FASB Statement No. 6

STATUS

Issued: January 1976

Effective Date: For balance sheets and statements of changes in financial position dated on or
after February 29, 1976

Affects: No other pronouncements

Affected by: No other pronouncements

FASB Interpretation No. 8
Classification of a Short-Term Obligation Repaid Prior to Being Replaced by a Long-Term Security

an interpretation of FASB Statement No. 6

INTRODUCTION

1. *FASB Statement No. 6*, "Classification of Short-Term Obligations Expected to Be Refinanced," specifies that a short-term obligation shall be excluded from current liabilities only if the enterprise intends to refinance the obligation on a long-term basis and before the balance sheet is issued has either (a) completed the refinancing by issuing a long-term obligation or by issuing equity securities or (b) has entered into a financing agreement that permits refinancing on a long-term basis. (See paragraphs 9-11 of the Statement.)

2. The FASB has been asked to clarify whether a short-term obligation should be included in or excluded from current liabilities if it is repaid after the balance sheet date and subsequently replaced by long-term debt before the balance sheet is issued. For example, assume that an enterprise has issued $3,000,000 of short-term commercial paper during the year to finance construction of a plant. At June 30, 1976, the enterprise's fiscal year end, the enterprise intends to refinance the commercial paper by issuing long-term debt. However, because the enterprise temporarily has excess cash, in July 1976 it liquidates $1,000,000 of the commercial paper as the paper matures. In August 1976, the enterprise completes a $6,000,000 long-term debt offering. Later during the month of August, it issues its June 30, 1976 financial statements. The proceeds of the long-term debt offering are to be used to replenish $1,000,000 in working capital, to pay $2,000,000 of commercial paper as it matures in September 1976, and to pay $3,000,000 of construction costs expected to be incurred later that year to complete the plant.

INTERPRETATION

3. The concept that a short-term obligation will not require the use of current assets during the ensuing fiscal year if it is to be excluded from current liabilities underlies *FASB Statement No. 6* (see paragraphs 1, 2, and 20 of the Statement). That concept is also fundamental to Chapter 3A, "Current Assets and Current Liabilities," of *ARB No. 43*, which was not changed by *FASB Statement No. 6* (except as specified in paragraph 16 of the Statement). Repayment of a short-term obligation *before* funds are obtained through a long-term refinancing requires the use of current assets. Therefore, if a short-term obligation is repaid after the balance sheet date and subsequently a long-term obligation or equity securities are issued whose proceeds are used to replenish current assets before the balance sheet is issued, the short-term obligation shall not be excluded from current liabilities at the balance sheet date.

4. In the example described in paragraph 2 above, the $1,000,000 of commercial paper liquidated in July would be classified as a current liability in the enterprise's balance sheet at June 30, 1976. The $2,000,000 of commercial paper liquidated in September 1976 but refinanced by the long-term debt offering in August 1976 would be excluded from current liabilities in balance sheets at the end of June 1976, July 1976, and August 1976.[1] It should be noted that the existence of a financing agreement at the date of issuance of the financial statements rather than a completed financing at that date would not change these classifications.

EFFECTIVE DATE

5. This Interpretation shall be effective February 29, 1976 and shall apply to balance sheets dated on or after that date and to related statements of changes in financial position. Reclassification in financial statements for periods ending prior to February 29, 1976 is permitted but not required.

This Interpretation was adopted by the unanimous vote of the seven members of the Financial Accounting Standards Board following submission to the members of the Financial Accounting Standards Advisory Council.

Marshall S. Armstrong,
Chairman
Oscar S. Gellein

Donald J. Kirk
Arthur L. Litke
Robert E. Mays

Walter Schuetze
Robert T. Sprouse

---

[1] At the end of August 1976, $2,000,000 of cash would be excluded from current assets or if included in current assets, a like amount of debt would be classified as a current liability. (See footnote 1 and paragraph 40 of *FASB Statement No. 6*.)

FIN9

FASB Interpretation No. 9
Applying APB Opinions No. 16 and 17 When a Savings and Loan Association or a Similar Institution Is Acquired in a Business Combination Accounted for by the Purchase Method

an interpretation of APB Opinions No. 16 and 17

STATUS

Issued: February 1976

Effective Date: For business combinations initiated on or after March 1, 1976

Affects: No other pronouncements

Affected by: Paragraphs 8 and 9 amended by FAS 72

FASB Interpretation No. 9
Applying APB Opinions No. 16 and 17 When a Savings and Loan Association or a Similar Institution Is Acquired in a Business Combination Accounted for by the Purchase Method

an interpretation of APB Opinions No. 16 and 17

INTRODUCTION

1. The FASB has been asked to explain how the provisions of *APB Opinions No. 16,* "Business Combinations," and *No. 17,* "Intangible Assets," should be applied to account for the acquisition of a savings and loan association[1] in a business combination accounted for by the purchase method. In this regard, the FASB has been asked (1) whether the *net-spread* method or the *separate-valuation* method is appropriate for determining the amounts assigned to the assets and liabilities of the acquired savings and loan association and (2) whether any cost not assigned to the identifiable assets acquired less liabilities assumed may be amortized using an accelerated method of amortization rather than the straight-line method of amortization.

2. Under the net-spread method, the acquisition of a savings and loan association is viewed as the acquisition of a leveraged whole rather than the acquisition of the separate assets and liabilities of the association. Therefore, if the spread between the rates of interest received on mortgage loans and the rates of interest (often called *dividends* in the industry) paid on savings accounts is normal for the particular market area, the acquired savings and loan association's principal assets and liabilities, i.e., its mortgage loan portfolio and savings accounts, are brought forward at the carrying amounts shown in the financial statements of the acquired association.

3. Under the separate-valuation method, each of the identifiable assets and liabilities of the acquired savings and loan association is accounted for in the consolidated financial statements at an amount based on fair value at the date of acquisition, either individually or by types of assets and types of liabilities.

INTERPRETATION

4. Paragraph 87 of *APB Opinion No. 16* states the general principle that "all identifiable assets acquired, either individually or by type, and liabilities assumed in a business combination . . . should be assigned a portion of the cost of the acquired company, normally equal to their fair values at date of acquisition." Because the net-spread method ignores fair value of individual assets and liabilities or types of assets and liabilities, that method is inappropriate under *APB Opinion No. 16.*

5. Paragraph 88 of *APB Opinion No. 16* provides "general guides for assigning amounts to the individual assets acquired and liabilities assumed, except goodwill." In paragraph 88(b), the general guide for receivables is "present values of amounts to be received determined at appropriate current interest rates, less allowances for uncollectibility and collection costs, if necessary." Ascertaining appropriate current interest rates (and the periods over which the receivables are to be discounted) requires an analysis of the many factors that determine the fair value of the portfolio of loans acquired.

6. In paragraph 88(e), the general guide for "intangible assets which can be identified and named, including contracts, patents, franchises, customer and supplier lists, and favorable leases" is "appraised values." A footnote to that paragraph states that "fair values should be ascribed to specific assets; identifiable assets should not be included in goodwill."

7. In paragraph 88(g), the general guide for "accounts and notes payable, long-term debt, and other claims payable" is "present values of amounts to be paid determined at appropriate current interest rates." That present value for savings deposits due on demand is their face amount plus interest accrued or accruable as of the date of acquisition. That present value for other liabilities assumed, e.g., time savings deposits, borrowings from a Federal Home Loan Bank, or other borrowings, shall be determined by using prevailing interest rates for similar liabilities at the acquisition date.

8. The purchase price paid for a savings and loan association may include an amount for one or more factors, such as the following:

a. Capacity of existing savings accounts and loan

---

[1]This Interpretation applies not only in the case of the acquisition of a savings and loan association but also in the case of the acquisition of a savings and loan association holding company, a savings and loan branch, or other financial institution having similar types of assets and liabilities.

accounts to generate future income,

b. Capacity of existing savings accounts and loan accounts to generate additional business or new business, and

c. Nature of territory served.

If the amount paid for any such factor can be determined, that amount shall not be included in goodwill. Rather, the amount paid for that separately identified intangible shall be recorded as the cost of the intangible and amortized over its estimated life as specified by *APB Opinion No. 17.* Any portion of the purchase price that cannot be assigned to specifically identifiable tangible and intangible assets acquired (see paragraph 6 above) less liabilities assumed shall be assigned to goodwill.

9. Paragraph 30 of *APB Opinion No. 17* requires that goodwill be amortized using the straight-line method "unless a company demonstrates that another systematic method is more appropriate." An accelerated method would be appropriate and may be used to amortize goodwill when a company demonstrates that (a) the amount assigned to goodwill represents an amount paid for factors such

as those listed in paragraph 8 but there is not a satisfactory basis for determining appraised values for the individual factors, and (b) the benefits expected to be received from the factors decline over the expected life of those factors. Unless both (a) and (b) are demonstrated, straight-line amortization shall be used.

EFFECTIVE DATE AND TRANSITION

10. This Interpretation shall be effective for business combinations initiated on or after March 1, 1976. Application to business combinations initiated before March 1, 1976 but consummated on or after that date is encouraged but not required. Application to a business combination consummated prior to March 1, 1976 is permitted if the annual financial statements for the fiscal year in which the business combination was consummated have not yet been issued; if applied to such a combination, financial statements for interim periods of that fiscal year shall be restated if subsequently presented. Previously issued annual financial statements shall not be restated.

This Interpretation was adopted by the unanimous vote of the seven members of the Financial Accounting Standards Board following submission to the members of the Financial Accounting Standards Advisory Council.

Marshall S. Armstrong, *Chairman*	Donald J. Kirk	Walter Schuetze
Oscar S. Gellein	Arthur L. Litke	Robert T. Sprouse
	Robert E. Mays	

FASB Interpretation No. 10
Application of FASB Statement No. 12
to Personal Financial Statements

an interpretation of FASB Statement No. 12

STATUS

Issued: September 1976

Effective Date: For annual and interim periods ending after October 15, 1976

Affects: No other pronouncements

Affected by: Superseded by FAS 83

(This page intentionally left blank.)

FASB Interpretation No. 11
Changes in Market Value after the Balance Sheet Date

an interpretation of FASB Statement No. 12

STATUS

Issued: September 1976

Effective Date: For annual and interim periods ending after October 15, 1976

Affects: No other pronouncements

Affected by: Superseded by FAS 115

Note: Although superseded by FAS 115, this pronouncement has not been removed from this volume because of the delayed effective date for FAS 115.

FASB Interpretation No. 11
Changes in Market Value after the Balance Sheet Date

an interpretation of FASB Statement No. 12

INTRODUCTION

1. Paragraphs 13 and 17[1] of *FASB Statement No. 12*, "Accounting for Certain Marketable Securities," specify in part that "an enterprise's financial statements shall not be adjusted for realized gains or losses or for changes in market prices with respect to marketable equity securities when such gains or losses or changes occur after the date of the financial statements but prior to their issuance, except for situations covered by paragraph 21." The Board has been requested to clarify the meaning of the qualification, *except for situations covered by paragraph 21.*

2. Paragraph 21 of *FASB Statement No. 12* states:

> For those marketable securities for which the effect of a change in carrying amount is included in stockholders' equity rather than in net income (including marketable securities in unclassified balance sheets), a determination must be made as to whether a decline in market value below cost as of the balance sheet date of an individual security is other than temporary. . . . If the decline is judged to be other than temporary, the cost basis of the individual security shall be written down to a new cost basis and the amount of the write-down shall be accounted for as a realized loss. The new cost basis shall not be changed for subsequent recoveries in market value.

The Board also has been asked to elaborate on the amount of the write-down that shall be accounted for as a realized loss when the "decline in market value below cost *as of the balance sheet date* of an individual security is other than temporary." (Emphasis added.)

INTERPRETATION

3. In the case of those marketable securities for which the effect of a change in carrying amount is included in stockholders' equity rather than in net income, the phrase "except for situations covered by paragraph 21" in paragraphs 13 and 17 refers to the provisions in paragraph 21 requiring a decline in market value below cost as of the balance sheet date of an individual security that is determined to be

other than temporary to be accounted for as a realized loss. In judging whether a decline in market value below cost at the balance sheet date is other than temporary, a gain or loss realized on subsequent disposition or changes in market price occurring after the date of the financial statements but prior to their issuance shall be taken into consideration along with other factors.

4. The amount of decline in market value below cost of an individual marketable equity security that is accounted for as a realized loss as of the balance sheet date because the decline is other than temporary shall not exceed the difference between market value at the balance sheet date and cost of the marketable equity security. Further declines in market value after the balance sheet date might indicate that the decline in market value below cost at the balance sheet date was other than temporary. However, those declines result from information, events, or changes in expectations occurring after the balance sheet date. Accordingly, if a decline in market value below cost as of the balance sheet date of an individual security is judged to be other than temporary, further declines in market value occurring after the date of the balance sheet shall not be included in the amount that is accounted for as a realized loss as of the balance sheet date. Recoveries in market value after the balance sheet date also result from information, events, or changes in expectations occurring after the balance sheet date, but they tend to indicate that a portion or all of the decline at the balance sheet date was in fact temporary. Accordingly, such recoveries shall be considered when estimating the amount of decline as of the balance sheet date that is judged to be other than temporary.

EFFECTIVE DATE AND TRANSITION

5. The provisions of this Interpretation shall be effective for financial statements for annual and interim periods ending after October 15, 1976. Earlier application is encouraged in financial statements for annual and interim periods ending before October 16, 1976 that have not been previously issued. This Interpretation shall not be applied retroactively for previously issued annual or interim financial statements.

---

[1]Paragraph 13 applies to enterprises in industries not having specialized accounting practices with respect to marketable securities, and paragraph 17 applies to enterprises in industries having specialized accounting practices with respect to marketable securities.

FASB Interpretation No. 12
Accounting for Previously Established
Allowance Accounts

an interpretation of FASB Statement No. 12

STATUS

Issued: September 1976

Effective Date: For annual and interim periods ending after October 15, 1976

Affects: No other pronouncements

Affected by: Superseded by FAS 115

Note: Although superseded by FAS 115, this pronouncement has not been removed from this volume because of the delayed effective date for FAS 115.

FASB Interpretation No. 12
Accounting for Previously Established Allowance Accounts

an interpretation of FASB Statement No. 12

INTRODUCTION

1. Paragraph 8 of *FASB Statement No. 12*, "Accounting for Certain Marketable Securities," specifies that the "carrying amount of a marketable equity securities portfolio shall be the lower of its aggregate cost or market value, determined at the balance sheet date." Paragraph 7(e) of *FASB Statement No. 12* defines "cost" of a marketable equity security as "original cost . . . unless a new cost basis has been assigned based on recognition of an impairment of value that was deemed other than temporary. . . . In such cases, the new cost basis shall be the cost. . . ."

2. Prior to the issuance of *FASB Statement No. 12*, some enterprises that carried marketable equity securities at cost had reduced the carrying amount of individual marketable equity securities to market value through an allowance account with a corresponding amount included in the determination of net income. In some of those cases, a new cost basis was not established for individual securities and the allowance account was expected to increase or decrease depending on fluctuations in the market price of the marketable equity security because the decline in market value below cost was assessed to be temporary. The Board has been asked to clarify whether, in those cases, the original cost of the individual securities or the original cost reduced by an existing allowance account should be used in applying paragraphs 7(e) and 8 of *FASB Statement No. 12*.

INTERPRETATION

3. The original cost of individual marketable equity securities shall be used in applying paragraphs 7(e) and 8 of *FASB Statement No. 12* by an enterprise that carried marketable equity securities at cost and that (a) had reduced the carrying amount of individual marketable equity securities through an allowance account with a corresponding amount included in the determination of net income prior to the effective date of the Statement and (b) expected the allowance account to increase or decrease in the future based on fluctuations in the market price of the security because the decline in market value below cost was assessed to be temporary. Any balance remaining in such an existing allowance account shall be eliminated and credited to income in the period in which this Interpretation is initially applied. The valuation allowance would then be determined in accordance with paragraph 8 of *FASB Statement No. 12*.

4. If, prior to the effective date of *FASB Statement No. 12*, a new cost basis had been assigned to a marketable equity security based on recognition of an impairment of value that was deemed other than temporary, the new cost basis shall be used in applying the provisions of *FASB Statement No. 12*.

EFFECTIVE DATE AND TRANSITION

5. The provisions of this Interpretation shall be effective for financial statements for annual and interim periods ending after October 15, 1976. Earlier application is encouraged in financial statements for annual and interim periods ending before October 16, 1976 that have not been previously issued. This Interpretation shall not be applied retroactively for previously issued annual or interim financial statements.

This Interpretation was adopted by the unanimous vote of the six members of the Financial Accounting Standards Board following submission to the members of the Financial Accounting Standards Advisory Council.

Marshall S. Armstrong,
    Chairman
Oscar S. Gellein

Donald J. Kirk
Arthur L. Litke

Robert E. Mays
Robert T. Sprouse

FASB Interpretation No. 13
Consolidation of a Parent and Its Subsidiaries
Having Different Balance Sheet Dates

an interpretation of FASB Statement No. 12

STATUS

Issued: September 1976

Effective Date: For annual and interim periods ending after October 15, 1976

Affects: No other pronouncements

Affected by: Superseded by FAS 115

Note: Although superseded by FAS 115, this pronouncement has not been removed from this volume because of the delayed effective date for FAS 115.

FASB Interpretation No. 13
Consolidation of a Parent and Its Subsidiaries
Having Different Balance Sheet Dates

an interpretation of FASB Statement No. 12

INTRODUCTION

1. Paragraphs 8, 9, and 15 of *FASB Statement No. 12,* "Accounting for Certain Marketable Securities," set forth the requirements of the portfolio basis for comparing cost and market value. The portfolio basis requires that marketable equity securities owned by enterprises that are consolidated and that do not follow specialized accounting practices with respect to marketable equity securities, or that are consolidated and follow the same specialized accounting practices with respect to marketable equity securities, shall be aggregated into separate portfolios according to the current or noncurrent classifications of the securities. The aggregate cost and aggregate market value of the portfolios are compared to determine carrying amount.

2. Paragraph 13 of *FASB Statement No. 12,* which applies to enterprises in industries not having specialized accounting practices with respect to marketable securities, states:

> An enterprise's financial statements shall not be adjusted for realized gains or losses or for changes in market prices with respect to marketable equity securities when such gains or losses or changes occur after *the date of the financial statements* but prior to their issuance, except for situations covered by paragraph 21. However, significant net realized and net unrealized gains and losses arising after *the date of the financial statements,* but prior to their issuance, applicable to marketable equity securities owned at the date of the most recent balance sheet shall be disclosed. (Emphasis added.)

Paragraph 17 of *FASB Statement No. 12,* which applies to enterprises in industries having specialized accounting practices with respect to marketable securities, is in substance identical to paragraph 13 of the Statement.

3. The financial statements of a subsidiary sometimes are consolidated with the financial statements of its parent even though the financial statements of the subsidiary are as of a date different from the financial statements of the parent. The use of different dates is permitted by paragraph 4 of *ARB No. 51,* "Consolidated Financial Statements," which states:

A difference in fiscal periods of a parent and a subsidiary does not of itself justify the exclusion of the subsidiary from consolidation. It ordinarily is feasible for the subsidiary to prepare, for consolidation purposes, statements for a period which corresponds with or closely approaches the fiscal period of the parent. However, where the difference is not more than about three months, it usually is acceptable to use, for consolidation purposes, the subsidiary's statements for its fiscal period; when this is done, recognition should be given by disclosure or otherwise to the effect of intervening events which materially affect the financial position or results of operations.

4. The Board has been requested to clarify application of the portfolio basis specified in *FASB Statement No. 12* when the financial statements of a subsidiary are as of a date different from that of its parent and are consolidated with the financial statements of its parent. Further, the Board has been asked to explain the meaning of "the date of the financial statements" in paragraphs 13 and 17 of *FASB Statement No. 12* when the financial statements of a subsidiary or investee are as of a date different from that of its parent or investor and are consolidated with or accounted for by the equity method in the financial statements of its parent or investor.

INTERPRETATION

5. To compute the amount of any valuation allowance(s) required by *FASB Statement No. 12* in the consolidated financial statements, aggregate cost and aggregate market value of the portfolio(s) shall be determined for each subsidiary that is consolidated as of the date of each subsidiary's balance sheet, and those aggregates shall be combined with aggregate cost and aggregate market value of the parent's portfolio(s) determined as of the parent's balance sheet date. For example, assume that consolidated financial statements dated December 31, 1976 and issued on March 1, 1977 include the financial statements of the parent as of December 31, 1976 and of the subsidiary as of October 31, 1976. The cost of the marketable equity securities owned by the subsidiary at October 31, 1976 is added to the cost of the marketable equity securities owned by the parent at December 31, 1976. The market values

at October 31, 1976 of the securities owned by the subsidiary and the market values at December 31, 1976 of the securities owned by the parent are aggregated in the same manner. The aggregate cost and aggregate market value of the portfolios are compared to determine the carrying amount in the consolidated financial statements.

6. For purposes of applying paragraphs 13 and 17 of *FASB Statement No. 12*, "the date of the financial statements" shall be for each subsidiary or investee the date of the financial statements that are consolidated with or accounted for by the equity method in the financial statements of its parent or investor. The last sentence in each of those paragraphs requires disclosure of significant net realized gains or losses and of significant net unrealized gains or losses arising after the date of the financial statements. Using the assumptions in the example in paragraph 5 above, aggregate amounts are computed as follows for possible disclosure: the net *realized* gains or losses arising after October 31, 1976 and prior to March 1, 1977 applicable to the marketable equity securities in the portfolio of the subsidiary at October 31, 1976 are aggregated with the net *realized* gains or losses arising after December 31, 1976 and prior to March 1, 1977 applicable to the marketable equity securities in the portfolio of the parent at December 31, 1976. Likewise, net *unrealized* gains or losses arising in the portfolio of the subsidiary after October 31, 1976 and prior to March 1, 1977 applicable to the marketable equity securities in the portfolio of the subsidiary at October 31, 1976 are aggregated with the net *unrealized* gains or losses arising after December 31, 1976 and prior to March 1, 1977 applicable to the marketable equity securities in the portfolio of the parent at December 31, 1976. If significant, each of the aggregate amounts shall be disclosed.

7. If the financial statements of a subsidiary are consolidated with the financial statements of its parent and the financial statements of the subsidiary are as of a date different from the financial statements of the parent, paragraph 4 of *ARB No. 51* requires that "recognition should be given by disclosure or otherwise to the effect of intervening events which materially affect the financial position or results of operations." In the case of the subsidiary in the example in paragraph 5 above, that requirement pertains to the period from October 31, 1976 to December 31, 1976. Accordingly, in addition to the disclosure required by paragraph 6 above, the net realized gains or losses and the net unrealized gains or losses arising after October 31, 1976 and prior to December 31, 1976 applicable to the marketable equity securities of the subsidiary shall be disclosed if they "materially affect the financial position or results of operations." Further, as required by paragraphs 13 and 17 of *FASB Statement No. 12*,[1] the subsidiary's financial statements shall not be adjusted for realized gains or losses or for changes in market prices with respect to its marketable equity securities occurring after October 31, 1976 and prior to December 31, 1976, unless the decline in market value below cost of an individual marketable equity security is determined to be other than temporary and, accordingly, shall be accounted for as a realized loss.

EFFECTIVE DATE AND TRANSITION

8. The provisions of this Interpretation shall be effective for financial statements for annual and interim periods ending after October 15, 1976. Earlier application is encouraged in financial statements for annual and interim periods ending before October 16, 1976 that have not been previously issued. This Interpretation shall not be applied retroactively for previously issued annual or interim financial statements.

This Interpretation was adopted by the unanimous vote of the six members of the Financial Accounting Standards Board following submission to the members of the Financial Accounting Standards Advisory Council.

Marshall S. Armstrong,	Donald J. Kirk	Robert E. Mays
Chairman	Arthur L. Litke	Robert T. Sprouse
Oscar S. Gellein		

---

[1] See also *FASB Interpretation No. 11*, "Changes in Market Value after the Balance Sheet Date: an interpretation of FASB Statement No. 12."

FASB Interpretation No. 14
Reasonable Estimation of the Amount of a Loss

an interpretation of FASB Statement No. 5

STATUS

Issued: September 1976

Effective Date: For annual and interim periods ending after October 15, 1976

Affects: No other pronouncements

Affected by: No other pronouncements

FASB Interpretation No. 14
Reasonable Estimation of the Amount of a Loss

an interpretation of FASB Statement No. 5

INTRODUCTION

1. The two conditions for accrual of an estimated loss from a loss contingency set forth in paragraph 8 of *FASB Statement No. 5,* "Accounting for Contingencies," are that "(a) information available prior to issuance of the financial statements indicates that it is probable that an asset had been impaired or a liability had been incurred at the date of the financial statements . . ." and "(b) the amount of loss can be reasonably estimated." In some situations in which condition (a) in paragraph 8 is met, a range of loss can be reasonably estimated but no single amount within the range appears at the time to be a better estimate than any other amount within the range. The Board has been asked to clarify whether, in those situations, condition (b) in paragraph 8 also is met and, if so, to explain what amount of loss should be accrued.

INTERPRETATION

2. As indicated in paragraph 59 of *FASB Statement No. 5,* the purpose of the two conditions in paragraph 8 of the Statement is "to require accrual of losses when they are reasonably estimable and relate to the current or a prior period." Condition (b) in paragraph 8, that "the amount of loss can be reasonably estimated," does not delay accrual of a loss until only a single amount can be reasonably estimated. To the contrary, when condition (a) in paragraph 8 is met, i.e., "it is probable that an asset had been impaired or a liability had been incurred," and information available indicates that the estimated amount of loss is within a range of amounts, it follows that some amount of loss has occurred and can be reasonably estimated.

3. When condition (a) in paragraph 8 is met with respect to a particular loss contingency and the reasonable estimate of the loss is a range, condition (b) in paragraph 8 is met and an amount shall be accrued for the loss. When some amount within the range appears at the time to be a better estimate than any other amount within the range, that amount shall be accrued. When no amount within the range is a better estimate than any other amount, however, the minimum amount in the range shall be accrued.[1] In addition, paragraph 9 of the Statement may require disclosure of the nature and, in some circumstances, the amount accrued, and paragraph 10 requires disclosure of the nature of the contingency and the additional exposure to loss if there is at least a reasonable possibility of loss in excess of the amount accrued.

4. As an example, assume that an enterprise is involved in litigation at the close of its fiscal year ending December 31, 1976 and information available indicates that an unfavorable outcome is probable. Subsequently, after a trial on the issues, a verdict unfavorable to the enterprise is handed down, but the amount of damages remains unresolved at the time the financial statements are issued. Although the enterprise is unable to estimate the exact amount of loss, its reasonable estimate at the time is that the judgment will be for not less than $3 million or more than $9 million. No amount in that range appears at the time to be a better estimate than any other amount. *FASB Statement No. 5* requires accrual of the $3 million at December 31, 1976, disclosure of the nature of the contingency and the exposure to an additional amount of loss of up to $6 million, and possibly disclosure of the amount of the accrual.

5. The same answer would result under the example in paragraph 4 above if it is probable that a verdict will be unfavorable even though the trial has not been completed before the financial statements are issued. In that situation, condition (a) in paragraph 8 would be met because information available to the enterprise indicates that an unfavorable verdict is probable. An assessment that the range of loss is between $3 million and $9 million would meet condition (b) in paragraph 8. If no single amount in that range is a better estimate than any other amount, *FASB Statement No. 5* requires an accrual of $3 million at December 31, 1976, disclosure of the nature of the contingency and the exposure to an additional amount of loss of up to $6 million, and possibly disclosure of the amount of the accrual. Note, however, that if the enterprise had assessed the verdict differently (e.g., that an unfavorable verdict was *not* probable but was only reasonably possible), condition (a) in paragraph 8 would not have been met and no amount of loss would be accrued but the nature of the contingency and any amount of loss that is reasonably possible would be disclosed.

---

[1]Even though the minimum amount in the range is not necessarily the amount of loss that will be ultimately determined, it is not likely that the ultimate loss will be less than the minimum amount.

6. Assume that in the examples given in paragraphs 4 and 5 above condition (a) in paragraph 8 has been met and a reasonable estimate of loss is a range between $3 million and $9 million but a loss of $4 million is a better estimate than any other amount in that range. In that situation, *FASB Statement No. 5* requires accrual of $4 million, disclosure of the nature of the contingency and the exposure to an additional amount of loss of up to $5 million, and possibly disclosure of the amount of the accrual.

7. As a further example, assume that at December 31, 1976 an enterprise has an investment of $1,000,000 in the securities of another enterprise that has declared bankruptcy, and there is no quoted market price for the securities. Condition (a) in paragraph 8 has been met because information available indicates that the value of the investment has been impaired, and a reasonable estimate of loss is a range between $300,000 and $600,000. No amount of loss in that range appears at the time to be a better estimate of loss than any other amount. *FASB Statement No. 5* requires accrual of the $300,000 loss at December 31, 1976, disclosure of the nature of the contingency and the exposure to an additional amount of loss of up to $300,000, and possibly disclosure of the amount of the accrual.

EFFECTIVE DATE AND TRANSITION

8. The provisions of this Interpretation shall be effective for financial statements for annual and interim periods beginning after October 15, 1976. Earlier application is encouraged in financial statements for annual and interim periods beginning before October 15, 1976 that have not been previously issued. An accrual for a loss contingency or an adjustment of an established accrual for a loss contingency resulting from application of this Interpretation shall be accounted for as a change in estimate in accordance with the requirements of paragraph 31 of *APB Opinion No. 20,* "Accounting Changes." This Interpretation shall not be applied retroactively for previously issued annual and interim financial statements.

This Interpretation was adopted by the unanimous vote of the six members of the Financial Accounting Standards Board following submission to the members of the Financial Accounting Standards Advisory Council.

Marshall S. Armstrong,	Donald J. Kirk	Robert E. Mays
Chairman	Arthur L. Litke	Robert T. Sprouse
Oscar S. Gellein		

FASB Interpretation No. 15
Translation of Unamortized Policy Acquisition
Costs by a Stock Life Insurance Company

an interpretation of FASB Statement No. 8

STATUS

Issued: September 1976

Effective Date: For annual and interim periods ending after December 15, 1976

Affects: No other pronouncements

Affected by: Superseded by FAS 52
　　　　　　Paragraphs 2 and 4 amended by FAS 60

FASB Interpretation No. 16
Clarification of Definitions and Accounting for Marketable Equity Securities That Become Nonmarketable

an interpretation of FASB Statement No. 12

STATUS

Issued: February 1977

Effective Date: For annual and interim periods ending after March 15, 1977

Affects: No other pronouncements

Affected by: Superseded by FAS 115

Note: Although superseded by FAS 115, this pronouncement has not been removed from this volume because of the delayed effective date for FAS 115.

FASB Interpretation No. 16

Clarification of Definitions and Accounting for Marketable Equity Securities That Become Nonmarketable

an interpretation of FASB Statement No. 12

INTRODUCTION

1. The FASB has been asked to clarify the definitions of the terms "marketable" and "restricted stock" as used in *FASB Statement No. 12,* "Accounting for Certain Marketable Securities," and to clarify whether paragraph 10 of *FASB Statement No. 12* requires a new cost basis to be assigned when a marketable equity security becomes nonmarketable if its market value is less than its cost at that time.

2. For purposes of applying paragraphs 8-13, 15, 17, and 19 of *FASB Statement No. 12,* the term "marketable" is defined in paragraph 7(b) of the Statement as follows:

> *Marketable,* as applied to an equity security, means an equity security as to which sales prices or bid and ask prices are currently available on a national securities exchange (i.e., those registered with the Securities and Exchange Commission) or in the over-the-counter market. In the over-the-counter market, an equity security shall be considered marketable when a quotation is publicly reported by the National Association of Securities Dealers Automatic Quotations System or by the National Quotations Bureau Inc. (provided, in the latter case, that quotations are available from at least three dealers). Equity securities traded in foreign markets shall be considered marketable when such markets are of a breadth and scope comparable to those referred to above. Restricted stock[3] does not meet this definition.

Footnote 3 to that paragraph defines restricted stock as follows:

> Restricted stock for purposes of this Statement shall mean securities for which sale is restricted by a governmental or contractual requirement except where such requirement terminates within one year or where the holder has the power by contract or otherwise to cause the requirement to be met within one year. Any portion of the stock which can reasonably be expected to qualify for sale within one year, such as may be the case under Rule 144 or similar

rules of the Securities and Exchange Commission, is not considered restricted [under *FASB Statement No. 12*].

3. Paragraph 10 of *FASB Statement No. 12* states:

> If there is a change in the classification of a marketable equity security between current and noncurrent, the security shall be transferred between the corresponding portfolios at the lower of its cost or market value at date of transfer. If market value is less than cost, the market value shall become the new cost basis, and the difference shall be accounted for as if it were a realized loss and included in the determination of net income.

INTERPRETATION

Definitions

4. For purposes of applying paragraphs 8-13, 15, 17, and 19 of *FASB Statement No. 12,* an equity security is not considered marketable if market price quotations specified by the Statement (see paragraph 2 above) are not available or if it is "restricted stock" as defined in the Statement (see paragraph 2 above) even though market price quotations are available for securities of the same class that are not restricted.

5. The determination of whether an equity security is marketable is made as of the balance sheet date,[1] but a temporary lack of trades or price quotations for an equity security at the balance sheet date does not make it nonmarketable for purposes of applying *FASB Statement No. 12* if the required market prices are available on days closely preceding and following the balance sheet date. In that situation, the market price of a security traded on a national securities exchange shall be determined from the sales or bid and ask prices on the first day following the balance sheet date that the information is available. If the lack of a publicly reported quotation by the National Association of Securities Dealers Automatic Quotations System or the lack of three quotations by the National Quotations Bureau Inc. is a mere temporary condition as described above for a security traded in the over-the-counter market, its market price shall be determined from:

---

[1]If the balance sheet date falls on a date that securities are not normally traded (e.g., Saturday or Sunday), the availability of market price quotations shall be determined as of the most recent business day preceding the balance sheet date.

a. The quotation publicly reported by the National Association of Securities Dealers Automatic Quotations System on the first day following the balance sheet date that a quotation is publicly reported, or

b. The quotation(s) reported by the National Quotations Bureau Inc. as of the balance sheet date if at least one quotation is available as of that date or on the first day following the balance sheet date that quotations are reported if no quotations are available on the balance sheet date.

6. If it can be reasonably expected that a security "for which sale is restricted by a governmental or contractual requirement" can qualify for sale within one year of the balance sheet date and market price quotations for unrestricted securities of the same class are available as of the balance sheet date, the security is considered marketable at the balance sheet date for purposes of applying *FASB Statement No. 12* (see paragraph 2 above). In this situation, market price quotations for unrestricted shares of the same class at the balance sheet date provide a surrogate market price for the restricted shares and shall be considered as the market price for the security. If the restricted security cannot qualify for sale within one year or market price quotations are not available for unrestricted shares of the same class, the security is considered nonmarketable for purposes of applying the Statement.

7. As an example of the application of paragraph 6 above, assume that an enterprise pledges a marketable equity security as collateral for a loan due in three years. Normally, debt agreements permit substitution for the collateral or sale of the collateral if the proceeds are used to repay the loan. However, if the debt agreement prohibits sale of or substitution for the collateral for the term of the loan, the pledged security becomes "restricted stock" and nonmarketable for purposes of applying *FASB Statement No. 12* at the time it is pledged and shall be excluded from the enterprise's portfolio of marketable equity securities from that date until one year before expiration of the long-term debt agreement.

8. As a further example, assume that an enterprise owns common stock that cannot be sold to the public, except pursuant to Rule 144 of the Securities and Exchange Commission (see explanation below), until a registration statement has been filed with the SEC and has become effective. Also assume that the stock is marketable at one balance sheet date pursuant to an effective registration statement. At the next balance sheet date, the registration statement is no longer effective and the enterprise does not have the power to cause another one to be filed within

one year. Then, only the portion of the stock that "can reasonably be expected to qualify for sale within one year . . . under Rule 144 . . . is not considered restricted" under *FASB Statement No. 12*. Rule 144 specifies that if certain conditions are met a security may be sold to the public without an effective registration statement on file with the SEC, subject to a limitation on the number of shares that may be sold during a given time period. The number of shares eligible for sale is based on the total number of shares of the security outstanding or the average weekly trading volume of the security for a stated past period. Changes in the number of shares outstanding or in trading volume change the number of shares that qualify for sale under Rule 144. The number of shares considered marketable for purposes of applying the Statement are those that "can reasonably be expected to qualify for sale within one year"; the determination of such number is a matter of judgment based on past trading volumes, the presently outstanding shares and plans for changes therein, and other relevant factors. The number of shares considered nonmarketable are those that cannot qualify for sale within one year under the preceding sentence.

Accounting

9. Paragraph 10 of *FASB Statement No. 12* applies to all transfers between current and noncurrent classifications of equity securities that are marketable, as that term is defined in the Statement (see paragraph 2 above). If the change in the classification of an equity security is coincident with a change in its status from marketable to nonmarketable or from nonmarketable to marketable, paragraph 10 of the Statement shall apply to the transfer between current and noncurrent classifications. Paragraph 10 of the Statement requires that if the market value of the security is less than its cost when it is transferred between current and noncurrent classifications, "the market value shall become the new cost basis, and the difference shall be accounted for as if it were a realized loss and included in the determination of net income." In that situation, market value shall be the security's last available market price if the transfer between classifications is coincident with a change in status from marketable to nonmarketable and the first available market price if the transfer between classifications is coincident with a change in status from nonmarketable to marketable.

10. The accounting for a nonmarketable security is outside of the scope of *FASB Statement No. 12*. When a marketable equity security becomes nonmarketable, the cost of that security shall be excluded from the portfolio of marketable equity securities of which it was a part for purposes of applying the Statement. When a nonmarketable

equity security becomes marketable, that security shall be included in the portfolio of marketable equity securities at cost. The term *cost* is defined in paragraph 7(e) of the Statement as "the original cost . . . unless a new cost basis has been assigned based on recognition of an impairment of value that was deemed other than temporary or as the result of a transfer between current and noncurrent classifications as described in paragraph 10 [of the Statement]. In such cases, the new cost basis shall be the cost for the purposes of this Statement."

EFFECTIVE DATE AND TRANSITION

11. The provisions of this Interpretation shall be effective for financial statements for annual and interim periods ending after March 15, 1977. Earlier application is encouraged in financial statements for annual and interim periods ending before March 16, 1977 that have not been previously issued. This Interpretation shall not be applied retroactively for previously issued annual or interim financial statements.

This Interpretation was adopted by the unanimous vote of the six members of the Financial Accounting Standards Board following submission to the members of the Financial Accounting Standards Advisory Council.

Marshall S. Armstrong, *Chairman*	Donald J. Kirk	Robert E. Mays
Oscar S. Gellein	Arthur L. Litke	Robert T. Sprouse

FASB Interpretation No. 17
Applying the Lower of Cost or Market Rule in Translated Financial Statements

an interpretation of FASB Statement No. 8

STATUS

Issued: February 1977

Effective Date: For annual and interim periods ending after March 15, 1977

Affects: No other pronouncements

Affected by: Superseded by FAS 52

(This page intentionally left blank.)

FASB Interpretation No. 18
Accounting for Income Taxes in Interim Periods

an interpretation of APB Opinion No. 28

STATUS

Issued: March 1977

Effective Date: For financial statements issued after March 31, 1977 for interim periods beginning after December 15, 1976

Affects: No other pronouncements

Affected by: Paragraph 4 superseded by FAS 71
Paragraphs 6, 16, 18, 40 through 43, 46 through 55, 58, 65, 66, and 68 and footnotes 2, 19, and footnote (*) of paragraph 47 amended by FAS 96 and FAS 109
Paragraph 8 amended by FAS 109
Paragraphs 14, 20, 23, 59 through 61, and 70 and footnotes 9 through 14, 18, 21 through 23, and 25 superseded by FAS 96 and FAS 109
Paragraph 15 amended by FAS 96
Paragraph 15 superseded by FAS 109
Footnote 5 superseded by FAS 111

Other Interpretive Pronouncements: FTB 79-9
FTB 86-1 (Superseded by FAS 96 and FAS 109)

CONTENTS

FASB Interpretation No. 18
Accounting for Income Taxes in Interim Periods

an interpretation of APB Opinion No. 28

INTRODUCTION AND BACKGROUND INFORMATION

1. The FASB has been asked to clarify the application of *APB Opinion No. 28*, "Interim Financial Reporting," with respect to accounting for income taxes in interim periods. In general, that Opinion requires that an estimated annual effective tax rate be used to determine interim period income tax provisions. Application of the general guideline to specific situations has resulted in differences in accounting for similar situations by different enterprises.

2. This Interpretation describes (a) the general computation of interim period income taxes (paragraphs 8 and 9), (b) the application of the general computation to specific situations (paragraphs 10-15), (c) the computation of interim period income taxes applicable to significant unusual or infrequently occurring items, discontinued operations, extraordinary items, and cumulative effects of changes in accounting principles (paragraphs 16-21), (d) special computations applicable to operations taxable in multiple jurisdictions (paragraph 22), (e) guidelines for reflecting the effects of new tax legislation in interim period income tax provisions (paragraphs 23 and 24), and (f) disclosure requirements (paragraph 25). Appendix A, "Excerpts from APB Opinions," quotes from *APB Opinion No. 28* on accounting for income taxes in interim financial reports and from the paragraphs of *APB Opinion No. 11*, "Accounting for Income Taxes," that prescribe the annual accounting for income taxes in certain situations. The computations described in paragraphs 10-24 are illustrated in Appendix C, "Examples of Computations of Interim Period Income Taxes."

3. An Exposure Draft of a proposed Interpretation on "Accounting for Income Taxes in Interim Periods" was issued October 7, 1976. The Board received 99 letters of comment in response to the Exposure Draft. This Interpretation incorporates a number of changes suggested by those respondents. Appendix E, "Summary of Consideration of Comments on Exposure Draft," describes certain of the comments and the FASB's consideration of them.

4. The Addendum to *APB Opinion No. 2*, "Accounting for the 'Investment Credit'," states that "differences may arise in the application of generally accepted accounting principles as between regulated and nonregulated businesses, because of the effect . . . of the rate-making process," and discusses the application of generally accepted accounting principles to regulated industries. FASB Statements and Interpretations should therefore be applied to regulated companies that are subject to the rate-making process in accordance with the provisions of the Addendum.

INTERPRETATION

Definition of Terms

5. As a matter of convenience of expression, certain terms are defined in this Interpretation as follows:

a. *"Ordinary" income (or loss)* refers to "income (or loss) from continuing operations before income taxes (or benefits)" excluding significant "unusual or infrequently occurring items." Extraordinary items, discontinued operations, and cumulative effects of changes in accounting principles are also excluded from this term.[1] The term is *not* used in the income tax context of ordinary income v. capital gain.

b. *Tax (or benefit)* is the total income tax expense (or benefit), including the provision (or benefit) for income taxes both currently payable and deferred.

Concept of APB Opinion No. 28

6. *APB Opinion No. 28* specifies that the tax (or benefit) for an interim period shall be determined under the provisions of *APB Opinion No. 11*, *APB Opinion No. 23*, "Accounting for Income Taxes-Special Areas," and *APB Opinion No. 24*, "Accounting for Income Taxes-Invesments in Common Stock Accounted for by the Equity Method (Other than Subsidiaries and Corporate Joint Ventures)."[2] The tax (or benefit) related to "ordinary" income (or loss) shall be computed at an estimated

---

[1] The terms used in this definition are described in *APB Opinion No. 20*, "Accounting Changes," and in *APB Opinion No. 30*, "Reporting the Results of Operations." See paragraph 8 of *APB Opinion No. 30* for *income (or loss) from continuing operations before income taxes (or benefits)* and *discontinued operations,* paragraph 10 for *extraordinary items,* and paragraph 26 for *unusual items* and *infrequently occurring items.* See paragraph 20 of *APB Opinion No. 20* for *cumulative effects of changes in accounting principles.*

[2] *APB Opinions No. 23* and *24* are not specifically described herein because no questions were raised regarding application of those Opinions for interim periods.

annual effective tax rate and the tax (or benefit) related to all other items shall be individually computed and recognized when the items occur. Application of this general guidance to specific situations is described in the following paragraphs and illustrated in Appendix C.

Tax (or Benefit) Applicable to "Ordinary" Income (or Loss)

7. Paragraphs 8 and 9 describe the computation of interim period tax (or benefit) related to "ordinary" income (or loss). Paragraphs 10-15 describe the application of paragraphs 8 and 9 to specific situations. Paragraphs 14 and 15 describe special limitations that apply to the computations in paragraphs 8 and 9 if an enterprise has a year-to-date "ordinary" loss or anticipates an "ordinary" loss for the fiscal year.

8. *Estimated annual effective tax rate.*[3] Paragraph 19 of *APB Opinion No. 28*[4] requires that an enterprise determine an estimated annual effective tax rate.[5] That rate "should reflect anticipated investment tax credits, foreign tax rates, percentage depletion, capital gains rates, and other available tax planning alternatives."[6] The rate is revised, if necessary, as of the end of each successive interim period during the fiscal year to the enterprise's best *current* estimate of its annual effective tax rate. In some cases, the rate will be the statutory rate modified as may be appropriate in particular circumstances. In other cases, the rate will be the enterprise's estimate of the tax (or benefit) that will be provided for the fiscal year, stated as a percentage of its estimated "ordinary" income (or loss) for

the fiscal year (see paragraphs 14 and 15 if an "ordinary" loss is anticipated for the fiscal year).[7]

9. *Computation of interim period tax (or benefit).* The estimated annual effective tax rate, described in paragraph 8 above, shall be applied to the year-to-date "ordinary" income (or loss) at the end of each interim period to compute the year-to-date tax (or benefit) applicable to "ordinary" income (or loss).[8] The interim period tax (or benefit) related to "ordinary" income (or loss) shall be the difference between the amount so computed and the amounts reported for previous interim periods of the fiscal year.

"Ordinary" income anticipated for fiscal year

10. *Year-to-date "ordinary" income.* If an enterprise has "ordinary" income for the year-to-date at the end of an interim period and anticipates "ordinary" income for the fiscal year, the interim period tax shall be computed as described in paragraph 9 above.

11. *Year-to-date "ordinary" loss.* If an enterprise has an "ordinary" loss for the year-to-date at the end of an interim period and anticipates "ordinary" income for the fiscal year, the interim period tax benefit shall be computed as described in paragraph 9 above, except that the year-to-date tax benefit recognized shall be limited to the amount determined in accordance with paragraphs 14 and 15 below.

"Ordinary" loss anticipated for fiscal year

12. *Year-to-date "ordinary" income.* If an enterprise has "ordinary" income for the year-to-date

---

[3]See also paragraph 22 below when the enterprise has operations taxable in multiple jurisdictions.

[4]See Appendix A, paragraph 28.

[5]Enterprises in some industries report certain items of "ordinary" income net of their related tax effect. For example, the AICPA Industry Audit Guide, "Audits of Stock Life Insurance Companies," illustrates a caption "Realized investment gains and losses, net of related income taxes of $. . ." in its suggested format of a stock life insurance company's statement of income. If an enterprise follows such an accepted industry practice, the item that will be reported net of tax and its related tax (or benefit) shall be excluded from the computation of the estimated annual effective tax rate and interim period tax (or benefit). A separate estimated annual effective tax rate shall be computed for the item, and applied to that item in accordance with paragraphs 9-15 below.

[6]Certain investment tax credits may be excluded from the estimated annual effective tax rate. If an enterprise includes allowable investment tax credits as part of its provision for income taxes over the productive life of acquired property and not entirely in the year the property is placed in service, amortization of deferred investment tax credits need not be taken into account in estimating the annual effective tax rate; however, if the investment tax credits are taken into account in the estimated annual effective tax rate, the amount taken into account shall be the amount of amortization that is anticipated to be included in income in the current year (see paragraphs 13 and 15 of *APB Opinion No. 2*). Further, paragraphs 43 and 44 of *FASB Statement No. 13*, "Accounting for Leases," specify that investment tax credits related to leases that are accounted for as leveraged leases shall be deferred and accounted for as return on the net investment in the leveraged leases in the years in which the net investment is positive. Footnote 25 of Statement No. 13 explains that the use of the term "years" is not intended to preclude application of the accounting described to shorter periods. If an enterprise accounts for investment tax credits related to leveraged leases in accordance with paragraphs 43 and 44 of Statement No. 13 for interim periods, those investment tax credits shall not be taken into account in estimating the annual effective tax rate.

[7]Estimates of the annual effective tax rate at the end of interim periods are, of necessity, based on evaluations of possible future events and transactions and may be subject to subsequent refinement or revision. If a reliable estimate cannot be made, the actual effective tax rate for the year-to-date may be the best estimate of the annual effective tax rate. If an enterprise is unable to estimate a part of its "ordinary" income (or loss) or the related tax (or benefit) but is otherwise able to make a reliable estimate, the tax (or benefit) applicable to the item that cannot be estimated shall be reported in the interim period in which the item is reported.

[8]One result of the year-to-date computation is that, if the tax benefit of an "ordinary" loss that occurs in the early portions of the fiscal year is not recognized because realization of the tax benefit is not assured, tax is not provided for subsequent "ordinary" income until the unrecognized tax benefit of the earlier "ordinary" loss is offset (see Appendix A, paragraph 32).

at the end of an interim period and anticipates an "ordinary" loss for the fiscal year, the interim period tax shall be computed as described in paragraph 9 above. The estimated tax benefit for the fiscal year, used to determine the estimated annual effective tax rate described in paragraph 8 above, shall not exceed the tax benefit determined in accordance with paragraphs 14 and 15 below.

13. *Year-to-date "ordinary" loss.* If an enterprise has an "ordinary" loss for the year-to-date at the end of an interim period and anticipates an "ordinary" loss for the fiscal year, the interim period tax benefit shall be computed as described in paragraph 9 above. The estimated tax benefit for the fiscal year, used to determine the estimated annual effective tax rate described in paragraph 8 above, shall not exceed the tax benefit determined in accordance with paragraphs 14 and 15 below. In addition to that limitation in the effective rate computation, if the year-to-date "ordinary" loss exceeds the anticipated "ordinary" loss for the fiscal year, the tax benefit recognized for the year-to-date shall not exceed the tax benefit determined, based on the year-to-date "ordinary" loss, in accordance with paragraphs 14 and 15 below.

Limitations applicable to losses

14. *Recognition of the tax benefit of a loss.* Paragraphs 44 and 45 of *APB Opinion No. 11*[9] require that the tax benefit of a loss shall not be recognized until it is realized, unless future realization is assured beyond any reasonable doubt at the time the loss occurs. Therefore, the estimated tax benefit of an "ordinary" loss for the fiscal year, used to determine the estimated annual effective tax rate described in paragraph 8 above, and the year-to-date tax benefit of a loss recognized at an interim date shall be limited to the tax benefit realized or assured of future realization beyond any reasonable doubt. Paragraph 47 of *APB Opinion No. 11*[10] describes circumstances that may assure future realization of the tax benefit of a loss for a fiscal year beyond any reasonable doubt. Assurance

beyond any reasonable doubt of future realization of the tax benefit of a loss at an interim date may also result from established seasonal patterns, as described in paragraph 20 of *APB Opinion No. 28.*[11] (See also paragraph 15 below.)

15. *Reversal of net deferred tax credits.* If an enterprise anticipates an "ordinary" loss for the fiscal year or has a year-to-date "ordinary" loss in excess of the anticipated "ordinary" loss for the fiscal year and all or a part of the tax benefit of the loss will not be realized or its realization is not assured beyond any reasonable doubt, existing deferred tax credits arising from timing differences shall be adjusted as required by paragraph 48 of *APB Opinion No. 11.*[12] The amount of the adjustment shall not exceed the lower of (a) the otherwise unrecognized tax benefit of the loss or (b) the amount of the net deferred tax credits that would otherwise be amortized during the carryforward period attributable to the loss. If the adjustment relates to an estimated "ordinary" loss for the fiscal year, the amount of the adjustment shall be considered additional current year tax benefit in the determination of the estimated annual effective tax rate described in paragraph 8 above.[13] If the adjustment relates to a year-to-date "ordinary" loss, the amount of the adjustment shall be considered additional tax benefit in computing the maximum tax benefit that shall be recognized for the year-to-date.[14]

Tax (or Benefit) Applicable to Significant Unusual or Infrequently Occurring Items, Discontinued Operations, or Extraordinary Items

16. *Basis of tax provision.* Paragraph 19 of *APB Opinion No. 28*[15] excludes taxes related to "significant unusual or extraordinary items that will be separately reported or reported net of their related tax effect"[16] from the estimated annual effective tax rate calculation. Paragraph 21 of *APB Opinion No. 28*[17] requires that those items be recognized in the interim period in which they occur. Paragraph 52 of *APB Opinion No. 11*[18] describes the method of ap-

---

[9]See Appendix A, paragraphs 29 and 30.

[10]See Appendix A, paragraph 31.

[11]See Appendix A, paragraph 32.

[12]See Appendix A, paragraph 33.

[13]See Appendix A, paragraph 34.

[14]Paragraph 48 of *APB Opinion No. 11* describes the reinstatement of previously eliminated deferred tax credits when the tax benefit of the loss is subsequently realized.

[15]See Appendix A, paragraph 28.

[16]In the context of paragraph 21 of *APB Opinion No. 28* (see Appendix A, paragraph 35), which is consistent with *APB Opinion No. 30*, this description includes unusual items, infrequently occurring items, discontinued operations, and extraordinary items.

[17]See Appendix A, paragraph 35.

[18]See Appendix A, paragraph 36.

plying tax allocation within a period. Under paragraph 52 of Opinion No. 11, the difference between the tax computed on income including an item described in footnote 16 below and the tax computed on income excluding that item is the tax related to the item. This computation shall be made using the estimated fiscal year "ordinary" income and the items described in footnote 16 below for the year-to-date.

17. *Financial statement presentation.* Extraordinary items and discontinued operations that will be presented net of related tax effects in the financial statements for the fiscal year shall be presented net of related tax effects in interim financial statements. Unusual or infrequently occurring items that will be separately disclosed in the financial statements for the fiscal year shall be separately disclosed as a component of pretax income from continuing operations, and the tax (or benefit) related to such items shall be included in the tax (or benefit) related to continuing operations. Paragraphs 18 and 19 describe the application of the above to specific situations.

18. *Recognition of the tax benefit of a loss.* If an enterprise has a significant unusual, infrequently occurring, or extraordinary loss or a loss from discontinued operations, the tax benefit of that loss shall not be recognized until it is realized or realization is assured beyond any reasonable doubt. Realization is assured beyond any reasonable doubt (a) by offsetting year-to-date "ordinary" income, (b) by offsetting taxable income from an unusual, infrequently occurring, or extraordinary item, or from discontinued operations, or items credited directly to stockholders' equity accounts, or (c) if the loss can be carried back (after any anticipated fiscal year "ordinary" loss is carried back). Realization beyond any reasonable doubt would also appear to be assured by future taxable income that is virtually certain to occur soon enough to provide realization during the carryforward period, including anticipated "ordinary" income for the current year expected to result from an established seasonal pattern of loss in early interim periods offset by income in later interim periods.[19] If previously recorded net deferred tax credits that would be amortized during the carryforward period of the loss are present and all or a portion of the tax benefit of the loss is not realized and future realization is not assured beyond any reasonable doubt, see paragraph 15 above. If all or a part of the tax benefit is not realized and future realization is not assured beyond any rea-

sonable doubt in the interim period of occurrence but becomes assured beyond any reasonable doubt in a subsequent interim period of the same fiscal year, the previously unrecognized tax benefit shall be reported in that subsequent interim period in the same manner that it would have been reported if realization had been assured beyond any reasonable doubt in the interim period of occurrence, i.e., as a tax benefit relating to continuing operations, discontinued operations, or an extraordinary item.

19. *Discontinued operations.* The computations described in paragraphs 16-18 shall be the basis for the tax (or benefit) related to both (a) the income (or loss) from operations of the discontinued segment[20] prior to the measurement date and (b) the gain (or loss) on disposal of discontinued operations (including any provision for operating loss subsequent to the measurement date). Income (or loss) from operations of the discontinued segment prior to the interim period in which the measurement date occurs will have been included in "ordinary" income (or loss) of prior periods and thus will have been included in the estimated annual effective tax rate and tax (or benefit) calculations described in paragraphs 8-15 above. The *total* tax (or benefit) provided in the prior interim periods shall not be recomputed but shall be divided into two components, applicable to the remaining "ordinary" income (or loss) and to the income (or loss) from operations of the discontinued segment as follows. A revised estimated annual effective tax rate and resulting tax (or benefit) shall be computed, in accordance with paragraphs 8-15 above, for the remaining "ordinary" income (or loss), based on the estimates applicable to such operations used in the original calculations for each prior interim period. The tax (or benefit) related to the operations of the discontinued segment shall be the total of (a) the difference between the tax (or benefit) originally computed for "ordinary" income (or loss) and the recomputed amount for the remaining "ordinary" income (or loss) and (b) the tax computed in accordance with paragraphs 16-18 above for any unusual or infrequently occurring items of the discontinued segment.

Using a Prior Year Operating Loss Carryforward

20. Paragraph 61 of *APB Opinion No. 11*[21] requires that the tax benefit of an operating loss carryforward recognized in a subsequent year be reported as an extraordinary item. Paragraph 19 of *APB Opinion No. 28*[22] excludes extraordinary items from the effective tax rate computation, and para-

---

[19]See paragraph 47 of *APB Opinion No. 11* (see Appendix A, paragraph 31) and paragraph 20 of *APB Opinion No. 28* (see Appendix A, paragraph 32).

[20]The term "discontinued segment" refers to a discontinued segment of the business as described in paragraph 13 of *APB Opinion No. 30*.

[21]See Appendix A, paragraph 38.

[22]See Appendix A, paragraph 28.

graph 21 of *APB Opinion No. 28*[23] specifies that extraordinary items should not be prorated over the balance of the year. Accordingly, the tax benefit of a prior year operating loss carryforward shall be recognized as an extraordinary item in each interim period to the extent that income in the period and for the year-to-date is available to offset the operating loss carryforward.

Cumulative Effects of Changes in Accounting Principles

21. *FASB Statement No. 3,* "Reporting Accounting Changes in Interim Financial Statements," specifies that the cumulative effect of a change in accounting principle on retained earnings at the beginning of the year shall be reported in the first interim period of the fiscal year. *APB Opinion No. 20,* "Accounting Changes," specifies that the related income tax effect of a cumulative effect type accounting change shall be computed as though the new accounting principle had been applied retroactively for all prior periods that would have been affected.

Operations Taxable in Multiple Jurisdictions

22. If an enterprise that is subject to tax in multiple jurisdictions pays taxes based on identified income in one or more individual jurisdictions, interim period tax (or benefit) related to consolidated "ordinary" income (or loss) for the year-to-date shall be computed in accordance with paragraphs 8-15 above using one overall estimated annual effective tax rate except that:

a. If in a separate jurisdiction an enterprise anticipates an "ordinary" loss for the fiscal year or has an "ordinary" loss for the year-to-date for which, in accordance with paragraphs 14 and 15 above, no tax benefit can be recognized, the enterprise shall exclude "ordinary" income (or loss) in that jurisdiction and the related tax (or benefit) from the overall computations of the estimated annual effective tax rate and interim period tax (or benefit). A separate estimated annual effective tax rate shall be computed for that jurisdiction and applied to "ordinary" income (or loss) in that jurisdiction in accordance with paragraphs 9-15 above.

b. If an enterprise is unable to estimate an annual effective tax rate in a foreign jurisdiction in dollars or is otherwise unable to make a reliable estimate of its "ordinary" income (or loss) or of the related tax (or benefit) for the fiscal year in a jurisdiction, the enterprise shall exclude "ordinary" income (or loss) in that jurisdiction and the related tax (or benefit) from the overall computations of the estimated annual effective tax rate and interim period tax (or benefit). The tax (or benefit) related to "ordinary" income (or loss) in that jurisdiction[24] shall be recognized in the interim period in which the "ordinary" income (or loss) is reported.

Effect of New Tax Legislation

23. Paragraph 20 of *APB Opinion No. 28*[25] states that changes resulting from new tax legislation shall be "reflected after the effective dates prescribed in the statutes." If new tax legislation prescribes changes that become effective during an enterprise's fiscal year, the tax effect of those changes shall be reflected in the computation of the estimated annual effective tax rate beginning with the first interim period that ends after the new legislation becomes effective. Paragraph 24 describes the determination of when new legislation becomes effective.

24. *Effective date.* Legislation generally becomes effective on the date prescribed in the statutes. However, tax legislation may prescribe changes that become effective during an enterprise's fiscal year that are administratively implemented by applying a portion of the change to the full fiscal year. For example, if the statutory tax rate applicable to calendar-year corporations were increased from 48 percent to 52 percent, effective January 1, the increased statutory rate might be administratively applied to a corporation with a fiscal year ending at June 30 in the year of the change by applying a 50 percent rate to its taxable income for the fiscal year, rather than 48 percent for the first six months and 52 percent for the last six months. In that case the legislation becomes effective for that enterprise at the beginning of the enterprise's fiscal year.

Disclosure

25. Application of the provisions of *APB Opinion No. 28* that are described in this Interpretation may result in a significant variation in the customary relationship between income tax expense and pretax accounting income. The reasons for significant variations in the customary relationship between income tax expense and pretax accounting income shall be disclosed if they are not otherwise apparent

---

[23]See Appendix A, paragraph 35.

[24]The tax (or benefit) related to "ordinary" income (or loss) in a jurisdiction may not be limited to tax (or benefit) in that jurisdiction. It might also include tax (or benefit) in another jurisdiction that results from providing taxes on unremitted earnings, foreign tax credits, etc.

[25]See Appendix A, paragraph 39.

from the financial statements or from the nature of the enterprise's business.[26]

Effective Date and Transition

26. The provisions of this Interpretation shall be effective for financial statements issued after March 31, 1977 for interim periods in fiscal years beginning after December 15, 1976. Earlier application is encouraged for any interim financial statements that have not been previously issued. This Interpretation shall not be applied retroactively for previously issued interim financial statements.

This Interpretation was adopted by the unanimous vote of the six members of the Financial Accounting Standards Board:

Marshall S. Armstrong,	Donald J. Kirk	Robert E. Mays
Chairman	Arthur L. Litke	Robert T. Sprouse
Oscar S. Gellein		

Appendix A

EXCERPTS FROM APB OPINIONS

27. This Appendix contains relevant excerpts from APB Opinions that relate to this Interpretation. It repeats the general guidance of *APB Opinion No. 28* on accounting for income taxes in interim financial reports and the specific paragraphs of *APB Opinion No. 11* that prescribe the annual accounting for income taxes in certain situations.

General Guidelines

28. Paragraph 19 of *APB Opinion No. 28* contains the following general guidelines for the computation of income tax provisions for interim periods:

In reporting interim financial information, income tax provisions should be determined under the procedures set forth in APB Opinion Nos. 11, 23, and 24. At the end of each interim period the company should make its best estimate of the effective tax rate expected to be applicable for the full fiscal year. The rate so determined should be used in providing for income taxes on a current year-to-date basis. The effective tax rate should reflect anticipated investment tax credits, foreign tax rates, percentage depletion, capital gains rates, and other available tax planning alternatives.

The paragraph continues with the following regarding the tax effects of unusual or extraordinary items:

However, in arriving at this effective tax rate no effect should be included for the tax related to significant unusual or extraordinary items that will be separately reported or reported net of their related tax effect in reports for the interim period or for the fiscal year. . . .

Recognition of the Tax Benefit of a Loss

29. Paragraph 44 of *APB Opinion No. 11* states the following with respect to tax benefits of loss carry-backs:

The tax effects of any realizable loss carry-*backs* should be recognized in the determination of net income (loss) of the loss periods. The tax loss gives rise to a refund (or claim for refund) of past taxes, which is both measurable and currently realizable; therefore the tax effect of the loss is properly recognizable in the determination of net income (loss) for the loss period. (Emphasis in original.)

30. Paragraph 45 of *APB Opinion No. 11* states the following with respect to tax benefits of loss carry-forwards:

The tax effects of loss carry*forwards* also relate to the determination of net income (loss) of the loss periods. However, a significant question generally exists as to realization of the tax effects of the carry*forwards,* since realization is dependent upon future taxable income. Accordingly, the Board [APB] has concluded that the tax benefits of loss carry*forwards* should not be recognized until they are actually realized, except in unusual circumstances when realization is *assured beyond any reasonable doubt* at the time the loss carry*forwards* arise. (Emphasis in original.)

31. Paragraph 47 of *APB Opinion No. 11* describes the circumstances that may assure future realization of the tax benefit of a loss carryforward beyond any reasonable doubt as follows:

Realization of the tax benefit of a loss carry*forward* would appear to be assured beyond any reasonable doubt when both of the following conditions exist: (a) the loss results from an iden-

---

[26]See Appendix A, paragraph 37.

tifiable, isolated and nonrecurring cause and the company either has been continuously profitable over a long period or has suffered occasional losses which were more than offset by taxable income in subsequent years, and (b) future taxable income is virtually certain to be large enough to offset the loss carry*forward* and will occur soon enough to provide realization during the carry*forward* period. (Emphasis in original.)

32. Paragraph 20 of *APB Opinion No. 28* states the following with respect to losses that arise in the early portion of a fiscal year:

> The tax effects of losses that arise in the early portion of a fiscal year (in the event carryback of such losses is not possible) should be recognized only when realization is assured beyond any reasonable doubt (paragraph 45 of APB Opinion No. 11). An established seasonal pattern of loss in early interim periods offset by income in later interim periods should constitute evidence that realization is assured beyond reasonable doubt, unless other evidence indicates the established seasonal pattern will not prevail. The tax effects of losses incurred in early interim periods may be recognized in a later interim period of a fiscal year if their realization, although initially uncertain, later becomes assured beyond reasonable doubt. When the tax effects of losses that arise in the early portions of a fiscal year are not recognized in that interim period, no tax provision should be made for income that arises in later interim periods until the tax effects of the previous interim losses are utilized. . . .

Reversal of Net Deferred Tax Credits

33. Paragraph 48 of *APB Opinion No. 11* states the following with respect to reversal in a loss year of existing net deferred tax credits arising from timing differences:

> Net deferred tax credits arising from timing differences may exist at the time loss carry*forwards* arise. In the usual case when the tax effect of a loss carry*forward* is not recognized in the loss period, adjustments of the existing net deferred tax credits may be necessary in that period or in subsequent periods. In this situation net deferred tax credits should be eliminated to the extent of the lower of (a) the tax effect of the loss carry*forward,* or (b) the amortization of the net deferred tax credits that would otherwise have occurred during the carry*forward* period. (Emphasis in original.)

34. Paragraph 46 of *APB Opinion No. 11* suggests that existing net deferred tax credits arising from timing differences that will be amortized during the carryforward period of a current year operating loss carryforward should be accounted for the same as if there were assurance of realization of the tax benefits of the loss carryforward beyond any reasonable doubt when it states:

> In those rare cases in which realization of the tax benefits of loss carry*forwards* is assured beyond any reasonable doubt, the potential benefits should be associated with the periods of loss and should be recognized in the determination of results of operations for those periods. Realization is considered to be assured beyond any reasonable doubt when conditions such as those set forth in paragraph 47 are present. (Also see paragraph 48.) (Emphasis in original.)

Tax (or Benefit) Applicable to Significant Unusual or Infrequently Occurring Items, Discontinued Operations, or Extraordinary Items

35. Paragraph 21 of *APB Opinion No. 28* states the following with respect to significant unusual or infrequently occurring items, discontinued operations, or extraordinary items:

> Extraordinary items should be disclosed separately and included in the determination of net income for the interim period in which they occur. In determining materiality, extraordinary items should be related to the estimated income for the full fiscal year. Effects of disposals of a segment of a business and unusual and infrequently occurring transactions and events that are material with respect to the operating results of the interim period but that are not designated as extraordinary items in the interim statements should be reported separately. . . . Extraordinary items, gains or losses from disposal of a segment of a business, and unusual or infrequently occurring items should not be prorated over the balance of the fiscal year.

Tax Allocation within a Period

36. Paragraph 52 of *APB Opinion No. 11* states the following concerning tax allocation within a period:

> The Board [APB] has concluded that tax allocation within a period should be applied to obtain an appropriate relationship between income tax expense and (a) income before extraordinary items, (b) extraordinary items, (c) adjustments of prior periods (or of the opening balance of retained earnings) and (d) direct entries to other stockholders' equity accounts. The income tax expense attributable to income before extraordinary items is computed by

determining the income tax expense related to revenue and expense transactions entering into the determination of such income, without giving effect to the tax consequences of the items excluded from the determination of income before extraordinary items. The income tax expense attributable to other items is determined by the tax consequences of transactions involving these items. If an operating loss exists before extraordinary items, the tax consequences of such loss should be associated with the loss.

Disclosure

37. Footnote 2 to paragraph 19 of *APB Opinion No. 28* states the following concerning the annual effective tax rate:

> Disclosure should be made of the reasons for significant variations in the customary relationship between income tax expense and pretax accounting income, if they are not otherwise apparent from the financial statements or from the nature of the entity's business (see APB Opinion No. 11, paragraph 63).

Paragraph 63 of *APB Opinion No. 11* requires disclosure of:

> Reasons for significant variations in the customary relationships between income tax expense and pretax accounting income, if they are not otherwise apparent from the financial state-

ments or from the nature of the entity's business.

Using a Prior Year Operating Loss Carryforward

38. Paragraph 61 of *APB Opinion No. 11* specifies:

> When the tax benefit of an operating loss carry*forward* is realized in full or in part in a subsequent period, and has not been previously recognized in the loss period, the tax benefit should be reported as an extraordinary item . . . in the results of operations of the period in which realized. (Emphasis in original.)

Effect of New Tax Legislation

39. Paragraph 20 of *APB Opinion No. 28* also contains the following guidance with respect to the effect of new tax legislation:

> Changes resulting from new tax legislation should be reflected after the effective dates prescribed in the statutes.

Appendix B

CROSS REFERENCE TABLE

40. This Appendix provides a cross reference from the paragraphs of this Intepretation to the paragraphs in Appendixes C and D that illustrate the application of those paragraphs.

Appendix C

EXAMPLES OF COMPUTATIONS OF INTERIM PERIOD INCOME TAXES

41. This Appendix provides examples of application of this Interpretation for some specific situations. In general, the examples illustrate matters

unique to accounting for income taxes at interim dates. The examples do not include consideration of the nature of tax credits and permanent differences or illustrate all possible combinations of circumstances.

42. Specific situations illustrated in this Appendix are:

Accounting for Income Taxes Applicable to "Ordinary" Income (or Loss) at an Interim Date If "Ordinary" Income Is Anticipated for the Fiscal Year

43. The following assumed facts are applicable to the examples of application of this Interpretation in paragraphs 44-47.

For the full fiscal year, an enterprise anticipates "ordinary" income of $100,000. All income is taxable in one jurisdiction at a 50 percent rate.

Anticipated tax credits for the fiscal year total $10,000. No permanent differences are anticipated. No changes in estimated "ordinary" income, tax rates, or tax credits occur during the year.

Computation of the estimated annual effective tax rate applicable to "ordinary" income is as follows:

Tax at statutory rate ($100,000 at 50%)	$ 50,000
Less anticipated tax credits	(10,000)
Net tax to be provided	$ 40,000
Estimated annual effective tax rate ($40,000 ÷ $100,000)	40%

Tax credits are generally subject to limitations, usually based on the amount of tax payable before the credits. In computing the estimated annual effective tax rate, anticipated tax credits are limited to the amounts that are expected to be realized or are expected to be assured of future realization beyond any reasonable doubt at year-end. An exception to this general rule occurs in the computation of deferred taxes resulting from timing differences. If tax credits are not realized but the credits would have been realized if timing differences were not present, the credits are accounted for as a tax benefit and included in the estimated annual effective tax rate. If an enterprise is unable to estimate the amount of its tax credits for the year, see footnote 7 to paragraph 8.

44. Assume the facts stated in paragraph 43. The enterprise has "ordinary" income in all interim periods. Quarterly tax computations are:

	"Ordinary" income		Estimated annual effective tax rate	Tax		
Reporting Period	Reporting period	Year-to-date		Year-to-date	Less previously provided	Reporting period
First quarter	$ 20,000	$ 20,000	40%	$ 8,000	$ —	$ 8,000
Second quarter	20,000	40,000	40%	16,000	8,000	8,000
Third quarter	20,000	60,000	40%	24,000	16,000	8,000
Fourth quarter	40,000	100,000	40%	40,000	24,000	16,000
Fiscal year	$100,000					$40,000

45. Assume the facts stated in paragraph 43. The enterprise has "ordinary" income and losses in interim periods; there is not an "ordinary" loss for the fiscal year-to-date at the end of any interim period. Quarterly tax computations are:

	"Ordinary" income (loss)		Estimated annual effective tax rate	Tax (or benefit)		
Reporting Period	Reporting period	Year-to-date		Year-to-date	Less previously provided	Reporting period
First quarter	$ 40,000	$ 40,000	40%	$16,000	$ —	$16,000
Second quarter	40,000	80,000	40%	32,000	16,000	16,000
Third quarter	(20,000)	60,000	40%	24,000	32,000	(8,000)
Fourth quarter	40,000	100,000	40%	40,000	24,000	16,000
Fiscal year	$100,000					$40,000

46. Assume the facts stated in paragraph 43. The enterprise has "ordinary" income and losses in interim periods, and there is an "ordinary" loss for the year-to-date at the end of an interim period. Established seasonal patterns assure the realization of the tax benefit of the year-to-date loss and realization of anticipated tax credits beyond any reasonable doubt. Quarterly tax computations are:

| | "Ordinary" income (loss) | | Estimated annual effective tax rate | Tax (or benefit) | | |
| | Reporting period | Year-to-date | | Year-to-date | Less previously provided | Reporting period |
Reporting Period						
First quarter	$ (20,000)	$ (20,000)	40%	$ (8,000)	$ —	$ (8,000)
Second quarter	10,000	(10,000)	40%	(4,000)	(8,000)	4,000
Third quarter	15,000	5,000	40%	2,000	(4,000)	6,000
Fourth quarter	95,000	100,000	40%	40,000	2,000	38,000
Fiscal year	$100,000					$40,000

47. Assume the facts stated in paragraph 43. The enterprise has "ordinary" income and losses in interim periods, and there is a year-to-date "ordinary" loss during the year. There is no established seasonal pattern, and realization of the tax benefit of the year-to-date loss and realization of the anticipated tax credits are not otherwise assured beyond any reasonable doubt. Quarterly tax computations are:

| | "Ordinary" income (loss) | | Estimated annual effective tax rate | Tax | | |
| | Reporting period | Year-to-date | | Year-to-date | Less previously provided | Reporting period |
Reporting Period						
First quarter	$ (20,000)	$ (20,000)	—*	$ —	$ —	$ —
Second quarter	10,000	(10,000)	—*	—	—	—
Third quarter	15,000	5,000	40%	2,000	—	2,000
Fourth quarter	95,000	100,000	40%	40,000	2,000	38,000
Fiscal year	$100,000					$40,000

*No benefit is recognized because realization of the tax benefit of the year-to-date loss is not assured beyond any reasonable doubt.

48. During the fiscal year, all of an enterprise's operations are taxable in one jurisdiction at a 50 percent rate. No permanent differences are anticipated. Estimates of "ordinary" income for the year and of anticipated credits at the end of each interim period are as shown below. Changes in the estimated annual effective tax rate result from changes in the ratio of anticipated tax credits to tax computed at the statutory rate. Changes consist of an unantic- ipated strike that reduced income in the second quarter, an increase in the capital budget resulting in an increase in anticipated investment tax credit in the third quarter, and better than anticipated sales and income in the fourth quarter. The enterprise has "ordinary" income in all interim periods. Computations of the estimated annual effective tax rate based on the estimate made at the end of each quarter are:

| | Estimated, end of | | | Actual fiscal year |
	First quarter	Second quarter	Third quarter	
Estimated "ordinary" income for the fiscal year	$100,000	$80,000	$80,000	$100,000
Tax at 50% statutory rate	$ 50,000	$40,000	$40,000	$ 50,000
Less anticipated credits	(5,000)	(5,000)	(10,000)	(10,000)
Net tax to be provided	$ 45,000	$35,000	$30,000	$ 40,000
Estimated annual effective tax rate	45%	43.75%	37.5%	40%

Quarterly tax computations are:

Reporting Period	"Ordinary" income Reporting period	"Ordinary" income Year-to-date	Estimated annual effective tax rate	Tax Year-to-date	Tax Less previously provided	Tax Reporting period
First quarter	$ 25,000	$ 25,000	45%	$11,250	$ —	$11,250
Second quarter	5,000	30,000	43.75%	13,125	11,250	1,875
Third quarter	25,000	55,000	37.5%	20,625	13,125	7,500
Fourth quarter	45,000	100,000	40%	40,000	20,625	19,375
Fiscal year	$100,000					$40,000

Accounting for Income Taxes Applicable to "Ordinary" Income (or Loss) at an Interim Date If an "Ordinary" Loss Is Anticipated for the Fiscal Year

49. The following assumed facts are applicable to the examples of application of this Interpretation in paragraphs 50-54.

For the full fiscal year, an enterprise anticipates an "ordinary" loss of $100,000. The enterprise oper- ates entirely in one jurisdiction where the tax rate is 50 percent. Anticipated tax credits for the fiscal year total $10,000. No permanent differences are antici- pated.

If realization of the tax benefit of the loss and real- ization of tax credits were assured beyond any rea- sonable doubt, computation of the estimated annual effective tax rate applicable to the "ordinary" loss would be as follows:

Tax benefit at statutory rate ($100,000 at 50%)	$(50,000)
Tax credits	(10,000)
Net tax benefit	$(60,000)
Estimated annual effective tax rate ($60,000 ÷ $100,000)	60%

The examples in paragraphs 50-54 state varying assumptions with respect to assurance of realization of the components of the net tax benefit. When the realization of a component of the benefit is not assured beyond any reasonable doubt, that compo- nent is not included in the computation of the esti- mated annual effective tax rate.

50. Assume the facts stated in paragraph 49. The enterprise has "ordinary" losses in all interim periods. Realization of the full tax benefit of the anticipated "ordinary" loss and realization of antici- pated tax credits are assured beyond any reasonable doubt because they will be carried back. Quarterly tax computations are:

Reporting Period	"Ordinary" loss Reporting period	"Ordinary" loss Year-to-date	Estimated annual effective tax rate	Tax benefit Year-to-date	Tax benefit Less previously provided	Tax benefit Reporting period
First quarter	$ (20,000)	$ (20,000)	60%	$(12,000)	$ —	$(12,000)
Second quarter	(20,000)	(40,000)	60%	(24,000)	(12,000)	(12,000)
Third quarter	(20,000)	(60,000)	60%	(36,000)	(24,000)	(12,000)
Fourth quarter	(40,000)	(100,000)	60%	(60,000)	(36,000)	(24,000)
Fiscal year	$(100,000)					$(60,000)

51. Assume the facts stated in paragraph 49. The enterprise has "ordinary" income and losses in interim periods and for the year-to-date. Realization of the full tax benefit of the anticipated "ordinary" loss and realization of the anticipated tax credits are assured beyond any reasonable doubt because they will be carried back. Realization of the full tax benefit of the maximum year-to-date "ordinary" loss is also assured beyond any reasonable doubt. Quarterly tax computations are:

Reporting period	"Ordinary" income (loss) Reporting period	"Ordinary" income (loss) Year-to-date	Estimated annual effective tax rate	Tax (or benefit) Year-to-date Computed	Tax (or benefit) Year-to-date Limited to	Less previously provided	Reporting period
First quarter	$ 20,000	$ 20,000	60%	$ 12,000		$ —	$ 12,000
Second quarter	(80,000)	(60,000)	60%	(36,000)		12,000	(48,000)
Third quarter	(80,000)	(140,000)	60%	(84,000)	$(80,000)*	(36,000)	(44,000)
Fourth quarter	40,000	(100,000)	60%	(60,000)		(80,000)	20,000
Fiscal year	$(100,000)						$(60,000)

---

*Because the year-to-date "ordinary" loss exceeds the anticipated "ordinary" loss for the fiscal year, the tax benefit recognized for the year-to-date is limited to the amount that would be recognized if the year-to-date "ordinary" loss were the anticipated "ordinary" loss for the fiscal year. The limitation is computed as follows:

Year-to-date "ordinary" loss times the statutory rate ($140,000 at 50%)	$(70,000)
Estimated tax credits for the year	(10,000)
Year-to-date benefit limited to	$(80,000)

52. In the examples in paragraphs 50 and 51, if neither realization of the tax benefit of the anticipated loss for the fiscal year nor realization of anticipated tax credits were assured beyond any reasonable doubt, the estimated annual effective tax rate for the year would be zero and no tax (or benefit) would be recognized in any quarter. That conclusion is not affected by changes in the mix of income and loss in interim periods during a fiscal year. However, see footnote 7 to paragraph 8 above.

53. Assume the facts stated in paragraph 49. The enterprise has an "ordinary" loss in all interim periods. Realization of the tax benefit of the loss is assured beyond any reasonable doubt only to the extent of $40,000 of prior income available to be offset by carryback ($20,000 of tax at the 50 percent statutory rate). Therefore the estimated annual effective tax rate is 20 percent ($20,000 benefit assured divided by $100,000 estimated fiscal year "ordinary" loss). Quarterly tax computations are:

Reporting period	"Ordinary" loss Reporting period	"Ordinary" loss Year-to-date	Estimated annual effective tax rate	Tax benefit Year-to-date	Tax benefit Less previously provided	Reporting period
First quarter	$ (20,000)	$ (20,000)	20%	$ (4,000)	$ —	$ (4,000)
Second quarter	(20,000)	(40,000)	20%	(8,000)	(4,000)	(4,000)
Third quarter	(20,000)	(60,000)	20%	(12,000)	(8,000)	(4,000)
Fourth quarter	(40,000)	(100,000)	20%	(20,000)	(12,000)	(8,000)
Fiscal year	$(100,000)					$(20,000)

54. Assume the facts stated in paragraph 49. The enterprise has "ordinary" income and losses in interim periods and for the year-to-date. Realization of the tax benefit of the anticipated "ordinary" loss is assured beyond any reasonable doubt only to the extent of $40,000 of prior income available to be offset by carryback ($20,000 of tax at the 50 percent statutory rate). Therefore the estimated annual effective tax rate is 20 percent ($20,000 benefit assured divided by $100,000 estimated fiscal year "ordinary" loss), and the benefit that can be recognized for the year-to-date is limited to $20,000 (the benefit that is assured of realization). Quarterly tax computations are:

| | "Ordinary" income (loss) | | Estimated annual | Tax (or benefit) | | | |
| | Reporting period | Year-to-date | effective tax rate | Year-to-date | | Less previously provided | Reporting period |
Reporting period				Computed	Limited to		
First quarter	$ 20,000	$ 20,000	20%	$ 4,000		$ —	$ 4,000
Second quarter	(80,000)	(60,000)	20%	(12,000)		4,000	(16,000)
Third quarter	(80,000)	(140,000)	20%	(28,000)	$(20,000)	(12,000)	(8,000)
Fourth quarter	40,000	(100,000)	20%	(20,000)		(20,000)	—
Fiscal year	$(100,000)						$(20,000)

55. The enterprise anticipates a fiscal year "ordinary" loss. The loss cannot be carried back, and future profits are not assured beyond any reasonable doubt. Net deferred tax credits arising from timing differences are present. A portion of the timing differences relating to those credits will reverse within the loss carryforward period. Computation of the estimated annual effective tax rate to be used is as follows:

Estimated fiscal year "ordinary" loss	$(100,000)
The tax benefit to be recognized is the lesser of: Tax effect of the loss carryforward ($100,000 at 50% statutory rate)	$50,000
Amount of the net deferred tax credits that would otherwise have been amortized during the carryforward period	$24,000
Estimated annual effective tax rate ($24,000 ÷ $100,000)	24%

Quarterly tax computations are:

| | "Ordinary" loss | | Estimated annual | Tax benefit | | |
Reporting Period	Reporting period	Year-to-date	effective tax rate	Year-to-date	Less previously provided	Reporting period
First quarter	$ (20,000)	$ (20,000)	24%	$ (4,800)	$ —	$ (4,800)
Second quarter	(20,000)	(40,000)	24%	(9,600)	(4,800)	(4,800)
Third quarter	(20,000)	(60,000)	24%	(14,400)	(9,600)	(4,800)
Fourth quarter	(40,000)	(100,000)	24%	(24,000)	(14,400)	(9,600)
Fiscal year	$(100,000)					$(24,000)

Note: Changes in the timing of the loss by quarter would not change the above computation.

Accounting for Income Taxes Applicable to Unusual, Infrequently Occurring, or Extraordinary Items

56. The examples of computations in paragraphs 57 and 58 illustrate the computation of the tax (or benefit) applicable to unusual, infrequently occurring, or extraordinary items when "ordinary" income is anticipated for the fiscal year. These examples are based on the facts and computations given in paragraphs 43-47 plus additional information supplied in paragraphs 57 and 58. The computation of the tax (or benefit) applicable to the "ordinary" income is not affected by the occurrence of an unusual, infrequently occurring, or extraordinary item; therefore, each example refers to one or more of the examples of that computation in

paragraphs 44-47 and does not reproduce the computation and the facts assumed. The income statement display for tax (or benefit) applicable to unusual, infrequently occurring, or extraordinary items is illustrated in Appendix D.

57. As explained in paragraph 56, this example is based on the computations of tax applicable to "ordinary" income that are illustrated in paragraph 44 above. In addition, the enterprise experiences a tax-deductible unusual, infrequently occurring, or extraordinary loss of $50,000 (tax benefit $25,000) in the second quarter. Because the loss can be carried back, the benefit of the loss is assured beyond any reasonable doubt at the time of occurrence. Quarterly tax provisions are:

| | | | Tax (or benefit) applicable to | |
Reporting period	"Ordinary" income	Unusual, infrequently occurring, or extraordinary loss	"Ordinary" income	Unusual, infrequently occurring, or extraordinary loss
First quarter	$ 20,000		$ 8,000	
Second quarter	20,000	$(50,000)	8,000	$(25,000)
Third quarter	20,000		8,000	
Fourth quarter	40,000		16,000	
Fiscal year	$100,000	$(50,000)	$40,000	$(25,000)

Note: Changes in assumptions would not change the timing of the recognition of the tax benefit applicable to the unusual, infrequently occurring, or extraordinary item as long as realization is assured beyond any reasonable doubt.

58. As explained in paragraph 56, this example is based on the computations of tax applicable to "ordinary" income that are illustrated in paragraphs 44 and 45 above. In addition, the enterprise experiences a tax-deductible unusual, infrequently occurring, or extraordinary loss of $50,000 (potential benefit $25,000) in the second quarter. The loss cannot be carried back, and the current projection of "ordinary" income is not considered sufficiently reliable to assure realization of the tax benefit of the year-to-date loss beyond any reasonable doubt. As a result, realization of the tax benefit of the unusual, infrequently occurring, or extraordinary loss is not assured beyond any reasonable doubt except to the extent of offsetting "ordinary" income for the year-to-date. Quarterly tax provisions under two different assumptions for the occurrence of "ordinary" income are:

| | | | Tax (or benefit) applicable to | | | | |
| | | | "Ordinary" income (loss) | | Unusual, infrequently occurring, or extraordinary loss | | |
Assumptions and reporting period	"Ordinary" income (loss)	Unusual, infrequently occurring, or extraordinary loss	Reporting period	Year-to-date	Year-to-date	Less previously provided	Reporting period
Income in all quarters:							
First quarter	$ 20,000		$ 8,000	$ 8,000			
Second quarter	20,000	$(50,000)	8,000	16,000	$(16,000)	$ —	$(16,000)
Third quarter	20,000		8,000	24,000	(24,000)	(16,000)	(8,000)
Fourth quarter	40,000		16,000	40,000	(25,000)	(24,000)	(1,000)
Fiscal year	$100,000	$(50,000)	$40,000				$(25,000)
Income and loss quarters:							
First quarter	$ 40,000		$16,000	$16,000			
Second quarter	40,000	$(50,000)	16,000	32,000	$ (25,000)	$ —	$ (25,000)
Third quarter	(20,000)		(8,000)	24,000	(24,000)	(25,000)	1,000
Fourth quarter	40,000		16,000	40,000	(25,000)	(24,000)	(1,000)
Fiscal year	$100,000	$(50,000)	$40,000				$ (25,000)

Using a Prior Year Operating Loss Carryforward

59. The examples of computations in paragraphs 60 and 61 illustrate the computation of the tax benefit that results from using a prior year operating loss carryforward. The examples are based on the following assumed facts.

For the full fiscal year, an enterprise anticipates "ordinary" income of $100,000. All income is taxable in one jurisdiction at a 50 percent rate. No tax credits or permanent differences are anticipated. If an operating loss carryforward is available, the estimated tax (or benefit) applicable to "ordinary" income (or loss) for the year is divided by the estimated "ordinary" income (or loss) for the year to arrive at an estimated annual effective tax rate. That rate is 50 percent in these examples. The estimated annual effective tax rate is applied to "ordinary" income (or loss) for the year-to-date to determine the year-to-date tax (or benefit) applicable to "ordinary" income (or loss), similar to the computations that are illustrated in paragraphs 44-47.

60. Assume the facts stated in paragraph 59. In addition, an operating loss carryforward is available that exceeds the estimated "ordinary" income for the year. Because *APB Opinion No. 28* required that an extraordinary item be recognized in the interim period of its occurrence and not spread over the year, the extraordinary credit recognized for the year-to-date at the end of each interim period is the amount that is realized by offsetting year-to-date taxable income. Quarterly tax provisions under various assumptions for the occurrence of "ordinary" income are:

Assumptions and reporting period	"Ordinary" income (loss)	Tax (or benefit)		Extraordinary charge (or credit)*		
		Reporting period	Year-to-date	Year-to-date	Less previously provided	Reporting period
Income in all quarters:						
First quarter	$ 20,000	$10,000	$10,000	$(10,000)	$ —	$(10,000)
Second quarter	20,000	10,000	20,000	(20,000)	(10,000)	(10,000)
Third quarter	20,000	10,000	30,000	(30,000)	(20,000)	(10,000)
Fourth quarter	40,000	20,000	50,000	(50,000)	(30,000)	(20,000)
Fiscal year	$100,000	$50,000				$(50,000)
Income and loss quarters; no year-to-date losses:						
First quarter	$ 40,000	$20,000	$20,000	$(20,000)	$ —	$(20,000)
Second quarter	40,000	20,000	40,000	(40,000)	(20,000)	(20,000)
Third quarter	(20,000)	(10,000)	30,000	(30,000)	(40,000)	10,000
Fourth quarter	40,000	20,000	50,000	(50,000)	(30,000)	(20,000)
Fiscal year	$100,000	$50,000				$(50,000)
Income and loss quarters and including year-to-date loss (realization of the tax benefit of the year-to-date "ordinary" loss and realization of anticipated tax credits are assured beyond any reasonable doubt by seasonal patterns):						
First quarter	$ (20,000)	$(10,000)	$(10,000)	$ —	$ —	$ —
Second quarter	10,000	5,000	(5,000)	—	—	—
Third quarter	15,000	7,500	2,500	(2,500)	—	(2,500)
Fourth quarter	95,000	47,500	50,000	(50,000)	(2,500)	(47,500)
Fiscal year	$100,000	$50,000				$(50,000)
Income and loss quarters, including year-to-date loss (realization of the tax benefit of the year-to-date "ordinary" loss and realization of anticipated tax credits are not assured beyond any reasonable doubt):						
First quarter	$ (20,000)	$ —	$ —	$ —	$ —	$ —
Second quarter	10,000	—	—	—	—	—
Third quarter	15,000	2,500	2,500	(2,500)	—	(2,500)
Fourth quarter	95,000	47,500	50,000	(50,000)	(2,500)	(47,500)
Fiscal year	$100,000	$50,000				$(50,000)

*Tax benefit resulting from using the operating loss carryforward.

61. Assume the facts stated in paragraph 59. In addition, an operating loss carryforward of $30,000 (tax benefit $15,000 at the 50 percent statutory rate) is available. Because *APB Opinion No. 28* requires that an extraordinary item be recognized in the interim period of its occurrence and not spread over the year, the extraordinary credit recognized for the year-to-date at the end of each interim period is the amount that is realized by offsetting year-to-date taxable income. Quarterly tax provisions are:

		Tax provision			Extraordinary credit	
					Less	
	"Ordinary"	Reporting	Year-to-	Year-to-	previously	Reporting
Reporting period	income	period	date	date	provided	period
First quarter	$ 20,000	$10,000	$10,000	$(10,000)	$ —	$(10,000)
Second quarter	20,000	10,000	20,000	(15,000)	(10,000)	(5,000)
Third quarter	20,000	10,000	30,000	(15,000)	(15,000)	—
Fourth quarter	40,000	20,000	50,000	(15,000)	(15,000)	—
Fiscal year	$100,000	$50,000				$(15,000)

Note: Differing patterns of occurrence of "ordinary" income and loss would result in computations similar to those in paragraph 60.

Accounting for Income Taxes Applicable to Income (or Loss) from Discontinued Operations at an Interim Date

62. An enterprise anticipates "ordinary" income for the year of $100,000 and tax credits of $10,000. The enterprise has "ordinary" income in all interim periods.The estimated annual effective tax rate is 40 percent, computed as follows:

Estimated pretax income	$ 100,000
Tax at 50% statutory rate	$ 50,000
Less anticipated credits	(10,000)
Net tax to be provided	$ 40,000
Estimated annual effective tax rate	40%

Quarterly tax computations for the first two quarters are:

| | "Ordinary" income | | Estimated annual | | Tax | |
| | Reporting | Year-to- | effective | Year-to- | Less previously | Reporting |
Reporting Period	period	date	tax rate	date	provided	period
First quarter	$20,000	$20,000	40%	$ 8,000	$ —	$ 8,000
Second quarter	25,000	45,000	40%	18,000	8,000	10,000

In the third quarter a decision is made to discontinue the operations of Division X, a segment of the business that has recently operated at a loss (before income taxes). The pretax income (and losses) of the continuing operations of the enterprise and of Division X through the third quarter and the estimated fourth quarter results are as follows:

| | Revised "ordinary" income from continuing operations | Division X | |
| | | Loss from operations | Provision for loss on disposal |
Reporting period			
First quarter	$ 25,000	$ (5,000)	
Second quarter	35,000	(10,000)	
Third quarter	50,000	(10,000)	$(55,000)
Fourth quarter	50,000*	—	—
Fiscal year	$160,000	$(25,000)	$(55,000)

---

*Estimated.

No changes have occurred in continuing operations that would affect the estimated annual effective tax rate. Anticipated annual tax credits of $10,000 included $2,000 of credits related to the operations of Division X. The revised estimated annual effective tax rate applicable to "ordinary" income from continuing operations is 45 percent, computed as follows:

Estimated "ordinary" income from continuing operations	$160,000
Tax at 50% statutory rate	$ 80,000
Less anticipated tax credits applicable to continuing operations	(8,000)
Net tax to be provided	$ 72,000
Estimated annual effective tax rate	45%

Quarterly computations of tax applicable to "ordinary" income from continuing operations are as follows:

	"Ordinary" income		Estimated annual effective tax rate	Tax		
Reporting Period	Reporting period	Year-to-date		Year-to-date	Less previously provided	Reporting period
First quarter	$ 25,000	$ 25,000	45%	$11,250	$ —	$11,250
Second quarter	35,000	60,000	45%	27,000	11,250	15,750
Third quarter	50,000	110,000	45%	49,500	27,000	22,500
Fourth quarter	50,000	160,000	45%	72,000	49,500	22,500
Fiscal year	$160,000					$72,000

Tax benefit applicable to Division X for the first two quarters is computed as follows:

	Tax applicable to "ordinary" income		Tax benefit applicable to Division X
Reporting period	Previously reported (A)	Recomputed (above) (B)	(A – B)
First quarter	$ 8,000	$11,250	$(3,250)
Second quarter	10,000	15,750	(5,750)
			$(9,000)

The third quarter tax benefits applicable to both the loss from operations and the provision for loss on disposal of Division X are computed based on estimated annual income with and without the effects of the Division X losses. Current year tax credits related to the operations of Division X have not been recognized. It is assumed that the tax benefit of those credits will not be realized because of the discontinuance of Division X operations. Any reduction in tax benefits resulting from recapture of previously recognized tax credits resulting from discontinuance or current year tax credits applicable to the discontinued operations would be reflected in the tax benefit recognized for the loss on disposal or loss from operations as appropriate. If, because of capital gains and losses, etc., the individually computed tax effects of the items do not equal the aggregate tax effects of the items, the aggregate tax effects are allocated to the individual items in the same manner that they will be allocated in the annual financial statements. The computations are as follows:

	Loss from operations Division X	Provision for loss on disposal
Estimated annual income from continuing operations	$160,000	$160,000
Loss from Division X operations	(25,000)	
Provision for loss on disposal of Division X		(55,000)
Total	$135,000	$105,000
Tax at 50% statutory rate	$ 67,500	$ 52,500
Anticipated credits from continuing operations	(8,000)	(8,000)
Tax credits of Division X and recapture of previously recognized tax credits resulting from discontinuance	—	—
Taxes on income after effect of Division X losses	59,500	44,500
Taxes on income before effect of Division X losses—see computation above	72,000	72,000
Tax benefit applicable to the losses of Division X	(12,500)	(27,500)
Amounts previously recognized—see computation above	(9,000)	—
Tax benefit recognized in third quarter	$ (3,500)	$ (27,500)

The resulting revised quarterly tax provisions are summarized as follows:

	Pretax income (loss)			Tax (or benefit) applicable to		
Reporting period	Continuing operations	Operations of Division X	Provision for loss on disposal	Continuing operations	Operations of Division X	Provision for loss on disposal
First quarter	$ 25,000	$ (5,000)		$11,250	$ (3,250)	
Second quarter	35,000	(10,000)		15,750	(5,750)	
Third quarter	50,000	(10,000)	$(55,000)	22,500	(3,500)	$(27,500)
Fourth quarter	50,000			22,500		
Fiscal year	$160,000	$(25,000)	$(55,000)	$72,000	$(12,500)	$(27,500)

Accounting for Income Taxes Applicable to the Cumulative Effect of a Change in Accounting Principle

63. The tax (or benefit) applicable to the cumulative effect of the change on retained earnings at the beginning of the fiscal year shall be computed the same as for the annual financial statements.

64. When an enterprise makes a cumulative effect type accounting change in other than the first interim period of the enterprise's fiscal year, paragraph 10 of *FASB Statement No. 3*, "Reporting Accounting Changes in Interim Financial Statements," requires that financial information for the pre-change interim periods of the fiscal year shall be restated by applying the newly adopted accounting principle to those pre-change interim periods. The tax (or benefit) applicable to those pre-change interim periods shall be recomputed. The restated tax (or benefit) shall reflect the year-to-date amounts and annual estimates originally used for the pre-change interim periods, modified only for the effect of the change in accounting principle on those year-to-date and estimated annual amounts.

Accounting for Income Taxes Applicable to "Ordinary" Income If an Enterprise Is Subject to Tax in Multiple Jurisdictions

65. An enterprise operates through separate corporate entities in two countries. Applicable tax rates are 50 percent in the United States and 20 percent in Country A. The enterprise has no unusual or extraordinary items during the fiscal year and anticipates no tax credits or permanent differences. (The effect of foreign tax credits and the necessity of providing tax on undistributed earnings are ignored because of

the wide range of tax planning alternatives available.) For the full fiscal year the enterprise anticipates "ordinary" income of $60,000 in the United States and $40,000 in Country A. The enterprise is able to make a reliable estimate of its Country A "ordinary" income and tax for the fiscal year in dollars. Computation of the overall estimated annual effective tax rate is as follows:

Anticipated "ordinary" income for the fiscal year:	
In the U.S.	$ 60,000
In Country A	40,000
Total	$100,000
Anticipated tax for the fiscal year:	
In the U.S. ($60,000 at 50% statutory rate)	$ 30,000
In Country A ($40,000 at 20% statutory rate)	8,000
Total	$ 38,000
Overall estimated annual effective tax rate ($38,000 ÷ $100,000)	38%

Quarterly tax computations are as follows:

Reporting Period	"Ordinary" income			Year-to-date	Overall estimated annual effective tax rate	Tax		
	U.S.	Country A	Total			Year-to-date	Less previously reported	Reporting period
First quarter	$ 5,000	$15,000	$ 20,000	$ 20,000	38%	$ 7,600	$ —	$ 7,600
Second quarter	10,000	10,000	20,000	40,000	38%	15,200	7,600	7,600
Third quarter	10,000	10,000	20,000	60,000	38%	22,800	15,200	7,600
Fourth quarter	35,000	5,000	40,000	100,000	38%	38,000	22,800	15,200
Fiscal year	$60,000	$40,000	$100,000					$38,000

66. Assume the facts stated in paragraph 65. In addition the enterprise operates through a separate corporate entity in Country B. Applicable tax rates in Country B are 40 percent. Operations in Country B have resulted in losses in recent years and an "ordinary" loss is anticipated for the current fiscal year in Country B. Realization of the tax benefit of those losses is not assured beyond any reasonable doubt; accordingly, no tax benefit is recognized for losses in Country B, and interim period tax (or benefit) is separately computed for the "ordinary" loss in Country B and for the overall "ordinary" income in the United States and Country A. The tax applicable to the overall "ordinary" income in the United States and Country A is computed as in paragraph 65. Quarterly tax provisions are as follows:

Reporting Period	"Ordinary" income (or loss)					Tax (or benefit)		
	U.S.	Country A	Combined excluding Country B	Country B	Total	Overall excluding Country B	Country B	Total
First quarter	$ 5,000	$15,000	$ 20,000	$ (5,000)	$15,000	$ 7,600	$ —	$ 7,600
Second quarter	10,000	10,000	20,000	(25,000)	(5,000)	7,600	—	7,600
Third quarter	10,000	10,000	20,000	(5,000)	15,000	7,600	—	7,600
Fourth quarter	35,000	5,000	40,000	(5,000)	35,000	15,200	—	15,200
Fiscal year	$60,000	$40,000	$100,000	$(40,000)	$60,000	$38,000	$ —	$38,000

67. Assume the facts stated in paragraph 65. In addition the enterprise operates through a separate corporate entity in Country C. Applicable tax rates in Country C are 40 percent in foreign currency. Depreciation in that country is large and exchange rates have changed in prior years. The enterprise is unable to make a reasonable estimate of its "ordinary" income for the year in Country C and

thus is unable to reasonably estimate its annual effective tax rate in Country C in dollars. Accordingly, tax (or benefit) in Country C is separately computed as "ordinary" income (or loss) occurs in Country C. The tax applicable to the overall "ordinary" income in the United States and Country A is computed as in paragraph 65. Quarterly computations of tax applicable to Country C are as follows:

Reporting period	Foreign currency amounts			Translated amounts in dollars	
	"Ordinary" income in reporting period	Tax (at 40% rate)		"Ordinary" income in reporting period	Tax
First quarter	FC 10,000	FC 4,000		$12,500	$ 3,000
Second quarter	5,000	2,000		8,750	1,500
Third quarter	30,000	12,000		27,500	9,000
Fourth quarter	15,000	6,000		16,250	4,500
Fiscal year	FC 60,000	FC 24,000		$65,000	$18,000

Quarterly tax provisions are as follows:

Reporting Period	"Ordinary" income					Tax		
	U.S.	Country A	Combined excluding Country C	Country C	Total	Overall excluding Country C	Country C	Total
First quarter	$ 5,000	$15,000	$ 20,000	$12,500	$ 32,500	$ 7,600	$ 3,000	$10,600
Second quarter	10,000	10,000	20,000	8,750	28,750	7,600	1,500	9,100
Third quarter	10,000	10,000	20,000	27,500	47,500	7,600	9,000	16,600
Fourth quarter	35,000	5,000	40,000	16,250	56,250	15,200	4,500	19,700
Fiscal year	$ 60,000	$40,000	$100,000	$65,000	$165,000	$38,000	$18,000	$56,000

Effect of New Tax Legislation

68. The following assumed facts are applicable to the examples of application of this Interpretation in paragraphs 69 and 70.

For the full fiscal year, an enterprise anticipates "ordinary" income of $100,000. All income is taxable in one jurisdiction at a 50 percent rate. Anticipated tax credits for the fiscal year total $10,000. No permanent differences are anticipated.

Computation of the estimated annual effective tax rate applicable to "ordinary" income is as follows:

Tax at statutory rate ($100,000 at 50%)	$ 50,000
Less anticipated tax credits	(10,000)
Net tax to be provided	$ 40,000
Estimated annual effective tax rate ($40,000 ÷ $100,000)	40%

69. Assume the facts stated in paragraph 68. In addition, assume that new legislation creating additional tax credits is enacted during the second quarter of the enterprise's fiscal year. The new legislation is effective on the first day of the third quarter. As a result of the estimated effect of the new legislation, the enterprise revises its estimate of its annual effective tax rate to the following:

Tax at statutory rate ($100,000 at 50%)	$ 50,000
Less anticipated tax credits	(12,000)
Net tax to be provided	$ 38,000
Estimated annual effective tax rate ($38,000 ÷ $100,000)	38%

The effect of the new legislation shall not be reflected until it is effective or administratively effective. Accordingly, quarterly tax computations are:

| | "Ordinary" income | | Estimated annual effective tax rate | | Tax | | |
Reporting Period	Reporting period	Year-to-date		Year-to-date	Less previously provided	Reporting period
First quarter	$ 20,000	$ 20,000	40%	$ 8,000	$ —	$ 8,000
Second quarter	20,000	40,000	40%	16,000	8,000	8,000
Third quarter	20,000	60,000	38%	22,800	16,000	6,800
Fourth quarter	40,000	100,000	38%	38,000	22,800	15,200
Fiscal year	$100,000					$38,000

70. Assume the facts stated in paragraph 68. In addition, assume that new legislation creating additional tax credits is enacted after the end of the third quarter of the enterprise's fiscal year but before the enterprise has reported the results of its operations for the third quarter. The new legislation is effective retroactive to the first day of the third quarter. The new legislation results in the following revised estimated annual effective tax rate:

Tax at statutory rate ($100,000 at 50%)	$ 50,000
Less anticipated tax credits	(12,000)
Net tax to be provided	$ 38,000
Estimated annual effective tax rate ($38,000 ÷ $100,000)	38%

Quarterly tax computations are:

| | "Ordinary" income | | Estimated annual effective tax rate | | Tax | | |
Reporting Period	Reporting period	Year-to-date		Year-to-date	Less previously provided	Reporting period
First quarter	$ 20,000	$ 20,000	40%	$ 8,000	$ —	$ 8,000
Second quarter	20,000	40,000	40%	16,000	8,000	8,000
Third quarter	20,000	60,000	38%	22,800	16,000	6,800
Fourth quarter	40,000	100,000	38%	38,000	22,800	15,200
Fiscal year	$100,000					$38,000

Appendix D

ILLUSTRATION OF INCOME TAXES IN INCOME STATEMENT DISPLAY

71. The following illustrates the location in an income statement display of the various tax amounts computed under this Interpretation:

*Net sales		$XXXX
*Other income		XXX
		XXXX
Costs and expenses:		
*Cost of sales	$XXXX	
*Selling, general, and administrative expenses	XXXX	
*Interest expense	XXX	
*Other deductions	XX	
Unusual items	XXX	
Infrequently occurring items	XXX	XXXX
Income (loss) from continuing operations before income taxes and other items listed below		XXXX
†Provision for income taxes (benefit)		XXXX
Income (loss) from continuing operations before other items listed below		XXXX
Discontinued operations:		
Income (loss) from operations of discontinued Division X (less applicable income taxes of $XXXX)	XXXX	
Income (loss) on disposal of Division X, including provision of $XXXX for operating losses during phase-out period (less applicable income taxes of $XXXX)	XXXX	XXXX
Income (loss) before extraordinary items and cumulative effect of a change in accounting principle		XXXX
Extraordinary items (less applicable income taxes of $XXXX)		XXXX
‡Cumulative effect on prior years of a change in accounting principle (less applicable income taxes of $XXXX)		XXXX
Net income (loss)		$XXXX

*Components of "ordinary" income (loss).

†Consists of the total of income taxes (or benefit) applicable to (a) "ordinary" income, (b) unusual items, and (c) infrequently occurring items

‡This amount is net of applicable income taxes. The amount of the applicable income taxes is usually separately disclosed but that is not required.

Appendix E

SUMMARY OF CONSIDERATION OF COMMENTS ON EXPOSURE DRAFT

72. The "Notice of Exposure and Request for Comments" accompanying the Exposure Draft issued October 7, 1976 for this Interpretation stated:

The Interpretation set forth in this EXPOSURE DRAFT explains, clarifies, and elaborates on the requirements of *APB Opinion No. 28,* "Interim Financial Reporting," which relies in part on *APB Opinion No. 11,* "Accounting for Income Taxes," and on other APB Opinions with respect to accounting for income taxes in interim periods.

The FASB currently has on its technical agenda a project entitled Interim Financial Reporting. As part of that project, the Board will examine possible methods of accounting for income taxes in interim periods. At the completion of that project, the Board expects to issue a comprehensive Statement specifying the financial accounting and reporting standards to be applied in interim financial reporting. The Board recognizes that some might prefer methods of accounting for income taxes in interim periods other than those required by the concepts of *APB Opinion No. 28.* However, the Board is of the view that any other methods should be considered as part of the FASB's technical agenda project on Interim Financial Reporting.

The FASB Rules of Procedure permit the

issuance of a final Interpretation without exposure for public comment but allow public exposure prior to final issuance when the Board deems such procedure to be advisable. The Board has reached that conclusion here and has also concluded that a public comment period extending to November 15, 1976 is appropriate.

73. In response to the request for comments on the Exposure Draft, the FASB received and considered 99 letters of comment. Certain of the comments and the FASB's consideration of them are summarized in paragraphs 74-85.

Issuance of the Interpretation

74. Many respondents recommended that the FASB not issue a final Interpretation on "Accounting for Income Taxes in Interim Periods" at this time. Some of those respondents recommended that the project be deferred until the FASB issues its comprehensive Statement on Interim Financial Reporting. Others questioned if the number of existing differences in accounting for similar situations was great enough to require an Interpretation at this time.

75. It is not likely that a final Statement for the Board's current agenda project on Interim Financial Reporting will be issued and effective before 1979. Comments received in respect of the Exposure Draft indicate that there is, currently, diversity of practice. The Board concluded that the provisions of *APB Opinion No. 28* are sufficiently clear to provide a basis for an Interpretation and that a final Interpretation should be issued.

Applicability to Annual Financial Statements

76. Some respondents stated that the proposed Interpretation and the examples in Appendix B implicitly included a number of interpretations of the application of *APB Opinion No. 11* to annual financial statements. They recommended that, if the Board intends to interpret Opinion No. 11, the intent should be stated. The Board does not intend to modify annual accounting practices in this Interpretation. Accordingly, specific guidance on those matters that appeared to imply interpretations of the application of *APB Opinion No. 11* to annual financial statements was deleted.

77. Some respondents asked if the example in paragraph 49 of Appendix C of this Interpretation was intended to change the annual accounting for investment tax credits. Paragraph 49 includes "tax credits" in the computed tax benefit of an

"ordinary" loss, but does not identify those "tax credits" as "investment tax credits." Various tax credits other than investment tax credits may be available to an enterprise. This Interpretation is not intended to change annual accounting for unrealized investment tax credits.

Applicability to Regulated Industries

78. A number of respondents stated that the proposed Interpretation should not apply to regulated industries. Some respondents noted that the Addendum to *APB Opinion No. 2* may provide an exemption from the Interpretation for certain enterprises in regulated industries. The Board is aware that differing applications of the Addendum exist in practice and has not addressed that issue.

Amortization of Deferred Investment Tax Credits

79. Several respondents recommended that the amortization of deferred investment tax credits be excluded from the estimated annual effective tax rate. Some stated that the rationale of *APB Opinion No. 2* requires those items to be allocated among interim periods on the same basis as depreciation expense for the property giving rise to the credit. Paragraph 13 of Opinion No. 2 states that "the . . . investment credit should be reflected in net income over the productive life of acquired property and not in the year in which it is placed in service."[27] Footnote 6 to paragraph 8 of this Interpretation was revised to indicate that amortization of deferred investment tax credits need not be taken into account in estimating the annual effective tax rate. However, if an enterprise elects to consider investment tax credits in estimating the annual effective tax rate, the amount to be taken into account shall be the estimated amount of the current year's amortization and not the amount that reduces income tax payable on the enterprise's tax return.

Tax Exempt Interest

80. A number of respondents recommended that tax-exempt interest income be excluded from "ordinary" income in estimating the annual effective tax rate and in computing the year-to-date tax (or benefit). A number of them stated that the tax effect of tax-exempt interest income must be reported on a discrete period basis to reflect the economic effects of tax-exempt investments. A few respondents noted that the practice of excluding tax-exempt interest income from "ordinary" income in estimating the annual effective tax rate and in computing interim period tax (or benefit) is followed by virtually all financial institutions. The Board noted

---

[27]That conclusion was amended by *APB Opinion No. 4,* "Accounting for the 'Investment Credit'." Paragraph 10 of Opinion No. 4 permits "the alternative method of treating the credit as a reduction of Federal income taxes of the year in which the credit arises. . . ."

that the accounting practice described above for tax-exempt interest income in interim periods appears to be uniform and concluded that it should not address the issue in this Interpretation.

Exchange Gains and Losses

81. Several respondents requested that the Board provide guidance on accounting for the tax effects of exchange gains and losses in interim periods. Paragraphs 166 and 192 of *FASB Statement No. 8,* "Accounting for the Translation of Foreign Currency Transactions and Foreign Currency Financial Statements," indicate that it would be rare that the timing, direction, and magnitude of future exchange rate changes and the enterprise's financial position at the time of an expected future exchange rate change could each be reasonably estimated. Footnote 7 to paragraph 8 has been expanded to explain that the tax (or benefit) applicable to an item that cannot be estimated shall be reported in the interim period in which the item is reported.

Estimated Annual Effective Tax Rate

82. Several respondents recommended that an estimated annual effective tax rate not be applied in various specific circumstances. Circumstances mentioned included (a) if the rate is extremely high or low, (b) if an "ordinary" loss is expected for the year, and (c) if an enterprise has a year-to-date "ordinary" income and anticipates an "ordinary" loss for the year. An example cited was an enterprise that experienced "ordinary" income in an early part of the year and anticipated offsetting "ordinary" losses in the balance of the year, resulting in zero estimated "ordinary" income and no tax (or benefit). Such unusual circumstances may result in significant variations in the customary relationship between income tax expense and pretax accounting income in interim periods and footnote 2 to paragraph 19 of Opinion No. 28 requires disclosure of the reasons for those variations. Footnote 7 to paragraph 8 of this Interpretation states that if a reliable estimate cannot be made the actual effective tax rate for the year-to-date may be the best estimate of the annual effective tax rate. What is and what is not a "reliable estimate" is a matter of judgment. In the break-even situation cited above, a small change in the enterprise's estimated "ordinary" income could produce a large change in the estimated annual effective tax rate. In those circumstances, a break-even estimate would not be reliable if a small change in the estimated "ordinary" income were considered

likely to occur.

Operations Taxable in Multiple Jurisdictions

83. Many respondents stated that the intent of Opinion No. 28 was to apply one overall estimated annual effective tax rate to "ordinary" income for the consolidated reporting entity. Several respondents stated that interrelationships between jurisdictions would make the use of separate rates impractical. Paragraph 22 was modified to indicate that one overall estimated annual effective tax rate shall be used with the two exceptions described in that paragraph and discussed further in paragraphs 84 and 85 below.

84. If an enterprise that operates in multiple jurisdictions has losses in one or more of the jurisdictions and realization of the tax benefit of the losses is not assured beyond any reasonable doubt, use of one overall estimated annual effective tax rate can result in the recognition of tax benefits for the year-to-date for those losses. Paragraph 20 of Opinion No. 28 states that "the tax effects of losses that arise in the early portion of a fiscal year (in the event carryback of such losses is not possible) should be recognized only when realization is assured beyond any reasonable doubt. . . ." Accordingly, a separate computation is necessary for the tax (or benefit) applicable to "ordinary" income (or loss) in those jurisdictions.

85. The effect of translating foreign currency financial statements may make it difficult to estimate an annual effective foreign currency tax rate in dollars. For example, depreciation is translated at historical exchange rates, whereas many transactions included in income are translated at current period average exchange rates. If depreciation is large in relation to earnings, a change in the estimated "ordinary" income that does not change the effective foreign currency tax rate can change the effective tax rate in the dollar financial statements. This result can occur with no change in exchange rates during the current year if there have been exchange rate changes in past years. If the enterprise is unable to estimate its annual effective tax rate in dollars or is otherwise unable to make a reliable estimate of its "ordinary" income (or loss) or of the related tax (or benefit) for the fiscal year in a jurisdiction, the tax (or benefit) applicable to "ordinary" income (or loss) in that jurisdiction shall be recognized in the interim period in which the "ordinary" income (or loss) is reported, as described in footnote 7 to paragraph 8.

FASB Interpretation No. 19
Lessee Guarantee of the Residual Value
of Leased Property

an interpretation of FASB Statement No. 13

STATUS

Issued: October 1977

Effective Date: For leasing transactions and revisions entered into on or after January 1, 1978

Affects: No other pronouncements

Affected by: No other pronouncements

Other Interpretive Pronouncement: FTB 79-18

FASB Interpretation No. 19
Lessee Guarantee of the Residual Value of Leased Property

an interpretation of FASB Statement No. 13

INTRODUCTION

1. The FASB has been asked to clarify whether a particular kind of lease provision constitutes a guarantee by the lessee of the residual value of leased property at the expiration of the lease term to be included in *minimum lease payments* in accordance with paragraph 5(j)(i)(b) of *FASB Statement No. 13,* "Accounting for Leases," and to clarify whether certain provisions in lease agreements and certain other circumstances limit the amount of a lessee guarantee to be included in minimum lease payments to an amount less than a stipulated residual value of the leased property at the end of the lease term. Paragraph 5(j)(i)(b) of the Statement states that minimum lease payments from the standpoint of the lessee shall include a "guarantee by the lessee . . . of the residual value at the expiration of the lease term, whether or not payment of the guarantee constitutes a purchase of the leased property. . . . When the lessee agrees to make up any deficiency below a stated amount in the lessor's realization of the residual value, the guarantee to be included in the minimum lease payments shall be the stated amount, rather than an estimate of the deficiency to be made up."

2. Specifically, the Board has been asked the following three questions:

a. Does a lease provision requiring the lessee to make up a residual value deficiency that is attributable to damage, extraordinary wear and tear, or excessive usage (e.g., excessive mileage on a leased vehicle) constitute a lessee guarantee of the residual value such that the estimated residual value of the leased property at the end of the lease term should be included in minimum lease payments under paragraph 5(j)(i)(b) of *FASB Statement No. 13?*

b. Some lease agreements limit the amount of a residual value deficiency that a lessee can be required to make up to an amount that is (1) less than the stipulated residual value of the leased property at the end of the lease term but (2) clearly in excess of any reasonable estimate of a deficiency that might be expected to arise in normal circumstances. In those cases, is the amount of the lessee's guarantee to be included in mini-

mum lease payments under paragraph 5(j)(i)(b) of *FASB Statement No. 13* limited to the specified maximum deficiency that the lessee can be required to make up, or is it the stipulated residual value of the leased property at the end of the lease term?

c. If a lessee who is obligated to make up a deficiency in the lessor's realization of the residual value obtains a guarantee of the residual value from an unrelated third party, may the lessee reduce the amount of his minimum lease payments under paragraph 5(j)(i)(b) of *FASB Statement No. 13* by the amount of the third-party guarantee?

INTERPRETATION

3. A lease provision requiring the lessee to make up a residual value deficiency that is attributable to damage, extraordinary wear and tear, or excessive usage is similar to contingent rentals in that the amount is not determinable at the inception of the lease.[1] Such a provision does not constitute a lessee guarantee of the residual value for purposes of paragraph 5(j)(i)(b) of *FASB Statement No. 13.*

4. If a lease limits the amount of the lessee's obligation to make up a residual value deficiency to an amount less than the stipulated residual value of the leased property at the end of the lease term, the amount of the lessee's guarantee to be included in minimum lease payments under paragraph 5(j)(i)(b) of *FASB Statement No. 13* shall be limited to the specified maximum deficiency the lessee can be required to make up. In other words, the "stated amount" referred to in the last sentence of paragraph 5(j)(i)(b) is the specified maximum deficiency that the lessee is obligated to make up. If that maximum deficiency clearly exceeds any reasonable estimate of a deficiency that might be expected to arise in normal circumstances, the lessor's risk associated with the portion of the residual in excess of the maximum may appear to be negligible. However, the fact remains that the lessor must look to the resale market or elsewhere rather than to the lessee to recover the unguaranteed portion of the stipulated residual value of the leased property. The lessee has not guaranteed full recovery of the residual value,

---

[1]Contingent rentals are not included in *minimum lease payments* as defined in paragraph 5(j) of *FASB Statement No. 13.* Contingent rentals are to be recognized as period costs when incurred (or revenue when receivable). (See paragraphs 12, 17(b), and 18(b) of Statement No. 13.)

and the parties should not base their accounting on the assumption that the lessee has guaranteed it. The 90 percent test specified in criterion (d) of paragraph 7 of Statement No. 13 is stated as a lower limit rather than as a guideline.

5. A guarantee of the residual value obtained by the lessee from an unrelated third party for the benefit of the lessor shall not be used to reduce the amount of the lessee's minimum lease payments under paragraph 5(j)(i)(b) of *FASB Statement No. 13* except to the extent that the lessor explicitly releases the lessee from obligation, including secondary obligation if the guarantor defaults, to make up a residual value deficiency. Amounts paid in consideration for a guarantee by an unrelated third party are executory costs and are not included in the lessee's minimum lease payments.

EFFECTIVE DATE AND TRANSITION

6. The provisions of this Interpretation shall be effective for leasing transactions and lease agreement revisions (see paragraph 9 of *FASB Statement No. 13*) entered into on or after January 1, 1978. Earlier application is encouraged. In addition, the provisions of this Interpretation shall be applied retroactively at the same time and in the same manner as the provisions of *FASB Statement No. 13* are applied retroactively (see paragraphs 49 and 51 of the Statement). Enterprises that have already applied the provisions of Statement No. 13 retroactively and have published financial statements based on the retroactively adjusted accounts before the effective date of this Interpretation may, but are not required to, apply the provisions of this Interpretation retroactively.

This Interpretation was adopted by the unanimous vote of the seven members of the Financial Accounting Standards Board:

Marshall S. Armstrong, *Chairman*	Donald J. Kirk	Robert T. Sprouse
	Arthur L. Litke	Ralph E. Walters
Oscar S. Gellein	Robert E. Mays	

FASB Interpretation No. 20
Reporting Accounting Changes under AICPA Statements of Position

an interpretation of APB Opinion No. 20

STATUS

Issued: November 1977

Effective Date: December 1, 1977

Affects: No other pronouncements

Affected by: Paragraph 5 amended by FAS 111

FASB Interpretation No. 20
Reporting Accounting Changes under AICPA Statements of Position

an interpretation of APB Opinion No. 20

CONTENTS

INTRODUCTION AND BACKGROUND INFORMATION

1. The Accounting Standards Division of the AICPA has asked the FASB to either reconsider certain provisions of *APB Opinion No. 20,* "Accounting Changes," or to clarify whether statements of position issued by the AICPA may specify how to report a change to adopt its recommendations for purposes of applying that Opinion.

2. Paragraph 4 of *APB Opinion No. 20* indicates that each APB Opinion specifies how to report a change to conform with the conclusions of the Opinion and further states:

> An industry audit guide prepared by a committee of the American Institute of Certified Public Accountants may also prescribe the manner of reporting a change in accounting principle. Accordingly, the provisions of this Opinion do not apply to changes made in conformity with such pronouncements issued in the past or in the future.

3. At the time *APB Opinion No. 20* was issued in July 1971, the Accounting Principles Board issued Opinions on financial accounting and reporting and various AICPA industry committees issued industry audit guides that dealt with both the specialized auditing procedures and the specialized accounting practices applicable to enterprises in those industries. Subsequently, specialized industry accounting practices were dealt with in a new series of industry accounting guides issued by the AICPA, each of

which specified how to report a change in accounting to conform with the conclusions of the guide. In July 1973, the FASB replaced the APB; the AICPA discontinued the industry accounting guides and its Accounting Standards Division began issuing statements of position[1] covering specialized industry accounting practices.

4. The FASB believes that in due course *APB Opinion No. 20* should be reconsidered. The FASB believes further, however, that pending that reconsideration, issuance of this Interpretation will result in improvements in financial accounting and reporting.

INTERPRETATION

5. For purposes of applying *APB Opinion No. 20,* an enterprise making a change in accounting principle to conform with the recommendations of an AICPA statement of position shall report the change as specified in the statement. If an AICPA statement of position does not specify the manner of reporting a change in accounting principle to conform with its recommendations, an enterprise making a change in accounting principle to conform with the recommendations of the statement shall report the change as specified by Opinion No. 20.

EFFECTIVE DATE

6. This Interpretation shall be effective December 1, 1977.

---

[1] In the introduction to previously issued statements of position, the AICPA indicates that "Statements of Position of the Accounting Standards Division are issued for the general information of those interested in the subject. They present the conclusions of at least a majority of the Accounting Standards Executive Committee, which is the senior technical body of the [AICPA] authorized to speak for the [AICPA] in the areas of financial accounting and reporting and cost accounting.

"The objective of Statements of Position is to influence the development of accounting and reporting standards in directions the Division believes are in the public interest. It is intended that they should be considered, as deemed appropriate, by bodies having authority to issue pronouncements on the subject. However, Statements of Position do not establish standards enforceable under the [AICPA's] Code of Professional Ethics."

This Interpretation was adopted by the affirmative votes of four members of the Financial Accounting Standards Board following submission to the members of the Financial Accounting Standards Advisory Council. Messrs. Armstrong, Kirk, and Mays dissented.

Messrs. Armstrong, Kirk, and Mays dissent from this Interpretation because they believe that the FASB should reconsider currently *APB Opinion No. 20* on its merit instead of permitting the AICPA to grant selective dispensations from the requirements of that Opinion.

Further, Mr. Mays dissents because he believes that this Interpretation, in effect, constitutes an unwarranted delegation of authority to the AICPA to establish standards of financial accounting and reporting.

Members of the Financial Accounting Standards Board:

Marshall S. Armstrong,
  Chairman
Oscar S. Gellein

Donald J. Kirk
Arthur L. Litke
Robert E. Mays

Robert T. Sprouse
Ralph E. Walters

FASB Interpretation No. 21
Accounting for Leases in a Business Combination

an interpretation of FASB Statement No. 13

STATUS

Issued: April 1978

Effective Date: For business combinations initiated on or after May 1, 1978

Affects: No other pronouncements

Affected by: No other pronouncements

Other Interpretive Pronouncement: FTB 79-18

FASB Interpretation No. 21
Accounting for Leases in a Business Combination

an interpretation of FASB Statement No. 13

Contents

INTRODUCTION AND BACKGROUND INFORMATION

1. The FASB has been asked to clarify the application of *FASB Statement No. 13*, "Accounting for Leases," in business combinations. Specifically, this involves the following questions:

a. Does the consummation of a business combination require the combined enterprise to treat leases of the combining companies as new leases to be classified according to the criteria set forth in Statement No. 13, based on conditions as of the date of the combination?
b. If the consummation of a business combination does not require enterprises to treat leases of the combining companies as new leases as of the date of the combination, how should Statement No. 13 be applied[1] to the leases of the combined enterprise?
c. How do the requirements of *APB Opinion No. 16*, "Business Combinations," for assigning amounts to the assets acquired and liabilities assumed in a business combination that is accounted for by the purchase method affect the application of Statement No. 13 by the combined enterprise to leases of the acquired company?

2. Paragraph 40 of *FASB Statement No. 13* requires the new lessee under a sublease or similar transaction to classify the lease in accordance with the criteria in Statement No. 13 and to account for it as a new lease. Subparagraphs (b) and (c) of paragraph 35 of Statement No. 13 describe the transactions similar to subleases that are subject to the requirements of paragraph 40 of the Statement as follows:

b. A new lessee is substituted under the original lease agreement. The new lessee becomes the primary obligor under the agreement, and the original lessee may or may not be secondarily liable.
c. A new lessee is substituted through a new agreement, with cancellation of the original lease agreement.

The question has been raised as to whether the provisions of paragraphs 35 and 40 ever require that leases in a business combination be treated as new leases by the combined enterprise.

3. In connection with a business combination, changes may be made in the provisions of existing leases of a combining enterprise. Paragraph 9 of *FASB Statement No. 13* discusses changes in the provisions of leases as follows:

> If at any time the lessee and lessor agree to change the provisions of the lease, other than by renewing the lease or extending its term, in a manner that would have resulted in a different classification of the lease under the criteria in paragraphs 7 and 8 had the changed terms been in effect at the inception of the lease, the revised agreement shall be considered as a new agreement over its term, and the criteria in paragraphs 7 and 8 shall be applied for purposes of classifying the new lease. Likewise, except when a guarantee or penalty is rendered inoperative as described in paragraphs 12 and 17(e), any action that extends the lease beyond the expiration of the existing lease term (see paragraph 5(f)), such as the exercise of a lease renewal option other than those already included in the lease term, shall be considered as a new agreement, which

---

[1]See paragraphs 49 and 51 of *FASB Statement No. 13* regarding retroactive application of Statement No. 13.

shall be classified according to the provisions of paragraphs 6-8. Changes in estimates (for example, changes in estimates of the economic life or of the residual value of the leased property) or changes in circumstances (for example, default by the lessee), however, shall not give rise to a new classification of a lease for accounting purposes.

4. Paragraph 88 of *APB Opinion No. 16* provides "general guides for assigning amounts to the individual assets acquired and liabilities assumed, except goodwill . . ." in a business combination that is accounted for by the purchase method. The guides in subparagraphs of paragraph 88 indicate the method of valuation to be used for various types of assets and liabilities. The concepts underlying *FASB Statement No. 13* that govern classification of leases differ in some respects from the concepts of prior APB Opinions on accounting for leases. Thus, the subparagraphs of paragraph 88 of Opinion No. 16 that were applied prior to Statement No. 13 may not be the appropriate subparagraphs to be applied under Statement No. 13. In addition, some provisions of Statement No. 13 (e.g., interest rates used) may suggest that certain of the general guidelines in paragraph 88 should be applied differently from the way they may have been applied in the past.

5. An Exposure Draft of a proposed Interpretation on "Accounting for Leases in a Business Combination" was issued on December 19, 1977. The Board received 27 letters of comment in response to the Exposure Draft. Certain of those comments and the Board's consideration of them are discussed in paragraphs 6-10 below.

6. One respondent requested that the Interpretation provide for circumstances in which determinations at the inception of the lease are not possible. The Board is aware that in some cases it is difficult to obtain accurate data relating to the remote past of an acquired enterprise but believes that reasonable estimates can be derived based on the information that is available.

7. Some respondents expressed the belief that the concept of purchase accounting in *APB Opinion No. 16* requires the acquiring enterprise to classify the acquired enterprise's leases as new leases at the date of a business combination that is accounted for by the purchase method and stated that the acquiring enterprise should apply the criteria of *FASB Statement No. 13* for classifying the acquired leases at the date of the acquisition. The Board does not believe that Opinion No. 16 requires reconsideration of the classification of existing leases that are already classified in conformity with Statement No. 13; rather, the Board views Opinion No. 16 as requiring valuation of the existing assets and obliga-

tions of the acquired company, including assets and obligations pertaining to leases, and allocation of cost to those assets and obligations. Also, the Board views the procedure suggested as contrary to Statement No. 13. Paragraph 8 below describes the basis for classification of a lease under Statement No. 13.

8. Paragraph 7 of *FASB Statement No. 13* states that "the criteria for classifying leases set forth in this paragraph and in paragraph 8 derive from the concept set forth in paragraph 60." Paragraph 60 of Statement No. 13 describes the underlying concept as follows:

> The provisions of this Statement derive from the view that a *lease that transfers* substantially all of the benefits and risks incident to the ownership of property should be accounted for as the acquisition of an asset and the incurrence of an obligation by the lessee and as a sale or financing by the lessor. All other leases should be accounted for as operating leases. . . . [Emphasis added.]

Statement No. 13 requires that the classification of a lease (an agreement between a lessee and a lessor) be determined at the inception of *the lease*. Once that determination is made, the classification of the lease is not reexamined unless either (a) both parties to the lease agree to a revision that would have resulted in a different classification of the lease had the changed terms been in effect at the inception of the lease or (b) the lease is extended or renewed. Paragraphs 36-40 of Statement No. 13 apply similar procedures with respect to classification to the parties affected by a sublease, as follows:

a. *The original lessor* retains the classification of the original lease unless it is replaced by a new agreement.
b. *The original lessee* retains the original classification of the original lease unless the original lessee is relieved of the primary obligation. (If the lessee is relieved of the primary obligation, the original lessor will have agreed to a revision.)
c. *The new lessee* has agreed to the terms of a lease, either with the original lessee (in effect, a sublease) or with the original lessor (a new lease). Accordingly, the new lessee is required to classify the new lease at the date of the new agreement.

Statement No. 13 applies the same rationale to an enterprise that purchases the lessor's interest in an existing lease from the original lessor. The Statement does not permit an enterprise that purchases property from a lessor while the property is leased to a third party lessee to classify the acquired lease as a new lease at the acquisition date. The lessee is not a party to the transaction and the original lessor ceases to be a party to the lease; thus, there has been no new agreement between a lessee and a lessor and the purchase date is not the inception of a new lease requiring classification at that date. The Board views the substance of a business combination that is accounted for under the purchase method to be the purchase of the lessor's or lessee's interest in an existing lease. The original lessor or lessee does not become a party to a new agreement; accordingly, there is no new agreement to be classified, and Statement No. 13 does not permit reclassification of the existing lease unless the provisions of the lease are modified. The Board is aware that the identity of a party to a lease may change in a business combination and that the lease may be modified to reflect that change. If the provisions of the lease are not changed (see paragraph 3 above), the modification does not represent a new agreement between the lessee and lessor in substance, and the lease should not be reclassified.

9. Some respondents suggested that the Board expand the scope of this Interpretation to address asset acquisitions that are not business combinations. As explained in paragraph 8 above, the Board believes that *FASB Statement No. 13* provides adequate guidance for those transactions.

10. Some enterprises have already applied the provisions of *FASB Statement No. 13* retroactively and have published financial statements based on the retroactively adjusted accounts. The Exposure Draft proposed that those enterprises would be permitted, but not required, to apply the provisions of this Interpretation retroactively. Some respondents' comments indicated that they interpreted the reference to "published financial statements" in the Exposure Draft to include financial summaries of interim results. The Board had intended the reference to "published financial statements" to exclude those summaries. Upon further consideration, the Board modified the wording of paragraph 18 to "published *annual* financial statements."

11. This Interpretation applies to the accounting for leases by combined enterprises at the date of and subsequent to a business combination.

INTERPRETATION

Summary

12. The classification of a lease in accordance with the criteria of *FASB Statement No. 13* shall not be changed as a result of a business combination unless

the provisions of the lease are modified. (See paragraph 13.)

Changes in the Provisions of the Lease

13. If in connection with a business combination, whether accounted for by the purchase method or by the pooling of interests method, the provisions of a lease are modified in a way that would require the revised agreement to be considered a new agreement under paragraph 9 of *FASB Statement No. 13,* the new lease shall be classified by the combined enterprise according to the criteria set forth in Statement No. 13, based on conditions as of the date of the modification of the lease.

Application of FASB Statement No. 13 in a Pooling of Interests

14. In a business combination that is accounted for by the pooling of interests method, each lease shall retain its previous classification under *FASB Statement No. 13* unless the provisions of the lease are modified as indicated in paragraph 13 above and shall be accounted for by the combined enterprise in the same manner that it would have been classified and accounted for by the combining enterprise.

Application of FASB Statement No. 13 in a Purchase Combination

15. In a business combination that is accounted for by the purchase method, the acquiring enterprise shall retain the previous classification in accordance with *FASB Statement No. 13* for the leases of an acquired enterprise unless the provisions of the lease are modified as indicated in paragraph 13 above.[2] The amounts assigned to individual assets acquired and liabilities assumed at the date of the combination shall be determined in accordance with the general guides for that type of asset or liability in paragraph 88 of *APB Opinion No. 16.* Subsequent to the recording of the amounts called for by Opinion No. 16, the leases shall thereafter be accounted for in accordance with Statement No. 13.[3] Paragraph 16 below explains the application of this paragraph to a leveraged lease by an enterprise that acquires a lessor.

16. In a business combination that is accounted for by the purchase method, the acquiring enterprise shall apply the following procedures to the acquired enterprise's investment as a lessor in a leveraged lease. The acquiring enterprise shall retain the classification of a leveraged lease at the date of the com-

---

[2]If the acquired enterprise has not applied *FASB Statement No. 13* retroactively at the date of the business combination, the acquiring enterprise shall classify the leases of the acquired enterprise as they would have been classified if the acquired enterprise had applied Statement No. 13 retroactively at that date.

[3]*FASB Statement No. 13* does not address the subsequent accounting for amounts recorded for favorable or unfavorable operating leases. Accordingly, present practice is not changed with respect to the amortization of those amounts.

bination. The acquiring enterprise shall assign an amount to the acquired net investment in the leveraged lease in accordance with the general guides in paragraph 88 of *APB Opinion No. 16*, based on the remaining future cash flows and giving appropriate recognition to the estimated future tax effects of those cash flows. Once determined, that net investment shall be broken down into its component parts, namely, net rentals receivable, estimated residual value, and unearned income including discount to adjust other components to present value. The acquiring enterprise thereafter shall account for that investment in a leveraged lease in accordance with the provisions of *FASB Statement No. 13*. Appendix A illustrates the application of this paragraph.

17. When an enterprise that has acquired another enterprise in a business combination accounted for by the purchase method prior to the effective date of this Interpretation applies the provisions of *FASB Statement No. 13* retroactively, leases acquired in the business combination shall be classified as they would have been classified if the acquired enterprise had applied Statement No. 13 retroactively at the date of the business combination. The amounts retroactively recorded for those leases shall be the amounts that would have been allocated under *APB Opinion No. 16* by the acquiring enterprise at the purchase date if the leases had been classified in accordance with the provisions of Statement No. 13 at that date. The following examples illustrate the application of this paragraph:

a. In the case of a lease for which the lessee's classification is changed by the retroactive application of Statement No. 13 from an operating lease to a capital lease, the favorable or unfavorable amount recorded under Opinion No. 16 at the date of the combination shall be restated to record an asset and a liability, each to be assigned an amount in accordance with Opinion No. 16. The net of the restated asset and liability may equal the amount previously recorded for a favorable or unfavorable operating lease. However, if the net of the restated asset and liability differs from the amount that was originally recorded under Opinion No. 16 for that lease, the difference is a retroactive adjustment of the allocation of the cost of the acquired enterprise with an offsetting retroactive adjustment, usually to goodwill.

b. In the case of a lease for which the lessor's classification is changed by the retroactive application of Statement No. 13 from an operating lease to a direct financing lease, the carrying amount of the leased asset and any favorable or unfavorable amount recorded under Opinion No. 16 at the date of the combination shall be restated to record a net investment in the direct financing lease determined in accordance with Opinion No. 16 and consisting of the gross receivable, residual value, and unearned income. If the restated amount allocated to the net investment in the direct financing lease differs from the net amount that was originally recorded for that lease, the difference is a retroactive adjustment of the allocation of the cost of the acquired enterprise with an offsetting retroactive adjustment, usually to goodwill.

Effective Date and Transition

18. The provisions of this Interpretation shall be effective for business combinations that are initiated[4] on or after May 1, 1978. Earlier application is encouraged. In addition, the provisions of this Interpretation shall be applied retroactively at the same time and in the same manner as the provisions of *FASB Statement No. 13* are applied retroactively (see paragraphs 49 and 51 of Statement No. 13). Enterprises that have already applied the provisions of Statement No. 13 retroactively and have published annual financial statements based on the retroactively adjusted accounts before the effective date of this Interpretation may, but are not required to, apply the provisions of this Interpretation retroactively.

This Interpretation was adopted by the unanimous vote of the seven members of the Financial Accounting Standards Board:

Donald J. Kirk,	John W. March	Robert T. Sprouse
Chairman	Robert A. Morgan	Ralph E. Walters
Oscar S. Gellein	David Mosso	

Appendix A

ILLUSTRATION OF THE ACCOUNTING FOR A LEVERAGED LEASE IN A PURCHASE COMBINATION

19. This Appendix illustrates one way that a lessor's investment in a leveraged lease might be valued by the acquiring enterprise in a business combination accounted for by the purchase method and the subsequent accounting for the investment in accordance with *FASB Statement No. 13*. The elements of accounting and reporting illustrated for this example are as follows:

1. Leveraged lease example—terms and assumptions, Schedule 1

---

[4]See paragraph 46(a) of *APB Opinion No. 16* for the definition of "initiated."

2. Acquiring enterprise's cash flow analysis by years, Schedule 2
3. Acquiring enterprise's valuation of investment in the leveraged lease, Schedule 3
4. Acquiring enterprise's allocation of annual cash flow to investment and income, Schedule 4
5. Journal entry for recording allocation of purchase price to net investment in the leveraged lease, Schedule 5
6. Journal entries for the year ending December 31, 1984 (year 10 of the lease), Schedule 6

SCHEDULE 1

Leveraged Lease Example Term and Assumptions

Cost of leased asset (equipment)	$1,000,000
Lease term	15 years, dating from January 1, 1975
Lease rental payments	$90,000 per year (payable last day of each year)
Residual value	$200,000 estimated to be realized one year after lease termination
Financing:	
Equity investment by lessor	$400,000
Long-term nonrecourse debt	$600,000, bearing interest at 9% and repayable in annual installments (on last day of each year) of $74,435.30
Depreciation allowable to lessor for income tax purposes	Seven-year ADR life using double-declining-balance method for the first two years (with the half-year convention election applied in the first year) and sum-of-years digits method for remaining life, depreciated to $100,000 salvage value
Lessor's income tax rate (federal and state)	50.4% (assumed to continue in existence throughout the term of the lease)
Investment tax credit	10% of equipment cost or $100,000 (realized by the lessor on last day of first year of lease)
Initial direct costs	For simplicity, initial direct costs have not been included in the illustration
Date of business combination	January 1, 1982
Tax status of business combination	Non-taxable transaction
Appropriate interest rate for valuing net-of-tax return on investment	4 1/2%

SCHEDULE 2

Acquiring Enterprise's Cash Flow Analysis by Years

Year	1 Gross lease rentals and residual value	2 Depreciation (for income tax purposes)	3 Loan interest payments	4 Taxable income (col. 1-2-3)	5 Income tax (charges) (col. 4 × 50.4%)	6 Loan principal payments	7 Annual cash flow (col. 1 − 3 + 5 − 6)
8	$ 90,000	—	$ 37,079	$ 52,921	$ (26,672)	$ 37,357	$(11,108)
9	90,000	—	33,717	56,283	(28,367)	40,719	(12,803)
10	90,000	—	30,052	59,948	(30,214)	44,383	(14,649)
11	90,000	—	26,058	63,942	(32,227)	48,378	(16,663)
12	90,000	—	21,704	68,296	(34,421)	52,732	(18,857)
13	90,000	—	16,957	73,043	(36,813)	57,478	(21,248)
14	90,000	—	11,785	78,215	(39,420)	62,651	(23,856)
15	90,000	—	6,145	83,855	(42,263)	68,290	(26,698)
16	200,000	$100,000	—	100,000	(50,400)	—	149,600
Totals	$920,000	$100,000	$183,497	$636,503	$(320,797)	$411,988	$ 3,718

SCHEDULE 3

Acquiring Enterprise's Valuation of Investment in the Leveraged Lease

Cash flow	Present value at 4 1/2% net-of-tax rate
1. Rentals receivable (net of principal and interest on the nonrecourse debt) ($15,564.70 at the end of each year for 8 years)	$ 102,663
2. Estimated residual value ($200,000 realizable at the end of 9 years)	134,581
3. Future tax payments (various amounts payable over 9 years— see Schedule 2)	(253,489)
Net present value	$ (16,245)

SCHEDULE 4

Acquiring Enterprise's
Allocation of Annual Cash Flow to Investment and Income

	1	2	3	4	5	6
			Annual Cash Flow		Components of Income[2]	
Year	Net investment at beginning of year	Total from Schedule 2, col. 7	Allocated to investment	Allocated to income[1]	Pretax income	Tax effect of pretax income
8	$ (16,245)	$ (11,108)	$ (11,108)	—	—	—
9	(5,137)	(12,803)	(12,803)	—	—	$ (5,206)
10	7,666	(14,649)	(14,973)	$ 324	$ 5,530	(15,395)
11	22,639	(16,663)	(17,621)	958	16,353	(27,383)
12	40,260	(18,857)	(20,561)	1,704	29,087	(41,363)
13	60,821	(21,248)	(23,822)	2,574	43,937	(57,577)
14	84,643	(23,856)	(27,439)	3,583	61,160	(76,250)
15	112,082	(26,698)	(31,443)	4,745	80,995	(97,623)
16	143,525	149,600	143,525	6,075	103,698	
Totals		$ 3,718	$ (16,245)	$19,963	$340,760	$(320,797)

[1]Lease income is recognized as 4.233% of the unrecovered investment at the beginning of each year in which the net investment is positive. The rate is that rate which when applied to the net investment in the years in which the net investment is positive will distribute the net income (net cash flow) to those years. The rate for allocation in this Schedule is calculated by a trial and error process. The allocation is calculated based upon an initial estimate of the rate as a starting point. If the total thus allocated to income (column 4) differs under the estimated rate from the net cash flow (column 2 less column 3) the estimated rate is increased or decreased, as appropriate, to derive a revised allocation. This process is repeated until a rate is selected which develops a total amount allocated to income that is precisely equal to the net cash flow. As a practical matter, a computer program is used to calculate Schedule 4 under successive iterations until the correct rate is determined.

[2]Each component is allocated among the years of positive net investment in proportion to the allocation of net income in column 4. Journal Entry 2 in Schedule 6 of this Appendix includes an example of this computation.

SCHEDULE 5

Illustrative Journal Entry for Recording Allocation of
Purchase Price to Net Investment in the Leveraged Lease

Rentals receivable (Schedule 2, total of column 1 less residual value,		
less totals of columns 3 and 6)	$124,515	
Estimated residual value (Schedule 1)	200,000	
Purchase price allocation clearing account (Schedule 3, present value)	16,245	
Unearned and deferred income (Schedule 3,		
present value, less total of rentals receivable		
and estimated residual value)		$340,760

SCHEDULE 6

Illustrative Journal Entries for Year Ending December 31, 1984

Third Year of Operation after the Business Combination (Year 10 of the Lease)

Journal Entry 1

Cash	$15,565	
Rentals receivable (Schedule 2, column 1 less columns 3 and 6)		$15,565
Collection of year's net rental		

Journal Entry 2

Unearned and Deferred Income	$ 5,530	
Income from Leveraged Leases (Schedule 4, column 5)		$ 5,530
Recognition of pretax income for the year allocated in the same		
proportion as the allocation of total income		

$$\left(\frac{\$\ 324}{\$19,963} \times \$340,760 = \$5,530 \right)$$

Journal Entry 3

Deferred taxes (Schedule 2, column 5, less Schedule 4, column 6)	$25,008	
Income tax expense (Schedule 4, column 6)	5,206	
Cash (Schedule 2, column 5)		$30,214

To record payment of tax for the year

FASB Interpretation No. 22
Applicability of Indefinite Reversal Criteria to Timing Differences

an interpretation of APB Opinions No. 11 and 23

STATUS

Issued: April 1978

Effective Date: For timing differences occurring in fiscal years beginning after June 15, 1978

Affects: No other pronouncements

Affected by: Paragraph 7 amended by FAS 60
Paragraph 8 superseded by FAS 71
Superseded by FAS 96 and FAS 109

(The next page is 600.)

(This page intentionally left blank.)

FASB Interpretation No. 23
Leases of Certain Property Owned by a
Governmental Unit or Authority

an interpretation of FASB Statement No. 13

STATUS

Issued: August 1978

Effective Date: For leasing transactions and revisions recorded as of December 1, 1978

Affects: No other pronouncements

Affected by: No other pronouncements

Other Interpretive Pronouncement: FTB 79-18

SUMMARY

This Interpretation clarifies that portion of paragraph 28 of *FASB Statement No. 13*, "Accounting for Leases," stating that leases of certain property owned by a governmental unit or authority shall be classified as operating leases.

The Interpretation describes six conditions that must be met for a lease of government owned property to be automatically classified as an operating lease. If all of the six conditions are not met, the criteria for classifying leases under Statement No. 13 that are applicable to leases generally are also applicable to leases involving government owned property.

FASB Interpretation No. 23
Leases of Certain Property Owned by a Governmental Unit or Authority

an interpretation of FASB Statement No. 13

CONTENTS

INTRODUCTION AND BACKGROUND INFORMATION

1. The FASB has been asked to clarify that portion of paragraph 28 of *FASB Statement No. 13*, "Accounting for Leases," stating that leases of certain property owned by a governmental unit or authority shall be classified as operating leases. That portion of paragraph 28 is as follows:

> Because of special provisions normally present in leases involving terminal space and other airport facilities owned by a governmental unit or authority, the economic life of such facilities for purposes of classifying the lease is essentially indeterminate. Likewise, the concept of fair value is not applicable to such leases. Since such leases also do not provide for a transfer of ownership or a bargain purchase option, they shall be classified as operating leases. Leases of other facilities owned by a governmental unit or authority wherein the rights of the parties are essentially the same as in a lease of airport facilities described above shall also be classified as operating leases. Examples of such leases may be those involving facilities at ports and bus terminals.

2. That provision of paragraph 28 was further explained in paragraph 106 of *FASB Statement No. 13* as follows:

> A number of respondents pointed out that leases of facilities such as airport and bus terminals and port facilities from governmental units or authorities contain features that render the criteria of paragraph 7 inappropriate for classifying such leases. Leases of such facilities do not transfer ownership or contain bargain purchase options. By virtue of its power to abandon a facility during the term of a lease, the governmental body can effectively control the lessee's continued use of the property for its intended purpose, thus making its economic life essentially indeterminate. Finally, since neither

the leased property nor equivalent property is available for sale, a meaningful fair value cannot be determined, thereby invalidating the 90 percent recovery criterion. For those reasons, the Board concluded that such leases shall be classified as operating leases by both the lessee and lessor.

3. The Board has been asked to clarify the conditions that shall cause leases of certain property owned by a governmental unit or authority to be classified as operating leases.

4. A draft of a proposed Interpretation on "Leases of Certain Property Owned by a Governmental Unit or Authority" was issued on April 7, 1978. The Board received 43 letters of comment in response to the proposed Interpretation. Some respondents disagreed with the proposed Interpretation because they believe that a lessee's classification of leases of government owned property should be determined by the same criteria as those applied to leases generally. A few respondents expressed neither overall agreement nor disagreement but offered comments or suggestions about specific matters. The remainder of the respondents expressed general agreement with the proposed Interpretation.

5. The Board also considered the possibility of amending *FASB Statement No. 13* to delete that portion of paragraph 28 that applies to leases of certain property owned by a governmental unit or authority. As stated in the proposed Interpretation that was released for comment, some Board members believe that a lessee's classification of leases of government owned property should be determined by the same criteria as those applied to leases generally. However, in the interest of a timely resolution of the matter, the Board concluded that further consideration of amending the applicable portion of paragraph 28 of Statement No. 13 should not delay the issuance of this Interpretation.

6. A number of respondents recommended that the Board clarify subparagraph 8(d) with respect to the

lessor's right to terminate the lease during the lease term. Some of those respondents stated that the existence of the termination right was the significant issue and that such a right can exist even though explicit reference to the right is not contained in the lease agreement. The Board did not intend that leases of government-owned property would be classified as operating leases merely because sovereign rights, such as the right of eminent domain, exist. Accordingly, the Board has modified subparagraph 8(d) to clarify its intent.

7. Some respondents suggested that the Board define the term "equivalent property in the same service area" as that term is used in subparagraph 8(f), and a footnote has been added to that subparagraph to provide additional guidance.

INTERPRETATION

8. The provisions of paragraph 28 of *FASB Statement No. 13* stating that certain leases shall be classified as operating leases are intended to apply to leases only if all of the following conditions are met:

a. The leased property is owned by a governmental unit or authority.
b. The leased property is part of a larger facility, such as an airport, operated by or on behalf of the lessor.
c. The leased property is a permanent structure or a part of a permanent structure, such as a building, that normally could not be moved to a new location.
d. The lessor, or in some cases a higher governmental authority, has the explicit right under the lease agreement or existing statutes or regulations applicable to the leased property to terminate the

lease at any time during the lease term, such as by closing the facility containing the leased property or by taking possession of the facility.
e. The lease neither transfers ownership of the leased property to the lessee nor allows the lessee to purchase or otherwise acquire ownership of the leased property.
f. The leased property or equivalent property in the same service area[1] cannot be purchased nor can such property be leased from a nongovernmental unit or authority.

9. Leases of property not meeting all of the conditions of paragraph 8 of this Interpretation are subject to the same criteria for classifying leases under *FASB Statement No. 13* that are applicable to leases not involving government owned property.

EFFECTIVE DATE AND TRANSITION

10. The provisions of this Interpretation shall be effective for leasing transactions recorded and lease agreement revisions (see paragraph 9 of *FASB Statement No. 13*) recorded as of December 1, 1978 or thereafter. Earlier application is encouraged. In addition, except as provided in the next sentence, the provisions of this Interpretation shall be applied retroactively at the same time and in the same manner as the provisions of Statement No. 13 are applied retroactively (see paragraphs 49 and 51 of Statement No. 13). Enterprises that have already applied the provisions of Statement No. 13 retroactively and have published annual financial statements based on the retroactively adjusted accounts before the effective date of this Interpretation may, but are not required to, apply the provisions of this Interpretation retroactively.

This Interpretation was adopted by the affirmative votes of six members of the Financial Accounting Standards Board following submission to the members of the Financial Accounting Standards Advisory Council and the Screening Committee on Emerging Problems. Mr. Walters dissented.

Mr. Walters cannot support further efforts to apply different capitalization criteria for leases of government owned property, and he believes that this Interpretation shows the futility of attempting to rationalize that position. Among the conditions cited in paragraph 8 of this Interpretation, the only

one that is relatively unique to leases of government property is the unilateral right to terminate the lease. Special consideration of this condition if termination is a remote contingency, in his view, denies the definition of "lease term" in paragraph 5(f) of *FASB Statement No. 13*.

Members of the Financial Accounting Standards Board:

Donald J. Kirk,	John W. March	Robert T. Sprouse
Chairman	Robert A. Morgan	Ralph E. Walters
Oscar S. Gellein	David Mosso	

---

[1]As used in this Interpretation, equivalent property in the same service area is property that would allow continuation of essentially the same service or activity as afforded by the leased property without any appreciable difference is economic results to the lessee.

FASB Interpretation No. 24
Leases Involving Only Part of a Building

an interpretation of FASB Statement No. 13

STATUS

Issued: September 1978

Effective Date: For leasing transactions and revisions recorded as of December 1, 1978

Affects: No other pronouncements

Affected by: No other pronouncements

Other Interpretive Pronouncement: FTB 79-18

SUMMARY

This Interpretation concerns that portion of *FASB Statement No. 13*, "Accounting for Leases," stating that "when the leased property is part of a larger whole, its cost (or carrying amount) and fair value may not be objectively determinable, as for example, when an office or a floor of a building is leased."

This Interpretation recognizes that reasonable estimates of the leased property's fair value might be objectively determinable from other information if sales of property similar to the leased property do not exist.

FASB Interpretation No. 24
Leases Involving Only Part of a Building

an interpretation of FASB Statement No. 13

CONTENTS

INTRODUCTION AND BACKGROUND INFORMATION

1. Paragraph 28 of *FASB Statement No. 13*, "Accounting for Leases," states that "when the leased property is part of a larger whole, its cost (or carrying amount) and fair value may not be objectively determinable, as for example, when an office or floor of a building is leased. If the cost and fair value of the leased property are objectively determinable, both the lessee and the lessor shall classify and account for the lease according to the provisions of paragraph 26." Paragraph 28 goes on to state that "if the fair value of the leased property is not objectively determinable, the lessee shall classify the lease according to the criterion of paragraph 7(c) only. . . ." Paragraph 5(c) of Statement No. 13 defines the fair value of leased property as "the price for which the property could be sold in an arm's-length transaction between unrelated parties."

2. The FASB has been asked if a fair value can be objectively determined for a lease involving only part of a building if there are no sales of property similar to the leased property to use as a basis for estimating the leased property's fair value for purposes of applying *FASB Statement No. 13*.

3. A draft of a proposed Interpretation on "Leases Involving Only Part of a Building" was issued on April 20, 1978. The Board received 29 letters of comment on the proposed Interpretation. The Board's consideration of certain of the respondents' comments is discussed in paragraphs 4 and 5 below.

4. A number of respondents questioned whether the proposed Interpretation would provide meaningful guidance. Some respondents noted that, in many cases, information providing a basis for a reasonable estimate of the leased property's fair value would not be available. Other respondents agreed that information providing a basis for a reasonable estimate of fair value might be obtained through an appraisal or other similar valuation. The Board does not intend to impose a requirement to obtain an appraisal or similar valuation as a general matter but does believe that kind of information should be obtained whenever possible if (a) classification as a capital lease seems likely and (b) the effects of capital lease classification would be significant to the financial statements of a lessee. Other respondents stated that the applicability of the Interpretation should be limited to lessees of a significant portion of a facility. Although that view was not adopted, the Board recognizes that a lessee's ability to make a reasonable estimate of the leased property's fair value will vary depending on the size of the leased property in relation to the entire facility. For example, obtaining a meaningful appraisal of an office or a floor of a multi-story building may not be possible whereas similar information may be readily obtainable if the leased property is a major part of that facility.

5. Some respondents stated that replacement cost measures costs of physical attributes but does not necessarily measure fair value. Two of those respondents stated that replacement cost would not reflect the value attributable to factors such as location of the leased property or traffic patterns of a larger complex. One respondent stated that a determination of replacement cost for only part of a building would require arbitrary cost allocations and subjective considerations. Paragraph 5(c)(ii) of *FASB Statement No. 13* states, in part, "when the lessor is not a manufacturer or dealer, the fair value of the property at the inception of the lease will ordinarily be its cost. . . ." That paragraph further provides that if there is a significant lapse of time between construction or acquisition of the property and inception of the lease, the determination of fair value shall be made in light of the market conditions at inception. The Board recognizes that replacement cost will not reflect the fair value of the leased property in all cases. However, if the leased facility has been recently constructed or acquired, cost estimates may provide a reasonable basis for estimating the property's fair value for purposes of applying the recovery criterion of paragraph 7(d) of Statement No. 13.

INTERPRETATION

6. For purposes of applying paragraph 28 of *FASB Statement No. 13* to leases involving only part of a building, other evidence may provide a basis for an objective determination of fair value even if there are no sales of property similar to the leased property. For example, reasonable estimates of the leased property's fair value might be objectively determined by referring to an independent appraisal of the leased property or to estimated replacement cost information.

EFFECTIVE DATE AND TRANSITION

7. The provisions of this Interpretation shall be effective for leasing transactions recorded and lease agreement revisions (see paragraph 9 of *FASB Statement No. 13*) recorded as of December 1, 1978 or thereafter. Earlier application is encouraged. In addition, except as provided in the next sentence, the provisions of this Interpretation shall be applied retroactively at the same time and in the same manner as the provisions of Statement No. 13 are applied retroactively (see paragraphs 49 and 51 of Statement No. 13). Enterprises that have already applied the provisions of Statement No. 13 retroactively and have published annual financial statements based on the retroactively adjusted accounts before the effective date of this Interpretation may, but are not required to, apply the provisions of this Interpretation retroactively.

This Interpretation was adopted by the affirmative votes of six members of the Financial Accounting Standards Board following submission to the members of the Financial Accounting Standards Advisory Council and the Screening Committee on Emerging Problems. Mr. Walters dissented.

Mr. Walters believes this is not a valid interpretation of *FASB Statement No. 13*. That Statement defines fair value as "the price for which the property could be sold in an arm's-length transaction between unrelated parties." Except for condominium or cooperative arrangements, fair value as defined does not exist for part of a building. Since it does not exist, it cannot be determined, objectively or otherwise. He believes this Interpretation contradicts the stated definition of fair value, and in effect selectively amends that definition as it relates to part of a building.

Members of the Financial Accounting Standards Board:

Donald J. Kirk,
Chairman
Oscar S. Gellein

John W. March
Robert A. Morgan
David Mosso

Robert T. Sprouse
Ralph E. Walters

FASB Interpretation No. 25
Accounting for an Unused Investment Tax Credit

an interpretation of APB Opinions No. 2, 4, 11, and 16

STATUS

Issued: September 1978

Effective Date: Prospectively for fiscal years beginning after December 15, 1978

Affects: No other pronouncements

Affected by: Paragraph 9 superseded by FAS 71
Footnote 5 superseded by FIN 32
Superseded by FAS 96 and FAS 109

Other Interpretive Pronouncements: FTB 81-2 (Superseded by FAS 96 and FAS 109)
FTB 86-1 (Superseded by FAS 96 and FAS 109)

(The next page is 613.)

FASB Interpretation No. 26
Accounting for Purchase of a Leased Asset by the Lessee during the Term of the Lease

an interpretation of FASB Statement No. 13

STATUS

Issued: September 1978

Effective Date: For purchases of leased property recorded as of December 1, 1978

Affects: No other pronouncements

Affected by: No other pronouncements

Other Interpretive Pronouncement: FTB 79-18

SUMMARY

This Interpretation clarifies the application of paragraph 14 of *FASB Statement No. 13,* "Accounting for Leases," to a termination of a capital lease that results from the purchase of a leased asset by the lessee.

The purchase by the lessee of property under a capital lease and the related lease termination are accounted for as a single transaction. The difference, if any, between the purchase price and the carrying amount of the lease obligation is recorded as an adjustment of the carrying amount of the asset. The Board also noted that Statement No. 13 does not prohibit recognition of a loss if a loss has been incurred.

FASB Interpretation No. 26
Accounting for Purchase of a Leased Asset by the Lessee during the Term of the Lease

an interpretation of FASB Statement No. 13

CONTENTS

INTRODUCTION AND BACKGROUND INFORMATION

1. The FASB has been asked to clarify whether a termination of a capital lease that results from the purchase of a leased asset by the lessee is the type of transaction contemplated by paragraph 14(c) of *FASB Statement No. 13,* "Accounting for Leases." That paragraph states that "a termination of a capital lease shall be accounted for by removing the asset and obligation, with gain or loss recognized for the difference."

2. A draft of a proposed Interpretation on "Accounting for Purchase of a Leased Asset by the Lessee during the Term of the Lease" was issued on April 28, 1978. The Board received 27 letters of comment in response to the proposed Interpretation. Certain of the comments received and the Board's consideration of them are discussed in paragraphs 3 and 4 below.

3. A number of respondents stated that the purchase of a leased asset by the lessee during the term of a capital lease gives rise to an early extinguishment of debt for which the accounting is prescribed in *APB Opinion No. 26,* "Early Extinguishment of Debt." The Board concluded that it should look to *FASB Statement No. 13* to clarify the accounting for the termination of a lease instead of Opinion No. 26. Statement No. 13 specifies different accounting for the termination of a capital lease for which the leased asset ceases to be carried on the enterprise's balance sheet and for a renewal or extension for which the leased asset continues to be carried on the enterprise's balance sheet. The Board views the purchase of the leased asset by the lessee during the term of the lease as a transaction for which similar rights for the same asset continue to be carried on the enterprise's balance sheet. The Board is aware that some extensions of capital leases and purchases of leased assets could be viewed as similar to early

extinguishments of debt. Other extensions of capital leases and purchases of leased assets could be viewed as nonmonetary transactions with an amount of monetary consideration of the type (exchanges of rights to productive assets not held for sale in the ordinary course of business) for which *APB Opinion No. 29,* "Accounting for Nonmonetary Transactions," does not permit recognition of gain. The Board considered the possible applicability of both Opinion No. 26 and Opinion No. 29 during its deliberations on the provisions of Statement No. 13 that address accounting for extensions and other terminations of capital leases. The subjectivity of an allocation of the purchase price between retirement of the lease obligation and acquisition of additional property rights was also a consideration in the determination that recognition of gain or loss should not be required if the asset continued to be carried on the enterprise's balance sheet.

4. Some respondents stated that this Interpretation should require recognition of a loss if a loss is indicated by the terms of the transaction. The Board noted that *FASB Statement No. 13* does not include a requirement for loss recognition on an extension of a capital lease. Therefore, an Interpretation of Statement No. 13 could not include such a requirement. However, the Board also noted that Statement No. 13 does not prohibit recognition of a loss if a loss has been incurred.

INTERPRETATION

5. The termination of a capital lease that results from the purchase of a leased asset by the lessee is not the type of transaction contemplated by paragraph 14(c) of *FASB Statement No. 13* but rather is an integral part of the purchase of the leased asset. The purchase by the lessee of property under a capital lease shall be accounted for like a renewal or extension of a capital lease that, in turn, is classified

as a capital lease,[1] that is, any difference between the purchase price and the carrying amount of the lease obligation shall be recorded as an adjustment of the carrying amount of the asset.

EFFECTIVE DATE AND TRANSITION

6. The provisions of this Interpretation shall be effective for purchases of leased property recorded as of December 1, 1978 or thereafter. Earlier application is encouraged. In addition, except as pro-

vided in the next sentence, the provisions of this Interpretation shall be applied retroactively at the same time and in the same manner as the provisions of *FASB Statement No. 13* are applied retroactively (see paragraphs 49 and 51 of Statement No. 13). Enterprises that have already applied the provisions of Statement No. 13 retroactively and have published annual financial statements based on the retroactively adjusted accounts before the effective date of this Interpretation may, but are not required to, apply the provisions of this Interpretation retroactively.

This Interpretation was adopted by the unanimous vote of the seven members of the Financial Accounting Standards Board following submission to the Financial Accounting Standards Advisory Council and the Screening Committee on Emerging Problems.

Members of the Financial Accounting Standards Board:

Donald J. Kirk,	John W. March	Robert T. Sprouse
Chairman	Robert A. Morgan	Ralph E. Walters
Oscar S. Gellein	David Mosso	

---

[1]Paragraph 14(b)(i) of *FASB Statement No. 13* refers to paragraph 14(a) of the Statement for the accounting for a renewal or an extension of a capital lease that is also classified as a capital lease.

FASB Interpretation No. 27
Accounting for a Loss on a Sublease

an interpretation of FASB Statement No. 13 and APB Opinion No. 30

STATUS

Issued: November 1978

Effective Date: For transactions with measurement dates on or after March 1, 1979

Affects: No other pronouncements

Affected by: No other pronouncements

Other Interpretive Pronouncements: FTB 79-15
FTB 79-18

SUMMARY

This Interpretation clarifies that recognition of a loss by an original lessee who disposes of leased property or mitigates the cost of an existing lease commitment by subleasing the property is not prohibited by *FASB Statement No. 13*, "Accounting for Leases."

This Interpretation also clarifies the treatment of a sublease that is part of a disposal of a segment. The determination of a gain or loss on disposal of the segment, under the provisions of *APB Opinion No. 30*, "Reporting the Results of Operations," comprehends amounts related to an original lease and a sublease entered into as part of the decision to dispose of the segment. Any gain or loss on the sublease becomes an indistinguishable part of the gain or loss on the disposal.

FASB Interpretation No. 27
Accounting for a Loss on a Sublease

an interpretation of FASB Statement No. 13 and APB Opinion No. 30

CONTENTS

INTRODUCTION

1. The FASB has been asked to clarify whether paragraph 39 of *FASB Statement No. 13,* "Accounting for Leases," prohibits the recognition of a loss by an original lessee[1] who disposes of property that was used in a discontinued operation or mitigates the cost of a lease commitment related to a discontinued operation by subleasing the property. In those circumstances, paragraphs 15-17 of *APB Opinion No. 30* may require recognition of a loss. Appendix A provides additional background information about this matter.

INTERPRETATION

2. Paragraph 39 of *FASB Statement No. 13* does not prohibit the recognition of a loss by an original lessee[2] who disposes of leased property or mitigates the cost of an existing lease commitment by subleasing the property.

3. If a sublease is entered into as part of a disposal of a segment of a business[3] as defined in paragraph 13 of *APB Opinion No. 30,* the anticipated future cash flows that will result from the original lease and

the sublease, as well as the carrying amount of any related recorded assets or obligations, shall be taken into account in determining the overall gain or loss on the disposal.

EFFECTIVE DATE AND TRANSITION

4. The provisions of this Interpretation shall be effective for estimates of losses on a disposal of a segment of a business recorded as of a measurement date[4] occurring on or after March 1, 1979 and for subleases recorded as of March 1, 1979 or thereafter. Earlier application is encouraged. In addition, except as provided in the next sentence, the provisions of this Interpretation shall be applied retroactively at the same time and in the same manner as the provisions of *FASB Statement No. 13* are applied retroactively (see paragraphs 49 and 51 of Statement No. 13). Enterprises that have already applied the provisions of Statement No. 13 retroactively and have published annual financial statements based on the retroactively adjusted accounts before the effective date of this Interpretation may, but are not required to, apply the provisions of this Interpretation retroactively.

This Interpretation was adopted by the unanimous vote of the seven members of the Financial Accounting Standards Board following submission to the Financial Accounting Standards Advisory Council and the Screening Committee on Emerging Problems.

Members of the Financial Accounting Standards Board:

Donald J. Kirk,	John W. March	Robert T. Sprouse
Chairman	Robert A. Morgan	Ralph E. Walters
Oscar S. Gellein	David Mosso	

---

[1] An "original lessee" is used in this Interpretation and in *FASB Statement No. 13* to include any lessee who acts as sublessor on a sublease.

[2] See Footnote 1.

[3] An AICPA Accounting Interpretation of APB Opinion No. 30, "Illustrations of the Application of APB Opinion No. 30," issued in November 1973, states that "the gain or loss on a sale of a portion of a line of business which is not a segment of a business . . . should be calculated using the same measurement principles as if it were a segment of a business (paragraphs 15-17 of the Opinion)."

[4] See paragraph 14 of *APB Opinion No. 30* for the definition of "measurement date."

Appendix A

BACKGROUND INFORMATION

5. Paragraph 39 of *FASB Statement No. 13* specifies the accounting by an original lessee for both an original lease and a sublease or similar transaction if the original lessee is not relieved of the primary obligation under the original lease. Under that paragraph, the original lessee accounts for a sublease as a sales-type, direct financing, or operating lease, based partly on the classification of the original lease and partly on the criteria of Statement No. 13 for those classifications. If the sublease is classified as an operating lease, the original lessee continues to account for the original lease as before. If the sublease is classified as a direct financing or sales-type lease, the unamortized balance of the asset under the original lease is treated as the cost of the subleased property, and the original lessee continues to account for the obligation related to the original lease as before. Paragraph 39 does not specifically address recognition of a loss on a sublease except when the sublease meets the criteria for classification as a sales-type lease.

6. Paragraphs 15-17 of *APB Opinion No. 30* describe how an enterprise determines a gain or loss on disposal of a segment of a business. Paragraph 17 of Opinion No. 30 states that "costs and expenses *directly* associated with the decision to dispose include items such as . . . future rentals on long-term leases to the extent they are not offset by sublease rentals." The provision for a loss on a sublease would be based on the net expected future cash disbursements if both the original lease and the sublease were classified as operating leases.

7. If an original lease was classified as a capital lease, a comparison of future rentals on the original lease with sublease rentals would not necessarily be indicative of the future loss on the sublease transaction. A loss, if any, would generally have to be measured based on other provisions of *APB Opinion No. 30.* Paragraph 15 of Opinion No. 30 states that "if it is expected that net losses from operations will be incurred between the measurement date and the expected disposal date, the computation of the gain or loss on disposal should also include an estimate of such amounts." Paragraph 16 of Opinion No. 30 states that "adjustments, costs, and expenses which (a) are clearly a *direct* result of the decision to dispose of the segment and (b) are clearly not the adjustments of carrying amounts or costs, or expenses that should have been recognized on a going-concern basis prior to the measurement date should be included in determining the gain or loss on disposal."

8. A draft of a proposed Interpretation on "Accounting for a Loss on a Sublease" was issued on April 28, 1978. The Board received 20 letters of comment in response to the proposed Interpretation. Certain of the comments received and the Board's consideration of them are discussed in paragraphs 9-11 below.

9. The proposed Interpretation was limited to subleases for which *APB Opinion No. 30* requires recognition of a loss. A number of respondents suggested that the proposed Interpretation be expanded to encompass all subleases. Paragraph 2 of this Interpretation is intended to clarify the Board's view that paragraph 39 of *FASB Statement No. 13* does not prohibit recognition of a loss on a sublease whether or not the sublease is part of a disposal of a segment. Paragraph 3 of this Interpretation is intended to indicate that determination of a gain or loss on disposal of a segment will comprehend amounts relating to an original lease and a sublease entered into as part of a decision to dispose of the segment. Any gain or loss on the lease or sublease becomes an indistinguishable part of the gain or loss on disposal. If a sublease is not entered into as part of a decision to dispose of the segment, Statement No. 13 does not specifically require recognition of an indicated loss except for a sales-type loss on a sales-type sublease. The Board has a possible amendment of Statement No. 13 under consideration that would specify the computation of an indicated loss to be recognized on a sublease that is not entered into as part of a disposal of a segment. However, the Board concluded that it should not delay issuance of this Interpretation pending a final decision on whether to proceed with that amendment.

10. A number of respondents stated that *FASB Statement No. 5,* "Accounting for Contingencies," requires recognition of a loss on a sublease. The Board views most subleases as outside the scope of Statement No. 5 by reason of the exclusion from the coverage of that Statement of write-downs of operating assets (paragraph 31 of Statement No. 5). In addition, if a sublease covered all of the remaining term of the original lease and no contingent rentals were involved, the only uncertainty would be the collectibility of the sublease rentals, and thus Statement No. 5 would not apply to the determination of any loss that would occur if all sublease rentals were collected.

11. A number of respondents suggested that the proposed Interpretation be expanded to address the application of *APB Opinion No. 30* to other specific matters. The essence of this Interpretation is that the application of Opinion No. 30 was not affected by the issuance of *FASB Statement No. 13.* Accordingly, the Board concluded that it should not expand the scope of this Interpretation to describe the application of Opinion No. 30.

FASB Interpretation No. 28
Accounting for Stock Appreciation Rights and Other Variable Stock Option or Award Plans

an interpretation of APB Opinions No. 15 and 25

STATUS

Issued: December 1978

Effective Date: For awards granted in fiscal years beginning after December 15, 1978

Affects: No other pronouncements

Affected by: Paragraph 6 amended by FIN 31

Other Interpretive Pronouncement: FTB 82-2

SUMMARY

This Interpretation clarifies aspects of accounting for compensation related to stock appreciation rights and other variable stock option or award plans. The Interpretation specifies that compensation should be measured at the end of each period as the amount by which the quoted market value of the shares of the enterprise's stock covered by a grant exceeds the option price or value specified under the plan and should be accrued as a charge to expense over the periods the employee performs the related services. Changes in the quoted market value should be reflected as an adjustment of accrued compensation and compensation expense in the periods in which the changes occur until the date the number of shares and purchase price, if any, are both known.

FASB Interpretation No. 28
Accounting for Stock Appreciation Rights and Other
Variable Stock Option or Award Plans

an interpretation of APB Opinions No. 15 and 25

CONTENTS

INTRODUCTION

1. The FASB has been asked to clarify whether the provisions of *APB Opinion No. 25,* "Accounting for Stock Issued to Employees," apply to stock appreciation rights and, if so, how the Opinion should be applied. Similar questions have been raised about awards under other stock compensation plans with variable terms, that is, plans for which the number of shares of stock the employee may receive, the price per share the employee must pay, or both the number of shares and the price are unknown at the date of grant or award. Appendix A provides additional background information about these matters. Appendix B illustrates applications of this Interpretation.

INTERPRETATION

2. *APB Opinion No. 25* applies to plans for which the employer's stock is issued as compensation or the amount of cash paid as compensation is determined by reference to the market price of the stock or to changes in its market price. Plans involving stock appreciation rights and other variable plan awards[1] are included in those plans dealt with by Opinion No. 25. When stock appreciation rights or other variable plan awards are granted, an enterprise shall measure compensation as the amount by which the quoted market value of the shares of the enterprise's stock covered by the grant exceeds the option price or value specified, by reference to a market price or otherwise, subject to any appreciation limitations under the plan. Changes, either increases or decreases, in the quoted market value of those shares between the date of grant and the measurement date[2] result in a change in the measure of compensation for the right or award.

3. Compensation determined in accordance with paragraph 2 shall be accrued as a charge to expense over the period or periods the employee performs the related services (hereinafter referred to as the "service period"). If the stock appreciation rights or other variable plan awards are granted for past services, compensation shall be accrued as a charge to expense of the period in which the rights or awards are granted. If the service period is not defined in the plan or some other agreement, such as an employment agreement, as a shorter or previous period, the service period shall be presumed to be the vesting period.[3]

4. Compensation accrued during the service period in accordance with paragraph 3 shall be adjusted in subsequent periods up to the measurement date[4] for

---

[1]Plans for which the number of shares of stock that may be acquired by or awarded to an employee or the price or both are not specified or determinable until after the date of grant or award are referred to in this Interpretation as "variable plan awards." However, plans described in paragraph 11(c) of Opinion No. 25 (see paragraph 12 in Appendix A of this Interpretation) and book value stock option, purchase, or award plans are not covered by this Interpretation. Plans under which an employee may receive cash in lieu of stock or additional cash upon the exercise of a stock option are variable plans for purposes of this Interpretation if the amount is contingent on the occurrence of future events.

[2]Paragraph 10 of Opinion No. 25 defines the measurement date as "the first date on which are known both (1) the number of shares that an individual employee is entitled to receive and (2) the option or purchase price, if any." Generally, the number of shares of stock that may be acquired or awarded under stock appreciation rights and many other variable plan awards are not known until the date that they are exercised.

[3]For purposes of this Interpretation, stock appreciation rights and other variable plan awards become vested when the employee's right to receive or retain shares or cash under the rights or awards is not contingent upon the performance of additional services. Frequently, the vesting period is the period from the date of grant to the date the rights or awards become exercisable.

[4]See footnote 2.

changes, either increases or decreases, in the quoted market value of the shares of the enterprise's stock covered by the grant but shall not be adjusted below zero. The offsetting adjustment shall be made to compensation expense of the period in which changes in the market value occur. Except as provided in paragraph 5, the accrued compensation for a right that is forfeited or cancelled shall be adjusted by decreasing compensation expense in the period of forfeiture, in accordance with paragraph 15 of *APB Opinion No. 25.*

5. For purposes of applying paragraph 11(h)[5] of *APB Opinion No. 25,* compensation expense for a combination plan[6] involving stock appreciation rights or other variable plan awards (including those that are granted after the date of grant of related stock options) shall be measured according to the terms the employee is most likely to elect based on the facts available each period. An enterprise shall presume that the employee will elect to exercise the stock appreciation rights or other variable plan awards, but the presumption may be overcome if past experience or the terms of a combination plan that limit the market appreciation available to the employee in the stock appreciation rights or other variable plan awards provide evidence that the employee will elect to exercise the related stock option. If an enterprise has been accruing compensation for a stock appreciation right or other variable plan award and a change in circumstances provides evidence that the employee will likely elect to exercise the related stock option, accrued compensation recorded for the right or award shall *not* be adjusted.[7] If the employee elects to exercise the stock option, the accrued compensation recorded for the right or award shall be recognized as a consideration for the stock issued. If all parts of the grant or award (e.g., both the option and the right or award) are forfeited or cancelled, accrued compensation shall be adjusted by decreasing compensation expense in that period.

6. Stock appreciation rights and other variable plan awards are common stock equivalents to the extent payable in stock for purposes of applying the provisions of *APB Opinion No. 15,* "Earnings per Share." Accrued compensation for those rights or awards shall be considered additional "proceeds" for purposes of applying the treasury stock method described in paragraph 36 of Opinion No. 15 for determining the dilutive effect of options in earnings per share computations. Stock appreciation rights and other variable plan awards payable only in cash are not common stock equivalents for the computation of earnings per share under that Opinion.

EFFECTIVE DATE AND TRANSITION

7. The provisions of this Interpretation shall be applied prospectively for stock appreciation rights and other variable plan awards granted in fiscal years beginning after December 15, 1978. Early application is encouraged for stock appreciation rights and other variable plan awards granted in fiscal years beginning before December 16, 1978 for which financial statements have not been previously issued. In addition, this Interpretation may be, but is not required to be, adopted for stock appreciation rights and other variable plan awards granted in fiscal years beginning before December 16, 1978 for which financial statements have been previously issued; if so adopted, an accrual of compensation expense or an adjustment of accrued compensation resulting from the application of this Interpretation for stock appreciation rights and other variable plan awards granted in fiscal years beginning before December 16, 1978 shall be accounted for as a change in estimate in the period of change (see paragraphs 31-33 of *APB Opinion No. 20*). This Interpretation shall not be applied retroactively for previously issued annual financial statements.

8. If early application is adopted in financial reports for interim periods of a fiscal year beginning before December 16, 1978, previously issued financial information for any interim periods of that fiscal year that precede the period of adoption shall be restated to give effect to the provisions of this Interpretation. Any subsequent presentation of that information shall be on the restated basis.

This Interpretation was adopted by the unanimous vote of the seven members of the Financial Accounting Standards Board following submission to the Financial Accounting Standards Advisory Council and the Screening Committee on Emerging Problems.

---

[5]See paragraph 13 in Appendix A of this Interpretation.

[6]See paragraph 10 in Appendix A of this Interpretation.

[7]A change in the circumstances may be indicated by market appreciation in excess of any appreciation limitations under the plan or the cancellation or forfeiture of the stock appreciation right or other variable plan award without a concurrent cancellation or forfeiture of the related stock option. A subsequent decrease in market value that reduces the appreciation to a level below the limitations under the plan would require adjustment of accrued compensation in accordance with paragraph 4 of this Interpretation if evidence then indicates that the employee will elect to exercise the stock appreciation right or other variable plan award.

Appendix A

BACKGROUND INFORMATION

9. Stock appreciation rights are awards entitling employees to receive cash, stock, or a combination of cash and stock in an amount equivalent to any excess of the market value of a stated number of shares of the employer company's stock over a stated price. The form of payment may be specified when the rights are granted or may be determined when they are exercised; in some plans the employee may choose the form of payment.

10. Stock appreciation rights are usually granted in combination with compensatory stock options but also may be granted separately. Combination plans usually provide that the rights are exercisable for the same period as the companion stock options and that the exercise of either cancels the other. In some combination plans, the enterprise may grant stock appreciation rights either when the options are granted or at a later date. In some cases the holder of stock options may apply to receive share appreciation in cash or stock with the approval of the enterprise, in lieu of exercising the options.

11. Paragraph 10 of *APB Opinion No. 25* specifies that "compensation for services that a corporation receives as consideration for stock issued through employee stock option, purchase, and award plans should be measured by the quoted market price of the stock at the measurement date less the amount, if any, that the employee is required to pay." Paragraphs 12-15 of Opinion No. 25 refer to accrual of compensation in periods for which service is rendered before issuance of stock. Paragraph 13 states that "the employer corporation should accrue compensation expense in each period in which the services are performed" and "if the measurement date is later than the date of grant or award, an employer corporation should record the compensation expense each period from date of grant or award to date of measurement based on the quoted market price of the stock at the end of each period." Paragraph 15 of Opinion No. 25 states that the effect of the change in estimated compensation expense should be accounted for in the period of change in accordance with paragraphs 31-33 of *APB Opinion No. 20*, "Accounting Changes."

12. Paragraph 11(c) of *APB Opinion No. 25* states that "the measurement date of an award of stock for current service may be the end of the fiscal period, which is normally the effective date of the award, instead of the date that the award to an employee is determined if (1) the award is provided for by the terms of an established formal plan, (2) the plan designates the factors that determine the total dollar amount of awards to employees for the period (for example, a percent of income), although the total amount or the individual awards may not be known at the end of the period, and (3) the award pertains to current service of the employee for the period.

13. Paragraph 11(h) of *APB Opinion No. 25* states that "compensation cost for a combination plan permitting an employee to elect one part should be measured according to the terms that an employee is most likely to elect based on the facts available each period." Although Opinion No. 25 principally addresses the measurement of compensation when stock is issued to an employee, the Opinion also addresses situations in which cash or stock is paid to an employee for appreciation in the market price of an enterprise's stock. Paragraph 32 of the Opinion states that "the terms of some plans, often called *phantom stock* or *shadow stock* plans, base the obligations for compensation on increases in market price of or dividends distributed on a specified or variable number of shares of stock of the employer corporation but provide for settlement of the obligation to the employee in cash, in stock of the employer corporation, or a combination of cash and stock."

14. A draft of a proposed Interpretation, "Accounting for Stock Appreciation Rights and Other Compensation Plans with Variable Terms Related to the Price of a Company's Stock," was released for comment August 17, 1978. The Board received 62 letters of comment in response to the proposed Interpretation. Certain of the comments received and the Board's consideration of them are discussed in paragraphs 15-18 below.

15. The proposed Interpretation required that compensation expense for stock appreciation rights and other variable plan awards be accrued to the extent that the quoted market value of the shares of the enterprise's stock covered by the grant exceeds the value specified. A majority of the respondents disagreed with that provision as a required allocation method and recommended that other methods be permitted for allocating compensation cost as an expense in the periods in which the related services

are performed. In adopting that recommendation, the Board concluded that the recommendation is consistent with the recognition principles underlying *APB Opinion No. 25.*

16. The proposed Interpretation specified that compensation expense for stock appreciation rights and other variable plan awards should be measured by the extent that the quoted market value of the shares of the enterprise's stock covered by the grant exceeds the value specified, by reference to a market price or otherwise. Several respondents recommended that the compensation expense be measured by using the average market price of the stock, the value of the right or award at the date of grant, or some other value. The Board considered those recommendations and concluded that the method of measuring compensation for stock appreciation rights and other variable plan awards should not be changed without a comprehensive reexamination of the measurement principles underlying *APB Opinion No. 25.* The Board plans such a reexamination in the future but has concluded that issuance of this Interpretation should not be delayed in the meantime.

17. Some respondents requested guidance on whether stock appreciation rights and other variable plan awards are common stock equivalents for purposes of computing earnings per share. Guidance in this regard is provided in paragraph 6 of this Interpretation.

18. The transition called for by the proposed Interpretation required that an accrual of compensation expense or an adjustment of accrued compensation resulting from initial application of the Interpretation should be accounted for as a change in estimate in the period of change. The proposed effective date was for annual periods *ending* after December 15, 1978. Several respondents recommended either prospective or retroactive application because, in their view, the application of the Interpretation would result in a change in accounting method for some enterprises. The Board concluded that the effective date and transition should be changed to prospective application for stock appreciation rights and other variable plan awards granted in fiscal years *beginning* after December 15, 1978. The Interpretation also provides an election that it may be applied to grants made in fiscal years

beginning before December 16, 1978 as a change in estimate in the period of the change.

Appendix B

ILLUSTRATION OF THE ACCOUNTING FOR STOCK APPRECIATION RIGHTS AND OTHER VARIABLE STOCK OPTION OR AWARD PLANS

19. This Appendix illustrates applications of this Interpretation in accounting for stock appreciation rights and other variable stock option or award plans when the service period is presumed to be the vesting period. The examples do not comprehend all possible combinations of circumstances nor do the examples illustrate the computation of deferred income taxes.

20. Provisions of the agreements:

Stock appreciation rights are granted in tandem with stock options for market value appreciation in excess of the option price. Exercise of the rights cancels the option for an equal number of shares and vice versa. Share appreciation is payable in stock, cash, or a combination of stock and cash at the enterprise's election.

Date of grant	January 1, 1979
Expiration date	December 31, 1988
Vesting	100% at the end of 1982
Number of shares under option	1,000
Option price	$10 per share
Quoted market price at date of grant	$10 per share

21. Market price assumptions:

Quoted market price per share at December 31 of subsequent years:

1979—$11
1980— 12
1981— 15
1982— 14
1983— 15
1984— 18

EXAMPLE 1

22. The following example illustrates the annual computation of compensation expense for the above described stock appreciation right plan.

Date	Market Price	Per Share	Compensation Aggregate (1)	Percentage Accrued (2)	Compensation Accrued to Date	\multicolumn{6}{c}{Accrual of Expense by Year (3)}
						1979	1980	1981	1982	1983	1984
12/31/79	$11	$1	$1,000	25%	$ 250	$250					
12/31/80	12	2	2,000	50	750 / 1,000		$750				
12/31/81	15	5	5,000	75	2,750 / 3,750			$2,750			
12/31/82	14	4	4,000	100	250 / 4,000				$250		
12/31/83	15	5	5,000	100	1,000 / 5,000					$1,000	
12/31/84	18	8	8,000	100	3,000 / $8,000						$3,000

Notes

(1) Aggregate compensation for unexercised shares to be allocated to periods service performed.

(2) The percentage accrued is based upon the four-year vesting period.

(3) A similar computation would be made for interim reporting periods.

EXAMPLE 2

23. If the stock appreciation rights vested 25 percent per year commencing in 1979, the computation of compensation expense in the preceding example would change as illustrated in the following examples.

24. Because 25 percent of the rights vest each year commencing in 1979, the service period over which compensation is accrued as a charge to expense is determined separately for each 25 percent portion. For example, the services for the 25 percent portion of the rights vesting in 1980 are performed in both 1979 and 1980 and the related compensation is accrued proportionately as a charge to expense in each year. Similarly, compensation for rights vesting in 1981 is proportionately accrued as a charge to expense in 1979, 1980, and 1981. In this way, compensation related to the portion of the rights vesting in 1979 is recognized in 1979, compensation related to the portion of the rights vesting in 1980 is recognized in 1979 and 1980, and so forth. The following schedule indicates the service period for each 25 percent portion of the rights and the computation of the *aggregate* percentage of compensation accrued by the end of each year of service (the vesting period). A similar computation would be made for interim reporting periods.

For Rights Vesting in	Service Period	Aggregate Percentage of Compensation Accrued by the End of Each Year of Service			
		1979	1980	1981	1982
1979	1 year	25%	25%	25%	25%
1980	2 years	12.5	25	25	25
1981	3 years	8.33	16.67	25	25
1982	4 years	6.25	12.5	18.75	25
Aggregate percentage accrued at the end of each year		52.08%	79.17%	93.75%	100%
Rounded for purposes of Examples 2 and 3		52%	79%	94%	100%

For periods ending after 1982, 100 percent of the aggregate compensation should be accrued.

25. Additional Assumptions:

On December 31, 1981, the employee exercises the right to receive share appreciation on 300 shares.
On March 15, 1982, the employee exercises the right to receive share appreciation on 100 shares; quoted market price $15 per share.
On June 15, 1983, the employee exercises the right to receive share appreciation on 100 shares; quoted market price $16 per share.
On December 31, 1983, the employee exercises the right to receive share appreciation on 300 shares.
On December 31, 1984, the employee exercises the right to receive share appreciation on 200 shares.

Date	Trans-action	Number of Shares	Market Price	Per Share	Aggregate (1)	Percentage Accrued (2)	Compensation Accrued to Date	1979	1980	1981	1982	1983	1984
12/31/79	A		$11	$1	$1,000	52%	$ 520	$520					
12/31/80	A		12	2	2,000	79	1,580		$1,060				
12/31/81	A		15	5	5,000	94	4,700			$3,120			
12/31/81	E	300	15	5	(1,500)	—	(1,500) 3,200						
3/15/82	E	100	15	5	(500)	—	(500) 2,700						
	A										$(300)		
12/31/82	A		14	4	2,400	100	2,400						
6/15/83	E	100	16	6	(600)	—	(400) 2,000					$200	
12/31/83	A		15	5	2,500	100	2,500					500	
12/31/83	E	300	15	5	(1,500)	—	(1,500) 1,000						
12/31/84	A		18	8	1,600	100	1,600						$600
12/31/84	E	200	18	8	(1,600)	—	(1,600) $ —						

Transaction Codes

A - Adjustment for changes in the market price of the stock.

E - Exercise of a stock appreciation right.

Notes

(1) Aggregate compensation for unexercised shares to be allocated to periods service performed.

(2) See the schedule in paragraph 24 of this Interpretation.

(3) A similar computation would be made for interim reporting periods.

EXAMPLE 3

26. If the plan limits the amount of share appreciation that the employee can receive to $5, the computation of compensation expense in Example 2 would change as illustrated in the following example.

27. When the quoted market price exceeds the appreciation limitation, the employee is more likely to exercise the related stock option rather than the stock appreciation right. Therefore, accrued compensation is *not* adjusted for changes in the quoted market price of the stock. The assumptions stated in paragraph 25 of this Interpretation are changed to the extent that on June 15, 1983 and December 31, 1984 the employee exercises the related stock option instead of the stock appreciation right. Accordingly, accrued compensation for the equivalent number of rights is recognized as part or all of the consideration for the stock issued in accordance with paragraph 5 of this Interpretation.

Date	Transaction	Number of Shares	Market Price	Per Share	Aggregate (1)	Percentage Accrued (2)	Compensation Accrued to Date	\<-- Accrual of Expense by Year (3) --> 1979	1980	1981	1982	1983	1984
12/31/79	A		$11	$1	$1,000	52%	$ 520	$520					
	A						1,060						
12/31/80	A		12	2	2,000	79	1,580		$1,060				
12/31/81	E	300	15	5	5,000	94	3,120			$3,120			
12/31/81	E		15	5	(1,500)	—	4,700						
							(1,500)						
3/15/82	E	100	15	5	(500)	—	3,200						
	E	100	15	5		—	(500)						
	A						2,700						
12/31/82	A		14	4	2,400	100	(300)				$(300)		
6/15/83	O	100	16	5	(500)	—	2,400						
	A						(400)						
							2,000					500	
12/31/83	E	300	15	5	2,500	100	500					$100	
12/31/83	E		15	5	(1,500)	—	2,500						
	NA						(1,500)						
							1,000						
							—						
12/31/84	O	200	18	5	1,000	100	1,000						
12/31/84	O		18	5	(1,000)	—	(1,000)						$ —
							$ —						

Transaction Codes

A - Adjustment for changes in the market price of the stock.
NA - No adjustment required because the market
     price exceeds the appreciation limitation.
E - Exercise of a stock appreciation right.
O - Exercise of the related stock option.

Notes

(1) Aggregate compensation for unexercised shares to be allocated to periods service performed.

(2) See the schedule in paragraph 24 of this Interpretation.

(3) A similar computation would be made for interim reporting periods.

FASB Interpretation No. 29
Reporting Tax Benefits Realized on Disposition of Investments in Certain Subsidiaries and Other Investees

an interpretation of APB Opinions No. 23 and 24

STATUS

Issued: February 1979

Effective Date: For dispositions of investments occurring after March 31, 1979

Affects: No other pronouncements

Affected by: Superseded by FAS 96 and FAS 109

(The next page is 633.)

(This page intentionally left blank.)

FASB Interpretation No. 30
Accounting for Involuntary Conversions of Nonmonetary Assets to Monetary Assets

an interpretation of APB Opinion No. 29

STATUS

Issued: September 1979

Effective Date: For fiscal years beginning after November 15, 1979

Affects: No other pronouncements

Affected by: Paragraph 5 amended by FAS 96 and FAS 109

SUMMARY

This Interpretation clarifies the accounting for involuntary conversions of nonmonetary assets (such as property or equipment) to monetary assets (such as insurance proceeds). Examples of such conversions are total or partial destruction or theft of insured nonmonetary assets and the condemnation of property in eminent domain proceedings. A diversity in practice exists in accounting for the difference between the cost of a nonmonetary asset that is involuntarily converted and the amount of monetary assets received. Generally, that difference has been recognized in income as a gain or loss. In other cases, that difference has been accounted for as an adjustment to the cost of subsequently acquired replacement property. This Interpretation requires that gain or loss be recognized when a nonmonetary asset is involuntarily converted to monetary assets even though an enterprise reinvests or is obligated to reinvest the monetary assets in replacement nonmonetary assets.

FASB Interpretation No. 30
Accounting for Involuntary Conversions of Nonmonetary Assets to Monetary Assets

an interpretation of APB Opinion No. 29

CONTENTS

INTRODUCTION

1. The FASB has been asked whether gain or loss results from an involuntary conversion of a nonmonetary asset to monetary assets if the monetary assets are subsequently reinvested in a similar nonmonetary asset.[1] Generally, if a nonmonetary asset is involuntarily converted, gain or loss for the difference between the cost[2] of the nonmonetary asset and the amount of monetary assets received has been recognized in income in the period of the involuntary conversion. In other cases, that difference has been accounted for as an adjustment to the cost basis of a nonmonetary asset that is subsequently acquired as replacement property.

INTERPRETATION

2. Involuntary conversions of nonmonetary assets to monetary assets are monetary transactions for which gain or loss shall be recognized even though an enterprise reinvests or is obligated to reinvest the monetary assets in replacement nonmonetary assets. As discussed in paragraph 11 of this Interpretation, however, the requirement to recognize gain does not apply to certain involuntary conversions of LIFO inventories.[3]

3. In some cases, a nonmonetary asset may be destroyed or damaged in one accounting period, and the amount of monetary assets to be received is not determinable until a subsequent accounting period. In those cases, gain or loss shall be recognized in accordance with FASB Statement No. 5, *Accounting for Contingencies.*

4. Gain or loss resulting from an involuntary conversion of a nonmonetary asset to monetary assets shall be classified in accordance with the provisions of APB Opinion No. 30, *Reporting the Results of Operations—Reporting the Effects of Disposal of a Segment of a Business, and Extraordinary, Unusual and Infrequently Occurring Events and Transactions.*

5. Gain or loss resulting from an involuntary conversion of a nonmonetary asset to monetary assets that is not recognized for income tax reporting purposes in the same period in which the gain or loss is recognized for financial reporting purposes is a timing difference for which comprehensive interperiod tax allocation, as described in APB Opinion No. 11, *Accounting for Income Taxes,* is required.

EFFECTIVE DATE AND TRANSITION

6. The provisions of this Interpretation shall be applied prospectively for involuntary conversions of nonmonetary assets to monetary assets occurring in fiscal years beginning after November 15, 1979. Earlier application is encouraged in financial statements for fiscal years beginning before November 16, 1979 that have not been previously issued.

Appendix A

BACKGROUND INFORMATION

7. APB Opinion No. 29, *Accounting for Nonmonetary Transactions,* concludes that the account-

---

[1]The terms "nonmonetary" and "monetary" as used in this Interpretation have the same meaning as those terms have in APB Opinion No. 29, *Accounting for Nonmonetary Transactions.*

[2]As used in this Interpretation, the term cost refers to the cost of a nonmonetary asset or to its carrying amount, if different.

[3]Paragraph 14(b) of APB Opinion No. 28, *Interim Financial Reporting,* provides an exception for the liquidation of a LIFO inventory at an interim date if replacement is expected by year-end. Accordingly, that exception applies to an involuntary conversion of a LIFO inventory if replacement is expected by year-end.

ing for nonmonetary transactions should generally be the same as for monetary transactions and that the basic principle of recognizing a gain or loss based on the fair values of the assets (or services) involved should be applied for nonmonetary transactions as for monetary transactions. However, in some cases, modifications of that basic principle are required. For example, paragraph 21 of Opinion 29 provides that an exchange of a nonmonetary asset for a similar nonmonetary asset that is not essentially the culmination of an earnings process should be accounted for based on the recorded amount of the nonmonetary asset relinquished.

8. Paragraph 4 of Opinion 29 states, in part:

> For purposes of applying this Opinion, events and transactions in which nonmonetary assets are involuntarily converted (for example, as a result of total or partial destruction, theft, seizure, or condemnation) to monetary assets that are then reinvested in other nonmonetary assets are monetary transactions *since the recipient is not obligated to reinvest the monetary consideration in other nonmonetary assets.* (Emphasis added.)

Paragraph 22 of Opinion 29 addresses exchanges of nonmonetary assets that involve some monetary consideration. That paragraph requires the recipient of monetary consideration to recognize a gain on the exchange to the extent that the amount of monetary receipt exceeds a proportionate share of the recorded amount of the asset surrendered.

9. A draft of a proposed Interpretation on *Accounting for Involuntary Conversions of Nonmonetary Assets to Monetary Assets* was released for comment on April 11, 1979. The Board received 31 letters of comment on the proposed Interpretation.

10. Some respondents disagreed with the proposed Interpretation, suggesting that the difference between the cost of a nonmonetary asset that is involuntarily converted and the amount of monetary assets received should be accounted for as an adjustment to the cost of subsequently acquired replacement property. For the most part, those respondents expressed the view that an involuntary conversion of a nonmonetary asset to monetary assets that are reinvested in replacement property is, in essence, an exchange transaction, as described in paragraph 21 of Opinion 29. Some of those respondents also noted that an involuntary conversion should be accounted for as an exchange transaction rather than as a monetary transaction if the recipient of monetary assets is obligated to reinvest the monetary assets in a nonmonetary asset similar to that which was destroyed. They contended that that position was consistent with paragraph 4 of Opinion 29, which states, in part, ". . . events and transactions in which nonmonetary assets are involuntarily converted . . . to monetary assets . . . are monetary transactions *since the recipient is not obligated to reinvest the monetary consideration in other nonmonetary assets.*" (Emphasis added.) However, the Board does not believe that an involuntary conversion of a nonmonetary asset to monetary assets and the subsequent reinvestment of the monetary assets is equivalent to an exchange transaction between an enterprise and another entity. In the Board's view, the conversion of a nonmonetary asset to monetary assets is a monetary transaction, whether the conversion is voluntary or involuntary, and such a conversion differs from exchange transactions that involve only nonmonetary assets. To the extent the cost of a nonmonetary asset differs from the amount of monetary assets received, the transaction results in the realization of a gain or loss that should be recognized. Furthermore, the cost of subsequently acquired nonmonetary assets should be measured by the consideration paid and not be affected by a previous transaction.

11. A question was raised as to the application of this Interpretation to an involuntary conversion of a LIFO inventory if the monetary assets are expected to be reinvested in replacement inventory. APB Opinion No. 28, *Interim Financial Reporting,* addresses that situation if the LIFO inventory replacement is expected before year-end, and footnote 3 has been added to provide an exception to conform with Opinion 28. If the LIFO inventory replacement is not made by year-end and a taxpayer does not recognize a gain for income tax reporting purposes, it has been asserted that application of this Interpretation might invalidate a taxpayer's LIFO election. The Board concluded that issuance of this Interpretation should not be delayed to resolve that matter and has exempted it from the provisions of this Interpretation. Accordingly, the requirement of this Interpretation with respect to gain recognition does not apply to an involuntary conversion of a LIFO inventory for which replacement is intended but not made by year-end and the taxpayer does not recognize gain for income tax reporting purposes.

This Interpretation was adopted by the affirmative votes of six members of the Financial Accounting Standards Board following submission to the members of the Financial Accounting Standards Advisory Council and the Screening Committee on Emerging Problems. Mr. Morgan dissented.

Mr. Morgan dissents because he believes that this Interpretation emphasizes form over substance. He disagrees with the statement in paragraph 10 that the conversion of a nonmonetary asset to monetary assets is a monetary transaction that differs from exchange transactions that involve only nonmonetary assets and that a gain should be recognized. He believes that the earnings process is not culminated simply because monetary assets are received if there is an economic incentive to reinvest the proceeds of

an involuntary conversion of a productive asset. He also believes that financial statements reporting improved earnings as a result of the destruction or incapacitation of significant productive assets are misleading and therefore fail to comply with the objectives of financial reporting as described in paragraph 32 *et seq* of FASB Concepts Statement No. 1, *Objectives of Financial Reporting by Business Enterprises.*

FASB Interpretation No. 31
Treatment of Stock Compensation Plans in
EPS Computations

an interpretation of APB Opinion No. 15 and a
modification of FASB Interpretation No. 28

STATUS

Issued: February 1980

Effective Date: For fiscal years beginning after December 15, 1979

Affects: Amends FIN 28, paragraph 6
Amends AIN-APB 15, Interpretation No. 82 and footnotes 38
through 42

Affected by: Footnote 1 amended by FAS 96 and FAS 109

SUMMARY

   Earnings per share data reflect the dilutive effect of outstanding stock options, including stock appreciation rights and other variable plan awards, computed by application of the treasury stock method under
APB Opinion No. 15, *Earnings per Share*. Under that method, earnings per share data are computed as if
the options were exercised at the beginning of the period (or at date of grant, if later) and as if the funds
obtained thereby were used to purchase common stock. This Interpretation specifies that the funds used in
applying the treasury stock method are the sum of the cash to be received on exercise, the compensation
related to the options to be charged to expense in the future, and any tax benefit to be credited to capital. The
Interpretation also provides guidance for how to include the effect of variable plans, combination plans, or
plans payable in cash or in stock in earnings per share computations.

FASB Interpretation No. 31
Treatment of Stock Compensation Plans in EPS Computations

an interpretation of APB Opinion No. 15 and
a modification of FASB Interpretation No. 28

CONTENTS

INTRODUCTION

1. The FASB received several requests to clarify the provisions of FASB Interpretation No. 28, *Accounting for Stock Appreciation Rights and Other Variable Stock Option or Award Plans,* that discuss the dilutive effect of stock appreciation rights and other variable plan awards in EPS computations. Some believed that FASB Interpretation 28 conflicted with earlier pronouncements with respect to the composition of funds obtained from the assumed exercise of stock options, including stock appreciation rights and other variable plan awards. Such funds are hereinafter referred to as "exercise proceeds."

2. This Interpretation modifies AICPA Interpretation No. 82 of APB Opinion No. 15, *Earnings per Share,* and supersedes the second sentence of paragraph 6 of FASB Interpretation 28. This Interpretation is not intended to alter the treatment of shares issuable contingent upon certain conditions being met, as discussed in paragraphs 61-64 of Opinion 15. Appendix A provides additional background information about this Interpretation. Appendix B illustrates applications of this Interpretation.

INTERPRETATION

3. In applying the treasury stock method of para-

graph 36 of Opinion 15 to stock options, including stock appreciation rights and other variable plan awards, the exercise proceeds of the options are the sum of the amount the employee must pay, the amount of measurable compensation ascribed to future services and not yet charged to expense (whether or not accrued), and the amount of any "windfall" tax benefit[1] to be credited[2] to capital. Exercise proceeds shall not include compensation ascribed to past services.

4. The dilutive effect of stock appreciation rights and other variable plan awards on primary earnings per share shall be computed using the average aggregate compensation and average market price for the period. The market price of an enterprise's stock and the resulting aggregate compensation used to compute the dilutive effect of stock appreciation rights and other variable plan awards in fully diluted earnings per share computations shall be the more dilutive of the market price and aggregate compensation at the close of the period being reported upon or the average market price and average aggregate compensation for that period.[3]

5. If an enterprise has a combination plan allowing the enterprise or the employee to make an election involving stock appreciation rights or other variable plan awards, earnings per share for a period shall be computed based on the terms used in the computation of compensation expense for that period.

---

[1]The "windfall" tax benefit is the tax credit resulting from a tax deduction for compensation in excess of compensation expense recognized for financial reporting purposes. Such credit arises from an increase in the market price of the stock under option between the measurement date (as defined in APB Opinion No. 25, *Accounting for Stock Issued to Employees*) and the date at which the compensation deduction for income tax purposes is determinable. The amount of the "windfall" tax benefit shall be determined by a "with-and-without" computation as described in paragraph 36 of APB Opinion No. 11, *Accounting for Income Taxes.*

[2]Paragraph 17 of Opinion 25 states that there may be instances when the tax deduction for compensation is less than the compensation expense recognized for financial reporting purposes. If the resulting difference in income tax will be deducted from capital in accordance with that paragraph, such taxes to be deducted from capital shall be treated as a reduction of exercise proceeds.

[3]If the rights or awards were granted during the period, the shares issuable must be weighted to reflect the portion of the period during which the rights or awards were outstanding.

6. If stock appreciation rights or other variable plan awards are payable in stock or in cash at the election of the enterprise or the employee, the decision of whether such rights or awards are common stock equivalents shall be made according to the terms most likely to be elected based on the facts available each period. It shall be presumed that such rights or awards will be paid in stock, but that presumption may be overcome if past experience or a stated policy provides a reasonable basis to believe that the rights or awards will be paid partially or wholly in cash.

This Interpretation was adopted by the unanimous vote of the seven members of the Financial Accounting Standards Board following submission to the Financial Accounting Standards Advisory Council and the Screening Committee on Emerging Problems.

Members of the Financial Accounting Standards Board:

Donald J. Kirk,	John W. March	Robert T. Sprouse
Chairman	Robert A. Morgan	Ralph E. Walters
Frank E. Block	David Mosso	

Appendix A

BACKGROUND INFORMATION

8. Paragraph 35 of Opinion 15 states that stock options "should be regarded as common stock equivalents at all times" and that ". . . earnings per share should reflect the dilution that would result from exercise . . . of these securities and use of the funds, if any, obtained." Paragraph 6 of FASB Interpretation 28 states that "stock appreciation rights and other variable plan awards are common stock equivalents to the extent payable in stock. . . ." Paragraph 36 of Opinion 15 discusses the treatment of stock options in earnings per share computations and provides that:

> . . . the amount of dilution to be reflected in earnings per share data should be computed by application of the "treasury stock" method. Under this method, earnings per share data are computed as if the options . . . were exercised at the beginning of the period (or at time of issuance, if later) and as if the funds obtained thereby were used to purchase common stock.
> . . .

The dilutive effect that would result from assumed exercise of stock options is reflected in the earnings per share computation by an increase in shares assumed to be outstanding equal to the number of shares issuable upon exercise of the stock options less the number of shares assumed to be purchased with the funds obtained from such exercise.

9. AICPA Interpretation 82 defines exercise pro-

EFFECTIVE DATE AND TRANSITION

7. The provisions of this Interpretation shall be effective for financial statements for fiscal years beginning after December 15, 1979. Earlier application is encouraged in financial statements for fiscal years beginning before December 16, 1979 that have not been previously issued. This Interpretation may be, but is not required to be, applied retroactively to previously issued financial statements.

ceeds as the sum of the amount the employee must pay, the unamortized deferred compensation, and the "windfall" tax benefit credited to capital surplus. That definition results in treating shares "earned" by past services as outstanding for earnings per share computations. The Board believes that definition is an appropriate interpretation of Opinion 15 and has accordingly adopted a similar definition of exercise proceeds in this Interpretation.

10. Stock appreciation rights are often granted in combination with stock options. Such combination plans usually provide that the rights are exercisable for the same period as the companion stock options and that the exercise of either cancels the other. Compensation expense and earnings per share for a period could differ depending on which terms (options or rights) were used in the computations. Paragraph 5 of FASB Interpretation 28 states that compensation expense for a combination plan "shall be measured according to the terms the employee is most likely to elect based on the facts available each period." The Board has concluded that earnings per share for a period should be computed according to the same terms used in the computation of compensation expense for that period.

11. A draft of a proposed Interpretation, *Treatment of Stock Compensation Plans in EPS Computations,* was released for comment October 1, 1979. The Board received 35 letters of comment in response to the proposed Interpretation. Certain of the comments received and the Board's consideration of them are discussed in paragraphs 12 and 13.

12. To simplify the EPS computation, the proposed Interpretation stated that "windfall" tax benefits

credited to capital are not part of exercise proceeds. Some respondents contended that "windfall" tax benefits should be included in the definition of exercise proceeds because they represent a potential future cash flow to the enterprise. The definition of exercise proceeds in paragraph 3 has been modified to include "windfall" tax benefits.

13. Some respondents requested clarification or guidance on how to treat stock appreciation rights that are payable in cash or in stock at the option of the enterprise or the employee in EPS computations. As noted in paragraph 8, stock appreciation rights and other variable plan awards are common stock equivalents to the extent payable in stock. The Board has decided that to provide a conservative estimate of potential dilution, such rights and awards should be presumed to be payable in stock unless there is a reasonable basis to believe that they will be paid in cash. That guidance is provided in paragraph 6 of this Interpretation.

Appendix B

ILLUSTRATION OF THE APPLICATION OF THE TREASURY STOCK METHOD FOR STOCK APPRECIATION RIGHTS AND OTHER VARIABLE STOCK OPTION AWARD PLANS

14. This appendix illustrates applications of this Interpretation in computing the dilutive effect on earnings per share of stock appreciation rights and other variable stock option or award plans when the service period is presumed to be the vesting period. The examples do not comprehend all possible combinations of circumstances. Amounts and quantities have been rounded down to whole units for simplicity.

15. Provisions of the agreements:

Stock appreciation rights are granted in tandem with stock options for market value appreciation in excess of the option price. Exercise of the rights cancels the options for an equal number of shares and vice versa. Share appreciation is payable in stock, cash, or a combination of stock and cash at the enterprise's election.

Date of grant	January 1, 1979
Expiration date	December 31, 1988
Vesting	100% at the end of 1982
Number of shares under option	1,000
Option price	$10 per share
Quoted market price at date of grant	$10 per share

16. Assumptions:

There are no circumstances in these three examples that would overcome the presumption that the rights are payable in stock.

The tax deduction for compensation will equal the compensation recognized for financial reporting purposes.

Quoted market price per share at December 31 of subsequent years:

1979 —	$11
1980 —	12
1981 —	15
1982 —	14
1983 —	15
1984 —	18

EXAMPLE 1

17. The following example illustrates the annual computation of incremental shares for the above described stock appreciation right plan. A single annual computation is shown for simplicity in this and the following examples. Normally, a computation would be done monthly or quarterly.

		COMPENSATION							FOR PRIMARY EARNINGS PER SHARE			FOR FULLY DILUTED EARNINGS PER SHARE		
Date	Market Price	Per Share	Aggregate (1)	Percentage Accrued (2)	Compensation Accrued to Date	Measurable Compensation Ascribed to Future Periods (3)	Amount to Be Paid by Employee	Exercise Proceeds	Shares Issuable (4)	Treasury Shares Assumed Repurchased (5)	Incremental Shares	Shares Issuable (6)	Treasury Shares Assumed Repurchased (7)	Incremental Shares
12/31/79	$11	$1	$1,000	25%	$ 250	$ 750	—	$ 750	47	35	12	90	68	22
12/31/80	12	2	2,000	50	1,000	1,000	—	1,000	130	76	54	166	83	83
12/31/81	15	5	5,000	75	3,750	1,250	—	1,250	259	83	176	333	83	250
12/31/82	14	4	4,000	100	4,000	—	—	—	310	43	267	285	—	285
12/31/83	15	5	5,000	100	5,000	—	—	—	310	—	310	333	—	333
12/31/84	18	8	8,000	100	8,000	—	—	—	393	—	393	444	—	444

Notes

(1) Aggregate compensation for unexercised shares to be allocated to periods service performed.
(2) The percentage accrued is based upon the four-year vesting period.
(3) Unaccrued compensation in this example.
(4) Average aggregate compensation divided by average market price.*
(5) Average exercise proceeds divided by average market price.*
(6) End-of-year aggregate compensation divided by market price as of year-end.
(7) End-of-year exercise proceeds divided by market price as of year-end.

Illustration of computation for one year (1982)

Date	Market Price	Aggregate Compensation	Exercise Proceeds	Shares Issuable	Treasury Shares Assumed Repurchased	Incremental Shares
12/31/81 (beginning of year)	$15	$5000	$1250	N/A	N/A	N/A
12/31/82 (end of year)	14	4000	—	285	—	285
Average	14.50	4500	625	310	43	267

If average incremental shares were higher than end-of-year incremental shares, average incremental shares would be used for both primary and fully diluted earnings per share computations.

*These computations could also be done using other methods of averaging.

EXAMPLE 2

18. If the stock appreciation rights vested 25 percent per year commencing in 1979, the annual computation of incremental shares for primary earnings per share in the preceding example would change as illustrated in the following example. Similar computations would be made for fully diluted earnings per share. The computation of compensation expense is explained in FASB Interpretation 28, Appendix B, Example 2.

19. Additional Assumptions:

On December 31, 1981, the employee exercises the right to receive share appreciation on 300 shares.

On March 15, 1982, the employee exercises the right to receive share appreciation on 100 shares; quoted market price $15 per share.

On June 15, 1983, the employee exercises the right to receive share appreciation on 100 shares; quoted market price $16 per share.

On December 31, 1983, the employee exercises the right to receive share appreciation on 300 shares.

On December 31, 1984, the employee exercises the right to receive share appreciation on 200 shares.

				COMPENSATION							ADDITIONAL SHARES FOR PRIMARY EARNINGS PER SHARE				
Date	Transaction	Number of Shares	Market Price	Per Share	Aggregate (1)	Percentage Accrued (2)	Compensation Accrued to Date	Measurable Compensation Ascribed to Future Periods (3)	Amount to Be Paid by Employee	Exercise Proceeds	Shares Issuable (4)	Treasury Shares Assumed Repurchased (5)	Incremental Shares	Weighted Average Shares Outstanding (6)	Total Shares
12/31/79			$11	$1	$1,000	52%	$ 520	$480	—	$480	47	22	25	—	25
12/31/80			12	2	2,000	79	1,580	420	—	420	130	39	91	—	91
12/31/81			15	5	5,000	94	4,700	300	—	300	259	26	233	—	233
12/31/81	E	300	15	5	(1,500)										
3/15/82	E	100	15	5	(500)	—									
12/31/82			16	4	2,400	100	2,400	—	—	—	193	10	183	126	309
6/15/83	E	100	16	6	(600)	—									
12/31/83			15	5	2,500	100	2,500	—	—	—	170	—	170	153	323
12/31/83	E	300	15	8	(1,500)	—									
12/31/84			18	8	1,600	100	1,600	—	—	—	78	—	78	270	348
12/31/84	E	200	18	8	(1,600)	—									

Transaction Code
E—Exercise of a stock appreciation right.

Notes
(1) Aggregate compensation for unexercised shares to be allocated to periods service performed.
(2) See the schedule in paragraph 24 of FASB Interpretation 28.
(3) Unaccrued compensation in this example.
(4) Average aggregate compensation divided by average market price, weighted for proportion of period during which rights were unexercised.
(5) Average exercise proceeds divided by average market price.
(6) Shares issued upon exercise of stock appreciation rights. These would be included in the enterprise's total weighted average shares outstanding.

Illustration of computation for one year (1982)

	Number of Shares	Average Market Price	Average Aggregate Compensation	Aggregate Shares Issuable	Weighing Factor	Shares Issuable
Rights outstanding entire year	600	$14.50	$2700	186	12/12	186
Rights outstanding 1/1-3/15	100	15.00	500	33	2.5/12	7
						193

643

EXAMPLE 3

20. If the plan limits the amount of share appreciation that the employee can receive to $5, the computation of additional shares in Example 2 would change as illustrated in the following example.

21. When the quoted market price exceeds the appreciation limitations, the employee is more likely to exercise the related stock option rather than the stock appreciation right. Therefore, accrued compensation is not adjusted for changes in the quoted market price of the stock. The assumptions stated in paragraph 19 of this Interpretation are changed to the extent that on June 15, 1983 and December 31, 1984 the employee exercises the related stock option instead of the stock appreciation right. In addition, it is assumed that the market price does not exceed $15 for substantially all of a three-month period until 1984. Therefore, for earnings per share purposes the incremental shares are computed based on assumed exercise of the stock appreciation rights prior to 1984 and on assumed exercise of the stock options in 1984.

			COMPENSATION							ADDITIONAL SHARES FOR PRIMARY EARNINGS PER SHARE (6)					
Date	Transaction	Number of Shares	Market Price	Per Share	Aggregate (1)	Percentage Accrued (2)	Compensation Accrued to Date	Measurable Compensation Ascribed to Future Periods (3)	Amount to Be Paid by Employee	Exercise Proceeds	Shares Issuable (4)	Treasury Shares Assumed Repurchased (5)	Incremental Shares	Weighted Average Shares Outstanding (7)	Total Shares
12/31/79			$11	$1	$1,000	52%	$ 520	$480	—	$480	47	22	25	—	25
12/31/80			12	2	2,000	79	1,580	420	—	420	130	39	91	—	91
12/31/81			15	5	5,000	94	4,700	300	—	300	259	26	233	—	233
12/31/81	E	300	15	5	(1,500)	—									
3/15/82	E	100	15	5	(500)	—									
12/31/82			14	4	2,400	100	2,400	—	—	—	193	10	183	126	309
6/15/83	O	100	16	5	(500)	—									
12/31/83			15	5	2,500	100	2,500	—	—	—	170	—	170	187	357
12/31/83	E	300	15	5	(1,500)	—									
12/31/84			18	5	1,000	100	1,000	—	$2,000	2,000	200	121	79	333	412
12/31/84	O	200	18	5	(1,000)	—									

Transaction Codes

E—Exercise of a stock appreciation right.
O—Exercise of the related stock option.

Notes

(1) Aggregate compensation for unexercised shares to be allocated to periods service performed.
(2) See the schedule in paragraph 24 of FASB Interpretation 28.
(3) Unaccrued compensation in this example.
(4) Average aggregate compensation divided by average market price, weighted for proportion of period during which options or rights were unexercised.
(5) Average exercise proceeds divided by average market price.
(6) Similar computations would be made for fully diluted earnings per share.
(7) Shares issued upon exercise of stock appreciation rights and stock options. These would be included in the enterprise's total weighted average shares outstanding.

FASB Interpretation No. 32
Application of Percentage Limitations in Recognizing Investment Tax Credit

an interpretation of APB Opinions No. 2, 4, and 11

STATUS

Issued: March 1980

Effective Date: For fiscal years beginning after December 15, 1979

Affects: Supersedes FIN 25, footnote 5

Affected by: Superseded by FAS 96 and FAS 109

Other Interpretive Pronouncement: FTB 86-1 (Superseded by FAS 96 and FAS 109)

(The next page is 656.)

(This page intentionally left blank.)

FASB Interpretation No. 33
Applying FASB Statement No. 34 to Oil and Gas Producing Operations Accounted for by the Full Cost Method

an interpretation of FASB Statement No. 34

STATUS

Issued: August 1980

Effective Date: For fiscal years beginning after December 15, 1979 and for interim periods within those years

Affects: No other pronouncements

Affected by: No other pronouncements

SUMMARY

FASB Statement No. 34, *Capitalization of Interest Cost*, establishes standards for capitalizing interest cost as part of the historical cost of acquiring certain assets. This Interpretation clarifies that the assets of an oil and gas producing operation accounted for by the full cost method that qualify for capitalization of interest are:

a. Those unusually significant investments in unproved properties and major development projects that are not being depreciated, depleted, or amortized currently and
b. Significant properties and projects in cost centers with no production,

provided that exploration or development activities on such assets are in progress.

FASB Interpretation No. 33
Applying FASB Statement No. 34 to Oil and Gas Producing Operations Accounted for by the Full Cost Method

an interpretation of FASB Statement No. 34

CONTENTS

INTRODUCTION

1. The FASB received several inquiries from oil and gas producing enterprises that use the full cost method of accounting asking how they should apply FASB Statement No. 34, *Capitalization of Interest Cost*, to their operations. Appendix A contains background information about those inquiries.

INTERPRETATION

2. For purposes of applying Statement 34 to oil and gas producing operations accounted for by the full cost method, assets whose costs are being currently depreciated, depleted, or amortized are assets in use in the earning activities of the enterprise and are not assets qualifying for capitalization of interest cost as defined in paragraph 9 of Statement 34. Unusually significant investments in unproved properties and major development projects that are not being currently depreciated, depleted, or amortized and on which exploration or development activities are in progress are assets qualifying for capitalization of interest cost. Similarly, in a cost center with no production, significant properties and projects on which exploration or development activities are in progress are assets qualifying for capitalization of interest cost.

EFFECTIVE DATE AND TRANSITION

3. The provisions of this Interpretation shall be effective for annual financial statements for fiscal years beginning after December 15, 1979 and for interim periods within those fiscal years, with earlier application encouraged. Enterprises that have applied Statement 34 in a manner contrary to this Interpretation in previously issued annual financial statements are encouraged, but are not required, to restate those financial statements and financial information for interim periods within those fiscal years to give effect to the provisions of this Interpretation. If those annual financial statements are not restated, the effect that the provisions of this Interpretation would have had in those financial statements shall be disclosed in the annual financial statements in which this Interpretation is first applied. Likewise, the effect that this Interpretation would have had on the financial information for interim periods within those years shall be disclosed whenever financial information for those interim periods is presented.

4. If the change to conform to the provisions of this Interpretation is made in *other than* the first interim period of an enterprise's fiscal year, financial information for the prechange interim periods of that fiscal year shall be restated by applying the newly adopted method of applying Statement 34 to those prechange interim periods. Whenever financial information that includes those prechange interim periods is presented, it shall be presented on the restated basis. In addition, the following disclosures shall be made for the interim period in which the provisions of this Interpretation are adopted:

a. The nature of the change in method of applying Statement 34;
b. The effect of the change on income from continuing operations. net income, and related per share amounts for each prechange interim period of that fiscal year; and
c. Income from continuing operations, net income, and related per share amounts for each prechange interim period restated in accordance with this Interpretation.

Appendix A

BACKGROUND INFORMATION

5. Paragraph 9 of Statement 34 states that interest shall be capitalized on "assets that are constructed

or otherwise produced for an enterprise's own use (including assets constructed or produced for the enterprise by others for which deposits or progress payments have been made)." Such assets are referred to as "qualifying assets." Paragraph 10 of Statement 34, however, states that interest shall not be capitalized on:

a. Assets that are in use or ready for their intended use in the earning activities of the enterprise
b. Assets that are not being used in the earning activities of the enterprise and that are not undergoing the activities necessary to get them ready for use.

6. Appendix B of FASB Statement No. 19, *Financial Accounting and Reporting by Oil and Gas Producing Companies*, discusses the full cost method. Paragraph 104 states that:

Under the full cost concept, all costs incurred in acquiring, exploring, and developing properties within a relatively large geopolitical (as opposed to geological) cost center (such as a country) are capitalized when incurred and are amortized as mineral reserves in the cost center are produced, subject to a limitation that the capitalized costs not exceed the value of those reserves.

Paragraph 107 further states that:

. . . acquisition, exploration, and development costs are sometimes included in the pool of capitalized costs associated with a cost center when incurred, so that if the cost center is producing, those costs are subject to amortization at once. In some cases, however, certain significant costs, such as those associated with off-shore U.S. operations, are deferred separately without amortization until the specific property to which they relate is found to be either productive or nonproductive, at which time those deferred costs and any reserves attributable to the property are included in the computation of amortization in the cost center.

Proponents of the full cost method have traditionally argued that all exploratory and development costs should be capitalized because such costs represent the historical cost of an enterprise's proved oil and gas reserves. As stated in paragraph 102 of Statement 19:

. . . all costs incurred in oil and gas producing activities are regarded as integral to the acquisition, discovery, and development of whatever reserves ultimately result from the efforts as a whole, and are thus associated with the company's reserves.

7. Securities and Exchange Commission (SEC) ASR No. 258, *Oil and Gas Producers—Full Cost Accounting Practices*, established "uniform requirements for financial accounting and reporting practices of oil and gas producers following the full cost method of accounting" and subject to SEC Rules. ASR 258 requires that costs to be amortized include "all capitalized costs, less accumulated amortization, other than the cost . . . of unusually significant investments in unproved properties and major development projects," plus certain other costs.

8. A proposed Interpretation, *Applying FASB Statement No. 34 to Oil and Gas Producing Operations Accounted for by the Full Cost Method*, was released for comment on January 28, 1980. The Board received 28 letters of comment to the proposed Interpretation. Certain of the comments received and the Board's consideration of them are discussed in paragraphs 9-15.

9. Two views have been expressed regarding what constitute the qualifying assets of an oil and gas producing operation accounted for by the full cost method. The first view is that major exploration or development projects constitute qualifying assets as long as exploration or development activities are in progress. Interest capitalization ends when those activities cease or when the property begins producing oil or gas, whichever comes first. Under this view, the qualifying assets of an oil and gas producing enterprise for purposes of capitalizing interest are the same regardless of whether the enterprise uses the successful efforts method or the full cost method.

10. Others argue that the first view fails to reflect the conceptual basis of the full cost method. Proponents of the full cost method have traditionally argued that the assets of an oil and gas producing company are not its individual properties, platforms, wells, and equipment, but are, rather, its underground oil and gas reserves. The historical acquisition cost of those reserves is the cumulative exploration and development expenditures of the enterprise and, accordingly, all exploration and development costs are capitalized. As reserves are produced, the costs of those reserves (the capitalized costs in the cost center) are amortized on a units-of-production basis. The cumulative capitalized costs in the cost center, therefore, represent the cost of one asset—proved oil and gas reserves—not an aggregation of the costs of separately identifiable assets each of which may or may not be ready for use. Once production begins, that asset is in use "in the earning activities of the enterprise" and is, therefore, not a qualifying asset for purposes of capitalizing interest. ASR 258 permits the costs of major nonproducing properties to be accounted for as separate assets excluded from the full cost pool and not

amortized because the reserves related to those costs are not yet known. Nonproducing properties whose costs are excluded from the full cost pool and are not being currently amortized are not in use "in the earning activities of the enterprise."

11. The Board believes that the view expressed in paragraph 10 is consistent with the conceptual basis of the full cost method. By contrast, the view expressed in paragraph 9, that the assets of an oil or gas producer that qualify for capitalization of interest should be the same regardless of the accounting method used, creates conceptual implementation problems. Assume that an oil and gas producer drills three exploratory wells on a property, that the first two wells are dry holes, and that the third well locates proved reserves. If the enterprise uses the successful efforts method, it will charge the costs of the first two wells to expense when they are determined to be dry holes and cease to capitalize interest on them. Under the view expressed in paragraph 9, an enterprise that uses the full cost method would capitalize interest as a cost of the wells and would stop capitalization of interest on the first two wells when they are determined to be dry holes. The full cost method, however, does not differentiate an exploratory dry hole from a successful exploratory well. All exploration costs are considered costs of locating proved reserves and the full cost method treats all exploration costs the same. Therefore, the arguments advanced in paragraph 9 would create a distinction between dry holes and successful wells that is incompatible with the full cost method.

12. Some respondents requested that the Board provide guidance to determine what constitute "unusually significant" investments and "major" projects. Those terms are taken from ASR 258, and enterprises subject to SEC rules have experience in applying those terms to their amortization policies. For enterprises not subject to SEC rules, the Board believes that judgments as to what constitute "unusually significant" investments and "major" projects should be determined by an enterprise and its auditors based upon the enterprise's facts and circumstances.

13. Some respondents suggested that the proposed Interpretation contradicted paragraph 18 of Statement 34, which states:

> The capitalization period shall end when the asset is substantially complete and ready for its intended use. Some assets are completed in parts, and each part is capable of being used independently while work is continuing on other parts. An example is a condominium. For such assets, interest capitalization shall stop on each part when it is substantially complete and ready for use. . . . Some assets cannot be used effectively until a separate facility has been completed. Examples are the oil wells drilled in Alaska before completion of the pipeline. For such assets, interest capitalization shall continue until the separate facility is substantially complete and ready for use.

Those respondents maintain that paragraph 18 of Statement 34 supports the view expressed in paragraph 9 of this appendix. Paragraph 18 of Statement 34, however, deals with the end of the capitalization period; it does not address what assets are qualifying assets. If an asset is not a qualifying asset for purposes of interest capitalization, then the duration of the capitalization period is not relevant.

14. The concept of assets completed in parts with each part capable of being used independently is compatible with this Interpretation. Interest may be capitalized as a part of the cost of unusually significant investments in unproved properties and major development projects that are not being currently depreciated, depleted, or amortized and on which exploration or development activities are in progress. Properties and projects whose costs are included in producing cost centers lose their separate identity, however, and are treated as part of a single, indivisible asset.

15. Some respondents found the effective date and transition provisions of the proposed Interpretation unclear. Other respondents objected to the requirement for enterprises that elected early implementation of Statement 34 in a manner not compatible with the proposed Interpretation to restate their previously issued financial statements or financial information. The effective date and transition section has been revised to encourage, but not require, restatement.

This Interpretation was adopted by the affirmative votes of six members of the Financial Accounting Standards Board following submission to the members of the Financial Accounting Standards Advisory Council and the Screening Committee on Emerging Problems. Mr. Mosso dissented.

Mr. Mosso dissents because he believes this Interpretation misapplies (1) the basic premise stated in paragraph 6 of Statement 34 that the cost of acquiring an asset includes interest as part of "the costs necessarily incurred to bring it to the *condition and location* necessary for its intended use" and (2) that part of paragraph 18 which reads "Some assets are completed in parts. . . . interest capitalization shall stop *on each part* when it is substantially complete and ready for use" (emphasis added).

The Interpretation hinges on rejection of the applicability of paragraph 18 of Statement 34 which deals with the end of the capitalization period for assets that are partly ready for use and partly not. Rejection of paragraph 18 requires a determination that a producing cost center for oil and gas reserves represents a single, indivisible asset, wholly ready for use when it satisfies an accounting test, current amortization. That determination, however, ignores the fact that readiness for use is defined in paragraph 6 of Statement 34 essentially in terms of satisfying physical tests, condition and location, and the further fact that similar physical tests are implicit in the SEC rule for full cost accounting.

The SEC rule for amortizing a full cost pool reads in part: "Costs to be amortized shall include . . . the estimated future expenditures . . . to be incurred in developing proved reserves. . . ." The fact that estimated future development costs are required to be included in the current amortization charge is clear recognition that some portions of proved reserves may not be physically ready for current production even though other portions are currently producing. It is recognition that a proved but undeveloped oil and gas field constitutes an incomplete part of a larger asset complex, the full cost pool. Interest in that context is as much a future development cost as any other kind of capitalizable cost.

Members of the Financial Accounting Standards Board:

FASB Interpretation No. 34
Disclosure of Indirect Guarantees
of Indebtedness of Others

an interpretation of FASB Statement No. 5

STATUS

Issued: March 1981

Effective Date: For fiscal years ending after June 15, 1981

Affects: No other pronouncements

Affected by: No other pronouncements

SUMMARY

This Interpretation clarifies that the disclosures that FASB Statement No. 5, *Accounting for Contingencies*, requires of guarantees of indebtedness of others also are required of indirect guarantees.

FASB Interpretation No. 34
Disclosure of Indirect Guarantees of Indebtedness of Others

an interpretation of FASB Statement No. 5

CONTENTS

INTRODUCTION

1. The Board has been asked to clarify the disclosures that are required of indirect guarantees of indebtedness of others. Paragraph 12 of FASB Statement No. 5, *Accounting for Contingencies*, requires disclosure of guarantees of indebtedness of others:

> Certain loss contingencies are presently being disclosed in financial statements even though the possibility of loss may be remote. The common characteristic of those contingencies is a guarantee, normally with a right to proceed against an outside party in the event that the guarantor is called upon to satisfy the guarantee. Examples include (a) guarantees of indebtedness of others. ... The Board concludes that disclosure of those loss contingencies, and others that in substance have the same characteristic, shall be continued. The disclosure shall include the nature and amount of the guarantee. Consideration should be given to disclosing, if estimable, the value of any recovery that could be expected to result, such as from the guarantor's right to proceed against an outside party.

INTERPRETATION

2. An indirect guarantee of the indebtedness of another arises under an agreement that obligates one entity to transfer funds to a second entity upon the occurrence of specified events, under conditions whereby (a) the funds are legally available to creditors of the second entity and (b) those creditors may enforce the second entity's claims against the first entity under the agreement. Examples of indirect guarantees include agreements to advance funds if a second entity's income, coverage of fixed charges, or working capital falls below a specified minimum.[1]

3. The term *guarantees of indebtedness of others* in paragraph 12 of Statement 5 includes indirect guarantees of indebtedness of others as described in paragraph 2 of this Interpretation.

EFFECTIVE DATE AND TRANSITION

4. This Interpretation shall be effective for financial statements for fiscal years ending after June 15, 1981. Earlier application is encouraged.

This Interpretation was adopted by the affirmative votes of six members of the Financial Accounting Standards Board following submission to the members of the Financial Accounting Standards Advisory Council. Mr. Morgan dissented.

Mr. Morgan dissents to issuance of this Interpretation because he believes that it is not needed. In his opinion, paragraph 12 of Statement 5 already requires disclosure of indirect guarantees of indebtedness of others.

One of the examples that paragraph describes is "guarantees of indebtedness of others" without explicitly referring to "indirect" guarantees. However, the paragraph's main point is that contingencies based on guarantees shall be disclosed, and it states that ". . . disclosure of those loss contingen-

cies, and *others that in substance have the same characteristic*, shall be continued" (emphasis added).

Mr. Morgan believes new financial accounting pronouncements should be issued only when GAAP is to be charged or expanded and should be avoided when earlier pronouncements seem clear to *most* concerned parties but lack the specificity that *some* parties desire. A trend toward more and more specificity in financial accounting pronouncements would seem to be a trend toward substituting the

---

[1] Disclosure of an indirect guarantee is not required by this Interpretation if it is otherwise disclosed in an entity's financial statements.

Board's judgment in place of the judgment of preparers and attestors who are most familiar with the

pertinent facts and circumstances.

The members of the Financial Accounting Standards Board:

Donald J. Kirk,
Chairman
Frank E. Block

John W. March
Robert A. Morgan
David Mosso

Robert T. Sprouse
Ralph E. Walters

Appendix A

BACKGROUND INFORMATION

5. The FASB released an Exposure Draft of a proposed Statement on March 31, 1980 titled *Disclosure of Guarantees, Project Financing Arrangements, and Other Similar Obligations* (March Exposure Draft), that would have amended Statement 5 to explicitly include in paragraph 12 both unconditional obligations and indirect guarantees of indebtedness of others. The FASB received 102 letters of comment on the March Exposure Draft. Based on the comments received, the content of the March Exposure Draft was separated into two documents that were exposed concurrently for comment on November 14, 1980: a proposed Interpretation, *Disclosure of Indirect Guarantees of Indebtedness of Others*, and a revised Exposure Draft, *Disclosure of Unconditional Obligations*.

6. The Board received 51 letters of comment on the proposed Interpretation. Certain of the comments received and the Board's consideration of them are discussed in paragraphs 7-10.

7. Some respondents stated that disclosure of indirect guarantees should not be required unless loss is probable. The approach suggested by those respondents would require an amendment of Statement 5, which requires disclosure of guarantees even though the possibility of loss may be remote. The Board does not believe those respondents have presented evidence sufficient to warrant an amendment.

8. Some respondents suggested that enterprises regulated on an individual-company-cost-of-service basis should be exempted from the requirements of

this Interpretation. They state that payments required under indirect guarantees usually would be recovered through the rate-making process, and no loss would result. Statement 5 requires disclosure of guarantees, however, even though the possibility of loss may be remote. The fact that the possibility of loss is remote for those regulated enterprises does not distinguish them or provide a basis for exemption.

9. Some respondents requested clarification of the definition of an indirect guarantee and the difference between direct and indirect guarantees of indebtedness of others. Both direct and indirect guarantees of indebtedness involve three parties: a debtor, a creditor, and a guarantor. In a direct guarantee, the guarantor states that if the debtor fails to make payment to the creditor when due, the guarantor will pay the creditor. If the debtor defaults, the creditor has a direct claim on the guarantor. Under an indirect guarantee, there is an agreement between the debtor and the guarantor requiring the guarantor to transfer funds to the debtor upon the occurrence of specified events. The creditor has only an indirect claim on the guarantor by enforcing the debtor's claim against the guarantor. After funds are transferred from the guarantor to the debtor, the funds become available to the creditor through its claim against the debtor.

10. The proposed Interpretation stated that a general partner's responsibility for the indebtedness of a partnership is an indirect guarantee. Several respondents suggested deleting that sentence for various reasons. A creditor has a direct claim against the general partners of a debtor partnership and, accordingly, a general partner's responsibility for the indebtedness of a partnership is not an indirect guarantee as discussed in paragraph 9. The Board, therefore, deleted the sentence.

FASB Interpretation No. 35
Criteria for Applying the Equity Method of Accounting for Investments in Common Stock

an interpretation of APB Opinion No. 18

STATUS

Issued: May 1981

Effective Date: For fiscal years beginning after June 15, 1981

Affects: No other pronouncements

Affected by: No other pronouncements

SUMMARY

This Interpretation clarifies the criteria for applying the equity method of accounting for investments of 50 percent or less of the voting stock of an investee enterprise (other than a corporate joint venture). APB Opinion No. 18, *The Equity Method of Accounting for Investments in Common Stock*, states that use of the equity method of accounting for the investment is required if the investor has the ability to exercise significant influence over operating and financial policies of the investee. Opinion 18 includes presumptions, based on the investor's percentage ownership, as to whether the investor has that ability, but those presumptions can be overcome by evidence to the contrary and do not override the need for judgment. If there is an indication that an investor owning 20 percent or more of an investee's voting stock is unable to exercise significant influence over the investee's operating and financial policies, all the facts and circumstances related to the investment shall be evaluated to determine whether the presumption of ability to exercise significant influence over the investee is overcome.

FASB Interpretation No. 35
Criteria for Applying the Equity Method of Accounting
for Investments in Common Stock

an interpretation of APB Opinion No. 18

CONTENTS

INTRODUCTION

1. The Board has been asked to clarify the provisions of APB Opinion No. 18, *The Equity Method of Accounting for Investments in Common Stock*, regarding application of that method to investments of 50 percent or less of the voting stock of an investee enterprise (other than a corporate joint venture).

INTERPRETATION

2. Opinion 18 requires that the equity method of accounting be followed by an investor whose investment in voting stock gives it the ability to exercise significant influence over operating and financial policies of an investee. The presumptions in paragraph 17 of Opinion 18 are intended to provide a reasonable degree of uniformity in applying the equity method. The presumptions can be overcome by predominant evidence to the contrary.

3. Evidence that an investor owning 20 percent or more of the voting stock of an investee may be unable to exercise significant influence over the investee's operating and financial policies requires an evaluation of all the facts and circumstances relating to the investment. The presumption that the investor has the ability to exercise significant influence over the investee's operating and financial policies stands until overcome by predominant evidence to the contrary.[1]

4. Examples of indications that an investor may be unable to exercise significant influence over the operating and financial policies of an investee include:

a. Opposition by the investee, such as litigation or complaints to governmental regulatory authorities, challenges the investor's ability to exercise significant influence.

b. The investor and investee sign an agreement under which the investor surrenders significant rights as a shareholder.[2]

c. Majority ownership of the investee is concentrated among a small group of shareholders who operate the investee without regard to the views of the investor.

d. The investor needs or wants more financial information to apply the equity method than is available to the investee's other shareholders (for example, the investor wants quarterly financial information from an investee that publicly reports only annually), tries to obtain that information, and fails.[3]

e. The investor tries and fails to obtain representation on the investee's board of directors.

This list is illustrative and is not all-inclusive. None of the individual circumstances is necessarily conclusive that the investor is unable to exercise significant influence over the investee's operating and financial policies. However, if any of these or similar circumstances exists, an investor with ownership of 20 percent or more shall evaluate all facts and circumstances relating to the investment to reach a judgment about whether the presumption that the investor has the ability to exercise significant influence over the investee's operating and financial policies is overcome. It may be necessary to evaluate the facts and circumstances for a period of time before reaching a judgment.

---

[1] Subject to the limitations on the use of the equity method identified in footnote 4 of Opinion 18. That footnote states that conditions that represent limitations on consolidation shall be applied as limitations to the use of the equity method.

[2] See paragraph 9 of this Interpretation for a discussion of such agreements.

[3] The subject of inability to obtain financial information also is addressed in the American Institute of Certified Public Accountants' *Codification of Statements on Auditing Standards*, AU Section 332, "Evidential Matter for Long-Term Investments," paragraph 9.

EFFECTIVE DATE AND TRANSITION

5. The provisions of this Interpretation shall be effective for fiscal years beginning after June 15, 1981, with earlier application encouraged. Changes in the method of accounting for investments required by this Interpretation shall be recorded in accordance with paragraphs 19(l) and (m) of Opinion 18, which provide that:

a. If the investor discontinues application of the equity method, the earnings and losses of the investee that were previously accrued shall remain as part of the carrying amount of the investment. The carrying amount of the investment shall not be adjusted retroactively.

b. If the investor begins applying the equity method, the investment, results of operations (current and prior periods presented), and retained earnings of the investor shall be adjusted retroactively.

This Interpretation was adopted by the unanimous vote of the seven members of the Financial Accounting Standards Board following submission to the Financial Accounting Standards Advisory Council.

Members of the Financial Accounting Standards Board:

Donald J. Kirk,	John W. March	Robert T. Sprouse
Chairman	Robert A. Morgan	Ralph E. Walters
Frank E. Block	David Mosso	

Appendix A

BACKGROUND INFORMATION AND BASIS FOR CONCLUSIONS

6. Paragraph 17 of Opinion 18 establishes standards for use of the equity method to account for investments in common stock other than subsidiaries and corporate joint ventures. It states that:

The [Accounting Principles] Board concludes that the equity method of accounting for an investment in common stock should also be followed by an investor whose investment in voting stock gives it the ability to exercise significant influence over operating and financial policies of an investee even though the investor holds 50% or less of the voting stock. Ability to exercise that influence may be indicated in several ways, such as representation on the board of directors, participation in policy making processes, material intercompany transactions, interchange of managerial personnel, or technological dependency. Another important consideration is the extent of ownership by an investor in relation to the concentration of other shareholdings, but substantial or majority ownership of the voting stock of an investee by another investor does not necessarily preclude the ability to exercise significant influence by the investor. The [Accounting Principles] Board recognizes that determining the ability of an investor to exercise such influence is not always clear and applying judgment is necessary to assess the status of each investment. In order to achieve a reasonable degree of uniformity in application, the [Accounting Principles] Board concludes that an investment (direct or indirect) of 20% or more of the voting stock of an investee should lead to a presumption that in the absence of evidence to the contrary an investor has the ability to exercise significant influence over an investee. Conversely, an investment of less than 20% of the voting stock of an investee should lead to a presumption that an investor does not have the ability to exercise significant influence unless such ability can be demonstrated. When the equity method is appropriate, it should be applied in consolidated financial statements and in parent-company financial statements prepared for issuance to stockholders as the financial statements of the primary reporting entity.

7. The basic question raised is how to decide when use of the equity method is appropriate; in particular, how much weight should be given to the statement that ". . . applying judgment is necessary to assess the status of each investment" and how much weight to the presumptions based on percentage ownership? The Board has been advised that some investors view the presumptions as rigid rules and believe that achievement of 20 percent ownership requires use of the equity method to account for the investment regardless of circumstances. This Interpretation clarifies that the presumptions are to be applied using judgment and may be overcome by predominant evidence to the contrary.

8. A related question involves how an investor owning 20 percent or more of the voting stock of an investee should account for the investment if the investee opposes the investor. That opposition might be in the form of the investee's filing a lawsuit against the investor or the investee's making allegations to appropriate governmental regulatory authorities. This Interpretation clarifies that opposition by the investee requires an assessment by the investor of all the facts and circumstances of the investment to determine whether they are sufficient to overcome the presumption.

9. A third question relates to the appropriateness of using the equity method if an investor and an investee have signed an agreement under which the investor agrees to limit its shareholding in the investee. (Because the investor usually agrees not to increase its current holdings, such agreements often are called "stand-still agreements.") Those agreements are commonly used to compromise disputes when an investee is fighting against a takeover attempt or an increase in an investor's percentage ownership. Depending on their provisions, the agreements may modify an investor's rights or may increase certain rights and restrict others compared with the situation of an investor without such an agreement. If the investor surrenders significant rights as a shareholder under the provisions of such an agreement, this Interpretation clarifies that the investor shall assess all the facts and circumstances of the investment to determine whether they are sufficient to overcome the presumption.

10. A proposed Interpretation, *Criteria for Applying the Equity Method of Accounting for Investments in Common Stock*, was released for comment on December 19, 1980. The Board received 45 letters of comment on the proposed Interpretation. Certain of the comments received and the Board's consideration of them are discussed in paragraphs 11-14.

11. Some respondents believed that the Board should not finalize the proposed Interpretation because the document did not provide guidance beyond that contained in Opinion 18. The Board believes that this Interpretation provides additional guidance in two respects:

a. It provides examples of indications that an investor may be unable to exercise significant influence over operating and financial policies of an investee.
b. It affirms that the presumptions in Opinion 18 may be overcome by contrary evidence.

12. Some respondents suggested that the Interpretation would strengthen investees relative to investors in takeover disputes by making it more difficult

for the investor to use the equity method to account for its investment. The Board disagrees with that suggestion for two reasons. First, the Board believes this Interpretation is a faithful interpretation of Opinion 18. The Board has not attempted to favor either investors or investees and does not believe that its role is to do so. The Board's role on this project is to faithfully interpret Opinion 18. Second, the Board notes that the actual cash returns on an investment and the income taxes that would be paid are unaffected by the method of accounting for the investment. Therefore, a decision not to proceed with an otherwise attractive investment simply because the equity method of accounting cannot be used would seem to be unlikely for the vast majority of companies. Conversely, an investment that is not otherwise attractive does not become so simply because the equity method will be used to account for that investment in the investor's financial statements.

13. Some respondents requested that the Interpretation explicitly provide guidance on accounting for investments of less than 20 percent. Paragraph 2 of this Interpretation states that the presumptions in paragraph 17 of Opinion 18 can be overcome. The Board believes that that statement plus the examples in Opinion 18 of ways an investor might indicate ability to exercise significant influence provide adequate guidance on accounting for investments of less than 20 percent.

14. Some respondents requested that the Interpretation provide more specific guidance, perhaps by providing some examples. The subject of "stand-still agreements" (paragraphs 4(b) and 9) was suggested as one for which guidance is particularly needed. The Board believes, as one respondent stated, that "every investor-investee relationship is unique. . . ." Even if the Board were to provide examples, they would not necessarily be applicable to unique facts and circumstances. Professional judgment would be required in any case. Accordingly, the Board has concluded that adding examples to this Interpretation would not reduce the degree of professional judgment required.

FASB Interpretation No. 36
Accounting for Exploratory Wells in Progress at the End of a Period

an interpretation of FASB Statement No. 19

STATUS

Issued: October 1981

Effective Date: For fiscal years beginning after December 15, 1981 and for interim periods within those years

Affects: No other pronouncements

Affected by: No other pronouncements

SUMMARY

FASB Statement No. 19, *Financial Accounting and Reporting by Oil and Gas Producing Companies*, requires that the costs of exploratory wells that do not locate proved oil and gas reserves (exploratory dry holes) be charged to expense. Questions have been raised about when to charge to expense the costs of an exploratory well in progress at the end of a period that is determined to be a dry hole before the financial statements for that period are issued. This Interpretation clarifies that the costs incurred through the end of the period shall be charged to expense for that period.

FASB Interpretation No. 36
Accounting for Exploratory Wells in Progress at the End of a Period

an interpretation of FASB Statement No. 19

CONTENTS

INTRODUCTION

1. The FASB has been asked to clarify certain provisions of FASB Statement No. 19, *Financial Accounting and Reporting by Oil and Gas Producing Companies,* relating to accounting for the costs of exploratory wells and exploratory-type stratigraphic test wells (both referred to generally as exploratory wells in this Interpretation) that are in progress at the end of a period and that are determined not to have found proved oil and gas reserves before issuance of the financial statements for the period. The Board has been advised that oil and gas producing enterprises are following differing accounting practices for those wells. Those practices are described in Appendix A.

INTERPRETATION

2. If an exploratory well or exploratory-type stratigraphic test well is in progress at the end of a period and the well is determined not to have found proved reserves before the financial statements for that period are issued, the costs incurred through the end of the period, net of any salvage value, shall be charged to expense for that period. Previously issued financial statements shall not be retroactively restated.

EFFECTIVE DATE AND TRANSITION

3. This Interpretation shall be effective for financial statements for fiscal years beginning after December 15, 1981 and for interim accounting periods within those fiscal years. Earlier application is encouraged but is not required.

This Interpretation was adopted by the affirmative votes of six members of the Financial Accounting Standards Board. Mr. Kirk dissented.

Mr. Kirk dissents to issuance of this Interpretation because, in his opinion, the positions stated in paragraphs 5(c) and 7 of this Interpretation, though rejected in this Interpretation, are consistent with the intention of Statement 19. Paragraph 11(d) of Statement 19 expressly defines costs incurred to "drill and equip wells that are not yet completed" as assets.

Mr. Kirk believes that while drilling is still in process, an exploratory well has value; industry experts indicate interests in uncompleted wells can be sold.

As of the balance sheet date, therefore, it is entirely appropriate to recognize the costs of an uncompleted well as an asset, though, if significant, disclosure of the subsequent determination that the well was unsuccessful may be required. Moreover, Mr. Kirk believes that Statement 19's intent was to avoid suggesting the need for an impairment of value assessment for the capitalized costs of exploratory wells in process, similar to the assessment explicitly required in Statement 19 (paragraph 28) for unproved properties.

The members of the Financial Accounting Standards Board:

Donald J. Kirk,	John W. March	Robert T. Sprouse
Chairman	Robert A. Morgan	Ralph E. Walters
Frank E. Block	David Mosso	

Appendix A

BACKGROUND INFORMATION

4. Paragraphs 19, 27, 31, 33, and 39 of Statement

19 are relevant to this matter. The substance of the relevant portions of paragraphs 19, 27, 31, and 33 is as follows:

a. The costs of drilling exploratory wells shall be capitalized as part of the enterprise's uncomplet-

ed wells, equipment, and facilities pending determination of whether the well has found proved reserves. That determination is usually made on or shortly after completion of drilling the well.
b. If the well has found proved reserves, the capitalized costs of drilling the well shall be reclassified as part of the enterprise's wells and related equipment and facilities.
c. If the well has not found proved reserves, the capitalized costs of drilling the well, net of any salvage value, shall be charged to expense.

Paragraph 39 states that:

Information that becomes available after the end of the period covered by the financial statements but before those financial statements are issued shall be taken into account in evaluating conditions that existed at the balance sheet date, for example, in assessing unproved properties (paragraph 28) and in determining whether an exploratory well or exploratory-type stratigraphic test well had found proved reserves (paragraphs 31-34).

5. The Board has been advised that three different accounting practices are now being followed for exploratory wells that are in progress at the end of a period and that are determined not to have found proved reserves before financial statements are issued.

a. Some enterprises believe the costs incurred on the well through the end of the period should be charged to expense. They believe that the determination, after the end of the period, that the exploratory well has not found proved reserves (is a "dry hole") confirms a condition that existed all the time. That condition is not affected by whether the well was completed at the end of the period. They believe, therefore, that paragraph 39 of Statement 19 requires charging the costs incurred through the end of the period to expense.
b. Other enterprises agree with the view in subparagraph (a) and in addition believe that the costs to complete the well should be accrued and charged to expense as of the end of the period. The subsequent determination that the well has not found proved reserves means that the total cost of the well represents a loss. They believe that the total loss, both already incurred and yet to be incurred, should be recognized at the end of the period. Those who hold the view stated in subparagraph (a) disagree because they feel continued drilling in the next period should not affect the results of the previous period. They believe that the costs of unsuccessful exploratory wells under Statement 19 are not comparable to costs of contractual commitments requiring recognition of losses.

c. A third group of enterprises capitalizes the costs incurred through the end of the period as uncompleted wells, equipment, and facilities. They believe that paragraphs 19, 27, 31, and 33 of Statement 19 require capitalization of the costs of an exploratory well until a determination is made of whether the well has found proved reserves. Because the determination cannot be made until the well is completed, the costs should not be charged to expense before the date of completion. They believe that paragraph 39 of Statement 19 is only applicable to exploratory wells that have been completed but not yet evaluated at the end of a period. Determination before issuance of financial statements that a completed well had not found proved reserves would result in charging the costs of the well to expense in the period of completion.

6. A draft of a proposed Interpretation, *Accounting for Exploratory Wells in Progress at the End of a Period,* was released for comment November 26, 1980. The Board received 48 letters of comment in response to the proposed Interpretation. Certain of the comments received and the Board's consideration of them are discussed in paragraphs 7-10.

7. Most of the respondents who disagreed with the proposed Interpretation believe that the proper method of accounting for an exploratory well in progress at the end of a period is that described in paragraph 5(c) of this Interpretation (i.e., that such costs should remain capitalized until the well is completed and determined to be dry). Those respondents relied heavily on the language in paragraph 19 of Statement 19, which provides that the cost of drilling an exploratory well shall be capitalized pending determination of whether the well has found proved reserves, and on paragraph 31, which addresses accounting when drilling of an exploratory well *is completed.* They believe that Statement 19 requires capitalization of the costs of an exploratory well until the well is completed, at which time an assessment is made and the cost of an unsuccessful well is charged to expense. They believe that paragraph 39 of Statement 19 does not apply to an exploratory well in progress at the end of a period.

8. Paragraph 198 of Statement 19 refers to capitalizing "the costs of drilling all exploratory wells *pending* determination of success or failure, that is, *pending* determination of whether proved reserves are found" (emphasis added). Paragraph 205 further explains that "the existence of future benefits is not known until the well is drilled. Future benefits depend on whether reserves are found." Also, that "an exploratory well must be assessed on its own, and the direct discovery of oil and gas reserves can be the sole determinant of whether future benefits exist and, therefore, whether an asset

should be recognized." The Board believes that the existence of future benefits is an essential characteristic of an asset. An exploratory well that is determined to be dry is not an asset. The timing of that determination has no bearing on the obligation to account for the nonexistence of the asset at the end of the period in yet-to-be issued financial statements for the period. A determination that is made after the end of the period but before financial statements for that period are issued is not an event that eliminates previously existing future benefits; the determination merely provides information as to whether future benefits did or did not exist at the end of the period and, therefore, whether an asset did or did not exist at that time.

9. Many respondents expressed concern that to finalize the proposed Interpretation would impair the comparability of financial statements of (a) different enterprises that issue their financial statements at different dates and (b) individual enterprises that issue financial statements at different times after the end of interim and annual accounting periods. They also believe that gathering data relating to exploratory wells in progress at the end of a period would be costly and might delay the release of financial statements. The Board believes these problems are not unique to this issue and exist for all contingencies that exist at the date of the financial statements.

10. A number of respondents requested that the Board define the term "before the issuance of financial statements" as it appears in this Interpretation. The Board did not do so because such a definition is beyond the scope of this Interpretation and is not unique to accounting for exploratory wells.

FASB Interpretation No. 37
Accounting for Translation Adjustments upon Sale of Part of an Investment in a Foreign Entity

an interpretation of FASB Statement No. 52

STATUS

Issued: July 1983

Effective Date: For partial sales investments after June 30, 1983

Affects: No other pronouncements

Affected by: No other pronouncements

SUMMARY

Upon sale or complete or substantially complete liquidation of an investment in a foreign entity, FASB Statement No. 52, *Foreign Currency Translation,* requires that the accumulated translation adjustment component of equity related to that investment be included in measuring the resulting gain or loss. Members of the Board's advisory group on implementation of Statement 52 and others have asked the Board to clarify the application of that requirement to a sale of part of an investment. This Interpretation indicates that the prescribed accounting applies to an enterprise's partial, as well as complete, disposal of its ownership interest.

This Interpretation is effective for transactions entered into after June 30, 1983.

FASB Interpretation No. 37
Accounting for Translation Adjustments upon Sale of
Part of an Investment in a Foreign Entity

an interpretation of FASB Statement No. 52

CONTENTS

INTRODUCTION

1. The Board has been asked to clarify the application of paragraph 14 of FASB Statement No. 52, *Foreign Currency Translation,* to the sale of part of an investment in a foreign entity. That paragraph states:

> Upon sale or upon complete or substantially complete liquidation of an investment in a foreign entity, the amount attributable to that entity and accumulated in the translation adjustment component of equity shall be removed from the separate component of equity and shall be reported as part of the gain or loss on sale or liquidation of the investment for the period during which the sale or liquidation occurs.

INTERPRETATION

2. If an enterprise sells part of its ownership interest in a foreign entity, a pro rata portion of the accumulated translation adjustment component of equity attributable to that investment shall be recognized in measuring the gain or loss on the sale.[1]

EFFECTIVE DATE AND TRANSITION

3. This Interpretation shall be applied to the sale of part of an investment after June 30, 1983. Earlier application is encouraged. Restatement of previously issued financial statements is permitted but is not required.

This Interpretation was adopted by the unanimous vote of the seven members of the Financial Accounting Standards Board.

Members of the Financial Accounting Standards Board:

Donald J. Kirk, *Chairman*	Victor H. Brown	Robert T. Sprouse
Frank E. Block	John W. March	Ralph E. Walters
	David Mosso	

Appendix

BACKGROUND INFORMATION

4. Paragraph 111 of Statement 52 explains the rationale for excluding translation adjustments from current operating results:

> Translation adjustments do not exist in terms of functional currency cash flows. Translation adjustments are solely a result of the translation process and have no direct effect on reporting currency cash flows. Exchange rate changes have an indirect effect on the net investment that may be realized upon sale or liquidation, but that effect is related to the net investment and not to the operations of the investee. Prior to sale or liquidation, that effect is so uncertain and remote as to require that translation adjustments arising currently should not be reported as part of operating results.

Upon sale or upon complete or substantially complete liquidation of an investment in a foreign entity, paragraph 14 of Statement 52 requires that the accumulated translation adjustment attributable to that investment be removed from equity and included in determining the gain or loss on sale or liquidation. Paragraph 119 of Statement 52 indicates that:

---

[1]Under APB Opinion No. 30, *Reporting the Results of Operations,* a gain or loss on disposal of part or all of a net investment may be recognized in a period other than that in which actual sale or liquidation occurs. Paragraph 14 of Statement 52 does not alter the period in which a gain or loss on sale or liquidation is recognized under existing generally accepted accounting principles.

. . . Sale and complete or substantially complete liquidation were selected because those events generally cause a related gain or loss on the net investment to be recognized in net income at that time. That procedure recognizes the "unrealized" translation adjustment as a component of net income when it becomes "realized."

5. Some members of the Board's advisory group on implementation of Statement 52 and others have questioned whether an enterprise's sale of part of its ownership interest in a foreign entity requires that a pro rata part of the accumulated translation adjustment attributable to that investment be recognized in measuring the gain or loss on the sale.

6. A proposed Interpretation, *Accounting for Translation Adjustments upon Sale of Part of an Investment in a Foreign Entity,* was released for public comment on February 16, 1983. The Board received 45 letters of comment on the proposed Interpretation. Certain of the comments received and the Board's consideration of them are discussed in paragraphs 7 and 8.

7. Respondents unanimously agreed with the Board's conclusion that the rationale stated in paragraph 119 of Statement 52 for recognition of translation adjustments in income when realized through sale of an investment requires proportionate recognition when an enterprise sells part of its ownership interest. However, some respondents believe that events other than a sale of some or all of an investor's ownership interest and complete or substantially complete liquidation of an investment

should require recognition of translation adjustments in net income. Views concerning which additional events should require such recognition included a subsidiary's sale of additional stock, liquidations of assets and liabilities by a subsidiary, and any reduction in an investor's net investment, including dividends and the payment of long-term intercompany accounts.

8. As discussed in paragraphs 110-119 of Statement 52, whether events other than an investor's sale of an ownership interest and complete or substantially complete liquidation should cause recognition of translation adjustments in net income was thoroughly considered by the Board before the issuance of that Statement. Information and developments that have come to the Board's attention since that time have not caused the Board to reconsider its conclusions with respect to that issue. For example, the Board is aware that a partial liquidation by a subsidiary may be considered to be similar to a sale of part of an ownership interest if the liquidation proceeds are distributed to the parent. However, extending pro rata recognition to such partial liquidations would require that their substance be distinguished from ordinary dividends. The Board is unconvinced that such a distinction is either possible or desirable. Further, paragraph 119 of Statement 52 states the Board's view that the information provided by recognizing "realized" translation adjustments in net income is probably marginal and gives the reasons for restricting recognition to sale and complete or substantially complete liquidation. Accordingly, this Interpretation is restricted to clarifying that a sale includes an investor's partial, as well as complete, disposal of its ownership interest.

FASB Interpretation No. 38
Determining the Measurement Date for Stock Option, Purchase, and Award Plans Involving Junior Stock

an interpretation of APB Opinion No. 25

STATUS

Issued: August 1984

Effective Date: For grants made to employees on or after March 14, 1984 under stock option, purchase, and award plans involving junior stock

Affects: No other pronouncements

Affected by: No other pronouncements

SUMMARY

APB Opinion No. 25, *Accounting for Stock Issued to Employees,* specifies that the measurement date for determining compensation cost in stock option, purchase, and award plans is the first date on which are known both (a) the number of shares that an individual employee is entitled to receive and (b) the option or purchase price, if any. Opinion 25 also specifies that the measurement date for a grant or award of convertible stock is the date on which the ratio of conversion is known unless other terms are variable at that date. Questions have been raised about determining the measurement date for stock option, purchase, and award plans involving junior stock, a separate class of stock issued to certain employees that is subordinate to an employer's regular common stock but is convertible into common stock if specified future events occur. This Interpretation clarifies that the measurement date for grants under stock option, purchase, and award plans involving junior stock is the date on which the number of shares of the employer's regular common stock that an employee is entitled to receive in exchange for the junior stock is known. This Interpretation is effective for grants made to employees on or after March 14, 1984 under stock option, purchase, and award plans involving junior stock.

FASB Interpretation No. 38

Determining the Measurement Date for Stock Option, Purchase, and Award Plans Involving Junior Stock

an interpretation of APB Opinion No. 25

CONTENTS

INTRODUCTION

1. The Board has been asked to clarify certain provisions of APB Opinion No. 25, *Accounting for Stock Issued to Employees,* relating to determining the measurement date for grants made to employees under stock option, purchase, and award plans involving junior stock. As used in this Interpretation, the term *junior stock* refers to a specific type of stock issued to employees that generally is subordinate to an employer's regular common stock with respect to voting, liquidation, and dividend rights and is convertible[1] into regular common stock if certain performance goals are achieved or if certain transactions occur. Junior stock generally is not transferable, except back to the issuing enterprise, and has a fair value lower than regular common stock because of its subordinate rights and the uncertainty of conversion to regular common stock.

INTERPRETATION

2. Stock option, purchase, and award plans involving junior stock are designed to provide that an employer ultimately will issue shares of regular common stock to employees. Those plans are variable plans because the number of shares of regular common stock that an individual employee is entitled to receive is not known until certain performance goals are achieved or certain transactions occur. There-

fore, for purposes of measuring compensation cost under Opinion 25, the measurement date for grants under stock option, purchase, and award plans involving junior stock is the first date on which are known both the number of shares of the employer's regular common stock that an employee is entitled to receive in exchange for the junior stock and the option or purchase price, if any.

3. In considering the convertible features of junior stock, paragraph 11(f) of Opinion 25 indicates that the measurement date for a grant or award of convertible stock is the date on which the ratio of conversion is known, unless other terms are variable at that date. Because conversion of junior stock to regular common stock generally is contingent on achieving certain performance goals or on certain transactions occurring, the conversion ratio[2] is not known with certainty until those future events occur. After those goals are achieved or those transactions occur, the conversion ratio is determinable and, accordingly, the number of shares of regular common stock that an individual is entitled to receive is known.

4. Compensation cost for stock option, purchase, and award plans involving junior stock shall be accrued according to the provisions of paragraphs 2-4 of FASB Interpretation No. 28, *Accounting for Stock Appreciation Rights and Other Variable Stock Option or Award Plans,* and paragraph 11(g) of

---

[1] Junior stock that is not convertible per se but that has restrictions that lapse (such as restrictions that lapse when certain performance goals are achieved) so that it ultimately becomes regular common stock is considered to be convertible for purposes of applying this Interpretation.

[2] If junior stock becomes convertible only to an equal number of shares of regular common stock upon achieving certain performance goals, the conversion ratio is either one-to-zero or one-to-one; some junior stock plans provide for different ratios of conversion depending on the level of performance attained.

Opinion 25. However, the provisions of paragraph 2 of Interpretation 28 shall be applied only when it becomes probable[3] that certain performance goals will be achieved or certain transactions will occur; that probability may or may not be present at the date junior stock is issued.

5. Stock option, purchase, and award plans involving junior stock generally are based on certain performance goals being achieved or certain transactions occurring within specific periods. Some plans, however, do not specify a period during which those future events must occur. If it is probable that the future event will occur at some time, compensation cost shall be charged to expense over the period from the date the future event becomes probable to the date the future event is most likely to occur or the end of any required service period.[4] Other plans provide for different ratios of conversion of junior stock to regular common stock within a specific period based on variable performance goals. If achieving more than one performance goal is probable, compensation cost shall be based on the highest ratio of conversion of junior stock to regular common stock attributable to those goals whose achievement is probable. However, the final measure of compensation cost shall be based on the ratio of conversion attributable to the performance goal achieved at the measurement date. For all plans, total compensation shall be based on the market price of the regular common stock as of the date compensation cost is determined.

6. Total compensation cost shall be the amount by which the market price at the measurement date of the employer's regular common stock that an employee is entitled to receive exceeds the amount that the employee paid or will pay for the junior stock. If vesting provisions cause junior stock to become convertible to regular common stock after the measurement date, compensation cost shall be recognized during the period from (a) the first date that it becomes probable that the future events will occur or the date the events have occurred to (b) the date that junior stock becomes convertible or the end of the service period, whichever occurs first. If junior stock does not become convertible to regular common stock but cash is paid to an employee to purchase previously issued junior stock, total compensation cost is the amount by which cash paid to the employee exceeds the amount initially paid by the employee for the junior stock.

7. Junior stock plans are variable plans for purposes of computing earnings per share under the provisions of APB Opinion No. 15, *Earnings per Share.* Paragraph 6 of Interpretation 28 provides that variable plan awards are common stock equivalents to the extent payable in stock. FASB Interpretation No. 31, *Treatment of Stock Compensation Plans in EPS Computations,* provides guidance in applying the treasury stock method of Opinion 15 to variable plan awards.

EFFECTIVE DATE AND TRANSITION

8. This Interpretation shall be applied to grants made to employees on or after March 14, 1984 under stock option, purchase, and award plans involving junior stock. Earlier application in financial statements that have not been previously issued is encouraged for grants made to employees before March 14, 1984.

This Interpretation was adopted by the affirmative votes of six members of the Financial Accounting Standards Board. Mr. Block dissented.

Mr. Block dissents from this Interpretation because he believes that most (but not all) junior stock issues are already a class of common stock and should be measured at the grant date if measurable. He believes that paragraph 29 of Opinion 25 shows that the intent was to delay measurement only when a reliable value could not be obtained at the grant date. The fact that junior stock is contingently convertible into another class of common stock does not create an uncertainty about the number of shares of junior stock given or sold to an employee.

In most cases, it can be properly valued at the grant date. The contingent conversion feature does add value to the junior stock and should be considered in estimating the price. If no value can be estimated at the grant date, Opinion 25 would dictate a later measurement date.

Mr. Block believes that all junior stock arrangements are not the same. Depending on circumstances, some may be variable and others not. This Interpretation, by inference, treats them all as variable plans.

Members of the Financial Accounting Standards Board:

Donald J. Kirk,	Frank E. Block	Victor H. Brown
Chairman	Raymond C. Lauver	John W. March
David Mosso	Robert T. Sprouse	

---

[3] *Probable* is used here, consistent with its use in FASB Statement No. 5, *Accounting for Contingencies,* to mean that it is likely that certain performance goals will be achieved or certain transactions will occur.

[4] The term *service period,* as used in this Interpretation, is defined in paragraph 16.

Appendix

**BACKGROUND INFORMATION AND
CONSIDERATION OF COMMENTS ON
EXPOSURE DRAFT**

Background Information

9. Paragraph 20 of Opinion 25 discusses the scope of that Opinion regarding arrangements between employers and employees and states:

> This Opinion applies to all stock option, purchase, award, and bonus rights granted by an employer corporation to an individual employee after December 31, 1972 under both existing and new arrangements. . . .

10. Footnote 2 to paragraph 8 of Opinion 25 states:

> All compensation arrangements involving stock, regardless of the name given, should be accounted for according to their substance.

11. Paragraph 10(b) of Opinion 25 addresses determination of the measurement date and states:

> *The measurement date* for determining compensation cost in stock option, purchase, and award plans is the first date on which are known both (1) the number of shares that an individual employee is entitled to receive and (2) the option or purchase price, if any. . . . the measurement date may be later than the date of grant or award in plans with variable terms that depend on events after date of grant or award.

12. Paragraph 11(f) of Opinion 25 addresses the measurement date for plans involving convertible stock and states:

> The measurement date for a grant or award of convertible stock (or stock that is otherwise exchangeable for other securities of the corporation) is the date on which the ratio of conversion (or exchange) is known unless other terms are variable at that date. . . . The higher of the quoted market price at the measurement date of (1) the convertible stock granted or awarded or (2) the securities into which the original grant or award is convertible should be used to measure compensation.

13. Paragraph 11(g) of Opinion 25 discusses purchasing stock previously issued to an employee under a compensation plan and states:

> Cash paid to an employee to settle an earlier award of stock or to settle a grant of option to

the employee should measure compensation cost. If the cash payment differs from the earlier measure of the award of stock or grant of option, compensation cost should be adjusted. . . . The amount that a corporation pays to an employee to purchase stock previously issued to the employee through a compensation plan is "cash paid to an employee to settle an earlier award of stock or to settle a grant of option" if stock is reacquired shortly after issuance. . . .

14. Paragraph 29 of Opinion 25 defines variable stock option, purchase, and award plans:

> . . . The characteristic that identifies plans in this group is that the terms prevent determining at the date of grant or award either the number of shares of stock that may be acquired by or awarded to an employee or the price to be paid by the employee, or both. . . .

15. Paragraph 2 of Interpretation 28 discusses measuring compensation cost for variable plans and states:

> . . . When stock appreciation rights or other variable plan awards are granted, an enterprise shall measure compensation as the amount by which the quoted market value of the shares of the enterprise's stock covered by the grant exceeds the option price or value specified, by reference to a market price or otherwise, subject to any appreciation limitations under the plan. Changes, either increases or decreases, in the quoted market value of those shares between the date of grant and the measurement date result in a change in the measure of compensation for the right or award. [Footnote reference omitted.]

16. Paragraphs 3 and 4 of Interpretation 28 discuss accruing compensation cost for variable plans and state:

> Compensation determined in accordance with paragraph 2 [of Interpretation 28] shall be accrued as a charge to expense over the period or periods the employee performs the related services (hereinafter referred to as the "service period"). . . . If the service period is not defined in the plan or some other agreement, such as an employment agreement, as a shorter or previous period, the service period shall be presumed to be the vesting period.
>
> Compensation accrued during the service period in accordance with paragraph 3 [of Interpretation 28] shall be adjusted in subsequent periods up to the measurement date for changes, either increases or decreases, in the quoted market value of the shares of the enterprise's stock covered by the grant but shall

not be adjusted below zero. The offsetting adjustment shall be made to compensation expense of the period in which changes in the market value occur. . . . [Footnote references omitted.]

17. Paragraphs 3 and 4 of Interpretation 31 discuss applying the treasury stock method of Opinion 15 to variable plans and state:

In applying the treasury stock method of paragraph 36 of Opinion 15 to stock options, including stock appreciation rights and other variable plan awards, the exercise proceeds of the options are the sum of the amount the employee must pay, the amount of measurable compensation ascribed to future services and not yet charged to expense (whether or not accrued), and the amount of any "windfall" tax benefit to be credited to capital. Exercise proceeds shall not include compensation ascribed to past services.

The dilutive effect of stock appreciation rights and other variable plan awards on primary earnings per share shall be computed using the average aggregate compensation and average market price for the period. The market price of an enterprise's stock and the resulting aggregate compensation used to compute the dilutive effect of stock appreciation rights and other variable plan awards in fully diluted earnings per share computations shall be the more dilutive of the market price and aggregate compensation at the close of the period being reported upon or the average market price and average aggregate compensation for that period. [Footnote references omitted.]

18. When the accounting for junior stock plans became an issue in 1981, the SEC staff allowed registrants to measure compensation as the difference between the value of the junior stock at date of grant and the amount the employee had to pay without considering the variable number of shares of common stock into which the junior stock was contingently convertible and the compensation that would be recognizable under Opinion 25 were it to be considered a variable plan.[5] Under that approach, compensation generally was not recognized. In 1983, the SEC staff became concerned about its position and, in November 1983, asked the FASB to clarify the accounting for junior stock plans. On December 16, 1983, the FASB staff released a proposed FASB Technical Bulletin, *Determining the Measurement Date for Stock Compensation Plans Involving Junior Stock,* to selected individuals and groups for comment, concluding that junior stock plans are variable plans under the provisions of Opinion 25.

19. Several of the respondents to the proposed Technical Bulletin stated that consideration of the accounting for junior stock plans should receive full Board due process procedures and urged that the issue be addressed in a Board pronouncement rather than in a staff Technical Bulletin. On March 14, 1984 the Board decided to address the accounting for junior stock plans in a proposed Interpretation of Opinion 25.

Consideration of Comments on Exposure Draft

20. A proposed Interpretation, *Determining the Measurement Date for Stock Option, Purchase, and Award Plans Involving Junior Stock,* was released for public comment on April 24, 1984. The Board received 31 letters of comment on the proposed Interpretation. Certain of the comments received and the Board's consideration of them are discussed in the following paragraphs.

21. Some respondents asserted that junior stock plans are not variable plans and that junior stock is an investment security that should be accounted for at its fair value at date of grant. They argue that junior stock is not subject to the provisions of paragraph 11(f) of Opinion 25 concerning convertible or exchangeable stock; instead, they focus solely on the issuance of junior stock. They point out that both the number of shares of junior stock that an employee is entitled to receive and the purchase price of the junior stock are known at the date of grant; therefore, they contend that a plan involving junior stock should measure compensation at the date of grant of the junior stock as the amount by which the value of the junior stock issued exceeds the amount paid or to be paid by the employee.

22. Even though junior stock possesses certain features of equity securities, the Board believes that the substance of junior stock plans is that they are compensation plans with the junior stock being a means for an employee ultimately to acquire regular common stock. Therefore, the Board's interpretation focuses on the number of shares of regular common stock that an individual employee is entitled to receive under a junior stock plan. Because the conversion of junior stock to regular common stock is contingent on certain performance goals being achieved or on certain transactions occurring, the number of shares of regular common stock that an employee is entitled to receive is not known until those future events occur. The number of shares of regular common stock that an employee is entitled to receive depends on events occurring after the date of grant of junior stock, thereby causing the plan to be variable under the provisions of paragraph 10(b) of Opinion 25.

[5]The term *variable plan,* as used in this Interpretation, is defined in paragraph 14.

23. The Board notes that contingent performance provisions generally cause stock option, purchase, and award plans to be accounted for as variable plans under Opinion 25. For example, paragraphs 23-26 of Opinion 25 describe plans that measure compensation cost at the date of grant. Included in those plans are plans that grant employees the right to purchase a fixed number of shares of stock at a stated price. Paragraphs 27-32 of Opinion 25 describe plans that measure compensation cost at dates other than the date of grant. Included in those plans are plans that grant employees the right to purchase shares of stock at a stated price, but the number of shares or the price may vary depending on such factors as levels of earnings of the employer or market performance of the stock. Therefore, contingent performance provisions cause a plan to be variable under the provisions of Opinion 25. The Board believes that contingent performance provisions also cause junior stock plans to be variable under the provisions of Opinion 25.

24. Some junior stock plans provide for conversion of junior stock to regular common stock on a share-for-share basis if certain performance goals are achieved or certain transactions occur. For purposes of determining the measurement date for those plans under paragraph 11(f) of Opinion 25, some respondents contend that the ratio of conversion is known at the date junior stock is granted. The Board believes that the ultimate ratio of conversion is not known for those plans until the performance goals are achieved or the transactions occur. That is, the ratio of conversion of junior stock to regular common stock is one-to-zero before those future events occur and changes to one-to-one when those events occur. Other junior stock plans may provide for different ratios of conversion depending on the level of performance attained; however, all junior stock plans have at least two possible ratios of conversion at the date junior stock is granted, thereby causing the ultimate ratio of conversion to be unknown at that date.

25. Some respondents stated that accounting for junior stock plans as variable plans under Opinion 25 recognizes compensation cost that is inconsistent with compensation cost recognized for other stock option, purchase, and award plans. For example, they point out that no compensation cost is recognized for a stock option plan that provides employees the right to purchase a fixed number of shares of common stock at a price equal to the market price of the common stock at the date of grant. They contend that it is inconsistent that a junior stock plan resulting in similar benefits to employees and similar costs to the employer as that stock option plan would result in compensation cost being recognized under this Interpretation. However, that distinction between fixed stock option plans and junior stock plans is the same as the distinction already drawn between fixed and variable plans in Opinion 25.

26. An FASB Interpretation is limited to clarifying, explaining, or elaborating on existing accounting principles. Some believe that the existing accounting principles of Opinion 25 do not result in a reasonable measure of compensation for stock option, purchase, and award plans involving junior stock. However, those principles can be changed only by either amending or superseding Opinion 25. On March 14, 1984, the Board added a project to its agenda to reconsider the underlying principles of Opinion 25. The Board concluded that any perceived inconsistencies in the existing principles of Opinion 25 should be addressed in the project involving a broad reconsideration of Opinion 25 and not through a narrow amendment that deals with only one specific type of stock option, purchase, or award plan, such as junior stock. The Board believes it is not appropriate to ignore the requirements of Opinion 25 for junior stock plans that have characteristics similar to variable plans covered by that Opinion.

27. Several respondents urged the Board to develop criteria to differentiate "legitimate" junior stock plans from "abusive" plans and apply the Interpretation only to the abusive plans. The Board believes that any attempt to distinguish between types of junior stock plans would involve an amendment of Opinion 25. As indicated in paragraph 26, the Board concluded that any proposed amendment of Opinion 25 should be addressed through the broad reconsideration of that Opinion.

28. Paragraphs 2-4 of Interpretation 28 discuss accruing compensation cost for variable plans and state that an enterprise should begin recognizing compensation cost for variable plans at the date of grant. Issuing regular common stock in stock option, purchase, and award plans involving junior stock is contingent on certain future events occurring. Some respondents stated that an enterprise should not be required to recognize compensation cost if it is unlikely that those future events will occur. The Board agrees and, accordingly, this Interpretation specifies that an enterprise should not begin recognizing compensation cost until occurrence of those future events becomes probable. The term *probable* is defined in FASB Statement No. 5, *Accounting for Contingencies*. Opinion 25 specifies, however, that the final measure of compensation cost is determinable only when those future events actually occur and the number of shares of regular common stock that an employee is entitled to receive is known.

FASB Interpretation No. 39
Offsetting of Amounts Related to Certain Contracts

an interpretation of APB Opinion No. 10 and
FASB Statement No. 105

STATUS

Issued: March 1992

Effective Date: For financial statements issued for periods beginning after December 15, 1993

Affects: Supersedes FTB 88-2

Affected by: Paragraph 7 amended by FAS 113

SUMMARY

APB Opinion No. 10, *Omnibus Opinion—1966,* paragraph 7, states that "it is a general principle of accounting that the offsetting of assets and liabilities in the balance sheet is improper except where a right of setoff exists." This Interpretation defines *right of setoff* and specifies what conditions must be met to have that right. It also addresses the applicability of that general principle to forward, interest rate swap, currency swap, option, and other conditional or exchange contracts and clarifies the circumstances in which it is appropriate to offset amounts recognized for those contracts in the statement of financial position. In addition, it permits offsetting of fair value amounts recognized for multiple forward, swap, option, and other conditional or exchange contracts executed with the same counterparty under a master netting arrangement.

This Interpretation is effective for financial statements issued for periods beginning after December 15, 1993.

FASB Interpretation No. 39

Offsetting of Amounts Related to Certain Contracts

an interpretation of APB Opinion No. 10 and FASB Statement No. 105

CONTENTS

INTRODUCTION

1. The FASB has been asked to clarify footnote i to the illustration in Appendix B of FASB Statement No. 105, *Disclosure of Information about Financial Instruments with Off-Balance-Sheet Risk and Financial Instruments with Concentrations of Credit Risk*. That footnote addresses the applicability of APB Opinion No. 10, *Omnibus Opinion—1966,* paragraph 7, and FASB Technical Bulletin No. 88-2, *Definition of a Right of Setoff,* to forward contracts, interest rate swaps, and currency swaps and discusses the circumstances in which amounts recognized for individual contracts may be offset against amounts recognized for other contracts and reported as a net amount in the statement of financial position. The fair value of those contracts or an accrued receivable or payable arising from those contracts, rather than the notional amounts or the amounts to be exchanged, is recognized in the statement of financial position.[1] Examples of other types of contracts for which the notional amounts or the amounts to be exchanged are not recognized in the statement of financial position include, but are not limited to, futures contracts and forward purchase-sale contracts.

2. Questions have also been raised about offsetting amounts recognized for contracts for which the fair value of those contracts, rather than the notional amounts or the items to be received or de-livered in a conditional exchange, is recognized in the statement of financial position. Examples of those contracts include, but are not limited to, financial options, interest rate caps, collars and floors, and swaptions.

3. The contracts described in paragraphs 1 and 2 are often referred to as *conditional* and *exchange* contracts. *Conditional contracts* are those whose obligations or rights depend on the occurrence of some specified future event that is not certain to occur and that could change the timing of the amounts or of the instruments to be received, delivered, or exchanged. *Exchange contracts* are those that require a future exchange of assets or liabilities rather than a one-way transfer of assets.

4. This Interpretation supersedes Technical Bulletin 88-2 as of the effective date of this Interpretation or its earlier application. The guidance in that Technical Bulletin is incorporated substantially unchanged in paragraphs 5-7 of this Interpretation primarily as a matter of convenience.

INTERPRETATION

General Principle

5. Opinion 10, paragraph 7, states that "it is a general principle of accounting that the offsetting

---

[1] For example, a forward foreign exchange contract may call for a party to deliver one million U.S. dollars in exchange for two million German marks at a specified future date. Under current reporting practice, the party would not record a receivable for the German marks or a payable for the U.S. dollars. Rather, a net amount reflecting the fair value of the position may be reported in the statement of financial position.

of assets and liabilities in the balance sheet is improper except where a right of setoff exists." A *right of setoff* is a debtor's legal right, by contract or otherwise, to discharge all or a portion of the debt owed to another party by applying against the debt an amount that the other party owes to the debtor.[2] A right of setoff exists when all of the following conditions are met:

a. Each of *two* parties owes the other determinable amounts.
b. The reporting party has the right to set off the amount owed with the amount owed by the other party.
c. The reporting party intends to set off.
d. The right of setoff is enforceable at law.

A debtor having a valid right of setoff may offset the related asset and liability and report the net amount.[3]

6. Generally, debts may be set off if they exist between mutual debtors each acting in its capacity as both debtor and creditor. In particular cases, however, state laws about the right of setoff may provide results different from those normally provided by contract or as a matter of common law. Similarly, the U.S. Bankruptcy Code imposes restrictions on or prohibitions against the right of setoff in bankruptcy under certain circumstances. Legal constraints should be considered to determine whether the right of setoff is enforceable.

Special Applications

7. Various accounting pronouncements specify accounting treatments in circumstances that result in offsetting or in a presentation in a statement of financial position that is similar to the effect of offsetting. This Interpretation does not modify the accounting treatment in the particular circumstances prescribed by any of the following pronouncements:

FASB Statements and Interpretations
APB Opinions
Accounting Research Bulletins
FASB Technical Bulletins
AICPA Accounting Interpretations
AICPA Audit and Accounting Guides
AICPA Industry Audit Guides
AICPA Statements of Position

Examples of those pronouncements are:

FASB Statement No. 13, *Accounting for Leases* (leveraged leases, paragraphs 42-47)
FASB Statement No. 60, *Accounting and Reporting by Insurance Enterprises* (reinsurance, paragraphs 38-40)
FASB Statement No. 87, *Employers' Accounting for Pensions* (accounting for pension plan assets and liabilities)
FASB Statement No. 106, *Employers' Accounting for Postretirement Benefits Other Than Pensions* (accounting for plan assets and liabilities)
FASB Statement No. 109, *Accounting for Income Taxes* (net tax asset or liability amounts reported)
APB Opinion No. 30, *Reporting the Results of Operations—Reporting the Effects of Disposal of a Segment of a Business, and Extraordinary, Unusual and Infrequently Occurring Events and Transactions* (reporting of discontinued operations)
AICPA Audit and Accounting Guides, *Audits of Brokers and Dealers in Securities* (trade date accounting for trading portfolio positions), and *Construction Contractors* and *Audits of Federal Government Contractors* (advances received on construction contracts)
AICPA Industry Audit Guide, *Audits of Banks* (reciprocal balances with other banks)

Applicability to Forward, Interest Rate Swap, Currency Swap, Option, and Other Conditional or Exchange Contracts

8. Unless the conditions in paragraph 5 are met, the fair value of contracts in a loss position should not be offset against the fair value of contracts in a gain position. Similarly, amounts recognized as accrued receivables should not be offset against amounts recognized as accrued payables unless a right of setoff exists.

9. When fair value or an amount receivable or payable related to conditional or exchange contracts of the reporting entity are recognized in the statement of financial position, the amount recognized represents an asset or a liability. The fair value of a contract in a gain position or an amount accrued as a receivable represents a probable future economic benefit controlled by the reporting entity under the contract. The fair value of a contract in a loss position or an amount accrued as a payable represents a probable future sacrifice of economic benefits aris-

---

[2]For purposes of this Interpretation, cash on deposit at a financial institution is to be considered by the depositor as cash rather than as an amount owed to the depositor.

[3]This Interpretation does not address derecognition or nonrecognition of assets and liabilities. Derecognition by sale of an asset or extinguishment of a liability results in removal of a recognized asset or liability and generally results in the recognition of gain or loss. Although conceptually different, offsetting that results in a net amount of zero and derecognition with no gain or loss are indistinguishable in their effects on the statement of financial position. Likewise, not recognizing assets and liabilities of the same amount in financial statements achieves similar reported results.

ing from the reporting entity's present obligations to transfer assets under the contract.

10. Without regard to the condition in paragraph 5(c), *fair value amounts*[4] recognized for forward, interest rate swap, currency swap, option, and other conditional or exchange contracts executed with the same counterparty under a master netting arrangement may be offset. The reporting entity's choice to offset or not must be applied consistently. A master netting arrangement exists if the reporting entity has multiple contracts, whether for the same type of conditional or exchange contract or for different types of contracts, with a single counterparty that are subject to a contractual agreement that provides for the net settlement of all contracts through a single payment in a single currency in the event of default on or termination of any one contract. Offsetting the fair values recognized for forward, interest rate swap, currency swap, option, and other conditional or exchange contracts outstanding with a single counterparty results in the net fair value of the position between the two counterparties being reported as an asset or a liability in the statement of financial position.

EFFECTIVE DATE AND TRANSITION

11. The provisions of this Interpretation are effective for financial statements issued for periods beginning after December 15, 1993. Earlier application is encouraged. Financial statements for fiscal years before the effective date may be restated to conform to the provisions of this Interpretation.

This Interpretation was adopted by the affirmative votes of five members of the Financial Accounting Standards Board. Mr. Swieringa dissented. Mr. Northcutt did not vote.

Mr. Swieringa disagrees with the exception in paragraph 10 that fair value amounts for certain contracts executed with the same counterparty under a master netting arrangement may be offset. The conditions in paragraph 5 specify that a right of setoff is necessary but not sufficient for offsetting assets and liabilities in a statement of financial position. To qualify for offsetting, that right must be unconditional and the reporting party must intend to set off.

Under a master netting arrangement, both the ability and intent to set off are conditional. That arrangement typically provides for the net settlement of cash flows that are payable at the same date and in the same currency, but it does not provide for the net settlement of cash flows that are payable at different dates and in different currencies. Moreover, that arrangement provides for the net settlement of gains and losses only in the event of default. The Board previously concluded that offsetting assets and liabilities in the statement of financial position is not representationally faithful if a party does not intend to set off (paragraph 45) and is inappropriate if a party has the legal right to set off only in the event of default (paragraph 49). Mr. Swieringa agrees with those conclusions and would not permit the exception in paragraph 10.

Mr. Northcutt joined the Board just before this Interpretation was issued and did not vote on it.

Members of the Financial Accounting Standards Board:

Dennis R. Beresford,
   Chairman
Joseph V. Anania

Victor H. Brown
James J. Leisenring
Robert H. Northcutt, Jr.

A. Clarence Sampson
Robert J. Swieringa

---

[4]The fair value recognized for some contracts may include an accrual component for the periodic unconditional receivables and payables that result from the contract; the accrual component included therein may also be offset for contracts executed with the same counterparty under a master netting arrangement.

Appendix

BACKGROUND INFORMATION AND BASIS FOR CONCLUSIONS

CONTENTS

Appendix

BACKGROUND INFORMATION AND BASIS FOR CONCLUSIONS

Introduction

12. This appendix summarizes considerations that Board members deemed significant in reaching the conclusions in this Interpretation. It includes reasons for accepting certain views and rejecting others. Individual Board members gave greater weight to some factors than to others.

Background Information

13. Many financial instruments and other contracts have been developed to manage risks, and their use has increased dramatically in recent years. Those instruments and contracts, sometimes referred to as off-balance-sheet instruments or derivative instruments, include forward contracts, interest rate swap contracts, currency swap contracts, and option contracts, among others. In the absence of definitive accounting standards for reporting assets and liabilities arising from those instruments and contracts, various financial reporting practices have developed. Certain amounts arising from the potential benefits of the rights and the potential sacrifices from the obligations under those contracts are sometimes recognized.

14. For example, for an interest rate swap contract, the fair value of the contract, or the net amounts receivable or payable as a result of the contract, may be recognized as an asset or a liability. Similarly, the premium paid or received, or the fair value of an option contract, may be recognized as an asset or a liability. Also, the fair value of a forward contract to exchange one item for another may be recognized in the statement of financial position.

15. The general principle that the offsetting of assets and liabilities is improper except where a right of setoff exists is usually thought of in the context of unconditional receivables from and payables to another party. That general principle also applies to conditional amounts recognized for contracts under which the amounts to be received or paid or items to be exchanged in the future depend on future interest rates, future exchange rates, future commodity prices, or other factors.

16. Footnote i to the illustration in Appendix B of Statement 105 addresses forward contracts, interest rate swaps, and currency swaps and states, "Netting of receivable and payable amounts when right of setoff does not exist is in contravention of APB Opinion No. 10, *Omnibus Opinion—1966,* paragraph 7, and FASB Technical Bulletin No. 88-2, *Definition of a Right of Setoff.*" Dealers in these contracts commonly report their holdings in trading accounts measured at their fair values. Some dealers in those contracts have reported the fair value of contracts with different parties as a net increase in or reduction of a trading account or other assets, arguing that the recognized fair values are valuation accounts rather than separate assets and liabilities.

Basis for Conclusions

17. Amounts recognized for forward, interest rate swap, currency swap, option, and other conditional or exchange contracts are not valuation accounts. The fair values recognized in the financial statements are measurements of the rights and obligations associated with the contracts already executed and, therefore, are assets and liabilities in their own right. FASB Concepts Statement No. 6, *Elements of Financial Statements,* paragraphs 34 and 43, states

the following about valuation accounts:

> A separate item that reduces or increases the carrying amount of an asset is sometimes found in financial statements. For example, an estimate of uncollectible amounts reduces receivables to the amount expected to be collected, or a premium on a bond receivable increases the receivable to its cost or present value. Those "valuation accounts" are part of the related assets and are neither assets in their own right nor liabilities.
>
> A separate item that reduces or increases the carrying amount of a liability is sometimes found in financial statements. For example, a bond premium or discount increases or decreases the face value of a bond payable to its proceeds or present value. Those "valuation accounts" are part of the related liability and are neither liabilities in their own right nor assets.

The fair values recognized for conditional or exchange contracts are not valuation accounts because valuation accounts exist only as part of a measurement of an asset or a liability, not as a complete measurement of an asset or a liability.

18. Paragraph 40 of FASB Statement No. 107, *Disclosures about Fair Value of Financial Instruments,* states:

> Fair values of financial instruments depict the market's assessment of the present value of net future cash flows directly or indirectly embodied in them, discounted to reflect both current interest rates and the market's assessment of the risk that the cash flows will not occur. Investors and creditors are interested in predicting the amount, timing, and uncertainty of future net cash inflows to an entity, as those are the primary sources of future cash flows from the entity to them. Periodic information about the fair value of an entity's financial instruments under current conditions and expectations should help those users both in making their own predictions and in confirming or correcting their earlier expectations.

19. While the fair value amount is a representation of the current market assessment of future events that will have cash flow consequences, the conditional nature of the contracts discussed in paragraph 10 means that the eventual cash flow consequences are often not discernable from the amounts reported in the statement of financial position. Statement 105 requires that additional information about the financial instruments that result from those contracts, even if they are recognized at fair value, be disclosed in the financial statements because of the practical limits on the information that is conveyed by the amounts reported in the body of the financial statements.

20. FASB Concepts Statement No. 1, *Objectives of Financial Reporting by Business Enterprises,* paragraph 37, states that ". . . financial reporting should provide information to help investors, creditors, and others assess the amounts, timing, and uncertainty of prospective net cash inflows to the related enterprise" (footnote reference omitted). The amount of credit risk exposure—the amount of accounting loss the entity would incur if the counterparties to forward, interest rate swap, currency swap, option, or other conditional or exchange contracts failed to perform in accordance with the terms of those contracts—is one indicator of the uncertainty of future cash flows from those instruments.

21. The Board decided to permit offsetting of the fair value recognized for forward, interest rate swap, currency swap, option, and other conditional or exchange contracts if they are executed with the same counterparty under a master netting arrangement. That arrangement effectively consolidates individual contracts into a single agreement between the parties. The failure to make one payment under the master netting arrangement would entitle the other party to terminate the entire arrangement and to demand the net settlement of all contracts. The Board believes that an exception to the requirement of paragraph 5(c) of this Interpretation, which states that "the reporting party intends to set off" is justified when a master netting arrangement exists because the net presentation discloses the amount of credit risk exposure under that arrangement. The Board decided that, given a master netting arrangement, presentation of the aggregate fair values of the individual contracts executed under that arrangement would not provide more information about the uncertainty of future cash flows from those contracts than net amounts would.

22. Paragraph 10 of this Interpretation applies only to *fair value amounts* recognized for conditional or exchange contracts executed with the same counterparty under a master netting arrangement. Paragraph 10 does not apply to other amounts recognized for other types of contracts executed under a master netting arrangement; however, those amounts could otherwise meet the conditions of paragraph 5 for a right of setoff. For example, unless the conditions in paragraph 5 are met, the amount recognized under a repurchase agreement may not be offset against the amount recognized under a reverse repurchase agreement

solely because the agreements are executed with the same counterparty under a master netting arrangement, nor may an accrued receivable be offset against an accrued payable on interest rate swaps that are not recognized at fair value solely because the swaps are executed with the same counterparty under a master netting arrangement. The Board concluded that the gross unconditional receivables and payables recognized in the statement of financial position for these types of assets and liabilities provide useful information about the timing and amount of future cash flows that would be lost if those amounts were offset.

23. The Board recognizes that under the existing mixed attribute measurement system, some amounts recognized in the statement of financial position provide more information about the uncertainties of future cash flows than other amounts do. Where information about the uncertainties of future cash flows is readily discernable from an unconditional receivable or payable recognized in the statement of financial position, the Board believes that information is useful to financial statement users and should not be offset unless the conditions in paragraph 5 for the right of setoff are satisfied.

24. This Interpretation permits, but does not require, offsetting of fair value amounts recognized for conditional or exchange contracts executed with the same counterparty under a master netting arrangement. The Board recognizes that optional accounting treatment of similar contracts adversely affects the comparability of financial statements. However, the Board is concerned that requiring offsetting may be costly for entities that do not have systems that separately identify the contracts that have been executed under each arrangement.

25. The Board decided to use the term *fair value* rather than *market value* in the final Interpretation. The concept of fair value is the same as that of market value as it was used in the Exposure Draft of a proposed Interpretation. The change was made to be consistent with the terminology used in Statement 107.

Comments on Exposure Draft

26. The Board issued a proposed Interpretation, *Offsetting of Amounts Related to Certain Contracts,* for comment on June 11, 1991 and received 59 letters of comment. Certain of the comments received and consideration of them are discussed in the following paragraphs.

27. Some respondents noted that the subject of offsetting is currently part of the Board's project on financial instruments and off-balance-sheet fi-

nancing and should be addressed there rather than in this Interpretation. This Interpretation is intended to provide interim guidance on the application of the general principle of a right of setoff and does not anticipate the conclusions to be reached in the financial instruments and off-balance-sheet financing project.

28. Some respondents asserted that the fair value of forward, interest rate swap, currency swap, option, and other conditional or exchange contracts are valuation accounts, not assets and liabilities, because they do not satisfy the definitions in Concepts Statement 6. The Board's reasons for concluding that the fair values recognized are assets and liabilities are discussed in paragraph 17.

29. Some respondents asserted that paragraph 253 of Concepts Statement 6, which addresses an estimated loss on a purchase commitment, seems to indicate that a valuation account may exist as a complete measurement of an asset or a liability. However, paragraphs 251-253 of Concepts Statement 6 acknowledge that the current accounting for estimated losses on purchase commitments is an expedient with no conceptual support. In concept, a valuation account decreases or increases the value of an asset or liability and has no existence apart from that asset or liability. Paragraph 251 differentiates between concept and expedient: "It [the estimated loss on a purchase commitment] is at best part of a liability and is not *by itself* an obligation to pay cash or otherwise sacrifice assets in the future. There is no asset from which it may be a deduction in present practice. . . . That predicament results, however, because estimated loss on purchase commitments is the recorded part of a series of transactions and events that are mostly unrecorded."

30. Some respondents reported that there has been a significant effort recently to develop *cross-product* master netting arrangements. A cross-product master netting arrangement consolidates a variety of types of contracts with a single counterparty and, in the event of default, entitles the nondefaulting party to terminate the entire arrangement and to demand net settlement of all contracts. The Board intended for the provisions of paragraph 10 to apply to conditional or exchange contracts executed with the same counterparty under a cross-product master netting arrangement. Thus, the Board revised the definition of master netting arrangement to clarify that a master netting arrangement exists when the reporting entity has multiple contracts, *whether for the same type of conditional or exchange contract or for different types of contracts,* with a single counterparty that are subject to a contractual agreement that provides for the net settlement of all contracts through a single payment in a single cur-

rency in the event of default on or termination of any one contract.

31. Some respondents commented that the proposed Interpretation seemed inconsistent in the list of financial instruments to which it applies. In particular, respondents cited the difference in the list of instruments included in paragraphs 1 and 2 and paragraph 10. Although paragraphs 1 and 2 were intended to be a more detailed list of financial instruments that raise the question of how to apply the conditions for right of setoff, they were not intended to be exhaustive. The Board believes that specifying an exhaustive list of instruments that are addressed by the Interpretation is not desirable and therefore has included *other conditional or exchange contracts* in paragraph 10 in the list of items to which this Interpretation applies so that the Interpretation will address not only those financial instruments that exist today but instruments that will result from future innovation.

32. Some respondents indicated that the provisions of paragraph 10 also should apply to repurchase and reverse repurchase agreements executed with the same counterparty under a master netting arrangement and to all interest rate swaps executed with the same counterparty under a master netting arrangement. For the reasons discussed in paragraph 22, the Board concluded that offsetting of these assets and liabilities is inappropriate unless those contracts otherwise satisfy the conditions in paragraph 5 for right of setoff.

33. Some respondents asserted that comparability will be adversely affected unless offsetting of fair value amounts for contracts executed under a master netting arrangement is mandatory. The Board acknowledges that respondents have valid concerns about comparability. However, the Board believes that the cost-benefit considerations, discussed in paragraph 24, that led the Board to permit, but not require, offsetting are valid.

34. Some respondents stated that an entity should be required to disclose whether it is offsetting fair value amounts so that financial statement users would be able to assess comparability between entities. This Interpretation does not affect the requirements of Statement 105 to disclose the extent, nature, and terms of financial instruments with off-balance-sheet risk and credit risk of financial instruments with off-balance-sheet credit risk. The Board believes that disclosure about whether an entity is offsetting fair value amounts under the provisions of paragraph 10 is not meaningful without also quantifying the effect of gross versus net presentation. Presumably an entity that reports gross amounts has determined that the cost-benefit of reporting net amounts is not justified; there-

fore, the Board concluded that the entity should not have to incur that same cost to make meaningful disclosures about the effect of choosing to report gross amounts.

35. Some respondents commented that having to apply the provisions of the proposed Interpretation would place U.S. financial institutions at a competitive disadvantage, thereby potentially reducing liquidity in the market. Other standard-setting organizations have issued guidance similar to the guidance in this Interpretation. For example, a joint Statement of Recommended Accounting Practice (SORP), *Off-Balance-Sheet Instruments and Other Commitments and Contingent Liabilities,* issued in November 1991 by the British Bankers' Association and the Irish Bankers' Federation, indicates that the value of interest rate, exchange rate, and market-price-related contracts should not be offset unless they are with the same counterparty and there is a legal right of setoff.

36. Some respondents indicated that paragraph 10 of this Interpretation seems inconsistent with the requirement in paragraph 5(c) that the reporting party intends to set off. Some respondents indicated that the requirement in paragraph 5(c) should be eliminated because intent is not relevant if the right and the ability to set off exist and because the requirement leads to noncomparability among financial statements. The Board concluded that a fundamental reconsideration of the requirements of paragraph 5 is beyond the scope of this Interpretation. The Board acknowledges the inconsistency between paragraph 10 and paragraph 5(c) and concluded, for the reasons stated in paragraph 21, that even if the reporting entity intends to set off only in the event of default or termination, it is appropriate to offset fair value amounts recognized for conditional or exchange contracts executed with the same counterparty under a master netting arrangement.

37. Some respondents commented that the effective date of this Interpretation should be delayed. In particular, banks requested a delay in the effective date to provide time to develop systems that can accumulate unrealized gains and losses on a counterparty basis and, thereby, permit offsetting of unrealized gains and losses for contracts executed under a master netting arrangement; to execute additional master netting arrangements; and to address capital adequacy concerns. Although the data required to implement the proposed Interpretation, gross unrealized gains and losses, are available and are currently disclosed under the requirements of Statement 105, the Board decided for practical reasons to delay the effective date of the Interpretation to provide adequate time for entities to resolve other implementation issues.

Background Information Incorporated from Technical Bulletin 88-2

38. This Interpretation supersedes FASB Technical Bulletin No. 88-2, *Definition of a Right of Setoff,* as of the effective date of this Interpretation or its earlier application. The guidance in that Technical Bulletin is incorporated substantially unchanged in paragraphs 5-7 of this Interpretation primarily as a matter of convenience. Some respondents to the proposed Interpretation suggested that the Background Information and Consideration of Comments Received on the Proposed Technical Bulletin section of Technical Bulletin 88-2 also be incorporated in this Interpretation. Respondents indicated that that information has been helpful in answering questions in practice and has provided preparers of financial statements with additional information to better understand the criteria needed for a right of setoff. Those sections of Technical Bulletin 88-2 have been reviewed and to the extent they are still relevant they have been incorporated as part of the basis for conclusions of this Interpretation in paragraphs 39-50. Those sections of this Interpretation have been brought forward from Technical Bulletin 88-2 essentially unchanged except for paragraph numbers; where applicable the word *Interpretation* has been substituted for the words *Technical Bulletin* and references to specific paragraphs of this Interpretation have been added.

39. FASB Statements No. 76, *Extinguishment of Debt,* and No. 77, *Reporting by Transferors for Transfers of Receivables with Recourse,* and FASB Technical Bulletin No. 85-2, *Accounting for Collateralized Mortgage Obligations (CMOs),* address extinguishment of recognized liabilities and derecognition of recognized assets. This Interpretation is based on the explanation in Statement 76 that offsetting is a display issue that does not presume the derecognition of recognized liabilities. Paragraph 40 of that Statement states:

> Several respondents to the revised Exposure Draft commented about offsetting assets against liabilities, though it was apparent that some respondents had confused *offsetting* with *extinguishment.* In the Board's view, *offsetting* is a display issue—how recognized assets and recognized liabilities should be presented in a balance sheet (or how other recognized elements should be displayed in a basic financial statement). In contrast, *extinguishment* is a recognition issue—whether an asset or a liability exists and whether continued recognition is warranted in the basic financial statements. This Statement addresses when debt ceases to be a liability that warrants continued recognition in the balance sheet.

Consideration of Comments Received Incorporated from Technical Bulletin 88-2

40. Some respondents to the proposed Interpretation suggested that the Consideration of Comments Received on the Proposed Technical Bulletin section of Technical Bulletin 88-2 also be incorporated in this Interpretation. Relevant portions of that section are contained herein in paragraphs 41-50.

41. A proposed Technical Bulletin, *Definition of a Right of Setoff,* was released for comment on April 14, 1988. Sixty letters of comment were received on the proposed Technical Bulletin. Certain of the comments received and consideration of them are discussed in the following paragraphs.

42. Some respondents questioned whether the proposed Technical Bulletin was intended to prohibit offsetting in circumstances in which offsetting is prescribed or permitted by various existing accounting pronouncements. They noted that such an objective would exceed the guidelines for a Technical Bulletin established in FASB Technical Bulletin No. 79-1 (Revised), *Purpose and Scope of FASB Technical Bulletins and Procedures for Issuance.* Paragraph 7 of this Interpretation clarifies that such a change is not intended.

43. Paragraph 2(a) of the proposed Technical Bulletin stated that the right of setoff "exists when each of *two* parties owes the other determinable amounts." Some respondents indicated that the number of entities involved in the transaction is not relevant to the decision to offset. The general principle of a right of setoff involves only two parties, and exceptions to that general principle should be limited to practices specifically permitted by the pronouncements indicated in paragraph 7 of this Interpretation.

44. Some respondents requested clarification of the requirement that each party owes the other determinable amounts. They specifically questioned whether those amounts need to be in the same currency, have the same maturities, and, if applicable, bear the same interest rate. If the parties meet the other criteria specified in the definition, specifying currency or interest rate requirements is unnecessary. However, if maturities differ, only the party with the nearer maturity could offset because the party with the longer term maturity must settle in the manner that the other party selects at the earlier maturity date.

45. Some respondents disagreed with the requirement that each party intend to set off and proposed that ability to set off should be sufficient. Those respondents further stated that the decision for net or gross settlement often is a matter of convenience or is tax motivated, would not be made until shortly

before settlement, and should not determine the presentation in a statement of financial position. Others indicated that intent is not a condition specified by Opinion 10 and that a new requirement should not be imposed. They also stated that intent is subjective, can exist in various degrees, and is difficult to substantiate, and that such a requirement will be applied inconsistently in practice. If a party does not intend to set off even though the ability to set off exists, an offsetting presentation in the statement of financial position is not representationally faithful. Acknowledgment of the intent to set off by the reporting party and, if applicable, demonstration of the execution of the setoff in similar situations meet the criterion of intent.

46. Other respondents supported requiring an intent to set off if the condition is limited to the party intending to set off. They observed that a reliable assessment of the other party's intent is impractical and that the lack of that intent is irrelevant if a unilateral legal right of setoff exists for one party. This Interpretation requires that only the reporting entity need have the intent to set off.

47. As used in the proposed Technical Bulletin, *enforceable by law* meant enforceable in a court proceeding by reason of statute or otherwise and demonstrable through examination of a contract. However, some respondents interpreted the requirement to mean the existence of a statute, and they cited situations in which the right of setoff is not specifically included in contractual agreements but was enforceable because of regulatory procedures or as part of normal business practice. The wording of the requirement in paragraph 5(d) of this Interpretation was revised to state *enforceable at law* in order to include those situations.

48. Some respondents opposed the bankruptcy protection requirement in paragraph 2(d) of the proposed Technical Bulletin as inconsistent with the going-concern concept. Commentators indicated that, as a general rule, accounting should reflect what is expected to occur in the normal course of business and protection in bankruptcy is not pertinent when the probability of bankruptcy is remote. Some respondents were concerned also about the difficulty of determining protection in

bankruptcy. They noted that the lack of a uniform bankruptcy law and the broad discretion provided to bankruptcy judges would make predicting the outcome of isolated transactions involved in a setoff situation extremely difficult. Those respondents also noted that legal opinions are costly, if obtainable at all, but would likely be required for management and auditors to determine if a right of setoff exists. Also, some banks pointed out that bankruptcy law generally is inapplicable to certain regulated industries due to regulatory intervention in insolvency. In light of these comments, the requirement of legal enforceability was deemed to be sufficient evidence of the right of setoff. This Interpretation does not include a separate requirement for protection in bankruptcy.

49. Some respondents questioned whether transactions involving a lender, a parent company, and its subsidiary could qualify under the proposed definition if all parties agree to the lender's unilateral right of setoff under a contractual arrangement. An example of that transaction is a loan by the foreign branch of a U.S. bank to a foreign subsidiary of a U.S. parent with the parent simultaneously depositing an amount equal to the loan in the U.S. bank for the same term. The deposit is collateral for the loan, and the bank has the legal right of setoff only in the event of default by the foreign subsidiary. Offsetting the collateral with the debt in that situation is inappropriate either in the bank's financial statements or in the consolidated financial statements of the parent and the foreign subsidiary.

50. Some respondents identified Statement 87 as an example in which plan assets are offset against the plan liabilities without meeting the criteria of the proposed Technical Bulletin. They indicated that other assets held in trust should be offset against the related liabilities in a manner similar to the reporting prescribed in Statement 87. Pension trusts are significantly different from most trusts and trusteed assets supporting other liabilities. The accounting and reporting for pensions was specifically considered by the Board in Statement 87. However, trusts established for other specified purposes, such as for decommissioning of a nuclear generating plant, would have to meet the conditions for setoff specified in paragraph 5.

FASB Interpretation No. 40
Applicability of Generally Accepted Accounting Principles to Mutual Life Insurance and Other Enterprises

an interpretation of FASB Statements No. 12, 60, 97, and 113

STATUS

Issued: April 1993

Effective Date: For financial statements issued for fiscal years beginning after December 15, 1994. Disclosure provisions effective for annual financial statements for fiscal years beginning after December 15, 1992.

Affects: No other pronouncements

Affected by: Paragraphs 4 and 5 amended by FAS 115

SUMMARY

This Interpretation clarifies that enterprises, including mutual life insurance enterprises, that issue financial statements described as prepared "in conformity with generally accepted accounting principles" are required to apply all applicable authoritative accounting pronouncements in preparing those statements. The Board recognizes that mutual life insurance enterprises, like a number of other regulated enterprises, prepare financial statements based on regulatory accounting practices that differ from generally accepted accounting principles and issue those financial statements to regulators. This Interpretation concludes that those financial statements should not be described as prepared "in conformity with generally accepted accounting principles."

This Interpretation is effective for financial statements issued for fiscal years beginning after December 15, 1994, except for the disclosure provisions, which are effective for fiscal years beginning after December 15, 1992. Earlier application is encouraged.

FASB Interpretation No. 40

Applicability of Generally Accepted Accounting Principles to Mutual Life Insurance and Other Enterprises

an interpretation of FASB Statements No. 12, 60, 97, and 113

CONTENTS

INTRODUCTION

1. The FASB has observed that some mutual life insurance enterprises are not following certain accounting pronouncements in financial statements that are described as prepared "in conformity with generally accepted accounting principles." This Interpretation clarifies the applicability of accounting pronouncements to mutual life insurance and other enterprises.

INTERPRETATION

2. Authoritative accounting pronouncements, such as FASB Statements and Interpretations and APB Opinions, apply to any enterprise (including mutual life insurance enterprises) that prepares financial statements that are intended to be in conformity with generally accepted accounting principles except to the extent that a pronouncement explicitly exempts that type of enterprise or that enterprise does not have the transaction, event, or circumstance addressed in the pronouncement.

3. The phrase *generally accepted accounting principles* embraces a number of sources of established accounting principles, in addition to pronouncements of the FASB, that are generally accepted in

the United States. Those sources are identified in AICPA Statement on Auditing Standards No. 69, *The Meaning of "Present Fairly in Conformity With Generally Accepted Accounting Principles" in the Independent Auditor's Report,* which provides the framework for auditors to judge the "fairness" of the overall presentation of financial statements intended to be in conformity with generally accepted accounting principles.

4. This Interpretation does not address or change the existing exemptions of mutual life insurance and other enterprises from FASB Statements No. 12, *Accounting for Certain Marketable Securities,* No. 60, *Accounting and Reporting by Insurance Enterprises,* No. 97, *Accounting and Reporting by Insurance Enterprises for Certain Long-Duration Contracts and for Realized Gains and Losses from the Sale of Investments,* and No. 113, *Accounting and Reporting for Reinsurance of Short-Duration and Long-Duration Contracts,*[1] which do not preclude those enterprises from applying the accounting guidance contained in those standards.

DISCLOSURE

5. Mutual life insurance enterprises, like all other business enterprises, are required to provide disclo-

---

[1] The FASB issued an Exposure Draft in September 1992, *Accounting for Certain Investments in Debt and Equity Securities,* that would supersede Statement 12 and would apply to mutual life insurance enterprises. The Board currently is redeliberating the issues in that Exposure Draft. In addition, the FASB has urged the AICPA to expeditiously complete its project on accounting by mutual life insurance enterprises for their insurance activities, which was the reason for the exemption of mutual life insurance enterprises in Statements 60, 97, and 113.

sures about significant accounting policies used to prepare financial statements that are intended to be in conformity with generally accepted accounting principles. APB Opinion No. 22, *Disclosure of Accounting Policies,* provides guidance on the content of those disclosures, which should include descriptions of accounting "principles and methods peculiar to the industry in which the reporting entity operates, even if such principles and methods are predominantly followed in that industry."[2] Because mutual life insurance enterprises are not required to apply Statements 12, 60, 97, and 113, those enterprises should specifically disclose the principles and methods used to account for marketable securities and insurance activities in accordance with Opinion 22.

6. Until the initial application of this Interpretation, annual financial statements for fiscal years beginning after December 15, 1992 shall provide a brief description of the Interpretation, including its effective date and transition provisions, and disclose that financial statements prepared on the basis of statutory accounting practices will no longer be described as prepared in conformity with generally accepted accounting principles after the effective date of the Interpretation.

EFFECTIVE DATE AND TRANSITION

7. The general provisions of this Interpretation are effective for financial statements issued for fiscal years beginning after December 15, 1994, and the disclosures specified in paragraphs 5 and 6 are effective for annual financial statements for fiscal years beginning after December 15, 1992. Earlier application is encouraged. The effect of initially applying this Interpretation shall be reported retroactively through restatement of all previously issued annual financial statements presented for comparative purposes for fiscal years beginning after December 15, 1992. Previously issued financial statements for any number of consecutive annual periods preceding that date may be restated to conform to the provisions of this Interpretation. The cumulative effect of adopting this Interpretation shall be included in the earliest year restated.

This Interpretation was adopted by the unanimous vote of the seven members of the Financial Accounting Standards Board:

Dennis R. Beresford,	Victor H. Brown	A. Clarence Sampson
Chairman	James J. Leisenring	Robert J. Swieringa
Joseph V. Anania	Robert H. Northcutt	

Appendix

BACKGROUND INFORMATION AND BASIS FOR CONCLUSIONS

Introduction

8. This appendix summarizes considerations that Board members deemed significant in reaching the conclusions in this Interpretation. Individual Board members gave greater weight to some factors than to others.

Background Information

9. In 1972, the AICPA published an Industry Audit Guide, *Audits of Stock Life Insurance Companies* (Guide). The Guide applies only to stock life insurance companies because a consensus was not reached at the time on the appropriate insurance accounting and reporting principles for mutual life insurance enterprises.[3] The AICPA Insurance Companies Committee subsequently formed a task force to address accounting and reporting by mutual life insurance enterprises but later suspended that project.

10. In 1982, the Board issued Statement 60, which extracted the specialized accounting practices from the Guide. Statement 60 specifically exempted mutual life insurance enterprises from its requirements but did not exempt those enterprises from any other accounting pronouncements. However, absent a definitive resolution of the issue of what insurance accounting and reporting principles should apply to mutual life insurance enterprises, many of them apparently considered themselves to be exempt from other pronouncements that establish generally accepted accounting principles.

---

[2]Opinion 22, par. 12(b).

[3]Although the Guide does not apply to mutual life insurance enterprises, its preface identifies certain sections that "should be used by auditors as a guide for audits of mutual life insurance companies." In addition, the preface states that "principal accounting policies and practices of mutual life insurance companies should be disclosed, as required by APB Opinion No. 22." That requirement is clarified by paragraph 5 of this Interpretation.

11. The FASB became aware that many mutual life insurance enterprises prepare financial statements based on statutory accounting practices, which differ from generally accepted accounting principles, and that those financial statements often are described as having been prepared in conformity with generally accepted accounting principles. In response to that information, the Board held an educational public meeting on July 8, 1992 with individuals who prepare or audit financial statements of mutual life insurance enterprises to discuss financial reporting by those enterprises.

12. At that meeting, the Board was informed that practice had evolved to consider statutory accounting practices as generally accepted accounting principles for mutual life insurance enterprises. Consequently, on July 15, 1992, the Board added to its agenda a limited-scope project to clarify that all applicable authoritative accounting pronouncements, such as those issued by the FASB, must be followed by a mutual life insurance enterprise to appropriately describe its financial statements as being in conformity with generally accepted accounting principles.

13. The Board issued a proposed Interpretation, *Applicability of Generally Accepted Accounting Principles to Mutual Life Insurance Enterprises,* for public comment on August 17, 1992. Concurrently, the Board urged the AICPA to reactivate and expeditiously complete its project on accounting and reporting by mutual life insurance enterprises for their insurance activities. The AICPA responded by submitting a project prospectus for the FASB's consideration, and the AICPA's Insurance Companies Committee established a special task force to address the application of Statements 60, 97, and 113 to the insurance activities of mutual life insurance enterprises.

14. Thirty-nine comment letters were received in response to the proposed Interpretation. The Board concluded that it could reach an informed decision without holding a public hearing but invited those who responded to the proposed Interpretation to participate in a public Board meeting in January 1993.

Basis for Conclusions

15. Accounting pronouncements that define generally accepted accounting principles usually apply to all enterprises that have the transaction, event, or circumstance addressed. However, certain enti-

ties may in some cases be explicitly exempted from a particular pronouncement. The Board believes that those situations do not change or override the applicability of other accounting pronouncements. Users of financial statements that are described as having been prepared in conformity with generally accepted accounting principles should expect that all appropriate accounting pronouncements have been applied.

16. The Board has observed the practice in the mutual life insurance industry of issuing financial statements using statutory accounting practices and not applying the accounting principles required for those statements to be described as "in conformity with generally accepted accounting principles." This Interpretation is specifically directed to mutual life insurance enterprises because the Board understands that other mutual entities either report on a comprehensive basis of accounting other than generally accepted accounting principles or follow all applicable accounting and disclosure requirements in accordance with generally accepted accounting principles. However, the Board intends this Interpretation to apply broadly to all entities that prepare financial statements that are described as having been prepared in conformity with generally accepted accounting principles and modified the title of the Interpretation to make that explicit.

17. The Board recognizes that mutual life insurance enterprises and other regulated enterprises may be required to prepare financial statements to be submitted to regulators based on accounting methods and practices prescribed or permitted by those regulators and that those methods and practices may differ from generally accepted accounting principles. AICPA Statement on Auditing Standards No. 62, *Special Reports,* provides guidance for reporting on financial statements prepared on a comprehensive basis other than generally accepted accounting principles.

18. This Interpretation does not preclude mutual life insurance enterprises from issuing financial statements prepared under statutory accounting practices but concludes that those financial statements should not be described as prepared "in conformity with generally accepted accounting principles." The Board understands that mutual life insurance enterprises that file their financial statements with the SEC are permitted by Regulation S-X, Rule 7-02(b) to file financial statements prepared in accordance with statutory accounting practices.[4]

---

[4]SEC Regulation S-X, Rule 7-02(b) states that "financial statements filed for mutual life insurance companies and wholly-owned stock insurance company subsidiaries of mutual life insurance companies may be prepared in accordance with statutory accounting requirements."

19. The Board believes that this Interpretation will improve comparability of financial reporting among insurance enterprises for transactions and events other than those specifically addressed in Statements 12, 60, 97, and 113 to the extent that mutual life insurance enterprises decide to prepare financial statements in conformity with generally accepted accounting principles and that it will assist users in understanding where financial statements are or are not comparable. The Board recognizes that comparability of financial reporting among insurance enterprises electing to adopt generally accepted accounting principles may not be achieved until a comprehensive model is developed for accounting for the insurance activities of mutual life insurance enterprises.

20. The Exposure Draft proposed that this Interpretation would be effective for fiscal years beginning after December 15, 1992. Many respondents urged the Board to delay the proposed effective date until the availability of guidance from the AICPA on accounting and reporting by mutual life insurance enterprises for their insurance activities. In its redeliberations, the Board discussed effective dates intended to allow mutual life insurance enterprises sufficient time to assimilate the Interpretation's requirements and to obtain the required information. The Board decided that a two-year delay of the proposed effective date to fiscal years beginning after December 15, 1994 would be adequate for that purpose and also would allow time for the AICPA to develop guidance for mutual life insurance enterprises on accounting and reporting for their insurance activities that could be concurrently effective.

21. The proposed Interpretation would have permitted, but not required, mutual life insurance enterprises to restate financial statements issued for fiscal years before the effective date. Several respondents to the Exposure Draft asked the Board to clarify how that provision would be applied when multiple accounting pronouncements, each specifying its own effective date and transition, are initially adopted when preparing financial statements pursuant to this Interpretation. Upon reconsideration, the Board decided to require a single method for reporting the effect of initially applying this Interpretation because the understandability and comparability of financial statements of mutual life insurance enterprises, both in the year of adoption and in subsequent periods, would be improved by a uniform transition method. For practical reasons, the Board decided that the Interpretation should not address detailed implementation issues that may result from that requirement.

22. Adoption of the provisions of this Interpretation may establish a fundamentally different basis of ac-

counting for mutual life insurance enterprises that currently prepare financial statements based on statutory accounting practices that differ significantly from generally accepted accounting principles. Therefore, the Board decided that retroactive restatement is the appropriate method for reporting the effect of initially applying this Interpretation. The Board also recognized that restatement of all years may be costly and may require information that mutual life insurance enterprises may no longer have or that their past procedures did not require. The Board concluded that transition is, to a significant extent, a practical matter and limited the requirement to restate previously issued annual financial statements that are presented for comparative purposes to fiscal years beginning after December 15, 1992. The combined effect of transition and of delaying the effective date of the Interpretation for a two-year period is to reflect its adoption in the period initially proposed by the Exposure Draft—fiscal years beginning after December 15, 1992—but to provide a two-year delay for implementation.

23. The Exposure Draft proposed an effective date of years beginning after December 15, 1992 and, therefore, did not address whether annual financial statements issued prior to the effective date of the Interpretation should disclose the impact it will have on the financial statements of mutual life insurance enterprises when adopted in a future period. In concluding to extend the effective date of this Interpretation by two years, the Board decided to require the disclosures specified in paragraph 6 because existing accounting and auditing literature is unclear as to whether any disclosure would be required of those mutual life insurance enterprises that do not intend or have not yet determined whether to prepare financial statements pursuant to this Interpretation. The Board believes that users of the statutory financial statements of mutual life insurance enterprises that currently are described as having been prepared in conformity with generally accepted accounting principles should be informed that those financial statements will no longer be described in that manner when the Interpretation becomes effective.

24. The Board recognizes that some mutual life insurance enterprises currently applying generally accepted accounting principles already may be in substantial compliance with the provisions of this Interpretation. This Interpretation would not preclude those enterprises from providing disclosures to that effect or from disclosing the status of their financial reporting practices. The effective date of the disclosure provisions of this Interpretation is the same as the effective date originally proposed for all provisions of the Exposure Draft.

(The next page is 1003.)

FASB Statements of
Financial Accounting Concepts

FASB CONCEPTS (CON)

TABLE OF CONTENTS

Statement of Financial Accounting Concepts No. 1 Objectives of Financial Reporting by Business Enterprises

STATUS

Issued: November 1978

Affects: No other pronouncements

Affected by: No other pronouncements

HIGHLIGHTS

[Best understood in context of full Statement]

- Financial reporting is not an end in itself but is intended to provide information that is useful in making business and economic decisions.

- The objectives of financial reporting are not immutable—they are affected by the economic, legal, political, and social environment in which financial reporting takes place.

- The objectives are also affected by the characteristics and limitations of the kind of information that financial reporting can provide.

  —The information pertains to business enterprises rather than to industries or the economy as a whole.

  —The information often results from approximate, rather than exact, measures.

  —The information largely reflects the financial effects of transactions and events that have already happened.

  —The information is but one source of information needed by those who make decisions about business enterprises.

  —The information is provided and used at a cost.

- The objectives in this Statement are those of general purpose external financial reporting by business enterprises.

  —The objectives stem primarily from the needs of external users who lack the authority to prescribe the information they want and must rely on information management communicates to them.

  —The objectives are directed toward the common interests of many users in the ability of an enterprise to generate favorable cash flows but are phrased using investment and credit decisions as a reference to give them a focus. The objectives are intended to be broad rather than narrow.

  —The objectives pertain to financial reporting and are not restricted to financial statements.

- The objectives state that:

  —Financial reporting should provide information that is useful to present and potential investors and creditors and other users in making rational investment, credit, and similar decisions. The information should be comprehensible to those who have a reasonable understanding of business and economic activities and are willing to study the information with reasonable diligence.

—Financial reporting should provide information to help present and potential investors and creditors and other users in assessing the amounts, timing, and uncertainty of prospective cash receipts from dividends or interest and the proceeds from the sale, redemption, or maturity of securities or loans. Since investors' and creditors' cash flows are related to enterprise cash flows, financial reporting should provide information to help investors, creditors, and others assess the amounts, timing, and uncertainty of prospective net cash inflows to the related enterprise.

—Financial reporting should provide information about the economic resources of an enterprise, the claims to those resources (obligations of the enterprise to transfer resources to other entities and owners' equity), and the effects of transactions, events, and circumstances that change its resources and claims to those resources.

- "Investors" and "creditors" are used broadly and include not only those who have or contemplate having a claim to enterprise resources but also those who advise or represent them.

- Although investment and credit decisions reflect investors' and creditors' expectations about future enterprise performance, those expectations are commonly based at least partly on evaluations of past enterprise performance.

- The primary focus of financial reporting is information about earnings and its components.

- Information about enterprise earnings based on accrual accounting generally provides a better indication of an enterprise's present and continuing ability to generate favorable cash flows than information limited to the financial effects of cash receipts and payments.

- Financial reporting is expected to provide information about an enterprise's financial performance during a period and about how management of an enterprise has discharged its stewardship responsibility to owners.

- Financial accounting is not designed to measure directly the value of a business enterprise, but the information it provides may be helpful to those who wish to estimate its value.

- Investors, creditors, and others may use reported earnings and information about the elements of financial statements in various ways to assess the prospects for cash flows. They may wish, for example, to evaluate management's performance, estimate "earning power," predict future earnings, assess risk, or to confirm, change, or reject earlier predictions or assessments. Although financial reporting should provide basic information to aid them, they do their own evaluating, estimating, predicting, assessing, confirming, changing, or rejecting.

- Management knows more about the enterprise and its affairs than investors, creditors, or other "outsiders" and accordingly can often increase the usefulness of financial information by identifying certain events and circumstances and explaining their financial effects on the enterprise.

* * * * *

Statement of Financial Accounting Concepts No. 1
Objectives of Financial Reporting by Business Enterprises

STATEMENTS OF FINANCIAL ACCOUNTING CONCEPTS

This is the first in a series of Statements of Financial Accounting Concepts. The purpose of the series is to set forth fundamentals on which financial accounting and reporting standards will be based. More specifically, Statements of Financial Accounting Concepts are intended to establish the objectives and concepts that the Financial Accounting Standards Board will use in developing standards of financial accounting and reporting.

The Board itself is likely to be the major user and thus the most direct beneficiary of the guidance provided by the new series. However, knowledge of the objectives and concepts the Board uses should enable all who are affected by or interested in financial accounting standards to better understand the content and limitations of information provided by financial accounting and reporting, thereby furthering their ability to use that information effectively and enhancing confidence in financial accounting and reporting. That knowledge, if used with care, may also provide guidance in resolving new or emerging problems of financial accounting and reporting in the absence of applicable authoritative pronouncements.

Unlike a Statement of Financial Accounting Standards, a Statement of Financial Accounting Concepts does not establish generally accepted accounting principles and therefore is not intended to invoke the application of Rule 203 of the Rules of Conduct of the Code of Professional Ethics of the American Institute of Certified Public Accountants (or successor rule or arrangement of similar scope and intent).* Like other pronouncements of the Board, a Statement of Financial Accounting Concepts may be amended, superseded, or withdrawn by appropriate action under the Board's *Rules of Procedure.*

The Board recognizes that in certain respects current generally accepted accounting principles may be inconsistent with those that may derive from the objectives and concepts set forth in this Statement and others in the series. In due course, the Board expects to reexamine its pronouncements, pronouncements of predecessor standard-setting bodies, and existing financial reporting practice in the light of newly enunciated objectives and concepts. In the meantime, a Statement of Financial Accounting Concepts does not (a) require a change in existing generally accepted accounting principles, (b) amend, modify, or interpret Statements of Financial Accounting Standards, Interpretations of the FASB, effective Opinions of the Accounting Principles Board, or effective Bulletins of the Committee on Accounting Procedure, or (c) justify either changing existing generally accepted accounting and reporting practices or interpreting the pronouncements listed in (b) based on personal interpretations of the objectives and concepts in the Statements of Financial Accounting Concepts.

To establish objectives and concepts will not, by itself, directly solve financial accounting and reporting problems. Rather, objectives and concepts are tools for solving problems. Moreover, although individual Statements of Financial Accounting Concepts may be issued serially, they will form a cohesive set of interrelated concepts and will often need to be used jointly.

The new series of Statements of Financial Accounting Concepts is intended and expected to serve the public interest within the context of the role of financial accounting and reporting in the economy—to provide evenhanded financial and other information that, together with information from other sources, facilitates efficient functioning of capital and other markets and otherwise assists in promoting efficient allocation of scarce resources in the economy.

---

*Rule 203 prohibits a member of the American Institute of Certified Public Accountants from expressing an opinion that financial statements conform with generally accepted accounting principles if those statements contain a material departure from an accounting principle promulgated by the Financial Accounting Standards Board, unless the member can demonstrate that because of unusual circumstances the financial statements otherwise would have been misleading.

Contents

This Statement contains no conclusions about matters expected to be covered in other Statements resulting from the Board's conceptual framework project, such as objectives of financial reporting by organizations other than business enterprises; elements of financial statements and their recognition, measurement, and display; capital maintenance; unit of measure; criteria for distinguishing information to be included in financial statements from that which should be provided by other means of financial reporting; and criteria for evaluating and selecting accounting information (qualitative characteristics).

INTRODUCTION AND BACKGROUND

1. This Statement establishes the objectives of general purpose external financial reporting by business enterprises. Its concentration on business enterprises is not intended to imply that the Board has concluded that the uses and objectives of financial reporting by other kinds of entities are, or should be, the same as or different from those of business enterprises. Those and related matters, including whether and, if so, how business enterprises and other organizations should be distinguished for the purpose of establishing objectives of and basic concepts underlying financial reporting, are issues in another phase of the Board's conceptual framework project.[1]

2. This Statement is the first of a planned series of publications in the Board's conceptual framework project. Later Statements are expected to cover the elements of financial statements and their recognition, measurement, and display as well as related matters such as capital maintenance, unit of

measure, criteria for distinguishing information to be included in financial statements from that which should be provided by other means of financial reporting, and criteria for evaluating and selecting accounting information (qualitative characteristics). Accordingly, this Statement contains no conclusions about matters such as the identity, number, or form of financial statements or about the attributes to be measured[2] or the unit of measure to be used. Thus, although designation in the objectives of certain information as relevant has implications for communicating the information, the Statement should not be interpreted as implying a particular set of financial statements. Nor should the Statement be interpreted as suggesting that the relative merits of various attributes, such as historical cost/historical proceeds or current cost/current proceeds, have been resolved. Similarly, references in it to measures in units of money should not be interpreted as precluding the possibility of measures in constant dollars (units of money having constant purchasing power).

3. This Statement also does not specify financial accounting standards prescribing accounting procedures or disclosure practices for particular items or events; rather it describes concepts and relations that will underlie future financial accounting standards and practices and in due course serve as a basis for evaluating existing standards and practices. Its effect on financial reporting will be reflected primarily in Statements of Financial Accounting Standards (please see "Statements of Financial Accounting Concepts" on the preceding page). Until the FASB reexamines its pronouncements, pronouncements of predecessor standard-setting bodies, and existing financial reporting practices,

---

[1]In August 1977, the Board announced its sponsorship of a research study on the objectives and basic concepts underlying financial reporting by organizations other than business enterprises. The Board published the research report, *Financial Accounting in Nonbusiness Organizations: An Exploratory Study of Conceptual Issues*, by Robert N. Anthony, in May 1978. It issued a *Discussion Memorandum*, "Objectives of Financial Reporting by Nonbusiness Organizations," in June 1978 and held public hearings in October and November 1978.

[2]"Attributes to be measured" refers to the traits or aspects of an element to be quantified or measured, such as historical cost/historical proceeds, current cost/current proceeds, etc. Attribute is a narrower concept than measurement, which includes not only identifying the attribute to be measured but also selecting a scale of measurement (for example, units of money or units of constant purchasing power). "Property" is commonly used in the sciences to describe the trait or aspect of an object being measured, such as the length of a table or the weight of a stone. But "property" may be confused with land and buildings in financial reporting contexts, and "attribute" has become common in accounting literature and is used in this Statement.

pronouncements such as *APB Statement No. 4,* "Basic Concepts and Accounting Principles Underlying Financial Statements of Business Enterprises," or the *Accounting Terminology Bulletins* will continue to serve their intended purpose—to describe objectives and concepts underlying standards and practices existing before the issuance of this Statement.

4. This Statement includes a brief exposition of the reasons for the Board's conclusions.[3] It therefore includes no separate Appendix containing a basis for conclusions. Appendix A to this Statement contains background information for the Statement.

Financial Statements and Financial Reporting

5. The objectives in this Statement pertain to financial reporting and are not restricted to information communicated by financial statements. Although financial reporting and financial statements have essentially the same objectives, some useful information is better provided by financial statements and some is better provided, or can only be provided, by means of financial reporting other than financial statements. The following paragraphs briefly describe some major characteristics of financial reporting and financial statements and give some examples, but they draw no clear distinction between financial reporting and financial statements and leave extremely broad the scope of financial reporting. The Board will draw boundaries, as needed, in other parts of the conceptual framework project or in financial accounting standards.

6. Financial statements are a central feature of financial reporting. They are a principal means of communicating accounting information to those outside an enterprise. Although financial statements may also contain information from sources other than accounting records, accounting systems are generally organized on the basis of the elements of financial statements (assets, liabilities, revenues, expenses, etc.) and provide the bulk of the information for financial statements. The financial statements now most frequently provided are (a) balance sheet or statement of financial position, (b) income or earnings statement, (c) statement of retained earnings, (d) statement of other changes in owners' or stockholders' equity, and (e) statement of changes in financial position (statement of sources and applications of funds). To list those examples from existing practice implies no conclusions about the identity, number, or form of financial statements because those matters are yet to be considered in the conceptual framework project (paragraph 2).

7. Financial reporting includes not only financial statements but also other means of communicating information that relates, directly or indirectly, to the information provided by the accounting system—that is, information about an enterprise's resources, obligations, earnings, etc. Management may communicate information to those outside an enterprise by means of financial reporting other than formal financial statements either because the information is required to be disclosed by authoritative pronouncement, regulatory rule, or custom or because management considers it useful to those outside the enterprise and discloses it voluntarily. Information communicated by means of financial reporting other than financial statements may take various forms and relate to various matters. Corporate annual reports, prospectuses, and annual reports filed with the Securities and Exchange Commission are common examples of reports that include financial statements, other financial information, and nonfinancial information. News releases, management's forecasts or other descriptions of its plans or expectations, and descriptions of an enterprise's social or environmental impact are examples of reports giving financial information other than financial statements or giving only nonfinancial information.

8. Financial statements are often audited by independent accountants for the purpose of enhancing confidence in their reliability. Some financial reporting by management outside the financial statements is audited, or is reviewed but not audited, by independent accountants or other experts, and some is provided by management without audit or review by persons outside the enterprise.

Environmental Context of Objectives

9. Financial reporting is not an end in itself but is intended to provide information that is useful in making business and economic decisions—for making reasoned choices among alternative uses of scarce resources in the conduct of business and economic activities. Thus, the objectives set forth stem largely from the needs of those for whom the information is intended, which in turn depend significantly on the nature of the economic activities and decisions with which the users are involved. Accordingly, the objectives in this Statement are affected by the economic, legal, political, and social environment in the United States. The objectives are also affected by characteristics and limitations of the information that financial reporting can provide (paragraphs 17-23).

---

[3]The Board has previously provided a more detailed discussion of the environment of financial reporting and the basis underlying the Board's conclusions on objectives of financial reporting by business enterprises in Chapters 1-3 of *Tentative Conclusions on Objectives of Financial Statements of Business Enterprises* (Stamford, CT: Financial Accounting Standards Board, December 2, 1976). The Board may reissue pertinent parts of that discussion, and perhaps other related material, in a more permanent publication.

10. The United States has a highly developed exchange economy. Most goods and services are exchanged for money or claims to money instead of being consumed by their producers. Most goods and services have money prices, and cash (ready money, including currency, coins, and money on deposit) is prized because of what it can buy. Members of the society carry out their consumption, saving, and investment decisions by allocating their present and expected cash resources.

11. Production and marketing of goods and services often involve long, continuous, or intricate processes that require large amounts of capital, which in turn require substantial saving in the economy. Savings are often invested through a complex set of intermediaries which offer savers diverse types of ownership and creditor claims, many of which can be freely traded or otherwise converted to cash.

12. Most productive activity in the United States is carried on through investor-owned business enterprises, including many large corporations that buy, sell, and obtain financing in national or multinational markets. Since investor-owners are commonly more interested in returns from dividends and market price appreciation of their securities than in active participation in directing corporate affairs, directors and professional managers commonly control enterprise resources and decide how those resources are allocated in enterprise operations. Management is accountable to owner-investors, both directly and through an elected board of directors, for planning and controlling enterprise operations in their interests, including gaining or maintaining competitive advantage or parity in the markets in which the enterprise buys, sells, and obtains financing and considering and balancing various other, often competing interests, such as those of employees, customers, lenders, suppliers, and government.

13. Business enterprises raise capital for production and marketing activities not only from financial institutions and small groups of individuals but also from the public through issuing equity and debt securities that are widely traded in highly developed securities markets. Numerous, perhaps most, transactions in those markets are transfers from one investor or creditor to another with no part of the exchange price going to the issuing enterprise. But those transactions set the market prices for particular securities and thereby affect an enterprise's ability to attract investment funds and its cost of raising capital. Those having funds to invest normally assess the expected costs, expected returns, and expected risks of alternative investment opportuni-

ties. They attempt to balance expected risks and returns and generally invest in high risk ventures only if they expect commensurately high returns and will accept low expected returns only if expected risk is commensurately low. A business enterprise is unlikely to be able to compete successfully in the markets for lendable or investment funds unless lenders and investors expect the enterprise to be able to sell its output at prices sufficiently in excess of its costs to enable them to expect a return from interest or dividends and market price appreciation commensurate with the risks they perceive. Thus, well-developed securities markets tend to allocate scarce resources to enterprises that use them efficiently and away from inefficient enterprises.

14. In the United States, productive resources are generally privately owned rather than government owned. Markets—which vary from those that are highly competitive, including many commodities and securities markets, to those that involve regulated monopolies, including markets for telephone service or electricity—are significant factors in resource allocation in the economy. However, government intervenes in the allocation process in many ways and for various purposes. For example, it intervenes directly by collecting taxes, borrowing, and spending for its purchases of goods and services for government operations and programs; by regulating business activities; or by paying subsidies. It intervenes less directly through broad tax, monetary, and fiscal policies. Government also has a broad interest in the impact of business enterprises on the community at large and may intervene to alter that impact. Many government interventions are expressly designed to work through market forces, but even government actions that are not so designed may significantly affect the balance of market forces.

15. Moreover, government is a major supplier of economic statistics and other economic information that are widely used by management, investors, and others interested in individual business enterprises and are commonly included in news reports and other statistics and analyses in ways that may broadly affect perceptions about business and economic matters. Although government statistics are primarily "macro" in nature (pertaining to the economy as a whole or to large segments of it) and do not generally disclose much about individual business enterprises, they are based to a considerable extent on information of the kind provided by financial reporting by individual business enterprises.

16. The effectiveness of individuals, enterprises, markets, and government in allocating scarce resources among competing uses is enhanced if

those who make economic decisions have information that reflects the relative standing and performance of business enterprises to assist them in evaluating alternative courses of action and the expected returns, costs, and risks of each. The function of financial reporting is to provide information that is useful to those who make economic decisions about business enterprises and about investments in or loans to business enterprises. Independent auditors commonly examine or review financial statements and perhaps other information, and both those who provide and those who use that information often view an independent auditor's opinion as enhancing the reliability or credibility of the information.

Characteristics and Limitations of Information Provided

17. The objectives of financial reporting are affected not only by the environment in which financial reporting takes place but also by the characteristics and limitations of the kind of information that financial reporting, and particularly financial statements, can provide. The information is to a significant extent financial information based on approximate measures of the financial effects on individual business enterprises of transactions and events that have already happened; it cannot be provided or used without incurring a cost.

18. The information provided by financial reporting is primarily financial in nature—it is generally quantified and expressed in units of money. Information that is to be formally incorporated in financial statements must be quantifiable in units of money. Other information can be disclosed in financial statements (including notes) or by other means, but financial statements involve adding, subtracting, multiplying, and dividing numbers depicting economic things and events and require a common denominator. The numbers are usually exchange prices or amounts derived from exchange prices. Quantified nonfinancial information (such as number of employees or units of product produced or sold) and nonquantified information (such as descriptions of operations or explanations of policies) that are reported normally relate to or underlie the financial information. Financial information is often limited by the need to measure in units of money or by constraints inherent in procedures, such as verification, that are commonly used to enhance the reliability or objectivity of the information.

19. The information provided by financial reporting pertains to individual business enterprises, which may comprise two or more affiliated entities, rather than to industries or an economy as a whole or to members of society as consumers. Financial reporting may provide information about industries and economies in which an enterprise operates but usually only to the extent the information is relevant to understanding the enterprise. It does not attempt to measure the degree to which the consumption of wealth satisfies consumers' wants. Since business enterprises are producers and distributors of scarce resources, financial reporting bears on the allocation of economic resources to producing and distributing activities and focuses on the creation of, use of, and rights to wealth and the sharing of risks associated with wealth.

20. The information provided by financial reporting often results from approximate, rather than exact, measures. The measures commonly involve numerous estimates, classifications, summarizations, judgments, and allocations. The outcome of economic activity in a dynamic economy is uncertain and results from combinations of many factors. Thus, despite the aura of precision that may seem to surround financial reporting in general and financial statements in particular, with few exceptions the measures are approximations, which may be based on rules and conventions, rather than exact amounts.

21. The information provided by financial reporting largely reflects the financial effects of transactions and events that have already happened. Management may communicate information about its plans or projections, but financial statements and most other financial reporting are historical. For example, the acquisition price of land, the current market price of a marketable equity security, and the current replacement price of an inventory are all historical data—no future prices are involved. Estimates resting on expectations of the future are often needed in financial reporting, but their major use, especially of those formally incorporated in financial statements, is to measure financial effects of past transactions or events or the present status of an asset or liability. For example, if depreciable assets are accounted for at cost, estimates of useful lives are needed to determine current depreciation and the current undepreciated cost of the asset. Even the discounted amount of future cash payments required by a long-term debt contract is, as the name implies, a "present value" of the liability. The information is largely historical, but those who use it may try to predict the future or may use the information to confirm or reject their previous predictions. To provide information about the past as an aid in assessing the future is not to imply that the future can be predicted merely by extrapolating past trends or relationships. Users of the information need to assess the possible or probable impact of factors that may cause change and form their own expectations about the future and its relation to the past.

22. Financial reporting is but one source of information needed by those who make economic decisions about business enterprises. Business enterprises and those who have economic interests in them are affected by numerous factors that interact with each other in complex ways. Those who use financial information for business and economic decisions need to combine information provided by financial reporting with pertinent information from other sources, for example, information about general economic conditions or expectations, political events and political climate, or industry outlook.

23. The information provided by financial reporting involves a cost to provide and use, and generally the benefits of information provided should be expected to at least equal the cost involved. The cost includes not only the resources directly expended to provide the information but may also include adverse effects on an enterprise or its stockholders from disclosing it. For example, comments about a pending lawsuit may jeopardize a successful defense, or comments about future plans may jeopardize a competitive advantage. The collective time needed to understand and use information is also a cost. Sometimes a disparity between costs and benefits is obvious. However, the benefits from financial information are usually difficult or impossible to measure objectively, and the costs often are; different persons will honestly disagree about whether the benefits of the information justify its costs.

Potential Users and Their Interests

24. Many people base economic decisions on their relationships to and knowledge about business enterprises and thus are potentially interested in the information provided by financial reporting. Among the potential users are owners, lenders, suppliers, potential investors and creditors, employees, management, directors, customers, financial analysts and advisors, brokers, underwriters, stock exchanges, lawyers, economists, taxing authorities, regulatory authorities, legislators, financial press and reporting agencies, labor unions, trade associations, business researchers, teachers and students, and the public. Members and potential members of some groups—such as owners, creditors, and employees—have or contemplate having direct economic interests in particular business enterprises. Managers and directors, who are charged with managing the enterprise in the interest of owners (paragraph 12), also have a direct interest. Members of other groups—such as financial analysts and advisors, regulatory authorities, and labor unions—have derived or indirect interests because they advise or represent those who have or contemplate having direct interests.

25. Potential users of financial information most directly concerned with a particular business enterprise are generally interested in its ability to generate favorable cash flows because their decisions relate to amounts, timing, and uncertainties of expected cash flows. To investors, lenders, suppliers, and employees, a business enterprise is a source of cash in the form of dividends or interest and perhaps appreciated market prices, repayment of borrowing, payment for goods or services, or salaries or wages. They invest cash, goods, or services in an enterprise and expect to obtain sufficient cash in return to make the investment worthwhile. They are directly concerned with the ability of the enterprise to generate favorable cash flows and may also be concerned with how the market's perception of that ability affects the relative prices of its securities. To customers, a business enterprise is a source of goods or services, but only by obtaining sufficient cash to pay for the resources it uses and to meet its other obligations can the enterprise provide those goods or services. To managers, the cash flows of a business enterprise are a significant part of their management responsibilities, including their accountability to directors and owners. Many, if not most, of their decisions have cash flow consequences for the enterprise. Thus, investors, creditors, employees, customers, and managers significantly share a common interest in an enterprise's ability to generate favorable cash flows. Other potential users of financial information share the same interest, derived from investors, creditors, employees, customers, or managers whom they advise or represent or derived from an interest in how those groups (and especially stockholders) are faring.

26. Some of the potential users listed in paragraph 24 may have specialized needs but also have the power to obtain information needed. For example, both the information needed to enforce tax laws and regulations and the information needed to set rates for public utilities are specialized needs. However, although both taxing authorities and rate-making bodies often use the information in financial statements for their purposes, both also have statutory authority to require the specific information they need to fulfill their functions and do not need to rely on information provided to other groups. Some investors and creditors or potential investors and creditors may also be able to require a business enterprise to provide specified information to meet a particular need—for example, a bank or insurance company negotiating with an enterprise for a large loan or private placement of securities can often obtain desired information by making the information a condition for completing the transaction.

27. Except for management, and to some extent directors, the potential users listed in paragraph 24 are commonly described as "external users," and accounting and reporting are sometimes divided conventionally into internal and external parts. That broad distinction more nearly suits the purposes of this Statement than does another common conventional distinction—that between managerial or management accounting (which is designed to assist management decision making, planning, and control at the various administrative levels of an enterprise) and financial accounting (which is concerned with accounting for an enterprise's assets, liabilities, revenues, expenses, earnings, etc.)[4] because management uses information provided by both management accounting and financial accounting. Management needs, in addition to financial accounting information, a great deal of management accounting information to carry out its responsibilities in planning and controlling operations. Much of that information relates to particular decisions or to particular cost or profit centers and is often provided in more detail than is considered necessary or appropriate for external financial reporting, even though the same accounting system normally accumulates, processes, and provides the information whether it is called managerial or financial or internal or external. Directors usually have access to at least some information available to management that is normally not provided outside an enterprise. Since management accounting is internal to an enterprise, it can usually be tailored to meet management's informational needs and is beyond the scope of this Statement.

General Purpose External Financial Reporting

28. The objectives in this Statement are those of general purpose external financial reporting by business enterprises. The objectives stem primarily from the informational needs of external users who lack the authority to prescribe the financial information they want from an enterprise and therefore must use the information that management communicates to them. Those potential users include most of the groups listed in paragraph 24.

29. Financial reporting has both an internal and an external aspect, and this Statement focuses on the external aspect. Management is as interested in information about assets, liabilities, earnings, and related elements as external users and, among its other requirements, generally needs the same kinds of information about those elements as external users (paragraph 25). Thus, management is a major user of the same information that is provided by external financial reporting. However, management's primary role in external financial reporting is that of communicating information for use by others. For that reason, it has a direct interest in the cost, adequacy, and understandability of external financial reporting.

30. General purpose external financial reporting is directed toward the common interest of various potential users in the ability of an enterprise to generate favorable cash flows (paragraph 25). Thus, the objectives in this Statement are focused on information for investment and credit decisions for reasons that are largely pragmatic, not to narrow their scope. The objectives need a focus to avoid being vague or highly abstract. Investors and creditors and their advisors are the most obvious prominent external groups who use the information provided by financial reporting and who generally lack the authority to prescribe the information they want. Their decisions and their uses of information have been studied and described to a much greater extent than those of other external groups, and their decisions significantly affect the allocation of resources in the economy. In addition, information provided to meet investors' and creditors' needs is likely to be generally useful to members of other groups who are interested in essentially the same financial aspects of business enterprises as investors and creditors.

31. For convenience, *financial reporting* is used in place of *general purpose external financial reporting by business enterprises* in the remainder of this Statement.

OBJECTIVES OF FINANCIAL REPORTING

32. The following objectives of financial reporting flow from the preceding paragraphs and proceed from the more general to the more specific. The objectives begin with a broad focus on information that is useful in investment and credit decisions; then narrow that focus to investors' and creditors' primary interest in the prospects of receiving cash from their investments in or loans to business enterprises and the relation of those prospects to the enterprise's prospects; and finally focus on information about an enterprise's economic resources, the claims to those resources, and changes in them, including measures of the enterprise's performance, that is useful in assessing the enterprise's cash flow prospects. The reasons for focusing the objectives of financial reporting primarily on investment, credit,

---

[4]That distinction between managerial and financial accounting is made, for example, by Eric L. Kohler, *A Dictionary for Accountants,* 5th ed. (Englewood Cliffs, NJ: Prentice-Hall, Inc., 1975), pp. 208 and 303, and by Sidney Davidson, James S. Schindler, Clyde P. Stickney, and Roman L. Weil, *Accounting: The Language of Business,* 3rd ed. (Glen Ridge, NJ: Thomas Horton and Daughters, Inc., 1977), pp. 24 and 34.

and similar decisions are given in paragraph 30. That focus and wording do not mean that the objectives apply only to investors and creditors and exclude everyone else. To the contrary, information that satisfies the objectives should be useful to all who are interested in an enterprise's future capacity to pay or in how investors or creditors are faring.

33. The objectives are those of financial reporting rather than goals for investors, creditors, or others who use the information or goals for the economy or society as a whole. The role of financial reporting in the economy is to provide information that is useful in making business and economic decisions, not to determine what those decisions should be. For example, saving and investing in productive resources (capital formation) are generally considered to be prerequisite to increasing the standard of living in an economy. To the extent that financial reporting provides information that helps identify relatively efficient and inefficient users of resources, aids in assessing relative returns and risks of investment opportunities, or otherwise assists in promoting efficient functioning of capital and other markets, it helps to create a favorable environment for capital formation decisions. However, investors, creditors, and others make those decisions, and it is not a function of financial reporting to try to determine or influence the outcomes of those decisions. The role of financial reporting requires it to provide evenhanded, neutral, or unbiased information. Thus, for example, information that indicates that a relatively inefficient user of resources is efficient or that investing in a particular enterprise involves less risk than it does and information that is directed toward a particular goal, such as encouraging the reallocation of resources in favor of a particular segment of the economy, are likely to fail to serve the broader objectives that financial reporting is intended to serve.

Information Useful in Investment and Credit Decisions

34. Financial reporting should provide information that is useful to present and potential investors and creditors and other users in making rational investment, credit, and similar decisions. The information should be comprehensible to those who have a reasonable understanding of business and economic activities and are willing to study the information with reasonable diligence.

35. This Statement uses the terms investors and creditors broadly. The terms include both those who deal directly with an enterprise and those who deal through intermediaries, both those who buy securities from other investors or creditors and those who buy newly issued securities from the enterprise or an underwriter, both those who commit funds for long periods and those who trade frequently, both those who desire safety of investment and those who are willing to accept risk to obtain high rates of return, both individuals and specialized institutions. The major groups of investors are equity securityholders and debt securityholders. The major groups of creditors are suppliers of goods and services who extend credit, customers and employees with claims, lending institutions, individual lenders, and debt securityholders.[5] The terms also may comprehend security analysts and advisors, brokers, lawyers, regulatory agencies, and others who advise or represent the interests of investors and creditors or who otherwise are interested in how investors and creditors are faring.

36. Individual investors, creditors, or other potential users of financial information understand to varying degrees the business and economic environment, business activities, securities markets, and related matters. Their understanding of financial information and the way and extent to which they use and rely on it also may vary greatly. Financial information is a tool and, like most tools, cannot be of much direct help to those who are unable or unwilling to use it or who misuse it. Its use can be learned, however, and financial reporting should provide information that can be used by all—nonprofessionals as well as professionals—who are willing to learn to use it properly. Efforts may be needed to increase the understandability of financial information. Cost-benefit considerations may indicate that information understood or used by only a few should not be provided. Conversely, financial reporting should not exclude relevant information merely because it is difficult for some to understand or because some investors or creditors choose not to use it.

Information Useful in Assessing Cash Flow Prospects

37. Financial reporting should provide information to help present and potential investors and creditors and other users in assessing the amounts, timing, and uncertainty of prospective cash receipts from dividends or interest and the proceeds from the sale, redemption, or maturity of securities or loans. The prospects for those cash receipts are affected by an enterprise's ability to generate enough cash to meet its obligations when due and its other cash operating needs, to reinvest in operations, and to pay cash

---

[5]Debt securityholders are included in both groups because they are investors as that term is commonly used as well as creditors by contract and usual legal definition. Moreover, it is often convenient to refer to them as investors without making a precise distinction between "investors in debt securities" and "investors in equity securities." That distinction is made if it is significant.

dividends and may also be affected by perceptions of investors and creditors generally about that ability, which affect market prices of the enterprise's securities. Thus, financial reporting should provide information to help investors, creditors, and others assess the amounts, timing, and uncertainty of prospective net cash inflows to the related enterprise.[6]

38. People engage in investing, lending, and similar activities primarily to increase their cash resources. The ultimate test of success (or failure) of those activities is the extent to which they return more (or less) cash than they cost.[7] A successful investor or creditor receives not only a return *of* investment but also a return *on* that investment (cash, goods, or services) commensurate with the risk involved. Moreover, investment, credit, and similar decisions normally involve choices between present cash and future cash—for example, the choice between the price of a security that can be bought or sold or the amount of a loan and rights to expected future cash receipts from dividends or interest and proceeds from resale or repayment. Investors, creditors, and others need information to help them form rational expectations about those prospective cash receipts and assess the risk that the amounts or timing of the receipts may differ from expectations, including information that helps them assess prospective cash flows to the enterprise in which they have invested or to which they have loaned funds.

39. Business enterprises, like investors and creditors, invest cash in noncash resources to earn more cash. The test of success (or failure) of the operations of an enterprise is the extent to which the cash returned exceeds (or is less than) the cash spent (invested) over the long run (footnote 7).[8] A successful enterprise receives not only a return *of* its invest-

ment but also a satisfactory return *on* that investment. The market's assessment of an enterprise's expected success in generating favorable cash flows affects the relative market prices of its securities, although the level of market prices of securities is affected by numerous factors—such as general economic conditions, interest rates, market psychology, and the like—that are not related to particular enterprises. Thus, since an enterprise's ability to generate favorable cash flows affects both its ability to pay dividends and interest and the market prices of its securities, expected cash flows to investors and creditors are related to expected cash flows to the enterprise in which they have invested or to which they have loaned funds.

Information about Enterprise Resources, Claims to Those Resources, and Changes in Them

40. Financial reporting should provide information about the economic resources of an enterprise, the claims to those resources (obligations of the enterprise to transfer resources to other entities and owners' equity), and the effects of transactions, events, and circumstances that change resources and claims to those resources.[9]

Economic Resources, Obligations, and Owners' Equity

41. Financial reporting should provide information about an enterprise's economic resources, obligations, and owners' equity. That information helps investors, creditors, and others identify the enterprise's financial strengths and weaknesses and assess its liquidity and solvency. Information about resources, obligations, and owners' equity also provides a basis for investors, creditors, and others to

---

[6]Several respondents to the Exposure Draft, "Objectives of Financial Reporting and Elements of Financial Statements of Business Enterprises," interpreted this objective as requiring "cash flow information," "current value information," or "management forecast information." However, the objective focuses on the purpose for which information provided should be useful—emphasizing the importance of cash to people and the activities they use to increase cash inflows that also help increase the productive resources and outputs of goods and services in an economy—rather than the kinds of information that may be useful for that purpose. The objective neither requires nor prohibits "cash flow information," "current value information," "management forecast information," or any other specific information. Conclusions about "current value information" and "management forecast information" are beyond the scope of this Statement. Paragraphs 42-44 show that information about cash receipts and disbursements is not usually considered to be the most useful information for the purposes described in this objective.

[7]Questions of measurement scale and unit of measure are beyond the scope of this Statement (paragraph 2). Therefore, the description in paragraphs 38, 39, and others ignore, for example, that a dollar of cash received as dividends, interest, or proceeds from resale or repayment is not necessarily equal in purchasing power to a dollar invested or loaned earlier, a dollar of cash collected from customers is not necessarily equal in purchasing power to a dollar spent earlier, and a dollar of cash paid to a creditor is not necessarily equal in purchasing power to a dollar received earlier.

[8]Descriptions of operations of business enterprises commonly describe a cycle that begins with cash outlays and ends with cash receipts. That description is not only straightforward and convenient but also generally fits manufacturing, merchandising, financial, and service enterprises whose operations comprise primarily activities such as acquiring goods and services, increasing their value by adding time, place, or form utility, selling them, and collecting the selling price. Cash receipts may precede cash payments, however, and commonly do in the operations of some service and financial enterprises. The order of cash flows does not affect the basic nature of operations but may complicate descriptions and analyses.

[9]Economic resources, claims to those resources, changes in resources and claims, and the elements that represent them in financial statements are the subject of the next phase in the Board's conceptual framework project on elements of financial statements of business enterprises.

evaluate information about the enterprise's performance during a period (paragraphs 42-48). Moreover, it provides direct indications of the cash flow potentials of some resources and of the cash needed to satisfy many, if not most, obligations. That is, some of an enterprise's resources are direct sources of cash to the enterprise, many obligations are direct causes of cash payments by the enterprise, and reasonably reliable measures of future net cash inflows or future net cash outflows are often possible for those resources and obligations. Many cash flows cannot be identified with individual resources (or some obligations), however, because they are the joint result of combining various resources in the enterprise's operations. Indirect measures of cash flow potential are widely considered necessary or desirable, both for particular resources and for enterprises as a whole. That information may help those who desire to estimate the value of a business enterprise, but financial accounting is not designed to measure directly the value of an enterprise.

Enterprise Performance and Earnings

42. Financial reporting should provide information about an enterprise's financial performance during a period. Investors and creditors often use information about the past to help in assessing the prospects of an enterprise. Thus, although investment and credit decisions reflect investors' and creditors' expectations about future enterprise performance, those expectations are commonly based at least partly on evaluations of past enterprise performance.[10]

43. The primary focus of financial reporting is information about an enterprise's performance provided by measures of earnings and its components. Investors, creditors, and others who are concerned with assessing the prospects for enterprise net cash inflows are especially interested in that information. Their interest in an enterprise's future cash flows and its ability to generate favorable cash flows leads primarily to an interest in information about its earnings rather than information directly about its cash flows. Financial statements that show only cash receipts and payments during a short period, such as a year, cannot adequately indicate whether or not an enterprise's performance is successful.

44. Information about enterprise earnings and its

components measured by accrual accounting generally provides a better indication of enterprise performance than information about current cash receipts and payments. Accrual accounting attempts to record the financial effects on an enterprise of transactions and other events and circumstances that have cash consequences for an enterprise in the periods in which those transactions, events, and circumstances occur rather than only in the periods in which cash is received or paid by the enterprise. Accrual accounting is concerned with the process by which cash expended on resources and activities is returned as more (or perhaps less) cash to the enterprise, not just with the beginning and end of that process. It recognizes that the buying, producing, selling, and other operations of an enterprise during a period, as well as other events that affect enterprise performance, often do not coincide with the cash receipts and payments of the period.

45. Periodic earnings measurement involves relating to periods the benefits from and the costs[11] of operations and other transactions, events, and circumstances that affect an enterprise. Although business enterprises invest cash to obtain a return *on* investment as well as a return *of* investment, the investment of cash and its return often do not occur in the same period. Modern business activities are largely conducted on credit and often involve long and complex financial arrangements or production or marketing processes. An enterprise's receivables and payables, inventory, investments, property, plant, equipment, and other noncash resources and obligations are the links between its operations and other transactions, events, and circumstances that affect it and its cash receipts and outlays. For example, labor is often used by an enterprise before it is paid for, requiring that salaries and wages payable be accrued to recognize the obligation and measure the effects on earnings in the period the labor is used rather than when the payroll checks are issued. Conversely, resources such as raw materials and equipment may be paid for by an enterprise in a period that does not coincide with their use, requiring that the resources on hand be recognized and that the effect on earnings be deferred until the periods the resources are used. Similarly, receivables and the related effects on earnings must often be accrued before the related cash is received, or obligations must be recognized when cash is received and the effects on earnings must be identified with the

---

[10]Investors and creditors ordinarily invest in or lend to enterprises that they expect to continue in operation—an expectation that is familiar to accountants as "the going concern" assumption. Information about the past is usually less useful in assessing prospects for an enterprise's future if the enterprise is in liquidation or is expected to enter liquidation. Then, emphasis shifts from performance to liquidation of the enterprise's resources and obligations. The objectives of financial reporting do not necessarily change if an enterprise shifts from expected operation to expected liquidation, but the information that is relevant to those objectives, including measures of elements of financial statements, may change.

[11]"Cost" is the sacrifice incurred in economic activities—that which is given up or foregone to consume, to save, to exchange, to produce, etc. For example, the value of cash or other resources given up (or the present value of an obligation incurred) in exchange for a resource is the cost of the resource acquired. Similarly, the expiration of future benefits caused by using a resource in production is the cost of using it.

periods in which goods or services are provided. The goal of accrual and deferral of benefits and sacrifices is to relate the accomplishments and the efforts so that reported earnings measures an enterprise's performance during a period instead of merely listing its cash receipts and outlays.[12]

46. Earnings and its components relate to an individual enterprise during a particular period. Over the life of an enterprise (or other very long period), total reported earnings equals the net cash receipts excluding those from capital changes (ignoring changes in value of money noted in footnote 7), but that relationship between earnings and cash flows rarely, if ever, holds for periods as short as a year. The major difference between periodic earnings measured by accrual accounting and statements of cash receipts and outlays is timing of recognition of the components of earnings.

47. Investors, creditors, and others often use reported earnings and information about the components of earnings in various ways and for various purposes in assessing their prospects for cash flows from investments in or loans to an enterprise. For example, they may use earnings information to help them (a) evaluate management's performance, (b) estimate "earning power" or other amounts they perceive as "representative" of long-term earning ability of an enterprise, (c) predict future earnings, or (d) assess the risk of investing in or lending to an enterprise. They may use the information to confirm, reassure themselves about, or reject or change their own or others' earlier predictions or assessments. Measures of earnings and information about earnings disclosed by financial reporting should, to the extent possible, be useful for those and similar uses and purposes.

48. However, accrual accounting provides measures of earnings rather than evaluations of management's performance, estimates of "earning power," predictions of earnings, assessments of risk, or confirmations or rejections of predictions or assessments. Investors, creditors, and other users of the information do their own evaluating, estimating, predicting, assessing, confirming, or rejecting. For example, procedures such as averaging or normalizing reported earnings for several periods and ignoring or averaging out the financial effects of "nonrepresentative" transactions and events are commonly used in estimating "earning power." However, both the concept of "earning power" and the techniques for estimating it are part of financial analysis and are beyond the scope of financial reporting.

Liquidity, Solvency, and Funds Flows

49. Financial reporting should provide information about how an enterprise obtains and spends cash, about its borrowing and repayment of borrowing, about its capital transactions, including cash dividends and other distributions of enterprise resources to owners, and about other factors that may affect an enterprise's liquidity or solvency. For example, although reports of an enterprise's cash receipts and cash outlays during a period are generally less useful than earnings information for measuring enterprise performance during a period and for assessing an enterprise's ability to generate favorable cash flows (paragraphs 42-46), information about cash flows or other funds flows may be useful in understanding the operations of an enterprise, evaluating its financing activities, assessing its liquidity or solvency, or interpreting earnings information provided. Information about earnings and economic resources, obligations, and owners' equity may also be useful in assessing an enterprise's liquidity or solvency.

Management Stewardship and Performance

50. Financial reporting should provide information about how management of an enterprise has discharged its stewardship responsibility to owners (stockholders) for the use of enterprise resources entrusted to it. Management of an enterprise is periodically accountable to the owners not only for the custody and safekeeping of enterprise resources but also for their efficient and profitable use and for protecting them to the extent possible from unfavorable economic impacts of factors in the economy such as inflation or deflation and technological and social changes. To the extent that management offers securities of the enterprise to the public, it voluntarily accepts wider responsibilities for accountability to prospective investors and to the public in general. Society may also impose broad or specific responsibilities on enterprises and their managements.

51. Earnings information is commonly the focus for assessing management's stewardship or accountability. Management, owners, and others emphasize enterprise performance or profitability in describing how management has discharged its stewardship accountability. A central question for owners, managers, potential investors, the public, and government is how an enterprise and its owners are faring. Since earnings and its components for a single period are often an insufficient basis for assessing management's stewardship, owners and others may

---

[12]The process described in this paragraph is commonly called the "matching of costs and revenues," and "matching" is a significant part of it, though not the whole. "Matching" is one of the subjects of the next phase in the conceptual framework project on elements of financial statements.

estimate "earning power" or other average they consider "representative" of long-term performance. As noted in paragraph 48, however, accrual accounting measures earnings for a period rather than "earning power" or other financial analysis concepts.

52. Financial reporting should provide information that is useful to managers and directors in making decisions in the interests of owners. Although this Statement is concerned primarily with providing information to external users, managers and directors are responsible to owners (and other investors) for enterprise performance as reflected by financial reporting and they are judged at least to some extent on the enterprise performance reported. Thus, how owners have fared during a period is of equal concern to managers and owners, and information provided should be useful to both in meeting their common goal.

53. Financial reporting, and especially financial statements, usually cannot and does not separate management performance from enterprise performance. Business enterprises are highly complex institutions, and their production and marketing processes are often long and intricate. Enterprise successes and failures are the result of the interaction of numerous factors. Management ability and performance are contributing factors, but so are events and circumstances that are often beyond the control of management, such as general economic conditions, supply and demand characteristics of enterprise inputs and outputs, price changes, and fortuitous events and circumstances. What happens to a business enterprise is usually so much a joint result of a complex interaction of many factors that neither accounting nor other statistical analysis can discern with reasonable accuracy the degree to which management, or any other factor, affected the joint result. Actions of past managements affect current periods' earnings, and actions of current management affect future periods' earnings. Financial reporting provides information about an enterprise during a period when it was under the direction of a particular management but does not directly provide information about that management's performance. The information is therefore limited for purposes of assessing management performance apart from enterprise performance.

Management Explanations and Interpretations

54. Financial reporting should include explanations and interpretations to help users understand financial information provided. For example, the usefulness of financial information as an aid to investors, creditors, and others in forming expectations about a business enterprise may be enhanced by management's explanations of the information. Manage-

ment knows more about the enterprise and its affairs than investors, creditors, or other "outsiders" and can often increase the usefulness of financial information by identifying certain transactions, other events, and circumstances that affect the enterprise and explaining their financial impact on it. In addition, dividing continuous operations into accounting periods is a convention and may have arbitrary effects. Management can aid investors, creditors, and others in using financial information by identifying arbitrary results caused by separating periods, explaining why the effect is arbitrary, and describing its effect on reported information. Moreover, financial reporting often provides information that depends on, or is affected by, management's estimates and judgment. Investors, creditors, and others are aided in evaluating estimates and judgmental information by explanations of underlying assumptions or methods used, including disclosure of significant uncertainties about principal underlying assumptions or estimates. Financial reporting may, of course, provide information in addition to that specified by financial accounting standards, regulatory rules, or custom.

THE CONCEPTUAL FRAMEWORK: A PERSPECTIVE

55. Paragraphs 40-54 focus the objectives of financial reporting by business enterprises on information about the economic resources of an enterprise, the claims to those resources, and the effects of transactions, events, and circumstances that change resources and claims to them. The paragraphs emphasize information about an enterprise's performance provided by measures of earnings and its components and also broadly describe other kinds of information that financial reporting should provide. The objectives lead to, but leave unanswered, questions such as the identity, number, and form of financial statements; elements of financial statements and their recognition, measurement, and display; information that should be provided by other means of financial reporting; and meanings and balancing or trading-off of relevance, reliability, and other criteria for evaluating and selecting accounting information (qualitative characteristics). Those matters are, as noted in paragraph 2, topics of other Statements that are expected to follow this Statement on objectives.

56. Financial statements are the basic means of communicating the information described in paragraphs 40-54 to those who use it. The elements of financial statements provide "... information about the economic resources of an enterprise, the claims to those resources (obligations of the enterprise to transfer resources to other entities and owners' equity), and the effects of transactions, events, and

circumstances that change resources and claims to those resources" (paragraph 40), including "... information about an enterprise's performance provided by measures of earnings and its components"

(paragraph 43). Thus, the next phase of the conceptual framework project pertains to the elements of financial statements.

This Statement was adopted by the unanimous vote of the seven members of the Financial Accounting Standards Board:

Donald J. Kirk, *Chairman*
Oscar S. Gellein
John W. March

Robert A. Morgan
David Mosso

Robert T. Sprouse
Ralph E. Walters

Appendix A

BACKGROUND INFORMATION

57. The need for a conceptual framework for financial accounting and reporting, beginning with consideration of the objectives of financial reporting, is generally recognized. The Accounting Principles Board issued *APB Statement No. 4,* "Basic Concepts and Accounting Principles Underlying Financial Statements of Business Enterprises," in 1970. When the Financial Accounting Standards Board came into existence, the Study Group on the Objectives of Financial Statements was at work, and its report, "Objectives of Financial Statements," was published in October 1973 by the American Institute of Certified Public Accountants.

58. The Financial Accounting Standards Board issued a Discussion Memorandum, "Conceptual Framework for Accounting and Reporting: Consideration of the Report of the Study Group on the Objectives of Financial Statements," dated June 6, 1974 and held a public hearing on September 23 and 24, 1974 on the objectives of financial statements. The Discussion Memorandum and the hearing were based primarily on the *Report of the Study Group on the Objectives of Financial Statements.* The Board received 95 written communications responding to the Discussion Memorandum, and 20 parties presented their views orally and answered Board Members' questions at the hearing.

59. On December 2, 1976, the Board issued three documents:

Tentative Conclusions on Objectives of Financial Statements of Business Enterprises,

FASB Discussion Memorandum, "Conceptual Framework for Financial Accounting and Reporting: Elements of Financial Statements and Their Measurement," and

Scope and Implications of the Conceptual Framework Project.

The same task force, with only one membership change, provided counsel in preparing both Discussion Memoranda. Eleven persons from academe, the financial community, industry, and public accounting served on the task force while the Discussion Memoranda were written.

60. The Board considered the 12 objectives of financial statements in the Study Group Report but has not attempted to reach conclusions on some of them—for example, reporting current value and changes in current value, providing a statement of financial activities, providing financial forecasts, determining the objectives of financial statements for governmental and not-for-profit organizations, and reporting enterprise activities affecting society. Some issues about reporting current values and changes in current values were discussed in the Discussion Memorandum, "Elements of Financial Statements and Their Measurement," and the Board has a project on supplementary disclosures of the effects of changing prices on business enterprises (paragraph 61). The Board also has a project on objectives of financial reporting by organizations other than business enterprises (footnote 1). The other matters may be dealt with in later phases of the conceptual framework project.

61. The Board held public hearings (a) August 1 and 2, 1977 on the *Tentative Conclusions on Objectives of Financial Statements* and Chapters 1-5 of the Discussion Memorandum concerning definitions of the elements of financial statements and (b) January 16-18, 1978 on the remaining chapters of the Discussion Memorandum concerning capital maintenance or cost recovery, qualities of useful financial information ("qualitative characteristics"), and measurement of the elements of financial statements.

62. The Board received 283 written communications on the subject of the August 1977 hearing, of which 214 commented on the objectives and 221 commented on the elements, and 27 parties presented their views orally and answered Board Members' questions at the hearing. The Board issued an Exposure Draft of a proposed Statement of Finan-

cial Accounting Concepts on "Objectives of Financial Reporting and Elements of Financial Statements of Business Enterprises," dated December 29, 1977 and received 135 letters of comment.

63. The major difference between this Statement and the Exposure Draft is the scope of the subject matter. "Elements of financial statements of business enterprises" and the brief comments on "qualitative characteristics" (paragraphs 41-66 and 69-75, respectively, of the Exposure Draft) have been omitted to be the subjects of separate exposure drafts. Other significant changes are (a) the "Highlights" preceding the text, (b) the subheadings in the third objective (paragraphs 40-54), and (c) reorganization of the "Introduction and Background" paragraphs, including the position of "characteristics and limitations of information provided" in the forepart of the Statement.

Statement of Financial Accounting Concepts No. 2
Qualitative Characteristics of Accounting Information

STATUS

Issued: May 1980

Affects: No other pronouncements

Affected by: Paragraph 4 and footnote 2 superseded by CON 6

SUMMARY OF PRINCIPAL CONCLUSIONS

The purpose of this Statement is to examine the characteristics that make accounting information useful. Those who prepare, audit, and use financial reports, as well as the Financial Accounting Standards Board, must often select or evaluate accounting alternatives. The characteristics or qualities of information discussed in this Statement are the ingredients that make information useful and are the qualities to be sought when accounting choices are made.

All financial reporting is concerned in varying degrees with decision making (though decision makers also use information obtained from other sources). The need for information on which to base investment, credit, and similar decisions underlies the objectives of financial reporting. The usefulness of information must be evaluated in relation to the purposes to be served, and the objectives of financial reporting are focused on the use of accounting information in decision making.

The central role assigned to decision making leads straight to the overriding criterion by which all accounting choices must be judged. The better choice is the one that, subject to considerations of cost, produces from among the available alternatives information that is most useful for decision making.

Even objectives that are oriented more towards stewardship are concerned with decisions. Stewardship deals with the efficiency, effectiveness, and integrity of the steward. To say that stewardship reporting is an aspect of accounting's decision making role is simply to say that its purpose is to guide actions that may need to be taken in relation to the steward or in relation to the activity that is being monitored.

A Hierarchy of Accounting Qualities

The characteristics of information that make it a desirable commodity can be viewed as a hierarchy of qualities, with usefulness for decision making of most importance. Without usefulness, there would be no benefits from information to set against its costs.

User-Specific Factors

In the last analysis, each decision maker judges what accounting information is useful, and that judgment is influenced by factors such as the decisions to be made, the methods of decision making to be used, the information already possessed or obtainable from other sources, and the decision maker's capacity (alone or with professional help) to process the information. The optimal information for one user will not be optimal for another. Consequently, the Board, which must try to cater to many different users while considering the burdens placed on those who have to provide information, constantly treads a fine line between requiring disclosure of too much or too little information.

The hierarchy separates user-specific qualities, for example, understandability, from qualities inherent in information. Information cannot be useful to decision makers who cannot understand it, even though it may otherwise be relevant to a decision and be reliable. However, understandability of information is related to the characteristics of the decision maker as well as the characteristics of the information itself and, therefore, understandability cannot be evaluated in overall terms but must be judged in relation to a specific class of decision makers.

Primary Decision-Specific Qualities

Relevance and *reliability* are the two primary qualities that make accounting information useful for decision making. Subject to constraints imposed by cost and materiality, increased relevance and increased reliability are the characteristics that make information a more desirable commodity—that is, one useful in making decisions. If either of those qualities is completely missing, the information will not be useful. Though, ideally, the choice of an accounting alternative should produce information that is both more reliable and more relevant, it may be necessary to sacrifice some of one quality for a gain in another.

To be relevant, information must be timely and it must have predictive value *or* feedback value or both. To be reliable, information must have representational faithfulness and it must be verifiable and neutral. Comparability, which includes consistency, is a secondary quality that interacts with relevance and reliability to contribute to the usefulness of information. Two constraints are included in the hierarchy, both primarily quantitative in character. Information can be useful and yet be too costly to justify providing it. To be useful *and* worth providing, the benefits of information should exceed its cost. All of the qualities of information shown are subject to a materiality threshold, and that is also shown as a constraint.

Relevance

- Relevant accounting information is capable of making a difference in a decision by helping users to form predictions about the outcomes of past, present, and future events or to confirm or correct prior expectations. Information can make a difference to decisions by improving decision makers' capacities to predict or by providing feedback on earlier expectations. Usually, information does both at once, because knowledge about the outcomes of actions already taken will generally improve decision makers' abilities to predict the results of similar future actions. Without a knowledge of the past, the basis for a prediction will usually be lacking. Without an interest in the future, knowledge of the past is sterile.
- Timeliness, that is, having information available to decision makers before it loses its capacity to influence decisions, is an ancillary aspect of relevance. If information is not available when it is needed or becomes available so long after the reported events that it has no value for future action, it lacks relevance and is of little or no use. Timeliness alone cannot make information relevant, but a lack of timeliness can rob information of relevance it might otherwise have had.

Reliability

- The reliability of a measure rests on the faithfulness with which it represents what it purports to represent, coupled with an assurance for the user that it has that representational quality. To be useful, information must be reliable as well as relevant. Degrees of reliability must be recognized. It is hardly ever a question of black or white, but rather of more reliability or less. Reliability rests upon the extent to which the accounting description or measurement is verifiable and representationally faithful. Neutrality of information also interacts with those two components of reliability to affect the usefulness of the information.
- Verifiability is a quality that may be demonstrated by securing a high degree of consensus among independent measurers using the same measurement methods. Representational faithfulness, on the other hand, refers to the correspondence or agreement between the accounting numbers and the resources or events those numbers purport to represent. A high degree of correspondence, however, does not guarantee that an accounting measurement will be relevant to the user's needs if the resources or events represented by the measurement are inappropriate to the purpose at hand.
- Neutrality means that, in formulating or implementing standards, the primary concern should be the relevance and reliability of the information that results, not the effect that the new rule may have on a particular interest. A neutral choice between accounting alternatives is free from bias towards a predetermined result. The objectives of financial reporting serve many different information users who have diverse interests, and no one predetermined result is likely to suit all interests.

Comparability and Consistency

- Information about a particular enterprise gains greatly in usefulness if it can be compared with similar information about other enterprises and with similar information about the same enterprise for some other period or some other point in time. Comparability between enterprises and consistency in the application of methods over time increases the informational value of comparisons of relative economic opportunities or performance. The significance of information, especially quantitative information, depends to a great extent on the user's ability to relate it to some benchmark.

Materiality

- Materiality is a pervasive concept that relates to the qualitative characteristics, especially relevance and reliability. Materiality and relevance are both defined in terms of what influences or makes a difference to a decision maker, but the two terms can be distinguished. A decision not to disclose certain information may be made, say, because investors have no need for that kind of information (it is not relevant) or because the amounts involved are too small to make a difference (they are not material). Magnitude by itself, without regard to the nature of the item and the circumstances in which the judgment has to be made, will not generally be a sufficient basis for a materiality judgment. The Board's present position is' that no general standards of materiality can be formulated to take into account all the considerations that enter into an experienced human judgment. Quantitative materiality criteria may be given by the Board in specific standards in the future, as in the past, as appropriate.

Costs and Benefits

- Each user of accounting information will uniquely perceive the relative value to be attached to each quality of that information. Ultimately, a standard-setting body has to do its best to meet the needs of society as a whole when it promulgates a standard that sacrifices one of those qualities for another; and it must also be aware constantly of the calculus of costs and benefits. In order to justify requiring a particular disclosure, the perceived benefits to be derived from that disclosure must exceed the perceived costs associated with it. However, to say anything precise about their incidence is difficult. There are costs of using information as well as of providing it; and the benefits from providing financial information accrue to preparers as well as users of that information.
- Though it is unlikely that significantly improved means of measuring benefits will become available in the foreseeable future, it seems possible that better ways of quantifying the incremental costs of regulations of all kinds may gradually be developed, and the Board will watch any such developments carefully to see whether they can be applied to financial accounting standards. The Board cannot cease to be concerned about the cost-effectiveness of its standards. To do so would be a dereliction of its duty and a disservice to its constituents.

Statement of Financial Accounting Concepts No. 2
Qualitative Characteristics of Accounting Information

STATEMENTS OF FINANCIAL ACCOUNTING CONCEPTS

This Statement of Financial Accounting Concepts is one of a series of publications in the Board's conceptual framework for financial accounting and reporting. Statements in the series are intended to set forth objectives and fundamentals that will be the basis for development of financial accounting and reporting standards. The objectives identify the goals and purposes of financial reporting. The fundamentals are the underlying concepts of financial accounting—concepts that guide the selection of transactions, events, and circumstances to be accounted for, their recognition and measurement, and the means of summarizing and communicating them to interested parties. Concepts of that type are fundamental in the sense that other concepts flow from them and repeated reference to them will be necessary in establishing, interpreting, and applying accounting and reporting standards.

The conceptual framework is a coherent system of interrelated objectives and fundamentals that is expected to lead to consistent standards and that prescribes the nature, function, and limits of financial accounting and reporting. It is expected to serve the public interest by providing structure and direction to financial accounting and reporting to facilitate the provision of evenhanded financial and related information that is useful in assisting capital and other markets to function efficiently in allocating scarce resources in the economy.

Establishment of objectives and identification of fundamental concepts will not directly solve financial accounting and reporting problems. Rather, objectives give direction, and concepts are tools for solving problems.

The Board itself is likely to be the most direct beneficiary of the guidance provided by the Statements in this series. They will guide the Board in developing accounting and reporting standards by providing the Board with a common foundation and basic reasoning on which to consider merits of alternatives.

However, knowledge of the objectives and concepts the Board will use in developing standards should also enable those who are affected by or interested in financial accounting standards to understand better the purposes, content, and characteristics of information provided by financial accounting and reporting. That knowledge is expected to enhance the usefulness of, and confidence in, financial accounting and reporting. Careful use of the concepts may also provide guidance in resolving new or emerging problems of financial accounting and reporting in the absence of applicable authoritative pronouncements.

Statements of Financial Accounting Concepts do not establish standards prescribing accounting procedures or disclosure practices for particular items or events, which are issued by the Board as Statements of Financial Accounting Standards. Rather, Statements in this series describe concepts and relations that will underlie future financial accounting standards and practices and in due course serve as a basis for evaluating existing standards and practices.*

The Board recognizes that in certain respects current generally accepted accounting principles may be inconsistent with those that may derive from the objectives and concepts set forth in Statements in this series. However, a Statement of Financial Accounting Concepts does not (a) require a change in existing generally accepted accounting principles, (b) amend, modify, or interpret Statements of Financial Accounting Standards, Interpretations of the FASB, Opinions of the Accounting Principles Board, or Bulletins of the Committee on Accounting Procedure that are in effect, or (c) justify either changing existing generally accepted accounting and reporting practices or interpreting the pronouncements listed in item (b) based on personal interpretations of the objectives and concepts in the Statements of Financial Accounting Concepts.

Since a Statement of Financial Accounting Concepts does not establish generally accepted accounting principles or standards for the disclosure of financial information outside of financial statements in published financial reports, it is not intended to invoke application of Rule 203 or 204 of the Rules of Conduct of the Code of Professional Ethics of the American Institute of Certified Public Accountants (or successor rules or arrangements of similar scope and intent). †

Like other pronouncements of the Board, a Statement of Financial Accounting Concepts may be

---

*Pronouncements such as APB Statement No. 4, *Basic Concepts and Accounting Principles Underlying Financial Statements of Business Enterprises,* and the Accounting Terminology Bulletins will continue to serve their intended purpose—they describe objectives and concepts underlying standards and practices existing at the time of their issuance.

†Rule 203 prohibits a member of the American Institute of Certified Public Accountants from expressing an opinion that financial statements conform with generally accepted accounting principles if those statements contain a material departure from an accounting principle promulgated by the Financial Accounting Standards Board, unless the member can demonstrate that because of unusual circumstances the financial statements otherwise would have been misleading. Rule 204 requires members of the Institute to justify departures from standards promulgated by the Financial Accounting Standards Board for the disclosure of information outside of financial statements in published financial reports.

amended, superseded, or withdrawn by appropriate action under the Board's *Rules of Procedure*.

FASB PUBLICATIONS ON CONCEPTUAL FRAMEWORK

Statements of Financial Accounting Concepts

No. 1, *Objectives of Financial Reporting by Business Enterprises* (November 1978)

Exposure Drafts Being (or Yet to Be) Considered by the Board

Elements of Financial Statements of Business Enterprises (December 28, 1979)

Objectives of Financial Reporting by Nonbusiness Organizations (March 14, 1980)

Discussion Memorandums and Invitations to Comment Having Issues Being Considered by the Board

Reporting Earnings (July 31, 1979)

Financial Statements and Other Means of Financial Reporting (May 12, 1980)

Other Projects in Process

Accounting Recognition Criteria
Funds Flows and Liquidity

CONTENTS

GLOSSARY OF TERMS

Bias

Bias in measurement is the tendency of a measure to fall more often on one side than the other of what it represents instead of being equally likely to fall on either side. Bias in accounting measures means a tendency to be consistently too high or too low.

Comparability
The quality of information that enables users to identify similarities in and differences between two sets of economic phenomena.

Completeness
The inclusion in reported information of everything material that is necessary for faithful representation of the relevant phenomena.

Conservatism
A prudent reaction to uncertainty to try to ensure that uncertainty and risks inherent in business situations are adequately considered.

Consistency
Conformity from period to period with unchanging policies and procedures.

Feedback Value
The quality of information that enables users to confirm or correct prior expectations.

Materiality
The magnitude of an omission or misstatement of accounting information that, in the light of surrounding circumstances, makes it probable that the judgment of a reasonable person relying on the information would have been changed or influenced by the omission or misstatement.

Neutrality
Absence in reported information of bias intended to attain a predetermined result or to induce a particular mode of behavior.

Predictive Value
The quality of information that helps users to increase the likelihood of correctly forecasting the outcome of past or present events.

Relevance
The capacity of information to make a difference in a decision by helping users to form predictions about the outcomes of past, present, and future events or to confirm or correct prior expectations.

Reliability
The quality of information that assures that information is reasonably free from error and bias and faithfully represents what it purports to represent.

Representational Faithfulness
Correspondence or agreement between a measure or description and the phenomenon that it purports to represent (sometimes called validity).

Timeliness
Having information available to a decision maker before it loses its capacity to influence decisions.

Understandability
The quality of information that enables users to perceive its significance.

Verifiability
The ability through consensus among measurers to ensure that information represents what it purports to represent or that the chosen method of measurement has been used without error or bias.

INTRODUCTION

1. The purpose of this Statement is to examine the characteristics of accounting information[1] that make that information useful. This Statement is one of a planned series of publications in the Board's conceptual framework project. It should be seen as a bridge between FASB Concepts Statement No. 1, *Objectives of Financial Reporting By Business Enterprises,* and other Statements to be issued covering the elements of financial statements and their recognition, measurement, and display. The Statement on objectives was concerned with the *purposes* of financial reporting. Later Statements will be concerned with questions about *how* those purposes are to be attained; and the standards that the Board has issued and will issue from time to time are also intended to attain those purposes. The Board believes that, in between the "why" of objectives and the "how" of other Statements and standards, it is helpful to share with its constituents its thinking about the characteristics that the information called for in its standards should have. It is those characteristics that distinguish more useful accounting information from less useful information.

2. Although those characteristics are expected to be stable, they are not immutable. They are affected by the economic, legal, political, and social environment in which financial reporting takes place and they may also change as new insights and new research results are obtained. Indeed, they ought to change if new knowledge shows present judgments to be outdated. If and when that happens, revised concepts Statements will need to be issued.

3. Although conventionally referred to as qualitative characteristics, some of the more important of the characteristics of accounting information that make it useful, or whose absence limit its usefulness, turn out on closer inspection to be quantitative in nature (for example, costliness) or to be partly quali-

[1]"Accounting information," "information provided by financial reporting," and variations on those descriptions are used interchangeably in this Statement.

tative and partly quantitative (for example, reliability and timeliness). While it will sometimes be important to keep those distinctions in mind, it will usually be convenient, and not misleading, to refer to all of the characteristics of information discussed in this Statement as "qualities" of information.

4. Although the discussion of the qualities of information and the related examples in this Statement refer primarily to business enterprises, the Board has tentatively concluded that similar qualities also apply to financial information reported by nonbusiness organizations. The Board intends to solicit views regarding its tentative conclusion.[2]

5. To maximize the usefulness of accounting information, subject to considerations of the cost of providing it, entails choices between alternative accounting methods. Those choices will be made more wisely if the ingredients that contribute to "usefulness" are better understood. The characteristics or qualities of information discussed in this Statement are, indeed, the ingredients that make information useful. They are, therefore, the qualities to be sought when accounting choices are made. They are as near as one can come to a set of criteria for making those choices.

The Nature of Accounting Choices

6. Accounting choices are made at two levels at least. At one level they are made by the Board or other agencies that have the power to require business enterprises to report in some particular way or, if exercised negatively, to prohibit a method that those agencies consider undesirable. An example of such a choice, made many years ago but still accepted as authoritative, is the pronouncement by the Committee on Accounting Procedure of the American Institute of Certified Public Accountants that ". . . the exclusion of all overheads from inventory costs does not constitute an accepted accounting procedure"[3] for general purpose external financial reporting.

7. Accounting choices are also made at the level of the individual enterprise. As more accounting standards are issued, the scope for individual choice inevitably becomes circumscribed. But there are now and will always be many accounting decisions to be made by reporting enterprises involving a choice between alternatives for which no standard has been promulgated or a choice between ways of implementing a standard.

8. Those who are unfamiliar with the nature of accounting are often surprised at the large number of choices that accountants are required to make. Yet choices arise at every turn. Decisions must first be made about the nature and definition of assets and liabilities, revenues and expenses, and the criteria by which they are to be recognized. Then a choice must be made of the attribute of assets to be measured—historical cost, current cost, current exit value, net realizable value, or present value of expected cash flows. If costs have to be allocated, either among time periods (for example, to compute depreciation) or among service beneficiaries (for example, industry segments), methods of allocation must be chosen. Further, choices must be made concerning the level of aggregation or disaggregation of the information to be disclosed in financial reports. Should a particular subsidiary company be consolidated or should its financial statements be presented separately? How many reportable segments should a company recognize? Choices involving aggregation arise at every point. Still other choices concern the selection of the terminal date of an enterprise's financial year, the form of descriptive captions to be used in its financial statements, the selection of matters to be commented on in notes or in supplementary information, and the wording to be used.

9. That list of choices, which is by no means comprehensive, illustrates some of the more important choices that arise in financial reporting. References throughout this Statement to alternative accounting policies, methods, or choices refer to the kinds of alternatives illustrated above.

10. If alternative accounting methods could be given points for each ingredient of usefulness in a particular situation, it would be an easy matter to add up each method's points and select the one (subject to its cost) that scored highest—so long, of course, as there were general agreement on the scoring system and how points were to be awarded. There are some who seem to harbor the hope that somewhere waiting to be discovered there is a comprehensive scoring system that can provide the universal criterion for making accounting choices. Unfortunately, neither the Board nor anyone else has such a system at the present time, and there is little probability that one will be forthcoming in the foreseeable future. Consequently, those who must choose among alternatives are forced to fall back on human judgment to evaluate the relative merits of

[2]The Board's consideration of aspects of the conceptual framework that pertain to nonbusiness organizations began later than its consideration of aspects that pertain to business enterprises. To date, the Board has sponsored and published a research study on the objectives and basic concepts underlying financial reporting by organizations other than business enterprises: FASB Research Report, *Financial Accounting in Nonbusiness Organizations,* by Robert N. Anthony; issued a Discussion Memorandum, *Conceptual Framework for Financial Accounting and Reporting: Objectives of Financial Reporting by Nonbusiness Organizations;* held public hearings on the Discussion Memorandum; and issued an Exposure Draft, *Objectives of Financial Reporting by Nonbusiness Organizations.* At its May 7, 1980 meeting, the Board authorized the staff to proceed with the consideration of concepts and standards issues relating to nonbusiness organizations that are beyond the scope of the existing nonbusiness objectives project.

[3]Accounting Research Bulletin No. 43, *Restatement and Revision of Accounting Research Bulletins,* Chapter 4, par. 5.

competing methods. If it were not so, there would be no need for a standard-setting authority; for by means of the comprehensive scoring system, agreement on the "best" methods would easily be secured.

11. That does not mean that nothing can be done to aid human judgment. By identifying and defining the qualities that make accounting information useful, this Statement develops a number of generalizations or guidelines for making accounting choices that are intended to be useful to the Board, to its staff, to preparers of financial statements, and to all others interested in financial reporting. For the Board and its staff, the qualities of useful accounting information should provide guidance in developing accounting standards that will be consistent with the objectives of financial reporting. This Statement also provides a terminology that should promote consistency in standard setting. For preparers of financial information, the qualities of useful accounting information should provide guidance in choosing between alternative ways of representing economic events, especially in dealing with situations not yet clearly covered by standards. This Statement also should be useful to those who use information provided by financial reporting. For them, its main value will be in increasing their understanding of both the usefulness and the limitations of the financial information that is provided by business enterprises and other organizations, either directly by financial reporting or indirectly through the commentaries of financial analysts and others. That increased understanding should be conducive to better-informed decisions.

12. The need for improved communication, especially between the Board and its constituents, provides much of the rationale for the whole conceptual framework project and particularly for this Statement. Indeed, improved communication may be the principal benefit to be gained from it. It is important that the concepts used by the Board in reaching its conclusions be understood by those who must apply its standards and those who use the results, for without understanding, standards become mere arbitrary edicts. Communication will also be facilitated if there is widespread use of a common terminology and a common set of definitions. The terminology used in this Statement is already widely, though not universally, used and its general adoption could help to eliminate many misunderstandings. The definitions of the principal terms used have been brought together in the glossary on pages 1025 and 1026.

13. It should perhaps be emphasized here that this Statement is not a standard. Its purpose is not to make rules but to provide part of the conceptual base on which rule making can stand. Unless that distinction is understood, this Statement may be invested with more authority than a discussion of concepts has a right to carry.

14. Whether at the level of the Board or the individual preparer, the primary criterion of choice between two alternative accounting methods involves asking which method produces the better—that is, the more useful—information. If that question can be answered with reasonable assurance, it is then necessary to ask whether the value of the better information sufficiently exceeds that of the inferior information to justify its extra cost, if any. If a satisfactory answer can again be given, the choice between the alternative methods is clear.

15. The qualities that distinguish "better" (more useful) information from "inferior" (less useful) information are primarily the qualities of relevance and reliability, with some other characteristics that those qualities imply. Subject to considerations of cost, the objective of accounting policy decisions is to produce accounting information that is relevant to the purposes to be served and is reliable. The meaning of those terms, the recognition that there are gradations of relevance and reliability, and the problems that arise if trade-offs between them are necessary all are matters discussed in later paragraphs of this Statement.

16. Accounting choices made by the Board and those made by individual statement preparers have this in common: they both aim to produce information that satisfies those criteria. Yet, though the objectives of the Board and of individual preparers are alike in that respect, the Board does not expect all its policy decisions to accord exactly with the preferences of every one of its constituents. Indeed, they clearly cannot do so, for the preferences of its constituents do not accord with each other. Left to themselves, business enterprises, even in the same industry, would probably choose to adopt different reporting methods for similar circumstances. But in return for the sacrifice of some of that freedom, there is a gain from the greater comparability and consistency that adherence to externally imposed standards brings with it. There also is a gain in credibility. The public is naturally skeptical about the reliability of financial reporting if two enterprises account differently for the same economic phenomena.

17. Throughout this Statement, readers should keep in mind the objectives of the Board in issuing accounting standards of widespread applicability and those of individual preparers who are concerned with the informational needs of a particular enterprise. Though the criteria by which information should be judged are the same whether the judgment is made by the Board or by a preparer, they cannot be expected always to produce agreement on a preferred choice of accounting method. The best accounting policies will provide information that best achieves the objectives of financial

reporting. But whatever information is provided, it cannot be expected to be equally useful to all preparers and users, for the simple reason that individual needs and objectives vary. The Board strives to serve the needs of all, knowing that in doing so some individual preferences are sacrificed. Like motorists who observe traffic laws in the interest of their own and general traffic safety, so long as others do the same, in general, those who have to subordinate their individual preferences to observe common accounting standards will, in the long run, gain more than they lose.

18. The analogy between accounting standards and traffic laws merits closer examination. Traffic laws impose certain minima or maxima in regulating behavior but still permit considerable flexibility in driving habits. A speed limit leaves slow drivers to choose their speed below the maximum and does not prohibit passing by other drivers. Even a requirement to drive on the right allows a driver to choose and to change lanes on all but very narrow roads. The point is that in most respects the traffic laws allow for considerable variations within a framework of rules. In setting accounting standards, the Board also strives to leave as much room as possible for individual choices and preferences while securing the degree of conformity necessary to attain its objectives.

19. This Statement must be seen as part of the larger conceptual framework, an important part of the foundations of which were laid with the publication of Concepts Statement 1. This Statement, with the proposed Statement on the elements of financial statements of business enterprises, is part of the second stage of the structure. With successive stages, the level of abstraction will give way to increasing specificity. The qualitative characteristics discussed in this document are formulated in rather general terms. As they are brought to bear on particular situations in subsequent pronouncements, however, those generalizations will give way to specific applications.

20. While this Statement concentrates on guidelines for making accounting choices, either by the Board or by those who provide financial information, its function is not to make those choices. Insofar as those choices lie within the Board's responsibility, some of them (for example, those relating to the attributes of assets and liabilities that should be measured and presented in financial statements) will be made in other parts of the conceptual framework project. Other choices will be made in the standards to be issued by the Board from time to time. The qualitative characteristics put forward in this Statement are intended to facilitate those choices and to

aid in making them consistent with one another.

The Objectives of Financial Reporting

21. The objectives of financial reporting underlie judgments about the qualities of financial information, for only when those objectives have been established can a start be made on defining the characteristics of the information needed to attain them. In Concepts Statement 1, the Board set out the objectives of financial reporting for business enterprises that will guide it. The information covered by that Statement was not limited to the contents of financial statements. "Financial reporting," the Statement said, "includes not only financial statements but also other means of communicating information that relates, directly or indirectly, to the information provided by the accounting system—that is, information about an enterprise's resources, obligations, earnings, etc. [paragraph 7]."

22. The objectives of financial reporting are summarized in the following excerpts from the Statement:

Financial reporting should provide information that is useful to present and potential investors and creditors and other users in making rational investment, credit, and similar decisions. The information should be comprehensible to those who have a reasonable understanding of business and economic activities and are willing to study the information with reasonable diligence [paragraph 34].

Financial reporting should provide information to help present and potential investors and creditors and other users in assessing the amounts, timing, and uncertainty of prospective cash receipts from dividends or interest and the proceeds from the sale, redemption, or maturity of securities or loans. The prospects for those cash receipts are affected by an enterprise's ability to generate enough cash to meet its obligations when due and its other cash operating needs, to reinvest in operations, and to pay cash dividends and may also be affected by perceptions of investors and creditors generally about that ability, which affect market prices of the enterprise's securities. Thus, financial reporting should provide information to help investors, creditors, and others assess the amounts, timing, and uncertainty of prospective net cash inflows to the related enterprise [paragraph 37].

Financial reporting should provide information about the economic resources of an enterprise, the claims to those resources (obligations of the enterprise to transfer resources to other entities and owners' equity), and the effects of transactions, events, and circumstances that change resources and claims to those resources [paragraph 40].

Financial reporting should provide information about an enterprise's financial performance during a period. Investors and creditors often use information about the past to help in assessing the prospects of an enterprise. Thus, although investment and credit decisions reflect investors' and creditors' expectations about future enterprise performance, those expectations are commonly based at least partly on evaluations of past enterprise performance [paragraph 42].

The primary focus of financial reporting is information about an enterprise's performance provided by measures of earnings and its components [paragraph 43].

Financial reporting should provide information about how an enterprise obtains and spends cash, about its borrowing and repayment of borrowing, about its capital transactions, including cash dividends and other distributions of enterprise resources to owners, and about other factors that may affect an enterprise's liquidity or solvency [paragraph 49].

Financial reporting should provide information about how management of an enterprise has discharged its stewardship responsibility to owners (stockholders) for the use of enterprise resources entrusted to it [paragraph 50].

Financial reporting should provide information that is useful to managers and directors in making decisions in the interests of owners [paragraph 52].

23. The Statement on objectives makes clear (paragraph 31) that *financial reporting* means *general purpose external financial reporting by business enterprises.* General purpose financial reporting attempts to meet "the informational needs of external users who lack the authority to prescribe the financial information they want from an enterprise and therefore must use the information that management communicates to them" (paragraph 28). General purpose statements are not all purpose statements, and never can be.

24. An analogy with cartography has been used to convey some of the characteristics of financial reporting, and it may be useful here. A map represents the geographical features of the mapped area by using symbols bearing no resemblance to the actual countryside, yet they communicate a great deal of information about it. The captions and numbers in financial statements present a "picture" of a business enterprise and many of its external and internal relationships more rigorously—more informatively, in fact—than a simple description of it. There are, admittedly, important differences between geography and economic activity and, therefore, between maps and financial statements. But the similarities may, nevertheless, be illuminating.

25. A "general purpose" map that tried to be "all purpose" would be unintelligible, once information about political boundaries, communications, physical features, geological structure, climate, economic activity, ethnic groupings, and all the other things that mapmakers can map were put on it. Even on a so-called general purpose map, therefore, the cartographer has to select the data to be presented. The cartographer, in fact, has to decide to serve some purposes and neglect others. The fact is that all maps are really special purpose maps, but some are more specialized than others. And so are financial statements. Some of the criticisms of financial statements derive from a failure to understand that even a general purpose statement can be relevant to and can, therefore, serve only a limited number of its users' needs.

26. The objectives focus financial reporting on a particular kind of economic decision—committing (or continuing to commit) cash or other resources to a business enterprise with expectation of future compensation or return, usually in cash but sometimes in other goods or services. Suppliers, lenders, employees, owners, and, to a lesser extent, customers commonly make decisions of that kind, and managers continually make them about an enterprise's resources. Concepts Statement 1 uses investment and credit decisions as prototypes of the kind of decisions on which financial reporting focuses. Nevertheless, as just noted, the Board, in developing the qualities in this Statement, must be concerned with groups of users of financial information who have generally similar needs. Those qualities do not necessarily fit all users' needs equally well.

THE CENTRAL ROLE OF DECISION MAKING

27. All financial reporting is concerned in varying degrees with decision making (though decision makers also use information obtained from other sources). The need for information on which to base investment, credit, and similar decisions underlies the objectives of financial reporting cited earlier.

28. Even objectives that are oriented more towards stewardship are concerned with decisions. The broader stewardship use of accounting, which is concerned with the efficiency, effectiveness, and integrity of the steward, helps stockholders or other financially interested parties (for example, bondholders) to evaluate the management of an enterprise. But that would be a pointless activity if

there were no possibility of taking action based on the results. Management is accountable to stockholders through an elected board of directors, but stockholders are often passive and do not insist on major management changes as long as an enterprise is reasonably successful. Their appraisals of management's stewardship help them to assess prospects for their investments, and stockholders who are dissatisfied with management's stewardship of those investments commonly sell their stock in the enterprise. Bondholders are concerned with management's compliance with bond indentures and may take legal action if covenants are broken. Thus, decision making and stewardship are interrelated accounting objectives. Indeed, the stewardship role of accounting may be viewed as subordinate to and a part of the decision making role, which is virtually all encompassing.

29. That view of the stewardship use of accounting in no way diminishes its importance, nor does it elevate the predictive value of accounting information above its confirmatory value. In its stewardship use, accounting compiles records of past transactions and events and uses those records to measure performance. The measurement confirms expectations or shows how far actual achievements diverged from them. The confirmation or divergence becomes the basis for a decision—which will often be a decision to leave things alone. To say that stewardship reporting is an aspect of accounting's decision making role is simply to say that its purpose is to guide actions that *may* need to be taken in relation to the steward or in relation to the activity that is being monitored.

30. The central role assigned here to decision making leads straight to the overriding criterion by which all accounting choices must be judged. The better choice is the one that, subject to considerations of cost, produces from among the available alternatives information that is most useful for decision making.[4]

31. So broad a generalization looks self-evident. Indeed, it says no more than the Board said in Concepts Statement 1 (paragraph 9): "Financial reporting is not an end in itself but is intended to provide information that is useful in making business and economic decisions. . . ." The challenge is to define in more detail what makes accounting information useful for decision making. If there is a serious difference of opinion, it is not over the general nature of characteristics such as relevance and reliability, which clearly occupy important places in the hierarchy of qualities that make information useful. There may indeed be some disagreement about their relative importance. But more serious disagreement

arises over the choice between two accounting methods (for example, methods of allocating costs or recognizing revenues) if the choice involves a judgment about which method will produce more relevant or more reliable results or a judgment about whether the superior relevance of the results of one method outweighs the superior reliability of the results of the other.

A HIERARCHY OF ACCOUNTING QUALITIES

32. The characteristics of information that make it a desirable commodity guide the selection of preferred accounting policies from among available alternatives. They can be viewed as a hierachy of qualities, with usefulness for decision making of most importance. Without usefulness, there would be no benefits from information to set against its costs. The hierarchy is represented in Figure 1.

Features and Limitations of the Chart

33. Before discussing the informational characteristics shown on the chart, some words of explanation are offered about what the chart attempts to convey. It is a limited device—limited, for example, by being in two dimensions only—for showing certain relationships among the qualities that make accounting information useful. The primary qualities are that accounting information shall be relevant and reliable. If either of those qualities is completely missing, the information will not be useful. Relevance and reliability can be further analyzed into a number of components. To be relevant, information must be timely and it must have predictive value *or* feedback value or both. To be reliable, information must have representational faithfulness and it must be verifiable and neutral (the meaning of these terms, like all the other terms used in the chart, will be discussed later). Comparability, including consistency, is a secondary quality that interacts with relevance and reliability to contribute to the usefulness of information. Finally, two constraints are shown on the chart, both primarily quantitative rather than qualitative in character. Information can be useful and yet be too costly to justify providing it. To be useful and worth providing, the benefits of information should exceed its cost. All of the qualities shown are subject to a materiality threshold, and that is also shown as a constraint. The requirement that information be reliable can still be met even though it may contain immaterial errors, for errors that are not material will not perceptibly diminish its usefulness. Similar considerations apply to the other characteristics of information shown on the chart.

---

[4]The divergence among individual needs was noted in paragraph 17. It needs to be considered here and throughout this Statement.

FIGURE 1

A HIERARCHY OF ACCOUNTING QUALITIES

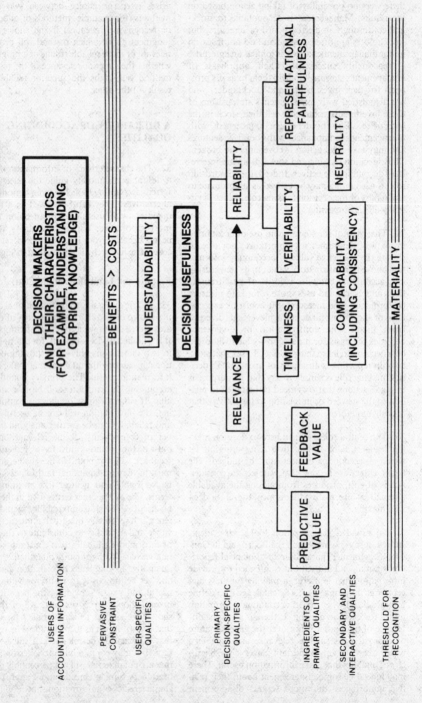

34. An important limitation of the hierarchy is that while it does distinguish between primary and other qualities, it does not assign priorities among qualities. That limitation is a salutary one, however, for the relative weight to be given to different qualities must vary according to circumstances. The hierarchy should be seen as no more than an explanatory device, the purpose of which is to clarify certain relationships rather than to assign relative weights. To be useful, financial information must have each of the qualities shown to a minimum degree. Beyond that, the rate at which one quality can be sacrificed in return for a gain in another quality without making the information less useful overall will be different in different situations.

35. Several characteristics that some would wish to see included in the hierarchy are not shown there. Rather than confuse a discussion of its positive features by explaining at this point why certain items have been excluded, discussion of that matter has been placed in Appendix B with other responses to comment letters that have been received by the Board.

Decision Makers and Their Characteristics

36. In the last analysis, each decision maker judges what accounting information is useful, and that judgment is influenced by factors such as the decisions to be made, the methods of decision making to be used, the information already possessed or obtainable from other sources, and the decision maker's capacity (alone or with professional help) to process the information. The optimal information for one user will not be optimal for another. Consequently, the Board, which must try to cater to many different users while considering the burdens placed on those who have to provide information, constantly treads a fine line between requiring disclosure of too much information and requiring too little.

37. The better informed decision makers are, the less likely it is that any new information can add materially to what they already know. That may make the new information less useful, but it does not make it less relevant to the situation. If an item of information reaches a user and then, a little later, the user receives the same item from another source, it is not less relevant the second time, though it will have less value. For that reason, relevance has been defined in this Statement (paragraphs 46 and 47) in terms of the capacity of information to make a difference (to someone who does not already have it) rather than in terms of the difference it actually does make. The difference it actually does make may be more a function of how much is already known (a condition specific to a particular user) than of the content of the new messages themselves (decision-specific qualities of information).

38. Thus, management in general and owners of small or closely held enterprises may find at least some information provided by external financial reporting to be less useful to them than it is to stockholders of large or publicly held enterprises. The latter must rely on financial reporting for information that the former has access to as a result of their intimate relationship to their enterprise.

39. Similarly, information cannot be useful to a person who cannot understand it. However, information may be relevant to a situation even though it cannot be understood by the person who confronts the situation. Its relevance will depend on its capacity to reduce uncertainty about the situation, even though it may call for more understanding to interpret it than its prospective user can command. For example, a hungry vegetarian traveling in a foreign country may experience difficulty in obtaining acceptable food when ordering from a menu printed in an unfamiliar language. The listing of items on the menu is relevant to the decision to be made but the traveler cannot use that information unless it is translated into another (understandable) language. Thus, the information may not be useful to a particular user even though it is relevant to the situation that the user faces. Information that cannot be understood, like information that is not available, may be relevant, but its relevance will be wasted because its capacity to make a difference cannot be utilized.

**Understandability and Other
User-Specific Qualities**

40. The Board said in Concepts Statement 1 (paragraph 34) that information provided by financial reporting should be comprehensible to those who have a reasonable understanding of business and economic activities and are willing to study the information with reasonable diligence. The Board elaborated as follows:

> Financial information is a tool and, like most tools, cannot be of much direct help to those who are unable or unwilling to use it or who misuse it. Its use can be learned, however, and financial reporting should provide information that can be used by all—nonprofessionals as well as professionals—who are willing to learn to use it properly. Efforts may be needed to increase the understandability of financial information. Cost-benefit considerations may indicate that information understood or used by only a few should not be provided. Conversely, financial reporting should not exclude relevant information merely because it is difficult for some to understand or because some investors or creditors choose not to use it [paragraph 36].

The benefits of information may be increased by

making it more understandable and, hence, useful to a wider circle of users. Understandability of information is governed by a combination of user characteristics and characteristics inherent in the information, which is why understandability and other user-specific characteristics occupy a position in the hierarchy of qualities as a link between the characteristics of users (decision makers) and decision-specific qualities of information. Other parts of the conceptual framework project that will deal with displays of financial information will have a contribution to make to this matter.

41. Understandability and similar qualities of information, for example, newness, are closely related to the characteristics of *particular* decision makers as well as *classes* of decision makers. However, the Board is concerned with qualities of information that relate to broad classes of decision makers rather than to particular decision makers. Understandability can be classified as relating to particular decision makers (does the decision maker speak that language?) or relating to classes of decision makers (is the disclosure intelligible to the audience for which it is intended?). Newness of information can be classified similarly to understandability. The Board can influence the newness of information to broad classes of decision makers, for example, by requiring the disclosure of relevant information that was not previously available. However, the newness to a particular decision maker of generally available information depends largely on the timing of the receipt of that information by the decision maker, and that timing is subject to the effects of many variables extraneous to accounting and financial reporting. The Board establishes concepts and standards for general purpose external financial reporting by considering the needs of broad classes of decision makers and cannot base its decisions on the specific circumstances of individual decision makers.

Relative Importance and Trade-Offs

42. Although financial information must be both relevant and reliable to be useful, information may possess both characteristics to varying degrees. It may be possible to trade relevance for reliability or vice versa, though not to the point of dispensing with one of them altogether. Information may also have other characteristics shown on the chart to varying degrees, and other trade-offs between characteristics may be necessary or beneficial.

43. The question has been raised whether the relative importance to be attached to relevance and reliability should be different in financial statements and in other means of financial reporting. The

issuance in September 1979 of FASB Statement No. 33, *Financial Reporting and Changing Prices,* calling for reporting by certain enterprises of supplementary information on both constant dollar and current cost bases outside of the primary financial statements, has brought into prominence the question of whether information reported outside financial statements should be allowed to be less reliable than what is reported in them.

44. Although there seems to be considerable support for the view that reliability should be the dominant quality in the information conveyed in financial statements, even at the expense of relevance, while the opposite is true of information conveyed outside the financial statements, that view has in it the seeds of danger. Like most potentially harmful generalizations, it does contain a germ of truth: almost everyone agrees that criteria for formally recognizing elements in financial statements call for a minimum level or threshold of reliability of measurement that should be higher than is usually considered necessary for disclosing information outside financial statements. But the remainder of the proposition does not follow. If it were carried to its logical conclusion and resulted in a downgrading of relevance of information in financial statements, the end would be that most really useful information provided by financial reporting would be conveyed outside the financial statements, while the audited financial statements would increasingly convey highly reliable but largely irrelevant, and thus useless, information. Those matters are germane to another part of the conceptual framework, the project on financial statements and other means of financial reporting.

45. This Statement discusses trade-offs between characteristics at several points. Those discussions apply generally to kinds of decisions and to groups of users of accounting information but do not necessarily apply to individual users. In a particular situation, the importance attached to relevance in relation to the importance of other decision specific qualities of accounting information (for example, reliability) will be different for different information users, and their willingness to trade one quality for another will also differ. The same thing is true of other considerations such as timeliness. That fact has an important bearing on the question of preferability, for it probably puts unanimity about preferences among accounting alternatives out of reach. Even though considerable agreement exists about the qualitative characteristics that "good" accounting information should have, no consensus can be expected about their relative importance in a specific situation because different users have or perceive themselves to have different needs and, therefore, have different preferences.

RELEVANCE

46. In discussions of accounting criteria, relevance has usually been defined in the dictionary sense, as pertaining to or having a bearing on the matter in question. That broad definition is satisfactory as far as it goes—information must, of course, be logically related to a decision in order to be relevant to it. Mistaken attempts to base decisions on logically unrelated information cannot convert irrelevant information into relevant information[5] any more than ignoring relevant information makes it irrelevant. However, the meaning of relevance for financial reporting needs to be made more explicit. Specifically, it is information's capacity to "make a difference" that identifies it as relevant to a decision.

47. To be relevant to investors, creditors, and others for investment, credit, and similar decisions, accounting information must be capable of making a difference in a decision by helping users to form predictions about the outcomes of past, present, and future events or to confirm or correct expectations. "Event" is a happening of consequence to an enterprise (Exposure Draft on elements, paragraph 67), and in this context can mean, for example, the receipt of a sales order or a price change in something the enterprise buys or sells. "Outcome" is the effect or result of an event or series of events and in this context can mean, for example, that last year's profit was $X or the expectation that this year's profit will be $Y. The event in question may be a past event the outcome of which is not already known, or it may be a future event the outcome of which can only be predicted.

48. Information need not itself be a prediction of future events or outcomes to be useful in forming, confirming, or changing expectations about future events or outcomes. Information about the present status of economic resources or obligations or about an enterprise's past performance is commonly a basis for expectations (Concepts Statement 1, paragraph 42).

49. Information may confirm expectations or it may change them. If it confirms them, it increases the probability that the results will be as previously expected. If it changes them, it changes the perceived probabilities of the previous possible outcomes. Either way, it makes a difference to one who does not already have that information. Decisions already made need not be changed, nor need a course of action already embarked on be altered by the information. A decision to hold rather than to sell an investment is a decision, and information that supports holding can be as relevant as information that leads to a sale. Information is relevant if the degree of uncertainty about the result of a decision that has already been made is confirmed or altered by the new information; it need not alter the decision.

50. One of the more fundamental questions raised by the search for relevance in accounting concerns the choice of attribute to be measured for financial reporting purposes. Will financial statements be more relevant if they are based on historical costs, current costs, or some other attribute? The question must be left for consideration in other parts of the conceptual framework project; but because of lack of experience with information providing measures of several of those attributes and differences of opinion about their relevance and reliability, it is not surprising that agreement on the question is so difficult to obtain.

Feedback[6] Value and Predictive Value as Components of Relevance

51. Information can make a difference to decisions by improving decision makers' capacities to predict or by confirming or correcting their earlier expectations. Usually, information does both at once, because knowledge about the outcome of actions already taken will generally improve decision makers' abilities to predict the results of similar future actions. Without a knowledge of the past, the basis for a prediction will usually be lacking. Without an interest in the future, knowledge of the past is sterile.

52. The same point can be made by saying that information is relevant to a situation if it can reduce uncertainty about the situation. Information that was not known previously about a past activity clearly reduces uncertainty about its outcome, and information about past activities is usually an indispensable point of departure for attempts to foresee the consequences of related future activities. Disclosure requirements almost always have the dual purpose of helping to predict and confirming or correcting earlier predictions. The reporting of business results by segments is a good example of accounting reports whose relevance is believed to lie both in the information they convey about the past performance of segments and in their contribution to an investor's ability to predict the trend of earnings of a diversified company. Another example is to be found in interim earnings reports, which provide both feedback on past performance and a basis for

---

[5]Information theorists assert that "relevant" as an adjective qualifying "information" is redundant, for irrelevant information is mere data. This Statement does not follow that usage.

[6]This inelegant term is used because no other single word has been found to comprehend both confirmation or corroboration and their opposites.

prediction for anyone wishing to forecast annual earnings before the year-end.

53. To say that accounting information has *predictive value* is not to say that it is itself a *prediction*. It may be useful here to draw an analogy between the financial information that analysts and others use in predicting earnings or financial position and the information that meteorologists use in forecasting weather. Meteorologists gather and chart information about actual conditions—temperatures, barometric pressures, wind velocities at various altitudes, and so on—and draw their conclusions from the relationships and patterns that they detect. Success in forecasting the weather has increased as new methods of gathering information have been developed. New kinds of information have become available, and with greater speed than was previously possible. To the simple sources of information available to our ancestors have been added satellite photographs, radar, and radiosondes to give information about the upper atmosphere. New information makes possible more sophisticated predictive models. When a meteorologist selects from among the alternative sources of information and methods of gathering information—about existing conditions, since future conditions cannot be known—those sources and methods that have the greatest predictive value can be expected to be favored. So it is with information about the existing financial state of a company and observed changes in that state from which predictions of success, failure, growth, or stagnation may be inferred. Users can be expected to favor those sources of information and analytical methods that have the greatest predictive value in achieving their specific objectives. Predictive value here means value as an *input* into a predictive process, not value directly as a prediction.

54. An important similarity and an important difference between predicting the weather and predicting financial performance may be noted. The similarity is that the meteorologist's information and the information derived from financial reporting both have to be fed into a predictive model[7] before they can throw light on the future. Financial predictions, like weather forecasts, are the joint product of a model and the data that go into it. A choice between alternative accounting methods on the basis of their predictive value can be made only if the characteristics of the model to be used are generally known. For example, the econometric models now used for economic forecasting are designed to use as data financial aggregates (among other things) as those aggregates are compiled at present. They might work less well if price-level adjusted data were

used. However, it might be possible to revise the model for use with that kind of data so that even better predictions could be made. The point is that the predictive value of information cannot be assessed in the abstract. It has to be transformed into a prediction, and the nature of the transformation as well as the data used determine the outcome.

55. The important difference between meteorological and financial predictions is that only exceptionally can meteorological predictions have an effect on the weather, but business or economic decision makers' predictions often affect their subjects. For example, the use of financial models to predict business failures looks quite successful judged in the light of hindsight by looking at the financial history of failed firms during their last declining years. But a prediction of failure can be self-fulfilling by restricting a company's access to credit. The prediction could also bring about a recovery by initiating action by managers or bankers to avert failure. Because information affects human behavior and because different people react differently to it, financial information cannot be evaluated by means of a simple tally of the correct predictions that are based on it. Nevertheless, predictive value is an important consideration in distinguishing relevant from irrelevant accounting information.

Timeliness

56. Timeliness is an ancillary aspect of relevance. If information is not available when it is needed or becomes available only so long after the reported events that it has no value for future action, it lacks relevance and is of little or no use. Timeliness in the present context means having information available to decision makers before it loses its capacity to influence decisions. Timeliness alone cannot make information relevant, but a lack of timeliness can rob information of relevance it might otherwise have had.

57. Clearly, there are degrees of timeliness. In some situations, the capacity of information to influence decisions may evaporate quickly, as, for example, in a fast-moving situation such as a take-over bid or a strike, so that timeliness may have to be measured in days or perhaps hours. In other contexts, such as routine reports by an enterprise of its annual results, it may take a longer delay to diminish materially the relevance and, therefore, the usefulness of the information. But a gain in relevance that comes with increased timeliness may entail sacrifices of other desirable characteristics of information, and as a result there may be an overall gain or loss in usefulness. It may sometimes be desirable, for example, to

---

[7]A model is no more than a simplified, scaled-down representation of a situation that is to be analyzed. Typically, sophisticated models are expressed in terms of mathematical equations.

sacrifice precision for timeliness, for an approximation produced quickly is often more useful than precise information that takes longer to get out. Of course, if, in the interest of timeliness, the reliability of the information is sacrificed to a material degree, the result may be to rob the information of much of its usefulness. What constitutes a material loss of reliability is discussed in later paragraphs. Yet, while every loss of reliability diminishes the usefulness of information, it will often be possible to approximate an accounting number to make it available more quickly without making it materially unreliable. As a result, its overall usefulness may be enhanced.

RELIABILITY

58. That information should be reliable as well as relevant is a notion that is central to accounting. It is, therefore, important to be clear about the nature of the claim that is being made for an accounting number that is described as reliable.

59. The reliability of a measure rests on the faithfulness with which it represents what it purports to represent, coupled with an assurance for the user, which comes through verification, that it has that representational quality. Of course, degrees of reliability must be recognized. It is hardly ever a question of black or white, but rather of more reliability or less.

60. Two different meanings of reliability can be distinguished and illustrated by considering what might be meant by describing a drug as reliable. It could mean that the drug can be relied on to cure or alleviate the condition for which it was prescribed, or it could mean that a dose of the drug can be relied on to conform to the formula shown on the label. The first meaning implies that the drug is effective at doing what it is expected to do. The second meaning implies nothing about effectiveness but does imply a correspondence between what is represented on the label and what is contained in the bottle.[8]

61. Effectiveness is indeed a quality that is necessary in information, but in an accounting context it goes by another name—relevance. It is not always easy to maintain a clear distinction between relevance and reliability, as in the drug illustration, yet it is important to try to keep the two concepts apart. Given at least a minimum acceptable level of reliability, the choice of a drug will depend on its effectiveness in treating the condition for which it is prescribed.

62. Use of the term reliability in this Statement implies nothing about effectiveness. Accounting information is reliable to the extent that users can depend on it to represent the economic conditions or events that it purports to represent. As indicated in paragraph 59, reliability of accounting information stems from two characteristics that it is desirable to keep separate, representational faithfulness and verifiability. Neutrality of information also interacts with those two characteristics to affect its usefulness.

Representational Faithfulness

63. Representational faithfulness is correspondence or agreement between a measure or description and the phenomenon it purports to represent. In accounting, the phenomena to be represented are economic resources and obligations and the transactions and events that change those resources and obligations.[9]

64. Clearly, much depends on the meaning of the words "purports to represent" in the preceding paragraphs. Sometimes, but rarely, information is unreliable because of simple misrepresentation. Receivables, for example, may misrepresent large sums as collectible that, in fact, are uncollectible. Unreliability of that kind may not be easy to detect, but once detected its nature is not open to argument. More subtle is the information conveyed by an item such as "goodwill." Does a balance sheet that shows goodwill as an asset purport to represent the company as having no goodwill except what is shown? An uninformed reader may well think so, while one who is familiar with present generally accepted accounting principles will know that nonpurchased goodwill is not included. The discussion of reliability in this Statement assumes a reasonably informed user (paragraphs 36-41), for example, one who understands that the information provided by financial reporting often results from approximate, rather than exact, measures involving numerous estimates, classifications, summarizations, judgments, and allocations. The following paragraphs elaborate on and illustrate the concept of representational faithfulness used in this Statement, including the considerations noted in this and the preceding paragraphs.

Degrees of Representational Faithfulness

65. The cost of acquiring assets is more often than not capable of being determined unambiguously,

---

[8]Perhaps, more accurately, there is also a third meaning—that the drug does not have hidden undesirable side effects. The alleged undesirable economic impact of certain FASB standards is perhaps an accounting analogue to side effects of drugs, which are, in essence, costs to be considered in a cost-benefit analysis.

[9]Representational faithfulness is closely related to what behavioral scientists call "validity," as in the statement that intelligence quotients are (or are not) a valid measure of intelligence. Validity is a more convenient term than representational faithfulness, but out of its scientific context it has too broad a connotation for it to be an appropriate substitute.

but that is by no means always the case. Thus, if a collection of assets is bought for a specified amount, the cost attributable to each individual item may be impossible to ascertain. The acquisition cost may also be difficult to determine if assets are acquired in exchange for assets other than cash, by issuing stock, or in transactions with related parties. If assets are converted into other assets within an enterprise, as when raw materials are converted into finished products, or buildings or equipment are constructed by an enterprise for its own use, the multiplicity of costing conventions that can be used, all within the boundaries of present generally accepted accounting principles, make it impossible to attach a unique cost to the finished asset. Thus, it may not be certain that the cost for the asset in the enterprise's records does faithfully represent its cost.

66. The problem of determining cost becomes more difficult if assets are fungible. If there have been several purchases at different prices and a number of disposals at different dates, only by the adoption of some convention (such as first-in, first-out) can a cost be attributed to the assets on hand at a particular date. Since what is shown as the assets' cost is only one of several alternatives, it is difficult to substantiate that the chosen amount does represent the economic phenomena in question.

67. In the absence of market prices for the assets in question, representational faithfulness of amounts purporting to be current costs or fair values of assets also involves the same kinds of difficulties as those already described. For example, unless there are markets for used equipment or partially processed products, the current costs or fair values of those assets can be determined only by means such as deducting estimated depreciation from current costs or fair values of similar new assets, applying price indexes to past acquisition costs, or combining the current costs of the materials, labor, and overhead used. The allocations required by those procedures inevitably cast at least some doubt on the representational faithfulness of the results.

68. As accounting concepts become more complex, assessing the faithfulness of accounting representations of economic phenomena becomes increasingly difficult, and separating relevance or effectiveness from reliability becomes much more difficult than in the drug example used earlier (paragraphs 60 and 61). Social scientists have much discussed the concept of representational faithfulness (which they call validity) in connection with educational testing, and though that field may seem remote from accounting, the difficulties that beset it in some respects bear a close resemblance to some of those encountered in accounting. If two students score 640 and 580, respectively, in a scholastic aptitude test of verbal skills, it is inferred that the first student has more

verbal aptitude than the second. But does the test really measure verbal aptitude? Is it, in other words, a valid test of verbal aptitude? That is a very difficult question to answer, for what is verbal aptitude? Without a definition of the quality to be measured, the validity of the test cannot be assessed. The problem of defining intelligence and of judging whether intelligence tests validly measure it may be even more difficult because of the many different manifestations of intelligence, the problems of separating innate and acquired abilities, standardizing for differences in social conditions, and many other things.

69. The nature of the problem just described can be clarified by means of an example. A spelling test is administered orally to a group of students. The words are read aloud by the tester, and the students are required to write down the test words. Some students, though they can usually spell well, fail the test. The reason, it turns out, is that they have hearing problems. The test score purports to measure ability to spell, whereas it, in fact, is partly measuring aural acuity. The test score lacks true representational faithfulness.

70. Another example, perhaps more closely related to accounting, may serve to further highlight some possible ways in which a representation may not be faithful to the economic phenomena that it purports to represent. The Consumer Price Index for All Urban Consumers (CPI-U) is an index of price level changes affecting consumers generally and is often used to measure changes in the general purchasing power of the monetary unit itself. However, if it were used as a measure of the price change of a specific asset, a purchase of a specific consumer, or an acquisition of a specific enterprise, it would not likely provide a faithful representation. The CPI-U is a "market basket" index, based on the average price a typical consumer would pay for a selection of consumer goods. Specific price changes experienced by specific consumers will differ from the index to the extent their consumption patterns are different from the selection of goods in the index market basket if the price changes on the goods they purchase are not perfectly correlated to the changes in the index. General price indexes, such as the CPI-U, cannot acknowledge individual differences, but they may provide a reasonable measure of the loss in the general purchasing power of the monetary unit. The index must be interpreted in the context of what it was designed to do and in view of the limitations of any averaging process.

71. The discussion in the preceding paragraph illustrates some of the problems that may arise when representations of economic phenomena are used in different contexts than those for which they were designed. Accounting information, for example, purports to reflect the activities of a particular

enterprise. However, aggregating the amounts reported by all businesses may not result in a faithful representation of total activity in the business sector, for that is not the purpose for which the accounting information was intended. Information that is representationally faithful in the context for which it was designed, therefore, may not be reliable when used in other contexts.

Precision and Uncertainty

72. Reliability does not imply certainty or precision. Indeed, any pretension to those qualities if they do not exist is a negation of reliability. Sometimes, a range within which an estimate may fall will convey information more reliably than can a single (point) estimate. In other cases, an indication of the probabilities attaching to different values of an attribute may be the best way of giving information reliably about the measure of the attribute and the uncertainty that surrounds it. Reporting accounting numbers as certain and precise if they are not is a negation of reliable reporting.

73. Different uses of information may require different degrees of reliability and, consequently, what constitutes a material loss or gain in reliability may vary according to use. An error in timekeeping of a few seconds a day will usually be acceptable to the owner of an ordinary wristwatch, whereas the same error would normally cause a chronometer to be judged unreliable. The difference is linked to use—a wristwatch is used for purposes for which accuracy within a few seconds (or perhaps a few minutes) is satisfactory; a chronometer is used for navigation, scientific work, and the like, uses for which a high degree of accuracy is required because an error of a few seconds or a fraction of a second may have large consequences. In everyday language, both the wristwatch and the chronometer are said to be reliable. By the standard of the chronometer, the wristwatch, in fact, is unreliable. Yet the watch's owner does not perceive it to be unreliable, for it is not expected to have the accuracy of a chronometer.

74. Fortunately, that is well understood by accountants. They recognize that a difference between an estimate and an accurate measurement may be material in one context and not material in another. The relationship between the concepts of reliability and materiality, including what constitutes *material* unreliability, will be discussed later in this Statement.

75. Reliability as a quality of a predictor has a somewhat different meaning from reliability as a quality of a measure. The reliability of a barometer should be judged in terms of the accuracy with which it measures air pressure and changes in air pressure. That is all that a barometer is constructed to do. Yet questions about its reliability are more likely to be couched in terms of its accuracy as a predictor of the weather, even though weather conditions in any location are the result of many factors besides air pressure in that location. Though much of the relevance of accounting information may derive from its value as input to a prediction model, the probability that it will lead to correct predictions does not determine its reliability as a set of measurements. The correctness of predictions depends as much on the predictive model used as on the data that go into the model. Thus, the result of a predictive process cannot be used to assess the reliability of the inputs into it any more than a run of successes by a barometer in forecasting the weather can tell us much about the accuracy with which it measures the pressure of the atmosphere.

76. The financial statements of a business enterprise can be thought of as a representation of the resources and obligations of an enterprise and the financial flows into, out of, and within the enterprise—as a model of the enterprise.[10] Like all models, it must abstract from much that goes on in a real enterprise. No model, however sophisticated, can be expected to reflect all the functions and relationships that are found within a complex organization. To do so, the model would have to be virtually a reproduction of the original. In real life, it is necessary to accept a much smaller degree of correspondence between the model and the original than that. One can be satisfied if none of the important functions and relationships are lost. Before an accounting model—either the one now used or an alternative—can be judged to represent an enterprise reliably, it must be determined that none of the important financial functions of the enterprise or its relationships have been lost or distorted. The mere fact that model works—that when it receives inputs it produces outputs—gives no assurance that it faithfully represents the original. Just as a distorting mirror reflects a warped image of the person standing in front of it or just as an inexpensive loudspeaker fails to reproduce faithfully the sounds that went into the microphone or onto the phonograph records, so a bad model gives a distorted representation of the system that it models. The question that accountants must face continually is how much distortion is acceptable. The cost of a perfect sound reproduction system puts it out of reach of most people, and perfect reliability of accounting information is equally unattainable.

---

[10]Nothing is implied here about the possible predictive uses of the model. While it is true that models are generally used to make predictions, they need not be so used. A model is no more than a representation of certain aspects of the real world.

Effects of Bias

77. Bias in measurement is the tendency of a measure to fall more often on one side than the other of what it represents instead of being equally likely to fall on either side. Bias in accounting measures means a tendency to be consistently too high or too low.

78. Accounting information may not represent faithfully what it purports to represent because it has one or both of two kinds of bias. The measurement method may be biased, so that the resulting measurement fails to represent what it purports to represent. Alternatively, or additionally, the measurer, through lack of skill or lack of integrity, or both, may misapply the measurement method chosen. In other words, there may be bias, not necessarily intended, on the part of the measurer. Those two kinds of bias are further discussed in the following paragraphs and in the next section on "verifiability." Intentional bias introduced to attain a predetermined result or induce a particular mode of behavior is discussed under "neutrality" (paragraphs 98-110).

Completeness

79. Freedom from bias, both in the measurer and the measurement method, implies that nothing material is left out of the information that may be necessary to insure that it validly represents the underlying events and conditions. Reliability implies completeness of information, at least within the bounds of what is material and feasible, considering the cost. A map that is 99 percent reliable but fails to show a bridge across a river where one exists can do much harm. Completeness, however, must always be relative, for neither maps nor financial reports can show everything.

80. Completeness of information also affects its relevance. Relevance of information is adversely affected if a relevant piece of information is omitted, even if the omission does not falsify what is shown. For example, in a diversified enterprise a failure to disclose that one segment was consistently unprofitable would not, before the issuance of FASB Statement No. 14, *Accounting for Segments of a Business Enterprise,* have caused the financial reporting to be judged unreliable, but that financial reporting would have been (as it would now be) deficient in relevance. Thus, completeness, within the bounds of feasibility, is necessary to both of the primary qualities that make information useful.

Verifiability

81. The quality of verifiability contributes to the usefulness of accounting information because the purpose of verification is to provide a significant degree of assurance that accounting measures represent what they purport to represent. Verification is more successful in minimizing measurer bias than measurement bias, and thus contributes in varying degrees toward assuring that particular measures represent faithfully the economic things or events that they purport to represent. Verification contributes little or nothing toward insuring that measures used are relevant to the decisions for which the information is intended to be useful.

82. Measurer bias is a less complex concept than measurement bias. In its simplest form, it arises from intentional misrepresentation. But even honest measurers may get different results from applying the same measurement method, especially if it involves a prediction of the outcome of a future event, such as the realization of an asset. Measurer bias can be detected and eliminated by having the measurement repeated with the same result. It is, therefore, a desirable quality of an accounting measure that it should be capable of replication. The Accounting Principles Board (APB) called this characteristic verifiability, and defined it in APB Statement No. 4, *Basic Concepts and Accounting Principles Underlying Financial Statements of Business Enterprises:* "Verifiable financial accounting information provides results that would be substantially duplicated by independent measurers using the same measurement methods" (paragraph 90).

83. The last five words of the APB's definition are significant for they imply that alternative methods may be available. Verification does not guarantee the appropriateness of the method used, much less the correctness of the resulting measure. It does carry some assurance that the measurement rule used, whatever it was, was applied carefully and without personal bias on the part of the measurer.

84. Verification implies consensus. Verifiability can be measured by looking at the dispersion of a number of independent measurements of some particular phenomenon. The more closely the measurements are likely to be clustered together, the greater the verifiability of the number used as a measure of the phenomenon.

85. Some accounting measurements are more easily verified than others. Alternative measures of cash will be closely clustered together, with a consequently high level of verifiability. There will be less unanimity about receivables (especially their net value), still less about inventories, and least about depreciable assets, for there will be disagreements about depreciation methods to be used, predictions of asset lives, and (if book values are based on historical cost) even which expenditures should be included in the investment base. More than one

empirical investigation has concluded that accountants may agree more about estimates of the market values of certain depreciable assets than about their carrying values. Hence, to the extent that verification depends on consensus, it may not always be those measurement methods widely regarded as "objective" that are most verifiable.

86. The elimination of measurer bias alone from information does not insure that the information will be reliable. Even though several independent measurers may agree on a single measurement method and apply it honestly and skillfully, the result will not be reliable if the method used is such that the measure does not represent what it purports to represent. Representational faithfulness of reported measurements lies in the closeness of their correspondence with the economic transactions, events, or circumstances that they represent.

87. Two further points about verifiability and representational faithfulness need to be emphasized. First, when accountants speak of verification they may mean either that an accounting measure itself has been verified or only that the procedures used to obtain the measure have been verified. For example, the price paid to acquire a block of marketable securities or a piece of land is normally directly verifiable, while the amount of depreciation for a period is normally only indirectly verifiable by verifying the depreciation method, calculations used, and consistency of application (paragraphs 65-67). Direct verification of accounting measures tends to minimize both personal bias introduced by a measurer (measurer bias) and bias inherent in measurement methods (measurement bias). Verification of only measurement methods tends to minimize measurer bias but usually preserves any bias there may be in the selection of measurement or allocation methods.

88. Second, measurement or allocation methods are often verifiable even if the measures they produce result in a very low degree of representational faithfulness. For example, before FASB Statement No. 5, *Accounting for Contingencies,* some enterprises that were "self-insured" recorded as an expense a portion of expected future losses from fire, flood, or other casualties. If an enterprise had a large number of "self-insured" assets, expectations of future losses could be actuarially computed, and the methods of allocating expected losses to periods could be readily verified. However, since uninsured losses occurred only when a casualty damaged or destroyed a particular asset or particular assets, the representational faithfulness of the resulting allocated measures was very low. In years in which no casualties were suffered by an enterprise, the allocated expenses or losses represented nonexistent transactions or events; while in years in which assets were actually damaged or destroyed, the allocated expenses or losses may have fallen far short of representing the losses.

89. In summary, verifiability means no more than that several measurers are likely to obtain the same measure. It is primarily a means of attempting to cope with measurement problems stemming from the uncertainty that surrounds accounting measures and is more successful in coping with some measurement problems than others. Verification of accounting information does not guarantee that the information has a high degree of representational faithfulness, and a measure with a high degree of verifiability is not necessarily relevant to the decision for which it is intended to be useful.

Reliability and Relevance

90. Reliability and relevance often impinge on each other. Reliability may suffer when an accounting method is changed to gain relevance, and vice versa. Sometimes it may not be clear whether there has been a loss or gain either of relevance or of reliability. The introduction of current cost accounting will illustrate the point. Proponents of current cost accounting believe that current cost income from continuing operations is a more relevant measure of operating performance than is operating profit computed on the basis of historical costs. They also believe that if holding gains and losses that may have accrued in past periods are separately displayed, current cost income from continuing operations better portrays operating performance. The uncertainties surrounding the determination of current costs, however, are considerable, and variations among estimates of their magnitude can be expected. Because of those variations, verifiability or representational faithfulness, components of reliability, might diminish. Whether there is a net gain to users of the information obviously depends on the relative weights attached to relevance and reliability (assuming, of course, that the claims made for current cost accounting are accepted).

Conservatism

91. Nothing has yet been said about conservatism, a convention that many accountants believe to be appropriate in making accounting decisions. To quote APB Statement 4:

> Frequently, assets and liabilities are measured in a context of significant uncertainties. Historically, managers, investors, and accountants have generally preferred that possible errors in measurement be in the direction of understatement rather than overstatement of net income and net assets. This has led to the convention of conservatism . . . [paragraph 171].

92. There is a place for a convention such as conservatism—meaning prudence—in financial accounting and reporting, because business and economic activities are surrounded by uncertainty, but it needs to be applied with care. Since a preference "that possible errors in measurement be in the direction of understatement rather than overstatement of net income and net assets" introduces a bias into financial reporting, conservatism tends to conflict with significant qualitative characteristics, such as representational faithfulness, neutrality, and comparability (including consistency). To be clear about what conservatism does not mean may often be as important as to be clear about what it means.

93. Conservatism in financial reporting should no longer connote deliberate, consistent understatement of net assets and profits. The Board emphasizes that point because conservatism has long been identified with the idea that deliberate understatement is a virtue. That notion became deeply ingrained and is still in evidence despite efforts over the past 40 years to change it. The convention of conservatism, which was once commonly expressed in the admonition to "anticipate no profits but anticipate all losses," developed during a time when balance sheets were considered the primary (and often only) financial statement, and details of profits or other operating results were rarely provided outside business enterprises. To the bankers or other lenders who were the principal external users of financial statements, understatement for its own sake became widely considered to be desirable, since the greater the understatement of assets the greater the margin of safety the assets provided as security for loans or other debts.

94. Once the practice of providing information about periodic income as well as balance sheets became common, however, it also became evident that understated assets frequently led to overstated income in later periods. Perceptive accountants saw that consistent understatement was difficult to maintain over a lengthy period, and the Committee on Accounting Procedure began to say so, for example, in ARB No. 3, *Quasi-Reorganization or Corporate Readjustment—Amplification of Institute Rule No. 2 of 1934:* "Understatement as at the effective date of the readjustment of assets which are likely to be realized thereafter, though it may result in conservatism in the balance-sheet, may also result in overstatement of earnings or of earned surplus when the assets are subsequently realized. Therefore, in general, assets should be carried forward as of the date of readjustment at a fair and not unduly conservative value." The Committee also formulated the "cost or market rule" in ARB No. 29, *Inventory Pricing,* in such a way that decreases in replacement costs do not result in writing down inventory unless (a) the expected selling price also

decreases or (b) costs to complete and sell inventory increase; unless those conditions are met, recognition of a loss by writing down inventory merely increases income in one or more later periods. (ARB 3 and 29 became, respectively, chapters 7A and 4 of ARB No. 43, *Restatement and Revision of Accounting Research Bulletins.*) Among the most recent admonitions on the point is that of the International Accounting Standards Committee (IASC) in International Accounting Standard No. 1, *Disclosure of Accounting Policies:* "Uncertainties inevitably surround many transactions. This should be recognized by exercising prudence in preparing financial statements. Prudence does not, however, justify the creation of secret or hidden reserves."

95. Conservatism is a prudent reaction to uncertainty to try to ensure that uncertainties and risks inherent in business situations are adequately considered. Thus, if two estimates of amounts to be received or paid in the future are about equally likely, conservatism dictates using the less optimistic estimate; however, if two amounts are not equally likely, conservatism does not necessarily dictate using the more pessimistic amount rather than the more likely one. Conservatism no longer requires deferring recognition of income beyond the time that adequate evidence of its existence becomes available or justifies recognizing losses before there is adequate evidence that they have been incurred.

96. The Board emphasizes that any attempt to understate results consistently is likely to raise questions about the reliability and the integrity of information about those results and will probably be self-defeating in the long run. That kind of reporting, however well-intentioned, is not consistent with the desirable characteristics described in this Statement. On the other hand, the Board also emphasizes that imprudent reporting, such as may be reflected, for example, in overly optimistic estimates of realization, is certainly no less inconsistent with those characteristics. Bias in estimating components of earnings, whether overly conservative or unconservative, usually influences the timing of earnings or losses rather than their aggregate amount. As a result, unjustified excesses in either direction may mislead one group of investors to the possible benefit or detriment of others.

97. The best way to avoid the injury to investors that imprudent reporting creates is to try to ensure that what is reported represents what it purports to represent. It has been pointed out in this Statement that the reliability of financial reporting may be enhanced by disclosing the nature and extent of the uncertainty surrounding events and transactions reported to stockholders and others. In assessing the prospect that as yet uncompleted transactions will be concluded successfully, a degree of skepticism is

often warranted. The aim must be to put the users of financial information in the best possible position to form their own opinion of the probable outcome of the events reported. Prudent reporting based on a healthy skepticism builds confidence in the results and, in the long run, best serves all of the divergent interests that are represented by the Board's constituents.

NEUTRALITY

98. Neutrality in accounting has a greater significance for those who set accounting standards than for those who have to apply those standards in preparing financial reports, but the concept has substantially the same meaning for the two groups, and both will maintain neutrality in the same way. Neutrality means that either in formulating or implementing standards, the primary concern should be the relevance and reliability of the information that results, not the effect that the new rule may have on a particular interest.

99. To say that information should be free from bias towards a predetermined result is not to say that standard setters or providers of information should not have a *purpose* in mind for financial reporting. Of course, information must be purposeful. But a predetermined purpose should not imply a predetermined result. For one thing, the purpose may be to serve many different information users who have diverse interests, and no one predetermined result is likely to suit them all.

100. Neutrality does not mean "without purpose," nor does it mean that accounting should be without influence on human behavior. Accounting information cannot avoid affecting behavior, nor should it. If it were otherwise, the information would be valueless—by definition, irrelevant—and the effort to produce it would be futile. It is, above all, the predetermination of a desired result, and the consequential selection of information to induce that result, that is the negation of neutrality in accounting. To be neutral, accounting information must report economic activity as faithfully as possible, without coloring the image it communicates for the purpose of influencing behavior in *some particular direction*.

101. Behavior will be influenced by financial information just as it is influenced and changed by the results of elections, college examinations, and sweepstakes. Elections, examinations, and sweepstakes are not unfair—nonneutral—merely because some people win and others lose. So it is with neutrality in accounting. The effect of "capitalization" of leases on enterprises in the leasing industry is a case in point. Recording of certain leases as assets and liabilities has been opposed by many of those enterprises on the grounds that, by making "off balance sheet" financing more difficult, it would make leasing less attractive to lessees, and that would have a detrimental effect on the business of lessors. Although it is at least debatable whether that kind of effect actually would result from lease capitalization, standard setters have not been indifferent to those fears. After carefully weighing the matter, various standard setters (including the Board) have generally concluded that those fears could not be allowed to stand in the way of what the Board and others considered to be a gain in the relevance and reliability of financial statements.

102. Some reject the notion of accounting neutrality because they think it is impossible to attain because of the "feedback effect." Information that reports on human activity itself influences that activity, so that an accountant is reporting not on some static phenomenon but on a dynamic situation that changes because of what is reported about it. But that is not an argument against neutrality in measurement. Many measurements relating to human beings—what they see when they step on a scale, what the speedometer registers when they drive a car, their performance in an athletic contest, or their academic performance, for example—have an impact on their behavior, for better or worse. No one argues that those measurements should be biased in order to influence behavior. Indeed, most people are repelled by the notion that some "big brother," whether government or private, would tamper with scales or speedometers surreptitiously to induce people to lose weight or obey speed limits or would slant the scoring of athletic events or examinations to enhance or decrease someone's chances of winning or graduating. There is no more reason to abandon neutrality in accounting measurement.

103. Another argument against the acceptance of neutrality as a necessary characteristic of accounting information is that it would inhibit the Board from working for the achievement of national goals. That view raises several issues. First, there would have to be agreement on national goals. For example, should the United States work to make energy cheap and plentiful or should it conserve natural resources for the benefit of posterity? Furthermore, governments come and go, and administrations change their political color and their policies. The Board concludes that it is not feasible to change financial accounting standards that accountants use every time governmental policy changes direction, even if it were desirable to do so. Moreover, only if accounting information is neutral can it safely be used to help guide those policies as well as to measure their results.

104. But more importantly, it is not desirable for the Board to tack with every change in the political wind, for politically motivated standards would quickly lose their credibility, and even standards that were defensible if judged against the criteria discussed in this Statement would come under suspicion because they would be tainted with guilt by association. The chairman of the SEC made the point in his statement on oil and gas accounting on August 29, 1978:

> If it becomes accepted or expected that accounting principles are determined or modified in order to secure purposes other than economic measurement—even such virtuous purposes as energy production—we assume a grave risk that confidence in the credibility of our financial information system will be undermined.[11]

105. For a standard to be neutral, it is not necessary that it treat everyone alike in all respects. A standard could require less disclosure from a small enterprise than it does from a large one without having its neutrality impugned, if the Board were satisfied that a requirement that was cost-effective if imposed on a large enterprise would be more burdensome than it was worth if imposed on a small one. Nevertheless, in general, standards that apply differentially need to be looked at carefully to ensure that the criterion of neutrality is not being transgressed.

106. While rejecting the view that financial accounting standards should be slanted for political reasons or to favor one economic interest or another, the Board recognizes that a standard-setting authority must be alert to the economic impact of the standards that it promulgates. The consequences of those standards will usually not be easy to isolate from the effects of other economic happenings, and they will be even harder to predict with confidence when a new standard is under consideration but before it has gone into effect. Nevertheless, the Board will consider the probable economic impact of its standards as best it can and will monitor that impact as best it can after a standard goes into effect. For one thing, a markedly unexpected effect on business behavior may point to an unforeseen deficiency in a standard in the sense that it does not result in the faithful representation of economic phenomena that was intended. It would then be necessary for the standard to be revised.

107. Neutrality in accounting is an important criterion by which to judge accounting policies, for information that is not neutral loses credibility. If information can be verified and can be relied on faithfully to represent what it purports to represent—*and if there is no bias in the selection of what is reported*—it cannot be slanted to favor one set of interests over another. It may in fact favor certain interests, but only because the information points that way, much as a good examination grade favors a good student who has honestly earned it.

108. The italicized words deserve comment. It was noted earlier in this Statement that reliability implies completeness of information, at least within the bounds of what is material and feasible, considering the cost. An omission can rob information of its claim to neutrality if the omission is material and is intended to induce or inhibit some particular mode of behavior.

109. Though reliability and the absence of bias in what is to be reported bring neutrality as a by-product, the converse is not true. Information may be unreliable even though it is provided without any intention on the part of the provider to influence behavior in a particular direction. Good intentions alone do not guarantee representational faithfulness.

110. Can information that is undeniably reliable produce undesirable consequences? The answer must be another question—consequences for whom? The consequences may indeed be bad for some interests. But the dissemination of unreliable and potentially misleading information is, in the long run, bad for all interests. It may be the responsibility of other agencies to intervene to take care of special interests that they think might be injured by an accounting standard. The Board's responsibility is to the integrity of the financial reporting system, which it regards as its paramount concern.

COMPARABILITY

111. Information about an enterprise gains greatly in usefulness if it can be compared with similar information about other enterprises and with similar information about the same enterprise for some other period or some other point in time. The significance of information, especially quantitative information, depends to a great extent on the user's ability to relate it to some benchmark. The comparative use of information is often intuitive, as when told that an enterprise has sales revenue of $1,000,000 a year, one forms a judgment of its size by ranking it with other enterprises that one knows. Investing and lending decisions essentially involve evaluations of alternative opportunities, and they

[11]Harold M. Williams, Chairman, Securities and Exchange Commission, "Accounting Practices for Oil and Gas Producers" (Washington, D.C., 1978), p. 12.

cannot be made rationally if comparative information is not available.

112. The difficulty in making financial comparisons among enterprises because of the use of different accounting methods has been accepted for many years as the principal reason for the development of accounting standards. Indeed, the only other possible reason for wanting accounting standards would be a belief that there was one right method among the available alternatives, and few people, if any, hold any such belief.

113. The purpose of comparison is to detect and explain similarities and differences. But, in comparing complex entities, such as human beings or business enterprises, it is useless to try to consider all similarities and differences at once, for to assess the significance of any one of them will then be impossible. Valid comparison, therefore, usually requires attention to be focused on one or two characteristics at a time. Other characteristics that are in no way correlated with those under inquiry can be ignored. Characteristics that are correlated with those under inquiry must be standardized to avoid affecting the comparison. For example, to find whether a man is overweight, one compares his weight with that of other men—not women—of the same height. That is, valid comparisons involve standardizing for gender and height because those characteristics are correlated with weight. It is not necessary to standardize for intelligence, for example, by comparing a man's weight with that of other males of similar height and intelligence because weight is not correlated with intelligence. Intelligence as a characteristic can be ignored.

114. Simple comparisons can often be made without the use of measurements expressed in units, but as the number of items to be compared increases, or if comparisons over an interval of time are desired, a unit of measure becomes indispensable. If valid comparisons are to be made over time, the unit of measurement used must be invariant. Units of money used in money measurement are not in one significant sense—their command over goods and services—invariant over time.

115. Defined in the broadest terms, comparability is the quality or state of having certain characteristics in common, and comparison is normally a quantitative assessment of the common characteristic. Clearly, valid comparison is possible only if the measurements used—the quantities or ratios—reliably represent the characteristic that is the subject of comparison. To cite a nonaccounting example, it may be desired to compare the fertility of land in Florida and Oregon. If that were done by comparing crop yields per acre, it should be obvious that crop yield is not a reliable representation of fer-

tility. Many other factors, such as climate and human efficiency, help to determine yields, and to use too broad a gauge to measure the characteristic of fertility invalidates the comparison.

116. While a particular datum, in some appropriate context, can be said to be relevant or reliable, it cannot be said to be comparable. Comparability is not a quality of information in the same sense as relevance and reliability are, but is rather a quality of the relationship between two or more pieces of information. Improving comparability may destroy or weaken relevance or reliability if, to secure comparability between two measures, one of them has to be obtained by a method yielding less relevant or less reliable information. Historically, extreme examples of this have been provided in some European countries in which the use of standardized charts of accounts has been made mandatory in the interest of interfirm comparability but at the expense of relevance and often reliability as well. That kind of uniformity may even adversely affect comparability of information if it conceals real differences between enterprises.

117. Generally, noncomparability is thought to arise because business enterprises do not use similar inputs, do not apply similar procedures, or do not use the same systems of classification of costs and revenues or assets and liabilities, and it is usually assumed that removal of those inconsistencies will make the results comparable. Certainly, comparability cannot be achieved without consistency of inputs and classification. For example, comparing liquidity between two enterprises by comparing their current ratios would usually not be valid if one enterprise valued its inventory on a last-in, first-out basis while the other valued inventory on first-in, first-out. The difference in practice would affect the comparison adversely to the first company, but its appearance of inferior liquidity would result from an invalid comparison, for the current value of its inventory may not have been less than that of the other company.

118. That kind of noncomparability imposes costs on users of financial statements and is best avoided, but it is relatively easy to diagnose and, with sufficient disclosure, can be rectified by a user of the information. A more difficult kind of noncomparability to deal with is the kind that results when ill-chosen or incomplete data inputs are used to generate information that fails one test of reliability—it does not truly represent what it purports to represent. If data inputs are ill-chosen or incomplete, the measures that result will not be truly comparable no matter how consistent the procedures are that are applied to them. For example, suppose it is desired to compare the performance of two investment managers. Each starts with the same

portfolio, but their portfolios at the end of the year are different as a result of trades during the year. Realized gains of the two managers are equal. The ending portfolio of one shows substantial unrealized gains, the other does not. To compare their performance by comparing only realized gains implies a definition of performance that many people would regard as incomplete and, therefore, as an unreliable representation.

119. To repeat what was said earlier, the purpose of comparison is to detect and explain similarities and differences. Comparability should not be confused with identity, and sometimes more can be learned from differences than from similarities if the differences can be explained. The ability to explain phenomena often depends on the diagnosis of the underlying causes of differences or the discovery that apparent differences are without significance. Much insight into the functioning of the capital market, for example, has been obtained from observing how market forces affect different stocks differently. Something has been learned, too, from observing that the market generally ignores apparent (cosmetic) differences among stocks that were formerly thought to be significant. Greater comparability of accounting information, which most people agree is a worthwhile aim, is not to be attained by making unlike things look alike any more than by making like things look different. The moral is that in seeking comparability accountants must not disguise real differences nor create false differences.

Consistency

120. Consistency in applying accounting methods over a span of time has always been regarded as an important quality that makes accounting numbers more useful. The standard form of an auditor's report states that the financial statements have been prepared "in conformity with generally accepted accounting principles consistently applied." The Accounting Principles Board stated in APB Opinion No. 20, *Accounting Changes,* that ". . . in the preparation of financial statements there is a presumption that an accounting principle once adopted should not be changed in accounting for events and transactions of a similar type. Consistent use of accounting principles from one accounting period to another enhances the utility of financial statements to users by facilitating analysis and understanding of comparative accounting data [paragraph 15]."

121. The same considerations apply whether comparisons involve time series data, with which discussions of consistency are mostly concerned, or cross-sectional data, which raise more general issues of comparability. Like comparability, consistency is a quality of the relationship between two accounting numbers rather than a quality of the numbers themselves in the sense that relevance and reliability are. The consistent use of accounting methods, whether from one period to another within a single firm, or within a single period across firms, is a necessary but not a sufficient condition of comparability. Consistency without genuine comparability is illustrated by time series data using units of money during periods of inflation. A 10-year summary of sales revenues covering a period when the purchasing power of the monetary unit has been declining may convey an exaggerated picture of growth unless the user of the information is accustomed to making purchasing power corrections. As before, it is the representational faithfulness of the measurements used, rather than simply the unchanging nature of the measurement rules or the classification rules, that results in true comparability over time.

122. Consistent use of accounting principles from one accounting period to another, if pushed too far, can inhibit accounting progress. No change to a preferred accounting method can be made without sacrificing consistency, yet there is no way that accounting can develop without change. Fortunately, it is possible to make the transition from a less preferred to a more preferred method of accounting and still retain the capacity to compare the periods before and after the change if the effects of the change of method are disclosed. If a change will bring only a small improvement, the trade-off between the improvement and the loss of consistency may make it hard to judge where the advantage lies. As in all trade-offs, it is a question of costs and benefits; and the costs include the psychological cost of adopting the change. If the cost of the added disclosure that will enable the user of accounting information to compare the prechange and post-change results is less than the expected benefits from making the change, the change should be made.

MATERIALITY

123. Those who make accounting decisions and those who make judgments as auditors continually confront the need to make judgments about materiality. Materiality judgments are primarily quantitative in nature. They pose the question: Is this item large enough for users of the information to be influenced by it? However, the answer to that question will usually be affected by the nature of the item; items too small to be thought material if they result from routine transactions may be considered material if they arise in abnormal circumstances.

124. Throughout this Statement, emphasis has been placed on relevance and reliability as the primary qualitative characteristics that accounting information must have if it is to be useful. Material-

ity is not a primary characteristic of the same kind. In fact, the pervasive nature of materiality makes it difficult to consider the concept except as it relates to the other qualitative characteristics, especially relevance and reliability.

125. Relevance and materiality have much in common—both are defined in terms of what influences or makes a difference to an investor or other decision maker. Yet the two concepts can be distinguished. A decision not to disclose certain information may be made, say, because investors have no interest in that kind of information (it is not relevant) or because the amounts involved are too small to make a difference (they are not material). But as was noted above, magnitude by itself, without regard to the nature of the item and the circumstances in which the judgment has to be made, will not generally be a sufficient basis for a materiality judgment.

126. Materiality judgments are concerned with screens or thresholds. Is an item, an error, or an omission large enough, considering its nature and the attendant circumstances, to pass over the threshold that separates material from immaterial items? An example of an applicant for employment who is negotiating with an employment agency will illustrate the relationship of the materiality concept to relevance and reliability. The agency has full information about a certain job for which the applicant is suited and will furnish any item of information about it. The applicant will certainly want information about the nature of the duties, the location of the job, the pay, the hours of work, and the fringe benefits. Information about vacations and job security may or may not be important enough to affect a decision concerning accepting the job. Further, the applicant may not be concerned at all with whether the office floor is carpeted or about the quality of the food in the cafeteria. All of those items are, in the broadest sense, relevant to an evaluation of the job. But some of them make no difference in a decision to accept it or not. The values placed on them by the applicant are too small for them to be material. They are not important enough to matter.

127. The employment agency example can also help to explain what is meant by a materiality threshold for reliability. Salary information accurate only to the nearest thousand dollars might not be acceptable to an applicant for an $8,000 a year job, but will almost certainly be acceptable if the job pays $100,000 a year. An error of a percentage point in the employee's rate of pension contribution would rarely make information about fringe benefits unac-

ceptable. An error of a year in the retirement date of someone who would block the applicant's advancement might be quite material. An error of a year in the applicant's mandatory retirement date will probably be immaterial to a person 20 years old, but quite material to a 63-year-old person.

128. The more important a judgment item[12] is, the finer the screen should be that will be used to determine whether it is material. For example:

a. An accounting change in circumstances that puts an enterprise in danger of being in breach of covenant regarding its financial condition may justify a lower materiality threshold than if its position were stronger.

b. A failure to disclose separately a nonrecurrent item of revenue may be material at a lower threshold than would otherwise be the case if the revenue turns a loss into a profit or reverses the trend of earnings from a downward to an upward trend.

c. A misclassification of assets that would not be material in amount if it affected two categories of plant or equipment might be material if it changed the classification between a noncurrent and a current asset category.

d. Amounts too small to warrant disclosure or correction in normal circumstances may be considered material if they arise from abnormal or unusual transactions or events.

129. Almost always, the relative rather than the absolute size of a judgment item determines whether it should be considered material in a given situation. Losses from bad debts or pilferage that could be shrugged off as routine by a large business may threaten the continued existence of a small one. An error in inventory valuation may be material in a small enterprise for which it cut earnings in half but immaterial in an enterprise for which it might make a barely perceptible ripple in the earnings. Some of the empirical investigations referred to in Appendix C throw light on the considerations that enter into materiality judgments.

130. Another factor in materiality judgments is the degree of precision that is attainable in estimating the judgment item. The amount of deviation that is considered immaterial may increase as the attainable degree of precision decreases. For example, accounts payable usually can be estimated more accurately than can contingent liabilities arising from litigation or threats of it, and a deviation considered to be material in the first case may be quite trivial in the second.

---

[12]A judgment item is whatever has to be determined to be material or immaterial. It may be an asset or liability item, a transaction, an error, or any of a number of things.

131. Some hold the view that the Board should promulgate a set of quantitative materiality guides or criteria covering a wide variety of situations that preparers could look to for authoritative support. That appears to be a minority view, however, on the basis of representations made to the Board in response to the Discussion Memorandum, *Criteria for Determining Materiality*. The predominant view is that materiality judgments can properly be made only by those who have all the facts. The Board's present position is that no general standards of materiality could be formulated to take into account all the considerations that enter into an experienced human judgment. However, that position is not intended to imply either that the Board may not in the future review that conclusion or that quantitative guidance on materiality of specific items may not appropriately be written into the Board's standards from time to time. That has been done on occasion already (for example, in the Statement on financial reporting by segments of a business enterprise), and the Board recognizes that quantitative materiality guidance is sometimes needed. Appendix C lists a number of examples of quantitative guidelines that have been applied both in the law and in the practice of accounting. However, whenever the Board or any other authoritative body imposes materiality rules, it is substituting generalized collective judgments for specific individual judgments, and there is no reason to suppose that the collective judgments are always superior. In any case, it must be borne in mind that if, to take one example, some minimum size is stipulated for recognition of a material item (for example, a segment having revenue equal to or exceeding 10 percent of combined revenues shall be recognized as a reportable segment), the rule does not prohibit the recognition of a smaller segment. Quantitative materiality guidelines generally specify minima only. They, therefore, leave room for individual judgment in at least one direction.

132. Individual judgments are required to assess materiality in the absence of authoritative criteria or to decide that minimum quantitative criteria are not appropriate in particular situations. The essence of the materiality concept is clear. The omission or misstatement of an item in a financial report is material if, in the light of surrounding circumstances, the magnitude of the item is such that it is probable that the judgment of a reasonable person relying upon the report would have been changed or influenced by the inclusion or correction of the item.

COSTS AND BENEFITS[13]

133. Accounting information must attain some minimum level of relevance and also some minimum level of reliability if it is to be useful. Beyond those minimum levels, sometimes users may gain by sacrificing relevance for added reliability or by sacrificing reliability for added relevance; and some accounting policy changes will bring gains in both. Each user will uniquely perceive the relative value to be attached to each quality. Ultimately, a standard-setting body has to do its best to meet the needs of society as a whole when it promulgates a standard that sacrifices one of those qualities for the other; and it must also be aware constantly of the calculus of costs and benefits.

134. Unless the benefits to be derived from a commodity or service exceed the costs associated with it, it will not be sought after. When a decision to acquire a commodity is being considered, the prospective buyer will compare the costs of acquisition and maintenance with the benefits of owning the commodity. Once the purchase has been made, the owner must decide—continually, from day to day—whether the opportunity cost of ownership, the sacrifice of the sale price that cannot be realized so long as ownership continues, is less than the benefits of continued ownership. Thus, both before and after acquisition, costs and benefits must be compared, though the comparison takes a somewhat different form according to whether the acquisition has or has not been consummated.

135. Financial information is unlike other commodities in certain important respects. While, in general, it will not be desired unless its benefits exceed its costs, what makes it different from other commodities, or at least from those that are traded in the marketplace, is that whereas those other commodities are private goods, to be enjoyed only by the buyer and those with whom the buyer chooses to share them, the benefits of information cannot always be confined to those who pay for it. If the whole government and private system by which the flow of financial information is regulated could now be dismantled, if information could be traded between buyers and sellers like other commodities and could be kept from those who did not pay for it, and if consumers of information were willing to rely on their own inquiries, the balance of costs and benefits could be left to the market. But in the real world the market for information is less complete than most other markets, and a standard-setting authority must concern itself with the perceived costs and benefits of the standards it sets—costs and benefits to both users and preparers of such information, to others, like auditors, who are also concerned with it, and to anyone else in society who may be affected.

---

[13]This section expands on the considerations mentioned in paragraph 23 of Concepts Statement 1.

136. Most of the costs of providing financial information fall initially on the preparers, while the benefits are reaped by both preparers and users. Ultimately, the costs and benefits are diffused quite widely. The costs are mostly passed on to the users of information and to the consumers of goods and services. The benefits also are presumably passed on to consumers by assuring a steady supply of goods and services and more efficient functioning of the marketplace. But, even if the costs and benefits are not traced beyond the preparers and users of information, to say anything precise about their incidence is difficult. There are costs of using information as well as of preparing it; and much published information would be compiled for the preparer's own use even if providing it to stockholders and others were not required. The preparer enjoys other benefits also, such as improved access to capital markets, favorable impact on the enterprise's public relations, and so on.

137. The costs of providing information are of several kinds, including costs of collecting and processing the information, costs of audit if it is subject to audit, costs of disseminating it to those who must receive it, costs associated with the dangers of litigation, and in some instances costs of disclosure in the form of a loss of competitive advantages vis-a-vis trade competitors, labor unions (with a consequent effect on wage demands), or foreign enterprises. The costs to the users of information, over and above those costs that preparers pass on to them, are mainly the costs of analysis and interpretation and may include costs of rejecting information that is redundant, for the diagnosis of redundancy is not without its cost.

138. Society needs information to help allocate resources efficiently, but the benefit to any individual or company from that source is not measurable. Nor is the spur to efficiency that comes from making managers account to stockholders capable of evaluation, either at the level of the enterprise or the economy. It is impossible to imagine a highly developed economy without most of the financial information that it now generates and, for the most part, consumes; yet it is also impossible to place a value on that information.

139. From the point of view of society, the loss of competitive advantage that is said to result from some disclosure requirements is clearly in a different category from the other costs involved. Although the loss to one business enterprise may be a gain to another, the Board is aware of and concerned about the economic effects of the possible discouragement of initiative, innovation, and willingness to take risks if a reward to risk taking is denied. That is another cost that is impossible to begin to quantify.

140. The burden of the costs and the incidence of benefits fall quite unevenly throughout the economy, and it has been rightly observed that ". . . the matter of establishing disclosure requirements becomes not only a matter of judgment but also a complex balancing of many factors so that all costs and benefits receive the consideration they merit. For example, a simple rule that any information useful in making investment decisions should be disclosed fails as completely as a rule that says disclosure should not be required if competitive disadvantage results."[14] The problem is to know how to accomplish that "complex balancing."

141. The Board has watched with sympathetic interest the efforts of the Cost Accounting Standards Board (CASB) to come to grips with the task of comparing the costs and benefits of its standards. The Report of the special group of consultants who were asked by the CASB to examine this matter was submitted on November 13, 1978. The conclusions were quite negative.

> Our conclusion is that no objective cost benefit calculation in aggregate quantitative terms is possible for CASB standards as a whole or for any of them individually. Reasonable people, with some experience in such matters, acting responsibly in a spirit of compromise, using such reliable information as can be gathered together, will make a "calculation," as they must if anything is to be done. But the calculation will be in ordinal rather than cardinal terms; it will be rough rather than precise; it will always be subject to revision, rather than fixed in stone. The situation is not different from that concerning the merits of many other laws, rules, regulations, and administrative decisions. Nor is our conclusion different from the conclusion reached by those concerned with the cost-benefit problem confronting the Paperwork Commission, for example.[15]

142. As the CASB's consultants point out, the reasons for that negative conclusion can be simply stated. The costs and benefits of a standard are both direct and indirect, immediate and deferred. They may be affected by a change in circumstances not foreseen when the standard was promulgated. There are wide variations in the estimates that different people make about the dollar values involved and the rate of discount to be used in reducing them to a

---

[14]R. K. Mautz and William G. May, *Financial Disclosure in a Competitive Economy* (New York: Financial Executives Research Foundation, 1978), p. 6.

[15]Robert N. Anthony et al., "Report to the Cost Accounting Standards Board by a Special Group of Consultants to Consider Issues Relating to Comparing Costs with Benefits" (1978), p. 1.

present value. "For these reasons," the consultants conclude, "the merits of any Standard, or of the Standards as a whole, can be decided finally only by judgments that are largely subjective. They cannot be decided by scientific test."

143. Despite the difficulties, the Board does not conclude that it should turn its back on the matter, for there are some things that it can do to safeguard the cost-effectiveness of its standards. Before a decision is made to develop a standard, the Board needs to satisfy itself that the matter to be ruled on represents a significant problem and that a standard that is promulgated will not impose costs on the many for the benefit of a few. If the proposal passes that first test, a second test may subsequently be useful. There are usually alternative ways of handling an

issue. Is one of them less costly and only slightly less effective? Even if absolute magnitudes cannot be attached to costs and benefits, a comparison between alternatives may yet be possible and useful.

144. Though it is unlikely that significantly improved means of measuring benefits will become available in the foreseeable future, it seems possible that better ways of quantifying the incremental costs of regulations of all kinds may gradually be developed, and the Board will watch any such developments carefully to see whether they can be applied to financial accounting standards. Even if that hope proves to be a vain one, however, the Board cannot cease to be concerned about the cost-effectiveness of its standards. To do so would be a dereliction of its duty and a disservice to its constituents.

This Statement was adopted by the unanimous vote of the seven members of the Financial Accounting Standards Board:

Donald J. Kirk, *Chairman*
Frank E. Block
John W. March

Robert A. Morgan
David Mosso

Robert T. Sprouse
Ralph E. Walters

Appendix A

BACKGROUND INFORMATION

145. The need for a conceptual framework for financial accounting and reporting, beginning with consideration of the objectives of financial reporting, is generally recognized. The Accounting Principles Board issued APB Statement No. 4 on basic concepts and accounting principles in 1970. When the Financial Accounting Standards Board came into existence, the Study Group on the Objectives of Financial Statements was at work, and its Report, *Objectives of Financial Statements,* was published in October 1973 by the American Institute of Certified Public Accountants. A chapter of that report briefly described "certain characteristics . . . [information should possess] to satisfy users' needs"—relevance and materiality, form and substance, reliability, freedom from bias, comparability, consistency, and understandability—which the Study Group called "qualitative characteristics of reporting."

146. The Financial Accounting Standards Board issued FASB Discussion Memorandum, *Conceptual Framework for Accounting and Reporting: Consideration of the Report of the Study Group on the Objectives of Financial Statements,* dated June 6, 1974, and held a public hearing on September 23 and 24, 1974 on the objectives of financial statements. The Discussion Memorandum and the hearing were based primarily on the Report of the Study Group on the Objectives of Financial State-

ments. The Discussion Memorandum asked respondents to comment on the acceptability of the seven qualitative characteristics in the Report and to suggest needed modifications. The Board received 95 written communications responding to the Discussion Memorandum, and 20 parties presented their views orally and answered Board members' questions at the hearing.

147. On December 2, 1976, the Board issued three documents:

Tentative Conclusions on Objectives of Financial Statements of Business Enterprises,

FASB Discussion Memorandum, *Conceptual Framework for Financial Accounting and Reporting: Elements of Financial Statements and Their Measurement,* and

Scope and Implications of the Conceptual Framework Project.

One chapter of the Discussion Memorandum was entitled, "Qualities of Useful Financial Information." Although it raised no specific issues, it asked respondents to explain what they meant by relevance, reliability, comparability, and other "qualitative characteristics" and to illustrate those meanings in responding to the issues about elements of financial statements and their measurement and by completing a set of matrixes designed to show trade-offs between various qualities or characteristics. The same task force, with one membership change, provided counsel in preparing both Discussion Memorandums. Eleven persons from academe, the financial community, industry, and public accounting served on the task force while the Discussion Memorandums were written.

148. The Board held public hearings (a) August 1 and 2, 1977 on the *Tentative Conclusions on Objectives of Financial Statements of Business Enterprises* and Chapters 1-5 of the Discussion Memorandum (December 1976) concerning definitions of the elements of financial statements and (b) January 16-18, 1978 on the remaining chapters of that Discussion Memorandum concerning capital maintenance or cost recovery, qualities of useful financial information ("qualitative characteristics"), and measurement of the elements of financial statements. The Board received 332 written communications on the Discussion Memorandum, of which 143 commented on the "qualitative characteristics." Twenty-seven parties presented their views orally and answered Board members' questions at the January 1978 hearing.

149. The Board issued an Exposure Draft of a proposed Statement of Financial Accounting Concepts, *Objectives of Financial Reporting and Elements of Financial Statements of Business Enterprises,* dated December 29, 1977, which included a very brief discussion of some "characteristics or qualities that make financial information useful," noting that those characteristics were to be the subject of another phase of the conceptual framework project. The Board received 135 letters of comment, of which 36 commented on the paragraphs discussing "qualitative characteristics." That discussion was not included in Concepts Statement 1.

150. The Board also issued FASB Discussion Memorandum, *Criteria for Determining Materiality,* on March 21, 1975 and held public hearings on it May 20 and 21, 1976. The Board received 96 written communications on the Discussion Memorandum, and 16 parties presented their views orally and answered Board members' questions at the hearing. The Board explored incorporating the conceptual aspects of the materiality project into the qualitative characteristics project during 1977 and 1978 and formally did so in October 1978.

151. Professor David Solomons, the Arthur Young Professor of Accounting at the Wharton School of the University of Pennsylvania, served as consultant to the Board and staff on the qualitative characteristics project.

Appendix B

PRINCIPAL RESPECTS IN WHICH THIS STATEMENT DIFFERS FROM THE EXPOSURE DRAFT AND OTHER RESPONSES TO LETTERS OF COMMENT ON THE EXPOSURE DRAFT

152. Of the changes made to the Exposure Draft that was issued on August 9, 1979, many were in response to suggestions that were made in the 89 comment letters received during the exposure period. One suggestion was that the definitions that were scattered throughout the Exposure Draft should be brought together in a glossary. That has now been done.

153. The chart that appears on page 1032 now distinguishes between primary qualities, ingredients of primary qualities, and secondary qualities that make information useful. The chart also now explicitly introduces decision makers and their characteristics as factors that help to determine what information will be useful in particular situations. Those characteristics include how much knowledge decision makers already have and how well they understand the significance of new information that comes to them. That makes it possible to view relevance as a quality that information has in relation to a situation or a decision rather than as a quality that depends on the personal characteristics of the decision maker. Thus, if information that is relevant to a decision were conveyed in a language that some decision makers did not understand, it would not be useful to them because of their lack of understanding. However, understandability of information is a prerequisite to the information being useful to particular decision makers.

154. The discussion of relevance has been further clarified by recognizing more explicitly the value of information about past activities as distinct from its value for predictive purposes. Thus, predictive value and feedback value are shown as coequal ingredients of relevance. To be relevant, information must have one of them or both, and it must be timely.

155. A clearer distinction is now drawn between the degree of reliability that can be achieved in a particular situation and the perceived need for more reliability or less. In terms of the chronometer-wristwatch analogy in paragraph 73, the wristwatch is not as reliable a timekeeper as the chronometer. It does not need to be. It is the perceived *need* for

reliability that is different because of the different uses to which the two instruments are put. That difference does not affect the *nature* of reliability but only the degree of reliability that may be needed for particular uses.

156. The discussion of materiality has been considerably recast, with much of the detail moved into Appendix C. Though the definition of materiality is not substantially changed, its quantitative character is now given a more central position, enabling the distinction between materiality and relevance to be stated more clearly. Though both qualities are present in information only if it "can make a difference" to a decision, relevance stems from the *nature* of the information while materiality depends on the *size* of the judgment item in particular circumstances.

157. Several of those who commented on the Exposure Draft doubted that the qualitative characteristics discussed in it were "operational" in the sense that they provided clear criteria for the selection of a preferred accounting method if two or more alternatives were available. Only in a few cases were other methods of selection proposed that were claimed to be more operational, and after careful review by the Board's staff, those claims had to be rejected as being unrealistic. The Board believes that the approach to preferability choices put forward in this Statement achieves as much operationality as is feasible in the present state of knowledge.The true test will be in the contributions that the criteria discussed here can make to the formulation of future standards. Unanimous acclaim for the Board's decisions is not to be expected; but the basis for those decisions should be better understood if they can be seen to be aimed at obtaining an optimal mix (as judged by the Board) of certain clearly defined informational characteristics.

158. A number of respondents urged the Board to include additional qualitative characteristics in its "hierarchy." All of the proposed additions had already been considered and excluded because they seemed to add little value to other characteristics that were already included. The more items are added, the more the impact of each is diluted. To earn a place, therefore, something really important must be added. None of the new candidates passed that test. For example, objectivity was mentioned by several respondents. Yet, verifiability better expresses the quality that those respondents were concerned with preserving. "Objective" means having an existence independent of the observer. That does not fit accounting measurements at all well, especially measurements such as profit, depreciation and other cost allocations, earnings per share, and others of like kind. Accounting terminology will be

improved if verifiability, which reflects what accountants do, replaces objectivity in the accountant's lexicon.

159. Feasibility was another candidate for inclusion in the hierarchy. That has been excluded because it adds nothing to the cost-benefit constraint. In accounting as in other fields, many things are feasible *at a cost*. But an accounting method that, though feasible, yields information that is worth less than it costs is not a good one to choose. For that reason, feasibility has not been included in the hierarchy.

160. Substance over form is an idea that also has its proponents, but it is not included because it would be redundant. The quality of reliability and, in particular, of representational faithfulness leaves no room for accounting representations that subordinate substance to form. Substance over form is, in any case, a rather vague idea that defies precise definition.

Appendix C

QUANTITATIVE MATERIALITY CONSIDERATIONS

161. Each Statement of Financial Accounting Standards issued by the Board has concluded by stating that: "The provisions of this Statement need not be applied to immaterial items." Rule 3-02 of the Securities and Exchange Commission's (SEC) Regulation S-X, "Form and Content of Financial Statements," states that if an "amount which would otherwise be required to be shown with respect to any item is not material, it need not be separately set forth."

162. Those who turn to SEC Regulation S-X for help in understanding the concept of materiality learn that a material matter is one "about which an average prudent investor ought reasonably to be informed" (Rule 1-02) and that material information is "such . . . information as is necessary to make the required statements, in the light of the circumstances under which they are made not misleading" (Rule 3-06). But those statements are not really definitions of materiality in that they provide only general guidance in distinguishing material from immaterial information.

163. The courts have stepped in to fill the gap. It is the impact of information on an investor's judgment that is at the heart of the distinction. To quote the Tenth Circuit Court of Appeals, information is material if ". . . the trading judgment of reasonable investors would not have been left untouched upon

receipt of such information."[16] That is very close to the definition of materiality adopted in the *BarChris* decision, in which the judge said that a material fact was one "which if it had been correctly stated or disclosed would have deterred or tended to deter the average prudent investor from purchasing the securities in question."[17] Both statements refer to one particular kind of user of information—a prudent investor—but, of course, the essential idea that they convey is applicable to other users also.

164. Statements by the Supreme Court have given added authority to that view of materiality. In the important case of *TSC Industries Inc.* v. *Northway Inc.,*[18] a case which concerned the omission of certain facts from a proxy statement, the Court held that:

> An omitted fact is material if there is a substantial likelihood that a reasonable shareholder would consider it important in deciding how to vote. This standard is fully consistent with the . . . general description of materiality as a requirement that "the defect have a significant *propensity* to affect the voting process." It does not require proof of a substantial likelihood that disclosure of the omitted fact would have caused the reasonable investor to change his vote. What the standard does contemplate is a showing of a substantial likelihood that, under all the circumstances, the omitted fact would have assumed actual significance in the deliberations of the reasonable shareholder. Put another way, there must be a substantial likelihood that the disclosure of the omitted fact would have been viewed by the reasonable investor as having significantly altered the "total mix" of information made available.

165. Until such time as the Supreme Court returns to this question, the *Northway* case provides the most authoritative judicial definition of what constitutes a material omitted fact. Examples, taken from earlier cases, of facts that have been held to be "material" are:[19]

1. Failure to disclose a greatly enhanced inventory value (carried on the corporation's financial statements at historical cost) and an intention to realize on it by liquidation. *Speed* v. *Transamerica Corp.,* 99 F. Supp. 808 (D. Del. 1951), *modified and aff'd.,* 235 F.2d 369 (3d Cir. 1956).

2. Failure to disclose pending negotiations to sell all of the assets of the corporation at a price per share substantially larger than that being paid to a selling shareholder. *Kardon* v. *National Gypsum Co.,* 69 F. Supp. 512 (E.D. Pa. 1946), *on the merits,* 73 F. Supp. 798 (E.D. Pa. 1947).

3. Failure to disclose the imminence of a highly profitable transaction by the corporation. *Northern Trust Co.* v. *Essaness Theatres Corp.,* 103 F. Supp. 954 (N.D. Ill. 1952).

4. Failure to disclose a readjustment of reported earnings from 85¢ per share for the first five months of the fiscal year to 12¢ per share for the first six months. *Financial Industrial Fund, Inc.* v. *McDonnell Douglas Corp.,* CCH Fed. Sec. L. Rep. ¶93,004 (D. Col. 1971).

5. Failure to disclose that investigations were pending by the SEC. *Hill York Corp.* v. *American International Franchises, Inc.,* 448 F.2d 680 (5th Cir. 1971).

6. Failure to disclose firm offers, in contrast to appraisals, greatly higher than the book value for the physical facilities of the acquired company which the acquiring company intended to liquidate as soon as possible. *Gerstle* v. *Gamble-Skogmo, Inc.,* 478 F2d 1281, 1295 (2d Cir. 1973).

7. Failure to disclose active negotiations by tender offeror to sell significant assets substantially below book value. *Chris Craft Industries, Inc.* v. *Piper Aircraft Corp.,* 480 F.2d 341, 367 (2d Cir. 1973).

166. The Discussion Memorandum on materiality cited some of the quantitative guides to materiality in authoritative statements issued by the SEC and other regulatory agencies and standard-setting bodies. It may be helpful to be reminded how certain specific situations have been dealt with in practice. Some of these examples of materiality are brought together again in the accompanying table.

---

[16]*Mitchell* v. *Texas Gulf Sulphur Co.,* 446 F.2D 90, at 99-100 (10th Circuit, 1971).

[17]*Escott et al.* v. *BarChris Construction Corporation et al.,* 283 Fed. Supp. (District Ct. S.D. New York, 1968), p. 681.

[18]CCH *Federal Securities Law Reports* ¶95,615 (US Sup Ct. June 14, 1976).

[19]The following list is taken from James O. Hewitt, "Developing Concepts of Materiality and Disclosure," *The Business Lawyer,* Vol. 32 (April 1977), pp. 910 and 911. A word of caution may be in order. The extreme brevity of the citations given here inevitably causes many important aspects of these cases to be omitted.

Table 1

EXAMPLES OF QUANTITATIVE MATERIALITY GUIDELINES

Subject	Authority	Materiality Guidelines
Dilution of earnings per share (EPS)	APB Opinion No. 15	Reduction of EPS of less than 3% in the aggregate not material.
Separate disclosure of balance sheet items	SEC Accounting Series Release No. 41	If 10% or more of their immediate category or more than 5% of total assets.
Receivables from officers and stockholders	SEC Regulation S-X, Rule 5-04	Disclose details of receivables from any officer or principal stockholder if it equals or exceeds $20,000 or 1% of total assets.
Segmental reporting: recognition of reportable segment	Statement of Financial Accounting Standards No. 14	Revenue equals or exceeds 10% of combined revenues, etc.
Gross rental expense under leases	SEC Accounting Series Release No. 147	Disclose total rental expense, etc., if gross rents exceed 1% of consolidated revenue.
Information on present value of lease commitments under noncapitalized financing leases	SEC Accounting Series Release No. 147	Disclose if present value is 5% or more of total of long-term debt, stockholders' equity, and present value of commitments, or if impact of capitalization on income is 3% or more of average net income for most recent 3 years.
Proved oil and gas reserves	SEC Accounting Series Release No. 258	Disclose quantities of proved oil and gas reserves and historical financial data unless, for each of the two most recent years, revenues and income from oil and gas producing activities and certain oil and gas capital values do not exceed 10% of the related company totals.

167. One approach in seeking guidance about what constitutes a material item or a material error is to examine current practice empirically. One study[20] investigated the factors that entered into judgments about the materiality of an error and found that the primary factor was the ratio of the error to current income before tax. The error took on special significance if it changed the trend in income. Another study[21] examined a sample of audit reports to try to determine the factors that caused auditors to render

---

[20]Sam M. Woolsey, "Materiality Survey," *The Journal of Accountancy* (September 1973), pp. 91 and 92.

[21]Paul Frishkoff, "An Empirical Investigation of the Concept of Materiality in Accounting," *Empirical Research in Accounting: Selected Studies* (1970), pp. 116-129.

qualified opinions when there was an accounting change. The effect on net income (as a percentage) was found to be the only significant variable, but there was little uniformity among auditors about when an accounting change was material. A much more extensive study, conducted for the Financial Executives Research Foundation[22] examined several kinds of materiality judgments. Perhaps its principal conclusion was that a "rule of thumb" of 5-10 percent of net income is widely used as a general materiality criterion.

168. A different approach looks to security prices to determine materiality norms. According to that view, "an observed association between extant security prices and reported accounting data (or changes therein) provides prima facie evidence as to the informational content of accounting numbers."[23] That means that the materiality of information released to the market can be tested by observing its impact on security prices. Of course, that can only be done after the event, whereas preparers and auditors have to make materiality judgments before information is released to the market. Presumably they are to act in the light of market behavior observed in similar circumstances.

169. Without doubt, observations of market behavior can improve understanding of what constitutes material information. But the market's anticipation of accounting information months before it is released and the dilution of accounting influences on prices by other factors acting concurrently make price fluctuations, in the present state of knowledge, too blunt an instrument to be depended on to set materiality guidelines.

170. It is already possible to simulate some aspects of the decision making processes of auditors by constructing a model that will bring into play many of the decision variables that enter into materiality judgments.[24] Those variables would normally include the nature and size of the judgment item in question (for example, an accounting change or a contingent liability), the size of the enterprise, its financial condition and recent changes in condition, present and recent profitability, and as many as possible of the other significant factors that affect materiality judgments. Further development of such models is perhaps the most promising line of research that needs to be pursued before accountants can hope to be relieved of the onerous duty of making materiality decisions. But, until further progress has been made, that duty must continue to be discharged by the exercise of judgment taking into account as many relevant considerations as possible.

---

[22]James W. Pattillo, *The Concept of Materiality in Financial Reporting* (New York: Financial Executives Research Foundation, 1976).

[23]Melvin C. O'Connor and Daniel W. Collins, "Toward Establishing User-Oriented Materiality Standards," *The Journal of Accountancy* (December 1974), p. 70.

[24]For an example, see "Policy-Capturing on Selected Materiality Judgments," by James R. Boatsman and Jack C. Robertson (*Accounting Review,* April 1974, pp. 342-352).

Statement of Financial Accounting Concepts No. 3
Elements of Financial Statements of Business Enterprises

STATUS

Issued: December 1980

Affects: No other pronouncements

Affected by: Superseded by CON 6

Concepts Statement No. 6 replaces Concepts Statement No. 3 expanding its scope to encompass not-for-profit organizations. Below is a cross-reference list showing where paragraphs that were in Concepts Statement No. 3 may now be found in Concepts Statement No. 6.

(This page intentionally left blank.)

Statement of Financial Accounting Concepts No. 4
Objectives of Financial Reporting by
Nonbusiness Organizations

STATUS

Issued: December 1980

Affects: No other pronouncements

Affected by: No other pronouncements

HIGHLIGHTS

[*Best understood in context of full Statement*]

- This Statement establishes the objectives of general purpose external financial reporting by nonbusiness organizations.

  —Based on its review of those objectives and the objectives set forth in FASB Concepts Statement No. 1, *Objectives of Financial Reporting by Business Enterprises,* the Board has concluded that it is not necessary to develop an independent conceptual framework for any particular category of entities.

  —The two sets of objectives will serve as the foundation of an integrated conceptual framework for financial accounting and reporting that, when completed, will have relevance to all entities while providing appropriate consideration of any different reporting objectives and concepts that may apply to only certain types of entities.

  —Pending resolution of the appropriate structure for setting financial accounting and reporting standards for state and local governmental units, the Board has deferred a final decision on whether the objectives in this Statement should apply to general purpose external financial reporting of those units. On the basis of its study to date, the Board is aware of no persuasive evidence that the objectives in this Statement are inappropriate for that type of financial reporting by state and local governmental units.

  —Based on its study, the Board believes that the objectives of general purpose external financial reporting for government-sponsored entities (for example, hospitals, universities, or utilities) engaged in activities that are not unique to government should be similar to those of business enterprises or other nonbusiness organizations engaged in similar activities.

- This Statement focuses on organizations that have predominantly nonbusiness characteristics that heavily influence the operations of the organization.

  —The major distinguishing characteristics of nonbusiness organizations include: (a) receipts of significant amounts of resources from resource providers who do not expect to receive either repayment or economic benefits proportionate to resources provided, (b) operating purposes that are primarily other than to provide goods or services at a profit or profit equivalent, and (c) absence of defined ownership interests that can be sold, transferred, or redeemed, or that convey entitlement to a share of a residual distribution of resources in the event of liquidation of the organization.

  —These characteristics result in certain types of transactions that are infrequent in business enterprises, such as contributions and grants, and in the absence of transactions with owners.

  —The line between nonbusiness organizations and business enterprises is not always sharp since the incidence and relative importance of those characteristics in any organization are different. This suggests that, for purposes of developing financial reporting objectives, a spectrum of organizations exists ranging from those with clearly dominant nonbusiness characteristics to those with wholly business characteristics.

—Examples of organizations that clearly fall outside the focus of this Statement include all investor-owned enterprises and other types of organizations, such as mutual insurance companies and other mutual cooperative entities that provide dividends, lower costs, or other economic benefits directly and proportionately to their owners, members, or participants.

—Examples of organizations that clearly fall within the focus of this Statement include most human service organizations, churches, foundations, and some other organizations, such as those private nonprofit hospitals and nonprofit schools that receive a significant portion of their financial resources from sources other than the sale of goods and services.

—Borderline cases may exist where organizations possess some of the distinguishing characteristics but not others. Examples are those private nonprofit hospitals and nonprofit schools that may receive relatively small amounts of contributions and grants but finance their capital needs largely from the proceeds of debt issues and their operating needs largely from service charges. As a result, the objectives of Concepts Statement 1 may be more appropriate for those organizations.

• The objectives in this Statement stem from the common interests of those who provide resources to nonbusiness organizations in the services those organizations provide and their continuing ability to provide services.

• Nonbusiness organizations generally have no single indicator of performance comparable to a business enterprise's profit. Thus, other indicators of performance usually are needed.

• The performance of nonbusiness organizations generally is not subject to the test of direct competition in markets to the extent that business enterprises are.

—Other kinds of controls introduced to compensate for the lesser influence of markets are a major characteristic of their operations and affect the objectives of their financial reporting. Controls, such as formal budgets and donor restrictions on the use of resources, give managers a special responsibility to ensure compliance. Information about departures from those mandates is important in assessing how well managers have discharged their stewardship responsibilities.

• The objectives in this Statement apply to general purpose external financial reporting by nonbusiness organizations.

—The objectives stem primarily from the needs of external users who generally cannot prescribe the information they want from an organization.

—In addition to information provided by general purpose external financial reporting, managers and, to some extent, governing bodies need a great deal of internal accounting information to carry out their responsibilities in planning and controlling activities. That information and information directed at meeting the specialized needs of users having the power to obtain the information they need are beyond the scope of this Statement.

• The objectives of financial reporting are affected by the economic, legal, political, and social environment in which financial reporting takes place.

—The operating environments of nonbusiness organizations and business enterprises are similar in many ways. Both nonbusiness organizations and business enterprises produce and distribute goods and services and use scarce resources in doing so.

—Differences between nonbusiness organizations and business enterprises arise in the ways they obtain resources. Noneconomic reasons are commonly factors in decisions to provide resources to particular nonbusiness organizations.

- The objectives also are affected by the characteristics and limitations of the kind of information that financial reporting can provide.

  —The information provided by financial reporting is primarily financial in nature: It is generally quantified and expressed in units of money. However, quantified information expressed in terms other than units of money and nonquantified information may be needed to understand the significance of information expressed in units of money or to help in assessing the performance of a nonbusiness organization.

  —The information provided by financial reporting pertains to individual reporting entities, often results from approximate rather than exact measures, largely reflects the effects of transactions and events that have already happened, is but one source of information needed by those who make decisions about nonbusiness organizations, and is provided and used at a cost.

- The objectives state that:

  —Financial reporting by nonbusiness organizations should provide information that is useful to present and potential resource providers and other users in making rational decisions about the allocation of resources to those organizations.

  —Financial reporting should provide information to help present and potential resource providers and other users in assessing the services that a nonbusiness organization provides and its ability to continue to provide those services.

  —Financial reporting should provide information that is useful to present and potential resource providers and other users in assessing how managers of a nonbusiness organization have discharged their stewardship responsibilities and about other aspects of their performance.

  —Financial reporting should provide information about the economic resources, obligations, and net resources of an organization, and the effects of transactions, events, and circumstances that change resources and interests in those resources.

  —Financial reporting should provide information about the performance of an organization during a period. Periodic measurement of the changes in the amount and nature of the net resources of a nonbusiness organization and information about the service efforts and accomplishments of an organization together represent the information most useful in assessing its performance.

  —Financial reporting should provide information about how an organization obtains and spends cash or other liquid resources, about its borrowing and repayment of borrowing, and about other factors that may affect an organization's liquidity.

  —Financial reporting should include explanations and interpretations to help users understand financial information provided.

- Background information relating to the development of this Statement is included in paragraphs 57-66. Paragraph 67 contains a comparison of the objectives in this Statement to those in Concepts Statement 1.

Statement of Financial Accounting Concepts No. 4
Objectives of Financial Reporting by Nonbusiness Organizations

Statements of Financial Accounting Concepts

This Statement of Financial Accounting Concepts is one of a series of publications in the Board's conceptual framework for financial accounting and reporting. Statements in the series are intended to set forth objectives and fundamentals that will be the basis for development of financial accounting and reporting standards. The objectives identify the goals and purposes of financial reporting. The fundamentals are the underlying concepts of financial accounting—concepts that guide the selection of transactions, events, and circumstances to be accounted for; their recognition and measurement; and the means of summarizing and communicating them to interested parties. Concepts of that type are fundamental in the sense that other concepts flow from them and repeated reference to them will be necessary in establishing, interpreting, and applying accounting and reporting standards.

The conceptual framework is a coherent system of interrelated objectives and fundamentals that is expected to lead to consistent standards and that prescribes the nature, function, and limits of financial accounting and reporting. It is expected to serve the public interest by providing structure and direction to financial accounting and reporting to facilitate the provision of evenhanded financial and related information that helps promote the efficient allocation of scarce resources in the economy and society, including assisting capital and other markets to function efficiently.

Establishment of objectives and identification of fundamental concepts will not directly solve financial accounting and reporting problems. Rather, objectives give direction and concepts are tools for solving problems.

The Board itself is likely to be the most direct beneficiary of the guidance provided by the Statements in this series. They will guide the Board in developing accounting and reporting standards by providing the Board with a common foundation and basic reasoning on which to consider merits of alternatives.

However, knowledge of the objectives and concepts the Board will use in developing standards also should enable those who are affected by or interested in financial accounting standards to understand better the purposes, content, and characteristics of information provided by financial accounting and reporting. That knowledge is expected to enhance the usefulness of, and confidence in, financial accounting and reporting. The concepts also may provide some guidance in analyzing new or emerging problems of financial accounting and reporting in the absence of applicable authoritative pronouncements.

Statements of Financial Accounting Concepts do not establish standards prescribing accounting procedures or disclosure practices for particular items or events, which are issued by the Board as Statements of Financial Accounting Standards. Rather, Statements in this series describe concepts and relations that will underlie future financial accounting standards and practices and in due course serve as a basis for evaluating existing standards and practices.*

The Board recognizes that in certain respects current generally accepted accounting principles may be inconsistent with those that may derive from the objectives and concepts set forth in Statements in this series. However, a Statement of Financial Accounting Concepts does not (a) require a change in existing generally accepted accounting principles; (b) amend, modify, or interpret Statements of Financial Accounting Standards, Interpretations of the FASB, Opinions of the Accounting Principles Board, or Bulletins of the Committee on Accounting Procedure that are in effect; or (c) justify either changing existing generally accepted accounting and reporting practices or interpreting the pronouncements listed in item (b) based on personal interpretations of the objectives and concepts in the Statements of Financial Accounting Concepts.

Since a Statement of Financial Accounting Concepts does not establish generally accepted accounting principles or standards for the disclosure of financial information outside of financial state-

---

*Generally accepted accounting principles for nonbusiness organizations are primarily set forth in publications of the American Institute of Certified Public Accountants (AICPA) and other bodies, such as the National Council on Governmental Accounting (NCGA). The Board has agreed to exercise responsibility, except as noted below, for all the specialized accounting and reporting principles and practices in AICPA Statements of Position and Guides that are neither superseded by nor contained in Accounting Research Bulletins, Accounting Principles Board Opinions, FASB Statements, and FASB Interpretations. The Board deferred similar action with regard to those specialized accounting and reporting principles and practices contained in the AICPA Industry Audit Guide, *Audits of State and Local Governmental Units*, and the three Statements of Position (75-3, *Accruals of Revenues and Expenditures by State and Local Governmental Units;* 77-2, *Accounting for Interfund Transfers of State and Local Governmental Units;* and 80-2, *Accounting and Financial Reporting by Governmental Units*) that supplement that Guide. In so doing, the Board noted that at the present time the accounting and reporting by such governmental units is addressed by the AICPA and the NCGA. The Board also noted that discussions are continuing among interested parties, including the AICPA, the Financial Accounting Foundation (FAF), and NCGA, as to what the appropriate structure for accounting standard setting for such governmental units should be. Until the matter is resolved, the FASB proposes no changes with respect to its involvement with pronouncements in that area (paragraphs 3-5).

ments in published financial reports, it is not intended to invoke application of Rule 203 or 204 of the Rules of Conduct of the Code of Professional Ethics of the American Institute of Certified Public Accountants (or successor rules or arrangements of similar scope and intent).*

Like other pronouncements of the Board, a Statement of Financial Accounting Concepts may be amended, superseded, or withdrawn by appropriate action under the Board's *Rules of Procedure.*

FASB PUBLICATIONS ON CONCEPTUAL FRAMEWORK

Statements of Financial Accounting Concepts

No.1, *Objectives of Financial Reporting by Business Enterprises* (November 1978)

No. 2, *Qualitative Characteristics of Accounting Information* (May 1980)

No. 3, *Elements of Financial Statements of Business Enterprises* (December 1980)

Discussion Memorandums and Invitations to Comment Having Issues Being (or Yet to Be) Considered by the Board

Elements of Financial Statements and Their Measurement (December 2, 1976)

Reporting Earnings (July 31, 1979)

Financial Statements and Other Means of Financial Reporting (May 12, 1980)

Reporting Funds Flows, Liquidity, and Financial Flexibility (December 15, 1980)

Other Projects in Process

Accounting Recognition Criteria

CONTENTS

---

*Rule 203 prohibits a member of the American Institute of Certified Public Accountants from expressing an opinion that financial statements conform with generally accepted accounting principles if those statements contain a material departure from an accounting principle promulgated by the Financial Accounting Standards Board, unless the member can demonstrate that because of unusual circumstances the financial statements otherwise would have been misleading. Rule 204 requires members of the Institute to justify departures from standards promulgated by the Financial Accounting Standards Board for the disclosure of information outside of financial statements in published financial reports.

INTRODUCTION AND BACKGROUND

Scope

General

1. This Statement establishes the objectives of general purpose external financial reporting by nonbusiness organizations. Those objectives, together with the objectives set forth in FASB Concepts Statement No. 1, *Objectives of Financial Reporting by Business Enterprises,* will serve as the foundation of the conceptual framework the Board is developing for financial accounting and reporting. Based on its review of the similarities and differences between those two sets of objectives, the Board has concluded that it is not necessary to develop an independent conceptual framework for any particular category of entities (e.g., nonbusiness organizations or business enterprises). Rather, its goal is to develop an integrated conceptual framework that has relevance to all entities and that provides appropriate consideration of any different reporting objectives and concepts that may apply to only certain types of entities. Consideration of the differences between the objectives of financial reporting set forth in this Statement and those in Concepts Statement 1 will be most useful in helping to identify those areas that may require unique treatment. Appendix A to this Statement provides background information. Appendix B compares the objectives of this Statement and Concepts Statement 1, noting the many areas of similarity and the few, but important, areas of difference (paragraph 9).

2. This Statement uses terminology that has been chosen carefully to avoid prejudging issues that may be subjects of other conceptual framework projects. For example, it uses the terms *resource inflows* and *outflows* rather than *revenues, expenses,* and *expenditures.* The reasons for the Board's conclusions are included in the text rather than in a separate appendix.

State and Local Governmental Units

3. From its outset, the project leading to this Statement has included governmental units in its scope, and the Exposure Draft included governmental examples. On the basis of its study to date, the Board is aware of no persuasive evidence that the objectives in this Statement are inappropriate for general purpose external financial reports of governmental units. Nonetheless, the appropriate structure for setting financial accounting and reporting standards for state and local governmental units continues to be discussed.[1] Pending resolution of that issue, the Board has deferred a final decision on whether the objectives set forth in this Statement should apply to general purpose external financial reporting by state and local governmental units.

4. If the responsibility for standard setting was ultimately given to the Financial Accounting Standards Board, the Board would expect to consider the findings of research in process by the National Council on Governmental Accounting (NCGA), the Council of State Governments (CSG) (paragraphs 65 and 66), and other intervening research. Before reaching a decision, it would also solicit additional views regarding the applicability of the conclusions in this Statement to general purpose external financial reporting of state and local governmental units.

5. Based on its study, the Board believes that the objectives of general purpose external financial reporting for government-sponsored entities (for example, hospitals, universities, or utilities) engaged in activities that are not unique to government should be similar to those of business enterprises or other nonbusiness organizations engaged in similar activities. Accordingly, examples of such government-sponsored organizations and activities are included in the sections of this Statement that discuss the environment in which nonbusiness organizations operate and the users of their financial reports.

Distinguishing Characteristics of Nonbusiness Organizations

6. The major distinguishing characteristics of nonbusiness organizations include:

a. Receipts of significant amounts of resources from resource providers who do not expect to receive either repayment or economic benefits proportionate to resources provided

b. Operating purposes that are other than to provide goods or services at a profit or profit equivalent

---

[1] The Board recognizes that standard setting for the federal government is not in question. Although the Board sees no conceptual reasons why the objectives in this Statement could not be applied to general purpose external financial reporting by the federal government, the Board acknowledges that determination is the responsibility of others.

c. Absence of defined ownership interests that can be sold, transferred, or redeemed, or that convey entitlement to a share of a residual distribution of resources in the event of liquidation of the organization.

These characteristics result in certain types of transactions that are largely, although not entirely, absent in business enterprises, such as contributions and grants,[2] and to the absence of transactions with owners, such as issuing and redeeming stock and paying dividends. Because the authoritative accounting literature has largely focused on problems commonly encountered in business enterprises, it has not dealt comprehensively with these unique areas in nonbusiness organizations.

7. This Statement focuses on organizations that have predominantly nonbusiness characteristics that heavily influence the operations of the organization. The line between nonbusiness organizations and business enterprises is not always sharp since the incidence and relative importance of those characteristics in any organization are different. This suggests that, for purposes of developing financial reporting objectives, a spectrum of organizations exists ranging from those with clearly dominant nonbusiness characteristics to those with wholly business characteristics. Examples of organizations that clearly fall outside the focus of this Statement include all investor-owned enterprises and other types of organizations, such as mutual insurance companies and other mutual cooperative entities that provide dividends, lower costs, or other economic benefits directly and proportionately to their owners, members, or participants. The objectives of financial reporting set forth in Concepts Statement 1 are appropriate for those types of organizations. Examples of organizations that clearly fall within the focus of this Statement include most human service organizations, churches, foundations, and some other organizations, such as those private nonprofit hospitals and nonprofit

schools that receive a significant portion of their financial resources from sources other than the sale of goods and services.[3] As happens with any distinction, there will be borderline cases. This will be true especially for organizations that possess some of the distinguishing characteristics of nonbusiness organizations but not others.

8. Some organizations have no ownership interests but are essentially self-sustaining from fees they charge for goods and services. Examples are those private nonprofit hospitals and nonprofit schools that may receive relatively small amounts of contributions and grants but finance their capital needs largely from the proceeds of debt issues and their operating needs largely from service charges rather than from private philanthropy or governmental grants. As a result, assessment of amounts, timing, and uncertainty of cash flows becomes the dominant interest of their creditors and other resource providers and profitability becomes an important indicator of performance. Consequently, the objectives of Concepts Statement 1 may be more appropriate for those organizations.[4]

9. The objectives in this Statement stem from the common interests of those who provide resources to nonbusiness organizations in the services those organizations provide and their continuing ability to provide services. In contrast, the objectives of financial reporting of Concepts Statement 1 stem from the interests of resource providers in the prospects of receiving cash as a return of and return on their investment.[5] Despite different interests, resource providers of all entities look to information about economic resources, obligations, net resources, and changes in them for information that is useful in assessing their interests. All such resource providers focus on indicators of organization performance and information about management stewardship. Nonbusiness organizations generally have no single indicator of performance comparable to a business enterprise's profit. Thus, other indicators of perfor-

---

[2]These types of transactions are classified in APB Statement No. 4, *Basic Concepts and Accounting Principles Underlying Financial Statements of Business Enterprises,* as nonreciprocal transfers. Nonreciprocal transfers are therein defined as "transfers in one direction of resources or obligations, either from the enterprise to other entities or from other entities to the enterprise" (paragraphs 62 and 182). Two types of such transfers noted are: (a) transfers between the enterprise and its owners and (b) transfers between the enterprise and entities other than owners. Transactions of the second type frequently are found in nonbusiness organizations.

[3]The FASB Research Report, *Financial Accounting in Nonbusiness Organizations,* distinguishes two types of nonprofit organizations based "on a difference in the source of the financial resources" (page 161). A Type A nonprofit organization is therein defined as "a nonprofit organization whose financial resources are obtained, entirely, or almost entirely, from revenues from the sale of goods and services" (page 162). A Type B nonprofit organization, in contrast, is defined as "a nonprofit organization that obtains a significant amount of financial resources from sources other than the sale of goods and services" (page 162). The Type B category corresponds to the type of organizations that clearly falls within the focus of this Statement.

[4]The organizations described in this paragraph correspond to the Type A category described in the preceding footnote. To the extent, however, that Type A organizations have the unique transactions described in paragraph 6, they naturally will be impacted by standards promulgated by the Board in those areas.

[5]Creditors of nonbusiness organizations are also interested in receiving cash. Because of the differences in environment (principally the motivations of other resource providers) and different indicators of the performance of a nonbusiness organization, creditors also look to information useful in assessing the services that type of organization provides and its ability to continue to provide services to satisfy their basic interest in the prospect for cash flows.

mance are usually needed. This Statement sets forth two performance indicators for nonbusiness organizations: information about the nature of and relation between inflows and outflows of resources and information about service efforts and accomplishments. Moreover, the performance of nonbusiness organizations generally is not subject to the test of direct competition in markets to the extent that business enterprises are. Other kinds of controls introduced to compensate for the lesser influence of markets are a major characteristic of their operations and affect the objectives of their financial reporting. Controls, such as formal budgets and donor restrictions on the use of resources, give managers a special responsibility to ensure compliance. Information about departures from those mandates that may impinge upon an organization's financial performance or its ability to provide a satisfactory level of services is important in assessing how well managers have discharged their stewardship responsibilities. Paragraphs 13-22 compare the environments of nonbusiness organizations and business enterprises and provide a basis for the similarities and differences noted in this section and elsewhere in this Statement.

General Purpose External Financial Reporting

10. The objectives in this Statement apply to general purpose external financial reporting by nonbusiness organizations. The aim of that type of financial reporting is limited. It does not attempt to meet all informational needs of those interested in nonbusiness organizations nor to furnish all the types of information that financial reporting can provide. For example, although managers and governing bodies of nonbusiness organizations are interested in the information provided by general purpose external financial reporting, they also need additional information to help them carry out their planning, controlling, and other stewardship responsibilities (paragraph 32). Nor is general purpose external financial reporting intended to meet specialized needs of regulatory bodies, some donors or grantors, or others having the authority to obtain the information they need (paragraph 31). Rather, general purpose external financial reporting focuses on providing information to meet the common interests of external users who generally cannot prescribe the information they want from an organization. Those users must use the information that is communicated to them by the organization. The most obvious and important users fitting that description in the nonbusiness environment are resource providers, such as members, taxpayers, contributors, and creditors (paragraph 36).

11. The objectives in this Statement are not restricted to information communicated by financial statements. Financial reporting includes not only financial statements but also other means of communicating information that relates, directly or indirectly, to the information provided by the accounting system, that is, information about an organization's resources and obligations.[6]

12. For convenience, *financial reporting* is used in place of *general purpose external financial reporting by nonbusiness organizations* in the remainder of this Statement.

Environmental Context of Objectives

13. Financial reporting is not an end in itself but is intended to provide information that is useful in making economic decisions—for making reasoned choices among alternative uses of scarce resources.[7] Thus, the objectives in this Statement stem largely from the needs of those for whom the information is intended. Those needs depend significantly on the activities of nonbusiness organizations and the decisions that users of the information make about them. Accordingly, the objectives in this Statement are affected by the economic, legal, political, and social environment within which those organizations function in the United States. The objectives are also affected by the characteristics and limitations of the information that financial reporting can provide (paragraphs 23-28).

14. The operating environments of nonbusiness organizations and business enterprises are similar in many ways. Both nonbusiness organizations and business enterprises produce and distribute goods or services and use scarce resources in doing so. They sometimes provide essentially the same goods or services. For example, both municipal transportation systems significantly subsidized by general tax revenues and private bus lines may carry passengers within a large city, and both private nonprofit organizations supported by significant philanthropy and investor-owned enterprises may operate theatri-

---

[6]Distinctions between financial reporting and financial statements are discussed at more length in Concepts Statement 1 (paragraphs 5-8), and are the subject of another phase of the Board's conceptual framework project.

[7]Economic decisions about nonbusiness organizations may take different forms depending on the factors that are evident in the resource allocation process affecting an organization. For example, if an element of compulsion is present as it is with members paying dues or taxpayers paying taxes, this Statement describes processes, such as approval of budgets, elections, referendums, and involvement in legislative processes, through which resource providers decide or influence decisions about matters that affect the amount and use of resources allocated to organizations. A member may discontinue membership or a taxpayer may choose to locate in one governmental jurisdiction rather than another as a result of assessment of their respective policies. That kind of action also represents, in part, the result of an economic decision.

cal, dance, and musical organizations.[8] Both nonbusiness organizations and business enterprises obtain resources from external sources and are accountable to those who provide resources or their representatives. Both are integral parts of the national economy and interrelate directly or indirectly with other organizations. Both own or control supplies of resources, some of which are used in current operations and some of which are held for use in future periods. Both incur obligations. Some nonbusiness organizations, as well as business enterprises, incur and pay taxes, and both are subject to governmental laws and regulations. Both must be financially viable: To achieve their operating objectives, they must, *in the long run*, receive at least as many resources as they need to provide goods and services at levels satisfactory to resource providers and other constituents.[9] Both generally obtain resources from the same pool of resource providers, and the resources available for use by all organizations are limited.

15. Differences between nonbusiness organizations and business enterprises arise principally in the ways they obtain resources. The following descriptions begin with areas of greatest similarity between nonbusiness organizations and business enterprises and end with the areas of greatest difference.

16. Both nonbusiness organizations and business enterprises obtain resources in exchange transactions in markets. Both obtain labor, materials, and facilities or their use by paying for them or agreeing to pay for them in the future.[10] Both may borrow funds through bank loans, mortgages, or other direct loans or through issuing debt securities to creditors who commonly may evaluate and compare the risks and returns of securities of both nonbusiness organizations and business enterprises.

17. Both nonbusiness organizations and business enterprises may obtain resources by charging a price or fee for goods or services they provide, but the purpose of sales of goods or services is different. Some nonbusiness organizations may sell goods or services at prices that equal or exceed costs, but many nonbusiness organizations commonly provide goods or services at prices less than costs. Nonbusiness organizations also commonly provide goods or

services free of charge. Moreover, those that charge prices sufficient to cover costs often use resources from those sales to subsidize other activities within the organization. For example, the football or basketball program at a college or university may finance both intercollegiate and intramural athletic programs. Although sales of goods or services may be important sources of financing for some nonbusiness organizations, nonbusiness organizations generally are not expected to and do not need to cover all costs, and perhaps earn profits, by sales because they rely significantly on other continuing sources of financing (paragraph 18). For example, some nonbusiness organizations have the power to assess dues, taxes, or other compulsory contributions, and others depend significantly on voluntary contributions. In contrast, business enterprises attempt to sell goods or services at prices that enable them to repay or compensate all resource providers, including owners and others who expect a monetary return for providing resources. Profit is the basis for compensating owners and others for providing resources, and expectations of profit are necessary to attract resources. Moreover, unprofitable business enterprises find it increasingly difficult to borrow or otherwise obtain resources. Sales of goods or services are not only significant sources of resources for business enterprises but also underlie their ability to obtain resources from other sources.

18. Members, contributors, taxpayers, and others who provide resources to nonbusiness organizations do so for reasons different from those of owners of business enterprises. All nonbusiness organizations obtain significant resources from resource providers who either expect no economic benefits or expect benefits received not to be proportionate to the resources provided. Those resources are often provided for charitable, humanitarian, religious, or other noneconomic reasons.[11] As a result, those who provide resources to a nonbusiness organization and those who benefit from the goods or services it provides may be different individuals or groups. Owners of business enterprises, in contrast, generally expect returns through dividends or price appreciation of their securities commensurate with the perceived risk.

19. As the preceding paragraphs indicate, non-

---

[8]Other nonprofit organizations (paragraph 8) lacking all the distinguishing characteristics of nonbusiness organizations also may provide the services described in this sentence.

[9]Some nonbusiness organizations are established for short-term purposes and are not intended to survive after completing their operating objectives, such as an organization established to erect a memorial.

[10]Nonbusiness organizations also may receive significant donations of labor, materials, and facilities or their use from resource providers.

[11]Contributors to nonbusiness organizations often provide resources, such as property, materials, and uncompensated volunteer labor, in addition to financial resources. In many nonbusiness organizations, such as charities and youth groups, these donated materials and services are significant factors in the organization's operations. In other nonbusiness organizations, especially those operated by religious bodies, services contributed by personnel at far less than their market value are equally significant. Such donated or contributed services and materials are rarely found in business enterprises.

economic reasons are commonly factors in decisions to provide resources to particular nonbusiness organizations. For example, contributors[12] to philanthropic organizations, such as charities, and to some membership organizations, such as churches, generally seek no direct economic benefits. Rather, their reasons for voluntarily providing resources relate to their interests in furthering the purpose and goals of the organization. The goals may involve a wide range of endeavors including those of a charitable, cultural, educational, economic, religious, scientific, social, or political nature. Some kinds of membership organizations, such as professional and trade associations, assess membership dues. Persons joining these organizations often seek noneconomic benefits, such as recognition or prestige, in addition to direct service benefits.

20. Nonbusiness organizations and business enterprises have different degrees of involvement with markets. Most transactions of business enterprises with other entities involve exchange prices in active markets; that market mechanism provides a measure of the utility and satisfaction of goods and services businesses buy and sell and of the overall performance of those enterprises. Nonbusiness organizations also borrow money and buy goods and services in markets and may or may not sell goods or services in markets. However, market transactions play a more limited role in the resource allocation process of nonbusiness organizations because those organizations do not finance their operations through equity markets and they commonly receive resources and provide goods or services in other than market transactions. Since market controls exist to a lesser degree for nonbusiness organizations than for business enterprises, other kinds of controls are introduced to compensate for their absence.

21. Resource providers or governing bodies may restrict or mandate the ways a nonbusiness organization may spend the resources provided. Spending mandates generally take one of two forms: specific budgetary appropriations or direct restrictions by donors or grantors. For example, a budgetary appropriation may limit the amount that a church may spend for its educational program or that a governmental unit may spend to subsidize its public transportation system, a donor or grantor may specify that a gift to a museum must be used to construct a new wing, or an agency of the federal government may specify that its grant to a university must be used for medical research. Those mandates give managers of nonbusiness organizations a special responsibility to ensure compliance. Although spending mandates also may exist in business

enterprises, they are less common. Their effects on the conduct and control of the activities of business enterprises are less pervasive than in nonbusiness organizations.

22. Budgets are particularly significant in the nonbusiness environment. Both business and nonbusiness organizations use budgets to allocate and control uses of resources. However, in nonbusiness organizations for which providing resources is compulsory (for example, many membership organizations and governmental units), budgets are significant factors not only in allocating resources within an organization but also in obtaining resources. For example, budgets in membership organizations and governmental units are often pivotal in establishing the level of dues, taxes, or fees to be imposed; the level of services to be provided; and the desired relation between the two. Members and taxpayers may have the opportunity, either by direct vote or through elected representatives, to participate in developing and approving budgets. Elections and referendums also offer opportunities to change policies and the amounts and uses of resources provided. In other kinds of nonbusiness organizations, budgets may be important to voluntary donors in deciding whether to provide resources to nonbusiness organizations and in establishing the level of their giving.

Characteristics and Limitations of Information Provided by Financial Reporting

23. The objectives of financial reporting by nonbusiness organizations are affected not only by the environment in which financial reporting takes place but also by the characteristics and limitations of the kind of information that financial reporting, and particularly financial statements, can provide. The information provided by financial reporting is primarily financial in nature: It is generally quantified and expressed in terms of units of money. Information that is to be incorporated formally in financial statements must be quantifiable in terms of units of money. Other information can be disclosed in financial statements (including notes) or by other means, but financial statements involve adding, subtracting, multiplying, and dividing numbers that depict economic things and events and require a common denominator. Quantified information expressed in terms other than units of money (such as number of employees or units of services or products provided) and nonquantified information (such as descriptions of operations or explanations of policies) that are reported normally relate to or underlie the financial information. Information that is not expressed in terms of units of money may be needed

---

[12]Contributors include donors and prospective donors, grantors and prospective grantors, and federated fund-raising organizations that solicit contributions and then redistribute those contributions to nonbusiness organizations after deducting fund-raising and other costs.

to understand the significance of information expressed in terms of units of money or to help in assessing the performance of a nonbusiness organization (paragraphs 47-53). Financial reporting by nonbusiness organizations, however, is limited in its ability to provide direct measures of the quality of goods and services provided in the absence of market-determined exchange prices or the degree to which they satisfy the needs of service beneficiaries and other consumers.

24. The information provided by financial reporting pertains to individual nonbusiness reporting entities. This Statement, however, does not include criteria for determining the appropriate reporting entity for purposes of financial reporting by nonbusiness organizations. That matter will need to be addressed by other projects.[13]

25. The information provided by financial reporting often results from approximate, rather than exact, measures. The measures commonly involve numerous estimates, classifications, summarizations, judgments, and allocations. Thus, despite the aura of precision that may seem to surround financial reporting in general and financial statements in particular, with few exceptions the measures are approximations which may be based on rules and conventions rather than exact amounts.

26. The information provided by financial reporting largely reflects the effects of transactions and events that have already happened. Governing bodies and managers may use budgets to communicate information about plans or projections, but most of the information provided by financial reporting is historical, including comparisons of actual results with previously approved budgets. The acquisition price of land and the current market price of a marketable equity security are other examples of historical data included in financial reports. No future amounts or events are involved. Estimates resting on expectations of the future are often needed in financial reporting, but their major use, especially of those formally incorporated in financial statements, is to measure financial effects of past transactions or events or the present status of an asset or liability.

27. Financial reporting is but one source of information needed by those who make economic decisions about nonbusiness organizations. They need to combine information provided by financial reporting with relevant social, economic, and political information from other sources.

28. The information provided by financial reporting involves a cost to provide and use. The cost includes not only the resources directly expended to provide the information but also may include adverse effects on an organization from disclosing it. For example, comments about a pending lawsuit may jeopardize a successful defense. The collective time needed to understand and use information is also a cost. Generally, the benefits of information provided should be expected to at least equal the cost involved.[14] However, the benefits and costs usually are difficult to measure. Different persons will honestly disagree about whether the benefits of the information justify its cost.

Types of Users and Their Interests

29. Many people base economic decisions on their relationships to and knowledge about nonbusiness organizations and, thus, are interested in the information provided by financial reporting. Among present and potential users are members, taxpayers, contributors, grantors, lenders, suppliers, creditors, employees, managers, directors and trustees, service beneficiaries, financial analysts and advisors, brokers, underwriters, lawyers, economists, taxing authorities, regulatory authorities, legislators, the financial press and reporting agencies, labor unions, trade associations, researchers, teachers, and students. The following groups are especially interested in information provided by the financial reporting of a nonbusiness organization:

a. *Resource providers.* Resource providers include those who are directly compensated for providing resources—lenders, suppliers, and employees (paragraph 16)—and those who are not directly and proportionately compensated—members, contributors, and taxpayers (paragraph 18).[15]

b. *Constituents.* Constituents are those who use and benefit from the services rendered by the organization. In some nonbusiness organizations, constituents include resource providers (for example, members who pay dues or taxpayers), and distinguishing constituents from

---

[13]A discussion of the reporting entity issue can be found in the FASB Research Report on financial accounting in nonbusiness organizations, pages 18-21.

[14]Paragraphs 133-144 of FASB Concepts Statement No. 2, *Qualitative Characteristics of Accounting Information,* expand on the cost/benefit considerations discussed in this paragraph. The Board intends to solicit views regarding its tentative conclusion that the qualities of information set forth in Concepts Statement 2 also apply to accounting information of nonbusiness organizations.

[15]Taxpayers provide resources to nonbusiness organizations both directly and indirectly. They pay taxes to all levels of government. Governments (especially federal and state), in turn, provide funding to other levels of government, government-sponsored entities, and private nonbusiness organizations.

resource providers may serve no function. However, resource providers and service beneficiaries are largely different groups or individuals in some organizations. The degree to which service beneficiaries are a distinctive part of a constituency depends largely on the extent of separation between those providing the resources and those using and receiving the service benefits.

c. *Governing and oversight bodies.* Governing and oversight bodies are those responsible for setting policies and for overseeing and appraising managers of nonbusiness organizations. Governing bodies include boards of trustees, boards of overseers or regents, legislatures, councils, and other bodies with similar responsibilities. Oversight bodies also are responsible for reviewing the organization's conformance with various laws, restrictions, guidelines, or other items of a similar nature. Oversight bodies include national headquarters of organizations with local chapters, accrediting agencies, agencies acting on behalf of contributors and constituents, oversight committees of legislatures, and governmental regulatory agencies. In some nonbusiness organizations, governing bodies commonly are elected representatives of a constituency that is largely comprised of resource providers. In other nonbusiness organizations, governing bodies may be self-perpetuating through election of their successors.

d. *Managers.* Managers of an organization are responsible for carrying out the policy mandates of governing bodies and managing the day-to-day operations of an organization. Managers include certain elected officials; managing executives appointed by elected governing bodies, such as school superintendents, agency heads, and executive directors; and staff, such as fund-raising and program directors.

30. Present and potential users of the information provided by financial reporting by a particular nonbusiness organization share a common interest in information about the services provided by the nonbusiness organization, its efficiency and effectiveness in providing those services, and its ability to continue to provide those services. Resource providers, such as members and contributors, may be interested in that information as a basis for assessing how well the organization has met its objectives and whether to continue support. Taxpayers may need similar information to help them assess whether governmental units and government-sponsored entities have achieved their operating objectives. In addition, they may want to know how the services provided by the governmental unit or government-sponsored entity are likely to affect the amount of taxes and fees they will be required to pay. Resource providers, such as lenders, suppliers, and employees, view a nonbusiness organization as a source of payment for the cash, goods, or services they supply. Their interest stems from concern about the organization's ability to generate cash flows for timely payment of the organization's obligations to them. Governing and oversight bodies also use information about services rendered to help them evaluate whether managers have carried out their policy mandates and to change or formulate new policies for the organization. That information also is important to managers in evaluating the accomplishment of the responsibilities for which they are accountable to governing bodies, resource providers, and other constituents. Constituents, including recipients and beneficiaries of services who as a group are distinct from resource providers, share a direct interest in similar information.

31. Some users have specialized needs but also have the power to obtain the information they need. For example, donors and grantors who restrict the use of resources they provide often stipulate that they be apprised periodically of the organization's compliance with the terms and conditions of the gift or grant. Creditors also may be able to stipulate that certain specialized types of information be provided. Special-purpose reports directed at those kinds of needs are beyond the scope of this Statement.

32. Managers and, to some extent, governing bodies commonly are described as "internal users." In addition to the information provided by financial reporting, they need a great deal of internal accounting information to carry out their responsibilities in planning and controlling activities. Much of that information relates to particular decisions or to managers' exercise of their stewardship responsibility to ensure that resources are used for their intended purposes. For example, governing bodies and managers need information to evaluate properly the competing requests for funding of capital projects. They also need information to assist them in complying or overseeing compliance with spending mandates established by budgetary appropriations or donor or grantor restrictions. They need to know how much of a budgetary appropriation or restricted grant is unspent or uncommitted. They need to know that restricted resources were expended or committed in compliance with related mandates. Generally, both the number of spending mandates and the detail about them required to meet the informational needs of managers are so great that the usefulness of general purpose external financial reports would be reduced significantly if they reported the status of compliance with each mandate (paragraph 41). Since the type of reporting described in this paragraph needs to be tailored to

meet the specialized needs of managers and governing bodies of particular organizations, it is beyond the scope of this Statement.

OBJECTIVES OF FINANCIAL REPORTING

33. The following objectives of financial reporting flow from the preceding paragraphs and proceed from the general to the specific. The objectives begin with a broad focus on information that is useful to resource providers and other users in making rational decisions about allocating resources to nonbusiness organizations. The focus is then narrowed to the needs of resource providers and other users for information about the services an organization provides and its ability to continue to provide those services. That directs their attention to information about the organization's performance and how its managers have discharged their stewardship responsibility. Finally, the objectives focus on the types of information financial reporting can provide to meet those needs. The reasons for focusing the objectives of financial reporting on decisions generally made by resource providers are given in paragraph 36. That focus and wording do not mean that the objectives apply to only resource providers. On the contrary, information that satisfies the objectives should be useful to all who are interested in a nonbusiness organization's present and future capacity to render service and achieve its operating goals.

34. The objectives are those of financial reporting rather than goals for resource providers or others who use the information or for the economy or society as a whole. The role of financial reporting in the economy and society is to provide information that is useful in making decisions about allocating scarce resources, not to determine what those decisions should be. For example, information that tries to indicate that a relatively inefficient user of resources is efficient or information that is directed toward a particular goal, such as encouraging the reallocation of resources in favor of certain programs or activities of nonbusiness organizations, is likely to fail to serve the broader objectives that financial reporting is intended to serve. The role of financial reporting requires it to provide neutral information.

Information Useful in Making
Resource Allocation Decisions

35. Financial reporting by nonbusiness organizations should provide information that is useful to present and potential resource providers and other users in making rational decisions about the allocation of resources to those organizations. The information should be comprehensible to those who have a reasonable understanding of an organization's activities and are willing to study the information with reasonable diligence.

36. Resource providers are important users of information provided by financial reporting who generally cannot prescribe the information they want. Their decisions significantly affect both nonbusiness organizations and the allocation of resources in society generally. In addition, information provided to meet the needs of present and potential resource providers is likely to be useful to others who are interested in essentially the same aspects of nonbusiness organizations as resource providers.

37. The potential users listed in paragraph 29 understand, to varying degrees, the environment within which a nonbusiness organization operates, the nature of its activities, and related matters. Their understanding of information provided by financial reporting and the extent to which they use and rely on it also varies greatly. Financial reporting information is a tool and, like most tools, cannot be of much direct help to those who are unable or unwilling to use it or who misuse it. Its use can be learned, however, and financial reporting should provide information that can be used by all who are willing to learn to use it properly. Efforts may be needed to increase the understandability of information provided by financial reporting. Cost/benefit considerations may indicate that information understood or used by only a few should not be provided.[16] Conversely, financial reporting should not exclude relevant information merely because it is difficult for some to understand or because some choose not to use it.

Information Useful in Assessing Services and
Ability to Provide Services

38. Financial reporting should provide information to help present and potential resource providers and other users in assessing the services[17] that a nonbusiness organization provides and its ability to continue to provide those services.[18] They are interested in that information because the services are the end for which the resources are provided. The relation of the services provided to the resources used to provide them helps resource providers and others assess the extent to which the organization is successful in

---

[16]See footnote 14.

[17]The term *services* in this context encompasses the goods as well as the services a nonbusiness organization may provide.

[18]An organization's ability to continue to provide services ultimately depends on its ability to obtain resources from resource providers. The ability to obtain sufficient resources normally is not discussed in general purpose external financial reports unless that ability is in doubt. Paragraphs 43-55 discuss the type of information financial reporting can provide to meet the objective in paragraph 38.

carrying out its service objectives.

39. Resources are the lifeblood of an organization in the sense that it uses resources to provide services. A nonbusiness organization cannot, in the long run, continue to achieve its operating objectives unless the resources made available to it at least equal the resources needed to provide services at levels satisfactory to resource providers and other constituents. Although decisions of potential and present resource providers to provide or continue to provide resources involve expectations about future services of an organization, those expectations commonly are based at least partly on evaluations of past performance. Thus, resource providers tend to direct their interest to information about the organization's resources and how it acquires and uses resources. The focus of that interest is information about the organization's performance and how its managers have discharged their stewardship responsibility during a period.

Information Useful in Assessing Management Stewardship and Performance

40. Financial reporting should provide information that is useful to present and potential resource providers and other users in assessing how managers of a nonbusiness organization have discharged their stewardship responsibilities and about other aspects of their performance. Managers of an organization are accountable to resource providers and others, not only for the custody and safekeeping of organization resources, but also for their efficient and effective use. Those who provide resources to nonbusiness organizations do not have a profit indicator to guide their resource allocation decisions and may not have an immediate choice about the amounts of their contributions. They must look to managers to represent their interests and to make operating cost/benefit judgments that achieve the objectives of the organizations with minimum use of resources. Managers also are accountable for compliance with statutory, contractual, or other limitations.

41. Information about an organization's performance (paragraphs 47-53) should be the focus for assessing the stewardship or accountability of managers of a nonbusiness organization. Users also need assurance that managers have exercised their special responsibilities to ensure that an organization uses resources in the manner specifically designated by resource providers. General purpose external financial reporting can best meet that need by disclosing failures to comply with spending mandates that may

impinge on an organization's financial performance or on its ability to continue to provide a satisfactory level of services.

42. Financial reporting is limited in its ability to distinguish the performance of managers from that of the organization itself. Nonbusiness organizations are often highly complex institutions, and the processes by which they acquire resources and render services often are long and intricate. Organizational successes and failures are the result of numerous factors. The ability and performance of managers are contributing factors, as are events and circumstances that often are beyond the control of managers. It is usually not possible to determine the degree to which managers, or any other specific factors, have affected the result. Actions of past managers affect current periods' performance, and actions of present managers affect future periods' performance.

Information about Economic Resources, Obligations, Net Resources, and Changes in Them

43. Financial reporting should provide information about the economic resources, obligations, and net resources of an organization and the effects of transactions, events, and circumstances that change resources and interests in those resources.[19] That type of information is useful in achieving each of the above objectives.

Economic Resources, Obligations, and Net Resources

44. Financial reporting should provide information about an organization's economic resources, obligations, and net resources. That information helps resource providers and others identify the organization's financial strengths and weaknesses, evaluate information about the organization's performance during a period (paragraphs 47-53), and assess its ability to continue to render services.

45. Information about an organization's economic resources, obligations, and net resources also provides direct indications of the cash flow potential of some resources and of the cash needed to satisfy many, if not most, obligations. The assessment of cash flow potential is important because it relates directly to the organization's ability to provide the goods and services for which it exists.

46. Resources provided to nonbusiness organizations often are restricted by providers as to time and for particular purposes (paragraph 21). Accord-

[19]In FASB Concepts Statement No. 3, *Elements of Financial Statements of Business Enterprises,* the Board has attempted to define many elements (for example, assets and liabilities) in a way that they could apply to all types of entities. In the near future, the Board expects to consider and solicit views about which, if any, of the definitions are inappropriate or may require modification for nonbusiness organizations and whether other elements are needed for financial statements of nonbusiness organizations.

ingly, information about restrictions on the use of resources is important for assessing the types and levels of services an organization is able to provide. That information is also important to creditors in assessing their prospects for receiving cash.[20]

Organization Performance

47. Financial reporting should provide information about the performance of an organization during a period. Periodic measurement of the changes in the amount and nature of the net resources of a nonbusiness organization and information about the service efforts and accomplishments of an organization together represent the information most useful in assessing its performance.

Nature of and relation between inflows and outflows

48. Financial reporting should provide information about the amounts and kinds of inflows and outflows of resources during a period. It should distinguish resource flows that change net resources, such as inflows of fees or contributions and outflows for wages and salaries, from those that do not change net resources, such as borrowings or purchases of buildings. It also should identify inflows and outflows of restricted resources.

49. Financial reporting should provide information about the relation between inflows and outflows of resources during a period. Those who provide resources to a nonbusiness organization and others want to know how and why net resources changed during a period. To meet that need, financial reporting must distinguish between resource flows that are related to operations and those that are not.[21] In this way, financial reporting may provide information that is useful in assessing whether the activities of a nonbusiness organization during a particular period have drawn upon, or have contributed to, past or future periods. Thus, it should show the relation of resources used in operations of a period to resource inflows available to finance those operations. Similarly, it should provide information about changes in resources that are not related to operations. For

example, resource providers to colleges or universities need information about changes in an organization's endowment and plant to understand more fully the changes in its net resources during a period.

50. The information described in paragraphs 47-49 measured by accrual accounting generally provides a better indication of an organization's performance than does information about cash receipts and payments.[22] Accrual accounting attempts to record the financial effects of transactions, events, and circumstances that have cash consequences for an organization in the periods in which those transactions, events, and circumstances occur rather than in only the periods in which cash is received or paid by the organization. Accrual accounting is concerned with the process by which cash is obtained and used, not with just the beginning and end of that process. It recognizes that the acquisition of resources needed to provide services and the rendering of services by an organization during a period often do not coincide with the cash receipts and payments of the period.[23]

Service efforts and accomplishments

51. Information about an organization's service efforts and accomplishments is useful to resource providers and others in assessing the performance of a nonbusiness organization and in making resource allocation decisions, particularly because:

a. The accomplishments of nonbusiness organizations generally cannot be measured in terms of sales, profit, or return on investment.
b. Resource providers often are not in a position to have direct knowledge of the goods or services provided when they also are not users or beneficiaries of those goods and services.

52. Financial reporting should provide information about the service efforts of a nonbusiness organization. Information about service efforts should focus on how the organization's resources (inputs such as money, personnel, and materials) are used in providing different programs or services. Techniques for measuring the costs of significant programs or ser-

---

[20]Issues that affect how, if at all, restricted resources are displayed in financial statements, for example, by using multi-column presentations or disclosure in the notes, are outside the scope of this Statement and may be the subject of future Board projects.

[21]Resource flows that are not related to operations have been described in various ways, for example, as "nonexpendable," "capital," or "restricted" flows. The Board's endorsement of distinguishing these types of flows is not intended to prejudge future determinations of (a) the criteria that should be used in making this distinction and (b) how and in what financial statements different types of flows might be displayed.

[22]In some relatively small organizations, the benefits of the better information obtained from accrual accounting may not justify the costs of obtaining that information (footnote 14).

[23]Accrual accounting is concerned with the timing of recognizing transactions, events, and circumstances that have financial effects on an organization. This paragraph is not intended to prejudge specific recognition and measurement issues involved in applying accrual accounting in the nonbusiness area. For example, whether certain inflows of financial resources, such as taxes, grants, and contributions, should be recognized in the period when a claim arises, when they are received, when they are appropriated for use, when they are used, or when other events occur, is beyond the scope of this Statement.

vices are well developed and this information normally should be included in financial statements.

53. Ideally, financial reporting also should provide information about the service accomplishments of a nonbusiness organization. Information about service accomplishments in terms of goods or services produced (outputs) and of program results[24] may enhance significantly the value of information provided about service efforts. However, the ability to measure service accomplishments, particularly program results, is generally undeveloped. At present, such measures may not satisfy the qualitative characteristics of accounting information identified in Concepts Statement 2. Research should be conducted to determine if measures of service accomplishments with the requisite characteristics of relevance, reliability, comparability, verifiability, and neutrality can be developed. If such measures are developed, they should be included in financial reports. In the absence of measures suitable for financial reporting, information about service accomplishments may be furnished by managers' explanations and sources other than financial reporting.

Liquidity

54. Financial reporting should provide information about how an organization obtains and spends cash or other liquid resources, about its borrowing and repayment of borrowing, and about other factors that may affect its liquidity. Information about those resource flows may be useful in understanding the operations of an enterprise, evaluating its financing activities, assessing its liquidity, or interpreting performance information provided. Information about performance and economic resources, obligations, and net resources also may be useful in assessing an enterprise's liquidity.

Managers' Explanations and Interpretations

55. Financial reporting should include explanations and interpretations to help users understand financial information provided. For example, the usefulness of financial information to resource providers and others may be enhanced by managers' explanations of the information. Since managers usually know more about the organization and its affairs than do resource providers or others outside the organization, they often can increase the usefulness of information provided by financial reporting by identifying certain transactions, events, and circumstances that affect the organization and by explaining their financial impact.[25] In addition, dividing continuous operations into accounting periods is a convention and may have arbitrary effects. Managers can enhance the usefulness of information contained in financial reports by identifying arbitrary results caused by allocations between periods and by describing the effects of those allocations on reported information. Moreover, financial reporting often provides information that depends on, or is affected by, managers' estimates and judgments. Users are aided in evaluating estimates and judgments by explanations of underlying assumptions and methods used, including disclosure of significant uncertainties about principal underlying assumptions or estimates.

THE NONBUSINESS OBJECTIVES PROJECT—A PERSPECTIVE

56. Paragraphs 43-54 focus on information that assists resource providers and other users in assessing an organization's financial viability, its performance, and how the organization's managers have discharged their stewardship responsibilities. Those paragraphs emphasize information about an organization's economic resources, obligations, and net resources and its performance during a period. The objectives lead to, but leave unanswered, questions such as the identity, number, and form of financial statements; elements of financial statements and their recognition, measurement, and display; and criteria for determining the reporting entity. The Board's approach to resolving those questions will be to integrate consideration of nonbusiness organizations into its series of conceptual framework projects. That integration may involve initiating new projects to deal with issues that may be more prevalent in or unique to nonbusiness organizations.

This Statement was adopted by the unanimous vote of the seven members of the Financial Accounting Standards Board:

Donald J. Kirk, *Chairman*	Robert A. Morgan	Robert T. Sprouse
Frank E. Block	David Mosso	Ralph E. Walters
John W. March		

---

[24]Service accomplishments generally may be viewed as the results of service efforts. The FASB Research Report, *Reporting of Service Efforts and Accomplishments,* distinguishes two possible measures of accomplishments, outputs and results. "*Outputs* usually are observable directly as a result of service delivery; they describe goods and services provided by service delivery but do not measure impact upon clients or problems. . . . *Results* . . . represent impact upon clients or problem situations" (page 7). In discussing this latter measure, this Statement uses the term *program results.*

[25]These discussions may include information about service efforts and accomplishments as described in paragraphs 51-53.

Appendix A

BACKGROUND INFORMATION

Brief History of FASB Nonbusiness Objectives Project

57. The Board's project on objectives of financial reporting by nonbusiness organizations is related to and part of its effort to develop a conceptual framework for financial reporting. The Board began its work on a conceptual framework in 1973 and used as a point of departure the Report of the Study Group on the Objectives of Financial Statements, *Objectives of Financial Statements* (Trueblood Report), published by the American Institute of Certified Public Accountants in October 1973. That report included governmental and not-for-profit organizations in its scope.

58. As more fully discussed in paragraphs 57-62 of Concepts Statement 1, the Board initially considered the 12 objectives of financial statements in the Trueblood Report but decided to concentrate its initial efforts on formulating objectives of financial reporting by business enterprises. Initially, therefore, the Board did not attempt to reach conclusions on the objectives of financial reporting for governmental and not-for-profit organizations.

59. The need to consider the objectives of general purpose external financial reporting by nonbusiness organizations generally is recognized. An increasing number of public officials and private citizens are questioning the relevance and reliability of financial accounting and reporting by nonbusiness organizations. That concern has been reflected in legislative initiatives and well-publicized allegations of serious deficiencies in the financial reporting of various types of nonbusiness organizations.

60. In response to those concerns, the Board, in August 1977, engaged Professor Robert N. Anthony of the Harvard Business School to prepare a research report aimed at identifying the objectives of financial reporting by organizations other than business enterprises. A 53-member advisory group was appointed to assist in that effort. When the Board began consideration of objectives of financial reporting by nonbusiness organizations in August 1977, significant progress already had been made on the objectives of financial reporting by business enterprises. Rather than delay progress on that project to include nonbusiness organizations in its scope, and to explore thoroughly the issues in the nonbusiness area, the Board proceeded with two separate objectives projects. The Board issued Concepts Statement 1 in November 1978. Paragraph 1 of Concepts Statement 1 states:

This Statement establishes the objectives of general purpose external financial reporting by business enterprises. Its concentration on business enterprises is not intended to imply that the Board has concluded that the uses and objectives of financial reporting by other kinds of entities are, or should be, the same as or different from those of business enterprises. Those and related matters, including whether and, if so, how business enterprises and other organizations should be distinguished for the purpose of establishing objectives of and basic concepts underlying financial reporting, are issues in another phase of the Board's conceptual framework project.

61. In May 1978, the Board published the FASB Research Report, *Financial Accounting in Nonbusiness Organizations,* prepared by Professor Anthony. The Board added the nonbusiness objectives project to its technical agenda on May 11, 1978 and directed the staff to prepare a Discussion Memorandum to solicit public comment. The Discussion Memorandum was issued on June 15, 1978. It focused on specific issues discussed in the Research Report and identified those on which the Board sought comments.

62. The Board held public hearings in Washington, D.C. on October 12 and 13, 1978; in San Francisco on October 19 and 20, 1978; and in Chicago on November 3, 1978. The Board received 87 written responses to the Discussion Memorandum, and 48 oral presentations were made at the public hearings.

63. The Board issued an Exposure Draft, *Objectives of Financial Reporting by Nonbusiness Organizations,* on March 14, 1980. In preparing the Exposure Draft, the Board deliberated the issues at meetings which were open to public observation. FASB Board and staff members have met with and maintained close liaison with various groups and individuals in the community of nonbusiness organizations since the outset of this project. In addition, persons from academe, public accounting, and various nonbusiness organizations provided counsel to the Board and its staff in preparing the Exposure Draft. The Board received 77 letters of comment on the Exposure Draft and considered the issues raised by respondents in those comment letters at meetings which were open to public observation.

64. The major differences between this Statement and the Exposure Draft are revisions to the scope of the document. The types of organizations to which the objectives in this document apply have been clarified (paragraph 1 of the Exposure Draft), and a discussion has been added concerning the relationship of this Statement to Concepts Statement 1.

Other significant changes are (a) the addition of examples of various types of nonbusiness organizations in the environment section (paragraphs 13-22); (b) greater emphasis on distinguishing flows that affect operations from those that do not (paragraph 49); (c) greater emphasis on the need for research to determine if measures of service accomplishments with the requisite characteristics of relevance, reliability, comparability, verifiability, and neutrality can be developed; and (d) acknowledgement that, in the absence of that financial reporting capability, information about service accomplishments may be furnished by managers' explanations and sources other than financial reporting.

State and Local Governmental Units

65. Others have been studying the objectives of financial reporting by governmental units during the period that the Board has been deliberating the issues and preparing this concepts Statement. The National Council on Governmental Accounting is sponsoring research in the broad area of a conceptual framework for governmental accounting, which includes the objectives of external financial reporting by state and local governmental units. A state accounting project that was commissioned by the Council of State Governments includes a study of objectives of accounting and financial reporting by state governments. The U.S. General Accounting Office is developing a statement of the objectives of financial reporting by the federal government and its agencies.

66. Since the publication of the Exposure Draft of this concepts Statement, the Board and its staff have monitored developments on the three pro-

jects discussed above. This monitoring has consisted of reviewing and analyzing working drafts of certain materials made available to the FASB by the NCGA and other researchers. On the basis of its study to date, the Board is aware of no persuasive evidence that the objectives in this Statement are inappropriate for general purpose external financial reports of governmental units.

Appendix B

COMPARISON OF OBJECTIVES IN THIS STATEMENT TO THOSE IN CONCEPTS STATEMENT 1

67. This Statement follows the *structure* of Concepts Statement 1. Both sets of objectives are based on the fundamental notion that financial accounting and reporting concepts and standards should be based on their decision usefulness. Thus, the objectives in this Statement and in Concepts Statement 1 focus on:

a. Types of users of the information provided by financial reporting and the types of decisions they make

b. The broad interests of the users identified and the information they need to assist them in making decisions

c. The type of information financial reporting can provide to help satisfy their informational needs.

The chart on pages 1078-1081 compares the similarities and differences of this Statement and Concepts Statement 1 in each of those areas.

(This page intentionally left blank.)

Purpose of Objectives	Nonbusiness Organizations Concepts Statement 4	Business Enterprises Concepts Statement 1	Comparison of Objectives
a. Identifies (1) the types of users that financial reporting should focus on in providing information and (2) the types of decisions those users make.	a. Financial reporting by nonbusiness organizations should provide information that is useful to present and potential resource providers and other users in making rational decisions about the allocation of resources to those organizations (paragraph 35).	a. Financial reporting should provide information that is useful to present and potential investors and creditors and other users in making rational investment, credit, and similar decisions (paragraph 34).	a(1) Investors and creditors are major resource providers to business enterprises. Thus, resource providers, as a type of user, include investors and creditors as well as the other groups identified in Concepts Statement 4. a(2) Both Statements focus on providing information useful in deciding whether to provide resources to an entity. The reasons for providing the resources, in each case, are quite different. Investors and creditors of business enterprises seek monetary repayment of and a return on resources they provide. Nonbusiness organizations, in contrast, obtain significant resources from resource providers who either expect no economic benefits or expect benefits that are not proportionate to the resources provided.
b. Identifies the broad interests of the users identified and the information they need to assist them in making the type of decisions described above.	b(1) Financial reporting should provide information to help present and potential resource providers and other users in assessing the services that a nonbusiness	b(1) Financial reporting should provide information to help present and potential investors and creditors and other users in assessing the amounts, timing, and	b(1) These two objectives reflect the different interests of the respective resource providers. Those different interests lead to the other major area of difference in the

organization provides and its ability to continue to provide those services (paragraph 38).

b(2) Financial reporting should provide information that is useful to present and potential resource providers and other users in assessing how managers of a nonbusiness organization have discharged their stewardship responsibilities and about other aspects of their performance (paragraph 40).

uncertainty of prospective cash receipts from dividends or interest and the proceeds from the sale, redemption, or maturity of securities or loans (paragraph 37).

b(2) Financial reporting should provide information about how management of an enterprise has discharged its stewardship responsibility to owners (stockholders) for the use of enterprise resources entrusted to it (paragraph 50).

objectives; the types of information financial reporting should provide about performance.

b(2) The substance of these two objectives is similar but their placement within the two Statements is different. In this concepts Statement, the objective is viewed as a basic information need of users. In concepts Statement 1, it was viewed as information financial reporting could provide to satisfy other basic information needs. That difference in placement arises from the importance of stewardship information in the environment of nonbusiness organizations. It is more important because the organization often is not self-sustaining (not profit oriented) and is dependent upon the continuing support of its resource providers. Consequently, there often is a more direct relationship between resource providers and the entity than for a business enterprise.

Purpose of Objectives	Nonbusiness Organizations Concepts Statement 4	Business Enterprises Concepts Statement 1	Comparison of Objectives
c. Identifies the type of information financial reporting can provide to help satisfy users' informational needs.	c. Financial reporting should provide information about the economic resources, obligations, and net resources of an organization and the effects of transactions, events, and circumstances that change resources and interests in those resources (paragraph 43).	c. Financial reporting should provide information about the economic resources of an enterprise, the claims to those resources (obligations of the enterprise to transfer resources to other entities and owners' equity), and the effects of transactions, events, and circumstances that change resources and claims to those resources (paragraph 40).	c. The objectives are similar except for differences in terminology that reflect one of the distinguishing characteristics of nonbusiness organizations—the lack of ownership interests entitled to a residual distribution in the event of liquidation.
	(1) Financial reporting should provide information about an organization's economic resources, obligations, and net resources (paragraph 44).	(1) Financial reporting should provide information about an enterprise's economic resources, obligations, and owners' equity (paragraph 41).	(1) Except for differences in terminology, these objectives are the same.
	(2) Financial reporting should provide information about the performance of an organization during a period. Periodic measurement of the changes in the amount and nature of the net resources of a nonbusiness organization and information about the service efforts and accomplishments of an organization together represent the information most useful in assessing its performance (paragraph 47).	(2) Financial reporting should provide information about an enterprise's financial performance during a period. The primary focus of financial reporting is information about an enterprise's performance provided by measures of earnings and its components (paragraphs 42 and 43).	(2) The goals of the two objectives are the same but, because of the distinguishing characteristics of nonbusiness organizations, somewhat different information is required to satisfy those goals. Both seek to measure the efforts and accomplishments of the entity but assessment of performance in nonbusiness lacks earnings as a focal measure. This creates the need for information on service efforts and accomplishments.

(3) Financial reporting should provide information about how an organization obtains and spends cash or other liquid resources, about its borrowing and repayment of borrowing, and about other factors that may affect its liquidity (paragraph 54).

(4) Financial reporting should include explanations and interpretations to help users understand financial information provided (paragraph 55).

(3) Financial reporting should provide information about how an enterprise obtains and spends cash, about its borrowing and repayment of borrowing, about its capital transactions, including cash dividends and other distributions of enterprise resources to owners, and about other factors that may affect an enterprise's liquidity or solvency (paragraph 49).

(4) Financial reporting should include explanations and interpretations to help users understand financial information provided (paragraph 54).

(3) Except for differences in terminology and circumstances that reflect the lack of ownership interests entitled to receive cash dividends and other distributions of entity resources in nonbusiness organizations, these objectives are the same.

(4) These objectives are the same.

Statement of Financial Accounting Concepts No. 5
Recognition and Measurement in Financial
Statements of Business Enterprises

STATUS

Issued: December 1984

Affects: No other pronouncements

Affected by: No other pronouncements

HIGHLIGHTS

[Best understood in context of full Statement]

- This Statement sets forth recognition criteria and guidance on what information should be incorporated into financial statements and when. The Statement provides a basis for consideration of criteria and guidance by first addressing financial statements that should be presented and their contribution to financial reporting. It gives particular attention to statements of earnings and comprehensive income. The Statement also addresses certain measurement issues that are closely related to recognition.

- Financial statements are a central feature of financial reporting—a principal means of communicating financial information to those outside an entity. Some useful information is better provided by financial statements and some is better provided, or can only be provided, by notes to financial statements, supplementary information, or other means of financial reporting. For items that meet criteria for recognition, disclosure by other means is not a substitute for recognition in financial statements.

- Recognition is the process of formally incorporating an item into the financial statements of an entity as an asset, liability, revenue, expense, or the like. A recognized item is depicted in both words and numbers, with the amount included in the statement totals.

- A full set of financial statements for a period should show:

  — Financial position at the end of the period

  — Earnings for the period

  — Comprehensive income for the period

  — Cash flows during the period

  — Investments by and distributions to owners during the period.

- Financial statements individually and collectively contribute to meeting the objectives of financial reporting. No one financial statement is likely to provide all the financial statement information that is useful for a particular kind of decision.

- The parts of a financial statement also contribute to meeting the objectives of financial reporting and may be more useful to those who make investment, credit, and similar decisions than the whole.

- Financial statements result from simplifying, condensing, and aggregating masses of data. As a result, they convey information that would be obscured if great detail were provided. Although those simplifications, condensations, and aggregations are both necessary and useful, the Board believes that it is important to avoid focusing attention almost exclusively on "the bottom line," earnings per share, or other highly simplified condensations.

- A statement of financial position provides information about an entity's assets, liabilities, and equity and their relationships to each other at a moment in time. The statement delineates the entity's resource structure—major classes and amounts of assets—and its financing structure—major classes and amounts of liabilities and equity.

- A statement of financial position does not purport to show the value of a business enterprise but, together with other financial statements and other information, should provide information that is useful to those who desire to make their own estimates of the enterprise's value. Those estimates are part of financial analysis, not of financial reporting, but financial accounting aids financial analysis.

- Statements of earnings and of comprehensive income together reflect the extent to which and the ways in which the equity of an entity increased or decreased from all sources other than transactions with owners during a period.

- The concept of earnings set forth in this Statement is similar to net income for a period in present practice; however, it excludes certain accounting adjustments of earlier periods that are recognized in the current period—cumulative effect of a change in accounting principle is the principal example from present practice. The Board expects the concept of earnings to be subject to the process of gradual change or evolution that has characterized the development of net income.

- Earnings is a measure of entity performance during a period. It measures the extent to which asset inflows (revenues and gains) associated with cash-to-cash cycles substantially completed during the period exceed asset outflows (expenses and losses) associated, directly or indirectly, with the same cycles.

- Comprehensive income is a broad measure of the effects of transactions and other events on an entity, comprising all recognized changes in equity (net assets) of the entity during a period from transactions and other events and circumstances except those resulting from investments by owners and distributions to owners.

- A variety of terms are used for net income in present practice. The Board anticipates that a variety of terms will be used in future financial statements as names for earnings (for example, net income, profit, or net loss) and for comprehensive income (for example, total nonowner changes in equity or comprehensive loss).

- Earnings and comprehensive income are not the same because certain gains and losses are included in comprehensive income but are excluded from earnings. Those items fall into two classes that are illustrated by certain present practices:

  — Effects of certain accounting adjustments of earlier periods that are recognized in the current period (already described)

  — Certain other changes in net assets (principally certain holding gains and losses) that are recognized in the period but are excluded from earnings, such as some changes in market values of investments in marketable equity securities classified as noncurrent assets, some changes in market values of investments in industries having specialized accounting practices for marketable securities, and foreign currency translation adjustments.

- The full set of financial statements discussed in this Statement is based on the concept of financial capital maintenance.

- Future standards may change what is recognized as components of earnings. Future standards may also recognize certain changes in net assets as components of comprehensive income but not of earnings.

- A statement of cash flows directly or indirectly reflects an entity's cash receipts classified by major sources and its cash payments classified by major uses during a period, including cash flow information about its operating, financing, and investing activities.

- A statement of investments by and distributions to owners reflects an entity's capital transactions during a period—the extent to which and in what ways the equity of the entity increased or decreased from transactions with owners *as owners.*

- An item and information about it should meet four fundamental recognition criteria to be recognized and should be recognized when the criteria are met, subject to a cost-benefit constraint and a materiality threshold. Those criteria are:

    - *Definitions.* The item meets the definition of an element of financial statements.

    - *Measurability.* It has a relevant attribute measurable with sufficient reliability.

    - *Relevance.* The information about it is capable of making a difference in user decisions.

    - *Reliability.* The information is representationally faithful, verifiable, and neutral.

- Items currently reported in the financial statements are measured by different attributes (for example, historical cost, current [replacement] cost, current market value, net realizable value, and present value of future cash flows), depending on the nature of the item and the relevance and reliability of the attribute measured. The Board expects use of different attributes to continue.

- The monetary unit or measurement scale in current practice in financial statements is nominal units of money, that is, unadjusted for changes in purchasing power of money over time. The Board expects that nominal units of money will continue to be used to measure items recognized in financial statements.

- Further guidance in applying the criteria for recognizing components of earnings is necessary because of the widely acknowledged importance of earnings as a primary measure of entity performance. Guidance for recognizing components of earnings is concerned with identifying which cycles are substantially complete and with associating particular revenues, gains, expenses, and losses with those cycles.

- In assessing the prospect that as yet uncompleted transactions will be concluded successfully, a degree of skepticism is often warranted. As a reaction to uncertainty, more stringent requirements have historically been imposed for recognizing revenues and gains as components of earnings than for recognizing expenses and losses. Those conservative reactions influence the guidance for applying the recognition criteria to components of earnings.

- Guidance for recognizing revenues and gains is based on their being:

    - *Realized or realizable.* Revenues and gains are generally not recognized as components of earnings until realized or realizable and

    - *Earned.* Revenues are not recognized until earned. Revenues are considered to have been earned when the entity has substantially accomplished what it must do to be entitled to the benefits represented by the revenues. For gains, being earned is generally less significant than being realized or realizable.

- Guidance for expenses and losses is intended to recognize:

    - *Consumption of benefit.* Expenses are generally recognized when an entity's economic benefits are consumed in revenue-earning activities or otherwise or

    - *Loss or lack of benefit.* Expenses or losses are recognized if it becomes evident that previously recognized future economic benefits of assets have been reduced or eliminated, or that liabilities have been incurred or increased, without associated economic benefits.

- In a limited number of situations, the Board may determine that the most useful information results from recognizing the effects of certain events in comprehensive income but not in earnings, and set standards accordingly. Certain changes in net assets that meet the fundamental recognition criteria may qualify for recognition in comprehensive income even though they do not qualify for recognition as components of earnings.

- Information based on current prices should be recognized if it is sufficiently relevant and reliable to justify the costs involved and more relevant than alternative information.

- Most aspects of current practice are consistent with the recognition criteria and guidance in this Statement, but the criteria and guidance do not foreclose the possibility of future changes in practice. When evidence indicates that information that is more useful (relevant and reliable) than information currently reported is available at a justifiable cost, it should be included in financial statements.

Statement of Financial Accounting Concepts No. 5
Recognition and Measurement in Financial Statements
of Business Enterprises

Statements of Financial Accounting Concepts

This Statement of Financial Accounting Concepts is one of a series of publications in the Board's conceptual framework for financial accounting and reporting. Statements in the series are intended to set forth objectives and fundamentals that will be the basis for development of financial accounting and reporting standards. The objectives identify the goals and purposes of financial reporting. The fundamentals are the underlying concepts of financial accounting—concepts that guide the selection of transactions, events, and circumstances to be accounted for; their recognition and measurement; and the means of summarizing and communicating them to interested parties. Concepts of that type are fundamental in the sense that other concepts flow from them and repeated reference to them will be necessary in establishing, interpreting, and applying accounting and reporting standards.

The conceptual framework is a coherent system of interrelated objectives and fundamentals that is expected to lead to consistent standards and that prescribes the nature, function, and limits of financial accounting and reporting. It is expected to serve the public interest by providing structure and direction to financial accounting and reporting to facilitate the provision of evenhanded financial and related information that helps promote the efficient allocation of scarce resources in the economy and society, including assisting capital and other markets to function efficiently.

Establishment of objectives and identification of fundamental concepts will not directly solve financial accounting and reporting problems. Rather, objectives give direction, and concepts are tools for solving problems.

The Board itself is likely to be the most direct beneficiary of the guidance provided by the Statements in this series. They will guide the Board in developing accounting and reporting standards by providing the Board with a common foundation and basic reasoning on which to consider merits of alternatives.

However, knowledge of the objectives and concepts the Board will use in developing standards also should enable those who are affected by or interested in financial accounting standards to understand better the purposes, content, and characteristics of information provided by financial accounting and reporting. That knowledge is expected to enhance the usefulness of, and confidence in, financial accounting and reporting. The concepts also may provide some guidance in analyzing new or emerging problems of financial accounting and reporting in the absence of applicable authoritative pronouncements.

Statements of Financial Accounting Concepts do not establish standards prescribing accounting procedures or disclosure practices for particular items or events, which are issued by the Board as Statements of Financial Accounting Standards. Rather, Statements in this series describe concepts and relations that will underlie future financial accounting standards and practices and in due course serve as a basis for evaluating existing standards and practices.*

The Board recognizes that in certain respects current generally accepted accounting principles may be inconsistent with those that may derive from the objectives and concepts set forth in Statements in this series. However, a Statement of Financial Accounting Concepts does not (a) require a change in existing generally accepted accounting principles; (b) amend, modify, or interpret Statements of Financial Accounting Standards, Interpretations of the FASB, Opinions of the Accounting Principles Board, or Bulletins of the Committee on Accounting Procedure that are in effect; or (c) justify either changing existing generally accepted accounting and reporting practices or interpreting the pronouncements listed in item (b) based on personal interpretations of the objectives and concepts in the Statements of Financial Accounting Concepts.

Since a Statement of Financial Accounting Concepts does not establish generally accepted accounting principles or standards for the disclosure of financial information outside of financial statements in published financial reports, it is not intended to invoke application of Rule 203 or 204 of

---

*Pronouncements such as APB Statement No. 4, *Basic Concepts and Accounting Principles Underlying Financial Statements of Business Enterprises,* and the Accounting Terminology Bulletins will continue to serve their intended purpose—they describe objectives and concepts underlying standards and practices existing at the time of their issuance.

the Rules of Conduct of the Code of Professional Ethics of the American Institute of Certified Public Accountants (or successor rules or arrangements of similar scope and intent).†

Like other pronouncements of the Board, a Statement of Financial Accounting Concepts may be amended, superseded, or withdrawn by appropriate action under the Board's *Rules of Procedure.*

CONTENTS

---

†Rule 203 prohibits a member of the American Institute of Certified Public Accountants from expressing an opinion that financial statements conform with generally accepted accounting principles if those statements contain a material departure from an accounting principle promulgated by the Financial Accounting Standards Board, unless the member can demonstrate that because of unusual circumstances the financial statements otherwise would have been misleading. Rule 204 requires members of the Institute to justify departures from standards promulgated by the Financial Accounting Standards Board for the disclosure of information outside of financial statements in published financial reports.

INTRODUCTION, SCOPE, AND LIMITATIONS

1. This Statement sets forth fundamental recognition criteria and guidance on what information should be formally incorporated into financial statements and when. It builds on the foundation laid by earlier concepts Statements, bringing those concepts together to apply them to broad recognition issues. As a basis for considering recognition criteria, the Statement first addresses financial statements that should be presented and how those financial statements contribute to the objectives of financial reporting. Both that discussion and the later discussion of recognition give particular attention to statements of earnings and comprehensive income.

2. The recognition criteria and guidance in this Statement are generally consistent with current practice and do not imply radical change. Nor do they foreclose the possibility of future changes in practice. The Board intends future change to occur in the gradual, evolutionary way that has characterized past change.

3. This Statement also addresses certain measurement issues that are closely related to recognition. Measurement involves choice of an attribute by which to quantify a recognized item and choice of a scale of measurement (often called "unit of measure"). The Statement notes that different attributes are currently used to measure different items in financial statements and that the Board expects the use of different attributes to continue. The Statement further notes that the measurement scale in current practice is nominal units of money (that is, unadjusted for changes in purchasing power over time) and that the Board expects use of nominal units to continue.

4. This Statement is not intended to apply to organizations other than business enterprises. Recognition criteria and guidance on what information should be formally incorporated into financial statements of nonbusiness organizations can be considered only after completion of another Board project that concerns significant underlying concepts upon which recognition criteria and guidance

are built. The Board issued its Exposure Draft, *Proposed Amendments to FASB Concepts Statements 2 and 3 to Apply Them to Nonbusiness Organizations,* on July 7, 1983 and held public hearings on that matter on November 14 and 15, 1983. Since that project is still in progress, all references in this Statement are to the original Statements, FASB Concepts Statements No. 2, *Qualitative Characteristics of Accounting Information,* and No. 3, *Elements of Financial Statements of Business Enterprises.*

FINANCIAL STATEMENTS

Financial Statements, Financial Reporting, and Recognition

5. Financial statements are a central feature of financial reporting—a principal means of communicating financial information to those outside an entity. In external general purpose financial reporting, a financial statement is a formal tabulation of names and amounts of money derived from accounting records that displays either financial position of an entity at a moment in time or one or more kinds of changes in financial position of the entity during a period of time. Items that are recognized in financial statements are financial representations of certain resources (assets) of an entity, claims to those resources (liabilities and owners' equity), and the effects of transactions and other events and circumstances that result in changes in those resources and claims. The financial statements of an entity are a fundamentally related set that articulate with each other and derive from the same underlying data.[1]

6. Recognition is the process of formally recording or incorporating an item into the financial statements of an entity as an asset, liability, revenue, expense, or the like. Recognition includes depiction of an item in both words and numbers, with the amount included in the totals of the financial statements. For an asset or liability, recognition involves recording not only acquisition or incurrence of the item but also later changes in it, including changes that result in removal from the financial statements.[2]

---

[1]FASB Concepts Statement No. 1, *Objectives of Financial Reporting by Business Enterprises,* pars. 6 and 18; Concepts Statement 3, pars. 6 and 14 and 15. *Financial position* and *changes in financial position* are used here in a broad sense and do not refer to specific financial statements. "Used broadly, financial position refers to state or status of assets or claims to assets at moments in time, and changes in financial position refers to flows or changes in assets or claims to assets over time" (Concepts Statement 3, par. 14, footnote 6). "Through the financial accounting process, the myriad and complex effects of the economic activities of an enterprise are accumulated, analyzed, quantified, classified, recorded, summarized, and reported as information of two basic types: (1) financial position, which relates to a point in time, and (2) changes in financial position, which relate to a period of time" (APB Statement No. 4, *Basic Concepts and Accounting Principles Underlying Financial Statements of Business Enterprises,* par. 10).

[2]Concepts Statement 3, pars. 83, 6, 25, 26, and 34 and 35.

7. Although financial statements have essentially the same objectives as financial reporting, some useful information is better provided by financial statements and some is better provided, or can only be provided, by notes to financial statements or by supplementary information or other means of financial reporting:[3]

a. Information disclosed in notes or parenthetically on the face of financial statements, such as significant accounting policies or alternative measures for assets or liabilities, amplifies or explains information recognized in the financial statements.[4] That sort of information is essential to understanding the information recognized in financial statements and has long been viewed as an integral part of financial statements prepared in accordance with generally accepted accounting principles.

b. Supplementary information, such as disclosures of the effects of changing prices, and other means of financial reporting, such as management discussion and analysis, add information to that in the financial statements or notes, including information that may be relevant but that does not meet all recognition criteria.[5]

8. The scope of this concepts Statement is limited to recognition (and measurement) in financial statements. That limitation on scope does not alter the status of notes, supplementary information, or other means of financial reporting; those types of information remain important and useful for the reasons discussed in the preceding paragraph. To clarify the scope of this concepts Statement, the diagram on the next page illustrates the types of information used in investment, credit, and similar decisions.

9. Since recognition means depiction of an item in both words and numbers, with the amount included in the totals of the financial statements, disclosure by other means is *not* recognition. Disclosure of information about the items in financial statements and their measures that may be provided by notes or parenthetically on the face of financial statements, by supplementary information, or by other means of financial reporting is not a substitute for recognition in financial statements for items that meet recognition criteria. Generally, the most useful information about assets, liabilities, revenues, expenses, and other items of financial statements and their measures (that with the best combination of relevance and reliability) should be recognized in the financial statements.

Financial Statements and Objectives of Financial Reporting

10. FASB Concepts Statement No. 1, *Objectives of Financial Reporting by Business Enterprises,* describes the broad purposes of financial reporting, including financial statements.[6] Financial reporting should provide:

Information that is useful to present and potential investors and creditors and other users in making rational investment, credit, and similar decisions (paragraphs 34-36)

Information to help investors, creditors, and others assess the amounts, timing, and uncertainty of prospective net cash inflows to the related enterprise because their prospects for receiving cash from investments in, loans to, or other participation in the enterprise depend significantly on its cash flow prospects (paragraphs 37-39)

Information about the economic resources of an enterprise, the claims to those resources (obligations of the enterprise to transfer resources to other entities and owners' equity), and the effects of transactions, events, and circumstances that change resources and claims to those resources (paragraph 40).

---

[3]Concepts Statement 1, par. 5.

[4]For example, notes provide essential descriptive information for long-term obligations, including when amounts are due, what interest they bear, and whether important restrictions are imposed by related covenants. For inventory, the notes provide information on the measurement method used—FIFO cost, LIFO cost, current market value, etc. For an estimated litigation liability, an extended discussion of the circumstances, counsel's opinions, and the basis for management's judgment may all be provided in the notes. For sales, useful information about revenue recognition policies may appear only in the notes (FASB Statement No. 47, *Disclosure of Long-Term Obligations;* ARB No. 43, Chapter 4, "Inventory Pricing," statement 8; FASB Statement No. 5, *Accounting for Contingencies,* par. 10; and APB Statement 4, par. 199).

[5]Concepts Statement 1, pars. 6, 7, and 22. Supplementary financial statements, complete or partial, may be useful, especially to introduce and to gain experience with new kinds of information. Criteria for including information in supplementary statements may have much in common with recognition criteria for primary statements discussed here, but the criteria discussed in this Statement apply specifically to primary financial statements.

[6]Paragraphs 8-33 of Concepts Statement 1 give needed background. They describe factors affecting the objectives of general purpose external financial reporting, such as characteristics of the environment in the United States, characteristics and limitations of information provided, potential users and their interests, and the nature of the objectives. For example, "financial reporting is but one source of information needed by those who make economic decisions about business enterprises" (par. 22).

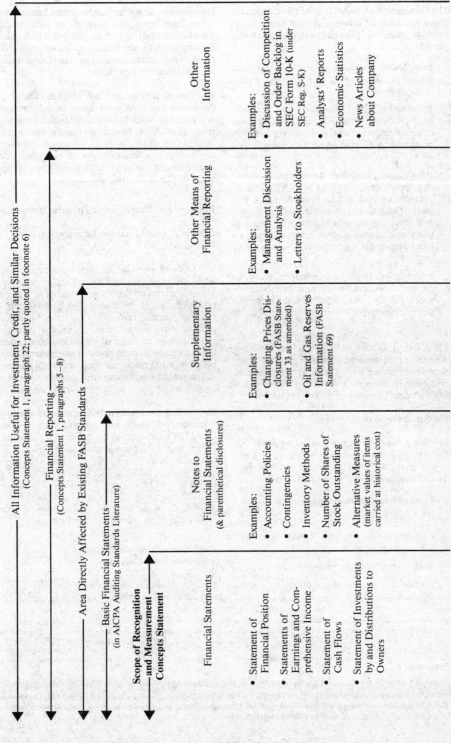

All Information Useful for Investment, Credit, and Similar Decisions
(Concepts Statement 1, paragraph 22; partly quoted in footnote 6)

Financial Reporting
(Concepts Statement 1, paragraphs 5–8)

Area Directly Affected by Existing FASB Standards

Basic Financial Statements
(in AICPA Auditing Standards Literature)

Scope of Recognition and Measurement Concepts Statement

Financial Statements

- Statement of Financial Position
- Statements of Earnings and Comprehensive Income
- Statement of Cash Flows
- Statement of Investments by and Distributions to Owners

Notes to Financial Statements
(& parenthetical disclosures)

Examples:
- Accounting Policies
- Contingencies
- Inventory Methods
- Number of Shares of Stock Outstanding
- Alternative Measures (market values of items carried at historical cost)

Supplementary Information

Examples:
- Changing Prices Disclosures (FASB Statement 33 as amended)
- Oil and Gas Reserves Information (FASB Statement 69)

Other Means of Financial Reporting

Examples:
- Management Discussion and Analysis
- Letters to Stockholders

Other Information

Examples:
- Discussion of Competition and Order Backlog in SEC Form 10-K (under SEC Reg. S-K)
- Analysts' Reports
- Economic Statistics
- News Articles about Company

11. Concepts Statement 1 also gives guidance about the kinds of information that financial reporting, including financial statements, should provide:

> Information about an enterprise's economic resources, obligations, and owners' equity (paragraph 41)
>
> Information about an enterprise's performance provided by measures of earnings and comprehensive income[7] and their components measured by accrual accounting (paragraphs 42-48)
>
> Information about how an enterprise obtains and spends cash, about its borrowing and repayment of borrowing, about its capital (equity) transactions, including cash dividends and other distributions of enterprise resources to owners, and about other factors that may affect an enterprise's liquidity or solvency (paragraph 49)
>
> Information about how management of an enterprise has discharged its stewardship responsibility to owners (stockholders) for the use of enterprise resources entrusted to it (paragraphs 50-53).

12. A full, articulated set of several financial statements that provide those various kinds of information about an entity's financial position and changes in its financial position is necessary to satisfy the broad purposes of financial reporting.

Full Set of Financial Statements

13. The amount and variety of information that financial reporting should provide about an entity require several financial statements. A full set of financial statements for a period should show:

> Financial position at the end of the period
>
> Earnings (net income)[8] for the period
>
> Comprehensive income (total nonowner changes in equity)[8] for the period
>
> Cash flows during the period
>
> Investments by and distributions to owners during the period.

Information about earnings, comprehensive income, cash flows, and transactions with owners have in common that they are different kinds of information about the effects of transactions and other events and circumstances that change assets and liabilities during a period.

14. This Statement does not consider details of displaying those different kinds of information and does not preclude the possibility that some entities might choose to combine some of that information in a single statement. In present practice, for example, a reconciliation of beginning and ending balances of retained earnings is sometimes appended to an income statement.

Purposes and Limitations of Financial Statements

General Purpose Financial Statements and Individual Users

15. General purpose financial statements, to which the objectives of financial reporting apply, are directed toward the common interest of various potential users in the ability of a business enterprise to generate favorable cash flows.[9] General purpose financial statements are feasible only because groups of users of financial information have generally similar needs. But "general purpose" does not mean "all purpose," and financial statements do not necessarily satisfy all users equally well.

16. Each decision maker judges what accounting information is useful, and that judgment is influenced by factors such as the decisions to be made, the methods of decision making to be used, the information already possessed or obtainable from other sources, and the decision maker's capacity (alone or with professional help) to process the information. Even users of financial statement information who make generally similar kinds of decisions differ from each other in those matters.[10]

Usefulness of Financial Statements, Individually and Collectively

17. Financial statements of an entity individually and collectively contribute to meeting the objec-

---

[7]Concepts Statement 3 used the term *comprehensive income* for the concept that was called *earnings* in Concepts Statement 1 and reserved the term *earnings* for possible use to designate a component part of comprehensive income (par. 1, footnote 1). Earnings, including its relationship to comprehensive income, is a major topic of this Statement.

[8]Pars. 33 and 40.

[9]Concepts Statement 1, par. 30.

[10]Concepts Statement 2, pars. 23-26 and 32-41. For example, information cannot be useful to decision makers who cannot understand it, even though it may otherwise be relevant to a decision and be reliable. Understandability of information is related to the characteristics of the decision maker as well as to the characteristics of the information itself.

tives of financial reporting. Component parts of financial statements also contribute to meeting the objectives.

18. Each financial statement provides a different kind of information, and, with limited exceptions (paragraph 14), the various kinds of information cannot be combined into a smaller number of statements without unduly complicating the information. Moreover, the information each provides is used for various purposes, and particular users may be especially interested in the information in one of the statements. Paragraphs 26-57 of this Statement summarize how individual financial statements provide the information listed in paragraph 13.

19. The following two sections first describe how classification and aggregation, if done and used with care, enhance the decision usefulness of financial statements and how financial statements complement each other.

Classification and aggregation in financial statements

20. Classification in financial statements facilitates analysis by grouping items with essentially similar characteristics and separating items with essentially different characteristics. Analysis aimed at objectives such as predicting amounts, timing, and uncertainty of future cash flows requires financial information segregated into reasonably homogeneous groups. For example, components of financial statements that consist of items that have similar characteristics in one or more respects, such as continuity or recurrence, stability, risk, and reliability, are likely to have more predictive value than if their characteristics are dissimilar.

21. Financial statements result from processing vast masses of data and involve needs to simplify, to condense, and to aggregate.[11] Real things and events that affect a dynamic and complex business enterprise are represented in financial statements by words and numbers, which are necessarily highly simplified symbols of the real thing. Real transactions and other events are voluminous and are interpreted, combined, and condensed to be reflected in financial statements. Numerous items and components are aggregated into sums or totals. The resulting financial statements convey information that would be obscured from most users if great detail, such as descriptions of each transaction or event, were provided.

22. Although those simplifications, condensations, and aggregations are both necessary and useful, the Board believes it is important to avoid focusing attention almost exclusively on "the bottom line," earnings per share, or other highly simplified condensations. Summary data, such as the amounts of net assets, comprehensive income, earnings, or earnings per share, may be useful as general indicators of the amount of investment or overall past performance and are often used in efforts to compare an entity with many other entities. But, in a complex business enterprise, summary amounts include many heterogeneous things and events. Components of a financial statement often reflect more homogeneous classes of items than the whole statement. The individual items, subtotals, or other parts of a financial statement may often be more useful than the aggregate to those who make investment, credit, and similar decisions.

Complementary nature of financial statements

23. Financial statements interrelate (articulate) because they reflect different aspects of the same transactions or other events affecting an entity.[12] Although each presents information different from the others, none is likely to serve only a single purpose or provide all the financial statement information that is useful for a particular kind of assessment or decision. Significant tools of financial analysis, such as rates of return and turnover ratios, depend on interrelationships between financial statements and their components.

24. Financial statements complement each other. For example:

a. Statements of financial position include information that is often used in assessing an entity's liquidity and financial flexibility,[13] but a statement of financial position provides only an incomplete picture of either liquidity or financial flexibility unless it is used in conjunction with at least a cash flow statement.

---

[11]". . . It is a very fundamental principle indeed that knowledge is always gained by the *orderly* loss of information, that is, by condensing and abstracting and indexing the great buzzing confusion of information that comes from the world around us into a form which we can appreciate and comprehend" (Kenneth E. Boulding, *Economics as a Science* [New York: McGraw-Hill Book Company, 1970], p. 2, emphasis added).

[12]Concepts Statement 3, pars. 14 and 15.

[13]Liquidity reflects an asset's or liability's nearness to cash. Financial flexibility is the ability of an entity to take effective actions to alter amounts and timing of cash flows so it can respond to unexpected needs and opportunities.

b. Statements of earnings and comprehensive income generally reflect a great deal about the profitability of an entity during a period, but that information can be interpreted most meaningfully or compared with that of the entity for other periods or that of other entities only if it is used in conjunction with a statement of financial position, for example, by computing rates of return on assets or equity.

c. Statements of cash flows commonly show a great deal about an entity's current cash receipts and payments, but a cash flow statement provides an incomplete basis for assessing prospects for future cash flows because it cannot show inter period relationships. Many current cash receipts, especially from operations, stem from activities of earlier periods, and many current cash payments are intended or expected to result in future, not current, cash receipts. Statements of earnings and comprehensive income, especially if used in conjunction with statements of financial position, usually provide a better basis for assessing future cash flow prospects of an entity than do cash flow statements alone.[14]

d. Statements of investments by and distributions to owners provide information about significant sources of increases and decreases in assets, liabilities, and equity, but that information is of little practical value unless used in conjunction with other financial statements, for example, by comparing distributions to owners with earnings and comprehensive income or by comparing investments by and distributions to owners with borrowings and repayments of debt.

Individual Financial Statements

25. This discussion summarizes how individual financial statements provide the information listed in paragraph 13. It also introduces recognition considerations, which are the subject of the sections following.

Statement of Financial Position

26. A statement of financial position provides information about an entity's assets, liabilities, and equity and their relationships to each other at a moment in time. The statement delineates the entity's resource structure—major classes and amounts of assets—and its financing structure—major classes and amounts of liabilities and equity.

27. A statement of financial position does not purport to show the value of a business enterprise[15] but, together with other financial statements and other information, should provide information that is useful to those who desire to make their own estimates of the enterprise's value. As a result of limitations stemming from uncertainty and cost-benefit considerations, not all assets and not all liabilities are included in a statement of financial position, and some assets and liabilities that are included are affected by events, such as price changes or accretion, that are not recognized. Statements of financial position also commonly use different attributes to measure different assets and liabilities.[16]

28. Uncertainty and related limitations of financial accounting put the burden of estimating values of business enterprises and of investments in them on investors, creditors, and others. Information about components of earnings and comprehensive income often plays a significant part in that analysis. For example, investors may use that information to help estimate "earning power," or other amounts that they perceive as representative of long-term earning ability of an enterprise, as a significant step in comparing the market price of an equity security with its "intrinsic value." Those estimates and analyses are part of financial analysis, not financial reporting,[17] but financial accounting facilitates financial analysis by, among other things, classifying financial statement information in homogeneous groups.[18]

29. Important uses of information about an entity's financial position include helping users to assess factors such as the entity's liquidity, financial flexibility, profitability, and risk. Comparisons among entities and computations of rates of return are enhanced to the extent that significant asset and liability groupings are homogeneous in general characteristics and measurement.

---

[14]Concepts Statement 1, pars. 42-46.

[15]Ibid., par. 41.

[16]The different attributes are defined and their current use illustrated in paragraphs 66-70 of this Statement.

[17]". . . [A]ccrual accounting provides measures of earnings rather than evaluations of management's performance, estimates of 'earning power,' predictions of earnings, assessments of risk, or confirmations or rejections of predictions or assessments. Investors, creditors, and other users of the information do their own evaluating, estimating, predicting, assessing, confirming, or rejecting. For example, procedures such as averaging or normalizing reported earnings for several periods and ignoring or averaging out the financial effects of 'nonrepresentative' transactions and events are commonly used in estimating 'earning power.' However, both the concept of 'earning power' and the techniques for estimating it are part of financial analysis and are beyond the scope of financial reporting" (Concepts Statement 1, par. 48).

[18]Pars. 20-22 of this Statement.

Statements of Earnings and Comprehensive Income

30. Statements of earnings and comprehensive income together reflect the extent to which and the ways in which the equity of an entity increased or decreased from all sources other than transactions with owners during a period. Investors, creditors, managers, and others need information about the causes of changes in an entity's assets and liabilities—including results of its ongoing major or central operations, results of its incidental or peripheral transactions, and effects of other events and circumstances stemming from the environment that are often partly or wholly beyond the control of the entity and its management.

31. Effects of an entity's various activities, transactions, and events differ in stability, risk, and predictability, indicating a need for information about various components of earnings and comprehensive income. That need underlies the distinctions between revenues and gains, between expenses and losses, between various kinds of gains and losses, and between measures found in present practice such as income from continuing operations and net income.[19]

32. Since the parts of a financial statement may be more useful to decision makers than the whole (paragraphs 20-22), this Statement emphasizes usefulness of components, interrelationships, and different perspectives as well as usefulness, collectively and individually, of financial statements.

Earnings

33. The concept of earnings described in this Statement is similar to net income in present practice. It includes almost all of what is in present net income for a period, and a statement of earnings based on it will be much like a present income statement. Present practice accepts a variety of terms for net income, and the Board anticipates that net income, profit, net loss, and other equivalent terms will continue to be used in financial statements as names for earnings. However, earnings is not exactly the same as present net income, and this Statement uses the term *earnings* in part to distinguish the concept described here from present net income.

34. Earnings does not include the cumulative effect of certain accounting adjustments of earlier periods that are recognized in the current period.[20] The principal example that is included in present net income but excluded from earnings is the cumulative effect of a change in accounting principle, but others may be identified in the future. Earnings is a measure of performance for a period and to the extent feasible excludes items that are extraneous to that period—items that belong primarily to other periods.[21] The following condensed statements show the similarities and major existing difference between earnings and present net income.

	Present Net Income		Earnings	
Revenues		100		100
Expenses		80		80
Gain from unusual source		(3)		(3)
Income from continuing operations		23		23
Loss on discontinued operations				
Income from operating discontinued segment	10		10	
Loss on disposal of discontinued segment	12	2	12	2
Income before extraordinary items				21
and effect of a change in accounting principle		21		
Extraordinary loss	6			6
Cumulative effect on prior years of a change in accounting principle	2	8		
Earnings				15
Net Income		13		

---

[19]Concepts Statement 3, pars. 61 and 151.

[20]That is, the cumulative effect on equity at the beginning of the period for which an earnings statement is provided, sometimes called a "catch-up adjustment."

[21]Prior period adjustments as defined in FASB Statement No. 16, *Prior Period Adjustments,* are not included in net income in present practice and are not, therefore, differences between earnings in this Statement and present net income. Statement 16 narrowed considerably the definition of prior period adjustments in APB Opinions No. 9, *Reporting the Results of Operations,* and No. 30, *Reporting the Results of Operations—Reporting the Effects of Disposal of a Segment of a Business, and Extraordinary, Unusual and Infrequently Occurring Events and Transactions.* Some items that were prior period adjustments under those Opinions are included in net income in present practice, and some argue that the existing definition is too narrow because as a result net income includes items that belong to other periods.

35. The Board expects the concept of earnings to be subject to the process of gradual change or evolution that has characterized the development of net income. Present practice has developed over a long time, and that evolution has resulted in significant changes in what net income reflects, such as a shift toward what is commonly called an "all-inclusive" income statement. Those changes have resulted primarily from standard-setting bodies' responses to several factors, such as changes in the business and economic environment and perceptions about the nature and limitations of financial statements, about the needs of users of financial statements, and about the need to prevent or cure perceived abuse(s) in financial reporting. Those factors sometimes may conflict or appear to conflict. For example, an all-inclusive income statement is intended, among other things, to avoid discretionary omissions of losses (or gains) from an income statement, thereby avoiding presentation of a more (or less) favorable report of performance or stewardship than is justified. However, because income statements also are used as a basis for estimating future performance and assessing future cash flow prospects, arguments have been advanced urging exclusion of unusual or nonrecurring gains and losses that might reduce the usefulness of an income statement for any one year for predictive purposes.

36. Earnings is a measure of performance during a period that is concerned primarily with the extent to which asset inflows associated with cash-to-cash cycles[22] substantially completed (or completed) during the period exceed (or are less than) asset outflows associated, directly or indirectly, with the same cycles. Both an entity's ongoing major or central activities and its incidental or peripheral transactions involve a number of overlapping cash-to-cash cycles of different lengths. At any time, a significant proportion of those cycles is normally incomplete, and prospects for their successful completion and amounts of related revenues, expenses, gains, and losses vary in degree of uncertainty. Estimating those uncertain results of incomplete cycles is costly and involves risks, but the benefits of timely financial reporting based on sales or other more relevant events, rather than on

cash receipts or other less relevant events, outweigh those costs and risks.

37. Final results of incomplete cycles usually can be reliably measured at some point of substantial completion (for example, at the time of sale, usually meaning delivery) or sometimes earlier in the cycle (for example, as work proceeds on certain long-term, construction-type contracts), so it is usually not necessary to delay recognition until the point of full completion (for example, until after receivables have been collected and warranty obligations have been satisfied). Guidance for applying recognition criteria to components of earnings (paragraphs 78-87) helps define earnings by aiding in making those determinations.

38. Earnings focuses on what the entity has received or reasonably expects to receive for its output (revenues) and what it sacrifices to produce and distribute that output (expenses). Earnings also includes results of the entity's incidental or peripheral transactions and some effects of other events and circumstances stemming from the environment (gains and losses).[23]

Comprehensive income

39. Comprehensive income is a broad measure of the effects of transactions and other events on an entity, comprising all recognized changes in equity (net assets) of the entity during a period from transactions and other events and circumstances except those resulting from investments by owners and distributions to owners.[24]

40. Just as a variety of terms are used for net income in present practice, the Board anticipates that total nonowner changes in equity, comprehensive loss, and other equivalent terms will be used in future financial statements as names for comprehensive income.

41. Components of comprehensive income other than those that are included in earnings present no recognition problems in addition to those involved in recognizing assets and liabilities, for which fundamental criteria are described later (paragraphs 58-77).

---

[22]The patterns of cash-to-cash cycles vary by industry. "Descriptions of operations of business enterprises commonly describe a cycle that begins with cash outlays and ends with cash receipts. That description . . . generally fits manufacturing, merchandising, financial, and service enterprises whose operations comprise primarily activities such as acquiring goods and services, increasing their value by adding time, place, or form utility, selling them, and collecting the selling price. Cash receipts may precede cash payments, however, and commonly do in the operations of some service and financial enterprises" (Concepts Statement 1, par. 39, footnote 8).

[23]Concepts Statement 3, paragraphs 50 and 63-73, defines revenues, expenses, gains, and losses.

[24]Ibid., pars. 50, 56-62, and 147-152.

Relationships between earnings and comprehensive income

42. Earnings and comprehensive income have the same broad components—revenues, expenses, gains, and losses—but are not the same because certain classes of gains and losses are included in comprehensive income but are excluded from earnings.[25] Those items fall into two classes that are illustrated by certain present practices:

a. Effects of certain accounting adjustments of earlier periods that are recognized in the period, such as the principal example in present practice—cumulative effects of changes in accounting principles—which are included in present net income but are excluded from earnings as set forth in this Statement (paragraphs 33 and 34)
b. Certain other changes in net assets (principally certain holding gains and losses) that are recognized in the period, such as some changes in market values of investments in marketable equity securities classified as noncurrent assets, some changes in market values of investments in industries having specialized accounting practices for marketable se-

curities, and foreign currency translation adjustments.[26]

Both classes and the items they comprise are subject to evolutionary change (paragraph 35).

43. Differences between earnings and comprehensive income require some distinguishing terms. The items in both classes described in paragraph 42 are gains and losses under the definitions in Concepts Statement 3 (paragraphs 67-73), but to refer to *some* gains and losses that are included in earnings and *other* gains and losses that are included in comprehensive income but are excluded from earnings is not only clumsy but also likely to be confusing. This Statement therefore uses *gains* and *losses* for those included in earnings and uses *cumulative accounting adjustments* and *other nonowner changes in equity* for those excluded from earnings but included in comprehensive income.

44. The relationships between earnings and comprehensive income described in the foregoing paragraphs mean that statements of earnings and comprehensive income complement each other something like this:[27]

+	Revenues	100	+ Earnings	15
−	Expenses	80	− Cumulative accounting adjustments	2
+	Gains	3	+ Other nonowner changes in equity	1
−	Losses	8		
=	Earnings	15	= Comprehensive income	14

Financial capital maintenance

45. The full set of articulated financial statements discussed in this Statement is based on the concept of financial capital maintenance.

46. An enterprise receives a return only after its capital has been maintained or recovered. The concept of capital maintenance, therefore, is critical in distinguishing an enterprise's return *on* investment from return *of* its investment. Both investors and

the enterprises in which they acquire an interest invest financial resources with the expectation that the investment will generate more financial resources than they invested.

47. A return on financial capital results only if the financial (money) amount of an enterprise's net assets at the end of a period exceeds the financial amount of net assets at the beginning of the period after excluding the effects of transactions with

---

[25]That possibility was noted in Concepts Statement 3: ". . . the reason for using *comprehensive income* rather than *earnings* in this Statement is that the Board has decided to reserve *earnings* for possible use to designate a different concept that is a component part of—that is, is narrower than or less than—comprehensive income. . . ." (par. 58, footnote reference omitted).

[26]FASB Statements No. 12, *Accounting for Certain Marketable Securities;* No. 60, *Accounting and Reporting by Insurance Enterprises;* and No. 52, *Foreign Currency Translation.* Changes in market values of marketable securities are included in earnings by some other entities having specialized accounting practices for marketable securities (for example, securities brokers and dealers and investment companies) and for some classes of marketable securities (for example, securities held in trading accounts of banks and futures contracts that are considered speculative [FASB Statement No. 80, *Accounting for Futures Contracts*]).

[27]Earnings and its components are the same as in the example in paragraph 34. Both *cumulative accounting adjustments* and *other nonowner changes in equity* may be either additions to or deductions from earnings. The signs used in the example are for illustration only.

owners. The financial capital concept is the traditional view and is the capital maintenance concept in present financial statements.[28] In contrast, a return on physical capital results only if the physical productive capacity of the enterprise at the end of the period (or the resources needed to achieve that capacity) exceeds the physical productive capacity at the beginning of the period, also after excluding the effects of transactions with owners. The physical capital maintenance concept can be implemented only if inventories and property, plant, and equipment (and perhaps other assets) are measured by their current costs, while the financial capital maintenance concept does not require measurement by a particular attribute.

48. The principal difference between the two capital maintenance concepts involves the effects of price changes during a period on assets while held and liabilities while owed. Under the financial capital concept, if the effects of those price changes are recognized, they are conceptually holding gains and losses (though they are commonly reported under other names)[29] and are included in the return on capital. Under the physical capital concept, those changes would be recognized but conceptually would be capital maintenance adjustments that would be included directly in equity and not included in return on capital. Both earnings and comprehensive income as set forth in this Statement, like present net income, include holding gains and losses that would be excluded from income under a physical capital maintenance concept.

Recognition implications of earnings

49. Although recognition involves considerations of relevance and comparability, recognition criteria, conventions, and rules are primarily intended to increase reliability—they are means of coping with the uncertainty that surrounds business and economic activities. Uncertainty in business and economic affairs is a continuum, ranging from mere lack of absolute sureness to a degree of vagueness that precludes anything other than guesswork. Since uncertainty surrounds an entity's incomplete cash-to-cash cycles in varying degrees, measuring progress reliably involves determining

whether uncertainty about future cash flows has been reduced to an acceptable level.

50. In response to uncertainty, there has been a general tendency to emphasize purchase and sale transactions and to apply conservative procedures in accounting recognition. Perceptions about characteristics such as realizability and volatility may also help to explain why some events are recognized in present practice while others are not. For example, revenues are sometimes recognized before sale if readily realizable (if sale is a more-or-less effortless or perfunctory activity, and uncertainty about amounts involved is reduced to an acceptable level by quoted prices for interchangeable units in active markets or other reliable measures).[30] Those characteristics may also help to explain certain special recognition rules. For example, so-called translation adjustments from translating foreign currency financial statements are excluded from net income but are reported separately in comprehensive income (paragraphs 39 and 42) because they are considered not only unrealized but also unrealizable short of sale or liquidation of the investment in the entity. Effects of exchange rate changes on the net investment are considered too uncertain and remote to be included in operating results.[31] Similarly, a reason commonly given for the same treatment for certain changes in market values of investments in marketable equity securities is that they may be temporary, and temporary fluctuations in market values of long-term investments should not be included in net income.[32]

51. Since earnings in this Statement is similar to net income for a period in present practice, criteria and guidance given in the Statement for recognizing components of earnings (paragraphs 58-87) are generally similar to revenue and expense recognition criteria or rules in present practice. Future standards may change what is recognized as components of earnings (paragraph 35). Moreover, because of the differences between earnings and comprehensive income, future standards also may recognize certain changes in net assets as components of comprehensive income but not as components of earnings.[33]

---

[28]Concepts Statement 3, par. 58. "Comprehensive income as defined in paragraph 56 is a return *on* financial capital" (Ibid.).

[29]For example, under the FIFO method in present practice, gains from price increases on inventory while held reduce cost of goods sold.

[30]ARB No. 43, Chapter 4, par. 16; FASB Statement 12, pars. 14-16, 27, and 28.

[31]Statement 52, pars. 111-113.

[32]Statement 12, pars. 21, 29, and 30.

[33]A possibility that has been suggested is the "inventory profits" that would result if cost of goods sold were reported on LIFO while inventories were reported on FIFO.

Statement of Cash Flows

52. A statement of cash flows directly or indirectly reflects an entity's cash receipts classified by major sources and its cash payments classified by major uses during a period. It provides useful information about an entity's activities in generating cash through operations to repay debt, distribute dividends, or reinvest to maintain or expand operating capacity; about its financing activities, both debt and equity; and about its investing or spending of cash. Important uses of information about an entity's current cash receipts and payments include helping to assess factors such as the entity's liquidity, financial flexibility, profitability, and risk.

53. Since neither earnings nor comprehensive income measured by accrual accounting is the same as cash flow from operations, cash flow statements provide significant information about amounts, causes, and intervals of time between earnings and comprehensive income and cash receipts and outlays. Users commonly consider that information in assessing the relationship between earnings or comprehensive income and associated cash flows.

54. Statements of cash flows present few recognition problems because all cash receipts and payments are recognized when they occur. Reporting cash flows involves no estimates or allocations and few judgments except regarding classification in cash flow statements.[34]

*Statement of Investments by and
Distributions to Owners*

55. A statement of investments by and distributions to owners reflects the extent to which and in what ways the equity of an entity increased or decreased from transactions with owners as owners[35] during a period. That is, it reflects the capital transactions[36] of the entity, in contrast to its income transactions—those with nonowners—which are reflected in statements of earnings and comprehensive income. Statements of comprehensive income and statements of transactions with owners together include all changes in equity (net assets) recognized during a period.

56. Investments by owners establish or increase ownership interests in the entity and may be received in the form of cash, goods or services, or satisfaction or conversion of the entity's liabilities. Distributions decrease ownership interests and include not only cash dividends when declared (or other cash withdrawals by owners of noncorporate entities) but also transactions such as reacquisitions of the entity's equity securities and distributions "in kind" of noncash assets. Information about those events is useful, in conjunction with other financial statement information, to investors, creditors, and other users as an aid in assessing factors such as the entity's financial flexibility, profitability, and risk.

57. Transactions with owners are now normally recognized when they occur. Recognition problems concerning them can be difficult; for example, problems sometimes arise in distinguishing transactions with owners from transactions with certain creditors, and investments and dividends in kind may present measurement problems.[37] However, the recognition implications of earnings that lead to special guidance do not apply to transactions with owners, and that sort of special guidance is not needed for them.

RECOGNITION CRITERIA

58. As noted in paragraphs 6-9, recognition is the process of formally recording or incorporating an item into the financial statements of an entity as an asset, liability, revenue, expense, or the like. A recognized item is depicted in both words and numbers, with the amount included in the statement totals. Recognition comprehends both initial recognition of an item and recognition of subsequent changes in or removal of a previously recognized item.

Purposes of Criteria

59. Criteria are set forth in this Statement to provide direction for resolving issues that involve accounting recognition. An entity's assets and liabilities and the effects of events on them and on its

---

[34]Determinations about the particular items to be reported within cash flow statements and the form of those statements are matters that may be developed further in Statements of Financial Accounting Standards or in practice.

[35]Rather than as its employees, suppliers, customers, lenders, or the like (Concepts Statement 3, par. 44); that Statement defines investments by and distributions to owners in paragraphs 52-55.

[36]Capital transactions are transactions with owners that affect ownership interests (equity) in an entity:
  Although *capital* is not a precise term in referring to ownership interests because it is also applied to assets and liabilities in various ways, it is used in this discussion because *capital* is part of so many terms commonly used to describe aspects of ownership interests; for example, investments by owners are commonly called capital contributions, distributions to owners are commonly called capital distributions, and discussions of comprehensive income and its components often refer to capital maintenance. [Concepts Statement 3, par. 144]

[37]Concepts Statement 3, par. 49, and APB Opinion No. 29, *Accounting for Nonmonetary Transactions*.

equity are candidates for recognition in its financial statements.

60. Some events that affect assets, liabilities, or equity are not recognized in financial statements at the time they occur. Some events that result in future benefits, for example, creation of product awareness by advertising and promotion, may perhaps never be recognized as separate assets. Other events, for example, a disaster loss of unknown dimension, are recognized only when sufficient information about the effects of the event has become available at a justifiable cost to reduce uncertainty to an acceptable level. Recognition criteria aid in making those determinations.

Structure of Recognition Criteria

61. The recognition criteria in this Statement are derived from the qualitative characteristics of financial information in Concepts Statement 2 and are helpful in making the definitions of elements of financial statements in Concepts Statement 3 operational in resolving financial reporting issues.

62. The fundamental criteria apply to all recognition decisions. Further guidance is provided in paragraphs 78-87 for applying the fundamental criteria to components of earnings.

Fundamental Recognition Criteria

63. An item and information about it should meet four fundamental recognition criteria to be recognized and should be recognized when the criteria are met, subject to a cost-benefit constraint and a materiality threshold. Those criteria are:

Definitions—The item meets the definition of an element of financial statements.

Measurability—It has a relevant attribute measurable with sufficient reliability.

Relevance—The information about it is capable of making a difference in user decisions.

Reliability—The information is representationally faithful, verifiable, and neutral.

All four criteria are subject to a pervasive cost-benefit constraint: the expected benefits from recognizing a particular item should justify perceived costs of providing and using the information.[38] Recognition is also subject to a materiality threshold: an item and information about it need not be recognized in a set of financial statements if the item is not large enough to be material and the aggregate of individually immaterial items is not large enough to be material to those financial statements.[39]

Definitions

64. The definitions are those in FASB Concepts Statement No. 3, *Elements of Financial Statements of Business Enterprises*.[40] To be recognized in financial statements, a resource must meet the definition of an asset, and an obligation must meet the definition of a liability. A change in equity must meet the definition of a revenue, expense, gain, or loss to be recognized as a component of comprehensive income.[41]

Measurability

65. The asset, liability, or change in equity must have a relevant attribute[42] that can be quantified in monetary units with sufficient reliability. Measurability must be considered together with both relevance and reliability.

Measurement attributes

66. Items currently reported in financial statements are measured by different attributes, depending on the nature of the item and the relevance and reliability of the attribute measured. The

---

[38]Concepts Statement 2, pars. 32 and 33 and 133-144.

[39]"Individual judgments are required to assess materiality. . . . The essence of the materiality concept is clear. The omission or misstatement of an item in a financial report is material if, in the light of surrounding circumstances, the magnitude of the item is such that it is probable that the judgment of a reasonable person relying upon the report would have been changed or influenced by the inclusion or correction of the item" (Concepts Statement 2, par. 132).

[40]Concepts Statement 3 does not define elements of cash flow statements but notes classes of items that may be called elements of financial statements, for example, cash provided by operations, cash provided by borrowing, cash provided by issuing equity securities, and so forth (par. 4). However, all items in cash flow statements involve cash receipts or payments, which for recognition purposes are covered by the definitions in that Statement.

[41]As already noted (pars. 42 and 43), the items called *cumulative accounting adjustments* and *other nonowner changes in equity* are gains and losses under the definitions in Concepts Statement 3.

[42]*Attribute* "refers to the traits or aspects of an element to be quantified or measured, such as historical cost/historical proceeds, current cost/current proceeds, etc. Attribute is a narrower concept than measurement, which includes not only identifying the attribute to be measured but also selecting a scale of measurement (for example, units of money or units of constant purchasing power)" (Concepts Statement 1, par. 2, footnote 2).

Board expects the use of different attributes to continue.

67. Five different attributes of assets (and liabilities) are used in present practice:

a. *Historical cost (historical proceeds).* Property, plant, and equipment and most inventories are reported at their historical cost, which is the amount of cash, or its equivalent, paid to acquire an asset, commonly adjusted after acquisition for amortization or other allocations. Liabilities that involve obligations to provide goods or services to customers are generally reported at historical proceeds, which is the amount of cash, or its equivalent, received when the obligation was incurred and may be adjusted after acquisition for amortization or other allocations.

b. *Current cost.* Some inventories are reported at their current (replacement) cost, which is the amount of cash, or its equivalent, that would have to be paid if the same or an equivalent asset were acquired currently.

c. *Current market value.* Some investments in marketable securities are reported at their current market value, which is the amount of cash, or its equivalent, that could be obtained by selling an asset in orderly liquidation. Current market value is also generally used for assets expected to be sold at prices lower than previous carrying amounts. Some liabilities that involve marketable commodities and securities, for example, the obligations of writers of options or sellers of common shares who do not own the underlying commodities or securities, are reported at current market value.

d. *Net realizable (settlement) value.* Short-term receivables and some inventories are reported at their net realizable value, which is the nondiscounted amount of cash, or its equivalent, into which an asset is expected to be converted in due course of business less direct costs, if any, necessary to make that conversion. Liabilities that involve known or estimated amounts of money payable at unknown future dates, for example, trade payables or warranty obligations, generally are reported at their net settlement value, which is the nondiscounted amounts of cash, or its equivalent, expected to be paid to liquidate an obligation in the due course of business, including direct costs, if any, necessary to make that payment.

e. *Present (or discounted) value of future cash flows.* Long-term receivables are reported at their present value (discounted at the implicit or historical rate), which is the present or discounted value of future cash inflows into which an asset is expected to be converted in due course of business less present values of cash outflows necessary to obtain those inflows. Long-term payables are similarly reported at their present value (discounted at the implicit or historical rate), which is the present or discounted value of future cash outflows expected to be required to satisfy the liability in due course of business.

68. The different attributes often have the same amounts, particularly at initial recognition. As a result, there may be agreement about the appropriate amount for an item but disagreement about the attribute being used. Present financial statements frequently are characterized as being based on the historical cost (historical proceeds) attribute. That no doubt reflects the fact that, for most enterprises, a great many of the individual events recognized in financial statements are acquisitions of goods or services for cash or equivalent that are recorded at historical cost. Although the "historical cost system" description may be convenient and describes well present practice for some major classes of assets (most inventories, property, plant, and equipment, and intangibles), it describes less well present practice for a number of other classes of assets and liabilities—for example, trade receivables, notes payable, and warranty obligations.

69. "Historical exchange price" is more descriptive of the quantity most generally reflected in financial statements in present practice (and "transaction-based system" would be a better description of the present accounting model than "historical cost system"). Amounts initially recorded for trade receivables and long-term notes payable, for example, generally fit the historical exchange price description. But some assets are acquired, and some liabilities are incurred, without exchanges—for example, assets found or received as contributions and income tax or litigation liabilities. There is no historical exchange price in those situations, and some other attribute must be used. Moreover, carrying amounts of assets (liabilities) are frequently reduced (increased) from historical exchange price to a lower (higher) current cost, current market value, or net realizable value, even though no subsequent exchange of the assets held or liabilities owed has occurred. And some assets are carried at current market value, independent of historical exchange price.

70. Rather than attempt to characterize present practice as being based on a single attribute with numerous major exceptions for diverse reasons, this concepts Statement characterizes present practice as based on different attributes. Rather than attempt to select a single attribute and force changes in practice so that all classes of assets and liabilities use that attribute, this concepts Statement suggests that use of different attributes will

continue, and discusses how the Board may select the appropriate attribute in particular cases.[43]

Monetary unit or measurement scale

71. The monetary unit or measurement scale in financial statements in current practice is nominal units of money, that is, unadjusted for changes in purchasing power of money over time. An ideal measurement scale would be one that is stable over time. At low rates of change in general purchasing power (inflation or deflation), nominal units of money are relatively stable. Also, preparation and use of financial statements is simpler with nominal units than with other units of measure, such as units of constant general purchasing power (used, for example, in supplementary disclosures of the effects of changing prices),[44] artificial monetary units (for example, the European Currency Unit or ECU), or units of a commodity (for example, ounces of gold). However, as rates of change in general purchasing power increase, financial statements expressed in nominal units of money become progressively less useful and less comparable.

72. The Board expects that nominal units of money will continue to be used to measure items recognized in financial statements. However, a change from present circumstances (for example, an increase in inflation to a level at which distortions became intolerable) might lead the Board to select another, more stable measurement scale.

Relevance

73. Relevance is a primary qualitative characteristic. To be relevant, information about an item must have feedback value or predictive value (or both) for users and must be timely.[45] Information is relevant if it has the capacity to make a difference in investors', creditors', or other users' decisions. To be recognized, the information conveyed by including an asset, liability, or change therein in the financial statements must be relevant.

74. The relevance of particular information about an item being considered for recognition cannot be determined in isolation. Relevance should be eval-

uated in the context of the principal objective of financial reporting: providing information that is useful in making rational investment, credit, and similar decisions.[46] Relevance should also be evaluated in the context of the full set of financial statements—with consideration of how recognition of a particular item contributes to the aggregate decision usefulness.

Reliability

75. Reliability is the other primary qualitative characteristic. To be reliable, information about an item must be representationally faithful, verifiable, and neutral.[47] To be reliable, information must be sufficiently faithful in its representation of the underlying resource, obligation, or effect of events and sufficiently free of error and bias to be useful to investors, creditors, and others in making decisions. To be recognized, information about the existence and amount of an asset, liability, or change therein must be reliable.

76. Reliability may affect the timing of recognition. The first available information about an event that may have resulted in an asset, liability, or change therein is sometimes too uncertain to be recognized: it may not yet be clear whether the effects of the event meet one or more of the definitions or whether they are measurable, and the cost of resolving those uncertainties may be excessive. Information about some items that meet a definition may never become sufficiently reliable at a justifiable cost to recognize the item. For other items, those uncertainties are reduced as time passes, and reliability is increased as additional information becomes available.

77. Unavailability or unreliability of information may delay recognition of an item, but waiting for virtually complete reliability or minimum cost may make the information so untimely that it loses its relevance. At some intermediate point, uncertainty may be reduced at a justifiable cost to a level tolerable in view of the perceived relevance of the information. If other criteria are also met, that is the appropriate point for recognition. Thus, recognition may sometimes involve a trade-off between relevance and reliability.

---

[43]This discussion of measurement attributes is based in part on the FASB Discussion Memorandum, *Conceptual Framework for Financial Accounting and Reporting: Elements of Financial Statements and Their Measurement* (December 2, 1976), paragraphs 388-574, which further describes and illustrates each of the attributes and remains a useful reference.

[44] FASB Statement No. 33, *Financial Reporting and Changing Prices,* as amended.

[45]Concepts Statement 2, pars. 46-57.

[46]Concepts Statement 1, pars. 34-40.

[47]Concepts Statement 2, pars. 58-110.

GUIDANCE IN APPLYING CRITERIA TO COMPONENTS OF EARNINGS

78. This section discusses the need for and provides further guidance in applying the fundamental criteria in recognizing components of earnings. Changes in net assets are recognized as components of earnings if they qualify under the guidance in paragraphs 83-87. Certain changes in net assets (discussed in paragraphs 42-44 and 49-51) that meet the four fundamental recognition criteria just described may qualify for recognition in comprehensive income even though they do not qualify for recognition as components of earnings based on that guidance.

79. Further guidance in applying the recognition criteria to components of earnings is necessary because of the widely acknowledged importance of information about earnings and its components as a primary measure of performance for a period. The performance measured is that of the entity, not necessarily that of its management, and includes the recognized effects upon the entity of events and circumstances both within and beyond the control of the entity and its management.[48] The widely acknowledged importance of earnings information leads to guidance intended in part to provide more stringent requirements for recognizing components of earnings than for recognizing other changes in assets or liabilities.

80. As noted in paragraph 36, earnings measures the extent to which asset inflows (revenues and gains) associated with substantially completed cash-to-cash cycles exceed asset outflows (expenses and losses) associated, directly or indirectly, with the same cycles. Guidance for recognizing components of earnings is concerned with identifying which cycles are substantially complete and with associating particular revenues, gains, expenses, and losses with those cycles.

81. In assessing the prospect that as yet uncompleted transactions will be concluded successfully,

a degree of skepticism is often warranted.[49] Moreover, as a reaction to uncertainty, more stringent requirements historically have been imposed for recognizing revenues and gains than for recognizing expenses and losses, and those conservative reactions influence the guidance for applying the recognition criteria to components of earnings.

82. The guidance stated here is intended to summarize key considerations in a form useful for guidance for future standard setting—guidance which also is consistent with the vast bulk of current practice. The following paragraphs provide guidance separately for recognition of revenues and gains and for expenses and losses as components of earnings.

Revenues and Gains

83. Further guidance for recognition of revenues and gains is intended to provide an acceptable level of assurance of the existence and amounts of revenues and gains before they are recognized. Revenues and gains of an enterprise during a period are generally measured by the exchange values of the assets (goods or services) or liabilities involved, and recognition involves consideration of two factors, (a) being realized or realizable and (b) being earned, with sometimes one and sometimes the other being the more important consideration.

a. *Realized or realizable.* Revenues and gains generally are not recognized until realized or realizable.[50] Revenues and gains are realized when products (goods or services), merchandise, or other assets are exchanged for cash or claims to cash. Revenues and gains are realizable when related assets received or held are readily convertible to known amounts of cash or claims to cash. Readily convertible assets have (i) interchangeable (fungible) units and (ii) quoted prices available in an active market that can rapidly absorb the quantity held by the entity without significantly affecting the price.

---

[48]"What happens to a business enterprise is usually so much a joint result of a complex interaction of many factors that neither accounting nor other statistical analysis can discern with reasonable accuracy the degree to which management, or any other factor, affected the joint result" (Concepts Statement 1, par. 53).

[49]Concepts Statement 2, par. 97.

[50]The terms *realized* and *realizable* are used in the Board's conceptual framework in precise senses, focusing on conversion or convertibility of noncash assets into cash or claims to cash (Concepts Statement 3, par. 83). *Realized* has sometimes been used in a different, broader sense: for example, some have used that term to include *realizable* or to include certain conversions of noncash assets into other assets that are also not cash or claims to cash. APB Statement 4, paragraphs 148-153, used the term *realization* even more broadly as a synonym for *recognition*.

b. *Earned*. Revenues are not recognized until earned. An entity's revenue-earning activities involve delivering or producing goods, rendering services, or other activities that constitute its ongoing major or central operations,[51] and revenues are considered to have been earned when the entity has substantially accomplished what it must do to be entitled to the benefits represented by the revenues. Gains commonly result from transactions and other events that involve no "earning process," and for recognizing gains, being earned is generally less significant than being realized or realizable.

84. In recognizing revenues and gains:

a. The two conditions (being realized or realizable and being earned) are usually met by the time product or merchandise is delivered or services are rendered to customers, and revenues from manufacturing and selling activities and gains and losses from sales of other assets are commonly recognized at time of sale (usually meaning delivery).[52]
b. If sale or cash receipt (or both) precedes production and delivery (for example, magazine subscriptions), revenues may be recognized as earned by production and delivery.
c. If product is contracted for before production, revenues may be recognized by a percentage-of-completion method as earned—as production takes place—provided reasonable estimates of results at completion and reliable measures of progress are available.[53]
d. If services are rendered or rights to use assets extend continuously over time (for example, interest or rent), reliable measures based on contractual prices established in advance are commonly available, and revenues may be recognized as earned as time passes.
e. If products or other assets are readily realizable because they are salable at reliably determinable prices without significant effort (for example, certain agricultural products, precious metals, and marketable securities), revenues and some

gains or losses may be recognized at completion of production or when prices of the assets change. Paragraph 83(a) describes readily realizable (convertible) assets.
f. If product, services, or other assets are exchanged for nonmonetary assets that are not readily convertible into cash, revenues or gains or losses may be recognized on the basis that they have been earned and the transaction is completed. Gains or losses may also be recognized if nonmonetary assets are received or distributed in nonreciprocal transactions. Recognition in both kinds of transactions depends on the provision that the fair values involved can be determined within reasonable limits.[54]
g. If collectibility of assets received for product, services, or other assets is doubtful, revenues and gains may be recognized on the basis of cash received.

Expenses and Losses

85. Further guidance for recognition of expenses and losses is intended to recognize consumption (using up) of economic benefits or occurrence or discovery of loss of future economic benefits during a period. Expenses and losses are generally recognized when an entity's economic benefits are used up in delivering or producing goods, rendering services, or other activities that constitute its ongoing major or central operations or when previously recognized assets are expected to provide reduced or no further benefits.

Consumption of Benefits

86. Consumption of economic benefits during a period may be recognized either directly or by relating it to revenues recognized during the period:[55]

a. Some expenses, such as cost of goods sold, are matched with revenues—they are recognized upon recognition of revenues that result directly and jointly from the same transactions or other events as the expenses.

---

[51]"Most types of revenue are the joint result of many profit-directed activities of an enterprise and revenue is often described as being 'earned' gradually and continuously by the whole of enterprise activities. *Earning* in this sense is a technical term that refers to the activities that give rise to the revenue—purchasing, manufacturing, selling, rendering service, delivering goods, allowing other entities to use enterprise assets, the occurrence of an event specified in a contract, and so forth. All of the profit-directed activities of an enterprise that comprise the process by which revenue is earned may be called the *earning process*" (APB Statement 4, par. 149). Concepts Statement 3, paragraph 64, footnote 31, contains the same concept.

[52]The requirement that revenue be earned before it is recorded "usually causes no problems because the earning process is usually complete or nearly complete by the time of [sale]" (APB Statement 4, par. 153).

[53]If production is long in relation to reporting periods, such as for long-term, construction-type contracts, recognizing revenues as earned has often been deemed to result in information that is significantly more relevant and representationally faithful than information based on waiting for delivery, although at the sacrifice of some verifiability. (Concepts Statement 2, paragraphs 42-45, describes trade-offs of that kind.)

[54]APB Opinion 29.

[55]Concepts Statement 3, pars. 84-89.

b. Many expenses, such as selling and administrative salaries, are recognized during the period in which cash is spent or liabilities are incurred for goods and services that are used up either simultaneously with acquisition or soon after.

c. Some expenses, such as depreciation and insurance, are allocated by systematic and rational procedures to the periods during which the related assets are expected to provide benefits.

Loss or Lack of Future Benefit

87. An expense or loss is recognized if it becomes evident that previously recognized future economic benefits of an asset have been reduced or eliminated, or that a liability has been incurred or increased, without associated economic benefits.

RECOGNITION OF CHANGES IN ASSETS AND LIABILITIES

88. Initial recognition of assets acquired and liabilities incurred generally involves measurement based on current exchange prices at the date of recognition. Once an asset or a liability is recognized, it continues to be measured at the amount initially recognized until an event that changes the asset or liability or its amount occurs and meets the recognition criteria.

89. Events that change assets and liabilities are of two types: (a) inflows (acquisitions of assets or incurrences of liabilities) and outflows (sale or other disposal or loss of assets and settlement or cancellation of liabilities) and (b) changes of amounts of assets while held or of liabilities while owed by the entity. The latter also are of two types: (i) changes in utility or substance and (ii) changes in price. Examples of changes in utility or substance that are recognized in current practice include use of assets in production, depreciation of assets used in administrative activities, and fire damage to assets.

90. Information based on current prices should be recognized if it is sufficiently relevant and reliable to justify the costs involved and more relevant than alternative information. The merits of recognizing changes in prices may be clear in certain cases, and, as already noted, some price changes are recognized in present practice. In other cases, the relative merits of information based on current prices and alternative information may be unclear or may be a matter of dispute. In considering the application of the fundamental recognition criteria, those relative merits must be evaluated in the light of the circumstances of each case.

SUMMARY

91. Most aspects of current practice are consistent with the recognition criteria and guidance in this Statement, but the criteria and guidance do not foreclose the possibility of future changes in practice. This Statement is intended to provide guidance for orderly change in accounting standards when needed. When evidence indicates that information about an item that is more useful (relevant and reliable) than information currently reported is available at a justifiable cost, it should be included in financial statements.

This Statement was adopted by the affirmative vote of six members of the Financial Accounting Standards Board. Mr. March dissented.

Mr. March dissents from this Statement because (a) it does not adopt measurement concepts oriented toward what he believes is the most useful single attribute for recognition purposes, the cash equivalent of recognized transactions reduced by subsequent impairments or loss of service value—instead it suggests selecting from several different attributes without providing sufficient guidance for the selection process; (b) it identifies all nonowner changes in assets and liabilities as comprehensive income and return on equity, thereby including in income, incorrectly in his view, capital inputs from nonowners, unrealized gains from price changes, amounts that should be deducted to maintain capital in real terms, and foreign currency translation adjustments; (c) it uses a concept of income that is fundamentally based on measurements of assets, liabilities, and changes in them, rather than adopting the Statement's concept of earnings as the definition of income; and (d) it fails to provide sufficient guidance for initial recognition and derecognition of assets and liabilities.

Mr. March would not, in general, recognize increases in prices of assets and decreases in prices of liabilities before they are realized. He believes present measurement practice can be characterized as largely using a single attribute, the cash equivalent of recognized transactions reduced by subsequent impairments or loss of service value, and that present practices that recognize revenues or gains from changes in prices before realization, such as the uses of current market values and net realizable values cited in paragraphs 67(c) and (d) and 69, are exceptions to the general use of that single attribute. Mr. March is concerned that the guidance in paragraph 90 would permit, and perhaps point toward, more recognition of changes in current prices before realization. He believes that income, recognition, and measurement concepts based largely on the single attribute that he proposes are most relevant to reporting capital committed, performance, and the investment and realization of resources.

Mr. March objects to comprehensive income, defined in Concepts Statement 3 and confirmed in this Statement, as a concept of income because it includes all recognized changes (including price changes) in assets and liabilities other than investments by owners and distributions to owners. He would exclude from income, and include in the amount of capital to be maintained (in addition to transactions with owners), what he would consider to be direct capital inputs to the enterprise from non-owner sources. Those include governmental and other capital contributions or grants and capital arising in reorganizations, recapitalizations, and extinguishments or restatements of debt capital.

Mr. March would also require that income must first deduct a provision for maintenance of capital in real terms (adjusted for changes in purchasing power of money over time, paragraphs 71-72). He believes that is necessary to avoid reporting a return of capital as income. Complex implementation should not be necessary to provide for the erosion of capital caused by the effects of inflation on the unit of measure. A "rubber yardstick" is a poor measuring tool. Mr. March would also exclude from income foreign currency translation adjustments (excluded from earnings but included in comprehensive income by paragraph 42(b)), which he believes are analogous to provisions for maintenance of capital in real terms.

The description of earnings (paragraphs 33-38) and the guidance for applying recognition criteria to components of earnings (paragraphs 78-87) is consistent with Mr. March's view that income should measure performance and that performance flows primarily from an entity's fulfillment of the terms of its transactions with outside entities that result in revenues, other proceeds on resource dispositions (gains), costs (expenses) associated with those revenues and proceeds, and losses sustained. However, Mr. March believes that those concepts are fundamental and should be embodied in definitions of the elements of financial statements and in basic income recognition criteria rather than basing income on measurements of assets, liabilities, and changes in them.

Disregarding the foregoing objections, Mr. March believes this Statement offers insufficient guidance for the near-term future work of the Board. To be useful, it needs to be supplemented with more specific guidance for selecting measurement attributes for specific assets, liabilities, and transactions and for deciding when the criteria require recognition or derecognition of an asset or a liability.

Members of the Financial Accounting Standards Board:

Appendix

BACKGROUND INFORMATION

92. The Board's study of recognition and measurement concepts has spanned several years. The need to develop those concepts was identified early in the conceptual framework project, and the first FASB concepts Statement, *Objectives of Financial Reporting by Business Enterprises,* listed them among several separate matters to be covered:

. . . Later Statements are expected to cover the elements of financial statements and their recognition, measurement, and display . . . , criteria for distinguishing information to be included in financial statements from that which should be provided by other means of financial reporting, and criteria for evaluating and selecting accounting information (qualitative characteristics). [paragraph 2]

93. During that period, three FASB Research Reports,[56] a Discussion Memorandum,[57] a concepts Statement,[58] and an Exposure Draft[59] have dealt in whole or in part with recognition and measure-

---

[56]*Recognition of Contractual Rights and Obligations: An Exploratory Study of Conceptual Issues,* by Yuji Ijiri, December 1980; *Survey of Present Practices in Recognizing Revenues, Expenses, Gains, and Losses,* by Henry R. Jaenicke, January 1981; and *Recognition in Financial Statements: Underlying Concepts and Practical Conventions,* by L. Todd Johnson and Reed K. Storey, July 1982.

[57]FASB Discussion Memorandum, *Conceptual Framework for Financial Accounting and Reporting: Elements of Financial Statements and Their Measurement,* December 2, 1976, Part III.

[58]FASB Concepts Statement No. 3, *Elements of Financial Statements of Business Enterprises,* pars. 16 and 17, 37-43, and 74-89.

[59]FASB Exposure Draft, *Reporting Income, Cash Flows, and Financial Position of Business Enterprises,* November 1981, pars. 13-16 and elsewhere. This Statement supersedes that Exposure Draft.

ment matters, and the Board has discussed those matters extensively.

94. The once-separate projects on recognition and on measurement were combined, principally because in the Board's view certain recognition questions, which are among the most important to be dealt with, are so closely related to measurement issues that it is not productive to discuss them separately. For example, the question of whether the appropriate attribute to measure a particular item is a past exchange price or a current exchange price is not easily separable from the question of whether events such as price changes should be recognized.

95. The Board issued an Exposure Draft, *Recognition and Measurement in Financial Statements of Business Enterprises,* on December 30, 1983 and received 104 letters of comment on it.

96. The changes made to the Exposure Draft were largely in response to suggestions in those comment letters and are intended to improve the clarity and organization of the ideas presented in the Exposure Draft. The Board believes that the substance of this Statement is not significantly changed from the Exposure Draft. Noteworthy changes made and changes suggested but not made are discussed below.

97. The discussion of financial statements, financial reporting, and recognition in paragraphs 5-12 has been expanded and reorganized in response to comments that the status of notes, supplementary information, and other means of financial reporting outside of financial statements (all of which are outside the scope of this concepts Statement) was unclear.

98. The term *full set* of financial statements has been used in paragraph 13 and elsewhere in response to comments that *complete set,* the term used in the Exposure Draft, implied that no further information beyond the listed financial statements was needed and to comments that *complete set* had been used in some standards in a different way.

99. A number of respondents inferred from the discussion of cash flow statements in the Exposure Draft that the Board had decided one or more specific issues about cash flow reporting. Those issues include the direct and indirect methods of presentation; whether or not "cash" should include equivalents to cash and, if so, what instruments qualify; whether or not the nonmonetary transactions currently reported in statements of changes in financial position should appear in cash flow statements; and the definitions of cash provided by (or used for) operations, financing activities, and investing activities. Those and other specific cash flow statement issues mentioned by respondents

are beyond the scope of this concepts Statement. The discussion of the statement of cash flows was revised to emphasize that.

100. Many respondents criticized the term *comprehensive income* and some criticized the term *earnings* as unwarranted innovations likely to cause confusion and legal difficulties. Those terms are not new. They were first used in their present senses in Concepts Statement 3, in which the Board defined comprehensive income as an element of financial statements and reserved the term *earnings* for possible later use to designate a component part of comprehensive income. This Statement carries forward the concept of comprehensive income and describes a concept for earnings. The Board retained the idea of two separate measures both to reflect present practice for the items discussed in paragraph 42(b) and to allow for the possibility that future standards may recognize some items, for example, the cumulative accounting adjustments discussed in paragraph 42(a), in comprehensive income but not in earnings.

101. The Board explored the alternative terms for *comprehensive income* and *earnings* suggested by respondents, as well as other possibilities suggested by its staff, but concluded that the other terms had disadvantages greater than those attaching to the terms originally selected. The Statement was revised to indicate that the Board anticipates that, as with net income in present practice, a variety of terms will be used in future financial statements as names for earnings (for example, net income, profit, or net loss) and for comprehensive income (for example, total nonowner changes in equity or comprehensive loss).

102. Some respondents urged the Board to clarify the concept of earnings. The discussion in paragraphs 36-38, the table in paragraph 44, and footnote 26 have been rewritten to explain more fully what the Board intended.

103. The materiality threshold for recognition, implicit in the conceptual framework, has been made explicit in paragraph 63 at the suggestion of several respondents. Some respondents suggested that materiality and cost-benefit considerations should be fundamental recognition criteria. No change was made because the Board believes that, while those considerations affect the application of the criteria, they are different in character from the four fundamental recognition criteria.

104. Several respondents urged the Board to include the question of the monetary unit or measurement scale within the scope of the Statement. The Exposure Draft described present practice as using nominal units of money but left the unit of measure

outside its scope. The Board clarified the matter by indicating in paragraph 72 that it expects that nominal units of money will continue to be used to measure items recognized in financial statements.

105. The discussion of measurement has been expanded, in response to the suggestions of several respondents, to explain and illustrate the different attributes more fully and to discuss why different attributes are needed to describe present practice and are expected to continue to be used to measure items in financial statements.

106. Some respondents expressed concern that the guidance in paragraph 84(e) (concerning circumstances under which revenue or gain may be recognized at completion of production or when prices of assets change) and the guidance in paragraph 87 (concerning recognition of losses when it becomes evident that assets have been reduced or eliminated or liabilities incurred or increased without associated benefits) meant significant change from present practice. Those paragraphs describe concepts that the Board believes underlie many current practices and standards, just as do the other parts of the guidance for recognition of components of earnings. They have been retained and clarified.

107. Several respondents urged the Board to address in this Statement certain specific recognition and measurement issues including definitive guidance for recognition of contracts that are fully executory (that is, contracts as to which neither party has as yet carried out any part of its obligations, which are generally not recognized in present practice) and selection of measurement attributes for particular assets and liabilities. Those issues have long been, and remain, unresolved on a general basis. As noted in the introductory statement to this and earlier concepts Statements (page 1085), establishment of objectives and identification of fundamental concepts will not directly solve specific financial accounting and reporting problems. Rather, objectives give direction, and concepts are tools for solving problems.

108. The Board and others who use this Statement will be guided and aided by the concepts it sets forth, but judgments, based on the particular circumstances of each case, will continue to play a major role in solving problems of recognition and measurement in financial statements. The Board believes that further development of recognition, measurement, and display matters will occur as the concepts are applied at the standards level.

Summary Index of Concepts Defined or Discussed

Statement of Financial Accounting Concepts No. 6
Elements of Financial Statements

a replacement of FASB Concepts Statement No. 3 (incorporating an amendment of FASB Concepts Statement No. 2)

STATUS

Issued: December 1985

Affects: Supersedes CON 2, paragraph 4 and footnote 2
Supersedes CON 3

Affected by: No other pronouncements

HIGHLIGHTS

[Best understood in context of full Statement]

- Elements of financial statements are the building blocks with which financial statements are constructed—the classes of items that financial statements comprise. The items in financial statements represent in words and numbers certain entity resources, claims to those resources, and the effects of transactions and other events and circumstances that result in changes in those resources and claims.

- This Statement replaces FASB Concepts Statement No.3, *Elements of Financial Statements of Business Enterprises,* expanding its scope to encompass not-for-profit organizations as well.

- This Statement defines 10 interrelated elements that are directly related to measuring performance and status of an entity. (Other possible elements of financial statements are not addressed.)

  — Assets are probable future economic benefits obtained or controlled by a particular entity as a result of past transactions or events.

  — Liabilities are probable future sacrifices of economic benefits arising from present obligations of a particular entity to transfer assets or provide services to other entities in the future as a result of past transactions or events.

  — Equity or net assets is the residual interest in the assets of an entity that remains after deducting its liabilities. In a business enterprise, the equity is the ownership interest. In a not-for-profit organization, which has no ownership interest in the same sense as a business enterprise, net assets is divided into three classes based on the presence or absence of donor-imposed restrictions—permanently restricted, temporarily restricted, and unrestricted net assets.

  — Investments by owners are increases in equity of a particular business enterprise resulting from transfers to it from other entities of something valuable to obtain or increase ownership interests (or equity) in it. Assets are most commonly received as investments by owners, but that which is received may also include services or satisfaction or conversion of liabilities of the enterprise.

  — Distributions to owners are decreases in equity of a particular business enterprise resulting from transferring assets, rendering services, or incurring liabilities by the enterprise to owners. Distributions to owners decrease ownership interest (or equity) in an enterprise.

— Comprehensive income is the change in equity of a business enterprise during a period from trans-actions and other events and circumstances from nonowner sources. It includes all changes in equity during a period except those resulting from investments by owners and distributions to owners.

— Revenues are inflows or other enhancements of assets of an entity or settlements of its liabilities (or a combination of both) from delivering or producing goods, rendering services, or other activities that constitute the entity's ongoing major or central operations.

— Expenses are outflows or other using up of assets or incurrences of liabilities (or a combination of both) from delivering or producing goods, rendering services, or carrying out other activities that constitute the entity's ongoing major or central operations.

— Gains are increases in equity (net assets) from peripheral or incidental transactions of an entity and from all other transactions and other events and circumstances affecting the entity except those that result from revenues or investments by owners.

— Losses are decreases in equity (net assets) from peripheral or incidental transactions of an entity and from all other transactions and other events and circumstances affecting the entity except those that result from expenses or distributions to owners.

• The Statement defines three classes of net assets of not-for-profit organizations and the changes in those classes during a period. Each class is composed of the revenues, expenses, gains, and losses that affect that class and of reclassifications from or to other classes.

— Change in permanently restricted net assets during a period is the total of (a) contributions and other inflows during the period of assets whose use by the organization is limited by donor-imposed stipulations that neither expire by passage of time nor can be fulfilled or otherwise removed by actions of the organization, (b) other asset enhancements and diminishments during the period that are subject to the same kinds of stipulations, and (c) reclassifications from (or to) other classes of net assets during the period as a consequence of donor-imposed stipulations.

— Change in temporarily restricted net assets during a period is the total of (a) contributions and other inflows during the period of assets whose use by the organization is limited by donor-imposed stipu-lations that either expire by passage of time or can be fulfilled and removed by actions of the organi-zation pursuant to those stipulations, (b) other asset enhancements and diminishments during the period subject to the same kinds of stipulations, and (c) reclassifications to (or from) other classes of net assets during the period as a consequence of donor-imposed stipulations, their expiration by passage of time, or their fulfillment and removal by actions of the organization pursuant to those stipulations.

— Change in unrestricted net assets during a period is the total change in net assets during the period less change in permanently restricted net assets and change in temporarily restricted net assets for the period. It is the change during the period in the part of net assets of a not-for-profit organization that is not limited by donor-imposed stipulations. Changes in unrestricted net assets include (a) rev-enues and gains that change unrestricted net assets, (b) expenses and losses that change unrestricted net assets, and (c) reclassifications from (or to) other classes of net assets as a consequence of donor-imposed stipulations, their expiration by passage of time, or their fulfillment and removal by actions of the organization pursuant to those stipulations.

• The Statement also defines or describes certain other concepts that underlie or are otherwise closely re-lated to the 10 elements and 3 classes defined in the Statement.

• Earnings is not defined in this Statement. FASB Concepts Statement 5 has now described earnings for a period as excluding certain cumulative accounting adjustments and other nonowner changes in equity that are included in comprehensive income for a period.

• The Board expects most assets and liabilities in present practice to continue to qualify as assets or liabili-ties under the definitions in this Statement. The Board emphasizes that the definitions neither require nor presage upheavals in present practice, although they may in due time lead to some evolutionary changes in practice or at least in the ways certain items are viewed. They should be especially helpful in understanding the content of financial statements and in analyzing and resolving new financial ac-counting issues as they arise.

- The appendixes are not part of the definitions but are intended for readers who may find them useful. They describe the background of the Statement and elaborate on the descriptions of the essential characteristics of the elements and classes, including some discussions and illustrations of how to apply the definitions.

- This Statement amends FASB Concepts Statement No. 2, *Qualitative Characteristics of Accounting Information,* to apply it to financial reporting by not-for-profit organizations.

Statement of Financial Accounting Concepts No. 6
Elements of Financial Statements

Statements of Financial Accounting Concepts

This Statement of Financial Accounting Concepts is one of a series of publications in the Board's conceptual framework for financial accounting and reporting. Statements in the series are intended to set forth objectives and fundamentals that will be the basis for development of financial accounting and reporting standards. The objectives identify the goals and purposes of financial reporting. The fundamentals are the underlying concepts of financial accounting—concepts that guide the selection of transactions, events, and circumstances to be accounted for; their recognition and measurement; and the means of summarizing and communicating them to interested parties. Concepts of that type are fundamental in the sense that other concepts flow from them and repeated reference to them will be necessary in establishing, interpreting, and applying accounting and reporting standards.

The conceptual framework is a coherent system of interrelated objectives and fundamentals that is expected to lead to consistent standards and that prescribes the nature, function, and limits of financial accounting and reporting. It is expected to serve the public interest by providing structure and direction to financial accounting and reporting to facilitate the provision of evenhanded financial and related information that helps promote the efficient allocation of scarce resources in the economy and society, including assisting capital and other markets to function efficiently.

Establishment of objectives and identification of fundamental concepts will not directly solve financial accounting and reporting problems. Rather, objectives give direction, and concepts are tools for solving problems.

The Board itself is likely to be the most direct beneficiary of the guidance provided by the Statements in this series. They will guide the Board in developing accounting and reporting standards by providing the Board with a common foundation and basic reasoning on which to consider merits of alternatives.

However, knowledge of the objectives and concepts the Board will use in developing standards also should enable those who are affected by or interested in financial accounting standards to understand better the purposes, content, and characteristics of information provided by financial accounting and reporting. That knowledge is expected to enhance the usefulness of, and confidence in, financial accounting and reporting. The concepts also may provide some guidance in analyzing new or emerging problems of financial accounting and reporting in the absence of applicable authoritative pronouncements.

Statements of Financial Accounting Concepts do not establish standards prescribing accounting procedures or disclosure practices for particular items or events, which are issued by the Board as Statements of Financial Accounting Standards. Rather, Statements in this series describe concepts and relations that will underlie future financial accounting standards and practices and in due course serve as a basis for evaluating existing standards and practices.*

The Board recognizes that in certain respects current generally accepted accounting principles may be inconsistent with those that may derive from the objectives and concepts set forth in Statements in this series. However, a Statement of Financial Accounting Concepts does not (a) require a change in existing generally accepted accounting principles; (b) amend, modify, or interpret Statements of Financial Accounting Standards, Interpretations of the FASB, Opinions of the Accounting Principles Board, or Bulletins of the Committee on Accounting Procedure that are in effect; or (c) justify either changing existing generally accepted accounting and reporting practices or interpreting the pronouncements listed in item (b) based on personal interpretations of the objectives and concepts in the Statements of Financial Accounting Concepts.

Since a Statement of Financial Accounting Concepts does not establish generally accepted accounting principles or standards for the disclosure of financial information outside of financial statements in published financial reports, it is not intended to invoke application of Rule 203 or 204 of the Rules of Conduct of the Code of Professional Ethics of the American Institute of Certified Pub-

---

*Pronouncements such as APB Statement No. 4, *Basic Concepts and Accounting Principles Underlying Financial Statements of Business Enterprises,* and the Accounting Terminology Bulletins will continue to serve their intended purpose—they describe objectives and concepts underlying standards and practices existing at the time of their issuance.

lic Accountants (or successor rules or arrangements of similar scope and intent). [†]

Like other pronouncements of the Board, a Statement of Financial Accounting Concepts may be amended, superseded, or withdrawn by appropriate action under the Board's *Rules of Procedure.*

CONTENTS

[†]Rule 203 prohibits a member of the American Institute of Certified Public Accountants from expressing an opinion that financial statements conform with generally accepted accounting principles if those statements contain a material departure from an accounting principle promulgated by the Financial Accounting Standards Board, unless the member can demonstrate that because of unusual circumstances the financial statements otherwise would have been misleading. Rule 204 requires members of the Institute to justify departures from standards promulgated by the Financial Accounting Standards Board for the disclosure of information outside of financial statements in published financial reports.

INTRODUCTION

Scope and Content of Statement

1. This Statement defines 10 elements of financial statements: 7 elements of financial statements of both business enterprises and not-for-profit organizations—assets, liabilities, equity (business enterprises) or net assets (not-for-profit organizations), revenues, expenses, gains, and losses—and 3 elements of financial statements of business enterprises only—investments by owners, distributions to owners, and comprehensive income.[1] It also defines three classes of net assets of not-for-profit organizations and the changes in those classes during a period—change in permanently restricted net assets, change in temporarily restricted net assets, and change in unrestricted net assets. The Statement also defines or describes certain other concepts that underlie or are otherwise related to those elements and classes (Summary Index, pages 1160 and 1161).

2. This Statement replaces FASB Concepts Statement No. 3, *Elements of Financial Statements of Business Enterprises,* extending that Statement's definitions to not-for-profit organizations.[2] It con-

firms conclusions in paragraph 2 of Concepts Statement 3 that (a) assets and liabilities are common to all organizations and can be defined the same for business and not-for-profit organizations, (b) the definitions of equity (net assets), revenues, expenses, gains, and losses fit both business and not-for-profit organizations, and (c) not-for-profit organizations have no need for elements such as investments by owners, distributions to owners, and comprehensive income. Thus, this Statement continues unchanged the elements defined in Concepts Statement 3, although it contains added explanations stemming from characteristics of not-for-profit organizations and their operations. It also defines three classes of net assets of not-for-profit organizations, distinguished by the presence or absence of donor-imposed restrictions, and the changes in those classes during a period—change in permanently restricted, temporarily restricted, and unrestricted net assets.

Other Possible Elements of Financial Statements

3. Although the elements defined in this Statement include basic elements and are probably those most commonly identified as elements of financial statements, they are not the only elements

---

[1] *Comprehensive income* is the name used in this Statement and in FASB Concepts Statement No. 3, *Elements of Financial Statements of Business Enterprises,* for the concept that was called *earnings* in FASB Concepts Statement No. 1, *Objectives of Financial Reporting by Business Enterprises,* and other conceptual framework documents previously issued (*Tentative Conclusions on Objectives of Financial Statements of Business Enterprises* [December 1976]; FASB Discussion Memorandum, *Elements of Financial Statements and Their Measurement* [December 1976]; FASB Exposure Draft, *Objectives of Financial Reporting and Elements of Financial Statements of Business Enterprises* [December 1977], and FASB Discussion Memorandum, *Reporting Earnings* [July 1979]). Concepts Statement 3 did not define *earnings* because the Board decided to reserve the term for possible use to designate a component part, then undetermined, of comprehensive income.

FASB Concepts Statement No. 5, *Recognition and Measurement in Financial Statements of Business Enterprises* (December 1984), has now described earnings for a period as excluding certain cumulative accounting adjustments and other nonowner changes in equity that are included in comprehensive income for a period.

[2] The term *not-for-profit organizations* in this Statement encompasses private sector organizations described in FASB Concepts Statement No. 4, *Objectives of Financial Reporting by Nonbusiness Organizations* (December 1980). Financial reporting by state and local governmental units is within the purview of the Governmental Accounting Standards Board (GASB), and the FASB has not considered the applicability of this Statement to those units.

of financial statements. The elements defined in this Statement are a related group with a particular focus—on assets, liabilities, equity, and other elements directly related to measuring performance and status of an entity. Information about an entity's performance and status provided by accrual accounting is the primary focus of financial reporting (FASB Concepts Statement No. 1, *Objectives of Financial Reporting by Business Enterprises,* paragraphs 40-48, and FASB Concepts Statement No. 4, *Objectives of Financial Reporting by Nonbusiness Organizations,* paragraphs 38-53). Other statements or focuses may require other elements.[3]

4. Variations of possible statements showing the effects on assets and liabilities of transactions or other events and circumstances during a period are almost limitless, and all of them have classes of items that may be called elements of financial statements. For example, a statement showing funds flows or cash flows during a period may include categories for funds or cash provided by (a) operations, (b) borrowing, (c) issuing equity securities, (d) sale of assets, and so forth. Other projects may define additional elements of financial statements as needed.

Elements and Financial Representations

5. Elements of financial statements are the building blocks with which financial statements are constructed—the classes of items that financial statements comprise. *Elements* refers to broad classes, such as assets, liabilities, revenues, and expenses. Particular economic things and events, such as cash on hand or selling merchandise, that may meet the definitions of elements are not elements as the term is used in this Statement. Rather, they are called *items* or other descriptive names. This Statement focuses on the broad classes and their characteristics instead of defining particular assets, liabilities, or other items. Although notes to financial statements are described in some authoritative pronouncements as an integral part of financial statements, they are not elements. They serve different functions, including amplifying or complementing information about items in financial statements.[4]

6. The items that are formally incorporated in financial statements are financial representations (depictions in words and numbers) of certain resources of an entity, claims to those resources, and the effects of transactions and other events and circumstances that result in changes in those resources and claims. That is, symbols (words and numbers) in financial statements stand for cash in a bank, buildings, wages due, sales, use of labor, earthquake damage to property, and a host of other economic things and events pertaining to an entity existing and operating in what is sometimes called the "real world."

7. This Statement follows the common practice of calling by the same names both the financial representations in financial statements and the resources, claims, transactions, events, or circumstances that they represent. For example, *inventory* or *asset* may refer either to merchandise on the floor of a retail enterprise or to the words and numbers that represent that merchandise in the entity's financial statements; and *sale* or *revenue* may refer either to the transaction by which some of that merchandise is transferred to a customer or to the words and numbers that represent the transaction in the entity's financial statements.[5]

Other Scope and Content Matters

8. Appendix A of this Statement contains background information. Appendix B contains explanations and examples pertaining to the characteristics of elements of financial statements of business enterprises and not-for-profit organizations.

Objectives, Qualitative Characteristics, and Elements

9. The focus of the FASB concepts Statements that underlie this one is usefulness of financial reporting information in making economic decisions—reasoned choices among alternative uses of scarce

---

[3]Some respondents to the 1977 Exposure Draft on elements of financial statements of business enterprises (par. 157) interpreted the discussion of other possible elements to mean that financial statements now called balance sheets and income statements might have elements other than those defined. However, the other elements referred to pertain to other possible financial statements. Although this Statement contains no conclusions about the identity, number, or form of financial statements, it defines all elements for balance sheets and income statements of business enterprises in their present forms, except perhaps *earnings* (par. 1, footnote 1), and for balance sheets and statements of changes in net assets of not-for-profit organizations in their present forms.

[4]Paragraphs 5-9 of Concepts Statement 5 discuss the role of notes and their relation to financial statements.

[5]The 1977 Exposure Draft on elements of financial statements of business enterprises attempted to distinguish the representations from what they represent by giving them different names. For example, *assets* referred only to the financial representations in financial statements, and *economic resources* referred to the real-world things that assets represented in financial statements. That aspect of the Exposure Draft caused considerable confusion and was criticized by respondents. The revised Exposure Draft, *Elements of Financial Statements of Business Enterprises* (December 28, 1979), reverted to the more common practice of using the same names for both, and this Statement adopts the same usage.

resources. Concepts Statement No. 1, *Objectives of Financial Reporting by Business Enterprises,* emphasizes usefulness to present and potential investors, creditors, and others in making rational investment, credit, and similar decisions. Concepts Statement No. 4, *Objectives of Financial Reporting by Nonbusiness Organizations,* emphasizes usefulness to present and potential resource providers and others in making rational decisions about allocating resources to not-for-profit organizations.[6] Concepts Statement No. 2, *Qualitative Characteristics of Accounting Information,* emphasizes that usefulness of financial reporting information for those decisions rests on the cornerstones of relevance and reliability.

10. The definitions in this Statement are of economic things and events that are relevant to investment, credit, and other resource-allocation decisions and thus are relevant to financial reporting.[7] Those decisions involve committing (or continuing to commit) resources to an entity. The elements defined are an entity's resources, the claims to or interests in those resources, and the changes therein from transactions and other events and circumstances involved in its use of resources to produce and distribute goods or services and, if it is a business enterprise, to earn a profit. Relevance of information about items that meet those definitions stems from the significance of an entity's resources and changes in resources (including those affecting profitability).

11. Economic resources or assets and changes in them are central to the existence and operations of an individual entity. Both business enterprises and not-for-profit organizations and are in essence resource or asset processors, and a resource's capacity to be exchanged for cash or other resources or to be combined with other resources to produce needed or desired scarce goods or services gives it utility and value (future economic benefit) to an entity.

12. Business enterprises and not-for-profit organizations obtain the resources they need from various sources. Business enterprises and some not-for-profit organizations sell the goods and services they produce for cash or claims to cash. Both buy goods and services for cash or by incurring liabilities to pay cash. Business enterprises receive resources from investments in the enterprise by owners, while not-for-profit organizations commonly receive significant amounts of resources from contributors who do not expect to receive either repayment or economic benefits proportionate to resources provided. Those contributions are the major source of resources for many not-for-profit organizations but are not significant for other not-for-profit organizations or for most business enterprises.[8]

13. A not-for-profit organization obtains and uses resources to provide certain types of goods or services to members of society, and the nature of those goods or services or the identity of the groups or individuals who receive them is often critical in donors' or other resource providers' decisions to contribute or otherwise provide cash or other assets to a particular organization. Many donors provide resources to support certain types of services or for the benefit of certain groups and may stipulate how or when (or both) an organization may use the cash or other resources they contribute to it. Those donor-imposed restrictions on a not-for-profit organization's use of assets may be either permanent or temporary.

14. Resources or assets are the lifeblood of a not-for-profit organization, and an organization cannot long continue to achieve its operating objec-

---

[6]Those who make decisions about allocating resources to not-for-profit organizations include both (a) lenders, suppliers, employees, and the like who expect repayment or other direct pecuniary compensation from an entity and have essentially the same interest in and make essentially the same kinds of decisions about the entity whether it is a not-for-profit organization or a business enterprise and (b) members, contributors, donors, and the like who provide resources to not-for-profit organizations for reasons other than expectations of direct and proportionate pecuniary compensation (Concepts Statement 4, pars. 15-19, 29).

[7]Decision usefulness of information provided about those relevant economic things and events depends not only on their relevance but also on the reliability (especially representational faithfulness) of the financial representations called assets, liabilities, revenues, expenses, and so forth in financial statements. Representational faithfulness depends not only on the way the definitions are applied but also on recognition and measurement decisions that are beyond the scope of this Statement (pars. 22 and 23).

[8]Concepts Statement 4 (par. 6) lists as the distinguishing characteristics of not-for-profit organizations (a) contributions from resource providers who do not expect pecuniary return, (b) operating purposes other than to provide goods or services at a profit, and (c) absence of ownership interests like those of business enterprises. Not-for-profit organizations have those characteristics in varying degrees. "The line between nonbusiness [not-for-profit] organizations and business enterprises is not always sharp since the incidence and relative importance of those characteristics in any organization are different. . . . As happens with any distinction, there will be borderline cases. . . . especially for organizations that possess some of the distinguishing characteristics of nonbusiness [not-for-profit] organizations but not others. Some organizations have no ownership interests but are essentially self-sustaining from fees they charge for goods and services. . . . the objectives of Concepts Statement 1 may be more appropriate for those organizations" (Concepts Statement 4, pars. 7 and 8).

tives unless it can obtain at least enough resources to provide goods or services at levels and of a quality that are satisfactory to resource providers. Organizations that do not provide adequate goods or services often find it increasingly difficult to obtain the resources they need to continue operations.

15. Economic resources or assets are also the lifeblood of a business enterprise. Since resources or assets confer their benefits on an enterprise by being exchanged, used, or otherwise invested, changes in resources or assets are the purpose, the means, and the result of an enterprise's operations, and a business enterprise exists primarily to acquire, use, produce, and distribute resources. Through those activities it both provides goods or services to members of society and obtains cash and other assets with which it compensates those who provide it with resources, including its owners.

16. Although the relation between profit of an enterprise[9] and compensation received by owners is complex and often indirect, profit is the basic source of compensation to owners for providing equity or risk capital to an enterprise. Profitable operations generate resources that can be distributed to owners or reinvested in the enterprise, and investors' expectations about both distributions to owners and reinvested profit may affect market prices of the enterprise's equity securities. Expectations that owners will be adequately compensated—that they will receive returns *on* their investments commensurate with their risks—are as necessary to attract equity capital to an enterprise as are expectations of wages and salaries to attract employees' services, expectations of repayments of borrowing with interest to attract borrowed funds, or expectations of payments on account to attract raw materials or merchandise.

17. Repayment or compensation of lenders, employees, suppliers, and other nonowners for resources provided is also related to profit or loss in the sense that profitable enterprises (and those that break even) generally are able to repay borrowing with interest, pay adequate wages and salaries, and pay for other goods and services received, while unprofitable enterprises often become less and less able to pay and thus find it increasingly difficult to obtain the resources they need to continue operations. Thus, information about profit and its components is of interest to suppliers, employees, lenders, and other providers of resources as well as to owners.

18. In contrast to business enterprises, not-for-profit organizations do not have defined ownership interests that can be sold, transferred, or redeemed, or that convey entitlement to a share of a residual distribution of resources in the event of liquidation of the organization. A not-for-profit organization is required to use its resources to provide goods and services to its constituents and beneficiaries as specified in its articles of incorporation (or comparable document for an unincorporated association) or by-laws and generally is prohibited from distributing assets as dividends to its members, directors, officers, or others.[10] Thus, not-for-profit organizations have operating purposes that are other than to provide goods or services at a profit or profit equivalent, and resource providers do not focus primarily on profit as an indicator of a not-for-profit organization's performance.[11]

19. Instead, providers of resources to a not-for-profit organization are interested in the services the organization provides and its ability to continue to provide them. Since profit indicators are not the focus of their resource-allocation decisions, resource providers need other information that is useful in assessing an organization's performance during a period and in assessing how its managers have discharged their stewardship responsibilities, not only for the custody and safekeeping of the organization's resources, but also for their efficient and effective use—that is, information about the amounts and kinds of inflows and outflows of resources during a period and the relations between them and information about service efforts and, to the extent possible, service accomplishments.[12]

---

[9]*Profit* is used in this and the following paragraphs in a broad descriptive sense to refer to an enterprise's successful performance during a period. It is not intended to have a technical accounting meaning or to imply resolution of classification and display matters that are beyond the scope of this Statement, and no specific relation between *profit* and either *comprehensive income* or *earnings* (par. 1, footnote 1) is implied. *Loss* as in *profit or loss* (in contrast to *gain or loss*) is also used in a broad descriptive sense to refer to negative profit or unsuccessful performance and is not intended to have a technical accounting meaning.

[10]Some not-for-profit organizations, for example, many membership organizations, may be permitted under law to distribute assets to members upon dissolution or final liquidation. However, assets of many other not-for-profit organizations are held subject to limitations (a) permitting their use only for religious, charitable, eleemosynary, benevolent, educational, or similar purposes or (b) requiring their return to donors or their designees if the organization is dissolved. Thus, upon dissolution of a not-for-profit organization, its assets, or a significant part of them, must often be transferred to another not-for-profit organization engaged in activities substantially similar to those of the dissolving organization, to donors, or, in some cases, to other unrelated entities.

[11]Concepts Statement 4, pars. 6-9.

[12]Concepts Statement 4, pars. 9, 38, 41, and 47-53.

FASB Statement of Concepts

Interrelation of Elements—Articulation

20. Elements of financial statements are of two different types, which are sometimes explained as being analogous to photographs and motion pictures. The elements defined in this Statement include three of one type and seven of the other. (Three of the latter apply only to business enterprises.) Assets, liabilities, and equity (net assets) describe levels or amounts of resources or claims to or interests in resources at a moment in time. All other elements describe effects of transactions and other events and circumstances that affect an entity during intervals of time (periods). In a business enterprise, the second type includes comprehensive income and its components—revenues, expenses, gains, and losses—and investments by owners and distributions to owners. In a not-for-profit organization, it includes revenues, expenses, gains, and losses.[13]

21. The two types of elements are related in such a way that (a) assets, liabilities, and equity (net assets) are changed by elements of the other type and at any time are their cumulative result and (b) an increase (decrease) in an asset cannot occur without a corresponding decrease (increase) in another asset or a corresponding increase (decrease) in a liability or equity (net assets). Those relations are sometimes collectively referred to as "articulation." They result in financial statements that are fundamentally interrelated so that statements that show elements of the second type depend on statements that show elements of the first type and vice versa.[14]

Definition, Recognition, Measurement, and Display

22. All matters of recognition, measurement, and display have purposely been separated from the definitions of the elements of financial statements in the Board's conceptual framework project. The definitions in this Statement are concerned with the essential characteristics of elements of financial statements. Other phases of the conceptual framework project are concerned with questions such as which financial statements should be provided; which items that qualify under the definitions should be included in those statements; when particular items that qualify as assets, liabilities, revenues, expenses, and so forth should be formally recognized in the financial statements; which attributes of those items should be measured; which unit of measure should be used; and how the information included should be classified and otherwise displayed.[15]

23. Definitions of elements of financial statements are a significant first screen in determining the content of financial statements. An item's having the essential characteristics of one of the elements is a necessary but not a sufficient condition for formally recognizing the item in the entity's financial statements. To be included in a particular set of financial statements, an item must not only qualify under the definition of an element but also must meet criteria for recognition and have a relevant attribute (or surrogate for it) that is capable of reasonably reliable measurement or estimate.[16] Thus, some items that meet the definitions may have to be excluded from formal incorporation in financial statements because of recognition or measurement considerations (paragraphs 44-48).

DEFINITIONS OF ELEMENTS

24. All elements are defined in relation to a particular entity, which may be a business enterprise, an

---

[13]The two types can also be distinguished as financial position and changes in financial position, without meaning to imply or describe particular financial statements. Used broadly, *financial position* refers to state or status of assets or claims to assets at moments in time, and *changes in financial position* refers to flows or changes in assets or claims to assets over time. In that sense, for example, both income statements and funds statements (now commonly called statements of changes in financial position for business enterprises) show changes in financial position in present practice. Other statements, such as statements of retained earnings or analyses of property, plant, and equipment, may show aspects of both financial position at the beginning and end of a period and changes in financial position during a period. The other possible elements of financial statements referred to in paragraphs 3 and 4 also fall into this second type. That is, they are changes in financial position, describing effects of transactions and other events and circumstances that affect assets, liabilities, or equity during a period, for example, acquisitions and dispositions of assets, borrowing, and repayments of borrowing. Financial statements of not-for-profit organizations may have different names from those of business enterprises but have the same distinctions between financial position and changes in financial position.

[14]The two relations described in this paragraph are commonly expressed as (a) balance at beginning of period + changes during period = balance at end of period and (b) assets = liabilities + equity. "Double entry," the mechanism by which accrual accounting formally includes particular items that qualify under the elements definitions in articulated financial statements, incorporates those relations.

[15]FASB Concepts Statement No. 5, *Recognition and Measurement in Financial Statements of Business Enterprises,* addresses those questions for business enterprises. Those conceptual questions as they relate to not-for-profit organizations and more detailed development of those concepts for all entities may be the subject of further concepts Statements or standards.

[16]Decisions about recognizing, measuring, and displaying elements of financial statements depend significantly on evaluations such as what information is most relevant for investment, credit, and other resource-allocation decisions and whether the information is reliable enough to be trusted. Other significant evaluations of the information involve its comparability with information about other periods or other entities, its materiality, and whether the benefits from providing it exceed the costs of providing it. Those matters are discussed in Concepts Statement 2, and criteria and guidance for business enterprises based on them are set forth in Concepts Statement 5.

educational or charitable organization, a natural person, or the like. An item that qualifies under the definitions is a particular entity's asset, liability, revenue, expense, or so forth. An entity may comprise two or more affiliated entities and does not necessarily correspond to what is often described as a "legal entity." The definitions may also refer to "other entity," "other entities," or "entities other than the enterprise," which may include individuals, business enterprises, not-for-profit organizations, and the like. For example, employees, suppliers, customers or beneficiaries, lenders, stockholders, donors, and governments are all "other entities" to a particular entity. A subsidiary company that is part of the same entity as its parent company in consolidated financial statements is an "other entity" in the separate financial statements of its parent.[17]

Assets

25. Assets are probable[18] future economic benefits obtained or controlled by a particular entity as a result of past transactions or events.

Characteristics of Assets

26. An asset has three essential characteristics: (a) it embodies a probable future benefit that involves a capacity, singly or in combination with other assets, to contribute directly or indirectly to future net cash inflows, (b) a particular entity can obtain the benefit and control others' access to it, and (c) the transaction or other event giving rise to the entity's right to or control of the benefit has already occurred. Assets commonly have other features that help identify them—for example, assets may be acquired at a cost[19] and they may be tangible, exchangeable, or legally enforceable. However, those features are not essential characteristics of assets. Their absence, by itself, is not sufficient to preclude an item's qualifying as an asset. That is, assets may be acquired without cost, they may be intangible, and although not exchangeable they may be usable by the entity in

producing or distributing other goods or services. Similarly, although the ability of an entity to obtain benefit from an asset and to control others' access to it generally rests on a foundation of legal rights, legal enforceability of a claim to the benefit is not a prerequisite for a benefit to qualify as an asset if the entity has the ability to obtain and control the benefit in other ways.

27. The kinds of items that qualify as assets under the definition in paragraph 25 are also commonly called economic resources. They are the scarce means that are useful for carrying out economic activities, such as consumption, production, and exchange.

28. The common characteristic possessed by all assets (economic resources) is "service potential" or "future economic benefit," the scarce capacity to provide services or benefits to the entities that use them. In a business enterprise, that service potential or future economic benefit eventually results in net cash inflows to the enterprise. In a not-for-profit organization, that service potential or future economic benefit is used to provide desired or needed goods or services to beneficiaries or other constituents, which may or may not directly result in net cash inflows to the organization. Some not-for-profit organizations rely significantly on contributions or donations of cash to supplement selling prices or to replace cash or other assets used in providing goods or services. The relationship between service potential or future economic benefit of its assets and net cash inflows to an entity is often indirect in both business enterprises and not-for-profit organizations.

29. Money (cash, including deposits in banks) is valuable because of what it can buy. It can be exchanged for virtually any good or service that is available or it can be saved and exchanged for them in the future. Money's "command over resources"—its purchasing power—is the basis of its value and future economic benefits.[20]

---

[17]The concept of a "reporting entity" for general-purpose external financial reporting is the subject of a separate Board project that includes consolidated financial statements, the equity method, and related matters.

[18]*Probable* is used with its usual general meaning, rather than in a specific accounting or technical sense (such as that in FASB Statement No. 5, *Accounting for Contingencies,* par. 3), and refers to that which can reasonably be expected or believed on the basis of available evidence or logic but is neither certain nor proved (*Webster's New World Dictionary of the American Language,* 2d college ed. [New York: Simon and Schuster, 1982], p. 1132). Its inclusion in the definition is intended to acknowledge that business and other economic activities occur in an environment characterized by uncertainty in which few outcomes are certain (pars. 44-48).

[19]*Cost* is the sacrifice incurred in economic activities—that which is given up or forgone to consume, to save, to exchange, to produce, and so forth. For example, the value of cash or other resources given up (or the present value of an obligation incurred) in exchange for a resource measures the cost of the resource acquired. Similarly, the expiration of future benefits caused by using a resource in production is the cost of using it.

[20]Money's command over resources, or purchasing power, declines during periods of inflation and increases during periods of deflation (increases and decreases, respectively, in the level of prices in general). Since matters of measurement, including unit of measure, are beyond the scope of this Statement, it recognizes but does not emphasize that characteristic of money.

30. Assets other than cash benefit an entity by being exchanged for cash or other goods or services, by being used to produce goods or services or otherwise increase the value of other assets, or by being used to settle liabilities. To carry out their operating purposes, both business enterprises and not-for-profit organizations commonly produce scarce goods or services that have the capacity to satisfy human wants or needs. Both create utility and value in essentially the same way—by using goods or services to produce other goods or services that their customers or constituents desire or need. Business enterprises expect customers to pay for the utility and value added, and they price their outputs accordingly. Many not-for-profit organizations also distribute some or all of their outputs of goods or services at prices that include the utility and value they have added. Other not-for-profit organizations commonly distribute the goods or services they produce to beneficiaries gratis or at nominal prices. Although that may make measuring the value of their outputs difficult, it does not deprive them of value.

31. Services provided by other entities, including personal services, cannot be stored and are received and used simultaneously. They can be assets of an entity only momentarily—as the entity receives and uses them—although their use may create or add value to other assets of the entity. Rights to receive services of other entities for specified or determinable future periods can be assets of particular entities.

Transactions and Events That Change Assets

32. Assets of an entity are changed both by its transactions and activities and by events that happen to it. An entity obtains cash and other assets from other entities and transfers cash and other assets to other entities. It adds value to noncash assets through operations by using, combining, and transforming goods and services to make other desired goods or services. Some transactions or other events decrease one asset and increase another. An entity's assets or their values are also commonly increased or decreased by other events and circumstances that may be partly or entirely beyond the control of the entity and its management, for example, price changes, interest rate changes, technological changes, impositions of taxes and regulations, discovery, growth or accretion, shrinkage,

vandalism, thefts, expropriations, wars, fires, and natural disasters.

33. Once acquired, an asset continues as an asset of the entity until the entity collects it, transfers it to another entity, or uses it up, or some other event or circumstance destroys the future benefit or removes the entity's ability to obtain it.

Valuation Accounts

34. A separate item that reduces or increases the carrying amount of an asset is sometimes found in financial statements. For example, an estimate of uncollectible amounts reduces receivables to the amount expected to be collected, or a premium on a bond receivable increases the receivable to its cost or present value. Those "valuation accounts" are part of the related assets and are neither assets in their own right nor liabilities.

Liabilities

35. Liabilities are probable[21] future sacrifices of economic benefits arising from present obligations[22] of a particular entity to transfer assets or provide services to other entities in the future as a result of past transactions or events.

Characteristics of Liabilities

36. A liability has three essential characteristics: (a) it embodies a present duty or responsibility to one or more other entities that entails settlement by probable future transfer or use of assets at a specified or determinable date, on occurrence of a specified event, or on demand, (b) the duty or responsibility obligates a particular entity, leaving it little or no discretion to avoid the future sacrifice, and (c) the transaction or other event obligating the entity has already happened. Liabilities commonly have other features that help identify them—for example, most liabilities require the obligated entity to pay cash to one or more identified other entities and are legally enforceable. However, those features are not essential characteristics of liabilities. Their absence, by itself, is not sufficient to preclude an item's qualifying as a liability. That is, liabilities may not require an entity to pay cash but to convey other assets, to provide or stand ready to provide services, or to use assets. And the identity of the recipient need not be known to the obligated

---

[21]*Probable* is used with its usual general meaning, rather than in a specific accounting or technical sense (such as that in Statement 5, par. 3), and refers to that which can reasonably be expected or believed on the basis of available evidence or logic but is neither certain nor proved (*Webster's New World Dictionary,* p. 1132). Its inclusion in the definition is intended to acknowledge that business and other economic activities occur in an environment characterized by uncertainty in which few outcomes are certain (pars. 44-48).

[22]*Obligations* in the definition is broader than *legal obligations.* It is used with its usual general meaning to refer to duties imposed legally or socially; to that which one is bound to do by contract, promise, moral responsibility, and so forth (*Webster's New World Dictionary,* p. 981). It includes equitable and constructive obligations as well as legal obligations (pars. 37-40).

entity before the time of settlement. Similarly, although most liabilities rest generally on a foundation of legal rights and duties, existence of a legally enforceable claim is not a prerequisite for an obligation to qualify as a liability if for other reasons the entity has the duty or responsibility to pay cash, to transfer other assets, or to provide services to another entity.

37. Most liabilities stem from human inventions—such as financial instruments, contracts, and laws—that facilitate the functioning of a highly developed economy and are commonly embodied in legal obligations and rights (or the equivalent) with no existence apart from them. Liabilities facilitate the functioning of a highly developed economy primarily by permitting delay—delay in payment, delay in delivery, and so on.[23]

38. Entities routinely incur most liabilities to acquire the funds, goods, and services they need to operate and just as routinely settle the liabilities they incur. For example, borrowing cash obligates an entity to repay the amount borrowed, usually with interest; acquiring assets on credit obligates an entity to pay for them, perhaps with interest to compensate for the delay in payment; using employees' knowledge, skills, time, and efforts obligates an enterprise to pay for their use, often including fringe benefits; selling products with a warranty or guarantee obligates an entity to pay cash or to repair or replace those that prove defective; and accepting a cash deposit or prepayment obligates an entity to provide goods or services or to refund the cash. In short, most liabilities are incurred in exchange transactions to obtain needed resources or their use, and most liabilities incurred in exchange transactions are contractual in nature—based on written or oral agreements to pay cash or to provide goods or services to specified or determinable entities on demand, at specified or determinable dates, or on occurrence of specified events.

39. Although most liabilities result from agreements between entities, some obligations are imposed on entities by government or courts or are accepted to avoid imposition by government or courts (or costly efforts related thereto), and some relate to other nonreciprocal transfers from an entity to one or more other entities. Thus, taxes, laws, regulations, and other governmental actions commonly require business enterprises (and sometimes not-for-profit organizations) to pay cash, convey other assets, or provide services either directly to specified governmental units or to others for purposes or in ways specified by government.

An entity may also incur liabilities for donations pledged to educational or charitable organizations or for cash dividends declared but not paid.

40. Similarly, although most liabilities stem from legally enforceable obligations, some liabilities rest on equitable or constructive obligations, including some that arise in exchange transactions. Liabilities stemming from equitable or constructive obligations are commonly paid in the same way as legally binding contracts, but they lack the legal sanction that characterizes most liabilities and may be binding primarily because of social or moral sanctions or custom. An equitable obligation stems from ethical or moral constraints rather than from rules of common or statute law, that is, from a duty to another entity to do that which an ordinary conscience and sense of justice would deem fair, just, and right—to do what one ought to do rather than what one is legally required to do. For example, a business enterprise may have an equitable obligation to complete and deliver a product to a customer that has no other source of supply even though its failure to deliver would legally require only return of the customer's deposit. A constructive obligation is created, inferred, or construed from the facts in a particular situation rather than contracted by agreement with another entity or imposed by government. For example, an entity may create a constructive obligation to employees for vacation pay or year-end bonuses by paying them every year even though it is not contractually bound to do so and has not announced a policy to do so. The line between equitable or constructive obligations and obligations that are enforceable in courts of law is not always clear, and the line between equitable or constructive obligations and no obligations may often be even more troublesome because to determine whether an entity is actually bound by an obligation to a third party in the absence of legal enforceability is often extremely difficult. Thus, the concepts of equitable and constructive obligations must be applied with great care. To interpret equitable and constructive obligations too narrowly will tend to exclude significant actual obligations of an entity, while to interpret them too broadly will effectively nullify the definition by including items that lack an essential characteristic of liabilities.

Transactions and Events That Change Liabilities

41. Liabilities of an entity are changed both by its transactions and activities and by events that happen to it. The preceding paragraphs note most major sources of changes in liabilities. An entity's liabilities are also sometimes affected by price

---

[23]A common feature of liabilities is interest—the time value of money or the price of delay.

changes, interest rate changes, or other events and circumstances that may be partly or wholly beyond the control of an entity and its management.

42. Once incurred, a liability continues as a liability of the entity until the entity settles it, or another event or circumstance discharges it or removes the entity's responsibility to settle it.

Valuation Accounts

43. A separate item that reduces or increases the carrying amount of a liability is sometimes found in financial statements. For example, a bond premium or discount increases or decreases the face value of a bond payable to its proceeds or present value. Those "valuation accounts" are part of the related liability and are neither liabilities in their own right nor assets.

Effects of Uncertainty

44. Uncertainty about economic and business activities and results is pervasive, and it often clouds whether a particular item qualifies as an asset or a liability of a particular entity at the time the definitions are applied. The presence or absence of future economic benefit that can be obtained and controlled by the entity or of the entity's legal, equitable, or constructive obligation to sacrifice assets in the future can often be discerned reliably only with hindsight. As a result, some items that with hindsight actually qualified as assets or liabilities of the entity under the definitions may, as a practical matter, have been recognized as expenses, losses, revenues, or gains or remained unrecognized in its financial statements because of uncertainty about whether they qualified as assets or liabilities of the entity or because of recognition and measurement considerations stemming from uncertainty at the time of assessment. Conversely, some items that with hindsight did not qualify under the definitions may have been included as assets or liabilities because of judgments made in the face of uncertainty at the time of assessment.

45. An effect of uncertainty is to increase the costs of financial reporting in general and the costs of recognition and measurement in particular. Some items that qualify as assets or liabilities under the definitions may therefore be recognized as expenses, losses, revenues, or gains or remain unrecognized as a result of cost and benefit analyses indicating that their formal incorporation in financial statements is not useful enough to justify the time and effort needed to do it. It may be possible, for example, to make the information more re-

liable in the face of uncertainty by exerting greater effort or by spending more money, but it also may not be worth the added cost.

46. A highly significant practical consequence of the features described in the preceding two paragraphs is that the existence or amount (or both) of most assets and many liabilities can be probable but not certain.[24] The definitions in this Statement are not intended to require that the existence and amounts of items be certain for them to qualify as assets, liabilities, revenues, expenses, and so forth, and estimates and approximations will often be required unless financial statements are to be restricted to reporting only cash transactions.

47. To apply the definitions of assets and liabilities (and other elements of financial statements) thus commonly requires assessments of probabilities, but degrees of probability are not part of the definitions. That is, the degree of probability of a future economic benefit (or of a future cash outlay or other sacrifice of future economic benefits) and the degree to which its amount can be estimated with reasonable reliability that are required to recognize an item as an asset (or a liability) are matters of recognition and measurement that are beyond the scope of this Statement. The distinction needs to be maintained between the definitions themselves and steps that may be needed to apply them. Matters involving measurement problems, effects of uncertainty, reliability, and numerous other factors may be significant in applying a definition, but they are not part of the definition. Particular items that qualify as assets or liabilities under the definitions may need to be excluded from formal incorporation in financial statements for reasons relating to measurement, uncertainty, or unreliability, but they are not excluded by the definitions. Similarly, the attitude commonly known as conservatism may be appropriate in applying the definitions under uncertain conditions, but conservatism is not part of the definitions. Definition, recognition, measurement, and display are separate in the Board's conceptual framework (paragraphs 22 and 23).[25]

48. All practical financial accounting and reporting models have limitations. The preceding paragraphs describe one limit that may affect various models—how recognition or measurement considerations stemming from uncertainty may result in not recognizing as assets or liabilities some items that qualify as such under the definitions or may result in postponing recognition of some assets or liabilities until their existence becomes more probable or their measures become more reliable.

---

[24]The meaning of *probable* in these paragraphs is described in paragraph 25, footnote 18, and paragraph 35, footnote 21.

[25]The Board's Concepts Statements 2 and 5 bear directly on the matter discussed in paragraphs 44-48.

Equity or Net Assets

49. Equity or net assets is the residual interest in the assets of an entity that remains after deducting its liabilities.

Equity of Business Enterprises and Net Assets of Not-for-Profit Organizations

50. The equity or net assets[26] of both a business enterprise and a not-for-profit organization is the difference between the entity's assets and its liabilities. It is a residual, affected by all events that increase or decrease total assets by different amounts than they increase or decrease total liabilities. Thus, equity or net assets of both a business enterprise and a not-for-profit organization is increased or decreased by the entity's operations and other events and circumstances affecting the entity.

51. A major distinguishing characteristic of the equity of a business enterprise is that it may be increased through investments of assets by owners who also may, from time to time, receive distributions of assets from the entity. Owners invest in a business enterprise with the expectation of obtaining a return on their investment as a result of the enterprise's providing goods or services to customers at a profit. Owners benefit if the enterprise is profitable but bear the risk that it may be unprofitable (paragraphs 11 and 12 and 15-17).

52. In contrast, a not-for-profit organization has no ownership interest or profit purpose in the same sense as a business enterprise and thus receives no investments of assets by owners and distributes no assets to owners. Rather, its net assets often is increased by receipts of assets from resource providers (contributors, donors, grantors, and the like) who do not expect to receive either repayment or economic benefits proportionate to the assets provided[27] but who are nonetheless interested in how the organization makes use of those assets and often impose temporary or permanent restrictions on their use (paragraphs 11-13, 18, and 19).

53. Since the interests of investor-owners of business enterprises and the interests of donors to not-for-profit organizations differ, this Statement discusses separately (a) equity of business enterprises (paragraphs 60-63) and the transactions and events that change equity (paragraphs 64-89) and (b) net assets of not-for-profit organizations (paragraphs 90-106) and the transactions and events that change net assets (paragraphs 107-133).

Equity and Liabilities

54. An entity's assets, liabilities, and equity (net assets) all pertain to the same set of probable future economic benefits. Assets are probable future economic benefits owned or controlled by the entity. Its liabilities are claims to the entity's assets by other entities and, once incurred, involve nondiscretionary future sacrifices of assets that must be satisfied on demand, at a specified or determinable date, or on occurrence of a specified event. In contrast, equity is a residual interest—what remains after liabilities are deducted from assets—and depends significantly on the profitability of a business enterprise or on fund raising or other major or central operations of a not-for-profit organization. A not-for-profit organization may provide goods or services to resource providers who are also employees, members, or beneficiaries, but except upon dissolution or final liquidation of the organization, it cannot distribute assets to members or other resource providers as owners. A business enterprise may distribute assets resulting from income to its owners, but distributions to owners are discretionary, depending on the volition of owners or their representatives after considering the needs of the enterprise and restrictions imposed by law, regulation, or agreement. An enterprise is generally not obligated to transfer assets to owners except in the event of the enterprise's liquidation. An enterprise's liabilities and equity are mutually exclusive claims to or interests in the enterprise's assets by entities other than the enterprise, and liabilities take precedence over ownership interests.

55. Although the line between equity and liabilities is clear in concept, it may be obscured in practice. Applying the definitions to particular situations may involve practical problems because several kinds of securities issued by business enterprises seem to have characteristics of both liabilities and equity in varying degrees or because the names given some securities may not accurately describe their essential characteristics. For example, convertible debt instruments have both liability and residual-interest characteristics, which may create problems in accounting for them. (APB Opinion No. 14, *Accounting for Convertible Debt and Debt Issued with Stock Purchase Warrants,* and APB Opinion No. 15, *Earnings per Share,* both discuss problems of that kind.) Preferred stock also often has both debt and equity characteristics, and some preferred stocks may effectively have maturity amounts and dates at which they must be redeemed for cash.

---

[26]This Statement generally applies the term *equity* to business enterprises, which is common usage, and the term *net assets* to not-for-profit organizations, for which the term *equity* is less commonly used. The two terms are interchangeable.

[27]Since, in common use, *grants* mean not only gifts but also exchange transactions in which the *grantor* expects to receive commensurate value, this Statement generally avoids those terms.

56. Similarly, the line between net assets and liabilities of not-for-profit organizations may be obscured in practice because donors' restrictions that specify the use of contributed assets may seem to result in liabilities, although most do not. The essence of a not-for-profit organization is that it obtains and uses resources to provide specific types of goods or services, and the nature of those goods or services is often critical in donors' decisions to contribute cash or other assets to a particular organization. Most donors contribute assets (restricted as well as unrestricted) to an organization to increase its capacity to provide those goods or services, and receipt of donated assets not only increases the assets of the organization but also imposes a fiduciary responsibility on its management to use those assets effectively and efficiently in pursuit of those service objectives.

57. That responsibility pertains to all of the organization's assets and does not constitute an equitable or constructive obligation as described in paragraphs 36-40. In other words, a not-for-profit organization's fiduciary responsibility to use assets to provide services to beneficiaries does not itself create a duty of the organization to pay cash, transfer other assets, or provide services to one or more creditors. Rather, an obligation to a creditor results when the organization buys supplies for a project, its employees work on it, and the like, and the organization therefore owes suppliers, employees, and others for goods and services they have provided to it.[28]

58. A donor's restriction focuses that fiduciary responsibility on a stipulated use for specified contributed assets but does not change the basic nature of the organization's fiduciary responsibility to use its assets to provide services to beneficiaries. A donor's gift of cash to be spent for a stipulated purpose or of another asset to be used for a stipulated purpose—for example, a mansion to be used as a museum, a house to be used as a dormitory, or a sculpture to be displayed in a cemetery—imposes a responsibility to spend the cash or use the asset in accordance with the donor's instructions. In its effect on the liabilities of the organization, a donor's restriction is essentially the same as management's designating a specified use for certain assets. That is, the responsibility imposed by earmarking assets for specified uses is fundamentally different, both economically and legally, from the responsibility imposed by incurring a liability, which involves a creditor's claim. Consequently, most donor-imposed restrictions on an organization's use of contributed assets do not create obligations that qualify as liabilities of the organization.

59. To determine whether liabilities or equity (net assets) result from issuing specific securities with both debt and equity characteristics or from specific donors' stipulations presents practical problems of applying definitions rather than problems of determining the essential characteristics of those definitions. Adequate definitions are the starting point. They provide a basis for assessing, for example, the extent to which a particular application meets the qualitative characteristic of representational faithfulness, which includes the notion of reporting economic substance rather than legal form (Concepts Statement 2, paragraphs 63-80 and 160).

Equity of Business Enterprises

Characteristics of Equity of Business Enterprises

60. In a business enterprise, the equity is the ownership interest.[29] It stems from ownership rights (or the equivalent)[30] and involves a relation between an enterprise and its owners *as owners* rather

---

[28]Most liabilities are legally enforceable, and the concepts of equitable and constructive obligations have a relatively narrow area of application. To assess all or most donor-restricted contributions to not-for-profit organizations as having the essential characteristics of liabilities is too broad an interpretation of the definition of liabilities. A not-for-profit organization's need to acquire goods and services to provide services to beneficiaries in the future, or to expand to provide new services, is analogous to a business enterprise's need to replace merchandise sold or raw materials or equipment used up (paragraph 200), or to buy new assets, not to its liability to provide magazines to customers who have paid in advance.

[29]This Statement defines equity of business enterprises only as a whole, although the discussion notes that different owners of an enterprise may have different kinds of ownership rights and that equity has various sources. In financial statements of business enterprises, various distinctions *within* equity, such as those between common stockholders' equity and preferred stockholders' equity, between contributed capital and earned capital, or between stated or legal capital and other equity, are primarily matters of display that are beyond the scope of this Statement.

[30]Other entities with proprietary or ownership interests in a business enterprise are commonly known by specialized names, such as stockholders, partners, and proprietors, and by more general names, such as investors, but all are also covered by the descriptive term *owners*. Equity of business enterprises is thus commonly known by several names, such as owners' equity, stockholders' equity, ownership, equity capital, partners' capital, and proprietorship. Some enterprises (for example, mutual organizations) do not have stockholders, partners, or proprietors in the usual sense of those terms but do have participants whose interests are essentially ownership interests, residual interests, or both.

than as employees, suppliers, customers, lenders, or in some other nonowner role.[31] Since equity ranks after liabilities as a claim to or interest in the assets of the enterprise, it is a residual interest: (a) equity is the same as net assets, the difference between the enterprise's assets and its liabilities, and (b) equity is enhanced or burdened by increases and decreases in net assets from nonowner sources as well as investments by owners and distributions to owners.

61. Equity sets limits, often legal limits, on distributions by an enterprise to its owners, whether in the form of cash dividends or other distributions of assets. Owners' and others' expectations about distributions to owners may affect the market prices of an enterprise's equity securities, thereby indirectly affecting owners' compensation for providing equity or risk capital to the enterprise (paragraph 16). Thus, the essential characteristics of equity center on the conditions for transferring enterprise assets to owners. Equity—an excess of assets over liabilities—is a necessary but not sufficient condition; distributions to owners are at the discretion and volition of the owners or their representatives after satisfying restrictions imposed by law, regulation, or agreements with other entities. Generally, an enterprise is not obligated to transfer assets to owners except in the event of the enterprise's liquidation unless the enterprise formally acts to distribute assets to owners, for example, by declaring a dividend.[32] Owners may sell their interests in an enterprise to others and thus may be able to obtain a return *of* part or all of their investments and perhaps a return *on* investments through a securities market, but those transactions do not normally affect the equity of an enterprise or its assets or liabilities.

62. An enterprise may have several classes of equity (for example, one or more classes each of common stock or preferred stock) with different degrees of risk stemming from different rights to participate in distributions of enterprise assets or different priorities of claims on enterprise assets in the event of liquidation. That is, some classes of owners may bear relatively more of the risks of an enterprise's unprofitability or may benefit relatively more from its profitability (or both) than other classes of owners. However, all classes depend at least to some extent on enterprise profitability for distributions of enterprise assets, and no class of equity carries an unconditional right to receive future transfers of assets from the enterprise except in liquidation, and then only after liabilities have been satisfied.

63. Equity is originally created by owners' investments in an enterprise and may from time to time be augmented by additional investments by owners. Equity is reduced by distributions by the enterprise to owners. However, the distinguishing characteristic of equity is that it inevitably is affected by the enterprise's operations and other events and circumstances affecting the enterprise (which together constitute comprehensive income—paragraph 70).

Transactions and Events That Change Equity of Business Enterprises

64. The diagram on the next page shows the sources of changes in equity (class B) and distinguishes them from each other and from other transactions, events, and circumstances affecting an entity during a period (classes A and C). Specifically, the diagram shows that (a) class B (changes in equity) comprises two mutually exclusive classes of transactions and other events and circumstances, B1 and B2, each of which has significant subclasses, and (b) classes B1, B2, and A are the sources of all increases and decreases in assets and liabilities of an enterprise; class C includes no changes in assets or liabilities. In the diagram, dashed lines rather than solid boundary lines separate revenues and gains and separate expenses and losses because of display considerations that are beyond the scope of this Statement. Paragraphs 78-89 of this Statement define and discuss revenues, expenses, gains, and losses as elements of financial statements but do not precisely distinguish between revenues and gains on the one hand or between expenses and losses on the other. Fine distinctions between revenues and gains and between expenses and losses, as well as other distinctions *within* comprehensive income, are more appropriately considered as part of display or reporting.

---

[31]Distinctions between liabilities and equity generally depend on the nature of the claim rather than on the identity of the claimant. The same entities may simultaneously be both owners and employees, owners and creditors, owners and customers, creditors and customers, or some other combination. For example, an investor may hold both debt and equity securities of the same enterprise, or an owner of an enterprise may also become its creditor by lending to it or by receiving rights to unpaid cash dividends that it declares. Wages due, products or services due, accounts payable due, and other amounts due to owners in their roles as employees, customers, suppliers, and the like are liabilities, not part of equity. Exceptions involve situations in which relationships between the parties cast doubts that they are liabilities in substance rather than investments by owners.

[32]A controlling interest or an interest that confers an ability to exercise significant influence over the operations of an enterprise may have more potential than other ownership interests to control or affect assets of the enterprise or distributions of assets to owners. Procedures such as consolidated financial statements and the equity method of accounting for intercorporate investments have been developed to account for the rights and relations involved.

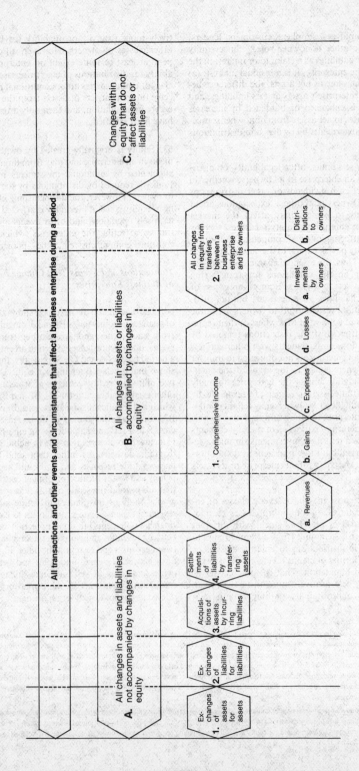

All transactions and other events and circumstances that affect a business enterprise during a period

C. Changes within equity that do not affect assets or liabilities

B. All changes in assets or liabilities accompanied by changes in equity

  2. All changes in equity from transfers between a business enterprise and its owners

    a. Investments by owners

    b. Distributions to owners

  1. Comprehensive income

    a. Revenues

    b. Gains

    c. Expenses

    d. Losses

A. All changes in assets and liabilities not accompanied by changes in equity

  1. Exchanges of assets for assets

  2. Exchanges of liabilities for liabilities

  3. Acquisitions of assets by incurring liabilities

  4. Settlements of liabilities by transferring assets

65. The full width of the diagram, represented by the two-pointed arrow labeled "All transactions and other events and circumstances that affect a business enterprise during a period," encompasses all potentially recordable events and circumstances affecting an entity. Moving from top to bottom of the diagram, each level divides the preceding level into classes that are significant for the definitions and related concepts in this Statement. (Size of classes does not indicate their relative volume or significance.)[33]

A. All changes in assets and liabilities not accompanied by changes in equity. This class comprises four kinds of exchange transactions that are common in most entities. (Exchanges that affect equity belong in class B rather than class A.)
  1. Exchanges of assets for assets, for example, purchases of assets for cash or barter exchanges
  2. Exchanges of liabilities for liabilities, for example, issues of notes payable to settle accounts payable or refundings of bonds payable by issuing new bonds to holders that surrender outstanding bonds
  3. Acquisitions of assets by incurring liabilities, for example, purchases of assets on account, borrowings, or receipts of cash advances for goods or services to be provided in the future
  4. Settlements of liabilities by transferring assets, for example, repayments of borrowing, payments to suppliers on account, payments of accrued wages or salaries, or repairs (or payments for repairs) required by warranties

B. All changes in assets or liabilities accompanied by changes in equity. This class is the subject of this section and comprises:
  1. Comprehensive income (defined in paragraph 70) whose components (broadly defined and discussed in paragraphs 78-89) are:
    a. Revenues
    b. Gains
    c. Expenses
    d. Losses

  2. All changes in equity from transfers between a business enterprise and its owners (defined in paragraphs 66 and 67):
    a. Investments by owners in the enterprise
    b. Distributions by the enterprise to owners

C. Changes within equity that do not affect assets or liabilities (for example, stock dividends, conversions of preferred stock into common stock, and some stock recapitalizations). This class contains only changes *within* equity and does not affect the definition of equity or its amount.

The definitions in paragraphs 70-89 are those in class B1—comprehensive income—and its subclasses—revenues, expenses, gains, and losses.[34]

Investments by and Distributions to Owners

66. Investments by owners are increases in equity of a particular business enterprise resulting from transfers to it from other entities of something valuable to obtain or increase ownership interests (or equity) in it. Assets are most commonly received as investments by owners, but that which is received may also include services or satisfaction or conversion of liabilities of the enterprise.

67. Distributions to owners are decreases in equity of a particular business enterprise resulting from transferring assets, rendering services, or incurring liabilities by the enterprise to owners. Distributions to owners decrease ownership interest (or equity) in an enterprise.[35]

Characteristics of Investments by and Distributions to Owners

68. Investments by owners and distributions to owners are transactions between an enterprise and its owners *as owners*. Through investments by owners, an enterprise obtains resources it needs to begin or expand operations, to retire debt securities or other liabilities, or for other business purposes; as a result of investing resources in the enterprise, other entities obtain ownership interests in the enterprise or increase ownership interests they already have.

---

[33]The diagram reflects the concept that value added by productive activities increases assets as production takes place, which is the basis for the common observation that revenues are *earned* by the entire process of acquiring goods and services, using them to produce other goods or services, selling the output, and collecting the sales price or fee. However, that value added is commonly *recognized* after production is complete, usually when product is delivered or sold but sometimes when cash is received or product is completed. The diagram does not, of course, settle recognition issues.

[34]The definitions of revenues, expenses, gains, and losses in paragraphs 78-89 also apply to the changes in net assets of not-for-profit organizations as discussed in paragraphs 107-113.

[35]Investments by owners are sometimes called capital contributions. Distributions to owners are sometimes called capital distributions; distributions of earnings, profits, or income; or dividends.

Not all investments in the equity securities of an enterprise by other entities are investments by owners as that concept is defined in this Statement. In an investment by owners, the enterprise that issues the securities acquired by an owner always receives the proceeds or their benefits; its net assets increase. If the purchaser of equity securities becomes an owner or increases its ownership interest in an enterprise by purchasing those securities from another owner that is decreasing or terminating its ownership interest, the transfer does not affect the net assets of the enterprise.

69. Distributions by an enterprise to its owners decrease its net assets and decrease or terminate ownership interests of those that receive them. Reacquisition by an entity of its own equity securities by transferring assets or incurring liabilities to owners is a distribution to owners as that concept is defined in this Statement. Since owners become creditors for a dividend declared until it is paid, an enterprise's incurrence of a liability to transfer assets to owners in the future converts a part of the equity or ownership interest of the enterprise into creditors' claims; settlement of the liability by transfer of the assets is a transaction in class A4 in the diagram in paragraph 64 rather than in class B2(b). That is, equity is reduced by the incurrence of the liability to owners, not by its settlement.

Comprehensive Income of Business Enterprises

70. Comprehensive income is the change in equity of a business enterprise during a period from transactions and other events and circumstances from nonowner sources. It includes all changes in equity during a period except those resulting from investments by owners and distributions to owners.

Concepts of Capital Maintenance

71. A concept of maintenance of capital or recovery of cost is a prerequisite for separating return *on* capital from return *of* capital because only inflows in excess of the amount needed to maintain capital are a return *on* equity. Two major concepts of capital maintenance exist, both of which can be measured in units of either money or constant purchas-

ing power: the financial capital concept and the physical capital concept (which is often expressed in terms of maintaining operating capability, that is, maintaining the capacity of an enterprise to provide a constant supply of goods or services). The major difference between them involves the effects of price changes on assets held and liabilities owed during a period. Under the financial capital concept, if the effects of those price changes are recognized, they are called "holding gains and losses" and are included in return on capital. Under the physical capital concept, those changes would be recognized but called "capital maintenance adjustments" and would be included directly in equity and would not be included in return on capital. Under that concept, capital maintenance adjustments would be a separate element rather than gains and losses.

72. The financial capital concept is the traditional view and is generally the capital maintenance concept in present primary financial statements. Comprehensive income as defined in paragraph 70 is a return *on* financial capital.[36]

Characteristics, Sources, and Components of Comprehensive Income

73. Over the life of a business enterprise, its comprehensive income equals the net of its cash receipts and cash outlays, excluding cash (and cash equivalent of noncash assets) invested by owners and distributed to owners (Concepts Statement 1, paragraph 46). That characteristic holds whether the amounts of cash and comprehensive income are measured in nominal dollars or constant dollars. Although the amounts in constant dollars may differ from those in nominal dollars, the basic relationship is not changed because both nominal and constant dollars express the same thing using different measuring units. Matters such as recognition criteria and choice of attributes to be measured[37] also do not affect the amounts of comprehensive income and net cash receipts over the life of an enterprise but do affect the time and way parts of the total are identified with the periods that constitute the entire life. Timing of recognition of revenues, expenses, gains, and losses is also a major difference between accounting

---

[36]Concepts Statement 5, paragraphs 45-48 adopted financial capital maintenance as the concept on which the full set of articulated financial statements it discusses is based.

[37]"'Attributes to be measured' refers to the traits or aspects of an element to be quantified or measured, such as historical cost/historical proceeds, current cost/current proceeds, etc. Attribute is a narrower concept than measurement, which includes not only identifying the attribute to be measured but also selecting a scale of measurement (for example, units of money or units of constant purchasing power). 'Property' is commonly used in sciences to describe the trait or aspect of an object being measured, such as the length of a table or the weight of a stone. But 'property' may be confused with land and buildings in financial reporting contexts, and 'attribute' has become common in accounting literature and is used in this Statement" (Concepts Statement 1, par. 2, footnote 2). The choice of measurement attribute, measurement unit, and recognition criteria are discussed in Concepts Statement 5.

based on cash receipts and outlays and accrual accounting. Accrual accounting may encompass various timing possibilities—for example, when goods or services are provided, when cash is received, or when prices change.

74. Comprehensive income of a business enterprise results from (a) exchange transactions and other transfers between the enterprise and other entities that are not its owners, (b) the enterprise's productive efforts,[38] and (c) price changes, casualties, and other effects of interactions between the enterprise and the economic, legal, social, political, and physical environment of which it is part. An enterprise's productive efforts and most of its exchange transactions with other entities are ongoing major activities that constitute the enterprise's central operations by which it attempts to fulfill its basic function in the economy of producing and distributing goods or services at prices that are sufficient to enable it to pay for the goods and services it uses and to provide a satisfactory return to its owners.

75. Comprehensive income is a broad concept. Although an enterprise's ongoing major or central operations are generally intended to be the primary source of comprehensive income, they are not the only source. Most entities occasionally engage in activities that are peripheral or incidental to their central activities. Moreover, all entities are affected by the economic, legal, social, political, and physical environment of which they are part, and comprehensive income of each enterprise is affected by events and circumstances that may be partly or wholly beyond the control of individual enterprises and their managements.

76. Although cash resulting from various sources of comprehensive income is the same, receipts from various sources may vary in stability, risk, and predictability. That is, characteristics of various sources of comprehensive income may differ significantly from one another, indicating a need for information about various components of comprehensive income. That need underlies the distinctions between revenues and gains, between expenses and losses, between various kinds of gains and losses, and between measures found in present practice such as income from continuing operations and income after extraordinary item and cumulative effect of change in accounting principle.

77. Comprehensive income comprises two related but distinguishable types of components. It consists of not only its basic components—revenues, expenses, gains, and losses—but also various intermediate components that result from combining the basic components. Revenues, expenses, gains, and losses can be combined in various ways to obtain several measures of enterprise performance with varying degrees of inclusiveness. Examples of intermediate components in business enterprises are gross margin, income from continuing operations before taxes, income from continuing operations, and operating income. Those intermediate components are, in effect, subtotals of comprehensive income and often of one another in the sense that they can be combined with each other or with the basic components to obtain other intermediate measures of comprehensive income.[39]

Revenues

78. Revenues are inflows or other enhancements of assets of an entity or settlements of its liabilities (or a combination of both) from delivering or producing goods, rendering services, or other activities that constitute the entity's ongoing major or central operations.

Characteristics of Revenues

79. Revenues represent actual or expected cash inflows (or the equivalent) that have occurred or will eventuate as a result of the entity's ongoing major or central operations. The assets increased by reve-

---

[38]An enterprise increases the values of goods or services it holds or acquires by adding time, place, or form utility. Thus, *productive efforts* and *producing and distributing activities* include not only manufacturing and other conversion processes but also other productive activities such as storing, transporting, lending, insuring, and providing professional services that might be overlooked if *producing* were narrowly equated with *manufacturing*.

[39]*Earnings* as adopted in Concepts Statement 5 and its relation to comprehensive income is discussed in paragraph 1, footnote 1.

nues[40] may be of various kinds—for example, cash, claims against customers or clients, other goods or services received, or increased value of a product resulting from production. Similarly, the transactions and events from which revenues arise and the revenues themselves are in many forms and are called by various names—for example, output, deliveries, sales, fees, interest, dividends, royalties, and rent—depending on the kinds of operations involved and the way revenues are recognized.[41]

Expenses

80. Expenses are outflows or other using up of assets or incurrences of liabilities (or a combination of both) from delivering or producing goods,[42] rendering services, or carrying out other activities that constitute the entity's ongoing major or central operations.

Characteristics of Expenses

81. Expenses represent actual or expected cash outflows (or the equivalent) that have occurred or will eventuate as a result of the entity's ongoing major or central operations. The assets that flow out or are used or the liabilities that are incurred[43] may be of various kinds—for example, units of product delivered or produced, employees' services used, kilowatt hours of electricity used to light an office building, or taxes on current income. Similarly, the transactions and events from which ex-

penses arise and the expenses themselves are in many forms and are called by various names—for example, cost of goods sold, cost of services provided, depreciation, interest, rent, and salaries and wages—depending on the kinds of operations involved and the way expenses are recognized.

Gains and Losses

82. Gains are increases in equity (net assets) from peripheral or incidental transactions of an entity and from all other transactions and other events and circumstances affecting the entity except those that result from revenues or investments by owners.

83. Losses are decreases in equity (net assets) from peripheral or incidental transactions of an entity and from all other transactions and other events and circumstances affecting the entity except those that result from expenses or distributions to owners.

Characteristics of Gains and Losses

84. Gains and losses result from entities' peripheral or incidental transactions and from other events and circumstances stemming from the environment that may be largely beyond the control of individual entities and their managements. Thus, gains and losses are not all alike. There are several kinds, even in a single entity, and they may be described or classified in a variety of ways that are not necessarily mutually exclusive.

---

[40]In concept, revenues increase assets rather than decrease liabilities, but a convenient shortcut is often to directly record reduction of liabilities. Production is essentially an asset conversion process to create future economic benefit (par. 30; par. 65, footnote 33; and par. 74, footnote 38). It adds utility and value to assets and is the primary source of revenue, which may be recognized (as noted in footnote 41) when product is delivered, when cash is received, or when production is completed rather than as production takes place. Production does not directly incur or settle liabilities but is often closely related to exchange transactions in which liabilities are incurred or settled. Entities acquire assets (economic benefits), not expenses or losses, to carry out their production operations, and most expenses are at least momentarily assets. Since many goods and services acquired are used either simultaneously with acquisition or soon thereafter, it is common practice to record them as expenses at acquisition. However, to record an expense as resulting from incurring a liability is a useful shortcut that combines two conceptually separate events: (a) an exchange transaction in which an asset was acquired and (b) an internal event (production) in which an asset was used up. The assets produced by operations may be used to settle liabilities (for example, by delivering product that has been paid for in advance). However, again, to record a liability as being directly reduced by recording revenue is a useful shortcut that combines two conceptually separate events: (a) an internal event (production) that resulted in an asset and revenue and (b) an exchange transaction in which the asset was transferred to another entity to satisfy a liability. In the diagram in paragraph 64, the exchange transactions are in class A, while the internal events (production) that result in revenues or expenses are in class B1.

[41]Timing of recognition of revenues—including existing recognition procedures, which usually recognize revenues when goods are delivered or services are performed but may sometimes recognize them when cash is received, when production is completed, or as production progresses—is a subject of Concepts Statement 5. This Statement contains no conclusions about recognition of revenues or of any other elements.

[42]If manufactured products are accounted for at accumulated costs until sold, as is common in present practice, production costs are recognized as expenses in the periods in which product is sold rather than in periods in which assets are used to produce output. For example, use of raw materials and depreciation of factory machinery are included in the cost of product and are recognized as expenses as part of the cost of goods sold. In contrast, if products are accounted for at net realizable value using a percentage-of-completion method, as output under construction contracts often is, production costs such as raw materials used and depreciation of construction equipment are recognized as expenses in the periods in which the assets are used to produce output.

[43]In concept, most expenses decrease assets rather than increase liabilities. They involve using (sacrificing) goods or services, not acquiring them. However, acquisition and use of many goods or services may occur simultaneously or during the same period, and a convenient shortcut is often to record directly increases of liabilities (par. 79, footnote 40). Taxes and other expenses resulting from nonreciprocal transfers to other entities commonly do result directly from incurring liabilities.

85. Gains and losses may be described or classified according to sources. Some gains or losses are net results of comparing the proceeds and sacrifices (costs) in peripheral or incidental transactions with other entities—for example, from sales of investments in marketable securities, from dispositions of used equipment, or from settlements of liabilities at other than their carrying amounts. Other gains or losses result from nonreciprocal transfers between an entity and other entities that are not its owners—for example, from gifts or donations,[44] from winning a lawsuit, from thefts, and from assessments of fines or damages by courts. Still other gains or losses result from holding assets or liabilities while their values change—for example, from price changes that cause inventory items to be written down from cost to market, from changes in market prices of investments in marketable equity securities accounted for at market values or at the lower of cost and market, and from changes in foreign exchange rates. And still other gains or losses result from other environmental factors, such as natural catastrophes—for example, damage to or destruction of property by earthquake or flood.

86. Gains and losses may also be described or classified as "operating" or "nonoperating," depending on their relation to an entity's major ongoing or central operations. For example, losses on writing down inventory from cost to market are usually considered to be operating losses, while major casualty losses are usually considered nonoperating losses.

Revenues, Expenses, Gains, and Losses

87. Revenues and gains are similar, and expenses and losses are similar, but some differences are significant in conveying information about an enterprise's performance. Revenues and expenses result from an entity's ongoing major or central operations and activities—that is, from activities such as producing or delivering goods, rendering services, lending, insuring, investing, and financing. In contrast, gains and losses result from incidental or peripheral transactions of an enterprise with other entities and from other events and circumstances affecting it. Some gains and losses may be considered "operating" gains and losses and may be closely related to revenues and expenses. Revenues and expenses are commonly displayed as gross inflows or outflows of net assets, while gains and losses are usually displayed as net inflows or outflows.

88. The definitions and discussion of revenues, expenses, gains, and losses in this Statement give broad guidance but do not distinguish precisely between revenues and gains or between expenses and losses. Distinctions between revenues and gains and between expenses and losses in a particular entity depend to a significant extent on the nature of the entity, its operations, and its other activities. Items that are revenues for one kind of entity may be gains for another, and items that are expenses for one kind of entity may be losses for another. For example, investments in securities that may be sources of revenues and expenses for insurance or investment companies may be sources of gains and losses in manufacturing or merchandising companies. Technological changes may be sources of gains or losses for most kinds of enterprises but may be characteristic of the operations of high-technology or research-oriented enterprises. Events such as commodity price changes and foreign exchange rate changes that occur while assets are being used or produced or liabilities are owed may directly or indirectly affect the *amounts* of revenues or expenses for most enterprises, but they are *sources* of revenues or expenses only for enterprises for which trading in foreign exchange or commodities is a major or central activity.

89. Since a primary purpose of distinguishing gains and losses from revenues and expenses is to make displays of information about an enterprise's sources of comprehensive income as useful as possible, fine distinctions between revenues and gains and between expenses and losses are principally matters of display or reporting (paragraphs 64, 219 and 220, and 228).

Net Assets of Not-for-Profit Organizations

Characteristics of Net Assets of Not-for-Profit Organizations

90. In a not-for-profit organization, as in a business enterprise, net assets (equity) is a residual, the difference between the entity's assets and its liabilities but, in contrast to equity of a business enterprise, it is not an ownership interest. Distinguishing characteristics of a not-for-profit organization include absence of ownership interest(s) in the same sense as a business enterprise, operating purposes not centered on profit, and significant receipts of contributions, many involving donor-imposed restrictions (paragraphs 11-15, 18 and 19, and 49-53).

---

[44]Gifts or donations received by not-for-profit organizations may be revenues or gains (pars. 111-113).

91. Net assets of not-for-profit organizations is divided into three mutually exclusive classes, permanently restricted net assets, temporarily restricted net assets, and unrestricted net assets.[45]

Classes of Net Assets

92. Permanently restricted net assets is the part of the net assets of a not-for-profit organization resulting (a) from contributions and other inflows of assets whose use by the organization is limited by donor-imposed stipulations that neither expire by passage of time nor can be fulfilled or otherwise removed by actions of the organization, (b) from other asset enhancements and diminishments subject to the same kinds of stipulations, and (c) from reclassifications from (or to) other classes of net assets as a consequence of donor-imposed stipulations.

93. Temporarily restricted net assets is the part of the net assets of a not-for-profit organization resulting (a) from contributions and other inflows of assets whose use by the organization is limited by donor-imposed stipulations that either expire by passage of time or can be fulfilled and removed by actions of the organization pursuant to those stipulations, (b) from other asset enhancements and diminishments subject to the same kinds of stipulations, and (c) from reclassifications to (or from) other classes of net assets as a consequence of donor-imposed stipulations, their expiration by passage of time, or their fulfillment and removal by actions of the organization pursuant to those stipulations.

94. Unrestricted net assets is the part of net assets of a not-for-profit organization that is neither permanently restricted nor temporarily restricted by donor-imposed stipulations—that is, the part of net assets resulting (a) from all revenues, expenses, gains, and losses that are not changes in permanently or temporarily restricted net assets and (b) from reclassifications from (or to) other classes of net assets as a consequence of donor-imposed stipulations, their expiration by passage of time, or their fulfillment and removal by actions of the organization pursuant to those stipulations. The only limits on unrestricted net assets are broad limits resulting from the nature of the organization and the purposes specified in its articles of incorporation (or comparable document for an unincorporated association) or bylaws and perhaps limits resulting

from contractual agreements—for example, loan covenants—entered into by the organization in the course of its operations.

Donor-imposed restrictions

95. The three classes of net assets reflect differences in, or absence of, donor-imposed restrictions on a not-for-profit organization's use of its assets. Thus, *restriction* and *restricted* in this Statement refer to limits placed on a not-for-profit organization's use of assets by donors' stipulations that are more specific than broad limits resulting from the nature of the organization and the purposes specified in its articles of incorporation (or comparable document for an unincorporated association) or bylaws. Restrictions generally do not create liabilities (paragraphs 56-58), but they do restrain the organization from using part of its resources for purposes other than those specified, for example, to settle liabilities, purchase goods, or provide services not within the scope of the restrictions.

96. Donors need not explicitly limit uses of contributed assets for a not-for-profit organization to classify the increase in net assets as restricted if circumstances surrounding those receipts make clear the donor's implicit stipulation of restricted use. For example, use of contributed assets is restricted despite absence of a donor's explicit stipulation about use if the assets are received in a fund-raising drive declared to be for a specific purpose, such as to add to the organization's endowment, to acquire a particular property, or to obtain resources for next year's operations.

97. Only donors' explicit, or clearly evident implicit, stipulations that limit a not-for-profit organization's use of its assets can result in permanently or temporarily restricted net assets (as this Statement uses those terms). Decisions, resolutions, appropriations, or the like by the directors, trustees, or managers of a not-for-profit organization may impose seemingly similar limits on the use of net assets that were not stipulated by donors. However, unless limits are imposed by donors' stipulations that place them beyond the organization's discretion to change, they differ substantively from donor-imposed limits that result in restricted net assets. For example, a voluntary resolution by the trustees of an organization to earmark a portion of its unrestricted net assets to function as an endow-

---

[45]This Statement does not use the terms *funds* and *fund balances* because the most common meanings of those terms refer respectively to a common group of assets and related liabilities within a not-for-profit organization and to the net amount of those assets and liabilities. This Statement classifies net assets, not assets or liabilities. While some not-for-profit organizations may choose to classify assets and liabilities into fund groups, information about those groupings is not a necessary part of general purpose external financial reporting. Issues that affect how, if at all, classifications of assets and liabilities may be displayed in financial statements, for example, by using multicolumn presentations or disclosure in the notes, are outside the scope of this Statement and may be the subject of future Board projects.

ment is a revocable internal designation that does not give rise to restricted net assets.[46] Only in the relatively few instances in which self-imposed limits become legally irrevocable are they substantively equivalent to donor-imposed restrictions and the cause of restricted net assets.

Temporary and permanent restrictions

98. Contributions (or other enhancements) of assets with donor-imposed limits on their use increase assets and net assets of a not-for-profit organization in the period in which it receives them, but they do not increase unrestricted net assets, nor are they generally available for payment to creditors, as long as the restriction remains. Donor-imposed restrictions on use of assets may be either temporary or permanent.[47]

99. Some donors stipulate that their contributions be used in a later period or after a specified date rather than be expended immediately; those are often called time restrictions. Other donors stipulate that their contributions be used for a specified purpose, such as sponsoring a particular program or service, acquiring a particular building, or settling a particular liability; those are often called purpose restrictions. Time and purpose restrictions have in common that they can be satisfied, either by passage of time or by actions of the organization, and that the contributed assets can be expended. Those restrictions are temporary. Once the stipulation is satisfied, the restriction is gone.

100. Still other donors stipulate that resources be maintained permanently—not used up, expended, or otherwise exhausted—but permit the organization to use up or expend the income (or other economic benefits) derived from the donated assets. That type of restricted gift is often called an endowment. The restriction lasts in effect forever. It cannot be removed by actions of the organization or passage of time. The donations do not increase the organization's unrestricted net assets in any period, and the donated assets are not available for payment to creditors.

Restrictions affect net assets rather than particular assets

101. Restrictions impose responsibilities on management to ensure that the organization uses donated resources in the manner stipulated by resource providers. Sometimes donor-imposed restrictions limit an organization's ability to sell or exchange the particular asset received. For example, a donor may give a painting to a museum stipulating that it must be publicly displayed, properly maintained, and never sold.

102. More commonly, donors' stipulations permit the organization to pool the donated assets with other assets and to sell or exchange the donated assets for other suitable assets as long as the economic benefits of the donated assets are not consumed or used for a purpose that does not comply with the stipulation. For example, a donor may contribute 100 shares of Security A to an organization's endowment, thereby requiring that the amount of the gift be retained permanently but not requiring that the specific shares be held indefinitely. Thus, permanently restricted net assets and temporarily restricted net assets generally refer to amounts of net assets that are restricted by donor-imposed limits, not to specific assets.

Maintenance of Net Assets

103. Although not-for-profit organizations do not have ownership interests or profit in the same sense as business enterprises, they nonetheless need a concept of capital maintenance or its equivalent to reflect "the relation between inflows and outflows of resources during a period."[48] The activities of an organization during a period may draw upon resources received in past periods or may add resources that can be used in future periods.

104. Unless a not-for-profit organization maintains its net assets, its ability to continue to provide services dwindles; either future resource providers must make up the deficiency or services to future beneficiaries will decline. For example, use of an asset such as a building to provide goods or serv-

---

[46]However, the nature and amounts of self-imposed limits on use of assets and of limits imposed by others as a condition of operating activities (for example, by debt covenants or other arrangements) may be significant information for financial statement users and may need to be disclosed.

[47]This Statement makes distinctions among resource flows based on the presence or absence of donor-imposed restrictions on their use. In the past, other distinctions have been made, for example, between "nonoperating" and "operating," "nonexpendable" and "expendable," "noncapital" and "capital," and "restricted" and "unrestricted." Those terms have been used by not-for-profit organizations in practice to name groups of resource flows that, while similar in many respects, have differed in important details.

[48]FASB Concepts Statement 4, par. 49. The Statement also says, "A nonbusiness [not-for-profit] organization cannot, in the long run, continue to achieve its operating objectives unless the resources made available to it at least equal the resources needed to provide services at levels satisfactory to resource providers and other constituents" (par. 39).

ices to beneficiaries consumes part of the future economic benefits or service potential constituting the asset, and that decrease in future economic benefits is one of the costs (expenses) of using the asset for that purpose.[49] The organization's net assets decrease as it uses up an asset unless its revenues and gains at least equal its expenses and losses, including the cost of consuming part of the asset during the period (depreciation). Even if that organization plans to replace the asset through future contributions from donors, and probably will be able to do so, it has not maintained its net assets during the current period.

105. Maintenance of net assets in not-for-profit organizations, as in business enterprises (paragraph 72), is based on the maintenance of financial capital—that is, a not-for-profit organization's capital has been maintained if the financial (money) amount of its net assets at the end of a period equals or exceeds the financial amount of its net assets at the beginning of the period.

106. Since donor-imposed restrictions affect the types and levels of service a not-for-profit organization can provide, whether an organization has maintained certain classes of net assets may be more significant than whether it has maintained net assets in the aggregate. For example, if net assets were maintained in a period only because permanently restricted endowment contributions made up for a decline in unrestricted net assets, information focusing on the aggregate change might obscure the fact that the organization had not maintained the part of its net assets that is fully available to support services in the next period.

Transactions and Events That Change Net Assets of Not-for-Profit Organizations

107. The diagram on the next page shows the sources of changes in the amount of or the restrictions on a not-for-profit organization's net assets and distinguishes them from each other and from other transactions, events, and circumstances affecting the organization during a period. While similar in many respects to the diagram in paragraph 64 for business enterprises, it reflects the different characteristics and financial reporting objectives of not-for-profit organizations. The importance to those organizations of donor-imposed restrictions on use of some assets focuses financial reporting information on changes in restrictions on net assets as well as on changes in the amount of net assets.

108. The full width of the diagram, represented by the two-pointed arrow labeled "All transactions and other events and circumstances that affect a not-for-profit organization during a period," encompasses all potentially recordable events and circumstances affecting a not-for-profit organization. Moving down the diagram, the next level is divided into three mutually exclusive classes that are the same as those of business enterprises (classes A, B, and C). Continuing down the diagram, however, classes B and C are divided differently from classes B and C in the business-enterprise diagram because not-for-profit organizations have no owners or transactions with owners in the same sense as business enterprises and because restrictions on net assets and changes in the restrictions are significant in not-for-profit organizations. (Size of classes does not indicate their relative volume or significance.)

A. All changes in assets and liabilities not accompanied by changes in net assets. This class comprises four kinds of exchange transactions that are common in most entities; paragraph 65 includes examples. (Exchanges that affect the amount of net assets belong in class B rather than A.)
   1. Exchanges of assets for assets
   2. Exchanges of liabilities for liabilities
   3. Acquisitions of assets by incurring liabilities
   4. Settlements of liabilities by transferring assets

B. All changes in assets or liabilities accompanied by changes in the amount of net assets. This class comprises four kinds of items that also exist for business enterprises:
   1. Revenues
   2. Gains
   3. Expenses
   4. Losses

C. All changes within net assets that do not affect assets or liabilities.
   1. Reclassifications between classes of net assets from changes in donor-imposed restrictions, for example, temporarily restricted net assets become unrestricted net assets when a donor-imposed time stipulation expires. This class comprises events that increase one class of net assets while decreasing another but do not change the amount of net assets.
   2. Changes within a class of net assets, for example, an internal designation by trustees to establish a working capital reserve from a portion of the entity's unrestricted net assets.

---

[49]Some assets—for example, land and endowment investments in securities—are generally not used up or consumed by productive use. The extent, if any, to which the future economic benefits or service potential of particular kinds of assets are used up by productive use involves measurement issues beyond the scope of this Statement.

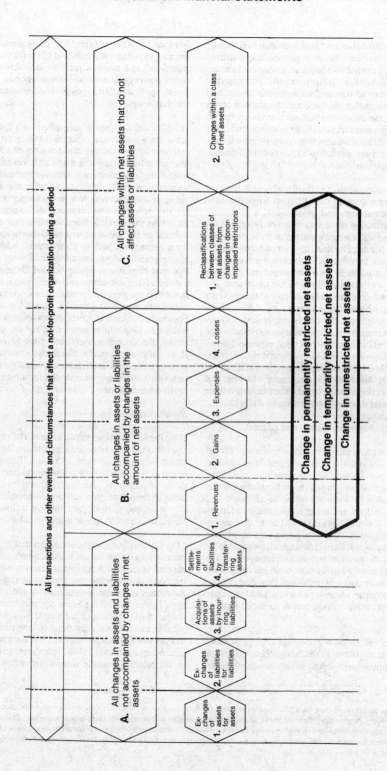

109. The shaded arrow* that is divided horizontally into three classes—change in permanently restricted net assets, change in temporarily restricted net assets, and change in unrestricted net assets—encompasses all transactions and other events and circumstances that change either the amount of net assets or the donor-imposed restrictions on net assets. It thus encompasses the transactions and other events and circumstances that comprise class B (revenues, expenses, gains, losses), and class C1 (reclassifications), combined.

110. In other words, the third and fourth levels of the diagram show in two different ways the same set of transactions and other events and circumstances affecting net assets of a not-for-profit organization and the composition of its three classes during a period. The third level emphasizes sources of changes in net assets—transactions or other events that result in revenues, expenses, gains, or losses or in reclassifications within net assets. The fourth level emphasizes the effects of those events on each of the three classes of net assets—permanently restricted net assets, temporarily restricted net assets, and unrestricted net assets. The components of class B—revenues, expenses, gains, and losses—are discussed collectively in paragraphs 111-113; reclassifications (class C1) are defined and discussed in paragraphs 114-116; and changes in classes of net assets (the fourth level) are defined and discussed in paragraphs 117-133.

Revenues, Expenses, Gains, and Losses

111. Revenues, expenses, gains, and losses are defined and discussed in paragraphs 78-89. Collectively, they include all transactions and other events and circumstances that change the amount of net assets of a not-for-profit organization. All resource inflows and other enhancements of assets of a not-for-profit organization or settlements of its liabilities that increase net assets are either revenues or, gains and have characteristics similar to the revenues or gains of a business enterprise. Likewise, all resource outflows or other using up of assets or incurrences of liabilities that decrease net assets are either expenses or losses and have characteristics similar to expenses or losses of business enterprises.

112. Net assets of a not-for-profit organization change as a result of (a) exchange transactions, (b) contributions and other nonreciprocal transfers from or to other entities, (c) the organization's service-providing efforts,[50] and (d) price changes, casualties, and other effects of interactions between the organization and the economic, legal, social, political, and physical environment of which it is a part.

113. A not-for-profit organization's service-providing efforts, most of its fund-raising activities, and most of its exchange transactions with other entities are generally ongoing major activities that constitute the organization's central operations by which it attempts to fulfill its basic function of providing goods or services to its constituency and thus are the sources of its revenues and expenses. Its gains and losses result from activities that are peripheral or incidental to its central operations and from interactions with its environment, which give rise to price changes, casualties, and other effects that may be partly or wholly beyond the control of individual organizations and their managements. Items that are revenues (or expenses) for one kind of organization may be gains (or losses) for another. For example, donors' contributions are revenues to many not-for-profit organizations but are gains to others that do not actively seek them and receive them only occasionally. Similarly, contributions such as those for endowments are usually gains because they occur only occasionally for most not-for-profit organizations.

Reclassifications

114. Reclassifications between classes of net assets result from donor-imposed stipulations, their expiration by passage of time, or their fulfillment and removal by actions of the organization pursuant to those stipulations. Reclassifications simultaneously increase one class and decrease another class of net assets; they do not involve inflows, outflows, or other changes in assets or liabilities.

115. Reclassifications include events that remove or impose restrictions on an organization's use of its existing resources. Restrictions are removed from temporarily restricted net assets when stipulated conditions expire or are fulfilled by the organization. Time-restricted net assets generally become unrestricted when the stipulated time arrives; for example, net assets that are restricted by contribution of assets during 1985 for use in 1986 become unrestricted on January 1, 1986. Purpose-restricted net assets generally become unrestricted when the or-

---

*Editor's Note: The arrow is highlighted in this edition by a boldfaced outline rather than by shading.

[50]A not-for-profit organization, like a business enterprise, increases the values of goods or services it acquires by adding time, place, or form utility. Thus, *service-providing efforts* and *producing and distributing activities* include conversion processes and other utility-adding activities such as storing, transporting, distributing, providing professional services, and many others. Since a not-for-profit organization may provide goods, services, or cash to its beneficiaries, the term *service-providing efforts* may refer to activities for producing and distributing goods or cash as well as services.

ganization undertakes activities pursuant to the specified purpose, perhaps over several periods, depending on the nature of donors' stipulations. The resulting reclassifications increase unrestricted net assets, often at the same time that the activities that remove the restrictions result in expenses that decrease unrestricted net assets (paragraphs 151 and 152). Temporarily restricted net assets may become unrestricted when an organization incurs liabilities to vendors or employees as it undertakes the activities required by donor stipulations, rather than at the time those liabilities are paid. Restrictions occasionally may be withdrawn by the donor or removed by judicial action.

116. A donor's gift may impose restrictions on otherwise unrestricted net assets. For example, some donors provide endowment gifts on the condition that the organization agree to "match" them by permanently restricting a stated amount of its unrestricted net assets. "Matching agreements" that are not reversible without donors' consent result in a reclassification of unrestricted net assets to permanently restricted net assets or to temporarily restricted net assets.

Changes in Classes of Net Assets of Not-for-Profit Organizations

117. Those who provide, or may provide, resources to a not-for-profit organization usually need information not only about sources of changes in its net assets—about transactions and other events that result in revenues, expenses, gains, and losses—but also about their effects, and the effects of events that change donor-imposed restrictions, on classes of net assets. Effects on classes of net assets often may be more significant to them than sources of changes because donor-imposed restrictions may significantly affect the types and levels of services that a not-for-profit organization can provide.

118. Events that result in reclassifications within net assets and revenues, expenses, gains, and losses together encompass the transactions and other events and circumstances that comprise change in permanently restricted net assets, change in temporarily restricted net assets, and change in unrestricted net assets (paragraphs 108-110).

Change in Permanently Restricted Net Assets

119. Change in permanently restricted net assets of a not-for-profit organization during a period is the total of (a) contributions and other inflows during the period of assets whose use by the organization is limited by donor-imposed stipulations that neither expire by passage of time nor can be fulfilled or otherwise removed by actions of the or-

ganization, (b) other asset enhancements and diminishments during the period that are subject to the same kinds of stipulations, and (c) reclassifications from (or to) other classes of net assets during the period as a consequence of donor-imposed stipulations.

Characteristics of change in permanently restricted net assets

120. Most increases in permanently restricted net assets of a not-for-profit organization are from its accepting contributions of assets that donors stipulate must be maintained in perpetuity. Receipt of a contribution increases permanently restricted net assets if the donor stipulates that the resources received must be maintained permanently and those resources are capable of providing future economic benefit indefinitely. Only assets that are not by their nature used up in carrying out the organization's activities are capable of providing economic benefits indefinitely. Gifts of cash, securities, or nonexhaustible property, such as land and art objects, to be added to an organization's endowment or collections are common examples of those types of assets.

121. Donors' permanent restrictions on the use of contributed assets may also extend to enhancements of those assets or to inflows that result from them. For example, increases in the value of endowment investments that by donor stipulation or law become part of endowment principal also increase permanently restricted net assets. Events that diminish permanently restricted net assets may also occur. Examples include destruction of or damage to a permanently restricted work of art by fire, flood, or vandalism; decline in value of endowment investments that by donor stipulation or law reduces endowment principal; or external mandate (by judicial or similar authority) to transfer endowment securities to another organization.

122. Reclassifications also may increase the amount of permanently restricted net assets or occasionally decrease it (paragraphs 114-116).

Change in Temporarily Restricted Net Assets

123. Change in temporarily restricted net assets of a not-for-profit organization during a period is the total of (a) contributions and other inflows during the period of assets whose use by the organization is limited by donor-imposed stipulations that either expire by passage of time or can be fulfilled and removed by actions of the organization pursuant to those stipulations, (b) other asset enhancements and diminishments during the period subject to the same kinds of stipulations, and (c) reclassifications to (or from) other classes of net assets during the

period as a consequence of donor-imposed stipulations, their expiration by passage of time, or their fulfillment and removal by actions of the organization pursuant to those stipulations.

Characteristics of change in temporarily restricted net assets

124. Most increases in temporarily restricted net assets of a not-for-profit organization are from its accepting contributions of assets that donors limit to use after a specified future time—for example, to be used for next year's operations or to be invested for 10 years before becoming available for operations—or for a specified purpose—for example, sponsoring a particular program activity or acquiring a particular building or piece of equipment. Temporary restrictions pertain to contributions with donor stipulations that expire or can be fulfilled and removed by using assets as specified. And, in contrast to permanent restrictions, which pertain to assets that can provide economic benefits indefinitely and must be maintained in perpetuity by the receiving organization, temporary restrictions pertain to assets that by their nature are spent or used up in carrying out the receiving organization's activities or, if capable of providing economic benefits indefinitely, need not be retained after a stipulated time.

125. Donors' restrictions on the use of contributed assets may also extend to enhancements of those assets or to inflows that result from them. For example, if a donor stipulates that interest income derived from investment of contributed assets is limited to use after a specified date or for a specified operating purpose, the interest income is a restricted inflow that increases temporarily restricted net assets. Events that diminish temporarily restricted net assets, other than expirations and removals of restrictions (next paragraph), may also occur and are much like those that affect permanently restricted net assets (paragraph 121).

126. Reclassifications are the most common source of decreases in temporarily restricted net assets. Events resulting in the expiration or removal of temporary restrictions result in reclassifications from temporarily restricted net assets to unrestricted net assets.

Change in Unrestricted Net Assets

127. Change in unrestricted net assets of a not-for-profit organization during a period is the total change in net assets during the period less change in permanently restricted net assets and change in temporarily restricted net assets for the period. It is the change during the period in the part of net assets of a not-for-profit organization that is not limited by donor-imposed stipulations.

Characteristics of change in unrestricted net assets

128. Changes in unrestricted net assets include (a) revenues and gains that change unrestricted net assets, (b) expenses and losses that change unrestricted net assets, and (c) reclassifications from (or to) other classes of net assets as a consequence of donor-imposed stipulations, their expiration by passage of time, or their fulfillment and removal by actions of the organization pursuant to those stipulations.

129. Revenues and gains that increase unrestricted net assets of a not-for-profit organization have characteristics similar to those of revenues and gains of business enterprises. Those revenues and gains and the transactions that give rise to them are in many forms and are called by various names—for example, fees for services, membership dues, unrestricted gifts or bequests, interest income, and gains on sales of marketable securities.

130. Expenses and losses that decrease unrestricted net assets of a not-for-profit organization have characteristics similar to those of expenses and losses of business enterprises. Except for diminishments of donor-restricted contributed assets that decrease either permanently restricted or temporarily restricted net assets, all types of transactions, other events, and circumstances that decrease net assets of an organization are expenses or losses that decrease unrestricted net assets (paragraphs 121 and 125). Those expenses and losses and the transactions that give rise to them are in many forms and are called by various names—for example, cost of services provided, cost of goods sold, salaries and wages, rent, supplies, interest expense, depreciation, flood damage, and gifts to other entities.[51]

---

[51]Information about the service efforts of a not-for-profit organization should focus on how the organization's resources are used in providing different programs or services (Concepts Statement 4, pars. 51-53). Accordingly, it may be useful to group and report separately the costs of providing various services or other activities for each significant program or supporting activity. However, whether expenses and unrestricted losses are reported by program or supporting activity, by kind (such as salaries and wages, rent, supplies, and other purchased services), or otherwise is a display matter beyond the scope of this Statement.

131. Reclassifications, although not changing the amount of net assets, may change the amount of unrestricted net assets. Reclassifications more commonly increase rather than decrease unrestricted net assets. Events resulting in the expiration or removal of temporary restrictions result in reclassifications from temporarily restricted net assets that increase unrestricted net assets.

132. A not-for-profit organization's activities that fulfill stipulated conditions and result in removing donor-imposed purpose restrictions on use of donated assets also commonly result in expenses that decrease unrestricted net assets. Activities undertaken pursuant to a specified purpose remove the related restriction, often as the organization pays cash or incurs liabilities to vendors or employees to carry out a stipulated activity (paragraph 115). Those transactions result in expenses either when cash is paid or liabilities are incurred or as the organization uses up assets acquired in the transactions.

133. Information about whether a not-for-profit organization has maintained particular classes of net assets may be more significant than whether it has maintained net assets in the aggregate (paragraph 106). Change in unrestricted net assets for a period indicates whether an organization has maintained the part of its net assets that is fully available—that is, free of donor-imposed restrictions—to support the organization's services to beneficiaries in the next period. The combined change in unrestricted net assets and change in temporarily restricted net assets for a period indicates whether an organization has maintained the part of its net assets that is now or can someday be available—that is, free of permanent restrictions—to support its services to beneficiaries in future periods.

ACCRUAL ACCOUNTING AND RELATED CONCEPTS

134. Items that qualify under the definitions of elements of financial statements and that meet criteria for recognition and measurement (paragraph 23) are accounted for and included in financial statements by the use of accrual accounting procedures. Accrual accounting and related concepts are therefore significant not only for defining elements of financial statements but also for understanding and considering other aspects of the conceptual framework for financial accounting and reporting. Paragraphs 135-152 define or describe several significant financial accounting and reporting concepts that are used in this Statement and other concepts Statements.

Transactions, Events, and Circumstances

135. This Statement commonly uses *transactions and other events and circumstances affecting an entity* to describe the sources or causes of changes in assets, liabilities, and equity or net assets. An event is a happening of consequence to an entity. It may be an internal event that occurs within an entity, such as using raw materials or equipment in production, or it may be an external event that involves interaction between an entity and its environment, such as a transaction with another entity, a change in price of a good or service that an entity buys or sells, a flood or earthquake, or an improvement in technology by a competitor.[52] Many events are combinations. For example, acquiring services of employees or others involves exchange transactions, which are external events; using those services, often simultaneously with their acquisition, is part of production, which involves a series of internal events (paragraph 79, footnote 40). An event may be initiated by an entity, such as a purchase of merchandise or use of a building, or it may be partly or wholly beyond the control of an entity and its management, such as an interest rate change, an act of vandalism or theft, the imposition of taxes, or the expiration of a donor-imposed time restriction.

136. Circumstances are a condition or set of conditions that develop from an event or a series of events, which may occur almost imperceptibly and may converge in random or unexpected ways to create situations that might otherwise not have occurred and might not have been anticipated. To see the circumstance may be fairly easy, but to discern specifically when the event or events that caused it occurred may be difficult or impossible. For example, a debtor's going bankrupt or a thief's stealing gasoline may be an event, but a creditor's facing the situation that its debtor is bankrupt or a warehouse's facing the fact that its tank is empty may be a circumstance.

137. A transaction is a particular kind of external event, namely, an external event involving transfer of something of value (future economic benefit) between two (or more) entities. The transaction may be an exchange in which each participant both receives and sacrifices value, such as purchases or sales of goods or services; or the transaction may

[52]In contrast, APB Statement No. 4, *Basic Concepts and Accounting Principles Underlying Financial Statements of Business Enterprises* (October 1970), paragraph 62, distinguishes external and internal events as follows: External events are "events that affect the enterprise and in which other entities participate," while internal events are "events in which only the enterprise participates." In that classification, so-called acts of God, such as floods and earthquakes, which are external events in this Statement, are internal events.

be a nonreciprocal transfer in which an entity incurs a liability or transfers an asset to another entity (or receives an asset or cancellation of a liability) without directly receiving (or giving) value in exchange. Nonreciprocal transfers contrast with exchanges (which are reciprocal transfers) and include, for example, investments by owners, distributions to owners, impositions of taxes, gifts, charitable or educational contributions given or received, and thefts.[53]

138. This Statement does not use the term *internal transaction* (which is essentially contradictory). Transferring materials to production processes, using plant and equipment whose wear and tear is represented by depreciation, and other events that happen within an entity are internal events, not internal transactions.

Accrual Accounting

139. Accrual accounting attempts to record the financial effects on an entity of transactions and other events and circumstances that have cash consequences for the entity in the periods in which those transactions, events, and circumstances occur rather than only in the periods in which cash is received or paid by the entity. Accrual accounting is concerned with an entity's acquiring of goods and services and using them to produce and distribute other goods or services. It is concerned with the process by which cash expended on resources and activities is returned as more (or perhaps less) cash to the entity, not just with the beginning and end of that process. It recognizes that the buying, producing, selling, distributing, and other operations of an entity during a period, as well as other events that affect entity performance, often do not coincide with the cash receipts and payments of the period (FASB Concepts Statement No. 1, *Objectives of Financial Reporting by Business Enterprises,* paragraph 44, and FASB Concepts Statement No. 4, *Objectives of Financial Reporting by Nonbusiness Organizations,* paragraph 50).

140. Thus, accrual accounting is based not only on cash transactions but also on credit transactions, barter exchanges, nonreciprocal transfers of goods or services, changes in prices, changes in form of assets or liabilities, and other transactions, events, and circumstances that have cash consequences for an entity but involve no concurrent cash movement. By accounting for noncash assets, liabilities, revenues, expenses, gains, and losses, accrual accounting links an entity's operations and other transactions, events, and circumstances that affect it with its cash receipts and outlays. Accrual accounting thus provides information about an entity's assets and liabilities and changes in them that cannot be obtained by accounting for only cash receipts and outlays.

Accrual and Deferral (Including Allocation and Amortization)

141. Accrual accounting attempts to recognize noncash events and circumstances as they occur and involves not only accruals but also deferrals, including allocations and amortizations. Accrual is concerned with expected future cash receipts and payments: it is the accounting process of recognizing assets or liabilities and the related liabilities, assets, revenues, expenses, gains, or losses for amounts expected to be received or paid, usually in cash, in the future. Deferral is concerned with past cash receipts and payments—with prepayments received (often described as collected in advance) or paid: it is the accounting process of recognizing a liability resulting from a current cash receipt (or the equivalent) or an asset resulting from a current cash payment (or the equivalent) with deferred recognition of revenues, expenses, gains, or losses. Their recognition is deferred until the obligation underlying the liability is partly or wholly satisfied[54] or until the future economic benefit underlying the asset is partly or wholly used or lost. Common examples of accruals include purchases and sales of goods or services on account, interest, rent (not yet paid), wages and salaries, taxes, and decreases and increases in marketable securities accounted for at lower of cost and market. Common examples of deferrals include prepaid insurance and unearned subscriptions.[55]

142. Allocation is the accounting process of assigning or distributing an amount according to a

---

[53]APB Statement 4, par. 62, and APB Opinion No. 29, *Accounting for Nonmonetary Transactions,* beginning with par. 5.

[54]For example, paragraph 79, footnote 40, explains how liabilities that result from customers' cash advances are later satisfied by delivery of goods or services.

[55]The expressions *accrued depreciation* or *to accrue depreciation* are sometimes used, but depreciation in present practice is technically the result of allocation or amortization, which are deferral, not accrual, techniques. Conversely, the expressions *unamortized debt discount or premium* and *to amortize debt discount or premium* are sometimes used, but accounting for debt securities issued (or acquired as an investment) at a discount or premium by the "interest" method is technically the result of accrual, not deferral or amortization, techniques (pars. 235-239 of this Statement). The "interest" method is described in APB Opinion No. 12, *Omnibus Opinion—1967,* paragraphs 16 and 17, and APB Opinion No. 21, *Interest on Receivables and Payables,* paragraphs 15 and 16.

plan or a formula. It is broader than and includes amortization, which is the accounting process of reducing an amount by periodic payments or write-downs. Specifically, amortization is the process of reducing a liability recorded as a result of a cash receipt by recognizing revenues or reducing an asset recorded as a result of a cash payment by recognizing expenses or costs of production. That is, amortization is an allocation process for accounting for prepayments and deferrals. Common examples of allocations include assigning manufacturing costs to production departments or cost centers and thence to units of product to determine "product cost," apportioning the cost of a "basket purchase" to the individual assets acquired on the basis of their relative market values, and spreading the cost of an insurance policy or a building to two or more accounting periods. Common examples of amortizations include recognizing expenses for depreciation, depletion, and insurance and recognizing earned subscription revenues.

Realization and Recognition

143. Realization in the most precise sense means the process of converting noncash resources and rights into money and is most precisely used in accounting and financial reporting to refer to sales of assets for cash or claims to cash. The related terms *realized* and *unrealized* therefore identify revenues or gains or losses on assets sold and unsold, respectively. Those are the meanings of realization and related terms in the Board's conceptual framework. Recognition is the process of formally recording or incorporating an item in the financial statements of an entity. Thus, an asset, liability, revenue, expense, gain, or loss may be recognized (recorded) or unrecognized (unrecorded). *Realization* and *recognition* are not used as synonyms, as they sometimes are in accounting and financial literature.[56]

Recognition, Matching, and Allocation

144. Accrual accounting recognizes numerous noncash assets, liabilities, and transactions and other events that affect them (paragraphs 139-141). Thus, a major difference between accrual accounting and accounting based on cash receipts and outlays is timing of recognition of revenues, expenses, gains, and losses. Investments by an entity in goods and services for its operations or other activities commonly do not all occur in the same period as revenues or other proceeds from selling the resulting products or providing the resulting services. Several periods may elapse between the time cash is invested in raw materials or plant, for example, and the time cash is re-

turned by collecting the sales price of products from customers. A report showing cash receipts and cash outlays of an enterprise for a short period cannot indicate how much of the cash received is return *of* investment and how much is return *on* investment and thus cannot indicate whether or to what extent an enterprise is successful or unsuccessful. Similarly, goods or services that a not-for-profit organization provides gratis to beneficiaries commonly result from using goods or services acquired with cash received and spent in earlier periods. A report showing cash receipts and outlays of the organization for a short period cannot tell much about the relation of goods or services provided to the resources used to provide them and thus cannot indicate whether or to what extent an organization is successful or unsuccessful in carrying out its service objectives. Cash receipts in a particular period may largely reflect the effects of activities of a business enterprise or a not-for-profit organization in earlier periods, while many of the cash outlays may relate to its activities and efforts expected in future periods.

145. Accrual accounting uses accrual, deferral, and allocation procedures whose goal is to relate revenues, expenses, gains, and losses to periods to reflect an entity's performance during a period instead of merely listing its cash receipts and outlays. Thus, recognition of revenues, expenses, gains, and losses and the related increments or decrements in assets and liabilities—including matching of costs and revenues, allocation, and amortization—is the essence of using accrual accounting to measure performance of entities. The goal of accrual accounting is to account in the periods in which they occur for the effects on an entity of transactions and other events and circumstances, to the extent that those financial effects are recognizable and measurable.

146. Matching of costs and revenues is simultaneous or combined recognition of the revenues and expenses that result directly and jointly from the same transactions or other events. In most entities, some transactions or events result simultaneously in both a revenue and one or more expenses. The revenue and expense(s) are directly related to each other and require recognition at the same time. In present practice, for example, a sale of product or merchandise involves both revenue (sales revenue) for receipt of cash or a receivable and expense (cost of goods sold) for sacrifice of the product or merchandise sold to customers. Other examples of expenses that may result from the same transaction and be directly related to sales revenues are transportation to customers, sales commissions, and perhaps certain other selling costs.

---

[56]Concepts Statement 5 uses the term *recognition* in the same way as does this Statement and distinguishes it from *realization*. It also uses *realized* in the same sense and defines the related concept *realizable* (par. 83 and footnote 50).

147. Many expenses, however, are not related directly to particular revenues but can be related to a period on the basis of transactions or events occurring in that period or by allocation. Recognition of those expenses is largely independent of recognition of particular revenues, but they are deducted from particular revenues by being recognized in the same period.[57]

148. Some costs that cannot be directly related to particular revenues are incurred to obtain benefits that are exhausted in the period in which the costs are incurred. For example, salesmen's monthly salaries and electricity used to light an office building usually fit that description and are usually recognized as expenses in the period in which they are incurred. Other costs are also recognized as expenses in the period in which they are incurred because the period to which they otherwise relate is indeterminable or not worth the effort to determine.

149. However, many assets yield their benefits to an entity over several periods, for example, prepaid insurance, buildings, and various kinds of equipment. Expenses resulting from their use are normally allocated to the periods of their estimated useful lives (the periods over which they are expected to provide benefits) by a "systematic and rational" allocation procedure, for example, by recognizing depreciation or other amortization. Although the purpose of expense allocation is the same as that of other expense recognition—to reflect the using up of assets as a result of transactions or other events or circumstances affecting an entity—allocation is applied if causal relations are generally, but not specifically, identified. For example, wear and tear from use is known to be a major cause of the expense called depreciation, but the amount of depreciation caused by wear and tear in a period normally cannot be measured. Those expenses are not related directly to either specific revenues or particular periods. Usually no traceable relationship exists, and they are recognized by allocating costs to periods in which assets

are expected to be used and are related only indirectly to the revenues that are recognized in the same period.

150. Some revenues and gains result from nonreciprocal transfers to an entity from other entities and thus relate to the period in which cash or other assets are received by the entity, or in which its liabilities are reduced. Recognition of those nonreciprocal transfers seldom involves allocation or matching procedures. For example, not-for-profit organizations commonly receive donations in cash, and timing of cash receipts is normally readily verifiable. Similarly, receipts of other assets, including receivables (promises by another entity to pay cash or transfer other assets), or of reductions or remissions of liabilities are also usually readily identifiable with the periods in which they occur, and there is nothing to allocate to other periods.

151. Nonreciprocal transfers to an entity rarely result directly and jointly from the same transactions as expenses. Most contributions and expenses are much more closely related to time periods than to each other. For example, the receipt by a not-for-profit organization of contributed assets that involve donor stipulations restricting their use to particular types of services may be a cause of the expenses incurred in providing those services; however, the receipt of contributed assets—revenues or gains—and the subsequent incurring of liabilities or reduction of assets in providing services—expenses—are separate events recognized in the periods in which they occur.

152. Removal of restrictions on temporarily restricted net assets of a not-for-profit organization is an event that often occurs at the same time as the incurring of particular expenses. The discussion of donor-imposed restrictions in this Statement contemplates that removals of restrictions on net assets—reclassifications—may be shown in financial statements in the same period(s) as the activities that remove the restrictions.

This Statement was adopted by the unanimous vote of the seven members of the Financial Accounting Standards Board:

Donald J. Kirk,	Victor H. Brown	Robert T. Sprouse
Chairman	Raymond C. Lauver	Arthur R. Wyatt
Frank E. Block	David Mosso	

---

[57]APB Statement 4 (pars. 154-161) describes "three pervasive expense recognition principles": associating cause and effect, systematic and rational allocation, and immediate recognition. Paragraphs 146-149 of this Statement describe generally the same three bases for recognizing expenses but not in the same order.

Guidance for recognition of expenses and losses, set forth for business enterprises in Concepts Statement 5 (pars. 85-87), is based in large part on the considerations in paragraphs 146-149.

Appendix A

BACKGROUND INFORMATION

153. The need for a conceptual framework for financial accounting and reporting, beginning with consideration of the objectives of financial reporting, is generally recognized. The Accounting Principles Board issued APB Statement No. 4, *Basic Concepts and Accounting Principles Underlying Financial Statements of Business Enterprises,* in 1970. When the Financial Accounting Standards Board came into existence, the Study Group on the Objectives of Financial Statements was at work, and its report, *Objectives of Financial Statements,* was published in October 1973 by the American Institute of Certified Public Accountants. Although that report focused primarily on business enterprises, it also included a brief discussion of "objectives of financial statements for governmental and not-for-profit organizations."

154. The Financial Accounting Standards Board issued a Discussion Memorandum, *Conceptual Framework for Accounting and Reporting: Consideration of the Report of the Study Group on the Objectives of Financial Statements,* dated June 6, 1974, and held a public hearing on September 23 and 24, 1974 on the objectives of financial statements.

155. The Board first concentrated on concepts of financial accounting and reporting by business enterprises and issued three documents on December 2, 1976: *Tentative Conclusions on Objectives of Financial Statements of Business Enterprises,* FASB Discussion Memorandum, *Conceptual Framework for Financial Accounting and Reporting: Elements of Financial Statements and Their Measurement,* and *Scope and Implications of the Conceptual Framework Project.* The same task force, with only one membership change, provided counsel in preparing both Discussion Memorandums. Eleven persons from academe, the financial community, industry, and public accounting served on the task force while the Discussion Memorandums were written.

156. The Board held public hearings (a) August 1 and 2, 1977 on the *Tentative Conclusions on Objectives of Financial Statements of Business Enterprises* and on Chapters 1-5 of the Discussion Memorandum concerning definitions of the elements of financial statements and (b) January 16-18, 1978 on the remaining chapters of the Discussion Memorandum concerning capital maintenance or cost recovery, qualities of useful financial information (qualitative characteristics), and measurement of the elements of financial statements.

157. The Board received 283 written communications on the subject of the August 1977 hearing, of which 221 commented on the elements, and 27 parties presented their views orally and answered Board members' questions at the hearing. The Board issued an Exposure Draft of a proposed Statement of Financial Accounting Concepts, *Objectives of Financial Reporting and Elements of Financial Statements of Business Enterprises,* dated December 29, 1977, and received 135 letters of comment.

158. During 1978, the Board divided the subject matter of the Exposure Draft. One part became FASB Concepts Statement No. 1, *Objectives of Financial Reporting by Business Enterprises,* which was issued in November 1978. A second part became the basis for the revised Exposure Draft, *Elements of Financial Statements of Business Enterprises,* issued December 28, 1979, on which the Board received 92 letters of comment. That Exposure Draft led in December 1980 to FASB Concepts Statement No. 3, *Elements of Financial Statements of Business Enterprises,* following FASB Concepts Statement No. 2, *Qualitative Characteristics of Accounting Information,* which was issued in May 1980.

159. The Board's work on concepts of financial accounting and reporting by not-for-profit organizations began in August 1977. Professor Robert N. Anthony of the Harvard Business School prepared an FASB Research Report, *Financial Accounting in Nonbusiness Organizations,* published in May 1978, which was followed by a related Discussion Memorandum and an Exposure Draft. FASB Concepts Statement No. 4, *Objectives of Financial Reporting by Nonbusiness Organizations,* was issued in December 1980.

160. The four concepts Statements described are part of a single conceptual framework for financial accounting and reporting by all entities. The Board noted in Concepts Statements 2 and 3 its expectation that the qualitative characteristics and definitions of elements of financial statements should apply to both business enterprises and not-for-profit organizations and its intent to solicit views on that matter.

161. The Board issued an Exposure Draft, *Proposed Amendments to FASB Concepts Statements 2 and 3 to Apply Them to Nonbusiness Organizations,* on July 7, 1983. In considering similarities and differences of business enterprises and not-for-profit organizations that may affect qualitative characteristics of accounting information and definitions of elements of financial statements, the Board had the counsel of a task force consisting of

32 members knowledgeable about not-for-profit organizations and their financial reporting. The Board received 74 letters of comment on the Exposure Draft, and 20 parties presented their views orally and answered Board members' questions at public hearings held on November 14 and 15, 1983.

162. That Exposure Draft was in two parts, and the Board made decisions on both. First, it reaffirmed the conclusion of the Exposure Draft that the qualitative characteristics of accounting information set forth in Concepts Statement 2 (relevance, reliability, comparability, and related qualities) apply to not-for-profit organizations as well as to business enterprises. Second, based on suggestions of respondents to the Exposure Draft and on its own further consideration of similarities and differences between business enterprises and not-for-profit organizations, the Board revised the proposed amendments to Concepts Statement 3 and issued a revised Exposure Draft, *Elements of Financial Statements,* on September 18, 1985. The following describe major changes from the 1983 Exposure Draft and identify major changes suggested but not made.

• This Statement does not define as elements of financial statements two that the 1983 Exposure Draft proposed: change in net assets (described as a concept equivalent to comprehensive income of business enterprises) and contributions. Instead, by identifying three broad classes of net assets of not-for-profit organizations—permanently restricted, temporarily restricted, and unrestricted net assets—and changes in those classes, it emphasizes the importance of donor-imposed restrictions on resources contributed to not-for-profit organizations and changes in both the amount and nature of net assets based on the presence or absence of donor restrictions. Numerous respondents, both those interested in not-for-profit organizations and those interested in business enterprises, questioned whether defining contributions separately from revenues and gains, though clearly possible, was either necessary or useful. This Statement notes that inflows of assets in nonreciprocal transfers from nonowners (contributions), like other transactions that increase net assets, result either in revenues (from ongoing major operating activities) or in gains (from peripheral or incidental transactions). It also notes that whether a particular contribution results in a revenue or a gain is often less important than whether it increases permanently restricted, temporarily restricted, or unrestricted net assets.
• A separate diagram now shows interrelationships between sources of changes in net assets of not-for-profit organizations (revenues, expenses, gains, and losses), reclassifications be-

tween classes of net assets, and changes in permanently restricted, temporarily restricted, and unrestricted net assets.
• This Statement reaffirms the conclusion in the 1983 Exposure Draft that under the definitions in Concepts Statement 3 (and this Statement) contributions or donations, whether or not subject to donor-imposed restrictions, generally increase net assets (equity) rather than liabilities. Several respondents had argued that purpose-restricted, and perhaps time-restricted, contributions result in (or should be considered to result in) liabilities.
• This Statement reaffirms the conclusion in the 1983 Exposure Draft that how an asset was acquired and whether and how it will be replaced are not germane to whether or not the entity's using it up results in an expense. Some respondents to the Exposure Draft had suggested that depreciation often should not be an expense (or cost) of a not-for-profit organization, in part because the related assets were, and their replacements are expected to be, funded by contributions or special assessments.
• Some respondents to the 1983 Exposure Draft had suggested that depreciation based on historical cost is not the most relevant way of measuring a not-for-profit organization's cost of using up of long-lived assets. However, how depreciation expense should be measured is a measurement issue beyond the scope of this Statement.
• This Statement takes note of Board decisions on matters that were still under consideration as part of other projects at the time Concepts Statement 3 and the 1983 Exposure Draft were issued, particularly the recognition, measurement, and display matters for business enterprises that are the subjects of Concepts Statement 5.
• Although financial statement display is beyond the scope of this Statement, the Board has attempted to respond at various points to requests by a number of respondents for more explanation of the significance of the proposed definitions for reporting by not-for-profit organizations.

163. The Board received 60 letters of comment on the revised Exposure Draft. Some respondents reiterated the arguments referred to in paragraph 162, while others expressed new concerns. The Board has considered those comments. The following describe and identify changes made to the revised Exposure Draft and identify changes suggested by respondents but not made.

• This Statement reaffirms the conclusion that financial reporting by not-for-profit organizations requires a concept of maintenance of net assets. Some respondents suggested that depreciation is often irrelevant to not-for-profit organizations because the related expenses need not be "matched" with revenues to measure income, which in their view is not important for not-for-profit organizations. However, this Statement describes depreciation as a cost of using assets, not as a technique for "matching" expenses with revenues.

- This Statement reaffirms the conclusion in the Exposure Drafts that most restrictions do not create obligations that qualify as liabilities. The discussion has been expanded (paragraphs 56-58) to clarify the point.
- Some respondents suggested that the revisions to the characteristics of assets and liabilities proposed in the revised Exposure Draft had changed the related definitions and expressed concern about the intent of the revisions. The troublesome aspects of the revisions have been reworded to alleviate those concerns. The revisions to the last sentences in paragraph 26 and in paragraph 36 are meant to avoid circularity in the use of the term *probable* in explaining probable future benefit and sacrifice, and clarify the intended point, that there are ways other than legal enforceability by which an entity may obtain an existing benefit or may be unable to avoid paying an existing obligation.

Appendix B

CHARACTERISTICS OF ASSETS, LIABILITIES, AND EQUITY OR NET ASSETS AND OF CHANGES IN THEM

Purpose and Summary of Appendix

164. This appendix elaborates on the descriptions of the essential characteristics that items must have to qualify under the definitions of elements of financial statements in this Statement. It includes some discussion and illustrations of how to assess the characteristics of items that are potential candidates for formal inclusion in financial statements and in general how to apply the definitions.

165. The remainder of this section briefly illustrates the relationship of the definitions to recognition, measurement, and display issues and the function and some consequences of the definitions. It is followed by a discussion of the characteristics of assets, liabilities, equity of business enterprises, comprehensive income of business

enterprises and its components, and net assets and changes in the classes of net assets of not-for-profit organizations.[58] The appendix concludes with a series of examples that are intended to illustrate the meanings of the definitions and the essential characteristics that form them.

166. This Statement emphasizes that the definitions of elements are not intended to answer recognition, measurement, or display questions.[59] The definitions are, however, a significant first step in determining the content of financial statements. They screen out items that lack one or more characteristics of assets, liabilities, revenues, expenses, or other elements of financial statements (paragraphs 22 and 23).

167. Thus, unless an item qualifies as an asset of an entity under the definition in paragraph 25, for example, questions do not arise about whether to recognize it as an asset of the entity, which of its attributes to measure, or how to display it as an asset in the financial statements of the entity. Although items that fail to qualify under the definitions of elements during a period do not raise recognition issues, they may nevertheless raise issues about whether and, if so, how and at what amounts they should be disclosed. For example, contingencies that have not yet, and may never, become assets or liabilities may need to be estimated and disclosed. Thus, the first question about each potential candidate for formal inclusion in financial statements is whether it qualifies under one of the definitions of elements; recognition, measurement, and display questions follow.

168. An item does not qualify as an asset or liability of an entity if it lacks one or more essential characteristics. Thus, for example, an item does not qualify as an asset of an entity under the definition in paragraph 25 if (a) the item involves no future economic benefit, (b) the item involves future economic benefit, but the entity cannot obtain it, or (c) the item involves future economic benefit that the entity may in the future obtain, but the events or circumstances that give the entity access to and control of the benefit have not yet occurred (or the entity in the past had the ability to obtain or control the future benefit, but events or circumstances have occurred to remove that ability). Similarly, an item does not qualify as a liability of an entity under the definition in paragraph 35 if (a) the item entails no future sacrifice of assets, (b) the

---

[58]As noted in paragraph 50, footnote 26, this Statement often uses *equity* and *net assets* interchangeably but generally applies *equity* to business enterprises and *net assets* to not-for-profit organizations.

[59]Those questions are a subject of FASB Concepts Statement No. 5, *Recognition and Measurement in Financial Statements of Business Enterprises*. Recognition, measurement, and display questions for not-for-profit organizations, and more detailed development of those concepts for all entities, may be the subject of further concepts or standards Statements.

item entails future sacrifice of assets, but the entity is not obligated to make the sacrifice, or (c) the item involves a future sacrifice of assets that the entity will be obligated to make, but the events or circumstances that obligate the entity have not yet occurred (or the entity in the past was obligated to make the future sacrifice, but events or circumstances have occurred to remove that obligation).

169. This appendix contains numerous examples of items that commonly qualify as assets or liabilities of an entity under the definitions in this Statement. It also includes several illustrations showing that items that may not qualify as assets may readily qualify as reductions (valuation accounts) of liabilities and that items that may not qualify as liabilities may readily qualify as reductions (valuation accounts) of assets. The following examples illustrate items that do not qualify as assets or liabilities of an entity under the definitions: (a) "dry holes" drilled by an exploration enterprise that has not yet discovered hydrocarbon, mineral, or other reserves are not assets (except to the extent of salvageable materials or equipment) because they provide no access to probable future economic benefit;[60] (b) estimated possible casualty losses from future floods or fires are not liabilities or impairments of assets because an event incurring a liability or impairing an asset has not occurred; (c) inventories or depreciable assets required (but not yet ordered) to replace similar items that are being or have been used up are not assets because no future economic benefits have been acquired, and the requirement to sacrifice assets to obtain them is not a liability because the entity is not yet obligated to sacrifice assets in the future; (d) deferrals relating to assets no longer held or liabilities no longer owed—such as a deferred loss on selling an asset for cash or a deferred gain on settling a liability for cash—are not assets or liabilities because they involve no future economic benefit or no required future sacrifice of assets; (e) receipts of grants of cash or other assets with no strings attached do not create liabilities because the entity is not required to sacrifice assets in the future; (f) other receipts of cash in return for which an entity is in no way required to pay cash, transfer other assets, or provide services do not create liabilities because the entity is not presently obligated to sacrifice assets in the future;[61] (g) "know-how" of NASA or other governmental agencies placed in the public domain is not an asset of an entity unless the entity spends funds or otherwise acts to secure benefits not freely availa-

ble to everyone; (h) estimated losses for two years from a decision to start up a new product line next year are not liabilities because the entity is not legally, equitably, or constructively obligated to sacrifice assets in the future; and (i) "stock dividends payable" are not liabilities because they do not involve an obligation to make future sacrifices of assets.

170. The Board expects most assets and liabilities in present practice to continue to qualify as assets or liabilities under the definitions in this Statement. That expectation is supported by the examples in the preceding paragraph as well as by those throughout this appendix. The Board emphasizes that the definitions in this Statement neither require nor presage upheavals in present practice, although they may in due time lead to some evolutionary changes in practice or at least in the ways certain items are viewed. They should be especially helpful, however, in understanding the content of financial statements and in analyzing and resolving new financial accounting issues as they arise.

Characteristics of Assets

171. Paragraph 25 defines assets as "probable future economic benefits obtained or controlled by a particular entity as a result of past transactions or events." Paragraphs 26-34 amplify that definition. The following discussion further amplifies it and illustrates its meaning under three headings that correspond to the three essential characteristics of assets described in paragraph 26: future economic benefits, control by a particular entity, and occurrence of a past transaction or event.

Future Economic Benefits

172. Future economic benefit is the essence of an asset (paragraphs 27-31). An asset has the capacity to serve the entity by being exchanged for something else of value to the entity, by being used to produce something of value to the entity, or by being used to settle its liabilities.

173. The most obvious evidence of future economic benefit is a market price. Anything that is commonly bought and sold has future economic benefit, including the individual items that a buyer obtains and is willing to pay for in a "basket purchase" of several items or in a business combination. Simi-

---

[60]Paragraph 247 notes an aspect of the cost of some "dry holes" in different circumstances.

[61]Examples (e) and (f) describe receipts of assets in nonreciprocal transfers to an entity, for example, contributions. Although restrictions may place limits on assets received, most donor-imposed restrictions do not create obligations that qualify as liabilities of the recipient. Moreover, the transaction necessarily is an exchange rather than a nonreciprocal transfer if an entity receives assets and incurs liabilities in the same transaction. Although restrictions on the use of donated assets may lead to the future use of cash (or other assets) to provide stipulated services, that future use of cash is not a required "sacrifice" of assets. Rather, it generally is a future exchange of assets to purchase goods or services from suppliers or employees (pars. 56-58, 137, and 150 and 151).

larly, anything that creditors or others commonly accept in settlement of liabilities has future economic benefit, and anything that is commonly used to produce goods or services, whether tangible or intangible and whether or not it has a market price or is otherwise exchangeable, also has future economic benefit.[62] Incurrence of costs may be significant evidence of acquisition or enhancement of future economic benefits (paragraphs 178-180).

174. To assess whether a particular item constitutes an asset of a particular entity at a particular time requires at least two considerations in addition to the general kinds of evidence just described: (a) whether the item obtained by the entity embodied future economic benefit in the first place and (b) whether all or any of the future economic benefit to the entity remains at the time of assessment.

175. Uncertainty about business and economic outcomes often clouds whether or not particular items that might be assets have the capacity to provide future economic benefits to the entity (paragraphs 44-48), sometimes precluding their recognition as assets. The kinds of items that may be recognized as expenses or losses rather than as assets because of uncertainty are some in which management's intent in taking certain steps or initiating certain transactions is clearly to acquire or enhance future economic benefits available to the entity. For example, business enterprises engage in research and development activities, advertise, develop markets, open new branches or divisions, and the like, and spend significant funds to do so. The uncertainty is not about the intent to increase future economic benefits but about whether and, if so, to what extent they succeeded in doing so. Certain expenditures for research and development, advertising, training, start-up and preoperating activities, development stage enterprises, relocation or rearrangement, and goodwill are examples of the kinds of items for which assessments of future economic benefits may be especially uncertain.

176. Since many of the activities described in the preceding paragraph involve incurring costs, the distinction between the items just listed and assets, such as prepaid insurance and prepaid rent, that are described in paragraph 181 is often difficult to draw because the two groups tend to shade into each other. Indeed, the distinction is not based on the definition of assets in paragraph 25 but rather on the practical considerations of coping with the effects of uncertainty. If research or development activities or advertising results in an entity's acquiring or increasing future economic benefit, that future economic benefit qualifies as an asset as

much as do the future benefits from prepaid insurance or prepaid rent. The practical problem is whether future economic benefit is actually present and, if so, how much—an assessment that is greatly complicated by the feature that the benefits may be realized far in the future, if at all.

177. Most assets presently included in financial statements qualify as assets under the definition in paragraph 25 because they have future economic benefits. Cash, accounts and notes receivable, interest and dividends receivable, investments in securities of other entities, and similar items so obviously qualify as assets that they need no further comment except to note that uncollectible receivables do not qualify as assets. Inventories of raw materials, supplies, partially completed product, finished goods, and merchandise likewise obviously fit the definition as do productive resources, such as property, plant, equipment, tools, furnishings, leasehold improvements, natural resource deposits, and patents. They are mentioned separately from cash, receivables, and investments only because they have commonly been described in accounting literature as "deferred costs" or occasionally as "deferred charges" to revenues. The point requires noting because comments received on the Discussion Memorandum and earlier Exposure Drafts have manifested some misunderstanding: some respondents apparently concluded that all or most deferrals of costs were precluded by the definition of assets.

Assets and costs

178. An entity commonly incurs costs to obtain future economic benefits, either to acquire assets from other entities in exchange transactions or to add value through operations to assets it already has (paragraph 32). An entity acquires assets in exchanges with other entities by sacrificing other assets or by incurring liabilities to transfer assets to the other entity later. An entity also incurs a cost when it uses an asset in producing or distributing goods or services—future economic benefits are partially or wholly used up to produce or acquire other assets, for example, product in process, completed product, or receivables from customers.

179. Although an entity normally incurs costs to acquire or use assets, costs incurred are not themselves assets. The essence of an asset is its future economic benefit rather than whether or not it was acquired at a cost. However, costs may be significant to applying the definition of assets in at least two ways: as evidence of acquisition of an asset or as a measure of an attribute of an asset.

---

[62]Absence of a market price or exchangeability of an asset may create measurement and recognition problems, but it in no way negates future economic benefit that can be obtained by use as well as by exchange.

180. First, since an entity commonly obtains assets by incurring costs, incurrence of a cost may be evidence that an entity has acquired one or more assets, but it is not conclusive evidence. Costs may be incurred without receiving services or enhanced future economic benefits. Or, entities may obtain assets without incurring costs—for example, from investment in kind by owners or contributions of securities or buildings by donors. The ultimate evidence of the existence of assets is the future economic benefit, not the costs incurred.

181. Second, cost may measure an attribute of future economic benefit. Costs of assets such as inventories, plant, equipment, and patents are examples of costs or unamortized costs of future benefits from present practice, as are prepayments such as prepaid insurance and prepaid rent, which are unamortized costs of rights to receive a service or use a resource.

182. Losses have no future economic benefits and cannot qualify as assets under the definition in paragraph 25. Stated conversely, items that have future economic benefits are not in concept losses, although practical considerations may sometimes make it impossible to distinguish them from expenses or losses.

Control by a Particular Entity

183. Paragraph 25 defines assets in relation to specific entities. Every asset is an asset of some entity; moreover, no asset can simultaneously be an asset of more than one entity, although a particular physical thing or other agent that provides future economic benefit may provide separate benefits to two or more entities at the same time (paragraph 185). To have an asset, an entity must control future economic benefit to the extent that it can benefit from the asset and generally can deny or regulate access to that benefit by others, for example, by permitting access only at a price.

184. Thus, an asset of an entity is the future economic benefit that the entity can control and thus can, within limits set by the nature of the benefit or the entity's right to it, use as it pleases. The entity having an asset is the one that can exchange it, use it to produce goods or services, exact a price for others' use of it, use it to settle liabilities, hold it, or perhaps distribute it to owners.

185. The definition of assets focuses primarily on the future economic benefit to which an entity has access and only secondarily on the physical things and other agents that provide future economic benefits. Many physical things and other agents are in effect bundles of future economic benefits that can be unbundled in various ways, and two or more entities may have different future economic benefits from the same agent at the same time or the same continuing future economic benefit at different times. For example, two or more entities may have undivided interests in a parcel of land. Each has a right to future economic benefit that may qualify as an asset under the definition in paragraph 25, even though the right of each is subject at least to some extent to the rights of the other(s). Or, one entity may have the right to the interest from an investment, while another has the right to the principal. Leases are common examples of agreements that unbundle the future economic benefits of a single property to give a lessee a right to possess and use the property and give a lessor a right to receive rents and a right to the residual value. Moreover, a mortgagee may also have a right to receive periodic payments that is secured by the leased property.

Control and legal rights

186. As some of the preceding discussion indicates, an entity's ability to obtain the future economic benefit of an asset commonly stems from legal rights. Those rights share the common feature of conferring ability to obtain future economic benefits, but they vary in other ways. For example, ownership, a contract to use, and a contract to receive cash confer different rights.

187. Although the ability of an entity to obtain the future economic benefit of an asset and to deny or control access to it by others rests generally on a foundation of legal rights, legal enforceability of a right is not an indispensable prerequisite for an entity to have an asset if the entity has the ability to obtain and control the benefit in some other way. For example, exclusive access to future economic benefit may be maintained by keeping secret a formula or process.

Noncontrolled benefits

188. Some future economic benefits cannot meet the test of control. For example, public highways and stations and equipment of municipal fire and police departments may qualify as assets of governmental units but they cannot qualify as assets of other entities under the definition in paragraph 25. Similarly, general access to things such as clean air or water resulting from environmental laws or requirements cannot qualify as assets of individual entities, even if the entities have incurred costs to help clean up the environment.

189. Those examples should be distinguished from similar future economic benefits that an individual entity can control and thus are its assets. For example, an entity can control benefits from a pri-

vate road on its own property, clean air it provides in a laboratory or water it provides in a storage tank, or a private fire department or a private security force, and the related equipment probably qualifies as an asset even if it has no other use to the entity and cannot be sold except as scrap. Equipment used to help provide clean air or water in the general environment may provide future economic benefit to the user, even if it has no other use and cannot be sold except as scrap. Moreover, a specific right to use a public highway from which the licensee might otherwise be excluded—for example, a license to operate a truck on the highways within a state—may have future economic benefit to the licensee even though it does not keep everyone else off the highway. Similarly, riparian rights and airspace rights may confer future economic benefits on their holders even though they do not keep others' boats off the river or prevent airplanes from flying overhead.

Occurrence of a Past Transaction or Event

190. The definition of assets in paragraph 25 distinguishes between the future economic benefits of present and future assets of an entity. Only present abilities to obtain future economic benefits are assets under the definition, and they become assets of particular entities as a result of transactions or other events or circumstances affecting the entity. For example, the future economic benefits of a particular building can be an asset of a particular entity only after a transaction or other event—such as a purchase or a lease agreement—has occurred that gives it access to and control of those benefits. Similarly, although an oil deposit may have existed in a certain place for millions of years, it can be an asset of a particular entity only after the entity either has discovered it in circumstances that permit the entity to exploit it or has acquired the rights to exploit it from whoever had them.

191. Since the transaction or event giving rise to the entity's right to the future economic benefit must already have occurred, the definition excludes from assets items that may in the future become an entity's assets but have not yet become its assets. An entity has no asset for a particular future economic benefit if the transactions or events that give it access to and control of the benefit are yet in the future. The corollary is that an entity still has an asset if the transactions or events that use up or destroy a particular future economic benefit or remove the entity's access to and control of it are yet in the future. For example, an entity does not acquire an asset merely by budgeting the purchase of a machine and does not lose an asset from fire until a fire destroys or damages some asset.

Characteristics of Liabilities

192. Paragraph 35 defines liabilities as "probable future sacrifices of economic benefits arising from present obligations of a particular entity to transfer assets or provide services to other entities in the future as a result of past transactions or events." Paragraphs 36-43 amplify that definition. The following discussion further amplifies that definition and illustrates its meaning under three headings that correspond to the three essential characteristics of liabilities described in paragraph 36: required future sacrifice of assets, obligation of a particular entity, and occurrence of a past transaction or event.

Required Future Sacrifice of Assets

193. The essence of a liability is a duty or requirement to sacrifice assets in the future. A liability requires an entity to transfer assets, provide services, or otherwise expend assets to satisfy a responsibility to one or more other entities that it has incurred or that has been imposed on it.

194. The most obvious evidence of liabilities are contracts or other agreements resulting from exchange transactions and laws or governmental regulations that require expending assets to comply. Although receipt of proceeds is not conclusive evidence that a liability has been incurred (paragraph 198), receipt of cash, other assets, or services without an accompanying cash payment is often evidence that a liability has been incurred. Evidence of liabilities may also be found in declarations of dividends, lawsuits filed or in process, infractions that may bring fines or penalties, and the like. Reductions in prices paid or offered to acquire an enterprise or a significant part of it to allow for items that a buyer must assume that require future transfers of assets or providing of services also may indicate the kinds of items that qualify as liabilities. Moreover, liabilities that are not payable on demand normally have specified or determinable maturity dates or specified events whose occurrence requires that they must be settled, and absence of a specified maturity date or event may cast doubt that a liability exists.

195. To assess whether a particular item constitutes a liability of a particular entity at a particular time requires at least two considerations in addition to the general kinds of evidence just described: (a) whether the entity incurred a responsibility to sacrifice assets in the future and (b) whether all or any of the responsibility remains unsatisfied at the time of assessment.

196. Most liabilities presently included in financial statements qualify as liabilities under the definition in paragraph 35 because they require an entity to sacrifice assets in the future. Thus, accounts and notes payable, wages and salaries payable, long-term debt, interest and dividends payable, and similar requirements to pay cash so obviously qualify as liabilities that they need no further comment. Responsibilities such as those to pay pensions, deferred compensation, and taxes and to honor warranties and guarantees also create liabilities under the definition. That they may be satisfied by providing goods or services instead of cash, that their amounts or times of settlement must be estimated, or that the identity of the specific entities to whom an entity is obligated is as yet unknown does not disqualify them under the definition, although some may not be recognized because of uncertainty or measurement problems (paragraphs 44-48).

197. Deposits and prepayments received for goods or services to be provided—"unearned revenues," such as subscriptions or rent collected in advance—likewise qualify as liabilities under the definition because an entity is required to provide goods or services to those who have paid in advance. They are mentioned separately from other liabilities only because they have commonly been described in the accounting literature and financial statements as "deferred credits" or "reserves." Comments on the Discussion Memorandum and earlier Exposure Drafts have manifested some misunderstanding: some respondents apparently concluded that all or most "deferred credits" and "reserves" were precluded by the definition of liabilities.

Liabilities and proceeds

198. An entity commonly receives cash, goods, or services by incurring liabilities (paragraph 38), and that which is received is often called proceeds, especially if cash is received. Receipt of proceeds may be evidence that an entity has incurred one or more liabilities, but it is not conclusive evidence. Proceeds may be received from cash sales of goods or services or other sales of assets, from cash contributions by donors, or from cash investments by owners, and entities may incur liabilities without receiving proceeds, for example, by imposition of taxes. The essence of a liability is a legal, equitable, or constructive obligation to sacrifice economic benefits in the future rather than whether proceeds were received by incurring it. Although proceeds received may be a useful attribute in measuring a liability incurred, proceeds themselves are not liabilities.

Obligation of a Particular Entity

199. Paragraph 35 defines liabilities in relation to specific entities. A required future sacrifice of assets is a liability of the particular entity that must make the sacrifice.

200. To have a liability, an entity must be obligated to sacrifice its assets in the future—that is, it must be bound by a legal, equitable, or constructive duty or responsibility to transfer assets or provide services to one or more other entities. Not all probable future sacrifices of economic benefits (assets) are liabilities of an entity. For example, an entity's need to replace merchandise sold or raw materials or equipment used up, no matter how pressing, does not by itself constitute a liability of the entity because no obligation to another entity is present.

201. Most obligations that underlie liabilities stem from contracts and other agreements that are enforceable by courts or from governmental actions that have the force of law,[63] and the fact of an entity's obligation is so evident that it is often taken for granted. To carry out its operations, an entity routinely makes contracts and agreements that obligate it to repay borrowing, to pay suppliers and employees for goods and services they provide, to provide goods or services to customers, or to repair or replace defective products sold with warranties or guarantees. Governmental units also routinely assess tax obligations against business enterprises and some not-for-profit organizations, and courts may impose obligations for damages or fines.

202. Equitable or constructive obligations may underlie liabilities as well as those that are legally enforceable. Legal obligations are much more common, and their existence may be more readily substantiated, but other kinds of obligations are sometimes liabilities. For example, the question, which has resulted in differences of opinion, of the extent to which future payments under a lease agreement are legally enforceable against lessees is not necessarily significant in determining whether the obligations under lease agreements qualify as liabilities.

203. An entity may incur equitable or constructive obligations by actions to bind itself or by finding

---

[63]Contracts and agreements and enforceability of agreements and statutes are necessary parts of the environment in which business and other economic activities and financial reporting take place. Business and other economic activities in the United States depend on flows of money and credit, and the fact that the participants largely keep their promises to pay money or provide goods or services is a necessary stabilizing factor. But the definitions in this Statement are not legal definitions and do not necessarily agree with legal definitions of the same or related terms (which have a propensity to have diverse meanings, often depending on the context or the branch of law that is involved). Nor is existence of a legally enforceable obligation inevitably required for an entity to have a liability (pars. 36-40).

itself bound by circumstances rather than by making contracts or participating in exchange transactions. An entity is not obligated to sacrifice assets in the future if it can avoid the future sacrifice at its discretion without significant penalty. The example of an entity that binds itself to pay employees vacation pay or year-end bonuses by paying them every year even though it is not contractually bound to do so and has not announced a policy to do so has already been noted (paragraph 40). It could refuse to pay only by risking substantial employee-relations problems.

204. Most liabilities are obligations of only one entity at a time. Some liabilities are shared—for example, two or more entities may be "jointly and severally liable" for a debt or for the unsatisfied liabilities of a partnership. But most liabilities bind a single entity, and those that bind two or more entities are commonly ranked rather than shared. For example, a primary debtor and a guarantor may both be obligated for a debt, but they do not have the same obligation—the guarantor must pay only if the primary debtor defaults and thus has a contingent or secondary obligation, which ranks lower than that of the primary debtor.

205. Secondary, and perhaps even lower ranked, obligations may qualify as liabilities under the definition in paragraph 35, but recognition considerations are highly significant in deciding whether they should formally be included in financial statements because of the effects of uncertainty (paragraphs 44-48). For example, the probability that a secondary or lower ranked obligation will actually have to be paid must be assessed to apply the definition.

Occurrence of a Past Transaction or Event

206. The definition of liabilities in paragraph 35 distinguishes between present and future obligations of an entity. Only present obligations are liabilities under the definition, and they are liabilities of a particular entity as a result of the occurrence of transactions or other events or circumstances affecting the entity.

207. Most liabilities result from exchange transactions in which an entity borrows funds or acquires goods or services and agrees to repay borrowing, usually with interest, or to pay for goods or services received. For example, using employees' services obligates an entity to pay wages or salaries and usually fringe benefits.

208. In contrast, the acts of budgeting the purchase of a machine and budgeting the payments required to obtain it result in neither acquiring an asset nor in incurring a liability. No transaction or event has occurred that gives the entity access to or control of future economic benefit or obligates it to transfer assets or provide services to another entity.

209. Many agreements specify or imply how a resulting obligation is incurred. For example, borrowing agreements specify interest rates, periods involved, and timing of payments; rental agreements specify rentals and periods to which they apply; and royalty agreements may specify payments relating to periods or payments relating to production or sales. The occurrence of the specified event or events results in a liability. For example, interest accrues with the passage of time (that is, providing loaned funds for another hour, day, week, month, or year), while royalties may accrue either with the passage of time or as units are produced or sold, depending on the agreement.

210. Transactions or events that result in liabilities imposed by law or governmental units also are often specified or inherent in the nature of the statute or regulation involved. For example, taxes are commonly assessed for calendar or fiscal years, fines and penalties stem from infractions of the law or failure to comply with provisions of laws or regulations, damages result from selling defective products, and restoring the land after strip-mining the mineral deposit is a consequence of removing the ground cover or overburden and ore. For those imposed obligations, as for obligations resulting from exchange transactions, no liability is incurred until the occurrence of an event or circumstance that obligates an entity to pay cash, transfer other assets, or provide services to other entities in the future.

211. A liability once incurred by an entity remains a liability until it is satisfied in another transaction or other event or circumstance affecting the entity. Most liabilities are satisfied by cash payments. Others are satisfied by the entity's transferring assets or providing services to other entities, and some of those—for example, liabilities to provide magazines under a prepaid subscription agreement—involve performance to earn revenues. Liabilities are also sometimes eliminated by forgiveness, compromise, incurring another liability, or changed circumstances.

Characteristics of Equity of Business Enterprises

212. Paragraph 49 defines equity or net assets as "the residual interest in the assets of an entity that remains after deducting its liabilities." Characteristics of equity of business enterprises are briefly discussed under two headings: residual interest, and invested and earned equity. Although *capital* is not a precise term in referring to equity because it is also applied to assets and liabilities in various ways, it is used in this discussion because *capital* is part of so many terms commonly used to describe

aspects of equity of business enterprises; for example, investments by owners are commonly called capital contributions, distributions to owners are commonly called capital distributions, and discussions of comprehensive income and its components often refer to capital maintenance. (The distinguishing characteristics of net assets of not-for-profit organizations are discussed in paragraphs 50-53 and 90-106.)

Residual Interest

213. Equity in a business enterprise is the ownership interest, and its amount is the cumulative result of investments by owners, comprehensive income, and distributions to owners. That characteristic, coupled with the characteristic that liabilities have priority over ownership interest as claims against enterprise assets, makes equity not determinable independently of assets and liabilities. Although equity can be described in various ways, and different recognition criteria and measurement procedures can affect its amount, equity always equals net assets (assets minus liabilities). That is why it is a residual interest.

Invested and Earned Equity

214. Equity is defined only in total in this Statement. Although equity of business enterprises is commonly displayed in two or more classes, usually based on actual or presumed legal distinctions, those classes may not correspond to the two sources of equity: investments by owners and comprehensive income. For example, a traditional classification for corporate equity is capital stock, other contributed capital, and retained or undistributed profit, with the first two categories described as invested or contributed capital and the third described as earned capital or capital from operations. That distinction holds reasonably well in the absence of distributions to owners or stock dividends; and cash dividends or dividends in kind that are "from profit" may not cause significant classification problems. However, transactions and events such as stock dividends (proportional distributions of an enterprise's own stock accompanied by a transfer of retained or undistributed profit to capital stock and other contributed capital) and reacquisitions and reissues of ownership interests (commonly called treasury stock transactions in corporations) mix the sources and make tracing of sources impossible except by using essentially arbitrary allocations. Thus, categories labeled invested or contributed capital or earned capital may or may not accurately reflect the sources of equity of an enterprise. However, those problems are problems of measurement and display, not problems of definition.

Characteristics of Comprehensive Income of Business Enterprises and Its Components

215. Paragraph 70 defines comprehensive income as "the change in equity of a business enterprise during a period from transactions and other events and circumstances from nonowner sources." It adds that "it includes all changes in equity during a period except those resulting from investments by owners and distributions to owners." Comprehensive income comprises four basic components—revenues, expenses, gains, and losses—that are defined in paragraphs 78-89.

216. The diagram in paragraph 64 shows that comprehensive income and investments by and distributions to owners account for all changes in equity (net assets) of a business enterprise during a period. The sources of comprehensive income are therefore significant to those attempting to use financial statements to help them with investment, credit, and similar decisions about the enterprise, especially since various sources may differ from each other in stability, risk, and predictability. Users' desire for information about those sources underlies the distinctions between revenues, expenses, gains, and losses as well as other components of comprehensive income that result from combining revenues, expenses, gains, and losses in various ways (paragraphs 73-77).

217. The principal distinction between revenues and expenses on the one hand and gains and losses on the other is the distinction between an entity's ongoing major or central operations and its peripheral and incidental transactions and activities. Revenues and expenses result from an entity's productive efforts and most of its exchange transactions with other entities that constitute the entity's ongoing major or central operations. The details vary with the type of entity and activities involved. For example, a manufacturing or construction enterprise buys or contracts to use labor, raw materials, land, plant, equipment, and other goods and services it needs. Its manufacturing or construction operations convert those resources into a product—output of goods—that is intended to have a greater utility, and therefore a higher price, than the combined inputs. Sale of the product should therefore bring in more cash or other assets than were spent to produce and sell it. Other kinds of enterprises earn more cash or other assets than they spend in producing and distributing goods or services through other kinds of operations—for example, by buying and selling goods without changing their form (such as retailers or wholesalers), by providing one or more of a wide variety of services (such as garages, professional firms, insurance companies, and banks), or by investing in securi-

ties of other entities (such as mutual funds, insurance companies, and banks). Some enterprises simultaneously engage in many different ongoing major or central activities.

218. Most entities also occasionally engage in activities that are peripheral or incidental to their ongoing major or central operations. For example, many entities invest in securities of other entities to earn a return on otherwise idle assets (rather than to control or influence the other entities' operations). Moreover, all entities are affected by price changes, interest rate changes, technological changes, thefts, fires, natural disasters, and similar events and circumstances that may be wholly or partly beyond the control of individual entities and their managements. The kinds of events and circumstances noted in this paragraph are commonly sources of gains and losses. Of course, the distinction between revenues and gains and between expenses and losses depends significantly on the nature of an entity and its activities (paragraphs 87 and 88).

Interest in Information about Sources of Comprehensive Income

219. Information about various components of comprehensive income is usually more useful than merely its aggregate amount to investors, creditors, managers, and others who are interested in knowing not only that an entity's net assets have increased (or decreased) but also *how* and *why*. The amount of comprehensive income for a period can, after all, be measured merely by comparing the ending and beginning equity and eliminating the effects of investments by owners and distributions to owners, but that procedure has never provided adequate information about an entity's performance. Investors, creditors, managers, and others need information about the causes of changes in assets and liabilities.

220. As the preceding paragraphs imply, financial accounting and reporting information that is intended to be useful in assessing an enterprise's performance or profitability focuses on certain components of comprehensive income. Ways of providing information about various sources of comprehensive income are matters of display that are beyond the scope of this Statement. Pertinent issues involve questions such as: Should all components of comprehensive income be displayed in a single financial statement or in two or more statements and, if the latter, which statements should be provided? What level of aggregation or disaggregation is needed for revenues, expenses, gains, and losses? Which intermediate components or measures resulting from combining those elements

should be emphasized and which, if any, should be emphasized to the extent of being the "bottom line" of a financial statement? Which, if any, intermediate component or components should be designated as *earnings?* Should some components of comprehensive income be displayed as direct increases or decreases of equity (net assets)?[64]

Characteristics of Net Assets and Changes in the Classes of Net Assets of Not-for-Profit Organizations

221. Paragraph 49 defines equity or net assets as "the residual interest in the assets of an entity that remains after deducting its liabilities." This Statement defines net assets of not-for-profit organizations in total and divides it into three classes—permanently restricted net assets, temporarily restricted net assets, and unrestricted net assets—based on the presence or absence of donor-imposed restrictions and the nature of those restrictions. The two restricted classes of net assets at any time reflect existing limits on the organization's use of assets resulting from donor stipulations. When the limiting conditions are met, expire, or are withdrawn, temporarily restricted net assets are reclassified as unrestricted net assets. Characteristics of net assets of a not-for-profit organization and the interests in information about changes in the classes of net assets are briefly discussed in the following paragraphs.

Residual Interest

222. Net assets in a not-for-profit organization is the cumulative result of changes in permanently restricted, temporarily restricted, and unrestricted net assets, each of which, in turn, is the result of revenues, gains, expenses, and losses and of reclassifications within net assets. That characteristic, coupled with the characteristic that net assets is subject to the priority of liabilities as claims against organization assets, makes net assets not determinable independently of assets and liabilities. Although equity or net assets can be described in various ways, and different recognition criteria and measurement procedures can affect its amount, it is always the amount that remains after deducting liabilities from assets. That is why it is a residual interest.

Interest in Information about Changes in Classes of Net Assets

223. Resource providers are interested in knowing not only that a not-for-profit organization's net assets has increased (or decreased) but also *how* and *why*. That stems from the common interests of

---

[64]Concepts Statement 5 addresses many of those matters and notes that those matters may be developed further at the standards level.

contributors, creditors, and others who provide resources to not-for-profit organizations in information about the services those organizations provide, their efficiency and effectiveness in providing those services, and their continuing ability to provide those services. Some resource providers, such as contributors and members, may be interested in that information as a basis for assessing how well the organization has met its objectives and for determining whether to continue their support. Other resource providers, such as lenders, suppliers, and employees, view a not-for-profit organization as a source of payment for the cash, goods, or services they supply and accordingly are interested in assessing the organization's ability to generate the cash needed for timely payment of the organization's obligations to them.[65]

224. Because the use of resources provided to not-for-profit organizations is often restricted by providers to a particular purpose or time, information about the restrictions on the use of resources and the amounts and kinds of inflows and outflows of resources that change its net assets is usually more useful to present and potential resource providers than merely the amount of change in net assets. The amount of change in net assets for a period can be measured by comparing the ending and beginning net assets, but that procedure alone does not provide adequate information for assessing (a) the services a not-for-profit organization provides, (b) its ability to continue to provide those services, or (c) how managers have discharged their stewardship responsibilities to contributors and others for use of its resources entrusted to them, all of which are important in assessing an organization's performance during a period.

225. Information about purpose restrictions may help assess the organization's ability to provide particular types of services or to make cash payments to creditors. Similarly, information about time restrictions may help creditors and others assess whether an organization has sufficient resources to provide

future services or to make cash payments when due. Information about the amounts and kinds of changes in those restrictions is useful in assessing the extent to which activities of a not-for-profit organization during a period may have drawn upon resources obtained in past periods or have added resources for use in future periods.

226. Information about permanent restrictions is useful in determining the extent to which an organization's resources may not be a source of cash for payments to present or prospective lenders, suppliers, or employees. Thus, information that distinguishes permanently restricted resource inflows from other kinds of changes in an organization's net assets is useful in identifying the resource inflows that are not directly available for providing its services or cash for paying creditors in that (or any other) period (even though they may be a source of future income or other continuing economic benefits).[66]

227. Information about the change in unrestricted net assets for a period is a useful indicator of whether an organization's activities have drawn upon, maintained, or added to the part of its net assets that is fully available—that is, free of donor-imposed restrictions—to support the organization's operating activities. Information about the combined change in unrestricted net assets and in temporarily restricted net assets for a period indicates whether an organization has maintained the part of its net assets that is now or, at some time will be, available to support its operating activities.

228. As the preceding paragraphs suggest, financial reporting information that is intended to be useful in assessing a not-for-profit organization's performance focuses on information about changes in the three classes of a not-for-profit organization's net assets, classes based on the effects of donor-imposed restrictions.[67] Ways of presenting information about the various sources of those changes—revenues, expense, gains, and losses—and of changes in donor-

---

[65]Concepts Statement 4, par. 30. Paragraphs 29, 31, and 32 also discuss the interest of other types of users of financial information, including those having specialized needs and those of internal users, such as managers and governing bodies, and explain that special-purpose reports and detailed information often required by those types of users is beyond the scope of general-purpose external financial reporting.

[66]Permanently restricted resource inflows (for example, endowment contributions) are sometimes said to resemble the "capital" inflows of a business enterprise—investments by its owners. However, as this Statement indicates, characteristics of and changes in net assets of not-for-profit organizations and equity of business enterprises are often more different than similar. For example, unlike investments by owners, donations of assets with permanent restrictions are not a source of cash for payment to creditors. Furthermore, the rights of owners and donors are fundamentally different. A not-for-profit organization that accepts a permanently restricted contribution is obligated only to comply with the restriction. It generally operates for the benefit of the recipients of its services—not for the financial benefit of its donors.

[67]Donors that provide restricted resources may have specific interests in how those resources are used. Information focused on donor-imposed restrictions may be useful to them; however, broad distinctions are not intended to provide external users with assurance that managers have exercised their responsibilities in the manner specifically designated by a particular resource provider. General purpose external financial reporting can best meet the need for information about managers' special responsibilities by disclosing any failures to comply with restrictions that may impinge on an organization's financial performance or on its ability to continue to provide a satisfactory level of services (Concepts Statement 4, par. 41).

imposed restrictions on net assets—reclassifications—are matters of display rather than problems of definition, and thus are beyond the scope of this Statement. Pertinent issues for later study involve questions such as: Should changes in classes of net assets be displayed in a single financial statement or in two or more statements? What level of aggregation or disaggregation is needed for revenues, expenses, gains, or losses? How should reclassifications of temporarily restricted net assets that become unrestricted be displayed?

Examples to Illustrate Concepts

229. The following paragraphs illustrate some possible applications of the definitions and related concepts. Two cautions apply. First, although the points involved are conceptually significant, they may be practically trivial—that is, the results may appear to make little difference in practice. However, since this Statement is part of the Board's conceptual framework project, it is intended to emphasize concepts and sound analysis and to foster careful terminology, classification, and disclosure. The illustrations are meant to focus on substance rather than form. They illustrate, among other things, (a) that the presence or absence of future economic benefit rather than whether or not an entity incurred a cost ultimately determines whether it has a particular kind of asset, (b) that the presence or absence of a legal, equitable, or constructive obligation entailing settlement by future sacrifice of economic benefit (assets) rather than whether or not an entity received proceeds ultimately determines whether it has a particular kind of liability, and (c) that debit balances are not necessarily assets and credit balances are not necessarily liabilities.

230. Second, the examples used are intended to illustrate concepts and are not intended to imply that the accounting illustrated or the display described should necessarily be adopted in practice. Statements of Financial Accounting Standards, not Statements of Financial Accounting Concepts, establish generally accepted accounting principles. Decisions about what should be adopted in practice involve not only concepts but also practical considerations, including the relative benefits and costs of procedures and the reliability of measures. For example, some of the kinds of items illustrated are significantly affected by the uncertainty that surrounds the activities of business enterprises and

not-for-profit organizations (paragraphs 44-48), and those effects should be considered in applying the definitions in this Statement.

231. A particular item to which the definitions may be applied may belong to either of two groups of elements:

First Group	Second Group
an asset,	a liability,
a reduction of a liability (liability valuation),[68]	a reduction of an asset (asset valuation),[68]
an expense, or	a revenue, or
a loss.	a gain.

(None of the examples involves investments by owners or distributions to owners, and only the last one involves equity; those elements are therefore omitted from the two groups.) The nature of the elements and the relations between them dictate that the same item can be, for example, either an asset or an expense or either a liability or a gain, but the same item cannot be, for example, either an asset or a liability or either an expense or a gain. (Those who are familiar with the mechanics of accounting will recognize that the first group includes "debits" and the second group includes "credits.") Thus, to apply the definitions involves determining the group to which an item belongs and the element within the group whose definition it fits.[69]

Deferred Gross Profit on Installment Sales

232. Deferred gross profit on installment sales falls into the second group. It is neither a revenue nor a gain; the recognition basis that results in deferred gross profit (in substance a cash receipts basis) permits no revenue or gain to be recognized at the time of sale, except to the extent of gross profit in a down payment. Designating the amount as "deferred gross profit" also indicates that it is not now a revenue or gain, although it may be in the future.

233. Nor is the deferred gross profit a liability. The selling entity is not obligated to pay cash or to provide goods or services to the customer, except perhaps to honor a warranty or guarantee on the item sold, but that is a separate liability rather than part of the deferred gross profit. The deferred gross profit resulted because of doubt about the collectibility of the sales price (installment receivable), not because of cash payments or other asset transfers that the seller must make.

---

[68]Valuation accounts are part of the assets or liabilities to which they pertain and are neither assets nor liabilities in their own right (pars. 34 and 43). That distinction is significant in several of the examples.

[69]The examples generally concern transactions and other events of business enterprises and are expressed in business terms. Since not-for-profit organizations may have similar transactions (except those related to ownership interests and perhaps those related to income taxes) these examples and the concepts they illustrate relate to those organizations as well.

234. The essence of the installment sale transaction (using the recognition basis involved) is that the sale resulted in an increase in installment receivables and a decrease in inventory of equal amounts—the receivable reflects the unrecovered cost of the inventory sold. Gross profit (revenue less the related cost of goods sold) is recognized as cash is collected on the installment receivable, and the receivable continues to reflect the unrecovered cost—as it should using a cash-receipts basis of recognition—if the deferred gross profit is deducted from it. Thus, no matter how it is displayed in financial statements, deferred gross profit on installment sales is conceptually an asset valuation— that is, a reduction of an asset.

Debt Discount, Premium, and Issue Cost

235. Unamortized or deferred debt discount belongs to the first group (paragraph 231) and was long commonly reported as an asset and amortized to interest expense by straight-line methods. APB Opinion No. 21, *Interest on Receivables and Payables,* changed that practice by requiring debt discount to be (a) deducted directly from the liability (as a "valuation account") and (b) "amortized" by the "interest" method using the effective interest or discount rate implicit in the borrowing transaction. That accounting reports the liability at the present value of the future cash payments for interest and maturity amount, discounted at the effective rate (which is higher than the nominal rate specified in the debt agreement), and reports interest expense at an amount determined by applying the effective rate to the amount of the liability at the beginning of the period.

236. The definitions in this Statement support the accounting required by Opinion 21. The debt discount is not an asset because it provides no future economic benefit. The entity has the use of the borrowed funds but it pays a price for that use— interest. A bond discount means that the entity borrowed less than the face or maturity amount of the debt instrument and therefore pays a higher actual (effective) interest rate than the rate (nominal rate) specified in the debt agreement. Conceptually, debt discount is a liability valuation—that is, a reduction of the face or maturity amount of the related liability.

237. Debt issue cost also falls into the first group of elements and is either an expense or a reduction of the related debt liability. Debt issue cost is not an asset for the same reason that debt discount is not—it provides no future economic benefit. Debt issue cost in effect reduces the proceeds of borrowing and increases the effective interest rate and thus may be accounted for the same as debt discount. However, debt issue cost may also be considered to be an expense of the period of borrowing.

238. Unamortized or deferred debt premium is the exact counterpart of unamortized or deferred debt discount, and Opinion 21 requires counterpart accounting. Unamortized debt premium is not itself a liability—it has no existence apart from the related debt—and is accounted for under the Opinion by being (a) added directly to the related liability and (b) "amortized" by the "interest" method using the effective interest or discount rate implicit in the borrowing transaction. The lower interest rate and lower interest cost result because the proceeds of borrowing exceeded the face or maturity amount of the debt. Conceptually, debt premium is a liability valuation, that is, an addition to the face or maturity amount of the related liability.

239. Terms such as *unamortized or deferred discount or premium* and *to amortize discount or premium* are carry-overs from the days when debt discount was considered to be an amortizable asset (paragraph 235) and do not describe accurately either the assets or liabilities and events involved or the interest method of accounting for them. Paragraphs 141 and 142 of this Statement define and describe accrual, deferral, and amortization. A simple example shows the distinction described in footnote 55: ". . . accounting for debt securities issued (or acquired as an investment) at a discount or premium by the 'interest' method is technically the result of accrual, not deferral or amortization, techniques."

The proceeds are $87 (ignoring debt issue costs) if a 2-year debt security with a $100 face amount and 7 percent interest (payable annually) is issued to yield 15 percent. The interest method gives this accounting (all amounts are rounded to nearest dollar) if the usual valuation account—debt discount—is omitted.

1/1/X1

Cash	$87	
Debt payable		$87

12/31/X1			**12/31/X2**		
Interest expense	$13		Interest expense	$14	
Interest payable (.15 × $87)		$13	Interest payable [.15 × ($87 + $6)]		$ 14
Interest payable	$ 7		Debt payable	$87	
Cash		$ 7	Interest payable	$20	
			Cash		$107

Thus, despite references to the *interest method of amortization* in Opinion 21 and APB Opinion No. 12, *Omnibus Opinion—1967,* the interest method that both Opinions describe is straightforward accounting for cash receipts and payments and accrual of interest expense and interest payable at the effective rate. It involves neither deferring costs nor amortizing deferred costs. Similarly, accounting for investments in debt securities by the interest method involves accruing interest income and receivable but involves no deferrals or amortizations.[70]

Deferred Income Tax Credits

240. One view of deferred income tax credits—the liability method—is that they are taxes payable in future periods, that is, they are obligations of an entity that entail future cash payments. Another view—the net-of-tax method—is that they are valuations related to the effects of taxability and tax deductibility on individual assets. Deferred tax credits belong in the second group (paragraph 231), and the two views just noted exhaust the possibilities—deferred tax credits cannot be revenues, or gains.[71] Both the liability method and the net-of-tax method are compatible with the definitions in this Statement.

241. Only the deferred method that is prescribed by APB Opinion No. 11, *Accounting for Income Taxes,* does not fit the definitions. Deferred income tax credits are neither liabilities nor reductions of assets in Opinion 11. That Opinion rejects the liability method and specifically denies that deferred tax credits are "payables in the usual sense" (paragraph 57). The Opinion also proscribes the net-of-tax method. It requires accounting for deferred tax credits as "tax effects of current timing differences [that] are deferred currently and allocated to income tax expense of future periods when the timing differences reverse" (paragraph 23) rather than either as accrued taxes to be paid in future periods when the timing differences reverse or as reductions in related assets.[72]

242. The compatibility of two of the three most widely suggested methods of accounting for tax effects of timing differences with the definitions in this Statement (and a possible compatible rationale for the results of the third method) is noted because several comments on the Discussion Memorandum and 1977 Exposure Draft had concluded, some with dismay and some with satisfaction, that the definitions ruled out deferred tax accounting or interperiod income tax allocation. However, the definitions are neutral on that recognition question: they affect only the method of allocation and neither require tax allocation nor rule it out.

Deferred Investment Tax Credits

243. Deferred investment tax credits were created by APB Opinion No. 2, *Accounting for the "Investment Credit,"* and the concept of deferred investment tax credits in that Opinion is the basis of this example. Those deferred credits fall into the second group (paragraph 231) and are not revenues, or gains. Deferred investment tax credits differ from deferred income tax credits in lacking a characteristic of liabilities that deferred income tax credits may have: deferred investment tax credits do not involve an obligation to pay taxes or otherwise sacrifice assets in the future. Conceptually, if investment tax credits are to be deferred and amortized over the life of the related assets, they are reductions of the acquisition costs of assets, not liabilities.

244. The Accounting Principles Board concluded in Opinion 2 that an investment tax credit was in substance a reduction of the cost of the related asset acquired and thereby a reduction of depreciation expense over the life of the asset rather than a reduction of income tax expense for the period of acquisition. The APB therefore concluded that "reflection of the allowable credit as a reduction in the net amount at which the acquired property is stated (either directly or by inclusion in an offsetting account)" was "preferable in many cases," and it permitted accounting for the credit as "de-

---

[70]The proceeds are $114.50 if the example is changed to a 15 percent security issued to yield 7 percent. Interest income and receivable accrued is $8.00 (.07 × $114.50) for the first year and $7.50 [.07 × ($114.50 − $7.00)] for the second. Accounting for cash received is:

12/31/X1		12/31/X2	
Cash	$15.00	Cash	$115.00
Interest receivable	$8.00	Interest receivable	$ 7.50
Investment	$7.00	Investment	$107.50

[71]Deferred tax charges are not discussed separately in this Statement. However, they are assets (prepaid taxes) in the liability method and reductions of related liabilities in the net-of-tax method.

[72]Some proponents of the deferred method hold that it is actually a variation of the net-of-tax method despite rejection of that method in Opinion 11. They view the deferred tax charges and credits as the separate display of the effects of interperiod tax allocation instead of as reductions of the related assets, liabilities, revenues, expenses, gains, and losses. They argue that separate display is necessary or desirable, but it is a matter of "geography" in financial statements rather than a matter of the nature of deferred income tax credits.

ferred income'' (a deferred credit) only if it were amortized over the productive life of the property (Opinion 2, paragraph 14). In other words, a deferred investment tax credit could be displayed as if it were a liability, and its amortization could be displayed as a reduction of income tax expense, but it must be accounted for as a reduction of an asset.[73]

245. The issue of whether the tax credit is a liability (deferred credit) or a reduction of the assets acquired is a significant conceptual question with a much less significant practical effect. Indeed, some consider the matter trivial because it does not affect reported profit. The issue of whether the investment tax credit is an asset valuation or a liability focuses, however, directly on the heart of the definition of liabilities. The essence of a liability is a legal, equitable, or constructive obligation to sacrifice economic benefits (assets) in the future, and a deferred investment tax credit based on the analysis in Opinion 2 wholly lacks that characteristic. If, therefore, liabilities were defined in a way that those deferred investment tax credits could qualify as liabilities, the concept would have virtually no meaning—almost any credit balance would qualify as a liability. A definition must set limits to be useful, and a definition broad enough to include deferred investment tax credits would be of little or no help in determining whether any other particular item was a liability of a particular entity.

Deferred Costs of Assets

246. Accountants, and others, are accustomed to describing costs incurred as assets, but costs incurred are at best evidence of the existence of assets (paragraphs 178–180). They result in assets only if an entity acquires or increases future economic benefits available to it in exchange transactions or through production. Once that conceptual point is made, however, it is obvious that cost incurred (acquisition cost or sometimes "historical cost") is commonly the attribute that is measured in financial reporting for many assets. Thus, inventories, plant, equipment, land, and a host of other future economic benefits are now represented in financial statements by some variation of costs incurred to acquire or make them.

247. Other "deferred costs" that are not themselves assets may be costs of the kinds of assets of an entity described in the preceding paragraph. For example, a procedure so long established that it rarely rates a second thought is to account for the costs (less salvage value, if any) of units normally spoiled in producing a product as additional costs of the salable units produced. Similarly, although a "dry hole" cannot by itself qualify as an asset, except perhaps for some salvageable materials or equipment, the costs of drilling a dry hole may be part of the cost of developing the future economic benefits of a mineral deposit that has been discovered.[74] Or, the legal and other costs of successfully defending a patent from infringement are "deferred legal costs" only in the sense that they are part of the cost of retaining and obtaining the future economic benefit of the patent.

248. The examples in the preceding paragraph illustrate costs that are accounted for in current practice as costs of other assets rather than as assets by themselves. The examples in this and the next two paragraphs illustrate costs that are of the same general nature but have sometimes been accounted for, and are commonly described, as if they were themselves assets. For example, entities that incur relocation, repair, training, advertising, or similar costs usually receive services (that is, something of value) in exchange for cash paid or obligations incurred. The question that needs to be answered to apply the definition of assets is whether the economic benefit received by incurring those costs was used up at the time the costs were incurred or shortly thereafter or future economic benefit remains at the time the definition is applied. Costs such as those of relocation, repair, training, or advertising services do not *by themselves* qualify as assets under the definition in paragraph 25 any more than do spoiled units, dry holes, or legal costs. The reason for considering the possibility that they might be accounted for as if they were assets stems from their possible relationship to future economic benefits.

249. Costs incurred for services such as research and development, relocation, repair, training, or advertising relate to future economic benefits in

---

[73]The definitions in this Statement do not bear on the question of whether an investment tax credit should be accounted for by the "deferral and amortization" method (which is described in this paragraph) or the "flow-through" method (which the Board also accepted in APB Opinion No. 4, *Accounting for the "Investment Credit,"* [amending Opinion 2]). That issue involves whether the tax credit reduces the cost of the asset and depreciation over its life or reduces income tax expense in the period of acquisition, which is a recognition or measurement question. The existence of an asset from whose cost the credit may be deducted is not in doubt.

[74]"The cost of a development well [in contrast to that of an exploratory well] is a part of the cost of a bigger asset—a producing system of wells and related equipment and facilities intended to extract, treat, gather, and store known reserves" (FASB Statement No. 19, *Financial Accounting and Reporting by Oil and Gas Producing Companies,* par. 205). The "full-costing" method incorporates the same notion—costs of dry holes are not themselves assets but are costs of mineral deposits.

one of two ways. First, costs may represent rights to unperformed services yet to be received from other entities. For example, advertising cost incurred may be for a series of advertisements to appear in national news magazines over the next three months. Those kinds of costs incurred are similar to prepaid insurance or prepaid rent. They are payments in advance for services to be rendered to the entity by other entities in the future. Second, they may represent future economic benefit that is expected to be obtained within the entity by using assets or in future exchange transactions with other entities. For example, prerelease advertising of a motion picture may increase the future economic benefits of the product, or repairs may increase the future economic benefits of a piece of equipment. Those kinds of costs may be accounted for as assets either by being added to other assets or by being disclosed separately. If costs are to be included in assets because they enhance future economic benefits of two or more assets, the only practical alternative to arbitrarily allocating them to those other assets may be to show them as separate assets.

250. The examples do not, of course, preclude accounting for the kinds of costs involved as expenses of the period in which they are incurred. Many, perhaps most, will not be shown as assets at all for practical reasons stemming from considerations of uncertainty or measurement (paragraphs 44-48 and 175 and 176).

Estimated Loss on Purchase Commitments

251. Estimated loss on purchase commitments belongs in the second group of elements (paragraph 231). It is not a revenue or gain because it results from a loss. It is at best part of a liability and is not *by itself* an obligation to pay cash or otherwise sacrifice assets in the future. There is no asset from which it may be a deduction in present practice. Thus, it seems not to fit in the second group, after all. That predicament results, however, because estimated loss on purchase commitments is the recorded part of a series of transactions and events that are mostly unrecorded.

252. A purchase commitment involves both an item that might be recorded as an asset and an item that might be recorded as a liability. That is, it involves both a right to receive assets and an obligation to pay.[75] A decrease in the price that leaves the committed buyer in the position of now being able to buy the assets cheaper were it not committed to

buy them at the former, higher price does not by itself create an obligation that was not already present. If both the right to receive assets and the obligation to pay were recorded at the time of the purchase commitment, the nature of the loss and the valuation account that records it when the price falls would be clearly seen. The obligation to pay has been unaffected by the price decrease—the full amount must be paid if the assets are accepted upon delivery, or damages must be paid if the assets are not accepted. However, the future economic benefit and value of the right to receive the assets has decreased because the market value of the assets to be received has declined, and the estimated loss on purchase commitment is in concept a reduction of that asset.

253. As long as the commitment transaction remains unrecorded, however, the only way to recognize the loss on the commitment is to do as is done in current practice—to recognize the valuation account for estimated loss on purchase commitments and include it among the assets or liabilities. Although it can be deducted from assets in some way, even though the asset to which it applies is not recorded, it is now sometimes shown among the liabilities.

Minority Interests and Stock Purchase Warrants

254. Minority interests in net assets of consolidated subsidiaries do not represent present obligations of the enterprise to pay cash or distribute other assets to minority stockholders. Rather, those stockholders have ownership or residual interests in components of a consolidated enterprise. The definitions in this Statement do not, of course, preclude showing minority interests separately from majority interests or preclude emphasizing the interests of majority stockholders for whom consolidated statements are primarily provided. Stock purchase warrants are also sometimes called liabilities but entirely lack the characteristics of liabilities. They also are part of equity.

Examples Do Not Govern Practice

255. The Board reiterates that the examples in paragraphs 232-254 are intended to illustrate the definitions and related concepts, not to establish standards for accounting practice (paragraph 230). The examples are intended to help readers understand the essential characteristics of the definitions and related concepts and thereby to help them understand the definitions in this Statement.

---

[75]Whether those rights and obligations might be accounted for as assets and liabilities is a question of recognition, criteria for which are established by Concepts Statement 5 and may be developed further as they are applied at the standards level. Although the definitions in this Statement do not exclude the possibility of recording assets and liabilities for purchase commitments, the Statement contains no conclusions or implications about whether they should be recorded.

Summary Index of Concepts Defined or Discussed

In addition to defining 10 elements of financial statements and 3 classes of net assets (of not-for-profit organizations) and changes in those classes during a period, this Statement defines or discusses other concepts, terms, or phrases that are used in the definitions or explanations or that are otherwise related to those elements and classes. This index identifies the paragraphs in which those elements and classes and certain other significant concepts, terms, or phrases are defined or discussed.

Paragraph
Numbers

AMENDMENT OF FASB CONCEPTS STATEMENT NO. 2, QUALITATIVE CHARACTERISTICS OF ACCOUNTING INFORMATION

As discussed in Appendix A (paragraphs 160-162) the Board has reaffirmed the conclusion that the qualitative characteristics of accounting information set forth in Concepts Statement 2 (relevance, reliability, comparability, and related qualities) apply to both not-for-profit organizations and business enterprises. Accordingly, paragraph 4 and footnote 2 of Concepts Statement 2 are superseded and replaced by the following:

4. The qualities of information discussed in this Statement apply to financial information reported by business enterprises and by not-for-profit organizations. Although the discussion and the examples in this Statement are expressed in terms commonly related to business enterprises, they generally apply to not-for-profit organizations as well. "Objectives of financial reporting by business enterprises," "investors and creditors," "investment and credit decisions," and similar terms are intended to encompass their counterparts for not-for-profit organizations, "objectives of financial reporting by not-for-profit organizations," "resource providers," "resource allocation decisions," and similar terms.[2]

[2]This paragraph is as amended by FASB Concepts Statement No. 6, *Elements of Financial Statements* (December 1985).

FASB Technical Bulletins

FASB TECHNICAL BULLETINS (FTB)

TABLE OF CONTENTS

Table of Contents

Table of Contents

Table of Contents

FASB Technical Bulletin No. 79-1
Purpose and Scope of FASB Technical Bulletins and Procedures for Issuance

STATUS

Issued: December 28, 1979

Effective Date: None stated; Technical Bulletins issued prior to June 30, 1984 indicate only the date of issuance.

Affects: No other pronouncements

Affected by: Superseded by FTB 79-1(R)

(This page intentionally left blank.)

FASB Technical Bulletin No. 79-1 (Revised)
Purpose and Scope of FASB Technical Bulletins
and Procedures for Issuance

STATUS

Issued: June 29, 1984

Effective Date: None stated; Technical Bulletins issued prior to June 30, 1984 indicate only the date of issuance.

Affects: Supersedes FTB 79-1

Affected by: No other pronouncements

FASB Technical Bulletin No. 79-1 (Revised)
Purpose and Scope of FASB Technical Bulletins
and Procedures for Issuance

1. The Financial Accounting Standards Board has authorized its staff to prepare FASB Technical Bulletins to provide guidance on certain financial accounting and reporting problems on a timely basis. This Bulletin describes the purpose and scope of FASB Technical Bulletins, the procedures for issuing them, and related background information. Those procedures have been approved by the Board.

Background

2. The scope of FASB Technical Bulletins and the procedures for issuing them were initially established following solicitation of the public's views through two documents, *Request for Written Comments on an FASB Proposal for Dealing with Industry Accounting Matters and Accounting Questions of Limited Application* issued on November 7, 1978 and *Information about FASB Technical Bulletins* issued on August 10, 1979. In August 1982, the Structure Committee of the Financial Accounting Foundation recommended in its report to the trustees that the Board develop a plan to provide more timely guidance for implementation questions and emerging issues. The Board appointed a task force, which solicited the public's views in an Invitation to Comment, *Timely Guidance on Emerging Issues and Implementation of FASB Standards,* issued in December 1982 and a public hearing held in March 1983. In its report to the Board, the task force recommended that the scope of Technical Bulletins be expanded to allow them to address more emerging problems, implementation issues, and specialized industry accounting questions. In December 1983, the Board issued an Invitation to Comment, *Proposed Procedures for Implementing Recommendations of the FASB Task Force on Timely Financial Reporting Guidance,* to solicit comments on the procedures it proposed to adopt. After consideration of the responses received, the Board decided to expand the scope of Technical Bulletins and to modify the procedures involved in their issuance. The new procedures require that all proposed Bulletins be made available for comment by interested parties. In addition, Board involvement with Technical Bulletins was modified to require Board consideration of *all* proposed Technical Bulletins at a public Board meeting.

Purpose and Scope of FASB Technical Bulletins and Procedures for Issuance

3. FASB Technical Bulletins provide guidance for applying standards in ARBs, APB Opinions, and FASB Statements and Interpretations and for resolving accounting issues not directly addressed in those standards. The following kinds of guidance may be provided in a Technical Bulletin:

a. The guidance in the Bulletin may clarify, explain, or elaborate upon an underlying standard.

b. The guidance in the Bulletin for a particular situation (usually in a specific industry) may differ from the general application required by the standard in an ARB, APB Opinion, or FASB Statement or Interpretation. For example, a Bulletin may specify that the standard does not apply to enterprises in a particular industry or may provide for a deferral of the effective date of a standard for that industry.

c. The guidance in the Bulletin may address areas not directly covered by existing standards.

4. An accounting or reporting problem that comes to the FASB's attention is analyzed by the staff to determine whether the problem might be resolved by issuing an FASB Technical Bulletin. Generally, a Technical Bulletin can provide guidance if the financial accounting and reporting problem can be resolved within the following guidelines:

a. The guidance is not expected to cause a major change in accounting practice for a significant number of entities.

b. The administrative cost that may be involved in implementing the guidance is not expected to be significant to most affected entities.

c. The guidance does not conflict with a broad fundamental principle or create a novel new accounting practice.

Generally, an FASB Statement or Interpretation would be more appropriate to provide guidance than a Technical Bulletin if any one of those guidelines is not met.

5. The director of research and technical activities will release all proposed Technical Bulletins to

selected knowledgeable persons or groups for comment prior to issuance. Further, the availability of proposed Bulletins will be publicized so that any interested party can obtain a copy on request to the FASB. Any party may comment in writing to the director of research and technical activities by a designated date that will not be less than 15 days after initial release of a proposed Bulletin. The FASB will maintain a public record of proposed Bulletins released and all written comments received. The public record will be available for public inspection on the same basis as those for other documents under the FASB's *Rules of Procedure.*

6. All matters proposed for FASB Technical Bulletins will be discussed by the Board at a public meeting and Board members will be provided with copies of all proposed Bulletins prior to their release for comment by interested parties. In addition, all Bulletins and a summary of comments received will be submitted for consideration by the Board at a public meeting prior to final issuance. A Bulletin will not be issued if a majority of the Board members object either to the guidance in it or to communicating that guidance in a Technical Bulletin.

7. The Board may support use of a Technical Bulletin because the nature of the accounting issue addressed and the guidance provided do not, in the Board's judgment, warrant more extensive due process. If the appropriateness of resolving a problem

by issuing an FASB Technical Bulletin is in doubt, the Board may choose to issue a Statement or Interpretation to resolve the problem or to take such other action as it deems appropriate.

8. Each Technical Bulletin will specify an effective date and transition provisions for its initial application. While the Board expects that most Technical Bulletins will be applied prospectively, Technical Bulletins may require retroactive application if that is determined to be appropriate in the circumstances.

9. The Board monitors the procedures for issuing FASB Technical Bulletins and, if deemed advisable, may modify the above procedures from time to time. Any modification will be announced publicly.

10. FASB Technical Bulletins are generally in question-and-answer format and are published with the following legend:

The Financial Accounting Standards Board has authorized its staff to prepare FASB Technical Bulletins to provide guidance on certain financial accounting and reporting problems on a timely basis, pursuant to the procedures described in FASB Technical Bulletin No. 79-1 (Revised), *Purpose and Scope of FASB Technical Bulletins and Procedures for Issuance.*

(This page intentionally left blank.)

FASB Technical Bulletin No. 79-2
Computer Software Costs

STATUS

Issued: December 28, 1979

Effective Date: None stated; Technical Bulletins issued prior to June 30, 1984 indicate only the date of issuance.

Affects: No other pronouncements

Affected by: Superseded by FAS 86

FTB79-3

FASB Technical Bulletin No. 79-3
Subjective Acceleration Clauses in
Long-Term Debt Agreements

STATUS

Issued: December 28, 1979

Effective Date: None stated; Technical Bulletins issued prior to June 30, 1984 indicate only the date of
    issuance.

Affects: No other pronouncements

Affected by: No other pronouncements

FASB Technical Bulletin No. 79-3
Subjective Acceleration Clauses in Long-Term Debt Agreements

Reference:

FASB Statement No. 6, *Classification of Short-Term Obligations Expected to Be Refinanced*

Question

1. Should long-term debt be classified as a current liability if the long-term debt agreement contains a subjective clause that may accelerate the due date?

Background

2. Statement 6 indicates that a subjective acceleration clause contained in a financing agreement that would otherwise permit a short-term obligation to be refinanced on a long-term basis would preclude that short-term obligation from being classified as long-term. Statement 6 does not address financing agreements other than those related to short-term obligations.

Response

3. In some situations, the circumstances (for example, recurring losses or liquidity problems) would indicate that long-term debt subject to a subjective acceleration clause should be classified as a current liability. Other situations would indicate only disclosure of the existence of such clauses. It would also seem that neither reclassification nor disclosure would be required if the likelihood of the acceleration of the due date were remote, such as when the lender historically has not accelerated due dates of loans containing similar clauses and the financial condition of the borrower is strong and its prospects are bright.

FASB Technical Bulletin No. 79-4
Segment Reporting of Puerto Rican Operations

STATUS

Issued: December 28, 1979

Effective Date: None stated; Technical Bulletins issued prior to June 30, 1984 indicate only the date of issuance.

Affects: No other pronouncements

Affected by: No other pronouncements

FASB Technical Bulletin No. 79-4
Segment Reporting of Puerto Rican Operations

Reference:

FASB Statement No. 14, *Financial Reporting for Segments of a Business Enterprise*, paragraphs 31-38

Question

1. Are Puerto Rican operations and operations relating to other areas under U.S. sovereignty or some type of American jurisdiction, such as the Virgin Islands and American Samoa, to be considered *foreign* operations and thus subject to the disclosure requirements of paragraphs 31-38 of Statement 14?

Background

2. Paragraphs 31-38 of Statement 14 require disclosure of information about an enterprise's foreign operations and export sales. Paragraph 31 states that "for purposes of this Statement, an enterprise's foreign operations include those revenue-producing operations . . . that (a) *are located outside the*

enterprise's home country (the United States for U.S. enterprises). . . ." (Emphasis added.)

Response

3. Statement 14 allows judgment (paragraph 83) to distinguish between domestic and foreign operations based on the features of the operation and the facts and circumstances of the enterprise (paragraph 31). Based on those guidelines the degree of interrelationship between the United States and Puerto Rico (as well as non-self-governing U.S. territories such as the Virgin Islands and American Samoa) is such that Puerto Rican operations of U.S. enterprises should be considered domestic operations. Factors such as proximity, economic affinity, and similarities in business environments also indicate this classification for the Puerto Rican operations of U.S. enterprises. It should be noted that the Statement does not prohibit additional disclosures about Puerto Rican operations that might be useful in analyzing and understanding an enterprise's financial statements.

FASB Technical Bulletin No. 79-5
Meaning of the Term "Customer" as It Applies to Health Care Facilities under FASB Statement No. 14

STATUS

Issued: December 28, 1979

Effective Date: None stated; Technical Bulletins issued prior to June 30, 1984 indicate only the date of issuance.

Affects: No other pronouncements

Affected by: No other pronouncements

FASB Technical Bulletin No. 79-5
Meaning of the Term "Customer" as It Applies to Health Care Facilities under FASB Statement No. 14

Reference:

FASB Statement No. 14, *Financial Reporting for Segments of a Business Enterprise*, paragraph 39

Question

1. Would an insuring entity (such as Blue Cross) be considered a "customer" of a health care facility as that term is defined in paragraph 39 of Statement 14?

Background

2. Paragraph 39 of Statement 14 requires that if 10 percent or more of an enterprise's revenue is derived from sales to any single customer, that fact and the amount of revenue from each such customer should be disclosed. A group of customers under common control is regarded as a single customer for purposes of that requirement.

Response

3. An insuring entity should not be considered the "customer" of a health care facility as that term is used in Statement 14. The fact that an insuring entity is a paying agent for the patient does not make the insuring entity the customer of the health care facility because the insuring entity does not decide which services to purchase and from which health care facility to purchase the services. The latter two factors are important in determining the customer.

FASB Technical Bulletin No. 79-6
Valuation Allowances Following Debt Restructuring

STATUS

Issued: December 28, 1979

Effective Date: None stated; Technical Bulletins issued prior to June 30, 1984 indicate only the date of issuance.

Affects: No other pronouncements

Affected by: Superseded by FAS 114

Note: Although superseded by FAS 114, this pronouncement has not been removed from this volume because of the delayed effective date for FAS 114.

FASB Technical Bulletin No. 79-6
Valuation Allowances Following Debt Restructuring

Reference:

FASB Statement No. 15, *Accounting by Debtors and Creditors for Troubled Debt Restructurings,* paragraphs 1 and 29

Question

1. Must the collectibility of a receivable whose terms have been modified and carrying basis adjusted in a troubled debt restructuring under Statement 15 be evaluated to determine the need for subsequent valuation allowances?

Background

2. Statement 15 addresses the accounting appropriate at the time that a restructuring occurs but does not specifically address the accounting for allowances for estimated uncollectible amounts.

Response

3. Statement 15 does not proscribe subsequent provisions for anticipated losses on assets adjusted or acquired in a troubled debt restructuring. Paragraphs 1, 29, 60, 90, and 91 and footnotes 18 and 34 of that Statement are relevant in this respect. Furthermore, FASB Statement No. 5, *Accounting for Contingencies,* requires recognition of anticipated losses whenever they are probable and reasonably estimable. Thus, an assessment of the collectibility of a receivable with modified terms is necessary for a troubled debt restructuring subject to Statement 15.

FASB Technical Bulletin No. 79-7
Recoveries of a Previous Writedown under a Troubled Debt Restructuring Involving a Modification of Terms

STATUS

Issued: December 28, 1979

Effective Date: None stated; Technical Bulletins issued prior to June 30, 1984 indicate only the date of issuance.

Affects: No other pronouncements

Affected by: Superseded by FAS 114

Note: Although superseded by FAS 114, this pronouncement has not been removed from this volume because of the delayed effective date for FAS 114.

FASB Technical Bulletin No. 79-7
Recoveries of a Previous Writedown under a Troubled Debt Restructuring Involving a Modification of Terms

Reference:

FASB Statement No. 15, *Accounting by Debtors and Creditors for Troubled Debt Restructurings*, paragraph 30 and footnote 17

Question

1. May a creditor reverse a previous direct write-down of a receivable when, under a restructuring of a troubled loan through a modification of terms, the future cash receipts exceed the recorded investment in the receivable?

Background

2. Paragraph 30 of Statement 15 discusses the accounting by a creditor for a restructuring involving only a modification of terms and states that the recorded investment in the receivable is not changed unless that amount exceeds the total future cash receipts specified by the new terms, in which case the investment is reduced to an amount equal to the total future cash receipts and a loss recognized. If the total future cash receipts exceed the recorded investment in the receivable, the excess is recognized as interest over the remaining term of the loan. Footnote 17 states that the recorded investment in the receivable is the face amount decreased by the amount of any previous direct writedown.

Response

3. The future cash receipts in excess of the recorded investment in the receivable shall be accounted for as interest income even if a previous direct write-down results in an unusually high effective interest rate on the recorded investment. The amount of the direct writedown should not be reversed.

4. Paragraph 40(a) of Statement 15 does not require disclosures related to a receivable whose terms have been modified if its effective interest rate is equal to or greater than the rate that the creditor was willing to accept for a new receivable with comparable risk; however, disclosure of the amount and source of interest income on such receivables is permitted.

FASB Technical Bulletin No. 79-8
Applicability of FASB Statements 21 and 33 to Certain Brokers and Dealers in Securities

STATUS

Issued: December 28, 1979

Effective Date: None stated; Technical Bulletins issued prior to June 30, 1984 indicate only the date of issuance.

Affects: No other pronouncements

Affected by: Paragraphs 1, 4, and 6 amended by FAS 89
Paragraph 3 superseded by FAS 89
Paragraphs 5 and 6 amended by FAS 111

FASB Technical Bulletin No. 79-8
Applicability of FASB Statements 21 and 33 to
Certain Brokers and Dealers in Securities

References:

FASB Statement No. 21, *Suspension of the Reporting of Earnings per Share and Segment Information by Nonpublic Enterprises,* paragraph 13
FASB Statement No. 33, *Financial Reporting and Changing Prices,* paragraph 22(h)

Question

1. Should closely held brokers or dealers in securities that file financial statements with the Securities and Exchange Commission (SEC) be considered nonpublic enterprises for purposes of applying Statements 21 and 33?

Background

2. Statement 21 suspends the requirements of FASB Statement No. 14, *Financial Reporting for Segments of a Business Enterprise,* and APB Opinion No. 15, *Earnings Per Share,* for nonpublic enterprises.

3. Statement 33 establishes standards for reporting effects of price changes by certain large, public enterprises.

4. To be considered a nonpublic enterprise under Statement 21, an enterprise must meet two specific conditions, one of which is that the enterprise is not required to file financial statements with the SEC. Reciprocally, Statement 33 states that an enterprise that is required to file financial statements with the SEC is a public enterprise.

5. All security brokers and dealers registered with the SEC must file complete sets of financial statements with the SEC for use by the SEC's Division of Market Regulation for regulatory purposes, whether they are closely held or publicly held. Although the statement of financial condition filed by a broker-dealer must be available for public inspection, the income statement and statement of changes in financial position may be treated as "confidential" if so requested by the broker-dealer. A publicly held broker-dealer that is subject to sections 12 and 13 of the Securities Exchange Act of 1934 must, in addition, file a complete set of financial statements and various forms with the SEC in the same manner as is required of other publicly held enterprises subject to those sections of the 1934 Act.

Response

6. The fact that financial statements are required to be filed for broker-dealer regulatory purposes with the SEC does not make an otherwise "nonpublic" enterprise public for purposes of Statements 21 and 33. Thus, the Statement 21 suspension applies to, and the Statement 33 definition of a public enterprise excludes, closely held broker-dealers that are required to file financial statements with the SEC only for use by its Division of Market Regulation, principally because the broker-dealer can cause a significant portion of those financial statements (that is, the income statement and statement of changes in financial position) to be unavailable for public inspection by requesting confidential treatment.

FASB Technical Bulletin No. 79-9
Accounting in Interim Periods for Changes in Income Tax Rates

STATUS

Issued: December 28, 1979

Effective Date: None stated; Technical Bulletins issued prior to June 30, 1984 indicate only the date of issuance.

Affects: No other pronouncements

Affected by: Paragraph 3 amended by FAS 96 and FAS 109

FASB Technical Bulletin No. 79-9
Accounting in Interim Periods for Changes in Income Tax Rates

Reference:

FASB Interpretation No. 18, *Accounting for Income Taxes in Interim Periods,* paragraph 24

Question

1. How should a company with a fiscal year other than a calendar year account during interim periods for the reduction in the corporate tax rate resulting from the Revenue Act of 1978?

Background

2. The Revenue Act of 1978, among other things, reduced the corporate income tax rate from 48 per-cent to 46 percent.

Response

3. Paragraph 24 of Interpretation 18 requires that the effect of a change in tax rates be reflected in a revised annual effective tax rate calculation in the same way that the change will be applied to the company's taxable income for the year. The revised annual effective tax rate would then be applied to pretax income for the year-to-date at the end of the current interim period. Paragraph 13 of FASB Statement No. 16, *Prior Period Adjustments,* indicates that previous interim periods of the company's current fiscal year would be restated by prior period adjustment if the effect is material.

FASB Technical Bulletin No. 79-10
Fiscal Funding Clauses in Lease Agreements

STATUS

Issued: December 28, 1979

Effective Date: None stated; Technical Bulletins issued prior to June 30, 1984 indicate only the date of issuance.

Affects: No other pronouncements

Affected by: No other pronouncements

FASB Technical Bulletin No. 79-10
Fiscal Funding Clauses in Lease Agreements

Reference:

FASB Statement No. 13, *Accounting for Leases,* paragraph 5(f)

Question

1. What effect, if any, should the existence of a fiscal funding clause in a lease agreement have on the classification of the lease under Statement 13?

Background

2. A fiscal funding clause is commonly found in a lease agreement in which the lessee is a governmental unit. A fiscal funding clause generally provides that the lease is cancelable if the legislature or other funding authority does not appropriate the funds necessary for the governmental unit to fulfill its obligations under the lease agreement.

Response

3. Paragraph 5(f) of Statement 13 requires that a cancelable lease, such as a lease containing a fiscal funding clause, be evaluated to determine whether the uncertainty of possible lease cancellation is a remote contingency. That paragraph states that "a lease which is cancelable (i) only upon occurrence of some *remote* contingency . . . shall be considered 'noncancelable' for purposes of this definition" of lease term. (Emphasis added.)

4. In discussing the likelihood of the occurrence of a future event or events to confirm a loss contingency, paragraph 3 of FASB Statement No. 5, *Accounting for Contingencies,* defines *remote* as relating to conditions when "the chance of the future event or events occurring is slight." The evaluation of the uncertainty of possible lease cancellation should be consistent with that definition.

5. The existence of a fiscal funding clause in a lease agreement would necessitate an assessment of the likelihood of lease cancellation through exercise of the fiscal funding clause. If the likelihood of exercise of the fiscal funding clause is assessed as being remote, a lease agreement containing such a clause would be considered a noncancelable lease; otherwise, the lease would be considered cancelable and thus classified as an operating lease.

FASB Technical Bulletin No. 79-11
Effect of a Penalty on the Term of a Lease

STATUS

Issued: December 28, 1979

Effective Date: None stated; Technical Bulletins issued prior to June 30, 1984 indicate only the date of issuance.

Affects: No other pronouncements

Affected by: Superseded by FAS 98

(This page intentionally left blank.)

FASB Technical Bulletin No. 79-12
Interest Rate Used in Calculating the Present Value
of Minimum Lease Payments

STATUS

Issued: December 28, 1979

Effective Date: None stated; Technical Bulletins issued prior to June 30, 1984 indicate only the date of
issuance.

Affects: No other pronouncements

Affected by: No other pronouncements

FASB Technical Bulletin No. 79-12
Interest Rate Used in Calculating the Present Value of Minimum Lease Payments

Reference:

FASB Statement No. 13, *Accounting for Leases,* paragraphs 5(l) and 7(d)

Question

1. May a lessee use its secured borrowing rate in calculating the present value of minimum lease payments in applying the provisions of Statement 13?

Background

2. Paragraph 7(d) of Statement 13 requires the lessee to use its incremental borrowing rate (or the lessor's implicit interest rate in certain circumstances) to calculate the present value of minimum lease payments. The incremental borrowing rate is defined in paragraph 5(l) as "the rate that . . . the lessee would have incurred to borrow over a similar term the funds necessary to purchase the leased asset."

Response

3. Paragraph 5(l) of Statement 13 does not proscribe the lessee's use of a secured borrowing rate as its incremental borrowing rate if that rate is determinable, reasonable, and consistent with the financing that would have been used in the particular circumstances.

FASB Technical Bulletin No. 79-13
Applicability of FASB Statement No. 13 to
Current Value Financial Statements

STATUS

Issued: December 28, 1979

Effective Date: None stated; Technical Bulletins issued prior to June 30, 1984 indicate only the date of issuance.

Affects: No other pronouncements

Affected by: No other pronouncements

FASB Technical Bulletin No. 79-13
Applicability of FASB Statement No. 13 to Current Value Financial Statements

Reference:

FASB Statement No. 13, *Accounting for Leases,* paragraphs 7 and 8

Question

1. Are financial statements prepared on a current value basis exempt from the provisions of Statement 13?

Response

2. Statement 13 would not be inapplicable merely because financial statements are prepared on a current value basis. For example, if at its inception a lease involving property meets one or more of the four criteria of paragraph 7 and both of the criteria of paragraph 8 of Statement 13, the lessor would classify the lease as a sales-type or direct financing lease, whichever is appropriate. Subsequently, the carrying amount of the recorded investment in the lease payments receivable would be adjusted in accordance with the valuation techniques employed in preparing the financial statements on a current value basis.

FASB Technical Bulletin No. 79-14
Upward Adjustment of Guaranteed Residual Values

STATUS

Issued: December 28, 1979

Effective Date: None stated; Technical Bulletins issued prior to June 30, 1984 indicate only the date of
issuance.

Affects: No other pronouncements

Affected by: No other pronouncements

FASB Technical Bulletin No. 79-14
Upward Adjustment of Guaranteed Residual Values

Reference:

FASB Statement No. 13, *Accounting for Leases,* paragraphs 17(d), 18(d), and 46

Question

1. Does the prohibition against upward adjustments of estimated residual values in Statement 13 also apply to upward adjustments that result from renegotiations of the guaranteed portions of residual values?

Background

2. Paragraphs 17(d), 18(d), and 46 of Statement 13 require the lessor to review annually the estimated residual value of sales-type leases, direct financing leases, and leveraged leases, respectively. Those paragraphs also contain a provision that prohibits any upward adjustment of the estimated residual value.

Response

3. The prohibitions of paragraphs 17(d), 18(d), and 46 of Statement 13 against upward adjustments to the leased property's estimated residual value are equally applicable to the guaranteed portion. If a lease initially transferred substantially all of the benefits and risks incident to the ownership of the leased property, it would not seem appropriate that the lessor could subsequently increase the benefits that were accounted for as having been retained initially.

4. Recording upward adjustments to the leased property's residual value would, in essence, result in recognizing a sale of the residual value interest. In this respect, the prohibition of an upward adjustment in the leased property's residual value is similar to the prohibition in paragraph 17 of FASB Statement No. 5, *Accounting for Contingencies,* of recognizing gain contingencies because to do so might be recognizing revenue before realization. Realization of the residual value interest might also be contingent on factors, such as the physical condition of the leased property or the requirements and related costs, if any, relating to remarketing agreements at the end of the lease term.

FASB Technical Bulletin No. 79-15
Accounting for Loss on a Sublease Not Involving the Disposal of a Segment

STATUS

Issued: December 28, 1979

Effective Date: None stated; Technical Bulletins issued prior to June 30, 1984 indicate only the date of issuance.

Affects: No other pronouncements

Affected by: No other pronouncements

FASB Technical Bulletin No. 79-15
Accounting for Loss on a Sublease Not Involving the Disposal of a Segment

References:

FASB Statement No. 13, *Accounting for Leases,*
paragraphs 35-39
FASB Interpretation No. 27, *Accounting for a Loss
on a Sublease*

Question

1. Should a loss on a sublease not involving the disposal of a segment be recognized and how is it determined?

Response

2. The general principle of recognizing losses on transactions and the applicability of that general principle to contracts that are expected to result in a loss are well established. Accordingly, if costs expected to be incurred under an operating sublease (that is, executory costs and either amortization of the leased asset or rental payments on an operating lease, whichever is applicable) exceed anticipated revenue on the operating sublease, a loss should be recognized by the sublessor. Similarly, a loss should be recognized on a direct financing sublease if the carrying amount of the investment in the sublease exceeds the total of rentals expected to be received and estimated residual value unless the sublessor's tax benefits from the transaction are sufficient to justify that result.

3. The absence of explicit reference to accounting for these transactions in Statement 13 does not affect the necessity to follow general principles of loss recognition.

(This page intentionally left blank.)

FASB Technical Bulletin No. 79-16
Effect of a Change in Income Tax Rate on the Accounting for Leveraged Leases

STATUS

Issued: December 28, 1979

Effective Date: None stated; Technical Bulletins issued prior to June 30, 1984 indicate only the date of issuance.

Affects: No other pronouncements

Affected by: Superseded by FTB 79-16(R)

FASB Technical Bulletin No. 79-16 (Revised)
Effect of a Change in Income Tax Rate on the Accounting for Leveraged Leases

STATUS

Issued: February 29, 1980

Effective Date: None stated; Technical Bulletins issued prior to June 30, 1984 indicate only the date of issuance.

Affects: Supersedes FTB 79-16

Affected by: Paragraph 4 amended by FAS 96 and FAS 109

FASB Technical Bulletin No. 79-16 (Revised)
Effect of a Change in Income Tax Rate on the Accounting for Leveraged Leases

Reference:

FASB Statement No. 13, *Accounting for Leases,* paragraph 46

Question

1. What effect, if any, does a change[1] in the income tax rate have on the accounting for leveraged leases under Statement 13?

Background

2. Paragraph 46 of Statement 13 provides that, when an important assumption changes, the rate of return and the allocation of income shall be recalculated from the inception of the lease, and the change in the recalculated balances of net investment shall be recognized as a gain or loss in the year in which the assumption is changed.

Response

3. The lessor's income tax rate is an important assumption in accounting for a leveraged lease. Accordingly, the income effect of a change in the income tax rate should be recognized in the first accounting period ending on or after the date on which the legislation effecting a rate change becomes law.[2]

4. If accounting for the effect on leveraged leases of the change in tax rates results in a significant variation from the customary relationship between income tax expense and pretax accounting income and the reason for that variation is not otherwise apparent, paragraph 63 of APB Opinion No. 11, *Accounting for Income Taxes,* requires that the reason for that variation should be disclosed.

---

[1]FASB Technical Bulletin No. 79-16 addressed the effect of a reduction in the corporate income tax rate from 48 percent to 46 percent. Because the response is applicable to increases as well as decreases in the tax rate, this revised Bulletin has been generalized to address the effect of all income tax changes on the accounting for leveraged leases.

[2]Bulletin 79-16 stated "ending on or after the *effective date of the rate change*." (Emphasis added.) This revised Bulletin clarifies the ambiguity of that phrase.

FASB Technical Bulletin No. 79-17
Reporting Cumulative Effect Adjustment from
Retroactive Application of FASB Statement No. 13

STATUS

Issued: December 28, 1979

Effective Date: None stated; Technical Bulletins issued prior to June 30, 1984 indicate only the date of
issuance.

Affects: No other pronouncements

Affected by: No other pronouncements

FASB Technical Bulletin No. 79-17
Reporting Cumulative Effect Adjustment from Retroactive Application of FASB Statement No. 13

Reference:

FASB Statement No. 13, *Accounting for Leases,* paragraph 51

Question

1. If a company presents in its annual report five annual income statements that were retroactively restated to apply the provisions of paragraphs 1-47 of Statement 13, must the cumulative effect of applying those provisions be included in determining net income of any period presented?

Background

2. Paragraph 49 of Statement 13 requires retroactive application of the provisions of that Statement in financial statements for fiscal years beginning after December 31, 1980. Financial statements presented for prior periods are to be restated. Paragraph 51 of that Statement requires that the

cumulative effect on the retained earnings at the beginning of the earliest period restated shall be included in determining the net income of that period.

Response

3. The cumulative effect of applying the provisions of paragraphs 1-47 of Statement 13 would *not* be included in net income of any period presented unless the year prior to the earliest year presented could not be restated. Paragraph 51 does not refer to the earliest period *presented* but rather refers to the earliest period *restated*. Thus, if income statements for five years are presented and the next prior year cannot be restated, the cumulative effect would be included in the determination of net income of the first year presented. In that same situation, if a company presented income statements only for the current year and the immediately preceding year, neither income statement would include a cumulative effect adjustment.

FASB Technical Bulletin No. 79-18
Transition Requirement of Certain FASB Amendments and Interpretations of FASB Statement No. 13

STATUS

Issued: December 28, 1979

Effective Date: None stated; Technical Bulletins issued prior to June 30, 1984 indicate only the date of issuance.

Affects: No other pronouncements

Affected by: No other pronouncements

FASB Technical Bulletin No. 79-18
Transition Requirement of Certain FASB Amendments and
Interpretations of FASB Statement No. 13

References:

FASB Statements 17, 22, 23, 26, 27, 28, and 29
FASB Interpretations 19, 21, 23, 24, 26, and 27
[All related to FASB Statement No. 13, *Accounting for Leases*]

Question

1. In applying the transition requirement of the amendments and interpretations of Statement 13, what is meant by the phrase "have published annual financial statements" and what disclosure is required to indicate that Statement 13 had been applied retroactively without restatement of the prior years' financial statements due to immateriality?

Background

2. The relevant portion of the transition requirement in FASB amendments and interpretations of Statement 13 states:

In addition, except as provided in the next sentence, the provisions of this [Interpretation/Statement] shall be applied retroactively at the same time and in the same manner as the provisions of FASB Statement No. 13 are applied retroactively (see paragraphs 49 and 51 of Statement No. 13). Enterprises that *have already applied the provisions of Statement No. 13 retroactively and have published annual financial statements* based on the retroactively adjusted accounts before the effective date of this [Interpretation/Statement] may, but are not required to, apply the provisions of this [Interpretation/Statement] retroactively. [Emphasis added.]

Response

3. The phrase "have published annual financial statements" generally refers to those financial statements that a company normally includes in its annual report to shareholders for its established 12-month reporting period (that is, its fiscal year). Inclusion of the word "published" in the transition requirement emphasizes that the annual financial statements should be those that are distributed to all shareholders. For a publicly held company, those financial statements would normally be accompanied by an independent auditor's opinion.

4. Although the phrase "have published annual financial statements" generally refers to the financial statements included in a company's annual reports to shareholders, other circumstances, such as in a filing under the requirements of the Federal Securities Act, may necessitate the issuance to all shareholders of complete financial statements for a company's established 12-month reporting period. For example, if a calendar-year company files a registration statement with the Securities and Exchange Commission in October 1978 and subsequently delivers a proxy statement containing complete financial statements for its year ended December 31, 1977 to all shareholders, the 1977 financial statements (which would include all footnotes contained in the annual report to shareholders) that are included in the proxy statement could constitute published annual financial statements as contemplated by the transition requirement of the amendments and interpretations of Statement 13.

5. On the other hand, the "have published annual financial statements" provision would not be met if the calendar-year company referred to in the above example included its 1977 financial statements, restated to adopt the requirements of Statement 13 retroactively, in the 1978 third quarter interim report to shareholders unless inclusion of its normal fiscal year financial statements is consistent with that company's previously established reporting practices. In addition, the issuance of complete financial statements for a 12-month period that is not the company's established fiscal year would not constitute published annual financial statements for purposes of satisfying the transition requirement in question.

6. Amendments and interpretations of Statement 13 should be applied retroactively as they become effective unless Statement 13 had been applied retroactively in published annual financial statements to shareholders at an earlier date. The retroactive application of Statement 13 would not necessarily require the recording of an adjustment in a company's accounting records when the effects of applying Statement 13 on a retroactive basis call for adjustments that are clearly immaterial. However, in those instances, it could be expected that the notes to the published annual financial statements would have included appropriate disclosure to indicate that the company had adopted Statement 13 retroactively and that prior years' financial statements were not restated because the effects of retroactive application were immaterial. The absence of such disclosures would indicate that Statement 13 had not yet been adopted retroactively. Similarly, if the notes to financial statements in an annual report to shareholders include the "as if" disclosures required by paragraph 50 of Statement 13, it would also be apparent that a company had not adopted the provisions of Statement 13 on a retroactive basis in those earlier financial statements.

FASB Technical Bulletin No. 79-19
Investor's Accounting for Unrealized Losses on Marketable Securities Owned by an Equity Method Investee

STATUS

Issued: December 28, 1979

Effective Date: None stated; Technical Bulletins issued prior to June 30, 1984 indicate only the date of issuance.

Affects: No other pronouncements

Affected by: Paragraph 1 amended by FAS 115
Paragraph 6 superseded by FAS 115

FASB Technical Bulletin No. 79-19
Investor's Accounting for Unrealized Losses on Marketable Securities Owned by an Equity Method Investee

References:

FASB Statement No. 12, *Accounting for Certain Marketable Securities,* paragraph 9 and footnote 5
APB Opinion No. 18, *The Equity Method of Accounting for Investments in Common Stock,* paragraph 19

Question

1. How should a parent or investor account for its share of the accumulated changes in the valuation allowance for marketable equity securities included in stockholders' equity of an investee accounted for under the equity method?

Background

2. Paragraph 9 of Statement 12 specifies in part that "the portfolios of marketable equity securities owned by an entity (subsidiary or investee) that is accounted for by the equity method shall not be combined with the portfolios of marketable equity securities owned by any other entity included in the financial statements. However, such an entity is, itself, subject to the requirements of this Statement." (Footnote reference omitted.)

3. Under Statement 12, if the aggregate cost of a portfolio of marketable equity securities exceeds the aggregate market value of the portfolio, the difference is accounted for as a valuation allowance and the securities are thereby carried at market value. For a portfolio of marketable equity securities classified as a noncurrent asset or included in an unclassified balance sheet, an amount equal to the accumulated changes in the valuation allowance is included in the equity section of the investee's balance sheet and shown separately. On the other hand,

for a portfolio of marketable equity securities classified as a current asset, an amount equal to the changes in the valuation allowance is included in the determination of net income by the investee and the parent or investor includes its proportionate share of the investee's earnings or losses in income.

4. Opinion 18 states in paragraph 19:

Applying the equity method. The difference between consolidation and the equity method lies in the details reported in the financial statements. Thus, an investor's net income for the period and its stockholders' equity at the end of the period are the same whether an investment in a subsidiary is accounted for under the equity method or the subsidiary is consolidated. . . . A transaction of an investee of a capital nature that affects the investor's share of stockholders' equity of the investee should be accounted for as if the investee were a consolidated subsidiary.

5. Footnote 5 of Statement 12 recognizes that exclusion of the securities owned by a subsidiary that is accounted for by the equity method from the parent company's portfolio of marketable equity securities may result in income different from that which would have resulted if that subsidiary had been consolidated rather than accounted for by the equity method because portfolios of consolidated subsidiaries are combined while portfolios of entities accounted for by the equity method are not combined. However, that footnote does not describe, as an exception to paragraph 19 of Opinion 18, any difference in stockholders' equity from applying the portfolio approach required by Statement 12.

Response

6. If a subsidiary or other investee that is accounted for by the equity method is required to include accumulated changes in a valuation allowance for a portfolio of marketable equity securities in the stockholders' equity section of its balance sheet pursuant to the provisions of Statement 12, the parent or investor shall reduce its investment in that investee by its proportionate share of the accumulated changes in the valuation allowance and a like amount shall be included in the stockholders' equity section of its balance sheet.

FASB Technical Bulletin No. 80-1
Early Extinguishment of Debt through Exchange for Common or Preferred Stock

STATUS

Issued: December 19, 1980

Effective Date: None stated; Technical Bulletins issued prior to June 30, 1984 indicate only the date of issuance.

Affects: No other pronouncements

Affected by: Paragraphs 1 through 4 amended by FAS 111

FASB Technical Bulletin No. 80-1
Early Extinguishment of Debt through Exchange for Common or Preferred Stock

References:

APB Opinion No. 26, *Early Extinguishment of Debt*
FASB Statement No. 4, *Reporting Gains and Losses from Extinguishment of Debt*
FASB Statement No. 15, *Accounting by Debtors and Creditors for Troubled Debt Restructurings*

Question

1. Does Opinion 26 apply to early extinguishments of debt effected by issuance of common or preferred stock, including redeemable and fixed-maturity preferred stock?

Background

2. Under Opinion 26, the conversion of debt to common or preferred stock is not an early extinguishment if the conversion represents the exercise of a conversion right contained in the terms of the debt issue. Other exchanges of common or preferred stock for debt before the scheduled maturity of the debt would constitute early extinguishment.

Response

3. All early extinguishments of debt must be accounted for in accordance with either Statement 15 or Opinion 26. Statement 15 applies to extinguishments effected in a troubled debt restructuring; Opinion 26 applies to all other early extinguishments of debt.

4. Thus, Opinion 26 applies to all early extinguishments of debt effected by issuance of common or preferred stock, including redeemable and fixed-maturity preferred stock, unless the extinguishment is a troubled debt restructuring or a conversion by the holder pursuant to conversion privileges contained in the original debt issue. Paragraph 20 of Opinion 26 requires the difference between the net carrying amount of the extinguished debt and the reacquisition price of the extinguished debt to be recognized currently in income of the period of extinguishment. Paragraph 8 of Statement 4 requires any such difference, if material, to be classified as an extraordinary item, net of related income tax effect. The reacquisition price of the extinguished debt is to be determined by the value of the common or preferred stock issued or the value of the debt—whichever is more clearly evident.

FASB Technical Bulletin No. 80-2
Classification of Debt Restructurings by Debtors and Creditors

STATUS

Issued: December 19, 1980

Effective Date: None stated; Technical Bulletins issued prior to June 30, 1984 indicate only the date of issuance.

Affects: No other pronouncements

Affected by: No other pronouncements

FASB Technical Bulletin No. 80-2
Classification of Debt Restructurings by
Debtors and Creditors

Reference:

FASB Statement No. 15, *Accounting by Debtors and Creditors for Troubled Debt Restructurings*

Question

1. In applying Statement 15, can a debt restructuring be a troubled debt restructuring for a debtor but not for the creditor?

Background

2. Paragraph 2 of Statement 15 states that "a restructuring of a debt constitutes a *troubled debt restructuring* for purposes of this Statement if the creditor for economic or legal reasons related to the debtor's financial difficulties grants a concession to the debtor that it would not otherwise consider." Paragraph 7 points out that a debt restructuring is not necessarily a troubled debt restructuring simply because the debtor is experiencing some financial difficulties. That paragraph states in part:

> For example, a troubled debt restructuring is not involved if (a) the fair value[2] of cash, other assets, or an equity interest accepted *by a creditor* from a debtor in full satisfaction of its receivable at least equals *the creditor's* recorded investment in the receivable;[3] (b) the fair value of cash, other assets, or an equity interest transferred *by a debtor* to a creditor in full settlement of its payable at least equals the *debtor's* carry-

ing amount of the payable; (c) the creditor reduces the effective interest rate on the debt primarily to reflect a decrease in market interest rates in general or a decrease in the risk so as to maintain a relationship with a debtor that can readily obtain funds from other sources at the current market interest rate; or (d) the debtor issues in exchange for its debt new marketable debt having an effective interest rate based on its market price that is at or near the current market interest rates of debt with similar maturity dates and stated interest rates issued by nontroubled debtors. [Emphasis added.]

---

[2]Defined in paragraph 13 [of Statement 15].
[3]Defined in footnote 17 [of Statement 15].

Response

3. Yes, a debtor may have a troubled debt restructuring under Statement 15 even though the related creditor does not have a troubled debt restructuring. The debtor and creditor must individually apply Statement 15 to the specific facts and circumstances to determine whether a troubled debt restructuring has occurred. Example (a) in paragraph 7 of Statement 15 identifies a type of debt restructuring that is *not* a troubled debt restructuring for purposes of the creditor's application of Statement 15; similarly, example (b) in paragraph 7 identifies a type of debt

restructuring that is *not* a troubled debt restructuring for purposes of the debtor's application of Statement 15. Thus, Statement 15 establishes tests for applicability that are not symmetrical as between the debtor and the creditor when the debtor's carrying amount and the creditor's recorded investment differ.

Illustration

4. Creditor A makes a $10,000 interest-bearing loan to Debtor X and, when Debtor X later encounters financial difficulties, sells its receivable from Debtor X to Creditor B for $4,000 on a nonrecourse basis. Following the sale, the carrying amount of the loan payable by Debtor X would still be $10,000 and the recorded investment of the loan by Creditor B would be $4,000. If Debtor X subsequently transfers to Creditor B assets with a fair value of $5,500 in full settlement of the loan, that transaction would be a troubled debt restructuring for Debtor X because the fair value of the assets is less than the carrying amount of the loan, whereas Creditor B would not have a troubled debt restructuring because the fair value of the assets received exceeds its recorded investment in the loan.

FASB Technical Bulletin No. 81-1
Disclosure of Interest Rate Futures Contracts and Forward and Standby Contracts

STATUS

Issued: February 6, 1981

Effective Date: None stated; Technical Bulletins issued prior to June 30, 1984 indicate only the date of issuance.

Affects: No other pronouncements

Affected by: Superseded by FAS 80

FASB Technical Bulletin No. 81-2
Accounting for Unused Investment Tax Credits Acquired in a Business Combination Accounted for by the Purchase Method

STATUS

Issued: February 6, 1981

Effective Date: None stated; Technical Bulletins issued prior to June 30, 1984 indicate only the date of issuance.

Affects: No other pronouncements

Affected by: Superseded by FAS 96 and FAS 109

FASB Technical Bulletin No. 81-3
Multiemployer Pension Plan Amendments Act of 1980

STATUS

Issued: February 6, 1981

Effective Date: None stated; Technical Bulletins issued prior to June 30, 1984 indicate only the date of issuance.

Affects: No other pronouncements

Affected by: Superseded by FAS 111

(The next page is 1224.)

FASB Technical Bulletin No. 81-4
Classification as Monetary or Nonmonetary Items

STATUS

Issued: February 6, 1981

Effective Date: None stated; Technical Bulletins issued prior to June 30, 1984 indicate only the date of issuance.

Affects: No other pronouncements

Affected by: Superseded by FAS 89

FASB Technical Bulletin No. 81-5
Offsetting Interest Cost to be Capitalized
with Interest Income

STATUS

Issued: February 6, 1981

Effective Date: None stated; Technical Bulletins issued prior to June 30, 1984 indicate only the date of
issuance.

Affects: No other pronouncements

Affected by: Superseded by FAS 62

FASB Technical Bulletin No. 81-6
Applicability of Statement 15 to Debtors
in Bankruptcy Situations

STATUS

Issued: November 30, 1981

Effective Date: None stated; Technical Bulletins issued prior to June 30, 1984 indicate only the date of issuance.

Affects: No other pronouncements

Affected by: No other pronouncements

FASB Technical Bulletin No. 81-6
Applicability of Statement 15 to Debtors
in Bankruptcy Situations

Reference:

FASB Statement No. 15, *Accounting by Debtors and Creditors for Troubled Debt Restructurings,* paragraph 10

Question

1. Does Statement 15 apply to troubled debt restructurings of debtors involved in bankruptcy proceedings?

Background

2. Some confusion has arisen about the interaction of paragraph 10 and footnote 4 of Statement 15. Paragraph 10 indicates that the Statement applies to troubled debt restructurings consummated under reorganization, arrangement, or other provisions of the Federal Bankruptcy Act or other federal statutes related thereto. However, footnote 4 to that paragraph states that the Statement does not apply ". . . if, under provisions of those Federal statutes or in a quasi-reorganization or corporate readjustment (*ARB No. 43,* Chapter 7, Section A, 'Quasi-Reorganization or Corporate Readjustment . . .') with which a troubled debt restructuring coincides, the debtor restates its liabilities generally."

Response

3. Statement 15 does not apply to debtors who, in connection with bankruptcy proceedings, enter into troubled debt restructurings that result in a general restatement of the debtor's liabilities, that is, when such restructurings or modifications accomplished under purview of the bankruptcy court encompass most of the amount of the debtor's liabilities.

4. For example, companies involved with Chapter XI bankruptcy proceedings frequently reduce all or most of their indebtedness with the approval of their creditors and the court in order to provide an opportunity for the company to have a fresh start. Such reductions are usually by a stated percentage so that, for example, the debtor owes only 60 cents on the dollar. Because the debtor would be restating its liabilities generally, Statement 15 would not apply to the debtor's accounting for such reduction of liabilities.

5. On the other hand, Statement 15 would apply to an isolated troubled debt restructuring by a debtor involved in bankruptcy proceedings if such restructuring did not result in a general restatement of the debtor's liabilities.

FASB Technical Bulletin No. 82-1
Disclosure of the Sale or Purchase of Tax Benefits through Tax Leases

STATUS

Issued: January 27, 1982

Effective Date: None stated; Technical Bulletins issued prior to June 30, 1984 indicate only the date of issuance.

Affects: No other pronouncements

Affected by: Paragraph 4 amended by FAS 95
Paragraph 5 superseded by FAS 96 and FAS 109
Paragraph 7 amended by FAS 96 and FAS 109

FASB Technical Bulletin No. 82-1
Disclosure of the Sale or Purchase of Tax Benefits through Tax Leases

References:

ARB No. 43, *Restatement and Revision of Accounting Research Bulletins,* Chapter 2A, paragraph 2

APB Opinion No. 11, *Accounting for Income Taxes,* paragraph 63

APB Opinion No. 22, *Disclosure of Accounting Policies*

APB Opinion No. 30, *Reporting the Results of Operations,* paragraph 26

FASB Statement No. 5, *Accounting for Contingencies*

Question

1. What disclosures are required for the sale or purchase of tax benefits through tax leases?

Background

2. The term *tax leases,* as used in this Bulletin, refers to leases that are entered into to transfer certain tax benefits as allowed by the leasing provisions of the Economic Recovery Tax Act of 1981. The tax benefits that can be transferred are deductions under the Accelerated Cost Recovery System and credits such as the investment tax credit and energy credit. Temporary Treasury regulations were issued on October 20, 1981, November 10, 1981, and December 28, 1981 that prescribe the conditions that must be met for a transaction to be characterized as a "safe harbor" lease for federal income tax purposes, thus enabling the parties to the transaction to transfer certain tax benefits between them.

3. The FASB issued an Exposure Draft of a proposed Statement, *Accounting for the Sale or Purchase of Tax Benefits through Tax Leases,* for public comment on October 29, 1981, and received over 160 letters of comment. At the December 16, 1981

Board meeting, the Board concluded that the provisions of that Exposure Draft should be revised and that it should be reexposed for public comment. In late December 1981, a need was identified for disclosure of transactions involving solely the sale or purchase of tax benefits through tax leases until the accounting issues related to those transactions are resolved.

Response

4. Opinion 22 requires disclosure of all significant accounting policies where alternative accounting principles or practices exist, including the methods of applying those accounting principles that materially affect the determination of financial position, changes in financial position, and results of operations. Because alternative accounting practices may exist until the FASB issues a final Statement addressing the sale or purchase of tax benefits through tax leases, the accounting policies or practices followed for those transactions should be disclosed in accordance with that Opinion. The disclosure should include the method of accounting for those transactions and the methods of recognizing revenue and allocating income tax benefits and asset costs to current and future periods.

5. Paragraph 63 of Opinion 11 requires disclosure of the reasons for significant variations in the customary relationships between income tax expense and pretax accounting income if they are not otherwise apparent from the financial statements or from the nature of the enterprise's business. Accordingly, any significant variation in the customary relationship between income tax expense and pretax accounting income resulting from transactions involving the sale or purchase of tax benefits through tax leases should be disclosed in accordance with Opinion 11.

6. Paragraph 26 of Opinion 30 requires disclosure of material events or transactions that are unusual in nature or occur infrequently as a separate component of income from continuing operations. If material and unusual or infrequent to the enterprise, the nature and financial effects of transactions involving the sale or purchase of tax benefits through tax leases should be disclosed on the face of the income statement or, alternatively, in notes to the financial statements in accordance with Opinion 30.

7. Disclosures in addition to those required by Opinions 11, 22, and 30 as discussed above also may

be appropriate depending on the circumstances involved. For example, if significant contingencies exist with respect to the sale or purchase of tax benefits, disclosures in accordance with Statement 5 may be warranted. Also, as referred to in paragraph 2 of Chapter 2A of ARB 43, if comparative financial statements are presented, disclosure should be made of any change in practice that significantly affects comparability.

8. This Bulletin does not address the accounting for the sale or purchase of tax benefits through tax leases.

FASB Technical Bulletin No. 82-2
Accounting for the Conversion of Stock Options into Incentive Stock Options as a Result of the Economic Recovery Tax Act of 1981

STATUS

Issued: March 31, 1982

Effective Date: None stated; Technical Bulletins issued prior to June 30, 1984 indicate only the date of issuance.

Affects: No other pronouncements

Affected by: No other pronouncements

Technical Bulletin No. 82-2
Accounting for the Conversion of Stock Options into Incentive Stock Options as a Result of the Economic Recovery Tax Act of 1981

References:

ARB No. 43, *Restatement and Revision of Accounting Research Bulletins,* Chapter 13B, "Compensation Involved in Stock Option and Stock Purchase Plans"
APB Opinion No. 25, *Accounting for Stock Issued to Employees*
FASB Interpretation No. 28, *Accounting for Stock Appreciation Rights and Other Variable Stock Option or Award Plans*

Question

1. What are the accounting implications for enterprises that convert previously issued stock options into incentive stock options (ISOs) as a result of the Economic Recovery Tax Act of 1981 (Act)?

Background

2. The Act includes provisions that grant favorable tax treatment to individuals who own incentive stock options. Enterprises can provide individuals with ISOs in two ways, by issuing new ISOs and by converting previously issued options into ISOs through changes to conform those options to the requirements of the Act. Accounting issues arise for enterprises with respect to plan modifications that are undertaken to convert existing options into ISOs.

3. One ISO requirement is that the option price must either equal or exceed the fair market value of the stock either at the date of grant or, if the option has been modified or renewed, at the date of the most recent amendment providing benefits to the option holder. This is commonly referred to as the "repricing" requirement of the Act. Enterprises electing to convert existing options into ISOs may be forced to raise option prices to meet the repricing requirement.

4. The Act allows enterprises to limit or eliminate the need to raise option prices by canceling certain prior plan amendments. For example, assume the option price and stock price at date of grant are $8 and $10, respectively, for a nonqualified plan and that a plan amendment is later introduced when the stock price is $17. By canceling the amendment, the option can be repriced at $10, resulting in $2 of additional cost to the employee; if the amendment is not canceled, the repricing is at $17 and the employee's additional cost is $9. In recent years, several stock option plans have been amended to add a tandem stock appreciation right (SAR). Therefore, if they are converting the underlying stock option into an ISO, some enterprises may elect to cancel SARs that were previously added through plan amendments.

5. ARB 43, Chapter 13B, states in paragraph 10 that ". . . in most cases . . . valuation should be made of the option as of the date of grant." Opinion 25 did not change that underlying principle for plans that do not have variable terms. Paragraph 29 of Opinion 25 defines plans with variable terms:

> . . . The characteristic that identifies plans in this group is that the terms prevent determining at the date of grant or award either the number of shares of stock that may be acquired by or awarded to an employee or the price to be paid by the employee, or both.

Regarding the determination of the measurement date, paragraph 10(b) of Opinion 25 states that:

> *The measurement date* for determining compensation cost in stock option, purchase, and award plans is the first date on which are known both (1) the number of shares that an individual employee is entitled to receive and (2) the option or purchase price, if any. . . . The measurement date may be later than the date of grant or award in plans with variable terms that depend on events after date of grant or award.

6. Paragraph 5 of Interpretation 28 addresses tandem plans and states that:

> . . . If an enterprise has been accruing compensation for a stock appreciation right or other variable plan award and a change in circumstances provides evidence that the employee will likely elect to exercise the related stock option, accrued compensation recorded for the right or award shall *not* be adjusted.[7] If the employee elects to exercise the stock option, the accrued compensation recorded for the right or award shall be recognized as a consideration for the stock issued. If all parts of the grant or award (e.g., both the option and the right or award) are

Accounting for the Conversion of Stock
Options into Incentive Stock Options as a Result of the   FTB82-2
Economic Recovery Tax Act of 1981

forfeited or cancelled, accrued compensation shall be adjusted by decreasing compensation expense in that period.

---

[7]A change in the circumstances may be indicated by . . . cancellation or forfeiture of the stock appreciation right or other variable plan award without a concurrent cancellation or forfeiture of the related stock option.

7. Paragraph 17 of Opinion 25 describes accounting for income tax benefits under stock option plans:

An employer corporation should reduce income tax expense for a period by no more of a tax reduction under a stock option, purchase, or award plan than the proportion of the tax reduction that is related to the compensation expense for the period. . . . The remainder of the tax reduction, if any, is related to an amount that is deductible for income tax purposes but does not affect net income. The remainder of the tax reduction should not be included in income but should be added to capital in addition to par or stated value of capital stock in the period of the tax reduction. Conversely, a tax reduction may be less than if recorded compensation expenses were deductible for income tax purposes. If so, the corporation may deduct the difference from additional capital in the period of the tax reduction to the extent that tax reductions under the same or similar compensatory stock option, purchase, or award plans have been included in additional capital.

Response

Repricing

8. Opinion 25 requires that an enterprise record compensation for services it receives for stock issued to employees through a stock option plan. That compensation is equal to the quoted market price of the stock on the measurement date less the amount the employee is required to pay. The compensation cost is charged to expense over the periods in which the employee performs the related services. Increasing the option price to meet the repricing requirement described in paragraph 3 of this Bulletin results in the enterprise's recapturing the compensation cost that arose when the option was granted. In recognition of that recapture, enterprises should reverse, in the period in which the option price is increased, the portion of total compensation cost that arose when the option was granted and has been charged to expense in subsequent periods.

9. A variable plan is a plan that has variable terms at its inception, as described in paragraph 5 of this Bulletin. A variable plan therefore differs from a plan with terms that are fixed at inception, modified once to increase the option price to conform to the Act, and remain fixed thereafter. A stock option plan that has fixed terms does not become a variable plan simply because the option price is raised to meet the repricing requirements of the Act. Accordingly, the increase in the option price to 100 percent of the fair market value at the date of grant to qualify an option under the Act does not result in a new measurement date.

Tandem Plans

10. *Presumption as to Exercise.* Interpretation 28 clarifies how compensation expense shall be recorded in connection with a combination or tandem stock option and SAR plan. Paragraph 5 of that Interpretation states that ". . . compensation expense . . . shall be measured according to the terms an employee is most likely to elect based on the facts available each period. An enterprise shall presume that the employee will elect to exercise the stock appreciation rights or other variable plan awards, but the presumption may be overcome. . . ." The fact that the Act grants more favorable tax treatment to holders of stock options does not invalidate the presumption of Interpretation 28 that the SAR will be exercised. However, it may be an important factor in evaluating what the employee is most likely to elect.

11. *Cancellation of SAR Only.* Interpretation 28 also discusses accounting for the cancellation of the SAR in a tandem SAR and stock option plan. Paragraph 5 and footnote 7 of that Interpretation (refer to paragraph 6 of this Bulletin) state that accrued compensation recorded for an SAR shall not be adjusted if cancellation or forfeiture of the SAR occurs without a concurrent cancellation or forfeiture of the related stock option. Enterprises that cancel SARs under the circumstances described in paragraph 4 of this Bulletin should look to paragraph 5 and footnote 7 of Interpretation 28 for guidance. Those sections of Interpretation 28 also include guidance concerning the ultimate disposition of the accrued compensation amount if the option is exercised, canceled, or forfeited.

Combination of Circumstances

12. A combination of certain of the circumstances described in the preceding paragraphs may exist. For example, the cancellation of a tandem SAR may be combined with the repricing of the underlying option. If that happens, the portion of total accrued compensation that relates to the repricing should be reversed as described in paragraph 8 of this Bulletin; the balance of accrued compensation relates to the cancellation of the SAR and should be accounted for under the provisions of paragraph 11 of this Bulletin. As an illustration, assume the following: (a) a

nonqualified option for $110 was granted when the market value of the stock was $130, (b) a tandem SAR was subsequently introduced through a plan amendment, (c) all compensation costs for the option and SAR relate to prior periods and have been charged to expense, and (d) the enterprise decides to cancel the SAR and reprice the stock option to a $130 option price when the market value of the stock is $180. The accounting result is that $20 of accrued compensation (computed $130 − $110) is reversed in the current period and the remaining $50 (computed $180 − $130) is retained as accrued compensation.

Taxes

13. Certain of the guidance in this Bulletin involves adjustments to compensation expense. For account-ing purposes, the tax effects of those adjustments should be determined in accordance with the general guidance concerning accounting for income tax benefits under stock option plans found in para-graph 17 of Opinion 25 (refer to paragraph 7 of this Bulletin). For example, a reversal of compensation expense in connection with a repricing as described in paragraph 8 of this Bulletin results in a corre-sponding reversal of the related deferred tax bene-fits. Likewise, if a tandem SAR is canceled as described in paragraph 11, the tax benefit is not adjusted, but is retained along with the accrued compensation that gave rise to it. Ultimately, depending on the employee's actions, the compensa-tion and tax benefit are disposed of in the same manner—together, they are either reversed or applied to additional paid-in capital.

FASB Technical Bulletin No. 83-1
Accounting for the Reduction in the Tax Basis of an Asset Caused by the Investment Tax Credit

STATUS

Issued: July 26, 1983

Effective Date: None stated; Technical Bulletins issued prior to June 30, 1984 indicate only the date of issuance.

Affects: No other pronouncements

Affected by: Superseded by FAS 96 and FAS 109

(The next page is 1240.)

FASB Technical Bulletin No. 84-1
Accounting for Stock Issued to Acquire the Results of a Research and Development Arrangement

STATUS

Issued: March 15, 1984

Effective Date: None stated; Technical Bulletins issued prior to June 30, 1984 indicate only the date of issuance.

Affects: No other pronouncements

Affected by: No other pronouncements

FASB Technical Bulletin No. 84-1
Accounting for Stock Issued to Acquire the Results of a Research and Development Arrangement

References:

FASB Statement No. 68, *Research and Development Arrangements,* paragraphs 11, 13, and 20
APB Opinion No. 16, *Business Combinations,* paragraph 67

Question

1. How should an enterprise account for stock issued to acquire the results of a research and development arrangement?

Background

2. Paragraph 20 of Appendix A of Statement 68 describes the usual contractual right of an enterprise to acquire the results of a research and development arrangement (that paragraph describes an arrangement between the enterprise and a partnership):

> Either as part of the partnership agreement or through contracts with the partnership, the enterprise usually has an option either to purchase the partnership's interest in or to obtain the exclusive rights to the entire results of the research and development in return for a lump sum payment or royalty payments to the partnership. Some arrangements contain a provision that permits the enterprise to acquire complete ownership of the results for a specified amount of the enterprise's stock or cash at some future time. In some of those purchase agreements, the partnership has the option to receive either the enterprise's stock or cash; in others, the enterprise makes the decision. Sometimes, warrants or similar instruments to purchase the enterprise's stock are issued in connection with the arrangement.

3. Paragraph 11 of Statement 68 describes the accounting for a purchase of the results of a research and development arrangement:

> If the enterprise's obligation is to perform research and development for others and the enterprise subsequently decides to exercise an option to purchase the other parties' interests in the research and development arrangement or to obtain the exclusive rights to the results of the research and

development, the nature of those results and their future use shall determine the accounting for the purchase transaction. [Footnote reference omitted.]

4. Paragraph 67 of Opinion 16 describes the general principles of historical cost accounting that are applied in determining the cost of an asset acquired by issuing shares of stock:

> c. An asset acquired by issuing shares of stock of the acquiring corporation is recorded at the fair value of the asset— that is, shares of stock issued are recorded at the fair value of the consideration received for the stock.

The general principles must be supplemented to apply them in certain transactions. For example, the fair value of an asset received for stock issued may not be reliably determinable, or the fair value of an asset acquired in an exchange may be more reliably determinable than the fair value of a noncash asset given up. Restraints on measurement have led to the practical rule that assets acquired for other than cash, including shares of stock issued, should be stated at "cost" when they are acquired and "cost may be determined either by the fair value of the consideration given or by the fair value of the property acquired, whichever is more clearly evident." . . . [Footnote references omitted.]

5. Paragraph 13 of Statement 68 describes the accounting for the issuance of warrants or similar instruments in connection with a research and development arrangement:

> If warrants or similar instruments are issued in connection with the arrangement, the enterprise shall report a portion of the proceeds to be provided by the other parties as paid-in capital. The amount so reported shall be the fair value of the instruments at the date of the arrangement.

Statement 68 does not address the accounting for a subsequent issuance of stock pursuant to the exercise of warrants or similar instruments issued in connection with a research and development arrangement.

Response

6. When an enterprise that is or was a party to a research and development arrangement acquires the results of the research and development arrangement in exchange for cash, common stock of the enterprise, or other consideration, the transaction is a purchase of tangible or intangible assets resulting from the activities of the research and development arrangement. Although such a transaction is not a business combination, paragraph 67 of Opinion 16 describes the general principles that apply in recording the purchase of such an asset.

7. Accordingly, when an enterprise that is or was a party to a research and development arrangement exchanges stock for the results of the research and development arrangement, whether pursuant to the exercise of warrants or similar instruments issued in connection with the arrangement or otherwise, the enterprise should record the stock issued at its fair value, or at the fair value of consideration received, whichever is more clearly evident. The transaction should be accounted for in this manner whether the enterprise exchanges stock for the results of the research and development arrangement, for rights to use the results, or for ownership interests in the arrangement or a successor to the arrangement. The fair value should be determined as of the date the enterprise exercises its option to acquire the results of the research and development arrangement.

FASB Technical Bulletin No. 84-2
Accounting for the Effects of the Tax Reform Act
of 1984 on Deferred Income Taxes Relating to
Domestic International Sales Corporations

STATUS

Issued: September 18, 1984

Effective Date: For financial statements issued after September 30, 1984 for fiscal years ending after
July 18, 1984 and for interim periods within such years

Affects: No other pronouncements

Affected by: Superseded by FAS 96 and FAS 109

FASB Technical Bulletin No. 84-3
Accounting for the Effects of the Tax Reform Act of 1984 on Deferred Income Taxes of Stock Life Insurance Enterprises

STATUS

Issued: September 18, 1984

Effective Date: For financial statements issued after September 30, 1984 for fiscal years ending after July 18, 1984 and for interim periods within such years

Affects: No other pronouncements

Affected by: Superseded by FAS 96 and FAS 109

(The next page is 1249.)

FASB Technical Bulletin No. 84-4
In-Substance Defeasance of Debt

STATUS

Issued: October 17, 1984

Effective Date: For debt incurred on or after September 12, 1984

Affects: No other pronouncements

Affected by: No other pronouncements

FASB Technical Bulletin No. 84-4
In-Substance Defeasance of Debt

Reference:

FASB Statement No. 76, *Extinguishment of Debt*

INSTANTANEOUS IN-SUBSTANCE DEFEASANCE

Question

1. May debt be extinguished through an in-substance defeasance (under paragraph 3(c) of Statement 76) if the debtor irrevocably places in trust assets that were acquired at about the time that the debt was incurred?

Background

2. Some have indicated to the FASB that, due to differences in interest rates in different markets, the opportunity exists for a company to borrow at one interest rate and concurrently invest in "essentially risk-free" assets that yield a higher interest rate. They have suggested certain structured transactions (so-called instantaneous defeasance transactions) in which those assets would be irrevocably placed in trust to effect an in-substance defeasance of the newly issued debt under Statement 76, thereby immediately recognizing a gain related to the concurrent differences in interest rates.

Response

3. No. Debt may not be extinguished through an in-substance defeasance if the assets that the debtor irrevocably places in trust were acquired at about the time that the debt was incurred or were acquired as part of a series of investment activities (for example, purchasing assets or entering into a purchase agreement or futures contract) initiated at about the time that the debt was incurred. Similarly, debt may not be extinguished through an in-substance defeasance if the debt was incurred pursuant to a forward contract entered into at about the time the debtor acquired the assets being irrevocably placed in trust.

4. Although the conceptual basis for recognizing an in-substance defeasance as an extinguishment of debt does not impose special conditions, such as restrictions on how the borrowed funds are used or on when the debtor acquires the assets being placed in the trust, certain structured transactions warrant special consideration in determining whether debt is extinguished under Statement 76.

5. Enterprises that borrow funds and concurrently purchase higher-yielding securities to be used in an in-substance defeasance, thereby recognizing a gain on the extinguishment, are essentially engaging in borrow-and-invest activities. The proximity of the borrowing and the acquisition of securities suggest a structured transaction in which the enterprise borrowed with the intent of executing an in-substance defeasance. The effect of considering such structured borrow-and-invest transactions as extinguishments is substantively different from the effect of considering in-substance defeasances of previously outstanding debt as extinguishments. Such borrow-and-invest activities, in effect, hedge the debtor against the risk of changes in interest rates. Any gain or loss on extinguishing previously outstanding debt reflects in large measure the effect of past changes in interest rates for the debtor, whereas the gain or loss related to borrow-and-invest activities reflects principally the concurrent differences in interest rates when the debt was issued. Statement 76 states in paragraph 22 that "the Board believes that, in general, recognizing the effect of in-substance defeasance transactions as extinguishing debt is reasonable because settlement in cash is not always feasible and *the effect of an in-substance defeasance is essentially the same.*" (Emphasis added.)

ASSESSING REMOTENESS OF RISK OF TRUST ASSETS

Question

6. In determining whether an in-substance defeasance transaction meets the requirement in paragraph 4(a) of Statement 76 that the cash inflows to the trust from its assets be essentially risk free, may a debtor use an assessment of the remoteness of the related risks?

Background

7. For an in-substance defeasance, paragraph 3(c) of Statement 76 requires that "the debtor irrevocably places cash or other assets in a trust to be used solely for satisfying scheduled payments of both interest and principal of a specific obligation and [that] the possibility that the debtor will be required to make future payments with respect to that debt is remote." Paragraph 4 addresses the nature of the assets that the debtor irrevocably places in trust and requires, among other things, that those assets be monetary assets "that are *essen-*

tially risk free as to the amount, timing, and collection of interest and principal.''

Response

8. No, in some circumstances; yes, in others. In requiring that the cash inflows to the trust in an in-substance defeasance be essentially risk free, Statement 76 establishes specific criteria with respect to certain aspects of the transaction but requires the use of judgment in assessing remoteness in other areas. The specified criteria of Statement 76 focus principally on the nature of the monetary assets placed in trust rather than on possible external events. For example, Statement 76 requires the following:

a. The monetary assets placed in the trust must be denominated in the currency in which the debt is payable. (Refer to paragraphs 4(a) and 32 of Statement 76.)
b. The monetary assets placed in the trust must be direct obligations of the sovereign government in whose currency the debt is payable or must be obligations collateralized by such government securities or guaranteed by that government. (Refer to paragraphs 4(a), 31, and 32 of Statement 76.)
c. Monetary assets that are callable (that is, can be prepaid) are not essentially risk free as to the timing of the interest and principal payments to be received by the trust and thus do not qualify for ownership by the trust. (Refer to paragraph 4(a) of Statement 76.)

Statement 76 does not permit variations from those requirements on the basis that any related risks are remote. Thus, a debtor may not justify use of assets denominated in differing currencies in combination with a forward exchange contract on the basis that the likelihood of default on the forward contract is remote. Similarly, a debtor may not use securities issued by a sovereign government but denominated in a currency other than its own (for example, French government securities denominated in Swiss francs used to defease Swiss franc debt) on the basis that the likelihood of the French government's being unable to obtain sufficient Swiss francs to make timely payments is remote. Likewise, securities that are callable may not be used in the trust on the basis that the likelihood is remote that the call provision will introduce any risk that the trust could have insufficient funds.

9. However, for areas not specifically covered, Statement 76 requires the debtor to assess the remoteness of various contingencies in determining whether the cash inflows to the trust from its assets are essentially risk free. For example, since any default by a sovereign government on its obligations held by the trust would cause the trust assets to be

insufficient to pay the defeased debt (thereby requiring the debtor to make up the deficiency), Statement 76 implicitly requires the debtor to conclude that the likelihood of a default by the sovereign government on its direct obligations is remote. Similarly, the likely resolution of other uncertainties that could affect the cash flows to the trust, such as the imposition of currency controls or withholding taxes through future legislation, needs to be assessed to determine whether it is remote that the debtor will be required to make further payments with respect to the debt.

IN-SUBSTANCE DEFEASANCE OF CALLABLE DEBT

Question

10. May a debt be extinguished through an in-substance defeasance if it is callable by the debtor?

Background

11. Paragraph 1 of Statement 76 states that the circumstances for an extinguishment of debt through an in-substance defeasance as described in paragraph 3(c) of the Statement ''apply only to debt with specified maturities and fixed payment schedules; consequently, those circumstances do not apply to debt with variable terms that do not permit advance determination of debt service requirements, such as debt with a floating interest rate.''

Response

12. Yes. Debt that is callable by the debtor can be extinguished through an in-substance defeasance. The debtor's retention of an option to purchase the debt through a call provision is not, in itself, an impediment to an in-substance defeasance; the mere existence of the option creates no risk that the debtor will be required to make further payments with respect to the debt because exercise of the option is at the debtor's discretion. Furthermore, the existence of the call option does not mitigate the debtor's previous surrender of control over the assets that were irrevocably placed in trust.

13. If exercise of the call option by the debtor prior to the debt's scheduled maturity is not remote, the debtor ordinarily would not be able to extinguish the debt through an in-substance defeasance because the possibility of future payments with respect to the debt would also not be remote, as required by paragraph 3(c) of Statement 76. However, if the debtor plans to exercise the call option at a specific date and takes the necessary action currently to effect the call irrevocably for that future date (thereby giving the debt a new, ear-

lier maturity date), extinguishment through an in-substance defeasance is possible provided the assets in the trust are structured to meet the cash flow requirements of the revised payment schedule and new maturity date.

14. Paragraph 33 of Statement 76 states that "if a debtor purchases its own debt securities that have previously been recognized as extinguished in an in-substance defeasance, the debtor is making an investment in the future cash flows from the trust and should report its investment as an asset in its balance sheet." Whether such debt securities are purchased in the open market or acquired through exercise of a call option, it is appropriate to account for them as an investment in the future cash flows to be distributed by the trust as originally scheduled. However, because the assets in the trust must "be used *solely* for satisfying *scheduled* payments of both interest and principal" (Statement 76, paragraph 3(c); emphasis added), the debtor could not use funds from the trust to purchase its debt securities; rather, the debtor would need to use other funds to acquire the debt securities as an investment. Exercise of the call option would not negate compliance with the requirement in Statement 76 that the assets be irrevocably placed in trust because the call option should not enable the debtor to invade the trust and re-acquire those assets prematurely.

EFFECTIVE DATE AND TRANSITION

15. The provisions of this Technical Bulletin are effective for debt incurred on or after September 12, 1984. Earlier application is encouraged for transactions in fiscal years for which annual financial statements have not previously been issued.

FASB Technical Bulletin No. 85-1
Accounting for the Receipt of Federal Home Loan
Mortgage Corporation Participating Preferred Stock

STATUS

Issued: March 18, 1985

Effective Date: For financial statements issued after March 31, 1985 for fiscal years ending after December 1, 1984 and for interim periods within such years

Affects: No other pronouncements

Affected by: Paragraph 3 amended by FAS 115

FASB Technical Bulletin No. 85-1
Accounting for the Receipt of Federal Home Loan Mortgage Corporation Participating Preferred Stock

References:

ARB No. 43, Chapter 7, "Capital Accounts," Section B, "Stock Dividends and Stock Split-ups," paragraph 1
APB Opinion No. 29, *Accounting for Nonmonetary Transactions,* paragraphs 18, 23, 25, and 26
APB Opinion No. 30, *Reporting the Results of Operations—Reporting the Effects of Disposal of a Segment of a Business, and Extraordinary, Unusual and Infrequently Occurring Events and Transactions,* paragraph 20
FASB Statement No. 12, *Accounting for Certain Marketable Securities*
FASB Concepts Statement No. 3, *Elements of Financial Statements of Business Enterprises,* paragraph 20

Question

1. On December 6, 1984, the Federal Home Loan Mortgage Corporation (FHLMC) created a new class of participating preferred stock (preferred stock) and distributed the preferred stock to the 12 district banks of the Federal Home Loan Banking System subject to the condition that the district banks subsequently distribute the stock to their member institutions (primarily savings and loan institutions) that owned stock in the district banks as of December 31, 1984. Until that time, the FHLMC had one class of capital stock outstanding that was callable at par and was owned by the 12 district banks. How should the members of the Federal Home Loan Banking System account for the receipt of the preferred stock?

Response

2. The distribution of preferred stock grants the member institutions an ownership right to the residual net assets of the FHLMC that they did not have

previously, directly or indirectly, since the only previously outstanding capital stock was redeemable at par. The preferred stock is a nonmonetary asset that should be recognized by member institutions at its fair value as of December 31, 1984, in accordance with Opinion 29 (as discussed in paragraph 12 below). The resulting income should be reported as an extraordinary item in accordance with Opinion 30.

3. The fair value of the preferred stock recognized as of December 31, 1984 becomes its cost. Since the stock is trading on the New York Stock Exchange, it is a marketable equity security that subsequently should be reported in accordance with Statement 12 (at the lower of cost or market).

4. The FHLMC resolution authorizing the distribution of the preferred stock requires that the preferred stock be distributed to the member institutions as a condition of the district banks' receipt of the stock. Because the district banks did not have the benefits of ownership of the preferred stock at any time, for financial reporting purposes the preferred stock was not an asset to them, and they should not report the receipt of the preferred stock as income or their distribution of the preferred stock as a dividend.

Effective Date and Transition

5. The provisions of this Technical Bulletin are effective for financial statements issued after March 31, 1985 for fiscal years ending after December 1, 1984, and for interim periods within such years. Earlier application is encouraged. If financial statements have been issued that did not report this transaction in December 1984 as required herein, those financial statements should be restated to conform to the provisions of this Technical Bulletin when subsequently reissued.

Appendix

BACKGROUND

6. On December 6, 1984, the board of directors of the FHLMC adopted resolutions establishing a new class of participating preferred stock to be distributed through the district banks to the member institutions. Prior to the creation of the preferred stock, the only outstanding capital stock of the FHLMC was $100,000,000 of $1,000 par, nonvoting, redeemable common stock held by the district banks. The district banks' only capital stock is $100 par redeemable common stock held by the member institutions.

7. The accounting by the member institutions for the preferred stock received has been the subject of some controversy. The Federal Home Loan Bank Board (FHLBB), as the governing body of the Federal Home Loan Bank System, requested an analysis of the transaction from several accounting firms in December 1984. The consensus of those firms was that the member institutions should record the preferred stock at its fair value based on an investment advisor's appraisal, resulting in income in 1984.

8. The FASB was asked by several interested parties to indicate its views on the accounting issues. On January 17 and 18, 1985, the FASB met jointly in public Board meetings with representatives of its Emerging Issues Task Force, the FHLBB, the FHLMC, and others to gather information regarding the transfer of preferred stock. A proposed Technical Bulletin, *Accounting for the Receipt of Federal Home Loan Mortgage Corporation Participating Preferred Stock,* was released for comment for 15 days on January 25, 1985, and 254 comment letters were received. Virtually all respondents agreed with the proposed Technical Bulletin as released for comment.

9. The threshold accounting issue is whether something of value has been received by the member institutions to which they previously were not entitled. One possibility was that the issuance of the preferred stock was simply a recognition of implicit existing ownership rights of member institutions. If so, it would follow that ARB 43, Chapter 7B provides relevant accounting guidance for this transaction. Although ARB 43, Chapter 7B does not apply to stock dividends of shares of a different class, the underlying concept would seem to apply if no new ownership rights were transferred. The following description of a stock dividend from ARB 43, Chapter 7B would seem to parallel this distribution:

1. The term *stock dividend* as used in this section refers to an issuance by a corporation of its own common shares to its common shareholders without consideration and under conditions indicating that such action is prompted mainly by a desire to give the recipient shareholders some ostensibly separate evidence of a part of their respective interests in accumulated corporate earnings without distribution of cash or other property which the board of directors deems necessary or desirable to retain in the business.

10. Another possibility was that the interrelationships among the FHLBB, the district banks, and the member institutions with regard to this transaction were such that the spinoff provisions of paragraph 23 of Opinion 29 should be applied. Under that approach, the member institutions would allocate the cost of district bank stock owned between the FHLMC stock received and the district bank stock and would not report income from receipt of the FHLMC stock.

11. Representatives of the FHLBB and the FHLMC have indicated that the distribution of preferred shares granted the member institutions additional legal rights to the net assets of the FHLMC that were not previously held by them. It follows that something of value was received by the member institutions to which they previously had no rights, somewhat like a grant from government.

12. Because something of value was transferred to the member institutions to which they previously had no rights, either directly or indirectly, the member institutions should recognize the fair value of the preferred stock under Opinion 29 if that fair value is determinable within reasonable limits. That Opinion establishes the following basic principle in paragraph 18:

. . . a nonmonetary asset received in a nonreciprocal transfer should be recorded at the fair value of the asset received.

That basic principle is modified, however, if fair value is not determinable within reasonable limits. Paragraphs 25 and 26 of Opinion 29 discuss the determination of fair values:

25. Fair value of a nonmonetary asset transferred to or from an enterprise in a nonmonetary transaction should be determined by referring to estimated realizable values in cash transactions of the same or similar assets, quoted market prices, independent appraisals, estimated fair values of assets or services received in exchange, and other available evidence.

26. Fair value should be regarded as not determinable within reasonable limits if major uncertainties exist about the realizability of the

value that would be assigned to an asset received in a nonmonetary transaction accounted for at fair value.

The FHLMC obtained an independent appraisal from an investment banker of the price range at which the preferred stock could be expected to trade. Trading began on the New York Stock Exchange on January 23, 1985.

13. Some believe that the member institutions should report the receipt of preferred stock as a dividend from the district banks and that it is not extraordinary since dividends have been periodically declared by the district banks. Others, relying on the two requirements for an extraordinary item in paragraph 20 of Opinion 30, believe that the receipt of the preferred stock is an extraordinary item because of its nature:

a. *Unusual nature*—the underlying event or transaction should possess a high degree of abnormality and be of a type clearly unrelated to, or only incidentally related to, the ordinary and typical activities of the entity, taking into account the environment in which the entity operates.

b. *Infrequency of occurrence*—the underlying event or transaction should be of a type that would not reasonably be expected to recur in the foreseeable future, taking into account the environment in which the entity operates.

The conclusion in paragraph 2 of this Technical Bulletin that the member institutions should report the distribution as an extraordinary item is based on two factors. First, the substance of the distribution is not a dividend in the usual sense from the district banks since they were merely a conduit for the distribution (as more fully discussed in paragraph 14). Second, the distribution recognizable by the member institutions represents a distribution of residual rights not previously held, either directly or indirectly, by the member institutions. Those residual rights can be distributed only *once,* and therefore the distribution is both unusual and cannot be expected to recur.

14. Some have evaluated the distribution of the preferred stock as the receipt of a dividend-in-kind by the district banks and then a dividend-in-kind by

those banks to their member institutions that should be recognized by the district banks at its fair value. Two questions are involved in determining the accounting by the district banks: first, whether the receipt of the preferred stock by the district banks constitutes an asset and therefore income to them and, second, if so, at what amount the asset should be recognized by the district banks. In response to the first question, the stock must first have been an asset of the district banks for them to distribute it as a dividend-in-kind. Concepts Statement 3 is relevant in identifying whether the stock had the essential characteristics of an asset to the district banks. Paragraph 20 states:

> An asset has three essential characteristics: (a) it embodies a probable future benefit that involves a capacity, singly or in combination with other assets, to contribute directly or indirectly to future net cash inflows, (b) a particular enterprise can obtain the benefit and control others' access to it, and (c) the transaction or other event giving rise to the enterprise's right to or control of the benefit has already occurred.

The district banks' receipt of the preferred stock was contingent upon its subsequent distribution, so the district banks did not have control of the stock and could not obtain benefit from it. Accordingly, the preferred stock was not an asset or income to the district banks. It was a transfer of a residual interest in the FHLMC through the district banks rather than a dividend from them to the member institutions. While the transaction demonstrates the limited rights of the district banks in the FHLMC and warrants disclosure of the newly defined relationship, it does not constitute a transaction that should affect income or equity of the district banks. In response to the second question, the preferred stock, while having a value to the member institutions, had no realizable value to the district banks as is required by paragraph 23 of Opinion 29 for value to be recognized by the district banks.

15. This Technical Bulletin does not address the accounting for the distribution of preferred stock by the FHLMC. The substance of this distribution is unique and the authoritative accounting literature does not appear to be specifically applicable. Further, the issues are limited to a single transaction by a single entity.

FASB Technical Bulletin No. 85-2
Accounting for Collateralized Mortgage Obligations (CMOs)

STATUS

Issued: March 18, 1985

Effective Date: For collateralized mortgage obligations issued after March 31, 1985

Affects: No other pronouncements

Affected by: Footnote 9 superseded by FAS 111

FASB Technical Bulletin No. 85-2
Accounting for Collateralized Mortgage Obligations (CMOs)

References:

ARB No. 51, *Consolidated Financial Statements,* paragraphs 1 and 2
APB Opinion No. 10, *Omnibus Opinion—1966,* paragraph 7
FASB Statement No. 57, *Related Party Disclosures,* paragraph 24
FASB Statement No. 65, *Accounting for Certain Mortgage Banking Activities,* paragraph 11
FASB Statement No. 76, *Extinguishment of Debt,* paragraphs 1, 3(c), and 4
FASB Statement No. 77, *Reporting by Transferors for Transfers of Receivables with Recourse,* paragraphs 3-5
FASB Technical Bulletin No. 84-4, *Extinguishment of Debt,* paragraph 3

Question

1. Certain types of bonds secured by mortgage-backed securities[1] or mortgage loans are structured so that all or substantially all of the collections of principal and interest from the underlying collateral are paid through to the holders of the bonds. The bonds are typically issued with two or more maturity classes; the actual maturity of each bond class will vary depending upon the timing of the cash receipts from the underlying collateral. These bonds are issued by a minimally capitalized special-purpose corporation (issuer) established by a sponsoring parent corporation and are commonly referred to as "collateralized mortgage obligations," or CMOs. The mortgage-backed securities or mortgage loans securing the obligation are acquired by the special-purpose corporation and then pledged

to an independent trustee until the issuer's obligation under the bond indenture has been fully satisfied. The investor can look only to the issuer's assets (primarily the trusteed assets) or third parties (such as insurers or guarantors) for repayment of the obligation. As a result, the sponsor and its other affiliates have no financial obligation under the instrument, although one of those entities may retain the responsibility for servicing the underlying mortgage loans. How should the special-purpose issuer account for this transaction?

Response

2. CMOs should be presumed to be borrowings that are reported as liabilities in the financial statements of the issuer unless all but a nominal[2] portion of the future economic benefits inherent in the associated collateral have been irrevocably passed to the investor and no affiliate[3] of the issuer can be required to make future payments with respect to the obligation. The existence of all of the following conditions at the date of issuance of the CMO would generally indicate that the borrowing presumption has been overcome, that the associated collateral should be eliminated from the issuer's financial statements, and that gain or loss should be recognized:

a. The issuer and its affiliates surrender the future economic benefits embodied in the collateral securing the obligation.
   (1) Neither the issuer nor its affiliates have the right or obligation to substitute collateral or obtain it by calling the obligation.[4]
   (2) The expected residual interest,[5] if any, in the collateral is nominal.[6]

---

[1] The term *mortgage-backed securities* is defined in Statement 65 as securities issued by a governmental agency or corporation (for example, the Government National Mortgage Association or the Federal Home Loan Mortgage Corporation) or by private issuers (for example, the Federal National Mortgage Association, banks, and mortgage banking enterprises). Mortgage-backed securities generally are referred to as mortgage participation certificates or pass-through certificates (PCs). A PC represents an undivided interest in a pool of specific mortgage loans.

[2] The term *nominal* is used in this Technical Bulletin to mean insignificantly small or trifling (The American Heritage Dictionary, 2d college ed. [Boston: Houghton Mifflin Company, 1982], p. 845) and implies a lower amount than that normally associated with materiality as defined in FASB Concepts Statement No. 2, *Qualitative Characteristics of Accounting Information.*

[3] The term *affiliate* is defined in Statement 57 as "a party that, directly or indirectly through one or more intermediaries, controls, is controlled by, or is under common control with an enterprise" and is used in the same sense in this Technical Bulletin.

[4] Some CMOs require or permit the issuer to call the obligation when the amount of the outstanding bonds is minor to keep the cost of servicing the underlying mortgage loans relative to their remaining outstanding balances from becoming unreasonable. If the amount of reacquired collateral is expected to be minor, the existence of this type of call provision alone does not preclude the collateral from being eliminated from the financial statements.

[5] The expected residual interest in the collateral should be computed using the present value of all amounts expected to revert to the issuer or its affiliates (including reinvestment earnings). Excess (above-normal) servicing fees should be considered to be part of the expected residual interest.

[6] This condition would not be met if an affiliate of the issuer retained a partial ownership interest in the mortgage-backed securities or mortgage loans securing the obligation.

b. No affiliate of the issuer can be required to make any future payments with respect to the obligation.[7]

(1) The investor can look only to the issuer's assets or third parties (such as insurers or guarantors) for repayment of both principal and interest on the obligation, and neither the sponsor of the issuer nor its other affiliates are secondarily liable.

(2) Neither the issuer nor its affiliates can be required to redeem the obligation prior to its stated maturity other than through the normal pay-through of collections from the collateral.

If the associated collateral is eliminated from the financial statements because all of the above conditions are met, any expected residual interest in the collateral should not be recognized as an asset. Rather, such residual interest should be recorded as it accrues to the benefit of the issuer or its affiliates. If servicing rights are retained by an affiliate of the issuer and the stated servicing fee rate is less than a current (normal) servicing fee rate,[8] the CMO proceeds should be adjusted to provide for a normal servicing fee in each subsequent servicing period. All transaction costs associated with the offering should be charged to expense when the associated collateral is eliminated from the financial statements.

3. Because a majority-owned entity formed to issue the CMO is merely a conduit for the sponsor, the financial statements of that entity should be consolidated with those of its sponsor.[9]

4. For CMOs recorded as liabilities, the pledging of collateral against the related liability is not tantamount to prepayment as it was contemplated by Opinion 10. Therefore, CMOs are not an exception to the general principle of accounting stated in paragraph 7 of that Opinion, and offsetting the collateral against the related liability in the balance sheet is not appropriate.

Effective Date and Transition

5. The provisions of this Technical Bulletin are effective for collateralized mortgage obligations issued after March 31, 1985. Earlier application is encouraged in annual or interim financial statements that have not been previously issued. Retroactive application to all CMOs issued during fiscal years for which annual financial statements have previously been issued is permitted.

The Financial Accounting Standards Board has authorized its staff to issue FASB Technical Bulletins to provide guidance on certain financial accounting and reporting problems on a timely basis. Although Board members are provided with copies of proposed Bulletins prior to issuance, the Board does not approve them. Copyright © 1985 by the Financial Accounting Standards Board.

Background

6. In determining the accounting for CMOs, some have viewed the issuer's receipt of cash in exchange for issuing the secured bonds to be substantively the same as the transfers of receivables with recourse contemplated by Statement 77. They believe that the conditions specified in paragraph 5 of that Statement should be used to determine whether the issuer should recognize the transaction as a sale of the underlying collateral to the bondholders or report it as a secured borrowing. Others believe that State- ment 76 is applicable and suggest that, if the collateral pledged to the trustee is "essentially risk free" and provides cash flows that approximately coincide with the interest and principal payments on the obligation (as described in paragraph 4 of that Statement), the issuer should account for the transaction as an in-substance defeasance of the liability created by issuing the CMOs. In addition, others have inquired as to (a) the proper consolidation policy to be followed for any majority-owned entity formed to issue the bonds, (b) the propriety of offsetting the collateral against the related liability in the balance

---

[7]The retention of servicing rights by an affiliate of the issuer does not, in itself, preclude the associated collateral from being eliminated from the financial statements.

[8]The term *current (normal) servicing fee rate* is defined in Statement 65 as "a servicing fee rate that is representative of servicing fee rates most commonly used in comparable servicing agreements covering similar types of mortgage loans" and is used in the same sense in this Technical Bulletin.

[9]Consistent with ARB 51, this Technical Bulletin does not require a parent company engaged in manufacturing operations to consolidate the accounts of an unconsolidated finance subsidiary that consolidates the CMO issuer.

sheet if the CMO is reported as a secured borrowing, and (c) how the gain or loss on the transaction should be computed if the issuer does not record the CMO as a liability.

7. Paragraphs 3 and 4 of Statement 77 describe the transactions to which the Statement is applicable:

> 3. This Statement establishes standards of financial accounting and reporting by transferors for transfers of receivables with recourse that *purport to be sales* of receivables. It also applies to participation agreements (that is, transfers of specified interests in a particular receivable or a pool of receivables) that provide for recourse, factoring agreements that provide for recourse, and sales or assignments with recourse of leases or property subject to leases that were accounted for as sales-type or direct financing leases. [Emphasis added; footnote reference omitted.]
>
> 4. This Statement does not address accounting and reporting of loans collateralized by receivables, for which the receivables and the loan are reported on the borrower's balance sheet.

8. Paragraph 1 of Statement 76 states that the conditions for an extinguishment of debt through an in-substance defeasance "apply only to debt with specified maturities and fixed payment schedules; consequently, those circumstances do not apply to debt with variable terms that do not permit advance determination of debt service requirements, such as debt with a floating interest rate."

Paragraph 4(a) further states:

> . . . [S]ome securities . . . can be paid prior to scheduled maturity and so are not essentially risk free as to the *timing* of the collection of interest and principal; thus, they do not qualify for ownership by the trust.

9. Therefore, neither Statement 77 nor Statement 76 directly specifies the initial accounting for CMOs:

a. In specifying the scope of Statement 77, the phrase *purport to be sales* and all the transactions enumerated in paragraph 3 refer only to those transfers structured as sales agreements. As a result, the provisions of Statement 77 do not apply to CMOs because they are not structured as sales agreements; rather, CMOs are debt instruments collateralized by mortgage-backed securities or mortgage loans.

b. Because of the lack of fixed payment schedules and because the monetary assets securing the obligation do not qualify as "essentially risk free" with respect to timing of the collection of principal and interest, CMOs do not meet the in-substance defeasance requirements described in paragraph 3(c) of Statement 76. Furthermore, Technical Bulletin 84-4 states that debt may not be extinguished through an in-substance defeasance by irrevocably placing in trust assets that were acquired at about the time the debt was incurred.

10. Paragraph 11 of Statement 65 states with respect to servicing arrangements:

> If mortgage loans are sold with servicing retained and the stated servicing fee rate differs materially from a current (normal) servicing fee rate, the sales price shall be adjusted, for purposes of determining gain or loss on the sale, to provide for the recognition of a normal servicing fee in each subsequent year.

11. ARB 51 provides guidance regarding the presentation of consolidated financial statements. Paragraph 1 states:

> There is a presumption that consolidated statements are more meaningful than separate statements and that they are usually necessary for a fair presentation when one of the companies in the group directly or indirectly has a controlling financial interest in the other companies.

Paragraph 2 further states that "the fact that the subsidiary has a relatively large indebtedness to bondholders or others is not in itself a valid argument for exclusion of the subsidiary from consolidation."

12. Paragraph 7 of Opinion 10 addresses offsetting and states, in part:

> It is a general principle of accounting that the offsetting of assets and liabilities in the balance sheet is improper except where a right of setoff exists. . . . The only exception to this general principle occurs when it is clear that a purchase of securities (acceptable for the payment of taxes) is in substance an advance payment of taxes that will be payable in the relatively near future, so that in the special circumstances the purchase is tantamount to the prepayment of taxes.

FASB Technical Bulletin No. 85-3
Accounting for Operating Leases with Scheduled Rent Increases

STATUS

Issued: November 14, 1985

Effective Date: For leasing transactions entered into after November 14, 1985

Affects: No other pronouncements

Affected by: No other pronouncements

Other Interpretive Pronouncement: FTB 88-1

FASB Technical Bulletin No. 85-3
Accounting for Operating Leases with Scheduled Rent Increases

References:

FASB Statement No. 13, *Accounting for Leases,* paragraphs 15 and 19(b)
FASB Statement No. 29, *Determining Contingent Rentals*

Question

1. Certain operating lease agreements specify scheduled rent increases over the lease term. Such scheduled rent increases may, for example, be designed to provide an inducement or "rent holiday" for the lessee, to reflect the anticipated effects of inflation, to ease the lessee's near-term cash flow requirements, or to acknowledge the time value of money. For operating leases that include scheduled rent increases, is it ever appropriate for lessees or lessors to recognize rent expense or rental income on a basis other than the straight-line basis required by Statement 13?

Response

2. The effects of those scheduled rent increases, which are included in minimum lease payments under Statement 13, should be recognized by lessors and lessees on a straight-line basis over the lease term unless another systematic and rational allocation basis is more representative of the time pattern in which the leased property is physically employed. Using factors such as the time value of money, anticipated inflation, or expected future revenues to allocate scheduled rent increases is inappropriate because these factors do not relate to the *time pattern* of the physical usage of the leased property. However, such factors may affect the periodic reported rental income or expense if the lease agreement involves contingent rentals, which are excluded from minimum lease payments and accounted for separately under Statement 13, as amended by Statement 29.

Effective Date and Transition

3. The provisions of this Technical Bulletin are effective for leasing transactions entered into after November 14, 1985. Earlier application of this Technical Bulletin is encouraged in annual or interim financial statements that have not been previously issued.

Appendix

BACKGROUND INFORMATION AND CONSIDERATION OF COMMENTS RECEIVED ON THE PROPOSED TECHNICAL BULLETIN

Background Information

4. Paragraph 15 of Statement 13 discusses the lessee's recognition of expense under an operating lease:

Normally, rental on an operating lease shall be charged to expense over the lease term as it becomes payable. If rental payments are not made on a straight-line basis, rental expense nevertheless shall be recognized on a straight-line basis unless another systematic and rational basis is more representative of the time pattern in which use benefit is derived from the leased property, in which case that basis shall be used.

Paragraph 19(b) discusses the lessor's recognition of income under an operating lease:

> Rent shall be reported as income over the lease term as it becomes receivable according to the provisions of the lease. However, if the rentals vary from a straight-line basis, the income shall be recognized on a straight-line basis unless another systematic and rational basis is more representative of the time pattern in which use benefit from the leased property is diminished, in which case that basis shall be used.

5. Notwithstanding the requirements in the above paragraphs, some have suggested that, under certain conditions, rentals should be recognized on a basis that is neither straight-line nor representative of the time pattern of the physical usage of the leased property. Such conditions include (a) granting "rent holidays" or reduced rentals in the early part of the lease term as an inducement for the lessee to sign the lease agreement and (b) scheduling rent increases that are designed to reflect the anticipated effects of inflation. Some have suggested that, under those conditions, rentals should be recognized in the period that the rental payment is due.

6. Others believe that, because a lease with scheduled rent increases typically requires rental payments in the early years in amounts less than the amount of rentals to be recognized as income or expense under Statement 13, such a lease implicitly involves a borrowing by the lessee of the difference, that is, the amounts charged to expense by the lessee but not paid to the lessor. Thus, they believe the lessee is obtaining the use of the leased asset as well as the temporary use of some cash in those early years of the lease term. Accordingly, they recommend that both the lessor and lessee impute interest on that borrowing from the lessor. They suggest that the time value of money should be recognized as follows: (a) a level rental schedule should be computed that has the same present value as the present value of the escalating lease payments, (b) the computed level rental amount should be recorded as rental expense or income, and (c) interest expense or income should be imputed on the deferred amount recorded on the balance sheet that results from the difference between actual payments and the computed level rental amounts. Such an interest imputation allocation approach would generally result in lower total expense or income (including both the rental and interest elements) in the early years and the closing years of the lease than would a straight-line allocation approach. Since the amount allocated to "rental" is recorded on a straight-line basis, proponents of such an approach argue that it meets the requirements of Statement 13.

Consideration of Comments Received on the Proposed Technical Bulletin

7. A proposed Technical Bulletin, *Accounting for Operating Leases with Scheduled Rent Increases,* was released for comment on June 24, 1985. Thirty-two letters of comment were received on the proposed Technical Bulletin. Certain of the comments received and consideration of them are discussed in the following paragraphs.

8. The proposed Technical Bulletin indicated that it is not appropriate to use the time value of money as a factor in recognizing rentals under an operating lease. Thus, the proposed Technical Bulletin indicated that the interest imputation allocation approach is unacceptable. A majority of the respondents who addressed that approach agreed with the guidance in the proposed Bulletin. However, some respondents supported the interest imputation allocation approach, arguing that it reflects the economic substance of the transaction. They also indicated that the time value of money is an economic reality that warrants recognition.

9. The time value of money is an important concept underlying the fundamental accounting in Statement 13. That Statement specifies criteria for identifying the leases (known as capital leases) for which the lessee must recognize an asset and a liability, the initial measurements of which are based on present value. However, that Statement also stipulates the accounting for the leases (known as operating leases) that do not meet those criteria. That accounting does not recognize a liability for the lessee's obligation to pay all the future minimum rentals under an operating lease, nor does it permit the time value of money to affect the accounting for those future rentals. Statement 13 views operating leases as executory contracts, not as financing transactions, for accounting purposes.

10. The proposed Technical Bulletin indicated that inducements in the form of rent abatements in the early part of the lease term do not warrant special accounting treatment that differs from the requirements of Statement 13. Thus, the proposed Bulletin effectively required inducements to be recognized over the term of the lease. Substantially all the respondents commenting on this issue supported the position in the proposed Technical Bulletin.

11. The proposed Technical Bulletin also indicated that scheduled rent increases designed to reflect the anticipated effects of inflation do not warrant special accounting treatment that differs from the requirements of Statement 13. A majority of the respondents who addressed that issue indicated support for the guidance in the proposed Bulletin.

However, some respondents opposed the proposed guidance and suggested that recognizing rent expense as paid would provide a better matching of revenues and expenses and be more representative of the economics of the lease agreements.

12. Recognizing scheduled rent increases as rent expense as paid would effectively account for those mandatory increases in the same manner as for contingent rentals. The accounting for operating leases under Statement 13, as amended by Statement 29, however, differentiates between (a) scheduled rent increases that are not dependent on future events and (b) increases or decreases in rentals that are dependent on future events such as future sales volume, future inflation, future property taxes, and so forth. The former are minimum lease payments to be accounted for under paragraphs 15 and 19(b) of Statement 13. The latter are contingent rentals that affect the measure of expense or income as accruable, as specified by Statement 29. Opponents of the guidance in the proposed Technical Bulletin asserted that the economic substance of contingent rentals and scheduled rent increases designed to reflect the anticipated effects of inflation are the same and should be accounted for similarly.

13. There is an important substantive difference between lease rentals that are contingent upon some specified future event and scheduled rent increases that are unaffected by future events; the accounting under Statement 13 reflects that difference. If the lessor and lessee eliminate the risk of variable payments inherent in contingent rentals by agreeing to scheduled rent increases, the accounting should reflect those different circumstances.

FASB Technical Bulletin No. 85-4
Accounting for Purchases of Life Insurance

STATUS

Issued: November 14, 1985

Effective Date: For insurance policies acquired after November 14, 1985

Affects: Supersedes AIN-Key-Man Life Insurance

Affected by: No other pronouncements

FASB Technical Bulletin No. 85-4
Accounting for Purchases of Life Insurance

References:

AICPA Accounting Interpretation, "Accounting for Key-Man Life Insurance"
FASB Concepts Statement No. 3, *Elements of Financial Statements of Business Enterprises,* paragraphs 19 and 123

Question

1. How should an entity[1] account for an investment in life insurance?

Response

2. The amount that could be realized under the insurance contract as of the date of the statement of financial position should be reported as an asset. The change in cash surrender or contract value during the period is an adjustment of premiums paid in determining the expense or income to be recognized under the contract for the period.

Effective Date and Transition

3. The provisions of this Technical Bulletin are effective for insurance policies acquired after November 14, 1985.

> The Financial Accounting Standards Board has authorized its staff to prepare FASB Technical Bulletins to provide guidance on certain financial accounting and reporting problems on a timely basis, pursuant to the procedures described in FASB Technical Bulletin No. 79-1 (Revised), *Purpose and Scope of FASB Technical Bulletins and Procedures for Issuance.* The provisions of Technical Bulletins need not be applied to immaterial items. Copyright © 1985 by the Financial Accounting Standards Board.

Appendix

BACKGROUND

4. In November 1970, the AICPA issued an Accounting Interpretation entitled "Accounting for Key-Man Life Insurance." That Accounting Interpretation identified the cash surrender value method as generally accepted accounting for purchases of life insurance. New types of life insurance contracts, new provisions in traditional contracts, and changes in the insurance industry have led some to question the 1970 Accounting Interpretation. In October 1984, the AICPA's Accounting Standards Executive Committee (AcSEC) approved an Issues Paper entitled "Accounting for Key-Person Life Insurance." In the Issues Paper, AcSEC reaffirmed support of the cash surrender value method as the only generally accepted method. The AcSEC position differed from the position of the AICPA Insurance Companies Committee, which supported use of a different method in certain circumstances. AcSEC was concerned that diversity would develop in practice because of the difference between those positions and requested that the FASB consider the matter.

5. A premium paid by a purchaser of life insurance serves a variety of purposes. A portion of the premium pays the insurer for assumption of mortality risk and provides for recovery of the insurer's contract acquisition, initiation, and maintenance costs. Another portion of the premium contributes to the accumulation of contract values. The relative amounts of premium payment credited to various contract attributes change over time as the age of the insured party increases and as earnings are credited to previously established contract values.

6. An insurance contract is significantly different from most investment agreements. The various attributes of the policy could be obtained separately through term insurance and purchase of invest-

---

[1] The provisions of this Technical Bulletin apply to all entities that purchase life insurance in which the entity is either the owner or beneficiary of the contract, without regard to the funding objective of the purchase. Such purchases would typically include those intended to meet loan covenants or to fund deferred compensation agreements, buy-sell agreements, or postemployment death benefits. Purchases of life insurance by retirement plans that are subject to FASB Statement No. 35, *Accounting and Reporting by Defined Benefit Pension Plans,* are not addressed by this Technical Bulletin.

ments. The combination of benefits and contract values could not, however, typically be acquired absent the insurance contract. Continued protection from mortality risk and realization of scheduled increases in contract accumulation usually requires payment of future premiums.

7. The payment of insurance premiums may take a number of different forms. The insurance contract may be purchased through payment of a single premium, as opposed to the typical series of future premiums. Alternatively, the premium payments may be made through loans from the insurance company that are secured by policy cash surrender values. The pattern of premium payments is a decision that does not alter the underlying nature of the insurance contract.

Consideration of Comments Received on Proposed Technical Bulletin

8. A proposed Technical Bulletin, *Accounting for Business-Owned Life Insurance,* was released for comment on June 28, 1985. Forty-seven letters of comment were received on the proposed Technical Bulletin. Certain of the comments received and consideration of them are discussed in the following paragraphs.

9. Some respondents view the dominant objective of a life insurance contract to be investment. Subject to certain criteria evidencing an intent to continue the contract, they maintain that the contract meets the definition of an asset established in paragraph 19 of Concepts Statement 3, which states, "Assets are probable future economic benefits obtained or controlled by a particular entity as a result of past transactions or events" (footnote reference omitted). Those who hold this view suggested that such contracts should be accounted for using methods that result in reporting the investment in life insurance at amounts different from those stipulated in the contract.

10. This Technical Bulletin does not take that view. The current capacity to realize contract benefits is limited to settlement amounts specified in the contract. Additional amounts in excess of cash surrender value, which would be reported as assets under the various alternative accounting methods suggested, are created by future events, which typically include premium payments and earnings credited to contract amounts.

11. Paragraph 123 of Concepts Statement 3 discusses the occurrence of past events and the role of future events in the recognition of assets.

> Since the transaction or event giving rise to the enterprise's right to the future economic benefit must already have occurred, the definition excludes from assets items that may in the future become an enterprise's as-

sets but have not yet become its assets. An enterprise has no asset for a particular future economic benefit if the transactions or events that give it access to and control of the benefit are yet in the future.

12. Some respondents asserted that reporting an insurance investment at its realizable value represents an accounting based on liquidation values. Those respondents suggested that the entity acquiring an insurance contract is, in many cases, economically or contractually committed to maintain the contract in force. They maintained that such a commitment virtually assures that benefits in excess of premiums paid would be realized and that the policy should be reported on a basis other than its cash surrender value.

13. This Technical Bulletin does not accept that view. The amount realizable under an insurance investment represents settlement values agreed to by an independent buyer and seller. The variety of yields and contract accumulation patterns available in the insurance marketplace provides the buyer and seller a variety of insurance and settlement options. There is no compelling justification to depart from the recording of such contracts based on agreed provisions. The commitment referred to by respondents is, in the staff's view, a commitment to ensure that assets are available to meet contractual obligations. The presence of such a commitment does not change the measurement of the asset that is expected to satisfy the obligation.

14. Some respondents asserted that policy features, most notably the business exchange rider, were significant factors in determining the proper accounting for the policy. The business exchange rider allows a company to use values in an existing policy to insure a different employee when the originally insured employee leaves the company. They maintain that this feature gives the employer the ability to transfer the contract freely and enhances the employer's ability to realize the future value of the investment. They further maintain that the increased probability of realizing future values should lead to the reporting of amounts in excess of cash surrender value.

15. This Technical Bulletin rejects that view. The business exchange rider is a significant development in the design of business insurance products and reduces additional policy costs if a covered employee leaves the company. Such a provision does not affect the realization of future benefits under the insurance contract, nor does it change the traditional underwriting decisions involved in insuring a new life. Instead, the provision only reduces the cost of obtaining those benefits by allowing a new employee to be insured without the costs that are typically associated with obtaining a new policy.

FASB Technical Bulletin No. 85-5

Issues Relating to Accounting for Business Combinations, Including

- Costs of Closing Duplicate Facilities of an Acquirer
- Stock Transactions between Companies under Common Control
- Downstream Mergers
- Identical Common Shares for a Pooling of Interests
- Pooling of Interests by Mutual and Cooperative Enterprises

STATUS

Issued: December 31, 1985

Effective Date: The provisions of paragraph 2 are effective for transactions consummated after June 5, 1985. Other provisions are effective for business combinations initiated after December 31, 1985.

Affects: No other pronouncements

Affected by: No other pronouncements

FASB Technical Bulletin No. 85-5
Issues Relating to Accounting for Business Combinations, Including
- **Costs of Closing Duplicate Facilities of an Acquirer**
- **Stock Transactions between Companies under Common Control**
- **Downstream Mergers**
- **Identical Common Shares for a Pooling of Interests**
- **Pooling of Interests by Mutual and Cooperative Enterprises**

COSTS OF CLOSING DUPLICATE FACILITIES OF AN ACQUIRER

Reference:

APB Opinion No. 16, *Business Combinations,* paragraphs 76 and 88

Question 1

1. Are the costs incurred to close duplicate facilities of an acquiring company recognized as part of the cost of acquisition in a business combination accounted for by the purchase method?

Response

2. No. Only the direct costs of an acquisition should be included in the cost of a purchased company in a business combination accounted for by the purchase method. Indirect expenses of an acquiring company, including costs incurred when the acquiring company closes some of its facilities because they duplicate facilities acquired in a purchase business combination, should be charged to expense in determining net income. Therefore, the disposition of the acquiring company's assets do not affect the accounting for assets acquired and liabilities assumed of the acquired company, and any gain or loss on disposal or other cost associated with the disposition of an existing asset of the acquiring company should be charged to income.

Background

3. Paragraph 76 of Opinion 16 states that:

> The cost of a company acquired in a business combination accounted for by the purchase method includes the direct costs of acquisition. . . . indirect and general expenses related to acquisitions are deducted as incurred in determining net income.

Costs incurred by an acquiring company to dispose of its assets are not *direct* costs of the acquisition and therefore are not to be considered in determining the amounts to be assigned to the assets acquired and liabilities assumed.

4. The treatment of the acquiring company's assets and those of the acquired company is different in a business combination. The acquiring company measures the cost of an acquisition at the fair value of the consideration paid to the selling parties and other direct costs of acquisition, whether that consideration involves assets, liabilities, or equity interests. In recording the acquisition, that cost is allocated to the individual assets acquired and liabilities assumed. No adjustments are made to the acquiring company's assets and liabilities because of a business combination other than to reflect the consideration paid by the acquiring company to the selling parties. Paragraph 88 of Opinion 16 provides guidance for allocating the cost of the acquisition by the acquiring company. Paragraph 88(i) states that "commitments and plant closing expense incident to the acquisition" are among factors that should be considered in allocating the purchase price. Plant closing expense is not part of the cost of the acquisition; it is one factor to be considered in allocating the cost of the acquired company to the individual assets acquired and liabilities assumed. Therefore, the reference to plant closing expense in paragraph 88(i) pertains only to the facilities of the acquired company. The cost of closing a facility of the *acquiring* company should not be similarly treated because the cost of the acquisition is not allocated to assets and liabilities of the acquiring company.

STOCK TRANSACTIONS BETWEEN COMPANIES UNDER COMMON CONTROL

References:

APB Opinion No. 16, *Business Combinations,* paragraphs 5 and 43
AICPA Accounting Interpretation 26, "Acquisition of Minority Interest," of Opinion 16
AICPA Accounting Interpretation 39, "Transfers and Exchanges between Companies under Common Control," of Opinion 16

Question 2

5. How should a parent company account for minority interest in an exchange of stock between two

of its subsidiaries if one or both of the subsidiaries are partially owned?

Response

6. The accounting depends on whether the minority shareholders are party to the exchange of shares. If some or all of the shares owned by minority shareholders are exchanged for shares of ownership in another subsidiary of the parent (or a new subsidiary formed by combining two or more subsidiaries of the parent), then the transaction is recognized by the parent company as the acquisition of shares from the minority interest, which according to paragraph 43 of Opinion 16 should be accounted for by the purchase method, that is, based on fair value. The original minority interest effectively is purchased, and a new minority interest in a different subsidiary is created. However, if the exchange lacks substance, it is not a purchase event and should be accounted for based on existing carrying amounts. That is, if the minority interest does not change and if in substance the only assets of the combined entity after the exchange are those of the partially owned subsidiary prior to the exchange, a change in ownership has not taken place, and the exchange should be accounted for based on the carrying amounts of the partially owned subsidiary's assets and liabilities.

7. If, however, minority shareholders are not party to an exchange of shares between two subsidiaries of the same parent (a partially owned subsidiary issues its shares in exchange for shares of another subsidiary previously owned by the same parent), the minority interest in the issuing subsidiary remains outstanding, and the transaction is an exchange of stock between companies under common control. In contrast to the acquisition of a minority interest, this transaction leaves all of the issuing subsidiary's minority interest outstanding, although the minority stockholders' interest in the net assets has changed in each case. Accounting Interpretation 39 of Opinion 16 indicates that the assets and liabilities transferred in such an exchange of shares should be accounted for at existing carrying amounts.

Background

8. In some circumstances, the transaction described in paragraph 10 may result in ownership interests of the parent and the minority shareholders that are similar or identical to the ownership interests that result from the transaction described in paragraph 11. Accounting Interpretations 26 and 39 (which interpret paragraphs 43 and 5 of Opinion 16) prescribe different accounting treatment for these transactions; how-ever, the similarity of results of the transactions has led to many questions and inconsistency in practice.

9. Paragraph 43 of Opinion 16 states:

> The acquisition . . . of some or all of the stock held by minority stockholders of a subsidiary—whether acquired by the parent, the subsidiary itself, or another affiliate—should be accounted for by the purchase method rather than by the pooling of interests method.

10. Accounting Interpretation 26 of Opinion 16 gives several examples of transactions that are, in substance, the acquisition of a minority interest. It states for one of those examples:

> Thus, purchase accounting applies when . . . (c) another subsidiary of the parent exchanges its common stock or assets or debt for common stock held by the minority shareholders of an affiliated subsidiary.

11. Accounting Interpretation 39 of Opinion 16 clarifies how an exchange of stock between two subsidiaries of a parent would be recorded:

> Also, a parent may exchange its ownership or the net assets of a wholly owned subsidiary for additional shares issued by the parent's partially owned subsidiary, thereby increasing the parent's percentage of ownership in the partially owned subsidiary but leaving all of the existing minority interest outstanding.
>
> None of the above transfers or exchanges is covered by APB Opinion No. 16. The assets and liabilities so transferred would be accounted for at historical cost in a manner similar to that in pooling of interests accounting.

12. Some transactions involve both an effective acquisition of a minority interest and an exchange of stock between companies under common control, which usually are accounted for differently. In those cases, the accounting depends on whether the minority shareholders are party to the exchange of shares. In transactions described in Accounting Interpretation 26 of Opinion 16, an exchange takes place involving the minority shareholders. In transactions described in Accounting Interpretation 39 of Opinion 16, an effective change in the equity interest of the minority shareholders arises, but no exchange takes place. The accounting for the above types of transactions depends on the nature of the exchange that takes place, not the apparent similarity of the results of different transactions.

DOWNSTREAM MERGERS

References:

APB Opinion No. 16, *Business Combinations,*
paragraphs 5 and 43
AICPA Accounting Interpretation 26, "Acquisition of Minority Interest," of Opinion 16
AICPA Accounting Interpretation 39, "Transfers
and Exchanges between Companies under Common Control," of Opinion 16

Question 3

13. Are there circumstances in which an exchange
by a partially owned subsidiary of its common
stock for the outstanding voting common stock of
its parent (a "downstream merger") can be accounted for like a pooling of interests?

Response

14. No. Accounting for this transaction is specifically addressed in Accounting Interpretation 26 of
Opinion 16.

> . . . Pooling is precluded in the exchange
> by a subsidiary of its common stock for the
> outstanding voting common stock of its
> parent (usually referred to as a "down-
> stream merger"). Instead, purchase ac-
> counting applies and the transaction should
> be accounted for as if the parent had ex-
> changed its common stock for common
> stock held by minority shareholders of its
> subsidiary. (Whether a parent acquires the
> minority or a subsidiary acquires its parent,
> the end result is a single shareholder group,
> including the former minority sharehold-
> ers, owning the consolidated net assets.)
> The same would be true if a new corpora-
> tion exchanged its common stock for the
> common stock of the parent and the com-
> mon stock of the subsidiary held by minor-
> ity shareholders.

Background

15. Some have observed that a downstream merger
is a transaction between companies under common
control. They cite Accounting Interpretation 39 of
Opinion 16 to support accounting for a downstream
merger like a pooling of interests. However, although a downstream merger is a transaction involving companies under common control, the accounting for that transaction is explicitly described
in Accounting Interpretation 26 of Opinion 16.

IDENTICAL COMMON SHARES FOR A POOLING OF INTERESTS

References:

APB Opinion No. 16, *Business Combinations,*
paragraphs 47(b) and 48(a)
AICPA Accounting Interpretation 11, "Use of Restricted Stock to Effect a Business Combination," of Opinion 16
AICPA Accounting Interpretation 13, "Two-Class
Common for Pooling," of Opinion 16

Question 4

16. Does the issuance in a business combination
of common shares that are identical to other outstanding common shares, except that the issuer retains a right of first refusal to repurchase the shares
issued in certain specific circumstances, preclude
the issuer from accounting for the business combination as a pooling of interests?

Response

17. Yes. Paragraph 47(b) of Opinion 16 states that
the shares that are issued by a combining company
to effect a business combination must have "rights
identical to those of the majority of its outstanding
voting common stock" in order for the combination to meet the requirements for pooling.

Background

18. Accounting Interpretation 13 of Opinion 16 includes guidance on the meaning of identical rights.

> *Interpretation*—Paragraph 47-b does not
> prohibit designating the common stock is-
> sued as a different class if it has *rights iden-
> tical* to those of the majority class of out-
> standing voting common stock. Thus, the
> different class must have the same voting,
> dividend, liquidation, preemptive, etc.,
> rights as the majority class with the stipula-
> tion that these rights cannot be changed un-
> less a corresponding change is made in the
> rights of the majority class.

19. Opinion 16 and Accounting Interpretations 11
and 13 of Opinion 16 specifically use the term *identical* to describe the type of shares to be issued in a
pooling of interests. A restriction imposed by the issuing corporation upon the sale of stock is discussed
in Accounting Interpretation 11 of Opinion 16:

> However, a restriction imposed *by the is-
> suing corporation* upon the sale of the stock

in the absence of a governmental regulation would probably create different rights between previously outstanding and newly issued stock. Such a restriction might also indicate the previously separate stockholder groups would not be sharing the same risks in the business combination (see paragraph 45 and introductory statements in paragraphs 46 and 47). Likewise, a restriction upon the sale of the stock to anyone other than the issuing corporation or an affiliate would not meet the "absence of planned transactions" condition specified in paragraph 48-a. [Emphasis added.]

20. Accounting Interpretation 11 of Opinion 16 describes one specific exception to the requirement that shares issued be identical. Temporary restrictions imposed by government regulations on the sale of the shares to the public does not cause the shares to be regarded as different for purposes of determining whether a business combination may be accounted for as a pooling of interests. That type of restriction is different from the type of restriction described in paragraph 17 of this Bulletin.

POOLING OF INTERESTS BY MUTUAL AND COOPERATIVE ENTERPRISES

Reference:

APB Opinion No. 16, *Business Combinations,* paragraphs 5 and 47(c)

Question 5

21. Does the conversion of a mutual or cooperative enterprise to stock ownership within two years before a plan of combination is initiated or between the dates a combination is initiated and consummated preclude accounting for the combination as a pooling of interests?

Response

22. No. The changes in the equity interests of the combining companies that are proscribed in a pooling of interests are those that might be used to circumvent the intent of Opinion 16—that the combination is effected through an exchange of voting interests. In the case of a conversion from mutual ownership to stock ownership, the change to stock ownership may be a necessary step to effect a combination, in which case it should not preclude accounting for a combination as a pooling.

Background

23. Paragraph 47(c) of Opinion 16 states that as a condition for pooling:

> c. None of the combining companies changes the equity interest of the voting common stock in contemplation of effecting the combination either within two years before the plan of combination is initiated or between the dates the combination is initiated and consummated; changes in contemplation of effecting the combination may include distributions to stockholders and additional issuances, exchanges, and retirements of securities.

24. Combinations of mutuals and cooperative enterprises were not specifically addressed in Opinion 16, although paragraph 5 indicates that Opinion 16 should be applied to a combination of two or more unincorporated businesses. The requirements of paragraph 47(c) of Opinion 16 were included to ensure that other provisions of Opinion 16 would not be circumvented. In the special case of a mutual or cooperative enterprise that converts to stock ownership for purposes of effecting a business combination, the conversion is not a shift of equity ownership from one group of equity owners to another. It is a shift from a form of organization that has no substantive equity ownership to one that has. This would not preclude accounting for the transaction as a pooling of interests. This exception to paragraph 47(c) of Opinion 16 applies exclusively to mutual and cooperative enterprises, which must meet all of the other requirements of Opinion 16 to qualify for a pooling of interests.

Consideration of Comments Received on the Proposed Technical Bulletin

25. A proposed Technical Bulletin, *Issues Relating to Accounting for Business Combinations, Including Costs of Settling Employee Stock Options and Awards, Costs of Closing Duplicate Facilities of an Acquirer, Stock Transactions between Companies under Common Control, Downstream Mergers, Identical Common Shares for a Pooling of Interests, and Pooling of Interests by Mutual and Cooperative Enterprises,* was released for comment on June 28, 1985. Forty-one letters of comment were received on the proposed Technical Bulletin. Certain of the comments received and consideration of them are discussed in the following paragraphs.

26. The proposed Technical Bulletin addressed the issue of whether costs incurred by a purchased company to settle an earlier award of stock or to settle a grant of option to an employee are part of the purchase price in a business combination accounted for by the purchase method. Some of the comments received on this issue indicated that the question and related response were not clear as to how they should apply in various circumstances. Because addressing all circumstances would significantly delay issuance of the final Technical Bulletin, it was decided that the issue should be referred to the FASB's Emerging Issues Task Force for further consideration. The issue is not included in this Technical Bulletin.

27. Several respondents questioned the significance of the June 5, 1985 effective date for the provisions of paragraph 2 (response to question 1). June 5, 1985 was the date the proposed Technical Bulletin was discussed at a public Board meeting, and that conclusion was publicly announced.

Effective Date and Transition

28. The provisions of paragraph 2 of this Technical Bulletin (response to question 1) are effective for transactions consummated after June 5, 1985. Other provisions of this Technical Bulletin are effective for business combinations initiated after December 31, 1985. Earlier application to transactions occurring in periods for which financial statements have not been issued is encouraged.

FASB Technical Bulletin No. 85-6
Accounting for a Purchase of Treasury Shares at a Price Significantly in Excess of the Current Market Price of the Shares and the Income Statement Classification of Costs Incurred in Defending against a Takeover Attempt

STATUS

Issued: December 31, 1985

Effective Date: Effective for transactions after December 31, 1985

Affects: No other pronouncements

Affected by: No other pronouncements

Accounting for a Purchase of Treasury Shares
and Costs Incurred in Defending against **FTB85-6**
a Takeover Attempt

FASB Technical Bulletin No. 85-6
Accounting for a Purchase of Treasury Shares at a Price Significantly in Excess of the Current Market Price of the Shares and the Income Statement Classification of Costs Incurred in Defending against a Takeover Attempt

References:

FASB Concepts Statement No. 6, *Elements of Financial Statements,* paragraph 28
APB Opinion No. 30, *Reporting the Results of Operations—Reporting the Effects of Disposal of a Segment of a Business, and Extraordinary, Unusual and Infrequently Occurring Events and Transactions,* paragraph 20
APB Opinion No. 26, *Early Extinguishment of Debt*
APB Opinion No. 25, *Accounting for Stock Issued to Employees,* paragraph 11(g)
APB Opinion No. 21, *Interest on Receivables and Payables,* paragraph 7
APB Opinion No. 16, *Business Combinations,* paragraph 72
APB Opinion No. 6, *Status of Accounting Research Bulletins,* paragraph 12
ARB No. 43, Chapter 1B, "Profits or Losses on Treasury Stock"

Question 1

1. How should a company account for a purchase of treasury shares at a stated price significantly in excess of the current market price of the shares?

Response

2. An agreement to purchase shares from a shareholder may also involve the receipt or payment of consideration in exchange for stated or unstated rights or privileges that should be identified to allocate properly the purchase price.

3. A purchase of shares at a price significantly in excess of the current market price creates a presumption that the purchase price includes amounts attributable to items other than the shares purchased. For example, the selling shareholder may agree to abandon certain acquisition plans, forego other planned transactions, settle litigation, settle employment contracts, or restrict voluntarily the ability to purchase shares of the company or its affiliates within a stated time period. If the purchase of treasury shares includes the receipt of stated or unstated rights, privileges, or agreements in addition to the capital stock, only the amount representing the fair value of the treasury shares at the date the major terms of the agreement to purchase the shares are reached should be accounted for as the cost of the shares acquired.

The price paid in excess of the amount accounted for as the cost of treasury shares should be attributed to the other elements of the transaction and accounted for according to their substance. If the fair value of those other elements of the transaction is more clearly evident, for example, because a company's shares are not publicly traded, that amount should be assigned to those elements and the difference recorded as the cost of treasury shares. If no stated or unstated consideration in addition to the capital stock can be identified, the entire purchase price should be accounted for as the cost of treasury shares. The allocation of amounts paid and the accounting treatment for such amounts should be disclosed.

Question 2

4. Should amounts paid by an enterprise to a shareholder or former shareholder attributed to an agreement precluding the shareholder or former shareholder from purchasing additional shares be capitalized as assets and amortized over the period of the agreement?

Response

5. No. Payments by an enterprise to a shareholder or former shareholder attributed, for example, to a "standstill" agreement, or any agreement in which a shareholder or former shareholder agrees not to purchase additional shares, should be expensed as incurred. Such payments do not give rise to assets of the enterprise as defined in Concepts Statement 6.

Question 3

6. Should the costs incurred by a company to defend itself from a takeover attempt or the cost attributed to a "standstill" agreement be classified as extraordinary items?

Response

7. No. Neither the costs incurred by a company to defend itself from a takeover attempt nor the costs incurred as part of a "standstill" agreement meet the criteria for extraordinary classification as discussed in paragraph 20 of Opinion 30. The *event* that gave rise to those costs—a takeover attempt—cannot be considered to be both *unusual* and *infrequent* as those terms are used in Opinion 30.

Effective Date and Transition

8. The provisions of this Technical Bulletin are effective for transactions after December 31, 1985.

Earlier application to transactions occurring in periods for which financial statements have not been issued is encouraged.

Appendix

BACKGROUND INFORMATION

9. Most transactions by an enterprise in shares of its own stock are solely capital transactions, that is, the transactions involve only the transfer of ownership of the enterprise's stock or rights associated with ownership of the stock. Those transactions do not result in recognition of income or expense by the enterprise. The accounting for transactions involving treasury stock purchases or reissuances is well established, as described in paragraph 12 of Opinion 6, which expanded on guidance in Chapter 1B of ARB 43. That guidance was first provided in 1938 by the AICPA Committee on Accounting Procedure, the predecessor of the Accounting Principles Board.

10. In some cases, however, a transaction involving shares of an enterprise's own stock may involve the receipt or payment of consideration in exchange for rights or privileges that may require recognition of income or expense by the enterprise. The Board and its predecessor, the Accounting Principles Board, have addressed several transactions of this type and concluded that recognition of income or expense is required. For example, paragraph 11(g) of Opinion 25 requires that compensation expense be recognized when an enterprise settles an earlier grant of stock to an employee by repurchasing the shares granted to the employee if the shares are reacquired shortly after issuance. Opinion 26 (as amended by FASB Statements No. 76, *Extinguishment of Debt*, and No. 84, *Induced Conversions of Convertible Debt)* requires recognition of gain or loss when debt of an enterprise is extinguished by the issuance of shares of the enterprise and the fair value of shares issued differs from the carrying amount of the debt.

11. Paragraph 7 of Opinion 21 describes the need to give accounting recognition to unstated rights or privileges that affect the interest rate on a note. Although Opinion 21 does not address transactions involving equity instruments, the need to give accounting recognition to unstated rights or privileges is a well-established concept in accounting. Frequently, transactions involve payment of an amount that must be allocated among assets acquired, liabilities settled, and expenses paid, because the prices paid for the individual assets, liabilities, and expenses are unstated. For example, it is often necessary to allocate the cost of real estate between land and buildings acquired in a single transaction.

12. The need to allocate cost among items acquired as a group is a common occurrence in accounting. Paragraph 72 of Opinion 16 states that "the same accounting principles apply to determining the cost of assets acquired individually, those acquired in a group, and those acquired in a business combination."

13. In an exchange transaction of other assets for marketable securities, the fair value of the securities typically is more clearly evident from the market prices of the same securities being traded in the market than is the fair value of other assets acquired or given up. In those transactions, the fair value of the securities is generally the best indication of the fair value of the other assets acquired or sold. A similar relationship holds true in a treasury stock transaction involving the receipt of consideration in addition to the capital stock; the quoted market price of the securities being traded in the market will frequently be the best indication of the fair value of the shares acquired.

**Accounting for a Purchase of Treasury Shares
and Costs Incurred in Defending against
a Takeover Attempt**   **FTB85-6**

14. An enterprise offering to repurchase shares only from a specific shareholder (or group of shareholders) suggests that the repurchase may involve more than the purchase of treasury shares. Also, when an enterprise repurchases shares at a price that is different from the price obtainable in transactions in the open market or transactions in which the identity of the selling shareholder is not important, some portion of the amount being paid presumably represents a payment for stated or unstated rights or privileges that should be given separate accounting recognition.

15. Transactions do arise, however, in which an acquisition of an enterprise's stock may take place at prices different from routine transactions in the open market. For example, to obtain the desired number of shares in a tender offer to all or most shareholders, the offer may need to be at a price in excess of the current market price. In addition, a block of shares representing a controlling interest will generally trade at a price in excess of market, and a large block of shares may trade at a price above or below the current market price depending on whether the buyer or seller initiates the transaction. A company's acquisition of its shares in those circumstances is solely a treasury stock transaction properly accounted for at the purchase price of the treasury shares. Therefore, in the absence of the receipt of stated or unstated consideration in addition to the capital stock, the entire purchase price should be accounted for as the cost of treasury shares.

16. The allocation of amounts described in paragraph 3 of this Technical Bulletin requires significant judgment and consideration of many factors that can significantly affect amounts recognized in the financial statements. Disclosure of the allocation of amounts and the accounting treatment for such amounts is necessary to enable the user of the financial statements to understand the nature of significant transactions that may affect, in part, the capital of the enterprise.

17. Paragraph 5 of this Technical Bulletin states that payments by an enterprise to a shareholder or former shareholder attributed to an agreement in which a shareholder or former shareholder agrees not to take specified actions for a specific period of time should be expensed as incurred. Payments to shareholders generally do not give rise to assets of an enterprise unless they meet the definition of an asset in Concepts Statement 6. According to paragraph 28 of Concepts Statement 6, the primary characteristic of an asset is the scarce capacity to provide services or benefits to the entities that use them:

> The common characteristic possessed by all assets (economic resources) is "service potential" or "future economic benefit," the scarce capacity to provide services or benefits to the entities that use them. In a business enterprise, that service potential or future economic benefit eventually results in net cash inflows to the enterprise.

FASB Technical Bulletin No. 86-1
Accounting for Certain Effects
of the Tax Reform Act of 1986

STATUS

Issued: October 27, 1986

Effective Date: October 22, 1986 for interim and annual periods ending on or after January 1, 1986

Affects: No other pronouncements

Affected by: Superseded by FAS 96 and FAS 109

(The next page is 1282.)

(This page intentionally left blank.)

FASB Technical Bulletin No. 86-2
Accounting for an Interest in the Residual Value of a Leased Asset:
- Acquired by a Third Party or
- Retained by a Lessor That Sells the Related Minimum Rental Payments

STATUS

Issued: December 17, 1986

Effective Date: December 17, 1986 for transactions entered into on or after June 18, 1986

Affects: No other pronouncements

Affected by: No other pronouncements

FASB Technical Bulletin No. 86-2
Accounting for an Interest in the Residual Value of a Leased Asset:

- **Acquired by a Third Party or**
- **Retained by a Lessor That Sells the Related Minimum Rental Payments**

References

FASB Statement No. 13, *Accounting for Leases*, paragraphs 17, 18, 42, and 99
FASB Concepts Statement No. 5, *Recognition and Measurement in Financial Statements of Business Enterprises*, paragraphs 83, 84(c), 84(d), and 84(f)
FASB Statement No. 33, *Financial Reporting and Changing Prices*, paragraph 47
APB Opinion No. 10, *Omnibus Opinion—1966*, paragraph 7

Question

1. How should an enterprise account for the acquisition from a lessor of the unconditional right to own and possess, at the end of the lease term, an asset subject to a lease? Also, how should an enterprise account for the acquisition of the right to receive all, or a portion, of the proceeds from the sale of a leased asset at the end of the lease term?

Response

2. At the date the rights are acquired, both transactions involve a right to receive, at the end of the lease term, all, or a portion, of any future benefit to be derived from the leased asset and should be accounted for as the acquisition of an asset. (Hereinafter, both transactions are referred to as the acquisition of an interest in the residual value of a leased asset.)

Question

3. How should an enterprise acquiring an interest in the residual value of a leased asset measure the cost of the acquisition?

Response

4. An interest in the residual value of a leased asset should be recorded as an asset at the amount of cash disbursed, the fair value of other consideration given, and the present value of liabilities assumed at the date the right is acquired. The fair value of the interest in the residual value of the leased asset at the date of the agreement should

be used to measure its cost if that fair value is more clearly evident than the fair value of assets surrendered, services rendered, or liabilities assumed.

Question

5. A lessor recognizes increases in the residual value of a leased asset accounted for as a sales-type or direct financing lease to its estimated value at the end of the lease term. How should an enterprise acquiring an interest in the residual value of a leased asset account for that asset during the lease term?

Response

6. An enterprise acquiring an interest in the residual value of any leased asset, irrespective of the classification of the related lease by the lessor, should not recognize increases to the asset's estimated value over the remaining term of the related lease, and the asset should be reported at no more than its acquisition cost until sale or disposition. If it is subsequently determined that the fair value of the residual value of a leased asset has declined below the carrying amount of the acquired interest and that decline is other than temporary, the asset should be written down to fair value, and the amount of the write-down should be recognized as a loss. That fair value becomes the asset's new carrying amount, and the asset should not be increased for any subsequent increase in its fair value prior to its sale or disposition.

Question

7. Do the foregoing provisions apply to lease brokers?

Response

8. Yes. An interest in the residual value of a leased asset acquired by a lease broker for cash, liabilities assumed, and the fair value of other consideration given, including services rendered, should be accounted for under the foregoing provisions.

Question

9. If a lessor sells substantially all of the minimum rental payments associated with a sales-type, direct financing, or leveraged lease and retains an interest in the residual value of the leased asset, how should the lessor account for that asset over the remaining lease term?

Response

10. A lessor retaining an interest in the residual value of the leased asset should not recognize increases in the value of the lease residual to its estimated value over the remaining lease term. The lessor should report any remaining interest thereafter at its carrying amount at the date of the sale of the lease payments. If it is subsequently determined that the fair value of the residual value of the leased asset has declined below the carrying amount of the interest retained and that decline is other than temporary, the asset should be written down to fair value, and the amount of the writedown should be recognized as a loss. That fair value becomes the asset's new carrying amount, and the asset should not be increased for any subsequent increase in its fair value prior to its sale or disposition.

Question

11. If an interest in the residual value of a leased asset is guaranteed, does the guarantee change the nature of the asset or the accounting?

Response

12. No. A guarantee does not change the nature of an interest in the residual value of a leased asset or its historical acquisition cost.

Effective Date and Transition

13. The provisions of this Technical Bulletin are effective December 17, 1986 for transactions entered into on or after June 18, 1986, the date the conclusions of this Technical Bulletin were first discussed at a public Board meeting. Earlier application to transactions occurring in periods for which financial statements have not been issued is encouraged. Financial information for transactions entered into on or after June 18, 1986 that was reported differently than specified by this Technical Bulletin should be restated to conform to its provisions when the interim or annual financial statements containing that information are subsequently presented.

Appendix

BACKGROUND INFORMATION AND CONSIDERATION OF COMMENTS RECEIVED ON THE PROPOSED TECHNICAL BULLETIN

Background Information

14. An enterprise can acquire an unconditional interest in a leased asset or a right to receive proceeds from the sale of a leased asset without also acquiring the related lease. For example, a lease broker may receive an interest in the residual value of a leased asset as a fee for services. An interest in the residual value of a leased asset can also be purchased directly from lessors. In addition, a lessor can sell the minimum rental payments associated with a lease and retain an interest in the residual value of the leased asset.

15. The accounting for an interest in the residual value of a leased asset has varied in practice. Some enterprises record the lease residual at its acquisition cost (or in the case of the lessor who retains an interest in the residual value of the leased asset, at its carrying amount at the date of the sale of the related lease) and carry it at that amount until ultimate disposition. Others increase the carrying amount of the lease residual to its estimated value over the remaining term of

the related lease. An AICPA Issues Paper, "Accounting by Lease Brokers," issued on June 20, 1980, states in paragraph 72 that "if the lease broker records the present value of his share of the estimated residual value of the leased assets at the beginning of the initial lease term, he should subsequently accrete the value over the term of the lease using the interest method." (The term *accrete* is used in that document to refer to a method of systematically increasing the carrying amount of a lease residual to its estimated value at the end of the related lease term.)

16. This Technical Bulletin addresses the accounting by a lease broker for an interest in the residual value of a leased asset acquired in exchange for services rendered and prohibits a lease broker from recognizing increases in the asset's estimated value over the remaining term of the lease. In that respect, it differs from the AICPA Issues Paper, "Accounting by Lease Brokers." It does not address other areas of fee recognition by lease brokers, or any other provisions of that Issues Paper.

Consideration of Comments Received on the Proposed Technical Bulletin

17. A proposed Technical Bulletin, *Accounting for an Interest in the Residual Value of a Leased Asset Acquired by a Third Party or Retained by a Lessor That Sells the Related Minimum Rental Payments*, was released for comment on September 25, 1986. Thirty-two letters of comment were received; the most significant comments are discussed in the following paragraphs.

18. Several respondents stated that the carrying amount of an acquired interest in the residual value of a leased asset should be increased to its estimated value and justify doing so by an analogy to paragraphs 17 and 18 of Statement 13, which require a lessor who enters into a sales-type or direct financing lease to recognize as income over the lease term the difference between the estimated residual value of the leased asset at the end of the lease term and its present value at the beginning of the lease term. However, sales-type and direct financing leases are financing transactions under Statement 13, and the estimated residual value of a leased asset is looked upon as the final payment, as stated in paragraph 99 of that Statement:

> . . . in the vast majority of leases, the estimated residual value is realized by a sale or re-lease of the property and, for that reason, the residual should be looked upon as a last payment similar to the minimum lease payments. In addition, . . .

presentation of the estimated residual value as part of the lease investment rather than as part of property, plant, and equipment is necessary to portray the proper relationship between the gross investment in leases and the related unearned income, since a portion of the unearned income relates to the residual value.

However, an analogy to the lessor's recognition of an increase in the residual value of a leased asset required in Statement 13 is not appropriate for an acquired interest in the residual value of a leased asset absent the related financing elements of the lease. Therefore, if substantially all of the related financing elements of a lease (the minimum rental payments) have been sold, any retained interest in the residual value of a leased asset cannot be looked upon as a final payment of the lease agreement.

19. Paragraph 83 of Concepts Statement 5 states, ". . . recognition [of revenues and gains] involves consideration of two factors, (a) being realized or realizable and (b) being earned. . . ." Some respondents commented that an increase in the value of an interest in the residual value of a leased asset is being earned over time. However, an interest in the residual value of a leased asset is not realized and cannot be considered realizable until its ultimate sale or disposition. Concepts Statement 5 acknowledges that revenue is sometimes recognized when earned even though not readily realizable, for example, when a product is contracted for before production, when rights to use assets extend continuously over time, and when assets are exchanged for nonmonetary assets that are not readily convertible into cash (paragraphs 84(c), 84(d), and 84(f)). Since none of those examples apply, the recognition of revenue or gain from holding an interest in the residual value of a leased asset is not appropriate.

20. Some respondents asserted that, in substance, a *guarantee* of an interest in a lease residual that is required to be sold fixes contract terms and changes the nature of the asset to a monetary asset, making it appropriate to recognize increases to the expected value. A monetary asset is defined in paragraph 47 of Statement 33 as "money or a claim to receive a sum of money the amount of which is fixed or determinable without reference to future prices of specific goods or services." While a guarantee limits the risk of not realizing the estimated value of the leased asset, it does not fix or determine the amount to be received by the acquirer at the end of the lease term because the acquirer of the lease residual may receive an amount that exceeds the guarantee. As a result, a guarantee does not change the nature of

the asset to a monetary asset and, therefore, does not make it appropriate to recognize increases to its expected value. Rather, a guarantee is *separate* from the asset and is obtained to reduce the risk of not realizing the estimated value of the leased asset, similar to insurance.

21. Some respondents expressed concern that paragraph 10 of the proposed Technical Bulletin would prohibit lessors from increasing the carrying amount of an interest in the residual value of a leased asset if they remove lease receivables from their balance sheet and retain an interest in the residual value of a leased asset, either (a) through sale of the related lease receivable or (b) by offsetting the lease receivable with nonrecourse debt. Some respondents who offset nonrecourse debt with the related lease receivable used as collateral apparently view the transaction, in substance, as a sale. Paragraph 10, however, only addresses those transactions structured as a sale of the related lease receivable and is not intended to consider any circumstance in which nonrecourse debt is collateralized by a lease receivable. In that circumstance, recognizing increases in the carrying amount of an interest in the residual value of a leased asset is appropriate under Statement 13. However, paragraph 7 of Opinion 10 states:

> It is a general principle of accounting that the offsetting of assets and liabilities in the balance sheet is improper except where a right of setoff exists.

Therefore, offsetting the lease receivable with nonrecourse debt is appropriate only in those circumstances in which a legal right of offset exists or when, at the inception of the lease, the lease meets all of the characteristics of paragraph 42 of Statement 13 and is appropriately classified as a leveraged lease. Otherwise, the guidance provided in paragraph 7 of Opinion 10 should be applied.

FASB Technical Bulletin No. 87-1
Accounting for a Change in Method of Accounting for Certain Postretirement Benefits

STATUS

Issued: April 9, 1987

Effective Date: Effective for fiscal years beginning after December 15, 1986

Affects: No other pronouncements

Affected by: Superseded by FAS 106 for accounting changes adopted on or after December 21, 1990

FASB Technical Bulletin No. 87-2
Computation of a Loss on an Abandonment

STATUS

Issued: December 31, 1987

Effective Date: For fiscal years beginning after December 15, 1987

Affects: Supersedes FAS 90, paragraphs 16 through 25

Affected by: Paragraphs 9 through 11, 13, and 22 through 33 and footnotes 4 and 8 superseded by
FAS 96 and FAS 109
Paragraph 18 amended by FAS 96 and FAS 109
Paragraphs 14, 34 through 36, 40, 45, and 46 amended by FAS 109

FASB Technical Bulletin No. 87-2
Computation of a Loss on an Abandonment

References

FASB Statement No. 90, *Regulated Enterprises—Accounting for Abandonments and Disallowances of Plant Costs*, paragraphs 3(b), 5, 6(b), 14, and 16-25
APB Opinion No. 11, *Accounting for Income Taxes*
FASB Statement No. 71, *Accounting for the Effects of Certain Types of Regulation*
FASB Statement No. 96, *Accounting for Income Taxes*

Question 1

1. The example in paragraphs 16-25 of Statement 90 illustrates the computations of a loss on an abandonment and subsequent accounting when the regulator allows recovery of cost without return on investment. Does that example correctly reflect the intent of Statement 90?

Background

2. Paragraph 3(b) of Statement 90 states that "the discount rate used to compute the present value shall be the enterprise's incremental borrowing rate. . . ." Paragraph 5 states that "during the period between the date on which the new asset is recognized and the date on which recovery begins, the carrying amount [of the asset resulting from the abandonment] shall be increased by accruing a carrying charge. The rate used to accrue that carrying charge shall be . . . the rate that was used to compute the present value." Paragraph 6(b) states that, during the recovery period, "the asset shall be amortized in a manner that will produce a constant return on the unamortized investment in the new asset equal to the rate at which the expected revenues were discounted." Paragraph 14 indicates that the tax effects of the transactions illustrated should be recognized when appropriate under Opinion 11 and that the examples assume that those tax effects may be recognized.

3. Some challenge the example in question. They observe that in the example the pretax earnings on the investment in the abandoned plant reduced by any deferred taxes related to that investment (here-

inafter referred to as "the net investment") increase from an initial rate of 11.26 percent ($3,699,582 earnings in the month following the abandonment on a net investment of $394,246,334)[1] to a rate of 13.94 percent when the final installment of recovery is collected ($65,529 earnings in month 120 on a net investment of $5,639,043).[2] The net investment is the amount on which a regulator usually would compute a return on investment if that return were allowed.[3]

Response

4. The example in paragraphs 16-25 of Statement 90 does not accurately reflect the intent of paragraphs 3(b), 5, 6(b), and 14 of Statement 90. The new asset in that example is not amortized in a manner that produces a constant return on the unamortized investment in the new asset equal to the rate at which net revenues were discounted.

Question 2

5. When a loss on abandonment is recognized, how should the amount of deferred income taxes related to the remaining asset be determined?

Background

6. While under construction, a utility's plant has a recorded cost that consists of the following three separate elements for income tax purposes:

a. Costs that will be deductible in the future, either as depreciation or (in the event that the plant is abandoned) as an abandonment loss
b. Costs that have been deducted in the past
c. Costs that are never deductible (the allowance for equity funds used during construction, hereinafter referred to as "equity AFUDC").

7. An abandonment loss generally is deductible for federal income tax purposes when the abandonment occurs. That tax deduction is allowed without regard to the rate-making treatment applied to the recorded cost of the abandoned plant.

8. When a regulator is expected to provide recovery of the cost of an abandoned plant without re-

---

[1] $394,246,334 is the total of the beginning recorded amount ($317,107,016) shown in Schedule 1 of Statement 90 and the deferred tax benefit ($77,139,318) computed in paragraph 19 of Statement 90.

[2] $5,639,043 is the total of the unamortized investment at the end of month 120 ($5,616,763) shown in Schedule 3 of Statement 90 and the remaining unreversed deferred tax benefit of $22,280 (34 percent of the $65,529 return shown in Schedule 3 of Statement 90).

[3] In some jurisdictions, certain deferred income taxes are considered cost-free capital in computing the weighted-average cost of capital. That procedure has approximately the same effect as basing return on investment on the net investment. Accordingly, the examples in this Technical Bulletin would also be appropriate in those jurisdictions.

turn on investment, Statement 90 requires a portion of the cost of the abandoned plant to be recognized as a loss, equivalent to the present value of the effective disallowance of return on investment.

9. Under Opinion 11 and Statement 71, some of the costs that had been deducted in the past have resulted in deferred income taxes, whereas others have not resulted in deferred income taxes because the benefit of that past tax deduction has been "flowed through" to customers[4] *and* it was probable that the regulator would set rates to recover the income tax cost that would result when those costs were later recovered. Effectively, Opinion 11 and Statement 71 allow an asset representing the revenue that will be provided for the payment of income taxes to be offset against the deferred income taxes that otherwise would have been provided.

10. Under Opinion 11, equity AFUDC is considered a permanent difference. The equity AFUDC is neither taxable when it is accrued nor deductible at any later time. However, recovery of that recorded amount does result in taxable income because no tax deduction offsets the revenue. Regulators treat the resulting income taxes as allowable costs when those income taxes become payable. Except for the fact that there was no previous tax benefit, the portion of the recorded costs of a utility's plant that represents equity AFUDC is like a timing difference for which the benefit has been "flowed through" to customers. There is an unrecognized liability (the future taxes that will become payable as a result of recovery of the recorded costs), and there is an unrecognized asset in an equal amount (the future revenue that will be provided for the payment of income taxes).

11. Under Opinion 11, deferred income taxes related to a plant abandonment are computed as the difference between (a) the income taxes (federal and state) computed on the tax returns (including any deduction that will be claimed for the abandonment loss) and (b) the income taxes that would result if the tax returns included a deduction for the accounting loss on the abandoned plant instead of the actual tax deduction claimed. Opinion 11 does not provide specific guidance as to the amount of the tax deduction that should be used

for the accounting loss in the computation in (b) above when the asset contains the elements described in paragraphs 6, 9, and 10 above.

12. Statement 96 supersedes Opinion 11. Statement 96 is effective for fiscal years beginning after December 15, 1988, with earlier application encouraged. Statement 96 requires that deferred income tax liabilities be recognized for the amount of income taxes that will result from recovery of the carrying amount of an enterprise's assets and settlement of its liabilities at their recorded amounts. Those income taxes are computed based on the enacted tax rates that will be in effect in each year of expected recovery and settlement. Paragraph 9 of Statement 71 requires that a new asset be recognized when those deferred income tax liabilities are recognized if receipt of future revenue through the regulatory process for payment of the deferred income tax liabilities is probable.

Response

13. Under Opinion 11, deferred income taxes for an originating timing difference (the situation illustrated in this Technical Bulletin) are recorded (or an increase to existing deferred income taxes is recorded) in an amount determined through the with-and-without calculation outlined in paragraph 11 above. The tax deduction used for the accounting loss in that calculation should be the total amount of the recognized pretax loss.

14. Under Statement 96, the deferred income tax liabilities related to the remaining asset will be (a) the amount of income taxes that will be payable in future years, based on the enacted tax law for those years at the measurement date, as a result of the recovery of the recorded amount of that remaining asset and (b) any additional income taxes that will result from recovery of a separate asset recognized to reflect the future revenue that is expected to be provided in rates by the regulator when the income taxes described both in (a) and (b) of this paragraph become payable.

Question 3

15. How should a regulated enterprise that meets the criteria for application of Statement 71[5] compute a loss on an abandonment, accrue a return on

---

[4]*"Flowed through" to customers* and *"flow-through" methods of rate making* are references in general use in regulated enterprises. When a regulator uses a realized tax benefit to reduce allowable costs for rate-making purposes, that tax benefit is effectively given to the regulated enterprise's customers as a reduction of the rates that would otherwise be payable. That procedure is generally referred to as a "flow-through" method of rate making because the regulator has "flowed" the benefit "through" the regulated enterprise to that enterprise's customers.

[5]The response to this question is based on both the guidance in Statement 90 (which applies only to enterprises that meet the criteria for application of Statement 71) and the nature of rate making in the regulatory process. Whether this approach would be appropriate in other circumstances is beyond the scope of this Technical Bulletin.

investment, and amortize the recorded asset when the regulator allows recovery of cost without return on investment?

Background

16. Paragraph 51 of Statement 90 describes the Board's intent when it specified the accounting for abandonments. The intent was (a) to recognize "the effect of the regulator's disallowance of future return on investment as a loss" and (b) to accrue a carrying charge that would have "the effect of maintaining the level of return on investment similar to what it would have been if there had been no disallowance [of return on investment]." The rate-making process generally allows a return on a utility's net investment in property (the recorded investment reduced by allocable deferred income tax amounts). In that situation, the computation in the example in question should result in pretax earnings of 14 percent (the assumed incremental borrowing rate) times the net investment. The present value of a net investment cannot be computed directly on a pretax basis because any write-off of the investment will also result in a write-off of an allocable amount of recorded deferred income taxes.

Response

17. Usually, the net loss on an abandonment should be computed by discounting the after-tax future revenues expected to be allowed by the regulator at an after-tax incremental borrowing rate and comparing the result to the recorded net investment in the abandoned plant. If that discounted present value is less than the recorded net investment, a net loss should be recognized. However, the present accounting model generally does not permit display of losses on a net-of-tax basis. As a result, the net loss on an abandonment is grossed up for display purposes.

18. Appendix A illustrates how the computations described in paragraph 17 should be done under Opinion 11. Appendix B illustrates how those computations should be done under Statement 96.

19. The computation of a loss on an abandonment is intended to approximate the economic effects of the regulator's rate actions. The response in paragraph 17 and the examples in Appendixes A and B are based on the following general assumptions about the rate-making methods used for income taxes:

a. Deferred income taxes are allocated to the assets that resulted in those deferred income taxes. Under that assumption, if certain assets are included in the rate base (that is, a return is allowed on those assets), the deferred income taxes allocated to those assets are deducted from the rate base in computing the investment on which a return will be allowed. Similarly, if certain assets are excluded from the rate base (that is, a return is not allowed on those assets), the deferred income taxes allocated to those assets are not deducted from the rate base in computing the investment on which a return will be allowed.[6]

b. Income taxes that result from recovery of the recorded cost of the abandoned plant will be treated as allowable costs when those income taxes become payable to the extent those income taxes do not represent repayment of an income tax benefit that has already accrued to the enterprise's shareholders.

20. If the rate-making methods used for an enterprise differ from the assumptions stated in paragraph 19, the computation used to compute the loss on the abandonment should be different from that described in paragraph 17 and illustrated in Appendixes A and B. The computation should be changed to reflect the different economics of those different rate-making methods. For example, if the regulator deducts *all* existing deferred income taxes from the rate base in determining the investment on which a return will be provided (instead of allocating deferred income taxes between items included in the rate base and items excluded from the rate base), the procedure effectively disallows a return on the gross investment in the abandoned plant instead of disallowing a return on the net investment, and the recognized loss should reflect a disallowance of a return on the gross investment in the abandoned plant.

Effective Date and Transition

21. The provisions of this Technical Bulletin are effective for fiscal years beginning after December 15, 1987 for all losses on abandonments recognized in accordance with Statement 90. Earlier application is encouraged. If Statement 90 was initially implemented[7] after October 31, 1987 and before the beginning of the enterprise's next fiscal year beginning after December 15, 1987, existing assets resulting from abandonments that have already been recognized in accordance with Statement 90 should be adjusted to comply with this

---

[6]Refer to footnote 3.

[7]The term *initially implemented* is used in this paragraph to refer to a decision to apply Statement 90 currently followed by a public announcement of that decision within a reasonably short period after the decision is made. In this context, a public announcement can be in the form of published financial statements including the reporting required by Statement 90 for a period, a press release announcing the effects of applying Statement 90, or some other action to inform the public of the application of Statement 90 and the effects of that application.

FTB87-2 — FASB Technical Bulletins

Technical Bulletin. If Statement 90 was initially implemented prior to November 1, 1987, existing assets resulting from abandonments that have already been recognized in accordance with Statement 90 may be, but are not required to be, adjusted to comply with this Technical Bulletin. This Technical Bulletin may be applied to existing assets that have already been recognized in accordance with Statement 90 either by retroactively restating the previously reported amounts or by an adjustment, in the year of application of this Technical Bulletin, for the cumulative effect of an accounting change with appropriate disclosure.

> The Financial Accounting Standards Board has authorized its staff to prepare FASB Technical Bulletins to provide guidance on certain financial accounting and reporting problems on a timely basis, pursuant to the procedures described in FASB Technical Bulletin No. 79-1 (Revised), *Purpose and Scope of FASB Technical Bulletins and Procedures for Issuance*. The provisions of Technical Bulletins need not be applied to immaterial items. Copyright © 1987 by the Financial Accounting Standards Board.

Appendix A

EXAMPLE OF THE COMPUTATION OF A LOSS ON AN ABANDONMENT UNDER STATEMENT 90 AND OPINION 11

22. This appendix illustrates how a loss on an abandonment should be computed under Statement 90 by an enterprise that has not yet applied Statement 96. The example is based on specific rate actions related to the abandonment and on the other assumptions stated in the example. The computations may need to be changed to reflect the economic effects of different fact situations.

23. The principal assumptions on which the example in this appendix is based are as follows:

a. Utility A decides to abandon a plant that has been under construction for some time. Although the possibility of abandoning the plant has been under consideration, abandonment was not considered probable before the actual decision was made. The recorded cost of the plant is $750.5 million.
b. For income tax purposes, the abandoned plant has a basis of $500 million at the date of the abandonment.
c. Existing deferred taxes on timing differences relating to the abandoned plant total $35 million.
d. Utility A will deduct the remaining tax basis of the abandoned plant ($500,000,000) as an abandonment loss on its income tax return in the year of the abandonment and will receive a tax benefit of 34 percent of that remaining tax basis ($170,000,000). Utility A operates in a state that has no state income taxes. The federal income tax rate is 34 percent.
e. Accounting pretax income before the loss on the abandonment and taxable income before any deduction for the loss on the abandonment both are $1,500,000,000. Utility A has no other timing differences or tax credits.
f. Utility A operates solely in a single-state jurisdiction.
g. In the past, Utility A's regulator has permitted recovery of amounts prudently invested in abandoned plants over an extended period of time without a return on unrecovered investment during the recovery period.
h. The normal practice of Utility A's regulator is to allocate deferred income taxes to assets on which return on investment is disallowed. Deferred taxes allocated to assets excluded from the rate base are not deducted from the rate base for purposes of computing allowable return on investment.
i. Utility A's regulator normally treats income taxes that were not previously provided as allowable costs if they result from recovery of other allowable costs.
j. Utility A's incremental borrowing rate at the date of the decision to abandon the plant is 14 percent, interest payable monthly.
k. Utility A believes that it is probable that recovery of cost without return on investment during the recovery period will be granted over a period that will not be less than 5 years nor more than 10 years, but it has no basis for estimating the exact time period that the regulator will select.
l. At the date of the abandonment, Utility A believes that it will take approximately 18 months to obtain a rate order covering the abandoned plant.

1292

m. No disallowance of recorded cost is expected.

n. A rate order covering the abandoned plant is received in the 18th month following the abandonment. There is no disallowance of recorded costs of the abandoned plant. Those recorded costs are to be recovered over 60 months commencing in the 19th month after abandonment.

24. Because the amount of deferred taxes related to the remaining investment is both (a) a component of the net investment on which return would be based in the regulatory process and (b) based on the amount of the accounting loss on the abandonment, which is also based on the present value of the net investment, the present value of the net investment cannot be derived through a simple present value calculation using a pretax rate. That present value could be derived through a series of iterative calculations, starting with an assumed loss and the resulting deferred tax amounts, then computing the accrual of return on investment and amortization by applying the pretax rate to the resulting net investment, and then computing the income tax effects of the resulting pretax income. Using the remaining asset at the end of the recovery period, the estimate of the loss could be refined until the accrual of a return, amortization, recovery of recorded costs, and the related tax effects resulted in a zero net asset at the end of the recovery period. Alternatively, the net loss can be initially computed based on a present value calculation using an after-tax rate. While the latter approach is used in this appendix, either approach will provide the same result. The following paragraphs illustrate how that approach can be used and the resulting computations of loss recognition, return to be accrued, and amortization.

25. Opinion 11 requires additional deferred taxes to be recognized, using a with-and-without calculation, for the tax benefit that results from the current deduction of a loss for tax purposes that is not recognized for accounting purposes. A direct calculation of the present value of the remaining net cash flows requires an initial calculation of deferred taxes as if no accounting loss were recognized. Then, a portion of those deferred taxes must be reversed as a percentage of the pretax loss. The latter step requires a calculation of the tax rate attributable to the accounting loss, because the Opinion 11 calculation can result in a rate other than the statutory rate. That calculation is made by estimating both a maximum and a minimum accounting loss that will result from the recognition of disallowance of return on investment and performing with-and-without calculations on both estimates. If the computed loss falls outside the range of the estimates, the calculation can be repeated using the actual loss to verify that the tax rate used is appropriate. For example, the pretax accounting loss might initially be estimated as a range from $400,000,000 to $100,000,000. Based on that range, the following with-and-without calculations would be performed:

	Tax Return	Accounting	
Before loss			
Taxable income		$1,500,000,000	
Resulting income tax		$ 510,000,000	(1)
Maximum loss within range			
Taxable income before abandonment	$1,500,000,000	$1,500,000,000	
Abandonment loss deduction	(500,000,000)	—	
Accounting abandonment loss	—	(400,000,000)	
Adjusted taxable income	$1,000,000,000	$1,100,000,000	
Resulting income tax	$ 340,000,000	$ 374,000,000	
Accounting tax expense:			
Current		$ 340,000,000	
Deferred		34,000,000	
Total		$ 374,000,000	(2)
Difference in tax expense resulting from $400,000,000 loss (1) − (2)		$ 136,000,000	
Rate ($136,000,000/$400,000,000)		34%	

Minimum loss within range

Taxable income before abandonment	$1,500,000,000	$1,500,000,000
Abandonment loss deduction	(500,000,000)	—
Accounting abandonment loss	—	(100,000,000)
Adjusted taxable income	$1,000,000,000	$1,400,000,000
Resulting income tax	$ 340,000,000	$ 476,000,000
Accounting tax expense:		
Current		$ 340,000,000
Deferred		136,000,000
Total		$ 476,000,000 (3)
Difference in tax expense resulting from		
$100,000,000 loss (1) − (3)		$ 34,000,000
Rate ($34,000,000/$100,000,000)		34%

Since the effective rate is 34 percent for both a $400,000,000 loss and a $100,000,000 loss, the rate would be 34 percent for any amount of loss between those estimates.

26. For a utility that meets the criteria for application of Statement 71, the result of the computation described in paragraph 25 will often be a rate equal to the statutory tax rate. That results from the deferral and amortization of investment tax credits and from the way that the process tracks individual timing differences. In some cases, the result of that computation will be different rates for the two estimated loss amounts used in the computations in paragraph 25. If the result is a rate equal to the statutory tax rate, the calculations in paragraphs 28-30 can be used to derive the amount of loss to be recognized. Otherwise, those calculations will only refine the estimate of loss so that the tax rate can be computed. Determining the appropriate tax rate to be used to calculate the net-of-tax discount rate, which will be used to calculate the present value of the after-tax revenues, may take several iterations.

27. Once the rate for this computation is determined, the actual tax benefit that results from the abandonment can be treated as additional deferred taxes, and the loss and corresponding reduction in deferred taxes can be computed directly, following the sequence of steps illustrated in this appendix.

28. When the abandonment becomes probable (in this case, at the date of the decision to abandon), Utility A should remove the recorded cost of the plant from the construction work-in-process accounts. Any disallowance of the recorded cost that is probable and can be reasonably estimated also should be recorded as a loss. There is none in this example. Utility A should record a separate new asset, representing the future revenues expected to result from the regulator's treatment of the cost of the abandoned plant, at the present value of those expected future revenues. To compute the amount of the new asset, Utility A should first compute its net investment in the abandoned plant because that is the investment on which the regulator would allow a return on investment if that return were allowed. That net investment should be computed as follows:

	Plant Cost	Deferred Taxes	Net Investment
Tax basis of plant (deducted for tax purposes at date of abandonment)	$500,000,000	$170,000,000[*]	
Interest component of AFUDC (deducted for tax purposes when incurred)	102,941,177	35,000,000[†]	
Equity component of AFUDC	147,558,823	0	
Totals per books	$750,500,000	$205,000,000	
Net investment			$545,500,000

---

[*]Tax benefit of current deduction of abandonment loss
[†]Prior years' accounting under Opinion 11

29. The cash flows provided to recover the asset should be estimated to begin in 19 months. For purposes of computing the present value of the net investment, the probable future after-tax revenues should be estimated at $9,091,667 per month for 5 years (based on an assumed straight-line recovery of the net investment over the 5-year minimum pe-riod within the range—$545,500,000/60). The discount rate used should be 9.24 percent (14 percent net of tax at the 34 percent rate computed in paragraph 25). The computation of the amount to be recorded for the new asset and of the loss resulting from the abandonment should be as follows:

Present value of $9,091,667 per month at 9.24% for 60 months, starting at the end of the 19th month (amount of new asset net of related deferred income taxes) (components computed in paragraph 30)	$379,361,954
Less net investment in abandoned plant (computed in paragraph 28)	545,500,000
Loss (net of related income taxes) to be recognized at time of decision to abandon the plant	$166,138,046

30. The net loss should be allocated between the new asset resulting from the abandonment and the existing deferred taxes based on the relationship between the investment (100 percent), deferred taxes (34 percent as computed in paragraph 25), and the net investment (66 percent). The computation should be as follows:

	Gross Investment	Deferred Taxes	Net Investment
Balances before loss recognition	$750,500,000	$205,000,000	$545,500,000
Loss to be recognized	(251,724,312)*	(85,586,266)†	(166,138,046)
Balances after loss recognition	$498,775,688	$119,413,734	$379,361,954

---

*Computed as $166,138,046/0.66

†Computed as $251,724,312 × 34%

31. Pending receipt of a rate order, Utility A should accrue carrying charges on the net recorded asset at a monthly rate of 1/12 of 14 percent. Taxes should be provided on those accrued carrying charges based on the with-and-without computation required by Opinion 11 for originating timing differences. Schedule 1 illustrates those computations.

Schedule 1

Mo. Comp.	(1) Asset *	(2) Beginning of Month Def. Taxes †	(3) Net Invest. [(1) − (2)]	(4) Carrying Charges Accrued [14%/12 × (3)]	(5) Deferred Inc. Taxes Accrued [34% × (4)]
1	$498,775,688	$119,413,734	$379,361,954	$4,425,889	$1,504,802
2	503,201,577	120,918,536	382,283,041	4,459,969	1,516,390
3	507,661,546	122,434,926	385,226,620	4,494,310	1,528,065
4	512,155,856	123,962,991	388,192,865	4,528,917	1,539,832
5	516,684,773	125,502,823	391,181,950	4,563,789	1,551,688
6	521,248,562	127,054,511	394,194,051	4,598,931	1,563,636
7	525,847,493	128,618,147	397,229,346	4,634,342	1,575,677
8	530,481,835	130,193,824	400,288,011	4,670,027	1,587,809
9	535,151,862	131,781,633	403,370,229	4,705,986	1,600,035
10	539,857,848	133,381,668	406,476,180	4,742,222	1,612,356
11	544,600,070	134,994,024	409,606,046	4,778,737	1,624,770
12	549,378,807	136,618,794	412,760,013	4,815,534	1,637,282
13	554,194,341	138,256,076	415,938,265	4,852,613	1,649,888
14	559,046,954	139,905,964	419,140,990	4,889,978	1,662,593
15	563,936,932	141,568,557	422,368,375	4,927,631	1,675,394
16	568,864,563	143,243,951	425,620,612	4,965,574	1,688,295
17	573,830,137	144,932,246	428,897,891	5,003,809	1,701,296
18	578,833,946	146,633,542	432,200,404	5,042,338	1,714,395
19	583,876,284	148,347,937	435,528,347		

Computations:

* Prior month (1) + prior month (4)
† Prior month (2) + prior month (5)

32. Based on the rate order (paragraph 23(n)), revenues actually allowed will be $13,775,253 per month ($826,515,152/60).[8] Of that monthly total, $1,266,919 ($76,015,152/60) will be provided to recover the income taxes that result from recovery of the recorded equity AFUDC and from the revenue provided to pay those income taxes, and $12,508,333 ($750,500,000/60) will be provided to recover the gross investment in the abandoned plant. In accordance with Statement 71 and Opinion 11, the $1,266,919 will be accrued as revenue and as income tax expense when the revenue is provided, so it should be ignored in computing earnings on the net investment. Earnings should continue to be recognized each month equal to 1/12 of 14 percent of the remaining net investment, and taxes should continue to be provided on those earnings at a 34 percent rate. Schedule 2 illustrates those computations.

33. Under the provisions of Opinion 11, changes in tax rates that occur subsequent to the initial loss recognition do not change the amount of the loss recognized or the amount of accumulated deferred income taxes at the date of the rate change. However, they will change the amounts of income tax expense recognized in each subsequent period because (a) existing deferred tax amounts are reduced by a rate that differs from the current tax rate, (b) income taxes are paid at the new tax rate, and (c) revenues may be changed to reflect the new tax rates.

---

[8]$826,515,152 is the total of the amount required to recover the total plant cost—$750,500,000, taxes of $50,170,000 that will result from recovery of $147,558,823 of the cost of the plant that had no tax basis, and additional taxes of $25,845,152 that will result from the revenue ($76,015,152) needed to recover $50,170,000 after taxes on that revenue.

Schedule 2

Mo. Comp.	(1) Asset *	(2) Beginning of Month Def. Taxes †	(3) Net Invest. [(1) − (2)]	(4) Return on Investment at 14% [14%/12 × (3)]	(5) Amortization of Asset ‡	(6) Income Tax Expense [34% × (4)]	(7) Reversal of Existing Def. Taxes §
19	$583,876,284	$148,347,937	$435,528,347	$5,081,164	$7,427,169	$1,727,596	$1,689,071
20	576,449,115	146,658,866	429,790,249	5,014,219	7,494,114	1,704,835	1,711,832
21	568,955,001	144,947,034	424,007,967	4,946,759	7,561,574	1,681,898	1,734,769
22	561,393,427	143,212,265	418,181,162	4,878,780	7,629,553	1,658,786	1,757,881
23	553,763,874	141,454,384	412,309,490	4,810,277	7,698,056	1,635,494	1,781,173
24	546,065,818	139,673,211	406,392,607	4,741,247	7,767,086	1,612,024	1,804,642
25	538,298,732	137,868,569	400,430,163	4,671,685	7,836,648	1,588,373	1,828,294
26	530,462,084	136,040,275	394,421,809	4,601,587	7,906,746	1,564,540	1,852,127
27	522,555,338	134,188,148	388,367,190	4,530,951	7,977,382	1,540,524	1,876,143
28	514,577,956	132,312,005	382,265,951	4,459,769	8,048,564	1,516,322	1,900,345
29	506,529,392	130,411,660	376,117,732	4,388,040	8,120,293	1,491,934	1,924,733
30	498,409,099	128,486,927	369,922,172	4,315,758	8,192,575	1,467,358	1,949,309
31	490,216,524	126,537,618	363,678,906	4,242,920	8,265,413	1,442,593	1,974,074
32	481,951,111	124,563,544	357,387,567	4,169,521	8,338,812	1,417,638	1,999,029
33	473,612,299	122,564,515	351,047,784	4,095,558	8,412,775	1,392,490	2,024,177
34	465,199,524	120,540,338	344,659,186	4,021,023	8,487,310	1,367,148	2,049,519
35	456,712,214	118,490,819	338,221,395	3,945,916	8,562,417	1,341,612	2,075,055
36	448,149,797	116,415,764	331,734,033	3,870,230	8,638,103	1,315,879	2,100,788
37	439,511,694	114,314,976	325,196,718	3,793,961	8,714,372	1,289,947	2,126,720
38	430,797,322	112,188,256	318,609,066	3,717,106	8,791,227	1,263,816	2,152,851
.	.	.	.	.	.	.	.
73	72,867,498	19,757,949	53,109,549	619,612	11,888,721	210,669	3,205,998
74	60,978,777	16,551,951	44,426,826	518,312	11,990,021	176,226	3,240,441
75	48,988,756	13,311,510	35,677,246	416,234	12,092,099	141,520	3,275,147
76	36,896,657	10,036,363	26,860,294	313,370	12,194,963	106,546	3,310,120
77	24,701,694	6,726,243	17,975,451	209,714	12,298,619	71,304	3,345,364
78	12,403,075	3,380,879	9,022,196	105,258	12,403,075	35,788	3,380,879

Computations:

* Prior month (1) − prior month (5)

† Prior month (2) − prior month (7)

‡ $12,508,333 − (4)

§ $(13,775,253 × 34%) − $1,266,919 − (6)

Appendix B

EXAMPLE OF THE COMPUTATION OF A LOSS ON AN ABANDONMENT UNDER STATEMENTS 90 AND 96

34. This appendix illustrates how a loss on an abandonment should be computed under Statement 90 by an enterprise that has applied Statement 96. Except for the method of accounting for income taxes, the example in this appendix is the same as the example in Appendix A. The example is based on specific rate actions related to the abandonment and on the other assumptions stated in the example. The computations may need to be changed to reflect the economic effects of different fact situations.

35. Upon initial application of Statement 96, an enterprise that meets the criteria for application of Statement 71 will adjust its deferred income tax liabilities as required by Statement 96. The details of initial application of Statement 96 are covered in that Statement. The example in this appendix is presented as though the enterprise has already ap-

plied Statement 96 prior to the date of the abandonment.

36. If an enterprise initially applies Statement 96 after a loss has been recognized on an abandonment and before the end of the recovery period for any recoverable costs, the amount of the previously recognized loss may change. The amount of that loss will change if the tax rate used in the initial net-of-tax discount rate under Statement 96 is different from that used under Opinion 11. Once Statement 96 is initially applied, the accounting for the abandonment should follow the approach described in this appendix.

37. The principal assumptions on which the example in this appendix is based are as follows:

a. Utility A decides to abandon a plant that has been under construction for some time. Although the possibility of abandoning the plant has been under consideration, abandonment was not considered probable before the actual decision was made.

b. Immediately before the abandonment, the recorded assets for the plant and related deferred income tax liabilities are as follows:

	Assets	Deferred Income Tax Liabilities
Recorded plant and related deferred income tax liabilities	$750,500,000	$ 85,170,000
Asset representing revenue that will be provided for payment of income taxes and related deferred income tax liabilities	76,015,152	25,845,152
Total	$826,515,152	$111,015,152

c. For income tax purposes, the abandoned plant has a basis of $500 million at the date of the abandonment.

d. Utility A will deduct the remaining tax basis of the abandoned plant ($500,000,000) as an abandonment loss on its income tax return in the year of the abandonment and will receive a tax benefit of 34 percent of the tax basis of the plant ($170,000,000). Utility A operates in a state that has no state income taxes. The federal income tax rate is 34 percent.

e. Accounting pretax income before the loss on the abandonment and taxable income before any deduction for the loss on the abandonment are both $1,500,000,000. Utility A has no other temporary differences or tax credits.

f. Utility A operates solely in a single-state jurisdiction.

g. In the past, Utility A's regulator has permitted recovery of amounts prudently invested in

abandoned plants over an extended period of time without a return on unrecovered investment during the recovery period.

h. The normal practice of Utility A's regulator is to allocate deferred income taxes to assets on which return on investment is disallowed. Deferred taxes allocated to assets excluded from the rate base are not deducted from the rate base for purposes of computing allowable return on investment.

i. Utility A's regulator normally treats income taxes that were not previously provided as allowable costs if they result from recovery of other allowable costs.

j. Utility A's incremental borrowing rate at the date of the decision to abandon the plant is 14 percent, interest payable monthly.

k. Utility A believes that it is probable that recovery of cost without return on investment during the recovery period will be granted over a period that will not be less than 5 years nor more than 10 years, but it has no basis for estimating the exact time period that the regulator will select.

l. At the date of the abandonment, Utility A believes that it will take approximately 18 months to obtain a rate order covering the abandoned plant.

m. No disallowance of recorded cost is expected.

n. A rate order covering the abandoned plant is received in the 18th month following the abandonment. There is no disallowance of recorded costs of the abandoned plant. Those recorded costs are to be recovered over 60 months commencing in the 19th month after abandonment.

38. Because the amount of deferred taxes related to the remaining investment is both (a) a component of the net investment on which return would be based in the regulatory process and (b) based on the amount of the accounting loss on the abandonment (which is based on the present value of the net investment), the present value of the net investment cannot be derived through a simple present value calculation using a pretax rate. That present value could be derived through a series of iterative calculations, starting with an assumed loss and the resulting deferred tax amounts, then computing the accrual of return on investment and amortization by applying the pretax rate to the resulting net investment, and then computing the income tax effects of the resulting pretax income. Using the remaining asset at the end of the recovery period, the estimate of the loss could be refined until the accrual of a return, amortization, recovery of recorded costs, and the related tax effects resulted in a zero net asset at the end of the recovery period. Alternatively, the net loss can be initially computed based on a present value calculation using an after-tax rate. While that approach is used in this appendix, either approach will provide the same result. The following paragraphs illustrate how that approach can be used and the resulting computations of loss recognition, return to be accrued, and amortization.

39. When the abandonment becomes probable (in this case, at the date of the decision to abandon), Utility A should remove the recorded cost of the plant from the construction work-in-process accounts. Any disallowance of the recorded cost that is probable and can be reasonably estimated should also be recorded as a loss. There is none in this example. Utility A should record a separate new asset, representing the future revenues expected to result from the regulator's treatment of the cost of the abandoned plant, at the present value of those expected future revenues.

40. The next step is to compute the deferred income tax liabilities that would be recorded if the tax consequences of the abandonment were recognized before any loss related to the disallowance of return on investment were recognized. When the tax basis of the abandoned plant is deducted as an abandonment loss on the current year's tax return, an additional $500,000,000 of the recorded cost of the asset will be without tax basis. Recovery of that additional amount will result in $500,000,000 of taxable income. The deferred income tax liability on that amount should be computed in accordance with Statement 96. Usually, that deferred income tax liability will be computed at the statutory rate. However, a different rate could result. For example, application of an alternative minimum tax may produce a different rate. This example assumes that the rate is the statutory rate of 34 percent and that Utility A should recognize additional deferred income tax liabilities of $170,000,000.

41. The amount of tax benefit that resulted from the current deduction of the abandonment loss is also $170,000,000, so no additional asset representing revenue that will be provided for the payment of income taxes should be recognized. Thus, the recorded balance sheet items related to the plant after the abandonment, but before any loss for disallowance of return on investment is recognized, and the resulting net investment should be as follows:

	Assets	Deferred Income Tax Liabilities
Recorded plant and related deferred income tax liabilities	$750,500,000	$255,170,000
Asset representing revenue that will be provided for payment of income taxes and related deferred income tax liabilities	76,015,152	25,845,152
Total assets	$826,515,152 (1)	
Total deferred income tax liabilities		$281,015,152 (2)
Net investment (1) − (2)		$545,500,000

42. If the computed additional deferred income tax liabilities did not equal the tax benefit that resulted from the abandonment loss, the difference should be recorded as an adjustment of the asset representing revenue that will be provided for the payment of income taxes.

43. The cash flows provided to recover the asset should be estimated to begin in 19 months. For purposes of computing the present value of the net investment, the probable future after-tax revenues should be estimated at $9,091,667 per month for 5 years (based on an assumed straight-line recovery of the net investment over the 5-year minimum period within the range—$545,500,000/60). The discount rate used should be 9.24 percent (14 percent net of tax at the rate computed in paragraph 40). The computation of the amount to be recorded for the new asset and of the loss resulting from the abandonment should be as follows:

Present value of $9,091,667 per month at 9.24% for 60 months, starting at the end of the 19th month (amount of new asset net of related deferred income taxes) (components computed in paragraph 44)	$379,361,954
Less net investment in abandoned plant (computed in paragraph 41)	545,500,000
Loss (net of related income taxes) to be recognized at time of decision to abandon the plant	$166,138,046

44. The net loss should be allocated between the new asset resulting from the abandonment and the existing deferred taxes based on the relationship between the investment (100 percent), deferred taxes (34 percent, computed as $281,015,152/ $826,515,152), and the net investment (66 percent). The computation should be as follows:

	Gross Investment	Deferred Taxes	Net Investment
Balances before loss recognition	$826,515,152	$281,015,152	$545,500,000
Loss to be recognized	(251,724,312)*	(85,586,266)[†]	(166,138,046)
Balances after loss recognition	$574,790,840	$195,428,886	$379,361,954

---

*Computed as $166,138,046/0.66

[†]Computed as $251,724,312 × 34%

45. Pending receipt of a rate order, Utility A should accrue carrying charges on the net recorded asset at a monthly rate of 1/12 of 14 percent. Taxes should be provided on those accrued carrying charges based on the rate required to adjust the accumulated deferred income tax liabilities to the amounts required by Statement 96. Usually, that rate will be the statutory rate. Schedule 3 illustrates those computations based on the statutory rate.

46. Based on the rate order (paragraph 37(n)), revenues actually allowed will be $13,775,253 per month ($826,515,152/60). Earnings should continue to be recognized each month equal to 1/12 of 14 percent of the remaining net investment, and taxes should continue to be provided on those earnings at the rate required to adjust the recorded deferred income tax liabilities to the amount required by Statement 96. Usually, that rate would be the statutory rate. Schedule 4 illustrates those computations using the 34 percent statutory rate.

47. In the event of a change in tax rates, the accumulated deferred income tax liabilities should be adjusted to the computed liability at the new rates. If the change in tax rates causes a reduction of the recorded deferred income tax liability, that reduction would usually result in a reduction of the recorded asset representing revenue that will be provided for payment of income taxes. If the change in tax rates causes an increase of the recorded deferred income tax liability, that increase would usually result in an increase of the recorded asset representing revenue that will be provided for payment of income taxes. However, the regulator's expected rate actions could change that result.

Schedule 3

Mo. Comp.	(1) Gross Investment *	(2) Deferred Charge	(3) Related Deferred Taxes †	(4) Net Investment	(5) Carrying Charges Accrued	(6) Inc. Tax Liability Accrued
		Beginning of Month	Beginning of Month	[(1) + (2) − (3)]	[14%/12 × (4)]	[34% × (5)]
1	$498,775,688	$76,015,152	$195,428,886	$379,361,954	$4,425,889	$1,504,802
2	503,201,577	76,015,152	196,933,688	382,283,041	4,459,969	1,516,390
3	507,661,546	76,015,152	198,450,078	385,226,620	4,494,310	1,528,065
4	512,155,856	76,015,152	199,978,143	388,192,865	4,528,917	1,539,832
5	516,684,773	76,015,152	201,517,975	391,181,950	4,563,789	1,551,688
6	521,248,562	76,015,152	203,069,663	394,194,051	4,598,931	1,563,636
7	525,847,493	76,015,152	204,633,299	397,229,346	4,634,342	1,575,677
8	530,481,835	76,015,152	206,208,976	400,288,011	4,670,027	1,587,809
9	535,151,862	76,015,152	207,796,785	403,370,229	4,705,986	1,600,035
10	539,857,848	76,015,152	209,396,820	406,476,180	4,742,222	1,612,356
11	544,600,070	76,015,152	211,009,176	409,606,046	4,778,737	1,624,770
12	549,378,807	76,015,152	212,633,946	412,760,013	4,815,534	1,637,282
13	554,194,341	76,015,152	214,271,228	415,938,265	4,852,613	1,649,888
14	559,046,954	76,015,152	215,921,116	419,140,990	4,889,978	1,662,593
15	563,936,932	76,015,152	217,583,709	422,368,375	4,927,631	1,675,394
16	568,864,563	76,015,152	219,259,103	425,620,612	4,965,574	1,688,295
17	573,830,137	76,015,152	220,947,398	428,897,891	5,003,809	1,701,296
18	578,833,946	76,015,152	222,648,694	432,200,404	5,042,338	1,714,395
19	583,876,284	76,015,152	224,363,089	435,528,347		

Computations:
* Prior month (1) + prior month (5)
† Prior month (3) + prior month (6)

Schedule 4

Mo. Comp.	(1) Gross Investment *	Beginning of Month (2) Deferred Charge †	Beginning of Month (3) Income Tax Liability ‡	(4) Net Investment [(1)+(2)−(3)]	(5) Return on Net Investment [14%/12 × (4)]	(6) Amortization of Gross Investment §	(7) Amortization of Deferred Charge	(8) Income Tax Expense [34% × (5)]	(9) Payment of Previously Recorded Income Tax Liability ‖
19	$583,876,284	$76,015,152	$224,363,089	$435,528,347	$5,081,164	$7,427,169	$1,266,919	$1,727,596	$2,955,990
20	576,449,115	74,748,233	221,407,099	429,790,249	5,014,219	7,494,114	1,266,919	1,704,835	2,978,751
21	568,955,001	73,481,314	218,428,348	424,007,967	4,946,759	7,561,574	1,266,919	1,681,898	3,001,688
22	561,393,427	72,214,395	215,426,660	418,181,162	4,878,780	7,629,553	1,266,920	1,658,786	3,024,801
23	553,763,874	70,947,475	212,401,859	412,309,490	4,810,277	7,698,056	1,266,919	1,635,494	3,048,092
24	546,065,818	69,680,556	209,353,767	406,392,607	4,741,247	7,767,086	1,266,919	1,612,024	3,071,561
25	538,298,732	68,413,637	206,282,206	400,430,163	4,671,685	7,836,648	1,266,919	1,588,373	3,095,213
26	530,462,084	67,146,718	203,186,993	394,421,809	4,601,587	7,906,746	1,266,919	1,564,540	3,119,046
27	522,555,338	65,879,799	200,067,947	388,367,190	4,530,951	7,977,382	1,266,920	1,540,524	3,143,063
28	514,577,956	64,612,879	196,924,884	382,265,951	4,459,769	8,048,564	1,266,919	1,516,322	3,167,264
29	506,529,392	63,345,960	193,757,620	376,117,732	4,388,040	8,120,293	1,266,919	1,491,934	3,191,652
30	498,409,099	62,079,041	190,565,968	369,922,172	4,315,758	8,192,575	1,266,919	1,467,358	3,216,228
31	490,216,524	60,812,122	187,349,740	363,678,906	4,242,920	8,265,413	1,266,919	1,442,593	3,240,993
32	481,951,111	59,545,203	184,108,747	357,387,567	4,169,521	8,338,812	1,266,920	1,417,638	3,265,949
33	473,612,299	58,278,283	180,842,798	351,047,784	4,095,558	8,412,775	1,266,919	1,392,490	3,291,096
34	465,199,524	57,011,364	177,551,702	344,659,186	4,021,023	8,487,310	1,266,919	1,367,148	3,316,438
35	456,712,214	55,744,445	174,235,264	338,221,395	3,945,916	8,562,417	1,266,919	1,341,612	3,341,975
.									
.									
.									
73	72,867,498	7,601,515	27,359,464	53,109,549	619,612	11,888,721	1,266,919	210,669	4,472,917
74	60,978,777	6,334,596	22,886,547	44,426,826	518,312	11,990,021	1,266,919	176,226	4,507,360
75	48,988,756	5,067,677	18,379,187	35,677,246	416,234	12,092,099	1,266,919	141,520	4,542,066
76	36,896,657	3,800,758	13,837,121	26,860,294	313,370	12,194,963	1,266,919	106,546	4,577,039
77	24,701,694	2,533,839	9,260,082	17,975,451	209,714	12,298,619	1,266,920	71,304	4,612,284
78	12,403,075	1,266,919	4,647,798	9,022,196	105,258	12,403,075	1,266,919	35,788	4,647,798

Computations:
* Prior month (1) − prior month (6)
† Prior month (2) − prior month (7)
‡ Prior month (3) − prior month (9)
§ $13,775,253 − (5) − (7)
‖ $4,683,586 − (8)

Appendix C

CONSIDERATION OF COMMENTS RECEIVED ON THE PROPOSED TECHNICAL BULLETIN

48. A proposed Technical Bulletin, *Computation of a Loss on an Abandonment*, was released for comment on October 26, 1987. Twenty-five letters of comment were received on the proposed Technical Bulletin. Certain of the comments received and consideration of them are discussed in the following paragraphs.

49. Several respondents urged that enterprises that have already applied Statement 90 not be required to apply the provisions of this Technical Bulletin. They noted that the actual disallowance, when a regulator provides recovery of the cost of an abandoned plant without return on investment during the recovery period, is the return on investment that would result from applying the weighted-average cost of the enterprise's capital to the investment during the recovery period. The weighted-average cost of capital that will be appropriate in the future is not known. Accordingly, the computation is merely an approximation. In their view, the difference between the approximation in this Technical Bulletin and the approximation in the original example does not warrant the reduction of investor confidence that could result from two restatements for the same item. Those suggestions were accepted. This Technical Bulletin need not be applied by enterprises that initially applied Statement 90 prior to November 1, 1987. November 1, 1987 is the date by which affected enterprises should have received a copy of the proposed Technical Bulletin.

50. Several respondents suggested that the examples of an explicit, but indirect, disallowance in Statement 90 and of a disallowance of return on investment in FASB Statement No. 92, *Regulated Enterprises—Accounting for Phase-in Plans*, should also be changed to conform to the example in this Technical Bulletin.

51. The requirements of Statement 90 concerning accounting for an abandonment on which no return on investment is provided are quite explicit. Statement 90's requirements concerning accounting for an explicit, but indirect, disallowance of plant costs are very general. The Statement states that "an equivalent amount of cost shall be deducted from the reported cost of the plant and recognized as a loss." For an indirect disallowance,

the Board's intent was to require estimation by the best method available. For example, the amount disallowed indirectly may be known and is thus the best estimate. For a short-term disallowance of return on investment, no new rate decisions may be expected during the period encompassed by the disallowance. In that case, the return on investment ordered in the same rate case probably would be the best estimate of the rate to use to compute the disallowance. Whether the rate used should be a pretax or an after-tax rate will depend on how the tax benefits attributable to the indirectly disallowed costs will be handled for rate-making purposes.

52. Some respondents to the proposed Technical Bulletin indicated that the examples were overly complex. Others indicated that the examples should be expanded to include the accounting for changes in estimates and discounting of cancellation charges payable, as was done in the original example in Statement 90. Still others indicated that additional explanation of the reason for the various computations would be helpful.

53. This Technical Bulletin attempts to illustrate fully the computation of a loss on an abandonment under Statement 90. Because of the inherent complexity of the computations, particularly when they involve two different approaches for accounting for income taxes, items not unique to the requirements of Statement 90 were omitted. Discounting is required by APB Opinion No. 21, *Interest on Receivables and Payables*, for items like cancellation charges that will be paid after an extended period. Accounting for changes in estimates is specified by APB Opinion No. 20, *Accounting Changes*. Both of those opinions have been in effect since 1971, so an illustration of their application was considered unnecessary.

54. Several respondents noted that tax rates in the United States have changed recently. In many cases, tax rate changes occurred after the date on which an abandonment became probable. Those respondents asked that the examples specify how the effects of changes in tax rates should be recognized.

55. The recognition of changes in tax rates required by Opinion 11 is explained in considerable detail in that Opinion and in various related pronouncements. The recognition of changes in tax rates required by Statement 96 is explained in detail in that Statement. Some references to those requirements have also been added in the examples in this Technical Bulletin.

FASB Technical Bulletin No. 87-3
Accounting for Mortgage Servicing Fees and Rights

STATUS

Issued: December 31, 1987

Effective Date: For transactions entered into on or after December 31, 1987

Affects: No other pronouncements

Affected by: No other pronouncements

FASB Technical Bulletin No. 87-3
Accounting for Mortgage Servicing Fees and Rights

References

FASB Statement No. 65, *Accounting for Certain Mortgage Banking Activities,* paragraphs 11, 16, 19, 34, and 45
FASB Statement No. 77, *Reporting by Transferors for Transfers of Receivables with Recourse,* paragraphs 6 and 12
FASB Technical Bulletin No. 85-2, *Accounting for Collateralized Mortgage Obligations (CMOs),* paragraph 2

APPLICATION OF THE DEFINITION OF A NORMAL SERVICING FEE RATE

Question 1

1. Federally sponsored secondary market makers for mortgage loans, such as Government National Mortgage Association (GNMA), Federal Home Loan Mortgage Corporation (FHLMC), and Federal National Mortgage Association (FNMA), set minimum servicing fee rates for transactions with them. For purposes of determining gain or loss on mortgage loans sold to those agencies with servicing retained, should mortgage servicers consider the servicing fee rates set by such agencies for transactions with them to be a *normal servicing fee rate* as that term is used in Statement 65?

Background

2. Enterprises that conduct mortgage banking activities buy or originate mortgage loans and may sell the loans but retain the right to service them (collect mortgage and escrow payments, maintain loan payment records, and so forth) in return for a fee. Those who make a market for loans establish minimum servicing fee rates that will be paid to the servicer from the underlying loans' cash flows. The fee is generally expressed as a percentage of the outstanding loan balance. Several alternatives are available to the seller-servicer on how the loans are packaged and to whom they are sold. The seller-servicer may (a) sell the whole loans to the federally sponsored secondary market makers or exchange the loans for pass-through certificates collateralized by such loans or (b) sell the whole loans to private-sector investors, including private secondary market makers, thrifts, pension funds, and insurance companies. Alternatively, the seller-servicer may sell participations in pools of loans either through brokers or directly to investors.

Response

3. Yes. The servicing fee rates set by GNMA,

FHLMC, and FNMA in servicing agreements should be considered a normal servicing fee rate for a transaction with those agencies. Statement 65 defines a *normal servicing fee rate* as a servicing fee rate that is representative of servicing fee rates *most* commonly used in comparable servicing agreements covering similar types of mortgage loans. The fact that federally sponsored secondary market makers specify minimum servicing fee rates for transactions with them indicates that the normal servicing fee rate for those transactions should be no less than those agencies' minimum servicing fee rates. In addition, if normal servicing fees are expected to be less than the estimated servicing costs over the estimated life of the mortgage loans, the expected loss on servicing the loans should be accrued as of the date the mortgage loans are sold.

Question 2

4. If a seller-servicer sells mortgage loans directly to private-sector investors and retains the servicing of those loans, what rate should the seller-servicer use as the servicing fee rate?

Response

5. As stated in paragraph 3 of this Technical Bulletin, Statement 65 defines a normal servicing fee rate as a servicing fee rate that is representative of servicing fee rates most commonly used in comparable servicing agreements covering similar types of mortgage loans. Implicit in the phrase "most commonly used in comparable servicing agreements" is the requirement to consider servicing fee rates that are customary in the secondary market. Consequently, the seller-servicer should consider the normal servicing fee rate that would have been specified in comparable servicing agreements if the loans had been sold to or securitized by one of the federally sponsored secondary market makers.

6. The seller-servicer should first select the federally sponsored secondary market maker whose servicing terms are most comparable to those specified in the servicing agreement. The seller-servicer should then select the rate used by that federally sponsored agency for loans similar to those sold under the servicing agreement. If the seller-servicer determines that the selected federally sponsored agency does not make a secondary market for the type of loans sold, the seller-servicer should use a similar process to select the predominant rate used by major private-sector secondary market makers as the normal servicing fee rate for similar loans.

7. If the stated servicing fee rate is not considered

a normal servicing fee rate, the seller-servicer should adjust the sales price of the loans for purposes of determining gain or loss on the sale, to provide for the recognition of a normal servicing fee in each subsequent year. The amount of the adjustment should be the difference between the actual sales price and the estimated sales price that would have been obtained if a normal servicing fee rate had been specified. The adjustment and any gain or loss to be recognized should be determined as of the date the mortgage loans are sold. In addition, if normal servicing fees are expected to be less than estimated servicing costs over the estimated life of the mortgage loans, the expected loss on servicing the loans should be accrued at that date.

ACCOUNTING FOR THE CAPITALIZED COST OF A PURCHASED SERVICING RIGHT WHEN MORTGAGE LOANS ARE REFINANCED

Question 3

8. When an enterprise that is servicing mortgage loans refinances a loan that is being serviced (resulting in prepayment of the old loan and origination of a new loan), should the enterprise consider the estimated future net servicing income (that is, servicing revenue in excess of servicing costs) from the new loan in determining how to amortize any capitalized cost related to acquiring the mortgage servicing right for the old loan?

Background

9. Statement 65 designates the right to service

mortgage loans for other than an enterprise's own account as an intangible asset that may be acquired separately, in a purchase of mortgage loans, or in a business combination. If a mortgage servicing right qualifies for capitalization, Statement 65 specifies that the asset should be amortized in proportion to, and over the period of, estimated net servicing income.

Response

10. No. The mortgage servicing right represents a contractual relationship between the servicer and the investor in the loan, not between the servicer and the borrower. The cost of the mortgage servicing right may require adjustment as a result of the refinancing transaction depending on the servicer's assumptions in recording the servicing asset. If the refinancing transaction represents prepayment activity anticipated by the servicer when the servicing asset was recorded, an adjustment would not be necessary. However, if actual prepayments differ from anticipated prepayments, an adjustment to the servicing asset would be required.

EFFECTIVE DATE AND TRANSITION

11. The provisions of this Technical Bulletin are effective for transactions entered into on or after December 31, 1987. Earlier application is encouraged for transactions occurring in periods for which financial statements have not been issued.

Appendix

BACKGROUND INFORMATION AND CONSIDERATION OF COMMENTS RECEIVED ON THE PROPOSED TECHNICAL BULLETIN

Background Information

12. The accounting for mortgage servicing fees and rights is addressed in Statement 65. Paragraph 11 of Statement 65 states that "if mortgage loans are sold with servicing retained and the stated servicing fee rate differs materially from a current (normal) servicing fee rate, the sales price shall be adjusted, for purposes of determining gain or loss on the sale, to provide for the recognition of a normal servicing fee in each subsequent year." The FASB has been informed that there are differences of opinion among enterprises performing mortgage banking activities as to what constitutes a normal servicing fee rate. Those differences can result in significantly different amounts of gain or loss on the sales, even though the loans being sold, the sales prices, and the servicing agreements are virtually identical. Generally, mortgage bankers originate loans to obtain the servicing rights; thus, many believe that the gain or loss on the sale of those loans is secondary to the enterprise's ability to establish profitable long-term servicing operations.

13. The primary issue in this Technical Bulletin is what constitutes a normal servicing fee rate when an enterprise sells loans with servicing retained. For example, an enterprise may determine that the stated servicing fee rate is less than a normal servicing fee rate. The enterprise should adjust the sales price of the loans for purposes of determining gain or loss on the sale, to provide for the recognition of a normal servicing fee in each subsequent year.

14. At a meeting of the Emerging Issues Task Force (the Task Force) on December 4, 1986, the question of what constitutes a normal servicing fee rate and related issues were discussed. The Task Force did not reach a consensus as to what constitutes a normal servicing fee rate; however, it did conclude that the rate should *not* be based on an enterprise's estimated cost of servicing. The Task Force requested that the FASB formally address the issues related to this topic.

15. This Technical Bulletin provides guidance on how to apply the definition of a normal servicing fee rate to many of the loan sale transactions in the secondary mortgage market. In addition, the Technical Bulletin provides guidance on whether an enterprise, when refinancing a loan that is being serviced, should consider the estimated future net servicing income from the new loan in determining how to amortize any capitalized mortgage servicing right of the old loan.

Consideration of Comments Received on the Proposed Technical Bulletin

16. A proposed Technical Bulletin, *Accounting for Mortgage Servicing Fees and Rights,* was released for comment on July 8, 1987. Fifty-one letters of comment were received; the most significant comments are discussed in the following paragraphs.

17. Many respondents stated that the servicing fee rates established by the federally sponsored secondary market makers vary among the different agencies, as well as within each agency. In addition, they stated that FHLMC and FNMA may specify different servicing fee rates for different servicers even though the servicing agreements involve identical assets and similar servicing requirements. GNMA requires 44 basis points as the minimum servicing fee rate for its servicing contracts, while FHLMC and FNMA require rates that range from 25 to 37 1/2 basis points. Generally, FHLMC and FNMA set the servicing fee rate in a servicing agreement based on the assets delivered by the seller-servicer (for example, conventional whole loans may require a rate of 37 1/2 basis points, while mortgage-backed securities may require a rate of 25 basis points). In addition, those agencies may negotiate with the seller-servicer in determining the stated servicing fee rate based on the size and experience of the servicer's operations. This Technical Bulletin requires that the seller-servicer use the rate specified in the servicing agreement with the federally sponsored secondary market maker. In addition, if the normal servicing fees are expected to be less than the estimated servicing costs over the estimated life of the mortgage loans, the expected loss on servicing the loans should be accrued as of the date the mortgage loans are sold.

18. Some respondents stated that GNMA's rate, which was established a number of years ago when the average outstanding balance of a loan was generally smaller, may not reflect the current market conditions in the mortgage loan servicing industry. GNMA's minimum servicing fee rate of 44 basis points is greater than the rates established by FHLMC and FNMA for several reasons. Unlike servicers for FHLMC and FNMA, GNMA servicers are required to (a) make timely principal and interest payments to certificate holders in the event of a borrower's default, (b) advance to GNMA one month of interest on the loans as additional security, and (c) submit detailed monthly servicing reports to GNMA. In

addition, many believe that the GNMA market is more established than those of the other agencies and, thus, a GNMA-backed security is a safer investment to the investor and should result in higher proceeds to the seller-servicer on the loan sale.

19. Some respondents indicated that the normal servicing fee rates established by the federally sponsored secondary market makers include a profit factor and questioned whether that portion of the rate should be excluded in determining a normal servicing fee rate. The federally sponsored secondary market makers include a profit factor in the normal servicing fee rate to protect the market and its investors and to encourage seller-servicers to fulfill their servicing responsibilities subsequent to the sale of the loans. The profit factors are not published and may vary among the various agencies; however, they are an integral part of the servicing fee rate. To separate the profit factor from the servicing fee rate would inappropriately produce a larger gain (or smaller loss) on the sale of loans while reducing the profitability of future servicing operations.

20. Many respondents asked what rate should be considered a normal servicing fee rate when a seller-servicer sells loans to a private-sector investor. Paragraphs 5-7 of this Technical Bulletin address that situation.

21. Some respondents stated that a normal servicing fee rate should be based on the servicer's expected cost of servicing the loan plus a reasonable profit factor. They believe that efficient servicers generally are able to provide servicing at a rate lower than the rate specified by the secondary market makers; thus, efficient servicers (compared with inefficient servicers) are penalized because the amount of the gain or loss recognized when loans are sold with servicing retained would be reduced or increased, respectively.

22. The gain or loss on the sale of loans should not include any portion of the proceeds from the sale that may relate to the future servicing responsibilities of the seller-servicer. A normal servicing fee rate should result in consistent financial reporting between enterprises that sell loans with servicing retained. Two lenders that sell identical loans for the same sales price under similar servicing agreements, including the specified servicing fee rate, should recognize the same gain or loss on the sale. If those lenders have different estimated servicing costs, the effect on reported income of those different levels of servicing efficiency should be recognized as those services are provided rather than at the time the loans are sold.

FASB Technical Bulletin No. 88-1
Issues Relating to Accounting for Leases:
- Time Pattern of the Physical Use of the Property in an Operating Lease
- Lease Incentives in an Operating Lease
- Applicability of Leveraged Lease Accounting to Existing Assets of the Lessor
- Money-Over-Money Lease Transactions
- Wrap Lease Transactions

STATUS

Issued: December 28, 1988

Effective Date: For transactions entered into after December 31, 1988

Affects: No other pronouncements

Affected by: No other pronouncements

FASB Technical Bulletin No. 88-1

Issues Relating to Accounting for Leases:
- **Time Pattern of the Physical Use of the Property in an Operating Lease**
- **Lease Incentives in an Operating Lease**
- **Applicability of Leveraged Lease Accounting to Existing Assets of the Lessor**
- **Money-Over-Money Lease Transactions**
- **Wrap Lease Transactions**

TIME PATTERN OF THE PHYSICAL USE OF THE PROPERTY IN AN OPERATING LEASE

References

FASB Statement No. 13, *Accounting for Leases,* paragraph 15
FASB Technical Bulletin No. 85-3, *Accounting for Operating Leases with Scheduled Rent Increases*

Question 1

1. A lease agreement may include scheduled rent increases designed to accommodate the lessee's projected physical use of the property. For example, rents may escalate in contemplation of the lessee's physical use of the property even though the lessee takes possession of or controls the physical use of the property at the inception of the lease, or rents may escalate under a master lease agreement as the lessee adds additional equipment to the leased property or requires additional space or capacity (hereinafter referred to as additional leased property). For operating leases that include those provisions, how should the rental payment obligation be recognized by the lessee and lessor in accordance with paragraph 15 of Statement 13 and Technical Bulletin 85-3?

Response

2. Both the lessee and the lessor should recognize the lease payments under Statement 13 and Technical Bulletin 85-3 as follows:

a. If rents escalate in contemplation of the lessee's physical use of the leased property, including equipment, but the lessee takes possession of or controls the physical use of the property at the beginning of the lease term, all rental payments, including the escalated rents, should be recognized as rental expense or rental revenue on a straight-line basis in accordance with paragraph 15 of Statement 13 and Technical Bulletin 85-3 starting with the beginning of the lease term.

b. If rents escalate under a master lease agreement because the lessee gains access to and control over additional leased property at the time of the escalation, the escalated rents should be considered rental expense or rental revenue attributable to the leased property and recognized in proportion to the additional leased property in the years that the lessee has control over the use of the additional leased property. The amount of rental expense or rental revenue attributed to the additional leased property should be proportionate to the relative fair value of the additional property, as determined at the inception of the lease, in the applicable time periods during which the lessee controls its use.

Background

3. This issue involves how to apply Technical Bulletin 85-3 to lease agreements that escalate rents in contemplation of the lessee's projected use of the property. The issue arises from paragraph 2 of Technical Bulletin 85-3, which states "... scheduled rent increases, which are included in minimum lease payments under Statement 13, should be recognized by lessors and lessees on a straight-line basis over the lease term *unless another systematic and rational allocation basis is more representative of the time pattern in which the leased property is physically employed*" (emphasis added).

4. This Technical Bulletin considers the right to control the use of the leased property as the equivalent of physical use. When the lessee controls the use of the leased property, recognition of rental expense or rental revenue should not be affected by the extent to which the lessee utilizes that property.

5. This Technical Bulletin makes a distinction between agreements that give the lessee the right to control the use of the leased property at the beginning of the lease term and those that do not. Escalated rents under agreements that give the lessee the right to control the use of the entire leased property at the beginning of the lease term should be included in the minimum lease payments and

recognized on a straight-line basis over the lease term. When the agreement provides that the lessee gains control over additional leased property, rental expense or rental revenue should be recognized based on the relative fair value of the additional property leased and the period during which the lessee has the right to control the use of the additional property. This is the intent of Statement 13 and Technical Bulletin 85-3.

LEASE INCENTIVES IN AN OPERATING LEASE

References

FASB Statement No. 13, *Accounting for Leases,* paragraphs 15, 19, and 35-40
FASB Technical Bulletin No. 79-15, *Accounting for Loss on a Sublease Not Involving the Disposal of a Segment*
FASB Technical Bulletin No. 85-3, *Accounting for Operating Leases with Scheduled Rent Increases*

Question 2

6. An operating lease agreement with a new lessor may include incentives for the lessee to sign the lease, such as an up-front cash payment to the lessee, payment of costs for the lessee (such as moving expenses), or the assumption by the lessor of the lessee's preexisting lease with a third party. For operating leases that include such incentives, should lessees or lessors ever recognize those incentives as rental expense or rental revenue other than on a straight-line basis in accordance with paragraph 15 of Statement 13 and Technical Bulletin 85-3?

Response

7. Payments made to or on behalf of the lessee represent incentives that should be considered reductions of rental expense by the lessee and reductions of rental revenue by the lessor over the term of the new lease. Similarly, losses incurred by the lessor as a result of assuming a lessee's preexisting lease with a third party should be considered an incentive by both the lessor and the lessee. Incentives should be recognized on a straight-line basis over the term of the new lease in accordance with paragraph 15 of Statement 13, Technical Bulletin 85-3, and paragraphs 1-5 above.

8. The lessee's immediate recognition of expenses or losses, such as moving expenses, losses on subleases, or the write-off of abandoned leasehold improvements, is not changed by this Technical Bulletin. Rather, this Technical Bulletin addresses the question of when to recognize the incentive re-

lated to the new lessor's assumption of that expense or loss. The new lessor and the lessee should independently estimate any loss attributable to the assumption of a preexisting lease with a third party. For example, the lessee's estimate of the incentive could be based on a comparison of the new lease with the market rental rate available for similar lease property or the market rental rate from the same lessor without the lease assumption, and the lessor should estimate any loss based on the total remaining costs reduced by the expected benefits from the sublease or use of the assumed leased property.

9. For example, in conjunction with an operating lease of property for eight years, the lessor assumes the lessee's preexisting lease with a third party that has four years remaining. Assume that the old lease payment is $800 per year and the new lease payment is $1,200 per year. Also assume that the lessor estimates the loss on the assumed lease of $1,000 over its remaining term based on the ability to sublease the property for $550 per year. The lessee estimates the incentive as $960 based on a comparison of the preexisting lease rate to current rates for similar property. The accounting for that incentive is as follows:

Lessor Accounting

At inception:

Incentive to lessee	1,000	
Liability on sublease assumed		1,000
To record deferred cost and liability related to loss on assumption of remaining lease		

Recurring journal entries in years 1-4:

Liability on sublease assumed (1,000/ 4 years)	250	
Sublease expense	550	
Cash		800
To record cash payment on sublease assumed and amortization of the liability on the sublease assumed		
Cash	550	
Sublease revenue		550
To record cash received from sublease of the property		

Recurring journal entries in years 1-8:

Cash	1,200	
Rental revenue		1,075
Incentive to lessee (1,000/ 8 years)		125
To record cash received on new lease and amortization of incentive over new lease term		

Lessee Accounting

At inception:

Loss on sublease assumed by lessor	960	
Incentive from lessor		960
To record loss on sublease assumed in conjunction with new lease agreement		

Recurring journal entries in years 1-8:

Lease expense	1,080	
Incentive from lessor (960/ 8 years)	120	
Cash		1,200
To record cash payment on new lease and amortization of incentive over the new lease term		

Background

10. Some have suggested that incentives paid to or incurred on behalf of the lessee by the lessor are not part of the normal lessee-lessor relationship and should be recognized in income by the lessee in the period paid or incurred by the lessor. This Technical Bulletin views those incentives as an inseparable part of the new lease agreement that must be recognized as reductions to rental expense and rental revenue on a straight-line basis over the term of the new lease in accordance with paragraph 15 of Statement 13, Technical Bulletin 85-3, and paragraph 2 above.

APPLICABILITY OF LEVERAGED LEASE ACCOUNTING TO EXISTING ASSETS OF THE LESSOR

References

FASB Statement No. 13, *Accounting for Leases,* paragraphs 6 and 42-46
FASB Statement No. 27, *Classification of Renewals or Extensions of Existing Sales-Type or Direct Financing Leases,* paragraph 7

Question 3

11. Paragraph 6(b)(ii) of Statement 13, as amended, requires that the cost or carrying amount, if different, and the fair value of the asset be the same at the inception of the lease for it to be classified as a direct financing lease. Paragraph 42(a) of Statement 13 requires that a lease qualify as a direct financing lease for the lessor to classify that lease as a leveraged lease. How does a lessor apply those requirements to leasing an asset the lessor has owned and had previously placed in service?

Response

12. Paragraphs 6(b)(ii) and 42(a) of Statement 13, as amended, should be applied literally. Although the carrying amount (cost less accumulated depreciation) of an asset previously placed in service may not be significantly different from its fair value, the two amounts will not likely be the same. Therefore, leveraged lease accounting will not be appropriate, generally, other than when an asset to be leased is acquired by the lessor. If the carrying amount of an existing asset of the lessor before any related write-down is equal to fair value as established in transactions by unrelated third parties, that asset could qualify for leveraged lease accounting. However, any write-down to the existing asset's fair value in contemplation of leasing the asset precludes the transaction from leveraged lease accounting.

Background

13. Paragraphs 6(b)(ii) and 42(a) of Statement 13, as amended, state:

Direct financing leases. Leases other than leveraged leases that do not give rise to manufacturer's or dealer's profit (or loss) to the lessor but that meet one or more of the criteria in paragraph 7 and both of the criteria in paragraph 8. In such leases, the cost or carrying amount, if different, and fair value of the leased property are the same at the inception of the lease.

Except for the exclusion of leveraged leases from the definition of a direct financing lease as set forth in paragraph 6(b)(ii), it otherwise meets that definition. Leases that meet the definition of sales-type leases set forth in paragraph 6(b)(i) shall not be accounted for as leveraged leases but shall be accounted for as prescribed in paragraph 17.

14. The FASB has received inquiries about the applicability of leveraged lease accounting to an existing asset of a lessor and whether the requirement in paragraphs 6(b)(ii), as amended, and 42(a) that the carrying amount of a leased asset must equal its fair value at the inception of the lease to qualify as a leveraged lease applies literally to a lease of a lessor's existing asset. Some may have interpreted that requirement to allow leveraged lease accounting for an asset whose carrying amount was not significantly different from its fair value or whose carrying amount after a recent write-down equaled its fair value. This Technical Bulletin reaffirms the requirement that the carrying amount of an existing asset before any write-down must equal its fair value, as that requirement is intended to be applied literally.

15. Regulated utilities have argued that the carrying amounts of certain of their assets always equal the fair value based on a utility's ability to recover that cost in conjunction with a franchise to sell a related service in a specified area. That argument is not valid when considering the value of the asset to a third-party purchaser who does not own that franchise, and it is not consistent with paragraphs 6(b)(ii) and 42(a) of Statement 13, as amended, or this Technical Bulletin.

MONEY-OVER-MONEY LEASE TRANSACTIONS

References

FASB Statement No. 13, *Accounting for Leases,* paragraphs 6-8 and 41-45
FASB Technical Bulletin No. 85-2, *Accounting for Collateralized Mortgage Obligations (CMOs)*
FASB Technical Bulletin No. 86-2, *Accounting for an Interest in the Residual Value of a Leased Asset: Acquired by a Third Party or Retained by a Lessor That Sells the Related Minimum Rental Payments,* paragraph 21

Question 4

16. An enterprise manufactures or purchases an asset, leases the asset to a lessee, and obtains nonrecourse financing in excess of the asset's cost using the leased asset and the future lease rentals as collateral (commonly referred to as a money-over-money lease transaction). Should the enterprise ever recognize any of the amount by which the cash received plus the present value of any estimated residual retained exceeds the carrying amount of the leased asset as profit on that transaction at the beginning of the lease term? If not, how should the enterprise account for the transaction?

Response

17. Other than the recognition of manufacturer's or dealer's profit in a sales-type lease, an enterprise should never recognize as income the proceeds from the borrowing in a money-over-money lease transaction at the beginning of the lease term. The enterprise should account for that transaction as (a) the manufacture or purchase of an asset, (b) the leasing of the asset under an operating, direct financing, or sales-type lease as required by paragraphs 6-8 of Statement 13, as amended, and (c) the borrowing of funds. The asset (if an operating lease) or the lease receivable (if a direct financing or sales-type lease) and the liability for the nonrecourse financing should not be offset in the statement of financial position unless a right of setoff exists.

Background

18. The FASB has received several inquiries about how paragraph 21 of Technical Bulletin 86-2 applies to a transaction in which the lease receivable used as collateral and the related nonrecourse debt are offset because the transaction is viewed as a sale. Apparently, some justify sales accounting for that transaction by applying the money-over-money lease provisions of the June 20, 1980 AICPA Issues Paper, *Accounting by Lease Brokers* (hereinafter referred to as the Issues Paper). Paragraph 11 of the Issues Paper defines a money-over-money lease transaction as a transaction "in which the lease broker purchases an asset, obtains a lessee, and sells or assigns, on a nonrecourse basis, his right to receive rentals for the leased asset to unrelated third party financers for an amount that exceeds his investment in the leased asset." The advisory conclusions in paragraphs 60 and 61 of the Issues Paper suggest that in a money-over-money lease transaction a lease broker may recognize income at the beginning of the lease term for the cash received in excess of the carrying amount of the leased asset (and the residual value retained) provided that the following criteria are met:

a. The financing is nonrecourse to the lease broker.
b. The lease broker receives more cash (excluding the amount recognized based on the residual value share) from third-party financers or lessees (both on a nonrecourse basis) than the lease broker paid for the leased asset.
c. All parties to the transaction are arranged for at the beginning of the initial lease term.
d. The leased asset is acquired at the same time the transaction is arranged.

19. Those criteria do not warrant an exemption to the traditional presentation of nonrecourse debt and lease income recognition. However, those and other nonrecourse debt issues may be reconsidered as part of the Board's project on financial instruments and off-balance-sheet financing.

20. The money-over-money lease transaction described in this Technical Bulletin is not structured to meet the requirements of Technical Bulletin 85-2, which allows a collateralized borrowing on a nonrecourse basis to be accounted for as the sale of the collateral. Those who support sale accounting for nonrecourse debt in lease transactions (as described in the advisory conclusions in the Issues Paper) suggest that the economics of the nonrecourse financing collateralized by the lease

receivable justifies sales accounting. The economics of nonrecourse financing in leasing transactions was considered during the deliberations on Statement 13. The Board concluded that some accelerated recognition of lease income and modification of the presentation of the nonrecourse debt and lease receivable in a statement of financial position were appropriate for leasing transactions that meet all of the criteria for leveraged leases but determined that lease accounting should not be modified in any other circumstance.

WRAP LEASE TRANSACTIONS

References

FASB Statement No. 13, *Accounting for Leases,* paragraphs 6, 32-36, and 107
FASB Statement No. 28, *Accounting for Sales with Leasebacks*
FASB Statement No. 66, *Accounting for Sales of Real Estate*
FASB Statement No. 98, *Accounting for Leases: Sale-Leaseback Transactions Involving Real Estate, Sales-Type Leases of Real Estate, Definition of the Lease Term, and Initial Direct Costs of Direct Financing Leases*

Question 5

21. An enterprise purchases an asset, leases the asset to a lessee, obtains nonrecourse financing using the lease rentals or the lease rentals and the asset as collateral, sells the asset subject to the lease and the nonrecourse debt to a third-party investor, and leases the asset back while remaining the substantive principal lessor under the original lease (commonly referred to as a wrap lease transaction). Other than as required by Statement 13, as amended by Statements 28, 66, and 98, should an enterprise ever recognize any profit on the wrap lease transaction at its inception? If not, how should the enterprise account for the transaction?

Response

22. If the property involved is real estate, the provisions of Statement 98 apply to the sale-leaseback transaction. If the property involved is not real estate, the enterprise should account for the transaction as a sale-leaseback transaction in accordance with paragraphs 32-34 of Statement 13, as amended, and the lease to the end user should be accounted for as a sublease in accordance with paragraph 36 of Statement 13. Under Statement 13 the asset should be removed from the books of the original enterprise, the leaseback should be classi-

fied in accordance with paragraph 6 of Statement 13, and any gain on the transaction should be recognized or deferred and amortized in accordance with paragraph 33 of Statement 13, as amended. The enterprise would also reflect the retained residual interest, gross sublease receivable, nonrecourse third-party debt, the leaseback obligation, and the note receivable from the investor in the statement of financial position. As in accounting for a money-over-money lease transaction (refer to paragraph 17 of this Technical Bulletin), the sublease asset and the related nonrecourse debt should not be offset in the statement of financial position unless a right of setoff exists.

Background

23. The Emerging Issues Task Force discussed the accounting for wrap lease transactions in EITF Issue No. 87-7, "Sale of an Asset Subject to a Lease and Nonrecourse Financing: 'Wrap Lease Transactions.'" The Task Force did not reach a consensus about whether the enterprise that sells the asset to the equity investor should recognize income at the inception of the leaseback for the amount by which the proceeds received from the sale (including any portion of the residual value of the leased asset retained) exceed the carrying amount of residual value of the asset sold. Some Task Force members commented that the wrap lease transaction is a sale-leaseback transaction and any income should be deferred and amortized over the lease term under the sale-leaseback provisions of Statement 13, as amended. Other Task Force members viewed the wrap lease transaction as a sale of the residual value and tax benefits associated with the leased asset and proposed that income should be recognized at the time of sale.

24. Paragraph 107 of Statement 13 acknowledges that sale-leaseback transactions initiated for tax purposes were anticipated in developing that standard.

> . . . *Most sale-leasebacks are entered into* as a means of financing, *for tax reasons,* or both and that the terms of the sale and the terms of the leaseback are usually negotiated as a package. Because of this interdependence of terms, no means could be identified for separating the sale and the leaseback that would be both practicable and objective. [Emphasis added.]

Therefore, a wrap lease transaction should be accounted for as a sale-leaseback transaction under Statement 13, as amended, or Statement 98, as appropriate.

EFFECTIVE DATE AND TRANSITION

25. The provisions of this Technical Bulletin are effective for transactions entered into[1] after December 31, 1988. Earlier application to transactions occurring in periods for which annual financial statements have not been issued is encouraged.

> The Financial Accounting Standards Board has authorized its staff to prepare FASB Technical Bulletins to provide guidance on certain financial accounting and reporting problems on a timely basis, pursuant to the procedures described in FASB Technical Bulletin No. 79-1 (Revised), *Purpose and Scope of FASB Technical Bulletins and Procedures for Issuance.* The provisions of Technical Bulletins need not be applied to immaterial items. Copyright © 1988 by the Financial Accounting Standards Board.

Appendix

BACKGROUND INFORMATION AND CONSIDERATION OF COMMENTS RECEIVED ON THE PROPOSED TECHNICAL BULLETIN

26. A proposed Technical Bulletin, *Issues Relating to Accounting for Leases,* was released for comment on April 14, 1988. Sixty-seven letters of comment were received on the proposed Technical Bulletin. Certain of the comments received and consideration of them are included in the following discussions of the specific issues to which they relate.

27. The proposed Technical Bulletin addressed three issues, "Lessee's Use of the Maximum Implicit Interest Rate," "Sales of Assets Subject to Operating Leases and 'Nondiscriminatory Remarketing Agreements,'" and "Delayed Equity Contributions in Leveraged Leases Using Recourse Debt," that are not included in this Technical Bulletin. Comments received indicated those issues may require consideration of additional issues that could not be done expeditiously. Therefore, those issues are not addressed here.

Time Pattern of the Physical Use of the Property in an Operating Lease

28. Some respondents to the issue "Time Pattern of the Physical Use of the Property in an Operating Lease" indicated that rent should be expensed only during the period that the lessee occupies or utilizes the leased property, irrespective of the time period the lessee actually has control over the property's use. Consistency with Technical Bulletin 85-3 was questioned because in the situations being discussed all of the space is not being fully employed. The Technical Bulletin clarifies that the right to control the use of the property is viewed as the same as the use of the property.

29. Some respondents requested clarification about how to account for situations in which the rental rate for the right to control the use of additional property is higher or lower than the rental rate for property already leased. This Technical Bulletin prescribes the recognition of rental revenue or rental expense based on the fair value of the leased property that the lessee controls, rather than rental recognition based on square footage.

---

[1] For the purpose of applying this Technical Bulletin, *entered into* is used in the context of the term *inception of the lease* as defined in paragraph 5(b) of Statement 13, as amended by FASB Statement No. 23, *Inception of the Lease.*

Lease Incentives in an Operating Lease

30. Some respondents to the issue "Lease Incentives in an Operating Lease" stated that the assumption by the lessor of any portion of the obligation of the lessee's preexisting lease with a third party should not be considered part of the new lease by either the lessor or the lessee. They contend that paragraphs 35-40 of Statement 13 prescribe the appropriate accounting for subleases for both the original lessee and the new lessee (the lessor who assumes the lease obligation) and require that the sublease be accounted for as a separate transaction. Although the sublease can be viewed as a second transaction, the assumption of the old lease by the lessor is the same as the lessor's making the lessee's remaining lease payments. Under this Technical Bulletin, any loss incurred by the lessor as a result of entering into a lease is an incentive for the lessee to sign the new lease and should be accounted for as part of the new lease transaction.

31. Some respondents noted that it is difficult and confusing to require the lessee to estimate the loss incurred by the lessor on the assumption of the preexisting lease with a third party as an incentive. Those respondents noted that the lessee would not normally possess that information. This Technical Bulletin presumes that a lessee can make a reasonable estimate of such an incentive; otherwise, negotiating payments due under the new lease would be impossible. A comparison of a lease without the assumption of the previous lease should provide an indication of the effect of that lease assumption. While such comparisons are not based on market transactions, the lessee should make its best estimate and account for the incentive under this Technical Bulletin.

Applicability of Leveraged Lease Accounting to Existing Assets of the Lessor

32. A number of respondents to the issue "Applicability of Leveraged Lease Accounting to Existing Assets of the Lessor" agreed with the literal reading of Statement 13, but they argued that accounting ignores the substance of the transaction. They stated that interpreting the word *same* to mean *exactly the same* is inappropriate and overly harsh for an existing asset when measurement of carrying value and fair value for that asset are based on approximations, that is, depreciation and appraisal. Another suggestion was to allow an acceptable range of amounts between cost and fair value. Those respondents also argued that a transaction with insignificant profit recognition is consistent with the cash flow concept on which leveraged leasing is based and should be allowed. Those views were not ac-

cepted because leveraged lease accounting is an exception to normal lease accounting, and the requirements are intended to be applied literally.

33. Certain respondents disagreed with proscribing leveraged lease accounting following an asset write-down to fair value in contemplation of the lease transaction. They noted the absence of any prohibition in Statement 13 and argued that write-downs that are not arbitrary should not preclude leveraged lease accounting. Statement 13 requires a leveraged lease to first qualify as a direct financing lease. Under Statement 13, sales-type and direct financing leases are similar except that a sales-type lease reports a gain or loss at the inception of the lease and a direct financing lease does not. This Technical Bulletin views a write-down in contemplation of a leveraged lease as a sales-type lease with a loss. Sales-type leases do not qualify for leveraged lease accounting as is specifically stated in paragraph 42(a) of Statement 13.

Money-Over-Money Lease Transactions

34. Several respondents to the issue "Money-Over-Money Lease Transactions" stated that accounting for the transactions as sales has been accepted in practice as being in accordance with generally accepted accounting principles, even though that accounting is contrary to the requirements of Statement 13. Several respondents also stated that sales accounting for a money-over-money lease transaction better reflects the economics of the transaction because the lessor's primary role is as an intermediary in the transaction. Those respondents stated that money-over-money lease transactions are analogous to extinguishments of debt and transfers of receivables provided for under FASB Statements No. 76, *Extinguishment of Debt,* and No. 77, *Reporting by Transferors for Transfers of Receivables with Recourse.* They stated the existence of nonrecourse debt in this transaction is more reflective of a full transfer of risks than occurs for transactions that receive favorable accounting under those Statements. However, those Statements were developed for certain fact-specific situations, and analogies to those Statements usually are not appropriate.

35. Some respondents proposed that the accounting for money-over-money lease transactions should follow leveraged lease accounting. Those respondents indicated that the money-over-money lease transaction is an extension of the leveraged lease concept, except that the lessor's net investment at the inception of the lease may be negative. Since leveraged lease accounting does not permit income recognition when the net investment is negative, those respondents questioned whether in-

come should be recognized in a manner consistent with income recognition for leveraged leases. The lessee's prepayment of operating lease revenues could also result in the lessor's negative net investment in a leased asset. In a money-over-money lease transaction, the lessor accomplishes the same effect as prepayment by borrowing from a third party at a lower financing cost than the lessor is charging on the lease. Thus, the lessor is only gaining by a financing transaction that should not result in immediate income recognition or be eligible for derecognition in the statement of financial position.

Wrap Lease Transactions

36. Some respondents to the issue "Wrap Lease Transactions" stated that the accounting should reflect the economic substance of the sale of tax benefits and residual interest. That argument was considered and rejected in the proposed Technical Bulletin as discussed in paragraphs 23 and 24 of this Technical Bulletin. Some respondents noted that the discussion of sale-leasebacks did not refer to the provisions of Statement 98 that would be applicable if the property leased back is real estate. A reference to that Statement has been added.

FASB Technical Bulletin No. 88-2
Definition of a Right of Setoff

STATUS

Issued: December 28, 1988

Effective Date: For transactions entered into after December 31, 1988

Affects: No other pronouncements

Affected by: Paragraph 4 amended by FAS 109
Superseded by FIN 39

Note: Although superseded by FIN 39, this pronouncement has not been removed from this volume because of the delayed effective date for FIN 39.

FASB Technical Bulletin No. 88-2
Definition of a Right of Setoff

Reference

APB Opinion No. 10, *Omnibus Opinion—1966,* paragraph 7

Question

1. Paragraph 7 of Opinion 10 states that "It is a general principle of accounting that the offsetting of assets and liabilities in the balance sheet is improper except where a right of setoff exists." What is meant by a *right of setoff* and what conditions must be met to have that right?

Response

2. A *right of setoff* is a debtor's legal right, by contract or otherwise, to discharge all or a portion of the debt owed to another party by applying against the debt an amount that the other party owes to the debtor.[1] A right of setoff exists when all of the following conditions are met:

a. Each of *two* parties owes the other determinable amounts.
b. The reporting party has the right to set off the amount owed with the amount owed by the other party.
c. The reporting party intends to set off.
d. The right of setoff is enforceable at law.

A debtor having a valid right of setoff may offset the related asset and liability and report the net amount.[2]

3. Generally, debts may be set off if they exist between mutual debtors each acting in its capacity as both debtor and creditor. In particular cases, however, state laws about the right of setoff may provide results different from those normally provided by contract or as a matter of common law. Similarly, the U.S. Bankruptcy Code imposes restrictions on or prohibitions against the right of setoff in bankruptcy under certain circumstances. Legal constraints should be considered to determine whether the right of setoff is enforceable.

4. Various accounting pronouncements specify accounting treatments in specific circumstances that result in offsetting or in a presentation in a statement of financial position that is similar to the effect of offsetting. This Technical Bulletin does not modify the accounting treatment in the particular circumstances prescribed by any of the following pronouncements:

FASB Statements and Interpretations
APB Opinions
Accounting Research Bulletins
FASB Technical Bulletins
AICPA Accounting Interpretations
AICPA Audit and Accounting Guides
AICPA Industry Audit Guides
AICPA Statements of Position

Examples of those pronouncements are:

FASB Statement No. 13, *Accounting for Leases* (leveraged leases, paragraphs 42-47)
FASB Statement No. 60, *Accounting and Reporting by Insurance Enterprises* (reinsurance, paragraphs 38-40)
FASB Statement No. 87, *Employers' Accounting for Pensions* (accounting for pension plan assets and liabilities)
FASB Statement No. 96, *Accounting for Income Taxes* (net tax asset or liability amounts reported)
APB Opinion No. 30, *Reporting the Results of Operations—Reporting the Effects of Disposal of a Segment of a Business, and Extraordinary, Unusual and Infrequently Occurring Events and Transactions* (reporting of discontinued operations)
AICPA Audit and Accounting Guides, *Audits of Brokers and Dealers in Securities* (trade date accounting for trading portfolio positions), and *Construction Contractors* and *Government Contractors* (advances received on construction contracts)
AICPA Industry Audit Guide, *Audits of Banks* (reciprocal balances with other banks)

---

[1]For purposes of this Technical Bulletin, cash on deposit at a financial institution is to be considered by the depositor as cash rather than as an amount owed to the depositor.

[2]This Technical Bulletin does not address derecognition or nonrecognition of assets and liabilities (refer to paragraphs 7, 8, and 12).

Effective Date and Transition

5. The provisions of this Technical Bulletin are effective for transactions entered into after December 31, 1988. Earlier application to transactions occurring in periods for which annual financial statements have not been issued is encouraged. Restatement of previously issued financial statements for periods prior to the effective date to conform to the provisions of this Technical Bulletin is also encouraged.

Appendix

BACKGROUND INFORMATION AND CONSIDERATION OF COMMENTS RECEIVED ON THE PROPOSED TECHNICAL BULLETIN

Background Information

6. Although the term *right of setoff* appears in paragraph 7 of Opinion 10, that term has never been defined. The intent of this Technical Bulletin is to define that term because questions often arise about whether offsetting is appropriate. These questions arise because (a) various accounting pronouncements have prescribed or permitted offsetting in specific circumstances for varying or unstated reasons, which has apparently blurred the understanding of when the general principle applies, and (b) new forms of financing transactions have been created that have been asserted to create a relationship that justifies offsetting certain assets and liabilities.

7. This Technical Bulletin clarifies the general principle by specifying the conditions necessary for a right of setoff to exist; it does not address derecognition or nonrecognition. The existence of a right of setoff would permit an enterprise to offset the specified asset and liability in its statement of financial position. Offsetting is the display of a recognized asset and a recognized liability as a net amount, which will result in no presentation in a statement of financial position if the asset and liability amounts are the same. Derecognition by sale of an asset or extinguishment of a liability results in removal of a recognized asset or liability and generally results in the recognition of gain or loss. Although conceptually different, offsetting that results in a net amount of zero and derecognition with no gain or loss are indistinguishable in their effects on the statement of financial position. Likewise, not recognizing assets and liabilities of the same amount in financial statements (often referred to as *off-balance-sheet financing*) achieves similar reported results.

8. FASB Statements No. 76, *Extinguishment of Debt,* and No. 77, *Reporting by Transferors for Transfers of Receivables with Recourse,* and FASB Technical Bulletin No. 85-2, *Accounting for Collateralized Mortgage Obligations (CMOs),* address extinguishment of recognized liabilities and derecognition of assets. This Technical Bulletin is based on the explanation in Statement 76 that offsetting is a display issue that does not presume the derecognition of recognized assets or extinguishment of recognized liabilities. Paragraph 40 of that Statement states:

Several respondents to the revised Exposure Draft commented about offsetting assets against liabilities, though it was apparent that some respondents had confused *offsetting* with *extinguishment*. In the Board's view, *offsetting* is a display issue—how recognized assets and recognized liabilities should be presented in a balance sheet (or how other recognized elements should be displayed in a basic financial statement). In contrast, *extinguishment* is a recognition issue—whether an asset or a liability exists and whether continued recognition is warranted in the basic financial statements. This Statement addresses when debt ceases to be a liability that warrants continued recognition in the balance sheet.

Consideration of Comments Received on the Proposed Technical Bulletin

9. A proposed Technical Bulletin, *Definition of a Right of Setoff,* was released for comment on April 14, 1988. Sixty letters of comment were received on the proposed Technical Bulletin. Certain of the comments received and consideration of them are discussed in the following paragraphs.

10. Several respondents questioned whether the proposed Technical Bulletin was intended to prohibit offsetting in circumstances prescribed or permitted by various existing accounting pronouncements. They noted that such an objective would exceed the guidelines for a Technical Bulletin established in FASB Technical Bulletin No. 79-1 (Revised), *Purpose and Scope of FASB Technical Bulletins and Procedures for Issuance.* Paragraph 4 clarifies that such a change is not intended.

11. Some respondents noted that offsetting is currently part of the Board's project on financial instruments and off-balance-sheet financing and should be addressed there rather than in this Technical Bulletin. This Technical Bulletin is intended to provide interim guidance on the application of the general principle of a right of setoff and does not anticipate the conclusions to be reached in the financial instruments and off-balance-sheet financing project.

12. Some respondents inquired whether this Technical Bulletin applies to unrecognized as well as recognized assets and liabilities, making reference to specific transactions, such as currency and interest rate swaps. This Technical Bulletin clarifies only the display issue of offsetting recognized assets and liabilities and, as stated in footnote 2, does not address derecognition or nonrecognition of assets and liabilities.

13. Paragraph 2(a) of the proposed Technical Bulletin stated that the right of setoff "exists when each of *two* parties owes the other determinable amounts." Some respondents indicated that the number of entities involved in the transaction is not relevant to the decision to offset. The general principle of a right of setoff involves only two parties and exceptions to that general principle should be limited to practices specifi-

cally permitted by the pronouncements indicated in paragraph 4.

14. Some respondents requested clarification of the requirement that each party owes the other determinable amounts. They specifically questioned whether those amounts need to be in the same currency, have the same maturities, and, if applicable, bear the same interest rate. If the parties meet the other criteria specified in the definition, specifying currency or interest rate requirements is unnecessary. However, if maturities differ, only the party with the nearer maturity could offset because the party with the longer term maturity must settle in the manner that the other party selects at the earlier maturity date.

15. Several respondents disagreed with the requirement that each party intend to set off and proposed that ability to set off should be sufficient. Those respondents further stated that the decision for net or gross settlement often is a matter of convenience or is tax motivated, would not be made until shortly before settlement, and should not determine the presentation in a statement of financial position. Others indicated that intent is not a condition specified by Opinion 10 and that a new requirement should not be imposed by a Technical Bulletin. They also stated that intent is subjective, can exist in various degrees, and is difficult to substantiate, and that such a requirement will be applied inconsistently in practice. If a party does not intend to set off even though the ability to set off exists, an offsetting presentation in the statement of financial position is not representationally faithful. Acknowledgment of the intent to set off by the reporting party and, if applicable, demonstration of the execution of the setoff in similar situations meet the criterion of intent.

16. Other respondents supported requiring an intent to set off if the condition is limited to the party intending to set off. They observed that a reliable assessment of the other party's intent is impractical and that the lack of that intent is irrelevant if a unilateral legal right of setoff exists for one party. This Technical Bulletin requires that only the reporting entity need have the intent to set off.

17. As used in the proposed Technical Bulletin, *enforceable by law* meant enforceable in a court proceeding by reason of statute or otherwise and demonstrable through examination of a contract. However, some respondents interpreted the requirement to mean the existence of a statute and they cited situations in which the right of setoff is not specifically included in contractual agreements but was enforceable because of regulatory

procedures or as part of normal business practice. The wording of the requirement in paragraph 2(d) of this Technical Bulletin was revised to state *enforceable at law* in order to include those situations.

18. Some respondents opposed the bankruptcy protection requirement in paragraph 2(d) of the proposed Technical Bulletin as inconsistent with the going-concern concept. Commentators indicated that, as a general rule, accounting should reflect what is expected to occur in the normal course of business and protection in bankruptcy is not pertinent when the probability of bankruptcy is remote.

19. Several respondents were concerned also about the difficulty of determining protection in bankruptcy. They noted that the lack of a uniform bankruptcy law and the broad discretion provided to bankruptcy judges would make predicting the outcome of isolated transactions involved in a setoff situation extremely difficult. Those respondents also noted that legal opinions are costly, if obtainable at all, but would likely be required for management and auditors to determine if a right of setoff exists. Also, some banks pointed out that bankruptcy law generally is inapplicable to certain regulated industries due to regulatory intervention in insolvency. In light of these comments, the requirement of legal enforceability was deemed to be sufficient evidence of the right of setoff. This Technical Bulletin does not include a separate requirement for protection in bankruptcy.

20. Some respondents questioned whether transactions involving a lender, a parent company, and its subsidiary could qualify under the proposed definition if all parties agree to the lender's unilateral right of setoff under a contractual arrangement. An example of that transaction is a loan by the foreign branch of a U.S. bank to a foreign subsidiary of a U.S. parent with the parent simultaneously depositing an amount equal to the loan in the U.S. bank for the same term. The deposit is collateral for the loan, and the bank has the legal right of setoff only in the event of default by the foreign subsidiary. Offsetting the collateral with the debt in that situation is inappropriate either in the bank's financial statements or in the consolidated financial statements of the parent and the foreign subsidiary.

21. Some respondents identified Statement 87 as an example in which plan assets are offset against the plan liabilities without meeting the criteria of the proposed Technical Bulletin. They indicated that other assets held in trust should be offset against the related liabilities in a manner similar to the reporting prescribed in Statement 87. Pension trusts are significantly different from most trusts and trusteed assets supporting other liabilities. The accounting and reporting for pensions was specifically considered by the Board in Statement 87. However, trusts established for other specified purposes, such as for decommissioning of a nuclear generating plant, would have to meet the conditions for setoff specified in paragraph 2.

FTB90-1

FASB Technical Bulletin No. 90-1
Accounting for Separately Priced Extended Warranty and Product Maintenance Contracts

STATUS

Issued: December 17, 1990

Effective Date: For contracts sold in fiscal years beginning after December 15, 1990

Affects: No other pronouncements

Affected by: No other pronouncements

FASB Technical Bulletin No. 90-1
Accounting for Separately Priced Extended Warranty and Product Maintenance Contracts

References

APB Opinion No. 20, *Accounting Changes,* paragraphs 19-21
FASB Statement No. 5, *Accounting for Contingencies,* paragraphs 4 and 24
FASB Statement No. 60, *Accounting and Reporting by Insurance Enterprises,* paragraphs 11, 13, 17, 29, and 32-34
FASB Statement No. 91, *Accounting for Nonrefundable Fees and Costs Associated with Originating or Acquiring Loans and Initial Direct Costs of Leases,* paragraph 6
FASB Concepts Statement No. 5, *Recognition and Measurement in Financial Statements of Business Enterprises,* paragraphs 83 and 84
FASB Concepts Statement No. 6, *Elements of Financial Statements,* paragraph 197

Question

1. How should revenue and costs from a separately priced extended warranty or product maintenance contract be recognized?

Background

2. An *extended warranty* is an agreement to provide warranty protection in addition to the scope of coverage of the manufacturer's original warranty, if any, or to extend the period of coverage provided by the manufacturer's original warranty. A *product maintenance contract* is an agreement to perform certain agreed-upon services to maintain a product for a specified period of time. The terms of the contract may take different forms, such as an agreement to periodically perform a particular service a specified number of times over a specified period of time, or an agreement to perform a particular service as the need arises over the term of the contract. Some contracts may provide both extended warranty coverage and product maintenance services. A contract is *separately priced* if the customer has the option to purchase the services provided under the contract for an expressly stated amount separate from the price of the product.

Response

3. Revenue from separately priced extended warranty and product maintenance contracts should be deferred and recognized in income on a straight-line basis over the contract period except in those circumstances in which sufficient historical evidence indicates that the costs of performing services under the contract are incurred on other than a straight-line basis. In those circumstances, revenue should be recognized over the contract period in proportion to the costs expected to be incurred in performing services under the contract.

4. Costs that are directly related to the acquisition of a contract and that would have not been incurred but for the acquisition of that contract (incremental direct acquisition costs) should be deferred and charged to expense in proportion to the revenue recognized. All other costs, such as costs of services performed under the contract, general and administrative expenses, advertising expenses, and costs associated with the negotiation of a contract that is not consummated, should be charged to expense as incurred.

5. A loss should be recognized on extended warranty or product maintenance contracts if the sum of expected costs of providing services under the contracts and unamortized acquisition costs exceeds related unearned revenue. Extended warranty or product maintenance contracts should be grouped in a consistent manner to determine if a loss exists. A loss should be recognized first by charging any unamortized acquisition costs to expense. If the loss is greater than the unamortized acquisition costs, a liability should be recognized for the excess.

Effective Date and Transition

6. The provisions of this Technical Bulletin are effective for separately priced extended warranty and product maintenance contracts sold in fiscal years beginning after December 15, 1990. Earlier application is permitted but not required. At initial application, this Technical Bulletin may (but is not required to) be applied to existing contracts by applying paragraphs 19-21 of Opinion 20, recognizing the cumulative effect of an accounting change and disclosing the effects of adopting this Technical Bulletin.

Appendix

BACKGROUND INFORMATION AND CONSIDERATION OF COMMENTS RECEIVED ON THE PROPOSED TECHNICAL BULLETIN

Background Information

7. Extended warranty and product maintenance contracts provide warranty protection or product services not included in the original price of the product covered by the contracts. The manner of recognizing revenue and costs under the contracts varies in practice depending on analogies drawn to existing literature and practice for other transactions. The FASB's Emerging Issues Task Force addressed certain aspects of the issue in Issue No. 89-17, "Accounting for the Retail Sale of an Extended Warranty Contract in Connection with the Sale of a Product." The Task Force concluded that recognizing all of the revenue at the time the contract is sold would be inappropriate but did not reach a consensus between deferring all or only a portion of the contract revenue, leaving diversity in practice among retailers, manufacturers, and other sellers of the contracts.

8. Warranties are explicitly included within the scope of Statement 5. However, that Statement addresses warranty obligations that are incurred in connection with the sale of the product, that is, obligations that are not separately priced or sold but are included in the sale of the product. This Technical Bulletin addresses extended warranty and product maintenance contracts that are priced and sold separately from the product and concludes that the accounting should recognize the sale of the product and the sale of the contract as separate transactions regardless of the seller's pricing and marketing strategy.

9. This Technical Bulletin concludes that accounting for extended warranty and product maintenance contracts should follow an approach similar to that described in Statement 60 for short-duration insurance contracts. Like short-duration insurance contracts, extended warranty and product maintenance contracts provide coverage against the risk of certain specified claim costs for a specified period. Those claim costs may take the form of repair costs if the product requires repair or service costs if the customer requests that a covered service be performed on the product. Paragraph 13 of Statement 60 indicates that premiums from short-duration insurance contracts should be recognized as revenue over the period of the contract in proportion to the amount of insurance protection provided. That generally results in premiums being recognized as revenue evenly over the contract period. This Technical Bulletin concludes that revenue on extended warranty and product maintenance contracts also should be recognized in income evenly over the contract period except for those circumstances in which sufficient historical evidence indicates that costs of providing services under the contract are incurred in some pattern other than straight line. The pattern of cost incurrence may vary depending on characteristics of the product or may be a function of the coverage provided under the contract. When the coverage under the contract varies, such as those situations in which the period of the extended warranty partially overlaps the period of the product's original warranty, or the extended warranty contains a graduating deductible, costs of providing services under the contract may vary proportionate to that coverage.

10. Paragraph 83 of Concepts Statement 5 states that revenue is not recognized until earned. Revenue is considered earned when the entity has substantially completed what it must do to be enti-

tled to the benefits represented by the revenue. This Technical Bulletin concludes that sellers of extended warranty or product maintenance contracts have an obligation to the buyer to perform services throughout the period of the contract and, therefore, revenue should be recognized in income over the period in which the seller is obligated to perform. This treatment is consistent with revenue recognition under Statement 60.

11. This Technical Bulletin concludes that costs of providing services under extended warranty and product maintenance contracts should be recognized in a manner similar to the approach required by Statement 60. Paragraph 17 of that Statement states that claim costs should be recognized when insured events occur.

12. Paragraph 29 of Statement 60 states that acquisition costs (such as commissions) should be capitalized and charged to expense in proportion to premium revenue recognized. Both Statements 60 and 91 provide guidance on identifying acquisition costs. This Technical Bulletin concludes that acquisition costs should be identified consistent with guidance in paragraph 6 of Statement 91, which defines acquisition costs in terms of incremental direct costs. Therefore, only the additional costs incurred because a contract is sold are incremental direct acquisition costs under this Technical Bulletin.

13. Paragraphs 32–34 of Statement 60 discuss the accounting for insurance contracts with premium deficiencies. In accounting for contracts with losses, paragraph 5 of this Technical Bulletin requires an approach similar to that described in Statement 60.

Consideration of Comments Received on the Proposed Technical Bulletin

14. A proposed Technical Bulletin, *Accounting for Separately Priced Extended Warranty and Product Maintenance Contracts,* was released for comment on August 15, 1990. Fifty-two letters of comment were received on the proposed Technical Bulletin. Certain of the comments received and consideration of them are discussed in the following paragraphs.

15. Some respondents supported recognizing all or deferring only a portion of the contract revenue at the time of sale. Those who supported full recognition commented that the contract revenue has been earned at the time of sale because the revenue is nonrefundable and contract costs are predictable and may be insignificant. Those who supported deferring only a portion of the revenue asserted that the sale of the product and the sale

of the contract are essentially a single planned transaction because sellers price their products expecting sales of contracts to a significant number of customers. Therefore, in their view, some of the contract revenue should be allocated to the product so that an equal gross profit margin is recognized on the product and on the contract. They commented that the stated contract price does not provide an appropriate basis for deferral. In their view, the amount deferred should include only an amount equal to expected costs under the contract plus a profit margin reflecting the combined sale.

16. This Technical Bulletin concludes that separately priced extended warranty and product maintenance contracts are not incidental to the sale of the product but rather are independent transactions under which the buyer agrees to purchase and the seller agrees to perform certain services. The buyer's decision to purchase a product alone does not entail any obligation to also purchase a contract, nor does it oblige the seller to provide any additional services. This Technical Bulletin acknowledges that some sellers may generally lower product prices in expectation of also selling contracts. However, it is the seller's obligation to perform services, not the seller's pricing and marketing strategy, that determines the appropriate financial reporting of the transactions. Because that obligation extends over a period of time, immediate revenue recognition is inappropriate. Furthermore, a seller's desire to sell a contract along with a product provides no basis for allocating revenue between the product and contract. Such an approach would result in recognizing different profit margins on identical products based on a buyer's independent decision to purchase or decline a contract.

17. Some respondents commented that deferring the stated contract price is inappropriate because expected costs under the contract are insignificant relative to the contract price. As a result, they commented that the balance sheet liability is significantly overstated. However, paragraph 197 of Concepts Statement 6 states that prepayments for services to be provided qualify as liabilities because an entity is required to provide services to those who paid in advance. This Technical Bulletin concludes that the stated price of the contract is the appropriate basis for deferral and rejects the viewpoint that revenue recognition should be accelerated because future contract costs are expected to be insignificant. Revenue is earned over the period in which the enterprise is required to provide services.

18. Some respondents indicated that deferring the contract revenue is misleading to financial

statement users because all of the cash from selling the contract has been received and is nonrefundable. This Technical Bulletin relies on a basic premise of generally accepted accounting principles that accrual accounting provides more relevant and useful information than cash basis accounting. Accrual accounting goes beyond cash transactions and recognizes the financial effects of transactions that have past or future cash consequences as those transactions occur, rather than only when cash is received or paid by an entity. This Technical Bulletin reaffirms the position that revenue has not been earned simply because cash has been received, even if nonrefundable. The cash received is, of course, given accounting recognition, but this Technical Bulletin concludes that this is one of many areas in which information about cash flows alone is not sufficient.

19. Paragraph 3 of the proposed Technical Bulletin stated that deferred revenue from separately priced extended warranty and product maintenance contracts should be "recognized in income on a straight-line basis over the contract period except for those circumstances in which the coverage under the contract varies according to a predetermined schedule." Some respondents stated that the proposed Technical Bulletin should not require straight-line amortization for contracts for which sufficient historical experience indicates that costs of providing services under the contracts are incurred on other than a straight-line basis. In their view, revenue recognition should reflect the amount of risk assumed by period, and such risk is best evidenced by the pattern of service costs expected to be incurred over the contract period. Paragraph 13 of Statement 60 discusses insurance contracts for which the period of risk differs significantly from the contract period. For those contracts, Statement 60 permits the recognition of revenue in proportion to the amount of risk assumed by period. Therefore, proportionately higher revenue is recognized in the periods of greatest risk assumption, as evidenced by increased claims activity. The proposed Technical Bulletin's requirement to recognize contract revenue on a straight-line basis was revised accordingly to include this "period of risk" concept provided sufficient historical evidence indicates a pattern of service costs that is other than straight line.

20. The proposed Technical Bulletin defined acquisition costs as those costs that "vary with and are primarily related to the acquisition of contracts." Some respondents questioned whether certain selling expenses, such as a portion of the salaries of employees who sell the contracts, are acquisition costs. This Technical Bulletin concludes that acquisition costs are incremental costs incurred as a result of acquiring a contract and would not have been incurred but for the acquisition of that contract. Therefore, such costs as employees' salaries, advertising, and general and administrative expenses that would have been incurred even if no contract was acquired are not acquisition costs. Paragraph 4 was revised to include the concept of incremental cost.

21. Several respondents questioned whether the proposed Technical Bulletin required loss recognition on an individual contract or a "pool of risk" basis. Paragraph 5 was revised to include the "pool of risk" concept from Statement 60.

22. Some respondents commented that the effective date of this Technical Bulletin should be delayed. Many of the retail entities affected by this Technical Bulletin have fiscal years that end in the first calendar quarter. The effective date was changed to contracts sold in fiscal years beginning after December 15, 1990 so those entities would not be required to adopt the provisions of this Technical Bulletin for the last few months of their current fiscal years. Others commented that entities should be permitted to change their method of accounting for the contracts by reporting the cumulative effect of an accounting change. This Technical Bulletin was revised to allow this option by application of Opinion 20.

FASB Technical Bulletin No. 94-1
Application of Statement 115 to Debt Securities Restructured in a Troubled Debt Restructuring

STATUS

Issued: April 20, 1994

Effective Date: For financial statements issued after April 30, 1994

Affects: No other pronouncements

Affected by: No other pronouncements

FASB Technical Bulletin No. 94-1
Application of Statement 115 to Debt Securities Restructured in a Troubled Debt Restructuring

References

FASB Statement No. 15, *Accounting by Debtors and Creditors for Troubled Debt Restructurings*
FASB Statement No. 114, *Accounting by Creditors for Impairment of a Loan,* paragraph 27
FASB Statement No. 115, *Accounting for Certain Investments in Debt and Equity Securities,* paragraph 3

Question

1. For a loan that was restructured in a troubled debt restructuring involving a modification of terms, does Statement 115 apply to the accounting by the creditor (that is, investor) if the restructured loan meets the definition of a *security* in Statement 115?

Background

2. Statement 15 specifies the accounting for troubled debt restructurings and has been amended by Statement 114, which has changed a creditor's accounting for troubled debt restructurings involving a modification of terms. However, Statement 114 grandfathered certain previous troubled debt restructurings; that is, it does not require loans restructured prior to its effective date to be retroactively remeasured upon adoption of that Statement. Paragraph 27 of Statement 114 states that "if a loan that was restructured in a troubled debt restructuring involving a modification of terms before the effective date of this Statement is not impaired based on the terms specified by the restructuring agreement, a creditor may continue to account for the loan in accordance with the provisions of Statement 15 prior to its amendment by this Statement." (Although the term *loan* is defined in Statement 114 to encompass both loans that are securities and loans that are not, paragraph 6(d) of Statement 114

excludes all debt securities from the scope of that pronouncement.) Some have perceived an inconsistency between paragraph 27 of Statement 114 and paragraph 3 of Statement 115, which indicates that Statement 115 applies to all investments in debt securities.

Response

3. Statement 115 applies to all loans that meet the definition of a *security* in that Statement. Thus, any loan that was restructured in a troubled debt restructuring involving a modification of terms, including those restructured before the effective date of Statement 114, would be subject to the provisions of Statement 115 if the debt instrument meets the definition of a *security*. Paragraph 137 of Statement 115 defines a *security* as follows:

> A share, participation, or other interest in property or in an enterprise of the issuer or an obligation of the issuer that (a) either is represented by an instrument issued in bearer or registered form or, if not represented by an instrument, is registered in books maintained to record transfers by or on behalf of the issuer, (b) is of a type commonly dealt in on securities exchanges or markets or, when represented by an instrument, is commonly recognized in any area in which it is issued or dealt in as a medium for investment, and (c) either is one of a class or series or by its terms is divisible into a class or series of shares, participations, interests, or obligations.

Effective Date and Transition

4. The provisions of this Technical Bulletin are effective for financial statements issued after April 30, 1994.

The Financial Accounting Standards Board has authorized its staff to prepare FASB Technical Bulletins to provide guidance on certain financial accounting and reporting problems on a timely basis, pursuant to the procedures described in FASB Technical Bulletin No. 79-1 (Revised), *Purpose and Scope of FASB Technical Bulletins and Procedures for Issuance.* The provisions of Technical Bulletins need not be applied to immaterial items.

Appendix

**BACKGROUND INFORMATION AND
CONSIDERATION OF COMMENTS
RECEIVED ON THE PROPOSED
TECHNICAL BULLETIN**

5. The perceived inconsistency between paragraph 27 of Statement 114 and paragraph 3 of Statement 115 was identified during the Board's discussion of the applicability of Statement 115 to "Brady bonds" that were received in a troubled debt restructuring. The phrase *Brady bonds* refers to bonds issued to financial institutions by foreign governments (such as Mexico and Venezuela) under a program designed by Treasury Secretary Nicholas Brady in the late 1980s to help developing countries refinance their debt to those institutions.

6. If Statement 115 were not to apply to a debt security that was restructured in a troubled debt restructuring involving a modification of terms prior to the effective date of Statement 114, then the impairment provisions of neither Statement 114 nor Statement 115 would apply. Instead, the security would be accounted for under the provisions of Statement 15, which do not recognize the relevance of the time value of money or the security's fair value. For example, restructured securities that otherwise would be classified as available-for-sale would be accounted for at amortized cost.

7. Proposed FASB Technical Bulletin No. 94-a, *Application of Statement 115 to Debt Securities Restructured in a Troubled Debt Restructuring,* was released for comment on January 4, 1994. Twelve comment letters were received on the proposed Technical Bulletin. Most of the comment letters expressed support for issuing the Technical Bulletin; a few suggested clarifications, which have been implemented.

(The next page is A-1.)

Appendix A

APPENDIX A

Schedule of AICPA Practice Bulletins, Audit and Accounting Guides, and Statements of Position (SOPs)

This appendix presents a current list (as of June 1, 1994) of AICPA Practice Bulletins, audit and accounting Guides, and Statements of Position other than those that (1) have been extracted by the FASB and issued as Statements of Financial Accounting Standards (FAS) or (2) relate to matters other than accounting. The list excludes those Guides and Statements of Position containing specialized accounting relating to governmental units. The establishment of governmental accounting standards is the responsibility of the Governmental Accounting Standards Board (GASB).

In January 1992 the AICPA issued Statement on Auditing Standards (SAS) No. 69, *The Meaning of "Present Fairly in Conformity With Generally Accepted Accounting Principles" in the Independent Auditor's Report*, which revises the GAAP hierarchy. (AICPA Practice Bulletins, audit and accounting Guides, and Statements of Position are included in categories *(b)* and *(c)* of the revised hierarchy.) SAS 69 *requires* an entity to adopt the accounting principles in pronouncements whose effective date is after March 15, 1992. An entity initially applying an accounting principle after March 15, 1992 (including those making an accounting change) must follow the applicable hierarchy set forth in SAS 69. An entity following an established accounting principle that was effective as of March 15, 1992 need not change its accounting until a new pronouncement on that subject is issued. SAS 69 provides special transition provisions for FASB Emerging Issues Task Force (EITF) consensus positions (category *c*). (Appendix D presents a list of all EITF issues discussed to date and their current status.)

Practice Bulletins

1 *Purpose and Scope of AcSEC Practice Bulletins and Procedures for Their Issuance*, November 1987
2 *Elimination of Profits Resulting from Intercompany Transfers of LIFO Inventories*, November 1987
4 *Accounting for Foreign Debt/Equity Swaps*, May 1988
5 *Income Recognition on Loans to Financially Troubled Countries*, July 1988
6 *Amortization of Discounts on Certain Acquired Loans*, August 1989
7 *Criteria for Determining Whether Collateral for a Loan Has Been In-Substance Foreclosed*, April 1990
8 *Application of FASB Statement No. 97, "Accounting and Reporting by Insurance Enterprises for Certain Long-Duration Contracts and for Realized Gains and Losses from the Sale of Investments," to Insurance Enterprises*, November 1990

9   *Disclosure of Fronting Arrangements by Fronting Companies*, December 1991
10 *Amendment to Practice Bulletin 7, "Criteria for Determining Whether Collateral for a Loan Has Been In-Substance Foreclosed,"* June 1992
11 *Accounting for Preconfirmation Contingencies in Fresh-Start Reporting*, March 1994

Audit and Accounting Guides

[**Note:** The AICPA has issued the Audit and Accounting Guide Loose-Leaf Service that contains all of the audit and accounting Guides, including those listed below. This edition includes certain changes made by the AICPA staff due to the issuance of authoritative pronouncements since the original Guides were issued.]

Audits of Agricultural Producers and Agricultural Cooperatives
Audits of Airlines
Audits of Banks
Audits of Brokers and Dealers in Securities
Audits of Casinos
Audits of Certain Nonprofit Organizations
Audits of Colleges and Universities
Audits of Credit Unions
Audits of Employee Benefit Plans
Audits of Entities with Oil and Gas Producing Activities
Audits of Federal Government Contractors
Audits of Finance Companies (including Independent and Captive Financing Activities of Other Companies)
Audits of Investment Companies
Audits of Property and Liability Insurance Companies
Audits of Providers of Health Care Services
Audits of Savings Institutions
Audits of Voluntary Health and Welfare Organizations
Common Interest Realty Associations
Construction Contractors
Personal Financial Statements Guide

Statements of Position of the Accounting Standards Division

74-8   *Financial Accounting and Reporting by Colleges and Universities*, August 1974
75-2   *Accounting Practices of Real Estate Investment Trusts*, June 1975
78-2   *Accounting Practices of Real Estate Investment Trusts*, May 1978
78-9   *Accounting for Investments in Real Estate Ventures*, December 1978

(The next page is B-1.)

Appendix B

APPENDIX B

Schedule of Amended and Superseded Accounting Pronouncements

The following schedule lists changes in Accounting Research Bulletins (ARB), APB Opinions (APB), AICPA Accounting Interpretations (AIN-ARB or AIN-APB), FASB Statements of Financial Accounting Standards (FAS), FASB Interpretations (FIN), and FASB Technical Bulletins (FTB) that are readily determinable as the result of subsequent pronouncements. It does not address changes that may have been made implicitly by subsequent pronouncements and cannot be directly related to paragraphs in specific prior pronouncements. Refer to Appendix C for the effective dates of all pronouncements.

Changes in Accounting Pronouncements

ARB	Chapter	Paragraph	
43	1A	1	Amended by FAS 111
43	1B		Amended by APB 6
43	2A	3	Amended by APB 20
43	2B		Superseded by APB 9
43	3A	4	Amended by FAS 115
43	3A	6(g)	Amended by APB 21 and FAS 111
43	3A	7	Amended by FAS 78
43	3A	8	Amended by FAS 6
43	3A	10	Amended by APB 6
43	3A	fn4	Superseded by FAS 6
43	3B		Superseded by APB 10
43	5	1-9	Superseded prospectively by APB 17
43	5	5, 6	Amended by APB 9
43	5	7	Amended by APB 6
43	5	8	Amended by APB 9 and FAS 44
43	5	10	Superseded prospectively by APB 16
43	5	10	Amended by FAS 44
43	5	fn1	Superseded by APB 9
43	6		Superseded by FAS 5
43	7A	10	Amended by FAS 111
43	7B	6	Amended by APB 6
43	7C	-	Superseded by ARB 48
43	8		Superseded by APB 9

Appendix B

ARB	Chapter	Paragraph	
43	8	fn1-fn5	Superseded by APB 9
43	9B		Superseded by APB 6
43	9C		Amended by APB 6
43	9C	5	Amended by FAS 96 and FAS 109
43	9C	11-13	Amended by APB 11
43	9C	11-13	Superseded by FAS 96 and FAS 109
43	10A	19	Amended by APB 9 and FAS 111
43	10B		Amended by APB 6
43	10B	15, 17	Amended by APB 9
43	10B		Superseded by APB 11, FAS 96, and FAS 109
43	11B	8	Superseded by APB 11, FAS 96, and FAS 109
43	11B	9	Amended by APB 9 and FAS 111
43	11B	fn3, fn4	Amended by APB 9
43	11B	fn3, fn4	Superseded by FAS 111
43	12	5	Amended by FAS 8 and FAS 52
43	12	7	Superseded by FAS 8 and FAS 52
43	12	8, 9	Superseded by FAS 94
43	12	10-22	Superseded by FAS 8 and FAS 52
43	12	12, 18	Amended by APB 6
43	12	21	Amended by APB 9
43	13A		Superseded by APB 8
43	13B		Amended by APB 25
43	14		Superseded by APB 5
43	15	7	Amended by APB 9
43	15	11	Amended by APB 11
43	15	12	Amended by APB 6
43	15	17	Amended by APB 9
43	15	fn1, fn2	Superseded by APB 26
43	15		Superseded by APB 26
44			Superseded by ARB 44 (Rev.)
44 (Rev.)		3	Amended by APB 20
44 (Rev.)		4, 5, 7	Superseded by APB 11
44 (Rev.)		8	Superseded by FAS 71
44 (Rev.)		9	Superseded by APB 6 and FAS 71
44 (Rev.)		10	Superseded by APB 11
44 (Rev.)			Superseded by FAS 96 and FAS 109

Appendix B

ARB	Chapter	Paragraph	
Letter, Dated April 15, 1959			Superseded by APB 11, FAS 96, and FAS 109
47			Superseded by APB 8
48		5, 6	Amended by APB 6
48		12	Amended by APB 10
48			Superseded by APB 16
49			Superseded by APB 9
50			Superseded by FAS 5
51		2, 3	Superseded by FAS 94
51		6	Amended by FAS 71
51		7, 8	Superseded by APB 16
51		10	Amended by FAS 58
51		16	Superseded by APB 23
51		17	Amended by APB 11
51		17	Superseded by FAS 96
51		17	Reinstated by FAS 109
51		19, 20	Amended by APB 10 and APB 18
51		19-21	Superseded by FAS 94
51		21	Amended by APB 18
51		fn1	Superseded by FAS 111

Appendix B

APB Opinion	Paragraph	
1	1, 5, 6	Amended by APB 11
1	7	Superseded by FAS 71
1	fn1	Amended by APB 11
1		Superseded by FAS 96 and FAS 109
2	13, 17	Amended by APB 4
2	16	Superseded by FAS 109
2	17	Superseded by FAS 71
2	Addendum	Superseded by FAS 71
3		Superseded by APB 19
5	14	Amended by APB 31
5	16-18	Superseded by APB 31
5	20	Amended by APB 31
5	21	Amended by APB 11
5	23	Amended by APB 31
5		Superseded by FAS 13
6	12(c)	Superseded by APB 16
6	15	Superseded by APB 17
6	16	Amended by FAS 111
6	18	Superseded by FAS 8 and FAS 52
6	19	Superseded by APB 26
6	20	Superseded by FAS 71 and FAS 109
6	21	Superseded by APB 11, FAS 96, and FAS 109
6	22	Superseded by APB 16
6	23	Superseded by APB 11, FAS 96, and FAS 109
6	fn7, fn8	Superseded by APB 11, FAS 96, and FAS 109
7	8	Amended by APB 27
7	12	Superseded by APB 27
7		Superseded by FAS 13
8	31	Amended by FAS 74
8	46	Superseded by FAS 36
8		Superseded by FAS 87
9	6	Amended by APB 13
9	17	Amended by APB 30 and FAS 111
9	18	Amended by APB 20 and FAS 16
9	20	Amended by APB 20

APB Opinion	Paragraph	
9	20-22	Superseded by APB 30
9	23, 24	Superseded by FAS 16
9	25	Superseded by APB 20
9	29, Exh. A-D	Superseded by APB 30
9	30-51, Exh. E	Superseded by APB 15
9	fn2	Superseded by APB 30
9	fn6-fn9	Superseded by APB 15
10	2-4	Superseded by APB 18
10	5	Superseded by APB 16
10	8, 9	Amended by APB 12
10	8, 9	Superseded by APB 14
10	11(b)	Amended by FAS 111
10	fn1-fn5	Superseded by APB 18
10	fn6	Superseded by APB 16
11	6	Amended by APB 28, FAS 60, and FAS 71
11	38, 39	Superseded by APB 23
11	40	Superseded by FAS 9
11	41	Superseded by APB 23
11	49	Amended by APB 16
11	57	Amended by FAS 37
11	fn14	Amended by APB 16
11		Superseded by FAS 96 and FAS 109
12	6	Amended by FAS 87 and FAS 106
12	11-15	Superseded by APB 14
12	fn1	Superseded by FAS 106 and FAS 111
12	fn2	Superseded by APB 14
15	5	Amended by FAS 111
15	13	Amended by APB 20 and APB 30
15	33	Amended by FAS 55
15	33	Superseded by FAS 85
15	35	Amended by FAS 85
15	45	Amended by FAS 21
15	fn8	Amended by APB 30
15	fn9, fn10	Superseded by FAS 85
15	fn10	Amended by FAS 55
15	App. C, Exh. B	Amended by FAS 111

Appendix B

APB Opinion	Paragraph	
15	App. D, "Cash Yield"	Superseded by FAS 85
16	6	Superseded by FAS 71
16	87	Amended by FAS 96 and FAS 109
16	88	Amended by FAS 38, FAS 87, FAS 96, FAS 106, and FAS 109
16	89	Superseded by FAS 96 and FAS 109
16	96	Amended by FAS 79
16	99	Amended by FAS 10
16	fn13	Superseded by FAS 87
17	6	Amended by FAS 2
17	7	Superseded by FAS 71
17	29, 30	Amended by FAS 72
17	30	Amended by FAS 96 and FAS 109
17	31	Amended by APB 30 and FAS 72
18	1	Amended by FAS 94
18	14	Superseded by FAS 94
18	15	Superseded by FAS 13
18	16, 17, 19, 19(a)	Amended by FAS 94
18	19(d)	Amended by APB 30
18	19(j)	Superseded by APB 23
18	19(l)	Amended by FAS 115
18	19(m)	Amended by FAS 58
18	20(c)	Superseded by FAS 94
18	20(d)	Amended by FAS 94
18	fn1, fn3, fn4	Superseded by FAS 94
18	fn5	Superseded by FAS 13
18	fn11	Superseded by APB 23
19	10	Amended by APB 30
19		Superseded by FAS 95
20	3	Amended by FAS 71 and FAS 95
20	4, 7, 9, 16	Amended by FAS 111
20	27	Amended by FAS 73
20	34	Amended by FAS 58
20	fn2	Superseded by FAS 111
20	fn4	Amended by FAS 111
20	fn5	Superseded by FAS 32 and FAS 111

APB Opinion	Paragraph	
20	fn9	Superseded by FAS 16
21	15, 16	Amended by FAS 34
21	fn8	Amended by FAS 96 and FAS 109
22	6, 7, 8, 12	Amended by FAS 95
22	13	Amended by FAS 2, FAS 8, and FAS 52
22	fn2	Amended by FAS 111
23	2	Amended by FAS 9
23	4	Superseded by FAS 71
23	9	Amended by FAS 96 and FAS 109
23	10	Amended by FAS 96
23	10	Superseded by FAS 109
23	11	Superseded by FAS 96 and FAS 109
23	13	Amended by FAS 96 and FAS 109
23	14	Superseded by FAS 96 and FAS 109
23	17	Amended by FAS 96
23	21	Amended by FAS 96 and FAS 109
23	23	Amended by FAS 109
23	24	Superseded by FAS 96 and FAS 109
23	26-30	Superseded by FAS 60
23	fn3	Superseded by FAS 109
23	fn4, fn6	Superseded by FAS 96 and FAS 109
23	fn7, fn9	Amended by FAS 96 and FAS 109
23	fn10	Superseded by FAS 96 and FAS 109
23	fn11	Superseded by FAS 60
24	3	Superseded by FAS 71
24		Superseded by FAS 96 and FAS 109
25	17	Amended by FAS 96 and FAS 109
26	2	Amended by FAS 15, FAS 71, and FAS 84
26	2	Superseded by FAS 76
26	3(a)	Amended by FAS 15
26	3(a)	Superseded by FAS 76
26	3(c)	Amended by FAS 76
26	19	Amended by FAS 76
26	20	Amended by APB 30 and FAS 4
26	21	Amended by FAS 76
27		Superseded by FAS 13
28	2	Amended by FAS 95
28	19, 20	Amended by FAS 96 and FAS 109

APB Opinion	Paragraph	
28	27	Superseded by FAS 3
28	31	Amended by FAS 3
28	33	Amended by FAS 95
28	fn2, fn3	Amended by FAS 96 and FAS 109
28	fn5	Superseded by FAS 3
29	4	Amended by FAS 71
29	27	Amended by FAS 96 and FAS 109
30	7	Amended by FAS 96 and FAS 109
30	20	Amended by FAS 4 and FAS 101
30	25	Amended by FAS 16
30	fn8	Amended by FAS 60 and FAS 83
30	fn8	Superseded by FAS 97
31		Superseded by FAS 13

AICPA
Interpretation
of   **No.**

AIN-Key-Man Life	1	Superseded by FTB 85-4
ARB 43, Ch.13B	1	Superseded by APB 25
ARB 51	1	Superseded by FAS 111
APB 4	4	Superseded by FAS 96 and FAS 109
APB 4	5	Superseded by FAS 111
APB 4	6	Superseded by FAS 96 and FAS 109
APB 7	1	Superseded by FAS 111
APB 8		Superseded by FAS 111
APB 9	1	Amended by APB 30
APB 9	2	Superseded by FAS 111
APB 11	4	Amended by FAS 71
APB 11		Superseded by FAS 96 and FAS 109
APB 15	Part I	Amended by FAS 111
APB 15	2	Amended by FAS 111
APB 15	10	Superseded by FAS 111
APB 15	13	Amended by FAS 21
APB 15	13, 16	Superseded by FAS 96 and FAS 109
APB 15	26, 30, 33	Amended by FAS 111
APB 15	34, 35, and fn21	Superseded by FAS 85
APB 15	36, 37	Amended by FAS 85
APB 15	38 and fn22	Superseded by FAS 111
APB 15	56	Amended by FAS 111
APB 15	82 and fn38-fn42	Amended by FIN 31
APB 15	92	Amended by FAS 111
APB 16	15-17, 24, 26	Amended by FAS 10
APB 16	30	Amended by FAS 111
APB 18	1	Amended by FAS 96 and FAS 109
APB 18	2	Amended by FAS 96, FAS 109, and FAS 111
APB 19	1-3	Superseded by FAS 95
APB 22	1	Superseded by FAS 111
APB 23	1	Superseded by FAS 96 and FAS 109
APB 25	1	Amended by FAS 96 and FAS 109
APB 26	1	Amended by FAS 111

Appendix B

Appendix B

FASB Statement	Paragraph	
13	12	Amended by FAS 29 and FAS 34
13	14	Amended by FAS 22
13	16(a)(iv)	Amended by FAS 29
13	17(a)	Amended by FAS 23 and FAS 98
13	17(b)	Amended by FAS 29
13	17(f)	Amended by FAS 22
13	17(f)(ii)	Amended by FAS 27
13	18(a)	Amended by FAS 23 and FAS 91
13	18(a)	Superseded by FAS 98
13	18(b)	Amended by FAS 29 and FAS 91
13	18(b)	Superseded by FAS 98
13	19	Amended by FAS 98
13	20	Amended by FAS 77
13	23(a)(i), (a)(iii)	Superseded by FAS 91
13	25	Amended by FAS 98
13	26(a)	Amended by FAS 98
13	26(a)(i)	Amended by FAS 23
13	26(a)(ii), (b)(i)(b)	Superseded by FAS 98
13	26(b)(ii)(b)	Amended by FAS 98
13	32, 33	Superseded by FAS 28
13	43(c)	Amended by FAS 23
13	47	Amended by FAS 96 and FAS 109
13	fn13	Superseded by FAS 29
14	3	Amended by FAS 95
14	4	Superseded by FAS 18
14	7	Amended by FAS 24 and FAS 95
14	27(c)	Amended by FAS 111
14	39	Superseded by FAS 30
14	41	Amended by FAS 18 and FAS 21
14	73	Superseded by FAS 18
14	fn15	Superseded by FAS 18
15	1	Amended prospectively by FAS 114
15	9	Superseded by FAS 71
15	30-32	Superseded prospectively by FAS 114
15	33-34	Amended prospectively by FAS 114
15	35-37, 40(a), 41	Superseded prospectively by FAS 114
15	42	Amended prospectively by FAS 114

Appendix B

FASB Statement	Paragraph	
15	fn18-fn19	Superseded prospectively by FAS 114
15	fn20	Superseded by FAS 111
15	fn21, fn24-fn25	Superseded prospectively by FAS 114
15	fn26	Amended by FAS 111
16	9	Superseded by FAS 71
16	11	Superseded by FAS 96 and FAS 109
16	13	Amended by FAS 96 and FAS 109
16	fn3, fn4	Amended by FAS 96 and FAS 109
16	fn5	Superseded by FAS 96 and FAS 109
17		Superseded by FAS 91
19	9	Superseded by FAS 71
19	48	Amended by FAS 25†
19	48-59	Superseded by FAS 69
19	61, 62	Amended by FAS 96 and FAS 109
19	63	Amended by FAS 25
19	271	Superseded by FAS 25
19	fn11, fn12	Superseded by FAS 25
20		Superseded by FAS 52
21	fn4	Amended by FAS 95
22	11	Superseded by FAS 71
22	fn1	Superseded by FAS 76
24	1, 5	Amended by FAS 95
24	fn2	Amended by FAS 95
25	6, 8	Superseded by FAS 111
26	7	Amended by FAS 66
26		Superseded by FAS 98
28	3, 23-25	Amended by FAS 66
29	13	Amended by FAS 98
31		Superseded by FAS 96 and FAS 109
32	App. A	Amended by FAS 45, FAS 48, FAS 49, FAS 50, FAS 51, FAS 53, FAS 56, FAS 60, FAS 63, FAS 65, FAS 66, FAS 67, FAS 76, FAS 77, and FAS 83
32	App. B	Amended by FAS 56, FAS 60, and FAS 67
32	App. B	Superseded by FAS 83
32		Superseded by FAS 111

†The effective date of certain paragraphs of FASB Statement 19 is suspended by FASB Statement 25 insofar as they pertain to a required form of successful efforts accounting.

FASB
Statement   **Paragraph**

33	22	Amended by FAS 70
33	22(c)	Superseded by FAS 70
33	23	Amended by FAS 54
33	29(a)	Amended by FAS 70
33	29(a)	Superseded by FAS 82
33	30(a-c)	Amended by FAS 39
33	30, 31	Amended by FAS 70
33	31, 33	Amended by FAS 82
33	34, 35	Amended by FAS 70
33	35(b)	Superseded by FAS 82
33	35(c)	Amended by FAS 39
33	36, 39	Amended by FAS 70
33	40	Amended by FAS 82
33	41	Amended by FAS 70
33	42-46	Amended by FAS 82
33	50	Amended by FAS 70
33	51(b)	Superseded by FAS 39 and FAS 69
33	52	Amended by FAS 39
33	52(b)	Superseded by FAS 39 and FAS 69
33	53	Superseded by FAS 39, FAS 40, and FAS 41
33	53	Amended by FAS 46 and FAS 70
33	53(a)	Superseded by FAS 69
33	56, 59, 66	Amended by FAS 70
33	66(a), 70, 224, 225, 227, 229, 239, 240	Amended by FAS 82
33		Superseded by FAS 89
34	5	Superseded by FAS 71
34	8, 9	Amended by FAS 42
34	9, 10	Amended by FAS 58
34	10, 13, 17	Amended by FAS 62
34	20	Amended by FAS 58
35	11	Amended by FAS 110
35	12	Superseded by FAS 110
35	30	Amended by FAS 59 and FAS 75
35	fn6	Superseded by FAS 110
36	8	Amended by FAS 95
36		Superseded by FAS 87

Appendix B

<table>
<tr><td>FASB
Statement</td><td>Paragraph</td><td></td></tr>
<tr><td>37</td><td></td><td>Superseded by FAS 96 and reinstated
by FAS 109</td></tr>
<tr><td>37</td><td>4, 17, 18, 26-29</td><td>Superseded by FAS 109</td></tr>
<tr><td>37</td><td>19-25</td><td>Amended by FAS 109</td></tr>
<tr><td>37</td><td>fn1-fn3, fn(*)
of par. 4</td><td>Superseded by FAS 109</td></tr>
<tr><td>38</td><td>2</td><td>Amended by FAS 96 and FAS 109</td></tr>
<tr><td>38</td><td>5</td><td>Amended by FAS 109</td></tr>
<tr><td>38</td><td>fn2</td><td>Amended by FAS 96</td></tr>
<tr><td>38</td><td>fn2</td><td>Superseded by FAS 109</td></tr>
<tr><td>39</td><td>10-12</td><td>Superseded by FAS 69</td></tr>
<tr><td>39</td><td>12</td><td>Superseded by FAS 40 and FAS 41</td></tr>
<tr><td>39</td><td>12</td><td>Amended by FAS 46</td></tr>
<tr><td>39</td><td></td><td>Superseded by FAS 89</td></tr>
<tr><td>40</td><td>6</td><td>Superseded by FAS 41 and FAS 69</td></tr>
<tr><td>40</td><td>6</td><td>Amended by FAS 46</td></tr>
<tr><td>40</td><td></td><td>Superseded by FAS 89</td></tr>
<tr><td>41</td><td>7</td><td>Amended by FAS 46</td></tr>
<tr><td>41</td><td>7</td><td>Superseded by FAS 69</td></tr>
<tr><td>41</td><td></td><td>Superseded by FAS 89</td></tr>
<tr><td>43</td><td>1</td><td>Amended by FAS 112</td></tr>
<tr><td>43</td><td>2</td><td>Superseded by FAS 112</td></tr>
<tr><td>43</td><td>3</td><td>Superseded by FAS 71</td></tr>
<tr><td>44</td><td>6</td><td>Amended by FAS 96 and FAS 109</td></tr>
<tr><td>46</td><td>8</td><td>Superseded by FAS 69</td></tr>
<tr><td>46</td><td></td><td>Superseded by FAS 89</td></tr>
<tr><td>49</td><td>7</td><td>Superseded by FAS 71</td></tr>
<tr><td>51</td><td>2</td><td>Superseded by FAS 71</td></tr>
<tr><td>52</td><td>22-24, 48</td><td>Amended by FAS 96 and FAS 109</td></tr>
<tr><td>54</td><td></td><td>Superseded by FAS 89</td></tr>
<tr><td>55</td><td></td><td>Superseded by FAS 111</td></tr>
<tr><td>56</td><td></td><td>Superseded by FAS 111</td></tr>
<tr><td>57</td><td>2</td><td>Amended by FAS 96 and FAS 109</td></tr>
<tr><td>57</td><td>fn2</td><td>Amended by FAS 95</td></tr>
<tr><td>59</td><td></td><td>Superseded by FAS 75</td></tr>
<tr><td>60</td><td>6</td><td>Amended by FAS 97</td></tr>
<tr><td>60</td><td>15</td><td>Superseded by FAS 97</td></tr>
<tr><td>60</td><td>38-40</td><td>Superseded by FAS 113</td></tr>
</table>

FASB Statement	Paragraph	
60	45-46	Superseded by FAS 115
60	47	Amended by FAS 114
60	49	Superseded by FAS 91
60	50	Amended by FAS 97 and FAS 115
60	51	Amended by FAS 115
60	55-58	Superseded by FAS 96 and FAS 109
60	59	Amended by FAS 109
60	60(f)	Superseded by FAS 113
60	60(i), 60(j)	Superseded by FAS 96 and FAS 109
60	fn7	Superseded by FAS 115
60	fn8	Superseded by FAS 96 and FAS 109
65	4-5	Amended by FAS 115
65	6	Amended by FAS 91 and FAS 115
65	7-8, 9(a), 9(c), 12	Amended by FAS 115
65	14	Superseded by FAS 91
65	17	Amended by FAS 115
65	21	Superseded by FAS 91
65	23	Amended by FAS 91
65	25-26	Superseded by FAS 91
65	28-29	Amended by FAS 115
65	fn2, fn7	Superseded by FAS 91
66	40	Superseded by FAS 98
66	fn34	Amended by FAS 98
67	2(b)	Amended by FAS 111
67	fn10	Amended by FAS 111
69	7, 8	Amended by FAS 95
69	26, 30(c)	Amended by FAS 96 and FAS 109
69	35-38	Superseded by FAS 89
69	40	Amended by FAS 96 and FAS 109
69	41	Amended by FAS 95, FAS 96, and FAS 109
69	fn3	Amended by FAS 95
69	fn10	Superseded by FAS 89
70	7, 8	Amended by FAS 82
70		Superseded by FAS 89
71	9	Amended by FAS 90 and FAS 92
71	10	Amended by FAS 90
71	13	Superseded by FAS 90 and FAS 92

Appendix B

FASB Statement	Paragraph	
71	14	Superseded by FAS 92
71	15	Amended by FAS 90
71	18	Superseded by FAS 96 and FAS 109
71	34	Amended by FAS 90
71	46	Amended by FAS 96 and FAS 109
71	fn6	Superseded by FAS 90
71	fn12	Superseded by FAS 96 and FAS 109
74		Superseded by FAS 88
76	7	Amended by FAS 111
77	9	Amended by FAS 105
80	5	Amended by FAS 115
81		Superseded by FAS 106
82		Superseded by FAS 89
83		Superseded by FAS 111
87	8	Amended by FAS 106
87	37	Amended by FAS 96 and FAS 109
87	fn3	Superseded by FAS 106
89	33, 96	Amended by FAS 96 and FAS 109
90	9(d)	Superseded by FAS 92
90	14	Amended by FAS 96 and FAS 109
90	16-25	Superseded by FTB 87-2
90	27	Amended by FAS 96 and FAS 109
91	3	Amended by FAS 115
91	14	Amended by FAS 114
91	25(a-c)	Superseded by FAS 98
91	27(a)	Amended by FAS 115
93	7	Amended by FAS 99
95	3	Amended by FAS 102 and FAS 117
95	13	Amended by FAS 104
95	15, 16(a), 16(b), 17(a), 17(b)	Amended by FAS 102
95	18-19	Amended by FAS 117
95	22(a), 23(a)	Amended by FAS 102
95	27(b), 28-30, 32, 130	Amended by FAS 117
95	147-148, 149(a)	Amended by FAS 102

FASB
Interpretation   **Paragraph**

95	fn4	Superseded by FAS 104
95	fn12	Amended by FAS 117
96	32	Amended by FAS 100, FAS 103, and FAS 108
96		Superseded by FAS 109
97	27	Superseded by FAS 113
97	28	Amended by FAS 115
100		Superseded by FAS 103, FAS 108, and FAS 109
101	19	Amended by FAS 109
102	8, fn4	Amended by FAS 115
103		Superseded by FAS 108 and FAS 109
105	6 and fn2-fn3	Amended by FAS 107
105	14(c)	Amended by FAS 111
107	8(a)	Amended by FAS 112
108		Superseded by FAS 109
109	36(b)	Amended by FAS 115

FASB Interpretation	Paragraph	
2		Superseded by FAS 15
3		Superseded by FAS 87
5		Superseded by FAS 7
6	3, 6, 8	Amended by FAS 86
6	7, 9	Superseded by FAS 86
9	8, 9	Amended by FAS 72
10		Superseded by FAS 83
11		Superseded by FAS 115
12		Superseded by FAS 115
13		Superseded by FAS 115
15	2, 4	Amended by FAS 60
15		Superseded by FAS 52
16		Superseded by FAS 115
17		Superseded by FAS 52
18	4	Superseded by FAS 71
18	6	Amended by FAS 96 and FAS 109
18	8	Amended by FAS 109
18	14	Superseded by FAS 96 and FAS 109
18	15	Amended by FAS 96
18	15	Superseded by FAS 109
18	16, 18	Amended by FAS 96 and FAS 109
18	20, 23	Superseded by FAS 96 and FAS 109
18	40-43, 46-55, 58	Amended by FAS 96 and FAS 109
18	59-61	Superseded by FAS 96 and FAS 109
18	65, 66, 68	Amended by FAS 96 and FAS 109
18	70	Superseded by FAS 96 and FAS 109
18	fn2	Amended by FAS 96 and FAS 109
18	fn5	Superseded by FAS 111
18	fn9-fn14, fn18, fn21-fn23, fn25	Superseded by FAS 96 and FAS 109
18	fn19, fn(*) of par. 47	Amended by FAS 96 and FAS 109
20	5	Amended by FAS 111
22	7	Amended by FAS 60
22	8	Superseded by FAS 71

FASB

Interpretation	Paragraph	
22		Superseded by FAS 96 and FAS 109
25	9	Superseded by FAS 71
25	fn5	Superseded by FIN 32
25		Superseded by FAS 96 and FAS 109
28	6	Amended by FIN 31
29		Superseded by FAS 96 and FAS 109
30	5	Amended by FAS 96 and FAS 109
31	fn1	Amended by FAS 96 and FAS 109
32		Superseded by FAS 96 and FAS 109
39	7	Amended by FAS 113
40	4-5	Amended by FAS 115

Appendix B

FASB
Concepts   **Paragraph**

2	4 and fn2	Superseded by CON 6
3		Superseded by CON 6

(The next page is C-1.)

Appendix C

APPENDIX C

Effective Dates of Pronouncements

This appendix lists effective dates of FASB Statements of Financial Accounting Standards (FAS), FASB Interpretations (FIN), certain FASB Technical Bulletins (FTB), APB Opinions (APB), and Accounting Research Bulletins (ARB), and the issue dates of AICPA Accounting Interpretations (AIN) and certain FASB Technical Bulletins.

Only the *principal* effective date is listed below. In many cases the provisions relating to the effective date are complex. Most pronouncements could be applied earlier than the date listed because application earlier than the effective date is usually encouraged. Any questions regarding effective dates should be resolved by referring to the effective date and transition provisions of the original pronouncement. For the convenience of the reader, the appendix presents the transition paragraphs of more recent pronouncements whose effective dates and transition provisions are such that they might be initially applied in annual financial statements issued on or after June 1, 1994.

Pronounce-ment	Effective Date
ARB	
43	June 1953 (replaced ARBs issued September 1939–January 1953)
44	October 1954
44 Rev.	July 1958
45	October 1955
46	February 1956
47	September 1956
48	January 1957
49	April 1958
50	October 1958
51	August 1959
APB	
1	November 1962
2	December 1962
3	October 1963
4	March 1964

Pronounce-ment	Effective Date

APB

5	September 1964
6	For fiscal periods beginning after December 31, 1965
7	For fiscal periods beginning after December 31, 1966
8	For fiscal periods beginning after December 31, 1966
9	For fiscal periods beginning after December 31, 1966
10	For fiscal periods beginning after December 31, 1966
11	For fiscal periods beginning after December 31, 1967
12	For fiscal periods beginning after December 31, 1967
13	For fiscal periods beginning after December 31, 1968
14	For fiscal periods beginning after December 31, 1966
15	For fiscal periods beginning after December 31, 1968
16	For business combinations initiated after October 31, 1970
17	For intangible assets acquired after October 31, 1970
18	For fiscal periods beginning after December 31, 1971
19	For fiscal periods ending after September 30, 1971
20	For fiscal years beginning after July 31, 1971
21	For transactions on or after October 1, 1971
22	For fiscal years beginning after December 31, 1971
23	For fiscal periods beginning after December 31, 1971
24	For fiscal periods beginning after December 31, 1971
25	For awards granted after December 31, 1972
26	For transactions on or after January 1, 1973
27	For transactions after December 31, 1972
28	For interim periods relating to fiscal years beginning after December 31, 1973
29	For transactions after September 30, 1973
30	For events and transactions after September 30, 1973
31	For fiscal periods ending on or after December 31, 1973

AIN-ARB

AIN (Key-Man Life Insurance)		November 1970
43	AIN #1	March 1971
51	AIN #1	February 1972

Pronouncement	Effective Date	
AIN-APB		
4	AIN #1	February 1972
	AIN #2 through 6	March 1972
7	AIN #1	November 1971
8	AIN (all)	1968
9	AIN #1	February 1971
	AIN #2	April 1971
11	AIN #1	July 1970
	AIN #2 through 23	1969
	AIN #24 and 25	March 1972
15	AIN #1 through 101	July 1970
	AIN #102	September 1971
16	AIN #1 through 7	December 1970
	AIN #8 through 17	April 1971
	AIN #18 through 23	September 1971
	AIN #24 and 25	November 1971
	AIN #26 through 33	December 1971
	AIN #34 and 35	January 1972
	AIN #36	Effective for combinations consummated after May 31, 1972
	AIN #37	November 1972
	AIN #38 and 39	March 1973
17	AIN #1	April 1971
	AIN #2	March 1973
18	AIN #1 and 2	November 1971
	AIN #3	February 1972
19	AIN #1 and 2	February 1972
	AIN #3	June 1972
20	AIN #1 and 2	March 1973
21	AIN #1	June 1972
22	AIN #1	November 1973
23	AIN #1	March 1973
25	AIN #1	June 1973
26	AIN #1	March 1973
30	AIN #1	November 1973

Pronounce-ment	Effective Date

FAS

1	For fiscal periods ending after November 30, 1973
2	For fiscal years beginning on or after January 1, 1975
3	For interim periods ending on or after December 31, 1974
4	For extinguishments after March 31, 1975
5	For fiscal years beginning on or after July 1, 1975
6	For fiscal periods ending on or after December 31, 1975
7	For fiscal periods beginning on or after January 1, 1976
8	For fiscal years beginning on or after January 1, 1976
9	For financial statements issued on or after December 1, 1975
10	November 1, 1975
11	For fiscal years beginning on or after July 1, 1975
12	For fiscal periods ending on or after December 31, 1975
13	For leasing transactions and revisions entered into on or after January 1, 1977
14	For fiscal years beginning after December 15, 1976 and interim periods within those years (but amended by FAS18, FAS21, and FAS24)
15	For troubled debt restructurings consummated after December 31, 1977
16	For fiscal years beginning after October 15, 1977
17	For leasing transactions and revisions entered into on or after January 1, 1978
18	December 1, 1977, retroactive to effective date of FAS14
19	For fiscal years beginning after December 15, 1978 and interim periods within those years (but amended by FAS25)
20	January 1, 1978
21	April 30, 1978, retroactive to fiscal years beginning after December 15, 1976
22	For lease agreement revisions entered into on or after July 1, 1978
23	For leasing transactions and revisions recorded as of December 1, 1978
24	January 1, 1979, retroactive to fiscal years beginning after December 15, 1976
25	For fiscal years beginning after December 15, 1978
26	For leasing transactions and revisions recorded as of August 1, 1979

Pronounce-ment	Effective Date

FAS

27	For lease agreement renewals and extensions recorded as of September 1, 1979
28	For leasing transactions and revisions recorded as of September 1, 1979
29	For leasing transactions and revisions recorded as of October 1, 1979
30	For fiscal years beginning after December 15, 1979
31	For annual or interim financial statements issued after September 30, 1979 for periods ending on or after July 26, 1979
32	October 31, 1979
33	For fiscal years ending on or after December 25, 1979
34	For fiscal years beginning after December 15, 1979
35	For plan years beginning after December 15, 1980 (but deferred indefinitely by FAS75 for plans sponsored by state or local governments)
36	For fiscal years beginning after December 15, 1979 and for complete interim statements issued after June 30, 1980 for interim periods within those fiscal years
37	For periods ending after December 15, 1980
38	For business combinations initiated after December 15, 1980
39	For fiscal years ending on or after December 25, 1980
40	For fiscal years ending on or after December 25, 1980
41	For fiscal years ending on or after December 25, 1980
42	For fiscal years beginning after December 15, 1979, unless enterprise had already adopted FAS34; if so, effective for fiscal years beginning after October 15, 1980
43	For fiscal years beginning after December 15, 1980
44	December 19, 1980 for financial statements for fiscal periods ending after December 15, 1980
45	For fiscal years beginning after June 15, 1981
46	For fiscal years ending on or after March 31, 1981
47	For fiscal years ending after June 15, 1981
48	For fiscal years beginning after June 15, 1981
49	For product financing arrangements entered into after June 15, 1981
50	For fiscal years beginning after December 15, 1981

Appendix C

Pronounce-ment	Effective Date
FAS	
51	For fiscal years beginning after December 15, 1981
52	For fiscal years beginning on or after December 15, 1982
53	For fiscal years beginning after December 15, 1981
54	January 27, 1982, retroactive to fiscal years ending on or after December 25, 1979
55	For convertible securities issued after February 28, 1982
56	For fiscal years beginning after December 31, 1981
57	For fiscal years ending after June 15, 1982
58	For investments made after June 30, 1982 but optional for investments contracted for but not yet made at that date
59	April 1982, retroactive to fiscal years beginning after December 15, 1980
60	For fiscal years beginning after December 15, 1982
61	For fiscal years beginning after December 15, 1982
62	For tax-exempt borrowing arrangements entered into and gifts or grants received after August 31, 1982
63	For fiscal years beginning after December 15, 1982
64	For extinguishments of debt occurring after September 30, 1982
65	For transactions entered into after December 31, 1982
66	For real estate sales transactions entered into after December 31, 1982
67	For costs of real estate incurred in fiscal years beginning after December 31, 1982
68	For research and development arrangements entered into after December 31, 1982
69	For fiscal years beginning on or after December 15, 1982
70	For fiscal years ending after December 15, 1982 for which an enterprise has applied FAS52
71	For fiscal years beginning after December 15, 1983
72	For business combinations initiated after September 30, 1982
73	For changes from retirement-replacement-betterment accounting to depreciation accounting made after June 30, 1983
74	For special termination benefits offered after June 30, 1983
75	November 1983, retroactive to fiscal years beginning after December 15, 1980
76	For transactions entered into after December 31, 1983

Appendix C

Pronounce-ment	Effective Date
FAS	

77   For transfers of receivables with recourse after December 31, 1983

78   For financial statements for fiscal years beginning after
        December 15, 1983 and for interim accounting periods within
        those fiscal years

79   For financial statements for fiscal years beginning after
        December 15, 1983

80   For futures contracts entered into after December 15, 1984

81   For financial statements issued for periods ending after
        December 15, 1984

82   For fiscal years ending on or after December 15, 1984

83   March 31, 1985

84   For conversions of convertible debt pursuant to inducements·
        offered after March 31, 1985

85   For convertible securities issued after March 31, 1985

86   For financial statements for fiscal years beginning after
        December 15, 1985

87   For fiscal years beginning after December 15, 1986

88   For events occurring in fiscal years beginning with the
        fiscal year in which FAS87 is first applied

89   For financial reports issued after December 2, 1986

90   For fiscal years beginning after December 15, 1987 and
        interim periods within those fiscal years

91   For lending and leasing transactions entered into and
        commitments granted in fiscal years beginning after
        December 15, 1987 and interim periods within those
        fiscal years

92   For fiscal years beginning after December 15, 1987 and interim
        periods within those fiscal years

93   For fiscal years beginning after May 15, 1988 (but amended by
        FAS99 to fiscal years beginning on or after January 1, 1990)

94   For fiscal years ending after December 15, 1988

95   For fiscal years ending after July 15, 1988

96   For fiscal years beginning after December 15, 1988 (but amended
        by FAS108 to allow initial application up to fiscal years
        beginning after December 15, 1992; at that time FAS96 is
        superseded by FAS109)

Appendix C

Pronounce- ment	Effective Date
FAS	
97	For fiscal years beginning after December 15, 1988
98	For transactions entered into after June 30, 1988
99	September 1988
100	December 15, 1988
101	For discontinuations of application of Statement 71 occurring in fiscal years ending after December 15, 1988
102	For financial statements issued after February 28, 1989
103	December 15, 1989
104	For fiscal years ending after June 15, 1990
105	For fiscal years ending after June 15, 1990
106	For fiscal years beginning after December 15, 1992
107	For fiscal years ending after December 15, 1992
108	December 16, 1991
109	For fiscal years beginning after December 15, 1992
110	For fiscal years beginning after December 15, 1992
111	November 30, 1992
112	For fiscal years beginning after December 15, 1993
113	For fiscal years beginning after December 15, 1992
114	For fiscal years beginning after December 15, 1994
115	For fiscal years beginning after December 15, 1993
116	For fiscal years beginning after December 15, 1994
117	For fiscal years beginning after December 15, 1994

Pronounce-ment	Effective Date

FIN

1	July 1, 1974
2	For transactions after June 30, 1974
3	December 31, 1974
4	For business combinations initiated after March 31, 1975
5	March 31, 1975 for fiscal periods beginning on or after January 1, 1975
6	For fiscal years beginning on or after April 1, 1975
7	For fiscal periods beginning on or after January 1, 1976
8	For balance sheets and statements of changes in financial position dated on or after February 29, 1976
9	For business combinations initiated on or after March 1, 1976
10	For annual and interim periods ending after October 15, 1976
11	For annual and interim periods ending after October 15, 1976
12	For annual and interim periods ending after October 15, 1976
13	For annual and interim periods ending after October 15, 1976
14	For annual and interim periods beginning after October 15, 1976
15	For annual and interim periods ending after December 15, 1976
16	For annual and interim periods ending after March 15, 1977
17	For annual and interim periods ending after March 15, 1977
18	For financial statements issued after March 31, 1977 for interim periods beginning after December 15, 1976
19	For leasing transactions and revisions entered into on or after January 1, 1978
20	December 1, 1977
21	For business combinations initiated on or after May 1, 1978
22	For timing differences occurring in fiscal years beginning after June 15, 1978
23	For leasing transactions and revisions recorded as of December 1, 1978
24	For leasing transactions and revisions recorded as of December 1, 1978
25	Prospectively for fiscal years beginning after December 15, 1978
26	For purchases of leased property recorded as of December 1, 1978
27	For transactions with measurement dates on or after March 1, 1979
28	For awards granted in fiscal years beginning after December 15, 1978

Appendix C

Pronouncement	Effective Date
FIN	
29	For dispositions of investments occurring after March 31, 1979
30	For fiscal years beginning after November 15, 1979
31	For fiscal years beginning after December 15, 1979
32	For fiscal years beginning after December 15, 1979
33	For fiscal years beginning after December 15, 1979 and for interim periods within those years
34	For fiscal years ending after June 15, 1981
35	For fiscal years beginning after June 15, 1981
36	For fiscal years beginning after December 15, 1981 and for interim periods within those years
37	For sale of part of an investment after June 30, 1983
38	For grants made to employees on or after March 14, 1984 under stock option, purchase, and award plans involving junior stock
39	For financial statements issued for periods beginning after December 15, 1993
40	For fiscal years beginning after December 15, 1994. Disclosure provisions effective for fiscal years beginning after December 15, 1992.

Pronounce-ment	Effective Date
FTB*	
79-1 through 79-19	December 28, 1979
79-1 Rev.	June 29, 1984
79-16 Rev.	February 29, 1980
80-1 and 80-2	December 19, 1980
81-1 through 81-5	February 6, 1981
81-6	November 30, 1981
82-1	January 27, 1982
82-2	March 31, 1982
83-1	July 26, 1983
84-1	March 15, 1984
84-2	For financial statements issued after September 30, 1984 for fiscal years ending after July 18, 1984 and for interim periods within such years
84-3	For financial statements issued after September 30, 1984 for fiscal years ending after July 18, 1984 and for interim periods within such years
84-4	For debt incurred on or after September 12, 1984
85-1	For financial statements issued after March 31, 1985 for fiscal years ending after December 1, 1984, and for interim periods within such years
85-2	For collateralized mortgage obligations issued after March 31, 1985
85-3	For leasing transactions entered into after November 14, 1985
85-4	For insurance policies acquired after November 14, 1985
85-5	Paragraph 2 effective for transactions consummated after June 5, 1985. Other provisions effective for business combinations initiated after December 31, 1985
85-6	For transactions after December 31, 1985
86-1	October 22, 1986 for interim and annual periods ending on or after January 1, 1986
86-2	December 17, 1986 for transactions entered into on or after June 18, 1986

---

*Note: Technical Bulletins (FTB) 79-1 through 84-1 have no stated effective date; the date indicated is the date issued.

Pronounce-ment	Effective Date

FTB*

87-1	For fiscal years beginning after December 15, 1986
87-2	For fiscal years beginning after December 15, 1987 for all losses on abandonments recognized in accordance with Statement 90
87-3	For transactions entered into on or after December 31, 1987
88-1	For transactions entered into after December 31, 1988
88-2	For transactions entered into after December 31, 1988
90-1	For contracts sold in fiscal years beginning after December 15, 1990
94-1	For financial statements issued after April 30, 1994

---

*Note: Technical Bulletins (FTB) 79-1 through 84-1 have no stated effective date; the date indicated is the date issued.

Appendix C

Effective Dates and Transition Provisions of Pronouncements That Might Initially Be Applied in Financial Statements Issued on or after June 1, 1994

Listed below are the transition paragraphs of more recent pronouncements whose effective dates and transitions are such that they might initially be applied in annual financial statements issued on or after June 1, 1994.

FAS106: Employers' Accounting for Postretirement Benefits Other Than Pensions

Except as noted in the following sentences of this paragraph and in paragraphs 114 and 115, this Statement shall be effective for fiscal years beginning after December 15, 1992. For plans outside the United States and for defined benefit plans of employers that (a) are nonpublic enterprises and (b) sponsor defined benefit postretirement plan(s) with no more than 500 plan participants in the aggregate, this Statement shall be effective for fiscal years beginning after December 15, 1994. Earlier application is encouraged. Restatement of previously issued annual financial statements is not permitted. If a decision is made in other than the first interim period of an employer's fiscal year to apply this Statement early, previous interim periods of that year shall be restated. [FAS106, ¶108]

If at the transition date an employer has excluded assets in a postretirement benefit fund from its statement of financial position and some or all of the assets in that fund do not qualify as plan assets as defined herein, the employer shall recognize in the statement of financial position the fair value of those nonqualifying assets as the employer's assets (not prepaid postretirement benefit cost) and an equal amount as an accrued postretirement benefit obligation pursuant to the transition to this Statement and before applying paragraph 110. Thereafter, those assets shall be accounted for in accordance with generally accepted accounting principles applicable to those types of assets, including their presentation in the employer's statement of financial position based on any restrictions on their use. The fair value of those assets at the transition date shall be used as their cost. [FAS106, ¶109]

For a defined benefit plan, an employer shall determine as of the measurement date (paragraph 72) for the beginning of the fiscal year in which this Statement is first applied (the transition date), the amounts of (a) the accumulated postretirement benefit obligation and (b) the fair value of plan assets plus any recognized accrued postretirement benefit cost or less any recognized prepaid postretirement benefit cost. The difference between those two amounts, whether it represents a transition obligation or a transition asset, may be recognized either immediately in net income of the period of the change (paragraph 111) as the effect of a change in accounting principle,[31] or on a delayed basis (paragraph 112) as a component of net periodic postretirement benefit cost. Any transition obligation related to a defined contribution plan shall be recognized in the same manner. A single method of transition shall be elected at the date this Statement is initially applied for all defined benefit and defined contribution postretirement plans. [FAS106, ¶110]

If immediate recognition of the transition obligation or asset is elected, the amount attributable to the effects of a plan initiation or any benefit improvements adopted after December 21, 1990 shall be treated as unrecognized prior service cost and excluded from the transition amount immediately recognized. In addition, an employer who chooses to immediately recognize the transition obligation or asset shall, at the date of transition, adjust as necessary the accounting for purchase business combinations consummated subsequent to December 21, 1990 to include in the assignment of the purchase price to assets acquired and liabilities assumed, recognition of the difference between the accumulated postretirement benefit obligation and the fair value of the plan assets, as described in paragraphs 87 and 88. If reliable information on which to base measurement of the assumed postretirement benefit obligation as of the date the business combination is consummated is not available, the purchaser shall retroactively adjust the purchase price allocation to recognize the obligation assumed or the asset acquired, using the best information available at the date of transition to this Statement. The cumulative effect on prior periods' income of that retroactive adjustment of the purchase price allocation, for example, increased amortization of goodwill associated with the business combination, and the amortization of prior service cost related to a plan initiation or amendment adopted after December 21, 1990, shall be recognized as part of the effect of the accounting change to adopt this Statement. [FAS106, ¶111]

If delayed recognition is elected, the transition obligation or asset shall be amortized on a straight-line basis over the average remaining service period of active plan participants, except that (a) if the average remaining service period is less than 20 years, the employer may elect to use a 20-year period, and (b) if all or almost all of the plan participants are inactive, the employer shall use the average remaining life expectancy period of those plan participants. [FAS106, ¶112]

Paragraph 6 and the related footnote of APB Opinion No. 12, *Omnibus Opinion—1967,* are amended effective for fiscal years beginning after March 15, 1991. The effect of the amendment on existing individual deferred compensation contracts, other than those providing postretirement health or welfare benefits, shall be recognized as the effect of a change in accounting principle in accordance with paragraphs 17-21 of APB Opinion No. 20, *Accounting Changes.* Individual de-

---

[31]The effect of the accounting change and the related income tax effect shall be presented in the statement of income between the captions "extraordinary items" and "net income." The per share information presented on the statement of income shall include the per share effect of the accounting change. [FAS106, ¶110, fn31]

ferred compensation contracts that provide postretirement health or welfare benefits shall be subject to the general transition provisions and effective dates of this Statement. [FAS106, ¶114]

Effective with the issuance of this Statement, FASB Technical Bulletin No. 87-1, *Accounting for a Change in Method of Accounting for Certain Postretirement Benefits,* is rescinded. If a change in method of accounting for postretirement benefits is adopted subsequent to the issuance of this Statement, the new method shall comply with the provisions of this Statement. [FAS106, ¶115]

Illustrations

This Statement provides two options for recognizing the transition obligation or asset in the statement of financial position and in the statement of income. An employer can phase in recognition of the transition obligation (asset) over future periods, as illustrated in Case 3A (paragraphs 432-434). [FAS106, ¶430]

Alternatively, an employer can recognize the transition obligation (asset) immediately in net income of the period of the change. However, if immediate recognition is elected, the amount attributable to the effects of a plan initiation or any benefit improvements adopted after December 21, 1990 is treated as prior service cost and excluded from the transition amount immediately recognized. In addition, an employer who chooses to immediately recognize its transition obligation shall, in accounting for any purchase business combination consummated after December 21, 1990, include in the purchase price allocation the unfunded accumulated postretirement benefit obligation assumed (paragraph 111). Case 3C (paragraphs 443-448) illustrates a situation in which those limitations apply. [FAS106, ¶431]

Case 3A—Measuring the Transition Obligation and Delayed Recognition

Company C adopts this Statement for its financial statements for the year beginning January 1, 1993. Prior to adopting this Statement, Company C accrued postretirement benefit costs and made contributions to the plan to the extent those contributions were tax deductible. At January 1, 1993, the company had accrued postretirement benefit cost of $150,000 and plan assets of $180,000. [FAS106, ¶432]

The transition obligation or asset is measured as the difference between (a) the accumulated postretirement benefit obligation and (b) the fair value of plan assets plus any recognized accrued postretirement benefit cost or less any recognized prepaid postretirement benefit cost as of the date of transition (paragraph 110). Company C's transition obligation is determined as follows:

Accumulated postretirement benefit obligation	$(465,000)
Plan assets at fair value	180,000
Accumulated postretirement benefit obligation in excess of plan assets	(285,000)
Accrued postretirement benefit cost	150,000
Transition obligation	$(135,000)

[FAS106, ¶433]

Company C elects to delay recognition of its transition obligation. Paragraph 112 permits straight-line amortization of the transition obligation or asset over the average remaining service period of plan participants or 20 years, if longer. Company C estimates the average remaining service period of its active employees who are plan participants at the date of transition to be 10 years. Therefore, Company C can elect to amortize its transition obligation of $135,000 on a straight-line basis over either the average remaining service period of 10 years or 20 years. That amortization (either $13,500 for 10 years or $6,750 for 20 years) is included as a component of net periodic postretirement benefit cost. However, amortization of the transition obligation is accelerated when the constraint on delayed recognition described in paragraph 112 applies. (Refer to Case 3B, paragraphs 435-442.) [FAS106, ¶434]

Case 3C—Limitation on Immediate Recognition of Transition Obligation

Company F plans to adopt this Statement for its financial statements for the year beginning January 1, 1993. Company F's postretirement defined benefit health care plan is presently accounted for on a pay-as-you-go basis. [FAS106, ¶443]

On January 1, 1991, Company F acquires Company G and accounts for the business combination as a purchase pursuant to APB Opinion No. 16, *Business Combinations.* Company G has a postretirement health care plan that Company F agrees to combine with its own plan. Company F assumes the accumulated postretirement benefit obligation of Company G's plan as part of the acquisition agreement. However, at the date the business combination is consummated, no liability is recognized for the postretirement benefit obligation assumed. [FAS106, ¶444]

On July 3, 1992, Company F amends its postretirement benefit plan to provide postretirement life insurance benefits to its employees; employees are given credit for their service prior to that date. At the date of the plan amendment, prior service cost is estimated at $250,000. Average remaining years of service to the full eligibility dates of the plan participants active at the date of the amendment is 25 years. [FAS106, ¶445]

At December 31, 1992, the accumulated postretirement benefit obligation is $2,000,000; there are no plan assets or accrued postretirement benefit cost. On January 1, 1993, when Company F adopts this Statement, it elects to recognize immediately the transition obligation. Because the plan amendment occurred after December 21, 1990, Company F must treat the effect of the amendment as unrecognized prior service cost (paragraph 111). Company F elects to recognize prior service cost on a straight-line basis over the average remaining years of service to full eligibility of the active plan participants as permitted by paragraph 53. Therefore, at December 31, 1992, the remaining prior service cost to be recognized over those plan participants' *future* years of service to their full eligibility dates is $245,000 ($250,000 less $5,000 retroactively recognized for the period from July 3, 1992 to December 31, 1992). [FAS106, ¶446]

Because the purchase business combination also occurred after December 21, 1990, Company F must retroactively reallocate the purchase price to the assets acquired and obligations assumed to reflect the postretirement benefit obligation assumed. Company F determines that the postretirement benefit obligation it assumed with the acquisition of Company G, measured as of the date of the acquisition, was $800,000. The cumulative effect on statements of income for the period January 1, 1991 to December 31, 1992 is the amortization of additional goodwill ($40,000), which Company F recognizes in 1993 as part of the effect of the change in accounting (paragraph 111). [FAS106, ¶447]

On January 1, 1993, Company F recognizes on its statement of financial position goodwill of $760,000 and an obligation for postretirement benefits of $1,755,000 ($2,000,000 unfunded postretirement benefit obligation less $245,000 unrecognized prior service cost). The difference of $995,000 ($1,755,000 − $760,000) is recognized in the statement of income as the effect of an accounting change and comprises the following:

Consequences of events affecting accumulated postretirement benefit obligation other than the business combination and plan amendment	$950,000
Amortization of goodwill for prior purchase business combination	40,000
Amortization of prior service cost for prior plan amendment	5,000
Effect of accounting change	$995,000

The unrecognized prior service cost ($245,000) will be recognized on a delayed basis over the remaining 24.5-year amortization period for the plan participants active at the date of the amendment. [FAS106, ¶448]

FAS107: Disclosures about Fair Value of Financial Instruments

This Statement shall be effective for financial statements issued for fiscal years ending after December 15, 1992, except for entities with less than $150 million in total assets in the current statement of financial position. For those entities, the effective date shall be for financial statements issued for fiscal years ending after December 15, 1995. Earlier application is encouraged. In the initial year of application of this Statement, it need not be applied to complete interim financial statements. [FAS107, ¶16]

Disclosures required by paragraphs 10-14 that have not previously been reported need not be included in financial statements that are being presented for comparative purposes for fiscal years ending before the applicable effective date of this Statement for an entity. For all subsequent fiscal years, the information required to be disclosed by this Statement shall be included for each year for which a statement of financial position is presented for comparative purposes. [FAS107, ¶17]

FAS112: Employers' Accounting for Postemployment Benefits

This Statement shall be effective for fiscal years beginning after December 15, 1993. Earlier application is encouraged. The effect of initially applying this Statement shall be reported as the effect of a change in accounting principle in a manner similar to the cumulative effect of a change in accounting principle (APB Opinion No. 20, *Accounting Changes,* paragraph 20). Pro forma effects of retroactive application (Opinion 20, paragraph 21) are not required. Previously issued financial statements shall not be restated. [FAS112, ¶12]

FAS114: Accounting by Creditors for Impairment of a Loan

This Statement shall be effective for financial statements for fiscal years beginning after December 15, 1994. Earlier application is encouraged. Previously issued annual financial statements shall not be restated. Initial application of this Statement shall be as of the beginning of an enterprise's fiscal year (that is, if the Statement is adopted prior to the effective date and during an interim period other than the first interim period, all prior interim periods of that fiscal year shall be restated). [FAS114, ¶26]

This Statement applies to all troubled debt restructurings involving a modification of terms. However, if a loan that was restructured in a troubled debt restructuring involving a modification of terms before the effective date of this Statement is not impaired based on the terms specified by the restructuring agreement, a creditor may continue to account for the loan in accordance with the provisions of Statement 15 prior to its amendment by this Statement. [FAS114, ¶27]

FAS115: Accounting for Certain Investments in Debt and Equity Securities

This Statement shall be effective for fiscal years beginning after December 15, 1993. Except as indicated in the following paragraph, initialapplication of this Statement shall be as of the beginning of an enterprise's fiscal year; at that date, investments in debt and equity securities owned shall be classified based on the enterprise's current intent. Earlier application as of the beginning of a fiscal year is permitted only in financial statements for fiscal years beginning after issuance of this Statement. This Statement may not be applied retroactively to prior years' financial statements. [FAS115, ¶23]

For fiscal years beginning prior to December 16, 1993, enterprises are permitted to initially apply this Statement as of the end of a fiscal year for which annual financial statements have not previously been issued. This Statement may not be applied retroactively to the interim financial statements for that year. [FAS115, ¶24]

The effect on retained earnings of initially applying this Statement shall be reported as the effect of a change in accounting principle in a manner similar to the cumulative effect of a change in accounting principle as described in paragraph 20 of APB Opinion No. 20, *Accounting Changes*. That effect on retained earnings includes the reversal of amounts previously included in earnings that would be excluded from earnings under this Statement (refer to paragraph 13). The unrealized holding gain or loss, net of tax effect, for securities classified as available-for-sale as of the date that this Statement is first applied shall be an adjustment of the balance of the separate component of equity. The pro forma effects of retroactive application (discussed in paragraph 21 of Opinion 20) shall not be disclosed. [FAS115, ¶25]

FAS116: Accounting for Contributions Received and Contributions Made

This Statement shall be effective for financial statements issued for fiscal years beginning after December 15, 1994 and interim periods within those fiscal years, except for not-for-profit organizations with less than $5 million in total assets and less than $1 million in annual expenses. For those organizations, the effective date shall be for fiscal years beginning after December 15, 1995. Earlier application is encouraged. [FAS116, ¶28]

Unless this Statement is applied retroactively under the provisions of paragraph 30, the effect of initially applying this Statement shall be reported as the effect of a change in accounting principle in a manner similar to the cumulative effect of a change in accounting principle (APB Opinion No. 20, *Accounting Changes,* paragraph 19). The amount of the cumulative effect shall be based on a retroactive computation, except that the provisions of paragraph 17 for recognition of expirations of restrictions may be applied prospectively. A not-for-profit organization shall report the cumulative effect of a change in accounting on each class of net assets in the statement of activities between the captions "extraordinary items," if any, and "change in unrestricted net assets," "change in temporarily restricted net assets," and "change in permanently restricted net assets." A business enterprise shall report the amount of the cumulative effect in the income statement between the captions "extraordinary items" and "net income" (Opinion 20, paragraph 20). [FAS116, ¶29]

This Statement may be applied retroactively by restating opening net assets for the earliest year presented or for the year this Statement is first applied if no prior years are presented. The provisions of paragraph 17 for recognition of expirations of restrictions may be applied prospectively. In the period that this Statement is first applied, a not-for-profit organization shall disclose the nature of any restatement and its effect on the change in net assets for each period presented. A business enterprise shall account for any restatement as a change in accounting principle applied retroactively (Opinion 20, paragraphs 27 and 28). [FAS116, ¶30]

For purposes of initial application of this Statement, entities are encouraged either to capitalize retroactively collections acquired in previous periods[4] or to capitalize collections on a prospective basis. Capitalization of selected collections or items is precluded. [FAS116, ¶12]

---

[4]Collections of works of art, historical treasures, and similar assets acquired in previous periods but not capitalized as assets may be retroactively capitalized at their cost or fair value at date of acquisition, current cost, or current market value, whichever is deemed most practical. [FAS116, ¶12, fn4]

FAS117: Financial Statements of Not-for-Profit Organizations

This Statement shall be effective for annual financial statements issued for fiscal years beginning after December 15, 1994, except for organizations with less than $5 million in total assets and less than $1 million in annual expenses. For those organizations, the effective date shall be for fiscal years beginning after December 15, 1995. Earlier application is encouraged. This Statement need not be applied in financial statements for interim periods in the initial year of application, but information for those interim periods shall be reclassified if reported with annual financial statements for that fiscal year. If comparative annual financial statements are presented for earlier periods, those financial statements shall be reclassified (or restated) to reflect retroactive application of the provisions of this Statement. In the year that this Statement is first applied, the financial statements shall disclose the nature of any restatements and their effect, if any, on the change in net assets for each year presented. [FAS117, ¶31]

FIN39: Offsetting of Amounts Related to Certain Contracts

The provisions of this Interpretation are effective for financial statements issued for periods beginning after December 15, 1993. Earlier application is encouraged. Financial statements for fiscal years before the effective date may be restated to conform to the provisions of this Interpretation. [FIN39, ¶11]

FIN40: Applicability of Generally Accepted Accounting Principles to Mutual Life Insurance and Other Enterprises

The general provisions of this Interpretation are effective for financial statements issued for fiscal years beginning after December 15, 1994, and the disclosures specified in paragraphs 5 and 6 are effective for annual financial statements for fiscal years beginning after December 15, 1992. Earlier application is encouraged. The effect of initially applying this Interpretation shall be reported retroactively through restatement of all previously issued annual financial statements presented for comparative purposes for fiscal years beginning after December 15, 1992. Previously issued financial statements for any number of consecutive annual periods preceding that date may be restated to conform to the provisions of this Interpretation. The cumulative effect of adopting this Interpretation shall be included in the earliest year restated. [FIN40, ¶7]

(The next page is D-1.)

Appendix D

APPENDIX D

Issues Discussed by the FASB Emerging Issues Task Force

The Emerging Issues Task Force was established in 1984 to aid the FASB in identifying implementation and emerging issues that may ultimately require action by the FASB. Makeup of the Task Force is designed to include persons in a position to be aware of emerging issues before they become widespread and before divergent practices regarding them become entrenched. After discussing the issues and the relevant accounting pronouncements, the group sometimes can reach a consensus on an issue, in which case no action by the FASB is usually needed. Because the application of EITF consensuses is mandatory under AICPA Statement on Auditing Standards (SAS) No. 69 (see Appendix A), a listing of all issues discussed to date (through May 19, 1994) is presented in this appendix. In addition, the Topical Index includes references to EITF issues.

The FASB publishes a summary of the proceedings of the Task Force in a loose-leaf service, *EITF Abstracts*. A separate Abstract is presented for each issue considered by the Task Force since its inception in 1984. A comprehensive topical index is included to facilitate quick identification of relevant issues that have been addressed by the Task Force.

Each Abstract summarizes the accounting issue involved and the results of the Task Force's discussion, including any consensus reached on the issue. The information in each Abstract is derived from the Issue Summary and related attachments, which are the discussion materials distributed to each Task Force member, and the official minutes of each Task Force meeting. Each Abstract also reports in its STATUS section subsequent developments on that issue, such as issuance of a relevant SEC Staff Accounting Bulletin or FASB Technical Bulletin. *EITF Abstracts* is also published each October in a bound version.

Copies of *EITF Abstracts*, the Issue Summary packages, and related meeting minutes can be obtained from the FASB Order Department. For information on prices and discounts, call (203) 847-0700, extension 555.

Issue Number and Topic	Status
84-1 Tax Reform Act of 1984: Deferred Income Taxes of Stock Life Insurance Companies	Resolved by FTB 84-3, which is superseded by FAS 96 and FAS 109.
84-2 Tax Reform Act of 1984: Deferred Income Taxes Relating to Domestic International Sales Corporations	Resolved by FTB 84-2, which is superseded by FAS 96 and FAS 109.
84-3 Convertible Debt "Sweeteners"	Resolved by FAS 84.
84-4 Acquisition, Development, and Construction Loans	Resolved by AICPA Notice to Practitioners, issued 2/10/86.

Issue Number and Topic		Status
84-5	Sale of Marketable Securities with a Put Option	Consensus reached. See Issue 85-40.
84-6	Termination of Defined Benefit Pension Plans	Consensus nullified by FAS 88.
84-7	Termination of Interest Rate Swaps	Consensus reached.
84-8	Variable Stock Purchase Warrants Given by Suppliers to Customers	Resolved by SEC Staff Accounting Bulletin No. 57.
84-9	Deposit Float of Banks	Consensus reached.
84-10	LIFO Conformity of Companies Relying on *Insilco* Tax Court Decision	No resolution.
84-11	Offsetting Installment Note Receivables and Bank Debt ("Note Monetization")	Consensus reached.
84-12	Operating Leases with Scheduled Rent Increases	Consensus nullified by FTB 85-3. Additional guidance provided by FTB 88-1.
84-13	Purchase of Stock Options and Stock Appreciation Rights in a Leveraged Buyout	Consensus reached.
84-14	Deferred Interest Rate Setting	Consensus reached.
84-15	Grantor Trusts Consolidation	No resolution.
84-16	Earnings-per-Share Cash-Yield Test for Zero Coupon Bonds	Resolved by FAS 85.
84-17	Profit Recognition on Sales of Real Estate with Graduated Payment Mortgages or Insured Mortgages	Consensus reached. See Issue 87-9.
84-18	Stock Option Pyramiding	To be addressed in FASB stock compensation project.
84-19	Mortgage Loan Payment Modifications	Consensus reached.
84-20	GNMA Dollar Rolls	Resolved by AICPA Statement of Position 85-2.
84-21	Sale of a Loan with a Partial Participation Retained	Consensus reached.
84-22	Prior Years' Earnings per Share Following a Savings and Loan Association Conversion and Pooling	Consensus reached.

Appendix D

Issue Number and Topic	Status
84-23 Leveraged Buyout Holding Company Debt	Guidance provided by SEC Staff Accounting Bulletin No. 73. Disclosure guidance provided by FAS 105. To be addressed in FASB project on consolidations.
84-24 LIFO Accounting Issues	Resolved by SEC Staff Accounting Bulletin No. 58.
84-25 Offsetting Nonrecourse Debt with Sales-Type or Direct Financing Lease Receivables	Resolved by FTB 86-2 and SEC Staff Accounting Bulletin No. 70.
84-26 Defeasance of Special-Purpose Borrowings	Resolved by FASB.
84-27 Deferred Taxes on Subsidiary Stock Sales	Resolved by FAS 96 which is superseded by FAS 109.
84-28 Impairment of Long-Lived Assets	FASB staff work in progress.
84-29 Gain and Loss Recognition on Exchanges of Productive Assets and the Effect of Boot	Consensus reached. See Issue 86-29.
84-30 Sales of Loans to Special-Purpose Entities	Disclosure guidance provided by SEC staff. See *EITF Abstracts*. To be addressed in FASB project on consolidations.
84-31 Equity Certificates of Deposit	Consensus reached.
84-32 (Not used)	N/A
84-33 Acquisition of a Tax Loss Carryforward— Temporary Parent-Subsidiary Relationship	Consensus reached.
84-34 Permanent Discount Restricted Stock Purchase Plans	To be addressed in FASB stock compensation project.
84-35 Business Combinations: Sale of Duplicate Facilities and Accrual of Liabilities	Resolved by FTB 85-5. Partially resolved by FAS 87 and SEC Staff Accounting Bulletin No. 61.
84-36 Interest Rate Swap Transactions	No resolution.
84-37 Sale-Leaseback Transaction with Repurchase Option	Partially resolved by FAS 98.
84-38 Identical Common Shares for a Pooling of Interests	Consensus nullified by FTB 85-5.

Issue Number and Topic	Status
84-39 Transfers of Monetary and Nonmonetary Assets among Individuals and Entities under Common Control	No resolution.
84-40 Long-Term Debt Repayable by a Capital Stock Transaction	Resolved by SEC. See *EITF Abstracts*.
84-41 Consolidation of Subsidiary after Instantaneous In-Substance Defeasance	Resolved by FAS 94.
84-42 Push-Down of Parent Company Debt to a Subsidiary	Guidance provided by SEC Staff Accounting Bulletin No. 73. To be addressed in FASB project on consolidations.
84-43 Income Tax Effects of Asset Revaluations in Certain Foreign Countries	Consensus nullified by FAS 96 which is superseded by FAS 109.
84-44 Partial Termination of a Defined Benefit Pension Plan	Resolved by FAS 88.
85-1 Classifying Notes Received for Capital Stock	Consensus reached.
85-2 Classification of Costs Incurred in a Takeover Defense	Consensus nullified by FTB 85-6.
85-3 Tax Benefits Relating to Asset Dispositions Following an Acquisition of a Financial Institution	Consensus nullified by FAS 96 which is superseded by FAS 109.
85-4 Downstream Mergers and Other Stock Transactions between Companies under Common Control	Resolved by FTB 85-5.
85-5 Restoration of Deferred Taxes Previously Eliminated by Net Operating Loss Recognition	Resolved by FAS 96 which is superseded by FAS 109.
85-6 Futures Implementation Questions	Resolved by FASB. See FASB *Highlights*, issued 6/85.
85-7 Federal Home Loan Mortgage Corporation Stock	Resolved by FTB 85-1.
85-8 Amortization of Thrift Intangibles	Consensus reached.

Issue Number and Topic		Status
85-9	Revenue Recognition on Options to Purchase Stock of Another Entity	Consensus reached. To be addressed in FASB project on financial instruments.
85-10	Employee Stock Ownership Plan Contribution Funded by a Pension Plan Termination	Consensus nullified by FAS 88.
85-11	Use of an Employee Stock Ownership Plan in a Leveraged Buyout	No resolution.
85-12	Retention of Specialized Accounting for Investments in Consolidation	Consensus reached.
85-13	Sale of Mortgage Service Rights on Mortgages Owned by Others	Consensus reached.
85-14	Securities That Can Be Acquired for Cash in a Pooling of Interests	Consensus reached.
85-15	Recognizing Benefits of Purchased Net Operating Loss Carryforwards	Consensus nullified by FAS 96 which is superseded by FAS 109.
85-16	Leveraged Leases • Real Estate Leases and Sale-Leaseback Transactions • Delayed Equity Contributions by Lessors	Consensus reached. Additional guidance provided by FAS 98.
85-17	Accrued Interest upon Conversion of Convertible Debt	Consensus reached.
85-18	Earnings-per-Share Effect of Equity Commitment Notes	Consensus reached.
85-19	(Not used)	N/A
85-20	Recognition of Fees for Guaranteeing a Loan	Consensus reached. Additional guidance provided by FAS 91 and SEC Staff Accounting Bulletin No. 60. Disclosure guidance provided by FAS 105.
85-21	Changes in Ownership Resulting in a New Basis of Accounting	To be addressed in FASB project on consolidations.

	Issue Number and Topic	Status
85-22	Retroactive Application of FASB Technical Bulletins	Resolved by FASB. See FASB *Status Report,* No. 175, issued 4/22/86.
85-23	Effect of a Redemption Agreement on Carrying Value of a Security	Consensus reached.
85-24	Distribution Fees by Distributors of Mutual Funds That Do Not Have a Front-End Sales Charge	Consensus reached.
85-25	Sale of Preferred Stocks with a Put Option	Consensus reached. See Issue 85-40.
85-26	Measurement of Servicing Fee under FASB Statement No. 65 When a Loan Is Sold with Servicing Retained	Resolved by FTB 87-3.
85-27	Recognition of Receipts from Made-Up Rental Shortfalls	Consensus reached.
85-28	Consolidation Issues Relating to Collateralized Mortgage Obligations	Consensus reached. Also addressed by FAS 94.
85-29	Convertible Bonds with a "Premium Put"	Consensus reached.
85-30	Sale of Marketable Securities at a Gain with a Put Option	Consensus reached. See Issue 85-40.
85-31	Comptroller of the Currency's Rule on Deferred Tax Debits	Consensus reached.
85-32	Purchased Lease Residuals	Consensus nullified by FTB 86-2.
85-33	Disallowance of Income Tax Deduction for Core Deposit Intangibles	Consensus nullified by FAS 96 which is superseded by FAS 109.
85-34	Bankers' Acceptances and Risk Participations	Resolved by SEC. See *EITF Abstracts.*
85-35	Transition and Implementation Issues for FASB Statement No. 86	Resolved by FASB. See FASB *Highlights,* issued 2/86.

Issue Number and Topic		Status
85-36	Discontinued Operations with Expected Gain and Interim Operating Losses	Consensus reached.
85-37	Recognition of Note Received for Real Estate Syndication Activities	Resolved by AICPA Statement of Position 92-1.
85-38	Negative Amortizing Loans	Resolved by FAS 91.
85-39	Implications of SEC Staff Accounting Bulletin No. 59 on Noncurrent Marketable Equity Securities	Resolved by SEC. See *EITF Abstracts*.
85-40	Comprehensive Review of Sales of Marketable Securities with Put Arrangements	Consensus reached.
85-41	Accounting for Savings and Loan Associations under FSLIC Management Consignment Program	Consensus reached.
85-42	Amortization of Goodwill Resulting from Recording Time Savings Deposits at Fair Values	Consensus reached.
85-43	Sale of Subsidiary for Equity Interest in Buyer	Consensus reached under Issue 86-29.
85-44	Differences between Loan Loss Allowances for GAAP and RAP	Consensus reached.
85-45	Business Combinations: Settlement of Stock Options and Awards	Consensus reached. May be addressed in FASB project on stock compensation.
85-46	Partnership's Purchase of Withdrawing Partner's Equity	No resolution.
86-1	Recognizing Net Operating Loss Carryforwards	Consensus nullified by FAS 96 which is superseded by FAS 109.
86-2	Retroactive Wage Adjustments Affecting Medicare Payments	Consensus reached.
86-3	Retroactive Regulations regarding IRC Section 338 Purchase Price Allocations	Consensus partially nullified by FAS 96 which is superseded by FAS 109.

Issue Number and Topic		Status
86-4	Income Statement Treatment of Income Tax Benefit for Employee Stock Ownership Plan Dividends	Consensus nullified by FAS 96 which is superseded by FAS 109.
86-5	Classifying Demand Notes with Repayment Terms	Consensus reached.
86-6	Antispeculation Clauses in Real Estate Sales Contracts	Consensus reached.
86-7	Recognition by Homebuilders of Profit from Sales of Land and Related Construction Contracts	Consensus reached.
86-8	Sale of Bad Debt Recovery Rights	Consensus reached.
86-9	IRC Section 338 and Push-Down Accounting	Consensus reached. Additional guidance provided by FAS 96 which is superseded by FAS 109.
86-10	Pooling with 10 Percent Cash Payout Determined by Lottery	Consensus reached.
86-11	Recognition of Possible 1986 Tax Law Changes	Resolved by FTB 86-1, which is superseded by FAS 96 and FAS 109.
86-12	Accounting by Insureds for Claims-Made Insurance Policies	Consensus reached.
86-13	Recognition of Inventory Market Declines at Interim Reporting Dates	Consensus reached.
86-14	Purchased Research and Development Projects in a Business Combination	Resolved by FASB. See *EITF Abstracts.*
86-15	Increasing-Rate Debt	Consensus reached. Additional guidance provided by SEC Staff Accounting Bulletin No. 77.
86-16	Carryover of Predecessor Cost in Leveraged Buyout Transactions	Consensus superseded by Issue 88-16.

Issue Number and Topic	Status
86-17 Deferred Profit on Sale-Leaseback Transaction with Lessee Guarantee of Residual Value	Consensus reached. Additional guidance provided by FAS 98.
86-18 Debtor's Accounting for a Modification of Debt Terms	Consensus reached.
86-19 Change in Accounting for Other Postemployment Benefits	Resolved by FTB 87-1, which is superseded by FAS 106.
86-20 Accounting for Other Postemployment Benefits of an Acquired Company	Consensus nullified by FAS 106.
86-21 Application of the AICPA Notice to Practitioners regarding Acquisition, Development, and Construction Arrangements to Acquisition of an Operating Property	Consensus reached.
86-22 Display of Business Restructuring Provisions in the Income Statement	Resolved by SEC Staff Accounting Bulletin No. 67.
86-23 (Not used)	N/A
86-24 Third-Party Establishment of Collateralized Mortgage Obligations	Consensus reached. Also will be addressed as part of the recognition phase of the FASB project on financial instruments.
86-25 Offsetting Foreign Currency Swaps	Consensus reached.
86-26 Using Forward Commitments as a Surrogate for Deferred Rate Setting	Resolved by SEC. See *EITF Abstracts*.
86-27 Measurement of Excess Contributions to a Defined Contribution Plan or Employee Stock Ownership Plan	Consensus reached.
86-28 Accounting Implications of Indexed Debt Instruments	Consensus reached.
86-29 Nonmonetary Transactions: Magnitude of Boot and the Exceptions to the Use of Fair Value	Consensus reached. See Issue 87-29.
86-30 Classification of Obligations When a Violation Is Waived by the Creditor	Consensus reached.

Issue Number and Topic	Status
86-31 Reporting the Tax Implications of a Pooling of a Bank and a Savings and Loan Association	Consensus reached. Additional guidance provided by FAS 96 which is superseded by FAS 109.
86-32 Early Extinguishment of a Subsidiary's Mandatorily Redeemable Preferred Stock	Consensus reached.
86-33 Tax Indemnifications in Lease Agreements	Consensus reached.
86-34 Futures Contracts Used as Hedges of Anticipated Reverse Repurchase Transactions	Consensus reached.
86-35 Debentures with Detachable Stock Purchase Warrants	Consensus reached.
86-36 Invasion of a Defeasance Trust	Consensus reached.
86-37 Recognition of Tax Benefit of Discounting Loss Reserves of Insurance Companies	Consensus nullified by FAS 96 which is superseded by FAS 109.
86-38 Implications of Mortgage Prepayments on Amortization of Servicing Rights	Consensus reached; consensus partially nullified by Issue 89-4.
86-39 Gains from the Sale of Mortgage Loans with Servicing Rights Retained	Consensus reached.
86-40 Investments in Open-End Mutual Funds That Invest in U.S. Government Securities	Consensus reached.
86-41 Carryforward of the Corporate Alternative Minimum Tax Credit	Consensus nullified by FAS 96 which is superseded by FAS 109. Also see Issue 87-8.
86-42 Effect of a Change in Tax Rates on Assets and Liabilities Recorded Net-of-Tax in a Purchase Business Combination	Consensus nullified by FAS 96 which is superseded by FAS 109.
86-43 Effect of a Change in Tax Law or Rates on Leveraged Leases	Consensus reached. See Issue 87-8.
86-44 Effect of a Change in Tax Law on Investments in Safe Harbor Leases	Consensus reached.

Appendix D

Issue Number and Topic	Status
86-45 Imputation of Dividends on Preferred Stock Redeemable at the Issuer's Option with Initial Below-Market Dividend Rate	Resolved by SEC Staff Accounting Bulletin No. 68. May be addressed in FASB project on financial instruments.
86-46 Uniform Capitalization Rules for Inventory under the Tax Reform Act of 1986	Consensus reached.
87-1 Deferral Accounting for Cash Securities That Are Used to Hedge Rate or Price Risk	No consensus reached. However, guidance provided by EITF and FASB. See *EITF Abstracts*.
87-2 Net Present Value Method of Valuing Speculative Foreign Exchange Contracts	Consensus reached.
87-3 (Not used)	N/A
87-4 Restructuring of Operations: Implications of SEC Staff Accounting Bulletin No. 67	Consensus reached.
87-5 Troubled Debt Restructurings: Interrelationship between FASB Statement No. 15 and the AICPA Savings and Loan Guide	Consensus nullified by FAS 114.
87-6 Adjustments Relating to Stock Compensation Plans	Consensus reached.
87-7 Sale of an Asset Subject to a Lease and Nonrecourse Financing: "Wrap Lease Transactions"	Consensus reached. Additional guidance provided by FTB 88-1.
87-8 Tax Reform Act of 1986: Issues Related to the Alternative Minimum Tax	Consensus partially nullified by FAS 96 which is superseded by FAS 109.
87-9 Profit Recognition on Sales of Real Estate with Insured Mortgages or Surety Bonds	Consensus reached.
87-10 Revenue Recognition by Television "Barter" Syndicators	Consensus reached.
87-11 Allocation of Purchase Price to Assets to Be Sold	Consensus reached.
87-12 Foreign Debt-for-Equity Swaps	Consensus reached.

Appendix D

Issue Number and Topic	Status
87-13 Amortization of Prior Service Cost for a Defined Benefit Plan When There Is a History of Plan Amendments	Resolved by FASB. See *EITF Abstracts*.
87-14 (Not used)	N/A
87-15 Effect of a Standstill Agreement on Pooling-of-Interests Accounting	Consensus reached.
87-16 Whether the 90 Percent Test for a Pooling of Interests Is Applied Separately to Each Company or on a Combined Basis	Consensus reached.
87-17 Spin-Offs or Other Distributions of Loans Receivable to Shareholders	Consensus reached.
87-18 Use of Zero Coupon Bonds in a Troubled Debt Restructuring	Consensus reached.
87-19 Substituted Debtors in a Troubled Debt Restructuring	Consensus reached.
87-20 Offsetting Certificates of Deposit against High-Coupon Debt	Consensus reached.
87-21 Change of Accounting Basis in Master Limited Partnership Transactions	Consensus reached.
87-22 Prepayments to the Secondary Reserve of the FSLIC	Consensus reached.
87-23 Book Value Stock Purchase Plans	Consensus reached. Also see Issue 88-6.
87-24 Allocation of Interest to Discontinued Operations	Consensus reached.
87-25 Sale of Convertible, Adjustable-Rate Mortgages with Contingent Repayment Agreement	No resolution.
87-26 Hedging of Foreign Currency Exposure with a Tandem Currency	Consensus reached.
87-27 Poolings of Companies That Do Not Have a Controlling Class of Common Stock	Consensus reached.
87-28 Provision for Deferred Taxes on Increases in Cash Surrender Value of Key-Person Life Insurance	Resolved by FAS 96 which is superseded by FAS 109.

Issue Number and Topic		Status
87-29	Exchange of Real Estate Involving Boot	Consensus reached.
87-30	Sale of a Short-Term Loan Made under a Long-Term Credit Commitment	Consensus reached.
87-31	Sale of Put Options on Issuer's Stock	Consensus reached.
87-32	(Not used)	N/A
87-33	Stock Compensation Issues Related to Market Decline	Consensus reached.
87-34	Sale of Mortgage Servicing Rights with a Subservicing Agreement	Consensus reached.
88-1	Determination of Vested Benefit Obligation for a Defined Benefit Pension Plan	Consensus reached.
88-2	(Not used)	N/A
88-3	Rental Concessions Provided by Landlord	Resolved by FTB 88-1.
88-4	Classification of Payment Made to IRS to Retain Fiscal Year	Consensus reached.
88-5	Recognition of Insurance Death Benefits	Consensus reached on principal issue. Guidance on second issue provided by FAS 96 Q&A and by FAS 109 which superseded FAS 96.
88-6	Book Value Stock Plans in an Initial Public Offering	Consensus reached.
88-7	(Not used)	N/A
88-8	Mortgage Swaps	Consensus reached.
88-9	Put Warrants	Consensus reached.
88-10	Costs Associated with Lease Modification or Termination	Consensus reached. Also see FTB 88-1.
88-11	Allocation of Recorded Investment When a Loan or Part of a Loan Is Sold	Consensus reached.
88-12	Transfer of Ownership Interest as Part of Down Payment under FASB Statement No. 66	Consensus reached.

Appendix D

Issue Number and Topic	Status
88-13 (Not used)	N/A
88-14 Settlement of Fees with Extra Units to a General Partner in a Master Limited Partnership	No resolution. Related issues addressed in AICPA Statement of Position 92-1.
88-15 Classification of Subsidiary's Loan Payable in Consolidated Balance Sheet When Subsidiary's and Parent's Fiscal Years Differ	No resolution. May be addressed in FASB project on consolidations.
88-16 Basis in Leveraged Buyout Transactions	Consensus reached.
88-17 Accounting for Fees and Costs Associated with Loan Syndications and Loan Participations	Consensus reached.
88-18 Sales of Future Revenues	Consensus reached.
88-19 FSLIC-Assisted Acquisitions of Thrifts	Consensus affected by FAS 109. Additional guidance provided by SEC Staff Accounting Bulletin No. 82.
88-20 Difference between Initial Investment and Principal Amount of Loans in a Purchased Credit Card Portfolio	Consensus reached. Disclosure guidance in Issue 92-5.
88-21 Accounting for the Sale of Property Subject to the Seller's Preexisting Lease	Consensus reached.
88-22 Securitization of Credit Card Portfolios	Consensus reached.
88-23 Lump-Sum Payments under Union Contracts	Consensus reached.
88-24 Effect of Various Forms of Financing under FASB Statement No. 66	Consensus reached.
88-25 Ongoing Accounting and Reporting for a Newly Created Liquidating Bank	Consensus reached. Additional guidance provided by SEC Staff Accounting Bulletin No. 82.
88-26 Controlling Preferred Stock in a Pooling of Interests	Consensus reached.

Issue Number and Topic	Status
88-27 Effect of Unallocated Shares in an Employee Stock Ownership Plan on Accounting for Business Combinations	Consensus reached. See Issue 93-2 for SEC staff position limiting application of consensus.
89-1 Accounting by a Pension Plan for Bank Investment Contracts and Guaranteed Investment Contracts	Resolved by FAS 110.
89-2 Maximum Maturity Guarantees on Transfers of Receivables with Recourse	Consensus reached.
89-3 Balance Sheet Presentation of Savings Accounts in Financial Statements of Credit Unions	Consensus reached.
89-4 Accounting for a Purchased Investment in a Collateralized Mortgage Obligation Instrument or in a Mortgage-Backed Interest-Only Certificate	Consensus reached. Consensus on Issue 3 modified by FAS 115 and Issue 93-18. See *EITF Abstracts*.
89-5 Sale of Mortgage Loan Servicing Rights	Consensus reached.
89-6 (Not used)	N/A
89-7 Exchange of Assets or Interest in a Subsidiary for a Noncontrolling Equity Interest in a New Entity	Consensus reached.
89-8 Expense Recognition for Employee Stock Ownership Plans	Consensus reached.
89-9 Accounting for In-Substance Foreclosures	Consensus affected. by FAS 114. See *EITF Abstracts*.
89-10 Sponsor's Recognition of Employee Stock Ownership Plan Debt	Consensus reached.
89-11 Sponsor's Balance Sheet Classification of Capital Stock with a Put Option Held by an Employee Stock Ownership Plan	Consensus reached.
89-12 Earnings-per-Share Issues Related to Convertible Preferred Stock Held by an Employee Stock Ownership Plan	Consensus reached.

Appendix D

Issue Number and Topic	Status
89-13 Accounting for the Cost of Asbestos Removal	Consensus reached.
89-14 Valuation of Repossessed Real Estate	Consensus reached.
89-15 Accounting for a Modification of Debt Terms When the Debtor Is Experiencing Financial Difficulties	Consensus reached.
89-16 Consideration of Executory Costs in Sale-Leaseback Transactions	Consensus reached.
89-17 Accounting for the Retail Sale of an Extended Warranty Contract in Connection with the Sale of a Product	Consensus nullified by FTB 90-1.
89-18 Divestitures of Certain Investment Securities to an Unregulated Commonly Controlled Entity under FIRREA	Consensus modified by FAS 115. See *EITF Abstracts*.
89-19 Accounting for a Change in Goodwill Amortization for Business Combinations Initiated Prior to the Effective Date of FASB Statement No. 72	Consensus reached.
89-20 Accounting for Cross Border Tax Benefit Leases	Consensus reached.
90-1 (Not used)	N/A
90-2 Exchange of Interest-Only and Principal-Only Securities for a Mortgage-Backed Security	Consensus reached.
90-3 Accounting for Employers' Obligations for Future Contributions to a Multiemployer Pension Plan	Consensus reached.
90-4 Earnings-per-Share Treatment of Tax Benefits for Dividends on Stock Held by an Employee Stock Ownership Plan	Consensus reached. Additional guidance in Issue 92-3.
90-5 Exchanges of Ownership Interests between Entities under Common Control	Consensus reached.
90-6 Accounting for Certain Events Not Addressed in Issue No. 87-11 Relating to an Acquired Operating Unit to Be Sold	Consensus reached.
90-7 Accounting for a Reload Stock Option	Consensus reached.
90-8 Capitalization of Costs to Treat Environmental Contamination	Consensus reached.

Issue Number and Topic		Status
90-9	Changes to Fixed Employee Stock Option Plans as a Result of Restructuring	Consensus reached.
90-10	Accounting for a Business Combination Involving a Majority-Owned Investee of a Venture Capital Company	No resolution.
90-11	Accounting for Exit and Entrance Fees Incurred in a Conversion from the Savings Association Insurance Fund to the Bank Insurance Fund	No resolution.
90-12	Allocating Basis to Individual Assets and Liabilities for Transactions within the Scope of Issue No. 88-16	Consensus reached.
90-13	Accounting for Simultaneous Common Control Mergers	Consensus reached.
90-14	Unsecured Guarantee by Parent of Subsidiary's Lease Payments in a Sale-Leaseback Transaction	Consensus reached.
90-15	Impact of Nonsubstantive Lessors, Residual Value Guarantees, and Other Provisions in Leasing Transactions	Consensus reached.
90-16	Accounting for Discontinued Operations Subsequently Retained	Consensus reached.
90-17	Hedging Foreign Currency Risks with Purchased Options	Consensus reached.
90-18	Effect of a "Removal of Accounts" Provision on the Accounting for a Credit Card Securitization	Consensus reached.
90-19	Convertible Bonds with Issuer Option to Settle for Cash upon Conversion	Consensus reached.
90-20	Impact of an Uncollateralized Irrevocable Letter of Credit on a Real Estate Sale-Leaseback Transaction	Consensus reached.
90-21	Balance Sheet Treatment of a Sale of Mortgage Servicing Rights with a Subservicing Agreement	Consensus reached.
90-22	Accounting for Gas-Balancing Arrangements	No resolution. Referred to AICPA industry group for consideration.

Appendix D

Issue Number and Topic		Status
91-1	Hedging Intercompany Foreign Currency Risks	Consensus reached.
91-2	Debtor's Accounting for Forfeiture of Real Estate Subject to a Nonrecourse Mortgage	Resolved by FASB. See *EITF Abstracts*.
91-3	Accounting for Income Tax Benefits from Bad Debts of a Savings and Loan Association	Resolved by FAS 109. Additional guidance provided by SEC staff. See *EITF Abstracts* and SEC Staff Accounting Bulletin No. 91.
91-4	Hedging Foreign Currency Risks with Complex Options and Similar Transactions	Resolved by SEC. See *EITF Abstracts*. Consensus reached on disclosure requirements.
91-5	Nonmonetary Exchange of Cost-Method Investments	Consensus reached.
91-7	Accounting for Pension Benefits Paid by Employers after Insurance Companies Fail to Provide Annuity Benefits	Consensus reached.
91-8	Application of FASB Statement 96 to a State Tax Based on the Greater of a Franchise Tax or an Income Tax	Consensus nullified by FAS 109.
91-9	Revenue and Expense Recognition for Freight Services in Process	Consensus reached.

Consensuses Reached after March 15, 1992*

91-6	Revenue Recognition of Long-Term Power Sales Contracts	Consensus reached.
91-10	Accounting for Special Assessments and Tax Increment Financing Entities	Consensus reached.
92-1	Allocation of Residual Value or First-Loss Guarantee to Minimum Lease Payments in Leases Involving Land and Building(s)	Consensus reached.

---

*For purposes of applying the requirements of SAS 69, those issues with consensuses reached after March 15, 1992 are listed below. (See the introduction to Appendix A for further information on SAS 69.)

Issue Number and Topic	Status
92-2 Measuring Loss Accruals by Transferors for Transfers of Receivables with Recourse	Consensus reached. Additional guidance provided by SEC staff. See *EITF Abstracts*.
92-3 Earnings-per-Share Treatment of Tax Benefits for Dividends on Unallocated Stock Held by an Employee Stock Ownership Plan (Consideration of the Implications of FASB Statement No. 109 on Issue 2 of EITF Issue No. 90-4)	Consensus reached.
92-4 Accounting for a Change in Functional Currency When an Economy Ceases to Be Considered Highly Inflationary	Consensus reached.
92-5 Amortization Period for Net Deferred Credit Card Origination Costs	Consensus reached.
92-6 (Not used)	N/A
92-7 Accounting by Rate-Regulated Utilities for the Effects of Certain Alternative Revenue Programs	Consensus reached.
92-8 Accounting for the Income Tax Effects under FASB Statement No. 109 of a Change in Functional Currency When an Economy Ceases to Be Considered Highly Inflationary	Consensus reached.
92-9 Accounting for the Present Value of Future Profits Resulting from the Acquisition of a Life Insurance Company	Consensus reached.
92-10 Loan Acquisitions Involving Table Funding Arrangements	Consensus reached.
92-11 (Not used)	N/A
92-12 Accounting for OPEB Costs by Rate-Regulated Enterprises	Consensus reached.
92-13 Accounting for Estimated Payments in Connection with the Coal Industry Retiree Health Benefit Act of 1992	Consensus reached.

Issue Number and Topic	Status
93-1 Accounting for Individual Credit Card Acquisitions	Consensus reached.
93-2 Effect of Acquisition of Employer Shares for/by an Employee Benefit Trust on Accounting for Business Combinations	Resolved by SEC. See *EITF Abstracts.*
93-3 Plan Assets under FASB Statement No. 106	Consensus reached.
93-4 Accounting for Regulatory Assets	Consensus reached. Impairment question may be addressed in FASB project on impairment of long-lived assets.
93-5 Accounting for Environmental Liabilities	Consensus reached.
93-6 Accounting for Multiple-Year Retrospectively Rated Contracts by Ceding and Assuming Enterprises	Consensus reached.
93-7 Uncertainties Related to Income Taxes in a Purchase Business Combination	Consensus reached.
93-8 Accounting for the Sale and Leaseback of an Asset That Is Leased to Another Party	Consensus reached.
93-9 Application of FASB Statement No. 109 in Foreign Financial Statements Restated for General Price-Level Changes	Consensus reached.
93-10 Accounting for Dual Currency Bonds	Resolved by SEC. See *EITF Abstracts.*
93-11 Accounting for Barter Transactions Involving Barter Credits	Consensus reached.
93-12 Recognition and Measurement of the Tax Benefit of Excess Tax-Deductible Goodwill Resulting from a Retroactive Change in Tax Law	Consensus reached.
93-13 Effect of a Retroactive Change in Enacted Tax Rates That Is Included in Income from Continuing Operations	Consensus reached.
93-14 Accounting for Multiple-Year Retrospectively Rated Insurance Contracts by Insurance Enterprises and Other Enterprises	Consensus reached.

Issue Number and Topic		Status
93-15	(Not used)	N/A
93-16	Application of FASB Statement No. 109 to Basis Differences within Foreign Subsidiaries That Meet the Indefinite Reversal Criterion of APB Opinion No. 23	Consensus reached.
93-17	Recognition of Deferred Tax Assets for a Parent Company's Excess Tax Basis in the Stock of a Subsidiary That Is Accounted for as a Discontinued Operation	Consensus reached.
93-18	Recognition of Impairment for an Investment in a Collateralized Mortgage Obligation Instrument or in a Mortgage-Backed Interest-Only Certificate	Consensus reached.
94-1	Accounting for Tax Benefits Resulting from Investments in Affordable Housing Projects	Further discussion pending.
94-2	(Not yet discussed by Task Force)	
94-3	Accounting for Restructuring Charges	Further discussion pending.
94-4	Classification of an Investment in a Mortgage-Backed Interest-Only Certificate as Held-to-Maturity	No resolution.

(The next page is T-1.)

Topical Index

INTRODUCTION TO THE TOPICAL INDEX

The topical index includes references to documents contained in the *Original Pronouncements* volumes, all sections of the *Current Text* volumes, matters discussed by the FASB Emerging Issues Task Force (EITF), and supplemental guidance published by the FASB in the form of question-and-answer *Highlights* and Special Reports.

Original Pronouncements References

For *Original Pronouncements,* the topical index generally excludes references to introductory paragraphs and those paragraphs that provide background information or bases for conclusions. However, if those paragraphs facilitate an understanding of an accounting standard, they are referenced. Superseded paragraphs and pronouncements are not indexed except for those superseded pronouncements with significantly delayed effective dates. The related pronouncements are also retained in the text but shaded to alert the reader that the material has been superseded. The effective date and transition paragraphs are also not indexed, but the principal effective dates are listed in Appendix C, "Effective Dates of Pronouncements."

Current Text References

The topical index provides references to specific paragraphs of all sections of the *Current Text.* It also includes references to all sections that have been superseded by pronouncements with significantly delayed effective dates; those superseded sections are presented in Appendix E of the *Current Text.*

EITF Issue References

References to issues discussed by the FASB Emerging Issues Task Force are also included in the topical index. In this volume, Appendix D presents a listing of all issues discussed to date and their status (through the May 19, 1994 meeting). Those matters are summarized by issue number in a separate publication, *EITF Abstracts.*

Other References

Also included in the topical index are references to supplemental guidance published by the FASB in the following documents:

- FASB *Highlights,* "Futures Contracts: Guidance on Applying Statement 80," June 1985 (Q&A.80)
- FASB *Highlights,* "Computer Software: Guidance on Applying Statement 86," February 1986 (Q&A.86)
- FASB Special Report, *A Guide to Implementation of Statement 87 on Employers' Accounting for Pensions: Questions and Answers* (Q&A.87)

- FASB Special Report, *A Guide to Implementation of Statement 88 on Employers' Accounting for Settlements and Curtailments of Defined Benefit Pension Plans and for Termination Benefits: Questions and Answers* (Q&A.88)
- FASB Special Report, *A Guide to Implementation of Statement 91 on Accounting for Nonrefundable Fees and Costs Associated with Originating or Acquiring Loans and Initial Direct Costs of Leases: Questions and Answers* (Q&A.91)
- FASB Special Report, *A Guide to Implementation of Statement 106 on Employers' Accounting for Postretirement Benefits Other Than Pensions: Questions and Answers* (Q&A.106)
- FASB Special Report, *A Guide to Implementation of Statement 109 on Accounting for Income Taxes: Questions and Answers* (Q&A.109)
- FASB Viewpoints, "Accounting for Reinsurance: Questions and Answers about Statement 113," FASB *Status Report,* February 26, 1993 (Q&A.113). [**Note:** For the convenience of the user, this article is reproduced in Topic No. D-34 of *EITF Abstracts.*]

Organization of the Topical Index

References in the topical index are made to the source documents in the following manner:

- *Current Text*—to the CT section and paragraph number
- *Original Pronouncements*—to the document and paragraph number
- EITF Issues—to the issue number or to Appendix D in *EITF Abstracts*
- Supplemental guidance—to the *Highlights* or FASB Special Report by the applicable FAS number and question number.

An example follows:

	OP	CT	EITF/Other
FUTURES CONTRACTS			
Hedges			
. . Ongoing Assessment of Correlation . .	FAS80, ¶11	F80.111	EITF.85-6
. . . .			Q&A.80 #20-21

The reference FAS80, ¶11 indicates paragraph 11 of FASB Statement No. 80, *Accounting for Futures Contracts.* F80.111 indicates paragraph .111 of the *Current Text* Section F80, "Futures Contracts." The reference to EITF.85-6 indicates EITF Issue No. 85-6, "Futures Implementation Questions." Q&A.80 #20-21 refers to questions 20 and 21 of the FASB *Highlights,* "Futures Contracts: Guidance on Applying Statement 80."

Multiple references on an individual topic are listed in alphabetical and numerical order and there is not necessarily a direct relationship between references listed on the same line.

Order Information on Source Material

Copies of *EITF Abstracts,* EITF Issue Summary packages and related meeting minutes, and the FASB *Highlights,* Viewpoints, and Special Reports listed above can be obtained from the FASB Order Department. The *Original Pronouncements* loose-leaf service also may be obtained from the FASB. In addition, for non-AICPA members, the *Current Text* loose-leaf service may be obtained from the FASB. For information call 203-847-0700, ext. 555.

AICPA members may obtain copies of the annual bound volumes of the *Current Text* and *Original Pronouncements,* as well as the *Current Text* loose-leaf service, from the American Institute of Certified Public Accountants. Members who wish to order copies of these publications should write or phone the Order Department, American Institute of CPAs, Harborside Financial Center, 201 Plaza III, Jersey City, NJ 07311. Call 1-800-862-4272.

Non-AICPA members may obtain copies of the annual bound volumes of the *Original Pronouncements* and *Current Text* from the Order Department, Richard D. Irwin, Inc., 1818 Ridge Road, Homewood, IL 60430. Call 1-800-634-3961.

	Original Pronouncements	Current Text	EITF and Other
ABANDONED PROPERTY			
See Oil and Gas Producing Activities			
See Real Estate: Costs and Initial Operations of Real Estate Projects			
See Regulated Operations			
ABANDONMENTS			
See Regulated Operations			
ABNORMAL COSTS			
See Extraordinary Items			
Inventory	ARB43, Ch.4, ¶5	I78.106	
Unusual or Infrequent Items	APB30, ¶26	I22.101	
ACCELERATED COST RECOVERY SYSTEM (ACRS)			
See Depreciation			
ACCELERATED DEPRECIATION			
See Depreciation			
ACCOUNTING CHANGES			
See Adjustments of Financial Statements for Prior Periods			
See Disclosure			
See Earnings per Share			
See Interim Financial Reporting			
AICPA Statements of Position (SOPs)	FAS111, ¶10	A06.127	
	FIN20, ¶5		
Accounting Policies	APB22, ¶14	A10.107	
Accounting Principles	APB20, ¶7-8	A06.105-106	
Amortization or Depreciation	APB20, ¶23-24	A06.119-120	
. . Oil and Gas Producing Activities	FAS19, ¶30	Oi5.121	
Audit and Accounting Guides			
. . Specialized Accounting and Reporting	FAS111, ¶7	A06.112	
Business Combinations			
. . Combined Enterprise, Pooling-of-Interests Method	APB16, ¶52	B50.111	
. . Disclosure	APB16, ¶64	B50.123	
Change for Tax Purposes	FAS37, ¶19-21	I27.205-207	
	FAS109, ¶287-288		
Change in Accounting Estimate	APB20, ¶10	A06.109	
	APB20, ¶31-33	A06.130-132	
. . Core Deposit Intangibles			EITF.85-33
Change in Accounting Principle			
. . Cumulative Effect	APB20, ¶18-20	A06.114-116	
. . Effected by Change in Accounting Principle	APB20, ¶11	A06.110	
. . Examples	APB20, ¶9	A06.107-108	
	FIN1, ¶5		
Change in Goodwill Amortization Method			
. . Business Combinations Initiated Prior to Effective Date of Statement 72			EITF.89-19
Changes Based on Tentative FASB Decision to Change GAAP			EITF.86-4

FAS–FASB Statements   FIN–FASB Interpretations   FTB–FASB Technical Bulletins
APB–APB Opinions   AIN–AICPA Interpretations   ARB–Accounting Research Bulletins
CON–FASB Concepts   EITF–EITF Issues   Q&A–FASB Special Reports

See "Terminology" for references to defined terms presented in various accounting pronouncements.

See the Introduction to the Topical Index for details on the use of this index.

	Original Pronouncements	Current Text	EITF and Other
ACCOUNTING CHANGES—continued			
Scope of Accounting and Reporting			
Requirements	APB20, ¶2-4	A06.101-103	
....	FAS111, ¶7		
Segment of Business Reporting...............	FAS14, ¶27	S20.133	
Specialized Accounting and Reporting........	APB20, ¶15-16	A06.111-112	
....	FAS111, ¶7	A06.127	
....	FAS111, ¶10		
....	FAS111, ¶17		
....	FIN20, ¶5		
Types...	APB20, ¶6	A06.104	
ACCOUNTING ESTIMATE CHANGES			
See Accounting Changes			
See Adjustments of Financial Statements for			
Prior Periods			
ACCOUNTING POLICIES			
See Disclosure			
Accounting Changes..........................	APB22, ¶14	A10.107	
Defined Benefit Pension Plans	FAS35, ¶27	Pe5.126	
Definition	APB22, ¶6	A10.401	
Description....................................	APB22, ¶6	A10.101	
Investments: Equity Method			
. . Disclosure..............................	APB18, ¶20	I82.110	
Scope of Accounting and Reporting			
Requirements	APB22, ¶8-10	A10.102-104	
....	FAS95, ¶152		
ACCOUNTING PRINCIPLE			
See Accounting Changes			
Definition	APB20, ¶7	A06.402	
ACCOUNTING PRINCIPLE CHANGES			
See Accounting Changes			
See Adjustments of Financial Statements for			
Prior Periods			
ACCOUNTING PRINCIPLES AND			
METHODS			
Choice of.....................................	CON2, ¶6-20		
ACCOUNTING TERMINOLOGY			
See Terminology			
ACCOUNTS PAYABLE (TRADE)			
See Balance Sheet Classification: Current			
Assets and Liabilities			
ACCOUNTS RECEIVABLE			
See Balance Sheet Classification: Current			
Assets and Liabilities			
See Receivables			
From Officers, Employees, or Affiliates.......	ARB43, Ch.1A, ¶5	R36.105	
ACCRUAL			
Balance Sheet Classification	ARB43, Ch.3A, ¶7	B05.108	
Definition	CON6, ¶141		

FAS–FASB Statements   FIN–FASB Interpretations   FTB–FASB Technical Bulletins
APB–APB Opinions   AIN–AICPA Interpretations   ARB–Accounting Research Bulletins
CON–FASB Concepts   EITF–EITF Issues   Q&A–FASB Special Reports

---

See "Terminology" for references to defined terms presented in various accounting pronouncements.

See the Introduction to the Topical Index for details on the use of this index.

	Original Pronouncements	Current Text	EITF and Other
ADJUSTMENTS OF FINANCIAL STATEMENTS FOR PRIOR PERIODS—continued			
Change from Unacceptable to Acceptable Accounting Principle	APB20, ¶13	A35.104	
	FAS111, ¶9		
Change in Accounting Principle			
. . Adopting LIFO Inventory Pricing			EITF.84-10
. . First Public Offering	APB20, ¶27	A35.114	
	APB20, ¶29		
. . From LIFO Inventory Pricing	APB20, ¶27	A35.114	
	APB20, ¶29		
. . From Retirement-Replacement-Betterment Accounting to Depreciation Accounting	FAS73, ¶2	A35.114	
	FAS73, ¶5-7		
. . Full Cost Method in Extractive Industries	APB20, ¶27	A35.114	
	APB20, ¶29		
. . Illustrations	APB20, ¶45-48	A35.116-119	
. . Long-Term Construction-Type Contracts	APB20, ¶27	A35.114	
. . Reporting Entity/Business Combinations	APB20, ¶34-35	A35.112-113	
Change in Estimates	APB20, ¶13	A35.104	
Comparative Financial Statements	APB9, ¶18	A35.106	
	FAS16, ¶16		
Correction of Errors	APB20, ¶13	A35.103-105	
	APB20, ¶37		
	FAS109, ¶288		
Disposal of a Segment of a Business See Income Statement Presentation: Discontinued Operations			
Earnings per Share	APB15, ¶18	E09.109	
Exclusions from Net Income	FAS109, ¶288	A35.103	
Extraordinary Items	FAS16, ¶16	I17.119	
Historical Summaries of Financial Data	APB9, ¶27	A35.108	
Implementation of an EITF Consensus			EITF.D-1
Interim Periods, Adjustments within Year	FAS16, ¶13	A35.109	
	FAS109, ¶288		
. . Disclosure	FAS16, ¶14-15	A35.110-111	
. . Effect of Tax Reform Act of 1986			EITF.86-11
. . Restatement	FAS16, ¶14	A35.110	
Investments: Equity Method	APB18, ¶19	I82.109	
Relation to Accounting Changes	FAS16, ¶12	A35.101	
Relation to Current Period Net Income	FAS16, ¶10	A35.102	
Restatement Reflected as Adjustments to Opening Retained Earnings	APB9, ¶18	A35.106-107	
	APB9, ¶26		
	FAS16, ¶16		
Retroactive Application of FASB Technical Bulletins			EITF.85-22

	Original Pronouncements	Current Text	EITF and Other
ADVANCE REFUNDING			
See Debt: Extinguishments			
See Leases			
AFFILIATES			
See Business Combinations			
See Consolidation			
See Related Parties			
AFFORDABLE HOUSING PROJECTS TAX BENEFITS			
See Income Taxes			
AGRICULTURE			
Inventory	ARB43, Ch.4, ¶16	I78.119	
AICPA			
See AICPA Practice Bulletins			
See AICPA Statement on Auditing Standards (SAS)			
See AICPA Statements of Position (SOPs)			
AICPA AUDIT AND ACCOUNTING GUIDES			
See Accounting Changes			
AICPA PRACTICE BULLETINS			
Accounting Changes	FAS111, ¶10	A06.127	
	FIN20, ¶5		
AICPA STATEMENT ON AUDITING STANDARDS (SAS)			
SAS No. 69			
. . Required Changes in Accounting Principle	FAS111, ¶7	A06.112	
AICPA STATEMENTS OF POSITION (SOPs)			
Accounting Changes	FAS111, ¶10	A06.127	
	FIN20, ¶5		
ALLOCATION OF COSTS			
See Accrual Basis of Accounting			
See Interim Financial Reporting			
See Segment of Business Reporting			
Definition	CON6, ¶142		
Matching of Costs and Revenues	CON6, ¶149		
ALLOCATION OF INCOME TAXES			
See Income Taxes			
ALLOWABLE COSTS			
See Regulated Operations			
Definition	FAS71, ¶1	Re6.111	
ALLOWANCE FOR DOUBTFUL ACCOUNTS			
See Valuation Allowances			
Sale of Bad-Debt Recovery Rights			EITF.86-8

See "Terminology" for references to defined terms presented in various accounting pronouncements.
See the Introduction to the Topical Index for details on the use of this index.

	Original Pronouncements	Current Text	EITF and Other
ALLOWANCE FOR EARNINGS ON SHAREHOLDERS' INVESTMENT			
See Regulated Operations			
ALTERNATIVE MINIMUM TAX (AMT)			
See Income Taxes			
Accounting for AMT.........................			EITF.87-8
Business Combinations			EITF.87-8
Leases.......................................			EITF.87-8
. . Leveraged Leases			EITF.86-43
Tax Credit Carryforwards....................			EITF.86-41
ALTERNATIVE TAX SYSTEMS			
See Income Taxes			
AMORTIZATION			
See Depreciation			
See Income Taxes			
See Intangible Assets			
See Lending Activities			
See Motion Picture Industry			
See Pension Costs			
See Postretirement Benefits Other Than Pensions			
Accounting Changes	APB20, ¶23-24	A06.119-120	
....	FAS19, ¶30	Oi5.121	
Accounting for Individual Credit Card Acquisitions..................................			EITF.93-1
Accounting Policy Disclosure.................	APB22, ¶13	A10.106	
Amortization Period for Net Deferred Credit Card Origination Costs.....................			EITF.92-5
Cable Television Industry	FAS51, ¶10	Ca4.108	
Core Deposit Intangibles of Thrifts	EITF.85-8		
Credit Cardholder Relationship			EITF.88-20
Definition	CON6, ¶142		
Goodwill			
. . Business Combinations Initiated Prior to Effective Date of Statement 72..........			EITF.89-19
Imputed Interest..............................	APB21, ¶16	I69.108	
Investment in Certain CMOs and Mortgage-Backed Interest-Only Certificates...........			EITF.89-4
Matching of Costs and Revenues	CON6, ¶149		
Methods for Debt Discount	CON6, ¶235-239		
Mortgage Servicing Rights...................			EITF.86-38
Negative Amortization of Loan Principle			
. . Applying Profit Recognition Criteria for Sale of Real Estate			EITF.84-17
. . Interest Income Recognition			EITF.85-38
. . Sale of Negative Amortizing Loans			EITF.85-38
Recognition Guidance	CON5, ¶86		
Unidentifiable Intangible Assets of Thrifts....			EITF.85-8
. . Business Combinations Initiated Prior to Effective Date of Statement 72..........			EITF.89-19

FAS–FASB Statements	FIN–FASB Interpretations	FTB–FASB Technical Bulletins
APB–APB Opinions	AIN–AICPA Interpretations	ARB–Accounting Research Bulletins
CON–FASB Concepts	EITF–EITF Issues	Q&A–FASB Special Reports

See "Terminology" for references to defined terms presented in various accounting pronouncements.
See the Introduction to the Topical Index for details on the use of this index.

	Original Pronouncements	Current Text	EITF and Other
ASSETS—continued			
Recognition of Changes in	CON5, ¶88-90		
Relation to Control............................	CON6, ¶183-189		
Relation to Costs...............................	CON6, ¶178-182		
Relation to Future Economic Benefits	CON6, ¶190-191		
Revaluation of Depreciable Basis for Tax			
Purposes			EITF.84-43
Service Potential	CON6, ¶28		
Transactions and Events Affecting	CON6, ¶32-33		
Uncertainty of Recognition	CON6, ¶44-48		
Valuation of Assets and Liabilities by			
Liquidating Bank			EITF.88-25
ASSOCIATED COMPANIES			
See Mortgage Banking Activities			
See Related Parties			
ATTRIBUTES			
See Measurement			
ATTRIBUTION			
See Postretirement Benefits Other Than			
Pensions			
AVERAGE COST			
Inventory......................................	ARB43, Ch.4, ¶6	I78.107-108	
AWARDS			
See Compensation to Employees: Stock			
Purchase and Stock Option Plans			
See Contributions			

(The next page is T-21.)

FAS–FASB Statements	FIN–FASB Interpretations	FTB–FASB Technical Bulletins
APB–APB Opinions	AIN–AICPA Interpretations	ARB–Accounting Research Bulletins
CON–FASB Concepts	EITF–EITF Issues	Q&A–FASB Special Reports

FAS–FASB Statements   FIN–FASB Interpretations   FTB–FASB Technical Bulletins
APB–APB Opinions   AIN–AICPA Interpretations   ARB–Accounting Research Bulletins
CON–FASB Concepts   EITF–EITF Issues   Q&A–FASB Special Reports

	Original Pronouncements	Current Text	EITF and Other
BALANCE SHEET CLASSIFICATION: CURRENT ASSETS AND LIABILITIES—continued			
Creditors	ARB43, Ch.3A, ¶7	B05.108	
Current Assets	ARB43, Ch.3A, ¶4-6	B05.105-107A	
	FAS115, ¶125		
. . Description and Examples	ARB43, Ch.3A, ¶4	B05.105	
	FAS115, ¶125		
Current Liabilities	ARB43, Ch.3A, ¶7	B05.108	
. . Compensated Absences	FAS43, ¶6	C44.104	
. . Deferred Taxes and Income Taxes	FAS37, ¶16	I27.204	
. . Description and Examples	ARB43, Ch.3A, ¶7-8	B05.108-109	
. . Employee Stock Purchase and Stock Option Plans	APB25, ¶13-15	C47.113-115	
. . Long-Term Obligations, Criteria for Inclusion	FAS78, ¶1	B05.109A-109B	EITF.86-5
	FAS78, ¶5		EITF.86-30
	FAS78, ¶13		
. . Long-Term Obligations, Grace Period within Which to Cure a Violation	FAS78, ¶5	B05.109A	EITF.86-30
Deferred Taxes	FAS109, ¶41-42	I27.140-141	
	FAS109, ¶288		
Definition			
. . Callable Obligations	FAS78, ¶1	B05.400	
. . Current Assets	ARB43, Ch.3A, ¶4	B05.401	
. . Current Liabilities	ARB43, Ch.3A, ¶7	B05.402	
. . Long-Term Obligations	FAS6, ¶2	B05.403	
. . Operating Cycle	ARB43, Ch.3A, ¶5	B05.404	
. . Short-Term Obligations	FAS6, ¶2	B05.405	
. . Subjective Acceleration Clause	FAS78, ¶10	B05.405A	
. . Working Capital	ARB43, Ch.3A, ¶3	B05.406	
Demand Notes			EITF.86-30
. . Obligations with Scheduled Repayment Terms			EITF.86-5
Investment Tax Credits	APB2, ¶14	I27.231	
Investments	ARB43, Ch.3A, ¶6	B05.107	
Long-Term Obligations	FAS6, ¶2	B05.111	
Marketable Securities	ARB43, Ch.3A, ¶4	B05.105	
	ARB43, Ch.3A, ¶9	B05.107A	
	FAS115, ¶125		
Mortgage Banking Activities			
. . Mortgage-Backed Securities and Loans	FAS65, ¶28	Mo4.129	
Motion Picture Industry			
. . Balance Sheet Classification	FAS53, ¶19-21	Mo6.118-120	
Noncurrent Assets	ARB43, Ch.3A, ¶6	B05.107	

See "Terminology" for references to defined terms presented in various accounting pronouncements.

See the Introduction to the Topical Index for details on the use of this index.

	Original Pronouncements	Current Text	EITF and Other
BALANCE SHEET CLASSIFICATION: CURRENT ASSETS AND LIABILITIES—continued			
Operating Cycle	ARB43, Ch.3A, ¶2	B05.103	
	ARB43, Ch.3A, ¶4-5	B05.106	
	ARB43, Ch.3A, ¶7	B05.108	
Prepaid Expenses	ARB43, Ch.3A, ¶4	B05.105	
Refinancing Agreements	FAS6, ¶2	B05.111	
Revolving Credit Agreement	FAS6, ¶14	B05.116	
Scope of Accounting and Reporting Requirements	FAS6, ¶7	B05.102	
Securities with a Put Option Held by an ESOP			EITF.89-11
Short-Term Debt	ARB43, Ch.3A, ¶7	B05.108	
Short-Term Obligations Expected to Be Refinanced	FAS6, ¶1-2	B05.110-117	
	FAS6, ¶8-14		
	FIN8, ¶3		
Sinking Fund Accruals	ARB43, Ch.3A, ¶6	B05.107	
Subjective Acceleration Clauses in Long-Term Debt Agreements	FAS78, ¶10	B05.405A	
	FTB79-3, ¶1-3	B05.501-503	
Unclassified Balance Sheet	FAS6, ¶7	B05.102	
	FAS78, ¶5	B05.118	
Unearned Discount	ARB43, Ch.3A, ¶9	B05.107A	
Working Capital	ARB43, Ch.3A, ¶3	B05.102	
	FAS6, ¶7	B05.104	
BALANCE SHEET CLASSIFICATION: DEBT VS. EQUITY			
Classifying Obligations			
. . Debt Repayable by a Capital Stock Transaction			EITF.84-40
BANKER'S ACCEPTANCES			
See Banking and Thrift Industries			
See Financial Instruments			
BANKING AND THRIFT INDUSTRIES			
See Collateralized Mortgage Obligations			
See Disclosure			
See Financial Instruments			
See Impairment: Loans			
See Lending Activities			
See Mortgage Banking Activities			
See Savings and Loan Associations			
Accounting for Individual Credit Card Acquisitions			EITF.93-1
Acquisition of a Banking or Thrift Institution	FAS72, ¶2-12	Bt7.102-115	
	FIN9, ¶1		
	FIN9, ¶4-5		
	FIN9, ¶7-9		

FAS—FASB Statements	FIN—FASB Interpretations	FTB—FASB Technical Bulletins
APB—APB Opinions	AIN—AICPA Interpretations	ARB—Accounting Research Bulletins
CON—FASB Concepts	EITF—EITF Issues	Q&A—FASB Special Reports

	Original Pronouncements	Current Text	EITF and Other
BANKING AND THRIFT INDUSTRIES—continued			
Acquisition of a Banking or Thrift Institution—continued			
. . Adjustments of Allocation of Original Purchase Price			EITF.85-3
. . Amortization of Unidentifiable Intangible Assets			EITF.85-8
. . FSLIC-Assisted Acquisitions of Thrifts			EITF.88-19
. . Goodwill			EITF.85-42
. . Identifiable Intangible Assets	FAS72, ¶4	Bt7.106	EITF.85-42
	FIN9, ¶8		
. . Net-Spread Method	FIN9, ¶1	Bt7.103	
	FIN9, ¶4		
. . Regulatory-Assisted Acquisitions of Thrifts			EITF.88-19
. . Regulatory-Assisted Combinations	FAS72, ¶3	Bt7.111-115	
	FAS72, ¶8-11		
. . Sale of Assets of Acquired Banking or Thrift Institution	FAS72, ¶7	Bt7.110	
. . Separate-Valuation Method	FIN9, ¶1	Bt7.103	
	FIN9, ¶4		
. . Unidentifiable Intangible Assets	FAS72, ¶5-7	Bt7.107-110	EITF.85-8
	FAS72, ¶12		EITF.85-42
. . Valuation of Assets	FIN9, ¶5	Bt7.104	
. . Valuation of Liabilities	FIN9, ¶7	Bt7.105	
Acquisition of a Savings and Loan Association by a Bank			
. . Accounting for Exit and Entrance Fees Incurred in a Conversion from the Savings Association Insurance Fund to the Bank Insurance Fund			EITF.90-11
. . Tax Implications of Excess Bad Debt Reserves			EITF.86-31
Acquisition, Development, and Construction Loans			EITF.84-4
			EITF.86-21
Amortization Period for Net Deferred Credit Card Origination Costs			EITF.92-5
Bad Debts			
. . Accounting for Income Tax Benefits from Bad Debts of a Savings and Loan Association			EITF.91-3
Banker's Acceptances			
. . Accounting for Risk Participations			EITF.85-34
Cash Flows Statement	FAS104, ¶7	C25.111A	
		Bt7.123	
Change in Accounting Estimate			
. . Core Deposit Intangibles			EITF.85-33
Collateralized Mortgage Obligations (CMOs)			
. . Purchased Investment			EITF.89-4
			EITF.93-18
Commitment Fees and Costs			
. . Loan Guarantees			EITF.85-20

See "Terminology" for references to defined terms presented in various accounting pronouncements.

See the Introduction to the Topical Index for details on the use of this index.

FAS—FASB Statements   FIN—FASB Interpretations   FTB—FASB Technical Bulletins
APB—APB Opinions   AIN—AICPA Interpretations   ARB—Accounting Research Bulletins
CON—FASB Concepts   EITF—EITF Issues   Q&A—FASB Special Reports

	Original Pronouncements	Current Text	EITF and Other
BANKING AND THRIFT INDUSTRIES—continued			
Federal Home Loan Mortgage Corporation (FHLMC)			
. . Accounting for Distribution of FHLMC Participating Preferred Stock	FAS115, ¶136		
	FTB85-1, ¶1-4	Bt7.501-504	
. . Disclosure of Relationship of District Banks and Member Banks	FTB85-1, ¶14	Bt7.505	
. . Receipt of FHLMC Participating Preferred Stock	FTB85-1, ¶1-4	Bt7.501-504	EITF.85-7
. . Relationship of District Banks and Member Banks	FTB85-1, ¶14	Bt7.505	
Federal Savings and Loan Insurance Corporation (FSLIC)			
. . FSLIC-Assisted Acquisitions of Thrifts			EITF.88-19
. . Management Consignment Program			EITF.85-41
. . Net Worth Certificates			EITF.85-41
. . Write-off of Prepayments to the Secondary Reserve			EITF.87-22
Financial Institutions Reform, Recovery, and Enforcement Act of 1989 (FIRREA)			
. . Divestiture of Certain Investment Securities			EITF.89-18
Flip Transactions			EITF.85-38
Futures Contracts, Hedges	FAS80, ¶63	F80.104	EITF.86-34
GNMA Dollar Rolls			EITF.84-20
Goodwill Amortization			
. . Business Combinations Initiated Prior to Effective Date of Statement 72			EITF.89-19
Hedging Reverse Repurchase Agreements			EITF.86-34
Hedging with Cash Securities			EITF.87-1
High-Risk Mortgage Security			EITF.D-39
Impairment			
. . Mortgage Obligation Instrument or Mortgage-Backed Interest-Only Certificate			EITF.93-18
Implementation of Statement 107			EITF.D-29
Intangible Assets			
. . Adjustments of Allocation of Original Purchase Price			EITF.85-3
. . Amortization of Unidentifiable Intangible Assets			EITF.85-8
. . Change in Amortization Method for Goodwill			EITF.89-19
. . Core Deposit Intangibles			EITF.85-33
. . Identifiable Intangible Assets			EITF.85-42
. . Unidentifiable Intangible Assets			EITF.85-8
			EITF.85-42
Interest Rate Swap Transactions			EITF.84-36
			EITF.88-8
. . Termination or Sale			EITF.84-7

See "Terminology" for references to defined terms presented in various accounting pronouncements.

See the Introduction to the Topical Index for details on the use of this index.

FAS—FASB Statements   FIN—FASB Interpretations   FTB—FASB Technical Bulletins
APB—APB Opinions   AIN—AICPA Interpretations   ARB—Accounting Research Bulletins
CON—FASB Concepts   EITF—EITF Issues   Q&A—FASB Special Reports

	Original Pronouncements	Current Text	EITF and Other
BANKING AND THRIFT INDUSTRIES—continued			
Mortgage Servicing Rights			
. . Recognition of Sale of Mortgage Servicing Rights			EITF.89-5
. . Sale of Mortgage Loan with Servicing Rights Retained			EITF.86-39
. . Sale of Mortgage Servicing Rights			EITF.85-13
. . . .			EITF.89-5
. . Sale of Mortgage Servicing Rights with Subservicing Agreement			EITF.87-34
. . . .			EITF.90-21
Mortgage Swaps			EITF.88-8
Participation in Future Payment Stream			
. . Unanticipated Mortgage Prepayments .			EITF.86-38
Receipt of FHLMC Participating Preferred Stock			EITF.85-7
Regulatory-Assisted Acquisitions of Thrifts			EITF.88-19
. . Disclosure Requirements			EITF.88-19
Relationship between Statement 15 and Savings and Loan Audit Guide			
. . Loan Loss Allowances			EITF.87-5
Reorganization of a Banking or Thrift Institution			
. . Regulatory-Assisted Combinations . . .			EITF.85-41
. . Valuation of Assets and Liabilities			EITF.85-41
Revenue Recognition			
. . Credit Card Portfolio Securitizations with a "Removal of Accounts" Provision			EITF.90-18
. . Fees Associated with Loan Syndications and Loan Participations			EITF.88-17
. . Sale of Convertible, Adjustable-Rate Mortgages with Contingent Repayment Agreement			EITF.87-25
. . Sale of Mortgage Loan with Servicing Rights Retained			EITF.86-39
. . Sale of Mortgage Servicing Rights			EITF.85-13
. . . .			EITF.89-5
. . Sale of Mortgage Servicing Rights with Subservicing Agreement			EITF.87-34
. . Sale of Short-Term Loan under Long-Term Credit Commitment			EITF.87-30
. . Sale with a Partial Participation Retained			EITF.84-21
. . Securitization of Credit Card Portfolio			EITF.88-22
Reverse Repurchase Agreements			EITF.84-20
Sale of Bad Debt Recovery Rights			EITF.86-8
Sale of Loan with a Partial Participation Retained			EITF.84-21
Sale of Short-Term Loan under Long-Term Credit Commitment			EITF.87-30

See "Terminology" for references to defined terms presented in various accounting pronouncements.

See the Introduction to the Topical Index for details on the use of this index.

FAS–FASB Statements   FIN–FASB Interpretations   FTB–FASB Technical Bulletins
APB–APB Opinions   AIN–AICPA Interpretations   ARB–Accounting Research Bulletins
CON–FASB Concepts   EITF–EITF Issues   Q&A–FASB Special Reports

See "Terminology" for references to defined terms presented in various accounting pronouncements.

See the Introduction to the Topical Index for details on the use of this index.

FAS–FASB Statements   FIN–FASB Interpretations   FTB–FASB Technical Bulletins
APB–APB Opinions   AIN–AICPA Interpretations   ARB–Accounting Research Bulletins
CON–FASB Concepts   EITF–EITF Issues   Q&A–FASB Special Reports

See "Terminology" for references to defined terms presented in various accounting pronouncements.

See the Introduction to the Topical Index for details on the use of this index.

	Original Pronouncements	Current Text	EITF and Other
BUSINESS			
COMBINATIONS—continued			
Definition—continued			
. . Contingent Consideration	APB16, ¶78	B50.402	
. . Goodwill	APB16, ¶87	B50.403	
. . Negative Goodwill	APB16, ¶87	B50.404	
. . Nonpublic Enterprise	FAS79, ¶5	B50.404A	
. . . .	FAS79, ¶16		
. . Pooling-of-Interests Method	APB16, ¶45	B50.405	
. . Preacquisition Contingencies	FAS38, ¶4	B50.406	
. . Purchase Method	APB16, ¶44	B50.407	
Different Tax and Accounting Bases for Acquired Assets and Liabilities	FAS109, ¶30	I27.129	
Different Tax and Accounting Bases for Depreciation of Property			
. . Unrecognized Tax Benefits			EITF.85-3
Divestiture	APB16, ¶46	B50.105	
Downstream Mergers	AIN-APB16, ¶26	B50.593-596	EITF.85-4
. . . .	FTB85-5, ¶13-14	B50.596E-596F	
Effect of Change in Tax Rate			EITF.86-42
Excess of Acquired Net Assets over Cost . .	APB16, ¶91-92	B50.160-161	
Exchange of Assets for Noncontrolling Equity Interest in New Entity			EITF.89-7
Exchange of Interest in Subsidiary for Noncontrolling Equity Interest in New Entity			EITF.89-7
Exchanges of Ownership Interests between Entities under Common Control			EITF.90-5
Federal Savings and Loan Insurance Corporation (FSLIC)			
. . FSLIC-Assisted Acquisitions of Thrifts			EITF.88-19
. . Management Consignment Program . .			EITF.85-41
Foreign Operations	FAS52, ¶101	F60.102	
Franchisor Acquisition of Franchisee's Business	FAS45, ¶19	Fr3.115	
Goodwill			
. . Amortization	APB16, ¶90	B50.159	
Guaranteed Future Value of Stock Issued by Acquirer			EITF.87-31
Initiation Date			
. . Description	APB16, ¶46	B50.105	
. . Effect of Terminating a Plan of Combination	AIN-APB16, #10	B50.528-529	
. . Notification to Stockholders	AIN-APB16, #2	B50.505-508	
. . Option to Exchange Shares	AIN-APB16, #29	B50.609-612	

FAS–FASB Statements   FIN–FASB Interpretations   FTB–FASB Technical Bulletins
APB–APB Opinions   AIN–AICPA Interpretations   ARB–Accounting Research Bulletins
CON–FASB Concepts   EITF–EITF Issues   Q&A–FASB Special Reports

	Original Pronouncements	Current Text	EITF and Other

BUSINESS
COMBINATIONS—continued
Initiation Date—continued

	Original Pronouncements	Current Text	EITF and Other
. . Ratio of Exchange	AIN-APB16, #1	B50.501-504	
Interim Financial Reporting	APB28, ¶21	I73.124	
Leveraged Buyout			
. . Allocating Basis to Individual Assets and Liabilities under Issue No. 88-16.			EITF.90-12
. . Carryover of Predecessor Cost			EITF.86-16
....			EITF.88-16
. . Financed by Loan to ESOP			EITF.85-11
. . Purchase of Stock Options and SARs by Target Company			EITF.84-13
. . Valuation of Shareholder's Interest ...			EITF.86-16
....			EITF.88-16
Loss Carryforwards			
. . Purchased			EITF.85-15
....			EITF.86-1
. . Realization of Income Tax Benefit			EITF.86-1
Master Limited Partnerships			
. . Carryover of Predecessor Cost			EITF.87-21
. . Recording Assets Acquired and Liabilities Assumed			EITF.87-21
Nonmonetary Transactions	APB29, ¶4	N35.101	EITF.85-43
....			EITF.86-29
. . Exchange of Assets for Noncontrolling Equity Interest in New Entity			EITF.89-7
. . Exchange of Interest in Subsidiary for Noncontrolling Equity Interest in New Entity			EITF.89-7
. . Nonmonetary Exchange of Cost-Method Investments			EITF.91-5
. . Transfer of Nonmonetary Assets to a New Corporation			EITF.84-39
. . Transfers between Entities under Common Control			EITF.84-39
Nonpublic Enterprises	FAS79, ¶6	B50.165	
Normal Dividends	APB16, ¶47	B50.106	
Operations Held for Sale after a Business Combination			
. . Disclosure by SEC Registrants			EITF.87-11
....			EITF.90-6
Part Purchase, Part Pooling	AIN-APB16, #15	B50.102	
....	APB16, ¶42	B50.545-548	
Personal Holding Enterprises			
. . Pooling by Subsidiary of	AIN-APB16, #28	B50.606-608	
Pooling-of-Interests Method			
. . Abnormal Dividends	APB16, ¶47	B50.106	
. . Absence of Controlling Class of Common Stock			EITF.87-27
....			EITF.88-26
. . Absence of Planned Transactions.....	APB16, ¶45	B50.104	
....	APB16, ¶48	B50.107	

See "Terminology" for references to defined terms presented in various accounting pronouncements.

See the Introduction to the Topical Index for details on the use of this index.

FAS–FASB Statements	FIN–FASB Interpretations	FTB–FASB Technical Bulletins
APB–APB Opinions	AIN–AICPA Interpretations	ARB–Accounting Research Bulletins
CON–FASB Concepts	EITF–EITF Issues	Q&A–FASB Special Reports

T-35

	Original Pronouncements	Current Text	EITF and Other

See "Terminology" for references to defined terms presented in various accounting pronouncements.

See the Introduction to the Topical Index for details on the use of this index.

	Original Pronouncements	Current Text	EITF and Other
BUSINESS COMBINATIONS—continued			
Pooling-of-Interests Method—continued			
. . Voting Common Stock	APB16, ¶47	B50.106	
. . Voting Ratio Maintained	APB16, ¶47	B50.106	
. . Warrants Acquired for Cash			EITF.85-14
. . Warrants May Defeat Pooling	AIN-APB16, #12	B50.534-538	
. . Wholly Owned Subsidiary, Use of Pooling	AIN-APB16, #18	B50.556-559	
	AIN-APB16, #36	B50.635-637	
Preacquisition Contingencies	FAS38, ¶4-6	B50.148-150	EITF.93-7
	FAS38, ¶23	C59.119	
Preacquisition Dividends of Subsidiary	ARB43, Ch.1A, ¶3	R70.102	
Preacquisition Earnings of Purchased Subsidiary	ARB51, ¶9	R70.101	
Prior Period Adjustments			
. . Change in Reporting Entity	APB20, ¶12	A35.112-113	
	APB20, ¶35		
Pro Forma Information	FAS79, ¶6	B50.165	
Purchase Method			
. . Accrual of Liabilities			EITF.84-35
. . Acquiring Assets, Accounting after Acquisition	APB16, ¶69	B50.127	
. . Acquiring Assets, Allocating Cost	APB16, ¶68	B50.126	EITF.87-8
. . Acquiring Assets, Principles	APB16, ¶67	B50.125	
. . Acquiring Enterprise, Characteristics and Identification	APB16, ¶70-71	B50.128-129	
. . Adjustments of Allocation of Original Purchase Price			EITF.85-3
. . Adjustments to Purchase Price Allocation under IRC Section 338			EITF.86-3
. . Allocating Basis to Individual Assets and Liabilities under Issue No. 88-16.			EITF.90-12
. . Allocating Cost to Assets to Be Sold			EITF.87-11
. . Allocating Cost to Assets to Be Sold When Sale Is Not Completed within Holding Period			EITF.90-6
. . Alternative Minimum Tax			EITF.87-8
. . Compensation in Contingent Agreements	APB16, ¶86	B50.144	
. . Contingent Consideration	APB16, ¶77-86	B50.135-144	
. . Contingent Consideration Based on Earnings	APB16, ¶80	B50.138	
. . Contingent Consideration Based on Security Prices	APB16, ¶81-83	B50.139-141	
. . Cost of an Acquired Enterprise			EITF.84-35
. . Costs of Acquisition	APB16, ¶76	B50.134	
. . Costs of Closing Duplicate Facilities of an Acquirer	FTB85-5, ¶1-4	B50.651-652	EITF.84-35
. . Determining Cost of an Acquired Enterprise	APB16, ¶72-75	B50.130-133	

FAS—FASB Statements   FIN—FASB Interpretations   FTB—FASB Technical Bulletins
APB—APB Opinions   AIN—AICPA Interpretations   ARB—Accounting Research Bulletins
CON—FASB Concepts   EITF—EITF Issues   Q&A—FASB Special Reports

T-37

See "Terminology" for references to defined terms presented in various accounting pronouncements.
See the Introduction to the Topical Index for details on the use of this index.

	Original Pronouncements	Current Text	EITF and Other
BUSINESS COMBINATIONS—continued			
Purchase Method—continued			
. . Transactions between Enterprises under Common Control			EITF.86-16
. . . .			EITF.88-16
. . Uncertainties Related to Income Taxes in a Purchase Business Combination .			EITF.93-7
. . Valuation of Assets and Liabilities Acquired	APB16, ¶88	B50.146	EITF.86-42
. . . .	FAS87, ¶74		
. . . .	FAS106, ¶86-88		
. . . .	FAS109, ¶288		
Push-down Accounting			EITF.85-21
. . . .			EITF.86-9
. . Parent Company's Debt to Subsidiary .			EITF.84-42
Recognition and Measurement of the Tax Benefit of Excess Tax-Deductible Goodwill Resulting from a Retroactive Change in Tax Law			EITF.93-12
Scope of Accounting and Reporting Requirements	APB16, ¶5	B50.101	
Separate Financial Statements of Acquired Company			
. . Push-down Accounting			EITF.86-9
Several Enterprises in a Single Business Combination	AIN-APB16, #38	B50.641-644	
Stock Options Acquired by Acquired Company with Assistance from Acquiring Company			EITF.85-45
Stock Options and SARs Purchased by Acquired Company			EITF.84-13
Takeover Attempt			
. . Costs Incurred in a Takeover Defense .			EITF.85-2
Transactions between Enterprises under Common Control	AIN-APB16, #39	B50.596A-596D	EITF.85-4
. . . .	FTB85-5, ¶5-7		
. . . .	FTB85-5, ¶12		
Transitional Matters			
. . Changes in Intercorporate Investments	AIN-APB16, #16	B50.549-551	
. . General Provisions	APB16, ¶99	B50.167-168	
. . Grandfather Clause for Subsidiaries . .	AIN-APB16, #24	B50.580-583	
. . Intercorporate Investment at October 31, 1970	AIN-APB16, #17	B50.552-555	
. . Part Purchase, Part Pooling	AIN-APB16, #15	B50.545-548	
BUSINESS ENTERPRISE			
Cash Flow Prospects	CON1, ¶39		
Compared to Not-for-Profit Organizations	CON4, ¶6-9		
. . . .	CON4, ¶14-22		

FAS–FASB Statements   FIN–FASB Interpretations   FTB–FASB Technical Bulletins
APB–APB Opinions   AIN–AICPA Interpretations   ARB–Accounting Research Bulletins
CON–FASB Concepts   EITF–EITF Issues   Q&A–FASB Special Reports

T-39

	Original Pronouncements	Current Text	EITF and Other

BUSINESS ENTERPRISE—continued
Earning Process .... CON1, ¶42-48
Performance Measurement .... CON1, ¶42-55
Return on Investment.................. CON1, ¶45
BUSINESS ENTERPRISE OBJECTIVES
Compared to Not-for-Profit
  Organizations' Objectives............. CON4, ¶67
BUSINESS INTERRUPTION
See Contingencies
BUSINESS SEGMENTS
See Segment of Business Reporting

(The next page is T-51.)

See "Terminology" for references to defined terms presented in various accounting pronouncements.

See the Introduction to the Topical Index for details on the use of this index.

	Original Pronouncements	Current Text	EITF and Other
CABLE TELEVISION INDUSTRY			
Amortization of Capitalized Costs	FAS51, ¶10	Ca4.108	
. . Franchise Costs	FAS51, ¶13	Ca4.111	
. . Hookup Revenue and Costs	FAS51, ¶11-12	Ca4.109-110	
. . Recoverability of Costs	FAS51, ¶14	Ca4.112	
Glossary	FAS51, ¶17	Ca4.401-404	
Prematurity Period			
. . Accounting during	FAS51, ¶6-9	Ca4.104-107	
. . Definition	FAS51, ¶17	Ca4.403	
. . Establishment by Management	FAS51, ¶4	Ca4.102	
. . Interest Capitalization	FAS51, ¶9	Ca4.107	
. . Portion of System in	FAS51, ¶5	Ca4.103	
Scope of Accounting and Reporting			
Requirements	FAS51, ¶1	Ca4.101	
CAPITAL			
Description	CON6, ¶212		
CAPITAL IN EXCESS OF PAR VALUE			
See Additional Paid-in Capital			
CAPITAL LEASES			
See Leases			
See Regulated Operations			
Definition	FAS13, ¶7	L10.102	
CAPITAL LOSSES			
See Quasi Reorganizations			
CAPITAL MAINTENANCE			
Concepts, Physical Capital and Financial			
Capital	CON5, ¶45-48		
. . . .	CON6, ¶71-72		
Disclosure in Cash Flows Statement	FAS95, ¶99	C25.115	
Maintenance of Net Assets			
. . Not-for-Profit Organizations	CON6, ¶103-106		
Relation to Price-Level Changes	CON6, ¶71		
Relation to Return on Investment			
(Business Enterprises)	CON6, ¶71		
CAPITAL STOCK			
See Earnings per Share			
CAPITAL STOCK: CAPITAL			
TRANSACTIONS			
See Business Combinations			
See Capital Stock: Dividends-in-Kind			
See Capital Stock: Preferred Stock			
See Capital Stock: Stock Dividends and			
Stock Splits			

FAS—FASB Statements	FIN—FASB Interpretations	FTB—FASB Technical Bulletins
APB—APB Opinions	AIN—AICPA Interpretations	ARB—Accounting Research Bulletins
CON—FASB Concepts	EITF—EITF Issues	Q&A—FASB Special Reports

T-51

	Original Pronouncements	Current Text	EITF and Other
CAPITAL STOCK: CAPITAL TRANSACTIONS—continued			
See Capital Stock: Treasury Stock			
See Debt: Convertible Debt and Debt with Stock Purchase Warrants			
See Disclosure			
Changes in Capital Accounts	APB12, ¶10	C08.102	
Contingent Stock Purchase Warrants			EITF.84-8
Costs Incurred in a Takeover Defense.....			EITF.85-2
Debt Exchanged for Common or Preferred Shares	FAS111, ¶8	D14.501-504	
....	FTB80-1, ¶1-4		
Debt Repayable by a Capital Stock Transaction........................			EITF.84-40
Detachable Stock Purchase Warrants Issued in Connection with Debt	APB14, ¶16	C08.104	
. . Includes Put for Stock Purchased			EITF.86-35
Development Stage Enterprises	FAS7, ¶11	De4.107	
....	FAS95, ¶151		
Employee Purchases at a Discount			
. . Employee Can Put Stock to Issuer....			EITF.84-34
. . Issuer Has Right of First Refusal			EITF.84-34
Exchanges of Ownership Interests between Entities under Common Control			EITF.90-5
Excluded from Income			
. . Retained Earnings Appropriations....	APB9, ¶28	C08.101	
. . Treasury Stock Transactions	APB9, ¶28	C08.101	
Nonmonetary Transactions	APB29, ¶4	N35.101	EITF.86-29
Notes Received for Capital Stock			EITF.85-1
Paid-in Capital	APB14, ¶16	C08.103-104	
....	ARB43, Ch.1A, ¶6		
Partnership Withdrawals			EITF.85-46
Redeemable Stock	FAS47, ¶9-10	C32.104-105	
....	FAS47, ¶31-32	C32.113-114	
. . Purchase by Parent Company			EITF.86-32
. . Sale of Put Options on Issuer's Stock .			EITF.87-31
Sale of Capital Stock by Subsidiary			EITF.84-27
Sale of Put Options on Issuer's Stock.....			EITF.87-31
Shareholder Appreciation Rights Program (SHARP)			EITF.87-31
Shareholder/Former Shareholder Payments			
. . Greenmail........................	FTB85-6, ¶3-5	C23.503-504	EITF.85-2
....	FTB85-6, ¶14-16	I60.507-508	
. . Payments for Precluding Further Share Purchases..................	FTB85-6, ¶4-7	I60.507-508	EITF.85-2
Stock Issued for Property and Subsequently Contributed Back to Enterprise........................	ARB43, Ch.1A, ¶6	C08.103	

See "Terminology" for references to defined terms presented in various accounting pronouncements.

See the Introduction to the Topical Index for details on the use of this index.

	Original Pronouncements	Current Text	EITF and Other
CAPITAL STOCK: CAPITAL TRANSACTIONS—continued			
Takeover Attempts	FTB85-6, ¶4-7	I17.509-510	
....		I60.507-508	
. . Costs Incurred in a Takeover Defense .			EITF.85-2
Variable Stock Purchase Warrants			EITF.84-8
Warrants Issued in Conjunction with Sales Agreement			EITF.84-8
CAPITAL STOCK: DIVIDENDS-IN-KIND			
See Capital Stock: Capital Transactions			
See Capital Stock: Preferred Stock			
See Capital Stock: Stock Dividends and Stock Splits			
See Capital Stock: Treasury Stock			
See Disclosure			
Distributions of Loans Receivable to Shareholders			EITF.87-17
Scope of Accounting and Reporting Requirements......................	APB29, ¶4	C11.101	
....	APB29, ¶18		
CAPITAL STOCK: PREFERRED STOCK			
See Capital Stock: Capital Transactions			
See Capital Stock: Dividends-in-Kind			
See Capital Stock: Stock Dividends and Stock Splits			
See Capital Stock: Treasury Stock			
See Disclosure			
Conversion to Common Stock	APB12, ¶10	C08.102	
Debt Repayable by a Capital Stock Transaction.........................			EITF.84-40
Disclosure Requirements	APB10, ¶10-11	C16.101-102	
....	APB15, ¶50		
Effect of a Redemption Agreement on Carrying Value of Investment.........			EITF.85-23
FHLMC Participating Preferred Stock . . Receipt of Stock...................			EITF.85-7
Foreign Currency Translation	FAS52, ¶48	F60.147	
Imputation of Dividends When Initial Dividend Rate Is Below Market........			EITF.86-45
Redeemable Stock	FAS47, ¶9-10	C32.104-105	
....	FAS47, ¶31-32	C32.113-114	
. . Purchase by Parent Company........			EITF.86-32
Redemption or Induced Conversion . . Calculation of Earnings per Share			EITF.D-42
CAPITAL STOCK: STOCK DIVIDENDS AND STOCK SPLITS			
See Capital Stock: Capital Transactions			
See Capital Stock: Dividends-in-Kind			
See Capital Stock: Preferred Stock			

FAS–FASB Statements   FIN–FASB Interpretations   FTB–FASB Technical Bulletins
APB–APB Opinions   AIN–AICPA Interpretations   ARB–Accounting Research Bulletins
CON–FASB Concepts   EITF–EITF Issues   Q&A–FASB Special Reports

	Original Pronouncements	Current Text	EITF and Other
CAPITAL STOCK: STOCK DIVIDENDS AND STOCK SPLITS—continued			
See Capital Stock: Treasury Stock			
Accounting by the Issuer			
. . Stock Dividends	ARB43, Ch.7B, ¶10-14	C20.103-107	
. . Stock Dividends of Subsidiaries	ARB51, ¶18	C20.110	
. . Stock Splits	ARB43, Ch.7B, ¶15-16	C20.108-109	
Accounting by the Recipient	ARB43, Ch.7B, ¶9	C20.102	
. . Distribution of FHLMC Participating Preferred Stock	FAS115, ¶136	Bt7.501-504	EITF.85-7
. . . .	FTB85-1, ¶1-4		
Definition			
. . Stock Dividend	ARB43, Ch.7B, ¶1	C20.401	
. . Stock Split	ARB43, Ch.7B, ¶2	C20.402	
Federal Home Loan Mortgage Corporation (FHLMC)			
. . Accounting for Distribution of FHLMC Participating Preferred Stock	FAS115, ¶136	Bt7.501-504	
. . . .	FTB85-1, ¶1-4		
Legal Requirements	ARB43, Ch.7B, ¶14	C20.107	
Nonmonetary Transactions	APB29, ¶4	N35.101	
Scope of Accounting and Reporting Requirements	ARB43, Ch.7B, ¶3	C20.101	
Shareholder Appreciation Rights Program (SHARP)			EITF.87-31
Special, Large, and Nonrecurring Dividends			EITF.90-9
CAPITAL STOCK: TREASURY STOCK			
See Capital Stock: Capital Transactions			
See Capital Stock: Dividends-in-Kind			
See Capital Stock: Preferred Stock			
See Capital Stock: Stock Dividends and Stock Splits			
See Disclosure			
Accounting for Treasury Stock in Leveraged Preferred Stock ESOPs			EITF.D-19
Business Combinations	AIN-APB16, #20	B50.106	
. . . .	APB16, ¶47	B50.562-568	
Dividends	ARB43, Ch.1A, ¶4	C23.101	
Earnings per Share	AIN-APB15, Exh.4	E09.910	
Effect of Acquisition of Employer Shares for/by an Employee Benefit Trust on Accounting for Business Combinations . .			EITF.93-2
Effect of Unallocated Shares on Applying Pooling-of-Interests Method to a Business Combination			EITF.88-27
Employer's Stock Contributed to Defined Contribution Plan			
. . Excess Assets Not Allocated to Participants			EITF.86-27
Employer's Stock Contributed to Employee Stock Ownership Plan			
. . Excess Assets Not Allocated to Participants			EITF.86-27

See "Terminology" for references to defined terms presented in various accounting pronouncements.

See the Introduction to the Topical Index for details on the use of this index.

	Original Pronouncements	Current Text	EITF and Other
CAPITAL STOCK: TREASURY STOCK—continued			
Held Not for Retirement	APB6, ¶12	C23.103	EITF.85-2
. . . .	ARB43, Ch.1A, ¶4	C23.501-503	
. . . .	FTB85-6, ¶1-3		
Investment by Subsidiary in Treasury Stock of Parent	ARB51, ¶13	C51.114	
Legal Requirements	APB6, ¶13	C23.104	
Purchase of Treasury Shares			
. . Price Significantly in Excess of the Current Market Price of the Shares . .	FTB85-6, ¶1-3	C23.501-504	EITF.85-2
. . . .	FTB85-6, ¶14-16		
Retirement	APB6, ¶12	C23.102	
Tainted Shares	AIN-APB16, #20	B50.567	EITF.88-27
. . . .			EITF.93-2
. . . .			EITF.D-19
Transactions Excluded from Income	APB9, ¶28	C08.101	
CAPITAL SURPLUS			
See Additional Paid-in Capital			
See Quasi Reorganizations			
CAPITAL TRANSACTIONS			
See Capital Stock: Capital Transactions			
CAPITALIZATION			
See Earnings per Share			
See Leases			
See Regulated Operations			
CAPITALIZATION OF INTEREST			
See Interest: Capitalization of Interest Costs			
See Oil and Gas Producing Activities			
CAPITALIZED COSTS			
Asbestos Treatment			EITF.89-13
Costs to Clean Up Environmental Contamination			EITF.90-8
Deferred Costs			
. . Development Stage Enterprises	FAS7, ¶10	De4.105	
. . Direct Loan Origination Costs	FAS91, ¶5-7	L20.104-106	
. . Loan Commitment Fees and Costs . . .	FAS91, ¶8-10	L20.107-109	
Regulated Operations	FAS71, ¶4	Re6.114	
. . . .	FAS71, ¶9-10	Re6.119-120	
. . . .	FAS90, ¶3-5	Re6.127A-127C	
. . Allowance for Earnings on Shareholders' Investment	FAS92, ¶8-9	Re6.125G	
. . Discontinuation of Accounting for the Effects of Certain Types of Regulation	FAS101, ¶5-7	Re6.204-206	
. . Phase-in Plan	FAS92, ¶4-5	Re6.125B-125C	
CAPITALIZED INTEREST			
See Interest: Capitalization of Interest Costs			
See Interest: Imputation of an Interest Cost			

FAS–FASB Statements   FIN–FASB Interpretations   FTB–FASB Technical Bulletins
APB–APB Opinions   AIN–AICPA Interpretations   ARB–Accounting Research Bulletins
CON–FASB Concepts   EITF–EITF Issues   Q&A–FASB Special Reports

T-55

	Original Pronouncements	Current Text	EITF and Other
CARRYFORWARDS AND CARRYBACKS			
See Income Taxes			
CARRYING AMOUNT			
See Banking and Thrift Industries			
See Debt: Restructurings			
See Investments: Marketable Securities			
Definition	FAS12, ¶7	Bt7.401	
....	FAS72, ¶5	I89.401	
Extinguished Debt	APB26, ¶19	D14.102	
Of Payables			
. . Definition	FAS15, ¶13	D22.401	
CASH			
See Financial Instruments			
Balance Sheet Classification	ARB43, Ch.3A, ¶4	B05.105	
Medium of Exchange...................	CON1, ¶10		
....	CON6, ¶29		
Restricted in Use.....................	ARB43, Ch.3A, ¶6	B05.107	
CASH BASIS OF ACCOUNTING			
Compared to Accrual Basis of Accounting	CON4, ¶50		
....	CON6, ¶139-140		
....	CON6, ¶144-145		
CASH FLOWS			
See Cash Flows Statement			
See Recognition and Measurement in Financial Statements			
Cash Flow per Share	FAS95, ¶33	C25.135	
....	FAS95, ¶125		
Information Useful in Assessing	CON1, ¶37-39		
Performance Measurement	CON1, ¶43-49		
Relation to Earnings..................	CON1, ¶43-49		
Statement of	CON5, ¶52-54		
Users' Needs for Information	CON1, ¶25		
....	CON1, ¶30		
CASH FLOWS STATEMENT			
See Disclosure			
Anticipatory Hedges	FAS104, ¶7	C25.112	
Banks, Savings Institutions, and Credit Unions	FAS104, ¶7	C25.111A	
Cash and Cash Equivalents	FAS95, ¶7-10	C25.105-108	
Cash Flow per Share	FAS95, ¶33	C25.135	
....	FAS95, ¶125		
Classification of Cash Receipts and Payments	FAS95, ¶14-24	C25.112-122B	
....	FAS102, ¶8-9	I80.117	

See "Terminology" for references to defined terms presented in various accounting pronouncements.

See the Introduction to the Topical Index for details on the use of this index.

FAS–FASB Statements   FIN–FASB Interpretations   FTB–FASB Technical Bulletins
APB–APB Opinions   AIN–AICPA Interpretations   ARB–Accounting Research Bulletins
CON–FASB Concepts   EITF–EITF Issues   Q&A–FASB Special Reports

	Original Pronouncements	Current Text	EITF and Other
CASH FLOWS			
STATEMENT—continued			
Operating Activities	FAS95, ¶27-30	C25.125-128	
. . Direct Method	FAS95, ¶27	C25.125	
....	FAS95, ¶29-30	C25.127-128	
. . Indirect Method	FAS95, ¶28-30	C25.126-128	
Scope and Purpose of Accounting and			
Reporting..........................	FAS95, ¶3-6	C25.101-104	
. . Employee Benefit Plans............	FAS102, ¶10	C25.101	
. . Investment Enterprises	FAS102, ¶10	C25.101	
. . Not-for-Profit	FAS117, ¶30	C25.101	
CASH SURRENDER VALUE			
Life Insurance			
. . Provision for Deferred Taxes on			
Increases in CSV			EITF.87-28
. . Temporary Differences	FAS109, ¶14	I27.113	
CASUALTY LOSSES			
See Extraordinary Items			
See Insurance Industry			
Loss Contingencies....................	FAS5, ¶4	C59.122	
Unasserted Claims	FAS5, ¶38	C59.144	
CATCH-UP ADJUSTMENT			
See Cumulative Accounting Adjustments			
CHANGE IN ACCOUNTING			
PRINCIPLES/ESTIMATES/ENTITY			
See Accounting Changes			
CHANGE IN BASIS OF ASSETS AND			
LIABILITIES			
See Business Combinations			
Adjustments for Payments during Rent-up			
Period of Real Estate................			EITF.85-27
Basis of Accounting under FSLIC			
Management Consignment Program			EITF.85-41
Exchanges of Ownership Interests between			
Entities under Common Control			EITF.90-5
Leveraged Buyout Transactions.........			EITF.86-16
....			EITF.88-16
. . Allocating Basis to Individual Assets			
and Liabilities under Issue No. 88-16.			EITF.90-12
Liquidation of a Banking Institution			
. . Valuation of Assets and Liabilities by			
Liquidating Bank................			EITF.88-25
Master Limited Partnership Transactions .			EITF.87-21
New Basis of Accounting Resulting from			
Change in Ownership			EITF.85-21
Push-down Accounting in Separate			
Statements of Acquired Entity.........			EITF.86-9
Push-down of Parent Company's Debt to			
Subsidiary			EITF.84-42

See "Terminology" for references to defined terms presented in various accounting pronouncements.

See the Introduction to the Topical Index for details on the use of this index.

FAS—FASB Statements	FIN—FASB Interpretations	FTB—FASB Technical Bulletins
APB—APB Opinions	AIN—AICPA Interpretations	ARB—Accounting Research Bulletins
CON—FASB Concepts	EITF—EITF Issues	Q&A—FASB Special Reports

T-59

See "Terminology" for references to defined terms presented in various accounting pronouncements.

See the Introduction to the Topical Index for details on the use of this index.

	Original Pronouncements	Current Text	EITF and Other

CLASSIFICATION OF ASSETS AND LIABILITIES
See Balance Sheet Classification: Current Assets and Liabilities
See Balance Sheet Classification: Debt vs. Equity

CLOSELY HELD COMPANIES
See Earnings per Share
See Mortgage Banking Activities
See Related Parties

CLOSING DUPLICATE FACILITIES OF AN ACQUIRER
See Business Combinations
Facilities of an Acquirer Duplicated by a Business Combination . . . . FTB85-5, ¶1-2   B50.651-652   EITF.84-35

CLUBS
See Not-for-Profit Organizations

CMOs
See Collateralized Mortgage Obligations

COAL INDUSTRY
Accounting for Estimated Payments in Connection with the Coal Industry Retiree Health Benefit Act of 1992 . . . . .   EITF.92-13

CO-BRANDING
See Lending Activities

COLLATERAL
See Financial Instruments
For Loans
. . Collateral-Dependent Loans . . . . FAS114, ¶13   I08.111
. . Loss Contingency . . . . FAS5, ¶18   C59.120

COLLATERALIZED MORTGAGE OBLIGATIONS (CMOs)
See Financial Instruments
Accounting by Issuer . . . . FTB85-2, ¶2   C30.502
Consolidation of Issuer with Sponsor . . . . . FTB85-2, ¶3   C30.503   EITF.85-28
Definition
. . Collateralized Mortgage Obligations . . FTB85-2, ¶1   C30.501
. . Nominal . . . . FTB85-2, ¶2   C30.502
Establishment through Third Party
. . Gain or Loss Recognition by Seller of Mortgages EITF.86-24
Offsetting Collateral against Liability . . . . . FTB85-2, ¶4   C30.504
Purchased Investment EITF.89-4
. . Impairment Recognition . . . . :   EITF.93-18

COLLECTIONS—WORKS OF ART, HISTORICAL TREASURES, AND SIMILAR ASSETS
Definition . . . . FAS116, ¶128   C67.111
. . . . FAS116, ¶209   C67.401
Examples of Contributed Collections . . . . . FAS116, ¶185-189   C67.137-141
Financial Statement Presentation and Disclosure . . . . FAS116, ¶26-27   C67.123-124
. . . . FAS116, ¶141   No5.142

FAS—FASB Statements   FIN—FASB Interpretations   FTB—FASB Technical Bulletins
APB—APB Opinions   AIN—AICPA Interpretations   ARB—Accounting Research Bulletins
CON—FASB Concepts   EITF—EITF Issues   Q&A—FASB Special Reports

T-61

	Original Pronouncements	Current Text	EITF and Other
COLLECTIONS—WORKS OF ART, HISTORICAL TREASURES, AND SIMILAR ASSETS—continued			
Optional Recognition and Capitalization of Contributed Collections	FAS116, ¶11-13	C67.111-113	
. . . .	FAS116, ¶135		
COMBINATIONS OF BUSINESSES			
See Business Combinations			
COMBINED FINANCIAL STATEMENTS			
See Consolidation			
Related Parties	ARB51, ¶22-23	C51.121-122	
COMMERCIAL BANKS			
See Banking and Thrift Industries			
COMMERCIAL PAPER			
See Financial Instruments			
Balance Sheet Classification	FAS6, ¶1	B05.110	
COMMITMENT FEES			
See Lending Activities			
See Loan Origination and Commitment Fees			
See Mortgage Banking Activities			
COMMITMENTS			
See Financial Instruments			
See Futures Contracts			
Contractor Accounting:			
Construction-Type Contracts	ARB45, ¶16	Co4.113	
Contributions Payable (Promises to Give) . .	FAS116, ¶18-21	C67.114-117	
Purchase, Losses—Qualification as a			
Liability	CON6, ¶251-253		
Recognition of Executory Contracts	CON6, ¶251-253		
COMMITMENTS: LONG-TERM OBLIGATIONS			
See Disclosure			
See Financial Instruments			
See Futures Contracts			
Glossary	FAS47, ¶23	C32.401-404	
Inventory			
. . Losses	ARB43, Ch.4, ¶17	I78.121-122	
Long-Term Debt			
. . Disclosure Requirements	FAS47, ¶10	C32.105	
Redeemable Stock	FAS47, ¶31-32	C32.113-114	
. . Accounting	FAS47, ¶9	C32.104	
. . Redemption Requirements	FAS47, ¶10	C32.105	
. . Sinking Fund Requirements for			
Long-Term Borrowings	FAS47, ¶10	C32.105	
. . Unconditional Purchase Obligations . .	FAS47, ¶10	C32.105	
Relation to Leases	FAS47, ¶6	C32.101	
Scope of Accounting and Reporting			
Requirements	FAS47, ¶1	C32.101	
. . . .	FAS47, ¶6		
Take-or-Pay Contract	FAS47, ¶29-32	C32.111-114	
Throughput Contract	FAS47, ¶24-28	C32.106-110	
Unconditional Purchase Obligations	FAS47, ¶1	C32.101	
. . . .	FAS47, ¶6		

See "Terminology" for references to defined terms presented in various accounting pronouncements.

See the Introduction to the Topical Index for details on the use of this index.

FAS—FASB Statements   FIN—FASB Interpretations   FTB—FASB Technical Bulletins
APB—APB Opinions   AIN—AICPA Interpretations   ARB—Accounting Research Bulletins
CON—FASB Concepts   EITF—EITF Issues   Q&A—FASB Special Reports

T-63

	Original Pronouncements	Current Text	EITF and Other
COMPARATIVE FINANCIAL STATEMENTS			
See Adjustments of Financial Statements for Prior Periods			
See Disclosure			
See Financial Statements: Comparative Financial Statements			
See Segment of Business Reporting			
Development Stage Enterprises	FAS7, ¶13	De4.109	
Earnings per Share	AIN-APB15, #23	E09.587-589	
COMPENSATION TO EMPLOYEES			
Lump-Sum Payments under Union Contracts			EITF.88-23
Recognition by Sponsor of Leveraged Employee Stock Ownership Plan (ESOP)			EITF.89-8
COMPENSATION TO EMPLOYEES: DEFERRED			
See Compensation to Employees: Paid Absences			
See Compensation to Employees: Stock Purchase and Stock Option Plans			
Deferred Compensation Agreements	APB12, ¶6-7	C38.101-102	
	FAS106, ¶13		
. . Illustrations	FAS106, ¶413-416	C38.103-106	
Qualification as a Liability	CON6, ¶196		
COMPENSATION TO EMPLOYEES: PAID ABSENCES			
See Disclosure			
Conditions for Accrual	FAS43, ¶6-7	C44.104-106	
	FAS43, ¶12	C44.109	
	FAS43, ¶18		
. . Disclosure If Criteria Met and Liability Not Accrued	FAS43, ¶6	C44.104	
. . Nonvesting Accumulating Rights to Receive Sick Pay Benefits	FAS43, ¶7	C44.108	
	FAS43, ¶15		
. . Nonvesting Rights	FAS43, ¶13	C44.107	
Definition	FAS43, ¶1	C44.401	
Regulated Operations	FAS71, ¶48-49	Re6.153-154	
Relation to Contingencies	FAS5, ¶7	C59.102	
Scope of Accounting and Reporting Requirements	FAS43, ¶1	C44.101-103	
	FAS43, ¶20		
	FAS112, ¶8-9		

See "Terminology" for references to defined terms presented in various accounting pronouncements.

See the Introduction to the Topical Index for details on the use of this index.

See "Terminology" for references to defined terms presented in various accounting pronouncements.
See the Introduction to the Topical Index for details on the use of this index.

FAS—FASB Statements	FIN—FASB Interpretations	FTB—FASB Technical Bulletins
APB—APB Opinions	AIN—AICPA Interpretations	ARB—Accounting Research Bulletins
CON—FASB Concepts	EITF—EITF Issues	Q&A—FASB Special Reports

	Original Pronouncements	Current Text	EITF and Other
COMPENSATION TO EMPLOYEES: STOCK PURCHASE AND STOCK OPTION PLANS—continued			
Stock Indemnification Rights			EITF.87-33
Stock Market Decline.			EITF.87-33
Stock Options Acquired by Acquired Company with Assistance from Acquiring Company			EITF.85-45
Stock Plans Established by a Principal Stockholder	AIN-APB25, #1	C47.501-506	
Stock-for-Stock Exercise of Stock Options			
. . Accounting for a Reload Stock Option			EITF.90-7
. . Phantom Stock-for-Stock Exercises . . .			EITF.87-6
. . Pyramiding.			EITF.84-18
Tandem Stock Plans.	APB25, ¶34	C47.137	
Use of Shares to Cover Tax Withholding . .			EITF.87-6
COMPLETED CONTRACT METHOD			
See Contractor Accounting: Construction-Type Contracts			
COMPLETENESS			
Definition	CON2, Glossary		
Relation to Representational Faithfulness .	CON2, ¶79-80		
COMPLETE SET OF FINANCIAL STATEMENTS			
Not-for-Profit Organizations	FAS117, ¶1-3	No5.104-105	
. . . .	FAS117, ¶6-7		
. . . .	FAS117, ¶70		
Segment of Business Reporting.	FAS14, ¶3	S20.104	
. . . .	FAS95, ¶152		
COMPREHENSIVE INCOME			
See Earnings			
See Investments: Marketable Securities			
See Losses			
See Revenues			
Change in Terms from Concepts Statement 1	CON5, ¶11		
Characteristics.	CON6, ¶73-77		
. . . .	CON6, ¶215-218		
Component of Full Set of Financial Statements	CON5, ¶13		
Components	CON6, ¶73-77		
Definition	CON6, ¶70		
Display Issues	CON6, ¶220		
Element of Financial Statements.	CON6, ¶70-77		
Equivalent Terms	CON5, ¶40		
Financial Capital Concept	CON6, ¶71-72		
Information about Sources	CON6, ¶219		

See "Terminology" for references to defined terms presented in various accounting pronouncements.

See the Introduction to the Topical Index for details on the use of this index.

	Original Pronouncements	Current Text	EITF and Other
COMPREHENSIVE INCOME—continued			
Relation to Price-Level Changes	CON6, ¶73-75		
Relation to Profit and Loss	CON6, ¶16		
Relationship between Earnings and Comprehensive Income	CON5, ¶42-44		
Statement of Comprehensive Income			
. . Complementary Relationship to Other Financial Statements	CON5, ¶24		
Statement of Earnings and Comprehensive Income	CON5, ¶30-32		
Total Nonowner Changes in Equity (or Equivalent Term)	CON5, ¶40		
COMPUTER SOFTWARE			
See Disclosure			
See Research and Development			
Amortization of Capitalized Software Costs	FAS86, ¶8	Co2.107	Q&A.86 #15-17
. . Estimated Useful Life of Product Enhancements			Q&A.86 #24
Capitalization of Costs	FAS86, ¶4-7	Co2.103-106	
Computer Software to Be Sold, Leased, or Otherwise Marketed			
. . Balance Sheet Presentation			Q&A.86 #21
. . Costs Incurred to Establish Technological Feasibility of Software Products	FAS86, ¶3-4	Co2.102-103	EITF.85-35
. . Created for Others under a Contractual Arrangement	FAS2, ¶2	Co2.101	
	FAS86, ¶2		
. . Development of Software to Be Used as a Product or Process	FAS86, ¶5	Co2.104	
	FIN6, ¶8	R50.117	
. . Evaluation of Capitalized Costs	FAS86, ¶10	Co2.109	Q&A.86 #22
. . Glossary	FAS86, ¶10	Co2.401-410	
	FAS86, ¶52		
. . Indirect Production Costs			Q&A.86 #11
. . Inventory Costs	FAS86, ¶9	Co2.108	
. . Maintenance and Customer Support Costs	FAS86, ¶6	Co2.105	Q&A.86 #12
	FAS86, ¶45		
. . Producing Product Masters	FAS86, ¶5	Co2.104	
. . Product Enhancement Costs			EITF.85-35
			Q&A.86 #23-25
. . Purchase of Computer Software to Be Used as Part of a Product or Process	FAS86, ¶5	Co2.104	Q&A.86 #13-14

See "Terminology" for references to defined terms presented in various accounting pronouncements.
See the Introduction to the Topical Index for details on the use of this index.

	Original Pronouncements	Current Text	EITF and Other
CONSERVATISM—continued			
Relation to Reliability	CON2, ¶91-97		
CONSISTENCY			
Accounting for Similar Circumstances	CON2, ¶16		
Definition	CON2, Glossary		
Relation to Comparability	CON2, ¶120-122		
Relation to Conservatism	CON2, ¶91-97		
CONSOLIDATED FINANCIAL STATEMENTS			
Classification of Subsidiary's Loan Payable in Consolidated Balance Sheet When Subsidiary's and Parent's Fiscal Years Differ			EITF.88-15
Fiscal Year of Parent and Subsidiary Differs			
. . Classification of Subsidiary's Loan Payable in Consolidated Balance Sheet			EITF.88-15
Specialized Accounting Principles of Subsidiaries			
. . Small Business Investment Company			EITF.85-12
. . Subsidiary Venture Capital Investment Company			EITF.85-12
CONSOLIDATION			
See Disclosure			
See Earnings per Share			
See Foreign Currency Translation			
See Interim Financial Reporting			
See Related Parties			
See Segment of Business Reporting			
Arbitrage Transactions of an Unconsolidated Subsidiary			EITF.84-41
Classification of Subsidiary's Loan Payable in Consolidated Balance Sheet When Subsidiary's and Parent's Fiscal Years Differ			EITF.88-15
Combined Statements			
. . Commonly Controlled Enterprises	ARB51, ¶22	C51.121	
. . Intercompany Balances and Transactions	ARB51, ¶23	C51.122	
Consolidated Tax Return	FAS109, ¶49	C51.108A	
Controlling Financial Interest	FAS94, ¶13	C51.102	
Definition	ARB51, ¶1	C51.401	
Development Stage Enterprises	FIN7, ¶4	De4.106	

FAS−FASB Statements   FIN−FASB Interpretations   FTB−FASB Technical Bulletins
APB−APB Opinions   AIN−AICPA Interpretations   ARB−Accounting Research Bulletins
CON−FASB Concepts   EITF−EITF Issues   Q&A−FASB Special Reports

See "Terminology" for references to defined terms presented in various accounting pronouncements.
See the Introduction to the Topical Index for details on the use of this index.

	Original Pronouncements	Current Text	EITF and Other
CONSOLIDATION—continued			
Separate vs. Consolidated Statements—continued			
. . Segment of Business Reporting	FAS14, ¶7	S20.108	
Shares of Parent Held by a Subsidiary	ARB51, ¶13	C51.114	
Special-Purpose Entities	FTB85-2, ¶3	C30.503	
. . Accounting for Lease Transactions . . .			EITF.90-15
. . Collateralized Mortgage Obligation Issuer			EITF.85-28
. . Grantor Trusts			EITF.84-15
. . Grantor Trusts Owned by a Subsidiary			EITF.84-40
. . Sale of Loans to Special-Purpose Entities			EITF.84-30
Step Acquisition			
. . Consolidation Procedure.	ARB51, ¶10-11	C51.111-112	
Subsidiary			
. . Acquired in Year	ARB51, ¶10-11	C51.111-112	
. . Allocating Consolidated Tax Provision			EITF.86-9
. . Disposed of in Year	ARB51, ¶12	C51.113	
. . Investment in Parent Treasury Stock . .	ARB51, ¶13	C51.114	
. . Stock Dividends	ARB51, ¶18	C51.117	
. . Unconsolidated	FAS14, ¶7	S20.108	
Subsidiary with No Equity Ownership			EITF.84-30
Temporary Control.	FAS94, ¶13	C51.102	
. . Sponsor Intends to Sell CMO Issuer . .			EITF.85-28
. . Subsidiary Acquired to Realize Parent's NOL Carryforward			EITF.84-33
Transactions Involving Special-Purpose Entities			EITF.D-14
Unconsolidated Subsidiaries in Consolidated Statements			
. . Disclosure about Formerly Unconsolidated Subsidiaries	FAS94, ¶14	C51.120A	
. . Limitations on Use of Equity Method .	FAS94, ¶13	C51.102	
Users' Needs for Information	FAS94, ¶14	C51.120A	
CONSTRUCTION CONTRACTS			
See Contractor Accounting: Construction-Type Contracts			
See Contractor Accounting: Government Contracts			
See Income Taxes			
Accounting Policy Disclosure	APB22, ¶13	A10.106	
Profit Recognition			
. . Construction of House on Builder's Lot			EITF.86-7
CONSTRUCTION LOANS			
Balance Sheet Classification	FAS6, ¶1	B05.110	

FAS—FASB Statements   FIN—FASB Interpretations   FTB—FASB Technical Bulletins
APB—APB Opinions   AIN—AICPA Interpretations   ARB—Accounting Research Bulletins
CON—FASB Concepts   EITF—EITF Issues   Q&A—FASB Special Reports

T-73

	Original Pronouncements	Current Text	EITF and Other
CONSTRUCTIVE OBLIGATIONS			
Definition	CON6, ¶40		
CONSUMER PRICE INDEX			
See Changing Prices: Reporting Their Effects in Financial Reports			
CONSUMPTION OF BENEFITS			
Guidance in Applying Recognition Criteria to Expenses.	CON5, ¶86		
CONTINGENCIES			
See Commitments: Long-Term Obligations			
See Disclosure			
See Financial Instruments			
See Impairment: Loans			
See Quasi Reorganizations			
See Receivables Sold with Recourse			
Accounting for Estimated Payments in Connection with the Coal Industry Retiree Health Benefit Act of 1992			EITF.92-13
Accounting for Multiple-Year Retrospectively Rated Contracts by Ceding and Assuming Enterprises			EITF.93-6
. . . .			EITF.D-35
See Insurance Industry			
Accounting for Multiple-Year Retrospectively Rated Insurance Contracts by Insurance Enterprises and Other Enterprises.			EITF.93-14
Accounting for Restructuring Charges			EITF.94-3
Business Combinations	AIN-APB16, #30-31	B50.106	
. . . .	APB16, ¶47	B50.135-144	
. . . .	APB16, ¶77-86	B50.148-150	
. . . .	FAS38, ¶5-6	B50.613-623	
. . . .	FAS38, ¶23		
Contingent Stock Purchase Warrants			EITF.84-8
Debt: Restructurings	FAS15, ¶22	D22.118	
. . . .	FAS15, ¶36	D22.132	
Definition			
. . Contingencies.	FAS5, ¶1	C59.401	
. . Indirect Guarantee of Indebtedness of Others.	FIN34, ¶2	C59.402	
. . Probable.	FAS5, ¶3	C59.403	
. . Reasonably Possible	FAS5, ¶3	C59.404	
. . Remote	FAS5, ¶3	C59.405	
Description of Term	FAS5, ¶1	C59.101	
Funded Catastrophe Covers			EITF.93-6
Gain Contingencies	FAS5, ¶17	C59.118	
General or Unspecified Business Risks	FAS5, ¶14	C59.116	
Interim Financial Reporting	APB28, ¶22	I73.125	
Lease Rentals	FAS29, ¶15-17	L10.164-166	
Loan Covenant Restrictions on Distribution	FAS5, ¶18-19	C59.120	
Loan Guarantees			
. . Recognition of Liability			EITF.85-20
. . Revenue Recognition of Fees			EITF.85-20

See "Terminology" for references to defined terms presented in various accounting pronouncements.

See the Introduction to the Topical Index for details on the use of this index.

	Original Pronouncements	Current Text	EITF and Other
CONTINGENCIES—continued			
Loss Contingencies....................	FAS5, ¶2	C59.105-107	
....	FAS5, ¶4	C59.121-151	
....	FAS5, ¶8		
....	FAS5, ¶21-45		
....	FAS113, ¶30		
....	FAS114, ¶21		
....	FIN14, ¶4-7		
. . Accounting by Insureds for Claims-Made Insurance Policies			EITF.86-12
. . Accounting for Environmental Liabilities			EITF.93-5
. . Appropriations of Retained Earnings .	FAS5, ¶15	C59.117	
. . Business Combinations, Contingent Consideration	APB16, ¶77	C59.119	
. . Business Combinations, Preacquisition Contingencies....................	APB16, ¶77	C59.119	
. . Business Interruption...............	FAS5, ¶29-30	C59.135-136	
. . Catastrophe Losses of Property and Casualty Insurance Enterprises	FAS5, ¶40-43	C59.146-149	
. . Catastrophe Losses of Property and Liability Insurance Enterprises......	FAS5, ¶4	C59.122	
. . Claims and Assessments	FAS5, ¶4	C59.122	
. . Damage to Property of Others	FAS5, ¶29-30	C59.135-136	
. . Examples	FAS5, ¶16	C59.103	
. . Expropriation of Assets.............	FAS5, ¶4	C59.122	
....	FAS5, ¶32	C59.138	
. . Future Injury to Others	FAS5, ¶29-30	C59.135-136	
. . Guarantees of Indebtedness	FAS5, ¶4	C59.122	
. . Guarantees of Indebtedness to Others .	FAS5, ¶12	C59.113	
. . Guarantees to Repurchase Receivables Sold...........................	FAS5, ¶4	C59.122	
. . Hazards Such as Fire or Explosion....	FAS5, ¶4	C59.122	
. . Indirect Guarantees of Indebtedness to Others........................	FIN34, ¶2-3	C59.114	
. . Litigation, Claims, and Assessments ..	FAS5, ¶33-39	C59.139-145	
. . Litigation, Pending or Threatened	FAS5, ¶4	C59.122	
. . Payments to Insurance Companies That May Not Involve Transfer of Risk...........................	FAS5, ¶44-45	C59.150-151	
....	FAS113, ¶18	In6.182	Q&A.113 #26
....	FAS113, ¶30		
. . Range of Loss	FIN14, ¶3-7	C59.107	
....		C59.124-127	
. . Receivables, Collectibility	FAS5, ¶4	C59.122	EITF.85-44
....	FAS5, ¶22-23	C59.128-129	EITF.87-5
....	FAS114, ¶21		
. . Relation to Estimates...............	FAS5, ¶2	C59.121	
. . Relation to Receivables	FAS5, ¶2	C59.121	
. . Return of Restricted Contribution	FAS116, ¶65-66	C67.107	
. . Risk of Loss or Damage of Enterprise Property......................	FAS5, ¶27-28	C59.133-134	
. . Sale of Marketable Securities with a Put Option.....................			EITF.84-5

FAS–FASB Statements	FIN–FASB Interpretations	FTB–FASB Technical Bulletins
APB–APB Opinions	AIN–AICPA Interpretations	ARB–Accounting Research Bulletins
CON–FASB Concepts	EITF–EITF Issues	Q&A–FASB Special Reports

T-75

	Original Pronouncements	Current Text	EITF and Other
CONTINGENCIES—continued			
Loss Contingencies—continued			
. . Standby Letters of Credit	FAS5, ¶4	C59.113	
	FAS5, ¶12	C59.122	
. . Subsequent Events	FAS5, ¶11	C59.112	
. . Warranties and Product Defects	FAS5, ¶4	C59.122	
	FAS5, ¶24-26	C59.130-132	
. . Write-down of Operating Assets	FAS5, ¶31	C59.137	
Loss Contingency Classifications			
. . Probable	FAS5, ¶3	C59.104	
. . Reasonably Possible	FAS5, ¶3	C59.104	
. . Remote	FAS5, ¶3	C59.104	
Loss Contingency on Debt Instruments with Contingent Payments			EITF.86-28
Losses			
. . Appropriations of Retained Earnings	FAS5, ¶15	R70.103	
Measuring Loss Accruals by Transferors for Transfers of Receivables with Recourse			EITF.92-2
Medicare Retroactive Wage Adjustments			EITF.86-2
Other Than Loss Contingencies			
. . Business Combinations	APB16, ¶77	C59.119	
	FAS38, ¶4		
. . Collateral for Loans and Commitments	FAS5, ¶19	C59.120	
. . Letters of Credit	FAS5, ¶18-19	C59.120	
Preacquisition Contingencies	FAS38, ¶4	C59.119	
Real Estate			
. . Future Improvement Costs	FAS66, ¶60	R10.154	
	FAS66, ¶75-76	Re1.173-174	
Regulated Operations	FAS71, ¶38-39	Re6.143-144	
Relation to Forms of Employee Compensation	FAS5, ¶7	C59.102	
	FAS112, ¶10		
Relation to Postemployment Benefits	FAS112, ¶10	C59.102	
Relation to Pension Costs	FAS5, ¶7	C59.122	
Restrictions on Dividend Distribution	FAS5, ¶18-19	C59.120	
Revenue Recognition When Right of Return Exists	FAS48, ¶7	R75.108	
Scope of Accounting and Reporting Requirements	FAS5, ¶6-7	C59.102	
	FAS5, ¶31		
	FAS5, ¶102		
	FAS112, ¶10		

CONTINGENCY RESERVES
See Contingencies
See Retained Earnings
CONTINGENT ASSETS/LIABILITIES
See Business Combinations
CONTINGENT CONSIDERATION
See Business Combinations
CONTINGENT LIABILITIES
See Contingencies
CONTINUATION OF BENEFITS
See Postemployment Benefits

See "Terminology" for references to defined terms presented in various accounting pronouncements.
See the Introduction to the Topical Index for details on the use of this index.

FAS—FASB Statements   FIN—FASB Interpretations   FTB—FASB Technical Bulletins
APB—APB Opinions   AIN—AICPA Interpretations   ARB—Accounting Research Bulletins
CON—FASB Concepts   EITF—EITF Issues   Q&A—FASB Special Reports

See "Terminology" for references to defined terms presented in various accounting pronouncements.

See the Introduction to the Topical Index for details on the use of this index.

	Original Pronouncements	Current Text	EITF and Other
CONTRIBUTIONS—continued			
Nonmonetary Transactions	FAS116, ¶5	C67.104	
. . . .	FAS116, ¶19	C67.115	
Promises to Give.	FAS116, ¶6	C67.105	
. . Conditional Promises to Give	FAS116, ¶22-23	C67.118-120	
. . Disclosures	FAS116, ¶24-25	C67.121-122	
. . . .	FAS116, ¶117		
. . Legal Enforceability	FAS116, ¶6	C67.105	
. . . .	FAS116, ¶108		
. . Present Value of Cash Flows	FAS116, ¶20	C67.116	
. . Unconditional Promises to Give	FAS116, ¶5-6	C67.104-105	
Recognition by Donee	FAS116, ¶8-11	C67.108-113	
. . . .	FAS116, ¶13-16	No5.143-145	
. . . .	FAS116, ¶123		
Recognition by Donor	FAS116, ¶18	C67.114	
Relation to Equity (Net Assets) and Liabilities	CON6, ¶56-59		
Scope of Accounting and Reporting Requirements	FAS116, ¶1	C67.101-103	
. . . .	FAS116, ¶3-4		
. . . .	FAS116, ¶49-51		
. . . .	FAS116, ¶53-54		
Unconditional Promises to Give	FAS116, ¶5-6	C67.104-105	
. . . .	FAS116, ¶24	C67.121	
CONTROL			
See Consolidation			
See Investments: Equity Method			
By a Particular Enterprise	CON6, ¶183-189		
Definition	FAS57, ¶24	R36.402	
Future Economic Benefits			
. . Relation to Legal Rights	CON6, ¶186-189		
CONVERSION			
See Capital Stock: Capital Transactions			
See Debt: Convertible Debt and Debt with Stock Purchase Warrants			
See Earnings per Share			
See Foreign Currency Translation			
Definition	FAS52, ¶162	F60.402	
CONVERSION FROM MUTUAL OWNERSHIP TO STOCK OWNERSHIP			
Savings and Loan Association			
. . Earnings per Share			EITF.84-22
CONVERSION OF DEBT			
See Debt: Convertible Debt and Debt with Stock Purchase Warrants			
See Earnings per Share			
Accrued Interest upon Conversion			EITF.85-17
Converted under Sweetened Terms			EITF.84-3
Induced Conversions			
. . Recognition of Expense upon Conversion			EITF.84-3

FAS—FASB Statements	FIN—FASB Interpretations	FTB—FASB Technical Bulletins
APB—APB Opinions	AIN—AICPA Interpretations	ARB—Accounting Research Bulletins
CON—FASB Concepts	EITF—EITF Issues	Q&A—FASB Special Reports

	Original Pronouncements	Current Text	EITF and Other
CONVERTIBLE DEBT			
See Capital Stock: Capital Transactions			
See Debt: Convertible Debt and Debt with Stock Purchase Warrants			
See Earnings per Share			
See Financial Instruments			
See Interest: Imputation of an Interest Cost			
Characteristics	CON6, ¶55		
Definition	APB14, ¶3	D10.101	
Recording a Premium Put Option			EITF.85-29
CONVERTIBLE PREFERRED STOCK			
See Capital Stock: Preferred Stock			
See Earnings per Share			
See Financial Instruments			
COOPERATIVES			
See Business Combinations			
Earnings per Share			
. . Exemption from Requirements	APB15, ¶6	E09.102	
CORPORATE JOINT VENTURES			
See Income Taxes			
Definition	APB18, ¶3	I82.401	
CORPORATE PENSION FUNDS			
See Pension Costs			
CORPORATE READJUSTMENTS			
See Quasi Reorganizations			
CORPORATE RETIREMENT PLANS			
See Pension Costs			
See Postretirement Benefits Other Than Pensions			
COST			
Definition	CON6, ¶26		
COST ALLOCATION			
See Business Combinations			
See Capital Stock: Stock Dividends and Stock Splits			
See Intangible Assets			
See Interest: Capitalization of Interest Costs			
See Interim Financial Reporting			
See Real Estate: Costs and Initial Operations of Real Estate Projects			
See Segment of Business Reporting			
COST-BENEFIT RELATIONSHIP			
Constraint	CON5, ¶63		
In FASB Standards	CON2, ¶143-144		
Not-for-Profit Organizations, Financial Information	CON4, ¶28		
Of Providing Information	CON2, ¶133-144		
COST METHOD OF CARRYING INVESTMENTS			
See Insurance Industry			
See Investment: Equity Method			

See "Terminology" for references to defined terms presented in various accounting pronouncements.

See the Introduction to the Topical Index for details on the use of this index.

	Original Pronouncements	Current Text	EITF and Other

FAS–FASB Statements FIN–FASB Interpretations FTB–FASB Technical Bulletins
APB–APB Opinions AIN–AICPA Interpretations ARB–Accounting Research Bulletins
CON–FASB Concepts EITF–EITF Issues Q&A–FASB Special Reports

T-81

	Original Pronouncements	Current Text	EITF and Other

See "Terminology" for references to defined terms presented in various accounting pronouncements.

See the Introduction to the Topical Index for details on the use of this index.

(The next page is T-97.)

FAS–FASB Statements	FIN–FASB Interpretations	FTB–FASB Technical Bulletins
APB–APB Opinions	AIN–AICPA Interpretations	ARB–Accounting Research Bulletins
CON–FASB Concepts	EITF–EITF Issues	Q&A–FASB Special Reports

FAS—FASB Statements	FIN—FASB Interpretations	FTB—FASB Technical Bulletins
APB—APB Opinions	AIN—AICPA Interpretations	ARB—Accounting Research Bulletins
CON—FASB Concepts	EITF—EITF Issues	Q&A—FASB Special Reports

	Original Pronouncements	Current Text	EITF and Other
DEBT—continued			
Equity Certificates of Deposit			
. . Recognizing Contingent Interest Expense			EITF.84-31
Equity Commitment Notes			
. . Earnings-per-Share Computations			EITF.85-18
Equity Contract Notes			
. . Earnings-per-Share Computations			EITF.85-18
Exchangeable for Stock of Unaffiliated Enterprise			EITF.85-9
Foreign Currency Swaps			
. . Offsetting			EITF.86-25
Foreign Debt-for-Equity Swaps			EITF.87-12
Holding Company Debt			
. . Leveraged Buyout Holding Company Debt			EITF.84-23
. . Push-down of Parent Company's Debt to Subsidiary			EITF.84-42
Indexed Debt Instruments			EITF.86-28
. . Convertible Bonds with Issuer Option to Settle for Cash upon Conversion			EITF.90-19
Interest Expense on Increasing-Rate Debt			EITF.86-15
Interest Rate Swap Transactions			EITF.84-7
			EITF.84-36
			EITF.88-8
Leveraged Employee Stock Ownership Plans (ESOPs)			
. . Recognition by Sponsor of ESOP Debt			EITF.89-10
. . Recognition of Compensation Expense When There Is Prepayment of Debt by Sponsor			EITF.89-8
Long-Term Debt			
. . Disclosure Requirements	FAS47, ¶10	C32.105	EITF.86-30
Modification of Debt Terms			EITF.86-18
			EITF.87-18
			EITF.87-19
			EITF.89-15
. . Debtor Experiencing Financial Difficulties			EITF.89-15
Mortgage Swaps			EITF.88-8
Nonrecourse Debt			
. . Debtor's Accounting for Forfeiture of Real Estate Subject to a Nonrecourse Mortgage			EITF.91-2
. . Grantor Trust			EITF.84-15
. . Offsetting with Lease Receivables			EITF.84-25
Offsetting			
. . Asset Puttable to Creditor to Satisfy Debt			EITF.84-11
. . Nonrecourse Debt with Lease Receivables			EITF.84-25
. . Note Monetization			EITF.84-11
Zero Coupon Bonds			
. . Cash Yield Test for Determining Common Stock Equivalents			EITF.84-16

See "Terminology" for references to defined terms presented in various accounting pronouncements.

See the Introduction to the Topical Index for details on the use of this index.

	Original Pronouncements	Current Text	EITF and Other
DEBT: CONVERTIBLE DEBT AND DEBT WITH STOCK PURCHASE WARRANTS			
See Capital Stock: Capital Transactions			
See Earnings per Share			
See Financial Instruments			
Conversion of Debt	AIN-APB26, #1	D10.501	
Conversion of Debt According to Terms of Issuance	AIN-APB26, #1	D10.103B	
	FAS84, ¶22-23	D10.501	
Convertible Bonds with Issuer Option to Settle for Cash upon Conversion			EITF.90-19
Convertible Debt	APB14, ¶3-4	D10.101-103	
	APB14, ¶7		
	APB14, ¶12		
. . Accrued Interest upon Conversion			EITF.85-17
. . Converted under Sweetened Terms			EITF.84-3
. . Definition	APB14, ¶3	D10.101	
. . Induced Conversions			EITF.84-3
. . Recording a Premium Put Option			EITF.85-29
Debt Exchangeable for Stock of Unaffiliated Enterprise			
. . Accounting for Exchangeability Feature			EITF.85-9
Debt with Put Warrants			EITF.88-9
Debt with Stock Purchase Warrants	APB14, ¶13	D10.104-106	
	APB14, ¶16-17		
. . Warrant Includes Put for Stock Purchased			EITF.86-35
Induced Conversions	FAS84, ¶2-4	D10.103A-103D	EITF.84-3
. . Examples of Computing Expense	FAS84, ¶7-13	D10.108-114	
. . Income Statement Display of Expense	FAS84, ¶3	D10.103C	
. . Measurement Date	FAS84, ¶4	D10.103D	
. . Recognition of Expense upon Conversion	FAS84, ¶3	D10.103C	
Other Types of Debt Securities	APB14, ¶18	D10.107	
Scope of Accounting and Reporting Requirements	FAS84, ¶2	D10.103A-103B	
	FAS84, ¶22-23		
	FAS84, ¶29		
	FAS84, ¶33		
DEBT DISCOUNT			
Qualification as an Asset	CON6, ¶235-236		
DEBT: EXTINGUISHMENTS			
See Debt: Convertible Debt and Debt with Stock Purchase Warrants			

FAS–FASB Statements	FIN–FASB Interpretations	FTB–FASB Technical Bulletins
APB–APB Opinions	AIN–AICPA Interpretations	ARB–Accounting Research Bulletins
CON–FASB Concepts	EITF–EITF Issues	Q&A–FASB Special Reports

T-99

See "Terminology" for references to defined terms presented in various accounting pronouncements.

See the Introduction to the Topical Index for details on the use of this index.

FAS—FASB Statements   FIN—FASB Interpretations   FTB—FASB Technical Bulletins
APB—APB Opinions   AIN—AICPA Interpretations   ARB—Accounting Research Bulletins
CON—FASB Concepts   EITF—EITF Issues   Q&A—FASB Special Reports

T-101

See "Terminology" for references to defined terms presented in various accounting pronouncements.

See the Introduction to the Topical Index for details on the use of this index.

FAS–FASB Statements	FIN–FASB Interpretations	FTB–FASB Technical Bulletins
APB–APB Opinions	AIN–AICPA Interpretations	ARB–Accounting Research Bulletins
CON–FASB Concepts	EITF–EITF Issues	Q&A–FASB Special Reports

	Original Pronouncements	Current Text	EITF and Other
DECISION USEFULNESS—continued			
Decision Makers and Their Characteristics	CON2, ¶36-39		
Not-for-Profit Organizations, Resource Allocation Decisions	CON4, ¶35-37		
Relation to Qualitative Characteristics	CON2, ¶36-39		
Role of Decision Making	CON2, ¶27-31		
DECLINING-BALANCE METHOD			
Depreciation	FAS109, ¶288	D40.104	
DEFEASANCE			
See Debt: Extinguishments			
DEFENSE CONTRACTS			
See Contractor Accounting: Government Contracts			
DEFERRAL			
Definition	CON6, ¶141		
DEFERRAL METHOD			
See Income Taxes			
DEFERRED COMPENSATION			
See Compensation to Employees: Deferred			
See Compensation to Employees: Stock Purchase and Stock Option Plans			
DEFERRED COSTS			
See Capitalized Costs			
Accounting for OPEB Costs by Rate-Regulated Enterprises			EITF.92-12
			EITF.93-4
Asbestos Treatment Costs Incurred in Anticipation of Sale of Property			EITF.89-13
Costs to Clean Up Environmental Contamination to Prepare a Property for Sale			EITF.90-8
Qualification as Assets	CON6, ¶177		
	CON6, ¶246-250		
DEFERRED CREDITS			
Qualification as Liabilities	CON6, ¶197		
DEFERRED INCOME			
See Contingencies			
See Deferred Revenue			
See Revenue Recognition			
DEFERRED INCOME TAX CREDITS			
Qualification as Liabilities	CON6, ¶240-242		
DEFERRED INTEREST RATE			
Deferred Interest Rate Setting Arrangement			EITF.84-14
DEFERRED REVENUE			
Amortization of Amount Received from Investor for Future Revenue			EITF.88-18
Franchise Fees	FAS45, ¶7	Fr3.103	
	FAS45, ¶11	Fr3.107	
	FAS45, ¶15	Fr3.111	
Loan, Commitment, and Syndication Fees	FAS91, ¶5-14	L20.104-113	
Motion Picture Industry	FAS53, ¶4	Mo6.103	

See "Terminology" for references to defined terms presented in various accounting pronouncements.

See the Introduction to the Topical Index for details on the use of this index.

	Original Pronouncements	Current Text	EITF and Other
DEFERRED TAXES			
See Accounting Changes			
See Balance Sheet Classification: Current Assets and Liabilities			
See Consolidation			
See Foreign Currency Translation			
See Income Taxes			
See Insurance Industry			
See Interim Financial Reporting			
See Investments: Equity Method			
Amortization of Acquired Goodwill	APB17, ¶30	I60.111	
	FAS109, ¶288		
Regulated Operations	FAS109, ¶288	Re6.128	
. . Abandonment of Assets	FTB87-2, ¶5	Re6.501-507	
	FTB87-2, ¶14-20		
DEFERRING GAIN AND LOSS RECOGNITION			
See Hedges			
Hedging with Cash Securities			EITF.87-1
DEFINED BENEFIT PENSION PLANS			
See Disclosure			
See Pension Costs			
See Postretirement Health Care and Life Insurance Benefits			
Accounting Policies	FAS35, ¶27	Pe5.126	
Accrual Basis of Accounting	FAS35, ¶9	Pe5.108	
Actuarial Present Value of Accumulated Plan Benefits	FAS35, ¶16-21	Pe5.115-120	
	FAS35, ¶134		
	FAS35, ¶153		
	FAS35, ¶156		
	FAS35, ¶184		
	FAS35, ¶198		
. . Changes in	FAS35, ¶23-26	Pe5.122-125	
	FAS35, ¶243		
. . Illustration of Measurement	FAS35, ¶283	Pe5.135	
. . Nonvested Benefits	FAS35, ¶22	Pe5.121	
	FAS35, ¶214		
. . Other Vested Benefits	FAS35, ¶22	Pe5.121	
	FAS35, ¶214		
. . Vested Benefits	FAS35, ¶22	Pe5.121	
	FAS35, ¶214		
Asset Reversions			EITF.84-6
Contribution of Excess Assets to ESOP upon Termination of Plan			EITF.85-10

FAS–FASB Statements   FIN–FASB Interpretations   FTB–FASB Technical Bulletins
APB–APB Opinions   AIN–AICPA Interpretations   ARB–Accounting Research Bulletins
CON–FASB Concepts   EITF–EITF Issues   Q&A–FASB Special Reports

T-105

	Original Pronouncements	Current Text	EITF and Other
DEFINED BENEFIT PENSION PLANS—continued			
Contributory Plan	FAS35, ¶28	Pe5.127	
....	FAS35, ¶252-253		
....	FAS35, ¶262-264		
....	FAS35, ¶267		
ERISA...............................	FAS35, ¶28	Pe5.127	
Financial Statement Information	FAS35, ¶5-8	Pe5.104-107A	
....	FAS35, ¶50		
....	FAS35, ¶60		
....	FAS35, ¶208		
....	FAS35, ¶232		
. . Accounting Policies	FAS35, ¶27	Pe5.126	
....	FAS35, ¶257		
. . Actuarial Present Value of Accumulated Plan Benefits	FAS35, ¶6	Pe5.105	
....	FAS35, ¶50	Pe5.121	
....	FAS35, ¶60		
....	FAS35, ¶214		
. . Benefit Information................	FAS35, ¶8	Pe5.107	
....	FAS35, ¶232		
. . Benefit Information Date	FAS35, ¶7	Pe5.106	
....	FAS35, ¶208		
. . Changes in Actuarial Present Value of Accumulated Plan Benefits	FAS35, ¶25-26	Pe5.124-125	
....	FAS35, ¶241		
....	FAS35, ¶243		
. . Changes in Net Assets Available for Benefits........................	FAS35, ¶236	Pe5.114	
....	FAS35, ¶238		
....	FAS35, ¶260		
. . Claims upon Plan Termination	FAS35, ¶28	Pe5.127	
. . Concentration of Investments........	FAS35, ¶28	Pe5.127	
....	FAS35, ¶252-253		
. . Contributions Receivable	FAS35, ¶10	Pe5.109	
....	FAS35, ¶90-91		
....	FAS35, ¶93		
. . Generally Accepted Accounting Principles	FAS35, ¶4	Pe5.103	
. . Illustration	FAS35, ¶281-282	Pe5.129-133	
. . Investments.......................	FAS35, ¶11	Pe5.110-112	
....	FAS35, ¶13		
....	FAS35, ¶104		
....	FAS110, ¶2		
....	FAS110, ¶7		
. . Net Assets Available for Benefits	FAS35, ¶6	Pe5.105	
....	FAS35, ¶9	Pe5.108	
....	FAS35, ¶60		
....	FAS35, ¶86		
. . Objectives........................	FAS35, ¶5	Pe5.104	
. . Operating Assets	FAS35, ¶14	Pe5.113	
....	FAS35, ¶128		

See "Terminology" for references to defined terms presented in various accounting pronouncements.

See the Introduction to the Topical Index for details on the use of this index.

FAS—FASB Statements FIN—FASB Interpretations FTB—FASB Technical Bulletins
APB—APB Opinions AIN—AICPA Interpretations ARB—Accounting Research Bulletins
CON—FASB Concepts EITF—EITF Issues Q&A—FASB Special Reports

	Original Pronouncements	Current Text	EITF and Other
DEFINED CONTRIBUTION POSTRETIREMENT PLAN			
See Postretirement Benefits Other Than Pensions			
DEFINITIONS			
See Terminology			
DEFLATION			
See Changing Prices: Reporting Their Effects in Financial Reports			
DELAYED EQUITY CONTRIBUTIONS BY LESSORS			
Leveraged Leases			EITF.85-16
DEMAND OBLIGATIONS			
Balance Sheet Classification	FAS78, ¶5	B05.109A-109B	EITF.86-5
	FAS78, ¶13		
DEPLETION			
See Oil and Gas Producing Activities			
DEPOSIT FLOAT			
See Banking and Thrift Industries			
DEPOSIT METHOD			
See Insurance Costs			
See Insurance Industry			
See Real Estate: Sales			
See Real Estate: Sales Other Than Retail Land Sales			
Definition	FAS60, ¶66	In6.408	
DEPOSITS			
Payment Made to IRS to Retain Fiscal Year			EITF.88-4
Qualification as Liabilities	CON6, ¶197		
DEPRECIATION			
See Disclosure			
Accelerated			
. . Temporary Differences, Regulated Operations	FAS109, ¶288	Re6.128	
Accounting Changes	APB20, ¶23-24	A06.119-120	
Accounting Policy Disclosure	APB22, ¶14	A10.106	
Applicability to Not-for-Profit Organizations	FAS93, ¶5-6	D40.101-101B	
	FAS93, ¶35-36		
Appraisals Not Allowed	APB6, ¶17	D40.102	
Basic Principle	APB6, ¶17	D40.101-102	
	ARB43, Ch.9C, ¶5	D40.104	
	FAS93, ¶5-6		
	FAS93, ¶35-37		
	FAS109, ¶288		
Deferred Tax Accounting			
. . Revaluation of Assets for Tax Purposes			EITF.84-43
Definition	ARB43, Ch.9C, ¶5	D40.401	

See "Terminology" for references to defined terms presented in various accounting pronouncements.

See the Introduction to the Topical Index for details on the use of this index.

	Original Pronouncements	Current Text	EITF and Other
DEPRECIATION—continued			
Fixed Assets to Be Recorded at Cost	APB6, ¶17	D40.102	
Historical Treasures	FAS93, ¶6	D40.101A-101C	
....	FAS93, ¶35-36		
Idle Facilities........................			EITF.84-28
Land	FAS93, ¶6	D40.101A	
....	FAS93, ¶34		
Method			
. . Annuity........................	FAS92, ¶37	D40.104	
. . Declining Balance	FAS109, ¶288	D40.104	
. . Sum-of-the-Years Digits	FAS109, ¶288	D40.104	
. . Units-of-Production			EITF.84-28
Recognition Guidance	CON5, ¶86		
Relation to Contingencies	FAS5, ¶2	C59.121	
Useful Life	ARB43, Ch.9C, ¶5	D40.101	
Works of Art.......................	FAS93, ¶6	D40.101A-101C	
....	FAS93, ¶35-36		
DEVALUATION			
See Foreign Currency Translation			
Extraordinary Item...................	APB30, ¶23	I17.110	
DEVELOPMENT STAGE ENTERPRISES			
See Disclosure			
Cash Inflows and Cash Outflows	FAS7, ¶11	De4.107	
....	FAS95, ¶151		
Comparative Financial Statements	FAS7, ¶13	De4.109	
Criteria for Expensing or Capitalization of			
Costs............................	FAS7, ¶10	De4.105	
. . When Enterprise Is Consolidated.....	FIN7, ¶4	De4.106	
Definition	FAS7, ¶8	De4.401	
Dormant Enterprise Reactivated........	FAS7, ¶11	De4.107	
End of Development Stage	FAS7, ¶29	De4.104	
Guidelines for Identification	FAS7, ¶8-9	De4.102-104	
....	FAS7, ¶29		
Identification of Financial Statements	FAS7, ¶12	De4.108	
Less Than Full Set of Statements	FAS7, ¶11	De4.107	
Nonmonetary Transactions	FAS7, ¶11	De4.107	
Periods Covered	FAS7, ¶11	De4.107	
Reporting When No Longer in			
Development Stage	FAS7, ¶13	De4.109	
Scope of Accounting and Reporting			
Requirements......................	FAS7, ¶4	De4.101	
Stockholders' Equity Transactions	FAS7, ¶11	De4.107	
Typical Activities	FAS7, ¶9	De4.103	
DEVELOPMENT WELLS			
Qualification as an Asset	CON6, ¶247		

FAS–FASB Statements   FIN–FASB Interpretations   FTB–FASB Technical Bulletins
APB–APB Opinions   AIN–AICPA Interpretations   ARB–Accounting Research Bulletins
CON–FASB Concepts   EITF–EITF Issues   Q&A–FASB Special Reports

	Original Pronouncements	Current Text	EITF and Other
DILUTION OF EARNINGS PER SHARE			
See Earnings per Share			
DIRECT FINANCING LEASE			
See Leases			
DISABILITY BENEFITS			
See Postemployment Benefits			
DISALLOWANCE OF COSTS			
See Regulated Operations			
DISC (DOMESTIC INTERNATIONAL SALES CORPORATION)			
Effects of the Tax Reform Act of 1984			EITF.84-2
DISCLOSURE			
See Financial Reporting			
See Management			
Accounting Changes....................	APB20, ¶17	A06.113	
....	APB20, ¶19	A06.115	
....	APB20, ¶21	A06.117	
....	APB20, ¶24-28	A06.120-124	
....	APB20, ¶33	A06.132-134	
....	APB20, ¶38-39		
....	FAS73, ¶2		
Accounting for Discontinued Operations Subsequently Retained			
. . Disclosure by SEC Registrants			EITF.90-16
Accounting for Environmental Liabilities			EITF.93-5
Accounting for Gas-Balancing Arrangements			
. . Disclosure by SEC Registrants			EITF.90-22
Accounting for Income Taxes			
. . Disclosure by SEC Registrants Prior to Adoption of Standard			EITF.D-28
Accounting for Postretirement Benefits Other Than Pensions			
. . Accounting by Rate-Regulated Enterprises			EITF.92-12
. . Accounting for Estimated Payments in Connection with the Coal Industry Retiree Health Benefit Act of 1992 ..			EITF.92-13
. . Disclosure Based on Current Substantive Plan			EITF.D-26
. . Disclosure Based on Probable Plan Amendment			EITF.D-26
. . Disclosure by SEC Registrants Prior to Adoption of Standard			EITF.D-26
Accounting Policies	APB22, ¶6	A10.101-102A	
....	APB22, ¶8	A10.105-108	
....	APB22, ¶12-15		
....	FAS95, ¶152		
....	FIN40, ¶5		

See ''Terminology'' for references to defined terms presented in various accounting pronouncements.

See the Introduction to the Topical Index for details on the use of this index.

	Original Pronouncements	Current Text	EITF and Other
DISCLOSURE—continued			
Adjustments of Financial Statements for			
Prior Periods	APB9, ¶18	A35.105-108	EITF.85-35
	APB9, ¶26-27	A35.111	
	APB20, ¶35	A35.113	
	APB20, ¶37	I73.145	
	FAS16, ¶15-16		
Amortization Period for Net Deferred Credit Card Origination Costs			EITF.92-5
Balance Sheet Classification: Current Assets and Liabilities	APB6, ¶14	B05.107	
	FAS6, ¶15	B05.109A	
	FAS78, ¶5	B05.118	
Banking and Thrift Industries	APB23, ¶25	Bt7.115	
	FAS72, ¶11	Bt7.120-121	
	FAS109, ¶288		
Broadcasting Industry	FAS63, ¶3	Br5.104	
	FAS63, ¶10	Br5.111	
Business Combinations	AIN-APB16, #23	B50.115-116	
	APB16, ¶56-57	B50.119-124	
	APB16, ¶60-65	B50.136	
	APB16, ¶78	B50.158F	
	APB16, ¶95-96	B50.164-166	
	FAS38, ¶10	B50.575-579	
	FAS72, ¶11		
	FAS79, ¶6		
Capital Stock: Capital Transactions	APB12, ¶10	C08.102	
Capital Stock: Dividends-in-Kind	APB29, ¶28	C11.102	
Capital Stock: Preferred Stock	APB10, ¶10-11	C16.101-102	
	APB15, ¶50		
Capital Stock: Treasury Stock	APB6, ¶12-13	C23.103-104	
	ARB43, Ch.1A, ¶4	C23.503	
	FTB85-6, ¶3		
Cash Flows Statement	FAS95, ¶25-33	C25.123-135	
	FAS117, ¶30		
Changing Prices: Reporting Their Effects in Financial Reports	FAS89, ¶3	C28.101	
	FAS89, ¶7-15	C28.103-111	
	FAS89, ¶20	C28.116	
Classification of In-Substance Foreclosed (ISF) Assets by SEC Registrants			EITF.D-37
Commitments: Long-Term Obligations	FAS47, ¶1	C32.101-102	
	FAS47, ¶6-7	C32.105	
	FAS47, ¶10		
Comparative Financial Statements	ARB43, Ch.2A, ¶2-3	F43.102-103	
Compensated Absences	FAS43, ¶6	C44.104	
Compensation to Employees: Stock Purchase and Stock Option Plans	APB25, ¶8	C47.108	
	APB25, ¶14	C47.114	
	ARB43, Ch.13B, ¶15	C47.123	
Computer Software	FAS2, ¶13	Co2.110-111	Q&A.86 #18
	FAS86, ¶11-12	R50.109	
Consolidation	ARB51, ¶4-5	C51.107-108	
	FAS94, ¶14	C51.119	

FAS—FASB Statements	FIN—FASB Interpretations	FTB—FASB Technical Bulletins
APB—APB Opinions	AIN—AICPA Interpretations	ARB—Accounting Research Bulletins
CON—FASB Concepts	EITF—EITF Issues	Q&A—FASB Special Reports

T-111

D *Topical Index*

	Original Pronouncements	Current Text	EITF and Other
DISCLOSURE—continued			
Contingencies	FAS5, ¶8-12	C59.108-113	
	FAS5, ¶17-19	C59.118	
		C59.120	
Contractor Accounting: Construction-Type Contracts	ARB45, ¶15-16	Co4.112-113	
Contractor Accounting: Government Contracts	ARB43, Ch.11A, ¶21-22	Co5.108-109	
	ARB43, Ch.11C, ¶18-23	Co5.116-121	
	ARB43, Ch.11C, ¶29	Co5.126	
Contributions	FAS116, ¶10	C67.110	
	FAS116, ¶24-25	C67.121-122	
	FAS116, ¶117		
	FAS116, ¶123		
. . Collections—Works of Art, Historical Treasures, and Similar Assets	FAS116, ¶26-27	C67.123-124	
	FAS116, ¶141	No5.142	
Debt: Extinguishments	FAS4, ¶8-9	D14.105	
	FAS64, ¶4	D14.107-108	
	FAS76, ¶6		
Debt: Restructurings	FAS15, ¶21	D22.117	
	FAS15, ¶25-26	D22.121-122	
	FAS15, ¶40-41	D22.136-137	
		D22.145	
Defined Benefit Pension Plans	FAS35, ¶7	Pe5.106	
	FAS35, ¶13-15	Pe5.112-114	
	FAS35, ¶22	Pe5.121	
	FAS35, ¶25-28	Pe5.124-127	
	FAS35, ¶208		
	FAS35, ¶214		
	FAS35, ¶238		
	FAS35, ¶241		
	FAS35, ¶243		
	FAS35, ¶252-253		
	FAS35, ¶257		
	FAS35, ¶260		
	FAS35, ¶262-264		
	FAS35, ¶267		
Depreciation	APB12, ¶5	D40.105	
Development Stage Enterprises	FAS7, ¶11-13	De4.107-109	
	FAS95, ¶151		
Earnings per Share	APB15, ¶4	E09.104	
	APB15, ¶13	E09.106-107	
	APB15, ¶15-16	E09.109-114	
	APB15, ¶18-23	E09.139	
	APB15, ¶48	E09.141	
	APB15, ¶50	E09.161	
	APB15, ¶70		
	APB20, ¶20		

See "Terminology" for references to defined terms presented in various accounting pronouncements.
See the Introduction to the Topical Index for details on the use of this index.

	Original Pronouncements	Current Text	EITF and Other
DISCLOSURE—continued			
Employee Stock Ownership Plans (ESOPs)			
. . Disclosures by SEC Registrants			EITF.89-8
Extraordinary Items	APB9, ¶6	I17.101-104	
. . . .	APB30, ¶11-12	I17.119	
. . . .	APB30, ¶25		
. . . .	FAS4, ¶9		
. . . .	FAS16, ¶16		
Financial Instruments.	FAS105, ¶16	F25.102	
. . . .	FAS105, ¶17-20	F25.105C	
. . . .	FAS105, ¶43-48	F25.112-115	
. . . .	FAS107, ¶9-15	F25.115C-115H	
. . . .	FAS107, ¶30-33	F25.135-140	
. . . .		F25.153-156	
. . Implementation of Statement 107.			EITF.D-29
Foreign Currency Translation	FAS52, ¶30-32	F60.140-143	
	FAS52, ¶142-144		
Foreign Operations.	ARB43, Ch.12, ¶5-6	F65.102-103	
Franchising	FAS45, ¶20-23	Fr3.116-119	
Futures Contracts	FAS80, ¶12	F80.112	Q&A.80 #30
. . . .	FAS80, ¶27		Q&A.80 #33
Hedging Anticipated Currency Transactions.			EITF.91-4
Impairment: Loans.	FAS114, ¶20	I08.118-119	
. . . .	FAS114, ¶65		
. . . .	FAS114, ¶74		
Income Statement Presentation:			
Discontinued Operations	APB30, ¶8-9	I13.104-109	
. . . .	APB30, ¶13		
. . . .	APB30, ¶18		
. . . .	APB30, ¶25		
. . . .	FAS16, ¶16		
Income Taxes	APB4, ¶11	I27.142-148	Q&A.109 #11
. . . .	APB23, ¶18	I27.219	Q&A.109 #18
. . . .	APB23, ¶25	I27.224	
. . . .	FAS109, ¶43-49	I27.229	
Infrequent Items.	APB30, ¶26	I22.101	

FAS–FASB Statements FIN–FASB Interpretations FTB–FASB Technical Bulletins
APB–APB Opinions AIN–AICPA Interpretations ARB–Accounting Research Bulletins
CON–FASB Concepts EITF–EITF Issues Q&A–FASB Special Reports

T-113

See "Terminology" for references to defined terms presented in various accounting pronouncements.

See the Introduction to the Topical Index for details on the use of this index.

	Original Pronouncements	Current Text	EITF and Other
DISCLOSURE—continued			
Investments: Marketable Securities.......	FAS12, ¶9	I89.101	
....	FAS12, ¶11-13	I89.103	
....	FAS12, ¶16-17	I89.105-107	
....	FAS12, ¶19-20	I89.110-111	
....	FIN40, ¶5	I89.113-114	
Leases	FAS13, ¶13	L10.112	
....	FAS13, ¶16	L10.119	
....	FAS13, ¶23	L10.125	
....	FAS13, ¶29	L10.130K-130L	
....	FAS13, ¶47	L10.149	
....	FAS91, ¶25		
....	FAS98, ¶17-18		
Mortgage Banking Activities	FAS65, ¶29-30	Mo4.130-131	
Motion Picture Industry	FAS53, ¶23	Mo6.122	
Nonmonetary Transactions	APB29, ¶28	N35.120	
Not-for-Profit Organizations	FAS116, ¶14	No5.110	
....	FAS116, ¶16	No5.112-113	
....	FAS117, ¶12	No5.120-123	
....	FAS117, ¶14-15	No5.143	
....	FAS117, ¶23-26	No5.145	
. . Collections—Works of Art, Historical Treasures, and Similar Assets	FAS116, ¶26-27	C67.123-124	
....	FAS116, ¶141	No5.142	
Oil and Gas Producing Activities	FAS69, ¶6-7	Oi5.156-157	
....	FAS69, ¶9-34	Oi5.159-186	
....	FAS69, ¶40-41		
....	FAS109, ¶288		
Operations Held for Sale after a Business Combination			
. . Disclosure by SEC Registrants			EITF.87-11
....			EITF.90-6
Pension Costs	FAS87, ¶54	P16.150	Q&A.87 #4
....	FAS87, ¶56	P16.153	Q&A.87 #33
....	FAS87, ¶65	P16.162	Q&A.87 #38
....	FAS87, ¶69	P16.166	Q&A.87 #70
....	FAS88, ¶17	P16.187	Q&A.87 #72-79
Postemployment Benefits	FAS112, ¶7	P32.105	
Postretirement Benefits Other Than Pensions...........................	FAS106, ¶74	P40.169	Q&A.106 #39-40
....	FAS106, ¶77-78	P40.172-173	
....	FAS106, ¶82-83	P40.178-179	
....	FAS106, ¶106	P40.198	
....	FAS106, ¶479-483	P40.276-280	
Postretirement Health Care and Life Insurance Benefits...................	FAS81, ¶6-7	P50.102-103	
....	FAS81, ¶28		
Quasi Reorganization.................	ARB43, Ch.7A, ¶4	Q15.105	
....	ARB43, Ch.7A, ¶10	Q15.111	
....	ARB46, ¶2		

FAS–FASB Statements	FIN–FASB Interpretations	FTB–FASB Technical Bulletins
APB–APB Opinions	AIN–AICPA Interpretations	ARB–Accounting Research Bulletins
CON–FASB Concepts	EITF–EITF Issues	Q&A–FASB Special Reports

T-115

	Original Pronouncements	Current Text	EITF and Other
DISCLOSURE—continued			
Real Estate	FAS66, ¶65	R10.159	
Real Estate: Sales	FAS66, ¶50	Re1.150	
	FAS66, ¶65	Re1.163	
Receivables Sold with Recourse	FAS77, ¶9	R20.109	
	FAS77, ¶39		
Record and Music Industry	FAS50, ¶13-14	Re4.108-109	
Regulated Operations	FAS71, ¶15	Re6.114	
	FAS71, ¶19-20	Re6.125	
	FAS71, ¶23	Re6.125F	
	FAS90, ¶13	Re6.127A	
	FAS92, ¶10-12	Re6.128-131B	
	FAS101, ¶8-9	Re6.207-208	
	FIN40, ¶5-6		
. . Accounting for OPEB Costs by Rate-Regulated Enterprises			EITF.92-12
Regulatory-Assisted Acquisitions of Thrifts			EITF.88-19
Related Parties	ARB43, Ch.1A, ¶5	R36.102-105	
	FAS57, ¶2-4		
	FAS109, ¶288		
Research and Development	FAS2, ¶13	R50.109	
Research and Development Arrangements	FAS68, ¶14	R55.112	
Restructuring of Business Operations			EITF.86-22
			EITF.87-4
Retained Earnings	FAS5, ¶15	R70.103	
Segment of Business Reporting	FAS14, ¶7	S20.103	
	FAS14, ¶20	S20.108	
	FAS14, ¶22-27	S20.126	
	FAS14, ¶30	S20.128-133	
	FAS14, ¶35-38	S20.136	
	FAS14, ¶40	S20.141-146	
	FAS21, ¶9		
	FAS30, ¶6		
	FAS95, ¶152		
Subsidiary's Loan Payable in Consolidated Balance Sheet When Subsidiary's and Parent's Fiscal Years Differ			EITF.88-15
Taxes: Real and Personal Property Taxes	ARB43, Ch.10A, ¶16	T10.106	
Title Plant	FAS61, ¶9	Ti7.109	
Valuation: Use of Valuation Allowances	APB12, ¶3	V18.102	
DISCONTINUED OPERATIONS			
See Income Statement Presentation: Discontinued Operations			
Accounting for Restructuring Charges			EITF.94-3
Recognition of Deferred Tax Assets for a Parent Company's Excess Tax Basis in the Stock of a Subsidiary That Is Accounted for as a Discontinued Operation			EITF.93-17
DISCOUNTED PRESENT VALUE OF FUTURE CASH FLOWS			
See Present Value			

See "Terminology" for references to defined terms presented in various accounting pronouncements.

See the Introduction to the Topical Index for details on the use of this index.

	Original Pronouncements	Current Text	EITF and Other
DISCOUNTING			
See Interest: Imputation of an Interest Cost			
See Present Value			
Accounting for Environmental Liabilities .			EITF.93-5
Broadcasting Industry	FAS63, ¶4	Br5.105	
Contributions Receivable and Payable	FAS116, ¶20	C67.116	
Defined Benefit Pension Plans			
. . Actuarial Present Value of			
Accumulated Plan Benefits	FAS35, ¶16-21	Pe5.115-120	
. . . .	FAS35, ¶134		
. . Investment Valuation	FAS35, ¶11	Pe5.110	
. . . .	FAS35, ¶104		
Foreign Currency Exchange Contracts			EITF.87-2
Loss Reserves of Insurance Companies . . .			EITF.86-37
Regulated Operations	FAS71, ¶33-34	Re6.127A	
. . . .	FAS90, ¶3	Re6.138-139	
DISPLAY			
Financial Statements	CON5, ¶13-14		
Relation to Elements of Financial Statements	CON6, ¶22-23		
Reporting Comprehensive Income	CON6, ¶220		
DISPOSAL OF A SEGMENT			
See Income Statement Presentation: Discontinued Operations			
Accounting for Discontinued Operations Subsequently Retained			EITF.90-16
. . Disclosure by SEC Registrants			EITF.90-16
Determination of Gains (Losses)			EITF.85-36
Expected Gain on Disposal with Interim Operating Losses			EITF.85-36
Operations Held for Sale after a Business Combination			EITF.87-11
. . . .			EITF.90-6
DISSENTERS' RIGHTS			
Effect on Pooling-of-Interests Accounting .			EITF.87-16
DISTRIBUTIONS TO OWNERS			
See Dividends			
Characteristics	CON6, ¶68-69		
Definition	CON6, ¶67		
Statement of Investments by and	CON5, ¶55-57		
DIVERSIFIED COMPANIES			
See Segment of Business Reporting			
DIVESTITURE			
See Business Combinations			
See Income Statement Presentation: Discontinued Operations			
See Leases			
Business Combinations	APB16, ¶46	B50.105	

FAS–FASB Statements	FIN–FASB Interpretations	FTB–FASB Technical Bulletins
APB–APB Opinions	AIN–AICPA Interpretations	ARB–Accounting Research Bulletins
CON–FASB Concepts	EITF–EITF Issues	Q&A–FASB Special Reports

	Original Pronouncements	Current Text	EITF and Other
DIVIDENDS			
See Capital Stock: Dividends-in-Kind			
See Capital Stock: Stock Dividends and Stock Splits			
Business Combinations	APB16, ¶47	B50.106	
	ARB43, Ch.1A, ¶3	R70.102	
Definition	APB18, ¶3	I82.403	
Disclosure	APB12, ¶10	C08.102	
	FAS5, ¶18-19	C59.120	
Disclosure in Cash Flows Statement	FAS95, ¶20	C25.118	
Per Share	APB15, ¶70	E09.161	
Pooling-of-Interests			
. . Abnormal	APB16, ¶47	B50.106	
Preferred Shares			
. . Dividend Rate Initially below Market Rate			EITF.86-45
Preferred Shares, Arrears	APB10, ¶11	C16.102	
	APB15, ¶50		
Prior to Enterprise Being Acquired	ARB43, Ch.1A, ¶3	R70.102	
Restrictions on Distribution	FAS5, ¶18	C59.120	
Treasury Stock	ARB43, Ch.1A, ¶4	C23.101	
DIVIDENDS TO POLICYHOLDERS			
See Insurance Industry			
Definition	FAS60, ¶66	In6.409	
DIVIDENDS-IN-KIND			
See Capital Stock: Dividends-in-Kind			
DOMESTIC SUBSIDIARIES			
See Segment of Business Reporting			
See Subsidiaries			
DONATIONS			
See Capital Stock: Capital Transactions			
See Contributions			
See Not-for-Profit Organizations			
See Real Estate: Costs and Initial Operations of Real Estate Projects			
DORMANT ENTERPRISE			
Accounting and Reporting Requirements	FAS7, ¶11	De4.107	
	FAS95, ¶151		
DOUBTFUL ACCOUNTS			
Valuation Allowances	APB12, ¶3	V18.102	
DOWNSTREAM MERGERS			
See Business Combinations			
DRY HOLE COSTS			
See Oil and Gas Producing Activities			
DUAL CURRENCY BONDS			
Accounting for Dual Currency Bonds			EITF.93-10
DUAL PRESENTATION			
See Earnings per Share			
Definition	APB15, App.D	E09.410	

(The next page is T-129.)

See "Terminology" for references to defined terms presented in various accounting pronouncements.
See the Introduction to the Topical Index for details on the use of this index.

	Original Pronouncements	Current Text	EITF and Other
EARLY EXTINGUISHMENT OF DEBT			
See Debt: Extinguishments			
Regulated Operations...............	FAS71, ¶36-37	Re6.141-142	
EARNING POWER			
Performance Measurement	CON1, ¶47-48		
....	CON1, ¶51		
....	CON5, ¶28		
EARNINGS			
Change in Use of Term from Concepts			
Statement 1	CON5, ¶11		
Description and Evolution of Concept....	CON5, ¶33-38		
Enterprise Performance...............	CON1, ¶42-48		
Measurement	CON1, ¶45-48		
Recognition Implications..............	CON5, ¶49-51		
Relation to Cash Flows	CON1, ¶43-49		
Relation to Comprehensive Income	CON5, ¶42-44		
....	CON6, ¶1		
....	CON6, ¶72		
EARNINGS OR LOSSES OF AN INVESTEE			
See Investments: Equity Method			
Definition	APB18, ¶3	I82.404	
EARNINGS PER SHARE			
See Disclosure			
Accounting Changes			
. . Catch-up Adjustment	AIN-APB20, #2	E09.511-514	
. . Restatement	AIN-APB20, #1	E09.503-510	
Adjustment of Income for Interest			
Expense	APB15, App.C	E09.167	
Antidilutive Securities	AIN-APB15, #5	E09.518	
....	AIN-APB15, Part I	E09.533-535	
Brokers and Dealers in Securities	FAS111, ¶8	E09.501-502	
....	FTB79-8, ¶1		
....	FTB79-8, ¶6		
Classification of Securities.............	AIN-APB15, Part I	E09.515-517	
Common Stock Contributed to Employee Stock Ownership Plan			
. . Excess Assets Not Allocated to			
Participants			EITF.86-27
Common Stock Equivalents	AIN-APB15, #2	E09.528	
....	FAS111, ¶8		
. . Junior Stock.....................	FIN38, ¶7	E09.130A	
. . Nonrecognition in Financial			
Statements	APB15, ¶39	E09.132	
Complex Capital Structure	AIN-APB15, #18	E09.164	
....	APB15, App.C	E09.168	
....	FAS111, ¶8	E09.571-573	
Computational Guidelines..............	APB15, ¶44	E09.137	
. . Business Combinations and			
Reorganization	APB15, ¶49	E09.140	EITF.84-22
. . Claims of Senior Securities	APB15, ¶50	E09.141	

FAS—FASB Statements	FIN—FASB Interpretations	FTB—FASB Technical Bulletins
APB—APB Opinions	AIN—AICPA Interpretations	ARB—Accounting Research Bulletins
CON—FASB Concepts	EITF—EITF Issues	Q&A—FASB Special Reports

E

Topical Index

See "Terminology" for references to defined terms presented in various accounting pronouncements.

See the Introduction to the Topical Index for details on the use of this index.

	Original Pronouncements	Current Text	EITF and Other
EARNINGS PER SHARE—continued			
Computational Guidelines, Convertible Securities—continued			
. . Convertible into Other Convertible Securities	AIN-APB15, #45	E09.661-665	
. . Definition of Same Terms	AIN-APB15, #31	E09.627-628	
. . If-Converted Method at Actual Conversion	AIN-APB15, #44	E09.657-660	
. . Issue Price Is Not a Term	AIN-APB15, #32	E09.629-630	
. . No Antidilution from Convertible Debt	AIN-APB15, #42	E09.649-651	
. . No Antidilution from Convertible Preferred Stock	AIN-APB15, #41	E09.646-648	
. . Original Issue Premium or Discount	AIN-APB15, #40	E09.644-645	
. . Property Included in Yield of Convertible Securities	AIN-APB15, #37 FAS85, ¶3	E09.639-641	
. . Put Warrants			EITF.88-9
. . Sold by Issuer from Securities Held as Treasury Securities	AIN-APB15, #33 FAS111, ¶8	E09.631-632	
. . Time of Issuance	AIN-APB15, #27	E09.608-612	
. . Yield of Convertible Securities in a Package	AIN-APB15, #36	E09.637-638	
Computations for Warrants Whose Proceeds Are Applied to Retire Debt			
. . Options and Warrants and Their Equivalents	AIN-APB15, #70	E09.786-789	
Contingently Issuable Shares under Equity Commitment and Contract Notes			EITF.85-18
Cooperatives			
. . Exemption from Requirements	FAS21, ¶12	E09.102	
Credit Unions			
. . Exemption from Requirements	FAS21, ¶12	E09.102	
Dilution Less Than Three Percent Test	AIN-APB15, #12	E09.554-559	
Dilutive Security	AIN-APB15, #4	E09.531-532	
Discontinued Operations	APB30, ¶9	I13.107	
Dual Presentation	AIN-APB15, #6	E09.536-538	
. . Dilution Less Than Three Percent	AIN-APB15, #11	E09.550-553	
Effects of Scheduled Changes			
. . Changing Exercise Prices and Conversion Rates	AIN-APB15, #94	E09.889-892	
Election to Classify Outstanding Securities			
. . Effect of New Issues of Common Stock Equivalents	AIN-APB15, #96	E09.893-894	
. . No Change for Options and Warrants	AIN-APB15, #97	E09.895-897	
. . Retroactive Restatement of Prior Periods	AIN-APB15, #99	E09.898-899	

FAS—FASB Statements   FIN—FASB Interpretations   FTB—FASB Technical Bulletins
APB—APB Opinions   AIN—AICPA Interpretations   ARB—Accounting Research Bulletins
CON—FASB Concepts   EITF—EITF Issues   Q&A—FASB Special Reports

	Original Pronouncements	Current Text	EITF and Other
EARNINGS PER SHARE—continued			
Fully Diluted Earnings per Share	AIN-APB15, #8	E09.541-542	
. . Antidilution	APB15, ¶40	E09.133	
. . When Required	APB15, ¶41-42	E09.134-135	
Glossary	APB15, App.D	E09.401-428	
	FAS21, ¶13		
	FAS85, ¶3		
Government-Owned Enterprises			
. . Exemption from Requirements	FAS21, ¶12	E09.102	
Historical Summaries			
. . Accounting Change	APB20, ¶39	A06.134	
If-Converted Method of Computation	APB15, ¶51-53	E09.142-144	
Illustrative Statements	APB15, App.C	E09.162	
Mutual Savings Bank			
. . Exemption from Requirements	FAS21, ¶12	E09.102	
Not-for-Profit Enterprises			
. . Exemption from Requirements	FAS21, ¶12	E09.102	
Options and Warrants and Their Equivalents	AIN-APB15, Part I	E09.521-524	
. . Antidilutive Exercise	AIN-APB15, #62	E09.745-754	
. . Antidilutive Options and Warrants Included	AIN-APB15, #72	E09.795-796	
. . Applying Ending and Average Market Prices	AIN-APB15, #60	E09.730-736	
. . Classification of	AIN-APB15, #46	E09.666-667	
. . Compensating Balances Excluded	AIN-APB15, #78	E09.815-816	
. . Computations May Differ for Primary and Fully Diluted	AIN-APB15, #81	E09.822-825	
. . Computations for Warrants Allowing Tendering of Debt	AIN-APB15, #69	E09.780-785	
. . Computations for Warrants Requiring the Tendering of Debt	AIN-APB15, #68	E09.778-779	
. . Computations for Warrants Whose Proceeds Are Applied to Retire Debt	AIN-APB15, #70	E09.786-789	
. . Debt Eligible Only While Outstanding	AIN-APB15, #80	E09.820-821	
. . Debt Purchased, Treasury-Stock Method	AIN-APB15, #77	E09.812-814	
. . Definition of "Period"	AIN-APB15, #58	E09.723-726	
. . Equivalents of	AIN-APB15, #48	E09.672-673	
. . Explanation of Twenty Percent Provision	AIN-APB15, #74	E09.799-805	
. . Fair Value If No Market Price	AIN-APB15, #56	E09.708-713	
. . Grouping	AIN-APB15, #49	E09.674-678	
. . Investments Assumed Purchased for Treasury-Stock Method	AIN-APB15, #79	E09.817-819	
. . Junior Stock Option, Purchase and Award Plans	FIN38, ¶7	E09.130A	

See "Terminology" for references to defined terms presented in various accounting pronouncements.
See the Introduction to the Topical Index for details on the use of this index.

FAS—FASB Statements   FIN—FASB Interpretations   FTB—FASB Technical Bulletins
APB—APB Opinions   AIN—AICPA Interpretations   ARB—Accounting Research Bulletins
CON—FASB Concepts   EITF—EITF Issues   Q&A—FASB Special Reports

See "Terminology" for references to defined terms presented in various accounting pronouncements.
See the Introduction to the Topical Index for details on the use of this index.

	Original Pronouncements	Current Text	EITF and Other
EARNINGS PER SHARE—continued			
Stock Compensation Plans in Earnings per Share Computations—continued			
. . Dilutive Effect	FIN31, ¶4	E09.130	
. . Junior Stock Option, Purchase and Award Plans	FIN38, ¶7	E09.130A	
. . Treasury-Stock Method	FIN31, ¶3	E09.129	
. . . .	FIN31, ¶14-21	E09.169-176	
Treasury-Stock Method	APB15, ¶36	E09.125	
Treatment of Tax Benefits for Dividends on Stock Held by an Employee Stock Ownership Plan			EITF.90-4
Two-Class Common Stock and Participating Securities			
. . Convertible Securities	AIN-APB15, #87	E09.847-851	
. . Nonconvertible Securities	AIN-APB15, #86	E09.842-846	
. . Treatment	AIN-APB15, #85	E09.836-841	
Two-Class Method for Warrants Issued by REITs	AIN-APB15, #102	E09.911-916	
Unaudited Financial Statements			
. . Applicability of Requirements	AIN-APB15, #14	E09.562-563	
Weighted Average Number of Shares	APB15, App.C	E09.165-166	
EARNINGS STATEMENTS			
See Income Statement			
See Income Statement Presentation: Discontinued Operations			
EARNINGS SUMMARIES			
Historical Summaries	APB20, ¶39	A06.134	
EARNOUT			
Business Combinations	APB16, ¶80	B50.138	
ECONOMIC LIFE			
See Depreciation			
See Intangible Assets			
Estimated Economic Life of Leased Property			
See Leases			
ECONOMIC RESOURCES			
Allocation in the Economy	CON1, ¶12-16		
Discussion	CON6, ¶11-15		
. . . .	CON6, ¶27-31		
Information about	CON1, ¶40-41		
Not-for-Profit Organizations	CON4, ¶43-54		

FAS—FASB Statements	FIN—FASB Interpretations	FTB—FASB Technical Bulletins
APB—APB Opinions	AIN—AICPA Interpretations	ARB—Accounting Research Bulletins
CON—FASB Concepts	EITF—EITF Issues	Q&A—FASB Special Reports

E

Topical Index

	Original Pronouncements	Current Text	EITF and Other

EFFECTIVE YIELD
See Earnings per Share

ELEMENTS OF FINANCIAL STATEMENTS
See Assets
See Expenses
See Gains
See Investments by Owners
See Liabilities
See Not-for-Profit Organizations
See Revenues

	Original Pronouncements		
Accrual Basis of Accounting	CON6, ¶134-152		
Articulation	CON6, ¶20-21		
Characteristics and Examples	CON6, ¶164-255		
Definition	CON6, ¶5		
Elements			
. . Assets	CON6, ¶25-34		
. . Comprehensive Income	CON6, ¶70-77		
. . Equity or Net Assets	CON6, ¶49-59		
. . Expenses	CON6, ¶80-81		
. . Gains and Losses	CON6, ¶82-89		
. . Investments by and Distributions to Owners	CON6, ¶66-69		
. . Liabilities	CON6, ¶35-43		
. . Revenues	CON6, ¶78-79		
Examples	CON6, ¶229-255		
Financial Representations	CON6, ¶5-7		
Relation to Objectives of Financial Reporting	CON6, ¶9-19		
Relation to Qualitative Characteristics	CON6, ¶9-19		
Relation to Recognition, Measurement, and Display	CON5, ¶64		
	CON6, ¶22-23		
Uncertainty	CON6, ¶44-48		

EMERGING ISSUES TASK FORCE (EITF)
See FASB Emerging Issues Task Force (EITF)

EMPLOYEE BENEFIT FUNDS
See Postretirement Health Care and Life Insurance Benefits

EMPLOYEE BENEFIT PLANS
See Pension Costs
See Postemployment Benefits
See Postretirement Benefits Other Than Pensions
See Postretirement Health Care and Life Insurance Benefits

			EITF and Other
Accounting for Estimated Payments in Connection with the Coal Industry Retiree Health Benefit Act of 1992			EITF.92-13
Accounting for Involuntary Termination Benefits			EITF.94-3

See "Terminology" for references to defined terms presented in various accounting pronouncements.

See the Introduction to the Topical Index for details on the use of this index.

	Original Pronouncements	Current Text	EITF and Other
EMPLOYEE STOCK OWNERSHIP PLANS (ESOPs)—continued			
Income Tax Benefits from Dividends Distributed			EITF.86-4
. . Earnings-per-Share Treatment			EITF.90-4
			EITF.92-3
Leveraged ESOPs			
. . Accounting for Treasury Stock in the Context of Pooling-of-Interests Business Combinations			EITF.D-19
. . Recognition by Sponsor of ESOP Debt			EITF.89-10
. . Sponsor's Balance Sheet Classification of Securities with a Put Option Held by an ESOP			EITF.89-11
Sale of Participant's Shares to Employer or to ESOP at Formula Price			EITF.87-23
Sponsor's Balance Sheet Classification of Securities with a Put Option Held by an ESOP			EITF.89-11
Use in a Leveraged Buyout			EITF.85-11
EMPLOYEE STOCK PURCHASE PLANS			
See Compensation to Employees: Stock Purchase and Stock Option Plans			
See Employee Stock Ownership Plans (ESOPs)			
EMPLOYEES			
See Compensation to Employees: Deferred			
See Defined Benefit Pension Plans			
See Pension Costs			
See Termination Benefits			
Definition	FAS35, ¶280	Pe5.410	
Receivables	ARB43, Ch.1A, ¶5	R36.105	
ENTITY			
Description	CON6, ¶24		
ENVIRONMENTAL CONTAMINATION			
Accounting for Environmental Liabilities			EITF.93-5
Asbestos Treatment Costs			EITF.89-13
Costs to Clean Up Environmental Contamination			EITF.90-8
ENVIRONMENTAL LIABILITIES			
See Environmental Contamination			
EQUIPMENT			
See Property, Plant, and Equipment			
EQUITABLE OBLIGATIONS			
Description	CON6, ¶202-203		
EQUITY (OR NET ASSETS)			
See Shareholders' Equity			
See Statement of Investments by and Distributions to Owners			
Characteristics			
. . Business Enterprises	CON6, ¶50-51		
	CON6, ¶60-63		
	CON6, ¶212-214		

See "Terminology" for references to defined terms presented in various accounting pronouncements.

See the Introduction to the Topical Index for details on the use of this index.

FAS—FASB Statements	FIN—FASB Interpretations	FTB—FASB Technical Bulletins
APB—APB Opinions	AIN—AICPA Interpretations	ARB—Accounting Research Bulletins
CON—FASB Concepts	EITF—EITF Issues	Q&A—FASB Special Reports

See "Terminology" for references to defined terms presented in various accounting pronouncements.

See the Introduction to the Topical Index for details on the use of this index.

	Original Pronouncements	Current Text	EITF and Other
EXTRACTIVE INDUSTRIES—continued			
Accounting Change			
. . From/To Full Cost Method	APB20, ¶27	A06.123	
Advances to Encourage Exploration,			
Imputed Interest	AIN-APB21, #1	I69.501	
Prior Period Adjustments			
. . Full Cost Method	APB20, ¶27	A35.114	
EXTRAORDINARY ITEMS			
See Disclosure			
See Income Statement Presentation:			
Discontinued Operations			
Abnormal Costs	APB30, ¶20-22	I17.108-109	
. . . .		I17.401	
Accounting for Estimated Payments in			
Connection with the Coal Industry			
Retiree Health Benefit Act of 1992			EITF.92-13
Asbestos Treatment Costs			EITF.89-13
Casualty Loss	APB30, ¶23	I17.111	
Costs Incurred in a Takeover Defense			EITF.85-2
Criteria	AIN-APB30, #1	I17.106-110	
. . . .	APB30, ¶19-23	I17.503-504	
. . Costs Incurred in Defending against a			
Takeover Attempt	FTB85-6, ¶6-7	I17.509-510	EITF.85-2
. . Examples That Do Not Meet Criteria .	AIN-APB9, #1	I17.501-502	EITF.85-2
. . . .	AIN-APB30, #1	I17.506-507	EITF.89-13
. . . .	FTB85-6, ¶6-7	I17.509-510	
. . Examples That Meet Criteria	AIN-APB30, #1	I17.505	
. . Losses Caused by Bankruptcy	AIN-APB9, #1	I17.501-502	
Debt: Extinguishments	FAS4, ¶8	D14.105-106	
. . . .	FAS4, ¶10		
Debt: Restructurings	FAS15, ¶21	D22.117	
Definition	APB30, ¶20	I17.401	
Devaluation	APB30, ¶23	I17.110	
Equity Method Investments	APB18, ¶19	I82.109	
Expropriation	APB30, ¶23	I17.111	
Extinguishment of Debt	FAS4, ¶8	I17.113	
. . . .	FAS64, ¶4		

FAS–FASB Statements   FIN–FASB Interpretations   FTB–FASB Technical Bulletins
APB–APB Opinions   AIN–AICPA Interpretations   ARB–Accounting Research Bulletins
CON–FASB Concepts   EITF–EITF Issues   Q&A–FASB Special Reports

T-141

	Original Pronouncements	Current Text	EITF and Other

(The next page is T-151.)

See "Terminology" for references to defined terms presented in various accounting pronouncements.
See the Introduction to the Topical Index for details on the use of this index.

	Original Pronouncements	Current Text	EITF and Other
FACTORING			
See Receivables Sold with Recourse			
FAIR VALUE			
See Impairment: Loans			
See Investments: Debt and Equity Securities			
See Leases			
See Pension Costs			
Basis in Leveraged Buyout Transactions...			EITF.86-16
....			EITF.88-16
Contributions	FAS116, ¶19-21	C67.115-117	
Debt Securities			
. . Determining Fair Value	FAS115, ¶110-112	I80.112	
Defined Benefit Pension Plans	FAS35, ¶11	Pe5.110	
....	FAS35, ¶104		
....	FAS110, ¶4		
....	FAS110, ¶7		
Definition	FAS67, ¶28	P16.422	
....	FAS87, ¶264	Re2.405	
Distributions of Loans Receivable to Shareholders			EITF.87-17
Dividends-in-Kind			EITF.87-17
Employee Benefit Plans			
. . Valuation of Investment Contracts with Noninsurance Entities.........			EITF.89-1
Equity Securities			
. . Determining Fair Value	FAS115, ¶110-111	I80.112	
. . Readily Determinable Fair Value	FAS115, ¶3	I80.101	
Exchange of Interest-Only and Principal-Only Securities for a Mortgage-Backed Security			EITF.90-2
Exchange of Real Estate Involving Boot ..			EITF.87-29
Exchanges of Ownership Interests between Entities under Common Control			EITF.90-5
Hedges.............................	FAS80, ¶5	F80.105	
....	FAS115, ¶129		
. . Anticipated Transactions............			EITF.86-28
. . Consistent Reporting for Hedged Instrument and Hedging Instrument .	FAS115, ¶115	I80.113	
. . Items Reported at Fair Value			EITF.86-28
. . Ongoing Assessment of Correlation...			EITF.86-28
Implementation of Statement 107........			EITF.D-29
In-Substance Foreclosure on Collateral ...			EITF.89-9
Liquidation of a Banking Institution			
. . Valuation of Assets and Liabilities by Liquidating Bank.................			EITF.88-25

FAS–FASB Statements	FIN–FASB Interpretations	FTB–FASB Technical Bulletins
APB–APB Opinions	AIN–AICPA Interpretations	ARB–Accounting Research Bulletins
CON–FASB Concepts	EITF–EITF Issues	Q&A–FASB Special Reports

See "Terminology" for references to defined terms presented in various accounting pronouncements.
See the Introduction to the Topical Index for details on the use of this index.

	Original Pronouncements	Current Text	EITF and Other
FEDERAL SAVINGS AND LOAN INSURANCE CORPORATION (FSLIC)—continued			
Liquidation of a Banking Institution			
. . Valuation of Assets and Liabilities by Liquidating Bank			EITF.88-25
Management Consignment Program			
. . Accounting for Newly Chartered Institutions			EITF.85-41
Net Worth Certificates			EITF.85-41
Secondary Reserve			
. . Write-off of Prepayments			EITF.87-22
FEEDBACK VALUE			
Component of Relevance	CON2, ¶51-52		
Definition	CON2, Glossary		
FEES			
See Franchising			
See Lending Activities			
See Mortgage Banking Activities			
FHLMC			
See Banking and Thrift Industries			
See Federal Home Loan Mortgage Corporation (FHLMC)			
FIFO (FIRST-IN, FIRST-OUT)			
Inventory Valuation Method			
See Inventory			
FINANCE CHARGES			
Balance Sheet Classification	ARB43, Ch.3A, ¶6	B05.107	
FINANCE COMPANIES			
See Lending Activities			
Nonrefundable Loan Fees and Costs	FAS91, ¶2	Fi4.102	
FINANCIAL CAPITAL MAINTENANCE CONCEPT			
See Capital Maintenance			
FINANCIAL FLEXIBILITY			
Definition	CON5, ¶24		
Use of Statement of Cash Flows in Assessing	CON5, ¶52		
Use of Statement of Financial Position in Assessing	CON5, ¶29		
FINANCIAL FUTURES			
See Financial Instruments			
See Futures Contracts			

FAS—FASB Statements FIN—FASB Interpretations FTB—FASB Technical Bulletins
APB—APB Opinions AIN—AICPA Interpretations ARB—Accounting Research Bulletins
CON—FASB Concepts EITF—EITF Issues Q&A—FASB Special Reports

T-153

See "Terminology" for references to defined terms presented in various accounting pronouncements.

See the Introduction to the Topical Index for details on the use of this index.

	Original Pronouncements	Current Text	EITF and Other
FINANCIAL INSTRUMENTS—continued			
Fair Value—continued			
. . Options	FAS107, ¶25	F25.148	
. . Practicability	FAS107, ¶14-15	F25.115G-115H	
. . Reporting Requirements	FAS107, ¶10-15	F25.105A	
	FAS107, ¶17	F25.115C-115H	
. . Scope	FAS107, ¶7-9	F25.105A-105C	
. . Trade Receivables and Payables	FAS107, ¶13	F25.115F	
Implementation of Statement 105			EITF.D-22
Implementation of Statement 107			EITF.D-29
Off-Balance-Sheet Risk			
. . Illustrations	FAS105, ¶40	F25.133-140	
	FAS105, ¶42-48		
. . Reporting Requirements	FAS105, ¶17-19	F25.112-114	
. . Scope	FAS105, ¶12-16	F25.101-105	
	FAS111, ¶8		
Offsetting of Amounts Related to Certain Contracts	FIN39, ¶8-10	B10.104-106	
Presentation of Market Values Recognized for Off-Balance-Sheet Financial Instruments			EITF.D-25
FINANCIAL POSITION			
See Balance Sheet Classification: Current Assets and Liabilities			
See Cash Flows Statement			
See Defined Benefit Pension Plans			
See Financial Statements: Comparative Financial Statements			
See Interim Financial Reporting			
See Statement of Financial Position			
Definition	APB18, ¶3	I82.404	
	CON6, ¶20		
FINANCIAL REPORTING			
Accrual Basis of Accounting	CON6, ¶134-152		
Character and Limitations of Information Provided	CON1, ¶17-23		
Characteristics	CON1, ¶5-8		
Compared to Management Reporting	CON1, ¶27		
Conservatism	CON2, ¶91-97		
General Purpose External Reporting, Objectives	CON1, ¶28-31		
Information about Claims on Resources, Changes	CON1, ¶40-41		
Information about Economic Resources, Changes	CON1, ¶40-41		

See "Terminology" for references to defined terms presented in various accounting pronouncements.

See the Introduction to the Topical Index for details on the use of this index.

	Original Pronouncements	Current Text	EITF and Other
FINANCIAL STATEMENTS: COMPARATIVE FINANCIAL STATEMENTS—continued			
See Disclosure			
See Earnings per Share			
See Not-for-Profit Organizations			
See Segment of Business Reporting			
Inconsistencies in Comparative Figures Disclosed	ARB43, Ch.2A, ¶3	F43.103	
Scope of Accounting and Reporting Requirements	ARB43, Ch.2A, ¶1-2	F43.101-102	
FINANCING			
See Balance Sheet Classification: Current Assets and Liabilities			
See Business Combinations			
See Capital Stock: Capital Transactions			
See Capital Stock: Preferred Stock			
See Consolidation			
See Debt: Convertible Debt and Debt with Stock Purchase Warrants			
See Debt: Product Financing Arrangements			
See Development Stage Enterprises			
See Franchising			
See Leases			
See Lending Activities			
See Quasi Reorganizations			
See Real Estate			
See Research and Development Arrangements			
See Retained Earnings			
Agreements			
See Balance Sheet Classification: Current Assets and Liabilities			
FINISHED GOODS			
See Inventory			
Balance Sheet Classification	ARB43, Ch.3A, ¶4	B05.105	
FIRE AND CASUALTY INSURANCE ENTERPRISES			
See Insurance Industry			
See Investments: Marketable Securities			
FISCAL FUNDING, LEASES			
See Leases			
FIXED ASSETS			
See Depreciation			
Cash Flows Reporting	FAS95, ¶15-17	C25.113-115	
	FAS95, ¶24	C25.122	

FAS–FASB Statements   FIN–FASB Interpretations   FTB–FASB Technical Bulletins
APB–APB Opinions   AIN–AICPA Interpretations   ARB–Accounting Research Bulletins
CON–FASB Concepts   EITF–EITF Issues   Q&A–FASB Special Reports

T-157

	Original Pronouncements	Current Text	EITF and Other
FIXED ASSETS—continued			
Duplicate Facilities following a Purchase Business Combination			
. . Costs of Closing Duplicate Facilities of an Acquirer	FTB85-5, ¶1-2	B50.651-652	EITF.84-35
Environmentally Contaminated Property			
. . Costs Incurred to Clean Up Environmental Contamination.			EITF.90-8
Idle Facilities.			EITF.84-28
Property with Asbestos			
. . Costs Incurred for Asbestos Treatment			EITF.89-13
Segment of Business Reporting.	FAS14, ¶27	S20.133	
Write-downs			
. . Operating Assets	FAS5, ¶31	C59.137	EITF.84-28
. . Relation to Contingencies	FAS5, ¶31	C59.102	
FIXED PRICE CONTRACTS			
See Contractor Accounting: Construction-Type Contracts			
See Contractor Accounting: Government Contracts			
FLOW-THROUGH METHOD			
See Income Taxes			
FOOTNOTES			
See Notes to Financial Statements			
FORECASTS			
See Development Stage Enterprises			
FORECLOSURE			
See Debt: Restructurings			
See Impairment: Loans			
Classification of In-Substance Foreclosed (ISF) Assets by SEC Registrants.			EITF.D-37
Valuation of Repossessed Real Estate			
. . Sale Accounted for under Installment or Cost Recovery Method.			EITF.89-14
FOREIGN CURRENCY			
See Foreign Currency Translation			
Accounting for a Change in Functional Currency When an Economy Ceases to Be Considered Highly Inflationary			EITF.92-4
. . Income Tax Effects			EITF.92-8
Definition	FAS52, ¶162	F60.401-423	
Transfer of Receivables in Which Risk of Foreign Currency Fluctuation Is Retained			EITF.D-13

See "Terminology" for references to defined terms presented in various accounting pronouncements.

See the Introduction to the Topical Index for details on the use of this index.

	Original Pronouncements	Current Text	EITF and Other
FOREIGN CURRENCY SWAPS			
See Financial Instruments			
Offsetting			EITF.86-25
FOREIGN CURRENCY TRANSLATION			
See Disclosure			
See Financial Instruments			
Accounting Changes	FAS52, ¶9	F60.113	
	FAS52, ¶45		
Accounting for a Change in Functional Currency When an Economy Ceases to Be Considered Highly Inflationary			EITF.92-4
. . Income Tax Effects			EITF.92-8
Accounting for Dual Currency Bonds			EITF.93-10
Currency Swaps	FAS52, ¶17	F60.124	
Devaluation			
. . Extraordinary Item	APB30, ¶23	I17.110	
Discounting			EITF.87-2
Exchange Rates	FAS52, ¶26	F60.136	
. . Criteria for Choice	FAS52, ¶27	F60.137	
. . Different Periods between Entities	FAS52, ¶28	F60.138	
. . Exchange Rates to Be Used	FAS52, ¶12	F60.118	
. . Lack of Convertibility	FAS52, ¶26	F60.136	
Foreign Currency Swaps			
. . Offsetting			EITF.86-25
Foreign Currency Transactions	FAS52, ¶15-16	F60.122-123	
	FAS52, ¶96		
	FAS52, ¶120		
Foreign Debt-for-Equity Swaps			EITF.87-12
Forward Exchange Contracts	FAS52, ¶17	F60.124	EITF.87-2
. . Computation of Gains (Losses)	FAS52, ¶18	F60.125	
. . Discount or Premium on	FAS52, ¶18	F60.125	
. . Reporting Hedges in Cash Flows Statement	FAS104, ¶7	C25.112	
		F60.126A	
. . Speculative Forward Contract	FAS52, ¶19	F60.126	
Functional Currency	FAS52, ¶5	F60.104	
. . Change in and Accounting for That Change	FAS52, ¶9	F60.113-114	
	FAS52, ¶46		
. . Classes of Foreign Operations	FAS52, ¶79-81	F60.106-108	
. . Management Judgment in Determining	FAS52, ¶8	F60.109	
	FAS52, ¶39		
	FAS52, ¶41		
. . Remeasurement Required If Books Not Maintained in Functional Currency	FAS52, ¶10	F60.115	

FAS–FASB Statements FIN–FASB Interpretations FTB–FASB Technical Bulletins
APB–APB Opinions AIN–AICPA Interpretations ARB–Accounting Research Bulletins
CON–FASB Concepts EITF–EITF Issues Q&A–FASB Special Reports

	Original Pronouncements	Current Text	EITF and Other

See "Terminology" for references to defined terms presented in various accounting pronouncements.
See the Introduction to the Topical Index for details on the use of this index.

	Original Pronouncements	Current Text	EITF and Other
FOREIGN CURRENCY			
TRANSLATION—continued			
Intercompany Balances and Transactions..	FAS52, ¶25	F60.135	
Inventories			
. . Application of Lower of Cost or Market Rule....................	FAS52, ¶49-53	F60.148-152	
Objectives of Translation...............	FAS52, ¶4	F60.103	
Remeasurement of Books of Record into Functional Currency			
. . Items to Be Measured Using Historical Rates........................	FAS52, ¶48	F60.147	
....	FAS109, ¶288		
. . Objectives........................	FAS52, ¶47	F60.146	
. . Rates to Be Used	FAS52, ¶47	F60.146	
Sale of Future Revenue			
. . Payment to Investor Denominated in Foreign Currency.................			EITF.88-18
Sale or Liquidation of an Investment in a Foreign Entity	FAS52, ¶14	F60.120	
....	FIN37, ¶2		
....	FIN37, ¶8		
Scope of Accounting and Reporting Requirements......................	FAS52, ¶2	F60.101	
. . Consolidation, Equity Investees, and Post-Business Combinations	FAS52, ¶101	F60.102	
Selection of Exchange Rate When Trading Is Temporarily Suspended............			EITF.D-12
Statement of Cash Flows			
. . Impact on......................	FAS95, ¶25	C25.142-152A	
....	FAS95, ¶136-146	F60.118A	
Translation Adjustments	FAS52, ¶13-14	F60.119-120	
....	FIN37, ¶2		
Translation of Operations in Highly Inflationary Economies	FAS52, ¶11	F60.116-117	
....	FAS52, ¶109		
Use of Averages or Other Methods of Approximation	FAS52, ¶133	F60.139	
FOREIGN ENTITY			
See Foreign Operations			
FOREIGN EXCHANGE			
See Foreign Currency Translation			
FOREIGN EXCHANGE CONTRACTS			
See Financial Instruments			
See Foreign Currency Translation			

FAS–FASB Statements FIN–FASB Interpretations FTB–FASB Technical Bulletins
APB–APB Opinions AIN–AICPA Interpretations ARB–Accounting Research Bulletins
CON–FASB Concepts EITF–EITF Issues Q&A–FASB Special Reports

T-161

	Original Pronouncements	Current Text	EITF and Other
FOREIGN EXCHANGE GAINS AND LOSSES			
See Foreign Currency Translation			
FOREIGN OPERATIONS			
See Consolidation			
See Disclosure			
See Foreign Currency Translation			
See Income Taxes			
See Oil and Gas Producing Activities			
See Pension Costs			
See Postretirement Benefits Other Than Pensions			
See Segment of Business Reporting			
Background to Requirements	ARB43, Ch.12, ¶1-3	F65.100A-100C	
Disclosure	ARB43, Ch.12, ¶5-6	F65.102-103	
Elimination of Write-ups on Depreciable Assets	APB6, ¶17	D40.102	
Interest: Capitalization of Interest Costs	FAS34, ¶14	I67.111	
Inventory			
. . Lower of Cost or Market	FAS52, ¶49-53	F60.148-152	
Recognition of Foreign Earnings	ARB43, Ch.12, ¶4	F65.101	
	ARB43, Ch.12, ¶6	F65.103	
. . Deferred Taxes	FAS37, ¶23-25	I27.209-211	
	FAS109, ¶287-288		
. . Earnings in Excess of Amounts Received in U.S.	ARB43, Ch.12, ¶5	F65.102	
FOREIGN TAXES			
See Foreign Currency Translation			
See Income Taxes			
FOREST PRODUCTS INDUSTRY			
See Timberlands and Growing Timber			
FORWARD COMMITMENTS			
See Financial Instruments			
See Foreign Currency Translation			
Hedges			EITF.86-26
Mortgage Swaps			EITF.88-8
Surrogate for Deferred Rate Setting			EITF.86-26
FORWARD CONTRACTS			
See Financial Instruments			
Comparison with Futures Contracts	FAS80, ¶34	F80.101	
FORWARD EXCHANGE CONTRACTS			
See Foreign Currency Translation			
FRANCHISE COSTS			
See Cable Television Industry			

See "Terminology" for references to defined terms presented in various accounting pronouncements.
See the Introduction to the Topical Index for details on the use of this index.

	Original Pronouncements	Current Text	EITF and Other

FRANCHISING

See Cable Television Industry
See Disclosure
Franchisors

. . Agency Sales......................	FAS45, ¶16	Fr3.112	
. . Area Franchise Fees................	FAS45, ¶8-9	Fr3.104-105	
. . Commingled Revenue	FAS45, ¶12-13	Fr3.108-109	
. . Continuing Franchise Fees, Revenue			
Recognition	FAS45, ¶14	Fr3.110	
. . Continuing Product Sales	FAS45, ¶15	Fr3.111	
. . Costs Relating to Franchise Sales	FAS45, ¶17	Fr3.113	
. . Disclosure........................	FAS45, ¶20-23	Fr3.116-119	
. . Individual Franchise Sales...........	FAS45, ¶5-7	Fr3.101-103	
. . Individual Franchise Sales, Initial			
Franchise Fees	FAS45, ¶7	Fr3.103	
. . Option to Repurchase Franchise......	FAS45, ¶11	Fr3.107	
. . Repossessed Franchises	FAS45, ¶18	Fr3.114	
Franchisors, Franchisees			
. . Business Combinations	FAS45, ¶19	Fr3.115	
. . Relationships	FAS45, ¶10-11	Fr3.106-107	
Glossary	FAS45, ¶26	Fr3.401-408	
Intangible Assets......................	APB17, ¶1	I60.101	

FREIGHT SERVICES

Revenue and Expense Recognition for			
Freight Services in Process			EITF.91-9

FRINGE BENEFIT PLANS

See Compensation to Employees: Stock
Purchase and Stock Option Plans
See Defined Benefit Pension Plans
See Employee Stock Ownership Plans
(ESOPs)
See Pension Costs
See Postemployment Benefits
See Postretirement Health Care and Life
Insurance Benefits

FULL ACCRUAL METHOD (REAL ESTATE)

See Real Estate: Sales Other Than Retail
Land Sales

FAS–FASB Statements	FIN–FASB Interpretations	FTB–FASB Technical Bulletins
APB–APB Opinions	AIN–AICPA Interpretations	ARB–Accounting Research Bulletins
CON–FASB Concepts	EITF–EITF Issues	Q&A–FASB Special Reports

T-163

	Original Pronouncements	Current Text	EITF and Other

FULL COST METHOD
See Accounting Changes
See Oil and Gas Producing Activities
FULL ELIGIBILITY DATE
See Postretirement Benefits Other Than
  Pensions
**FULLY DILUTED EARNINGS PER
  SHARE**
See Earnings per Share
**FUNCTIONAL CLASSIFICATION OF
  EXPENSES**
See Not-for-Profit Organizations
FUNCTIONAL CURRENCY
See Foreign Currency Translation

| Definition | FAS52, ¶162 | F60.415 | |

FUNDING REQUIREMENTS
See Pension Costs
FUNDS FLOWS
See Cash Flows
FUNDS STATEMENT
See Cash Flows Statement
FUTURE ECONOMIC BENEFITS

Discussion	CON6, ¶26-30		
	CON6, ¶172-182		
Relation to Assets	CON6, ¶190-191		

FUTURES CONTRACTS
See Disclosure
See Financial Instruments
See Foreign Currency Translation

Anticipatory Hedges	FAS80, ¶26	F80.109	
	FAS80, ¶54	F80.112A	
	FAS104, ¶7	F80.123	

Classification
. . Deferred Future Gains and Losses,
    Firm Commitments and Anticipated

Transactions	FAS80, ¶9-10	F80.109-110	Q&A.80 #16-17
. . Margin Deposits			Q&A.80 #15
Daily Limits on Change in Market Price . .			Q&A.80 #2
Difference between Options and Futures . .	FAS80, ¶32	F80.101	
Estimates of Value	FAS80, ¶11	F80.111	Q&A.80 #26
Examples	FAS80, ¶16	F80.113	
. . Hedge of Financial Instruments Held			
for Sale	FAS80, ¶22-24	F80.119-121	
. . Hedge of an Anticipated Purchase	FAS80, ¶19-21	F80.116-118	
. . Hedge of the Interest Expense Related			
to Short-Term Deposits	FAS80, ¶25-26	F80.122-123	

See "Terminology" for references to defined terms presented in various accounting pronouncements.
See the Introduction to the Topical Index for details on the use of this index.

	Original Pronouncements	Current Text	EITF and Other
FUTURES CONTRACTS—continued			
Examples—continued			
. . Nonhedge Contract	FAS80, ¶17-18	F80.114-115	
Exclusion of Forward Contracts, Foreign Currency Futures, and Options	FAS80, ¶1	F80.101	Q&A.80 #1
	FAS80, ¶34		
Glossary	FAS80, ¶4	F80.401-404	
	FAS80, ¶15		
Hedges	FAS80, ¶42	F80.103	
. . Amortization of Deferred Gains and Losses	FAS80, ¶7	F80.107	Q&A.80 #18-19
. . Anticipated Liabilities			EITF.86-34
. . Anticipated Transactions	FAS80, ¶54	F80.109-110	
	FAS80, ¶56-57		
. . Classification in Cash Flows Statement	FAS104, ¶7	C25.112	
		F80.112A	
. . Commodity Dealers	FAS80, ¶8	F80.108	
. . Criteria	FAS80, ¶4	F80.104	Q&A.80 #3-7
	FAS80, ¶62		
. . Cross-Hedging with Financial Futures			EITF.85-6
			Q&A.80 #14
. . Designation as a Hedge			EITF.85-6
			Q&A.80 #8-11
. . Existing Assets, Liabilities, and Firm Commitments	FAS80, ¶50	F80.106-108	
. . Financial Institutions	FAS80, ¶63	F80.104	
. . Financial Instruments Held to Maturity	FAS80, ¶4	F80.104	
. . Foreign Currency Exposure and a Tandem Currency			EITF.87-26
. . Initial Assessment of Probability of Correlation	FAS80, ¶4	F80.104	Q&A.80 #7
. . Items Reported at Fair Value	FAS80, ¶5	F80.105	
	FAS115, ¶129		
. . Measures of Correlation	FAS80, ¶4	F80.104	Q&A.80 #22-23
. . Of LIFO Inventories	FAS80, ¶8	F80.108	Q&A.80 #13
. . Ongoing Assessment of Correlation	FAS80, ¶11	F80.111	EITF.85-6
			Q&A.80 #20-21
			Q&A.80 #25
. . Probability of Occurrence of an Anticipated Transaction	FAS80, ¶9	F80.109	Q&A.80 #12
. . Reverse Repurchase Agreements			EITF.86-34
. . Subsequent to Termination			Q&A.80 #31-32
. . Termination of a Hedge			EITF.85-6
			Q&A.80 #27-30
Implementation Issues			EITF.85-6

FAS—FASB Statements	FIN—FASB Interpretations	FTB—FASB Technical Bulletins
APB—APB Opinions	AIN—AICPA Interpretations	ARB—Accounting Research Bulletins
CON—FASB Concepts	EITF—EITF Issues	Q&A—FASB Special Reports

T-165

	Original Pronouncements	Current Text	EITF and Other
FUTURES CONTRACTS—continued			
Interest Rate Swap Transactions			EITF.84-7
. . . .			EITF.84-36
. . . .			EITF.88-8
Mortgage Swaps			EITF.88-8
Recognition of Changes in Market Value . .	FAS80, ¶3	F80.103	
. . Daily Limits			Q&A.80 #2
Risk Assessment of Items to Be Hedged			
. . Ongoing Assessment	FAS80, ¶11	F80.111	Q&A.80 #24-25
. . Risk of the Business Unit	FAS80, ¶4	F80.104	Q&A.80 #4-5
. . Risk of the Enterprise	FAS80, ¶4	F80.104	Q&A.80 #3
. . Time Frame	FAS80, ¶4	F80.104	Q&A.80 #6
Scope of Accounting and Reporting			
Requirements	FAS80, ¶1-2	F80.101-102	
. . . .	FAS80, ¶35		
. . Comparison with Forward Contracts . .	FAS80, ¶1	F80.101	
. . . .	FAS80, ¶34		
. . Comparison with Futures Contracts			
for Foreign Currencies	FAS80, ¶1	F80.101	
. . Comparison with Options	FAS80, ¶32	F80.101	

(The next page is T-171.)

See "Terminology" for references to defined terms presented in various accounting pronouncements.
See the Introduction to the Topical Index for details on the use of this index.

	Original Pronouncements	Current Text	EITF and Other

GAIN CONTINGENCIES
See Contingencies
GAIN OR LOSS
See Contingencies
See Debt: Extinguishments
See Debt: Restructurings
See Extraordinary Items
See Foreign Currency Translation
See Gains
See Holding Gains (Losses)
See Income Statement Presentation:
   Discontinued Operations
See Income Taxes
See Inventory
See Investments: Debt and Equity
   Securities
See Investments: Equity Method
See Investments: Marketable Securities
See Leases
See Losses
See Nonmonetary Transactions
See Pension Costs
See Postretirement Benefits Other Than
   Pensions
See Quasi Reorganizations
See Recognition and Measurement in
   Financial Statements

	Original Pronouncements	Current Text	EITF and Other
Unusual or Infrequent Items	APB30, ¶26	I22.101	

GAINS
See Recognition and Measurement in
   Financial Statements

Characteristics	CON6, ¶84-89		
Component of Comprehensive Income	CON6, ¶73-77		
Definition	CON6, ¶82		
Elements of Financial Statements	CON6, ¶82-89		
Holding	CON6, ¶71		
Operating vs. Nonoperating			
. . Business Enterprises	CON6, ¶86		
. . Not-for-Profit Organizations	CON6, ¶87-89		
	CON6, ¶111-113		
Recognition Criteria			
. . Guidance in Application	CON5, ¶83-84		
Relation to Revenues	CON6, ¶87-89		
Unrealized	CON6, ¶143		

GENERAL AND ADMINISTRATIVE EXPENSES

Contractor Accounting	ARB45, ¶10	Co4.107	

FAS–FASB Statements   FIN–FASB Interpretations   FTB–FASB Technical Bulletins
APB–APB Opinions   AIN–AICPA Interpretations   ARB–Accounting Research Bulletins
CON–FASB Concepts   EITF–EITF Issues   Q&A–FASB Special Reports

T-171

See "Terminology" for references to defined terms presented in various accounting pronouncements.

See the Introduction to the Topical Index for details on the use of this index.

	Original Pronouncements	Current Text	EITF and Other
GOVERNMENT-OWNED ENTERPRISES			
See Earnings per Share			
Utilities	FAS71, ¶5	Re6.115	
GOVERNMENTAL UNIT			
See Leases			
Defined Benefit Pension Plans, Application of Accounting Requirements			
. . Effective Date		Pe5.102	
Fiscal Funding Clauses			
. . Leases	FTB79-10, ¶1-5	L10.501-505	
GRACE PERIOD			
Callable Obligations	FAS78, ¶5	B05.109A	
Classifying Obligations (Current vs. Noncurrent)			
. . Covenant Violation Waived by Creditor			EITF.86-30
GRANTOR TRUST			
Consolidation			EITF.84-15
. . Grantor Trusts Owned by a Subsidiary			EITF.84-40
GRANTS			
See Contributions			
GREENMAIL			
See Capital Stock: Capital Transactions			
GROSS PROFIT METHOD			
See Interim Financial Reporting			
GUARANTEED INVESTMENT CONTRACTS (GICs)			
Definition	FAS110, ¶2	Pe5.413B	
Employee Benefit Plans	FAS110, ¶2	Pe5.110	EITF.89-1
GUARANTEES AND WARRANTIES			
See Contingencies			
See Financial Instruments			
See Related Parties			
Business Combinations	APB16, ¶48	B50.107	
Fee Recognition			EITF.85-20
Guaranteed Future Value of Stock Issued by Acquirer in a Business Combination			EITF.87-31
Impact of an Uncollateralized Irrevocable Letter of Credit on a Sale-Leaseback Transaction Involving Real Estate			EITF.90-20
Recognition of Liability			EITF.85-20
Residual Value of Leased Asset	FTB79-14, ¶1-4	L10.514-517	
	FTB86-2, ¶11-12	L10.538-539	
Sponsor's Recognition of Employee Stock Ownership Plan Debt			EITF.89-10
Unsecured Guarantee by Parent of Subsidiary's Lease Payments			EITF.90-14

(The next page is T-179.)

	Original Pronouncements	Current Text	EITF and Other

HEALTH CARE PROVIDERS
See Not-for-Profit Organizations
See Segment of Business Reporting
HEDGES
See Financial Instruments
See Foreign Currency Translation
See Futures Contracts

	Original Pronouncements	Current Text	EITF and Other
Classification in Cash Flows Statement . . .	FAS104, ¶7	C25.112	
. . . .		F80.112A	
Consistent Reporting for Hedged Instrument and Hedging Instrument	FAS115, ¶115	I80.113	
Cross-Hedging with Financial Futures			EITF.85-6
Designation as a Hedge			EITF.85-6
Disclosures Required for Hedges of Anticipated Currency Transactions			EITF.91-4
Foreign Currency Options			EITF.D-16
Futures Contracts Implementation Issues . .			EITF.85-6
Hedging Currency Risks with Complex Options and Similar Transactions			EITF.91-4
Hedging Foreign Currency Risks of Future Net Income, Revenues, or Costs			EITF.D-16
Hedging Foreign Currency Risks with Purchased Options			EITF.90-17
Hedging Foreign Currency with Tandem Currency.			EITF.87-26
Hedging Intercompany Foreign Currency Risks.			EITF.91-1
Indexed Debt Instruments			EITF.86-28
Interest Costs through Forward Commitments			EITF.86-26
Interest Costs through a Deferred Rate Setting Arrangement			EITF.84-14
Interest Rate Swap Transactions			EITF.84-36
. . . .			EITF.88-8
. . Termination or Sale			EITF.84-7
Mortgage Swaps			EITF.88-8
Ongoing Assessment of Correlation			EITF.85-6
Termination of a Hedge . . . . , ...			EITF.85-6
Using Cash Securities			EITF.87-1

FAS—FASB Statements   FIN—FASB Interpretations   FTB—FASB Technical Bulletins
APB—APB Opinions   AIN—AICPA Interpretations   ARB—Accounting Research Bulletins
CON—FASB Concepts   EITF—EITF Issues   Q&A—FASB Special Reports

	Original Pronouncements	Current Text	EITF and Other
HIGHLY INFLATIONARY ECONOMIES			
See Foreign Currency Translation			
HISTORICAL COST (HISTORICAL PROCEEDS)			
Recognition and Measurement			
. . Measurement Attribute	CON5, ¶67-69		
HISTORICAL COST FINANCIAL STATEMENTS			
Conceptual Framework	CON1, ¶2		
HISTORICAL SUMMARIES OF FINANCIAL INFORMATION			
Accounting Changes	APB20, ¶39	A06.134	
HISTORICAL TREASURES			
Depreciation	FAS93, ¶6	D40.101A-101C	
. . . .	FAS93, ¶35-37		
HOLDING COMPANY			
See Consolidation			
HOLDING GAINS (LOSSES)			
See Changing Prices: Reporting Their Effects in Financial Reports			
Recognition and Measurement in Financial Statements			
. . Financial Capital Maintenance	CON5, ¶48		
HOLIDAY PAY			
See Compensation to Employees: Paid Absences			

(The next page is T-185.)

See "Terminology" for references to defined terms presented in various accounting pronouncements.

See the Introduction to the Topical Index for details on the use of this index.

See "Terminology" for references to defined terms presented in various accounting pronouncements.

See the Introduction to the Topical Index for details on the use of this index.

FAS–FASB Statements   FIN–FASB Interpretations   FTB–FASB Technical Bulletins
APB–APB Opinions   AIN–AICPA Interpretations   ARB–Accounting Research Bulletins
CON–FASB Concepts   EITF–EITF Issues   Q&A–FASB Special Reports

See "Terminology" for references to defined terms presented in various accounting pronouncements.

See the Introduction to the Topical Index for details on the use of this index.

FAS–FASB Statements FIN–FASB Interpretations FTB–FASB Technical Bulletins
APB–APB Opinions AIN–AICPA Interpretations ARB–Accounting Research Bulletins
CON–FASB Concepts EITF–EITF Issues Q&A–FASB Special Reports

	Original Pronouncements	Current Text	EITF and Other
INCOME TAXES—continued			
Business Combinations—continued			
. . Occurring in Years Not Restated for			
Effects of Statement 109	FAS109, ¶51		Q&A.109 #22-24
	FAS109, ¶53-56		
. . Purchase Price Allocations under IRC			
Section 338			EITF.86-3
. . Subsequent Realization of Unrecognized			
Tax Benefits	FAS109, ¶30	I27.129	EITF.85-3
	FAS109, ¶268	I27.195	
. . Subsequent Recognition of an Acquired			
Enterprise's Carryforward	FAS109, ¶30	I27.129	Q&A.109 #13
	FAS109, ¶268	I27.195	
. . Subsequent Recognition of an Acquiring			
Enterprise's Carryforward	FAS109, ¶30	I27.129	Q&A.109 #14
. . Taxable Combinations	FAS109, ¶261-263	I27.188-190	
	FAS109, ¶272	I27.199	
. . Tax Basis of Acquired Assets and			
Liabilities	FAS109, ¶30	I27.129	Q&A.109 #17
	FAS109, ¶36	I27.135	
	FAS109, ¶261	I27.188	
	FAS109, ¶272	I27.199	
	FAS109, ¶288		
. . Tax Deductible Goodwill	FAS109, ¶9	I27.108	
	FAS109, ¶30	I27.129	
	FAS109, ¶262-263	I27.189-190	
. . "Tax-to-Tax" Differences			EITF.D-31
. . Timing of Recognition of Tax Benefits for			
Pre-reorganization Temporary			
Differences and Carryforwards			EITF.D-33
. . Uncertainties Related to Income Taxes in			
a Purchase Business Combination			EITF.93-7
Carrybacks (Operating Losses and			
Tax Credits)	FAS109, ¶21	I27.120	
	FAS109, ¶37	I27.136	
	FAS109, ¶240	I27.167	
	FAS109, ¶245	I27.172	
	FAS109, ¶289	I27.401	
. . Change in Tax Rates	FAS109, ¶233-235	I27.160-162	
Carryforwards (Operating Losses and			
Tax Credits)	FAS109, ¶37	I27.136	
	FAS109, ¶240	I27.167	
	FAS109, ¶275	I27.202	
	FAS109, ¶289	I27.402	
. . Acquired in a Business Combination	FAS109, ¶30	I27.129	Q&A.109 #13
. . Assurance beyond Any Reasonable			
Doubt			EITF.85-15
. . Business Combinations	FAS109, ¶264-272	I27.191-199	
. . Business Combinations That Are Not			
Remeasured	FAS109, ¶51		Q&A.109 #23-24
	FAS109, ¶53-56		
. . Investment Tax Credit	FAS109, ¶288	I27.230	

See "Terminology" for references to defined terms presented in various accounting pronouncements.
See the Introduction to the Topical Index for details on the use of this index.

	Original Pronouncements	Current Text	EITF and Other
INCOME TAXES—continued			
Carryforwards (Operating Losses and Tax Credits)—continued			
. . Purchased in a Business Combination			EITF.84-33
			EITF.85-15
			EITF.86-1
. . Quasi Reorganizations	FAS109, ¶39	I27.138	
. . Recognition of Carryforwards as Offsets to Deferred Tax Credits			EITF.85-5
. . Recognition of Tax Benefits.	FAS109, ¶30	I27.129	Q&A.109 #13-14
	FAS109, ¶51	I27.168-171	Q&A.109 #18
	FAS109, ¶241-244	I27.199	
	FAS109, ¶272	I27.202	
	FAS109, ¶275		
. . Reporting of Tax Benefits	FAS109, ¶37	I27.136	
	FAS109, ¶45	I27.144	
	FAS109, ¶245	I27.172	
	FAS109, ¶275	I27.202	
. . Timing of Recognition of Tax Benefits for Pre-reorganization Temporary Differences and Carryforwards			EITF.D-33
Cash Surrender Value of Life Insurance	FAS109, ¶14	I27.113	
	FAS109, ¶251	I27.178	
Change in Tax Laws or Rates	FAS109, ¶27	I27.126	
	FAS109, ¶35	I27.134	
	FAS109, ¶234-235	I27.161-162	
. . Change in Tax Status That Results from Change in Tax Law	FAS109, ¶28	I27.127	Q&A.109 #11
. . Effect of a Retroactive Change in Enacted Tax Rates That Is Included in Income from Continuing Operations			EITF.93-13
. . Effects of the Tax Reform Act of 1986 . . .			EITF.86-11
. . Initial Catch-up Adjustment for a Change in Accounting Method for Tax Purposes			Q&A.109 #5-6
. . Phased-in Change in Tax Rates	FAS109, ¶18	I27.117	Q&A.109 #1
	FAS109, ¶233-234	I27.160-161	
. . Recognition of Effects of Changes Prior to Enactment			EITF.86-11
			EITF.D-7
			EITF.D-30
. . Tax Benefit of Excess Tax-Deductible Goodwill Resulting from a Retroactive Change in Tax Law			EITF.93-12
Change in Tax Status.	FAS109, ¶28	I27.127	Q&A.109 #11-12
	FAS109, ¶35	I27.134	Q&A.109 #28
	FAS109, ¶45	I27.144	
Comprehensive Income Excluded from Net Income.	FAS109, ¶36	I27.135	
	FAS109, ¶276	I27.203	
	FAS115, ¶133		
Consolidated Tax Return	FAS109, ¶40	I27.139	
	FAS109, ¶49	I27.148	

FAS–FASB Statements   FIN–FASB Interpretations   FTB–FASB Technical Bulletins
APB–APB Opinions   AIN–AICPA Interpretations   ARB–Accounting Research Bulletins
CON–FASB Concepts   EITF–EITF Issues   Q&A–FASB Special Reports

T-191

See "Terminology" for references to defined terms presented in various accounting pronouncements.

See the Introduction to the Topical Index for details on the use of this index.

	Original Pronouncements	Current Text	EITF and Other
INCOME TAXES—continued			
Deferred Taxes—continued			
. . Effect of a Retroactive Change in Enacted Tax Rates That Is Included in Income from Continuing Operations			EITF.93-13
. . Increases in Cash Surrender Value of Life Insurance.................................			EITF.87-28
. . Increases in Net Loan Value of Life Insurance.................................			EITF.88-5
. . Recognition of Deferred Tax Assets for a Parent Company's Excess Tax Basis in the Stock of a Subsidiary That Is Accounted for as a Discontinued Operation			EITF.93-17
. . Special Deductions.........................	FAS109, ¶231-232	I27.157-158	
. . Stock Life Insurance Enterprises..........			EITF.84-1
. . Subsidiary Stock Sales			EITF.84-27
. . Tax Benefit of Excess Tax-Deductible Goodwill Resulting from a Retroactive Change in Tax Law			EITF.93-12
Defined Benefit Pension Plans			
. . Tax Status	FAS35, ¶28	Pe5.127	
....	FAS35, ¶264		
Definition	FAS109, ¶289	I27.410	
Depreciable and Amortizable Assets	FAS109, ¶229	I27.155	Q&A.109 #2
Different Tax Jurisdictions	FAS109, ¶17	I27.116	Q&A.109 #1
....	FAS109, ¶19	I27.118	Q&A.109 #3
....	FAS109, ¶21	I27.120	
....	FAS109, ¶41-42	I27.140-141	
....	FAS109, ¶223	I27.149	
Disallowance of Deduction			
. . Core Deposit Intangibles of Banking or Thrift Institutions			EITF.85-33
. . Liability for			Q&A.109 #4
....			Q&A.109 #17
DISC (Domestic International Sales Corporation)			
. . Effects of the Tax Reform Act of 1984....			EITF.84-2
Discontinued Operations			
. . Recognition of Deferred Tax Assets for a Parent Company's Excess Tax Basis in the Stock of a Subsidiary That Is Accounted for as a Discontinued Operation			EITF.93-17
Equity Method Investments			
. . Excess of the Tax Basis over the Amount for Financial Reporting	FAS109, ¶34	I27.133	
....	FAS109, ¶288	I27.214	
. . Undistributed Earnings....................	APB18, ¶19	I27.130	
....	FAS109, ¶31	I82.109	
ESOP (Employee Stock Ownership Plan)	FAS109, ¶35-36	I27.134-135	
. . Benefit from Distribution of Dividends to Employees			EITF.86-4

FAS–FASB Statements	FIN–FASB Interpretations	FTB–FASB Technical Bulletins
APB–APB Opinions	AIN–AICPA Interpretations	ARB–Accounting Research Bulletins
CON–FASB Concepts	EITF–EITF Issues	Q&A–FASB Special Reports

See "Terminology" for references to defined terms presented in various accounting pronouncements.

See the Introduction to the Topical Index for details on the use of this index.

	Original Pronouncements	Current Text	EITF and Other
INCOME TAXES—continued			
Oil and Gas Producing Activities	FAS19, ¶60-62	Oi5.139-141	
....	FAS109, ¶231-232	I27.157-158	
Permanent Differences			
. . Different Tax and Accounting Carrying			
Bases......................................			EITF.84-43
. . Discounting Loss Reserves of Insurance			
Companies..............................			EITF.86-37
. . Subsidiary Stock Sales			EITF.84-27
Pooling-of-Interests	FAS109, ¶36	I27.135	
....	FAS109, ¶270-272	I27.197-199	
Quasi Reorganizations	FAS109, ¶36	I27.135	Q&A.109 #9-10
....	FAS109, ¶39	I27.138	
. . Tax Benefits.................................	FAS109, ¶36	I27.135	
....	FAS109, ¶39	I27.138	
Regulated Operations	FAS109, ¶29	I27.128	
....	FAS109, ¶252-255	I27.179-182	
....	FAS109, ¶288	Re6.128	
. . Abandonments of Assets	FTB87-2, ¶5	Re6.501-507	
....	FTB87-2, ¶14-20		
. . Comptroller of the Currency's Rule on			
Deferred Tax Debits.....................			EITF.85-31
Reorganization Carryforwards			EITF.D-33
Restoration of Deferred Tax Credits			
Previously Offset by NOL Carryforward ...			EITF.85-5
Sale or Purchase of Tax Benefits through			
Tax Leases	FAS109, ¶288	I27.501-506	
....	FTB82-1, ¶1-2		
....	FTB82-1, ¶4		
....	FTB82-1, ¶6-8		
. . Effect of Change in Tax Law..............			EITF.86-44
Savings and Loan Associations			
. . Accounting for Income Tax Benefits from			
Bad Debts of a Savings and Loan			
Association..............................			EITF.91-3
. . Comptroller of the Currency's Rule on			
Deferred Tax Debits.....................			EITF.85-31
. . Percentage-of-Taxable-Income Bad-Debt			
Deduction................................	FAS109, ¶231-232	I27.157-158	Q&A.109 #8
. . Tax Bad-Debt Reserves	APB23, ¶19-21	I27.220-224	
....	APB23, ¶23	I27.130-131	
....	APB23, ¶25	I27.133	
....	FAS109, ¶31-32	I27.143	
....	FAS109, ¶34		
....	FAS109, ¶44		
....	FAS109, ¶288		
. . Tax Implications of Conversion to Bank ..			EITF.86-31
Scheduling	FAS109, ¶236	I27.163	Q&A.109 #1
Scope of Accounting and Reporting	FAS109, ¶1	I27.101-104	
....	FAS109, ¶3-5		
S Corporations	FAS109, ¶28	I27.127	Q&A.109 #12
....			Q&A.109 #28

See "Terminology" for references to defined terms presented in various accounting pronouncements.
See the Introduction to the Topical Index for details on the use of this index.

	Original Pronouncements	Current Text	EITF and Other
INCOME TAXES—continued			
Separate Financial Statements of a Subsidiary	FAS109, ¶40	I27.139	
	FAS109, ¶49	I27.148	
Special Deductions	FAS109, ¶231-232	I27.157-158	
State and Local Income Taxes	FAS109, ¶4	I27.103	Q&A.109 #7
. . Calculation of Deferred Taxes	FAS109, ¶17	I27.116	Q&A.109 #3
. . State Tax Based on the Greater of a Franchise Tax or an Income Tax			EITF.91-8
Statutory Depletion	FAS109, ¶231	I27.157	
Steamship Companies (U.S.)	FAS109, ¶9	I27.108	
	FAS109, ¶32	I27.131	
	FAS109, ¶44	I27.143	
Stock Life Insurance Enterprises			
. . Deferred Taxes	FAS109, ¶288	I27.225	
		In6.161	
. . Effects of the Tax Reform Act of 1984			EITF.84-1
. . Policyholders' Surplus	FAS60, ¶59	I27.226	
	FAS109, ¶8	I27.107	
	FAS109, ¶31	I27.130	
	FAS109, ¶44	I27.143	
	FAS109, ¶288		
Tax Benefits			
. . Investments in Qualified Affordable Housing Projects			EITF.94-1
Tax Holidays	FAS109, ¶183-184	I27.127	
Tax Indemnifications Related to a Change in Tax Law			
. . Leases			EITF.86-33
Tax Leases Used to Transfer Tax Benefits	FAS109, ¶288	I27.501-506	
	FTB82-1, ¶1-2		
	FTB82-1, ¶4		
	FTB82-1, ¶6-8		
. . Effect of Change in Tax Law			EITF.86-44
. . Income Recognition for Cross Border Tax Benefit Leases			EITF.89-20
Tax-Planning Strategies	FAS109, ¶21-22	I27.120-121	
	FAS109, ¶246-251	I27.173-178	
	FAS109, ¶289	I27.418	
. . Criteria	FAS109, ¶22	I27.121	
	FAS109, ¶246	I27.173	
	FAS109, ¶251	I27.178	
. . Deferred Tax Liabilities	FAS109, ¶251	I27.178	
. . Effects of Qualifying Strategies	FAS109, ¶246-248	I27.173-175	
	FAS109, ¶250	I27.177	
. . Elections for Tax Purposes	FAS109, ¶22	I27.121	Q&A.109 #25
	FAS109, ¶246	I27.173	
. . Expense or Loss Associated with Implementing a Strategy	FAS109, ¶22	I27.121	
	FAS109, ¶249-250	I27.176-177	
. . Management Intent to Implement a Strategy	FAS109, ¶246	I27.173	
. . Recognition of Qualifying Strategies Not Elective	FAS109, ¶22	I27.121	Q&A.109 #26

FAS–FASB Statements	FIN–FASB Interpretations	FTB–FASB Technical Bulletins
APB–APB Opinions	AIN–AICPA Interpretations	ARB–Accounting Research Bulletins
CON–FASB Concepts	EITF–EITF Issues	Q&A–FASB Special Reports

	Original Pronouncements	Current Text	EITF and Other
INCOME TAXES—continued			
Tax-Planning Strategies—continued			
. . S Corporation Status, Not a Strategy	FAS109, ¶28	I27.127	Q&A.109 #28
. . Search for Qualifying Strategies			Q&A.109 #27
. . Valuation Allowance	FAS109, ¶21-22	I27.120-121	Q&A.109 #26
	FAS109, ¶250-251	I27.177-178	
"Tax-to-Tax" Differences			EITF.D-31
Temporary Differences........................	FAS109, ¶10-15	I27.109-114	
	FAS109, ¶289	I27.419	
. . Allocated Negative Goodwill	FAS109, ¶30	I27.129	Q&A.109 #15
	FAS109, ¶259	I27.186	
. . Application of Statement 109 in Foreign Financial Statements Restated for General Price-Level Changes			EITF.93-9
. . Application of Statement 109 to Inside Basis Differences of Foreign Subsidiaries			EITF.93-16
. . Asset Revaluation in Foreign Countries...			EITF.84-43
. . Cash Surrender Value of Life Insurance...	FAS109, ¶14	I27.113	
	FAS109, ¶251	I27.178	
. . Comprehensive Income Reported Directly in Stockholders' Equity	FAS109, ¶35-36	I27.134-135	
	FAS109, ¶276	I27.203	
	FAS115, ¶133		
. . Deductible Temporary Differences	FAS109, ¶13	I27.112	
	FAS109, ¶17	I27.116	
	FAS109, ¶224-225	I27.150-151	
	FAS109, ¶248	I27.175	
	FAS109, ¶289	I27.404	
. . Deferred State Income Tax Asset or Liability.................................	FAS109, ¶17	I27.116	Q&A.109 #3
			Q&A.109 #7
. . Deferred Taxable Income	FAS109, ¶15	I27.114	Q&A.109 #5-6
. . Depreciable and Amortizable Assets	FAS109, ¶229	I27.155	Q&A.109 #2
. . Disallowance of Tax Deductions			Q&A.109 #4
			Q&A.109 #17
. . Foreign Tax Assets and Liabilities	FAS109, ¶230	I27.156	
. . Foreign Currency Translation	FAS52, ¶22-24	F60.132-134	
. . Future Originating and Reversing Temporary Differences..................	FAS109, ¶21	I27.120	Q&A.109 #1-2
	FAS109, ¶229	I27.155	
	FAS109, ¶236	I27.163	
	FAS109, ¶244	I27.171	
	FAS109, ¶248	I27.175	
. . Goodwill	FAS109, ¶9	I27.108	
	FAS109, ¶30	I27.129	
	FAS109, ¶259	I27.186	
	FAS109, ¶261-263	I27.188-190	
. . Increase in Cash Surrender Value of Life Insurance................................			EITF.87-28
			EITF.88-5
. . Intangible Assets	FAS109, ¶30	I27.129	Q&A.109 #16
. . Inventory Costs			EITF.86-46

See "Terminology" for references to defined terms presented in various accounting pronouncements.
See the Introduction to the Topical Index for details on the use of this index.

	Original Pronouncements	Current Text	EITF and Other
INCOME TAXES—continued			
Temporary Differences—continued			
. . Inventory or Other Assets Transferred			
between Affiliated Companies	FAS109, ¶9	I27.108	
. . Involuntary Conversions	FIN30, ¶5	N35.119	
. . Leases			Q&A.109 #1
. . LIFO Inventory Differences	FAS109, ¶228	I27.154	EITF.D-31
. . Marketable Securities	FAS109, ¶36	I27.135	
. . . .	FAS115, ¶133		
. . Net-of-Tax Assets and Liabilities			
Acquired in a Business Combination . . .	FAS109, ¶54-56		Q&A.109 #22
. . Nonmonetary Transactions	APB29, ¶27	N35.113	
. . Obsolete Inventory Reserves	FAS109, ¶248	I27.175	
. . Offset of Taxable Deductible Amounts . . .	FAS109, ¶227	I27.153	
. . Regulated Operations	FAS109, ¶29	Re6.128	
. . . .	FAS109, ¶252-255	I27.179-182	
. . . .	FAS109, ¶288		
. . Reorganization Carryforwards			EITF.D-33
. . Subsidiary Company, Book Basis			
Exceeds Tax Basis of Parent's			
Investment	FAS109, ¶31-33	I27.130-132	
. . . .	FAS109, ¶251	I27.178	
. . Subsidiary Stock Sales			EITF.84-27
. . Taxable Temporary Difference	FAS109, ¶13	I27.112	
. . . .	FAS109, ¶17	I27.116	
. . . .	FAS109, ¶289	I27.416	
. . Tax Bad-Debt Reserves of a Savings and			
Loan Association	APB23, ¶19-21	I27.130-131	Q&A.109 #8
. . . .	APB23, ¶23	I27.133	Q&A.109 #12
. . . .	APB23, ¶25	I27.143	
. . . .	FAS109, ¶31-32	I27.220-224	
. . . .	FAS109, ¶34		
. . . .	FAS109, ¶44		
. . . .	FAS109, ¶288		
. . Tax Benefit of Excess Tax-Deductible			
Goodwill Resulting from a Retroactive			
Change in Tax Law			EITF.93-12
Temporary IRS Regulations			
. . Recognizing Effect in Financial			
Statements			EITF.86-3
Transition	FAS109, ¶50-59		Q&A.109 #20-23
Undistributed Earnings of a Subsidiary			
. . Change in Income Tax Rate			EITF.D-7
. . Change in Investment	APB23, ¶13	I27.216	
. . . .	FAS109, ¶33	I27.132	
. . . .	FAS109, ¶288		
. . Indefinite Reversal Criterion	APB23, ¶12	I27.215	
. . . .	FAS109, ¶31	I27.130	
. . Temporary Differences	APB23, ¶9	I27.212-213	
. . . .	FAS109, ¶31-34	I27.130-133	
. . . .	FAS109, ¶251	I27.178	
. . . .	FAS109, ¶287-288		
Uniform Cost Capitalization Rules			Q&A.109 #5

FAS–FASB Statements   FIN–FASB Interpretations   FTB–FASB Technical Bulletins
APB–APB Opinions   AIN–AICPA Interpretations   ARB–Accounting Research Bulletins
CON–FASB Concepts   EITF–EITF Issues   Q&A–FASB Special Reports

T-199

See "Terminology" for references to defined terms presented in various accounting pronouncements.

See the Introduction to the Topical Index for details on the use of this index.

I

Topical Index

See "Terminology" for references to defined terms presented in various accounting pronouncements.

See the Introduction to the Topical Index for details on the use of this index.

	Original Pronouncements	Current Text	EITF and Other
INSURANCE INDUSTRY—continued			
Investment Contracts.........................	FAS97, ¶7	In6.107A	
....	FAS97, ¶15	In6.107C	
....	FAS113, ¶12	In6.176	
Investments	FAS60, ¶12	In6.112	
....	FAS60, ¶47-48	In6.151-157	
....	FAS60, ¶50-51		
....	FAS97, ¶26		
....	FAS97, ¶28		
....	FAS115, ¶127		
....	FAS115, ¶131		
Investments in Debt and Equity Securities....	FAS115, ¶4	I80.102	
Life Insurance Contracts	FAS60, ¶4	In6.104	
....	FAS60, ¶8	In6.108	
Life Insurance Enterprises			
. . Deferred Income Taxes...................	FAS109, ¶288	In6.161	
. . Deferred Recognition of Realized Gains and Losses			EITF.87-1
. . Policyholders' Surplus	FAS60, ¶59	In6.165	
Life-Contingent Payments	FAS97, ¶8	In6.107B	
Limited Payment Contracts	FAS97, ¶9	In6.108A	
. . Liability for Policy Benefits...............	FAS97, ¶16	In6.132A	
Long-Duration Contract Accounting			
. . Acquisition Costs	FAS60, ¶11	In6.111	
....	FAS60, ¶28-29	In6.134-135	
....	FAS60, ¶31	In6.137	
. . Characteristics	FAS60, ¶4-5	In6.104-105	
....	FAS60, ¶7	In6.107	
. . Examples of Contracts	FAS60, ¶8	In6.108	
. . Liability for Claim Adjustment Expenses .	FAS60, ¶10	In6.110	
....	FAS60, ¶20	In6.120	
. . Liability for Future Policy Benefits	FAS60, ¶10	In6.110	
....	FAS60, ¶21-26	In6.127-132C	
....	FAS97, ¶16-18		
. . Liability for Unpaid Claims...............	FAS60, ¶10	In6.110	
....	FAS60, ¶17-18	In6.117-118	
. . Premium Deficiency	FAS60, ¶32	In6.138	
....	FAS60, ¶35-37	In6.141-143	
. . Premium Revenue Recognition	FAS60, ¶4-5	In6.104-105	
....	FAS60, ¶10	In6.110	
....	FAS60, ¶16	In6.115-116	
....	FAS97, ¶30		
. . Premium Revenue Recognition, Description.............................	FAS60, ¶2	In6.102	
. . Reinsurance	FAS113, ¶12-16	In6.176-180	
....	FAS113, ¶19-20	In6.183-184	
....	FAS113, ¶26	In6.190	
....	FAS113, ¶73		
....	FAS113, ¶76		
....	FAS113, ¶111		
Marketable Securities.........................	FAS12, ¶14	I89.108	

FAS–FASB Statements   FIN–FASB Interpretations   FTB–FASB Technical Bulletins
APB–APB Opinions   AIN–AICPA Interpretations   ARB–Accounting Research Bulletins
CON–FASB Concepts   EITF–EITF Issues   Q&A–FASB Special Reports

Note: The Q&A 113 text is reproduced in *EITF Abstracts* as Topic No. D-34.

See "Terminology" for references to defined terms presented in various accounting pronouncements.

See the Introduction to the Topical Index for details on the use of this index.

Note: The Q&A 113 text is reproduced in *EITF Abstracts* as Topic No. D-34.

FAS–FASB Statements   FIN–FASB Interpretations   FTB–FASB Technical Bulletins
APB–APB Opinions   AIN–AICPA Interpretations   ARB–Accounting Research Bulletins
CON–FASB Concepts   EITF–EITF Issues   Q&A–FASB Special Reports

Note: The Q&A 113 text is reproduced in *EITF Abstracts* as Topic No. D-34.

See "Terminology" for references to defined terms presented in various accounting pronouncements.

See the Introduction to the Topical Index for details on the use of this index.

Note: The Q&A 113 text is reproduced in *EITF Abstracts* as Topic No. D-34.

FAS–FASB Statements	FIN–FASB Interpretations	FTB–FASB Technical Bulletins
APB–APB Opinions	AIN–AICPA Interpretations	ARB–Accounting Research Bulletins
CON–FASB Concepts	EITF–EITF Issues	Q&A–FASB Special Reports

See "Terminology" for references to defined terms presented in various accounting pronouncements.

See the Introduction to the Topical Index for details on the use of this index.

	Original Pronouncements	Current Text	EITF and Other
INTANGIBLE ASSETS—continued			
Goodwill—continued			
. . Change in Amortization Method for Business Combinations Initiated Prior to the Effective Date of Statement 72 ...			EITF.89-19
. . Deferred Taxes	FAS109, ¶30	I27.129	
. . Recognition of Purchased NOL Carryforwards			EITF.85-15
. . Reduction for Realized Operating Loss Carryforward			EITF.86-1
Motor Carriers			
. . Allocation among Types	FAS44, ¶3-4	I60.125-126	
. . Intangible Assets Other Than Interstate Operating Rights	FAS44, ¶7	I60.129	
. . Interstate Operating Rights	FAS44, ¶5-6	I60.127-128	
. . Motor Carrier Act of 1980	FAS44, ¶1	I60.124	
. . Write-off as Extraordinary Item	FAS44, ¶6	I60.128	
Patents	APB17, ¶1	I60.101	
Regulated Operations	FAS71, ¶29-30	Re6.134-135	
Step Acquisition	AIN-APB17, #2	I60.503-505	
Trademarks	APB17, ¶1	I60.101	
Types	APB17, ¶1	I60.101	
INTANGIBLE DRILLING AND DEVELOPMENT COSTS			
See Oil and Gas Producing Activities			
INTERCOMPANY BALANCES AND TRANSACTIONS			
See Consolidation			
See Foreign Operations			
See Segment of Business Reporting			
Business Combinations	APB16, ¶56	B50.115	
. . Downstream Mergers	AIN-APB16, #26	B50.593-596	EITF.85-4
	FTB85-5, ¶13-14	B50.596E-596F	
. . Stock Transactions between Companies under Common Control	AIN-APB16, #26	B50.596A-596D	
	AIN-APB16, #39	B50.645-648	
	FTB85-5, ¶5-7		
	FTB85-5, ¶12		
Definition			
. . Intercompany Profit/Regulated Operations	FAS71, ¶16	Re6.126	
Dividends-in-Kind	APB29, ¶4	C11.101	
Equity Method Investments	AIN-APB18, #1	I82.109	
	APB18, ¶19	I82.501-507	
Foreign Currency Translation	FAS52, ¶20	F60.127	
	FAS52, ¶25	F60.135	
Hedging Intercompany Foreign Currency Risks			EITF.91-1
Interest: Capitalization of Interest Costs	FAS58, ¶6	I67.106	
Regulated Operations	FAS71, ¶16-17	Re6.126-127	
. . Consolidation	ARB51, ¶6	C51.109	

FAS–FASB Statements	FIN–FASB Interpretations	FTB–FASB Technical Bulletins
APB–APB Opinions	AIN–AICPA Interpretations	ARB–Accounting Research Bulletins
CON–FASB Concepts	EITF–EITF Issues	Q&A–FASB Special Reports

T-209

See "Terminology" for references to defined terms presented in various accounting pronouncements.

See the Introduction to the Topical Index for details on the use of this index.

	Original Pronouncements	Current Text	EITF and Other
INTEREST EXPENSE			
Accounting for Dual Currency Bonds			EITF.93-10
Accrued Interest Expense upon Conversion of Convertible Debt..........................			EITF.85-17
Allocation to Assets Held for Sale after Business Combination			EITF.87-11
. . Sale Not Completed within Holding Period...................................			EITF.90-6
Allocation to Discontinued Operations			EITF.87-24
Contingent Interest Expense Recognition			
. . Equity Certificates of Deposit.............			EITF.84-31
Deferred Interest Rate Setting.................			EITF.84-14
. . Forward Commitments as a Surrogate for Deferred Rate Setting			EITF.86-15
Increasing-Rate Debt.........................			EITF.86-15
Indexed Debt................................			EITF.86-28
Interest Rate Swap Transactions			EITF.84-36
....			EITF.88-8
. . Termination of Sale			EITF.84-7
Mortgage Swaps			EITF.88-8
Participating Mortgages......................			EITF.86-28
INTEREST: IMPUTATION OF AN INTEREST COST			
Amortization of Discount and Premium			
. . Interest Method	APB21, ¶15	I69.108	
Contributions Receivable and Payable	FAS116, ¶20	C67.116	
Determining an Appropriate Rate			
. . Considerations	APB21, ¶14	I69.107	
. . Objectives................................	APB21, ¶13	I69.106	
Disclosure...................................	APB21, ¶16	I69.109	
Eligibility for Interest Capitalization..........	FAS34, ¶2	I69.110	
Examples of Determining Present Value	APB21, ¶18-20	I69.111-115	
Notes Exchanged for Cash or for Cash and Rights or Privileges	APB21, ¶7	I69.104	
....	APB21, ¶11		
Notes Exchanged for Property, Goods, or Services....................................	APB21, ¶12	I69.105	
Pipeline Enterprises			
. . Advances to Encourage Exploration	AIN-APB21, #1	I69.501-502	
Scope of Accounting and Reporting Requirements	APB21, ¶2-4	I69.101-103	
Statement Presentation of Discount and Premium	APB21, ¶16	I69.109	
INTEREST INCOME			
Graduated Payment Mortgages			EITF.85-38
Interest Rate Swap Transactions			EITF.84-36
. . Termination or Sale			EITF.84-7
Negative Amortizing Loan....................			EITF.85-38
Required Use of the Interest Method			EITF.D-10
Sale of Loan with a Share of Interest Retained...................................			EITF.84-21
Shared Appreciation Mortgages..............			EITF.86-21

FAS – FASB Statements	FIN – FASB Interpretations	FTB – FASB Technical Bulletins
APB – APB Opinions	AIN – AICPA Interpretations	ARB – Accounting Research Bulletins
CON – FASB Concepts	EITF – EITF Issues	Q&A – FASB Special Reports

See "Terminology" for references to defined terms presented in various accounting pronouncements.

See the Introduction to the Topical Index for details on the use of this index.

	Original Pronouncements	Current Text	EITF and Other

FAS–FASB Statements   FIN–FASB Interpretations   FTB–FASB Technical Bulletins
APB–APB Opinions   AIN–AICPA Interpretations   ARB–Accounting Research Bulletins
CON–FASB Concepts   EITF–EITF Issues   Q&A–FASB Special Reports

T-213

See "Terminology" for references to defined terms presented in various accounting pronouncements.

See the Introduction to the Topical Index for details on the use of this index.

FAS–FASB Statements	FIN–FASB Interpretations	FTB–FASB Technical Bulletins
APB–APB Opinions	AIN–AICPA Interpretations	ARB–Accounting Research Bulletins
CON–FASB Concepts	EITF–EITF Issues	Q&A–FASB Special Reports

T-215

	Original Pronouncements	Current Text	EITF and Other
INVENTORY—continued			
Lower of Cost or Market	ARB43, Ch.4, ¶9	I78.110	
	ARB43, Ch.4, ¶11-13	I78.113-116	
. . Damage, Obsolescence, or Deterioration	ARB43, Ch.4, ¶8	I78.109	
. . Foreign Currency Translation	FAS52, ¶49-53	F60.148-152	
. . Net Realizable Value	ARB43, Ch.4, ¶9	I78.110	
. . Price Declines during Interim Reporting			
Periods			EITF.86-13
. . Replacement Cost	ARB43, Ch.4, ¶9	I78.111	
. . Retail Inventory Method	ARB43, Ch.4, ¶10	I78.112	
. . Seasonal Price Fluctuations during			
Interim Reporting Periods			EITF.86-13
. . Unusual Losses	ARB43, Ch.4, ¶14	I78.117	
Measurement Attributes Used			
. . Historical Cost, Current Cost, Net			
Realizable Value	CON5, ¶67		
Motion Picture Industry	FAS53, ¶16	Mo6.115	
Overhead	ARB43, Ch.4, ¶5	I78.106	
Precious Metals	ARB43, Ch.4, ¶16	I78.119	
Purchase Commitments			
. . Losses	ARB43, Ch.4, ¶17	I78.121-122	
Scope of Accounting and Reporting			
Requirements	ARB43, Ch.4, ¶2	I78.101	
Spoilage	ARB43, Ch.4, ¶5	I78.106	
Standard Costs	ARB43, Ch.4, ¶6	I78.108	
Valuation Methods			
. . Average	ARB43, Ch.4, ¶6	I78.107-108	
. . First-In, First-Out (FIFO)	ARB43, Ch.4, ¶6	I78.107-108	
. . Last-In, First-Out (LIFO)	ARB43, Ch.4, ¶6	I78.107-108	
. . Retail Inventory	ARB43, Ch.4, ¶6	I78.108	
	ARB43, Ch.4, ¶10	I78.112	
INVESTMENT ENTERPRISES			
See Financial Instruments Equity Method			
. . Investment Company Act of 1940	APB18, ¶2	I82.101	
Exemption from the Requirement to Provide			
a Statement of Cash Flows	FAS102, ¶6-7	C25.135B-135C	
		In8.103	
Investments in Debt and Equity Securities	FAS115, ¶4	I80.102	
Marketable Securities	FAS12, ¶14	I89.108	
Specialized Accounting and Reporting			
. . Retention in Consolidation			EITF.85-12
INVESTMENT TAX CREDITS			
See Income Taxes			
Deferred, Qualification as a Liability	CON6, ¶243-245		
INVESTMENTS			
See Balance Sheet Classification: Current			
Assets and Liabilities			
See Financial Instruments			
See Investments: Debt and Equity Securities			
See Investments: Equity Method			
See Investments: Marketable Securities			
Classification of Interest-Only Securities as			
Held-to-Maturity			EITF.94-4

See "Terminology" for references to defined terms presented in various accounting pronouncements.

See the Introduction to the Topical Index for details on the use of this index.

	Original Pronouncements	Current Text	EITF and Other
INVESTMENTS—continued			
Divestiture of Certain Securities to an Unregulated Commonly Controlled Entity under FIRREA			EITF.89-18
Exchanges of Ownership Interests between Entities under Common Control			EITF.90-5
Investments in Qualified Affordable Housing Projects			
. . Accounting for Tax Benefits			EITF.94-1
Nonmonetary Exchange of Cost-Method Investments			EITF.91-5
Purchase of Collateralized Mortgage Obligation Instruments or Mortgage-Backed Interest-Only Certificates			EITF.89-4
. . Impairment Recognition			EITF.93-18
Reclassification of Securities in Anticipation of Adoption of Statement 115 by SEC Registrants			EITF.D-38
Reverse Repurchase Agreements			
. . GNMA Dollar Rolls			EITF.84-20
Securities Acquired for Cash in a Pooling of Interests			EITF.85-14
INVESTMENTS BY OWNERS			
See Capital Stock: Capital Transactions			
See Capital Stock: Dividends-in-Kind			
See Capital Stock: Preferred Stock			
See Capital Stock: Treasury Stock			
Characteristics	CON6, ¶68		
Definition	CON6, ¶66		
Element of Financial Statements	CON5, ¶13		
	CON6, ¶66-69		
Partnerships			
. . Withdrawals			EITF.85-46
Statement of	CON5, ¶55-57		
INVESTMENTS: DEBT AND EQUITY SECURITIES			
Accounting for	FAS115, ¶6-18	I80.103-117	
	FAS115, ¶110-111		
	FAS115, ¶113		
	FAS115, ¶117		
Accounting for Debt Securities Reported as Loans			EITF.D-39
Adjustments for Holding Gains and Losses as Related to the Implementation of Statement 115			EITF.D-41
Available-for-Sale Securities	FAS115, ¶12-16	I80.109-111	
		I80.114-115	
Amortized Cost	FAS115, ¶7	I80.104	
Asset-Liability Management	FAS115, ¶10	I80.107	
Brady Bonds			EITF.D-39
Cash Flows Statement	FAS115, ¶18	I80.117	
Classification of	FAS115, ¶6	I80.103	
. . Change in Classification	FAS115, ¶15	I80.114	
	FAS115, ¶22	I80.121	

FAS–FASB Statements	FIN–FASB Interpretations	FTB–FASB Technical Bulletins
APB–APB Opinions	AIN–AICPA Interpretations	ARB–Accounting Research Bulletins
CON–FASB Concepts	EITF–EITF Issues	Q&A–FASB Special Reports

	Original Pronouncements	Current Text	EITF and Other
INVESTMENTS: DEBT AND EQUITY SECURITIES—continued			
Classification of Interest-Only Securities as Held-to-Maturity.............................			EITF.94-4
Consolidation			
. . Investee's Unrealized Losses on Marketable Securities..................	FAS115, ¶135	I80.501-502	
....	FTB79-19, ¶1		
Current/Noncurrent, Classified Balance Sheet.....	FAS115, ¶17	I80.116	
Determining Fair Value	FAS115, ¶110-111	I80.112	
Dividend Income.............................	FAS115, ¶14	I80.111	
Fair Value			
. . Decline in	FAS115, ¶16	I80.115	
....	FAS115, ¶113		
. . Readily Determinable.....................	FAS115, ¶3	I80.101	
. . Reporting Changes in	FAS115, ¶13-14	I80.110-111	
Financial Statement Presentation..............	FAS115, ¶17-18	I80.116-117	
....	FAS115, ¶117		
Glossary......................................	FAS115, ¶3	I80.401-406	
....	FAS115, ¶137		
Held-to-Maturity Securities..................	FAS115, ¶7-11	I80.104-108	
....	FAS115, ¶14-16	I80.111	
....	FAS115, ¶59	I80.114-115	
....	FAS115, ¶71-72		
....	FAS115, ¶74		
....	FAS115, ¶76		
. . Maturities	FAS115, ¶11	I80.108	
....	FAS115, ¶66		
. . Sale or Transfer of	FAS115, ¶8-9	I80.105-106	
....	FAS115, ¶15	I80.114	
....	FAS115, ¶22	I80.121	
....	FAS115, ¶59		
....	FAS115, ¶71-72		
....	FAS115, ¶74		
....	FAS115, ¶76		
Hedging of Investments at Fair Value	FAS115, ¶115	I80.113	
Impairment of Securities......................	FAS115, ¶16	I80.115	
....	FAS115, ¶113		
. . Other Than Temporary	FAS115, ¶16	I80.115	
Income Taxes			
. . Unrealized Gains (Losses)	FAS115, ¶13	I80.110	
Interest Income...............................	FAS115, ¶14	I80.111	
Mortgage-Backed Securities	FAS115, ¶12	I80.109	
Mortgage Derivative Product			
. . Effect of Potential Designation as a High-Risk Security......................			EITF.D-39
Realized Gains and Losses....................	FAS115, ¶14	I80.111	
. . Inclusion in Determination of Earnings ...	FAS115, ¶14	I80.111	
Reclassification of Securities in Anticipation of Adoption of Statement 115 by SEC Registrants			EITF.D-38
Restricted Stock..............................	FAS115, ¶3	I80.101	

See "Terminology" for references to defined terms presented in various accounting pronouncements.

See the Introduction to the Topical Index for details on the use of this index.

	Original Pronouncements	Current Text	EITF and Other

INVESTMENTS: DEBT AND EQUITY SECURITIES—continued

Scope of Accounting and Reporting
Requirements .... ARB43, Intro., ¶5 — I80.101-102

.... FAS91, ¶3 — I80.503-504

.... FAS115, ¶1

.... FAS115, ¶3-4

.... FAS115, ¶115

.... FTB94-1, ¶1

.... FTB94-1, ¶3

Shareholder's Equity

.. Separate Component of .... FAS115, ¶13 — I80.110

.... FAS115, ¶15-16 — I80.114-115

Trading Securities......................... FAS115, ¶12-15 — I80.109-111

.... FAS115, ¶115 — I80.113-114

Transfers between Categories of Investments. FAS115, ¶8 — I80.105

.... FAS115, ¶15 — I80.114

.... FAS115, ¶71-72

.... FAS115, ¶74

.... FAS115, ¶76

Troubled Debt Restructuring.................. FTB94-1, ¶1 — I80.503-405

.... FTB94-1, ¶3

Unrealized Holding Gains and Losses .... FAS115, ¶13 — I80.110

.... FAS115, ¶15 — I80.114

INVESTMENTS: EQUITY METHOD

See Disclosure

See Oil and Gas Producing Activities

Application to

.. Accounting Changes .... APB18, ¶19 — I82.109

.. Capital Transactions by Investee .... APB18, ¶19 — I82.109

.. Difference between Cost and Underlying
Equity.................................. APB18, ¶19 — I82.109

.. Difference in Year-End from Investor .... APB18, ¶19 — I82.109

.. Extraordinary Items .... APB18, ¶19 — I82.109

.. Income Taxes on Undistributed Earnings . APB18, ¶19 — I82.109

.. Intercompany Transactions and Balances . AIN-APB18, #1 — I82.109

.... APB18, ¶19 — I82.501-507

.... FAS94, ¶15

.. Investees Subject to Repurchase Option .. — — EITF.84-33

.. Losses, Earnings of Investee .... APB18, ¶19 — I82.109

.. Partnerships and Unincorporated (Joint)
Ventures................................ AIN-APB18, #2 — I82.508-512

.. Preferred Stock of Investee................ APB18, ¶19 — I82.109

.. Prior Period Adjustments.................. APB18, ¶19 — I82.109

.. Sale of Investment .... APB18, ¶19 — I82.109

.. Subsidiaries under Temporary Control ... — — EITF.84-33

.. Temporary Decline in Value................ APB18, ¶19 — I82.109

.. Unconsolidated Subsidiaries .... — C51.118

.. Unrealized Losses on Marketable
Securities Owned by Investee........... FAS115, ¶135 — I82.513-514

.... FTB79-19, ¶1

.... FTB79-19, ¶6

Capitalization of Interest...................... FAS34, ¶9 — I67.105

FAS–FASB Statements   FIN–FASB Interpretations   FTB–FASB Technical Bulletins
APB–APB Opinions   AIN–AICPA Interpretations   ARB–Accounting Research Bulletins
CON–FASB Concepts   EITF–EITF Issues   Q&A–FASB Special Reports

See "Terminology" for references to defined terms presented in various accounting pronouncements.

See the Introduction to the Topical Index for details on the use of this index.

FAS–FASB Statements	FIN–FASB Interpretations	FTB–FASB Technical Bulletins
APB–APB Opinions	AIN–AICPA Interpretations	ARB–Accounting Research Bulletins
CON–FASB Concepts	EITF–EITF Issues	Q&A–FASB Special Reports

Topical Index

	Original Pronouncements	Current Text	EITF and Other
INVESTORS			
Information Needs	CON1, ¶41		
Interest in Financial Reporting	CON1, ¶32-39		
INVOLUNTARY CONVERSION			
See Nonmonetary Transactions			
IRREGULARITIES			
See Adjustments of Financial Statements for Prior Periods			

(The next page is T-245.)

See "Terminology" for references to defined terms presented in various accounting pronouncements.

See the Introduction to the Topical Index for details on the use of this index.

	Original Pronouncements	Current Text	EITF and Other
JOINT VENTURES			
See Income Taxes			
See Investments: Equity Method			
JUNIOR STOCK OPTION, PURCHASE AND AWARD PLANS			
See Compensation to Employees: Stock Purchase and Stock Option Plans			
KEY-PERSON LIFE INSURANCE			
See Life Insurance			
Provision for Deferred Taxes on Increases in Cash Surrender Value			EITF.87-28

(The next page is T-247.)

FAS—FASB Statements	FIN—FASB Interpretations	FTB—FASB Technical Bulletins
APB—APB Opinions	AIN—AICPA Interpretations	ARB—Accounting Research Bulletins
CON—FASB Concepts	EITF—EITF Issues	Q&A—FASB Special Reports

	Original Pronouncements	Current Text	EITF and Other
LAND			
Balance Sheet Classification	ARB43, Ch.3A, ¶7	B05.107	
Depreciation	FAS93, ¶6	D40.101A	
	FAS93, ¶34		
Interest: Capitalization of Interest Costs	FAS34, ¶10	I67.106	
Leases	FAS13, ¶25-26	L10.121-122	
LAND SALES (REAL ESTATE)			
See Real Estate			
See Real Estate: Retail Land Sales			
LEASE BROKERS			
See Leases			
Accreting Lease Residuals			EITF.85-32
LEASES			
See Disclosure			
See Income Taxes			
Accruing Bad-Debt Expense at Inception			EITF.D-8
Allocation of Residual Value or First-Loss Guarantee to Minimum Lease Payments in Leases Involving Land and Building(s)			EITF.92-1
Amortization and Depreciation			
. . Capital Leases	FAS13, ¶11-12	L10.107-108	
. . Operating Leases	FAS13, ¶19	L10.115	
Bargain Purchase Option			
. . Effect on Classification	FAS13, ¶7	L10.103	
. . Effect on Lease Term	FAS98, ¶22	L10.414	
. . Effect on Minimum Lease Payments	FAS13, ¶5	L10.417	
Bargain Renewal Option			
. . Effect on Lease Term	FAS98, ¶22	L10.414	
. . Effect on Minimum Lease Payments	FAS13, ¶5	L10.417	
Business Combinations			
. . Accounting When Lease Provisions Are Unchanged	FIN21, ¶12	L10.137	
. . Change in Lease Provisions	FIN21, ¶13	L10.138	
. . Leveraged Leases—Purchase Method	FIN21, ¶16	L10.141	
	FIN21, ¶19	L10.161	
. . Pooling-of-Interests Method	FIN21, ¶14	L10.139	
. . Purchase Method	FIN21, ¶15-16	L10.140-142	
Capital Leases			
. . Accounting for Lease Obligation	FAS13, ¶12	L10.108-109	
	FAS13, ¶14		
	FAS22, ¶14		
	FIN26, ¶5		
. . Amortization of Capitalized Asset	FAS13, ¶11-12	L10.107-108	
. . Calculation of Capitalized Amount	FAS13, ¶10	L10.106	
	FIN23, ¶8		
. . Change in Lease Provisions	FAS13, ¶9	L10.105	
	FAS13, ¶14	L10.109	
	FAS22, ¶14		

FAS–FASB Statements FIN–FASB Interpretations FTB–FASB Technical Bulletins
APB–APB Opinions AIN–AICPA Interpretations ARB–Accounting Research Bulletins
CON–FASB Concepts EITF–EITF Issues Q&A–FASB Special Reports

T-247

	Original Pronouncements	Current Text	EITF and Other
LEASES—continued			
Capital Leases—continued			
. . Contingent Rentals	FAS29, ¶13	L10.108	
. . Criteria for Classification	FAS13, ¶7	L10.103	
. . Executory Costs	FAS13, ¶7	L10.103	
. . Extinguishment of Lease Debt	FAS22, ¶12	L10.110	
. . . .	FAS22, ¶17	L10.162-163	
. . Gains or Losses	FAS13, ¶14	L10.109-110	
. . . .	FAS22, ¶12		
. . . .	FAS22, ¶14		
. . . .	FIN26, ¶5		
. . Guarantee of Residual Value	FAS13, ¶11-12	L10.107-108	
. . Illustrations for Lessees	FAS13, ¶121-122	L10.150-153	
. . Interest Expense	FAS13, ¶12	L10.108	
. . Purchase of a Leased Asset by Lessee .	FIN26, ¶5	L10.109	
. . Refunding of Tax-Exempt Debt	FAS22, ¶12	L10.110	
. . . .	FAS22, ¶17	L10.162-163	
. . Renewals or Extensions	FAS13, ¶9	L10.105	
. . . .	FAS13, ¶12	L10.108-109	
. . . .	FAS13, ¶14		
. . . .	FAS22, ¶14		
. . Sale-Leaseback Transactions	FAS28, ¶2-3	L10.128-129	
. . Termination of Capital Lease	FAS13, ¶14	L10.109	
Classifying Leases (Other Than Leveraged Leases)			
. . Changes in Estimates or Provisions for Lessees and Lessors	FAS13, ¶9	L10.105	
. . Illustrations for Lessees and Lessors . .	FAS13, ¶121-122	L10.150-153	
. . Lessee Criteria	FAS13, ¶6-7	L10.102-103	
. . Lessor Criteria	FAS13, ¶6-8	L10.102-104	
. . . .	FAS27, ¶6-7		
. . . .	FAS98, ¶22		
Collateral			
. . Money-Over-Money Lease Transactions	FTB88-1, ¶16-17	L10.542-543	
. . Sale of Leased Property	FAS13, ¶22	L10.118	
. . Wrap Lease Transactions	FTB88-1, ¶21-22	L10.544-545	
Computer Software			
. . Cost Incurred to Lease Software	FIN6, ¶5	R50.114	
Concentrations of Credit Risk on Operating Leases			EITF.D-22
Consolidation			
. . Related-Party Leases	FAS13, ¶30	L10.126	
Contingent Rentals			
. . Capital Leases	FAS29, ¶13	L10.108	
. . Direct Financing Leases	FAS98, ¶22	L10.114	
. . Exclusion from Minimum Lease Payments	FAS13, ¶5	L10.417	
. . . .	FAS29, ¶10		

See "Terminology" for references to defined terms presented in various accounting pronouncements.

See the Introduction to the Topical Index for details on the use of this index.

	Original Pronouncements	Current Text	EITF and Other
LEASES—continued			
Contingent Rentals—continued			
. . Illustration of Calculation	FAS29, ¶15-17	L10.164-166	
. . Operating Leases with Scheduled Rent Increases	FTB85-3, ¶1-2	L10.525-527B	
	FTB85-3, ¶12-13		
	FTB88-1, ¶1-2		
. . Sales-Type Leases	FAS29, ¶13	L10.113	
Current Value Financial Statements	FTB79-13, ¶1-2	L10.512-513	
Debt: Restructuring			
. . Exemption from Requirements	FAS15, ¶8	D22.102	
Direct Financing Leases			
. . Accounting	FAS13, ¶18	L10.114	
	FAS98, ¶22		
. . Allowance for Doubtful Accounts	FAS98, ¶22	L10.104	
. . Calculation of Gross Investment	FAS98, ¶22	L10.114	
. . Calculation of Net Investment	FAS98, ¶22	L10.114	
. . Change in Lease Provisions	FAS13, ¶9	L10.105	
	FAS22, ¶14		
	FAS27, ¶6-7		
. . Compared with Leveraged Leases	FAS13, ¶42	L10.144	
. . Contingent Rentals	FAS98, ¶22	L10.114	
. . Criteria for Classification	FAS13, ¶6	L10.102	
	FAS13, ¶8	L10.104	
	FAS27, ¶7		
	FAS98, ¶22		
. . Executory Costs	FAS98, ¶22	L10.114	
. . Gains or Losses	FAS13, ¶18	L10.114	
	FAS98, ¶22		
. . Governmental Units	FAS22, ¶12	L10.113	
. . Guarantee of Residual Value	FAS13, ¶18	L10.114	
. . Income Determination	FAS13, ¶18	L10.114	
	FAS98, ¶22		
. . Initial Direct Costs	FAS98, ¶22	L10.114	
. . Involving Real Estate	FAS13, ¶25-26	L10.121-122	
	FAS98, ¶22		
. . Offsetting Nonrecourse Debt with Lease Receivables	FIN39, ¶5-7	B10.101A-101B	EITF.84-25
	FTB88-1, ¶16-17	B10.107	
	FTB88-1, ¶21-22	L10.542-545	
. . Penalty for Failure to Renew Lease	FAS13, ¶18	L10.114	
. . Sale of Leased Property	FAS13, ¶20	L10.116	
. . Sale or Assignment of Lease Receivable with Recourse	FAS13, ¶20	L10.116	
	FAS77, ¶3	R20.102	
	FAS77, ¶10		

FAS–FASB Statements   FIN–FASB Interpretations   FTB–FASB Technical Bulletins
APB–APB Opinions   AIN–AICPA Interpretations   ARB–Accounting Research Bulletins
CON–FASB Concepts   EITF–EITF Issues   Q&A–FASB Special Reports

See ''Terminology'' for references to defined terms presented in various accounting pronouncements.

See the Introduction to the Topical Index for details on the use of this index.

	Original Pronouncements	Current Text	EITF and Other
LEASES—continued			
Extinguishment of Lease Debt—continued			
. . Money-Over-Money Lease Transactions	FTB88-1, ¶16-17	L10.542-543	
. . Wrap Lease Transactions	FTB88-1, ¶21-22	L10.544-545	
Fair Value of Leased Property			
. . Appraisal Value	FIN24, ¶4	L10.124	
. . Effect on Lease Classification	FAS13, ¶7	L10.103	
. . Inception of the Lease	FAS23, ¶8	L10.122	
. . Leased Property Not Constructed	FAS23, ¶8	L10.106	
. . . .		L10.122	
. . Part of a Building	FAS13, ¶28	L10.124	
. . . .	FIN24, ¶4		
. . . .	FIN24, ¶6		
. . Real Estate	FAS13, ¶28	L10.124	
. . . .	FIN24, ¶4		
. . . .	FIN24, ¶6		
. . Sale-Leaseback Transactions	FAS28, ¶3	L10.129	
Fiscal Funding Clauses	FTB79-10, ¶1-5	L10.501-505	
Gains or Losses			
. . Capital Leases	FAS13, ¶14	L10.109-110	
. . . .	FAS22, ¶12		
. . . .	FAS22, ¶14		
. . . .	FIN26, ¶5		
. . Direct Financing Leases	FAS13, ¶18	L10.114	
. . . .	FAS98, ¶22		
. . Disposal of a Segment	FIN27, ¶2-3	L10.135	
. . . .	FTB79-15, ¶1-3	L10.518-520	
. . Illustration	FAS22, ¶17	L10.162-163	
. . Lease Incentives in Operating Leases . .	FTB88-1, ¶6-9	L10.527C-527F	
. . Leveraged Leases	FAS13, ¶45-46	L10.147-148	
. . Losses Not Involving Disposal of a Segment	FTB79-15, ¶1-3	L10.518-520	
. . Modification or Termination of Operating Leases	FTB79-15, ¶1-3	L10.518-520	EITF.88-10
. . Money-Over-Money Lease Transactions	FTB88-1, ¶16-17	L10.542-543	
. . Operating Leases Involving Real Estate	FAS98, ¶22	L10.115	
. . Refunding of Tax-Exempt Debt	FAS22, ¶12	L10.110	
. . . .	FAS22, ¶17	L10.113-114	
. . Related-Party Transactions	FAS13, ¶20-22	L10.116-118	
. . . .	FAS13, ¶29-30	L10.125-126	
. . . .	FAS77, ¶10		

FAS—FASB Statements
APB—APB Opinions
CON—FASB Concepts

FIN—FASB Interpretations
AIN—AICPA Interpretations
EITF—EITF Issues

FTB—FASB Technical Bulletins
ARB—Accounting Research Bulletins
Q&A—FASB Special Reports

	Original Pronouncements	Current Text	EITF and Other
LEASES—continued			
Gains or Losses—continued			
. . Sale of Property Subject to Seller's Preexisting Lease			EITF.88-21
. . Sale or Assignment to Third Party	FAS13, ¶20-22	L10.116-118	
. . . .	FAS77, ¶10		
. . Sale-Leaseback Transactions	FAS28, ¶2-3	L10.128-129	EITF.84-37
. . Sale-Leaseback Transactions Involving Real Estate	FAS98, ¶7-8	L10.130B-130D	
. . . .	FAS98, ¶70		
. . Sales-Type Leases	FAS13, ¶17	L10.113	
. . . .	FAS22, ¶15		
. . . .	FAS27, ¶8		
. . Subleases	FAS13, ¶38-39	L10.134-135	
. . . .	FIN27, ¶2-3		
. . Wrap Lease Transactions	FTB88-1, ¶21-22	L10.544-545	
Glossary	FAS13, ¶1	L10.401-424	
. . . .	FAS13, ¶5-7		
. . . .	FAS13, ¶10		
. . . .	FAS23, ¶6		
. . . .	FAS29, ¶11		
. . . .	FAS91, ¶24		
. . . .	FAS98, ¶22		
. . . .	FAS98, ¶70		
. . . .	FTB88-1, ¶16		
. . . .	FTB88-1, ¶21		
Government-Owned Facilities	FAS13, ¶28	L10.124	
. . . .	FIN23, ¶6		
. . . .	FIN23, ¶8-9		
. . Effect of Fiscal Funding Clauses	FTB79-10, ¶1-5	L10.501-505	
Guarantees			
. . Effect on Capital Lease Asset	FAS13, ¶11-12	L10.107-108	
. . Effect on Minimum Lease Payments . .	FAS13, ¶5	L10.417	
. . . .	FIN19, ¶3-5		
. . Effect on Sale-Leaseback Involving Real Estate	FAS98, ¶11-12	L10.130G-130H	
Impact of Nonsubstantive Lessors, Residual Value Guarantees, and Other Provisions in Leasing Transactions			EITF.90-15
Impairment: Loans			
. . Exemption from Requirements	FAS114, ¶6	I08.104	
Implicit Interest Rate			
. . Illustration of Calculation	FAS13, ¶121	L10.150	
Inception of Lease			
. . Leased Property Not Constructed	FAS23, ¶7-8	L10.104	
. . . .		L10.106	
. . . .		L10.122	
Income Recognition for Cross Border Tax Benefit Leases			EITF.89-20
Incremental Borrowing Rate			
. . Example of Computation	FAS13, ¶121	L10.150	

See "Terminology" for references to defined terms presented in various accounting pronouncements.

See the Introduction to the Topical Index for details on the use of this index.

	Original Pronouncements	Current Text	EITF and Other
LEASES—continued			
Incremental Borrowing Rate—continued			
. . Use of a Specific Borrowing Rate	FTB79-12, ¶1-3	L10.509-511	
Initial Direct Costs			
. . Direct Financing Leases	FAS98, ¶22	L10.114	
. . Leveraged Leases	FAS13, ¶43	L10.145	
. . Operating Leases	FAS13, ¶19	L10.115	
. . Sales-Type Leases	FAS13, ¶17	L10.113	
Interest Expense and Interest Method			
. . Capital Leases	FAS13, ¶12	L10.108	
. . Direct Financing Leases	FAS13, ¶18	L10.114	
. . Interest Rate Implicit in Lease	FAS13, ¶5	L10.412	
. . Leveraged Leases	FAS13, ¶43-44	L10.145-146	
. . Minimum Lease Payments	FTB79-12, ¶1-3	L10.509-511	
. . Nonapplicability to Operating Leases	FAS13, ¶15	L10.111	
	FTB85-3, ¶1-2	L10.525-527B	
	FTB85-3, ¶12-13		
	FTB88-1, ¶1-2		
. . Refunding of Tax-Exempt Debt	FAS22, ¶12	L10.110	
		L10.113-114	
. . Sales-Type Leases	FAS13, ¶17	L10.113	
Interest in Residual Value			
. . Acquired by Selling Leased Asset and Retaining Interest in Residual Value			EITF.87-7
Investment Tax Credits	AIN-APB4, #3	I27.507-508	
. . Accounting by Lessee or Lessor	AIN-APB4, #3	I27.507-508	
. . Deferral Method of Accounting	AIN-APB4, #3	I27.509	
. . Impact on Implicit Interest Rate	FAS13, ¶5	L10.412	
. . Leveraged Leases	FAS13, ¶42-43	L10.144-145	
Lease Incentives in an Operating Lease	FTB88-1, ¶6-9	L10.527C-527F	
Lease Payments			
. . Allocation between Interest and Principal	FAS13, ¶12	L10.108	
. . Allocation between Land and Buildings	FAS13, ¶26	L10.122	
. . Contingent Rentals	FAS29, ¶13	L10.108	
	FAS91, ¶25		
. . Escalating Rents	FAS13, ¶15	L10.111	
	FAS13, ¶19	L10.115	
	FTB85-3, ¶1-2	L10.525-527B	
	FTB85-3, ¶12-13		
	FTB88-1, ¶1-2		
. . Escalation Clauses	FAS23, ¶8	L10.106	
		L10.122	
. . Executory Costs	FAS13, ¶5	L10.106	
	FAS13, ¶10	L10.417	

FAS–FASB Statements   FIN–FASB Interpretations   FTB–FASB Technical Bulletins
APB–APB Opinions   AIN–AICPA Interpretations   ARB–Accounting Research Bulletins
CON–FASB Concepts   EITF–EITF Issues   Q&A–FASB Special Reports

	Original Pronouncements	Current Text	EITF and Other
LEASES—continued			
Lease Payments—continued			
. . Lease Incentives	FTB88-1, ¶6-9	L10.527C-527F	EITF.88-3
. . Lease Modification or Termination . . .			EITF.88-10
. . Lessor Estimate of Collectibility	FAS98, ¶22	L10.104	
. . Scheduled Rent Increases (Also Time Pattern of Physical Use of Leased Property)	FAS13, ¶15	L10.111	
	FAS13, ¶19	L10.115	
	FTB85-3, ¶1-2	L10.525-527B	
	FTB85-3, ¶12-13		
	FTB88-1, ¶1-2		
. . Unsecured Guarantee by Parent of Subsidiary's Lease Payments			EITF.90-14
Leased Property Not Constructed			
. . Determining Fair Value	FAS23, ¶8	L10.106	
. . Estimated Residual Value	FAS23, ¶9-10	L10.114	
		L10.145	
. . Inception of the Lease	FAS23, ¶7	L10.104	
. . Land and Buildings	FAS23, ¶8	L10.122	
. . Lessor Classification	FAS23, ¶7	L10.104	
Leveraged Leases			
. . Accounting	FAS13, ¶42-47	L10.104	
	FAS23, ¶10	L10.144-149	
	FAS98, ¶22		
. . Alternative Minimum Tax (AMT)			EITF.87-8
. . Applicability to Existing Assets of the Lessor	FTB88-1, ¶11-12	L10.540-541	
. . Business Combination—Purchase Method	FIN21, ¶16	L10.141	
	FIN21, ¶19	L10.161	
. . Changes in Important Assumptions	FAS13, ¶46	L10.148	
. . Compared with Direct Financing Leases	FAS13, ¶42	L10.144	
. . Deferred Taxes	FAS109, ¶256-258	L10.148A-148B	
. . Delayed Equity Contributions by Lessors			EITF.85-16
. . Description	FAS13, ¶6	L10.102	
	FAS13, ¶42	L10.144	
. . Effect of Change in Income Tax Rate	FAS109, ¶288	L10.521-524	EITF.86-43
	FTB79-16(R), ¶1-4		
. . Gains or Losses	FAS13, ¶45-46	L10.147-148B	
	FAS109, ¶256-258		
. . Illustration of Accounting	FAS13, ¶123	L10.154	
. . Initial Direct Costs	FAS13, ¶43	L10.145	
	FAS91, ¶24		
. . Investment Tax Credit	FAS13, ¶42-43	L10.144-145	

See "Terminology" for references to defined terms presented in various accounting pronouncements.

See the Introduction to the Topical Index for details on the use of this index.

FAS–FASB Statements FIN–FASB Interpretations FTB–FASB Technical Bulletins
APB–APB Opinions AIN–AICPA Interpretations ARB–Accounting Research Bulletins
CON–FASB Concepts EITF–EITF Issues Q&A–FASB Special Reports

See "Terminology" for references to defined terms presented in various accounting pronouncements.

See the Introduction to the Topical Index for details on the use of this index.

	Original Pronouncements	Current Text	EITF and Other
LEASES—continued			
Penalty—continued			
. . Effect on Minimum Lease Payments . .	FAS13, ¶5	L10.417	
Property			
. . Amortization and Depreciation	FAS13, ¶11	L10.107	
. . . .	FAS13, ¶19	L10.115	
. . Calculation of Capitalized Amount . . .	FAS13, ¶10	L10.106	
. . . .	FAS23, ¶8		
. . Economic Life	FAS13, ¶5	L10.406	
. . Fair Value	FAS13, ¶5	L10.409	
. . Government-Owned	FAS13, ¶28	L10.124	
. . . .	FIN23, ¶6		
. . . .	FIN23, ¶8-9		
. . Leased with Land.	FAS13, ¶26	L10.122	EITF.85-16
. . . .	FAS98, ¶22		
. . Money-Over-Money Lease Transactions.	FTB88-1, ¶16-17	L10.542-543	
. . Purchase of Leased Property	FIN26, ¶5	L10.109	
. . Sale of Leased Property	FAS13, ¶20-22	L10.116-118	
. . Wrap Lease Transactions.	FTB88-1, ¶21-22	L10.544-545	
Purchase of Leased Property			
. . Accounting by Lessee	FIN26, ¶5	L10.109	
. . Accounting by Lessor	FAS13, ¶20-22	L10.116-118	
Real Estate	FAS13, ¶24	L10.120	
. . Allocation of Residual Value or First-Loss Guarantee to Minimum Lease Payments in Leases Involving Land and Building(s).			EITF.92-1
. . Classification as Leveraged Lease.			EITF.85-16
. . Delayed Equity Contributions in a Leveraged Lease			EITF.85-16
. . Fair Value Determination	FAS13, ¶28	L10.124	
. . . .	FIN24, ¶4		
. . . .	FIN24, ¶6		
. . Government-Owned	FAS13, ¶28	L10.124	
. . . .	FIN23, ¶6		
. . . .	FIN23, ¶8-9		
. . Land and Buildings	FAS13, ¶26	L10.122	
. . . .	FAS98, ¶22		
. . Land Only	FAS13, ¶25	L10.121	
. . . .	FAS98, ¶22		
. . Part of a Building	FAS13, ¶28	L10.124	
. . . .	FIN24, ¶4		
. . . .	FIN24, ¶6		
. . Qualifying as a Sales-Type Lease	FAS98, ¶22	L10.102	
. . . .		L10.104	
Real Estate and Equipment	FAS13, ¶27	L10.123	
Refunding of Tax-Exempt Debt			
. . Illustration of Accounting.	FAS22, ¶17	L10.162-163	
. . Lessee Accounting	FAS22, ¶12	L10.110	

FAS–FASB Statements   FIN–FASB Interpretations   FTB–FASB Technical Bulletins
APB–APB Opinions   AIN–AICPA Interpretations   ARB–Accounting Research Bulletins
CON–FASB Concepts   EITF–EITF Issues   Q&A–FASB Special Reports

T-257

See "Terminology" for references to defined terms presented in various accounting pronouncements.

See the Introduction to the Topical Index for details on the use of this index.

	Original Pronouncements	Current Text	EITF and Other
LEASES—continued			
Residual Value—continued			
. . Annual Review of Estimate	FAS13, ¶17-18	L10.113-114	
....	FAS13, ¶46	L10.148	
. . Decline in Estimated Value	FAS13, ¶17-18	L10.113-114	
....	FAS13, ¶46	L10.148	
. . Direct Financing Leases.............	FAS13, ¶18	L10.114	
....	FAS98, ¶22		
. . Estimate for Leased Property Not			
Constructed	FAS23, ¶9-10	L10.114	
....		L10.145	
. . Estimated Residual Value of Leased			
Property	FAS13, ¶5	L10.407	
. . Guaranteed by Lessee	FAS13, ¶5	L10.417	
. . Included in Minimum Lease Payments	FAS13, ¶5	L10.108	
....	FAS13, ¶12	L10.417	
. . Leveraged Leases	FAS13, ¶43	L10.145	
....	FAS13, ¶46	L10.148	
....	FAS23, ¶10		
. . Sales-Type Leases	FAS13, ¶17	L10.113	
....	FAS23, ¶9		
. . Unguaranteed Residual Value	FAS13, ¶5	L10.422	
. . Upward Adjustment of Guaranteed			
Residual Values	FTB79-14, ¶1-4	L10.514-517	
Restrictions of Lease Agreement.........	FAS13, ¶16	L10.112	
Safe Harbor Leases Used to Transfer Tax			
Benefits			
. . Disclosure of Sale or Purchase of Tax			
Benefits........................	FAS109, ¶288	I27.501-506	
....	FTB82-1, ¶1-2		
....	FTB82-1, ¶4		
....	FTB82-1, ¶6-8		
. . Effect of Change in Tax Law			EITF.86-44
Sale of Lease Receivable			
. . Direct Financing or Sales-Type Leases .	FAS13, ¶20	L10.116	
....	FAS77, ¶3	R20.102	
....	FAS77, ¶10		
. . Interest in Residual Value Retained by			
Lessor.........................	FTB86-2, ¶9-10	L10.536-537	
. . Money-Over-Money Lease			
Transactions....................	FTB88-1, ¶16-17	L10.542-543	
. . Wrap Lease Transactions............	FTB88-1, ¶21-22	L10.544-545	
Sale of Leased Property			
. . Collateral	FAS13, ¶22	L10.118	
. . Money-Over-Money Lease			
Transactions....................	FTB88-1, ¶16-17	L10.542-543	
. . Recognition	FAS13, ¶20-22	L10.116-118	
. . Sale and Leaseback of an Asset			
That Is or Will Be Leased to			
Another Party			EITF.93-8
. . Sale of Property Subject to Seller's			
Preexisting Lease			EITF.88-21

FAS–FASB Statements	FIN–FASB Interpretations	FTB–FASB Technical Bulletins
APB–APB Opinions	AIN–AICPA Interpretations	ARB–Accounting Research Bulletins
CON–FASB Concepts	EITF–EITF Issues	Q&A–FASB Special Reports

See "Terminology" for references to defined terms presented in various accounting pronouncements.

See the Introduction to the Topical Index for details on the use of this index.

FAS–FASB Statements	FIN–FASB Interpretations	FTB–FASB Technical Bulletins
APB–APB Opinions	AIN–AICPA Interpretations	ARB–Accounting Research Bulletins
CON–FASB Concepts	EITF–EITF Issues	Q&A–FASB Special Reports

T-261

	Original Pronouncements	Current Text	EITF and Other
LEASES—continued			
Sales-Type Leases—continued			
. . Allowance for Doubtful Accounts	FAS98, ¶22	L10.104	
. . Calculation of Gross Investment	FAS13, ¶17	L10.113	
. . Calculation of Net Investment	FAS13, ¶17	L10.113	
	FAS29, ¶13		
. . Change in Lease Provisions	FAS13, ¶9	L10.105	
	FAS22, ¶15		
	FAS23, ¶9		
	FAS27, ¶6-8		
. . Collectibility	FAS98, ¶22	L10.104	
. . Contingent Rentals	FAS29, ¶13	L10.113	
. . Criteria for Classification	FAS13, ¶8	L10.102	
	FAS27, ¶7	L10.104	
	FAS98, ¶22		
. . Definition	FAS98, ¶22	L10.102	
. . Executory Costs	FAS13, ¶17	L10.113	
. . Gains or Losses	FAS13, ¶17	L10.113	
	FAS22, ¶15		
	FAS27, ¶8		
. . Income Determination.	FAS13, ¶17	L10.113	
	FAS22, ¶12		
	FAS22, ¶15		
	FAS23, ¶9		
	FAS29, ¶13		
. . Initial Direct Costs.	FAS13, ¶17	L10.113	
. . Involving Real Estate.	FAS13, ¶25-26	L10.121-122	
	FAS98, ¶22		
. . Lessor Accounting for Initial Direct Costs.	FAS13, ¶17	L10.113	
. . Offsetting Nonrecourse Debt with Lease Receivables			EITF.84-25
. . Penalty for Failure to Renew Lease . . .	FAS13, ¶17	L10.113	
. . Purchase of Leased Property	FAS13, ¶20	L10.116	
. . Residual Guarantee Contained in Lease.	FAS13, ¶17	L10.113	
. . Sale of Leased Property	FAS13, ¶20	L10.116	
. . Sale of Lease Receivable	FAS13, ¶20	L10.116	
	FAS77, ¶3	R20.102	
	FAS77, ¶10		
. . Termination	FAS13, ¶17	L10.113	
. . Unearned Income.	FAS13, ¶17	L10.113	
Scheduled Rent Increases Related to Physical Use.	FTB88-1, ¶1-2	L10.527A-527B	
Scope of Accounting and Reporting Requirements.	FAS13, ¶1	L10.101	

See "Terminology" for references to defined terms presented in various accounting pronouncements.

See the Introduction to the Topical Index for details on the use of this index.

	Original Pronouncements	Current Text	EITF and Other
LEASES—continued			
Special-Purpose Entities			
. . Accounting for Lease Transactions....			EITF.90-15
Subleases and Similar Transactions			
. . Accounting by New Lessee	FAS13, ¶40	L10.136	
. . Accounting by Original Lessee	FAS13, ¶38-39	L10.134-135	
....	FIN27, ¶2-3		
. . Accounting by Original Lessor	FAS13, ¶36-37	L10.132-133	
. . Accounting for Losses on Subleases...	FTB79-15, ¶1-3	L10.518-520	
. . Lease Incentives...................	FTB88-1, ¶6-9	L10.527C-527F	
. . Recognition of Gain or Loss.........	FAS13, ¶38-39	L10.134-135	EITF.88-10
....	FIN27, ¶2-3	L10.518-520	
....	FTB79-15, ¶1-3		
. . Sale and Leaseback of an Asset That Is or Will Be Leased to Another Party			EITF.93-8
. . Types of Subleases and Similar Transactions.....................	FAS13, ¶35	L10.131	
. . Wrap Lease Transactions............	FTB88-1, ¶21-22	L10.544-545	
Tax			
. . Sale or Purchase of Tax Benefits	FAS109, ¶288	I27.501-506	
....	FTB82-1, ¶1-2		
....	FTB82-1, ¶4		
....	FTB82-1, ¶6-8		
Tax Indemnification Related to a Change in Tax Law			EITF.86-33
Tax Leases Used to Transfer Tax Benefits			
. . Effect of Change in Tax Law			EITF.86-44
. . Income Recognition for Cross Border Tax Benefit Leases...............			EITF.89-20
Termination			
. . Payment to Terminate an Operating Lease..........................	FTB88-1, ¶6-9	L10.527C-527F	EITF.88-10
. . Termination of a Capital Lease.......	FAS13, ¶14	L10.109	
. . Termination of a Direct Financing Lease..........................	FAS13, ¶18	L10.114	
. . Termination of a Sales-Type Lease....	FAS13, ¶17	L10.113	
Transactions Involving Special-Purpose Entities............................			EITF.90-15
....			EITF.D-14
Uncertainties			
. . Collectibility of Lease Receivables	FAS98, ¶22	L10.104	
. . Contingent Rentals	FAS29, ¶11	L10.404	
. . Effect on Lease Classification........	FAS13, ¶8	L10.104	
. . Executory Costs	FAS13, ¶8	L10.104	
. . Fair Value Determination	FAS13, ¶5	L10.409	
. . Unreimbursable Costs..............	FAS13, ¶8	L10.104	
Unearned Income			
. . Direct Financing Lease	FAS98, ¶22	L10.114	
. . Leveraged Leases..................	FAS13, ¶43	L10.145	
. . Sales-Type Leases	FAS13, ¶17	L10.113	
Unguaranteed Residual Value			
. . Direct Financing Leases.............	FAS98, ¶22	L10.114	
. . Leveraged Leases..................	FAS13, ¶43	L10.145	
. . Sales-Type Leases	FAS13, ¶17	L10.113	

FAS–FASB Statements   FIN–FASB Interpretations   FTB–FASB Technical Bulletins
APB–APB Opinions   AIN–AICPA Interpretations   ARB–Accounting Research Bulletins
CON–FASB Concepts   EITF–EITF Issues   Q&A–FASB Special Reports

See "Terminology" for references to defined terms presented in various accounting pronouncements.

See the Introduction to the Topical Index for details on the use of this index.

	Original Pronouncements	Current Text	EITF and Other
LENDING ACTIVITIES—continued			
Loan Acquisitions Involving Table Funding Arrangements			EITF.92-10
Loan Guarantees			
. . Revenue Recognition of Fees			EITF.85-20
Loan Origination Fees and Costs	FAS91, ¶5-7	L20.104-106	Q&A.91 #30
. . . .	FAS91, ¶36		Q&A.91 #60
. . Direct Costs	FAS91, ¶6	L20.105	Q&A.91 #12
. . . .			Q&A.91 #16-20
			Q&A.91 #24
. . Inclusions in Loans Sold to Affiliated Enterprises			Q&A.91 #60
. . Method of Determining Direct Costs . .			Q&A.91 #21-23
. . Other Lending Related Costs	FAS91, ¶7	L20.106	Q&A.91 #13-15
. . Third-Party Costs	FAS91, ¶6	L20.105	Q&A.91 #9-11
. . . .			Q&A.91 #13
Purchase of Loan or Group of Loans	FAS91, ¶15-16	L20.114-115	Q&A.91 #35
Restatement of Financial Statements			Q&A.91 #62
. . . .			Q&A.91 #64
Revenue Recognition			
. . Credit Card Portfolio Securitizations with a "Removal of Accounts" Provision			EITF.90-18
. . Fees Associated with Loan Syndications and Loan Participations			EITF.88-17
. . Sale of Convertible, Adjustable-Rate Mortgages with Contingent Repayment Agreement			EITF.87-25
. . Sale of Short-Term Loan under Long-Term Credit Commitment.			EITF.87-30
. . Securitization of Credit Card Portfolio			EITF.88-22
Revolving Credit Agreement	FAS91, ¶20	L20.119	
Scope.	FAS91, ¶2-4	L20.101-103	Q&A.91 #1-8
. . . .	FAS115, ¶130		
Shared Appreciation Mortgages			EITF.86-21
Syndication Fees.	FAS91, ¶11	L20.110	Q&A.91 #34-35
. . Fees Associated with Loan Syndications and Loan Participations			EITF.88-17
LESSEE			
See Leases			
LESSOR			
See Leases			
LETTERS OF CREDIT			
See Contingencies			
See Financial Instruments			
LEVERAGED BUYOUT			
Allocating Basis to Individual Assets and Liabilities under Issue No. 88-16			EITF.90-12
Carryover of Predecessor Cost			EITF.86-16
. . . .			EITF.88-16
Financed by Loan to ESOP.			EITF.85-11
Leveraged Buyout Holding Company Debt			EITF.84-23

FAS—FASB Statements   FIN—FASB Interpretations   FTB—FASB Technical Bulletins
APB—APB Opinions   AIN—AICPA Interpretations   ARB—Accounting Research Bulletins
CON—FASB Concepts   EITF—EITF Issues   Q&A—FASB Special Reports

T-265

See "Terminology" for references to defined terms presented in various accounting pronouncements.

See the Introduction to the Topical Index for details on the use of this index.

FAS–FASB Statements FIN–FASB Interpretations FTB–FASB Technical Bulletins
APB–APB Opinions AIN–AICPA Interpretations ARB–Accounting Research Bulletins
CON–FASB Concepts EITF–EITF Issues Q&A–FASB Special Reports

T-267

See "Terminology" for references to defined terms presented in various accounting pronouncements.

See the Introduction to the Topical Index for details on the use of this index.

	Original Pronouncements	Current Text	EITF and Other

LOANS—continued

Collateralized Mortgage Obligations (CMOs)

. . Consolidation of Issuer with Sponsor . — — EITF.85-28

Debtor's Accounting for Forfeiture of Real Estate Subject to a Nonrecourse Mortgage . . . . — — EITF.91-2

International Loan Swaps

. . Requirements for Loss Recognition . . . — — EITF.D-3

Loan Acquisitions Involving Table Funding Arrangements . . . . — — EITF.92-10

Mortgage Loan Payment Modifications. . . — — EITF.84-19

Negative Amortization of Principal

. . Applying Profit Recognition Criteria for Sale of Real Estate. . . . . — — EITF.84-17

. . Interest Income Recognition . . . . — — EITF.85-38

. . Sale of Negative Amortizing Loans . . . — — EITF.85-38

Originating Loans with Intent to Sell . . . . . — — EITF.D-2

Participating Mortgage . . . . — — EITF.86-28

Payment Modifications Involving Forgiveness of Principal . . . . — — EITF.84-19

Sale of Bad-Debt Recovery Rights . . . . — — EITF.86-8

Sale of Interest-Only Cash Flows from Loans Receivable

. . Determination of Gain or Loss. . . . . . . — — EITF.88-11

. . Determination of Remaining Recorded Investment for Portion of Loan Retained . . . . — — EITF.88-11

Sale of Mortgage Loan by CMO Established through Third Party . . . . — — EITF.86-24

Sale of Mortgage Loan with Servicing Rights Retained . . . . — — EITF.86-39

Sale of Mortgage Servicing Rights . . . . — — EITF.85-13

Sale of Principal-Only Cash Flows from Loans Receivable

. . Determination of Gain or Loss. . . . . . . — — EITF.88-11

. . Determination of Remaining Recorded Investment for Portion of Loan Retained . . . . — — EITF.88-11

Sale of Short-Term Loan under Long-Term Credit Commitment . . . . — — EITF.87-30

Sale to Special-Purpose Entities . . . . — — EITF.84-30

Sale with a Partial Participation Retained . — — EITF.84-21

. . . . — — EITF.86-38

U.S. Dollar Loans to Argentine Private Sector . . . . — — EITF.D-4

LOANS RECEIVABLE/PAYABLE

See Balance Sheet Classification: Current Assets and Liabilities

See Impairment: Loans

See Lending Activities

See Loans

See Receivables

FAS—FASB Statements   FIN—FASB Interpretations   FTB—FASB Technical Bulletins
APB—APB Opinions   AIN—AICPA Interpretations   ARB—Accounting Research Bulletins
CON—FASB Concepts   EITF—EITF Issues   Q&A—FASB Special Reports

T-269

	Original Pronouncements	Current Text	EITF and Other

LOAN SWAPS
See Financial Instruments
See Loans

LOCAL CURRENCY
See Foreign Currency Translation

Definition .... FAS52, ¶162   F60.416

LONG-TERM CONTRACTS
See Accounting Changes
See Adjustments of Financial Statements
  for Prior Periods
See Commitments: Long-Term Obligations
See Contractor Accounting:
  Construction-Type Contracts
See Contractor Accounting: Government
  Contracts
See Debt: Product Financing
  Arrangements
See Oil and Gas Producing Activities

LONG-TERM DEBT
See Balance Sheet Classification: Current
  Assets and Liabilities
See Collateralized Mortgage Obligations
See Commitments: Long-Term Obligations
See Debt
See Debt Issue Cost
See Debt: Convertible Debt and Debt with
  Stock Purchase Warrants
See Debt: Extinguishments
See Debt: Product Financing
  Arrangements
See Debt: Restructurings
See Disclosure
See Financial Instruments

LONG-TERM INVESTMENTS
See Financial Instruments
See Investments: Debt and Equity
  Securities
See Investments: Equity Method
See Investments: Marketable Securities

Balance Sheet Classification .... ARB43, Ch.3A, ¶6   B05.107

LONG-TERM OBLIGATIONS
See Balance Sheet Classification: Current
  Assets and Liabilities
See Balance Sheet Classification: Debt vs.
  Equity
See Commitments: Long-Term Obligations
See Debt: Convertible Debt and Debt with
  Stock Purchase Warrants
See Debt: Extinguishments
See Debt: Product Financing
  Arrangements
See Debt: Restructurings
See Financial Instruments

See "Terminology" for references to defined terms presented in various accounting pronouncements.

See the Introduction to the Topical Index for details on the use of this index.

	Original Pronouncements	Current Text	EITF and Other
LONG-TERM OBLIGATIONS—continued			
See Long-Term Contracts			
Conversion to Capital Stock	APB12, ¶10	C08.102	
Definition			
. . Long-Term Obligations	FAS6, ¶2	B05.403	
LOSS CARRYBACKS AND CARRYFORWARDS			
See Income Taxes			
Benefit of Carryforward Realized			
. . Recognition of Purchased NOL or Own NOL			EITF.86-1
. . Reinstatement of Previously Eliminated Deferred Taxes			EITF.85-5
Business Combinations			
. . Purchased Loss Carryforwards.			EITF.84-33
. . . .			EITF.85-15
. . . .			EITF.86-1
LOSS CONTINGENCIES			
See Contingencies			
LOSS RESERVES			
See Contingencies			
See Insurance Industry			
LOSSES			
See Gain or Loss			
See Income Taxes			
Characteristics.	CON6, ¶84-89		
Component of Comprehensive Income . . .	CON6, ¶73-77		
. . . .	CON6, ¶215-220		
Definition	CON6, ¶83		
Element of Financial Statements.	CON6, ¶83-89		
Holding	CON6, ¶71		
Not-for-Profit Organizations	CON6, ¶111-113		
Operating vs. Nonoperating	CON6, ¶86		
Purchase Commitments			
. . Qualification to Be Included as	CON6, ¶251-253		
Recognition Criteria			
. . Guidance in Application	CON5, ¶85		
. . Guidance in Application, Loss or Lack of Future Benefit	CON5, ¶87		
Relation to Expenses	CON6, ¶87-89		
LOSSES (CATASTROPHE)			
See Insurance Industry			

FAS—FASB Statements   FIN—FASB Interpretations   FTB—FASB Technical Bulletins
APB—APB Opinions   AIN—AICPA Interpretations   ARB—Accounting Research Bulletins
CON—FASB Concepts   EITF—EITF Issues   Q&A—FASB Special Reports

T-271

(The next page is T-279.)

See "Terminology" for references to defined terms presented in various accounting pronouncements.

See the Introduction to the Topical Index for details on the use of this index.

	Original Pronouncements	Current Text	EITF and Other
MACHINERY AND EQUIPMENT			
See Property, Plant, and Equipment			
MAJOR CUSTOMERS			
See Segment of Business Reporting			
Concentrations of Credit Risk	FAS105, ¶20	F25.115	
MAJORITY-OWNED SUBSIDIARIES			
See Consolidation			
See Related Parties			
See Subsidiaries			
MANAGEMENT			
Definition	FAS57, ¶24	R36.404	
Discussion			
. . Foreign Currency Translation	FAS52, ¶144	F60.143	
Need for Operational Information	CON1, ¶27		
Relation to Enterprise Performance	CON1, ¶50-53		
Reporting	CON1, ¶54		
. . Not-for-Profit Organizations	CON4, ¶55		
Representations in Business Combinations	APB16, ¶47	B50.106	
Stewardship	CON1, ¶50-53		
. . Not-for-Profit Organizations	CON4, ¶40-42		
MANAGEMENT CONSIGNMENT PROGRAM			
Basis of Accounting under FSLIC Program			EITF.85-41
MANUFACTURER OR DEALER LESSORS			
See Leases			
MARKET RISK			
See Financial Instruments			
MARKET VALUE			
See Current Market Value			
See Fair Value			
MARKETABLE SECURITIES			
See Financial Instruments			
See Investments: Debt and Equity Securities			
See Investments: Marketable Securities			
Balance Sheet Classification	ARB43, Ch.3A, ¶4	B05.105	
MASTER LIMITED PARTNERSHIPS			
Carryover of Predecessor Cost			EITF.87-21
Roll-up of Limited Partnerships into an MLP			
. . Gain Recognition on MLP Units Received in Exchange for Future Fees			EITF.88-14
MATCHING OF COSTS AND REVENUES			
Consumption of Benefits	CON5, ¶86		

FAS–FASB Statements FIN–FASB Interpretations FTB–FASB Technical Bulletins
APB–APB Opinions AIN–AICPA Interpretations ARB–Accounting Research Bulletins
CON–FASB Concepts EITF–EITF Issues Q&A–FASB Special Reports

T-279

See "Terminology" for references to defined terms presented in various accounting pronouncements.

See the Introduction to the Topical Index for details on the use of this index.

See "Terminology" for references to defined terms presented in various accounting pronouncements.

See the Introduction to the Topical Index for details on the use of this index.

FAS–FASB Statements   FIN–FASB Interpretations   FTB–FASB Technical Bulletins
APB–APB Opinions   AIN–AICPA Interpretations   ARB–Accounting Research Bulletins
CON–FASB Concepts   EITF–EITF Issues   Q&A–FASB Special Reports

See "Terminology" for references to defined terms presented in various accounting pronouncements.

See the Introduction to the Topical Index for details on the use of this index.

	Original Pronouncements	Current Text	EITF and Other
MORTGAGE INSURANCE			
Federal Housing Administration (FHA) Insurance			
. . Effect on Profit Recognition by Seller			EITF.87-9
Veterans Administration (VA) Mortgage Guarantee			
. . Effect on Profit Recognition by Seller			EITF.87-9
MORTGAGES			
See Loans			
MORTGAGE SERVICING RIGHTS			
Balance Sheet Treatment of a Sale of Mortgage Servicing Rights with a Subservicing Agreement			EITF.90-21
Gain from Sale of Mortgage Loan with Servicing Rights Retained			EITF.86-39
Loan Acquisitions Involving Table Funding Arrangements			EITF.92-10
Normal Servicing Fee	FTB87-3, ¶1-7	Mo4.501-507	EITF.85-26
Rights Sold But Loan Retained			EITF.84-21
Sale of Rights			
. . Participation in Future Payment Stream			EITF.85-13
. . Revenue Recognition			EITF.89-5
. . With Concurrent Subservicing Agreement			EITF.87-34
			EITF.90-21
Unanticipated Mortgage Prepayments			
. . Effect on Amortization of Servicing Rights			EITF.86-38
MOTION PICTURE INDUSTRY			
See Disclosure			
Balance Sheet Classification			
. . Classified and Unclassified Balance Sheets	FAS53, ¶20	Mo6.119	
. . Film Costs to Be Realized from Secondary Television and Other Exploitations	FAS53, ¶21	Mo6.120	
. . License Agreement for Sale of Film Rights for Television Exhibition	FAS53, ¶19	Mo6.118	
Changing Prices Information	FAS89, ¶25	C28.121	
Costs and Expenses			
. . Exploitation Costs	FAS53, ¶15	Mo6.114	
. . Individual Film Forecast Method of Amortization	FAS53, ¶11-12	Mo6.110-111	
. . Interim Financial Statements	FAS53, ¶16	Mo6.115	
. . Inventory Valuation	FAS53, ¶16	Mo6.115	
. . Participation	FAS53, ¶14	Mo6.113	
. . Periodic Table Method of Amortization	FAS53, ¶13	Mo6.112	
. . Production Costs	FAS53, ¶10	Mo6.109	
. . Story Costs and Scenarios	FAS53, ¶17	Mo6.116	

	Original Pronouncements	Current Text	EITF and Other
MOTION PICTURE INDUSTRY—continued			
Disclosure	FAS53, ¶23	Mo6.122	
Films Licensed to Movie Theaters			
. . Deferred Revenue	FAS53, ¶4	Mo6.103	
Glossary	FAS53, ¶26	C28.410	
	FAS89, ¶44	Mo6.401-413	
Home Viewing Market	FAS53, ¶22	Mo6.121	
Investments in Films Produced by Independent Producers	FAS53, ¶18	Mo6.117	
Revenue	FAS53, ¶37-39	Mo6.123-125	
. . Films Licensed to Movie Theaters	FAS53, ¶3-4	Mo6.102-103	
. . Films Licensed to Television	FAS53, ¶5-9	Mo6.104-108	
. . Individual Film Forecast Method of Amortization	FAS53, ¶40-41	Mo6.126-127	
Scope of Accounting and Reporting Requirements	FAS53, ¶1	Mo6.101	
MOTOR CARRIERS			
Extraordinary Items	FAS44, ¶7	I17.114-115	
Interstate Operating Rights			
. . Disposition and Amortization	FAS44, ¶1	I60.124-129	
	FAS44, ¶3-7		
Revenue and Expense Recognition for Freight Services in Process			EITF.91-9
MOVING COSTS			
Change from One Leased Property to Another			EITF.88-10
Reimbursements by Lessor			EITF.88-3
MULTIEMPLOYER AND MULTIPLE-EMPLOYER PENSION PLANS			
See Pension Costs			
See Postretirement Benefits Other Than Pensions			
MULTIEMPLOYER BENEFIT PLAN			
Accounting for Estimated Payments in Connection with the Coal Industry Retiree Health Benefit Act of 1992			EITF.92-13
MULTIEMPLOYER PENSION PLAN AMENDMENTS ACT OF 1980			
See Pension Costs			
MULTINATIONAL ENTERPRISES			
See Foreign Currency Translation			
MULTINATIONAL OPERATIONS			
See Foreign Currency Translation			
See Foreign Operations			
See Segment of Business Reporting			

See "Terminology" for references to defined terms presented in various accounting pronouncements.

See the Introduction to the Topical Index for details on the use of this index.

	Original Pronouncements	Current Text	EITF and Other
MUNICIPAL BOND FUNDS			
See Investment Enterprises			
MUSIC PUBLISHING			
See Record and Music Industry			
MUTUAL ENTERPRISES (MUTUAL FUNDS)			
See Business Combinations			
See Investment Enterprises			
Fees Paid to Distributors			EITF.85-24
Stock Market Decline			
. . Subsequent Events Disclosure........			EITF.D-11
U.S. Government Securities Only Held in Fund			
. . Accounting by Investor in Mutual Fund.........................			EITF.86-40
MUTUAL FUND DISTRIBUTORS			
Fees Received from No-Load Funds......			EITF.85-24
MUTUAL INSURANCE ENTERPRISE			
See Insurance Costs			
MUTUAL LIFE INSURANCE ENTERPRISES			
See Insurance Industry			
MUTUAL SAVINGS BANKS			
See Banking and Thrift Industries			
See Earnings per Share			
See Investments: Marketable Securities			
See Lending Activities			
Conversion to Stock Ownership			EITF.84-22

(The next page is T-291.)

FAS–FASB Statements   FIN–FASB Interpretations   FTB–FASB Technical Bulletins
APB–APB Opinions   AIN–AICPA Interpretations   ARB–Accounting Research Bulletins
CON–FASB Concepts   EITF–EITF Issues   Q&A–FASB Special Reports

T-287

	Original Pronouncements	Current Text	EITF and Other
NATURAL RESOURCES			
See Extractive Industries			
Balance Sheet Classification	ARB43, Ch.3A, ¶6	B05.107	
NEGATIVE GOODWILL			
See Business Combinations			
See Intangible Assets			
NET ASSETS			
See Equity (or Net Assets)			
See Not-for-Profit Organizations			
NET INCOME PER SHARE			
See Earnings per Share			
NET OPERATING LOSS CARRYFORWARDS			
See Income Taxes			
Allocating Basis to Individual Assets and Liabilities under Issue No. 88-16			EITF.90-12
Business Combinations			
. . Allocating Cost to Assets to Be Sold ..			EITF.87-11
Loan Loss Allowances			
. . Applying Savings and Loan Audit Guide			EITF.87-5
NET REALIZABLE VALUE			
See Inventory			
Definition	FAS53, ¶26	Mo6.410	
....	FAS67, ¶28	Re2.410	
Recognition and Measurement			
. . Measurement Attribute	CON5, ¶67		
NET-OF-TAX METHOD			
See Income Taxes			
NEUTRALITY			
Definition	CON2, Glossary		
Financial Reporting	CON1, ¶33		
Relation to Relevance and Reliability	CON2, ¶98-110		
NEW BASIS ACCOUNTING			
See Change in Basis of Assets and Liabilities			
NINETY PERCENT RULE			
See Business Combinations			
NOMINAL			
Definition	FTB85-2, ¶2	C30.502	
NOMINAL DOLLAR ACCOUNTING			
Measurement Scale....................	CON5, ¶71-72		
NONBUSINESS ORGANIZATIONS			
See Not-for-Profit Organizations			

FAS–FASB Statements   FIN–FASB Interpretations   FTB–FASB Technical Bulletins
APB–APB Opinions   AIN–AICPA Interpretations   ARB–Accounting Research Bulletins
CON–FASB Concepts   EITF–EITF Issues   Q&A–FASB Special Reports

T-291

See "Terminology" for references to defined terms presented in various accounting pronouncements.

See the Introduction to the Topical Index for details on the use of this index.

	Original Pronouncements	Current Text	EITF and Other
NONMONETARY TRANSACTIONS—continued			
Common Stock Contributed to Employee Stock Ownership Plan			
. . Excess Assets Not Allocated to Participants			EITF.86-27
Development Stage Enterprises	FAS7, ¶11	De4.107	
Disclosure	APB29, ¶28	N35.120	
Dividends-in-Kind			
. . Distributions of Loans Receivable to Shareholders			EITF.87-17
Equity Investments			EITF.85-43
			EITF.86-29
Exchange of Assets for Noncontrolling Equity Interest in New Entity			EITF.89-7
Exchange of Interest in Subsidiary for Noncontrolling Equity Interest in New Entity			EITF.89-7
Exchanges of Real Estate Involving Boot			EITF.87-29
Fair Value Not Determinable	APB29, ¶20	N35.107	
	APB29, ¶26	N35.112	
Federal Home Loan Mortgage Corporation (FHLMC)			
. . Distribution of FHLMC Participating Preferred Stock	FTB85-1, ¶2	Bt7.502	EITF.85-7
Glossary	APB29, ¶1	N35.401-407	
	APB29, ¶3		
Guidance in Recognizing Revenues and Gains	CON5, ¶84		
Involuntary Conversions	FIN30, ¶1	N35.114	
. . Gain or Loss	FIN30, ¶4-5	N35.118-119	
. . LIFO Inventories	FIN30, ¶11	N35.115	
. . Nonmonetary Asset Destroyed or Damaged	FIN30, ¶3	N35.117	
. . Temporary Differences	FAS109, ¶287	N35.119	
	FIN30, ¶5		
Joint Ventures			EITF.86-29
Modifications	APB29, ¶19	N35.106	
Nonmonetary Exchange of Cost-Method Investments			EITF.91-5
Nonreciprocal Transfers to Other Than Owners	APB29, ¶6	N35.103	
Nonreciprocal Transfers to Owners	APB29, ¶5	N35.102	
	APB29, ¶23	N35.110	

FAS–FASB Statements   FIN–FASB Interpretations   FTB–FASB Technical Bulletins
APB–APB Opinions   AIN–AICPA Interpretations   ARB–Accounting Research Bulletins
CON–FASB Concepts   EITF–EITF Issues   Q&A–FASB Special Reports

	Original Pronouncements	Current Text	EITF and Other
NONMONETARY TRANSACTIONS—continued			
Property Held for Sale			EITF.86-29
Receipt of FHLMC Participating			
Preferred Stock			EITF.85-7
Sale of Subsidiary			EITF.85-43
Same Line of Business			EITF.84-29
. . . .			EITF.85-43
. . . .			EITF.86-29
Scope of Accounting and Reporting			
Requirements	APB29, ¶4	N35.101	
Similar Productive Assets			EITF.84-29
. . . .			EITF.85-43
. . . .			EITF.86-29
Temporary Differences	APB29, ¶27	N35.113	
. . . .	FAS109, ¶287		
Transfer of Nonmonetary Assets to a New			
Corporation			EITF.84-39
Transfers between Entities under Common			
Control			EITF.84-39
NONOWNER CHANGES IN EQUITY			
See Comprehensive Income			
NONPROFIT ENTERPRISES			
See Not-for-Profit Organizations			
NONPUBLIC ENTERPRISE			
Definition	FAS21, ¶8	B50.404A	
. . . .	FAS21, ¶13	E09.417	
. . . .	FAS79, ¶5	S20.407	
. . . .	FAS79, ¶16		
NONRECIPROCAL TRANSFERS			
See Contributions			
See Depreciation			
See Nonmonetary Transactions			
Definition	APB29, ¶3	N35.405	
. . . .	CON6, ¶137		
Description	CON6, ¶150-151		
Dividends-in-Kind	APB29, ¶18	C11.101	
NONRECOURSE DEBT			
See Financial Instruments			
Debtor's Accounting for Forfeiture of			
Real Estate Subject to a Nonrecourse			
Mortgage			EITF.91-2
Grantor Trust			EITF.84-15
Leases			
. . Delayed Equity Contributions by			
Leveraged Lessors			EITF.85-16

See "Terminology" for references to defined terms presented in various accounting pronouncements.

See the Introduction to the Topical Index for details on the use of this index.

	Original Pronouncements	Current Text	EITF and Other
NONRECOURSE DEBT—continued			
Leases—continued			
. . Offsetting Nonrecourse Debt with			
Lease Receivables			EITF.84-25
NONRECURRING ITEMS			
See Extraordinary Items			
NOT-FOR-PROFIT ORGANIZATIONS			
See Cash Flows Statement			
See Collections—Works of Art, Historical			
Treasures, and Similar Assets			
See Contributions			
See Disclosure			
Accounting Policies	APB22, ¶9	A10.103	
Accrual vs. Cash Basis of Accounting	CON4, ¶50		
Balance Sheet	FAS117, ¶9-16	No5.107-114	
. . . .	FAS117, ¶85-86	No5.131	
. . . .	FAS117, ¶93		
. . . .	FAS117, ¶156		
. . Classification of Assets and Liabilities.	FAS117, ¶11-12	No5.109-110	
Budgets	CON4, ¶21-22		
Change in Permanently Restricted			
Net Assets	CON6, ¶119-122	No5.117	
. . . .	FAS117, ¶19		
Change in Temporarily Restricted			
Net Assets	CON6, ¶123-126	No5.117	
. . . .	FAS117, ¶19		
Change in Unrestricted Net Assets	CON6, ¶127-133	No5.117	
. . . .	FAS117, ¶19		
Changes in Classes of Net Assets	CON6, ¶117-133	No5.116-117	
. . . .	CON6, ¶223-227		
. . . .	FAS117, ¶18-19		
Characteristics.	CON4, ¶6-9		
Characteristics of Information Provided . .	CON4, ¶23-28		
Characteristics of Net Assets	CON6, ¶90-102		
. . . .	CON6, ¶221-222		
Classes of Net Assets	CON6, ¶91-102	No5.111-114	
. . . .	FAS117, ¶13-16		
Classification of Revenues, Expenses,			
Gains, and Losses	FAS116, ¶14-16	No5.118-120	
. . . .	FAS117, ¶20	No5.143-145	
. . . .	FAS117, ¶22-23		
. . . .	FAS117, ¶129		
Comparison to Business Enterprise			
Objectives.	CON4, ¶67		
Comparison with Business Enterprises	CON4, ¶6-9		
. . . .	CON4, ¶14-22		

FAS—FASB Statements	FIN—FASB Interpretations	FTB—FASB Technical Bulletins
APB—APB Opinions	AIN—AICPA Interpretations	ARB—Accounting Research Bulletins
CON—FASB Concepts	EITF—EITF Issues	Q&A—FASB Special Reports

	Original Pronouncements	Current Text	EITF and Other
NOT-FOR-PROFIT ORGANIZATIONS—continued			
Contributions Received			
. . Required Classification	FAS116, ¶14-16	No5.143-145	
. . Expiration of Donor-imposed Restrictions	FAS116, ¶17	No5.146-147	
	FAS116, ¶166		
Deferred Taxes	FAS109, ¶4	I27.103	
Donor-imposed Restrictions	CON6, ¶95-102		
. . As Basis for Classification of Net Assets	CON6, ¶101-102	No5.111-113	
	FAS117, ¶13-15		
. . As Basis for Classification of Revenues	FAS116, ¶14-16	No5.118-119	
	FAS117, ¶20	No5.143-145	
	FAS117, ¶22		
Economic Resources, Obligations, Net Resources, and Changes in Them	CON4, ¶43-54		
Elements of Financial Statements			
. . Applicability	CON6, ¶1-2		
Environmental Context, Objectives	CON4, ¶13-22		
Examples of Characteristics of Not-for-Profit Organizations	CON4, ¶7-8		
Exemption from Earnings-per-Share Requirements	APB15, ¶6	E09.102	
Expiration of Donor-imposed Restrictions	FAS116, ¶17	No5.146-147	
	FAS116, ¶166		
Functional Classification of Expenses	FAS117, ¶26-28	No5.123-125	
General Purpose External Financial Reporting	CON4, ¶10-12		
General Purpose External Financial Statements			
. . Comparative Financial Statements	FAS117, ¶70	No5.105	
	FAS117, ¶153	No5.127	
. . Illustrative Statements and Notes	FAS117, ¶153-167	No5.127-141	
. . Requirements for Complete Set	FAS117, ¶6	No5.104	
. . Statement of Activities	FAS116, ¶14-16	No5.115-125	
	FAS117, ¶17-20	No5.132-134	
	FAS117, ¶22-28	No5.137-141	
	FAS117, ¶129	No5.143-145	
	FAS117, ¶138		
	FAS117, ¶157-159		
	FAS117, ¶163-167		
. . Statement of Cash Flows	FAS117, ¶29	No5.126	
	FAS117, ¶160	No5.135	
. . Statement of Financial Position	FAS117, ¶9-16	No5.107-114	
	FAS117, ¶85-86	No5.131	
	FAS117, ¶93		
	FAS117, ¶100		
	FAS117, ¶156		
. . Statement of Functional Expenses	FAS117, ¶26-28	No5.123-125	
	FAS117, ¶161	No5.136	
Glossary	FAS116, ¶209	No5.402-414	

See "Terminology" for references to defined terms presented in various accounting pronouncements.

See the Introduction to the Topical Index for details on the use of this index.

	Original Pronouncements	Current Text	EITF and Other
NOT-FOR-PROFIT ORGANIZATIONS—continued			
Glossary—continued			
....	FAS117, ¶168		
Illustrations of Financial Statements of Not-for-Profit Organizations	FAS116, ¶141	No5.127-142	
....	FAS117, ¶100		
....	FAS117, ¶114		
....	FAS117, ¶153-167		
Information about Gross Amounts of Revenues and Expenses...............	FAS117, ¶24-25	No5.121-122	
....	FAS117, ¶138		
Information Useful in Assessing Services and Ability to Provide Service	CON4, ¶38-39	No5.123-125	
....	FAS117, ¶26-28		
Information Useful in Making Resource Allocation Decisions	CON4, ¶35-37		
Interfund Balances	FAS117, ¶85	No5.109	
Intermediate Measure of Operations	FAS117, ¶23	No5.120	
....	FAS117, ¶163-167	No5.137-141	
Limitations of Information Provided.....	CON4, ¶23-28		
Liquidity	CON4, ¶54	No5.110	
....	FAS117, ¶12		
....	FAS117, ¶93		
Management Stewardship	CON4, ¶40-42		
Managers' Explanations and Interpretations	CON4, ¶55		
Nature of Resources...................	CON4, ¶14-22		
Netting Gains and Losses..............	FAS117, ¶25	No5.122	
Netting Revenues and Expenses			
. . Investment Revenues and Related Expenses.......................	FAS117, ¶24	No5.121	
. . Special Events	FAS117, ¶138	No5.122	
Nonbusiness Organizations			
. . Change in Terminology	CON6, ¶2		
Objectives of Financial Reporting........	CON4, ¶10-12		
....	CON4, ¶33-55		

FAS—FASB Statements   FIN—FASB Interpretations   FTB—FASB Technical Bulletins
APB—APB Opinions   AIN—AICPA Interpretations   ARB—Accounting Research Bulletins
CON—FASB Concepts   EITF—EITF Issues   Q&A—FASB Special Reports

See "Terminology" for references to defined terms presented in various accounting pronouncements.

See the Introduction to the Topical Index for details on the use of this index.

(The next page is T-301.)

FAS–FASB Statements	FIN–FASB Interpretations	FTB–FASB Technical Bulletins
APB–APB Opinions	AIN–AICPA Interpretations	ARB–Accounting Research Bulletins
CON–FASB Concepts	EITF–EITF Issues	Q&A–FASB Special Reports

	Original Pronouncements	Current Text	EITF and Other

OBJECTIVES OF FINANCIAL REPORTING
See Not-for-Profit Organizations
Accrual Accounting and Cash Flows ..... CON1, ¶44-49
Amount, Timing, and Uncertainty of
  Cash Receipts........................ CON1, ¶37-39
Business Estimates by Users .... CON1, ¶48
Characteristics and Limitations.......... CON1, ¶17-23
Comparison between Not-for-Profit and
  Business Enterprises .... CON4, ¶67
Description .... CON1, ¶32-54
Earnings and Enterprise Performance .... CON1, ¶44-48
Environmental Context .... CON1, ¶9-16
Financial Reporting, General Purpose
  External .... CON1, ¶28-31
Information for Users .... CON1, ¶34-36
Liquidity, Solvency, and Funds Flow ..... CON1, ¶49
Management Performance.............. CON1, ¶50-53
Management Reporting .... CON1, ¶54
Not-for-Profit Organizations .... CON4, ¶1
  .... CON4, ¶10-12
  .... CON4, ¶33-55
Relation to Elements of Financial
  Statements .... CON6, ¶9-19
Relation to Qualitative Characteristics .... CON2, ¶21-26
Relation to Recognition and Measurement CON5, ¶10-12
Resources, Claims, and Changes in Them . CON1, ¶40-41
Users, Interests .... CON1, ¶24-27
OBLIGATIONS
See Balance Sheet Classification: Current
  Assets and Liabilities
See Commitments: Long-Term Obligations
See Contingencies
See Debt
See Debt: Product Financing
  Arrangements
See Financial Instruments
See Franchising
See Leases
Definition .... CON6, ¶35
Description .... CON6, ¶200-205
Not-for-Profit Organizations .... CON4, ¶43-54
OBSOLESCENCE
See Contingencies
See Impairment
See Inventory
See Property, Plant, and Equipment
OFF-BALANCE-SHEET FINANCING
See Commitments: Long-Term Obligations
See Consolidation
See Financial Instruments
OFF-BALANCE-SHEET RIGHTS AND OBLIGATIONS
See Financial Instruments

FAS—FASB Statements	FIN—FASB Interpretations	FTB—FASB Technical Bulletins
APB—APB Opinions	AIN—AICPA Interpretations	ARB—Accounting Research Bulletins
CON—FASB Concepts	EITF—EITF Issues	Q&A—FASB Special Reports

See "Terminology" for references to defined terms presented in various accounting pronouncements.

See the Introduction to the Topical Index for details on the use of this index.

	Original Pronouncements	Current Text	EITF and Other
OFFSETTING—continued			
Offsetting Securities against Taxes Payable	APB10, ¶7	B10.102-103	
Securities Purchased by Third Party with Funds Loaned by Issuer			EITF.86-18
. . . .			EITF.87-20
Treatment in Specific Circumstances	FIN39, ¶7	B10.107	
OIL AND GAS PRODUCING ACTIVITIES			
See Disclosure			
See Extractive Industries			
Accounting at Time Costs Are Incurred			
. . Acquisition of Properties.	FAS19, ¶15	Oi5.106	
. . Capitalization of Interest.	FIN33, ¶2	I67.108	
. . Development	FAS19, ¶21-22	Oi5.112-113	
. . Exploration.	FAS19, ¶16-18	Oi5.107-109	
. . Exploratory Wells.	FAS19, ¶19	Oi5.110	
. . Geological and Geophysical Costs in Exchange for an Interest	FAS19, ¶20	Oi5.111	
. . Production Costs	FAS19, ¶23-25	Oi5.114-116	
. . Support Equipment and Facilities	FAS19, ¶26	Oi5.117	
Accounting Changes.	FAS25, ¶4	Oi5.102	
Accounting for Gas-Balancing Arrangements			EITF.90-22
. . Disclosure by SEC Registrants			EITF.90-22
. . Entitlements Method			EITF.90-22
. . Sales Method			EITF.90-22
Capitalizing Interest under Full Cost Method.	FIN33, ¶2	I67.108	
Definition			
. . Complete Set of Financial Statements .	FAS69, ¶1	Oi5.400	
. . . .	FAS95, ¶152		
. . Development Well	FAS19, ¶274	Oi5.401	
. . Exploratory Well	FAS19, ¶274	Oi5.402	
. . Field	FAS19, ¶272	Oi5.403	
. . Foreign Geographic Area	FAS69, ¶12	Oi5.403A	
. . Industry Segment	FAS69, ¶8	Oi5.403B	
. . Oil and Gas Producing Activities	FAS19, ¶1	Oi5.403C	
. . Proved Area	FAS19, ¶275	Oi5.404	
. . Proved Reserves	FAS25, ¶34	Oi5.405	
. . Publicly Traded Enterprise	FAS69, ¶1	Oi5.405A	
. . Reservoir.	FAS19, ¶273	Oi5.406	
. . Service Well	FAS19, ¶274	Oi5.407	
. . Stratigraphic Test Well	FAS19, ¶274	Oi5.408	
Disposition of Capitalized Costs	FAS19, ¶27	Oi5.118	
. . Accounting When Drilling of an Exploratory Well Is Completed	FAS19, ¶31-32	Oi5.122-123	
. . Accounting When Drilling of an Exploratory-Type Stratigraphic Well Is Completed	FAS19, ¶33-34	Oi5.124-125	
. . Assessment of Unproved Properties. . .	FAS19, ¶28	Oi5.119	
. . Costs Relating to Oil and Gas Reserves Produced Jointly	FAS19, ¶38	Oi5.129	
. . Dismantlement Costs and Salvage Values	FAS19, ¶37	Oi5.128	

FAS—FASB Statements   FIN—FASB Interpretations   FTB—FASB Technical Bulletins
APB—APB Opinions   AIN—AICPA Interpretations   ARB—Accounting Research Bulletins
CON—FASB Concepts   EITF—EITF Issues   Q&A—FASB Special Reports

See "Terminology" for references to defined terms presented in various accounting pronouncements.

See the Introduction to the Topical Index for details on the use of this index.

	Original Pronouncements	Current Text	EITF and Other

OPERATING INCOME
See Changing Prices: Reporting Their
  Effects in Financial Reports
See Income Statement Presentation:
  Discontinued Operations
See Oil and Gas Producing Activities
See Segment of Business Reporting

OPERATING LEASES
See Leases

**OPERATING LOSS CARRYBACKS
  AND CARRYFORWARDS**
See Extraordinary Items
See Income Taxes

OPERATING LOSSES
See Income Taxes

OPTIONS
See Compensation to Employees: Stock
  Purchase and Stock Option Plans
See Earnings per Share
See Financial Instruments
See Stock Options

	Original Pronouncements	Current Text	EITF and Other
Business Combinations	AIN-APB16, #32	B50.624-626	
Call Options on Debt Securities			
. . Fee for Waiving Call Provision			EITF.86-18
Comparison with Futures Contracts	FAS80, ¶32	F80.101	
Convertible Debt with a Premium Put			EITF.85-29
Currency Options			
. . Hedging Currency Risks with Complex Options and Similar Transactions			EITF.91-4
. . Hedging Foreign Currency Risks with Purchased Options			EITF.90-17
Definition	APB15, App.D	E09.418	
Nonapplicability of Futures Contracts Accounting and Reporting Requirements	FAS80, ¶32	F80.101	
Put Option for Stock Purchased with Warrants			EITF.86-35
Put Option to Satisfy Debt with Asset			EITF.84-11
Real Estate Purchases	FAS66, ¶7	R10.110	
	FAS66, ¶26	R10.128	
	FAS66, ¶32	R10.135	
		Re1.107	
		Re1.126	
		Re1.132	
Real Estate Sales			EITF.86-6
Repurchase Options			
. . Sale-Leaseback Transactions Involving Real Estate	FAS98, ¶11	L10.130G	EITF.84-37
Sale of Put Options on Issuer's Stock			EITF.87-31

FAS–FASB Statements FIN–FASB Interpretations FTB–FASB Technical Bulletins
APB–APB Opinions AIN–AICPA Interpretations ARB–Accounting Research Bulletins
CON–FASB Concepts EITF–EITF Issues Q&A–FASB Special Reports

	Original Pronouncements	Current Text	EITF and Other

ORGANIZATION COSTS
See Development Stage Enterprises
ORIGINATION COSTS
See Mortgage Banking Activities
OTHER MEANS OF FINANCIAL REPORTING
Relation to Recognition in Financial
Statements . . . .   CON5, ¶7-9
OTHER NONOWNER CHANGES IN EQUITY
See Comprehensive Income
OTHER POSTEMPLOYMENT BENEFITS
See Postemployment Benefits
Not Included in Accounting for
Postretirement Benefits Other Than
Pensions . . . .   FAS106, ¶1   P40.101
. . . .   FAS112, ¶4
OUTSTANDING SHARES
See Capital Stock: Preferred Stock
See Capital Stock: Stock Dividends and
Stock Splits
See Earnings per Share
OVERFUNDED PENSION PLANS
See Pension Costs
OVERSEAS OPERATIONS
See Foreign Currency Translation
See Foreign Operations
See Segment of Business Reporting
OWNERS' EQUITY
See Shareholders' Equity

(The next page is T-311.)

See ''Terminology'' for references to defined terms presented in various accounting pronouncements.
See the Introduction to the Topical Index for details on the use of this index.

	Original Pronouncements	Current Text	EITF and Other

PAID ABSENCES
See Compensation to Employees: Paid
  Absences
PAID-IN CAPITAL
See Additional Paid-in Capital
See Capital Stock: Capital Transactions
See Compensation to Employees: Stock
  Purchase and Stock Option Plans
PAID-IN SURPLUS
See Additional Paid-in Capital
See Capital Stock: Capital Transactions
See Compensation to Employees: Stock
  Purchase and Stock Option Plans
PAR VALUE
See Capital Stock: Capital Transactions
See Capital Stock: Preferred Stock
See Capital Stock: Stock Dividends and
  Stock Splits
See Capital Stock: Treasury Stock
PARENT COMPANY
Purchase of Subsidiary's Preferred Stock .   EITF.86-32

	Original Pronouncements	Current Text	EITF and Other
Related Parties	FAS57, ¶1	R36.101	

PARENT COMPANY STATEMENTS
See Consolidation
See Earnings per Share
See Investments: Equity Method
PARITY ADJUSTMENT

	Original Pronouncements	Current Text	EITF and Other
Changing Prices Information	FAS89, ¶39	C28.135	
	FAS89, ¶95	C28.190	
Definition	FAS89, ¶44	C28.411	

PART PURCHASE/PART POOLING
See Business Combinations
PARTICIPATING SECURITIES
See Earnings per Share
See Financial Instruments
PARTICIPATION LOAN AGREEMENTS
See Financial Instruments
See Lending Activities
See Loans
See Mortgage Banking Activities
PARTNERSHIPS
See Investments: Equity Method
Accounting for Tax Benefits Resulting
  from Investments in Qualified
  Affordable Housing Projects EITF.94-1
Classification of Payment Made to IRS to
  Retain Fiscal Year EITF.88-4
Election to Retain Fiscal Year
. . Classification of Payment Made to
   IRS EITF.88-4

FAS–FASB Statements   FIN–FASB Interpretations   FTB–FASB Technical Bulletins
APB–APB Opinions   AIN–AICPA Interpretations   ARB–Accounting Research Bulletins
CON–FASB Concepts   EITF–EITF Issues   Q&A–FASB Special Reports

T-311

	Original Pronouncements	Current Text	EITF and Other

See "Terminology" for references to defined terms presented in various accounting pronouncements.

See the Introduction to the Topical Index for details on the use of this index.

	Original Pronouncements	Current Text	EITF and Other
PENSION COSTS—continued			
Accumulated Benefit Obligation.........	FAS87, ¶18	P16.112	Q&A.87 #47-49
....	FAS87, ¶47-48	P16.143-144	Q&A.87 #59
....			Q&A.87 #64
Actuarial Cost Method			
. . Projected-Unit Credit	FAS87, ¶40	P16.134	
. . Unit Credit.......................	FAS87, ¶40	P16.134	
. . Unit Credit with Service Prorate	FAS87, ¶40	P16.134	
Additional Minimum Liability	FAS87, ¶36-38	P16.130-133	Q&A.87 #30
....	FAS87, ¶49	P16.145	Q&A.87 #34
....	FAS87, ¶52	P16.148	Q&A.87 #36-43
....	FAS109, ¶287		Q&A.87 #78
Annuity Contracts	FAS87, ¶54	P16.150	Q&A.87 #82
....	FAS87, ¶57-62	P16.154-159	Q&A.88 #6-13
....	FAS88, ¶5	P16.178-179	Q&A.88 #16-17
....	FAS88, ¶10		Q&A.88 #44
. . Insurance Companies Fail to Provide Annuity Benefits			EITF.91-7
Asset Reversions from Termination of a Defined Benefit Pension Plan.........			EITF.86-27
Asset Reversions of a Defined Benefit Pension Plan	FAS88, ¶20	P16.188	Q&A.88 #38
....			Q&A.88 #65
....			Q&A.88 #67-70
Assumptions.........................	FAS87, ¶13-14	P16.107-108	
....	FAS87, ¶43-48	P16.137-144	
....	FAS87, ¶174		
....	FAS87, ¶196		
....	FAS87, ¶198-201		
. . Anticipation of Retroactive Plan Amendments	FAS87, ¶41	P16.135	Q&A.87 #13
....			Q&A.87 #53
. . Benefit Limitations	FAS87, ¶46-48	P16.142-144	Q&A.87 #63-64
. . Discount Rates....................	FAS87, ¶44	P16.138	Q&A.87 #55-61
....	FAS106, ¶186		Q&A.88 #32-33
....	FAS106, ¶188		
. . Expected Long-Term Rate of Return on Plan Assets	FAS87, ¶44-45	P16.138	Q&A.87 #60
....		P16.141	Q&A.87 #62
. . Future Compensation Levels	FAS87, ¶46	P16.142	Q&A.87 #54
Attribution	FAS87, ¶15	P16.109	
....	FAS87, ¶40-42	P16.134-136	
....	FAS87, ¶127		
....	FAS87, ¶168		
. . Benefit/Years-of-Service Approach ...	FAS87, ¶40	P16.134	
Automatic Benefit Increases	FAS87, ¶48	P16.144	
Basic Elements of Pension Accounting ...	FAS87, ¶13-19	P16.106-113	
....	FAS87, ¶95		
....	FAS87, ¶191		

FAS—FASB Statements FIN—FASB Interpretations FTB—FASB Technical Bulletins
APB—APB Opinions AIN—AICPA Interpretations ARB—Accounting Research Bulletins
CON—FASB Concepts EITF—EITF Issues Q&A—FASB Special Reports

	Original Pronouncements	Current Text	EITF and Other
PENSION COSTS—continued			
Business Combinations	FAS87, ¶74-75	B50.146	Q&A.87 #15
. . . .			Q&A.87 #35
. . . .			Q&A.87 #39-40
. . . .			Q&A.87 #74
. . . .			Q&A.87 #88-94
Combining/Dividing Pension Plans			Q&A.87 #80-81
Components (of Net Periodic Pension Cost of a Defined Benefit Pension Plan)			
. . Actual Return on Plan Assets	FAS87, ¶16	P16.110	
. . . .	FAS87, ¶20	P16.114	
. . Gain or Loss (Component)	FAS87, ¶16	P16.110	
. . . .	FAS87, ¶20	P16.114	
. . Interest (Cost)	FAS87, ¶16	P16.110	Q&A.87 #6
. . . .	FAS87, ¶20-22	P16.114-116	Q&A.87 #45
. . . .	FAS87, ¶54	P16.150	
. . Service Cost (Component)	FAS87, ¶16	P16.110	
. . . .	FAS87, ¶20-21	P16.114-115	
. . . .	FAS87, ¶54	P16.150	
. . Unrecognized Net Obligation or Net Asset	FAS87, ¶20	P16.114	
. . Unrecognized Prior Service Cost	FAS87, ¶16	P16.110	
. . . .	FAS87, ¶20	P16.114	
Contractual Termination Benefits	FAS88, ¶15	P16.185	Q&A.88 #59-60
Curtailment (of a Defined Benefit Pension Plan)			
. . Accounting for	FAS88, ¶6-8	P16.173-175	Q&A.88 #27-29
. . . .	FAS88, ¶12-14	P16.182-184	Q&A.88 #39-41
. . . .			Q&A.88 #47-58
. . . .			Q&A.88 #63-64
. . Occurrence of	FAS88, ¶6-7	P16.173-174	Q&A.88 #14-15
. . . .			Q&A.88 #18-24
. . . .			Q&A.88 #26
Death and Disability Benefits			Q&A.87 #2
Deferred Compensation Contracts	FAS87, ¶7	P16.101	Q&A.87 #3
Defined Contribution Plan	FAS87, ¶63-66	P16.160-163	EITF.86-27
Delayed Vesting	FAS87, ¶42	P16.136	
Discount Rate	FAS87, ¶44	P16.138	
. . . .	FAS87, ¶49	P16.145	
. . . .	FAS87, ¶54	P16.150	
. . . .	FAS106, ¶186		
. . . .	FAS106, ¶188		
. . Guidance for SEC Registrants			EITF.D-36
Disposal of a Business Segment			Q&A.87 #100
. . Curtailment			Q&A.88 #15
. . . .			Q&A.88 #27-28
. . . .			Q&A.88 #39
. . Gain (Loss) from a Settlement or Curtailment of a Defined Benefit Pension Plan	FAS88, ¶16	P16.186	Q&A.88 #25

See "Terminology" for references to defined terms presented in various accounting pronouncements.

See the Introduction to the Topical Index for details on the use of this index.

	Original Pronouncements	Current Text	EITF and Other
PENSION COSTS—continued			
Disposal of a Business Segment—continued			
. . Settlement of a Pension Benefit Obligation			Q&A.88 #15
. . . .			Q&A.88 #27-28
. . . .			Q&A.88 #37
. . . .			Q&A.88 #39
. . Special Termination Benefits			Q&A.88 #61
. . Termination Indemnities			Q&A.88 #60
Early Application of Statement 87			Q&A.87 #60
. . . .			Q&A.87 #90-92
. . . .			Q&A.87 #94-97
Effective Dates of Statement 87			Q&A.87 #90-92
. . . .			Q&A.87 #94
. . . .			Q&A.87 #99
. . . .			Q&A.87 #101
Employers with Two or More Plans	FAS87, ¶55-56	P16.152-153	Q&A.87 #26
. . . .			Q&A.87 #49
. . . .			Q&A.87 #70
. . . .			Q&A.87 #73
. . . .			Q&A.87 #80-81
Excess Benefit (Top-Hat) Pension Plan . . .	FAS87, ¶46	P16.142	Q&A.87 #49
. . . .			Q&A.87 #73
Excise Tax			
. . Excess Plan Assets	FAS88, ¶20	P16.188	Q&A.88 #66
Federal Executive Agencies			Q&A.87 #1
Flat-Benefit Pension Plan	FAS87, ¶10	P16.134	Q&A.87 #44
. . . .			Q&A.87 #51
Funded Status Reconciliation	FAS87, ¶54	P16.150	
. . (Additional) Minimum Liability	FAS87, ¶54	P16.150	
. . Projected Benefit Obligation	FAS87, ¶54	P16.150	
. . Unrecognized Net Gain or Loss	FAS87, ¶54	P16.150	
. . Unrecognized Net Obligation or Net Asset	FAS87, ¶54	P16.150	
. . Unrecognized Prior Service Cost	FAS87, ¶54	P16.150	
Future Compensation Levels	FAS87, ¶46	P16.142	
Gains and Losses	FAS87, ¶29-34	P16.123-128	
. . Immediate Recognition			Q&A.87 #33
. . Minimum Amortization	FAS87, ¶32-33	P16.126-127	Q&A.87 #16-18
. . . .			Q&A.87 #31-32
. . Substantive Commitment			Q&A.87 #13
Glossary	FAS87, ¶57	P16.401-466	
. . . .	FAS87, ¶264		
. . . .	FAS88, ¶3		
. . . .	FAS88, ¶5-6		

FAS—FASB Statements   FIN—FASB Interpretations   FTB—FASB Technical Bulletins
APB—APB Opinions   AIN—AICPA Interpretations   ARB—Accounting Research Bulletins
CON—FASB Concepts   EITF—EITF Issues   Q&A—FASB Special Reports

T-315

See "Terminology" for references to defined terms presented in various accounting pronouncements.
See the Introduction to the Topical Index for details on the use of this index.

	Original Pronouncements	Current Text	EITF and Other
PENSION COSTS—continued			
Measurement of Cost and Obligations—continued			
. . Projected Benefit Obligation Less Than Accumulated Benefit Obligation	FAS87, ¶42	P16.136	Q&A.87 #48
. . Substantive Commitment	FAS87, ¶41	P16.135	Q&A.87 #13
			Q&A.87 #52
Multiemployer Pension Plans	FAS87, ¶67-70	P16.164-167	Q&A.87 #86-87
. . Accounting for Employers' Obligations for Future Contributions			EITF.90-3
. . Withdrawal from			Q&A.88 #26
Multiple-Employer Plans	FAS87, ¶71	P16.168	
Net Periodic Pension Income	FAS87, ¶16	P16.110	Q&A.87 #7-9
	FAS87, ¶20	P16.114	
Non-U.S. Pension Plans	FAS87, ¶56	P16.153	Q&A.87 #2
	FAS87, ¶72-73	P16.169-170	Q&A.87 #94
			Q&A.87 #96
			Q&A.87 #99
Nonbenefit Liabilities	FAS87, ¶54	P16.150	Q&A.87 #72
Nonpublic Enterprise			Q&A.87 #99
Nonqualified Pension Plan			Q&A.87 #11
			Q&A.87 #49
			Q&A.87 #73
Plan Amendments	FAS87, ¶24-28	P16.118-122	Q&A.87 #14-15
			Q&A.87 #44
. . Adding Health Care and Life Insurance Benefits			EITF.86-19
. . Amortization of Prior Service Cost	FAS87, ¶24-26	P16.118-120	Q&A.87 #14
			Q&A.87 #16-21
. . Anticipation of Plan Amendments	FAS87, ¶27	P16.121	Q&A.87 #13
	FAS87, ¶41	P16.135	Q&A.87 #52-53
. . History of Regular Plan Amendments	FAS87, ¶27	P16.121	Q&A.87 #20
. . Negative Amendment (Reduced Benefits)	FAS87, ¶28	P16.122	Q&A.87 #21-23
. . Recognition of Prior Service Cost in a Curtailment	FAS88, ¶3-4	P16.172-174	Q&A.88 #47-48
. . Successor Pension Plan	FAS88, ¶6-7	P16.182	Q&A.88 #14
	FAS88, ¶12		Q&A.88 #23
			Q&A.88 #26
Plan Assets	FAS87, ¶19	P16.113	
. . Asset Gains and Losses	FAS87, ¶31	P16.125	
	FAS87, ¶54	P16.150	
. . Classes of Assets	FAS87, ¶30	P16.124	Q&A.87 #27
. . Employer-Issued Securities	FAS87, ¶19	P16.113	Q&A.87 #10
. . Employer-Issued Securities Withdrawn from Pension Plan	FAS88, ¶9	P16.187	Q&A.88 #34
. . Expected (Long-Term Rate of) Return on Plan Assets	FAS87, ¶30	P16.124	
	FAS87, ¶45	P16.141	
	FAS87, ¶54	P16.150	

FAS—FASB Statements   FIN—FASB Interpretations   FTB—FASB Technical Bulletins
APB—APB Opinions   AIN—AICPA Interpretations   ARB—Accounting Research Bulletins
CON—FASB Concepts   EITF—EITF Issues   Q&A—FASB Special Reports

See "Terminology" for references to defined terms presented in various accounting pronouncements.

See the Introduction to the Topical Index for details on the use of this index.

	Original Pronouncements	Current Text	EITF and Other
PENSION COSTS—continued			
Related Party Transaction—continued			
....			Q&A.88 #17
Scope of Accounting and Reporting			
Requirements.......................	FAS87, ¶7-8	P16.101-104	
....	FAS87, ¶10-11	P16.171	
....	FAS88, ¶2		
....	FAS88, ¶45		
....	FAS106, ¶14		
Selection of Discount Rate to Be Used to Measure Obligation.................			EITF.D-36
Service Cost Component (of Net Periodic Pension Cost)....................	FAS87, ¶46	P16.142	
Settlement of a Defined Benefit Pension Plan			
. . Accounting for....................	FAS88, ¶5	P16.177-181	Q&A.88 #17
....	FAS88, ¶9-11		Q&A.88 #27-46
....	FAS88, ¶21		Q&A.88 #63-64
....	FAS88, ¶34		
. . Accounting for Pension Benefits Paid by Employers after Insurance Companies Fail to Provide Annuity Benefits........................			EITF.91-7
. . Occurrence of....................	FAS88, ¶3-4	P16.172	Q&A.88 #1-3
....			Q&A.88 #6-15
....			Q&A.88 #40
Significant Reduction of Expected Years of Future Service of Present Employees			
. . Threshold for....................	FAS88, ¶6	P16.447	Q&A.88 #18
Spinoff............................			Q&A.88 #40
State and Local Governmental Units.....			Q&A.87 #1
Successor Pension Plan................	FAS88, ¶7	P16.174	Q&A.88 #14
....			Q&A.88 #23-24
....			Q&A.88 #26
Temporary Suspension of Pension Benefit Accruals..........................			Q&A.88 #20
....			Q&A.88 #49
Termination Benefits of a Defined Benefit Pension Plan			
. . Accounting for....................	FAS88, ¶15	P16.185	Q&A.88 #54
....			Q&A.88 #57-63
Termination Indemnities..............	FAS87, ¶73	P16.170	Q&A.88 #60
Termination of a Defined Benefit Pension Plan			
. . Asset Reversions Contributed to Defined Contribution Plan.........			EITF.86-27
. . Asset Reversions Contributed to ESOP..........................			EITF.86-27
. . Between Measurement Date and Financial Report Date............			Q&A.88 #28
. . Contribution of Excess Plan Assets to Defined Contribution Pension Plan .			Q&A.88 #29
. . Employees Continue to Work for Employer.......................			Q&A.88 #48

FAS–FASB Statements	FIN–FASB Interpretations	FTB–FASB Technical Bulletins
APB–APB Opinions	AIN–AICPA Interpretations	ARB–Accounting Research Bulletins
CON–FASB Concepts	EITF–EITF Issues	Q&A–FASB Special Reports

T-319

	Original Pronouncements	Current Text	EITF and Other
PENSION COSTS—continued			
Termination of a Defined Benefit Pension Plan—continued			
. . Employer-Issued Securities Withdrawn from Pension Plan			Q&A.88 #34
. . Extraordinary Item			Q&A.88 #64
. . Pension Plan Amended to Provide for Its Termination or Suspension			Q&A.88 #56
. . Regulatory Approval			Q&A.88 #1-2
. . Settlement and Curtailment Effects Recognized in Different Periods			Q&A.88 #27
. . Successor Pension Plan			Q&A.88 #14
. . . .			Q&A.88 #23-24
. . . .			Q&A.88 #26
Transfer of a Pension Benefit Obligation or Plan Assets	FAS88, ¶3-4	P16.172-173	Q&A.88 #15
. . . .	FAS88, ¶6		Q&A.88 #40
Transition Requirements	FAS87, ¶20	P16.114	Q&A.88 #58
. . . .	FAS87, ¶77	P16.177	Q&A.88 #62
. . . .	FAS88, ¶9	P16.188	Q&A.88 #65
. . . .	FAS88, ¶20-21		Q&A.88 #67-70
Types of Pension Plans	FAS87, ¶17	P16.111	
. . Career-Average-Pay	FAS87, ¶17	P16.111	
. . . .	FAS87, ¶40-41	P16.134-135	
. . Contributory Pension Plan			Q&A.87 #16
. . Final-Average-Pay	FAS87, ¶17	P16.111	
. . Final-Pay	FAS87, ¶17	P16.111	
. . . .	FAS87, ¶40	P16.134	
. . Flat-Benefit (Non-Pay-Related)	FAS87, ¶17	P16.111	
. . . .	FAS87, ¶40-41	P16.134-135	
. . Pay-Related	FAS87, ¶17	P16.111	
. . Target Benefit	FAS87, ¶66	P16.163	
Unfunded Accrued or Prepaid Pension Costs	FAS87, ¶35	P16.129	Q&A.87 #34
			Q&A.87 #103
Unfunded Accumulated Benefit Obligation	FAS87, ¶36	P16.130	
Unrecognized Net Asset or Net Obligation at Transition to Statement 88	FAS88, ¶9	P16.177	Q&A.88 #35-36
. . . .	FAS88, ¶12-13	P16.182-183	Q&A.88 #50-53
. . . .	FAS88, ¶20	P16.188	Q&A.88 #68-69
Unrecognized Net Asset/Obligation at Date of Initial Application of Statement 87			
. . Amortization	FAS87, ¶24-26	P16.114	Q&A.87 #16-18
. . . .	FAS87, ¶32	P16.118-120	Q&A.87 #102
. . . .	FAS87, ¶77	P16.126	Q&A.87 #105-107

See "Terminology" for references to defined terms presented in various accounting pronouncements.

See the Introduction to the Topical Index for details on the use of this index.

FAS—FASB Statements	FIN—FASB Interpretations	FTB—FASB Technical Bulletins
APB—APB Opinions	AIN—AICPA Interpretations	ARB—Accounting Research Bulletins
CON—FASB Concepts	EITF—EITF Issues	Q&A—FASB Special Reports

T-321

	Original Pronouncements	Current Text	EITF and Other
PENSION FUNDS			
See Defined Benefit Pension Plans			
PENSION LIABILITIES			
See Pension Costs			
PENSION PLANS			
See Defined Benefit Pension Plans			
See Employee Benefit Plans			
See Pension Costs			
See Postretirement Health Care and Life Insurance Benefits			
See Related Parties			
Definition	FAS35, ¶280	Pe5.419	
PENSION REFORM ACT OF 1974			
See Defined Benefit Pension Plans			
See ERISA			
PENSION TRUSTS			
See Pension Costs			
PERCENTAGE-OF-COMPLETION METHOD			
See Contractor Accounting: Construction-Type Contracts			
See Real Estate: Sales Other Than Retail Land Sales			
PERFORMANCE			
See Earnings			
See Earnings Summaries			
See Financial Reporting			
See Management			
See Return on Investment			
Not-for-Profit Organizations	CON4, ¶47-53		
PER SHARE DIVIDENDS			
See Capital Stock: Dividends-in-Kind			
See Capital Stock: Stock Dividends and Stock Splits			
See Dividends			
See Earnings per Share			
PER SHARE EARNINGS			
See Earnings per Share			

See "Terminology" for references to defined terms presented in various accounting pronouncements.

See the Introduction to the Topical Index for details on the use of this index.

	Original Pronouncements	Current Text	EITF and Other

PERSONAL HOLDING COMPANY
See Business Combinations
See Investments: Marketable Securities
PERSONAL PROPERTY TAXES
See Tax
PERSONNEL COSTS
See Compensation to Employees: Deferred
See Compensation to Employees: Paid
  Absences
See Compensation to Employees: Stock
  Purchase and Stock Option Plans
PERSONNEL RETIREMENT PLANS
See Defined Benefit Pension Plans
See Pension Costs
PETROLEUM INDUSTRY
See Oil and Gas Producing Activities
PHANTOM STOCK PLANS
See Compensation to Employees: Stock
  Purchase and Stock Option Plans
PHASE-IN PLAN
See Regulated Operations
PHYSICAL CAPITAL MAINTENANCE
  CONCEPT
See Capital Maintenance
PILOT PLANT
See Research and Development
PIPELINE ENTERPRISES
See Oil and Gas Producing Activities
Advances to Encourage Exploration
. . Interest: Imputation of an Interest

	Original Pronouncements	Current Text	EITF and Other
Cost	AIN-APB21, #1	I69.501	

See "Terminology" for references to defined terms presented in various accounting pronouncements.

See the Introduction to the Topical Index for details on the use of this index.

	Original Pronouncements	Current Text	EITF and Other
POSTRETIREMENT BENEFITS OTHER THAN PENSIONS			
See Disclosure			
Accounting Change			
. . Amortization Method	FAS106, ¶59-60	P40.154-155	Q&A.106 #32
. . Changing from One-Plan Accounting to Two-Plan Accounting	FAS106, ¶76	P40.171	Q&A.106 #42
. . Effect of Implementation Guidance for Employers that Previously Adopted Statement 106	FAS106, ¶108	P40.141	Q&A.106 #55
. . . .	FAS106, ¶110		
. . Transition Method	FAS106, ¶110	P40.141	Q&A.106 #58
Accounting for Estimated Payments in Connection with the Coal Industry Retiree Health Benefit Act of 1992			EITF.92-13
Accounting for OPEB Costs by Rate-Regulated Enterprises.			EITF.92-12
. . . .			EITF.93-4
Accounting for the Transfer of Excess Pension Assets to a Retiree Health Care Benefits Account			EITF.D-27
Accumulated Postretirement Benefit Obligation	FAS106, ¶21	P40.114	
. . . .	FAS106, ¶168		
. . Assumed in a Business Combination . .	FAS106, ¶86	B50.146	
. . Benefits Covered by Insurance Contracts	FAS106, ¶67	P40.162	
. . Illustration	FAS106, ¶392-396	P40.204-208	
. . . .	FAS106, ¶418-419	P40.226-227	
. . Measurement of	FAS106, ¶21	P40.114	
. . . .	FAS106, ¶28	P40.121	
. . . .	FAS106, ¶30-31	P40.123-126	
. . . .	FAS106, ¶33	P40.128	
. . . .	FAS106, ¶48	P40.143	
. . . .	FAS106, ¶50	P40.145	
. . . .	FAS106, ¶174		
. . . .	FAS106, ¶194-195		
. . Reduction of.	FAS106, ¶55	P40.150	Q&A.106 #24-25
. . . .	FAS106, ¶98-99	P40.190-191	
. . Settlement of	FAS106, ¶93	P40.185	
Administration Costs	FAS106, ¶36	P40.131	
Aggregating Data for Measurement Purposes.	FAS106, ¶75-76	P40.170-171	
. . . .	FAS106, ¶357		
Assumptions (Actuarial)	FAS106, ¶19	P40.112	
. . . .	FAS106, ¶29-42	P40.122-137	
. . . .	FAS106, ¶73	P40.168	
. . . .	FAS106, ¶194-195		
. . Active Employee Contributions	FAS106, ¶30	P40.123	Q&A.106 #9
. . . .	FAS106, ¶35	P40.130	
. . Administration Costs	FAS106, ¶36	P40.131	

FAS–FASB Statements   FIN–FASB Interpretations   FTB–FASB Technical Bulletins
APB–APB Opinions   AIN–AICPA Interpretations   ARB–Accounting Research Bulletins
CON–FASB Concepts   EITF–EITF Issues   Q&A–FASB Special Reports

	Original Pronouncements	Current Text	EITF and Other
POSTRETIREMENT BENEFITS OTHER THAN PENSIONS—continued			
Assumptions (Actuarial)—continued			
. . (Assumed) per Capita Claims Cost			
(by Age)	FAS106, ¶30	P40.123	
. . . .	FAS106, ¶34-38	P40.129-133	
. . . .	FAS106, ¶41	P40.136	
. . . .	FAS106, ¶197		
. . Discount Rates	FAS106, ¶30-31	P16.138	Q&A.106 #8
. . . .	FAS106, ¶42	P40.123	Q&A.106 #40
. . . .	FAS106, ¶48	P40.126	
. . . .	FAS106, ¶186	P40.137	
. . . .	FAS106, ¶188	P40.143	
. . Effects of Changes in Assumptions . . .	FAS106, ¶45-46	P40.140-141	
. . . .	FAS106, ¶56	P40.151	
. . . .	FAS106, ¶59-60	P40.154-155	
. . Expected Long-Term Rate of Return			
on Plan Assets	FAS106, ¶32	P40.127	
. . . .	FAS106, ¶56-58	P40.151-153	
. . Future Compensation Levels	FAS106, ¶30	P40.123	
. . . .	FAS106, ¶33	P40.128	
. . . .	FAS106, ¶42	P40.137	
. . Health Care Cost Trend Rates	FAS106, ¶30	P40.123	Q&A.106 #11
. . . .	FAS106, ¶36-39	P40.131-134	
. . . .	FAS106, ¶41-42	P40.136-137	
. . Medicare Reimbursement	FAS106, ¶40	P40.135	Q&A.106 #13
. . Unique to Postretirement Health Care			
Benefits.	FAS106, ¶34-42	P40.129-137	
Attribution	FAS106, ¶19	P40.112	Q&A.106 #14-22
. . . .	FAS106, ¶29	P40.122	
. . . .	FAS106, ¶43-44	P40.138-139	
. . . .	FAS106, ¶47	P40.142	
. . . .	FAS106, ¶135		
. . . .	FAS106, ¶200		
. . . .	FAS106, ¶227		
. . Accrual of Annual Service Cost	FAS106, ¶44	P40.139	Q&A.106 #12
. . . .	FAS106, ¶46-47	P40.141-142	Q&A.106 #21
. . Change in Credited Service Period	FAS106, ¶44	P40.139	Q&A.106 #14
. . . .	FAS106, ¶55	P40.150	Q&A.106 Ex. 5
. . . .	FAS106, ¶96-99	P40.188-191	
. . Determining the Attribution Period or			
Pattern	FAS106, ¶9	C38.101-101A	Q&A.106 #4-5
. . . .	FAS106, ¶13	P40.105	Q&A.106 #14-22
. . . .	FAS106, ¶43-44	P40.138-139	
. . . .	FAS106, ¶47	P40.142	
. . . .	FAS106, ¶411-412	P40.223-224	
. . Determining the Full Eligibility Date . .	FAS106, ¶21	P40.114	Q&A.106 #15-17
. . . .	FAS106, ¶43-44	P40.138-139	
. . Frontloaded Plan	FAS106, ¶21	P40.114	Q&A.106 #17-18
. . . .	FAS106, ¶43-44	P40.138-139	
. . . .	FAS106, ¶412	P40.224	
. . Effect of Nontrivial Incremental			
Benefits.	FAS106, ¶21	P40.114	Q&A.106 #15
. . . .	FAS106, ¶43-44	P40.138-139	Q&A.106 #17
. . . .	FAS106, ¶398-401	P40.210-213	

See "Terminology" for references to defined terms presented in various accounting pronouncements.

See the Introduction to the Topical Index for details on the use of this index.

	Original Pronouncements	Current Text	EITF and Other
POSTRETIREMENT BENEFITS OTHER THAN PENSIONS—continued			
Attribution—continued			
. . Illustration	FAS106, ¶409-412	P40.221-228	
. . Nominal Credited Service Period	FAS106, ¶44	P40.139	Q&A.106 #21-22
	FAS106, ¶47	P40.142	Q&A.106 Ex. 5
Automatic Benefit Changes	FAS106, ¶28	P40.121	
Basic Elements of Accounting for Postretirement Benefits	FAS106, ¶19-22	P40.112-115	
Basis for Accounting	FAS106, ¶23	P40.118	
Benefit Formula	FAS106, ¶18	P40.111	
	FAS106, ¶43-44	P40.138-139	
Benefits Covered by Insurance Contracts	FAS106, ¶67-71	P40.162-166	
Business Combinations	FAS106, ¶86-88	B50.146	Q&A.106 #45
. . Adjustment of Purchase Price at Date of Adoption of Statement 106	FAS106, ¶110-111	P40.141	Q&A.106 #63
. . Unfunded Vested Obligations			EITF.86-20
Change in Accounting Method			EITF.86-19
Collectively Bargained Plan	FAS106, ¶25	P40.118	Q&A.106 #3
Components of Net Periodic Postretirement Benefit Cost	FAS106, ¶22	P40.115	
	FAS106, ¶46	P40.141	
. . Actual Return on Plan Assets	FAS106, ¶49	P40.144	
	FAS106, ¶58	P40.153	
	FAS106, ¶295		
. . Amortization of Unrecognized Prior Service Cost	FAS106, ¶50-55	P40.145-150	
. . Amortization of Unrecognized Transition Obligation or Transition Asset	FAS106, ¶110	P40.141	
	FAS106, ¶112-113	P40.200-201	
. . Gain or Loss	FAS106, ¶56-62	P40.151-157	
. . Interest Cost	FAS106, ¶31	P40.126	
	FAS106, ¶48	P40.143	
. . Service Cost	FAS106, ¶28-31	P40.121-123	
	FAS106, ¶47	P40.126	
	FAS106, ¶70	P40.142	
		P40.165	
Consideration of the Impact of Bankruptcy in Determining Plan Assets under FASB Statement No. 106			EITF.93-3
Consolidated Omnibus Budget Reconciliation Act of 1985 (COBRA)			Q&A.106 #2
Contributory Plans			
. . Changing a Plan to Require Contribution			Q&A.106 Ex. 1
. . Cost of Retirees' Benefits Reduced by Active Employee Contributions	FAS106, ¶35	P40.130	Q&A.106 #9
. . Retiree-Pay-All	FAS106, ¶35	P40.130	Q&A.106 #10
. . Temporary Deviation from the Substantive Plan	FAS106, ¶61	P40.156	Q&A.106 #33
			Q&A.106 #35

FAS—FASB Statements FIN—FASB Interpretations FTB—FASB Technical Bulletins
APB—APB Opinions AIN—AICPA Interpretations ARB—Accounting Research Bulletins
CON—FASB Concepts EITF—EITF Issues Q&A—FASB Special Reports

T-327

See "Terminology" for references to defined terms presented in various accounting pronouncements.

See the Introduction to the Topical Index for details on the use of this index.

FAS–FASB Statements   FIN–FASB Interpretations   FTB–FASB Technical Bulletins
APB–APB Opinions   AIN–AICPA Interpretations   ARB–Accounting Research Bulletins
CON–FASB Concepts   EITF–EITF Issues   Q&A–FASB Special Reports

See "Terminology" for references to defined terms presented in various accounting pronouncements.

See the Introduction to the Topical Index for details on the use of this index.

	Original Pronouncements	Current Text	EITF and Other
POSTRETIREMENT BENEFITS OTHER THAN PENSIONS—continued			
Interest Cost Component (of Net Periodic Postretirement Benefit Cost)	FAS106, ¶22	P40.115	
....	FAS106, ¶31	P40.126	
....	FAS106, ¶46	P40.141	
....	FAS106, ¶48	P40.143	
Interim Financial Reporting	FAS106, ¶73	P40.168	
....	FAS106, ¶113	P40.201	
. . Illustration	FAS106, ¶442	P40.245	
Life Insurance Benefits (Outside a Pension Plan)......................	FAS106, ¶6	P40.102	
Measurement Date	FAS106, ¶31	P40.126	
....	FAS106, ¶39	P40.134	
....	FAS106, ¶65	P40.141	
....	FAS106, ¶72-73	P40.160	
....	FAS106, ¶110	P40.167-168	
. . Illustration	FAS106, ¶456	P40.253	
Measurement of Cost and Obligations	FAS106, ¶15	P40.108	
....	FAS106, ¶23-44	P40.116-139	
....	FAS106, ¶183		
....	FAS106, ¶194-195		
. . Accounting for the Substantive Plan ..	FAS106, ¶23-28	P40.116-121	
. . Administration Costs..............	FAS106, ¶36	P40.131	
. . Aggregating Data.................	FAS106, ¶75-76	P40.170-171	
....	FAS106, ¶357		
. . Assumptions......................	FAS106, ¶29-42	P40.122-137	Q&A.106 #8-13
....	FAS106, ¶194-195		
. . Attribution	FAS106, ¶43-44	P40.138-139	
....	FAS106, ¶135		
....	FAS106, ¶200		
....	FAS106, ¶227		
. . Automatic Benefit Changes..........	FAS106, ¶28	P40.121	
. . Benefit Limitations	FAS106, ¶33	P40.128	
. . Contributions by Active and Retired Employees	FAS106, ¶20	P40.113	Q&A.106 #9-10
....	FAS106, ¶24-25	P40.117-118	
....	FAS106, ¶27	P40.120	
....	FAS106, ¶35	P40.130	
. . Discount Rates....................	FAS106, ¶31	P40.126	
....	FAS106, ¶42	P40.137	
....	FAS106, ¶186		
. . Employers with Two or More Plans ...	FAS106, ¶75-76	P40.170-171	
....	FAS106, ¶357		
. . Expected Long-Term Rate of Return on Plan Assets	FAS106, ¶32	P40.127	
....	FAS106, ¶57-58	P40.152-153	
. . Health Care Benefits	FAS106, ¶34-42	P40.129-137	
. . Illustration of Limits on Benefits or Obligation	FAS106, ¶472-478	P40.269-275	
. . Limits on Benefits or Obligation	FAS106, ¶17	P40.110	
....	FAS106, ¶33	P40.128	
. . Monetary Benefits	FAS106, ¶26	P40.119	
. . Pay-Related Plans	FAS106, ¶33	P40.128	

FAS–FASB Statements	FIN–FASB Interpretations	FTB–FASB Technical Bulletins
APB–APB Opinions	AIN–AICPA Interpretations	ARB–Accounting Research Bulletins
CON–FASB Concepts	EITF–EITF Issues	Q&A–FASB Special Reports

See "Terminology" for references to defined terms presented in various accounting pronouncements.

See the Introduction to the Topical Index for details on the use of this index.

FAS−FASB Statements   FIN−FASB Interpretations   FTB−FASB Technical Bulletins
APB−APB Opinions   AIN−AICPA Interpretations   ARB−Accounting Research Bulletins
CON−FASB Concepts   EITF−EITF Issues   Q&A−FASB Special Reports

See "Terminology" for references to defined terms presented in various accounting pronouncements.
See the Introduction to the Topical Index for details on the use of this index.

	Original Pronouncements	Current Text	EITF and Other
POSTRETIREMENT BENEFITS OTHER THAN PENSIONS—continued			
Substantive Plan	FAS106, ¶23-28	P40.116-121	Q&A.106 #6-7
. . Determination of	FAS106, ¶8	P40.104	Q&A.106 #3
	FAS106, ¶16-17	P40.109-110	Q&A.106 #6-7
	FAS106, ¶23-26	P40.116-119	Q&A.106 #23
			Q&A.106 #57
. . Deviation from	FAS106, ¶61	P40.156	
. . Purchase Business Combination	FAS106, ¶86	B50.146	
. . Temporary Deviation from	FAS106, ¶61	P40.156	Q&A.106 #33-35
Successor Plan	FAS106, ¶100	P40.192	Q&A.106 #44
Termination Benefits	FAS106, ¶6	P40.102	Q&A.106 #47-48
	FAS106, ¶101-102	P40.193-194	
	FAS106, ¶333		
. . Illustration	FAS106, ¶507-511	P40.302-308	
Transition	FAS106, ¶108	P40.141	Q&A.106 #55-64
	FAS106, ¶110-112		
. . Discontinued Operations			Q&A.106 #60-61
. . Effect of Implementation Guidance for Employers that Previously Adopted Statement 106			Q&A.106 #55
. . Effect on Transition Amount of a Negative Plan Amendment in Year of Adoption			Q&A.106 #57
. . Electing a Transition Method			Q&A.106 #56
			Q&A.106 #58-60
			Q&A.106 #62
. . Employer with More Than One Plan			Q&A.106 #56
			Q&A.106 #59
			Q&A.106 #62
. . Financial Statement Presentation of Transition Amount			Q&A.106 #61
. . Foreign Plans			Q&A.106 #62
. . Immediate Recognition of Transition Amount			Q&A.106 #55-56
			Q&A.106 #58-59
			Q&A.106 #62-63
. . Investor and Equity Method Investee Electing Different Transition Methods			Q&A.106 #51
. . Parent and Subsidiary Electing Different Transition Methods			Q&A.106 #56
. . Transition Period			Q&A.106 #64
. . Write-off of Goodwill Included in Cumulative Effect Adjustment			Q&A.106 #63
Transition Obligation or Asset	FAS106, ¶110	P40.141	
. . Illustration	FAS106, ¶418-419	P40.226-227	
	FAS106, ¶430	P40.238-245	
	FAS106, ¶435-437		
	FAS106, ¶439-442		

FAS–FASB Statements   FIN–FASB Interpretations   FTB–FASB Technical Bulletins
APB–APB Opinions   AIN–AICPA Interpretations   ARB–Accounting Research Bulletins
CON–FASB Concepts   EITF–EITF Issues   Q&A–FASB Special Reports

	Original Pronouncements	Current Text	EITF and Other

POSTRETIREMENT BENEFITS OTHER THAN PENSIONS—continued

Unfunded Plans

.. Aggregating Data for Measurement
  Purposes...... FAS106, ¶75-76 · P40.170-171
  ...... FAS106, ¶357

Unrecognized Net Gain or Loss .... FAS106, ¶59-60 · P40.154-155 · Q&A.106 #32
...... FAS106, ¶62 · P40.157
...... FAS106, ¶92-93 · P40.184-185
...... FAS106, ¶98 · P40.190

.. Amortization of ...... FAS106, ¶22 · P40.115
...... FAS106, ¶46 · P40.141
...... FAS106, ¶59-60 · P40.154-155

.. Corridor Approach ...... FAS106, ¶59 · P40.154
.. Illustration ...... FAS106, ¶455-471 · P40.252-268

Unrecognized Prior Service Cost...... FAS106, ¶50-55 · P40.145-150 · Q&A.106 #27-30
...... FAS106, ¶96-99 · P40.188-191

.. Amortization of ...... FAS106, ¶22 · P40.115
...... FAS106, ¶46 · P40.141
...... FAS106, ¶52-53 · P40.147-148

.. Illustration ...... FAS106, ¶449-454 · P40.246-251

Unrecognized Transition Obligation or Transition Asset

.. Accounting for a Curtailment ...... FAS106, ¶96-99 · P40.188-191 · Q&A.106 #27 / Q&A.106 #30

.. Additional Recognition Required..... FAS106, ¶55 · P40.150
...... FAS106, ¶60 · P40.155
...... FAS106, ¶93 · P40.185
...... FAS106, ¶97-98 · P40.189-190
...... FAS106, ¶113 · P40.201

.. Amortization of ...... FAS106, ¶22 · P40.115
...... FAS106, ¶46 · P40.141
...... FAS106, ¶112 · P40.200

.. Illustration ...... FAS106, ¶430 · P40.238-245
...... FAS106, ¶435-437
...... FAS106, ¶439-442

Unwritten Plans ...... FAS106, ¶8 · P40.104 · Q&A.106 #3
Use of Reasonable Approximations ...... FAS106, ¶15 · P40.108

See "Terminology" for references to defined terms presented in various accounting pronouncements.
See the Introduction to the Topical Index for details on the use of this index.

FAS–FASB Statements   FIN–FASB Interpretations   FTB–FASB Technical Bulletins
APB–APB Opinions   AIN–AICPA Interpretations   ARB–Accounting Research Bulletins
CON–FASB Concepts   EITF–EITF Issues   Q&A–FASB Special Reports

	Original Pronouncements	Current Text	EITF and Other
PREMATURITY COSTS AND PERIOD			
See Cable Television Industry			
PREMIUM ON DEBT			
See Interest: Imputation of an Interest Cost			
PREOPERATING COSTS			
See Development Stage Enterprises			
PREPAID EXPENSES			
Balance Sheet Classification	ARB43, Ch.3A, ¶6	B05.107	
PREPAYMENT OF DEBT			
See Debt: Extinguishments			
PREPAYMENTS			
Qualification as Assets	CON6, ¶176		
PREPRODUCTION COSTS			
See Research and Development			
PRESENT VALUE			
See Contributions			
See Defined Benefit Pension Plans			
See Discounting			
See Impairment: Loans			
See Interest: Imputation of an Interest Cost			
See Leases			
Accounting for the Present Value of Future Profits Resulting from the Acquisition of a Life Insurance Company			EITF.92-9
Definition			
. . Actuarially Computed Value	FAS87, ¶264	P16.403	
Foreign Currency Exchange Contracts			EITF.87-2
Recognition and Measurement			
. . Measurement Attribute	CON5, ¶67		
PRETAX ACCOUNTING INCOME			
See Income Taxes			
Definition	APB23, ¶21	Bt7.405	
PRICE CONTROLS			
Regulated Operations	FAS71, ¶8	Re6.118	
PRICE INDEXES			
See Changing Prices: Reporting Their Effects in Financial Reports			
PRICE LEVEL CHANGES			
See Changing Prices: Reporting Their Effects in Financial Reports			
Monetary Unit or Measurement Scale			
. . Effect on	CON5, ¶71-72		
Relation to Capital Maintenance	CON6, ¶71		
Relation to Comprehensive Income	CON6, ¶73-75		
PRICE RENEGOTIATION			
See Contractor Accounting: Government Contracts			
PRIMARY EARNINGS PER SHARE			
See Earnings per Share			
Definition	APB15, App.D	E09.419	

See "Terminology" for references to defined terms presented in various accounting pronouncements.

See the Introduction to the Topical Index for details on the use of this index.

FAS–FASB Statements   FIN–FASB Interpretations   FTB–FASB Technical Bulletins
APB–APB Opinions   AIN–AICPA Interpretations   ARB–Accounting Research Bulletins
CON–FASB Concepts   EITF–EITF Issues   Q&A–FASB Special Reports

	Original Pronouncements	Current Text	EITF and Other
PRODUCTION COSTS			
See Cable Television Industry			
See Computer Software			
See Motion Picture Industry			
See Oil and Gas Producing Activities			
See Record and Music Industry			
PROFIT AND LOSS			
Definition	CON6, ¶16		
Relation to Comprehensive Income	CON6, ¶16		
PROFIT AND LOSS STATEMENT			
See Income Statement			
See Income Statement Presentation: Discontinued Operations			
PROFIT-SHARING PLANS			
See Compensation to Employees: Deferred			
See Earnings per Share			
See Pension Costs			
PROPERTY AND CASUALTY INSURANCE ENTERPRISES			
See Insurance Industry			
PROPERTY DIVIDENDS			
See Capital Stock: Dividends-in-Kind			
PROPERTY, PLANT, AND EQUIPMENT			
See Depreciation			
Cash Flows Reporting	FAS95, ¶15-17	C25.113-115	
	FAS95, ¶24	C25.122	
Duplicate Facilities following a Purchase Business Combination			
. . Costs of Closing Duplicate Facilities of an Acquirer	FTB85-5, ¶1-2	B50.651-652	EITF.84-35
Environmentally Contaminated Property			
. . Costs Incurred to Clean Up Environmental Contamination			EITF.90-8
Idle Facilities			EITF.84-28
Property with Asbestos			
. . Costs Incurred for Asbestos Treatment			EITF.89-13
Segment of Business Reporting	FAS14, ¶27	S20.133	
Write-downs			
. . Of Operating Assets	FAS5, ¶31	C59.137	EITF.84-28
. . Relation to Contingencies	FAS5, ¶31	C59.102	
PROPERTY TAXES			
Accounting for Special Assessments and Tax Increment Financing Entities (TIFEs)			EITF.91-10
PROPORTIONATE CONSOLIDATION			
See Consolidation			
See Oil and Gas Producing Activities			

See "Terminology" for references to defined terms presented in various accounting pronouncements.

See the Introduction to the Topical Index for details on the use of this index.

	Original Pronouncements	Current Text	EITF and Other
PUBLIC UTILITIES			
See Regulated Operations			
PUBLICLY TRADED ENTERPRISE			
See Interim Financial Reporting			
Definition	FAS69, ¶1	Oi5.405A	
PURCHASE ACCOUNTING (ACQUISITIONS)			
See Business Combinations			
See Earnings per Share			
PURCHASE COMMITMENTS			
See Commitments: Long-Term Obligations			
PURCHASE METHOD			
See Business Combinations			
See Income Taxes			
See Intangible Assets			
Definition	APB16, ¶44	B50.407	
PURCHASE OF OWN CAPITAL STOCK			
See Capital Stock: Treasury Stock			
PURCHASE OF OWN DEBT			
See Debt: Extinguishments			
PURCHASE OF TREASURY STOCK			
See Capital Stock: Treasury Stock			
See Earnings per Share			
PURCHASED RESEARCH AND DEVELOPMENT			
See Research and Development			
PURCHASING POWER GAIN OR LOSS ON NET MONETARY ITEMS			
See Changing Prices: Reporting Their Effects in Financial Reports			
PUSH-DOWN ACCOUNTING			
See Business Combinations			
See Change in Basis of Assets and Liabilities			
Debt of Parent Company.			EITF.84-23
. . . .			EITF.84-42
IRC Section 338 and Push-Down Accounting.			EITF.86-9
Subsidiaries			
. . New Basis of Accounting Resulting from Change in Ownership			EITF.85-21
PUT OPTIONS			
See Financial Instruments			
See Options			
Convertible Debt with a Premium Put			EITF.85-29
Effect of a Redemption Agreement on Carrying Value of Investment.			EITF.85-23
Indexed Debt Instruments			EITF.86-28
Issuance of Debt with Put Warrants			EITF.88-9

	Original Pronouncements	Current Text	EITF and Other
PUT OPTIONS—continued			
Sale of Marketable Securities That Are Puttable to Seller			EITF.84-5
....			EITF.85-30
....			EITF.85-40
Sale of Preferred Stocks That Are Puttable to Seller			EITF.85-25
Sale of Put Options on Issuer's Stock......			EITF.87-31
Securities with a Put Option Held by an ESOP			
. . Sponsor's Balance Sheet Classification			EITF.89-11
Stock Purchased at Discount Puttable to Issuer			EITF.84-34
PUT WARRANTS			
See Financial Instruments			
Balance Sheet Classification			EITF.88-9
Effect on Earnings-per-Share Calculation .			EITF.88-9
PYRAMIDING OF STOCK OPTIONS			
See Compensation to Employees: Stock Purchase and Stock Option Plans			

(The next page is T-345.)

See "Terminology" for references to defined terms presented in various accounting pronouncements.

See the Introduction to the Topical Index for details on the use of this index.

	Original Pronouncements	Current Text	EITF and Other
QUALITATIVE CHARACTERISTICS			
Choice between Accounting Methods.....	CON2, ¶6-20		
Comparability........................	CON2, ¶111-122		
Conservatism	CON2, ¶91-97		
Costs and Benefits	CON2, ¶133-144		
Decision Making......................	CON2, ¶36-39		
Exposure Draft Comments and Responses	CON2, ¶152-160		
Glossary	CON2, Glossary		
Hierarchy of Accounting Qualities	CON2, ¶32-45		
Materiality..........................	CON2, ¶123-132		
Nature of Accounting Choices	CON2, ¶6-20		
Neutrality	CON2, ¶98-110		
Recognition Criteria Derived from	CON5, ¶61		
Relation to Elements of Financial Statements	CON6, ¶9-19		
Relation to Objectives of Financial Reporting.........................	CON2, ¶21-26		
Relation to Recognition, Measurement, and Display	CON6, ¶23		
Relation to Role of Decision Making	CON2, ¶27-31		
Relative Importance and Trade-offs	CON2, ¶42-45		
Relevance	CON2, ¶46-57		
Reliability	CON2, ¶58-97		
Representational Faithfulness	CON2, ¶63-80		
Timeliness..........................	CON2, ¶56-57		
Understandability.....................	CON2, ¶40-41		
Verifiability	CON2, ¶81-89		
QUARTERLY FINANCIAL STATEMENTS			
See Interim Financial Reporting			
QUASI REORGANIZATIONS			
See Capital Stock: Capital Transactions			
See Debt: Restructurings			
See Disclosure			
See Income Taxes			
Readjustments	ARB43, Ch.7A, ¶2-3	Q15.102	
....		Q15.104	
. . Accounting after, Additional Paid-in Capital	ARB43, Ch.7A, ¶11	Q15.112	
. . Accounting after, Retained Earnings ..	ARB43, Ch.7A, ¶10	Q15.111	
....	ARB46, ¶2		
. . Accounting after, Similar to New Enterprise........................	ARB43, Ch.7A, ¶9	Q15.110	
. . Charge to Retained Earnings, Additional Paid-in Capital	ARB43, Ch.7A, ¶6	Q15.107	
. . Effective Date of Readjustment	ARB43, Ch.7A, ¶8	Q15.109	
. . Fair Value of Assets Carried Forward .	ARB43, Ch.7A, ¶4	Q15.105	
. . Losses, Provision for...............	ARB43, Ch.7A, ¶5	Q15.106	
. . Retained Earnings of Subsidiaries	ARB43, Ch.7A, ¶7	Q15.108	
. . Scope of Accounting and Reporting Requirements...................	ARB43, Ch.7A, ¶12	Q15.103	

FAS–FASB Statements	FIN–FASB Interpretations	FTB–FASB Technical Bulletins
APB–APB Opinions	AIN–AICPA Interpretations	ARB–Accounting Research Bulletins
CON–FASB Concepts	EITF–EITF Issues	Q&A–FASB Special Reports

	Original Pronouncements	Current Text	EITF and Other
QUASI REORGANIZATIONS—continued			
Reorganization of Financial Affairs of			
Enterprise.........................	ARB43, Ch.7A, ¶1	Q15.101	
Tax Benefits........................	FAS109, ¶39	I27.138	
....		Q15.113	

(The next page is T-351.)

See "Terminology" for references to defined terms presented in various accounting pronouncements.

See the Introduction to the Topical Index for details on the use of this index.

T-346

	Original Pronouncements	Current Text	EITF and Other
RAILROAD ENTERPRISES			
Retirement-Replacement-Betterment (RRB) Accounting			
See Adjustments of Financial Statements for Prior Periods			
RATE-MAKING PROCESS			
See Regulated Operations			
RATE REGULATED INDUSTRIES			
See Regulated Operations			
RAW MATERIALS			
See Inventory			
Balance Sheet Classification	ARB43, Ch.3A, ¶4	B05.105	
REACQUIRED STOCK			
See Capital Stock: Treasury Stock			
READJUSTMENTS			
See Quasi Reorganizations			
REAL AND PERSONAL PROPERTY TAXES			
See Tax			
REAL ESTATE			
See Disclosure			
See Leases			
See Real Estate Enterprises			
See Real Estate: Sales Other Than Retail Land Sales			
Accounting for Special Assessments and Tax Increment Financing Entities (TIFEs)			EITF.91-10
Accounting for Tax Benefits Resulting from Investments in Qualified Affordable Housing Projects			EITF.94-1
Acquisition, Development, and Construction Loans			EITF.84-4
			EITF.86-21
Basis of Assets			
. . Adjustments for Payments during Rent-up Period			EITF.85-27
Condominium Units	FAS66, ¶37	R10.140	
Cost Recovery Method of Profit Recognition	FAS66, ¶22-24	R10.125-127	
	FAS66, ¶32	R10.135	
	FAS66, ¶35	R10.138	
	FAS66, ¶62-64	R10.156-158	
Debtor's Accounting for Forfeiture of Real Estate Subject to a Nonrecourse Mortgage			EITF.91-2
Decision Trees for Accounting and Reporting	FAS66, ¶123	R10.178	
		Re1.196	

	Original Pronouncements	Current Text	EITF and Other
REAL ESTATE—continued			
Deposit Method of Profit Recognition....	FAS66, ¶20-22	R10.123-125	EITF.86-7
....	FAS66, ¶28	R10.131	
....	FAS66, ¶32	R10.135	
....	FAS66, ¶37	R10.140	
....	FAS66, ¶65-67	R10.159-161	
. . Sale-Leaseback Transaction	FAS98, ¶30-33	L10.160D-160G	
Disclosure	FAS66, ¶65		
Exchanges Involving Boot			EITF.87-29
Financing Method			
. . Sale-Leaseback Transaction	FAS98, ¶34-39	L10.160H-160M	
Financing, Leasing, or Profit-Sharing Arrangements	FAS66, ¶26-29	R10.129-132	
Foreclosure			
. . Valuation When Sale Was Accounted for under Installment or Cost Recovery Method			EITF.89-14
Full Accrual Method of Profit Recognition	FAS66, ¶3-18	R10.106-121	
....	FAS66, ¶53-54	R10.147-148	
. . Antispeculation Clause			EITF.86-6
. . Buyer's Initial and Continuing Investment			EITF.87-9
....			EITF.88-12
. . Graduated Payment Mortgages			EITF.84-17
. . Mortgage Insurance/Guarantee			EITF.87-9
Income-Producing			
. . Changing Prices Information	FAS89, ¶25	C28.121	
Installment Method of Profit Recognition.	FAS66, ¶22-23	R10.125-126	
....	FAS66, ¶35	R10.138	
....	FAS66, ¶56-61	R10.150-155	
....	FAS66, ¶90	R10.177	
. . Antispeculation Clause			EITF.86-6
. . Sale-Leaseback Transaction	FAS98, ¶28-29	L10.160B-160C	
Leveraged Leases of Real Estate			EITF.85-16
Lines of Credit	FAS66, ¶9	R10.112	
Management Services			
. . Compensation Imputed.............	FAS66, ¶31	R10.134	
Partial Sales Transactions	FAS66, ¶33-36	R10.136-139	
Percentage-of-Completion Method of Profit Recognition..................	FAS66, ¶37	R10.140	EITF.86-7
....	FAS66, ¶41-42	R10.144-145	
....	FAS66, ¶75	R10.154	
Profit Recognition			
. . Antispeculation Clause			EITF.86-6
. . Collateral Securing Buyer's Note			EITF.88-12
. . Construction of House on Builder's Lot			EITF.86-7
. . Contract Sales for House and Lot			EITF.86-7

See "Terminology" for references to defined terms presented in various accounting pronouncements.
See the Introduction to the Topical Index for details on the use of this index.

FAS–FASB Statements	FIN–FASB Interpretations	FTB–FASB Technical Bulletins
APB–APB Opinions	AIN–AICPA Interpretations	ARB–Accounting Research Bulletins
CON–FASB Concepts	EITF–EITF Issues	Q&A–FASB Special Reports

T-353

See "Terminology" for references to defined terms presented in various accounting pronouncements.

See the Introduction to the Topical Index for details on the use of this index.

	Original Pronouncements	Current Text	EITF and Other
REAL ESTATE: RETAIL LAND SALES—continued			
Percentage-of-Completion Method of Profit Recognition..................	FAS66, ¶46	R10.154	
....	FAS66, ¶61	Re1.146	
....	FAS66, ¶73-75	Re1.171-173	
....	FAS66, ¶91-95	Re1.189-193	
Profit Recognition	FAS66, ¶44	Re1.144	
. . Illustrations	FAS66, ¶91-97	Re1.189-195	
Scope of Accounting and Reporting Requirements......................	FAS66, ¶1-2	Re1.101-102	
REAL ESTATE: SALES			
Buyer's Initial Investment			
. . Effect of Various Forms of Financing .			EITF.88-24
Cost Recovery Method of Profit Recognition			
. . Effect of Various Forms of Financing .			EITF.88-24
Installment Method of Profit Recognition			
. . Effect of Various Forms of Financing .			EITF.88-24
REAL ESTATE: SALES OTHER THAN RETAIL LAND SALES			
See Disclosure			
Buyer's Initial Investment			
. . Collateral Securing Buyer's Note			EITF.88-12
. . Compliance with FHA or VA Program Requirements...................			EITF.87-9
. . Effect of Various Forms of Financing .			EITF.88-24
. . Mortgage Insurance...............			EITF.84-17
....			EITF.87-9
. . Pledging of Ownership Interest as Part of Down Payment...............			EITF.88-12
. . Surety Bonds			EITF.87-9
Condominium Units..................	FAS66, ¶37	Re1.137	
Cost Recovery Method of Profit Recognition	FAS66, ¶22-24	Re1.122-124	
....	FAS66, ¶32	Re1.132	
....	FAS66, ¶35	Re1.135	
....	FAS66, ¶62-64	Re1.160-162	
. . Effect of Various Forms of Financing .			EITF.88-24
Deposit Method of Profit Recognition....	FAS66, ¶20-22	Re1.120-122	
....	FAS66, ¶28	Re1.128	
....	FAS66, ¶32	Re1.132	
....	FAS66, ¶37	Re1.137	
....	FAS66, ¶65-67	Re1.163-165	
. . Construction of House on Builder's Lot			EITF.86-7

	Original Pronouncements	Current Text	EITF and Other
REAL ESTATE: SALES OTHER THAN RETAIL LAND SALES—continued			
Deposit Method of Profit Recognition—continued			
. . Effect of Various Forms of Financing .			EITF.88-24
. . Sale-Leaseback Transaction	FAS98, ¶30-33	L10.160D-160G	
Description	FAS66, ¶101	Re1.101	
Exchange Involving Boot.			EITF.87-29
Financing, Leasing, or Profit-Sharing Arrangements	FAS66, ¶26-29	Re1.126-129	
Financing Method			
. . Sale-Leaseback Transaction	FAS98, ¶34-39	L10.160H-160M	
Full Accrual Method of Profit Recognition	FAS66, ¶3-18	Re1.103-118	
. . . .	FAS66, ¶53-54	Re1.151-152	
. . Antispeculation Clause			EITF.86-6
. . Buyer's Initial and Continuing Investment			EITF.87-9
			EITF.88-12
Installment Method of Profit Recognition.	FAS66, ¶22-23	Re1.122-123	
. . . .	FAS66, ¶35	Re1.135	
. . . .	FAS66, ¶56-61	Re1.154-159	
. . . .	FAS66, ¶90	Re1.188	
. . . .	FAS66, ¶96	Re1.194	
. . Antispeculation Clause			EITF.86-6
. . Effect of Various Forms of Financing .			EITF.88-24
. . Sale-Leaseback Transaction	FAS98, ¶28-29	L10.160B-160C	
Partial Sales Transactions	FAS66, ¶33-36	Re1.133-136	
Percentage-of-Completion Method of Profit Recognition.	FAS66, ¶37	Re1.137	EITF.86-7
. . . .	FAS66, ¶41	Re1.141	
Profit Recognition			
. . Antispeculation Clause			EITF.86-6
. . Buyer's Initial and Continuing Investment			EITF.87-9
. . Collateral Securing Buyer's Note			EITF.88-12
. . Construction of House on Builder's Lot			EITF.86-7
. . Full Accrual Method Inappropriate . . .	FAS66, ¶19-39	Re1.119-143	
. . . .	FAS66, ¶41-43	Re1.175-188	
. . . .	FAS98, ¶23		
. . Graduated Payment Mortgages			EITF.84-17
. . Illustrations	FAS66, ¶77-90	Re1.175-188	
. . Mortgage Insurance/Guarantee			EITF.84-17
			EITF.87-9
. . Mortgages with Initial Negative Amortization			EITF.84-17

See "Terminology" for references to defined terms presented in various accounting pronouncements.
See the Introduction to the Topical Index for details on the use of this index.

	Original Pronouncements	Current Text	EITF and Other
REAL ESTATE: SALES OTHER THAN RETAIL LAND SALES—continued			
Profit Recognition—continued			
. . Pledging of Ownership Interest as Part of Down Payment			EITF.88-12
. . Sale of Property Subject to Seller's Preexisting Lease			EITF.88-21
Reduced Profit Method of Profit Recognition	FAS66, ¶23	Re1.123	
	FAS66, ¶68-69	Re1.166-167	
Sale of Property Improvements Involves Land Lease	FAS66, ¶38-39	Re1.138-139	
Sale-Leaseback Transaction	FAS98, ¶6-14	L10.130A-130M	
	FAS98, ¶17-19	L10.155-160M	
	FAS98, ¶23	Re1.140	
. . Loans to Buyers by Sellers			EITF.84-37
. . Rental Shortfall Agreements			EITF.84-37
. . Repurchase Options			EITF.84-37
. . Residual Value Guarantee			EITF.86-17
. . Sale of Property Subject to Seller's Preexisting Lease			EITF.88-21
. . Short Initial Lease Term with Renewal Options			EITF.84-37
. . Subleases			EITF.84-37
Time-Sharing Interests	FAS66, ¶37	Re1.137	
REALIZATION			
Definition	CON6, ¶143		
Revenues and Gains			
. . Guidance in Applying Recognition Criteria	CON5, ¶83-84		
REASONABLY POSSIBLE EVENTS			
See Contingencies			
RECAPITALIZATION			
See Debt: Restructurings			
See Quasi Reorganizations			
Changes to Fixed Employee Stock Option Plans as a Result of Equity Restructuring			EITF.90-9
RECEIVABLES			
See Balance Sheet Classification: Current Assets and Liabilities			
See Contingencies			
See Financial Instruments			
See Impairment: Loans			
See Interest: Imputation of an Interest Cost			
See Loans			
See Receivables Sold with Recourse			
See Related Parties			

FAS—FASB Statements   FIN—FASB Interpretations   FTB—FASB Technical Bulletins
APB—APB Opinions   AIN—AICPA Interpretations   ARB—Accounting Research Bulletins
CON—FASB Concepts   EITF—EITF Issues   Q&A—FASB Special Reports

T-357

	Original Pronouncements	Current Text	EITF and Other
RECEIVABLES—continued			
See Valuation Allowances			
Acquisition, Development, and Construction Loans................			EITF.84-4
....			EITF.86-21
Balance Sheet Classification	ARB43, Ch.3A, ¶4	B05.105	
....	ARB43, Ch.3A, ¶6	B05.107	
. . Notes Received for Capital Stock			EITF.85-1
Credit Card Portfolio Securitizations with a "Removal of Accounts" Provision....			EITF.90-18
From Officers, Employees, or Affiliates ..	ARB43, Ch.1A, ¶5	R36.105	
Graduated Payment Mortgages..........			EITF.84-17
....			EITF.85-38
In-Substance Foreclosure on Collateral ...			EITF.89-9
Loan Loss Allowances			
. . Applying Savings and Loan Audit Guide			EITF.87-5
. . Differences between GAAP and RAP .			EITF.85-44
Loan Payment Modifications			EITF.84-19
Maximum Maturity Guarantees on Transfers with Recourse			EITF.89-2
Measuring Loss Accruals by Transferors for Transfers of Receivables with Recourse........................			EITF.92-2
Negative Amortizing Loan			EITF.85-38
Offsetting Nonrecourse Debt with Lease Receivables.......................			EITF.84-25
Offsetting Note Receivables with Debt			
. . Note Puttable to Creditor to Satisfy Debt			EITF.84-11
Operating Real Estate as Collateral.......			EITF.86-21
Sale of Bad-Debt Recovery Rights			EITF.86-8
Sale of Credit Card Portfolio with Partial Interest Retained			EITF.88-22
Sale of Interest-Only Cash Flows or Principal-Only Cash Flows from Loans Receivable			
. . Determination of Gain or Loss.......			EITF.88-11
. . Determination of Remaining Recorded Investment for Portion of Loan Retained			EITF.88-11
Sale with a Partial Participation Retained .			EITF.84-21
Sale with Recourse to Special-Purpose Entity			EITF.84-30
Shared Appreciation Mortgages			EITF.86-21
Transfer in Which Risk of Foreign Currency Fluctuation Is Retained			EITF.D-13
Valuation Allowances.................	APB12, ¶3	V18.101-103	

See "Terminology" for references to defined terms presented in various accounting pronouncements.
See the Introduction to the Topical Index for details on the use of this index.

	Original Pronouncements	Current Text	EITF and Other
RECEIVABLES SOLD WITH RECOURSE			
See Disclosure			
See Financial Instruments			
Description of Types of Transactions	FAS77, ¶1	R20.101	
....	FAS77, ¶15		
Glossary	FAS77, ¶12	R20.401-404	
Maximum Maturity Guarantees on Transfers with Recourse			EITF.89-2
Measuring Loss Accruals by Transferors for Transfers of Receivables with Recourse.........................			EITF.92-2
Scope of Accounting and Reporting Requirements......................	FAS77, ¶3-4	R20.102-104	
....	FAS77, ¶20		
Transactions Involving Special-Purpose Entities............................			EITF.84-30
....			EITF.D-14
Transfer Recognized as a Liability	FAS77, ¶8	R20.108	
Transfer Recognized as a Sale			
. . Criteria for Recognition	FAS77, ¶5-7	R20.105-107	
....	FAS77, ¶22-26		
....	FAS77, ¶28		
....	FAS77, ¶30-31		
....	FAS77, ¶34		
RECIPROCAL TRANSFERS			
See Nonmonetary Transactions			
RECOGNITION			
See Recognition and Measurement in Financial Statements			
Cost-Benefit Constraints	CON5, ¶63		
Criteria	CON5, ¶62		
. . Asset and Liability Changes	CON5, ¶85-88		
. . Asset and Liability Changes, Use of Current Prices	CON5, ¶90		
. . Fundamental	CON5, ¶63-64		
. . Guidance in Application to Components of Earnings	CON5, ¶79-84		
. . Guidance in Application to Expenses and Losses	CON5, ¶85-87		
. . Guidance in Application to Revenues and Gains.......................	CON5, ¶83-84		
. . Purposes.........................	CON5, ¶59-60		
. . Relevance	CON5, ¶73-74		
. . Reliability	CON5, ¶75-77		
. . Structure........................	CON5, ¶61-62		
Definition	CON5, ¶6		
....	CON6, ¶143		
Discussion..........................	CON5, ¶58		
Elements Definitions	CON5, ¶64		
Financial Reporting	CON5, ¶5-6		

	Original Pronouncements	Current Text	EITF and Other

RECOGNITION—continued

See "Terminology" for references to defined terms presented in various accounting pronouncements.

See the Introduction to the Topical Index for details on the use of this index.

	Original Pronouncements	Current Text	EITF and Other

RECOGNITION AND MEASUREMENT IN FINANCIAL STATEMENTS—continued
Financial Statements—continued
. . Notes to Financial Statements and Supplementary Information . . . . CON5, ¶7-9
. . Other Nonowner Changes in Equity . . CON5, ¶43
. . Recognition Implications of Earnings . CON5, ¶49-51
. . Relation to Other Means of Financial Reporting . . . . CON5, ¶7-9
. . Statement of Cash Flows, Nature and Recognition Considerations . . . . CON5, ¶52-54
. . Statement of Financial Position, Nature and Recognition Considerations . . . . CON5, ¶26-29
. . Statement of Investments by and Distributions to Owners: Nature, Recognition . . . . CON5, ¶55-57
. . Statements of Earnings and Comprehensive Income: Nature, Recognition . . . . CON5, ¶30-51
. . Usefulness of Financial Statements, Individually and Collectively . . . . CON5, ¶17-19
Gains and Losses . . . . CON5, ¶42
Not-for-Profit Organizations
. . Nonapplicability to . . . . CON5, ¶4
Objectives of Financial Reporting
. . Relationship . . . . CON5, ¶10-12
Other Nonowner Changes in Equity
. . Description . . . . CON5, ¶43

RECORD AND MUSIC INDUSTRY
See Disclosure
Advance Royalty . . . . FAS50, ¶10 — Re4.105
. . . . FAS50, ¶12 — Re4.107
Artist Compensation Cost . . . . FAS50, ¶10 — Re4.105
Glossary . . . . FAS50, ¶18 — Re4.401-405
Licensee Accounting . . . . FAS50, ¶15 — Re4.110
Record Masters
. . Cost . . . . FAS50, ¶11 — Re4.106
. . Valuation . . . . FAS50, ¶11 — Re4.106
Revenue Recognition
. . Licensor Accounting . . . . FAS50, ¶8 — Re4.103

RECOURSE ARRANGEMENTS
See Receivables Sold with Recourse
REDEEMABLE STOCK
See Financial Instruments

FAS–FASB Statements   FIN–FASB Interpretations   FTB–FASB Technical Bulletins
APB–APB Opinions   AIN–AICPA Interpretations   ARB–Accounting Research Bulletins
CON–FASB Concepts   EITF–EITF Issues   Q&A–FASB Special Reports

See "Terminology" for references to defined terms presented in various accounting pronouncements.

See the Introduction to the Topical Index for details on the use of this index.

	Original Pronouncements	Current Text	EITF and Other
REGULATED OPERATIONS—continued			
See Disclosure			
See Insurance Costs			
Abandonments of Assets	FAS90, ¶3-6	Re6.127A-127D	
. . Adjustment of Carrying Value	FAS90, ¶4	Re6.127B	
. . Amortization during Recovery Period	FAS90, ¶6	Re6.127D	
. . Before Recovery Begins	FAS90, ¶5	Re6.127C	
. . Carrying Charges	FAS90, ¶5	Re6.127C	
. . Computation of a Loss	FTB87-2, ¶5	Re6.501-507	
	FTB87-2, ¶14-20		
. . Deferred Income Taxes	FTB87-2, ¶5	Re6.501-507	
	FTB87-2, ¶14-20		
. . Discount Rate Used	FAS90, ¶3	Re6.127A	
. . Full Return on Investment Expected	FAS90, ¶3-6	Re6.127A-127D	
. . Illustrations	FTB87-2, ¶34-47	Re6.508-521	
. . Partial or No Return on Investment Expected	FAS90, ¶3-6	Re6.127A-127D	
	FTB87-2, ¶15-20	Re6.503-507	
Accounting by Rate-Regulated Utilities for the Effects of Certain Alternative Revenue Programs			EITF.92-7
Accounting Changes	FAS71, ¶31-32	Re6.136-137	
Accounting for OPEB Costs by Rate-Regulated Enterprises			EITF.92-12
			EITF.93-4
Allowable Costs	FAS71, ¶1-3	Re6.111-113	
Allowance for Earnings on Shareholders' Investment Capitalized for Rate-Making Purposes Only	FAS92, ¶5	Re6.125B	
	FAS92, ¶8-9	Re6.125G	
	FAS92, ¶40-41	Re6.198-199	
. . As Related to Disallowance	FAS92, ¶42-43	Re6.200-201	
. . As Related to Phase-in Plan	FAS92, ¶44-45	Re6.202-203	
Allowance for Funds Used during Construction	FAS71, ¶15	Re6.125	
. . Capitalization Criteria	FAS90, ¶9	Re6.125	
	FAS90, ¶66-68		
. . Prudence Investigation	FAS90, ¶68	Re6.125	
Application of Authoritative Accounting Pronouncements	FAS71, ¶7	Re6.117	
Asset			
. . Impairment by Actions of Regulator	FAS71, ¶10	Re6.120	
	FAS90, ¶9		
. . Reasonable Assurance of Existence	FAS71, ¶9	Re6.119	
	FAS90, ¶9		
Capitalization of Cost	FAS71, ¶4	Re6.114	
	FAS71, ¶9	Re6.119	
	FAS90, ¶9		
. . Allowance for Earnings on Shareholders' Investment	FAS92, ¶8-9	Re6.125G	

FAS–FASB Statements   FIN–FASB Interpretations   FTB–FASB Technical Bulletins
APB–APB Opinions   AIN–AICPA Interpretations   ARB–Accounting Research Bulletins
CON–FASB Concepts   EITF–EITF Issues   Q&A–FASB Special Reports

	Original Pronouncements	Current Text	EITF and Other
REGULATED OPERATIONS—continued			
Capitalization of Cost—continued			
. . Phase-in Plan	FAS92, ¶4-5	Re6.125B-125C	
Capitalization of Interest	FAS34, ¶10	I67.106	
. . . Allowance for Funds Used during Construction	FAS71, ¶15	Re6.125	
	FAS90, ¶9		
	FAS90, ¶66-68		
Changing Prices Information	FAS89, ¶31	C28.127	
Compensated Absences	FAS71, ¶48-49	Re6.153-154	
Contingencies	FAS71, ¶38-39	Re6.143-144	
Deferred Cost	FAS71, ¶4	Re6.114	
. . Allowance for Earnings on Shareholders' Investment	FAS92, ¶8-9	Re6.125G	
. . Phase-in Plan	FAS92, ¶4-5	Re6.125B-125C	
Deferred Taxes	FAS109, ¶29	I27.128	
	FAS109, ¶252-255	I27.179-182	
Definition			
. . Allowable Costs	FAS71, ¶1	Re6.401	
. . Capitalize	FAS71, ¶4	Re6.402	
. . Incurred Cost	FAS71, ¶9	Re6.403	
. . Intercompany Profit	FAS71, ¶16	Re6.404	
. . Phase-in Plan	FAS92, ¶2	Re6.404A	
. . Probable	FAS90, ¶9	Re6.405	
. . Regulatory Lag	FAS92, ¶39	Re6.406	
Differences between GAAP and RAP			EITF.85-44
Disallowance of Costs of Recently Completed Plants	FAS90, ¶7	Re6.127E	
	FAS90, ¶60-62	Re6.176-178	
. . Excess Capacity	FAS90, ¶60	Re6.176	
. . Hidden, Indirect Disallowance	FAS90, ¶62	Re6.178	
. . Illustrations of Disallowance Due to "Cost Cap"	FAS90, ¶28-31	Re6.169-172	
. . Illustrations of Disallowance of Plant Costs	FAS90, ¶26-27	Re6.167-168	
. . Illustrations of Explicit, but Indirect, Disallowance	FAS90, ¶32-34	Re6.173-175	
. . Value-Based Ratemaking	FAS90, ¶61	Re6.177	
Disallowance of Plant Cost			
. . As Related to Allowance for Earnings on Shareholders' Investment Capitalized for Rate-Making Purposes Only	FAS92, ¶42-43	Re6.200-201	
. . As Related to Phase-in Plan	FAS92, ¶7	Re6.125E	
. . Capitalized for Rate-Making Purposes Only	FAS92, ¶42-43	Re6.200-201	

See "Terminology" for references to defined terms presented in various accounting pronouncements.
See the Introduction to the Topical Index for details on the use of this index.

	Original Pronouncements	Current Text	EITF and Other
REGULATED OPERATIONS—continued			
Discontinuation of Accounting for the Effects of Certain Types of Regulation . .	FAS101, ¶5-7	Re6.204-206	
. . Illustrations of Specific Situations	FAS101, ¶13-20	Re6.209-216	
. . Income Statement Presentation of Net Effect	FAS101, ¶6	Re6.205	
. . . .	FAS101, ¶9-10	Re6.208	
Divestiture of Certain Investment Securities to an Unregulated Commonly Controlled Entity under FIRREA			EITF.89-18
Early Extinguishment of Debt	FAS71, ¶35-37	Re6.140-142	
Financial Statements Prepared Based on Statutory Accounting Practices Instead of GAAP	FIN40, ¶18	Re6.114	
Income Taxes	FAS109, ¶29	I27.128	
. . . .	FAS109, ¶252-255	I27.179-182	
. . . .	FAS109, ¶288	Re6.128	
. . . .	FTB87-2, ¶5	Re6.501-507	
. . . .	FTB87-2, ¶14-20		
Intangible Assets	FAS71, ¶29-30	Re6.134-135	
Intercompany Profit	FAS71, ¶16-17	Re6.126-127	
Leases	FAS71, ¶40-43	Re6.145-148	
Liability			
. . Eliminated by Regulator	FAS71, ¶12	Re6.122	
. . Imposed by Regulator	FAS71, ¶11	Re6.121	
Modification of Debt Terms When Debtor Is Experiencing Financial Difficulties . . .			EITF.89-15
Nonutility Generators (NUGs)			EITF.91-6
Pension Costs	FAS87, ¶210	Re6.155	
Phase-in Plan			
. . As Related to Disallowance	FAS92, ¶7	Re6.125E	
. . Background	FAS92, ¶48-50	Re6.114A-114B	
. . Criteria	FAS92, ¶5	Re6.125C	
. . Definition	FAS92, ¶3	Re6.125A	
. . Illustrations of Specific Situations	FAS92, ¶21-45	Re6.179-203	
. . Modifications of/Supplement to	FAS92, ¶6	Re6.125D	
. . Plants Completed at Different Times and Sharing Facilities			EITF.D-21
Postretirement Benefits Other Than Pensions	FAS106, ¶364	Re6.155	EITF.92-12
. . . .			EITF.93-4
Price Controls	FAS71, ¶8	Re6.118	
Recovery of Costs with Return on Investment			
. . Abandoned Assets	FAS90, ¶3-6	Re6.127A-127D	
Recovery of Costs without Return on Investment	FAS71, ¶20	Re6.131	
. . . .	FAS71, ¶33-34	Re6.138-139	
. . Abandoned Assets	FAS90, ¶3-6	Re6.127A-127D	
. . . .	FTB87-2, ¶15-20	Re6.503-507	
. . Phase-in Plan	FAS92, ¶9	Re6.125G	
Reduced Rates	FAS71, ¶11	Re6.121	

FAS–FASB Statements   FIN–FASB Interpretations   FTB–FASB Technical Bulletins
APB–APB Opinions   AIN–AICPA Interpretations   ARB–Accounting Research Bulletins
CON–FASB Concepts   EITF–EITF Issues   Q&A–FASB Special Reports

	Original Pronouncements	Current Text	EITF and Other
REGULATED OPERATIONS—continued			
Refunds to Customers	FAS71, ¶11	Re6.121	
....	FAS71, ¶19	Re6.130	
....	FAS71, ¶44-47	Re6.149-152	
Regulatory Accounting	FAS71, ¶5	Re6.115	
Regulatory-Assisted Acquisitions of Thrifts...........................			EITF.88-19
. . Disclosure Requirements			EITF.88-19
Revenue Collected Subject to Refund.....	FAS71, ¶44-45	Re6.149-150	
Revenue Recognition of Long-Term Power Sales Contracts of Nonutility Generators (NUGs)...........................			EITF.91-6
Sale-Leaseback Transactions	FAS98, ¶14-16	Re6.125H-125J	
Scope of Accounting and Reporting Requirements......................	FAS71, ¶5-8	Re6.115-118A	
....	FAS90, ¶2		
....	FAS92, ¶2		
. . Discontinuation of Accounting for the Effects of Certain Types of Regulation	FAS101, ¶1	Re6.117A-117B	
....	FAS101, ¶4		
Write-down or Write-off of Abandoned Nuclear Power Plant.................			EITF.D-5
REGULATORY ACCOUNTING PRINCIPLES			
Differences between GAAP and RAP			
. . Loan Loss Allowances..............			EITF.85-44
REINSURANCE			
See Insurance Industry			
Definition	FAS60, ¶66	In6.428	
Funded Catastrophe Covers			EITF.93-6
Multiple-Year Retrospectively Rated Contracts (RRCs)			EITF.93-6
....			EITF.D-35
See Insurance Industry			
RELATED PARTIES			
See Disclosure			
See Interest: Imputation of an Interest Cost			
See Investments: Equity Method			
See Leases			
See Research and Development Arrangements			
Arm's-Length Basis Transactions	FAS57, ¶3	R36.103	
Common Control.....................	FAS57, ¶4	R36.104	EITF.86-16
....			EITF.88-16
Consolidation of Special-Purpose Entity without Equity Ownership			EITF.84-30
Defined Benefit Pension Plan and Employer	FAS35, ¶28	Pe5.127	
....	FAS57, ¶1	R36.101	
Glossary	FAS57, ¶24	R36.401-406	
Leases	FAS13, ¶29-30	L10.125-126	
Receivables from Employees, Officers, or Affiliated Enterprises	ARB43, Ch.1A, ¶5	R36.105	

See "Terminology" for references to defined terms presented in various accounting pronouncements.

See the Introduction to the Topical Index for details on the use of this index.

	Original Pronouncements	Current Text	EITF and Other
RELATED PARTIES—continued			
Scope of Accounting and Reporting Requirements	FAS57, ¶1	R36.101	
RELEVANCE			
Criterion for Recognition	CON5, ¶74		
Definition	CON2, Glossary		
Feedback Value	CON2, ¶51-52		
Predictive Value	CON2, ¶53-55		
Primary Qualitative Characteristic	CON2, ¶46-57		
Relation to Neutrality	CON2, ¶98-110		
Relation to Reliability	CON2, ¶90		
Relation to Timeliness	CON2, ¶56-57		
Role in Financial Reporting	CON1, ¶36		
RELIABILITY			
Criterion for Recognition	CON5, ¶75-77		
Definition	CON2, Glossary		
Degree of	CON2, ¶65-71		
Financial Statements, Nature of Audit	CON1, ¶8		
Precision and Uncertainty	CON2, ¶72-76		
Primary Qualitative Characteristic	CON2, ¶58-97		
Relation to Conservatism	CON2, ¶91-97		
Relation to Neutrality	CON2, ¶98-110		
Relation to Relevance	CON2, ¶90		
Relation to Representational Faithfulness	CON2, ¶63-80		
Relation to Substance vs. Form	CON2, ¶160		
Relation to Uncertainty	CON6, ¶45-48		
Relation to Verifiability	CON2, ¶81-89		
RELIGIOUS ORGANIZATIONS			
See Not-for-Profit Organizations			
RELOCATION COSTS			
See Moving Costs			
REMOTELY POSSIBLE EVENTS			
See Contingencies			
RENEGOTIATION			
See Contractor Accounting: Construction-Type Contracts			
RENEWAL OPTIONS			
See Leases			
RENTAL CONCESSIONS			
Accounting by Tenant (Lessee)			EITF.88-3
RENTALS			
See Leases			
REORGANIZATIONS			
See Debt: Restructurings			
See Quasi Reorganizations			
Accounting for Restructuring Charges			EITF.94-3
Classification of Restructuring Gain or Loss			EITF.86-22
			EITF.87-4
Income Taxes			
. . Carryforwards			EITF.D-33
. . Temporary Differences			EITF.D-33

FAS–FASB Statements   FIN–FASB Interpretations   FTB–FASB Technical Bulletins
APB–APB Opinions   AIN–AICPA Interpretations   ARB–Accounting Research Bulletins
CON–FASB Concepts   EITF–EITF Issues   Q&A–FASB Special Reports

T-367

	Original Pronouncements	Current Text	EITF and Other
REPLACEMENT COST			
See Changing Prices: Reporting Their Effects in Financial Reports			
See Measurement			
REPORTING ENTITY CHANGES			
See Adjustments of Financial Statements for Prior Periods			
REPRESENTATIONAL FAITHFULNESS			
Definition	CON2, Glossary		
Relation to Bias	CON2, ¶77-78		
Relation to Completeness	CON2, ¶79-80		
Relation to Precision	CON2, ¶72-76		
Relation to Reliability	CON2, ¶63-80		
Relation to Uncertainties	CON2, ¶72-76		
REPURCHASE AGREEMENTS			
See Financial Instruments			
GNMA Dollar Rolls			EITF.84-20
REPURCHASED STOCK			
See Capital Stock: Treasury Stock			
RESEARCH AND DEVELOPMENT			
See Computer Software			
See Disclosure			
Accounting	FAS2, ¶12	R50.108	
Acquired in Business Combination	FAS2, ¶34	B50.151-152	
	FIN4, ¶4-5		
Elements of Costs to Be Identified with	FAS2, ¶11	R50.107	
Examples of Activities Typically Excluded	FAS2, ¶10	R50.112	
Examples of Activities Typically Included	FAS2, ¶9	R50.111	
Glossary	FAS2, ¶8	R50.401-402	
Performed by Venture Capital Subsidiaries			EITF.85-12
Process	FIN6, ¶4	R50.105	
Purchased in a Business Combination			EITF.86-14
Qualification as an Asset	CON6, ¶176		
Scope of Accounting and Reporting Requirements	FAS2, ¶1-3	R50.101-103	
RESEARCH AND DEVELOPMENT ARRANGEMENTS			
See Disclosure			
Loan or Advance to Other Parties	FAS68, ¶12	R55.110	
Obligation Is a Liability	FAS68, ¶4-9	R55.102-107	
Obligation Is to a Person			
.. Contractual Services	FAS68, ¶10-11	R55.108-109	
Related Parties	FAS68, ¶8	R55.106	
Scope of Accounting and Reporting Requirements	FAS68, ¶3	R55.101	
Stock Issued to Acquire Results of a Research and Development Arrangement	FTB84-1, ¶1-2	R55.501-504	

See "Terminology" for references to defined terms presented in various accounting pronouncements.

See the Introduction to the Topical Index for details on the use of this index.

	Original Pronouncements	Current Text	EITF and Other
RESEARCH AND DEVELOPMENT ARRANGEMENTS—continued			
Stock Issued to Acquire Results of a Research and Development Arrangement—continued			
. . . .	FTB84-1, ¶6-7		
Warrants or Similar Instruments Issued . . .	FAS68, ¶13	R55.111	
RESERVE FOR BAD DEBTS			
Valuation Allowance	APB12, ¶2	V18.102	
RESERVES			
See Contingencies			
See Extractive Industries			
Qualification as Liabilities	CON6, ¶197		
RESIDUAL INTEREST			
See Equity (or Net Assets)			
Characteristics	CON6, ¶49-53		
. . . .	CON6, ¶213		
. . . .	CON6, ¶222		
RESIDUAL VALUE			
See Leases			
RESOURCES			
See Economic Resources			
RESTATEMENTS			
See Adjustments of Financial Statements for Prior Periods			
RESTATE-TRANSLATE METHOD			
See Changing Prices: Reporting Their Effects in Financial Reports			
RESTRICTED FUNDS			
See Not-for-Profit Organizations			
Not-for-Profit Organizations	CON4, ¶21		
. . . .	CON4, ¶46		
Relation to Net Assets	CON6, ¶191		
RESTRICTED SECURITIES			
See Investments: Marketable Securities			
RESTRUCTURING OF BUSINESS OPERATIONS			
Accounting for Restructuring Charges			EITF.94-3
Changes to Fixed Employee Stock Option Plans as a Result of Equity Restructuring . .			EITF.90-9
Classification of Resulting Gain or Loss . .			EITF.86-22
. . . .			EITF.87-4
RESTRUCTURING OF DEBT			
See Debt: Restructurings			
RESULTS OF OPERATIONS			
See Adjustments of Financial Statements for Prior Periods			
See Extraordinary Items ·			
See Income Statement			
See Income Statement Presentation: Discontinued Operations			
See Interim Financial Reporting			
See Not-for-Profit Organizations			
See Oil and Gas Producing Activities			

FAS—FASB Statements	FIN—FASB Interpretations	FTB—FASB Technical Bulletins
APB—APB Opinions	AIN—AICPA Interpretations	ARB—Accounting Research Bulletins
CON—FASB Concepts	EITF—EITF Issues	Q&A—FASB Special Reports

	Original Pronouncements	Current Text	EITF and Other
RETAILERS			
Inventory Valuation	ARB43, Ch.4, ¶6	I78.108	
. . . .	ARB43, Ch.4, ¶10	I78.112	
RETAIL LAND SALES			
See Real Estate: Retail Land Sales			
RETAINED EARNINGS			
See Disclosure			
See Financial Statements: Comparative Financial Statements			
See Quasi Reorganizations			
See Statement of Investments by and Distributions to Owners			
Appropriations	APB9, ¶28	C08.101	
Appropriations for Loss Contingencies . . .	FAS5, ¶15	C59.117	
. . . .		R70.103	
Charges against	FAS5, ¶15	R70.103	
Preacquisition Dividends of Purchased Subsidiary	ARB43, Ch.1A, ¶3	R70.102	
Preacquisition Earnings of Purchased Subsidiary	ARB51, ¶9	R70.101	
Prior Period Adjustments	APB9, ¶26	A35.106-107	
. . . .	FAS16, ¶16		
RETIREE HEALTH CARE COSTS			
See Postretirement Benefits Other Than Pensions			
RETIREE MEDICAL BENEFITS			
See Postretirement Benefits Other Than Pensions			
RETIREMENT OF DEBT			
See Debt: Extinguishments			
RETIREMENT OF STOCK			
See Capital Stock: Capital Transactions			
RETIREMENT PLANS			
See Defined Benefit Pension Plans			
See Pension Costs			
See Postretirement Benefits Other Than Pensions			
See Postretirement Health Care and Life Insurance Benefits			
RETIREMENT-REPLACEMENT-BETTERMENT (RRB) ACCOUNTING			
See Adjustments of Financial Statements for Prior Periods			
RETURN ON INVESTMENT			
Accrual vs. Cash Basis of Accounting	CON1, ¶45-48		
Prospects for	CON1, ¶37-39		

See "Terminology" for references to defined terms presented in various accounting pronouncements.

See the Introduction to the Topical Index for details on the use of this index.

	Original Pronouncements	Current Text	EITF and Other
RETURN ON INVESTMENT—continued			
Relation to Capital Maintenance.........	CON6, ¶71		
RETURNS			
See Revenue Recognition			
REVENUE AND EXPENSE MATCHING			
See Matching of Costs and Revenues			
REVENUE RECOGNITION			
See Interest Income			
See Leases			
See Real Estate: Sales Other Than Retail Land Sales			
See Sales			
Accounting for Barter Transactions Involving Barter Credits			EITF.93-11
Amortization of Amount Received from Investor for Future Revenue...........			EITF.88-18
Banking and Thrift Industries			
. . Sale of Convertible, Adjustable-Rate Mortgages with Contingent Repayment Agreement			EITF.87-25
. . Sale of Mortgage Loan with Servicing Rights Retained			EITF.86-39
. . Sale of Servicing Rights on Mortgages Owned by Others.................			EITF.85-13
. . Sale with a Partial Participation Retained........................			EITF.84-21
Credit Card Portfolio Securitization......			EITF.88-22
....			EITF.90-18
Defeasance of Special-Purpose Borrowings........................			EITF.84-26
Definition			
. . Revenues........................	FAS14, ¶10	S20.411	
Extended Warranty and Product Maintenance Contracts			
. . Definitions	FTB90-1, ¶2	R75.502	
....	FTB90-1, ¶4	R75.504	
. . Incremental Direct Acquisition Costs .	FTB90-1, ¶4	R75.504	
....	FTB90-1, ¶12		
. . Loss Recognition	FTB90-1, ¶5	R75.505	
. . Recognition of Revenues and Costs ...	FTB90-1, ¶1-5	R75.501-505	EITF.89-17
Franchisors			
. . Cost Recovery Method	FAS45, ¶6	Fr3.102	
. . Installment Recovery Method........	FAS45, ¶6	Fr3.102	
GNMA Dollar Rolls...................			EITF.84-20
Grantor Trust			
. . Sales between Trust and Company....			EITF.84-15
Guidance for Applying Recognition Criteria...........................	CON5, ¶84		
Installment Method of Accounting.......	APB10, ¶12	R75.103	
Invasion of a Defeasance Trust			EITF.86-36
Leases			
. . Offsetting Nonrecourse Debt with Lease Receivables			EITF.84-25

FAS–FASB Statements	FIN–FASB Interpretations	FTB–FASB Technical Bulletins
APB–APB Opinions	AIN–AICPA Interpretations	ARB–Accounting Research Bulletins
CON–FASB Concepts	EITF–EITF Issues	Q&A–FASB Special Reports

	Original Pronouncements	Current Text	EITF and Other
REVENUE RECOGNITION—continued			
Leases—continued			
. . Recognition of Receipts from Made-up Rental Shortfalls			EITF.85-27
. . Sale-Leaseback with Guaranteed Residuals			EITF.86-17
. . Sale-Leaseback with Repurchase Option			EITF.84-37
Loan, Commitment, and Syndication Fees			
. . Fees Associated with Loan Syndications and Loan Participations...................			EITF.88-17
. . Interest Method	FAS91, ¶17-20	L20.116-119	
Loan Guarantee Fees			EITF.85-20
Loan Sales			
. . Sale of Bad Debt Recovery Rights			EITF.86-8
. . Sale of Convertible, Adjustable-Rate Mortgages with Contingent Repayment Agreement			EITF.87-25
. . Sale of Loan to Special-Purpose Entity			EITF.84-30
. . Sale of Loan with a Partial Participation Retained			EITF.84-21
. . Sale of Mortgage Loan with Servicing Rights Retained			EITF.86-39
. . Third-Party Establishment of CMOs..			EITF.86-24
Long-Term Power Sales Contracts of Nonutility Generators (NUGs).........			EITF.91-6
Master Limited Partnership (MLP)			
. . Gain Recognition on MLP Units Received in Exchange for Future Fees............................			EITF.88-14
Mutual Fund Distributors			
. . Fees Received from No-Load Funds ..			EITF.85-24
Nonmonetary Transactions			
. . Exchange of Assets for Noncontrolling Equity Interest in New Entity.......			EITF.89-7
. . Use of Fair Value			EITF.86-29
Options			
. . Options to Purchase Stock of Another Entity			EITF.85-9
. . Repurchase Option in Sale-Leaseback Transaction.....................			EITF.84-37
Preferred Stock			
. . Acquisition of a Subsidiary's Mandatorily Redeemable Stock			EITF.86-32
Product Financing Arrangements	FAS49, ¶6	D18.104	
Profit Recognition	ARB43, Ch.1A, ¶1	R75.101	
....	APB10, ¶12		
....	FAS111, ¶8		

See "Terminology" for references to defined terms presented in various accounting pronouncements.

See the Introduction to the Topical Index for details on the use of this index.

	Original Pronouncements	Current Text	EITF and Other
REVENUE RECOGNITION—continued			
Real Estate			
. . Antispeculation Clause in Sales Contract			EITF.86-6
. . Construction of House on Builder's Lot			EITF.86-7
. . Recognition of Receipts from Made-up Rental Shortfalls			EITF.85-27
. . Sale of Builder's Land and Related Construction Contract			EITF.86-7
. . Sale with Graduated Payment Mortgage or Insured Mortgage			EITF.84-17
. . Sale-Leaseback with Repurchase Option			EITF.84-37
. . Syndication Fees			EITF.85-37
Relation to Contractor Accounting: Construction-Type Contracts	ARB45, ¶4-6	Co4.103-110	
	ARB45, ¶9-12		
	ARB45, ¶15		
Relation to Contractor Accounting: Government Contracts	ARB43, Ch.11A, ¶19-20	Co5.106-107	
Relation to Franchising: Accounting by Franchisors	FAS45, ¶12-14	Fr3.108-110	
Revenue and Expense Recognition for Freight Services in Process			EITF.91-9
Sale of Marketable Securities with a Put Option			EITF.84-5
			EITF.85-30
			EITF.85-40
Sale of Preferred Stocks with a Put Option			EITF.85-25
Sale of Real Estate			
. . Antispeculation Clause in Sales Contract			EITF.86-6
. . Negative Amortization			EITF.84-17
			EITF.85-38
Sale of Rights to Service Mortgage Loans			EITF.89-5
Sale of Servicing Rights on Mortgages Owned by Others			EITF.85-13
Sale of Subsidiary for Equity Interest in Buyer			EITF.85-43
Seasonal Revenue			
. . Interim Financial Reporting	APB28, ¶18	I73.110	
Television Barter Syndicators			
. . Advertising Time for Television Programming			EITF.87-10
Unrealized Profits			
. . Nonrecognition	ARB43, Ch.1A, ¶1	R75.102	
When Right of Return Exists	FAS48, ¶6-8	R75.107-109	

FAS–FASB Statements	FIN–FASB Interpretations	FTB–FASB Technical Bulletins
APB–APB Opinions	AIN–AICPA Interpretations	ARB–Accounting Research Bulletins
CON–FASB Concepts	EITF–EITF Issues	Q&A–FASB Special Reports

T-373

	Original Pronouncements	Current Text	EITF and Other
REVENUE			
RECOGNITION—continued			
When Right of Return Exists—continued			
. . Scope of Accounting and Reporting			
Requirements	FAS48, ¶3-4	R75.105-106	
REVENUES			
See Revenue Recognition			
Characteristics	CON6, ¶79		
Component of Comprehensive Income . . .	CON6, ¶73-77		
Definition	CON6, ¶78		
Element of Financial Statements	CON6, ¶78-81		
Guidance in Applying Recognition			
Criteria	CON6, ¶87-89		
Not-for-Profit Organizations	CON6, ¶111-113		
Relation to Gains	CON6, ¶87-89		
REVERSE REPURCHASE			
AGREEMENTS			
See Financial Instruments			
GNMA Dollar Rolls			EITF. 84-20
Hedging with Futures Contracts			EITF.86-34
REVERSE STOCK SPLIT			
See Earnings per Share			
REVOLVING CREDIT AGREEMENT			
See Balance Sheet Classification: Current			
Assets and Liabilities			
See Lending Activities			
RIGHT OF RETURN			
See Revenue Recognition			
RIGHT OF SETOFF			
See Offsetting			
Definition	FIN39, ¶5	B10.101A	
RIGHTS			
See Debt: Convertible Debt and Debt with			
Stock Purchase Warrants			
See Debt: Extinguishments			
See Earnings per Share			
See Franchising			
See Leases			
See Mortgage Servicing Rights			
See Oil and Gas Producing Activities			
See Options			
Conversion			
See Debt: Convertible Debt and Debt			
with Stock Purchase Warrants			
See Debt: Extinguishments			
See Earnings per Share			

See "Terminology" for references to defined terms presented in various accounting pronouncements.

See the Introduction to the Topical Index for details on the use of this index.

(The next page is T-393.)

FAS—FASB Statements   FIN—FASB Interpretations   FTB—FASB Technical Bulletins
APB—APB Opinions   AIN—AICPA Interpretations   ARB—Accounting Research Bulletins
CON—FASB Concepts   EITF—EITF Issues   Q&A—FASB Special Reports

	Original Pronouncements	Current Text	EITF and Other
S CORPORATIONS			
See Income Taxes			
Classification of Payment Made to IRS to Retain Fiscal Year			EITF.88-4
Election to Retain Fiscal Year			
. . Classification of Payment Made to IRS			EITF.88-4
SABBATICAL LEAVE			
See Compensation to Employees: Paid Absences			
SAFE HARBOR LEASES			
See Leases			
SALE			
Loan with a Partial Participation Retained . . Income Recognition.			EITF.84-21
SALE-LEASEBACK TRANSACTIONS			
See Leases			
See Real Estate: Sales Other Than Retail Land Sales			
SALE VS. FINANCING			
Collateralized Mortgage Obligations Established through a Third Party			
. . Gain or Loss Recognition by Seller of Mortgages			EITF.86-24
Effect of a "Removal of Accounts" Provision on the Accounting for a Credit Card Securitization			EITF.90-18
GNMA Dollar Rolls			
. . Reverse Repurchase Agreements			EITF.84-20
Sale of Bad Debt Recovery Rights			EITF.86-8
Sale of Convertible, Adjustable-Rate Mortgages with Contingent Repayment Agreement			EITF.87-25
Sale of Credit Card Portfolio with Partial Interest Retained			EITF.88-22
Sale of Future Revenue			EITF.88-18
Sale of Marketable Securities with a Put Option			EITF.84-5
. . . .			EITF.85-30
. . . .			EITF.85-40
Sale of Mortgage Servicing Rights with Subservicing Agreement			EITF.87-34
. . Balance Sheet Treatment			EITF.90-21
Sale of Preferred Stocks with a Put Option . .			EITF.85-25
Sale of Short-Term Loan under Long-Term Credit Commitment			EITF.87-30
SALES			
See Contractor Accounting: Government Contracts			
See Leases			
See Nonmonetary Transactions			

FAS–FASB Statements   FIN–FASB Interpretations   FTB–FASB Technical Bulletins
APB–APB Opinions   AIN–AICPA Interpretations   ARB–Accounting Research Bulletins
CON–FASB Concepts   EITF–EITF Issues   Q&A–FASB Special Reports

See "Terminology" for references to defined terms presented in various accounting pronouncements.

See the Introduction to the Topical Index for details on the use of this index.

FAS—FASB Statements   FIN—FASB Interpretations   FTB—FASB Technical Bulletins
APB—APB Opinions   AIN—AICPA Interpretations   ARB—Accounting Research Bulletins
CON—FASB Concepts   EITF—EITF Issues   Q&A—FASB Special Reports

See "Terminology" for references to defined terms presented in various accounting pronouncements.

See the Introduction to the Topical Index for details on the use of this index.

FAS—FASB Statements   FIN—FASB Interpretations   FTB—FASB Technical Bulletins
APB—APB Opinions   AIN—AICPA Interpretations   ARB—Accounting Research Bulletins
CON—FASB Concepts   EITF—EITF Issues   Q&A—FASB Special Reports

T-397

	Original Pronouncements	Current Text	EITF and Other
SEGMENT OF BUSINESS REPORTING—continued			
Reportable Segments—continued			
. . Selection Criteria	FAS14, ¶15-18	S20.119-124	
	FAS14, ¶103-104		
. . Voluntary Disclosure of Detailed Information	FAS14, ¶21	S20.127	
Restatement of Previously Reported Information	FAS14, ¶40	S20.146	
Scope of Accounting and Reporting Requirements	FAS14, ¶4	S20.101-103	
	FAS21, ¶9		
	FAS21, ¶12		
	FAS21, ¶14-15		
SIC Codes	FAS14, ¶91-98	S20.149-156	
SELF-INSURANCE			
See Contingencies			
See Insurance Costs			
SELLING, GENERAL AND ADMINISTRATIVE EXPENSES			
See Interim Financial Reporting			
SENIOR SECURITIES			
See Earnings per Share			
SERVICE CONTRACTS			
See Revenue Recognition			
SERVICE EFFORTS AND ACCOMPLISHMENTS			
Not-for-Profit Organizations	CON4, ¶51-53		
SERVICE INDUSTRIES			
Revenue Recognition	FAS48, ¶4	R75.106	
SERVICE POTENTIAL			
Definition	CON6, ¶28		
Discussion	CON6, ¶26-30		
	CON6, ¶172-173		
SERVICING FEES			
See Mortgage Banking Activities			
See Mortgage Servicing Rights			
See Receivables Sold with Recourse			
SETOFF			
See Offsetting			
SETTLEMENTS (OF DEFINED BENEFIT PENSION PLANS)			
See Pension Costs			
SETTLEMENTS (OF POST-RETIREMENT BENEFIT PLANS)			
See Postretirement Benefits Other Than Pensions			

See "Terminology" for references to defined terms presented in various accounting pronouncements.

See the Introduction to the Topical Index for details on the use of this index.

	Original Pronouncements	Current Text	EITF and Other
SEVERANCE PAY			
See Income Statement Presentation: Discontinued Operations			
See Postemployment Benefits			
Accounting for Involuntary Termination Benefits..........................			EITF.94-3
SHADOW STOCK PLANS			
See Compensation to Employees: Stock Purchase and Stock Option Plans			
SHAREHOLDERS' EQUITY			
See Additional Paid-in Capital			
See Business Combinations			
See Capital Stock: Capital Transactions			
See Capital Stock: Dividends-in-Kind			
See Capital Stock: Preferred Stock			
See Capital Stock: Stock Dividends and Stock Splits			
See Capital Stock: Treasury Stock			
See Foreign Currency Translation			
See Retained Earnings			
See Statement of Investments by and Distributions to Owners			
Development Stage Enterprises..........	FAS7, ¶11	De4.107	
Nonreciprocal Transfers................	APB29, ¶5	N35.102	
Separate Component for Unrealized Gains (Losses) of Investments in Debt and Equity Securities	FAS115, ¶13	I80.110	
Valuation Allowances for Marketable Securities	FAS12, ¶11	I89.105	
SHAREHOLDERS/OWNERS			
See Shareholders' Equity			
SHARES OUTSTANDING			
See Capital Stock: Preferred Stock			
See Capital Stock: Stock Dividends and Stock Splits			
See Earnings per Share			
SHORT-TERM DEBT			
Balance Sheet Classification	ARB43, Ch.3A, ¶7	B05.108	
SICK PAY			
See Compensation to Employees: Paid Absences			
SIGNIFICANT INFLUENCE			
See Investments: Equity Method			
SINKING FUNDS			
See Capital Stock: Preferred Stock			
See Commitments: Long-Term Obligations			
See Debt: Extinguishments			
Balance Sheet Classification	ARB43, Ch.3A, ¶6	B05.107	
Redeemable Stock	FAS47, ¶10	C32.105	
SOFTWARE			
See Computer Software			

	Original Pronouncements	Current Text	EITF and Other
SOLVENCY			
Information about	CON1, ¶49		
SPECIAL ASSESSMENTS			
Accounting for Special Assessments and Tax Increment Financing Entities (TIFEs)			EITF.91-10
SPECIALIZED ACCOUNTING AND REPORTING			
See Accounting Changes			
See AICPA Statements of Position (SOPs)			
See Banking and Thrift Industries			
See Broadcasting Industry			
See Cable Television Industry			
See Contractor Accounting: Construction-Type Contracts			
See Contractor Accounting: Government Contracts			
See Defined Benefit Pension Plans			
See Development Stage Enterprises			
See Employee Benefit Funds			
See Finance Companies			
See Franchising			
See Insurance Industry			
See Investment Enterprises			
See Mineral Reserves			
See Mortgage Banking Activities			
See Motion Picture Industry			
See Not-for-Profit Organizations			
See Oil and Gas Producing Activities			
See Real Estate Enterprises			
See Record and Music Industry			
See Regulated Operations			
See Title Plant			
Retention in Consolidation			EITF.85-12
SPECIAL-PURPOSE BORROWINGS			
Gain or Loss Recognition on Defeasance			EITF.84-26
SPECIAL-PURPOSE ENTITIES			
Accounting for Special Assessments and Tax Increment Financing Entities (TIFEs)			EITF.91-10
Consolidation without Equity Ownership			EITF.84-30
Impact of Nonsubstantive Lessors, Residual Value Guarantees, and Other Provisions in Leasing Transactions			EITF.90-15
Receivables Sold with Recourse . . Sales to Special-Purpose Entity			EITF.84-30
Sales Recognition on Transfers of Assets by Sponsor			EITF.84-30
Transactions Involving Special-Purpose Entities			EITF.D-14

See "Terminology" for references to defined terms presented in various accounting pronouncements.
See the Introduction to the Topical Index for details on the use of this index.

	Original Pronouncements	Current Text	EITF and Other
SPECIAL TERMINATION BENEFITS PAID TO EMPLOYEES			
See Pension Costs			
See Postretirement Benefits Other Than Pensions			
SPINOFF			
Changes to Fixed Employee Stock Option Plans as a Result of Equity Restructuring			EITF.90-9
Description	APB29, ¶5	N35.102	
Distributions of Loans Receivable to Shareholders			EITF.87-17
SPOILAGE			
Inventory.	ARB43, Ch.4, ¶5	I78.106	
SPOT RATE			
See Foreign Currency Translation			
Definition	FAS52, ¶162	F60.419	
STANDARD COSTS			
See Inventory			
STANDARD INDUSTRIAL CLASSIFICATION (SIC) CODES			
See Segment of Business Reporting			
STANDARDIZED MEASURE OF DISCOUNTED FUTURE NET CASH FLOWS			
See Oil and Gas Producing Activities			
STANDARDS, FINANCIAL ACCOUNTING			
Relation to Concepts	CON1, ¶3		
STANDSTILL AGREEMENTS			
Costs Incurred in a Takeover Defense.			EITF.85-2
Effect on Subsequent Pooling of Interests .			EITF.87-15
Limit on Investors	FIN35, ¶9	I82.108	
Takeover Attempts	FTB85-6, ¶4-7	I17.509-510	
. . . .		I60.507-508	
. . Costs Incurred in a Takeover Defense .			EITF.85-2
START-UP COSTS			
See Development Stage Enterprises			
STATE AND LOCAL GOVERNMENTAL UNITS			
Application of Conceptual Framework . . .	CON4, ¶65-66		
. . . .	CON6, ¶2		
Compensated Absences			
. . Limitation of Accounting and Reporting Requirements	FAS43, ¶2	C44.102	

FAS–FASB Statements	FIN–FASB Interpretations	FTB–FASB Technical Bulletins
APB–APB Opinions	AIN–AICPA Interpretations	ARB–Accounting Research Bulletins
CON–FASB Concepts	EITF–EITF Issues	Q&A–FASB Special Reports

See "Terminology" for references to defined terms presented in various accounting pronouncements.
See the Introduction to the Topical Index for details on the use of this index.

	Original Pronouncements	Current Text	EITF and Other
STATEMENT OF INVESTMENTS BY AND DISTRIBUTIONS TO OWNERS			
See Shareholders' Equity			
Component of Full Set of Financial Statements	CON5, ¶13		
Description, Nature, and Recognition Considerations	CON5, ¶55-57		
STATEMENT OF RETAINED EARNINGS			
See Retained Earnings			
STATEMENT OF STOCKHOLDERS' EQUITY			
See Shareholders' Equity			
See Statement of Investments by and Distributions to Owners			
STATEMENTS OF EARNINGS AND COMPREHENSIVE INCOME			
See Comprehensive Income			
See Earnings			
Components of Full Set of Financial Statements	CON5, ¶13		
Description, Nature, and Recognition Considerations	CON5, ¶30-41		
Relationship between Earnings and Comprehensive Income	CON5, ¶42-44		
STATEMENTS OF NET ASSETS AVAILABLE FOR BENEFITS			
See Defined Benefit Pension Plans			
STATEMENTS OF POSITION (SOPs)			
Accounting Changes	FAS111, ¶10	A06.127	
	FIN20, ¶5		
STEAMSHIP COMPANIES (U.S.)			
Income Taxes	FAS109, ¶9	I27.108	
	FAS109, ¶32	I27.131	
STEP ACQUISITIONS			
See Consolidation			
See Intangible Assets			
Basis in Leveraged Buyout Transactions			EITF.86-16
			EITF.88-16
. . Allocating Basis to Individual Assets and Liabilities under Issue No. 88-16.			EITF.90-12
STOCK APPRECIATION RIGHTS			
Compensation Expense Relating to Cancellation			EITF.D-18
Definition	FIN28, ¶9	C47.403	
Description	FIN28, ¶2-5	C47.119-122	
	FIN28, ¶19-27	C47.138-146	
Purchase by Target Company in Leveraged Buyout			EITF.84-13

FAS–FASB Statements   FIN–FASB Interpretations   FTB–FASB Technical Bulletins
APB–APB Opinions   AIN–AICPA Interpretations   ARB–Accounting Research Bulletins
CON–FASB Concepts   EITF–EITF Issues   Q&A–FASB Special Reports

T-403

	Original Pronouncements	Current Text	EITF and Other
STOCK APPRECIATION **RIGHTS**—continued			
Pyramid Stock Option Plans............			EITF.84-18
STOCK BONUS OR AWARD PLANS			
See Compensation to Employees: Stock Purchase and Stock Option Plans			
STOCK DEPRECIATION RIGHTS			
See Compensation to Employees: Stock Purchase and Stock Option Plans			
See Stock Options			
STOCK DIVIDENDS			
See Capital Stock: Capital Transactions			
See Capital Stock: Dividends-in-Kind			
See Capital Stock: Stock Dividends and Stock Splits			
See Consolidation			
See Earnings per Share			
Definition	ARB43, Ch.7B, ¶1	C20.401	
STOCK DIVIDENDS SUBSIDIARIES			
See Consolidation			
STOCK INDEMNIFICATION RIGHTS			
See Compensation to Employees: Stock Purchase and Stock Option Plans			
See Stock Options			
STOCK ISSUED TO EMPLOYEES			
See Compensation to Employees: Stock Purchase and Stock Option Plans			
See Earnings per Share			
STOCK LIFE INSURANCE **ENTERPRISES**			
See Insurance Industry			
STOCK OPTION AND STOCK **PURCHASE PLANS**			
See Compensation to Employees: Stock Purchase and Stock Option Plans			
See Earnings per Share			
STOCK OPTIONS			
See Compensation to Employees: Stock Purchase and Stock Option Plans			
See Employee Stock Ownership Plans (ESOPs)			

See "Terminology" for references to defined terms presented in various accounting pronouncements.

See the Introduction to the Topical Index for details on the use of this index.

	Original Pronouncements	Current Text	EITF and Other
STOCK SPLITS—continued			
See Capital Stock: Stock Dividends and Stock Splits			
Definition	ARB43, Ch.7B, ¶2	C20.402	
STOCK SUBSCRIPTIONS			
See Capital Stock: Capital Transactions			
STOCKBROKERAGE INDUSTRY			
See Earnings per Share			
See Investments: Debt and Equity Securities			
See Investments: Marketable Securities			
See Segment of Business Reporting			
Unclassified Balance Sheet	FAS6, ¶7	B05.102	
STOCKHOLDERS' EQUITY			
See Shareholders' Equity			
STOCKHOLDERS/OWNERS			
See Shareholders' Equity			
SUBCHAPTER S CORPORATIONS			
See Earnings per Share			
SUBCONTRACTORS			
See Contractor Accounting: Construction-Type Contracts			
See Contractor Accounting: Government Contracts			
SUBJECTIVE ACCELERATION CLAUSE			
See Balance Sheet Classification: Current Assets and Liabilities			
SUBLEASE			
See Leases			
SUBSCRIPTIONS			
Qualification as Liabilities..............	CON6, ¶197		
SUBSEQUENT EVENTS			
See Contingencies			
See Foreign Currency Translation			
See Investments: Marketable Securities			
See Nonmonetary Transactions			
Change in Value of Marketable Securities .	FAS12, ¶13	I89.107	
SUBSIDIARIES			
See Consolidation			
See Discontinued Operations			
See Earnings per Share			
See Foreign Currency Translation			
See Income Taxes			
Business Combinations	AIN-APB16, #18	B50.556-559	

See "Terminology" for references to defined terms presented in various accounting pronouncements.

See the Introduction to the Topical Index for details on the use of this index.

	Original Pronouncements	Current Text	EITF and Other
SUBSIDIARIES—continued			
Business Combinations—continued			
....	AIN-APB16, #36	B50.635-637	
Definition	APB18, ¶3	I82.408	
Exchanges of Ownership Interests between Entities under Common Control			EITF.90-5
Fiscal Year of Parent and Subsidiary Differs			
. . Classification of Subsidiary's Loan Payable in Consolidated Balance Sheet...........................			EITF.88-15
Income Tax Provision			
. . Allocating Consolidated Tax Provision			EITF.86-9
Preacquisition Earnings................	ARB51, ¶9	R70.101	
Push-down Accounting			EITF.86-9
Push-down of Parent Company Debt			EITF.84-42
Related Parties	FAS57, ¶1	R36.101	
Sale of Capital Stock by Subsidiary			
. . Recognizing Income Tax Effect			EITF.84-27
Separate Financial Statements			
. . Push-down Accounting.............			EITF.85-21
. . Push-down of Parent Company Debt .			EITF.84-23
Unconsolidated......................	FAS14, ¶27	C51.102-103	
....	FAS94, ¶13	I82.102	
....	FAS94, ¶15	S20.133	
SUBSTANCE VS. FORM			
Relation to Reliability	CON2, ¶160		
SUCCESSFUL EFFORTS METHOD			
See Oil and Gas Producing Activities			
SUMMARY OF ACCOUNTING POLICIES			
See Accounting Policies			
SUM-OF-THE-YEARS DIGITS METHOD			
Depreciation	FAS109, ¶288	D40.104	
SUPPLEMENTAL FINANCIAL INFORMATION			
See Changing Prices: Reporting Their Effects in Financial Reports			
See Earnings per Share			
See Oil and Gas Producing Activities			
See Segment of Business Reporting			
Relation to Recognition in Financial Statements	CON5, ¶7-9		
SUPPLEMENTAL UNEMPLOYMENT BENEFITS			
See Postemployment Benefits			

	Original Pronouncements	Current Text	EITF and Other

SURPLUS (CAPITAL/ CONTRIBUTED/PAID-IN)
See Additional Paid-in Capital
See Capital Stock: Capital Transactions
See Statements of Investments by and
  Distributions to Owners

SWAPS
See Financial Instruments
Foreign Currency Swaps

. . Offsetting			EITF.86-25
Foreign Debt-for-Equity (Investor's Perspective)			EITF.87-12
Hedged by Cash Security			EITF.87-1
Interest Rate Swap Transactions			EITF.84-36
. . . .			EITF.88-8
. . Termination or Sale			EITF.84-7
Mortgage Swaps			EITF.88-8

SYNDICATION FEES

Fees Associated with Loan Syndications . .			EITF.88-17
Real Estate Syndicators			
. . Revenue Recognition of Syndication Fees			EITF.85-37

SYNDICATION OF REAL ESTATE

Recognition of Receipts from Made-up Rental Shortfalls			EITF.85-27

(The next page is T-421.)

See "Terminology" for references to defined terms presented in various accounting pronouncements.
See the Introduction to the Topical Index for details on the use of this index.

	Original Pronouncements	Current Text	EITF and Other

TAKE-OR-PAY CONTRACTS
Definition . . . . FAS47, ¶23   C32.403
Illustration. . . . . FAS47, ¶29-32   C32.111-114
TAKEOVER ATTEMPTS
Costs Incurred in a Takeover Defense. EITF.85-2
Issues Relating to . . . . FTB85-6, ¶1-7   C23.501-503
                                    I17.509-510
                                    I60.507-508
TANDEM PLANS
See Compensation to Employees: Stock
  Purchase and Stock Option Plans
TAX
See Income Taxes
See Interim Financial Reporting
Definition . . . . FIN18, ¶5   I73.403
Real and Personal Property. . . . . ARB43, Ch.10A, ¶10-14   T10.101-108
. . Balance Sheet and Income Statement
   Disclosure. . . . . ARB43, Ch.10A, ¶16-18   T10.106-108
TAXABLE INCOME
See Income Taxes
Definition . . . . APB23, ¶21   Bt7.408
                                    FAS109, ¶289   I27.415
TAX-EXEMPT BORROWINGS
See Interest: Capitalization of Interest Costs
TAX-EXEMPT SECURITIES
See Leases
See Municipal Bond Interest

FAS–FASB Statements   FIN–FASB Interpretations   FTB–FASB Technical Bulletins
APB–APB Opinions   AIN–AICPA Interpretations   ARB–Accounting Research Bulletins
CON–FASB Concepts   EITF–EITF Issues   Q&A–FASB Special Reports

T-421

See "Terminology" for references to defined terms presented in various accounting pronouncements.

See the Introduction to the Topical Index for details on the use of this index.

	Original Pronouncements	Current Text	EITF and Other
TERMINATION BENEFITS			
See Pension Costs			
See Postemployment Benefits			
See Postretirement Benefits Other Than Pensions			
See Special Termination Benefits Paid to Employees			
Accounting for Involuntary Termination Benefits..........................			EITF.94-3
TERMINATION OF PENSION PLAN			
See Pension Costs			
TERMINATION RATE			
See Insurance Industry			
Definition	FAS60, ¶66	In6.435	
TERMINOLOGY			
Accounting Changes..................	APB20, ¶6	A06.401	
Accounting Policies	APB22, ¶6	A10.401	
Accounting Principle	APB20, ¶7	A06.402	
Accrual	CON6, ¶139-141		
Accumulated Benefit Obligation	FAS87, ¶264	P16.401	
Accumulated Plan Benefits	FAS35, ¶280	Pe5.401	
Accumulated Postretirement Benefit Obligation	FAS106, ¶518	P40.401	
Acquisition Costs	FAS60, ¶66	In6.401	
Active Plan Participant	FAS106, ¶518	P40.402	
Actual Return on Plan Assets Component (of Net Periodic Pension Cost).........	FAS87, ¶264	P16.402	
Actual Return on Plan Assets Component (of Net Periodic Postretirement Benefit Cost).............................	FAS106, ¶518	P40.403	
Actuarial Present Value	FAS87, ¶264	P16.403	
....	FAS106, ¶518	P40.404	
Actuarial Present Value of Accumulated Plan Benefits	FAS35, ¶280	Pe5.403	
Advance Royalty......................	FAS50, ¶18	Re4.401	
Affiliated Enterprise...................	FAS65, ¶34	Mo4.401	
Affiliates	FAS57, ¶24	R36.401	
Allocated Contract	FAS87, ¶264	P16.404	
Allocation	CON6, ¶142		
Allocation Period	FAS38, ¶4	B50.401	
Allowable Costs	FAS71, ¶1	Re6.401	
Amenities	FAS67, ¶28	Re2.401	
Amortization	CON6, ¶142	P16.405	
....	FAS87, ¶264		
....	FAS106, ¶518	P40.405	
Annual Effective Tax Rate..............	APB28, ¶19	I73.401	
Annuity Contract	FAS60, ¶66	In6.402	
....	FAS87, ¶57	P16.406	
....	FAS87, ¶264		
....	FAS88, ¶5		
Area Franchise	FAS45, ¶26	Fr3.401	
Articulation.........................	CON6, ¶20-21		
Assessment Enterprise	FAS60, ¶66	In6.403	
Assets..............................	CON6, ¶25		
Assumed per Capita Claims Cost (by Age)	FAS106, ¶518	P40.406	

FAS–FASB Statements	FIN–FASB Interpretations	FTB–FASB Technical Bulletins
APB–APB Opinions	AIN–AICPA Interpretations	ARB–Accounting Research Bulletins
CON–FASB Concepts	EITF–EITF Issues	Q&A–FASB Special Reports

	Original Pronouncements	Current Text	EITF and Other
TERMINOLOGY—continued			
Assuming Enterprise	FAS113, ¶121	In6.403A	
Assumptions	FAS87, ¶264	P16.407	
	FAS106, ¶518	P40.407	
Attribute	CON6, ¶65-67	F60.401	
	FAS52, ¶162		
Attribution	FAS87, ¶264	P16.408	
	FAS106, ¶518	P40.408	
Attribution Period	FAS106, ¶518	P40.409	
Bargain Purchase	FAS45, ¶26	Fr3.402	
Bargain Purchase Option	FAS13, ¶5	L10.401	
Bargain Renewal Option	FAS13, ¶5	L10.402	
Barter	FAS63, ¶14	Br5.401	
Benefit	FIN18, ¶5	I73.403	
Benefit Formula	FAS87, ¶264	P16.409	
	FAS106, ¶518	P40.410	
Benefit Information	FAS35, ¶280	Pe5.404	
Benefit Information Date	FAS35, ¶280	Pe5.405	
Benefit Security	FAS35, ¶280	Pe5.406	
Benefit/Years-of-Service Approach	FAS87, ¶264	P16.411	
Benefits	FAS35, ¶280	P16.410	
	FAS87, ¶264	Pe5.407	
	FAS106, ¶518	P40.411	
Bias	CON2, Glossary		
Broadcaster	FAS63, ¶14	Br5.402	
Cable Television Plant	FAS51, ¶17	Ca4.401	
Call Price	APB15, App.D	E09.401	
Callable Obligations	FAS78, ¶1	B05.400	
Capital Leases	FAS13, ¶7	L10.403	
Capital Maintenance	CON6, ¶71		
Capitalize	FAS71, ¶4	Re6.402	
Captive Insurer	FAS87, ¶264	P16.412	
	FAS106, ¶518	P40.412	
Career-Average-Pay Formula (Career-Average-Pay Plan)	FAS87, ¶264	P16.413	
Carrybacks	FAS109, ¶289	I27.401	
Carryforwards	FAS109, ¶289	I27.402	
Carrying Amount	FAS12, ¶7	Bt7.401	
	FAS72, ¶5	I89.401	
Carrying Amount of the Payable	FAS15, ¶13	D22.401	
Cash Equivalents	FAS95, ¶8	C25.106	
Ceding Enterprise	FAS113, ¶121	In6.403B	
Change in Permanently Restricted Net Assets	CON6, ¶119		
Change in Temporarily Restricted Net Assets	CON6, ¶123		
Change in Unrestricted Net Assets	CON6, ¶127		
Changes in Financial Position	CON6, ¶20		
Circumstances (Affecting an Entity)	CON6, ¶136		
Claim Adjustment Expenses	FAS60, ¶66	In6.405	
Claims	FAS60, ¶66	In6.404	
Coding	FAS86, ¶52	Co2.401	

See "Terminology" for references to defined terms presented in various accounting pronouncements.

See the Introduction to the Topical Index for details on the use of this index.

FAS–FASB Statements	FIN–FASB Interpretations	FTB–FASB Technical Bulletins
APB–APB Opinions	AIN–AICPA Interpretations	ARB–Accounting Research Bulletins
CON–FASB Concepts	EITF–EITF Issues	Q&A–FASB Special Reports

	Original Pronouncements	Current Text	EITF and Other
TERMINOLOGY—continued			
Current Assets	ARB43, Ch.3A, ¶4	B05.401	
Current Cost/Constant Purchasing Power	FAS89, ¶44	C28.401	
Current Exchange Rate	FAS52, ¶162	F60.404	
Current Liabilities	ARB43, Ch.3A, ¶7	B05.402	
Current Market Value	FAS89, ¶44	C28.402	
Current Tax Expense or Benefit	FAS109, ¶289	I27.403	
Curtailment	FAS87, ¶264	P16.415	
	FAS88, ¶6	P16.447	
Curtailment (of a Postretirement Benefit Plan)	FAS106, ¶518	P40.416	
Customer Support	FAS86, ¶52	Co2.402	
Daypart	FAS63, ¶14	Br5.403	
Debt	FAS15, ¶4	D22.402	
Debt Security	FAS115, ¶137	I80.401	
Deductible Temporary Difference	FAS109, ¶289	I27.404	
Defeasance	FAS76, ¶14	D14.102A	
Deferral	CON6, ¶141		
Deferred Tax Asset	FAS109, ¶289	I27.405	
Deferred Tax Expense or Benefit	FAS109, ¶289	I27.406	
Deferred Tax Liability	FAS109, ¶289	I27.407	
Defined Benefit Pension Plan	FAS35, ¶280	P16.416	
	FAS87, ¶264	Pe5.409	
Defined Benefit Postretirement Plan	FAS106, ¶518	P40.417	
Defined Contribution Pension Plan	FAS87, ¶264	P16.417	
Defined Contribution Postretirement Plan	FAS106, ¶518	P40.418	
Dependency Status	FAS106, ¶518	P40.419	
Deposit Method	FAS60, ¶66	In6.408	
Depreciation Accounting	ARB43, Ch.9C, ¶5	D40.401	
Detail Program Design	FAS86, ¶52	Co2.403	
Development	FAS2, ¶8	R50.401	
Development Stage Enterprises	FAS7, ¶8	De4.401	
Development Well	FAS19, ¶274	Oi5.401	
Dilution (Dilutive)	APB15, App.D	E09.409	
Direct Financing Leases	FAS13, ¶6	L10.405	
Direct Selling Costs	FAS51, ¶17	Ca4.402	
Discontinued Operations	APB30, ¶8	I13.401	
Discount Rate	FAS87, ¶264	P16.418	
	FAS106, ¶518	P40.420	
Discount or Premium on a Forward Contract	FAS52, ¶162	F60.405	
Disposal Date	APB30, ¶14	I13.402	
Distributions to Owners	CON6, ¶67		
Distributor	FAS53, ¶26	Mo6.401	
Dividends	APB18, ¶3	I82.403	
Dividends to Policyholders	FAS60, ¶66	In6.409	

See "Terminology" for references to defined terms presented in various accounting pronouncements.

See the Introduction to the Topical Index for details on the use of this index.

	Original Pronouncements	Current Text	EITF and Other
TERMINOLOGY—continued			
Donor-imposed Condition.............	FAS116, ¶209	C67.404	
Donor-imposed Restriction............	FAS116, ¶209	C67.405	
....	FAS117, ¶168	No5.402	
Dual Presentation......................	APB15, App.D	E09.410	
ERISA..............................	FAS35, ¶280	Pe5.411	
....	FAS87, ¶264		
Earned................................	CON5, ¶83		
Earnings	CON5, ¶33		
Earnings or Losses of an Investee........	APB18, ¶3	I82.404	
Earnings per Share.....................	APB15, App.D	E09.411	
Economic Resources	CON6, ¶27		
Effective Yield	FAS85, ¶3	E09.123A	
Elements of Financial Statements........	CON6, ¶5		
Employee..............................	FAS35, ¶280	Pe5.410	
Endowment Contract....................	FAS60, ¶66	In6.410	
Endowment Fund.......................	FAS117, ¶168	No5.403	
Enterprise	FAS52, ¶162	F60.406	
Entity................................	CON6, ¶24	F60.407	
....	FAS52, ¶162		
Equitable Obligations...................	CON6, ¶40		
Equity	CON6, ¶49-50		
Equity Method Investments.............	APB18, ¶6	I82.405	
....	APB18, ¶11		
Equity Security........................	FAS12, ¶7	I89.403	
....	FAS115, ¶137	I80.402	
Estimated Economic Life of Leased Property...........................	FAS13, ¶5	L10.406	
Estimated Residual Value of Leased Property...........................	FAS13, ¶5	L10.407	
Event.................................	FAS109, ¶289	I27.408	
Events	CON6, ¶135		
Exchange (Exchange Transactions).......	APB29, ¶3	N35.401	
....	CON6, ¶137		
Executory Costs	FAS13, ¶7	L10.408	
....	FAS13, ¶10		
Exercise Price	APB15, App.D	E09.412	
Expected Long-Term Rate of Return on Plan Assets........................	FAS87, ¶264	P16.419	
....	FAS106, ¶518	P40.421	
Expected Postretirement Benefit Obligation	FAS106, ¶518	P40.422	
Expected Return on Plan Assets.........	FAS87, ¶264	P16.420	
....	FAS106, ¶518	P40.423	
Expenses	CON6, ¶80		
Explicit (Approach to) Assumptions......	FAS87, ¶264	P16.421	
....	FAS106, ¶518	P40.424	
Exploitation Costs	FAS53, ¶26	Mo6.402	
Exploratory Well.......................	FAS19, ¶274	Oi5.402	
Extended Warranty Contracts...........	FTB90-1, ¶2	R75.502	
Extraordinary Items...................	APB30, ¶20	I17.401	

FAS–FASB Statements   FIN–FASB Interpretations   FTB–FASB Technical Bulletins
APB–APB Opinions   AIN–AICPA Interpretations   ARB–Accounting Research Bulletins
CON–FASB Concepts   EITF–EITF Issues   Q&A–FASB Special Reports

See "Terminology" for references to defined terms presented in various accounting pronouncements.

See the Introduction to the Topical Index for details on the use of this index.

	Original Pronouncements	Current Text	EITF and Other
TERMINOLOGY—continued			
Funding Policy	FAS35, ¶280	P16.426	
. . . .	FAS87, ¶264	Pe5.413	
. . . .	FAS106, ¶518	P40.429	
Funds or Fund Balances	CON6, ¶91		
Future Economic Benefits	CON6, ¶28		
. . . .	CON6, ¶172		
Futures Contract.	FAS80, ¶15	F80.403	
Gain or Loss	FAS87, ¶264	P16.427	
. . . .	FAS106, ¶518	P40.430	
Gain or Loss Component (of Net Periodic Pension Cost).	FAS87, ¶264	P16.428	
Gain or Loss Component (of Net Periodic Postretirement Benefit Cost)	FAS106, ¶518	P40.431	
Gains	CON6, ¶82		
Gains and Losses Included in Comprehensive Income but Excluded from Net Income	FAS109, ¶289	I27.409	
Gap Commitment.	FAS65, ¶34		
General Reserve	APB23, ¶19	Bt7.402	
Goodwill	APB16, ¶87	B50.403	
Government National Mortgage Association (GNMA)	FAS65, ¶34	Mo4.406	
Gross Eligible Charges	FAS106, ¶518	P40.432	
Gross Premium.	FAS60, ¶66	In6.412	
Group Insurance.	FAS60, ¶66	In6.413	
Guaranteed Interest Contract	FAS110, ¶2	Pe5.413A	
Guaranteed Investment Contract	FAS110, ¶2	Pe5.413B	
Health Care Benefits	FAS81, ¶5	P50.401	
Health Care Cost Trend Rates.	FAS106, ¶518	P40.433	
Historical Cost	FAS89, ¶44	C28.403	
Historical Cost/Constant Purchasing Power	FAS89, ¶44	C28.404	
Holding Gain or Loss.	FAS115, ¶137	I80.404	
Home Viewing Market.	FAS53, ¶26	Mo6.405	
Identifiable Assets	FAS14, ¶10	S20.405	
If-Converted Method	APB15, App.D	E09.414	
Immediate Family.	FAS57, ¶24	R36.403	
Inactive Employees.	FAS112, ¶1	P32.401	
Inception of the Lease	FAS23, ¶6	L10.410	
Incidental Operations.	FAS67, ¶28	Re2.406	
Income from Continuing Operations	FAS89, ¶44	C28.405	
Income-Producing Real Estate	FAS89, ¶44	C28.406	
Income Taxes	FAS109, ¶289	I27.410	
Income Taxes Currently Payable (Refundable)	FAS109, ¶289	I27.411	

FAS—FASB Statements   FIN—FASB Interpretations   FTB—FASB Technical Bulletins
APB—APB Opinions   AIN—AICPA Interpretations   ARB—Accounting Research Bulletins
CON—FASB Concepts   EITF—EITF Issues   Q&A—FASB Special Reports

T-429

	Original Pronouncements	Current Text	EITF and Other
TERMINOLOGY—continued			
Income Tax Expense (Benefit)	FAS109, ¶289	I27.412	
Incremental Costs of Incidental Operations	FAS67, ¶28	Re2.407	
Incremental Direct Acquisition Costs	FTB90-1, ¶4	R75.504	
Incremental Direct Costs	FAS91, ¶80	L20.403	
Incremental Revenue from Incidental Operations	FAS67, ¶28	Re2.408	
Incurred but Not Reported Claims	FAS60, ¶66	In6.414	
Incurred Claims Cost (by Age)	FAS106, ¶518	P40.434	
Incurred Cost	FAS71, ¶9	Re6.403	
Independent Producer	FAS53, ¶26	Mo6.406	
Indirect Guarantee of Indebtedness of Others	FIN34, ¶2	C59.402	
Indirect Project Costs	FAS67, ¶28	Re2.409	
Industry Segment	FAS14, ¶10	Oi5.403B	
	FAS69, ¶8	S20.406	
Initial Direct Costs	FAS91, ¶24	L10.411	
Initial Franchise Fee	FAS45, ¶26	Fr3.407	
Initial Services	FAS45, ¶26	Fr3.408	
Instantaneous In-Substance Defeasance	FTB84-4, ¶2	D14.401A	
In-Substance Defeasance	FAS76, ¶14	D14.401B	
	FAS76, ¶22		
Insurance Contract	FAS106, ¶518	P40.435	
Insurance Risk	FAS113, ¶121	In6.414A	
Intercompany Profit	FAS71, ¶16	Re6.404	
Interest Cost Component (of Net Periodic Pension Cost)	FAS87, ¶264	P16.429	
Interest Cost Component (of Net Periodic Postretirement Benefit Cost)	FAS106, ¶518	P40.436	
Interest Rate	FAS87, ¶264	P16.430	
Interest Rate Implicit in the Lease	FAS13, ¶5	L10.412	
Internal Events	CON6, ¶135		
	CON6, ¶138		
Internal Reserve Method	FAS65, ¶34	Mo4.407	
Internal Transactions	CON6, ¶138		
Inventory	ARB43, Ch.4, ¶3	I78.401	
Investee	APB18, ¶3	I82.406	
Investment Value	APB15, App.D	E09.415	
Investments by Owners	CON6, ¶66		
Investor	APB18, ¶3	I82.407	
Junior Stock	FIN38, ¶1	C47.400	
Lease	FAS13, ¶1	L10.413	
Lease Term	FAS98, ¶22	L10.414	
Lessee's Incremental Borrowing Rate	FAS13, ¶5	L10.415	
Leveraged Lease	FAS13, ¶6	L10.416	
Liabilities	CON6, ¶35		
Liability for Claim Adjustment Expenses	FAS60, ¶66	In6.415	
Liability for Future Policy Benefits	FAS60, ¶66	In6.416	
Liability for Unpaid Claims	FAS60, ¶66	In6.417	

See "Terminology" for references to defined terms presented in various accounting pronouncements.

See the Introduction to the Topical Index for details on the use of this index.

	Original Pronouncements	Current Text	EITF and Other
TERMINOLOGY—continued			
License Agreement for Program Material .	FAS63, ¶14	Br5.404	
License Agreement for Television Program Material	FAS53, ¶26	Mo6.407	
License Agreements	FAS50, ¶18	Re4.402	
Life Insurance Enterprises	FAS60, ¶66	In6.418	
Liquidity	CON5, ¶24		
Local Currency	FAS52, ¶162	F60.416	
Long-Term Interest-Bearing Assets	FAS72, ¶5	Bt7.403	
Long-Term Obligations	FAS6, ¶2	B05.403	
Loss	CON6, ¶16	P16.431	
. . . .	FAS87, ¶264		
Losses	CON6, ¶83		
Lower of Cost or Market (Rule)	ARB43, Ch.4, ¶9	I78.403	
Maintenance	FAS86, ¶52	Co2.404	
Maintenance Costs	FAS60, ¶66	In6.419	
Maintenance of Net Assets	CON6, ¶105		
Management	FAS57, ¶24	R36.404	
Market	ARB43, Ch.4, ¶9	I78.404	
. . . .	FAS53, ¶26	Mo6.408	
Marketable Equity Security	FAS12, ¶7	I89.404	
. . . .	FIN16, ¶5		
Market Parity	APB15, App.D	E09.416	
Market Price	FAS12, ¶7	I89.405	
. . . .	FIN16, ¶5		
Market-Related Value of Plan Assets	FAS87, ¶264	P16.432	
. . . .	FAS106, ¶518	P40.437	
Market Risk	FAS105, ¶7	F25.403	
Market Value	FAS12, ¶7	I89.406	
Master Netting Arrangement	FIN39, ¶10	B10.106	
Materiality	CON2, Glossary		
Measurement Date	APB25, ¶10	C47.401	
. . . .	FAS87, ¶264	P16.433	
. . . .	FAS106, ¶518	P40.438	
Measurement Date of a Disposal	APB30, ¶14	I13.403	
Medicare Reimbursement Rates	FAS106, ¶518	P40.439	
Mineral Resource Assets	FAS89, ¶44	C28.407	
Minimum Guarantee	FAS50, ¶18	Re4.403	
Minimum Lease Payments	FAS13, ¶5	L10.417	
. . . .	FAS29, ¶10		
Monetary Assets	APB29, ¶3	C28.408	
. . . .	FAS89, ¶44	N35.402	
Monetary Liabilities	APB29, ¶3	C28.409	
. . . .	FAS89, ¶44	N35.402	
Money-Over-Money Lease Transactions . .	FTB88-1, ¶16	L10.417B	
Morbidity	FAS60, ¶66	In6.420	
Mortality	FAS60, ¶66	In6.421	
Mortality Rate	FAS87, ¶264	P16.434	
Mortgage Banking Enterprise	FAS65, ¶34	Mo4.409	
Mortgage Guaranty Insurance Enterprise .	FAS60, ¶66	In6.422	
Mortgage-Backed Securities	FAS65, ¶34	Mo4.408	
Motion Picture Films	FAS53, ¶26	C28.410	
. . . .	FAS89, ¶44	Mo6.409	

FAS—FASB Statements   FIN—FASB Interpretations   FTB—FASB Technical Bulletins
APB—APB Opinions   AIN—AICPA Interpretations   ARB—Accounting Research Bulletins
CON—FASB Concepts   EITF—EITF Issues   Q&A—FASB Special Reports

	Original Pronouncements	Current Text	EITF and Other
TERMINOLOGY—continued			
Multiemployer Plan	FAS87, ¶264	P16.435	
	FAS106, ¶518	P40.440	
Multiple-Employer Plan	FAS87, ¶264	P16.436	
	FAS106, ¶518	P40.441	
Negative Goodwill	APB16, ¶87	B50.404	
Net Asset Information	FAS35, ¶280	Pe5.414	
Net Assets	CON6, ¶49-50		
Net Assets Available for Benefits	FAS35, ¶280	Pe5.415	
Net Carrying Amount	APB26, ¶3	D14.402	
Net Incurred Claims Cost (by Age)	FAS106, ¶518	P40.442	
Net Periodic Pension Cost	FAS87, ¶264	P16.437	
Net Periodic Postretirement Benefit Cost	FAS106, ¶518	P40.443	
Net Premium	FAS60, ¶66	In6.423	
Net Realizable Value	FAS53, ¶26	Co2.405	
	FAS67, ¶28	Mo6.410	
	FAS86, ¶10	Re2.410	
Net Receivables	FAS77, ¶12	R20.402	
Net Unrealized Gain or Loss	FAS12, ¶7	I89.407	
Net-Spread Method	FIN9, ¶2	Bt7.404	
Network Affiliation Agreement	FAS63, ¶14	Br5.405	
Neutrality	CON2, Glossary		
Nominal	FTB85-2, ¶2	C30.502	
Nonforfeiture Benefits	FAS60, ¶66	In6.424	
Nonmonetary Assets	APB29, ¶3	N35.403	
Nonmonetary Liabilities	APB29, ¶3	N35.403	
Nonmonetary Transactions	APB29, ¶1	N35.404	
Nonparticipating Annuity Contracts	FAS87, ¶264	P16.438	
Nonparticipating Insurance Contract	FAS106, ¶518	P40.444	
Nonpublic Enterprise	FAS21, ¶13	B50.404A	
	FAS79, ¶5	E09.417	
	FAS79, ¶16	S20.407	
	FAS87, ¶264	I27.413	
	FAS109, ¶289		
Nonreciprocal Transfer	APB29, ¶3	C67.406	
	CON6, ¶137	N35.405	
	FAS116, ¶209		
Nonrecourse Financing	FAS98, ¶70	L10.417C	
Normal Servicing Fee Rate	FAS65, ¶34	Mo4.402	
	FAS77, ¶12	R20.401	
Not-for-Profit Organizations	FAS116, ¶209	C67.407	
	FAS117, ¶168	No5.405	
Obligations	CON6, ¶35		
Oil and Gas Producing Activities	FAS19, ¶1	Oi5.403C	
Operating Cycle	ARB43, Ch.3A, ¶5	B05.404	
Operating Lease	FAS13, ¶6	L10.418	
Operating Profit or Loss	FAS14, ¶10	S20.408	
Operating Right	FAS44, ¶3	I60.402	

See "Terminology" for references to defined terms presented in various accounting pronouncements.

See the Introduction to the Topical Index for details on the use of this index.

	Original Pronouncements	Current Text	EITF and Other
TERMINOLOGY—continued			
Option	APB15, App.D	E09.418	
Ordinary Income or Loss	FIN18, ¶5	I73.402	
Origination Fees	FAS91, ¶80	L20.404	
PBGC (Pension Benefit Guaranty Corporation)	FAS35, ¶280	Pe5.417	
	FAS87, ¶264		
Parity Adjustment	FAS89, ¶44	C28.411	
Participant	FAS35, ¶280	P16.439	
	FAS87, ¶264	Pe5.416	
Participating Annuity Contract	FAS87, ¶264	P16.440	
Participating Insurance	FAS60, ¶66	In6.425	
Participating Insurance Contract	FAS106, ¶518	P40.445	
Participation	FAS53, ¶26	Mo6.411	
Participation Right	FAS87, ¶264	P16.441	
	FAS106, ¶518	P40.446	
Pay-Related Plan	FAS106, ¶518	P40.447	
Penalty in Lease Arrangement	FAS98, ¶22	L10.418A	
Pension Benefit Formula (Plan's Benefit Formula or Benefit Formula)	FAS87, ¶264	P16.442	
Pension Benefits	FAS35, ¶280	P16.443	
	FAS87, ¶264	Pe5.418	
Pension Plans	FAS35, ¶280	Pe5.419	
Per Capita Claims Cost by Age	FAS106, ¶518	P40.448	
Permanent Investor	FAS65, ¶34	Mo4.410	
Permanent Restriction	FAS117, ¶168	No5.406	
Permanently Restricted Net Assets	CON6, ¶92	No5.407	
	FAS117, ¶168		
Phase	FAS67, ¶28	Re2.411	
Phase-in Plan	FAS92, ¶3	Re6.404A	
Physical Capital Maintenance Concept	CON5, ¶47		
Plan	APB25, ¶4	C47.402	
	FAS35, ¶280	Pe5.420	
	FAS106, ¶518	P40.449	
Plan Administrator	FAS35, ¶280	Pe5.421	
Plan Amendment	FAS87, ¶264	P16.444	
	FAS106, ¶518	P40.450	
Plan Assets	FAS87, ¶264	P16.445	
	FAS106, ¶518	P40.451	
Plan Assets Available for Benefits	FAS87, ¶264	P16.446	
Plan Curtailment	FAS87, ¶264	P16.447	
	FAS88, ¶6		
Plan Demographics	FAS106, ¶518	P40.452	
Plan Participant	FAS106, ¶518	P40.453	
Plan Termination	FAS106, ¶518	P40.454	
Plan Termination/Reestablishment	FAS87, ¶264	P16.449	
Plan's Benefit Formula	FAS87, ¶264	P16.448	
Pooling-of-Interests Method	APB16, ¶45	B50.405	
Postemployment	FAS81, ¶1	P50.402	
Postemployment Benefits	FAS112, ¶1	P32.402	
Postretirement	FAS81, ¶1	P50.403	

	Original Pronouncements	Current Text	EITF and Other
TERMINOLOGY—continued			
Postretirement Benefit Plan............	FAS106, ¶518	P40.455	
Postretirement Benefits	FAS106, ¶518	P40.456	
Postretirement Benefits Other Than Pensions...........................	FAS106, ¶518	P40.457	
Postretirement Health Care Benefits......	FAS106, ¶518	P40.458	
Preacquisition Contingencies............	FAS38, ¶4	B50.406	
Preacquisition Costs...................	FAS67, ¶28	Re2.412	
Predictive Value	CON2, Glossary		
Prematurity Period....................	FAS51, ¶17	Ca4.403	
Prepaid Pension Cost..................	FAS87, ¶264	P16.450	
Pretax Accounting Income	APB23, ¶21	Bt7.405	
Primary Earnings per Share	APB15, App.D	E09.419	
Principal Owners	FAS57, ¶24	R36.405	
Prior Service Cost....................	FAS87, ¶264	P16.451	
....	FAS106, ¶518	P40.459	
Probable	CON6, ¶25	C59.403	
....	CON6, ¶35	Re6.405	
....	FAS5, ¶3		
....	FAS90, ¶9		
Probable Adjustments	FAS77, ¶12	R20.403	
Probable Mineral Reserves in Extractive Industries Other Than Oil and Gas	FAS89, ¶44	C28.412	
Producer	FAS53, ¶26	Mo6.412	
Product Design.......................	FAS86, ¶52	Co2.406	
Product Enhancement	FAS86, ¶52	Co2.407	
Product Financing Arrangements........	FAS49, ¶3	D18.401	
Product Maintenance Contracts	FTB90-1, ¶2	R75.502	
Product Masters	FAS86, ¶52	Co2.408	
Production Costs	FAS53, ¶26	Mo6.413	
Productive Assets.....................	APB29, ¶3	N35.406	
Profit..............................	CON6, ¶16		
Project Costs........................	FAS67, ¶28	Re2.413	
Project Financing Arrangements.........	FAS47, ¶23	C32.401	
Projected Benefit Obligation............	FAS87, ¶264	P16.452	
Promise to Give	FAS116, ¶209	C67.408	
Property and Liability Insurance Enterprise........................	FAS60, ¶66	In6.426	
Prospective Reinsurance	FAS113, ¶121	In6.426A	
Proved Area	FAS19, ¶275	Oi5.404	
Proved Mineral Reserves in Extractive Industries Other Than Oil and Gas	FAS89, ¶44	C28.413	
Proved Reserves	FAS25, ¶34	Oi5.405	
Public Enterprise	FAS109, ¶289	I27.414	
Publicly Traded Enterprise.............	FAS69, ¶1	Oi5.405A	
Purchase Method	APB16, ¶44	B50.407	
Purchaser's Incremental Borrowing Rate..	FAS47, ¶23	C32.402	
Purchasing Power Gain or Loss	FAS89, ¶44	C28.414	
Reacquisition Price of Debt.............	APB26, ¶3	D14.403	
Realization	CON6, ¶143		

See "Terminology" for references to defined terms presented in various accounting pronouncements.
See the Introduction to the Topical Index for details on the use of this index.

	Original Pronouncements	Current Text	EITF and Other
TERMINOLOGY—continued			
Realized Gain (Loss)	FAS12, ¶7	I89.408	
Realized, Realizable	CON5, ¶83		
	CON6, ¶143		
Reasonably Possible....................	FAS5, ¶3	C59.404	
Reciprocal or Interinsurance Exchange ...	FAS60, ¶66	In6.427	
Recognition...........................	CON5, ¶6		
	CON6, ¶143		
Record Master	FAS50, ¶18	Re4.404	
Recorded Investment in the Receivable ...	FAS15, ¶28	D22.403	
Recourse	FAS77, ¶12-14	R20.404	
Recoverable Amount	FAS89, ¶44	C28.415	
Redemption Price......................	APB15, App.D	E09.420	
Regulatory Lag........................	FAS92, ¶39	Re6.406	
Reinsurance...........................	FAS60, ¶66	In6.428	
Reinsurance Receivables	FAS113, ¶121	In6.428A	
Reinsurer	FAS113, ¶121	In6.428B	
Related Parties	FAS13, ¶5	L10.419	
	FAS57, ¶24	R36.406	
Relative Fair Value before Construction...	FAS67, ¶28	Re2.414	
Relevance	CON2, Glossary		
Reliability	CON2, Glossary		
Remote	FAS5, ¶3	C59.405	
Renewal or Extension of a Lease	FAS13, ¶6	L10.420	
Reporting Currency	FAS52, ¶162	F60.417	
Reporting Date........................	FAS35, ¶280	Pe5.423	
Reporting Enterprise	FAS52, ¶162	F60.418	
Representational Faithfulness	CON2, Glossary		
Research	FAS2, ¶8	R50.402	
Reserve for Bad Debts	APB23, ¶19	Bt7.406	
Reservoir	FAS19, ¶273	Oi5.406	
Restate-Translate......................	FAS89, ¶44	C28.416	
Restricted Stock	FAS12, ¶7	I89.409	
	FAS115, ¶3	I80.405	
Restricted Support	FAS116, ¶209	C67.409	
		No5.408	
Retirees	FAS106, ¶518	P40.460	
Retroactive Benefits	FAS87, ¶264	P16.453	
Retroactive Reinsurance...............	FAS113, ¶121	In6.428C	
Return on Plan Assets	FAS87, ¶264	P16.454	
Revenue..............................	CON6, ¶78		
Right of Setoff	FIN39, ¶5	B10.101A	
Risk	FAS80, ¶4	F80.404	
Risk of Accounting Loss	FAS105, ¶7	F25.404	
Risk of Adverse Deviation..............	FAS60, ¶66	In6.429	
Royalties	FAS50, ¶18	Re4.405	
Sale-Leaseback Accounting	FAS98, ¶70	L10.420A	
Sales Recognition	FAS98, ¶70	L10.420B	
Sales-Type Lease	FAS13, ¶6	L10.421	
Salvage	FAS60, ¶66	In6.430	
Security	APB15, App.D	E09.421	
	FAS115, ¶137	I80.406	
Segment of a Business	APB30, ¶13	I13.404	

FAS—FASB Statements	FIN—FASB Interpretations	FTB—FASB Technical Bulletins
APB—APB Opinions	AIN—AICPA Interpretations	ARB—Accounting Research Bulletins
CON—FASB Concepts	EITF—EITF Issues	Q&A—FASB Special Reports

T-435

	Original Pronouncements	Current Text	EITF and Other
TERMINOLOGY—continued			
Senior Security	APB15, App.D	E09.422	
Separately Priced Contracts	FTB90-1, ¶2	R75.502	
Separate-Valuation Method	FIN9, ¶3	Bt7.407	
Service	FAS35, ¶280	P16.455	
	FAS87, ¶264	Pe5.424	
Service Cost Component (of Net Periodic Pension Cost)	FAS87, ¶264	P16.456	
Service Cost Component (of Net Periodic Postretirement Benefit Cost)	FAS106, ¶518	P40.461	
Service Period	FIN28, ¶3	C47.402A	
Service Potential	CON6, ¶28		
Service Providing Efforts	CON6, ¶112		
Service Well	FAS19, ¶274	Oi5.407	
Servicing	FAS65, ¶34	Mo4.411	
Settlement (of a Postretirement Benefit Plan)	FAS106, ¶518	P40.462	
Settlement Period	FAS113, ¶121	In6.430A	
Settlements	FAS87, ¶264	P16.457	
	FAS88, ¶3		
Short-Term Obligations	FAS6, ¶2	B05.405	
Similar Productive Assets	APB29, ¶3	N35.407	
Single-Employer Plan	FAS87, ¶264	P16.458	
	FAS106, ¶518	P40.463	
Sponsor	FAS35, ¶280	Pe5.425	
Spot Rate	FAS52, ¶162	F60.419	
Standby Commitment	FAS65, ¶34		
Statutory Accounting Practices	FAS60, ¶66	In6.431	
Stock Appreciation Rights	FIN28, ¶9	C47.403	
Stock Dividend	ARB43, Ch.7B, ¶1	C20.401	
Stock Split	ARB43, Ch.7B, ¶2	C20.402	
Stratigraphic Test Well	FAS19, ¶274	Oi5.408	
Subjective Acceleration Clause	FAS78, ¶10	B05.405A	
Subrogation	FAS60, ¶66	In6.432	
Subscriber Related Costs	FAS51, ¶17	Ca4.404	
Subsidiary	APB18, ¶3	I82.408	
Substantive Plan	FAS106, ¶518	P40.464	
Supplemental Actuarial Value	FAS35, ¶280	Pe5.426	
Supplementary Earnings per Share	APB15, App.D	E09.423	
Suspension	FAS87, ¶264	P16.459	
Take-or-Pay Contract	FAS47, ¶23	C32.403	
Tax	FIN18, ¶5	I73.403	
Taxable Income	APB23, ¶21	Bt7.408	
	FAS109, ¶289	I27.415	
Taxable Temporary Difference	FAS109, ¶289	I27.416	
Tax Consequences	FAS109, ¶289	I27.417	

See "Terminology" for references to defined terms presented in various accounting pronouncements.

See the Introduction to the Topical Index for details on the use of this index.

	Original Pronouncements	Current Text	EITF and Other
TERMINOLOGY—continued			
Tax-Planning Strategy	FAS109, ¶289	I27.418	
Temporarily Restricted Net Assets	CON6, ¶93	No5.409	
	FAS117, ¶168		
Temporary Difference	FAS109, ¶289	I27.419	
Temporary Restriction	FAS117, ¶168	No5.410	
Termination	FAS60, ¶66	In6.434	
Termination Benefits	FAS106, ¶518	P40.465	
Termination Rate	FAS60, ¶66	In6.435	
Term Life Insurance	FAS60, ¶66	In6.433	
Testing	FAS86, ¶52	Co2.409	
Throughput Contract	FAS47, ¶23	C32.404	
Time of Issuance	APB15, App.D	E09.424	
Time of Restructuring	FAS15, ¶6	D22.404	
Timeliness	CON2, Glossary		
Title Insurance Enterprise	FAS60, ¶66	In6.436	
Title Plant	FAS61, ¶1	Ti7.401	
Transaction	CON6, ¶137		
Transaction Date	FAS52, ¶162	F60.420	
Transaction Gain (Loss)	FAS52, ¶162	F60.421	
Transition Asset	FAS106, ¶518	P40.466	
Transition Obligation	FAS106, ¶518	P40.467	
Translate-Restate	FAS89, ¶44	C28.417	
Translation	FAS52, ¶162	F60.422	
Translation Adjustment	FAS52, ¶162	C28.418	
	FAS89, ¶44	F60.423	
Treasury-Stock Method	APB15, App.D	E09.425	
Troubled Debt Restructuring	FAS15, ¶2	D22.405	
Turnover	FAS87, ¶264	P16.460	
Two-Class Method	APB15, App.D	E09.426	
Uncertainty	CON6, ¶44		
Unconditional Promise to Give	FAS116, ¶209	C67.410	
		No5.411	
Understandability	CON2, Glossary		
Unfunded Accrued Pension Cost	FAS87, ¶264	P16.461	
Unfunded Accumulated Benefit Obligation	FAS87, ¶264	P16.462	
Unfunded Accumulated Postretirement Benefit Obligation	FAS106, ¶518	P40.468	
Unguaranteed Residual Value	FAS13, ¶5	L10.422	
Unrealized	CON6, ¶43		
Unrecognized Net Gain or Loss	FAS87, ¶264	P16.463	
	FAS106, ¶518	P40.469	

	Original Pronouncements	Current Text	EITF and Other
TERMINOLOGY—continued			
Unrecognized Prior Service Cost.........	FAS87, ¶264	P16.464	
....	FAS106, ¶518	P40.470	
Unrecognized Transition Asset	FAS106, ¶518	P40.471	
Unrecognized Transition Obligation	FAS106, ¶518	P40.472	
Unrelated Parties	FAS13, ¶5	L10.423	
Unrestricted Net Assets	CON6, ¶94	No5.412	
....	FAS117, ¶168		
Unrestricted Support	FAS116, ¶209	C67.411	
....		No5.413	
Valuation Allowance	FAS12, ¶7	I27.420	
....	FAS109, ¶289	I89.410	
....	CON6, ¶34	V18.401	
Value in Use	FAS89, ¶44	C28.419	
Variable Annuity Contract..............	FAS60, ¶66	In6.437	
Variable Stock Option, Purchase and Award Plans	APB25, ¶29	C47.405	
Verifiability..........................	CON2, Glossary		
Vested Benefit Obligation	FAS87, ¶264	P16.465	
Vested Benefits	FAS35, ¶280	P16.466	
....	FAS87, ¶264	Pe5.427	
Voluntary Health and Welfare Organizations......................	FAS117, ¶168	No5.414	
Warrant..............................	APB15, App.D	E09.427	
Weighted Average Number of Shares	APB15, App.D	E09.428	
Whole-Life Contract	FAS60, ¶66	In6.438	
Working Capital.......................	ARB43, Ch.3A, ¶3	B05.406	
Working Model........................	FAS86, ¶52	Co2.410	
Wrap Lease Transactions	FTB88-1, ¶21	L10.424	
THREE PERCENT RULE			
See Earnings per Share			
THRIFT INDUSTRY			
See Banking and Thrift Industries			
THROUGHPUT CONTRACTS			
See Financial Instruments			
Definition	FAS47, ¶23	C32.404	
Illustration..........................	FAS47, ¶24-28	C32.106-110	
TIMBERLANDS AND GROWING TIMBER			
Changing Prices Information	FAS89, ¶25-26	C28.121-122	
TIMELINESS			
Definition	CON2, Glossary		
Relation to Usefulness and Relevance	CON2, ¶56-57		
TIME-SHARING INTERESTS (REAL ESTATE)			
See Real Estate: Sales Other Than Retail Land Sales			

See "Terminology" for references to defined terms presented in various accounting pronouncements.

See the Introduction to the Topical Index for details on the use of this index.

	Original Pronouncements	Current Text	EITF and Other
TITLE INSURANCE ENTERPRISE			
See Insurance Industry			
See Title Plant			
Definition	FAS60, ¶66	In6.436	
TITLE PLANT			
See Disclosure			
Capitalization	FAS61, ¶3-6	Ti7.103-106	
Definition	FAS61, ¶1	Ti7.401	
Description	FAS61, ¶1	Ti7.101	
Impairment of Value	FAS61, ¶6	Ti7.106	
Maintenance and Title Searches	FAS61, ¶7	Ti7.107	
Sale of Asset	FAS61, ¶9	Ti7.109	
Scope of Accounting and Reporting Requirements	FAS61, ¶2	Ti7.102	
Storage and Retrieval	FAS61, ¶8	Ti7.108	
TOTAL NONOWNER CHANGES IN EQUITY			
See Comprehensive Income			
TRADEMARKS			
Intangible Assets	APB17, ¶1	I60.101	
TRADE PAYABLES/RECEIVABLES			
See Balance Sheet Classification: Current Assets and Liabilities			
See Financial Instruments			
TRANSACTIONS			
See Events and Transactions			
TRANSACTIONS WITH AFFILIATES			
See Related Parties			
TRANSFERS, NONRECIPROCAL AND RECIPROCAL			
See Nonmonetary Transactions			
TRANSLATE-RESTATE METHOD			
See Changing Prices: Reporting Their Effects in Financial Reports			
TRANSLATION			
See Foreign Currency Translation			
Definition	FAS52, ¶162	F60.422	
TRANSLATION ADJUSTMENTS			
See Changing Prices: Reporting Their Effects in Financial Reports			
See Foreign Currency Translation			
Definition	FAS52, ¶162	F60.423	
TREASURY BONDS			
See Debt: Extinguishments			
TREASURY STOCK			
See Capital Stock: Treasury Stock			
TREASURY-STOCK METHOD			
See Earnings per Share			
Definition	APB15, App.D	E09.425	

FAS—FASB Statements   FIN—FASB Interpretations   FTB—FASB Technical Bulletins
APB—APB Opinions   AIN—AICPA Interpretations   ARB—Accounting Research Bulletins
CON—FASB Concepts   EITF—EITF Issues   Q&A—FASB Special Reports

	Original Pronouncements	Current Text	EITF and Other
TROUBLED DEBT RESTRUCTURING			
See Debt: Restructurings			
See Impairment: Loans			
Definition	FAS15, ¶2	D22.405	
TRUSTS			
Acquisition of Employer Shares for/by an			
Employee Benefit Trust			EITF.93-2
Assets in Defeasance Trust Reacquired			EITF.86-36
Consideration of the Impact of			
Bankruptcy in Determining Plan Assets			
under FASB Statement No. 106			EITF.93-3
Financial Statements of Common Trust			
Funds			
. . Exemption from the Requirement to			
Provide a Statement of Cash Flows . .	FAS102, ¶6-7	C25.135B-135C	
Related Parties	FAS57, ¶1	R36.101	
TWENTY PERCENT RULE			
See Earnings per Share			
TWO-CLASS COMMON STOCK			
See Earnings per Share			

(The next page is T-453.)

See "Terminology" for references to defined terms presented in various accounting pronouncements.
See the Introduction to the Topical Index for details on the use of this index.

	Original Pronouncements	Current Text	EITF and Other

UNAMORTIZED DISCOUNT
See Debt: Extinguishments
See Debt: Restructurings
See Interest: Imputation of an Interest
  Cost
UNASSERTED CLAIMS
See Insurance Industry
UNAUDITED FINANCIAL
  STATEMENTS

| Accounting Policies | APB22, ¶10 | A10.104 | |
| Earnings per Share | AIN-APB15, #14 | E09.562-563 | |

UNBILLED RECEIVABLES
See Contractor Accounting: Government
  Contracts
UNCERTAINTIES
See Accounting Changes
See Adjustments of Financial Statements
  for Prior Periods
See Contingencies
See Franchising
See Pension Costs
Actuarial Assumptions
  See Defined Benefit Pension Plans

Effects of	CON6, ¶44-48		
Relation to Assets	CON6, ¶175		
Relation to Recognition of Assets and Liabilities	CON6, ¶48		
Relation to Reliability	CON6, ¶45-48		
Relation to Representational Faithfulness	CON2, ¶72-76		

UNCONSOLIDATED SUBSIDIARIES
See Consolidation
See Investments: Equity Method
See Segment of Business Reporting
UNDERSTANDABILITY

| Definition | CON2, Glossary | | |
| User-Specific Characteristic | CON2, ¶40-41 | | |

UNDEVELOPED PROPERTIES
See Oil and Gas Producing Activities
UNDISTRIBUTED EARNINGS OF
  SUBSIDIARIES
See Income Taxes
UNEARNED DISCOUNTS

| Balance Sheet Classification | ARB43, Ch.3A, ¶4 | B05.105 | |

UNEARNED REVENUES
See Revenue Recognition

| Qualification as Liabilities | CON6, ¶197 | | |

UNFUNDED PAST (PRIOR) SERVICE
  COST
See Pension Costs

FAS–FASB Statements   FIN–FASB Interpretations   FTB–FASB Technical Bulletins
APB–APB Opinions   AIN–AICPA Interpretations   ARB–Accounting Research Bulletins
CON–FASB Concepts   EITF–EITF Issues   Q&A–FASB Special Reports

	Original Pronouncements	Current Text	EITF and Other
UNFUNDED PENSION PLANS			
See Defined Benefit Pension Plans			
See Pension Costs			
UNINCORPORATED VENTURES			
See Investments: Equity Method			
UNINSURED RISKS			
See Contingencies			
Accounting by Insureds for Claims-Made Insurance Policies			EITF.86-12
UNIT OF PRODUCTION METHOD			
See Oil and Gas Producing Activities			
Depreciation			EITF.84-28
UNIVERSITIES AND COLLEGES			
See Not-for-Profit Organizations			
UNPROVED PROPERTIES			
See Oil and Gas Producing Activities			
UNREALIZED			
Definition	CON6, ¶143		
UNREALIZED PROFITS			
See Inventory			
See Revenue Recognition			
UNSTATED RIGHTS OR PRIVILEGES			
That Affect Interest Rate on a Note	APB21, ¶7	I69.104	
UNUSUAL ITEMS			
See Defined Benefit Pension Plans			
See Extraordinary Items			
See Income Statement Presentation: Discontinued Operations			
See Interim Financial Reporting			
Disclosure	APB30, ¶26	I22.101	
Scope of Accounting and Reporting Requirements	APB30, ¶26	I22.101	
USEFUL LIFE			
See Depreciation			
See Intangible Assets			
USEFULNESS			
Choice between Accounting Methods	CON2, ¶10-11		
	CON2, ¶14-15		
	CON2, ¶17		
Financial Statements			
. . Classification and Aggregation in	CON5, ¶20-22		
. . Individually and Collectively	CON5, ¶17-19		
Information for Assessing Cash Flow Prospects	CON1, ¶37-39		
Information for Investment and Credit Decisions	CON1, ¶34-36		
Relation to Timeliness	CON2, ¶56-57		
USERS OF FINANCIAL INFORMATION			
Description	CON1, ¶24-27		
External Users	CON1, ¶25-27		

See "Terminology" for references to defined terms presented in various accounting pronouncements.

See the Introduction to the Topical Index for details on the use of this index.

	Original Pronouncements	Current Text	EITF and Other

USERS OF FINANCIAL INFORMATION—continued

General Purpose Financial Statements .... CON5, ¶15-16

.... CON5, ¶28-30

Management .... CON1, ¶27

Not-for-Profit Organizations .... CON4, ¶29-32

Understanding Financial Accounting ..... CON2, ¶36-41

UTILITIES

See Insurance Costs

See Regulated Operations

(The next page is T-461.)

	Original Pronouncements	Current Text	EITF and Other
VACATION PAY			
See Compensation to Employees: Paid Absences			
VALUATION ALLOWANCES			
See Bad-Debt Allowances			
See Disclosure			
See Impairment: Loans			
See Income Taxes			
Deferred Profit on Repossessed Real Estate			EITF.89-14
Definition	CON6, ¶34	I89.410	
	CON6, ¶43	V18.401	
	FAS12, ¶7		
Examples			
. . Bad Debts	APB12, ¶2	V18.102	
. . Depreciation, Depletion	APB12, ¶2-3	V18.102	
. . Losses on Investments	APB12, ¶2-3	V18.102	
Following Debt Restructurings			EITF.87-5
Loan Loss Allowances			
. . Applying Savings and Loan Audit Guide			EITF.87-5
. . Differences between GAAP and RAP			EITF.85-44
Mortgage Loans, Mortgage-Backed Securities	FAS65, ¶4	Mo4.105	
	FAS115, ¶128		
VALUATION METHODS			
Last-In, First-Out (LIFO)			EITF.84-24
VARIABLE STOCK OPTION PLANS			
See Compensation to Employees: Stock Purchase and Stock Option Plans			
VENTURE CAPITAL COMPANY			
Accounting for a Business Combination Involving a Majority-Owned Investee of a Venture Capital Company			EITF.90-10
VERIFIABILITY			
Component to Reliability	CON2, ¶81-89		
Definition	CON2, Glossary		
VESTED BENEFIT OBLIGATION (VBO)			
See Pension Costs			
Benefits Payable Immediately			EITF.88-1
COLA-Adjusted from Termination to Normal Retirement Date			EITF.88-1
Effect When VBO Exceeds Accumulated Benefit Obligation			EITF.88-1
VETERANS ADMINISTRATION (VA)			
Mortgage Guarantee			
. . Effect on Profit Recognition by Seller			EITF.87-9
VOLUNTARY HEALTH AND WELFARE ORGANIZATIONS			
See Not-for-Profit Organizations			
Definition	FAS117, ¶168	No5.414	
VOTING STOCK			
See Capital Stock: Capital Transactions			

(The next page is T-465.)

	Original Pronouncements	Current Text	EITF and Other
WAGES			
See Compensation to Employees: Deferred			
See Compensation to Employees: Paid Absences			
WAR CONTRACTS			
See Contractor Accounting: Government Contracts			
WARRANTIES			
See Contingencies			
See Related Parties			
Extended Warranty and Product Maintenance Contracts			
. . Recognition of Revenues and Costs . . .	FTB90-1, ¶1-5	R75.501-505	EITF.89-17
	FTB90-1, ¶8-9		
	FTB90-1, ¶12		
Recognition of Revenues and Costs Associated with Extended Warranty Contracts			EITF.89-17
Revenue Recognition	FAS48, ¶4	R75.106	
WARRANTS			
See Debt: Convertible Debt and Debt with Stock Purchase Warrants			
See Financial Instruments			
Business Combinations	AIN-APB16, #12	B50.534-538	
Contingent Stock Purchase Warrants			EITF.84-8
Exchangeable Debt			EITF.85-9
Issued in Connection with Research and Development Costs	FAS68, ¶13	R55.111	
Issued in Connection with Sales Agreements			EITF.84-8
Issued with Debt	APB14, ¶16	C08.104	EITF.85-9
			EITF.86-35
Put Warrants			
. . Balance Sheet Classification			EITF.88-9
. . Effect on Earnings-per-Share Calculation			EITF.88-9
WHOLLY OWNED SUBSIDIARIES			
See Consolidation			
See Related Parties			
WORK-IN-PROCESS			
See Inventory			
Balance Sheet Classification	ARB43, Ch.3A, ¶4	B05.105	
WORKERS' COMPENSATION			
See Compensation to Employees: Deferred			
See Compensation to Employees: Paid Absences			
See Contingencies			
See Postemployment Benefits			
WORKING CAPITAL			
Definition	ARB43, Ch.3A, ¶3	B05.406	
WORKS OF ART			
Depreciation	FAS93, ¶6	D40.101A-101C	

	Original Pronouncements	Current Text	EITF and Other
WORKS OF ART—continued			
Depreciation—continued			
....	FAS93, ¶35-37		
WRAP LEASE TRANSACTIONS			
See Leases			
WRITE-DOWNS			
See Contingencies			
See Debt: Restructurings			
See Fixed Assets			
See Impairment			
See Impairment: Loans			
See Lower of Cost or Market			
See Property, Plant, and Equipment			
See Write-offs			
Operating Assets.......................	FAS5, ¶31	C59.137	
WRITE-OFFS			
See Extraordinary Items			
See Write-downs			
Intangible Assets.......................	ARB43, Ch.5, ¶8-9	I60.121-122	
....	FAS44, ¶4		
WRITE-UPS			
See Depreciation			
Foreign Assets........................	APB6, ¶17	D40.102	

(The next page is T-471.)

See "Terminology" for references to defined terms presented in various accounting pronouncements.

See the Introduction to the Topical Index for details on the use of this index.

	Original Pronouncements	Current Text	EITF and Other

YIELD
See Earnings per Share
ZERO COUPON BONDS
See Financial Instruments
Cash Yield Test for Determining Common
   Stock Equivalents EITF.84-16
Use in a Troubled Debt Restructuring EITF.87-18

FAS–FASB Statements   FIN–FASB Interpretations   FTB–FASB Technical Bulletins
APB–APB Opinions   AIN–AICPA Interpretations   ARB–Accounting Research Bulletins
CON–FASB Concepts   EITF–EITF Issues   Q&A–FASB Special Reports

T-471

TO USERS OF THE *ORIGINAL PRONOUNCEMENTS/CURRENT TEXT* (1994/1995 EDITION)

To assist us in improving the quality of the topical index, please complete this form and return it to the Financial Accounting Standards Board. Thank you.

- If you have had difficulty locating a particular topic in the index, please indicate that topic below.

  _____

- List the paragraph(s) in the source material that cover(s) this topic.

  _____

- Please indicate your suggested reference terms for locating this topic in the index.

  (Primary heading) _____

  (First subheading) _____

  (Second subheading) _____

- If you think the topic should be listed under more than one primary heading, please indicate where.

  _____

- Please list any other suggestions for changes that would make this volume more useful to you.

  _____

(Optional information):

Name _____

Firm/Organization _____

Address _____

City/State/Zip _____

( ) _____
Telephone

Send the completed form to:

Financial Accounting Standards Board
Attn: Judith A. Noë
401 Merritt 7
P.O. Box 5116
Norwalk, CT 06856-5116